Experience and Eternity in Spinoza

Spinoza Studies
Series editor: Filippo Del Lucchese, Brunel University London

Seminal works devoted to Spinoza that challenge mainstream scholarship
This series aims to broaden the understanding of Spinoza in the Anglophone world by making some of the most important work by continental scholars available in English translation for the first time. Some of Spinoza's most important themes – that right is coextensive with power, that every political order is based on the power of the multitude, the critique of superstition and the rejection of the idea of providence – are explored by these philosophers in detail and in ways that will open up new possibilities for reading and interpreting Spinoza.

Editorial Advisory board
Saverio Ansaldi, Etienne Balibar, Chiara Bottici, Laurent Bove, Mariana de Gainza, Moira Gatens, Thomas Hippler, Susan James, Chantal Jaquet, Mogens Laerke, Beth Lord, Pierre Macherey, Nicola Marcucci, Alexandre Matheron, Dave Mesing, Warren Montag, Pierre-François Moreau, Vittorio Morfino, Antonio Negri, Susan Ruddick, Martin Saar, Pascal Sévérac, Hasana Sharp, Diego Tatián, Dimitris Vardoulakis, Lorenzo Vinciguerra, Stefano Visentin, Manfred Walther, Caroline Williams

Books available
Affects, Actions and Passions in Spinoza: The Unity of Body and Mind, Chantal Jaquet, translated by Tatiana Reznichenko
The Spinoza-Machiavelli Encounter: Time and Occasion, Vittorio Morfino, translated by Dave Mesing
Politics, Ontology and Knowledge in Spinoza, Alexandre Matheron, translated and edited by Filippo Del Lucchese, David Maruzzella and Gil Morejón
Spinoza, the Epicurean: Authority and Utility in Materialism, Dimitris Vardoulakis
Spinoza and the Politics of Freedom, Dan Taylor
Experience and Eternity in Spinoza, Pierre-François Moreau, edited and translated by Robert Boncardo

Forthcoming
Affirmation and Resistance in Spinoza: Strategy of the Conatus, Laurent Bove, translated and edited by Émilie Filion-Donato and Hasana Sharp
Spinoza's Political Philosophy, Riccardo Caporali, translated by Fabio Gironi
Spinoza and Contemporary Biology: Lectures on the Philosophy of Biology and Cognitivism, Henri Atlan, translated by Inja Stracenski
Spinoza's Paradoxical Conservatism, François Zourabichvili, translated by Gil Morejón

Visit our website at www.edinburghuniversitypress.com/series/SPIN

Experience and Eternity in Spinoza

Pierre-François Moreau

Edited and translated by Robert Boncardo

EDINBURGH
University Press

Edinburgh University Press is one of the leading university presses in the UK. We publish academic books and journals in our selected subject areas across the humanities and social sciences, combining cutting-edge scholarship with high editorial and production values to produce academic works of lasting importance. For more information visit our website: edinburghuniversitypress.com

© Presses universitaires de France/Humensis, *Spinoza. L'expérience et l'éternité*
English translation © Robert Boncardo, 2021, 2022

Edinburgh University Press Ltd
The Tun – Holyrood Road, 12(2f) Jackson's Entry, Edinburgh EH8 8PJ

First published in hardback by Edinburgh University Press 2021

Typeset in 10/12 Goudy Old Style by
Servis Filmsetting Ltd, Stockport, Cheshire

A CIP record for this book is available from the British Library

ISBN 978 1 4744 3890 2 (hardback)
ISBN 978 1 4744 3893 3 (paperback)
ISBN 978 1 4744 3891 9 (webready PDF)
ISBN 978 1 4744 3892 6 (epub)

The right of Pierre-François Moreau to be identified as the author of this work has been asserted in accordance with the Copyright, Designs and Patents Act 1988, and the Copyright and Related Rights Regulations 2003 (SI No. 2498).

This book has been published with the support of the IHRIM
(*Institut d'histoire des représentations et des idées dans les modernités*).

Contents

Can't Stop the Feeling (of Being Eternal)   vii
   Robert Boncardo

Abbreviations   xxiii

Introduction   1

I *Certitudo*: The Journey of Philosophy

1. The Status of the Prologue   17
2. The Stages of Certainty   73
3. Common Life and Perishable Goods   113
4. The True Good   157
5. The 'Animus' and Love   177
6. The Circles of Experience   200

II *Experientia*: Determination and Fields of Experience

7. Determinations and Limits of Experience   235
8. Fields of Experience: Language   318
9. Fields of Experience: The Passions   390
10. Fields of Experience: History   477

III *Aeternitas*: The Experience of Eternity

11. A Metaphysical Experience?   499

Conclusion: The Constitution of Spinoza's System   560

An Infinite Internal to the Finite: An Interview with Pierre-François
Moreau on *Experience and Eternity in Spinoza*   569

Bibliography   601
Index of Names   650
Index of Concepts   652
Index Locorum   654

Can't Stop the Feeling (of Being Eternal)
Robert Boncardo

What could it mean to *feel* eternal? Could eternity be something we *experience*? Philosophers have long sought to produce knowledge of eternity, whether of our own eternity or the eternity of all or part of what is. Yet, to *know* that we are eternal is not the same as *feeling* or *experiencing* our eternity. For one, feelings can be misleading, even mutilated: more often than not, they fail to provide any clear insight into what exactly has caused them. Thus, to say that we *feel* eternal might well be a case of our consciousness making extravagant or fraudulent claims about itself – out of pride, for instance. In the European tradition, the seventeenth-century Dutch philosopher Baruch Spinoza is well-known as a severe critic of the testimony of first-person experience. Most famously, Spinoza rails against the idea that if we feel free, then we indubitably are. For Spinoza, the feeling of freedom marks nothing more than our ignorance of the complex web of causes that actually govern our actions. If philosophy is to make any headway at all, it must refuse to take consciousness at its word and instead seek to understand the forces that produce consciousness and its affective experiences. Along this path, philosophy might well discover that the feeling of being eternal, like the feeling of freedom, is an experience that obscures or misrepresents the mechanisms that produce it, thereby diverting us from knowledge of our irremediable finitude.

And yet, as Pierre-François Moreau reminds us in his monumental work *Experience and Eternity in Spinoza*, it is precisely Spinoza who says, in the Scholium to Proposition 23 of Book V of the *Ethics*, that 'we feel and know by experience that we are eternal' (CWS I, 607–8). Moreau's book is devoted to making sense of this most enigmatic and surprising of Spinoza's claims, which has confounded the philosopher's readers for centuries. Moreau takes an unexpected route to this Holy Grail of Spinoza scholarship: rather than focus on the concept of eternity or its correlates, he examines what the

Ethics says gives us access to our eternity: namely, *experience* and the feelings that accompany it. Moreau's central claim is that Spinoza's philosophy mobilises a conception of experience that interacts with and reinforces the results of his far more famous geometrical method. In this introduction, I will sketch out the main structure of Moreau's book and highlight some of its essential contributions to Spinoza studies. While the length and complexity of the book makes it impractical to offer anything but the most superficial summary, my hope is that by pointing out some of its key landmarks, readers will find the prospect of engaging with Moreau's enormous and erudite work less intimidating.

*

Spinoza: L'expérience et l'éternité began life as Moreau's *doctorat d'État*, which he wrote under the supervision of Jean-Toussaint Desanti.[1] In the French system of the time, a *doctorat d'État* was an extensive doctoral thesis that took at least seven years to prepare and gave successful candidates access to the most senior posts in the university system. The size and scope of Moreau's book attests to the pressures exerted by this most exigent of academic exercises, which has since been replaced by a shorter thesis and an *habilitation*, which allows academics to supervise their own students' theses. Moreau defended his *doctorat d'État* in 1991 in front of a jury that included such luminaries as Didier Deleule, Pierre Magnard, and Alexandre Matheron. It was then published with slight modifications by PUF in 1994 in the series 'Épiméthée', directed by the phenomenologist Jean-Luc Marion.[2] Before this date, however, Moreau was already recognised as a formidable interpreter of Spinoza and of early modern philosophy. He had authored no fewer than four scholarly monographs,[3] edited one collection,[4] and written ten articles and chapters on Spinoza alone.[5] Almost twenty years before the appearance of *Spinoza: L'expérience et l'éternité*, Moreau's first book, titled simply *Spinoza*,

---

[1] For an introduction to Desanti's work and its relation to French Spinozism, see Knox Peden's *Spinoza Contra Phenomenology: French Rationalism from Cavaillès to Deleuze*, Stanford: Stanford University Press, 2014.

[2] *Spinoza: L'expérience et l'éternité*, Paris: PUF, 1994.

[3] *Spinoza*, Paris: Seuil, 1975; *Fernand Deligny et les idéologies de l'enfance*, Paris: Retz, 1978; *Le Récit utopique: droit naturel et roman de l'Etat*, Paris: PUF, 1982; *Hobbes: philosophie, science, religion*, Paris: PUF, 1989.

[4] *Les racines du libéralisme, une anthologie*, Paris: Seuil, 1978.

[5] See the bibliography at the end of this work. Moreau cites his own, invariably excellent work throughout *Experience and Eternity in Spinoza* – something not many doctoral students can say of their own theses.

was published in the famous Seuil series *Écrivains de toujours*. Moreau's *doctorat d'État*, then, was not only the work of an academic who had achieved the highest possible grade in the French university system; it was a milestone in the career of one of France's preeminent Spinoza interpreters, a match for the likes of Desanti and Matheron themselves.

Beyond the academic context in which it was produced, *Spinoza: L'expérience et l'éternité* speaks to much broader trends in French thought in the twentieth century. In his ground-breaking 2014 study, *Spinoza Contra Phenomenology*,[6] Knox Peden has argued that French philosophers from Cavaillès to Althusser drew on Spinoza's work to counter the perceived dominance of phenomenology. Against phenomenology's focus on – and indeed basis in – consciousness, these philosophers turned to Spinoza's rationalism as a way of puncturing the illusions of the self at the same time as giving philosophy access to a world that constituted consciousness, rather than being constituted by it. Alongside these philosophers' appeal to rationalism went a denigration of lived experience as the site of imagination, illusion and error. As Peden presents it, this reading of Spinoza was one chapter in a century-long struggle in France between philosophies of the subject and philosophies of the concept, as Foucault once famously described his country's thought – with Spinoza's thought positioned firmly on the side of the concept.

Moreau's work on Spinoza, however, is devoted precisely to experience, a term most often aligned with philosophies of the subject like existentialism. In the context of twentieth-century French philosophy, what makes *Experience and Eternity in Spinoza* remarkable is that it demonstrates how Spinoza, far from denigrating experience, actually gave it a central place in his thought. Instead of seeing experience as external to Reason, Spinoza conceived of it as a domain with its own unique rationality. Moreau's wager is that it is possible to find something of a synthesis between what Foucault identified as the two strands of French thought, not by building some third doctrine, as we might understand some of Sartre's later work to do, or Bourdieu's, but simply by being more attentive to the arch-rationalist himself, Spinoza.

Structurally speaking, *Experience and Eternity in Spinoza* is something of a lopsided work. Almost the whole of the book's first half is devoted to a reading of the first eleven paragraphs of the *Treatise on the Emendation of the Intellect* (*TdIE*), which Moreau studies in unprecedented detail: he performs extensive genealogies of almost every key term in the text; compares the

---

[6] Knox Peden, *Spinoza Contra Phenomenology*.

various translations of the work over the centuries and in many different languages; engages with the syntactical complexities of Spinoza's writing; and carefully characterises Spinoza's text in terms of existing philosophical and literary genres. The remainder of the book then explores the rest of Spinoza's œuvre in light of this interpretation of the opening to Spinoza's first *Treatise*. Moreau's project is thus confidently revisionist in nature: by reading as closely as possible a text that is normally either dismissed because of its status as a work of youth or ignored because of its posthumous publication, Moreau claims that we can radically reorient our conception of Spinoza's thought as a whole. Let us track the stages of Moreau's argument, starting with his close reading of the 'prologue' to the *TdIE*.

*

In the first chapter, 'The Status of the Prologue', Moreau begins his exhaustive analysis of the opening eleven paragraphs of the *TdIE* by reflecting on the reception of the text since Spinoza's time. As he discovers, it was only in the nineteenth and early twentieth centuries, in particular with the works of German readers like Schopenhauer, Gebhardt and Wenzel, that the prologue to the *TdIE* began to be treated with the philosophical seriousness it deserved. Prior to this, the prologue was seen as sitting awkwardly alongside works like the *TTP* and the *Ethics*, whose systematic style contrasted sharply with the intensely personal content of these pages. Yet even after Schopenhauer, that sombre Romantic, lauded the prologue's emotional insight, the text was still treated as something of an extra-philosophical curiosity: a record of one individual's singular trajectory, not an essential contribution to systematic philosophy. Moreau thus sets himself the task of restoring the prologue's properly philosophical significance and unpacking the conceptual content latent in the term 'experience' from its first sentence.

Intriguingly, Moreau's *philosophical* reading of the prologue passes by way of a *literary* analysis of its rhetorical features, its borrowings from pre-existing genres, and its unique treatment of the narrative subject. Moreau aligns the prologue with two traditional genres that recount a similar drama: the conversion narrative and the protreptic. He then goes on to show how Spinoza decisively innovates with respect to these two structures. First, while the narrator's trajectory is cut in two, as it would be in a conversion narrative, this division occurs without any recourse to a Big Other, whether divine or not. Instead, as in a philosophical protreptic, it is the world of common life that provides the narrator with sufficient reasons for pursuing philosophical reflection. However, unlike in a protreptic, the prologue to the *TdIE* recounts a strictly individual journey, not a dialogue between a philosopher and a layman. If the narrator is in dialogue with anything, then, as Moreau shows, it is with *experience* as such: that is, with an ensemble of typical situations, each with its own latent and potentially unbearable tension; situations that have been lived through by others and recorded in well-known texts and quotations. This leads to Moreau's final literary critical point about the prologue: the narrator who speaks is strictly anonymous. They are neither Spinoza himself nor an individual singularised by their purely personal traits. In fact, if the narrator has any distinguishing features at all, then these derive solely from the journey they undertake. This journey, while marked by experiences whose site is by definition an individual subject, is structured by a series of exemplary deadlocks produced by common life itself. And it is the attempt to resolve these deadlocks – and not some singular genius or destiny, let alone the external intervention of God or a philosopher – that leads the narrator towards philosophy.

But what are these deadlocks? How precisely is the narrator's journey of experience structured? While Moreau is unwavering in his attention to the intertextual references Spinoza mobilises, he refuses to treat the prologue to the *TdIE* as if it were the mere sum of its various borrowings. Instead, he shows how Spinoza places his references to tropes such as the three goods of pleasure, honour and wealth within a wholly novel philosophical framework. The first element of this framework concerns the way the three goods are transformed in the course of the narrator's journey. In Chapter 2, 'The Stages of Certainty', Moreau demonstrates that the real time of the narrator's trajectory – and not the time of the prologue's own textual unfolding – begins with the three goods appearing as *certain* in the sense of being always close at hand. Then, since these goods invariably engender some form of sadness in the narrator – whether through their loss, the narrator's failure to attain them, or the conflicts with others that their pursuit produces – these goods come to be seen as *certain* in the sense of *certain evils*. Since this new sense of certainty also means that the narrator's own life is now at risk, it becomes essential for him to pursue a true good; a good whose key property of being 'fixed' initially arises in contrast with the perishable nature of pleasure, honour and wealth.

Where a hasty reader would see only a reprise of traditional motifs, Moreau thus identifies a strictly Spinozist philosophical substructure that constitutes the prologue's true motor. It is this substructure that is experience itself. In Chapter 3, 'Common Life and Perishable Goods', Moreau continues his reading strategy by first tracking the history of the motif of the three goods since Aristotle and Seneca, before pinpointing the unique twist that Spinoza gives this trope. Where in the ethical tradition pleasure, honour and wealth are condemned from the outset, Spinoza analyses these goods in a rigorously amoral fashion: it is only when they pose a risk to the narrator's efforts at self-preservation that they come to be seen as evil. Concomitantly, these goods are not judged in the light of some Sovereign Good that pre-exists the narrator's experience; rather, the true good that becomes their measure progressively emerges in the course of the journey that the prologue recounts.

But how can we speak of a true, transcendent good in the context of Spinoza's rigorously naturalistic philosophy? Moreau devotes Chapter 4, 'The True Good', to this question. His answer turns on his demonstration that each of the three perishable goods ends up lending something of its own nature to the conception of the true good that the narrator steadily constructs. Where the three perishable goods promise, respectively, a state of peace without any ensuing sadness (pleasure), a form of happiness engendered through relations with others (honours), and a sense of infinite usefulness (wealth), they all fail in various ways to keep these promises. The true good is thus the ideal synthesis of those properties promised by the three perishable goods.

Having established the structure of the prologue and the nature of the goods, both perishable and true, in Chapter 5, 'The *Animus* and Love', Moreau re-examines the narrator's trajectory to determine what kind of *subject* it presupposes. As is unsurprising in a Spinozist context, this subject is buffeted about by forces outside of its control, with little to no interiority to retreat to. Nevertheless, this subject is, crucially, minimally capable of thought and of drawing consequences from its encounters with the three kinds of perishable goods. What is most significant is the kind of *knowledge* this subject comes to possess. For the prologue is not written in the same geometrical style as the *Ethics*, nor does its dramatic structure resemble the tight argumentation of the *Treatises*. Its subject *witnesses* more than it *deduces* – and when it does deduce it is only after having retraced its steps and rendered explicit something that it initially lived in a state of confusion and obscurity. Nevertheless, Moreau argues, the conclusions the subject draws possess a force of necessity that is just as strong as the necessity driving the Demonstrations of the *Ethics* or other works written *more geometrico*.

The final chapter to Part I, 'The Circles of Experience', summarises Moreau's findings about the register of experience as it is operative in – and indeed determining for – the prologue to the *TdIE*. Experience is not a series of random occurrences, even if it is the domain of chance, or rather of what appears to the subject as chance. Experience is also not a name for what is ineffable in the subject's life, even if it is strictly correlated with what an individual goes through *qua* individual. Moreau's discovery is that experience is a structured trajectory that occurs within and because of the most basic features of common life: the presence of and encounter with the three goods, their ambivalent effects on the subject, and their progressively revealed limitations. This trajectory brings the subject to the threshold of philosophy, but it is not philosophy itself. Moreau stresses that while experience has a clear and systematic meaning, it will always remain sub- or pre-philosophical: there is no way of directly engendering the content of the remainder of the *TdIE* – let alone the Axioms, Postulates or Propositions of the *Ethics* – from experience. The impression that many readers of the *TdIE* have of a rupture occurring between paragraphs 11 and 12 is therefore justified. At best, experience can prepare – or, better, produce – the philosopher for philosophy. As Moreau convincingly argues, this is where the analogy breaks down between Spinoza's journey and what is perhaps its closet cousin in the work of another systematic philosophy: Hegel's account of the figures of consciousness in *The Phenomenology of Spirit*. In Spinozism, there is a definite rupture between experience and philosophy, not a single, spiralled line leading from the beginning to the end of the adventures of Spirit.

*

In offering this very schematic summary of the movement of Part I, I have missed much of the rich detail of Moreau's analyses of the prologue. As readers will discover, in addition to presenting a new account of these famous yet enigmatic paragraphs, Moreau systematically compares Spinoza's thought to contemporaneous thinkers like Descartes, Hobbes and Pascal. He also takes up the question of the evolution of Spinoza's views on experience from the *TdIE* to the *Ethics* to the *Political Treatise*. It is in Part II of his book, however, that Moreau addresses the question of the place of experience in Spinoza's thought in its fullness. Where in Part I Moreau engages in a minute textual analysis of a mere eleven paragraphs from an apparently minor work, in the four chapters that make up Part II he ranges widely over Spinoza's most famous writings, showing the various roles played by experience in the two major political *Treatises*, the *Hebrew Grammar* and the *Ethics*. As Moreau's reading demonstrates, the concept of experience does not appear and disappear with the *TdIE*; rather, it lends the power of its unique form of thinking to works where the geometrical method has hitherto seemed to dominate uncontested.

The opening chapter of Part II, 'Determinations and Limits of Experience', begins with a genealogy of the position diametrically opposed to Moreau's own. In the French context, Moreau traces the claim that

Spinoza either neglected or disparaged experience back to Emile Saisset's work in the nineteenth century. A disciple of Victor Cousin, Saisset not only produced the first complete translation of Spinoza's works into French, he also put forward the first systematic critique of the philosopher's thought; a critique whose effects continued to be felt well into the twentieth century, including in the works of Brunschvicg and Alain. At the core of Saisset's argument was the idea that Spinoza had violently subordinated the testimony of consciousness, of first-person experience, to the extrinsic demands of deductive reasoning. For Saisset, Spinoza was ever-ready to sacrifice even the most obvious of facts on the altar of his *a priori* constructions. Far from saving appearances, Spinoza replaced them with the Axioms and Definitions of his system. Spinoza's philosophy thus contrasted unfavourably with the philosophy of France's favourite son, Descartes, whose method had the advantage of being built on the firm ground of the indubitable experience of the self.

As powerful as Saisset's reading is, and as undeniable as its effects have been in the French context, as Peden's work indirectly shows, for Moreau it is based on the illegitimate amalgamation of a number of distinct notions. The most serious confusion Saisset is guilty of is between what Spinoza calls *experientia vaga* – vague or errant experience – and experience *tout court*. As Moreau notes, Saisset should have noticed this distinction, if only because Spinoza consistently critiques the limits of *experientia vaga* while referring to experience as such in almost exclusively positive terms. In Spinoza's later works, Moreau underscores, experience almost always denotes some stock of truths that are known or available to all, with or without the mediation of philosophy. Thus, where in the case of *experientia vaga* I derive false universals from the superficial effects of my body's encounters with external bodies, experience as such actually prevents me from doing so by closing off certain paths of inquiry or orienting me towards the truth. This also means that experience is to be distinguished from scientific experimentation. Through a detailed discussion of Spinoza's exchange with Oldenburg on the subject of Boyle's experiments with nitre, Moreau shows that where experimentation concerns the future – it involves constructing an apparatus that yields as yet unknown results – experience refers to the past, to what has already been adequately established. Finally, experience is not to be confused with mystical experience. On this point, Moreau offers a convincing refutation of those interpretations of Book V of the *Ethics* that read it as advocating a form of mystical insight conceived as an alternative path to knowledge. I will return to Moreau's own interpretation of Book V further on; for the moment, suffice to say that the experience of eternity – as Spinoza describes it in the

Scholium to Proposition 23 – is not a sudden and intuitive illumination, as the mystic would wish it, but rather an experience that is indissociable from the temporal thickness of one's past. Furthermore, this experience is not an experience of knowledge at all; rather, it is only a kind of spur to knowledge grounded in the distinction between our awareness of the reign of eternal necessity and the finitude of our own existence, much like the true good in contrast to the perishable goods of the *TdIE*.

Having circumscribed the limits of experience relative to other proximate domains, Moreau lists three distinct functions that experience performs in Spinoza's philosophy. First, it *confirms* the results arrived at by reason, even if it does not include the reason for these results – that is, the actual lines of causality that lead to them: this is the sense of experience that is closest to the one we find in the prologue to the *TdIE*. Second, experience is *constitutive* of certain domains where the existence of certain entities and the contours of their individuality cannot be deduced from their essence. We see this most prominently in the domains of language, the passions, and history. Third, experience plays an *indicative* role in that it moves the mind to seek out knowledge of particular essences. For Moreau, this is the function of experience in Book V of the *Ethics*. As can already be guessed, it also partly characterises the role of experience in the prologue to the *TdIE*.

Chapters 8, 9 and 10 in Part II explore the way experience operates in its first two guises – confirmative and constitutive – in Spinoza's philosophy of language, his account of the passions, and his conception of fortune in history. What unites these three domains is that they are populated by objects whose existence is distinct from their essence, as per the second of experience's functions. To both know that these objects exist and to know the singular form their existence takes, we have to pass by way of experience. Let us begin with the case of language. As Moreau reminds us, there exists a Spinozist critique of language that would seem to disqualify it as a proper object of study for the philosopher. Insofar as language is rooted in the imaginary – that is, in the network of associations woven between the various modifications of the body – it is the site of inadequation, error, and the confusion between the internal and the external. On this account, Spinoza's critique of language seems so extreme that it excludes even the possibility of philosophy itself as an at least partly linguistic exercise. Nonetheless, Spinoza studied language with extreme care at both its lexical, grammatical and rhetorical levels. Moreau gives us a compelling reason for why this is the case. For Spinoza, words are a species of image. Their specificity, however, lies in the fact that they tie together two images that refer to the same idea. To use a famous example from the *Ethics*, the word 'apple' unites a phonic or graphic image with the visual image of the fruit, with the whole construction referring to the idea of the apple. Crucially, as Spinoza recognizes, the link between the first two images is rooted only in the practices of a given community. As such, communication is not impossible, only limited by reference to this collective practice. Understanding language, then, requires an attention to the particularities of a people and their use of words. Yet, if we are to discover what this use is, it is not enough to employ a deductive method alone. In fact, deduction leads us right to the point where, having identified the arbitrary link between language's two images, we then have to seek out what in effect binds them together – and this can only be discovered through experience. Reason, here, points to its own incompleteness and demands that another procedure supplement it. Spinoza's studies of language thus place at their centre the concept of 'use'. While certain properties of language can be deduced *a priori*, a community's use of words is the final arbiter of their effective meaning. As Moreau demonstrates, when determining the meaning of a word or the structure of a language's syntax, Spinoza very rarely invokes *a priori* considerations concerning the supposedly logical basis of language or the existence of a universal grammar. Instead, he systematically refers to a list of accepted meanings at a given time and place. Spinoza's study of language thus hits upon a kind of contingent fact, at once specifically linguistic but also institutional: a culture. Moreau shows that this hermeneutic horizon is also operative for Spinoza in his interpretation of Scripture in a way that gives a unique twist to the requirement that Scripture be interpreted solely by reference to itself.

The necessity of exploring phenomena whose individuality cannot be deduced *a priori* is also present, Moreau shows, in Spinoza's analyses of the passions. Here, recourse to experience is most essential when it is a matter of identifying the singular disposition of the affects characteristic of an individual: their *ingenium*. Yet Spinoza also turns to experience in its *confirmative* guise in his deduction of the affects. In Book III of the *Ethics*, for instance, Spinoza's example of children's imitative practices *confirms* what has just been rationally demonstrated, while his example of the soldiers and sailors who enjoy recounting their narrow escape from past dangers shows how certain laws are at work even in cases that seem to contradict them. Experience, here, enjoins the reader to recognize the efficacy of laws where we sometimes see only an absence of reason. When it comes to the study of an individual's *ingenium*, however, experience does not simply double the results of reason but rather *constitutes* the very domain that reason comes to analyse. Such variables as an individual's capacity for courage, their susceptibility to affects like pride or despondency, their relative ambition or stubbornness, and so on, have such complex and indeed singular causes that they constitute a limit to the power of deduction alone. As Moreau shows, Spinoza extends the same idea to the study of composite individuals like a state or people. Where reason can deduce the various affects and describe their nature, the specific composition of these affects – the weight given to some rather than others, the complete absence of certain affects and the dominance of one all-powerful affect – can only be captured by experience. Thus, with regard to the Hebrews, their historical experience of servitude meant that they were predisposed to monotheism since obedience to a unique and transcendent figure implied they were no longer under the whip of any human individual. By contrast, the polytheism of the Romans lead to their characteristic violence, both internal and external, with their overly large number of gods determining that they could neither devote themselves with sufficient intensity to one god, nor agree on how to worship the many that they had. In short, while violence and devotion are universally effective or at least possible dispositions, it is the singularity of a people's historical experience that establishes which of these affects will come to dominate.

The philosophy of history is the third and final domain Moreau explores where experience plays a constitutive role. Here, in the midst of an analysis of Spinoza's concept of fortune and its distinction from various models of fortune from the tradition, Moreau points to a short circuit that occurs between experience in its confirmative and constitutive guises. Not only do we require experience to teach us about how individuals and states have dealt with the force of fortune, historical experience has presented us with an *exhaustive* list of all the possible ways of responding to and governing chance in history. In other words, what experience teaches us in this domain is *all there is to know* – even if we can also know this deductively.

Readers will find much more in these three chapters than I have hinted at above. For instance, they will find Moreau responding, in a number of subordinate arguments, to several sensitive points of Spinoza scholarship: he intervenes into the status of Spinoza's remarks on scientific method and on the physics and chemistry of his time; he compares Spinoza's exegesis of the Bible with those of his contemporaries; he offers an extensive discussion of the question of the individuality of the state; and he again compares Spinoza's philosophical commitments to those of his contemporaries, in particular Descartes and Hobbes. On occasion, readers might have the impression that the theme of experience functions more as a convenient thread that allows Moreau to bind together his forceful interventions into the scholarship, and less as the book's central concern.

One of these interventions, however, is key to his overall assessment of the status of experience in Spinoza. This is Moreau's reading of the enigmatic formula from Book V, Proposition 23, Scholium:

> And though it is impossible that we should recollect that we existed before the Body – since there cannot be any traces of this in the body, and eternity can neither be defined by time nor have any relation to time – still, we feel and know by experience that we are eternal (*CWS* I, 607–8).

It is worthwhile spending some time with Moreau's arguments for how best to read this Scholium. The first step is to say exactly what eternity is. For Spinoza, on Moreau's account, eternity is defined by a specific conjunction of necessity and existence. While everything is a product of necessity, not everything is eternal. Finite modes, for instance, are on the one hand caught in chains of causality – and are thus necessary – while on the other hand they exist only for a limited amount of time. Reciprocally, something can be eternal yet not actually exist. As Moreau reminds us, Spinoza distinguishes between eternal truths and eternal things: the essence of a finite mode is an eternal truth, while its existence in the form of that mode is not itself eternal, for this mode must be brought into being by something else and will also eventually be destroyed. What is truly eternal, by contrast, exists necessarily solely by virtue of its own essence. Put differently, an eternal thing is something that cannot be prevented from existing. We can thus understand why in the above Scholium Spinoza says that eternity is not defined by time: while an eternal thing might exist at all times, this is but a consequence of its definition, not a core component of it.

Having defined eternity, Moreau can now turn to another controversial aspect of the Scholium: the rupture with parallelism that it seems to imply. As Spinoza writes in Proposition 23:

> The human soul[7] cannot be destroyed with the body, but something of it remains which is eternal.

---

[7] As Moreau will explain in his introduction, for the most part he uses the term 'soul' – or 'âme' in French – to translate the Latin 'mens', which English commentators, including Curley, render as 'mind'. There are occasions, however, when Moreau uses the term 'esprit' to refer to a similar agency. I have followed his use throughout, translating any instance of 'âme' as 'soul' and 'esprit' as 'mind'.

Moreau's way of resolving this controversy is to show that it is possible for an eternal mode to correspond to a perishable mode. Thus, while the essence of a finite extended mode is not eternal, the idea of this extended mode's essence is not only an eternal truth, it is also an eternal mode – but a mode *only of the attribute of thought*. Thought thus has capacities that extension does not. The rupture between the two attributes of thought and extension is consecrated by the eternity of certain modes of thought.

Now, insofar as we are a body, the eternity Spinoza is referring to in this Scholium corresponds to that part of our soul that is linked to the essence of this extended mode. But what does it mean to have an *experience* of this eternity, indeed to *feel* it? Note that Spinoza says that *we* feel that *we* are eternal, not that we feel that any mode whatsoever is eternal. The experience of eternity is thus an experience of the *self*. But here we encounter the obstacle mentioned in the opening paragraph to this introduction: how can we trust such a first-person experience? What makes it different to the illusory experience of freedom, for instance?

For Moreau, the experience of eternity is actually the experience of a difference. It marks our apprehension of the difference between ourselves as irremediably finite and our capacity to grasp what is absolutely essential and thus eternal. Note that the experience of eternity, conceived in this way, is not a matter of knowledge. While it is always correlated with some adequate idea, what counts is not this knowledge per se but rather the abyss separating the eternity of what is essential from the finitude of the self. The experience of eternity thus proves nothing by itself. Instead, it motivates us to escape the realm of finitude by seeking ever more adequate knowledge of Nature. It is also not a determinate experience with precise contours but only ever the experience of the difference between *one* individual's singular experience of their finitude and their encounter with the knowledge of necessity. Indeed, this is why Spinoza says that *everyone* can have this experience, from the common person to the philosopher: the basis for the third kind of knowledge is found in every individual; all are susceptible to having their lives wrenched apart by the knowledge of Nature.

We can see now how Moreau's book comes full circle, with his reading of Proposition 23 linking up with his interpretation of the prologue to the *TdIE*. For there, too, the experience of eternity was the experience of a difference at the heart of the finite. It was through the dissatisfactions of common life that the narrator moved towards philosophy. With this dovetailing between one of Spinoza's earliest pieces of writing and one of his last, Moreau can claim to have identified a conceptual continuity at the heart of Spinoza's system: the concept of experience, which plays a hitherto unrecognized yet crucial role in his thought.

*

Moreau's style is typical of academic French, indeed of a *doctorat d'État* specifically. What makes his work stand out, however, is its truly international scope. While Moreau's work on Spinoza began within a distinctly French context – his first book was written in the wake of the publication of Gueroult, Matheron and Deleuze's ground-breaking studies from the late 1960s – it came into its own after the series of international conferences on Spinoza in 1977 marking 300 years since the philosopher's death. Since this time, Moreau has maintained a consistent and productive dialogue with Spinozists the world over. His work carries the trace of these encounters. For instance, in *Experience and Eternity in Spinoza*, Moreau engages with scholarship in no fewer than eight languages: Latin, Dutch, English, French, German, Italian, Portuguese and Spanish. If Moreau's book challenges our reading habits at this level, it also invites us to ask what a truly international philosophical community might look like.

Moreau's work is equally unique at the level of its methodology. Where before him French studies of Spinoza were typically austere affairs philosophically, with a focus on identifying the fundamental structures of Spinoza's thought, Moreau introduces an historical, indeed philological, sensibility to Spinoza studies. He is as attentive to questions of historicity and textuality as he is to the properly philosophical meaning of Spinoza's ideas. Indeed, it is not an exaggeration to say that *Experience and Eternity in Spinoza* is a defence-in-act of a certain way of doing philosophy, one that was marginalised at the time in the French academy. This also helps explain certain unmissable features of Moreau's text. Readers will encounter a number of what are essentially literature reviews, which punctuate the book whenever Moreau addresses a controversial point of scholarship. They will also find detailed discussions of methodology, both of Moreau's own and of those he has chosen not to adopt. At times Moreau embeds his own argument within lengthy discussions of centuries' worth of competing interpretations; at others he summarises vast tracts of Spinoza's corpus in a few punchy sentences. All of these features point to Moreau attempting to justify – at the same time as he carries out – his new approach to Spinoza. Readers will no doubt find it useful to engage with his work at this meta-theoretical level as well.

On matters of translation, I have tried to produce a text that is as readable and clear as possible. This has often meant breaking up Moreau's long and sinuous sentences, whose many parts are corralled together by an army of colons and semi-colons. Less frequently, it has meant substantially re-working his syntax. With regards to secondary scholarship, I have translated into English those quotations that Moreau himself translates, but have not translated what he leaves in its original language. The only exceptions to this are those passages in French from the secondary literature found in the main body of the text: I have translated these for ease of reading and to maintain the flow of the text. When it comes to key quotations from Descartes, I have used the three volumes of Cottingham, Stoothoff, Murdoch and Kenny's edition of *The Philosophical Writings of Descartes* published by Cambridge University Press. I have also kept Moreau's original references to the Adam and Tannery volumes of the *Œuvres de Descartes*. Whenever Moreau quotes important philosophers from outside of France in French, I have used up-to-date and accessible English editions, which I indicate in the footnotes. As for citing Spinoza himself, I have used Curley's two-volume translation of the *Complete Works* and Maurice J. Bloom's translation of the *Hebrew Grammar*. Nevertheless, since Moreau so scrupulously cites Gebhardt's four volume edition of the *Opera*, I have also kept these references in place and simply supplemented them with references in square brackets to Curley's edition of the *Collected Works*.

Before bringing this introduction to a close, I must acknowledge the indispensable help and support of a number of people without whom this project would never have begun, let alone been brought to completion. A first round of thanks must go to Filippo Del Lucchese, for initially proposing this translation and for the extraordinary energy he has brought to making foreign-language works on Spinoza available to an Anglophone audience; and to Carol Macdonald from Edinburgh University Press, for her unwavering support and expert advice. I must also thank Jennifer Milam for her stewardship of 'The Enlightenment and its Impact' programme at the University of Sydney. In 2017, I was exceedingly fortunate to be a Junior Research Fellow under the aegis of this programme, and this allowed me to complete a substantial amount of work on this translation. I also spent that year re-reading Spinoza's *Ethics* line by line with my close friend and colleague, Cat Moir, whose impact on my understanding of the great Dutch philosopher has been profound. Throughout the translation process I have had the support and inspiration of a not-so-small circle of Australian Spinozists, including Justin Clemens, Moira Gatens, Joe Hughes, Genevieve Lloyd, Janice Richardson, Jon Roffe, Jon Rubin, Inja Stracenski, Bahar Teymouri, Anthony Uhlmann and Dimitris Vardoulakis. While many of these remarkable scholars made suggestions as to how I could improve the translation, I am solely responsible for the faults and infelicities that remain. I encourage readers to get in contact if they find any mistakes. Much of the work would have been impossible without the moral and intellectual support of Claudia Hill, while my colleagues and friends at the University of Sydney, Anthony Coxeter, Shima Shahbazi, Nicole Fidalgo and Victoria Souliman, never failed to keep me both motivated and caffeinated. My family – Guy, Debra, Philip and Felicity Boncardo – remain an inspiration. A final thanks must go to Christian R. Gelder for his continued comradely support of my intellectual endeavours, and to Bryan Cooke, from whom I hope to continue learning about The Spiny One.

Abbreviations

Spinoza
CWS I   *The Collected Writings of Spinoza Volume I*
CWS II *The Collected Writings of Spinoza Volume II*
CM   *Cogitata Metaphysica*
HG   *Compendium Grammatices Linguae Hebraeae*
KV   *Short Treatise*
PP   *Descartes' Principles of Philosophy*
TdIE   *Treatise on the Emendation of the Intellect*
TP   *Political Treatise*
TTP   *Theological-Political Treatise*

Descartes
PWD I   *The Philosophical Writings of Descartes Volume I*
PWD II *The Philosophical Writings of Descartes Volume II*
PWD III *The Philosophical Writings of Descartes Volume III*

Introduction

'Sentimus experimurque nos aeternos esse'. This enigmatic formula (*Ethics*, Book V, Proposition 23, Scholium) has divided commentators. Does it mark Spinoza's abandonment of the theses from Book I of the *Ethics*? Does it reveal his secret yet consistent mysticism, a mysticism hitherto hidden by the *Ethics*' geometrical form? Or does it refer to a pure epiphenomenon of knowledge of the true idea? This phrase has, in fact, two virtues:

- it concentrates all of the interpretative difficulties raised by Book V, including whether or not this Book coheres with the rest of Spinoza's œuvre;
- it points to the essential role played by *experience*, a notion found throughout Spinoza's writings but which scholars have rarely studied, either because they have assumed it could be reduced to scientific experimentation, or because they have supposed that Spinoza's 'absolute rationalism' necessarily neglected experience, tied as it is to both imagination and error.

In the present work, I propose to re-evaluate the status of experience in Spinoza's thought, to study the different fields in which experience functions, and finally to apply the conclusions of this analysis to a reading of certain passages from Book V. In doing so I aim less to add one more domain to those already routinely studied in Spinoza scholarship; instead, I seek to bring to light the mutual imbrication of the geometrical and the experiential in Spinoza's thought. My claim is that this will allow us to better understand Spinoza's way of thinking. What is proper to a philosophy is not only the set of theses it advances; it is also the procedures by which it establishes these theses and convinces the reader of their validity. Typically Spinoza's logic has been reduced to, and identified with, the geometrical method, which itself has been represented in the exclusive form of deductive demonstrations. By contrast, what I hope to show is that while mathematics does indeed provide the model of intelligibility for Spinoza's system, in reality Spinoza's analyses and expositions combine both geometrical and experiential modes of reasoning. The latter is neither a simple pedagogical substitute for the former nor an admission of Reasons' defeat. Rather, each mode has a role to play – a role assigned to it by the order of reasons itself.

My reading of Spinoza's system is thus deliberately incomplete. I will deal neither with God, nor the infinite, nor even with eternity as such. If I nevertheless discuss certain of these notions, it will be only insofar as they have consequences for, or are apprehended by, experience. As for experience itself, I will not study in detail each of the possible fields in which it operates. Instead, I will reveal the procedures by which these fields are constituted. If, thanks to this work, the reader has the impression of better understanding Spinoza's various modes of reasoning – both in terms of the detail and the movement of certain arguments – then my efforts will not have been in vain.

In studying the constitution of Spinoza's system, I have employed the well-established methods of *structural analysis*. Analysing a system of thought's structure means showing how its concepts are organised, what arguments introduce them and give them their meaning, and finally how this thought at once shapes and transforms the materials it has inherited from elsewhere – whether from past philosophical systems, other theoretical disciplines, or everyday language. I have nevertheless supplemented this structural analysis with two additional procedures: reception history, and the micro-analysis of certain texts. *Reception history* complements the exposition of the system's constitution by refusing to reduce the successive readings of a text to a series of misunderstandings. Instead, it helps demonstrate how, by virtue of their distinct frameworks, these successive readings refract the various logical possibilities that animate the system itself and its articulated ensemble of concepts. For its part, the *micro-analysis* of texts helps draws out the differences between these readings insofar as each deals with a single, privileged experience. This is why, if chosen strategically, it is possible to use a single text, if not to sum up Spinoza's system (for a text is not a system in miniature), then at least to indicate how this system bends and buckles under the weight of what it inherits from, or shares with, other texts. Identity exists only through the play of demarcations; the more precise these demarcations, the more violent they are. What counts is choosing the right text to study; and the right text is often the one where the system attempts to think its other. For in such texts the system either seeks to engage with human experience in its most general form, or to show how one can pass from this experience to philosophy as such. Indeed, it is when philosophy appears in its least architectonic guise that its systematic nature is at its most intense: at this point, philosophy appears non-technical and unsystematic; and yet, thanks to the accumulated effects of patient technical work, it shines brightest precisely where its technicity seems to disappear and thought attempts to be as faithful as possible to the common gaze.

Allow me to briefly point out a few translation choices I have made. Like Appuhn, I have rendered *affectus* as 'affect' [*affection*]. When referring to *affectio*, I have translated it by 'modification' [*modification*] (save in the expression 'the affects of the body' [*les affections du corps*], which is unlikely to cause confusion). While this distinction is perhaps not ideal, it has the advantage of avoiding any ambiguity. For the same reason, *ingenium* has been translated as 'complexion' [*complexion*]. The translations of *mens* and *animus* vary according to context and period: for the beginning of the *TdIE*, I have translated *mens* as 'thought' [*pensée*], while for the *Ethics* I have translated it as 'soul' [*âme*], following the use established by Appuhn.

Spinoza's works are cited using the Gebhardt edition (noted by the letter G followed by the volume and page number), with the exception of the *Short Treatise*, which is cited in the Mignini edition (noted by the letter M, followed by the page number). For the *Treatise on the Emendation of the Intellect*, I have also included the numbered paragraphs established by Bruder, which Koyré follows. In the majority of cases the translations I have used come from Appuhn (noted A), but many have been reworked for reasons of uniformity. The titles of certain works have been abbreviated: *TdIE* (*Tractatus de Intellectus Emendatione*), KV (*Korte Verhandeling*), TTP (*Tractatus theologico-politicus*), TP (*Tractatus politicus*), CM (*Cogitata metaphysica*). Descartes is quoted by reference to the volumes of Adam and Tannery (AT), while quotations from Hobbes come from the Molesworth edition (*Opera latina*: OP; *English Works*: EW); Pascal is quoted from the 'Intégrale' edition published by *Seuil*. However, in the case of *Les Pensées*, the classification number from the Brunschvicg edition is given after the number from the Lafuma edition. The Greek and Hebrew have been transliterated. With respect to the Hebrew, I have followed Spinoza's method, which is somewhat onerous but has the advantage of avoiding diacritical marks.

This book reprises the essential elements of a *doctorat d'Etat* defended in Paris on 1 December 1991. The jury was presided over by Didier Deleule and was composed of Jean-Marie Beyssade, Jean-Toussaint Desanti, Pierre Magnard, Jean Margain and Alexandre Matheron.

It remains for me to thank my thesis supervisor, Jean-Toussaint Desanti, who was kind enough to take on the supervision of my research, and to whom I am indebted not only for the many fruitful discussions we had on 'theoretical spaces', but also for the stimulating example he set of epistemological rigour in both teaching and writing. I also wish to thank each of my teachers, in particular Alexandre Matheron, who read and discussed a first version of this work and always allowed me to reap the benefits of his perfect understanding of Spinozism. Anne Lagny was present at all stages of this work and I wish to express my gratitude to her. My thanks also go to Marie-Hélène Belin-Capon, Jacqueline Lagrée, Jean Margain, Marianne Taourel, each of whom read all or part of the work. And to Jacqueline Lagrée, for many long years of work done in common.

I

Certitudo: The Journey of Philosophy

'After experience had taught me that all the things which regularly occur in common life are empty and futile . . .'.[1]

Spinoza's reflections begin with a narrative written in the past tense and the first person. It is worthwhile pausing over this first line from what is the first book – or one of the first books[2] – that Spinoza ever wrote. The author (or at least the narrator) recounts his hesitations in his search for the true Good. He speaks to the reader, laying out his reasons for rejecting the goods that have been presented to him; why he hesitated before putting his decision into action; and how, finally, he recognised the means by which he could overcome his uncertainties. The first eleven paragraphs of the *Treatise on the Emendation of the Intellect* thus describe a journey whose first stage – indicated by the text's first substantive – is that of *experientia*. One rarely encounters the term *experientia* in commentators' writings on Spinoza's system. Most are persuaded that a rationalist doctrine can give only a marginal place to experience.[3] When they are not reducing it to

---

[1] 'Postquam me experientia docuit, omnia, quae in communi vita frequenter occurrunt, vana, & futilia esse', *TdIE*, § 1, G II, p. 5, l. 6–8 [*TdIE*, 5; CWS I, 7].

[2] As Jarig Jelles noted in his preface to the *Nagelate Schriften* (NS), 'De Handeling van de Verbetering van't Verstand enz. is een van des Schrijvers eerste werken geweest, gelijk zijn stijl en gedachten zelfs getuigen.' On the question of the anteriority of the *TdIE* relative to the *Short Treatise*, I refer the reader to the works of F. Mignini and to the discussions they have inspired.

[3] An example: Saisset, drawing on the *TdIE* and on the letter to Simon de Vries, writes that for Spinoza 'l'expérience, sous sa double forme, ne peut fournir une connaissance philosophique; car elle donne des images confuses et le philosophe cherche des idées; elle n'atteint que les accidents des choses, et la science néglige l'accident pour s'attacher à l'essence. L'expérience est donc absolument proscrite, sans restriction et sans réserve, du domaine de la métaphysique', *Introduction critique*, Volume One of the *Œuvres de Spinoza*, trans. Emile Saisset, Paris: Charpentier, 1861, p. 21. On the

the strict form of scientific experimentation, commentators suppose that experience is synonymous with imagination, chance, and irrationality. By contrast, in this work I propose to demonstrate the key role that experience plays in Spinoza's system, and to analyse both its importance and its various fields of signification. In doing so, the reader will perhaps come to a better understanding of how a philosophy establishes a relation with its outside – and thereby constitutes itself. Given that the opening pages to the *TdIE* introduce this register of the outside – and with it the narrator's reflections – I will begin by exploring the content of these pages with a view to elucidating their argumentative procedures. However, this is possible only by first bringing to light a certain number of concepts and questions, which will then serve to guide us in the examination of the rest of Spinoza's system.

At this point, however, the following objection could be raised: why should we once again read such a famous and well-studied text?[4] Indeed, all of the scholarly works that deal with the *TdIE*[5] include a study of its prologue. There also exist articles[6] – and even an entire book[7] – specially devoted to it. Without disregarding the monumental work of historical and conceptual clarification that scholars have accomplished, I am here presupposing that it is possible to find a different way of reading the prologue

---

ensemble of Saisset's analysis and on the meaning of this apparent rejection of experience in the Cousinian interpretation of Spinoza, see below, Chapter 7.

[4] As O. Proietti notes, 'Le célèbre début du *TdIE* a fait l'objet d'un nombre si considérable de commentaires qu'il semble difficile de pouvoir en donner encore une lecture susceptible d'en cerner des aspects nouveaux et signifiants', '*Lettres à Lucilius*: une source de *De Intellectus Emendatione*', *Travaux et documents du Groupe de recherches spinozistes*, 1, 'Lire et traduire Spinoza', PUPS, 1989, p. 40. Proietti makes this remark at the beginning of one of the most fruitful studies in recent Spinoza research.

[5] Cf. the commentaries by Elbogen (1898), Gebhardt (1905), Jaochim (1940), Klever (1986).

[6] E. Villa, 'La conversione di Spinoza. Commento alle prime pagine del *De Intellectus Emendatione*', *Rivista di filosofia*, 3 (1927); G. Dufour-Kowalska, 'Un itinéraire fictif. Le traité de la *Réforme de l'Entendement* et de la meilleure voie à suivre pour parvenir à la vraie connaissance des choses', *Studia philosophica*, 35 (1975), pp. 58–80; R. Violette, 'Méthode inventive et méthode inventée dans l'introduction au *De Intellectus Emendatione* de Spinoza', *Revue philosophique de la France et de l'étranger*, 102 (1977), pp. 303–22; H. Giannini, 'Autobiografia y sistema (a proposito de las primeras lineas de la *Reforma del Entendimiento*)', *Revista de Filosofia*, 15/2 (1977), pp. 87–95.

[7] Theo Zweerman, *L'Introduction à la philosophie de Spinoza: une analyse structurelle de l'Introduction du* Traité de la réforme de l'entendement *suivie d'un commentaire de ce texte*, Louvain: Presses Universitaires de Louvain, and Assen-Maastricht: Van Gorcum, 1993. See our analysis of this thesis in the *Bulletin de l'Association des amis de Spinoza*, 14 (1984), pp. 13–16.

to the *TdIE* to those that have hitherto been proposed. I will analyse the 'Prologue' by seeking to discern a certain type of perspective in it, one that first becomes perceptible through a certain *tone*. Without failing to recall the text's sources or the relation between its concepts and those we find elsewhere in Spinoza's œuvre, I will attend to the prologue's own specific procedures – to what might be called its specific materials [*sa donne*] and the play [*jeu*] that it produces on the basis of these materials.

I must nevertheless begin by pointing out a difficulty, one to which these terms 'materials' [*donne*] and 'play' [*jeu*] are meant to offer a solution, albeit only a metaphorical one. The difficulty is that the *TdIE* cannot be read as if it were a page from the *Ethics* – even if, by virtue of what it will help us discover, it can show us how to better interpret certain aspects of the *Ethics*. In fact, the text's narrative is not presented according to the rules of the geometrical order; indeed, it is written as if it were an inversion of this order. This inversion concerns both the text's chronology and its arguments: as a narrative recounting a decision informed by conceptual arguments, the 'Prologue' is written following the order of the decision and not that of the concept; more precisely, it is written according to the order of a decision that has already been taken. As such, what in a chronological explanation would be at the beginning is not necessarily to be found there, while the reasons the narrator gives for his decision are not presented with reference to their conceptual foundations, but only insofar as they are moments in the subject's practical reasoning. Such an expository procedure might be disorienting for a reader used to the geometrical order. Yet it is no less analogous to what happens at other moments in Spinoza's other treatises. This does not meant that the text's conceptual progression lacks rigour, only that its rigour is not exhibited for itself. At the same time, the text's themes are not linked one to the other beneath the reader's gaze according to causal laws: the reader encounters them only in the order that they come to play a role in what the narrator either feels or calculates. As a consequence, one and the same conceptual object can appear at many different places and in many different guises. We therefore run the risk of misunderstanding a notion if we identify it with its first appearance. If we want to think the various meanings of a concept as a totality, we must seek these meanings out at different places in the text before finally gathering them together;[8] and since their

---

[8] We could compare the procedure used here with the one that Spinoza recommends for reading one of the levels of the Holy Scriptures. Having noted that 'Scripture does not give definitions of the things of which it speaks, any more than nature does', he deduces from this that the absent definitions should be sought, as is done

dispersion is not the product of chance, it is necessary to ask what aspects of a concept appear at each point, given both the context and the movement of the demonstration. The meaning of each concept will thus follow from its content and from the different registers in which it is used. Finally, it will only be at the end of the analysis that we will be better able to master this process of imbrication itself.

I will begin by proposing a translation[9] of the text to be studied.[10] This translation aims less at ease of reading than at preci-

---

for natural things, 'from the different narratives occurring in the Texts concerning them'. ('Denique Scriptura rerum, de quibus loquitur, definitiones non tradit, ut nec etiam natura. Quare quemadmodum ex diversis naturae actionibus definitiones rerum naturalium concludendae sunt, eodem modo hae ex diversis narrationibus, quae de unaquque re in Scriptis occurrunt, sunt elicienade', *TTP*, chap. VII, G III, p. 99, II. 25–9 A, p. 140 [*TTP* VII, 13; *CWS* II, 172]). This principle of distribution leads to a rule for the ordered collection of terms ('Sententias uniuscujusque libri colligere debet, easque ad summa capita redigere, ut sic omnes, quae de eadem re reperiuntur, in promptu habere possimus', ibid., p. 100, II. 8–10 [*TTP* VII, 16; *CWS* II, 173]), which seems applicable to every coherent book that is not written in a mathematical form. This in no way means that we can uniformly apply the Spinozist method for the interpretation of the Scriptures to Spinoza's own texts, as we will see in detail further on. But here, within the limits of this narrative, this rule seems applicable.

[9] Translator's note: Moreau offers his own original French translation of Spinoza's text. I have included it in full below opposite an English version, which I have adapted from Curley's translation published in Volume One of the *Collected Works of Spinoza*, Princeton: Princeton University Press, 1985, pp. 7–10. I will include Moreau's footnotes to his translation in the English translation, along with additional footnotes of my own that will serve to indicate the most significant modifications of Curley's translation that I have made so as to better capture Moreau's own translation choices in English. I will not explain these choices, however, as their meaning will become clear as Moreau's study progresses.

[10] The main points on which my translation differs from previous translations are the following: it gives to *distrahere* the meaning of 'to tear' [*déchirer*]; it adopts 'institution' [*institution*] to translate *institutum*, since in classical French we speak of 'the institution of life' [*l'institution de la vie*]; the passive form of *videre* is translated by 'to appear' [*apparaître*] and not by 'to seem' [*sembler*], which is possible with the Latin (cf. Ernout's notes to his translation of Lucretius) and corresponds more precisely to the meaning of the text; *animus* and *mens* have been translated respectively by 'mind' [*esprit*] and 'thought' [*pensée*], even if these two terms appear almost synonymous: where *animus* designates the place where different desires confront each other, *mens*, by contrast, marks the continuity of reflection. Finally, I have systematically avoided introducing terms that are not found in the text, and I have also avoided inscribing certain terms in places other than the ones they already occupy, even when an ellipsis or a difficulty rendering neutral pronouns seemed to force me to do so. The lesser evil seemed to

sion,[11] for certain phrases will have to be taken up word for word further on. The Latin annotations added by Spinoza, which can be found in the *Opera Posthuma (OP)* in italics at the bottom of the page, have been indicated in the footnotes, along with any significant variations from the *Nagelate Schriften (NS)*.[12] The two sentence fragments which, in the original, are in italics have been placed in quotation marks in the translation, given that they are themselves quotations.[13]

[1] After experience had taught me that everything that regularly occurs in common life[14] is vain and futile; and while I saw that everything[15] that was the cause or object of my fear had nothing good or bad in itself, except insofar as [my] mind was moved by it, I resolved at last to try to	[1] Après que l'expérience m'eut enseigné que tout ce qui arrive fréquemment dans la vie commune est vain et futile; alors que je voyais que tout ce que je craignais, ou par quoi j'éprouvais de la crainte, n'avait en soi rien de bon ni rien de mauvais, si ce n'est dans la mesure où il suscitait un mou

consist in placing the necessary clarifications in square brackets, and even this I did sparingly (whereas Koyré, for instance, does not hesitate to insert the non-Spinozist notion of 'false goods' into the text). To the extent that these paragraphs function thanks to their progression and the way in which they determine this progression, my main concern was to preserve the tone and the semantic equilibriums that characterise the text.

[11] I will not systematically compare here the choices that have been made in translating this prologue.

[12] This survey in no way claims to be an exhaustive critical comparison (for instance, I admit to being indifferent when faced with the choice between *possem* and *possim*, above all since the editors recognise that the agreement between verbal times 'parum diligenter a nostro observatur', and since this neglect is particularly frequent in the case of the verb *posse*; cf. Leopold's remarks on the Van Vloten-Land edition, *Ad Spinozae Opera Posthuma*, pp. 2–3, as well as Gebhardt, *Textgestaltung*, G II, p. 322), nor does it reprise Gebhardt's hypotheses concerning a prior text whose existence the NS apparently attests to. What's at stake is simply trying to understand how Spinoza's text was first received – that is, how those closest to Spinoza understood his text, and what they might have found troubling in it. I would simply note the difficulty felt by the NS in translating the term *distrahere* (the translator tries three different terms successively, two of which are grouped together); the extension of *ding* and *gemeen*; and the rigour of the distinction between the terms *gemoed* and *geest* (on the the only occasion where this distinction is not respected, the translators correct the Latin text). Too attentive by half to seeking out the *Urtext*, Gebhardt's *Textgestaltung* pays too little attention to these questions.

[13] Moreover, these quotations are actually self-quotations: Spinoza reprises one of his own formulations in order to explain the content and clarify the conditions of his text – the first time at a few lines distance, the second at the end of a page.

[14] Translator's note: Curley translates *communi vita* by 'ordinary life'.

[15] The NS translates the first *omnia* by *alles* ('everything', *tout*), the second by *alle de dingen* ('all things', *toutes les choses*).

find out whether there was anything which would be the true good, capable of communicating itself,[16] and which alone would affect the mind, all others being rejected – whether there was something which, once discovered and possessed, would eternally give me a continuous and supreme joy.

[2] I say that *I resolved at last* – for at first glance it seemed ill-advised to be willing to lose something certain for something then uncertain. I saw, of course, the advantages[17] that honor and wealth bring, and that I would be forced to abstain from seeking them, if I wished to devote myself seriously to something new and different; and if by chance the greatest happiness lay in them, I saw that I should have to do without it. But if it did not lie in them, and I devoted my energies only to acquiring them, then I would equally go without it.

[3] So I wondered whether perhaps it would be possible to reach this new institution – or at least the certainty of attaining it – without changing the conduct and common[18] institution[19] of my life which I shared with other men. Often I tried this, but in vain. For what occurs most often[20] in life,[21] and which, to judge from their actions, men think to be the sovereign

vement dans mon esprit; je résolus enfin de chercher s'il existait quelque chose qui fût un bien véritable et capable de se communiquer et par quoi seulement l'esprit pût être affecté, une fois tout le reste rejeté; bien plus: s'il existait quelque chose dont la découverte et la possession me feraient jouir éternellement d'une joie continue et suprême.

[2] Je dis 'je résolus enfin': car à première vue il semblait inconsidéré, pour une chose encore incertaine, de vouloir en abandonner une certaine: je voyais bien quels avantages se tirent de l'honneur et des richesses, et qu'il me fallait cesser de les rechercher si je voulais m'appliquer sérieusement à cette entreprise nouvelle et différente; si par hasard la félicité suprême était contenue en eux [honneur et richesses], il me faudrait, je l'apercevais bien, en être privé; si en revanche elle ne s'y trouvait pas, et que je m'appliquais à les rechercher, dans ce cas aussi je serais privé de la suprême félicité.

[3] J'agitais donc dans mon esprit la question de savoir si par hasard il était possible de parvenir à cette nouvelle institution ou du moins à la certitude [*ipsius*; la concernant ou : qu'elle comporte] sans bouleverser l'ordre et l'institution commune de ma vie; je l'ai tenté maintes fois, mais en vain. En effet, ce qui arrive le plus souvent dans la vie et ce que les hommes, comme

---

[16] The NS translates this by *t welk het waar mededeelbar goet is* ('which was the true communicable good', *qui fût le vrai bien communicable*), and indicates in the margin: *Bonum verum communicabile* (a Latin text that is slightly different from the text of the OP).

[17] The NS renders *commoda* by *gemakken en voordelen* ('the opportunities and advantages', *les facilités et les avantages*).

[18] Translator's note: Curley does not include the adjective 'common' before 'life' in this paragraph; rather, he writes: 'the conduct and plan of life'.

[19] The NS renders the first *institutum* by *ooggemerk*, the second by *gesteltenis*.

[20] The NS renders *plerumque* by *gemenelijk* ('most often', *communément*), which echoes *gemeen*, a translation of *communis*.

[21] Translator's note: Curley translates this as 'For most things which present themselves in life . . .'.

good,[22] may be reduced to these three: wealth, honor, and pleasure. Thought[23] is so torn[24] by these three it cannot give the slightest thought to any other good.

[4] For as far as pleasure is concerned, the mind is so caught up in it, as if at rest[25] in a good, that it is quite prevented from thinking of anything else. But after the enjoyment of pleasure is past, the greatest sadness follows. If this does not completely engross, still it thoroughly confuses and dulls thought. Thought[26] is also torn[27] greatly by the pursuit of honors and wealth, particularly when[28] the latter is sought only for its own sake, because it is assumed to be the sovereign good.[29]

[5] But thought is far more torn[30] by honor. For this is always assumed to be good through itself and the ultimate end toward which everything is directed. Nor do honor and wealth have, as pleasure does, repentance as a natural consequence. The more each of these is possessed, the more joy is increased, and hence the more we are spurred on to increase them. But if our hopes should chance to be frustrated, we experience the greatest sadness. And

[4] Dans ce qui regarde le plaisir en effet, l'esprit y est retenu autant que s'il trouvait le repos dans quelque bien; il est donc au plus haut point empêché de réfléchir à un autre [bien] ; mais après la jouissance du plaisir suit une extrême tristesse qui, si elle ne retient pas la pensée, du moins la trouble et l'émousse. La pensée est grandement déchirée aussi lorsqu'elle poursuit les honneurs et les richesses, surtout lorsque celles-ci ne sont cherchées que pour elles-mêmes, parce qu'alors elles sont mises à la

[5] Quant à l'honneur, il déchire la pensée bien plus encore : on suppose en effet toujours que c'est un bien en soi, et comme une fin ultime vers quoi tout converge. En outre ces derniers [honneurs et richesses] ne portent pas en eux-mêmes leur propre regret, comme le fait le plaisir ; mais plus on possède de l'un et de l'autre, plus la joie en est accrue ; et par conséquent on est de plus en plus incité à accroître l'un et l'autre : or, si en quelque occasion nous sommes frustrés

on peut l'inférer de leurs actions, estiment comme étant le souverain bien, se ramène à ces trois chefs: les richesses, l'honneur, le plaisir. La pensée [mens] est tellement déchirée par eux qu'il lui est impossible de réfléchir à quelque autre bien.

---

[22] Translator's note: Curley uses 'highest good'.
[23] Translator's note: Curley uses 'mind'.
[24] NS: *afgetrokken*: 'pulled', 'torn' 'diverted', *tirée, arrachée, détournée*. [Translator's note: Curley's chosen term, by contrast, is 'distracted'].
[25] Translator's note: Curley's term is 'peace', but Moreau's French term 'repos' is better rendered as 'rest'.
[26] Translator's note: Curely uses 'The mind'.
[27] NS: *opgehouden* ('interrupted', *interrompue*) *en afgetrokken*.
[28] Spinoza's note A: 'This could be explained more fully and clearly by making a distinction between wealth that is sought for its sake, for the sake of honour, for sensual pleasure, for health, or for the advancement of the sciences and the arts. But this is reserved for its proper place, such a detailed investigation being inappropriate here.'
[29] Translator's note: Curley uses the term 'highest good'.
[30] NS: *afgetrokken en vervoert* ('carried away', *emporté*).

finally, honor is a great impediment:[31] to pursue it, we must direct our lives according to other men's powers of understanding – fleeing what they commonly[32] flee and seeking what they commonly seek.

[6] Since I saw that all of these things stood in the way of my working toward this new institution,[33] indeed were so opposed to it that one or the other must be given up, I was forced to ask what would be more useful to me. For as I say, I seemed to be willing to lose the certain good for the uncertain one. But after I had considered the matter a little, I first found that, if I devoted myself to this new institution, and gave up the old, I would be giving up a good by its nature uncertain (as we can clearly infer from what has been said) for one uncertain not by its nature (for I was seeking a permanent good) but only in respect to its attainment.[34]

[7] By persistent meditation, however, I came to the conclusion that, if only I could deliberate thoroughly, I would be giving up certain evils for a certain good. For I saw that I was in the greatest danger, and that I was forced to seek a remedy with all my strength, however uncertain it might be – like a man suffering from a fatal illness, who, foreseeing certain death unless he employs a remedy, is forced to seek it, however uncertain, with all his

dans notre espoir, alors en prend naissance une extrême tristesse. Enfin l'honneur est une grande source d'empêchement, en ce que pour l'atteindre il faut nécessairement diriger sa vie selon la compréhension des hommes, c'est-à-dire fuir ce qu'ils fuient couramment, et rechercher ce que couramment ils recherchent.

[6] C'est pourquoi, alors que je voyais combien tout cela faisait obstacle à ce que je m'applique à une nouvelle institution; bien plus, combien tout cela y était opposé – à tel point qu'il fallait nécessairement renoncer soit à l'un soit à l'autre; je fus contraint de rechercher ce qui m'était le plus utile; en effet, je l'ai dit, je semblais vouloir abandonner un bien certain pour un bien incertain. Mais, après m'être penché quelque peu sur cette question, je découvris d'abord que si je rejetais ces biens et me disposais à une nouvelle institution, j'allais rejeter un bien qui était incertain par sa nature, comme nous pouvons l'inférer clairement de ce qui vient d'être dit, en échange d'un bien incertain, qui cependant est incertain non point par sa nature (car c'est quelque chose de constant que je cherchais) mais seulement quant à son acquisition.

[7] Or par une méditation assidue je parvins à voir que dans ces conditions, pourvu que je puisse délibérer à fond, j'abandonnais des maux certains pour un bien certain. Je me voyais en effet plongé dans le plus grand péril et contraint de chercher de toutes mes forces un remède, si incertain fût-il; de même un malade souffrant d'une affection mortelle, qui, lorsqu'il prévoit une mort certaine s'il n'utilise un remède, est contraint de le chercher de toutes ses

---

[31] Translator's note: Curley translates this as 'And finally, honor has this great disadvantage . . .'.
[32] NS: *vulgo* is translated twice by *gemenelijk*.
[33] NS: *novum institutum* is given in the margin, and translated by *nieu ooggemerk*.
[34] In the NS, the entire last part of this phrase is part of the parenthesis.

strength. For all his hope lies there. But all those things³⁵ men ordinarily strive for,³⁶ not only provide no remedy to preserve our being, but in fact hinder that preservation, often cause the destruction of those who possess them,³⁷ and always cause the destruction of those who are possessed by them.³⁸

[8] There are a great many examples of people who have suffered persecution to the death on account of their wealth, or have exposed themselves to so many dangers to acquire wealth that they have at last paid the penalty for their folly with their life. Nor are there fewer examples of people who, to attain or defend honor, have suffered most miserably. And there are innumerable examples of people who have hastened³⁹ their death through too much pleasure.

[9] Furthermore, these evils⁴⁰ appeared⁴¹ to have arisen from the fact that all happiness or unhappiness was placed in the quality of the object to which we cling with love. For strife⁴² will never arise on account of what is not loved, nor will there be sadness if it perishes, nor envy if it is possessed by another, nor fear, nor hatred – in a word, no disturbances of the mind. Indeed, all

forces, si incertain soit-il: car c'est en lui que se trouve son espoir tout entier; or tous ces [biens] que la foule poursuit, non seulement ne fournissent aucun remède pour conserver notre être, mais encore l'empêchent: ils causent la perte, souvent, de qui les possède et, toujours, de qui est possédé par eux.

[8] Il existe en effet beaucoup d'exemples d'hommes qui ont souffert la persécution jusqu'à la mort à cause de leurs richesses, ainsi que de gens qui, pour s'enrichir, se sont exposés à tant de périls qu'ils payèrent enfin leur bêtise de leur vie. Il n'y a pas moins d'exemples d'hommes qui ont souffert fort misérablement pour obtenir ou conserver l'honneur. Il existe enfin d'innombrables exemples d'hommes qui ont hâté leur mort par l'excès du plaisir.

[9] Ces maux en outre apparaissaient provenir de ce que notre félicité ou notre infélicité tout entière se trouve en cela seul: la qualité de l'objet auquel nous adhérons par l'amour. En effet, pour un objet qui n'est point aimé, jamais ne naîtront de différends; on n'éprouvera aucune tristesse s'il périt, aucune jalousie si c'est un autre haine, et, pour le dire d'un mot, aucun

---

³⁵ The NS once again translates *omnia* by *alle de dingen*.
³⁶ NS: 'alle die dingen, naar de welken wy gemenelijk tracthen'.
³⁷ Spinoza's note B: 'This is to be demonstrated at greater length'; the NS displaces this note to the following page.
³⁸ The NS again renders *frequenter* by *gemenelijk*, then adds a parenthesis to the first proposition and a precise agent complement in the second: 'en gemenelijk d'oorzaak van d'ondergang der bezitters, (indien men dus mag spreken) en altijt van de genen, die van de rijkdom bezeten worden' ('and are commonly the loss of the possessors, if I may express it in this way, and always of those who are possessed by riches', *et sont communément la perte des possesseurs, si l'on peut s'exprimer ainsi, et toujours de deux qui sont possédés par la richesse*).
³⁹ The NS translates this by the common expression *op de hals halen*.
⁴⁰ *Haec mala*: NS: *deze dingen*.
⁴¹ Translator's note: Curly uses 'seemed'.
⁴² *Lites*: NS: *twisten en geschillen* ('quarrels and differends', *querelles et différends*).

these things happen only in the love of those things that can perish, as all the things we have just spoken of can do.

[10] But love toward the eternal and infinite thing feeds the mind[43] with a joy entirely exempt from sadness. This is greatly to be desired, and to be sought with all our strength. But not without reason did I use these words *if only I could deliberate thoroughly*.[44] For though I perceived these things [NS: this evil] so clearly in my thought, I still could not, on that account, put aside all desire of wealth, pleasure, and glory.

[11] I saw this, however: that so long as my thought was turned toward these objects, it was turned away from those things, and was thinking seriously about the new institution. That was a great comfort to me. For I saw that those evils would not refuse to yield to remedies. And although in the beginning these intervals were rare, and lasted a very short time, nevertheless, after the true good became more and more known to me, the intervals[45] became more frequent and longer – especially after I saw that the acquisition of money, pleasure, and glory are only harmful[46] so long as they are sought for their own sakes, and not as means to other things. But if they are sought as means, then they will have a limit, and will not be harmful at all. On the contrary, they will be of great use in attaining the end on account of which they are sought, as we will show in its place.

trouble de l'esprit; tout cela au contraire survient dans l'amour des choses périssables, comme le sont toutes celles dont nous venons de parler.

[10] Mais l'amour envers une chose éternelle et infinie repaît l'esprit de joie seulement, et cette joie est totalement exempte de tristesse; ce qu'il faut désirer au plus haut point et chercher de toutes ses forces. Pourtant ce n'est pas sans raison que j'ai usé de ces mots 'pourvu que je puisse délibérer à fond'. Si clairement en effet que ma pensée perçût cela, cependant je ne pouvais pour autant renoncer au désir des richesses, au plaisir et à la gloire.

[11] Je voyais seulement que, tant que ma pensée était plongée dans ces réflexions, elle restait détournée de [ces trois objets] et réfléchissait sérieusement à la nouvelle institution; ce qui me fut d'une grande consolation, car je voyais que ces maux n'étaient pas d'une condition telle qu'ils se refusent à céder aux remèdes. Et bien qu'au début ces intervalles aient été rares, et n'aient duré qu'un espace de temps extrêmement limité, au fur et à mesure cependant que j'appris à connaître de mieux en mieux le bien véritable, ces intervalles devinrent plus fréquents et plus longs; surtout après que j'eus vu que l'acquisition de l'argent, le plaisir et la gloire ne sont nuisibles qu'autant qu'on les cherche pour eux-mêmes et non pas comme moyens en vue d'autre chose; mais si on les cherche comme des moyens, ils conservent une certain mesure et ne sont pas nuisibles; bien au contraire: ils contribuent beaucoup à nous conduire à la fin que nous cherchons, comme nous le montrerons en son lieu.

---

[43] The NS indicates in the margin *mens* (and not *animus*, which is nevertheless in the text from the OP) and translates *de geest* in conformity with the coherence of its lexicon.
[44] The NS renders *penitus* from §7 and *serio* from the self-quotation as *gantschelijk*.
[45] OP: *intervalla*; NS: *intermittentia*.
[46] Translator's note: here Curley says that 'money, pleasure, and glory are only obstacles . . .'.

1
The Status of the Prologue

I began by recalling how famous these pages were and how they had inspired numerous commentaries.[1] It is worthwhile noting that their fame can in fact be historically dated. In the history of Spinozism, the *TdIE* did not immediately attract readers' attention: incomplete and unpublished during its author's lifetime, then published without fanfare in the *Posthumous Works*, it remained invisible during the great controversies of the seventeenth and eighteenth centuries, hidden behind those two great and scandalous works, the *TTP*[2]

---

[1] To simplify things, I will henceforth refer to these pages using the collective noun 'prologue' or 'proemium'. Likewise, I will conventionally reserve the adjective 'Spinozan' [*spinozien*] for the themes and expressions that are characteristic of this prologue, while keeping 'Spinozist' [*spinoziste*] for the constituted system of Spinoza. In doing so, I will presuppose neither an identity nor an opposition between the two: this distinction serves only to avoid two long periphrases.

[2] The different parts of the *TTP* have themselves received unequal attention, relative to the exigencies of different polemics: the properly political analyses of the final chapters of the *TTP* – and the *TP* in its entirety – initially had less impact than the analyses of the Holy Scriptures (cf. on this point Jacqueline Lagrée, 'Une traduction française du *Traité théologico-politique* de Spinoza au XVIIIème siècle', *Travaux et documents du Groupe de recherches spinozistes*, 1, 'Lire et traduire Spinoza', PUPS, 1989, pp. 109–23; J. Lagrée et P.-F. Moreau, 'La lecture de la Bible dans le cercle de Spinoza', in *Le Grand Siècle et la Bible*, sous la direction de J.-R. Armogathe [BTLT, vol. VI], Paris: Beauchesne, 1989, pp. 97–116, in particular pp. 97–9). By contrast, in the nineteenth century, this tendency was reversed: the impetus for a specialised science devoted to the Old Testament, established on a new basis, softened the subversive force of the first chapters of the *TTP* but appeared to exclude them from philosophy as such, before making them seem out-dated; while Semler re-edited L. Meyer's book in 1776 with a new preface in the context of his own critical textual enterprise, and while Hegel mentioned Spinoza's research into the Holy Scriptures – while treating them as part of a specialised science of which it was no longer necessary to speak – nineteenth-century *Bibelwissenschaft*, sure both of itself and of its method, erased all

and the *Ethics*.³ The only commentators who accorded it any importance – and who did so, moreover, without explicitly citing it – were Tschirnhaus,⁴ who transmitted certain of its qualities to the *Aufklärung*, and Van Balen.⁵ Yet both of these commentators considered only the text's methodological elements. Bayle failed to mention it,⁶ and it was through Bayle's refutation that Enlightenment thinkers learnt to read Spinoza. The situation changed

   memory of previous research; to the point that Karppe, while himself well-informed, could write in 1902: 'Spinoza has almost never been studied from this perspective [that of biblical criticism]. On the one hand, the philosopher has been unjustly celebrated over and against the exegete and the critic: that is, Spinoza's philosophical works have to a degree meant the *Tractatus* has been marginalised. The general relations between the *Tractatus* and Spinoza's philosophical works have been well-studied, as have the political conceptions – not to mention the conceptions of religious philosophy – that this philosophy contains. Yet everything in this treatise that concerns biblical criticism and exegesis has been almost entirely neglected', *Essais de critique d'histoire de la philosophie*, Paris: Alcan, 1902, pp. 143–4.
³ Similarly, the first polemics bore above all on the unity of substance affirmed in Book I and on what was thought to be immoral in Book IV. It is only with Hemsterhuis that we find a real attempt to take into account the themes from Book II (cf. P. Vernière, *Spinoza et la pensée française avant la Révolution*, Paris: PUF, 1954, p. 669). On Hemsterhuis, see the recent volume *Frans Hemsterhuis. Waarneming en werkelijkheid*. Uitgegeven, ingeleid en van aantekeningen voorzien door M. J. Petry, Baarn: Ambo, 1990, in the collection 'Geschiedenis van de wijsbegeerte in Nederland'. Allow me to point out once and for all the importance and usefulness of this collection for whomsoever may be interested in the intellectual history of the Netherlands, in particular as regards Spinoza's contemporaries and his reception.
⁴ In the last letter he wrote to Spinoza, Tschirnhaus asks when the treatise on method will be published. In his *Medicina Mentis*, Tschirnhaus uses the *TdIE* in an original way, but without naming it. See the works of J.-P. Wurtz, S. Wollgast, E. Winter, P. Cristofolini; cf. my review of Wurtz's translation of the *Medicina Mentis*, *Bulletin de bibliographie spinoziste*, III, pp. 13–14. On the subject of Tschirnhaus' influence on Wolff, specifically on this question of method, the reader can refer to the classic work of Mariano Campo, *Cristiano Wolff e il razionalismo precritico*, Milan: Pubblicazioni dell'Università Cattolica del S. Cuore, series 1, vol. XXX, 1939, reprinted in Christian Wolff, *Gesammelte Werke*, III. Abt.: *Materialien und Dokumente*, B 9, Hildesheim: Olms, 1980, vol. I, chaps. 1 through 3.
⁵ P. Van Balen, *De Verbetering der Gedagten ontrent waarheit en valsheit, of waare logica*, Rotterdam, 1684. On Van Balen, see M. J. Van den Hoven, *Petrus van Balen en Spinoza over de verbetering van het verstand*, MVHS 55, Leiden: Brill, 1988. Van den Hoven also published an edition of annotated extracts (Baarn: Ambo, 1988, in the collection 'Geschiedenis van de wijsbegeerte in Nederland'). There, he points out that Van Balen only cites Spinoza once regarding the *Hebrew Grammar*. Indeed he praises him, but does not name him.
⁶ Cf. Pierre Bayle, *Ecrits sur Spinoza*, choisis et présentés, F. Charles-Daubert and P.-F. Moreau, Paris: Berg International, 1983.

in the nineteenth century, however, and what is remarkable is that this change was not initially a consequence of any progress in erudition.[7] It was Spinoza's importance for philosophy that his first readers had remarked upon – and even then they did so more in terms of his philosophy's intensity than its content. Certainly, up to this point interest in Spinozism had been doubled by a fascination for Spinoza as an individual, including among detractors of his doctrine. Yet this fascination was tied to the figure of the 'virtuous atheist'. Then, following an inversion of interpretative horizons during the *Pantheismusstreit*, it became linked to the figure of Spinoza as a 'mystic drunk on God'. These two figures resemble each other to the extent that they both bring out Spinoza's effective positivity, whether this be the positivity of his conduct or his mysticism. By contrast, from the nineteenth century onwards, a new schema for adhering to Spinozism was established, which made his human authenticity appear as the source of what made him endearing. In Spinoza's writings, readers found the value of suffering, of inner conflict, but also the possibility of overcoming them. The prologue to the *TdIE* plays a key role in establishing this new image, and its promotion in the history of essential Spinozist texts is no doubt linked to this shift.

It is in *The World as Will and as Representation* that we find the the first mention of just how extraordinary the opening pages of the Treatise are.[8] At the end of the Fourth Book, Schopenhauer says that he believes he has shown for the first time *in the abstract* the essence of renunciation and of voluntary mortification; and yet, he adds, this essence had already been grasped intuitively and expressed in action by the saints and the ascetics, and that whoever sought to understand this essence must come to know it by way of examples drawn from experience and reality (examples that are, he clarifies, quoting from the last phrase of the *Ethics*, very rare). Schopenhauer then proceeds to name some of these examples; and between Madame Guyon and the *Confessions of a Beautiful Soul* included in

---

[7] Even if it is undeniable that the new possibility of accessing the ensemble of Spinoza's texts – a possibility that existed since Paulus and the editions that followed him, right up to Van Vloten's edition – played the role of a substrata, if not a motor, of these new readings. On the Paulus edition, on which Hegel collaborated, see the study of H.-C. Lucas, 'Hegel et l'édition de Spinoza par Paulus', *Cahiers Spinoza*, IV (1983), pp. 127–38.

[8] This was in opposition to the remainder of the text: 'in jenem herrlichen Eingang zu seiner sehr ungenügenden Abhandlung', *Die Welt as Wille und Vorstellung*, I, IV, § 68 (*Sämtliche Werke*, hrg. von Wolfgang Frhr v. Löhneysen, Frankfurt a. M.: Insel-Cotta, 1960, vol. 1, p. 523).

Wilhelm Meister, he includes the life of Spinoza.[9] To understand Spinoza's biography, however, Schopenhauer argues that its secrets must be unlocked using the introduction to the *TdIE*, which Schopenhauer recommends as 'the strongest means' he knows of 'for calming the storm of the passions'.[10] The *proemium* is thus given pride of place and becomes the object of philosophical meditation; it is said to be 'sublime' (*herrlich*), but less so for reasons of its systematic content and more for its capacity to communicate a vital moment in the confrontation with suffering. Schopenhauer's reading becomes the new point of departure for interpreting Spinoza's text. It is only after his intervention that the great philological explanations and commentaries on Spinoza come into alignment:[11] in one way or another, all of them – even if they do not share Schopenhauer's opposition to the rest of Spinoza's system – will reread the first pages of the *TdIE* in the 'passionate' register that we have just delineated. This is the case with Freudenthal: after noting that 'the *TdIE* is not one of Spinoza's most important works' since almost all of what it contains can be found elsewhere – and sometimes in a different form – Freudenthal adds that it is nevertheless one of Spinoza's most moving works, and that it allows us 'an in-depth look into his soul and into the motives for his actions'.[12] Gebhardt writes that 'nowhere else in Spinoza's work do we find the philosopher in such an unmediated form – in all of his sublimity and purity of his feelings';[13] and he follows this statement by citing Schopenhauer's formula. Even Alfred Wenzel, whose work *Die Weltanschauung Spinozas*

---

[9] 'Gewissermaßen könnte man als ein hierhergehöriges Beispiel sogar die bekannte französische Biographie Spinozas betrachten', ibid. Similarly, Goethe's text is only mentioned by way of the reference to the woman he took for his model – Suzanne de Klettenberg – and of whom he speaks directly in *Dichtung und Warheit*.

[10] 'Das wirksamste, mir bekkant gewordene Besänftigungsmittel des Sturms des Leidenschaften', ibid.

[11] The first work entirely devoted to the *TdIE* is Elbogen's (1898), but all of the great scholars of the end of the nineteenth century and the beginning of the twentieth devote a chapter to it.

[12] 'Aber sie ist eine der liebenswürdigsten Schriften Spinozas, weil sie uns einen tiefen Einblick in seine Seele und die Motive seines Handelns tun läßt', *Spinoza Leben und Lehre. Zweiter Teil: Die Lehre Spinozas auf Grund des Nachlasses von J. Freudenthal bearbeitet von Carl Gebbardt*, Heidelberg: Carl Winter, 1927, p. 96.

[13] 'Es gibt wohl kaum eine Stelle in den Schriften Spinozas, in der uns der Philosoph in der ganzen Erhabenheit und Lauterkeit seiner Gesinnung so unmittelbar entgegentritt wie in der Einleitung des tractatus de intellectus emendatione', *Spinozas Abhandlung über die Verbesserung des Verstandes. Eine entwicklungsgeschichtliche Untersuchung*, Heidelberg: Carl Winter, 1905, p. 54.

is devoted to the system in its totality, begins by remarking that 'the consoling force of Spinoza's writings has not yet been exhausted'. He then proceeds to cite the 'Prologue' in its entirety, and comments on it as follows: 'I could not stop myself from inserting here this entire passage since it permits us a close look into the soul of our philosopher, and constitutes in many ways the best commentary that exists on his writings. Such a confession could not have been written by an enemy of man, by a fanatic [Schwärmer] foreign to the world, or by an ideologist contemptuous of action. Spinoza knew life. He had passed through the fire. And a long time was needed, as he himself admits, for his wounds to be healed. This is why his poignant confessions are at the same time a human document of exemplary importance.'[14] A look into the soul, confessions, wounds: we are here in a register where thought is in close communication with its roots in what is most intimate and painful in life. A certain quality of lived experience is supposed to ground the truth of what is subsequently expressed theoretically, at the same time as it speaks more directly than geometry does to the reader's soul. Historiographers will continue down this path, reading the prologue as an immediate and authentic document of human suffering; the only additions they will make will come from their erudition. This interpretation will then be extended in three directions: the search for a biographical origin for the text; the discernment of its conceptual and (more recently) rhetorical influences; and finally the attempt to relate it to the rest of the system. I will return to this further on, but it is worthwhile pausing for a moment to consider the meaning of Schopenhauer's discovery. It was doubtless not by chance that a philosopher who accorded such a decisive place to suffering and to the question of its overcoming was drawn to the text that makes Spinozism irreducible to

---

[14] 'Ich konnte nicht unterlassen, diesen ganzen Passus hier anzuführen, weil er uns gestattet, einen tiefen Blick in die Seele unseres Philosophen zu tun und in mancher Hinsicht der beste Kommentar zu seinen Schriften ist. Solche Selbstbekenntnisse schreibt kein Menschenfeind, kein weltfremder Schwärmer, kein tatenverachtender Ideologe. Spinoza kannte das Leben. Er hatte mitten im Feuer gestanden. Und lange hat es, wie er selbst verrät, gedauert, bis die Wunden, die er davongetragen, vernarbten. Daher sind jene liebenswürdigen Selbstbekenntnisse zugleich documents humains von typischer Bedeutung', *Die Weltanschauung Spinozas*, 1 (einziger) Band: *Spinozas Lehre von Gott, von der menschlichen Erkenntis und von dem Wesen der Dinge*, Leipzig, 1907, Aalen: Neudruck Scientia, 1983, p. 24. I cannot agree in this context that the term *liebenswürdig* (a term used both by Freudenthal and by Wenzel, like the expression 'a look into the soul') should be translated by 'lovable' [*aimable*]. The formula on *die tröstende Kraft* is found on page 18.

an intellectual pantheism.¹⁵ Before this, the text was available, of course, yet it remained literally unreadable for those interpreters who began from the principle that Spinozism reduced creatures to the status of illusions and dissolved them in the unique substance.¹⁶ The philosophy itself thus produced the means of its own reception. But there was a price to be paid for this: on the one hand, the intensity of Spinoza's text seems to demand an explanation; it seems to communicate directly with its author's life¹⁷ and with the reader's conscience; on the other hand, Schopenhauer was also the philosopher who criticised Spinoza for having identified *causa* and *ratio* and who reproached him for his 'metaphysical optimism'.¹⁸ Together, these

---

¹⁵ On Schopenhauer and Spinoza, see the survey of the principal texts in Max Grunewald, *Spinoza in Deutschland*, Berlin, 1897, Aalen: Neudruck Scientia, 1986, V. Abschnitt, § 109, pp. 247–53, as well as Samuel Rappaport's dissertation, *Schopenhauer und Spinoza*, Halle/Wittemberg, 1899. There is nothing to be found in the book by Hong Han-Ding, *Spinoza und die deutsche Philosophie*, Aalen: Neudruck Scientia, 1989, nor in the otherwise illuminating exposition by Manfred Walther from the Colloque de Fontenay, 'Spinoza en Allemagne: Histoire des problèmes et de la recherche', *Cahiers de Fontenay*, 36–38 (1985): *Spinoza entre Lumières et Romantisme*, pp. 13–44. Italian commentators have often developed useful and detailed comparisons between Spinozist and Schopenhauerian motifs, in particular T. Moretti-Costanzi, *Spinoza*, Rome: Editrice Universitas, 1946, p. 173 sq; G. Semerari, *I Problemi dello Spinozismo*, Trani: Vecchi, 1952, chap. II, pp. 94, 103, 109–10.

¹⁶ To give but one example among others, one that nevertheless comes from a significant historian in the history of Spinozism: 'Aber nach Spinoza existiert das Endliche als Endliche gar nicht', J.-E. Erdmann, *Malebranche, Spinoza und die Skeptiker und Mystiker des siebzenten Jahrhunderts*, Leipzig: Eduard Frantzen, 1836, p. 64. From the other side of the Rhine, an extreme (and polemical version) can be found in Nourrisson's work: 'Cependant, imaginons que l'on étudie ce que c'est que cette substance unique. Encore un coup, que devient le monde? Un tissu régulier d'apparences. Que devient l'homme? Un ridicule et fantasmagorique Sosie, pas même un phénomène substantifié', *Spinoza et le naturalisme contemporain*, Paris: Didier, 1866, p. 232.

¹⁷ On Giordano Bruno and Spinoza, Schopenhauer speaks of their 'kümmerliches Daseyn und Sterben', *Die Welt . . .*, Anhang: 'Kritik der Kantischen Philosophie', vol. 1, p. 571.

¹⁸ This is not the place to summarise everything that Schopenhauer said about Spinoza; all the same, and despite theoretical divergences, we can note the hagiographic tone of the evocation of Spinoza in the conclusion to *On the Will in Nature*. Like Cleanthes, Spinoza knew how to prefer truth to institutions, even if he had to win his daily bread by the sweat of his brow. This is a way of opposing the authenticity of his life to the inauthenticity of the lives of anti-Schopenhauerian professors. It also responds to the temptation of reading the intensity of the *TdIE* in light of its author's authenticity: 'For assuredly he who makes love to this nude beauty, to this fascinating syren, to this portionless bride, will have to forego the good fortune of becoming a Government and University professor. [. . .] Better to grind spectacle-glasses like Spinoza or draw water like Cleanthes.'

two features fail to prepare the reader for thinking the intensity identified in the *proemium* theoretically.[19]

In any event, the following point warrants reflection: it is as much for reasons of its tone as its content that this prologue has been inscribed in the history of philosophy. Yet, we should not be too hasty here and see in Spinoza's text the manifestation of an extra-philosophical enthusiasm. The mark of a properly philosophical text cannot be limited to its conceptual content; its order of reasons can also be expressed through its tone, the situations it evokes, or the genres it reprises and reworks. A Platonic dialogue uses different procedures for establishing truth than Aristotle's didactic expositions; and it is not insignificant that Cartesian thought is presented in the form of *Principles* or *Meditations*. When reading doxographies, one often has the impression that all of these genres are equivalent and ultimately nothing but more or less suitable substitutes for dogmatic treatises. If we ignore the epigones, the style of philosophical expression is, on the contrary, essential to what it expresses, and there can be systematic reasons for choosing such-and-such a form of exposition for a system. If philosophical innovation does not always occur by introducing new concepts, it can also occur by accentuating different aspects of a well-known problem, by changing the tone with which a certain topos is treated, or by establishing a new relation between a series of concepts and their extra-philosophical correlates. The way in which these novelties emerge in thought can be based on the *form* of an inaugural piece of writing just as much as on its *content*.

For these reasons, my reading of the 'Prologue' will begin with these formal features: it is by evaluating them that we will have the best chance of understanding the register in which this text was written. I will therefore make a certain number of observations without rushing to interpret them,

---

[19] To complete the portrait, it would also be necessary to cite Schopenhauer's attitude during the affair of Kuno Fischer's destitution ('Das Ministerium in Baden hat Recht getan dem Menschen das Handwerk zu legen'), an attitude that gives a certain flavour to the preceding quotation. The man Schopenhauer sees as 'the last Hegelian and martyr for his lack of judgement' is guilty in his eyes of having sought not the man in Spinoza, but the speculative truth of the system; and, moreover, for having conceived this system from a Hegelian perspective: this is precisely what proves the difference between the two interpretative aims – aims expressed quite brutally in Schopenhauer's letter to Julius Frauenstadt from 28 January 1854 (*Gesammelte Briefe*, hrg. v. Arthur Hübscher, Bonn: Bouvier Verlag, 1987, 2nd edition, letter No. 316, pp. 329–31). On this matter, cf. H. Falkenheim, 'Spinoza und Kuno Fischer', *Chronicon Spinozanum*, II (1922), pp. 220–32, as well as Thomas E. Willey, 'The Harassed Hegelian', in *Back to Kant: The Revival of Kantianism in German Social and Historical Thought, 1860–1914*, Detroit: Wayne State University Press, 1978, pp. 59–63.

remaining for as long as possible at the level of reading. How does Spinoza express himself in these pages? What scene does he describe? Where does he draw its elements from? Thus: the tone, the situation, the substrata.

1. The Tone

First of all, it is necessary to underscore the particular *tone* struck by the *pro-emium*, both in its relation to the work it introduces – the *Treatise on the Emendation of the Intellect* – and in relation to the rest of Spinoza's œuvre. The text's tone can be characterised by three traits: *simplicity*, *tension* and *singularity*.

The tone is manifest above all in the text's lexicon: in these pages the great concepts of Spinozist philosophy – or at least those conveyed using specialist terms – are nowhere to be found. There is no mention of substance, of attributes, or of modes, of immanent cause or of the idea of the idea. Certainly, nothing can prevent a commentator from finding these concepts in an implicit form in the text, or relating the phrases from which these concepts are absent to passages from Spinoza's œuvre where, by contrast, these concepts are at work. But nothing can contradict the following radical observation: no technical term disturbs this text's smooth surface; better still, no term that has an exclusively philosophical meaning is to be found here, not even one from outside of Spinoza's system. Some commentators have sought signs of Descartes' influence in these pages, or the influence of other philosophers.[20] Yet whatever the truth of these theses, all of the prologue's words belong to the most common form of Latin;[21] and the simplicity of its words corresponds to the simplicity of the objects it speaks of: life and goods, sadness and joy, life and happiness. Everything the text's words speak of can be interpreted, at least superficially, by a reader who is not yet a professional philosopher. Such a reader can interpret the prologue in relation to his or her own life, or his or her own literary culture. To be convinced of the originality of this trait, one need only recall that what follows in the *Treatise* draws on, at least implicitly, a mathematical culture. Moreover, the *Treatise* will discuss in technical terms theses that originate in Cartesian or Scholastic philosophy, and it will introduce terminological distinctions that

---

[20] For Descartes, cf. below our reference to Elbogen's analyses.
[21] Even the expression *summum bonum* is much less technical than 'sovereign good' [*souverain bien*] is in English – all the more so since it is introduced at the beginning of a series of terms that progressively aligns it with *bonum* and *verum bonum*, which allows the reader to hear in the expression the two simple words that compose it rather than the fixed conceptual term suggested by the English translation.

still divide Spinoza's interpreters. In the prologue, by contrast, the problems evoked are those that every reader has experienced: wealth, pleasure and power – both their enjoyment and their loss, along with the joy and sadness that these goods engender. It is therefore not simply a matter of lexical sobriety (Spinoza's famous 'scarcity of words'[22]), nor of sobriety at the level of presentation (a concern for popularisation). It might be said that from the outset the text's vocabulary and what it evokes place the reader in the domain of the *familiar*. By the term 'familiar', I mean a world that is at once vague yet close to each potential reader. When we read these passages, we immediately understand what they are talking about, without requiring any particular education (though this does not mean no education at all). This trait suffices to distinguish these pages from both the philological discussions of the *TTP*'s first chapter, as from the demonstrations from Book I of the *Ethics*, as well as from the tightly argued analyses of political regimes at the end of the *TTP* or the end of the *TP*. This familiarity is the mark of the deliberate presence of the *communis vita* evoked in the text's first line – a domain that is presupposed as a point of reference and complemented by a language that corresponds to it. This *communis vita* is common in the sense that it is woven from events lived in common, but also in the sense that it is something that everyone shares – or that is at least shared by the author and reader. The former therefore speaks to the latter only of what both are familiar with, even if the author will proceed to draw consequences from these events that the reader is not yet aware of. It could be said that this familiarity is a sort of universality in a practical state.

This relation to the reader leads us to a second particularity of the tone used in these eleven paragraphs: namely, their extraordinary tension. The familiarity of what these paragraphs convey in no way softens the violence of the vision. On the contrary, it only makes this violence more insistent. Spinoza seems to want to communicate to the reader the feeling of making a final, decisive choice, but also a sense of extreme danger and extreme determination. The passionate nature of these paragraphs[23] contrasts with

---

[22] On this topic, cf. the admirable works of F. Akkerman, in particular 'Spinoza's tekort an woorden', *Mededelingen XXXVI vanwege het Spinozahuis*, Leiden: Brill, 1977; for the French translation, see A. van de Lindt and J. Lagrée, 'La pénurie des mots de Spinoza', *Travaux et documents du Groupe de recherches spinozistes*, 1, 'Lire et traduire Spinoza', PUPS, 1989, pp. 9–37.

[23] On this point F. Pollock speaks of an 'ardent disquiet' to characterise one of the striking traits that in his eyes most distinguishes the *TdIE* from the *Discourse on Method* – two texts whose kinship he elsewhere underscores (*Spinoza: His Life and Philosophy*, London: Duckworth, 1880, 1912, 2nd edition, p. 116).

the simplicity of their vocabulary. Everything happens as if common life, at once so close and so present, reveals, as soon as one interrogates it – even minimally – the worst of all possible perils and anxieties; as if the simplest words had only to be combined in a grammatical game of restrictives and superlatives to make the scenes evoked seem inescapable. On a number of occasions in these paragraphs, what is at stake are the risks that the narrator has run; indeed, the situation described is identified with a mortal illness. What makes this situation even more intense is that it is linked to the narrator's responsibility: the mortal illness is described as if its outcome were not entirely fixed in advance, since the illness will be fatal only if the narrator makes the wrong choice. The process is therefore described at the moment the narrator must make a final decision:[24] everything has been compromised, yet everything can still be saved, for it is indeed a question of life or death. This impression is again reinforced by the abundance of superlatives concerning quality and quantity, an abundance that is remarkable considering how economical Spinoza's style usually is. In addition to *summum bonum*, there appears successively *summa laetitia*,[25] *summa felicitas*[26] (along with the threat of being deprived of it!), *summa tristitia*[27] and *summum periculum*,[28] for which it is necessary to seek a remedy *summis viribus*.[29] As for examples of persecution and death, to which perishable goods lead, they are *permulta*, *neque pauciora* and *innumeranda*.[30] And when we suffer in this way, it is *miserrime*.[31] We should also add the play of the exclusive adjectives and pronouns *omnis*, *solus* and *totus*, whose frequency reinforces the impression that there exists no middle ground: in the space of a few lines, the first paragraph alone states that *all*[32] of the goods or events of common life are vain and futile; that *all*[33] things that cause fear do so only by virtue of their action on the soul; and that when the true good is found it will be necessary to reject *all*[34] the

---

[24] 'Veluti aeger lethali morbo laborans, qui ubi mortem certam praevidet, ni adhibeatur remedium, illud ipsum, quamvis incertum, summis viribus cogitur quaerere', § 7, G II, p. 7, ll. 2–5 [*TdIE* 7; *CWS* I, 9].
[25] § 1, G II, p. 5, ll. 15–16 [*TdIE* 1; *CWS* I, 7].
[26] § 2, G II, p. 1, ll. 20–1 and again at ll. 22–3 [*TdIE* 2; *CWS* I, 7].
[27] § 4, G II, p. 6, l. 5 and again at ll. 15–16 [*TdIE* 4; *CWS* I, 8].
[28] § 7, G II, p. 6, l. 32 [*TdIE* 7; *CWS* I, 9].
[29] § 7, G II, p. 7, l. 1 and again at l. 4 [*TdIE* 7; *CWS* I, 9].
[30] § 8, G II, p. 7, respectively ll. 9, 13 and 15 [*TdIE* 8; *CWS* I, 9].
[31] § 9, G II, p. 7, l. 14 [*TdIE* 9; *CWS* I, 9].
[32] § 1, G II, p. 5, l. 7 [*TdIE* 1; *CWS* I, 7].
[33] § 1, G II, p. 5. ll. 9–10 [*TdIE* 1; *CWS* I, 7].
[34] 'Rejectis caeteris omnibus', § 1, G II, p. 5, l. 14 [*TdIE* 1; *CWS* I, 7].

others. The same term *omnia* is used throughout the following paragraphs,[35] where it is said that the mind will be moved *only* by the true good ('a quo *solo*'[36]). As for the ultimate remedy, it is said that the sick person's hope is *entirely* invested in it ('in eo *tota* ejus spes est sita'[37]). A more complex formula takes up *totus* and *solus* in order to tie felicity and infelicity to the nature of love: '*tota* felicitas, atque infelicitas, in hoc *solo* sita est . . .';[38] a series of adjectives and adverbs – also exclusive but this time negative – evacuate what is not related to love (*nunquam . . . nulla . . . nullus . . . nullae*).[39] This tendency continues right up to the extraordinary phrase that states that love for an eternal and infinite thing nourishes the soul *only* with joy (or with joy *exclusively*, *sola laetitia*), that this joy is exempt from *all* sadness (*omnis tristitiae*), and that it is something one must seek with *all* one's might (*totis viribus*).[40] This formula, which brings together so many terms of exclusion, seems to negate the possibility of any outcome that resembles a mere half measure or compromise. The reader is thus placed in an all-or-nothing situation, and Spinoza explicitly underscores that this is indeed the case. It is necessary to renounce either one or the other[41] of the two possible ends; and this choice is presented as a painful choice since the narrator feels within himself the impossibility of renunciation. It is clear that the tone adds to the text's arguments: it determines that this is not an abstract problem but the site of a vital decision whose inescapability is made obvious to the reader and associated with the narrator's anxiety through all of the effects of the text's *mise en scène*.

Finally, such an effect would be much more difficult to achieve were the

---

[35] § 5, G II, p. 6, l. 11 [*TdIE* 5; *CWS* I, 8]; § 6, p. 6, l. 21 [*TdIE* 6; *CWS* I, 8]; § 7, p. 7, l. 5 [*TdIE* 7; *CWS* I, 9]; § 9, p. 7, l. 22 [*TdIE* 9; *CWS* I, 9]; and once again at l. 23 [*TdIE* 9; *CWS* I, 9]; and at § 10: 'omnem avaritiam, libidinem atque gloriam deponere', G II, p. 7. ll. 29–30 [*TdIE* 10; *CWS* I, 10].

[36] § 1, G II, p. 5, l. 13 [*TdIE* 1; *CWS* I, 7].

[37] § 7, G II, p. 7, ll. 4–5 [*TdIE* 7; *CWS* I, 9].

[38] 'Videbantur porro ex eo haec orta esse mala, quod tota felicitas, aut infelicitas in hoc solo sita est; videlicet, in qualitate objecti, cui adhaeremus amore', § 9, G II, p. 7, ll. 16–18 [*TdIE* 9; *CWS* I, 9].

[39] 'Nam propter illud, quod non amatur, nunquam orientur lites, nulla erit tristitia, si pereat, nulla invidia, is ab alio possideatur, nullus timor, nullum odium, et, ut verbo dicam, nulla commotiones animi', § 9 G II, p. 7, ll. 19–22 [*TdIE* 9; *CWS* I, 9].

[40] 'Sed amor erga rem aeternam, et infinitam *sola* laetitia pascit animum, ipsaque *omnis* tristitiae est expers; quod valde est desiderandum, *totisque* viribus quaerendum', § 10, G II, p. 7, ll. 24–6 [*TdIE* 10; *CWS* I, 9].

[41] 'Ab uno, aut altero necessario esset abstinendum', § 6, G II, p. 6, ll. 22–3 [*TdIE* 6; *CWS* I, 8].

narrative presented using the cold objectivity of the third person. It is therefore necessary to take into account the final characteristic of the text's tone, one that is indicated from its very beginning: we are here in the presence of a first-person narrative. The personal pronoun appears in the accusative mode from the second word of the first sentence: 'postquam *me* experientia docuit'. Incidentally, this is a familiar expression in Spinoza, since the same formula appears often in the *Ethics* and in the *TTP*, albeit in a depersonalised form: 'experientia docet', 'experientia et ratio docent', etc. The twist that the *TdIE* gives this formula places the emphasis on the person learning the lesson; it is no longer an abstract statement, accessible to all. We can now discern its function: it gives a name to the singularity. The function of the 'I' is not simply to present a series of events by indicating who lived them and who is narrating them; it brings even more powerfully into focus the specific speech situation and the singularity tied to it. To be convinced of this specificity, it suffices to survey the rest of Spinoza's writings. This is not, in fact, the only place in his œuvre that Spinoza says 'I'; it is not even the only place he says 'I' in the past tense. But in no other instance does the past tense of the first person have the same tonality that it possesses here. Typically, these first-person statements do not implicate the singularity of the person speaking. When Spinoza says 'I' in the *Ethics*, his statements have two very precise functions: an assertive function in the Definitions and a re-assertive one in the Scholia. The Definitions rarely indicate a personal choice, nor do they presuppose the past of the person who presents them: they simply make explicit certain technical choices.[42] These choices certainly have important

---

[42] The assertive function states what will be used in the chain of demonstrations; the re-assertive function underlines the validity of what has been demonstrated in the face of potential adversaries. This distinction seems to translate into a difference between two ways of indicating the first-person singular in Latin: by the mere verbal flexion in the first case, by an explicit pronoun in the second. The 'I' appears in the inflexion of the verbs: *intelligo* (for example, all of the Definitions from Book I, except Definitions 2 and 7: 'per causam sui, intelligo', 'per substantiam intelligo', etc.); *dico* (Explanation to Definition 6: 'dico absolute infinitum, non autem in suo genere . . .'); *dubito* (which introduces not a doubt but a certainty, since it is in the negative form: 'non dubito quin . . .', Scholium 2, Proposition 8). It also appears in all of the letters whenever the author is stating his opposition to those who forge fictions – yet here the *ego* is hardly subjective since it is characterised only by the *demonstravi* that mark out the distinction between author and addressee (Scholium 1 to Proposition 15: 'ego saltem satis clare, meo quidem judicio, demonstravi . . .'; the context shows that the formula 'meo quidem judicio' in no way nuances the validity of the Demonstration: on the contrary, it determines the *satis* of the reassertion; the reservation ultimately bears only on the time that it is necessary to devote to persuading those for whom

metaphysical consequences, yet they are presented to the reader without feeling and with the sobriety proper to the geometrical method.[43] As for the 'I' of the Scholia, this 'I' does not mark a singularity in the form of a site of passion and torment, but rather the singularity of a deliberate demarcation: *I have demonstrated, I have already said, in my judgement*. Rather than introduce new arguments, it reprises those that others either do not want to – or cannot – understand. The 'I' has the same function in the *TTP*.[44] Here it would be necessary only to add an apotropaic *I*, where the avowal of ignorance and incomprehension serves more to refuse discussion than to indicate the humility or weakness of the person writing. It might be thought

demonstrative clarity does not suffice); or when it is a case of recalling that the author has already responded to the arguments that could be opposed to him (same Scholium: 'Verum enim vero, si quis recte attendat, me ad haec jam respondisse comperiet' – this addition responds precisely to the *meo quidem judicio* from the preceding page: the uncertainty ultimately bears only on the attention that the interlocutor devotes to verifying what has already been established; the intervention of the *I* is therefore not a sign of a delay in the demonstration: it marks no more than a para-demonstrative detour, which ends when the writer places the uncertainty back on those who are responsible for it: 'So the weapon they aim at us, really they turn against themselves', '*quare telum, quod in nos intendunt, in se ipsos revera conjiciunt*'; it should not be surprising that the Scholium ends with 'satis superque'): in total, the *Ethics* count forty-nine pronouns in the first-person singular, of which nine are *ego*, thirty-five *me* and five *mihi*, as we learn from the useful instruments developed by M. Guéret, A. Robinet, and P. Tombeur (*Spinoza. Ethica. Concordances, index, listes de fréquences, tables comparatives*, Louvain-la-Neuve: CETEDOC, 1977, p. 378, col. 1 and 2).

[43] This is why I cannot share André Robinet's formulations from the study that closes the volume cited in the previous note: 'Car qui parle dans l'*Ethique*? quelle est cette émergence de la première personne, que nous receuillons avec tant d'ampleur, *ordine informatico*, mais dont le statut n'est nulle part prononcé, *ordine geometrico*?', ibid., 'Postface', p. 529). These verbs and pronouns cannot all be reduced to the emergence of the 'conatus de l'individu Spinoza' or of 'la substance en chair et en os'. Even with respect to the series that we have designated as being re-assertive, while it may mark a state of impatience, this feeling is theoretical, not psychological.

[44] We find the same assertive function in the *TTP*: it states in the first person definitions or equivalencies: 'By *God's guidance* I understand the fixed and immutable order of nature, *or* the connection of natural things' ('per Dei directionem intelligo fixum illum et immutabilem naturae ordinem', *TTP*, chap. III, G III, p. 45, ll. 34–5 [*TTP* III; *CWS* II, 112]). We also find the same re-assertive function: the personal pronoun recalls what the author has demonstrated and allows him to take his distance from those who disqualify themselves by denying what is obvious, as well as from those who 'extort from Scripture Aristotelian rubbish and their own inventions. Nothing seems to me more ridiculous' ('nam nihil aliud curaverunt, quam nugas aristotelicas et sua propria figmenta ex Scriptura extorquere; quo mihi quidem nihil magis riduculum videtur', *TTP*, chap. I, G III, p. 19, ll. 31–3; A, p. 36 [*TTP* I; *CWS* II, 82]).

that the singularity is reinforced when Spinoza speaks in the past tense: he does so at moments where he is retracing the history of an interpretation[45] and even of the abandonment of a hypothesis that he himself had previously adopted ('to this opinion I myself once inclined', he says on the subject of the historical circumstances of the Decalogue, and now I think that it is impossible without doing violence to the text).[46] Elsewhere he also admits to uncertainties, delays and difficulties (as in his last letter to Tschirnhaus[47]). Nonetheless, this past is the past of an objective chronology of research, and these delays are not presented as if they put into question the vital situation of the subject who experiences them. This past is either reabsorbed into a choice that subsequently grounds knowledge (one interpretative solution is chosen over another for such-and-such a passage of the Scriptures), or it is destined to be so reabsorbed (once the theory of motion is 'put in order', nothing will remain of this provisional state of uncertainty). In short, this is a purely chronological past, devoid of any theoretical or affective depth. By contrast, at the beginning of the *TdIE*, the past brings with it a supplementary trait: it has not been reabsorbed; it preserves the full weight of its status as a challenge, obstacle, or provocation. Here, the past fact remains constitutive of the present. It retains an implicit potentiality, and it is from recalling the past that the philosophical project draws its force. It is also how this project implicitly communicates the force of the past to the reader, insofar as a narrative of conversion is also and always at the same time a call

---

[45] 'I know that previously I have noted other things of this kind, but at the moment I cannot recall them', he says with respect to alterations of the biblical text ('et ad hunc modum scio me antehac alia notavisse, quae impraesentiarum non occurrunt', *TTP*, chap. IX, G III, p. 136, A, p. 36 [*TTP* IX; *CWS* II, 218].

[46] Certain Jews think that the words of the Decalogue were not proffered by God: 'Quod ego etiam aliquando suspicatus sum [. . .]. Attamen nisi Scripturae vim inferre velimus, omnino concedendum est, Israelitas veram vocem audivisse', *TTP*, chap. I, G III, p. 18 [*TTP* I; *CWS* II, 80]. Likewise, in the *Hebrew Grammar*, Spinoza evokes a hypothesis concerning accents that he has since abandoned: 'Equidem credo hoc non sine aliqua causa factum fuisse, imo aliquando animo volvebam, num eorum inventor eosdem introduxerat [. . .] ad animi affectus exprimendum. [. . .] Suspicatus igitur sum, num Hebraeorum accentuum inventor huic communi defectui subvenire voluit; sed postea eosdem examinado nihil minus invenire potui', *Compendium Grammatices Linguae hebraeae*, chap. IV, G I, pp. 294–5 [*HG* 18].

[47] 'But perhaps I will pursue these matters more clearly with you some other time, if life lasts. For up till now I have not been able to set out anything concerning them in an orderly way' ('Sed de his forsan aliquando, si vita suppetit, clarius tecum agam. Nam huc usque nihil de his ordine disponere mihi licuit', Letter 83, G IV, p. 334, ll. 26–8, A, pp. 353–4 [*Ep.* LXXXIII [to Tschirnhaus]; *CWS* II, 487]).

to conversion. The tension described and suggested by the text still possesses a power, even if it is no longer present. It is, in a certain sense, irreducible. And it is *singular* in two senses: on the one hand, its site is that of a singular individual, who lives this past and suffers from it, who feels the weight of a decision on his shoulders (and on his shoulders alone), in addition to the weight of everything that depends on it. This individual is the one who says *I*. On the other hand, the individual's past cannot be erased as if it were an illusion or a particularity, or even a memory of a past crisis. For as soon as common life exists, this tension can be engendered by the mere consideration of 'omnia quae frequenter occurrunt'; it can therefore arise again, and indeed with the same traits, in another individual who will say *I* in turn and who will come to occupy the place designated by this singular fold in the *vita communis*. This point allows me to highlight another of the prologue's traits: paradoxically, this singularity is anonymous. Since the perils this singularity faces are described only in vague terms (they are serious, but they are measured more by their consequences than by their determinate content), the past can immediately become the present again for any reader who relives it in turn. This neutrality of the *I* prohibits the reader from identifying the narrator with 'Spinoza': the narrator is whoever has travelled down this path, and the reader is whoever is assigned to it.

Familiarity, tension, singularity – these three constitutive traits come together around the following point: before the reader even considers the text's arguments, these traits indicate that the narrator's situation is at once intolerable and (at first glance) unsurpassable. Better still, the text not only indicates this situation; it both assumes this situation and shares it. It assumes it insofar as the form of the narration makes the scene much more present – above all, it makes it far more compelling than any description in the third person, such as those we find in Books III and IV of the *Ethics* – and it shares it insofar as the reader is invited, both by the familiarity of the subjects evoked and by the neutral modality of the *I*, to identify with the narrator and to see in his perils their own. While the *Ethics* leads its reader 'as if by the hand' to beatitude, in the *TdIE* it is less a matter of leading the reader than of making them enter a certain situation by force – a situation that the text shows is their own situation, albeit one that first appears as a despair-inducing labyrinth. We catch a glimpse here of what could be called the *tragic tone* of Spinozism.

The term I have just used will perhaps surprise the reader, or lead them down the path of typical misunderstandings. I must therefore explain myself: what do I mean by the term 'tragic'? I am not referring here, as some commentators do, to an explanation of Spinozism in terms of an existential attitude that would somehow constitute the hidden truth of the system.[48] However, I do want to highlight the fact that at a certain level of the system the effects of the laws of nature are felt by the individual as a contradiction that poses an apparently insoluble challenge to the purpose of their life. This contradiction takes the form of a problem whose impossible yet necessary solution will determine their existence. On the other hand, I also want to point out that this argument is, from a certain point of view (yet it is no less necessary for this), anterior to the exposition of the system. The beautiful pages where Sylvain Zac writes that 'a deterministic philosophy leaves no place for a feeling of the tragic'[49] are well known. To be clear, however, Zac's impeccable demonstration seems to me to show that the system in its entirety excludes the possibility that the tragic be its ultimate truth: the order of necessity, the preservation of our being and the development of our power to act – all these ideas define, in the final analysis, a quite different conception of ethics. But this does not prevent the 'feeling of the tragic' from appearing at certain moments in human development.[50] My analysis of the different elements of the *proemium*'s tone means that I cannot reduce the tragic to something else or conceive of it as an artifice. It is in no way a matter of pitting the tragic against the rational; instead, it is necessary to determine the precise place assigned to the tragic by the order of reasons.

Simplicity and familiarity, an urgency that rises to the point of passionate tension, the deliberate singularity of the narrative – all of these traits confer upon these few pages an absolutely original status in Spinoza's œuvre. Gebhardt already underscored this point[51] and remarked on the

---

[48] An example can be found in V. Bent's book *Spinoza, el límite humano*, Caracas: Mediciencia Editora, 1987: 'Pocos han resentido la contradicciòn existencial con una violencia tal que obligue a suprimir uno de sus términos – la contingencia, es decir el tiempo y el sentimiento de alienaciòn', p. 4; 'Lo vemos ahora claramente: la beatitud no es una recompensa, sino un a priori existencial que Spinoza trata de revelar', p. 188.

[49] 'une philosophie déterministe ne laisse pas une place au sentiment du tragique', *L'idée de vie dans la philosophie de Spinoza*, Paris: PUF, 1963, p. 202.

[50] In any case, S. Zac recognises this when he writes: 'Le sentiment du tragique n'est donc pas fondé', ibid., p. 203. If it is not founded, then this is at the very least because it has appeared as one of the facets of a singular reality. The same goes for the other two 'tones' of individuality that Sylvain Zac mentions at the same point in his book: namely, satire and melancholy. These are moments that the *conatus* passes through in certain circumstances (and where certain *conatus* remain fixed). These moments are not illusory, but they would be if one sought to explain the world from their perspective.

[51] Cf. the phrase already quoted above: 'Es gibt wohl kaum eine Stelle in den Schriften Spinozas, in der uns der Philosoph in der ganzen Erhabenheit und Lauterkeit seiner

obvious contrast with the theory of method that immediately follows these pages in the *TdIE*. Nevertheless, it is not enough to remark on the tone of this scene; it is also necessary to account both for what makes it possible and for what it itself makes possible. Gebhardt explained this contrast, along with the unusual length of the prologue, by the fact that these pages are not the introduction to the *TdIE* so much as the introduction to the system in its entirety.[52] Even if this thesis could be proven (and Gebhardt does prove it to a certain extent; it is necessary only to agree on the meaning of the term 'introduction': the *proemium* does indeed constitute an introduction *to the reading* of the *TdIE*, but it privileges the introduction of the *reader* into the system), this thesis nevertheless does not absolve us from analysing the immediate effects of the *proemium*'s tone. The tonality of a text, if it has philosophical implications, does not possess these implications all by itself; it possesses them by virtue of what it stages: the situation into which it introduces the reader, and the emphasis or interpretation that frames this content. It is therefore to this situation that I will now turn.

2. The Situation

Without yet entering into the logical articulations of Spinoza's reasoning, I have so far attempted to discern what constitutes the irreducibly tragic tone of this passage: its sense of familiarity, its tragic tension, and the way it plays with the category of singularity. As we have seen, all of these effects converge to induce in the reader a strong sense of identification with this narrative of an ineluctable trajectory. The text's enunciation stages an existential choice, one that the narrator himself has not yet made, even if everything indicates that it is a choice that must be made as a matter of priority. At the same time, everything points to the fact that this extraordinary sense of necessity originates in the most ordinary features of our lives. To go further, we must now interrogate the meaning of these traits: what structure do

---

Gesinnung so unmittelbar entgegentritt wie in der Einleitung des tractatus de intellectus emendatione'. Gebhardt continues: 'Allerdings, vergleicht man diese von innerster Wärme beseelte Einleitung mit der verhältnismässig kühlen und sachlichen Methodenlehre, so konnte man wohl einen Gegensatz finden, und man konnte auch die allzu große räumliche Ausdehnung der Einleitung constatieren', *Spinozas Abhandlung über die Verbesserung des Verstandes*, p. 54.

[52] 'Aber man darf nicht vergessen, daß sie nicht nur zur Methodenlehre, sondern zum System selbst hinführen sollte. Hier wollte Spinoza die Pforte errichten, durch die die Welt eintreten sollte in seine Lehre', ibid., pp. 54–5.

they confer upon Spinoza's reasoning? How do they determine the situation described by the text? Towards what type of interpretation do they orient the reader? In a word: what sort of *situation* do they invite the reader to enter into so that they too can understand what is being narrated? It is not simply a matter of giving a name to these rhetorical and theoretical gestures, but of knowing what kind of scene is being described here. Leaving aside provisionally the first trait – the choice of the familiar over the technical – I will now ask what the conjunction of the other two traits signifies.

As we have seen, the text's narrative form allows the discourse to transcend the bounds of simple argumentation. Its dramatic tension produces a temporality that escapes linear time to become concentrated around a single instant of radical change, where the narrator's relation to the world is suddenly overturned. Thus, the ideas that the text stages, along with the triumph of one idea over the other, are presented to the reader in the course of a temporal unfolding that coincides with an individual's life. Reciprocally, the story of this life is not a simple accumulation of facts, for what the text recounts – from the nature of goods to the dangers faced and resolutions made – comes into focus only insofar as it explains, delays, and ultimately makes possible this final choice. The individual's history is meaningful only by virtue of the cut that occurs within it; a cut that turns the individual away from seeking out certain goods and launches them on a different quest. The narrative is nothing other than the narrative of this turn – that is, etymologically speaking, of this conversion.

We are therefore dealing with a pre-existing form, one that our text does not invent, even if it thoroughly transforms it for its own ends. The points of reference for this form include biblical texts, along with the narratives of Saint Augustine:[53] a reader from the classical age could not help but be reminded of these. More precisely, rather than explicit associations, the

---

[53] For example, we find in Saint Augustine's writings the same oscillation between aspiration and hesitation. See the summary that Augustine gives of his path in 392 in *On the Advantage of Believing*: 'For as I left you and crossed the sea, now delaying, now hesitating, as to what I should hold and what I should discard (for my vacillation kept ever increasing from day to day from the time that I heard that man who, as you know, had been promised at his coming as one sent from heaven to solve all our difficulties, and found him, except for a certain eloquence, just like the others), I planned and deliberated much, now that I am established in Italy, not as to whether I should remain in that sect into which I now regretted having fallen, but in what way the truth had to be found . . .' (*The Immortality of the Soul, The Magnitude of the Soul, On Music, The Advantage of Believing, On Faith in Things Unseen*, Washington DC: Catholic University of America Press, 2002, pp. 415–16).

text's form and these points of reference together constitute a framework of reception through which any narrative that relates such a trajectory can be read.[54] The pregnancy of this form is all the more powerful since it makes a significant return in the sixteenth and seventeenth centuries[55] in the midst of religious scissions that demanded each person make a spiritual choice for themselves – a choice that could no longer be a matter of unquestioned inheritance[56] or of something automatically assumed by the mere fact of belonging to some collectivity.[57] The conversion narrative is a literary genre that includes a certain number of obligatory passages: the organisation of time around a foundational instant, the crucial difference between the 'before' and the 'after', the uncertainties that precede the decision, and the repose of the soul that follows it. These obligatory passages are not the mere effects of imitation or inheritance but the necessary consequence of the genre's structure[58] – that is, of the way it organises its foundational choices.[59]

---

[54] As an additional proof of this, the term 'conversion' occurs quite naturally in the writings of many commentators, and they are not wrong to use it; in fact, their only fault – if they have one – lies in their belief that this term counts as a response to a question, whereas it actually raises a question. To my mind it is not legitimate to refuse the term 'conversion' from the outset in the name of our text's originality; nevertheless, the term should be used in the context of a generic comparison that identifies where, precisely, the text's originality begins. Such a comparison would moreover be better placed to measure the text's effects and understand how they are produced. In sum, I propose to use a generic analysis to grasp the text as a texture.

[55] See the volume *La conversion au XVIIe siècle*, Actes du XXIe colloque de Marseille, CMR 17, Marseille, 1983, in particular L. Desgraves' study, 'Un aspect des controverses entre catholiques et protestants, les récits de conversion (1598–1628)', pp. 89–110.

[56] The spiritual situation in the Netherlands allowed the choice of one's religion to occur with the minimum of external constraints. A. Th. Van Deursen brings out the originality and the limits of this situation in the first part, titled 'Hel en Hemel', of his work *Het Kopergeld van de Gouden Eeuw*, Assen: Van Gorcum, 1980, vol. IV, pp. 1–3.

[57] In addition to the passage from one religion to another, it can also be a matter of the passage from the 'world' to spiritual devotion – a passage that can occur within one and the same belief system. We can think here of the role played by the idea of conversion in Jansenism and of Saint-Cyran's theorisation of it. We can also compare this with Pascal's crises of evolution, called 'conversions' since at least Sainte-Beuve, even though Pascal himself never uses this term. See J. Mesnard, 'Les conversions de Pascal', in *Pascal, l'homme et l'œuvre*, Cahiers de Royaumont, No. 1, Paris: Editions de Minuit, 1956, pp. 46–77.

[58] We find exactly the same structures in a Pietist context in the wake of the first conversion narrative, that of Franck, which is entirely organised on the basis of the *plötzlich*: 'God suddenly answered me.'

[59] I have elsewhere tried to show what the exigencies of a particular philosophical genre are and how they can be translated into a text with more certainty and consistency

I will now attempt to draw out these fundamental elements; in doing so, I will clarify in what sense Spinoza's writing is carried along by this current or tradition and in what sense it resists it. It is a matter not of locating 'sources' but of following the vectors suggested by the reading and writing of the text. Such vectors are the carriers of a tradition that one can choose to follow at the same time as modifying them, with these modifications nevertheless taking on their meaning only by virtue of this very tradition.

This structure is dominated by the division of a singularity. To be convinced of this, we need only follow the thread of Saint Augustine's texts.[60] The conversion narrative is less the narrative of an individual's life and more the narrative of this life's transformation;[61] it recounts the interpellation and the development of the *I*. There is always something essentially singular about a conversion: a people cannot be converted, even if they can be baptised by force. Moreover, this transformation is something that is assumed: that is, the subject bears witness to itself, at once to justify what has taken place, to make the conversion more efficacious still by reliving it, and to allow it to occur again by encouraging the reader to follow the same path for the same reasons.[62] The narrative therefore has a

---

than the text's contents. See P. F. Moreau, *Le récit utopique. Droit naturel et roman de l'Etat*, Paris: PUF, 1982.

[60] See *The Confessions*, naturally, in particular Book VIII, but also what P. Courcelles has named 'Augustine's first confessions', where we sometimes see the narrative's mechanisms operating in a more pure form since they do not suffer from the passage of time. See also, for example, the texts from Cassiciacum such as *De vita beata*. See P. Courcelles, 'Les premières confessions de saint Augustin', *Revue des études latines*, 22 (1945), pp. 155–74. In his study on Saint Augustine's conversion (*La fin du paganisme*, Paris: Hachette, 1898, livre III, Chapter 3, t.1, pp. 291–325), Gaston Boissier already pointed out the differences between the two types of text, but by insisting above all on their properly literary dimension ('Le cicéronisme des dialogues de Cassiciacum', pp. 316–19).

[61] In biblical texts this transformation is accompanied by the transformation of the individual's name, as if a new individual had been born (Genesis 17:5). In his historical novel, Berthold Auerbach will apply this to Spinoza himself: Olympia, the daughter of Van den Enden, will make him change his name in reference to the name changes undergone by the Patriarchs (B. Auerbach, *Spinoza, Ein Denkerleben*, 1837, 1854, reprinted by Schwäbische Verlagsgesellschaft, 1980, vol. 1, Chapter 10, pp. 183–97: 'Benedictus sit'). On this reading of Spinoza's biography in the context of the struggles and the worldview of liberal Judaism, cf. A. Lagny, 'Spinoza personnage de roman', in *Spinoza au XXe siècle*, a volume published under the direction of Olivier Bloch, Paris: PUF, 1993.

[62] On this point, G. Boissier compares the finality of the *Confessions* with public acts of penance: the invocation of God is at the same time an evocation of and for others: 'Il

dialogical horizon: the reader, who is mute, is the addressee of an evocation that aims neither at their pleasure nor at simply informing them, but which functions – at least potentially – as a means of persuading them. In order to bear witness in this way, such a narrative fundamentally must be written in the first person, and even when it appears not to be it is generally recorded by someone who shares the same values as the converted person, who belongs to their community, and who repeats their words or transmits a tradition that these words have inaugurated.[63] In one way or another, the narrative is rooted in their experience. This experience involves the confrontation with a frontier: this frontier is a limit, but one that can also be traversed. It is defined in three ways: in terms of objects (from the goods that were initially desired to those that are truly desirable), in terms of time (the 'before', which is rendered insignificant, and the 'after', which alone has real significance),[64] and in terms of the ego (which transitions from a figure of disquiet to one of peace).[65] Yet this line of division, while affirmed as being decisive in its essence,[66] is nevertheless in actual fact a blurred line, for the distinction between the 'before' and the 'after' projects in advance its shadow onto the 'before', constituting it as a zone of uncertainty where desire is not immediately transformed into effort and where the movement that will eventually help the protagonist cross the frontier is characterised by multiple false

---

lui rappelle toutes les erreurs de sa jeunesse, non pas pour les lui faire connaître – qui les sait mieux qui lui? – mais pour apprendre au pécheur par son exemple, et en lui montrant de quel abîme il a lui-même été tiré, qu'on ne doit jamais perdre courage et dire: je ne peux pas', *La fin du paganisme*, pp. 202–3.

[63] In this sense, biblical narratives from Abraham's calling to Saul's conversion can be inscribed retrospectively in this genre.

[64] It is not by chance that Augustine's *De Vita beata* concludes on a discussion of the lexicon of *plenitudo* (IV, 23–36).

[65] Traditionally represented by a stormy sea and by the calm of a port. Thus Augustine begins *De Vita beata* by recalling that we are thrown by chance into a tumultuous sea ('in quoddam procellosum salum') and that we arrive at the port of philosophy, from where we can advance on the solid ground of the happy life ('ad philosophiae portum, a quo jam in beatae vitae regionem solumque proceditur'); he then identifies the three kinds of men on the path to beatitude with three kinds of navigators. On this thematics of the sea voyage as a metaphor for human destiny, see H. Blumenberg, *Schiffbruch mit Zuschauer. Paradigma einer Daseinsmetaphor*, Frankfurt: Suhrkamp, 1979. In the text from *De Utilitate credendi* cited above, it is the image of the unpassable forest that represents the state of uncertainty of the one who seeks truth without having the means of finding it alone: 'Occurebat igitur inexplicabilis silva, cui demum inseri multum pigebat' (VIII, 20).

[66] 'La conversion signifie passer en un instant de rien, et pour ainsi dire de moins que rien, à plus que tout', writes J. Beaude in *La conversion au XVIIe siècle*, p. 313.

starts,[67] illusions, and regressions motivated by the protagonist's attachment to false goods.[68] What emerges, finally, from this topography of the singular is that the singularity's own forces and choices are insufficient by themselves to overcome these intermittencies.[69] This topography therefore implicitly includes a place for the intervention of the other;[70] appealing to this other will help the protagonist overcome their oscillations. The key point on this path is less the supernatural as such and more the demand for an authority who will break the circle of the ego.[71]

---

[67] 'But there was no lack of clouds to confound my course . . .' (*quibus confundetur cursus meus*), Saint Augustine, *On the Happy Life: St. Augustine's Cassiciacum Dialogues*, trans. Michael Foley (New Haven: Yale University Press, 2019), p. 20.

[68] 'for a long time the Academics held the helm of my ship as it resisted every gale in the midst of the waves', ibid.

[69] It is for this reason that Steno, in his letter to Spinoza (a letter that is in many ways a meditation on conversion), considers as 'the greatest of miracles' – that is, as the clearest case of divine intervention – the instantaneous passage of the soul from one state to another: 'ubi miraculi effectum animae alicuius a vitiis ad virtutes perfectam conversionem videmus, omnium virtutum authori iure illud adscribimus', *Nicolai Stenonis ad novae philosophiae reformatorem de vera philosophie epistola*, Florence, 1675, reproduced in the *Chronicon spinozanum*, I, 1921, p. 36 ['Whenever we see that the effect of a miracle is the perfect conversion of someone's soul from vices to virtues, we rightly ascribe that to the author of all virtues', *Ep*. LXVII [from Steno]; *CWS* II, 455]. Cf. the study by A. Ziggelaar on Stenone's conversion (where we see that this conversion will set off numerous others; the letter to Spinoza is therefore not an isolated effort) in *Niccolo Stenone 1638–1686*, Florence: Le S. Olschki, 1988. The most complete biography on Stenone can be found in the volume *Niels Stensen, Anatom, Geologe und Bischof*, by Max Bierbaum, Adolf Faller and Josef Traeger, Münster: Aschendorff, 1989. W. Klever has recently published a useful survey in the *Studia Spinozana*, VI, 1990, pp. 303–16.

[70] *Alius*: this is the term with which Augustine purposefully refers to the divine in the dialogues of Cassiciacum; this term occurs, precisely, in *De Vita beata*, not in the initial narrative but in a passage where the person who organises the discussion (which is compared to spiritual nourishment offered to friends) underscores the fact that the dialogue will take a new turn and escape him (III 17: 'Sed quid vobis praeparatum sit, ego quoque vobiscum nescio. Alius est enim qui omnibus cum omnes tum maxime tales epulas praebere non cessat . . .'). J. Doignon, the editor of the text in the Bibliothèque augustinienne, sees here a theme from Plotinus (p. 89). But it could be said that Epictetus also frequently refers to God, or rather to divine intervention, using this term *alius*, and that he does so in passages that recount a change of plan (*Discourses*, I, 25; I, 30, etc.). Thus, rather than being a matter of influence, we should see here the necessary expression of a procedure where aspiration is insufficient as a means of carrying out the conversion.

[71] This is why, if the image of the stormy seas translates the period of uncertainty, that of the violent and swift gust of wind signifies, by contrast, the movement, arising from

This ego is in no way the psychological ego in the modern sense of the term; it is not a matter of being attentive to the diversity and irreducibility of each person as a site of emotions.[72] The fluctuations that the ego undergoes are perhaps less those of an interiority than they are of a topography. These fluctuations, which can be expressed through images, are absorbed in their objects; the singularity that emerges from them is not an 'individual' but rather the site of a double appeal – the appeal of earthly goods, and the appeal of the true Good to which the singular individual is converted. This 'individual' has few individualised traits; moreover, when these are present at all they are swiftly rejected as errors.[73] This is doubtless why the individual's states are so easily objectified in the form of regions. As forms, images are better suited to a species of narration entirely oriented towards a foundational instant – better, that is, than the glittering of individual differences staged by other genres in which the ego flourishes.[74] Here, the ego – or rather the I – takes the form of a determinate figure only insofar as it is suspended at a precise moment, that of conversion. Yet this is a moment that will strip this ego's particularities of any significance they might have had. Certainly, the

an external origin, that leads – almost against their will – the voyager to port. The latter desires to go there, but he does not know how to get there; he has mistaken the route, and therefore has had to harness the wind as if by force so that it can lead him where he wants to go: few would have been able to find the right direction by themselves ('quotusquisque cognosceret, quo sibi nitendum esset quave redeundum, nisi aliquando et invitos contraque obnitentes aliqua tempestas, quae stultis videtur adversa, in optatissimam terram nescientes errantesque compingeret', I, 1); further on, Augustine applies an identical image to himself: 'Quid ergo restabat aliud, nisi ut immoranti mihi superfluis tempestas, quae putatur adversa, succurreret?' (I, 4).

[72] Thus, when in De Utilitate credendi Augustine discovers that the true method escapes the human mind, he concludes that it is necessary to seek something beyond it: 'eundemque ipsum modum ab aliqua divina auctoritate esse sumendum' (VIII, 20).

[73] In the case of Augustine's texts, it is precisely here that the distinction is strongest between the Confessions and the earlier texts, for the aim of the Confessions is different from the latter: marks of individuality are present in the Confessions since its project is no longer to simply narrate a conversion; rather, it also includes a kind of illustration of the paths of providence. The individual is presented here less as an interior gaze and more as the site at which divine action exerts itself.

[74] Examples could include the personal diary, the modern autobiography (so long as we are careful not to use this term as a catch-all term that refers to all first-person narratives), and even a type of psychological novel associated with the names of Benjamin Constant or Formentin. On the autobiography and its related genres, see the works of Ph. Lejeune, in particular Le pacte autobiographique, Paris: Seuil, 1975; Je est un autre, Paris: Seuil, 1980. For classical references, there are stimulating ideas in the work that Arnaldo Momigliano devotes to a broader topic: Lo sviluppo della biografia greca, Turin: Einaudi, 1974.

presence of a differentiated individuality is more or less prominent relative to different narratives, but even when biographical and psychological material is taken into account this material seems to fade into the background the closer one gets to the moment of conversion. The ego's individuality is no longer significant except insofar as it delays the conversion process or is an obstacle to it. The reader's gaze passes through these biographical and psychological facts without attending to their properties, and sees only the promised transparency of what is already beginning to no longer exist. The nuance that separates the 'no longer' from the 'almost no longer' marks a gap in which there can come to exist a description of what, at the heart of the ego, continues to resonate with the past's seductions; yet these resonances are evoked only to be immediately abolished. In Augustine's case, one might be tempted to explain this characteristic by reference to the classical tradition, which accorded little place to the subject's interiority.[75] But it owes its consistency much more to a generic trait: namely, that the only consistency possessed by the *I* is that of its division, for once it has resolved to convert, it is in some sense emptied of itself, for this 'self' was made up of false goods. Its life is now so radically transformed that its past becomes unrecognisable.[76] As such, the conversion narrative becomes, at the limit of its possibilities, the memory of what cannot be remembered.[77]

But we must go further: it is precisely this absence or exteriority of psy-

---

[75] Cf. J. de Romilly, *'Patience mon cœur!' L'essor de la psychologie dans la littérature grecque classique*, Paris: Belles Lettres, 1984; in particular pp. 220–1, where the author shows that, if the description of interiority progresses between the fifth and sixth centuries, it regresses in other periods, notably because of the development of Christianity, which 'offre l'image d'un retour à l'extériorité et aux interventions sacrées'. Cf. also Mikhaïl Bakhtin's remarks, 'Formes du temps et du chronotope dans le roman, § III: Biographie et autobiographie antiques', in *Esthétique et théorie du roman*, Paris: NRF, 1978, pp. 278–92.

[76] The phenomenon of conversion 'carr[ies] with it the conviction that the slate has been wiped clean', as E. R. Dodds remarks regarding the idea of 'regeneration' in late Antiquity (*Pagan and Christian in an Age of Anxiety*, Cambridge: Cambridge University Press, 1965, p. 77). Likewise, with regard to the Pietistic *Durchbruch*, R. Ayrault remarks on 'l'importance qu'y revêt l'entrée dans le temps, un certain jour, à une certaine heure, de cet événement qui non seulement change l'être mais, le restituant à sa destination éternelle, abolit pour lui le temps', *La genèse du romantisme allemand*, Paris: Aubier, 1961, vol. II, p. 409.

[77] Cf. J. Beaude's remarks on the Berrullian interpretation of Mary Magladene: 'Le regard sur le passé de Madeleine ne serait pas seulement une vaine curiosité mais une erreur [. . .] son péché n'est pas simplement effacé, il devient, pour ainsi dire, immémorable'; further on, he writes: 'en ce moment commence comme un présent sans passé', *La conversion au XVIIe siècle*, p. 312.

chological traits that subtracts the moment of conversion from the order of facts, making it a foundational instant. Without this erasure, this neutralisation of individual qualities, we would remain in a homogeneous order where character traits and the tendencies of interior life could be reinforced by anecdotes and events occurring in exterior space. It is because the ego has no physiognomy that the division from which it emerges can confer a meaning on the broken totality of a biographical trajectory. The conversion narrative thus appears fundamentally to be based on this particular form of singularity: it is this form that makes possible the narrative's temporal scansions, which organise the division between goods and the passage from one to the next; and it is ultimately this form that ensures that the disciple can in turn recognise themselves in the mirror that is proffered to them. Despite any variations it might undergo, the strong unity of this genre is above all reducible to the consistent specificity of such a gaze.

With two exceptions, these same motifs structure Spinoza's text: the narrator initially experiences dissatisfactions and aspirations, and he hesitates to cross the frontier and so face the difficulties this crossing implies. Yet he remains attached to false goods, even if he has begun to renounce them; most importantly, he errs in his method. There comes a time when he has understood that resolving to convert is something essential, but he has not yet committed to doing so.[78] This state of irresolution then leads to even more suffering. The 'persistent meditation' by means of which he travels down the path leading from decision to effectuation is also perfectly inscribed in the tradition of conversion narratives. Furthermore, the mirror relation between the converted and their addressee, which lies at the heart of the conversion narrative, can also be clarified by the above remarks. Spinoza also reduces biographical facts to their bare minimum: they are mere temptations and signs of the incompleteness of the protagonist's trajectory. Moreover, the ego that submits to the trajectory and strips itself of these temptations does not gain any determinate physiognomy; it exists only insofar as it appears as the site of a debate between different goods. We are therefore indeed dealing with the narrative of a divided ego – of an ego that can be reduced to its very division. Thanks to everything that makes these features effective and that prolongs the tradition in which they are inscribed, the prologue to the *TdIE* possesses all of the formal traits of a conversion narrative. Indeed, it draws much of its power from this genre's intense treatment of the demarcation

---

[78] 'Nam quamvis haec mente adeo clare perciperem, non poteram tamen ideo omnem avaritiam, libidinem atque gloriam deponere', § 10, G II, p. 7, ll. 28–30 [*TdIE* 10; *CWS* I, 10].

between past and present; from the irreducibly singular feeling of the turn once it has been accomplished; from the vital urgency of, precisely, this turn's accomplishment; and finally from the way this genre addresses the reader and traces out a path for them to take.

Whatever the similarities, there is nevertheless one major difference – not the obvious external difference, which is that Spinoza's text does not recount a conversion to orthodoxy, but an internal difference. It is this difference that is decisive. The conversion Spinoza recounts is integrally *natural.* It appeals to no external agency, to no superior authority; and even if it orients itself towards a Supreme Good, which the system will teach us consists in knowledge of God, it must be noted that the word 'God' does not appear even once in these pages. This should surprise us, particularly since we are dealing with a philosopher whose principal work will have for the title of its first section *De Deo.*

Nevertheless, when formulated in this way, this difference is seen only from its negative side. Yet this side is the reverse side of a *positive* difference – and this difference is revealed by the first trait I provisionally left aside above: the familiar universe that the text evokes. This universe not only excludes supernatural intervention; more fundamentally still, it excludes any place for external intervention *tout court* – for the intervention of what is foreign to the *communis vita.* The true conversion narrative has no need of miracles: it is the conversion itself that is the sole miracle since it wrenches a person away from everyday life – from a life that leaves them dissatisfied but to which they are still attached. With Spinoza, by contrast, there is no escape from everyday life; or rather, if there were such an escape, it could occur only by subverting the many kinds of escapism that everyday life has already offered us. Given this, in Spinoza we can no longer represent the consistency of the singular as something that is suspended, by virtue of its very emptiness, to the appeal to the other. The familiar universe subverts the relation of the singularity to itself; it does not exclude division, but formulates it in an entirely different manner. It both requires and makes possible that the subject find a way of overcoming common life from within the very logic of common life itself.

We can now ask ourselves whether Spinoza's text does not borrow certain of its effects from another theoretical genre, one that presents a number of affinities[79] with the conversion narra-

---

[79] Above all, the noun *protrepein* signifies 'to turn' or 'to turn towards'; both uses have for their second meaning 'to exhort' (in Aristotle's *Rhetoric, protropè* and *apotropè* are the two species of a deliberative genre (I, Chapter 3, 1358b)). As for the specific meaning

tive:⁸⁰ namely, the protreptic, or the exhortation to philosophy, such as we find it in Plato's *Euthydemus*,⁸¹ in Aristotle's work,⁸² in Cicero's *Hortensius*,⁸³ in Seneca's *Letters to Lucilius*, or indeed in Jamblique's work.⁸⁴ These texts present the model of a genre of persuasion that consists in enumerating the reasons for philosophising.⁸⁵ The affinities between the two genres are clear: in both cases it is a matter of choosing the true life – a life that is also that of the love of wisdom. The problem is therefore to leave a life of insignificance and enter one that has meaning: the individual's consistency, manifested by their happiness, depends on the choice of life they will make. Here, too, there are hesitations to overcome and reasons to accumulate for making the change. But these affinities are laid out in a mirror-like manner: the

of the word *conversio*, we know that it developed on the basis of the word *converti* (to enter into religion) in the course of an encounter with one of the semantic fields of *conversatio* (cf. Christine Mohrmann, *Etudes sur le latin des Chrétiens*, vol. II, Rome: Edizioni di Storia e Letteratura, 1961, p. 341–5).

⁸⁰ Certain commentators have indeed used this term to refer to the whole of the *TdIE*. Thus, Wim Klever, when noting that the *Short Treatise* constitutes the accomplishment of the *TdIE* insofar as it truly carries out the latter's aim, adds that the person in the *TdIE* who will become a philosopher is 'interpellated, persuaded, and elevated' towards the recognition of the unique foundation of salvation (namely: *la cognitio unionis, quam mes cum tota Natura habet*): 'Inhoudelijk gezien is de KV het vervolgverhaal van de *TdIE*, waarin de beoeling van de *TdIE* (koersverbetering van het verstand) geëffectueerd wordt. Men kan ook omgerkeerd zeggen, dat de *TdIE* de spinozistische "Protreptikos" is, waarin de kandidaat-filosoof aangesproken, overreed en opgetrokken wordt tot de erkenning van het alleenzaligmakende beginsel [. . .]', *De Methodologische functie van de Godsidee*, Medelingen XLVIII vanwege het Spinozahuis, Leiden: Brill, 1986. On other aspects of Klever's reading from his otherwise often illuminating commentary, see *Spinoza. Verhandeling over de verbetering van het verstand. Tekst en uitleg*, Baarn: Ambo, 1986, about which I expressed my punctual reservations in a review for the *Bulletin de bibliographie spinoziste*, IX, *Archives de Philosophie*, vol. 50 (1987/7), pp. 10–11.

⁸¹ It could even be said that the *Euthydemus* contains two protreptics – a false one and a true one – since the Socratic exhortation (278e–282e, and again at 288d ff.) presents itself as a critique by way of the example of a sophistical exhortation.

⁸² Ingemar Düring, *Aristotle's Protrepticus: An Attempt at Reconstruction*, Göteborg: Acta Universitatis Gothoburgensis, 1961; B. Dumoulin, *Recherches sur le premier Aristote (Eudème De la Philosophie, Protréptique)*, Paris: Vrin, 1981, pp. 113–58; R. Brague, *Aristote et la question du monde*, Paris: PUF, 1988, pp. 57–110.

⁸³ M. Ruch, *L'Hortensius de Cicéron, histoire et reonstitution*, Paris: Belles Lettres, 1958; A Grilli, M. *Tulli Ciceronis Hortensius*, Milan/Varese: Istituto editoriale cesalpino, 1962; D. Turkowska, *L'Hortensius de Cicéron et le Protreptique d'Aristote*, Wroclaw: Polska Akademia Nauk, 1965.

⁸⁴ *Protréptique*, texte établi et traduit par E. des Places, s. j., Paris: Belles Lettres, 1989.

⁸⁵ Cf. for the Greek historical tradition sketched by I. Düring, *Aristotle's Protrepticus*, pp. 19–24 and 33–5 (with, notably, the role of Isocrates).

protreptic takes the form of an exhortation and not of a narrative; it speaks to the future and not to the past as it situates the desired object in a future that is still to come; and the frontier, while drawn in a similar fashion, has nevertheless not yet been crossed. Finally, as the arguments can only be advanced by someone who already knows what is on the other side, the 'proficiens' cannot state them himself. There necessarily has to be a division in the reasoning, where instead of being centred on an *I* the reasoning will be turned either implicitly or explicitly towards a *you*. This explains why the fundamental structure of the protreptic determines that it so often takes the form of a letter or a dialogue.[86] In the place of a temporal division internal to the ego, in the protreptic we have a temporal division between two egos. The dialogical structure that exists on the horizon of the conversion narrative comes to the fore in the protreptic and leaves its mark on the work. While in the conversion narrative the reader could convert themselves in turn by way of adhesion and repetition, in the protreptic he enters into the text in the guise of a respondent or correspondent.[87]

Once again we find synthesised – albeit articulated in different ways – the structures of time and singularity.[88] However, the interest proper to the

---

[86] This does not exclude – quite to the contrary – that the exhortation turns into a monologue at its end, with the proficiens having by this point nothing more to prove. It is in this way, it seems, that the *Hortensius* ends, if we follow A. Grilli's reconstruction of the text: after the dialogue on the comparative merits of poetry, eloquence and philosophy, and the defence of philosophy against the attacks of Hortensius, the text proceeds to a *pars construens* where Cicero monopolises the discussion: 'Si tratta infatti, a un certo punto, di far un passo inanzi, oltre la semplice difesa della filosofia, conquale invitare gli uomini cui si rivolge il prottrettico a partecipare alla filosofia e alla vita cui essa induce', M. *Tulli Ciceronis Hortensius*, pp. 93–4.

[87] In addition to formal analogies, it is necessary to point out the slippage of certain works from one genre to another by means of the ambiguity of the terms and, more generally, of their intersection: the *Protreptic* of Clement of Alexandria is a call to join the true religion, conceived as the truth of philosophy. Origen's protreptic, for its part, is an exhortation to martyrdom. The narratives of Augustine speak of a conversion to philosophy (though it is true that in a Christian milieu it is Christianity itself that is considered as the true philosophy) and use the *Hortensius* as a reference (see also in the *Confessions*, III, 4).

[88] Here it would be necessary to analyse the extraordinary path of Saint Bonaventura, which supposes both a conversion of the soul and the imitation of a model, the path of the soul having for its point of departure the meditation on divine intervention in the case of St Francis of Assisi: 'Cum igitur exemplo beatissimi patris Francisci hanc pacem anhelo spiritu quaererem, ego peccator, qui loco ipsius patris beatissimi post eius transitum, septimus in generali fratrum ministerio per omnia indignus succedo; contigit, ut nutu divino circa Beatu ipsius transitum, anno trigesimo tertio ad montem

genre of the protreptic lies in its one major difficulty: as a philosophical work, it cannot presuppose philosophy since it must be an *introduction* to it. This difficulty is reinforced by the fact that, as is most often the case, the philosopher who wants to draw others towards the search for wisdom speaks in the name of a particular system that determines their own resolve to engage in this search. Yet the philosopher can no more presuppose this system – even if it is the site where his arguments typically take on their proper meaning – than he can presuppose 'philosophy' in general. This not only means that he cannot presuppose any knowledge of this system in his readers, but above all that he is not able to presuppose the *conditions* for this knowledge.

Such an absence of presuppositions does not constitute a simple expository difficulty: it raises the question of the constitutive difference of philosophical discourse as such. For this discourse cannot, in fact, distinguish itself from opinion or from everyday discourse except by arming itself with a strong rationality, one exhibited in definite concepts, specific procedures, and an architectonic – in short, in everything that makes a philosophy into a system. It is therefore paradoxical to claim to introduce someone to this philosophy by abandoning all of these guarantees of rigour. In this sense, an exhortation to philosophy is not at all the same thing as an introduction to, for instance, law or grammar, for while these disciplines certainly have a specific language, they are not organised from the outset in the form of a system with a completed architecture.[89] We can thus glimpse the reasons

Alvernae tanquam ad locum quietum amore quaerendi pacem spiritus declinarem, ibique existens, dum mente tractarem aliquas mentales ascensiones in Deum, inter alia occurrit miraculum, quod in praedicto loco contigit ipso beato Francisco, de visione scilicet Seraph alati ad instar Crucifixi. In cuius consideratione statim visum est mihi, quod visio illa praetenderet ipsius patris suspensionem in contemplando et viam per quam perventitur ad eam', Opera, Ad Claras Aquas, vol. V, *Opuscula varia theologica*, 1891, p. 291. 'Inspired by the example of our blessed Father, Francis, I wanted to seek after this peace with yearning soul, sinner that I am and all unworthy, yet seventh successor as Minister to all the brethren in the place of the blessed father after his death; it happened that, thirty-three years after the death of the Saint, about the time of his passing, moved by divine impulse, I withdrew to Mount Alverno, as to a place of quiet, there to satisfy the yearning of my soul for peace. While I dwelt there, pondering on certain spiritual ascents to God, I was struck, among other things, by that miracle which in this very place had happened to the blessed Francis, that is, the vision he received of the winged seraph in the form of the Crucified. As I reflected on this marvel, it immediately seemed to me that this vision might suggest the rising of Saint Francis into contemplation and point out the way by which that state of contemplation may be reached.' Bonaventure, *The Journey of the Mind to God*, trans. Philotheus Boehner (Indianapolis: Hackett, 1993), p. 1.

[89] On the necessity of being systematic as a condition for philosophy, one can do no

the question 'Why philosophise?' has a quite exceptional status among philosophical questions; put simply, it has the following particularity: it is, by rights, anterior to every system. Neither in its procedures nor its arguments can this question make use of the forms of rationality proper to the philosopher who poses it – or, if it does use them, at the very least it cannot expect them to have any *a priori* persuasive value. It is not possible to draw on Cartesian or Spinozist concepts in order to try and demonstrate to someone who is not yet a philosopher why they must turn to philosophy, or even enter into a philosophical system, whether Cartesian or Spinozist, for that would be to grant that the problem has already been solved. It is therefore necessary for the philosopher to do without their system. But is this even possible? Can a philosopher situate themselves on the border of their architectonic as if, at least provisionally, they weren't in the least concerned by it? If it is not to be an arbitrary passage, then the passage from everyday rationality to philosophical rationality must confront a double difficulty: it is necessary to find within common life arguments that suggest one should leave it – arguments that do not presuppose that determinate philosophical choices have already been made (for example, one cannot say that it is necessary to enter into philosophy in order to attain the third kind of knowledge, or to raise oneself up to the level of ideas, or to resolve the problem of the union of the soul and the body). If these arguments are based on values, then these values must themselves emerge in a certain fashion from common life. Finally, the mode of transition to philosophy must not be disqualified by this very philosophy itself once it has been constructed; that is, the system, with its order of reasons, must leave room for common life to lead to it. On the other hand, the

better than to refer to the analyses of Martial Gueroult in his 'Dianoématique', cf. book II: *Philosphie de l'histoire de la philosophie*, Paris: Aubier, 1979. It could certainly be objected that the history of philosophy has known other forms of thought, but it seems to me that when examined closely the systematic exigency is always there, even if the form of exposition can sometimes obscure it. In any case, there is no doubt about this as far as the great systems of the seventeenth century are concerned, in particular Spinoza's. This obviously does not absolve one from thinking the relation between the system and its exterior – indeed, this is one of the goals of the present piece of research. On the word and idea of the 'system' in the seventeenth century, in particular from Galileo to Regis, see R. Sasso, '*Système* and philosophical discourse in the 17th century', *Recherches sur le XVIIème siècle*, CNRS, No. 2 (1978), pp. 123–32. On the 'systematists' (Timpler, Keckermann, etc.), see the chapter on them in Wilhelm Risse's book *Logik der Neuzeit*, Bd. I, Stuttgart: Frommann-Holzboog, 1964, and for their influence in the Netherlands, P. Dibon, *La Philosophie néerlandaise au siècle d'or*, vol. 1, *L'enseignement philosophique dans les universités à l'époque précartésienne (1575–1650)*, Paris/Amsterdam: Elsevier, 1954, *passim*.

description that is given of philosophy must nevertheless map out for the reader a path leading to something else – to the other side. The values of common life cannot be judged by any other lights than its own, even if these values must ultimately give rise to *something else*. The problem takes on a different form, perhaps, in a philosophy that draws its justifications from the sciences or from religion; but in the case of a system that adopts the values of apodictic evidence and radicality, the most radical radicality is to be found precisely at the point where it is a question of philosophy's beginning.[90]

It is indeed in this way that Socrates proceeds in the *Euthydemus*. He begins from a point that is recognised by all, one internal to the affirmations of common life. Interrogating the young Clinias, he asks: 'Do we all wish to do well in the world? Or perhaps this is one of the questions which I feared you might laugh at, for it is foolish, no doubt, even to ask such things. Who in the world does not wish to do well? – Not a single one, said Clinias.'[91] Socrates insists on his naivety, on the simplicity of the series of questions he is posing. There is no irony in this, for in the course of a full page[92] Socrates effectively aligns a whole series of endoxal propositions: we all want to be happy; being happy means possessing a large number of goods; the list of goods is made by accumulation – wealth, health, beauty, knowledge (*sophia*), luck, and so on. The reduction begins only with the identification of luck with knowledge, and then, by the intermediary of the double distinction between possession and use and between correct and incorrect use, it proceeds by identifying all other goods with knowledge. At this point it becomes necessary to seek

---

[90] One will recognise here the premises of a problem that, in an altogether different context, Hegel ceaselessly confronted: cf. everything his prefaces say about the impossibility of a preface; the theme of the 'path of the natural consciousness' ('der Weg des natürlichen Bewusstein', *Werke*, Frankfurt: Suhrkamp, vol. 3, 1986, p. 73 [*Phenomenology of Spirit*, trans. A. V. Miller, Oxford, 1977, p. 49]) in the introduction to the *Phenomenology*; and the distinction in the *Encyclopedia* between the inexistent beginning of philosophy and the beginning for the philosophising subject ('Auf diese Weise sich die Philosophie als ein in sich zurückgehender Kreis, der keinen Anfang im Sinne anderer Wissenschaften hat, so daß der Anfang nur eine Beziehung auf das Subjekt, als welches sich entschli eßen will zu philosophieren, nicht aber auf die Wissenschaft als solche hat', *Werke*, 1986, vol. 8, p. 63. 'In this way, philosophy shows itself as a circle that goes back into itself; it does not have a beginning in the same sense as the other sciences, so that the beginning only has a relation to the subject, who takes the decision to philosophise, but not to the science as such.' *The Encylopedia Logic* (Indianapolis: Hackett, 1991), p. 41.

[91] Plato, *Euthydemus*, in *The Collected Dialogues of Plato* (New York: Pantheon Books, 1961), p. 392.

[92] Until the beginning of 279d.

knowledge – that is, to use Socrates' words, 'it is necessary to love wisdom'.[93] We have thus moved towards the desire for philosophy on the basis of a desire common to all people, a desire initially analysed on the basis of examples drawn from the shared opinions of the interlocutors.[94] The principle of the text's movement is to be found in the tension between the many forms taken by legitimate common desires, on the one hand, and the necessity, if one wishes to be truly happy, of giving oneself the means of luck and of correct use on the other. The disqualification of certain aspects of common life is thus provided by the exigencies of common life itself.

It seems to me that Spinoza is responding here to two exigencies – precisely those that I have grouped under the headings of familiarity and tension. On the one hand, Spinoza draws on nothing other than common life and the language through which it expresses itself; a glance at his vocabulary and examples suffices to show that we do indeed remain within the sphere of the familiar. Spinoza does not reason from within his own metaphysical system, or at least he remains on the threshold of this system, expressing himself in a way that is at once comprehensible and rationally admissible for someone unfamiliar with his lexicon – someone who does not yet accept his procedures of reasoning. On the other hand, however, he shows how, by way of their internal dynamic, the values of common life cannot satisfy the narrator and how they must therefore be transcended in the direction of a more dependable Good. The double foundational radicality is indeed at work here.

All the same, it is clear that the prologue is not a protreptic in the strict sense of the term: it presents itself as a narrative and not as an exhortation; furthermore, the word 'philosophy' is nowhere to be found in it. Nevertheless, Spinoza's text does introduce into the conversion narrative genre – specifically, into the gap opened up by the exclusion of the Other – the efficacy proper to the protreptic: the force of the familiar, understood as a point of departure that replaces the summoning of the singular. Even if it is not immediately visible, everything revolves around the harmonics of the *I*. It is here that the intellectual mechanism that produces the text's radically irreducible tone and situation is concentrated, not by an accumulation of

---

[93] Ibid., p. 396.

[94] R. Brague's analysis of Aristotle's *Protreptic* seems to lead to an analogous conclusion: Aristotle begins from the common notion of life and interprets it as harbouring a tension between what is most common in life and what is rarest. Without entering into the implications of this 'ambiguity', we can retain the idea that philosophy justifies itself by claiming that it achieves the precise goals all people share, but that it does so better, or differently.

stylistic effects but above all by establishing a definite relation between the singular, time, and the organisation of the world that unfolds at the singularity's call and that calls to it in turn in order to define it. It this relation that makes the stylistic effects that manifest this relation possible; and these stylistic effects can be read even before this relation has been posited.

I do not mean to say here that Spinoza sets out to construct a collage of procedures and fragments borrowed from different genres. On the contrary, through his mode of writing Spinoza constitutes a new genre whose effects efface those of its predecessors, all the while replacing them with new ones in the reader's mind. I have referred on a number of occasions to this reader; but who are they exactly? To this question, Alexandre Matheron answered: the Cartesians.[95] Others have said: the heterodox.[96] I would be tempted to say, by contrast, that the text constitutes its reader. But it does not constitute them out of nothing. It institutes a reader by taking a position. In fact, we can define the reader in broad terms as the text's *potential public*. In a stricter sense, we can define the reader as the character that the text itself awakens in the public's conscience. The potential public, whose composition we can get a sense of by way of the sociology and history of ideas, is without doubt made up of people similar to those Spinoza was in discussion with and whom he frequented: cultured people, even if they had different degrees of enculturation (though for the most part this diversity had for its lowest common denominator Latin scholastic culture),[97] people who were interested in the new sciences (and thus in Descartes, but also in Bacon or other innovators), as well as in their salvation (they are for the most part adepts of the 'Second Reformation' – but not necessarily; they are simply men who thought that their salvation would come from a personal quest more so than from belonging to a Church).[98] Within these limits, there is room for quite a large and diverse group of figures. However, the character brought to life by the text, extracted from this potential public, learns through their reading in what framework they can come to understand what is being said to them; the very form of the text signifies to them what strata of their culture they

---

[95] See the studies cited below.
[96] This is what R. Popkin suggests in the course of a quite complex argument, which also draws on P. Balling's work *Het Licht op den kandelaar* (R. Popkin and M. A. Signer, *Spinoza's Earliest Publication?*, Assen: Van Gorcum, 1987, pp. 12–13).
[97] This does not mean that they could all write in Latin. Yet all, or most, could read it. In any case, those exceptions who could not read Latin would have had it translated for them (this seems to have been the case with Jarig Jelles).
[98] For example those that L. Kolakowski calls 'coccéiens cartésiens', *Chrétiens sans Eglise*, Paris: NRF, 1969, p. 309 sq.

must reactualise. This is why determining the text's genre is not a question of etiquette. The genre that is used or constructed by the text predetermines its relation to the reader and orients the type of argumentation that will be deemed valid. To convince oneself of this, it suffices to take into account the diversity of Spinoza's writings. The *TTP*, for instance, is part of a debate. It intervenes into a polemical tradition where all of the arguments already exist. In this sense, its preface resembles those of Ludowijk Meyer's[99] and Lucius Antistius Constans' books:[100] it places the reader within the debate and in the midst of its key issues, commonplaces, and solemn warnings. In fact, the *TTP* will give the problematic into which it intervenes a radical shake-up; but it can only do so by first establishing itself within this problematic and by placing the reader on the 'wave-length' of the mix of dialectical, scriptural, historical and geometrical arguments that is proper to it. While the *Ethics* is written for a specialist audience, this is not the case for the *TdIE*. It presupposes a reader who has a specular relation with the author – an author who at once shows the reader why he has travelled down the path he has, and who points out this path so that the reader may follow it in turn and join up with him.

3. The Register

When faced with such a text, it is not enough to simply identify its tonalities before associating them with one or many literary genres. We must ultimately determine *what* Spinoza is talking about in this text. There exist two opposing lines of interpretation with regards to the meaning to be conferred on the *proemium*. As we will see, the discussion bears on the register these pages should be related to. This question is not simply a matter of classification: it indicates *where* we should seek out the text's true intention, if we are not to confuse what it takes from the tradition with the reasons it takes these things, not to mention with the means by which it makes them its own. Is the *proemium* an autobiographical narrative? Is it, on the contrary, a reprise of commonplaces from the philosophical tradition? This debate has long nourished the secondary literature, and we can hardly avoid it.

When we are dealing with a narrative where the author says 'I' and recounts the events that have led them to turn towards philosophy, the simplest approach consists in seeing the text as an autobiographical narrative.

---

[99] *Philosophia S. Sacrae Scripturae Interpres*, Amsterdam, 1666, trans. J. Lagrée and P.-F. Moreau, *La philosophie interprète de l'Ecriture sainte*, Paris: Intertextes, 1988.

[100] *De Jure ecclesiasticorum liber Singularis*, Amsterdam: Alethopoli, 1665.

The author reports to us what he has lived through; in turn, we can put a name and a date to the text's allusions and elliptical formulations. The text thus seems to find its truth in the life of the person who wrote it. If it is an autobiography, then we must decipher within the text the transcription of the young Spinoza's torments. In this vein, Dunin-Borkowski speaks of a 'Selbstbekenntnis' and seeks to identify the problems faced by Spinoza in the year 1656 with the first part of the description from the *TdIE*.[101] We find the same tendency in Feuer, who goes further still by 'identifying' concrete facts.[102] Indeed, we can clearly see in what sense a number of passages from the text might make us think of what we know of Spinoza's life (indeed, if we insist a little, we can see such indications in *each* passage): this is why it is not only 'classic'[103] biographical elements, but also all of those discovered by the nineteenth century,[104] or those that have more recently been brought

---

[101] 'Die Lebensperiode Despinozas, welche uns eben beschäftigt, zeigt ihn uns offenbar auf jener esrsten Stufe', *Der junge Despinoza*, Münster, 1910 (*Spinoza*, Bd I, 1933), p. 247. Further on (p. 465): 'Die Seelenschwankungen, welche nach dem Zeugnis der Selbstbekenntnisse nur seltene und kurze Augenblicke aufkommen ließen, ebneten sich mehr und mehr' (there follows the citation: 'Als mir das wahre Gut volkommener einleuchtete . . .'; and an attempt at dating the supposed 'rules of life').

[102] 'But Bento was meanwhile beginning to undergo a deep spiritual crisis. [. . .] A life devoted to the pursuit of riches began to seem futile and vacuous, as vain as a life spent in seeking fame or indulging the senses'; this sentence is followed by the quotation on danger; and then: 'The pursuit of money seemed to him akin to madness'; the author continues, likening this to a quotation from the *Ethics* IV, App. 29 (the role of money in the mind of the multitude); and then: 'Finally, in March 1656, Bento d'Espinosa began to retire from business' (Samuel Lewis Feuer, *Spinoza and the Rise of Liberalism*, Boston: Beacon Press, 1958, 1964, pp. 17–18). Notice, first, the way in which the quotations and allusions to the text are slipped in between episodes – whether real or conjectural – from the philosopher's life, without us knowing whether the first are meant to explain the latter, or vice versa; second, notice how this operation allows one to give an autobiographical charge even to a formula from the *Ethics* which is nevertheless strictly situated in the midst of an impersonal analysis; third, notice the strange work that it is necessary to perform on the text to make it say precisely *this*: given that the *TdIE* cites three 'false goods' while Spinoza's biography (and remember: Spinoza was a shopkeeper and not a magistrate!) clearly presents only one false good to the interpreter, the latter must resolve to give them different roles and to make the latter two mere points of comparison (*as vain as* . . .). The libido is lost in the story, but page 19 reassures us with a brief appearance of Clara Maria Van den Enden (attached to a late admission from Spinoza himself).

[103] Namely, the first five documents from the tradition: Lucas, Colerus, Bayle-Halma, Kortholt, the travel diary of Stolle-Hallman. On these sources, cf. our notes in the Meinsma volume: *Spinoza et son cercle*, Paris: Vrin, 1984.

[104] Namely, the works of Auerbach, Freudenthal, Meinsma, etc.

to light,[105] that might seem to be *illustrated* by these pages – by the difficulties these pages reveal and by the aspirations they indicate. As historiographical research has progressed and new details have emerged, we are tempted to find in this material new keys for unlocking this all-too-polished text. Thus, conflicts in the Jewish community or popular memories from the Inquisition, messianic or millenarian aspirations, the life of commerce or the despair induced by love, the shock of Cartesianism or the discovery of mathematics – all of these in turn become so many candidates for the truth of the *TdIE*.

We should underscore the fact that such tendencies in the scholarship are not simply a function of historiographical enthusiasm; the concern (which, moreover, is legitimate, and whose results are often illuminating) to establish the facts that constitute the cultural backdrop to Spinoza's life is also reinforced by another concern: the concern for human truth. By associating each movement – indeed each word – of the prologue with the fact it is meant to transcribe, we feel as if we are giving meaning to suffering, to uncertainty, to a truth finally found. In this sense, the Schopenhauerian reading of the *proemium* does not contradict the one advanced by scholars: on the contrary, it gives it a *raison d'être*. More generally, once we have remarked on the intensity of the text, we are tempted to reduce this intensity to an emotional intensity and to seek its foundation in the recollection of a set of specifically emotional experiences. This method is not necessarily false, particularly if it refuses to exclude the recollection of theoretical experiences; after all, other writings from the classical age – those of Uriel da Costa[106] or

---

[105] Namely, the documents discovered by Vaz Dias and Van der Tak, by Gebhardt, Revah, Petry, etc. I am not including Jelles-Meyer's preface to the *Opera Posthuma*, which is still well known but was long underestimated as a biographical document until Hubbeling-Akkerman's re-evaluation of it. See also the more general studies of the Iberian Jewish community (Revah, Nahon, Méchoulan, Saraiva, H. P. Salomon), the 'churchless' Christian community (Francès, Kolakowski) and the messianic and millenarian community (Popkin).

[106] Cf. Jean-Pierre Osier, *D'Uriel da Costa à Spinoza*, Paris: Berg International, 1983; Gabriel Albiac, *La Sinagoga vacia, un estudio de la fuentes marranas del espinosismo*, Madrid: Hiperion, 1987. Uriel's writings were collected by Gebhardt in 1922 (Carl Winter Verlag). I am leaving aside here the question of the authenticity of the *Exemplar humanae vitae*, such as it is posited for example by A. M. Vaz Dias, *Uriel da Costa, nieuwe bijdrage tot diens levensgeschiedenis*, Leiden: Brill, 1936 (MVHS, No. 2). What seems noteworthy to me is that in the *Exemplar*, such as we are familiar with it, and such as Limborch annexed it in his discussion with Orobio de Castro, the different stages of Uriel's path are identified by their content, something which is indissociably an act of biographical detective work and the evolution of a theoretical position: the narrator says both that he had such-and-such an entanglement with the

Hobbes,[107] for instance – appeal to such a connection, and it is likely that Spinoza was familiar with them.

Nevertheless, there are three objections to this interpretation:

1. In contradistinction to Uriel da Costa or Hobbes, Spinoza himself in no way invites the reader to undertake an autobiographical reading of the text; he makes no explicit links between the life of the individual 'Spinoza' and the theoretical and affective events that lead the narrator towards the search for the true good.

2. If one insists on the idea that a biographical document is not something that evokes already-known facts but is rather a document that *by itself* teaches us at least one biographical fact (even if we then relate this fact to other facts, whether concordant or discordant),[108] it is still necessary to admit that the beginning of the *TdIE does not teach us a single precise fact*. If we have the impression of reading these facts between the lines, then it is because we already know them; if we knew nothing of the content of other documents, we could identify none of the events that we believe we find in the text – unless these are extremely vague moments of intellectual history.[109] The best critique of the 'biographical' reading of the *TdIE* was

---

Catholic Church, the Jewish community, some contradictor, and that he chose the Old Testament over the New, the text of Scripture against the oral Law, and finally natural law. All of the discussions that have taken place on the question of knowing why he never speaks of his mother have a meaning (insofar as they do have one) only because he speaks so much of others: it is clear that we cannot ask such a question of Spinoza. Seeking the biographical grounding of Uriel's biographical narrative is thus a procedure that poses problems of method but finds its ultimate support in the text; it is difficult to say the same of the *TdIE*.

[107] Hobbes incessantly rewrote his biography, centred notably on the foundational scene where he enters a room in the centre of which there was an open copy of Euclid. Cf. Jean Bernhardt, *Hobbes*, Paris: PUF, 1989, pp. 12–13.

[108] This is the rule correctly formulated by J.-P. Osier at the beginning of the work cited above: 'Veut-on savoir qui était réellement Abélard? Il faut alors confronter son autobiographie (l'*Historia Calamitatum*) avec les lettres d'Héloïse et les témoignages contemporains. Journaux intimes, correspondances, romans, invitent de nos jours le lecteur à de semblables mises en rapport. Ici un texte où l'on se raconte, là une réalité' (*D'Uriel da Costa à Spinoza*, p. 17). Such a rule introduces us not only to an autobiographical dimension, but to the autobiographical as such: all genres that participate in this live off this relation between what is known of reality – of an individualised reality – including when this relation is one of torsion, negation, or apology.

[109] 'Vague' as biographical facts, naturally; as conceptual facts, they are, on the contrary, very precise, but they draw this precision from the rigour of the problematic in which they are inserted, not from some external real whose history they would present to us.

formulated by Antonio Banfi, who argued that this 'generic' biography could be adapted to the life of almost any philosopher.[110] Indeed, this claim can be tested: if these pages had remained unpublished and were discovered only today, would we attribute them with any certainty to Spinoza? Do they not also match the lives of Descartes or Hobbes? Both of these philosophers experienced uncertainties and reversals of fortune and aspired to leave the state that for a time they had found themselves in. One should take Banfi's thesis even further: at least in terms of its point of departure, this biography does not concern philosophers to the exclusion of others; if what we have said of the familiarity of the text's universe and the anonymity of its singularity is correct, then this autobiography merits the title[111] of 'everybody's autobiography'.

3. More serious still is the fact that in this text we can identify, on the one hand, a certain number of influences and conceptual reminiscences, and on the other hand the permanence of certain rhetorical structures that seem to exist prior to their present content. Thus, Pollock,[112] who Elbogen follows, highlights the analogies between the search for the true Good and the introduction to the *Discourse on Method*.[113] Gebhardt, for his part, mentions in passing a similarity with Marcus Aurelius.[114] Carla Gallicet-Calvetti, in a

---

[110] 'Il *De Emendatione* ha una introduzione di tono apparentemente autobiografico, ma la biografia è generica e potrebbe adattarsi a qualsiasi filosofo', *Spinoza e il suo tempo*, Florence: Vallecchi, 1969, p. 165.

[111] Stolen from Gertrude Stein, who used this title in a different sense.

[112] For whom the *TdIE* was 'probably [written] on the suggestion of Descartes' *Discourse on Method*', *Spinoza: His Life and Philosophy*, London: Kegan Paul, 1880, 1912, p. 114.

[113] He also remarks on the differences between the two texts – differences that at root come down to a question of degree: Spinoza advances directly to his goal while Descartes is more detailed: 'Freilich führt uns nicht Spinoza wie Descartes in dem berühmten Monolog am Beginn seines *Discours de la Méthode* seinen ganzen inneren Kampf und die Summe allen Erfahrungen vor, die ihn die Welt und ihre scheinbare Güter 'Reichtum, Sinnenlust une Ehre' als Übel erkennen liessen; in wohlüberlegten Sätzen gehr er direkt auf sein Ziel los, dem Menschen mit der Lösung des Erkenntnisproblems zugleich eine Lebenrichtung zu bieten', Elbogen, *Der Tractatus de Intellectus Emendationie Spinozas und seine Stellung in der Philosohie Spinozas*, Breslau, 1898, p. 4. With Pollock, it is a more of an attachment to an older tradition: put simply, Spinoza only ever gains some degree of autonomy with respect to a source reference by falling back on another: 'Following a more ancient course of thought than that struck out by Descartes, he is impelled by the futility of earthly [!] desires to set forth on the quest of man's true and perfect good', *Spinoza: His Life and Philosophy*, p. 117.

[114] 'Ähnlicher Gedankengang bei Marc Aurel, VIII, 1', in the notes to his translation of the *TdIE* in the *Philosophische Bibliothek*, Meiner, 1907 (republished with an

book where she takes up a thread begun by Couchoud,[115] Solmi,[116] Gentile[117] and Gebhardt,[118] seeks traces of Leo the Hebrew in the discussion of perishable goods and reads the division of goods into three groups, the relation between satiety and sensual desire, and the appreciation of wealth, as so many traits that one can already find in the first of the *Dialoghi d'Amore*.[119] Some have even gone back further still and shown the mark of the *Letters to Lucilius* in these opening pages. Long ago Akkerman noted that the Latin edition of these letters, along with their Danish translation by Glazemaker, were found in Spinoza's library,[120] yet he concluded that their influence on Books III and IV of the *Ethics* was superficial.[121] More recently Proietti has

introduction by K. Hammacher, 1977), p. 182. Gebhardt follows here a point made by Dilthey: 'Wie die Stoa verwirft auch Spinoza die gewöhnlichen Lebensgüter als Selbstzwecke. Der dies darstellende Anfang von de int. emend. stimmt genau überein mit Marc Aurel 8, 1' (Die Autonomie des Denkens im 17. Jahrundert ..., *Archiv für Geschichte der Philosophie*, VII/1 (1893), pp. 28–91; republished in *Gesammelte Schriften*, vol. II, Leipzig/Berlin: Teubner, 1914, pp. 246–96), p. 287. The passage from *Meditations* is the one in which we find the apostrophe: 'for you know by experience how many byways you have strayed along without ever discovering the good life. It lies neither in subtleties of argument, nor in riches, nor in glory, nor in sensual pleasure, nor anywhere at all; so where does it lie? In doing what human nature requires', Marcus Aurelius, *Meditations* 8, 1 (Oxford: Oxford University Press, 2016).

[115] P.-L. Couchoud, *Benoît de Spinoza*, Paris: Alcan, 1902, 2nd edition, 1924.
[116] E. Solmi, *Benedetto Spinoza e Leone Ebreo. Studio su una fonte dimenticata della spinozismo*, Modena: Vincenzi, 1903.
[117] G. Gentile, 'Leone Ebreo e Spinoza', in *Studi sul Rinascimento*, Florence: Vallecchi, 1923.
[118] C. Gebhardt, 'Spinoza und der Platonismus', *Chronicon spinozanum* I, 1921. Gebhardt had moreover procured an edition of Leon the Hebrew, Leon Ebre's work *Dialoghi d'Amore – Hebräische Gedicthe*, hrg mit einer Darstellung des Lebens und des Werkes Leones [...] von Carl Gebhardt, Heidelberg: Carl Winter, 1929.
[119] Carla Gallicet-Calvetti, *Benedetto Spinoza di fronte a Leone Ebreo (Jehudah Abarbanel). Problemi etico-religiosi e 'amor Dei intellectualis'*, Milan: CUSL, 1982.
[120] van de Lindt and Lagrée, 'La pénurie des mots de Spinoza', pp. 24–7.
[121] Akkerman has since returned more specifically to the first pages of the *TdIE* in a conference paper from 1986, where he makes the argument that the style of these pages is closer to L. Meyer's than to Spinoza's habitual style ('La latinité de Spinoza et l'authenticité du texte *Tractatus de intellectus emendatione*', *Revue des sciences philosophiques et théologiques*, 1 (1987), pp. 23–30). He concludes from this that Meyer rewrote a text for the publication of the *Opera Posthuma* that Spinoza's friends judged to be insufficient relative to its original redaction. It seems to me that we can distinguish two levels in this analysis: 1. the remarks, which are absolutely convincing, on the vocabulary, word play, and the stylistic differences with the rest of the œuvre; and 2. the explanation that is given for all of this. It could just as well be argued that Spinoza is expressing himself differently because he has something different to say.

returned to the first pages of the *TdIE* and has updated a certain number of relatively certain associations: the figure of the *proficiens* from letter 72 seems to provide the narrator who is on the path to philosophy with a certain number of traits.[122] Finally, Theo Zweerman has shown the presence of traditional rhetorical structures in the text, which he demonstrates is governed by classical methods for attracting the attention of the reader and which therefore cannot in any way be assimilated with a simple 'slice of life'.[123]

In these conditions, it is difficult to continue treating as a biography a text where the author does not declare that they are recounting their life, where no distinct biographical fact is ever clearly cited, and where a large part of what is recounted seems to come from previously existing models and to be governed by rhetorical laws more than by a concern to fix historically dated events. Whatever the pressure exerted by biographical researches in Spinoza studies, in the case of the *TdIE* this approach absolutely cannot offer us the essential interpretative rule we need.

Should we then go in the exact opposite direction? We can at least draw a first conclusion from all of this: if the *proemium* is constituted, at least in part, by Spinoza reprising a certain number of remembered readings, then we can assign ancestors[124] to these themes and juxtapose historico-thematic research with biographical research. This solution has the advantage of taking into account the evident rhetorical tenor of the text; but do we not thereby risk reducing it to this rhetorical tenor?[125] Must we conclude from the historico-thematic research that Spinoza is content to imitate Seneca, Abarbanel, or Descartes? If so, we would then run a different risk, one symmetrical to the preceding one: instead of seeking the truth of what

---

The divergence is extraordinary only if we are concerned to ensure at any price a homogeneous tone in all of Spinoza's writings.

[122] Thus, in letter 72, Seneca speaks to the sage by saying: 'laetitia fruitur maxima, continua, sua'; he opposes common life to the *studium sapientiae* and speaks of the procrastination of the person who takes the path towards philosophy.

[123] Th. Zweerman, *Spinoza's inleiding tot de filosofie. Een vertaling en structuuranalyse van de inleiding der Tractatus de intellectus emendatione; benevens een commentaar bij deze tekst*, Leuven: Catholic University of Leuven, 1983, *passim*.

[124] This is Gebhardt's solution.

[125] Thus, Gabrielle Dufour-Kowalska writes: 'Que Spinoza ne fasse que répéter un discours que la tradition philosophique prononce depuis toujours n'enlève rien à la séduction d'un texte [. . .]', 'Un itinéraire fictif', *Studia philosophica*, 35 (1975), pp. 58–80, p. 58; and further on: 'Ecoutons encore ce langage très ancien. Il raconte le surgissement de la conscience philosophique, l'éveil de l'âme à l'éternité d'un souverain bien, sa naissance à la sagesse' (p. 60).

is said in what has happened, we would seek it in what has previously been said.[126] Here, too, we would encounter the temptation of emotion: if we are nevertheless touched by a text whose thematic interpretation reduces it to a patchwork of quotations, then it is because beneath the words what seduces us is the authenticity of its intention.[127] Finally, the biographical interpretation and the search for sources or procedures are less contradictory than complementary, and both are perhaps nourished by the attempt to determine the origins of the *alterity* of the text – that is, by the attempt to *reduce* this alterity in some way. I would nevertheless wish to point out, first of all, what prevents me from adhering entirely to the solution offered by an appeal to sources, whatever its interest might be:

1. It is not enough to identify links to pre-existing texts for these links to have, all by themselves, any explanatory power. On the one hand, certain links are purely verbal: it is not enough for two authors to use the same term for these distinct uses to have any conceptual similarity.[128] On the other hand, terms that are indeed borrowed from a tradition can be taken up and have their sense bent, twisted, or pulled in the direction of some other signification. This does not mean that the search for similarities is useless; it means it is fruitful only if it serves to reveal differences. If Spinoza reprises the classical descriptions of the *falsa gaudia*, it is all the more surprising that he never uses the expression 'false goods'. If he says 'I' as Descartes does, it is likely that he does not use it in the same sense as Descartes. Finally, certain commonplaces no doubt refer more to the exigencies of the genre than they do to a heritage of shared contents. All of this implies that even true similarities must be accompanied by a close analysis of the process of transformation that accompanies the exportation of a term, notion, or image.

2. The text gives the reader the impression that it possesses a strong unity; it therefore cannot be reduced to a harlequin's coat.[129] This is the same as

---

[126] This is what Wolfson does for the *Ethics*.

[127] Cf. the terms 'séduction' and 'l'éveil de l'âme' in the preceding quotation.

[128] Martial Gueroult has shown this definitively with respect to certain of Wolfson's approximations. In the final analysis, *The Philosophy of Spinoza* is typical of a certain way of writing history.

[129] Is it necessary to recall the annoyance certain critics feel when faced with 'die entwicklungsgeschichtliche Methode'? Loewenhardt compared those who reduced Spinoza to Descartes, Bruno, or Heereboord to someone who has discovered a fragment of marble from Carrara and who then affirms that they have found the source stone from which the Venus de Medicis was cut (*Benedict Spinoza in seinem Verhältnis zur Philosophie und Naturfoschung der neuren Zeit*, Berlin, 1872, p. 384). This methodological position

saying that its arguments and examples are in fact hierarchised according to the text's global structure; one must therefore not only judge similarities in terms of their original context but also according to the place – that is to say, the function – that they come to occupy in their new context. The quotation from Marcus Aurelius opposes, in the context of a short dialogue (this is a rule of the diatribe genre), false goods and conformity with nature; Spinoza's text, by contrast, not only fails to reprise the exact same terms, it also opposes familiar terms to a term it claims to be seeking out – a term it seeks precisely as a function of its dissatisfaction with other, existing terms. What in the *Meditations* is a polarity appears in the *TdIE* as a path. And while it could be said that the Stoic is also on a quest, a quest that similarly requires a certain degree of tension, he nevertheless seeks to conquer something that he already knows (for he can define it), while his path is merely an effort to change this knowledge into will. Spinoza's narrator, by contrast, seeks above all to know what he aspires to, and his uncertainty affects the foundation of his quest, not simply the means by which he carries it out.

3. Finally, it should be noted that just as Spinoza does not explicitly cite any fact from his biography in these pages, he also does not name any precursors or adversaries at the strictly theoretical level. In fact, the text distances itself from those passages where Spinoza comments on or refutes Descartes, Bacon, Democritus or Epicurus. Moreover, contrary to many other Spinozist texts, the *TdIE* is not even implicitly polemical.[130] The conflict is internal to the

---

has nevertheless exerted some influence on the history of the secondary literature on Spinoza: Wenzel cites it and reprises it for his own ends (*Die Weltanschauung Spinozas*, vol. 1: *Spinozas Lehre von Gott, von der menschlichen Erkenntnis und von dem Wesen der Dinge*, Leipzig, 1907; Aalen: Neudruck Scientia, 1983, pp. 28–9), while Dunin-Borkowski violently critiques it by rectifying the significance of the comparison, at the same time as he presents his own method (*Spinoza*, Münster: Aschendorf, 1933–1936, vol. 1, pp. 167–8: 'Nicht ein beliebiges Marmorstück kann den richtigen Vergleichungspunkt bilden. Das ist freilich keine Quelle. Wer aber an einer gleichzeitigen Statue, an der das Auge des Schöpfers der Venus gehaftet, eine Armbeugung, einen Zug an der Stirne und um den Mund, eine Fußstellung entdeckt, die sich in der medizeischen Göttin wiederfindet, hat der Kunstgeschichte einen schönen Dienst geleistet und des Bidlhauers Ruhm nicht geschmälert').

[130] It is often said that Spinoza rarely cites others. This is true: it suffices to be convinced of this to compare his way of writing with that of certain of his contemporaries, including those close to him. L. Meyer's *La philosophie interprète de l'Ecriture sainte*, for instance, contains a veritable deluge of citations and authorities. Nevertheless, Spinoza often polemicises implicitly: without naming his adversary, and without, perhaps, even having a particular adversary in view, he sets out his thought (and invites

path and to the one following it; it is not a conflict between philosophers. The familiarity of the tone excludes systematic technicity, even if the latter is in the background and can come to the fore as soon as the writing changes style.[131] This is why it does not seem to me that these paragraphs lend themselves to a search for properly philosophical sources. On the other hand, its description of human life and its procedures of persuasion might remind us of the force of a rhetorical tradition conceived not only as an ensemble of procedures, but also as a repertoire of familiar topoi, both modifiable and modified – topoi that can be drawn on less to enrich a demonstration and more to evoke the universe of the familiar. This is the incontestable merit of the works of Leopold, Wirzubski, Akkerman, Zweerman and Proietti, for these works emphasise precisely this cultural component. The question we must ask, then, is: why does Spinoza cite other works? Is it because he expects his readers to recognise these citations? This would mean that the movement of the text makes use of them. Perhaps, then, Spinoza cites others as an appeal to authority? Yet this is hardly Spinoza's habit, even though he does occasionally do this in the *TTP*.[132] Perhaps it is to refute an opposing doctrine? Yet these pages hardly have the tone of a polemic. I would be tempted to reply that none of the real similarities are there in the form of a theoretical citation, for Spinoza's goal is neither to debate Aristotle or Seneca's theses, nor to rework their logic so as to introduce their concepts into his own architectonic.[133] That said, in a text like a protreptic, it is not inconceivable that the author would take care to place the text within a tradition of persuasion.[134] There is therefore a necessary and profitable disequilibrium in the search for sources; the heritage of 'contexts' must take priority over that of concepts.

If a text's totality is not seen as the ultimate key for understanding its details, then it is because this totality is not of an explicitly systematic type. After

> the reader to understand it) through differences and distinctions. Cf. P.-F. Moreau, *Spinoza*, Paris: Seuil, 1975, p. 26 ff.
>
> [131] As it will from paragraph 12 onwards, when the first-person narrative ends.
> [132] Cf. J. Lagrée, 'La citation dans le Traité théologico-politique', in F. Akkemann and P. Steenbakker (eds.), *Spinoza to the Letter*, Leiden: Brill, 2005.
> [133] Conversely, we can legitimately pose this question when it comes to 'common notions'. Cf. M. Gueroult, *Spinoza*, vol. II, *L'Ame*, Paris: Aubier, 1974, appendice, No. 12, pp. 581–2.
> [134] On the complex relation between philosophy and persuasion, one can find stimulating details in Jeff Mason, *Philosophical Rhetoric: The Function of Indirection in Philosophical Writing*, Abingdon: Routledge, 1989, in particular on the use of figurative language, p. 98 sqq. On the other hand, the section devoted to Spinoza (pp. 143–4) is disappointing.

all, there is no shortage of texts by Descartes in which we find signs of his reading of the scholastics, nor of texts by Leibniz that discuss, whether explicitly or not, Descartes and Spinoza; and no one has ever thought of dismembering these texts because of this presence of the other within them. This is because the discussion occurs within a Cartesian or Leibnizian framework: the philosophers' major concepts are there, present in person, and their efficacy remains undiminished by the fact that they have antecedents or contradictors. By contrast, it is clear that what is missing from the opening to the *TdIE*, such that it cannot be said to possess this kind of systematic unity, is an (apparent) conceptual progression. The reader would be more at home if the concepts of substance and modes appeared, for then the reader would have no trouble organising possible historical references under the rubric of examples. But the reader is disoriented by this apparent absence of concepts, by this form of reflection that occurs in such close proximity to common life. They might then attempt what certain commentators have done, and not the least of them – namely, to seek out in the rest of Spinoza's œuvre a principle of order that would give the beginning of the *TdIE* a coherence that it fails to explicitly manifest. Delbos, for instance, in passages that are at once stunning yet strangely violent with respect to the letter of the text, produced a commentary in which he makes the categories from the *Ethics* enter as if by force into the *TdIE*.[135] It is the idea of life that allows him to organise the text, for this idea makes it possible to tie the experience of human life to the relations between the *conatus* and Reason. Delbos begins by remarking that 'The dogmatism of Spinoza's doctrine not only implies that reason affirms being, but also, and above all, that reason realises life. This is why Spinoza poses the essential problem of his philosophy in a human and personal form.'[136] Delbos then cites the first few sentences of the prologue and the analysis of the narrator's uncertainty (who is said to be Spinoza). Delbos' commentary continues: 'It is essential, then, when one desires the sovereign good, to return into oneself; and this act of reflection, far from stopping life, marks the moment where life begins to grasp itself and govern itself. This act implies, fundamentally, the affirmation that the desire for happiness is as legitimate as it is indestructible; it is only that it requires the negation of the ordinary means by which human beings seek – in vain

---

[135] *Le problème moral dans la philosophie de Spinoza et dans l'histoire du spinozisme*, Paris: Alcan, 1893, chap. 1, p. 15 ff.

[136] 'Le dogmatisme de sa doctrine n'implique pas seulement que la raison affirme l'être, mais encore et surtout que la raison réalise la vie. De là la forme humaine et personnelle sous laquelle il pose le problème essentiel de sa philosophie', ibid., p. 15.

– the fulfilment of this desire.'[137] There is nothing false in this analysis; it presents us with an explanation that is in perfect conformity with the spirit of the system, such as we find it in Books III to V of the *Ethics* in particular. It should nevertheless be noted that, to achieve this end, Delbos makes the term 'life' take on a dynamic sense, one that is obviously absent from the text he is commenting on: to speak of 'stopping life' is to signify that one sees life as a flux, a continuous effort, a sum of individual tendencies – and not as the frame within which individuals' actions are inscribed. In other words, in Delbos' work the term 'life' becomes just another name for the *conatus*; and since we know that 'Reason demands nothing against nature' but allows the realisation of the individual's positive tendencies better than the passions do, it is easy to find the oscillation between the 'affirmation' of the need for infinite happiness and the 'negation' of the ordinary means by which we realise this goal imperfectly. As for the solution Delbos proposes, it conforms with Book V, and again by means of the same concept: once the destructive character of finite goods has been identified, unstable and exclusive as these goods are – for they lead us astray and disperse our fundamental drives – then 'the unity of the drive within us can only be reconstituted by the unity of its object; or, better still, it is only through the immediacy, whether natural or constructed, of this drive and its object that we can find the supreme certainty of life'.[138] Having arrived at this point, all that remains to be done is to indicate the equivalence between the love that is attached to something infinite and eternal and the love of God in the strict sense, which the *TTP* speaks of.[139] Absolutely none of this is incompatible with Spinozism. With respect to the architectonic side of Spinoza's thought, Martial Gueroult was right to say that 'Delbos is never wrong'. And yet, one is tempted to add, if Delbos is never wrong when it comes to the system, he is sometimes mistaken about individual texts. The logic at work here has the effect of

---

[137] 'Il faut donc, quand on désire le souverain bien, faire un retour sur soi, et cet acte de réflexion, loin d'arrêter la vie, marque le moment où elle commence à se ressaisir et à se gouverner. Il implique, au fond, l'affirmation que ce besoin de bonheur est légitime autant qu'indéstructible; il implique seulement la négation des moyens ordinaires par lesquels les hommes cherchent vainement à contenter ce besoin', ibid., p. 17.

[138] 'l'unité de la tendance qui est en nous ne peut se reconstituer que par l'unité de son objet; ou, pour mieux dire, c'est seulement dans l'immédiation, naturelle ou reconquise, de la tendance et de son objet que peut être la suprême certitude de la vie', ibid., p. 18.

[139] 'Amor erga rem aeternam et infinitam', *TdIE*, § 10 [*TdIE* 10; CWS I, 9]; 'L'amour de Dieu, comme le veut la tradition religieuse, est toute la loi; il est aussi tout le salut' (Delbos, *Le problème moral*, p. 18, with the reference to the *TTP*, chap. IV).

making the problematic specific to the prologue disappear by explaining it away; what takes the form of a path and an interrogation is transformed into a deduction. By substituting the *conatus* for 'life', Delbos is able to construct a positive theory of the essence of the individual. He thus ends up reading the love of God in a text that never mentions it.[140] The logic of all of these slippages is clear: it makes the *proemium*'s interrogative movement disappear. It also leads to the erasure of certain ideas specific to this text: thus, Delbos reads the few lines devoted to the libido in the following way: 'The pleasure that seems to overwhelm us soon leaves us weary and abandons us to ourselves, at once troubled and disenchanted.'[141] It is as if Spinoza were denouncing the illusory – and thus deceptive – character of pleasures (they '*seem* to overwhelm us'). One can then conclude that reason, insofar as it becomes conscious of this lie,[142] directs itself towards a higher realisation of its hope for unity. But does Spinoza say this? If we reread the text without projecting onto it the universe of the *Ethics*, then on the contrary what we are struck by is the fact that the text underscores not the illusory character of the passions, but rather their efficacy. The question that is posed just prior to this paragraph is: can one reconcile the pursuit of the goods of common life with the search for this other good to which we aspire? Spinoza's answer

---

[140] Freudenthal comes to the same conclusion as Delbos, albeit by a slightly different path: he insists less on the positivity of the individual and more on his aspiration to perfection, and concludes that God's love is the only goal which we should seek if we want to truly be happy – with God the only eternal and infinite being – for this good frees us of all other evils and offers us uninterrupted happiness ('Ein ewiges und unendliches Wesent ist allein Gott: die Liebe zu ihm also kann allein das Ziel sein, das wir erstreben müßen, wenn wir glücklich sein wollen; denn dies Gut bringt uns Befreiung von allen Ubeln und dauernde Glücseligkeit', *Die Lehre Spinoza . . .*, p. 98).

[141] 'Le plaisir qui semble nous prendre tout entiers nous lasse bientôt et nous abandonne à nous-mêmes, troublés, désenchantés', *Le problème moral*, p. 17. This constitutes Delbos' paraphrase of paragraph 4: 'Nam quod ad libidinem attinet, ea adeo suspenditur animus, ac si in aliquo bono quiesceret; quo maxime impeditur, ne de alio cogitet; sed post illius fruitonem summa sequitur tristitia, quae, si non suspendit mentem, tamen pertubat et hebetat' [*TdIE* 3; *CWS* I, 8].

[142] Moreover, Delbos calls finite goods 'misleading goods' [*biens mensongers*], which Spinoza does not do. He thus reinscribes the text in the tradition of the critique of false goods. If one were to seek out such an expression, then it would instead be in Malebranche that one would find it; there it would precisely be tied to the thematic of false rest (and thus of illusion): 'Car il vaut infiniment mieux chercher avec inquiétude la vérité et le bonheur qu'on ne possède pas, que de demeurer dans un faux repos en se contentant du mensonge et des faux biens dont on se repaît ordinairement', *Recherche de la Vérité*, IV. chap. III, § 1, *Œuvres*, Paris: Pléiade, édition établie par G. Rodis-Lewis avec la collaboration de G. Malbreil, vol. 1, p. 404.

is a general one: no, this is not possible, for the first kind of goods preoccupy thought to such an extent that thought is no longer capable of thinking of any other good. It is therefore this real power of preoccupation that is the topic of the following sentence, where the first example, that of the libido, is dealt with. In a first moment, the libido overwhelms us entirely (this is not an illusion, as Delbos' paraphrase interprets it), and it is this total possession that seems to prevent us from seeking anything else. The second moment, that of satiety, is then described not in terms of deception but as a kind of stupor that numbs (*hebetat*) the power of thought. In other words, the positive power of action is not situated in some *conatus* that is absent from the text; rather, it is to be found in the finite goods themselves, which have the power to stop us thinking of anything but else them. Is this just another way of saying the same thing? Whatever the case may be, this is how Spinoza chose to express himself here, and we obscure his mode of expression if we reduce it to the conceptual problematic of the *Ethics*.[143]

Must we therefore renounce the project of accounting philosophically for these pages? Can we not conceive of a rhetorical structure that would be in the service of philosophical conceptuality?

We find ourselves confronting a dilemma for which there seems to be no satisfactory solution. We will discover one only if we find a way of taking into account the particularity of these singular passages, situated as they are halfway between rhetoric and philosophy.

One way of making progress is perhaps via Theo Zweerman's hermeneutical approach.[144] The use Zweerman makes in his thesis of the methods of reception history and the analysis of literary structures is of great interest to us, since it brings out the production of meaning, which he conceives of as a specific process. Zweerman sums up his method as follows: 'This is the key hypothesis I aim to test in this study: given the role that the motif of attention plays, whether implicitly or explicitly, it is fruitful to study the introduction to the *Treatise* as a *rhetorical text*. What I mean by this is that Spinoza's argument contains irreducibly rhetorical moments, and, as such, demands a specifically rhetorical analysis. Destined as it is to introduce an exposition of method and Spinoza's philosophy in the form it had at this point, this texts deals above all with the problematic of the *transition* from a non-philosophical perspective to a philosophical perspective. Secondly, it deals with a problematic that is closely tied to this first one: that of how to

---

[143] On Delbos and Spinozism, see also Claude Troisfontaines, Maurice Blondel and Victor Delbos, *Revue philosophique de la France et de l'étranger*, 4 (1986), pp. 467–83.
[144] *Spinoza's inleiding tot de filosofie*, cf. in particular pp. 10–19.

persuade the reader to make this passage with the author.'[145] But Zweerman's goal (one that he attains, by the way) consists in showing in what sense the object of the prologue is irreducible: namely, to attract the reader's attention (*aandacht*). For my part, I also want to show what the *proemium* has in common with a number of passages from the *Ethics* and the treatises. It is necessary to recognise both the particularity of its procedures as well as what it teaches us about the rest of the system.

Another approach would consist in conceiving of the text in strategic terms, as Alexandre Matheron does.[146] Matheron identifies 'the very particular perspective adopted by this text'[147] by reference to three conditions: first, Spinoza 'describes an intellectual experience through which he has successfully passed, and thanks to which he became a Spinozist'; next, he 'seeks for his readers to go through this same experience', and thus 'takes them as they are'; and finally, 'as could be shown by reference to the language that he uses, in the *TdIE* Spinoza addresses readers who are for the most part Cartesians'.[148] Spinoza thus uses a series of arguments destined for this audience, and he has them reason according to principles that do not directly contradict those they already hold (for instance, instead of directly introducing the identity of method and the reflexive idea through the principle of the integral intelligibility of the real, he does so via one of its consequences: namely, the parallelism between formal reality and the objective reality of ideas; this is a consequence that can be admitted psychologically to the degree that its implications are not all immediately developed). Spinoza thus follows more of a pedagogical than an axiomatic path. This also explains why, even if he had already elaborated his own specific concept of 'common notions', Spinoza could not refer to these in the *TdIE*.[149] It seems to me that such a method of analysis – a method, moreover, that Matheron has applied to other works – is particularly illuminating and well-suited to the desire to grasp what one could call the semi-geometrical passages of the *TdIE*: namely, those passages where Spinoza reasons on the basis of principles and

---

[145] 'Het overhalen van lezers om met de auteur die overgang mee te maken', ibid., p. 10.
[146] See his article 'Pourquoi le *Tractatus de Intellectus Emendatione* est-il resté inachevé?', *Revue des sciences philosophiques et théologiques*, 71/1 (1987), pp. 45–54. One can also refer to his study on 'Les modes de connaissance du *Traité de la Réforme de l'Entendement* et les genres de connaissance de l'*Ethique*', in *Spinoza, Science et Religion*, Lyon: Actes du Colloque interdisciplinaire d'études épistémologiques, 1988, pp. 98–108.
[147] 'Pourquoi le *Tractatus*', p. 45.
[148] 'décrit une expérience intellectuelle par laquelle il est lui-même passé avec succès, grâce à laquelle il est lui-même devenu Spinoziste', ibid.
[149] Matheron, 'Les modes de connaissance', p. 104.

not axioms of experience – passages that make up practically the whole of the text from paragraph 18 onwards. Nevertheless, it seems to me that this method is hardly applicable in the case of the *proemium*, for there Spinoza never lays claim to any principles, but simply refers to experience.

It seems to me that it is precisely this term – *experientia* – and the register it implies that can help us escape from this aporia.[150] To understand what *experientia* means, at least on a first approach – that is, before we explore any of its implications – it suffices to read what the text says. There can be no doubt that Spinoza is speaking here to a certain extent of himself, saying 'I' and with this 'I' being irreducible to a simple grammatical procedure. We saw above what essential role the *I* played in the text. By drawing on the evocative power of the subject of conversion narratives and by disclosing the world and life in its own singular way, the *I* brings the efficacy of these themes into a discourse of introduction to philosophy. It is by virtue of the *I*'s force that such an introduction transcends the form of a purely theoretical discourse. The *I*'s power lies in its ability to simultaneously evoke and express. Indeed, this is what distinguishes the prologue to the *TdIE* from the rest of Spinoza's corpus, at the same time as it gives it the tragic intensity that readers and commentators have found so striking.

At the same time, however, the procedure by which the text simultaneously evokes and expresses is a depersonalising one: it empties the *I* of any concrete references and alludes to facts whose proper content is never presented.[151] How, then, can the text hope to convince anyone? We must now

---

[150] Here, again, it is Banfi who indicated the solution – and it is certain that his phenomenological horizon had something to do with his success: 'Non si fa la storia dei fatti personali, ma si porta una esperienza sul piano filosofico', 'Il De Emendatione', p. 165.

[151] Gebhardt noted this with respect to a possible Cartesian inspiration for the text: 'Das Ich, in dessen geistige Entwicklung und in dessen innere Kämpfe der Discours [de la Méthode] uns einführt, ist das indivduelle Ich Descartes; wir erfahren von der Erziehung in La Flèche, von den Reisen und Kriegsdiensten, von Winterquartier in Neuburg u.s.w. Anders dagegen im Tractatus de intellectus emendatione. Hier ist das Ich der typische Vertreter der Menschheit, dessen Entwicklungsgang von vorbildlicher Bedeutung ist.' Moreover, Gebhardt refers to this demarcation when he distances himself from a 'biographical' interpretation such as Freudenthal's, instead opting for a rapprochement with the *KV* as containing a universal description of the path of knowledge: 'deshalf müssen wir uns auch hüten, aus der Einleitung Folgerungen zu ziehen, die den Lebensgang Spinozas selbst erhellen sollen, wie dies neuerdings Freudenthal getan hat. Das ist schon deshalb unzulässig, weil der dort dargestellte Entwicklungsgang nu das ins Concrete umgesetzte Aufsteigen von den niederen Erkenntnisarten zur höchsten aus dem Tractatus brevis ist', 'Spinoza und der Platonismus', p. 66.

find the theoretical key of what I referred to above as the text's *familiarity*. The response, I believe, comes down to the following: the text subtracts from the narrative only what would personalise it such that it would refer *exclusively* to the life of the narrator, and not the life of the reader; the text therefore retains what is common to *both* narrator and reader. This is what the first sentence of the text presents us with: namely, *experience*, the terrain common to all individual lives, a terrain that is in a certain sense recorded in the memory of all individuals, even if it has been populated for each in a distinct way. One person was a businessman in the Jewish community of Amsterdam, the other a Lutheran, a doctor, and a theatre director, the third a German nobleman and mathematician ... Yet all have seen, or become familiar with, or suffered from, honours, pleasures and money. All, one could say, 'know what to expect' from them, to use an expression that has the merit of being at once very affirmative and very vague; for when we say that someone 'knows what to expect', we have said all there is to say. This expression does not mean that the person possesses technical knowledge, but rather that they have the means to judge a certain history or a certain activity. It does not say how they have obtained these means, but we assume that it was by frequenting such phenomena or analogous phenomena, and that his understanding of them has perhaps been reinforced by information or confidences given to him by others. But above all, what is essential is precisely not the question of the acquisition of this knowledge, of this information; the emphasis is placed more on the almost natural presence of this knowledge – natural not in the sense of necessary (for there are people who do not 'know what to expect'), but in the sense that, once it exists, the problem of how to demonstrate or verify this knowledge becomes irrelevant. We must therefore bring together what we said above about the text's familiarity with the anonymity of its singular subject: the *I* is the site at which experience circulates between individuals; it is what is lived singularly without being individual; it is what everyone can identify as the common backdrop both to their own life and to the lives of others, but without necessarily drawing rational, universal conclusions from this fact. Let me give an example: the formula 'to judge from their actions' (end of paragraph 3) signals the enumeration of the three types of finite goods; we shift abruptly from what appeared to be a personal narrative to what appears as an objective description of others. But in fact, two of the *haec tria* that are referred to in this vision of others' actions have already been mentioned in the first-person narrative; there is therefore something of a circulation between individual experience and the experience of others. This is what justifies the term I employed above: the 'autobiography of everyone'.

What remains is to work out how all of this is possible. The text does not give us an explicit answer to this question, but we can deduce one from the text's own procedures. In a word, this 'autobiography of everyone' is made possible by erasing the precise content of actions, by giving details only in the form of examples, and by being more attentive to the description of the mechanisms of the passions than to the way in which they are specified in the individual soul.[152] This is not a process of abstraction, however, and it is precisely the presence of the *I* that stops it from being one. Experience presents neither laws nor causes – and not even false causes. Already we can see that experience is not strictly a knowledge but rather a teaching. Finally, it should also be emphasised that experience is the subject of the first phrase of the text: the *I* is more the terrain where experience's lessons are learnt, and less the pioneer of knowledge in its own right.

We can concede to the partisans of rhetoric that in writing the prologue Spinoza situates himself within a tradition; but this tradition is present only because experience itself implies it: if it is common to others, then it is also common to those who presently feel it and those who have spoken of it in the past.[153] Citations, references, allusions – all of these are automatically part of the language of experience. Far from being a brute given, experience expresses itself best when it uses the very formulations that the classics have introduced. This is why the language of experience – which is also the language of citation – is juxtaposed to mathematical language as its counterpoint. The author, or the narrator, shares a culture with their reader – specifically, classical Latin culture, whether scholastic or not. This culture

---

[152] I should immediately underscore a point to which I will return further on: the list of the three goods is significant by how economical it is. While the majority of authors in the tradition can hardly resist the temptation to extend this list, to give supplementary examples, Spinoza limits himself, from the beginning to the end of these paragraphs, and with a rare sobriety, to the *haec tria*.

[153] This, moreover, is what the humanistic tradition says. At the beginning of his letter to Posterity – a fascinating text on many levels, since the history of culture is viewed here in an inverted form, with the one who will be cited speaking to those who will cite him – Petrarch notes that experience ends up confirming what we already knew through reading: 'Adolescentia me fefellit, iuventa corripuit, senecta autem correxit, experimentoque perdocuit verum illud quod diu ante perlegeram' (*Lettera ai posteri*, ed. Gianni Villani, Rome: Salerno Editrice, 1989, p. 34). When Descartes' dream presents him with the following crucial question: 'Quod vitae sectabor iter?', this is a quotation from Asone (cf. Baillet, *Vie de Descartes*, vol. I, pp. 82–4. The dreams from autumn 1619 are quoted and analysed by H. Gouhier, *La Pensée religieuse de Descartes*, Paris: Vrin, 1924, p. 45 ff., and by G. Rodis-Lewis, *Descartes textes et débats*, Paris: Hachette, 1984, pp. 49–57).

forms a common language in the same way Latin does. Everyone recognises the words, expressions and anecdotes that need only be referred to in order to be understood. This common culture does not necessarily include philosophers, and certainly not Greek philosophers. But it does include poets, historians, and those diffusers of culture that were Cicero and Seneca.[154] Experience is not the unsayable but rather the already-said. What remains is to work out how it is still possible *not* to know in certain circumstances what we know in this experiential way; how we can lose for an instant (the very instant that concerns us) what we seemed to have acquired forever. In short, how can this thing that is so well known be misrecognised? In any case, this already-said is said by an anonymous memory, more so than by a system. It is therefore important to point out that what we find of literary references in the prologue are present not to incarnate certain doctrines but rather to represent a common terrain on which everyone recognises the truth of what they have experienced. Experience is less a knowledge than it is the sign, in a particularly clear form, of what everyone has felt or lived.

Experience can thus be read at three levels: what I have lived; what I have seen others live; and what we have learnt together about what others have lived and transmitted to us, and which repeats in our own lives. Experience's language is one of familiarity – a familiarity that is not the exclusive property of the person speaking.[155]

---

[154] Seneca himself writes in this way. The style of his letters has been characterised as follows: 'Seneca usa rivestire I motivi diatribici della veste della sua personale esperienza. Non, perciò, che questa non sia esperienza sua, ma essa viene a sovrapporsi ad elementi di tradizione', A. Grilli, *Il Problema della vita contemplativa nel mondo greco-romano*, Milan/Rome: Bocca, 1953, p. 261, note.

[155] Here again, Petrarch can serve as an illustration. At the beginning of *De Vita solitaria* (a work included in Spinoza's library), he announces to his interlocutor that this treatise is written on the basis of his experience ('In hoc autem tractatu magna ex parte solius experientie ducatum habui'), that he will speak of a subject that he knows well ('multimode familiariterque notissima'), and that in writing it he will use a true and common language ('sententiis veris atque comunibus et sermone domestico contentus'). He thus underscores the fact that he has not referred to the treatises of the *sancti viri* on the matter (specifically, that of Pierre Damien), and, more generally, that he has not consulted the works of others to compose his own. The citations that are incorporated into the rest of the text show clearly that experience here does not exclude books; however, it draws on their heritage only by appropriating them in the form of its own language: the formulas of Ovid, Horace or Juvenal that follow are spontaneously included moments from the familiar world, something that would not occur with the study of a specialised treatises (cf. Francesco Petrarca, *Prose*, ed. G. Martellotti e di P. G. Ricci, E. Carrara, E. Bianchi, Milan/Naples: Ricciardi, 1955, p. 298 ff.). The page that P. Vuillard devotes to the 'antithesis' and 'analogy' between

We can see this more clearly still by comparing the *TdIE* with those texts by Descartes mentioned above, which Elbogen and Gebhardt also cite. These texts will interest us for the time being less for their explicit theoretical content (doubt, method and the scientific project) and more for their rhetorical dimension[156] and the presence within them of a narrator who speaks in the first person.[157] Descartes' text has been characterised precisely by 'the way he solves one of the touchiest problems of philosophical writing – to protect the vital individuality of philosophical inquiry without betraying the anonymity of reason'.[158] As far as the *Discourse* is concerned, it is clear that the status of the singular subject therein is not the same as the one implied by Spinozist experience: it is a determinate individual who speaks,[159]

Petrarch and Spinoza (*Spinoza d'après les livres de sa bibliothèque*, Paris: Chacornac, 1934, pp. 90–1) does not address this question.

[156] This question has been brought to light by H. Gouhier, 'La résistance au vrai et le problème cartésian d'une philosophie sans rhétorique', in *Retorica e barocco*, Atti del III Congresso Internazionale di Studi Umanistici, Rome, 1956, pp. 85–97; cf. in particular p. 90 on the relation to the reader: 'l'intention d'écrire suppose que celui qui n'est pas philosophe peut et doit le devenir: il faut donc parler à cet "autre" de telle manière qu'il cesse d'être "autre que philosophe". N'est-ce pas retrouver, dans une philosophie sans rhétorique, le problème auquel la rhétorique devait son existence?'; more recently by M. Fumaroli, 'Ego scriptor: rhétorique et philosophie dans le *Discoure de la Méthode*', in *Problématiques et réception du 'Discors de la Méthode' et des 'Essais'*, textes réunis par H. Méchoulan, Paris: Vrin, 1988, pp. 31–46; and by M. Miwa, 'Rhétorique et dialectique dans le *Discours de la Méthode*', ibid., pp. 47–55.

[157] The similarity on this point is remarked upon explicitly by H. A. Wolfson, who draws almost no consequences from it (*The Philosophy of Spinoza*, Cambridge, MA: Harvard University Press, 1934, 1958, vol. I, p. 39). I should add that it is not rare in the seventeenth century to see an author of a theoretical work begin with a 'history of his mind' (cf. O. Bloch, *La Philosophie de Gassendi*, The Hague: Martinus Nijhoff, 1971, pp. 30–1).

[158] H. G. Frankfurt, *Demons, Dreamers and Madmen: The Defense of Reason in Descartes's Meditations*, Princeton: Princeton University Press, 2008, p. 4. Very logically, the author is led to compare the writing of the *Meditations* to a conversion narrative: 'While the purpose of such writing is to instruct and initiate others, the method is not essentially didactic. The author strives to teach more by example than by precept. In a broad way the *Meditations* is a work of this sort', ibid., p. 5.

[159] 'My present aim, then, is not to teach the method which everyone must follow in order to direct his reason correctly, but only to reveal how I have tried to direct my own', AT, VI, p. 4 [PWD I, 112]. Cf. also the letter from March 1637: 'I have not put *Treatise on the Method* but *Discourse on the Method*, which means *Preface or Notice on the Method*, in order to show that I do not intend to teach the method but only to discuss it', AT, I, p. 349 [PWD III, 53]. From this perspective the *Discourse* is strictly continuous with what Baillet teaches us of the *Studium Bonae Mentis*: on the desire for knowledge, the sciences, wisdom, 'son dessen était de frayer un chemin tout nouveau;

an individual with a precise biography of which he offers a few carefully chosen yet recognisable fragments. Certainly, the subject speaks to other individuals by proposing that they join him on his path;[160] but at no point is there any circulation of the subject of the statement itself: it cannot be said that each person is invited to undertake the same journey, even if everyone is invited to enjoy its fruits.[161] The presence of a determinate biography legitimates Descartes' theoretical[162] statements, but it prevents the individual reader from identifying with this figure of singularity and anonymity. In Spinoza, by contrast, the individual is assumed without being described. The two texts are therefore both concerned with the insertion of the narrator's identity in the register of the universal, albeit in two entirely different ways. In the case of the *Meditations*, the problem contracts and the evaluation of its distinction from the prologue is all the more instructive for this reason: in Descartes, the *I* who speaks presents itself as exemplary;[163] it is no longer weighed down with individual qualitative determinations that give it one

---

mais il prétendait ne travailler que pour lui-même, et pour l'ami à qui il adressait son traité sous le nom de MUSAEUs', A. Baillet, *La vie de Monsieur Des-Cartes*, 1691, vol. II, p. 406 (AT, vol. X, p. 191).

[160] 'Mais ne proposant cet écrit que comme une histoire, ou, si vous l'aimez mieux, que comme une fable, en laquelle, parmi quelques exemples qu'on peut imiter, on en trouvera peut-être aussi plusieurs autres qu'on aura raison de ne pas suivre, j'espère qu'il sera utile à quelques-uns sans être nuisible à personne, et que tous me sauront gré de ma franchise', AT, VI, p. 4 ['But I am presenting this work only as a history or, if you prefer, a fable in which, among certain examples worthy of imitation, you will perhaps also find many others that it would be right not to follow; and so I hope it will be useful for some without being harmful to any, and that everyone will be grateful to me for my frankness', PDW I, 112].

[161] 'Le récit de 1637 rapporte l'histoire d'un esprit, remarquable mais isolé', notes J.-M. Beyssade, who adds: 'Ces démarches restent contingentes et individuelles, tant dans leur objet que dans leur légitimité. [. . .] [L]'histoire qui nous est relatée n'a aucune valeur d'exemple: l'humanité se compose presque entièrement de deux familles d'esprits pour qui l'imitation est déconseillée, les imprudents qui se perdraient par trop d'audance, et les modestes qui préfèrent la sécurité du disciple au périlleux honneur d'inventer', *La Philosophie première de Descartes*, Paris: Flammarion, 1979, pp. 30–1.

[162] In a study that draws out strong structural analogies between the *Confessions* and the *Discourse* ('Saint Augustin et les philosophes au XVIIe siècle: ontologie et autobiographie', *XVIIe siècle*, 135 (1982), pp. 121–32), P. Cahné argues: 'Chez Descartes comme chez saint Augustin, le récit autobiographique est nécessaire en ce qu'il fonde la légitimité du Moi auteur du dire fondateur', p. 128.

[163] 'Ce qui fut la trame d'une histoire singulière est devenu la première partie de la science parfaite: les raisons de doute mettent en cause les premiers principes de toute connaissance possible. Le doute hyberbolique, même s'il reste périlleux, devient par là exemplaire', Beyssade, *La Philosophie première de Descartes*, p. 33.

particular empirical figure as opposed to another; it is described in such a way that each person, so long as they make the effort, can come to reiterate Descartes' doubt, his discovery, and the consequences he draws. Better still, each person, if they desire to understand, must effectively undertake this journey. The tension that comes through at the beginning of the *TdIE* also seems to be present in the *Meditations*: disarray and uncertainty accompany doubt, at least at certain moments.[164] However, we can also trace a line of demarcation between the two texts, one that has to do with the familiarity we have identified in the universe of the prologue. In the *Meditations*, far from remaining close to the world of the everyday, we instead set out on an extraordinary if anonymous experience; the subject's singularity, which it has lost at the level of its identity, is refound in the identity of its act, while the essence of the *I* is expressed insofar as it withdraws from common activity. Moreover, if, in Descartes, we go beyond the experience of everyday life, then it is because our point of departure was not – or was not only – everyday life. By contrast, the Spinozist narrator is in some sense constrained to reflect on the true Good by 'omnia, quae in communi vita frequenter occurrunt'; but in this *omnia*, science is not included: it does not seem to immediately figure among the common ends of human beings (we will see it emerge only in a mediated form, in terms of the *commoda* that it can give us). On the other hand, the Cartesian narrator is already individuated by the fact that he has a determinate goal when the curtain rises: if he undergoes the experience of doubt, then it is with the intention of 'establishing something firm and constant in the sciences'. And there is, perhaps, an even more fundamental difference than this one – a difference that conditions it: in Descartes, the *I* has a positive content from the outset; it chooses and decides; and if it has not taken this path earlier, then this was only because it had decided it would do so one day.[165] While Descartes might experience moments of theoretical disorientation in the course of his journey,[166] he does not experience them

---

[164] 'It feels as if I have fallen unexpectedly into a deep whirlpool which tumbles me around so that I can neither stand on the bottom nor swim to the top', *PWD* II, 16.

[165] 'But the task looked an enormous one, and I began to wait until I should reach a mature enough age to ensure that no subsequent time of life would be more suitable for tackling such inquiries', *PWD* II, 12. Where the Spinozist narrator sees the delay as a failure ('quod saepe frustra tentavi'), Descartes sees the possibility of a fault – but one that he avoids.

[166] These moments are, moreover, few and far between: at the beginning of the *Second Meditation*, the passage on very deep water is almost immediately followed by the reference to the 'fixed and certain' Archimedean point and the 'high hopes' that are expected of it.

at the beginning. On the contrary, the Spinozist narrator is not even individuated by reference to his resolve since the latter comes only at the end; and it is perhaps this lack of will that makes Spinoza's text more experiential and less experimentational. The narrator has available to him only what is part of common use, and when he has succeeded in constructing something else he disappears in favour of this very construction. His path is not the first stage of science: it is an introduction *to* science, which is then abolished. In Descartes, the path of the *I* is so little abolished that it is repeated at the beginning of the exposition of the *Principia*.

I have now identified the three registers of experience; what remains to be done is to identify the notions by which experience presents itself. How should we proceed? I will now reconstitute the 'givens' of each of the actors in the prologue – common life, the true good, the *animus* – by asking what, precisely, is said of each. I will leave aside the text's biographical foundations and, at least provisionally, any doctrinal connections. That said, I will not prohibit myself from repeating certain commonplaces, but will do so only to ask what Spinoza makes of them; I will never consider their simple presence as explanation enough. Similarly, I will compare the *proemium* to other texts by Spinoza on precise points, but without supposing that there exists a doctrinal identity between them. The comparisons will serve to clarify (by similarity or difference) the possible meaning of a term and to mark out those limit points where a problem is transformed. However, I will always turn to the identification of these similarities and differences only once I have analysed the procedure proper to the prologue.[167]

---

[167] In particular, everything that concerns the comparison between the possible meanings of the relativity of goods is left to Chapter 6, after I have completed the analysis of the procedure proper to the *proemium*, while from Chapter 3 onwards I will analyse the theme of the three goods given that it is an anonymous topos that concerns rhetoric more than architectonics. The analysis of analogies with the *Short Treatise*, along with their limitations, is also left to Chapter 6, though this does not exclude at other moments associating the use of a Latin term with its Dutch correspondent.

2
The Stages of Certainty

A. Empiricist Reading, Experiential Reading

It is not enough to read the *proemium* from the perspective of experience; we must also interpret how experience is presented within it. Is experience a mere collection of disorganised data, in the midst of which we find feelings and familiar allusions, or does it have a structure that must be brought out?

It seems to me that many commentators – for reasons more of conviction than negligence – have implicitly chosen the first solution. Take the following example: in an exegesis that recognises the key role played by *experientia* along with its transindividual character,[1] we read the following summary: 'Spinoza rejects finite goods (*divitias, honor, libido*) for the following reasons: they provoke great sadness (*summa tristitia*), which disturbs and dulls the spirit; they distort all knowledge, since we consider them to be ultimate ends – that is, they distract thought such that it becomes incapable of thinking of another good; and they reduce us to slavery, since these are not goods that we possess, but rather that possess us. . . .' Lastly, finite goods constitute 'the negation of everything that Spinoza will consider as essential to an authentically human existence: joy, thought, freedom, and, above all, the preservation of one's own existence'.[2] This is a remarkable paragraph,

---

[1] 'Spinoza habla de sì mismo y expresa su propia experiencia. Pero al mismo tiempo – y en ello muestra su permanente tendencia a la totalización – va en su propia experiencia la experiencia de todos los hombres', César Tejedor Campomanes, *Una Antropologia del Conocimiento. Estudio sobre Spinoza*, Madrid: Publicaciones de la Universidad pontificia Comillas, 1981, p. 22.

[2] 'Spinoza *rechaza los bienes finitos* (*divitias, honor, libido*) por los siguientes motivos: provocan una gran tristeza (*summa tristitia*) que perturba y embota el espiritu; falsean todo conocimiento, puesto que se le considera como fines últimos, es decir,

for each element on its own is accurate (each is drawn from the text itself) while together the whole that these elements constitute is false (no element is in the correct place). It is true that Spinoza rejects finite goods, yet these goods are not initially known as such. At the beginning, the fact that these goods distort knowledge is not considered a reason to reject them, for at this point knowledge is not assumed to be an unconditioned value – no more so, that is, than freedom or thought (thought, for its part, appears up until paragraph 10 in the guise of a means more than an end). The classical opposition between the goods that we possess and those that possess us is nowhere to be found in Spinoza's text. What we do find, by contrast, is a progression that leads from one good to the next. Moreover, these goods together produce effects that are not opposed to one another but are rather mutually reinforcing.[3] What explains these errors of interpretation is the fact that the very reality of the narrator's journey has been overlooked: it is considered to be a mere artifice of presentation that can be ignored by summarising the facts, feelings and reminiscences that the reader discovers in the narrative. The value of these elements is seen to arise not from the place they occupy in the text but from the fact that the reader *recognises* them. We could call such a reading an empiricist reading, in the sense that it takes textual facts as they come yet fails to perceive the broader horizon within which they take on their meaning. This empiricist reading does not, however, leave these facts in a state of total disorder. Rather, it goes beyond them and relates what Spinoza says to what can be found in other sources, from the *Korte Verhandeling*[4] to Pascal,[5] Aristippus[6] and Marcus Aurelius.[7] We saw above that Delbos' reading interpreted the *TdIE*'s prologue as possessing the same strong conceptual coherence as a text like the *Ethics*. By contrast, in the case of the more common empiricist reading, the prologue is inserted into

---

distraen la mente de tal manera que se hace incapaz de pensar en cualquier otro bien y nos someten a su esclavitud, ya que en vez de tratarse de bienes que poseemos, son ellos los que nos poseen [. . .] Son, pues, la negación misma de todo lo que Spinoza considerarà essencial a una existencia auténticamente humana: la alegría, el pensamiento, la libertad, y, en suma, la conservacíon de la propia existencia', ibid., pp. 18–19.

[3] 'Frequenter sunt causa interitus eorum, qui ea possident, et semper causa interitus eorum, qui ab iis possidentur', § 7, G II, p. 7, ll. 7–9 [*TdIE* 7; *CWS* I, 9].

[4] C. T. Campomanes, *Una Antropologia del Conocimiento*, p. 19.

[5] 'Se trata de un *salto en el vacío* que recuerda a Pascal, Jacobi y Kierkegaard', ibid., p. 18.

[6] We can trace the opposition between 'possessing' and 'to be possessed' back to Aristippus, as Appuhn remarks in the notes to *Œuvres de Spinoza*, Garnier, vol. I, p. 536.

[7] Cf. above the comparison made by Gebhardt.

a much less determinate context, that of the moral tradition – a tradition that thinks it finds its own arguments in the *TdIE* and silently readies itself to lend the text its own order as soon as the prologue's proper order has been abandoned.

To such a reading, we must oppose another reading that subordinates the dynamics of recognition to the determination of the *place* of what is recognised. Above all, it is essential to bring out the specific structure of the prologue's journey – the whole in the context of which both the text's terms and its arguments take on their precise meaning. It is this journey that constitutes the woof and weave of experience, while each fact that the text refers to must be clarified by reference to the existential descriptions of which it is the object. Understanding these descriptions means determining at what moment, and to what end, each of them is situated. Of course, the articulation of these moments is not identical to the succession of the narrative's sentences, for the narrative itself is part of a persuasive structure whose that does not fundamentally follow a chronological order. In this sense, the narrative both reveals and delays the temporality of experience: the latter must therefore be reconstituted not by following the course of the narrative, but by way of its indications. In doing so we can account for what is perhaps the most striking feature of these pages: their radicality – a feature that is both the text's most powerful characteristic at the same time as it is what is most obscured by those interpretations that are quick to confuse it with human profundity. This radicality consists in presupposing, in this meditation that will lead to the transcendence of common life, nothing that is beyond the limits of common life itself. To bring out the prologue's radicality, we must now seek a thread to follow that will allow us to grasp the structure of experience.

B. Certainty as Criteria

There is a word in the text that has even greater priority than *experientia* or *me*: namely, *postquam*.[8] The narrative begins with a reference to time. This reference should not surprise us in a narrative that borrows some of its contours from the conversion narrative. For the text divides time in two in a very classical manner – into a 'before' and an 'after'. Prior to this foundational instant (the instant of the decision, which is strictly delimited by the *constitui*), the narrator is trapped in a world that the narrative describes by reference to negative traits – vanity, futility, then fear; and then, further

[8] § 1, G II, p. 5, l. 6 [*TdIE* 1; CWS I, 7].

on, sadness and the risk of death. After this same instant, a path opens up, one marked, at least in terms of its goal, by positive traits, beginning with the promise of an 'eternal and supreme joy'.[9] The story of the *animus* and its decision is thus given in its reality in the form of a fold that reorganises the totality of things according to a clear division between a 'before' and an 'after'. What we find here is thus a veritable inversion of the givens of the world, for in the instauration of the *postquam* we pass from sadness and its correlates to joy, from the promise of death to eternity. However, if we consider the text closely, things are not as simple as they appear: everything is indeed organised according to this division, but this division alone does not suffice to account for the totality of what it organises. The 'before' itself is divided again, as evidenced by the term *tandem*,[10] which announces the final decision – a *tandem* that is made explicit in what follows[11] as being the culmination of a series of intermediate stages, which are indicated by the expressions *primo enim intuitu*,[12] *postquam* (again)[13] and *primo*, etc.,[14] not to mention by the two formulations that mark the stages that we can suppose to have lasted quite a long time: 'Often I tried this, but in vain',[15] and 'By persistent meditation, however, I came to the conclusion . . .'.[16] The narrative therefore immediately presents itself not only as the staging of a division of time, but also, in the unfolding of this division, as the scansion of a history.

Now, as we saw above, this history is not made up of anecdotes drawn from an individual's life, even though these can be inscribed within it. This is, moreover, why the scansions of this history do not cancel out the division into two times, but on the contrary extend it and are subordinated to it. These scansions do not introduce a completely different division, but rather determine the moments of the 'before' – aspirations, hesitations and deliberations – as a function of their relation to the 'after'. They thereby articulate all of the elements of the narrator's choice without dissolving that choice, giving it an existential weight which, while not biographical, nevertheless still possesses an undeniable consistency. Thus, if anecdotes

---

[9] 'Continua ac summa fruerer laetitia', § 1, G, II, p. 5, ll. 15–16 [*TdIE* 1; *CWS* I, 7].
[10] § 1, G II, p. 5, l. 12 [*TdIE* 2; *CWS* I, 7].
[11] 'Dico, me tandem constituisse', § 2, G II, p. 5, l. 16 [*TdIE* 2; *CWS* I, 7].
[12] § 2, G II, p. 5, l. 16 [*TdIE* 2; *CWS* I, 7].
[13] 'Postquam aliquantulum huic rei incubueram', § 6 G II, p. 6, ll. 25–6 [*TdIE* 6; *CWS* I, 8].
[14] 'Inveni primo . . .', § 6, G II, p. 6, l. 26 [*TdIE* 6; *CWS* I, 8].
[15] 'Quod saepe frustra tentavi', § 3 G II, p. 5, ll. 25–6 [*TdIE* 3; *CWS* I, 7].
[16] 'Assidua autem meditatione eo perveni . . .', § 7, G II, p. 6, l. 30 [*TdIE* 7; *CWS* I, 8].

do not offer the key to the narrative's evolution, there must exist another principle for the text's scansions. What justifies the passage from one stage to the next? No detail, no means of dating events – which would allow us to identify the text's content from an external perspective – is given to the reader. We know nothing of the narrative's location (whereas in Augustine's narratives the passage from Africa to Italy is at least mentioned), nor do we know the identity of the doctrines that the narrator had adopted prior to his final decision, if indeed he had adopted any at all (Augustine, by contrast, speaks of the Manicheans and the Academicians, explains why their views are seductive, and refutes, at least allusively, their theses). We do not even know the exact personal content of the goods that the narrator has rejected (the examples stated in paragraphs 4 and 5, and then in paragraph 8, as vague as they are, are not spoken of in the first person). Can we get any grip on what constitutes the temporality of this text?

Spinoza does give us an indication of how to orient ourselves in the movement of his text. The narrative of the trajectory erases the external givens that would have lent a concrete form to the different stages of certainty; consequently, there is no way of measuring the unfolding of the stages of this trajectory other than by the note of certainty they strike. Finally, the most determinate trait that is indicated on each occasion as a reason for the narrator's hesitations, and which then initiates the overcoming of these hesitations, is the reference – different at each stage – to the domains of the certain and the uncertain. The text's scansions are therefore constituted by the labyrinth of certainty, as is shown above all by the almost obsessive repetition of the terms *certam/incertam*,[17] *certitudinem*,[18] *bonum certum pro incerto*,[19] *bonum sua natura incertum*,[20] *incerto quoad ipsius consecutionem*.[21] One cannot but be struck by the forceful insistence on the term 'certainty' and related words – words that are represented from the very first sentence by two adjectives that illustrate the faults of uncertainty:[22] *vana* and *futilia*. However, it is not only a matter of lexical quantity: what is most important

---

[17] 'Propter rem tunc incertam certam amittere velle', § 2, G II, p. 5, l. 17 [*TdIE* 2; *CWS* I, 7].

[18] 'Ad ipsius certitudinem pervenire', § 3, G II, p. 5, l. 24 [*TdIE* 3; *CWS* I, 7].

[19] 'Bonum certum pro incerto amittere velle', § 6, G II, p. 6, ll. 24–5 [*TdIE* 6; *CWS* I, 8].

[20] § 6, G II, p. 6, l. 27 [*TdIE* 6; *CWS* I, 8]. This is reprised in the form of an opposition in 1, 28: 'incerto, non quidem sua natura' [*TdIE* 6; *CWS* I, 8].

[21] 'Incerto [. . .] tantum quoad ipsius consecutionem', § 6, G II, p. 6, ll. 28–30 [*TdIE* 6; *CWS* I, 8].

[22] We will see further on that they only illustrate it relatively – for they can indeed coexist with a certain type of certainty.

is that the term 'certainty' occurs at key points in the text's argument, and that these occurrences help us pass from one stage of the journey to the next. The first given of experience, at least with respect to the narrative's order, is the 'vain and futile' tonality of what occurs in common life. By contrast, with respect to the internal order of common life itself – that is, before the revelation of its futility – what comes first is the unquestioned security and certainty attached to the goods that one encounters there. What sets the meditation in motion is thus a tension between an initial certainty and a sense of futility. Then, what prevents the narrator from immediately making a decision is the weaker sense of certainty that initially qualifies the *verum bonum*. What gives rise to his final decision is therefore the inversion of this qualification: what was initially certain has now become uncertain, and what caused the narrator to hesitate for reasons of its uncertainty appears, at the end, as more certain than whatever had barred access to it. Ultimately, then, it is indeed the internal transformation of this certainty that plays the same determining role that the intervention of the other plays in classical conversion narratives, or the teachings of the master in the protreptic genre. Moreover, as we will now see, this internal transformation – whether we interpret it in terms of the acquisition of goods or their nature – successively plays the role of a brake and a motor. It is the obstacle that stops movement while also motivating the effort to overcome the obstacle.

In the final analysis, then, it is the term *certitudo* that gives consistency to the narrative's temporality. The significance of this term cannot be overstated: *certitudo* is now revealed to be the bearer of the entire narrative novelty of the *proemium*. I noted above how Spinoza had forged a new philosophical genre by erasing the differences between the conversion narrative and the exhortation to philosophy. We can now see how this erasure occurs: in the term *certitudo* there is concentrated everything that makes this journey different, which is that it first appears as necessary and then as possible. . On its own, however, this essential term does not offer the key to its interpretation. For Spinoza does not define what he means here by the words 'certain' and 'certainty'. Like most terms in the prologue, these two words are borrowed from common language and are supposed to immediately evoke something in the reader. It is therefore necessary to determine their meaning on the basis of their place in the text – that is, in terms of the text's internal coherence – and by reference to the terms with which they are associated. It is true that these words can be found elsewhere in Spinoza's work, and they obviously make the reader think of the terms of Cartesian philosophy. But if we wish to avoid being overly hasty in identifying the word 'certainty' with the correlative Cartesian concept, it is preferable to explore each individual use of the term in the prologue. Only then can we compare them to Descartes' usage. In any case, we can immediately note that the adjective 'certain' refers to goods, not to knowledge. Or rather, if knowledge is at stake,[23] then it is knowledge considered initially as a good – that is, in terms of its acquisition, loss and enjoyment. Likewise, Spinoza never says 'I' am certain or 'I' am uncertain: it is the vagaries of certainty itself that allow the narrator to progress. Far from being their subject, the narrator is at best their observer and the site at which a certain reversal occurs.

1. Determinations of the Certain

This reversal structures the dynamics of the text. But how precisely does it do this? To determine how, we must reconstitute the stages of certainty. But before we explore the specific content of each of these stages, we must establish the limits of the various meanings of the term *certitudo*.

This first determination, provided by the two moments that bookend the process, brings out two fundamental dimensions of the idea of certainty: the inscription of its initial form in a sequence that occurs prior to the journey,[24] and the emergence of its second form as the result of a transformation of what is evident in experience. The two extreme points represented by paragraphs 2 and 7 show this in dramatic fashion. As we discover in the course of the argument, there are two types of certainty – or, more precisely, two forms of the opposition between the certain and the uncertain. In one sense, the argument consists precisely in this shift in perspective. The first opposition is an opposition with two terms (the certain goods that we possess versus the uncertain good in the name of which we would dare not sacrifice these certain goods). It is by way of this opposition that the world of the *vita communis* most immediately manifests a resistance to the project, which has only just begun to be elaborated, of leaving, precisely, the *vita communis*.

---

[23] In paragraph 13 – that is, after the interruption of the journey – the reader will learn, by anticipation, that the nature of the sovereign good one will come to enjoy is that it is a knowledge (*cognitio*); before this, the prologue had used the term 'good' (*bonum*) or the very general word 'thing' (*res*).

[24] [Translator's note: Moreau refers to the text's 'journey' as an 'itinéraire'; thus, he uses the term 'pré-itératif' to refer to what occurs prior to this 'journey'. Since I have chosen to use the word 'journey' to translate 'itinéraire', I have not used 'pre-iterative' to translate 'pré-itératif'. Nevertheless, I have included the following note that Moreau uses to explain his lexical choice]. The reader will forgive me this unusual use, which I have chosen in order to avoid a periphrasis designating what is present prior to the path. It is also justified by the fact that the reader can repeat the path.

Only a moment's reflection is required to see the power of this opposition: it is there *from the very beginning*. For this reason, at the slightest solicitation this opposition can become explicit and present overwhelming evidence in favour of its argument *primo enim intuitu*. Well before it appears as a response to the first challenge, this opposition is immediately apparent in the course of the *vita communis* itself. The challenge (that is, the perception of vanity and futility) serves merely to bring it to light. When it appears, this opposition discloses both the course of common life itself and the implicit doctrine of certainty on which it is based; a doctrine that common life presents only when it is forced to do so – that is, when it is challenged. This implicit doctrine could be summed up by the formula: 'a bird in the hand is worth two in the bush'.[25] Whoever doubts this doctrine risks missing their prey and catching only at shadows. It is perhaps not by accident that the weight of evidence that supports this implicit doctrine can so easily be reduced to the form of proverbs, for they participate in the same quasi-theoretical consciousness of common life and therefore constitute a barrier to discussion.

Next, we move to the second opposition, which reveals the principle of the first – a principle that is invisible from the perspective of the first opposition. This principle is the secret identity between the nature of a good and its mode of acquisition. Certain goods – or rather those considered at this initial stage to be certain – are goods that are close at hand; uncertain ones are those that are far away, sometimes so far that their very existence cannot be definitively determined. The source of the subject's disquiet is thus that they imagine seeing something that was previously close become distant, while in its place they find a good that might not exist. The inversion that moves the subject to the second perspective, while still conserving the vocabulary of the first, leads them to reconsider and indeed deepen this opposition, and thus to suppress the causes of their disquiet by discovering that, contrary to what they had spontaneously assumed, the nature of certainty is not reducible to the mode of a good's acquisition. Thus, those goods that had originally been close at hand will fall first into the category of the uncertain, and then into the category of definitively evil goods. I will return to these notions of the 'nature' and the 'mode of acquisition' of certainty. For the time being I will limit myself to the idea that it is the play of these notions that causes the transition from the narrator's hesitations to his overcoming of these hesitations. In other words, the two dimensions of certainty that we have just identified by examining the two moments that bookend the process – the evidence that precedes the journey and the re-working

---

[25] 'Un bon tient vaut mieux que deux tu l'auras' [Translator's note].

of this same evidence – suffice to reveal the temporality proper to the narrator's path. This temporality involves a progression that is at once logical and lived and which expresses in a quite specific mode a transformation in what is taken to be evident. It is only by going through the stages of this temporality that later on one can rightfully engage in the inquiry that forms the object of the *Treatise on the Emendation of the Intellect*. This temporality is irreducible; any reader who makes it vanish or reduces it risks effacing what is most specific to the procedure of the *proemium*.

If we now wish to go beyond this first determination and enter into the different stages of certainty in terms of their effective content, we cannot rest content with simply following the text's progression. As I have already remarked, the prologue does not present us with the journey's chronology in its proper order. The main verb from the first sentence indicates what happens at the *end* of the trajectory: namely, the narrator's final decision. As for the other stages, these are referred to very briefly in the first paragraphs and then reprised in the form of examples and explanations that mix clarifications with chronological developments. The proof of this difficulty lies in the three types of transition or articulation that govern the text as a whole: the temporal terms (*tandem*, etc.), which I have already cited; the explanatory terms (*nam, enim*) whose field of application is not always easy to determine with precision; and finally the self-citations, which restate the argument and together form a narrative that presents the journey's stages and their description less in terms of when they appear and more as a function of the moment at which they are overcome. It cannot be automatically supposed, then, that when two sentences follow one another, the second describes events that follow in time those that are described in the first. On the contrary, the second sentence might render explicit the first sentence's content or enumerate its causes. This is why, in retracing the real content of each stage, it will be necessary to understand the structure of their scansions by referring to the prologue's first sentence, which in a certain way synthesises the entirety of the process, and to then seek the content of each stage in the paragraphs that develop the term *tandem*.

It seems to me that Spinoza's translators have not always understood this first sentence. Consequently, commentators who share these translators' implicit hypotheses on the structure of the prologue's reasoning have also failed to understand it. Now, the first problem of comprehension involves the interpretation of the journey as a whole. The term *postquam* is not only a temporal indication, as an adverb would be: it is a conjunction of time. In contrast to *tandem* or *primum*, it indicates less a moment and more the logical structure of a relation between moments. The precise evaluation of this relation can help us put the stages that the narrative groups together back in their proper order. The first sentence attests to a rhetorical composition that is at once subtle and resolute. This should tell us that the narrative's 'opening' will perhaps give us the key to what follows. The second part of the sentence describes the decision (the conjugated verb *constitui*) and renders explicit its content (the infinitive *inquirere* and its complement *an aliquid daretur*, which is repeated with great intensity).[26] What interests us here, however, is the first part of the sentence: it is composed of two subordinate phrases that parallel each other in terms of their function, situation, and structure. They are parallel as regards their function since both are attached to the principal verb *constitui*; and they are parallel in terms of their situation, for as the adverb *tandem* proves, both describe a state of affairs that precedes the main action of the text; and finally, they are parallel in terms of their structure: both are composed of a kernel that is introduced by a preposition (*postquam* in the first case, *cum* in the second), followed by an infinitive complement of the verb of this central kernel, before the inscription of a relative clause that determines the subject of the infinitive (this is the same word in both cases: namely, *omnia*). This double structure could be represented as follows:[27]

Postquam me experientia docuit	(A_1)
omnia [. . .] vana et futilia esse	(B_1)
quae in communi vita frequenter occurrunt	(C_1)
Cum viderem	(A_2)
omnia [. . .] neque boni neque mali in se habere	(B_2)
a quibus et quae timebam	(C_2)

It is not enough to merely note this parallelism: we must pass from its formal aspects to its signification. More precisely, since this parallelism bears upon those clauses that refer to time, we must determine whether it should be interpreted as the expression of a simultaneity. The question that arises concerns the relation between the facts described by the two subordinate clauses. We will not be able to understand the chronology that undergirds the text if we fail to elucidate the relation between the events introduced by *postquam* and those introduced by *cum*. Allow me to mark out my interpre-

---

[26] 'An aliquid daretur [. . .]; imo, an aliquid daretur [. . .]', § 1, G II, p. 5, ll. 12 and 14–15 [*TdIE* 1; *CWS* I, 7].

[27] I am leaving out of this table the restriction 'nisi quatenus ab iis animus movebatur', which does not affect the general structure of this part of the sentence.

tation: these two subordinate clauses seem to me to refer to two *successive* stages on the path of certainty. The parallelism is thus not a parallelism of time but of causation. The unity of the sentence is not there to show that the two events took place together; on the contrary, it serves to embed the final decision in the network marked at its extremities by two events of inverse meaning but between which there is a relation of necessity. The path can therefore be recomposed in the following way:

a) the stage of the *communis vita* as it is given (and evoked by the first relative clause);
b) the stage of experience's teaching: experience teaches the narrator that the *omnia* (B_1), rendered explicit by the first relative, are 'vain and futile'; the narrator therefore aspires to something else – to a good that would be neither vain nor futile;
c) the stage of prevarication: at this point, *primo intuitu*, the narrator fears abandoning what is certain (the certain goods that are close at hand); he is undecided as to the determination of his happiness; and so he seeks, albeit in vain, a middle road;
d) finally, the stage of resolution: the narrator realises that the fears born in the third stage refer to a false appreciation of what is said in the relative clause: the *omnia* (B_2) are decisive only insofar as they provoke movements of the mind; the narrator then makes the resolute decision to seek the true Good.

If this schema is correct, then the two subordinate clauses are in no way situated at the same level. The one that begins with *postquam* corresponds to the second stage (while the relative clause it includes refers to the first stage); it conditions the emergence of a new aspiration. The clause that begins with *cum*, by contrast, corresponds to the fourth stage (while the relative clause within it belongs to the third) and indicates the final condition that justifies the decision the narrator is finally ready to make, for it removes the final obstacle.

This schema, by which we can read the prologue's first sentence and the paragraphs that follow, thus places a strong emphasis on the disjunction between the aspiration to the true good and the decision to seek it out. There are, in a sense, two 'realisations', each of which is preceded by an anterior moment where the *I* is dominated by the order of the given – in the first, by untroubled enjoyment, and in the second, by unresolved prevarications. It is the organisation of these four moments that gives Spinoza's quest its specificity. Now, this schema of reading is in no way the only possible one. It could even be said that the majority of the *TdIE*'s readers have chosen a different one. I will consider their reasons for doing so further on. Everything comes down to the interpretation of the initial parallelism: it is by identifying *two* causes in this parallelism – causes that are temporally distinct – that we can best analyse the narrator's interrupted trajectory. By contrast, Koyré, like many translators, sees in this parallelism the clear construction of an expression of simultaneity; he aligns the second subordinate clause with the first so closely that he effectively erases the second.[28] Such a reading seems to have behind it the authority of a tradition,[29] one that is nevertheless not wholly dominant.[30] It seems that for the followers of this tradition two concomitant events occur, situated at the same moment in the preparation of the decision to seek the true Good. An advantage of reducing the circumstances of the crisis to the same level is that one obviously simplifies the text's chronology. In my view, however, this choice is untenable, for it makes us misrecognise what is at stake in the path being described. It thereby leads us to reassociate the text with those traditions from which it is attempting to extract itself. In fact, it leads to the following two alternatives:

— *Either* the content of the two subordinate clauses must be situated at the beginning of the process, in which case there is no longer any theoretical place for the narrator's hesitations; for these hesitations, to the extent that they are mentioned in the text, appear in the form of a simple delay in the process of his holding firm to the decision. As such, the enumeration of the three goods and of their effects, when read as a denunciation of their lack of being, is naturally presented as the starting point of the text's journey. Yet this reading goes against the letter of the text. Furthermore, on this hypothesis one wonders where the fears mentioned in the second subordinate clause come from: are they inherent to the *communis vita*? This is a trait of the moral tradition that precedes Spinoza, and Spinoza mentions it briefly

---

[28] And he replaces it by 'et que': 'Après que l'expérience m'eut appris que tout ce qui arrive communément dans la vie ordinare est vain et futile, et que je vis [etc.]', B. de Spinoza, *Traité de la Réforme de l'Entendement* [. . .], texte, traduction et notes par A. Koyré, Paris: Vrin, 6th edition, 1979, p. 4.

[29] Saisset: 'L'expérience m'ayant appris à reconnaître que tous les événements ordinaires de la vie commune sont choses vaines et futiles, et que tous les objets de nos craintes n'ont rien en soi de bon ni de mauvais . . .', *Œuvres de Spinoza*, Paris: Charpentier, 1861, vol. III, p. 297.

[30] In the *Nagelate Schriften*, the *cum* is translated as *dewijl* – that is, by 'while' [*alors que*] – and thus marks a distinction between *dewijl* and *nadat*, the translation of *postquam* (NS, p. 407). Appuhn is prudent in his translation by placing two independent propositions in the place of the two subordinates, thereby avoiding the question of their relation.

in what follows. But he in no way makes it the paradigm for the agitations of the soul.[31] It is at the very least a risk to bring together in a single moment both the attachment to goods in their futility and in the fear they induce, and, again in a single moment, the critical consideration of these goods' futility and the liberation from fear; for in doing so one risks reading the narrator's decision as the *immediate* consequence of a sudden revelation: there is no longer any hesitation, let alone a journey. One therefore cannot explain the *tandem*, which now brings an inexistent journey to an end. In fact, such a reading empties out the content of the intermediate period, which is that of the acquisition of certainty. It applies the schema of the conversion narrative[32] to Spinoza's text, without attending to the way he modifies it.[33]

— *Or* the two subordinate clauses must be situated at the end of the process. But why, then, did the process begin in the first place? It becomes impossible to understand the beginning of the *TdIE* unless we suppose that there exists in the soul an innate and ever-present aspiration towards a Sovereign Good, with the narrator's decision bearing only on his own effective search for it. This latter solution seems impossible to me, unless we suppose that an external intervention has occurred and convinced the subject of the necessity of giving in to his own most profound tendencies. This second reading therefore also effaces the time proper to the journey, and applies the schema of the protreptic to Spinoza's narrative.[34]

---

[31] In fact, in paragraph 9, he situates fear on the same level as envy, hatred and sadness.

[32] This is what P. Martinetti does at the beginning of the chapter 'La conoscenza e il metodo' from his great posthumous work *Spinoza*, a cura di Franco Alessio, Naples: Bibliopolis, 1987: 'La filosofia di Spinoza è, nelle sui origini e nella sua tendenza generale, aspirazione religiosa e pratica verso l'unità divina delle cose. Le prime pagine del *De intellectus emendatione* rappresentano, nella loro commossa brevità, il racconto di una conversione personale dai beni fallaci della vita commune al bene eterno, che solo può riempire l'anima d'un gaudio immutabile e pura' (p. 139). This remark does not detract in any way from the fecundity of the dialogue with Spinozism that Martinetti engaged in throughout his theoretical life, and which nourished his own philosophy. Cf. F. Mignini, 'La *Spinoza* di Piero Martinetti', *Rivista di Filosofia*, LXXX, 1 (1989), pp. 127–52, as well as A.-M. Moschetti, 'Lo spinozaismo di Piero Martinetti', in *Itinerari e prospettive del Personalismo. Scritti in onore di Giovanni Giulietti*, Milan: Istituto propaganda libraria, 1986, pp. 465–97.

[33] One can even undertake such a reduction without adding the moment of the conversion: the path is then simply suppressed and human misery directly founds an ethics accessible to all 'normal and reflective members of our species', Robert J. McShea, 'Spinoza in the History of Ethical Theory', *Giornale critico della filosofia italiana*, 8 (1977), p. 431.

[34] A quite common way of doing so consists in directly introducing the representation of the superior form of human nature, which is evoked in paragraph 13. This superior

Both of these readings are incompatible with the prologue since both refuse to give meaning to what constitutes the substance of the text:[35] namely, the narrator's immanent hesitations, which occur and assert themselves in their own time and are transcended through their own movement.[36] The illusory advantage one gains from simplifying the chronology of the text in this manner comes at the price of a major 'inconvenience': the disappearance of what makes Spinoza's text irreducible to its predecessors.

We must therefore reject the interpretation implicit in Koyré's translation and return to our four-stage schema so as to clarify the content of each stage and identify what follows in the text with what occurs at each stage.

2. The Four Stages

A. The first stage is that of the naive enjoyment of the *communis vita*. What does this involve? Paragraph 2 tells us: we seek (*quaerere*)[37] certain goods. This does not mean that we necessarily possess them or can obtain them. Nevertheless, these goods are within reach and are advantageous (*com-*

---

form then plays, in a displaced form, the role of the master. This is what W. Lehrke does in his study 'Sozialerfahrung und Vernunftsautonomie – zwei Voraussentzungen spinozistischer Moralbegründung', *Wissenschaftliche Zeitschfrit der Karl-Marx-Universität Leipzig*, 1 (1977), pp. 57–64 (see, in particular, p. 59).

[35] By contrast, R. Violette shows clearly the irreducibility of the journey. However, as his study is founded on the opposition between two methods separated precisely by the difference between a process and a sudden revelation, all that remains is to reproach Spinoza for having failed to write a conversion narrative: 'Ayant proposé ces règles, Spinoza nous dit qu'il peut "se mettre en route". Et cette expression, à elle seule, montre qu'il va s'agir de méthode inventée. Car, nous le savons, là où règne la méthode inventive, on se jette à l'eau: il y a une conversion brusque à réaliser qui ne saurait s'accommoder d'une route, d'un chemin d'approche.' See also a little further on: 'Spinoza n'a donc pas encore bien compris que la vérité ne s'obtient pas au bout d'un cheminement visant un certain but: la vérité, du moins celle du panthéisme de l'*Ethique*, est découverte par une conversion, comme l'a éprouvé Romain Rolland. Et cette conversion est brusque', 'Méthode inventive et méthode inventée dans l'introduction au *De Intellectus Emendatione* de Spinoza', *Revue philosophique*, 167/3 (1977), pp. 310–11.

[36] The order of this procedure as a whole is analysed in remarkable terms by Otto Pfersmann, 'Spinoza et l'anthropologie du savoir', in *Spinoza, science et religion*, Paris: Vrin, 1988, pp. 55–62, in particular the distinction, analysed on p. 56, between the 'crise' and the 'retour en arrière', which allows us to put into perspective 'l'arrêt de la ligne 16', that is, the reprise 'dico, *me tandem constituisse*'.

[37] 'et quod ab iis quaerendis cogebar abstinere . . .', § 3 G II, p. 5, l. 19 [*TdIE* 3; CWS I, 7]. It is also possible to think that it is explicitly a question here of the *commoda*. In any case, these *commoda* themselves arise from the *acquirere* (ibid.).

moda) to us.[38] It is their accessibility and their visible efficacy – and not our immediate possession of them – that constitutes their certainty. Altogether this makes up an 'ordo et institutum commune vitae'. This is not a mere sum of goods and of the activities destined to acquire and use them, but rather a network by which these goods form a common figure and can be considered as a unity. Common life thus constitutes itself as a universe with its own certainty – a certainty that is fundamentally the certainty of what already exists, of what comes first. This certainty is strong enough to reconstitute itself even when it is contested, as is shown by what follows in the prologue. Such a situation cannot but recall the one described by Descartes at the end of the *First Meditation*.[39] And this is not by chance: despite differences in aim, in both cases it is a matter of an enterprise undertaken against a pre-existing environment, at once stubborn and insistent.

The vocabulary in which all of this is expressed is worth noting. The most general formula that designates, not so much the goods themselves but the ensemble of events referred to – the goods, the activity of obtaining them, and the feelings they invoke in us: in a word, what is most proximate to the text's backdrop – is, on two occasions, *occurrunt*.[40] These events happen, they appear, they occur. It is not necessary for the subject to seek them out; they occur whether the subject would like them to or not. This vocabulary of 'occurrence' is opposed to the vocabulary used to refer to the *verum bonum*, which it is necessary to seek out (*inquirere*),[41] to find (*invenire*) and to procure (*acquiere*).[42] There are two senses to this difference: on the one hand, the goods are already there, while the *verum bonum* is distant and out of reach; on the other hand, the goods are readily found – the web of life is all around me, before I have begun to reflect on it – while I must make a voluntary and methodical effort to find the true good. The world of occurrences, by contrast, seems instead to be made up of chance encounters.

---

[38] § 2, G II, p. 5, l. 18 [*TdIE* 2; *CWS* I, 7].

[39] With respect to the difficulties of maintaining an attitude of doubt: 'assidue enim recurrunt consuetae opiniones, occupantque credulitatem meam tanquam longo usu et familiaritatis jure sibi devinctam, fere etiam me invito', AT, VII, p. 22 [*PWD* II, 15: 'My habitual opinions keep coming back, and, despite my wishes, they capture my belief, which is as it were bound over to them as a result of long occupation and the law of custom']. The following is the translation by the Duke of Luynes: 'Car ces anciennes et ordinaires opinions me reviennent encore souvent en la pensée, le long et familier usage qu'elles ont eu avec moi leur donnant droit d'occuper mon esprit contre mon gré et de se rendre presque maîtresses de ma créance', AT, IX, p. 17.

[40] § 1, G II, p. 5, l. 7 [*TdIE* 1; *CWS* I, 7] and § 3, G II, p. 5, l. 26 [*TdIE* 3; *CWS* I, 7].

[41] 'Constitui tandem inquierere . . .' § 1, G II, p. 5, l. 12 [*TdIE* 1; *CWS* I, 7].

[42] 'Quo invento et acquisito', § 1, G II, p. 5, l. 15 [*TdIE* 1; *CWS* I, 7].

Their presence prior to the journey and their chance-like ordering unite to characterise the world of the given. In this world we nevertheless find purposeful activities that involve seeking – activities that bear on the *commoda* and on the advantages accorded by such-and-such a good. These activities are also examples of acquisition, just like the search for the true good is, even if the latter is external to the order of the *communis vita*. These activities do not occur without being sought out. Thus, the activities internal to the world of the given do not have quite the same status as the world itself: each one of the *commoda*, even if it is available to me, is not, generally speaking, in my grasp more often than the true good is. But this non-availability does not exclude availability, precisely because the *commoda* are all part of the web of the *communis vita*. On the one hand, then, they are, according to their own determinations, at once sought-after and acquired objects; they are what voluntary activity aims for. On the other hand, as part of the backdrop of common life within which they are formed, they are part of the order of chance occurrences – without there being any contradiction between these two determinations. Take an example from one of the categories that will be distinguished further on: with respect to honours, there exist legal authorities and, more generally, those with responsibilities (to give a concrete example, take the *parnassim*, the administrators or professors at Heidelberg). If I wish to obtain an honour, or, having obtained one, if I wish to retain my position, I must make an effort to acquire it, whether this involves acquiring or acquiring the right to retain it. Yet, whether or not I seek it out or obtain it, I cannot make such a position *not* exist, *not* be present – whether to me or to others. And even if some specific position does not present itself, another will. The way the position presents itself or when it does is never entirely determined by the person who will try to acquire it. As such, the position *occurs* in the world, irrespective of the strategies used by people to accommodate themselves to this occurrence and to take advantage of it. In the *Ethics*, we can know deductively why this is the case;[43] here in the prologue it is enough to say that this dual aspect of things is taken for granted, without needing to be thematised. The web of life in which we seek out and acquire goods is formed by what occurs and what we do not seek out. The *communis vita* can thus be reduced to the form of a backdrop that is always, already there; which is not itself something that is acquired; and which, finally, is the site where we must choose to pursue such-and-such a set of advantages.

---

[43] Cf. Propositions 3 and 4 in Book IV, whose demonstrations are focused on the passions, though the argument is valid for all human activities.

As for the goods themselves, the terms which concern them are *quaerere*, *prosequi* and *assequi*, all of which belong to the same register and influence the text's meaning by way of their derivatives and compounds. Consider for a moment the family of terms around *quaerere*. *Quaerere* is opposed, here, to its compounds *inquirere* and *acquirere*. The primitive meaning of this verb is to seek out an object and to seek to obtain it. *Inquiro*, on the contrary, has an immediately intellectual meaning: it means to seek to discover, to examine (and, by extension, to investigate). *Acquiro* means to procure or acquire something additional – and thus to break out of the circle of what one already has. There are obviously two ways of breaking this circle: either by increasing the current sum of one's possessions – that is, to *acquirere* new goods (and thus to remain within the web of common life) – or to exit the very circle of this *acquisitio* in order to *acquirere* the *verum bonum*. There is thus a real coherence to Spinoza's chosen lexicon.

To say that this first certainty is 'given' implies the following additional remark: its form is the form of what occurs 'frequently' (*frequenter*) or 'most often' (*plerumque*).[44] We can expect this greater frequency to concern not only the goods themselves (this is a response to the question: what sort of things present themselves?) but also the perspective from which they are given (this is a response to the question: how does this presentation occur?). Things can present themselves to us from a perspective that is not that of their essential content but which is nevertheless unavoidable as a first certainty – a first dimension that will subsequently be relativised or placed within certain limits, but which will still possess the spark of its first appearance. There is also, then, running concurrently to the narrator's path, a passage from one appearance of the thing to another, a passage that marks the discovery of the thing's other determinations. With respect to a specific thing, it is possible to identify the passage from the first certainty to the thing's essential dimension by way of the vocabulary that refers to it. In paragraph 3, Spinoza names the three sorts of goods that appear;[45] he then refers to them again alongside other variations, which we can leave aside for the moment. But in paragraph 17 – and thus at a moment in the argument where we are no longer in the midst of the *communis vita* – he names what appears as the goods' 'truth': health, relations of communication with others, and money. It thus becomes necessary to explain the difference

---

[44] 'Omnia quae in communis vita frequenter occurunt', § 1, G II, p. 5, l. 8 [*TdIE* 1; *CWS* I, 7]; 'quae plerumque in vita occurrunt', § 3, G II, p. 5, l. 26 [*TdIE* 3; *CWS* I, 7].

[45] 'Divitas scilicet, honorem atque libidinem', § 3, G II, p. 5, l. 28 [*TdIE* 3; *CWS* I, 7]; p. 6, l. 1 [*TdIE* 3; *CWS* I, 7].

between the goods' 'truth' and their appearance. In fact, money remains *nummi*, while everything else changes. It turns out, then, that the goods from paragraph 3 were the first form of the appearance of rational objects, whose first certainty presented only one aspect of them, or one dimension only. It could be said that those who do not wish to leave the *communis vita* remain at the level of this first certainty, while the ascetic who purely and simply refuses the use of these goods has also, fundamentally, remained at this stage. The first certainty is therefore (though we do not know this yet) the site of a possible opposition between two behaviours that appear to be opposed but which are in fact founded on the same relation to the dimension of the given. By comparing the terms used in the first paragraphs with those that come later, we thus learn that the first certainty of health is pleasure, the first certainty of relation is honour, while the first certainty of money is money. At this stage, things themselves tell us how they are given. This must be our starting point: 'the background context of experiences' or, at least, the first elements of this context 'that must have been constituted before there can develop the understanding that will form the basis of a decision'.[46]

B. We now come to the teachings of experience. How do we come to realise that the things that occur in life are *vana* and *futilia*? The use of these terms will not surprise the reader, for an entire tradition invites them to meditate on the vanity of the goods of this world. This is why empiricist readers of the prologue have hardly felt the need to elucidate the structural meaning of these two words. Or rather, when they have done so, it has been to immediately 'recognise' something familiar in them. These readers rush to identify characteristics that they think are present in the text, but which a close analysis does not permit us to retain as essential elements. If we want to avoid giving in to this tendency, it is above all necessary to note that it is not a matter here of goods 'of this world', for at this moment – and leaving aside later moments – we do not know if 'the world' is '*this*' world'. Moreover, it cannot be through their comparison with the Sovereign Good that the futility of these goods appears, for these goods are neither known nor even imagined as different from themselves. We must advance prudently here, for on the one hand the goods that are vain continue to remain certain in the first sense of the term once they have been recognised as vain and futile. The proof of this is that they conserve their power of attraction in the third stage,

---

[46] 'Een zeker fonds van ervaringen moest gevormd worden vóór een inzicht kon groeien, op basis waarvan een besluit genomen kon worden', Th. Zweerman, *Spinoza's inleiding tot de filosofie*, pp. 51–2.

where their certainty is counterbalanced by the uncertainty that still besets the true good. On the other hand, we must not confuse this vanity with the reflection on these goods that occurs later. It is only in what follows – that is, at the moment of compromise and failure[47] – that these goods' powers of distraction and disorientation will be mentioned. These powers are certainly present in them at the beginning, yet they are not initially conceived of as negative. They are thought of in this way only when we have begun to aspire to the true good and realise that, in a multitude of ways, these goods turn us away from it. This realisation can thus only occur against the backdrop of an opposition between two sorts of goods that has already been perceived and constituted, even if attempts at compromise have sought to reduce it. It is therefore not this realisation that is at the origin of the aspiration itself. What remains, then, as a principal characteristic of this vanity? It seems to me that if we wish to identify it – not by way of literary references but by the function assigned to it in Spinoza's journey – then we must see that this vanity is constituted by the unity of two determinations: one concerns the nature of goods, the other their effect on the *animus*. This effect is exerted at both intra- and inter-individual levels.

The first determination, and the one that is primary, comes down to these goods' disappearance – that is, to their perishable nature. In fact, in what follows, this is the sole general characteristic that is associated with them,[48] while the good that we eventually seek out will be described, by contrast, in terms of its 'fixity'.[49] The term 'perishable' must be understood in two senses: such a good can perish absolutely, but it can also escape our grasp by never coming into our possession or by being taken by another. In order to include these goods in the category of the perishable, it is therefore not necessary to undertake a philosophical reflection on becoming or finitude. The category of perishability reveals itself in the midst of everyday life by the simple fact that we do not necessarily acquire the goods we desire – even if they are accessible (*quoad consecutionem*). And if we can access them, we can always lose them as well. At this stage, experience shows us a new dimension of the given, of what is there from the outset: that of loss. It is essential to point out that it is not yet a matter of our own loss (this will only come later, and its possibility will, moreover, play a central role, but at a very precise moment

---

[47] 'quod saepe frustra tentavi. *Nam* [my emphasis] quae plerumque in vita occurrunt [. . .]. His tribus adeo distrahitur mens, ut etc.', § 3, G II, p. 5, l. 25 [*TdIE* 3; *CWS* I, 7]; p. 6, l. 1 [*TdIE* 3; *CWS* I, 7].
[48] 'Eorum, quae perire possunt', § 9, G II, p. 7, l. 23 [*TdIE* 9; *CWS* I, 9].
[49] 'Fixum enim bonum quaerebam', § 6 G II, p. 6, l. 29 [*TdIE* 6; *CWS* I, 8].

of the argument). It is also not a matter in the pure disappearance of things. Rather, it is a matter of goods' disappearance *relative to us*. We might think that goods disappear for us because they are in themselves capable of disappearing. However, experience shows the contrary: these are not things, but goods; in other words, we perceive in what sense the first form of certainty is not incompatible with vanity. It is certainty itself that reveals this vanity. On the one hand, there are accessible objects that we fail to acquire (even if we can always hope that we will), while on the other hand there are those that we do possess but which escape us. Whence the dream – and it is still a dream – of an object that would keep the promises that perishable objects make but do not live up to. At this stage, we form an aspiration for such an object, yet we do not set out to find it. In fact, without yet being sure of it, we presume that there exists a 'true good' that is in itself communicable. 'Communicable' no doubt has two meanings: this 'true good' can be obtained, and it can be shared. We know nothing of it, and conceive of it only by way of its difference with the world of the given – with the apparently unsurpassable play of what is imposed upon us from the outset.[50]

[50] In his article 'Le texte du *Tractatus de intellectus emendatione* et sa transmission', F. Mignini remarks that the genitive *sui* has no equivalent in the text of the NS. From this absence, and by means of a theoretical argument (the Spinozist good is a being of reason and is therefore incapable of being communicated), Mignini deduces that Spinoza doubtless did not write this word, and that, for once, it is the Dutch translator who is closer to the original, while the person who prepared the Latin version for printing automatically added the term which completes the scholastic expression (*sui communicabile*, or *diffusivum sui*), which he had in his memory, thus drawing Spinoza's doctrine back to a heritage that it contradicts. Such an observation cannot be taken lightly, for it comes from a researcher whose work on the edition of the TdIE tends more often than not to follow the Latin text of the OP against the Dutch version (and against Gebhardt, who witnessed a first version). Mignini's argument has a certain credibility, yet two objections can be raised against it: (a) the suppression of the *sui* takes nothing away from the theoretical argument: to be 'communicable' is already a significant predicate for a being of reason, and the proof of this is that the term, even when deprived of its complement, does not appear again in the *Ethics*; and (b) above all, it is not necessary for the narrator, at the moment where he forms the aspiration to the true good, to already be in possession of the Spinozist doctrine of a relative good; in fact it is essential that he *not* possess it, for if he did then his hesitations would not take place. The true question is knowing if at the moment of his decision (*tandem* . . .) he can still conserve this vision: this seems possible, to the degree that only the system will provide the determinations of the true good and that, while waiting, he can only imagine these determinations by way of their similarity with perishable goods and the difference with the latter's limitations. See F. Mignini, 'Le texte du *Tractatus de intellectus emendatione* et sa transmission' in F. Akkerman and P. Steenbakkers, *Spinoza to the Letter: Studies in Words, Texts and Books*, Leiden: Brill, 2005, pp. 189–207.

It is therefore clear that it is not by comparison with the true good that perishable goods are characterised as such.[51] On the contrary, it is the play of their promises and betrayals, which they organise in the midst of common life, that gives rise to the aspiration for a true good about which we know almost nothing for the time being, for its image is formed only by its difference with those that we do know.

Almost nothing, but not nothing at all – for we can at least hope that the effects the true good will have on the soul will be the opposite of perishable goods. By their loss, these goods trouble us. They provoke commotions of the mind such as sadness, envy, fear, and hatred. These feelings will only be mentioned in paragraph 9, where they will be referred to as things that the subject is already familiar with (what is novel in this later paragraph is not the discovery of these feelings but the explanation that is given for them). It can thus legitimately be asked when these feelings first appear in the field of reflection. The response must be: at this second stage, where the narrator remarks in himself the effect that the loss of perishable goods has on him. In fact, to the degree that Spinoza does not introduce any external moral judgement or any explicit norm that distinguishes between events, the exigency of radicality means that it becomes necessary to explain why this loss is felt as negative. The answer is that it is felt as negative precisely because of its consequences. These consequences occur, moreover, at two levels, if we follow the indications given in paragraph 9: at the intra-individual level (the *commotiones animi*), and at inter-individual level, which is governed at once objectively by the fact that people seek the same good – which they therefore cannot share – and emotionally by the fact that certain of the *commotiones animi* imply a specific type of conduct towards others: this is the case essentially for *invidia* and *odium*, and at least in part for *timor* – whence the inter-human conflicts that can arise due to perishable goods. This, then, is the second dimension of vanity and futility.

These two dimensions are inseparable. For if, in the final stage (which will be analysed in paragraph 9), the link between unhappiness and love for perishable things will be seen in its essence, for the time being this link has not yet been understood in terms of its consequences. This, moreover, is why at the beginning of the text the expression that refers to the general character of goods (*quae perire possunt*) does not appear here. Perishable goods

---

[51] Contrary to what R. McShea affirms ('Spinoza in the History of Ethical Theory', p. 428): 'Spinoza's ensuing critique of the claims of riches, fame and pleasure to be "real goods" hinges on his assumption that the end of life is "continuous, supreme and unending happiness".'

are given in their plurality, which is also the multiple ways in which they are lost, along with the plurality of negative emotions they provoke in and between us. Experience teaches me that each of the goods that remain on my horizon and that I try to acquire or conserve escape me or can escape me. Their disappearance – or the possibility of their disappearance, or, again, the efforts that I go to in order to prevent their disappearance – provoke feelings of sadness, fear, hatred, jealousy, and conflict. It is this lesson that is summed up in the words *vana* and *futilia*.

Why does Spinoza use these two words? *Futilis* is a *hapax* in Spinoza's lexicon.[52] *Vanus*, on the other hand, can be found elsewhere in his work: the *Ethics* speaks of vainglory[53] and of vain superstition,[54] while the first two pages of the *TTP* include five occurrences of the term.[55] In all of these cases, 'vain' does not mean inexistent or illusory, as its etymology would suggest: the object is not empty of content but rather deprived of a purely adequate cause. This implies that it has other causes – causes that produce negative effects: absurd effort, dissension, the search for the crowd's approbation.[56] Two uses are of particular interest: Chapter 2 from the *TTP* cites *Ecclesiastes*[57] in a context that attributes to Solomon the merit of having spoken according to an innate reason: '[Solomon] taught that all Fortune's favours to mankind are vanity, that humanity has no nobler gift than wisdom.'[58] This passage stands out because it places the word 'vain' in relation to scripture, which in turn gives 'vain' the meaning it has in the phil-

---

[52] It appears neither in Emilia Giancotti's *Lexicon* nor in the digital index of the *Ethics* and the *Political Treatise*.

[53] *Ethics* IV, 58, Schol., G II, p. 253, l. 3 [CWS I, 578. Curley in fact refers to an 'empty' form of 'esteem'].

[54] *Ethics* IV, 37, Schol. 1, G II, p. 236, l. 35 [CWS I, 566] (with respect to the prohibition on killing animals) [Curley uses the term 'empty superstition'].

[55] G III, p. 5, l. 15 [*TTP* I; CWS II, 66] (*vanum* is a part of a series including *ineptum* and *absurdum*), 29 [*TTP* I; CWS II, 66], and 30–1 [*TTP* I; CWS II, 66] (the superstitious call reason 'vain' because it cannot indicate a certain path towards the things that they seek), p. 6, l. 13 [*TTP* I; CWS II, 66], and p. 7, l. 1 [*TTP* I; CWS II, 66] (*vana religio*, which is then opposed to *vera*, but in order to show that they are surrounded by the same cult whose purpose is to inspire respect).

[56] 'Unde fit, ut qui vulgi opinione gloriatur, quotidiana cura anxius nitatur, faciat, experiatur, ut famam conservet', notes the Scholium of Proposition 58 from Book IV as an effect of vain glory.

[57] It is more an allusion to the first verse and a summary of the general spirit of the passage.

[58] 'Omnia fortunae bona mortalibus vana esse docuit (vide *Eccl.*) et nihil homines intellectu praestantius habere', G III, p. 41, ll. 25–6 [*TTP* II, 48; CWS II, 107].

osophical tradition that postdates the *Vulgate*, rather than the meaning that classical Latin gives it. Moreover, this passage also immediately undertakes to translate this tradition. Thus, the adjective 'vain' is, once again, and this time more immediately so than at the beginning of the *TdIE*, given the task of qualifying goods – or at least those goods that are other than the understanding. We also find here the equivalent of the vocabulary of occurrences in the term *fortuna*, which, as we will see, is closely linked to the lexicon of experience. The other revealing text is Letter XXX, which inscribes the term 'vain' in the following series: *vana, inordinata, absurda*,[59] in the course of a judgement I will return to when we look at Spinoza's evolution. Finally, we should note that the term can be found in Descartes' *Discourse on Method*, coupled with another term that is not far from 'futile'. Here these terms refer to human activities, but activities apprehended not at a certain moment of a journey but rather as the object of a critical gaze, a gaze that does not seem to be determined by time.[60] It is not impossible that these two remembrances – the text of the Scriptures[61] and the Cartesian expression – colour the formula used at the beginning of the *TdIE*. What is essential is that this formula receives from its own context the function of marking a milestone in the subject's attachment to and distance from the order of occurrences. As we have seen, this function allows us to extract finite goods from the secular condemnation that refers to their lack of being within a paradigm where only a single authentic good exists. If they are overcome, in Spinoza's text it is through the very play of certainty that these goods themselves produce. The *TdIE* thus substitutes an ontology of the promise for an ontology of corruption.

C. We turn now to the stage of prevarication. It is made up of three distinct moments. In the first, the subject's new aspiration does not succeed in becoming an *institutum*. Rather, the subject is weighed down by a struggle between certainties, while their object is constituted in an exclusively negative fashion. The mind thus fears abandoning its present object for a

[59] G IV, p. 166, ll. 17–18 [*Ep.* XXX [to Henry Oldenburg]; *CWS* II, 14].
[60] 'Et que regardant d'un œil de Philosophe les diverses actions et entreprises de tous les hommes, il n'y en ait quasi aucune qui ne me semble vaine et inutile', AT, VI, p. 3 [*PWD* I, 112]. The Latin of the *Specimina* says the same thing: 'Et dum varias hominum curas oculo philosophico intueor, vix ullae unquam occurrant quae non vanae et inutiles videantur', AT, VI, p. 541. Note the *occurrere* which renders the 'there is'.
[61] The comparison (by the intermediary of the phrase from Chapter II of the *TTP*) is made by Lelio Fernández and Jean-Paul Margot in their commentary on the translation of the *TdIE* (*Tratado de la Reforma del Entendimiento y otros escritos*, Bogotá: Universidad nacional de Colombia, 1984, p. 109).

pure illusion. The effort that the mind could draw on seems *inconsultum*. This term is important: it refers to a rational calculation whose result is to indefinitely defer the search for the true good. This calculation is therefore not – or at least not exclusively – a passion: it is a still-incomplete analysis of Reason. The person engaged with common life is capable of calculating what their interests are. We could compare this passage to those passages in Hobbes where he describes the state of nature; for there, too, the onset of war has something rational about it. It is not a pure passion (like malice, for instance) that makes me attack the other: it is the calculation that, if the other attacks me by surprise, I will be defeated and will not be able to persevere in my being. This calculation, which is rational to the extent that I know that no sovereign force can interpose itself between me and the other, incites me to attack him first.[62] Similarly, in the soul's state of nature, which is the world of the given, it seems reasonable not to lose what one currently possesses in favour of a good whose existence one cannot prove.[63]

The second moment is the subject's realisation of their ignorance of happiness.[64] This moment detaches the abstract term from those objects that the *animus* has enjoyed up to this point. It thus introduces something of a dynamic between the subject's enjoyment of what they had previously sought and successfully obtained and what they had actually sought: the *frui* no longer perfectly coincides with the *invenire* and the *acquirere*. The formal conditions are now in place for the couple *felicitas/infelicitas* to be associated – two pages further on and in almost identical terms[65] – not with an object but rather with a quality of the object. In the meantime, this second moment subtly introduces the temptation of a compromise: if I am no longer sure either of the one or the other, why not try both at once?

The third moment refers to the subject's effective attempt at making this

---

[62] 'And from this diffidence of one another, there is no way for any man to secure himselfe, so reasonable, as Anticipation; that is, by force, or wiles, to master the persons of all men he can, so long, till he see no other power great enough to endanger him: And this is no more than his own conservation requireth, and is generally allowed', *Leviathan*, I, London: Penguin, 2017, p. 64.

[63] That the first stage of the development of reason consists in placing oneself at the service of a biological egotism is also noted in the *Ethics*, albeit from a genetic point of view (IV, pr. 19–22). Cf. A. Matheron, *Individu et communauté chez Spinoza*, Paris: Editions de Minuit, 1969, p. 243 ff. Matheron notes moreover that, 'séparées de leur contexte, les propositions 19–22 pourrait fort bien être contresignées par Hobbes', ibid., p. 247.

[64] 'Et si forte felicitas in iis esset sita . . .', § 2, G II, p. 5, ll. 20–1 [*TdIE* 2; *CWS* I, 7].

[65] 'Quod tota felicitas, aut infelicitas in hoc solo sita est . . .', § 9, G II, p. 7, ll. 17–18 [*TdIE* 9; *CWS* I, 8].

compromise. The narrator sets out in search of the true good, but without upending his life's order. He thereby hopes to conserve the *commoda* which arise from the goods that are already available to him, all the while adding a new element to his quest for happiness. This results in failure, the causes of which are three inhibitions, of which Spinoza makes a detailed list. The, *Nam*[66] develops the term *frustra*: the traits proper to the goods that arise in common life explain how each one of them prevents the subject from thinking of something else. Note that while the presentation of everything preceding this section has been elliptical, the description now becomes detailed. Up to this point, Spinoza had limited himself to *recalling* what experience had taught the narrator. Now, we enter into the details of the *description* of experience itself. It is remarkable that this description occurs by way of an explosion of goods into multiple categories. When it was a matter of simply indicating these goods' presence or referring to their vanity, these goods could be evoked in a single breath. Yet, evoking the memory of the subject's singular encounters with these goods, in which these goods' power is inscribed, cannot be done without distinguishing them in terms of their different effects. It is thus necessary for each perishable good to indicate why it makes the realisation of the compromise impossible:

- a positive inhibition: *occupation*. The perishable good occupies the subject's attention, and occupies it completely. This is the case for whoever is absorbed in pleasure or honours. There remains no time for *cogitare*. This indicates in passing that *cogitare* is the mode in which one seeks the true good[67] (this is not necessarily the case for the other goods);
- a negative inhibition: *sadness*, which we are led to either by the realisation of pleasure or by the loss of wealth and honours, both of which also stop us from *cogitare* (being able to);
- an *imitative* inhibition: those who seek honours must moreover think *ad captum vulgi*. Note that the crowd's influence represents the second

---

[66] § 3, G II, p. 5, q. 26 [*TdIE* 3; *CWS* I, 7].

[67] Here, too, we find ourselves faced with what the *Ethics* will present as a conclusion, and which is here only a fact of experience. Propositions 26 and 27 from Book IV establish that the only thing that is useful – and which is therefore certainly known as good – is that which leads us *ad intelligendum* (G II, p. 227 [*Ethics* IV, 26, 27; *CWS* I, 558]). The beginning of the Demonstration of Proposition 9 from Book V deduces from this that 'An affect is only evil, *or* harmful, insofar as it prevents the mind from being able to think', 'quatenus mens ab eo impeditur quominus possit cogitare', G II, p. 286 [*Ethics* V, 9, Dem.; *CWS* I, 601].

occurrence of the other in the *I*'s trajectory (the first was when the *I* had to take into consideration the aspirations of others to the same good – aspirations that were positive in terms of sharing, negative in terms of rivalry).[68]

By identifying these inhibitory effects, we can now see the root of the problem: the narrator was uncertain, and he attempted to prolong this indecision in the practical form of a compromise solution. This solution revealed itself to be an impasse, first on the practical level (*frustra*), then through an explanatory analysis (*nam*), which showed that it was useless to prolong this vain effort: a choice had to be made. This entire stage has not, then, been entirely useless. While it has not resolved the problem, it has, through its internal movement, revealed the necessity of making a decision.[69] In other words, it has brought the subject to the extreme point of their crisis – to a point where they can no longer remain. This crisis, too, arises out of experience, for it is precisely the history of the subject's efforts at compromise that leads them to draw the conclusion that such efforts are doomed to fail. Yet this crisis is a strata of experience, which, by virtue of the place it occupies in the subject's journey, produces results that are at once better informed and more constraining than the subject's first aspirations, which had emerged solely from their commerce with perishable goods.

D. There now comes the moment where the meaning of certainty is inverted and the subject has to make a decision. This moment occurs in two stages and leads to the moment evoked by the *tandem* from the prologue's opening phrase. First, the subject's meditation radically transforms the terms of the problem they had identified in the previous phrase. Certainty is the first term to be divided: what was certain with respect to the acquisition of goods is not necessarily so as regards their nature. At this point, the two sorts of goods are equivalent. But now the narrator's 'assiduous meditation' upsets this equilibrium. From the point of view of their nature, perishable goods are not uncertain goods: they are certain evils. Henceforth the focus is no longer on the goods' destiny and their effects on the narrator, as it was initially, but instead on the destiny of the narrator himself. The reader realises that the pursuit

---

[68] The positive aspiration is mentioned from the first phrase (*communicabile*); the threat tied to rivalry appears only, as we have seen, in paragraph 9, but if one accepts our analysis of the chronology, this threat was perceived, if not understood, earlier on.

[69] 'Imo adeo esse opposita, ut ab uno, aut alterio necessario esset abstinendum', § 6, G II, p. 6, ll. 22–3 [*TdIE* 6; *CWS* I, 8]. Whence the necessity of asking oneself 'quid mihi esset utilius', ibid., l. 24 [*TdIE* 6; *CWS* I, 8].

of these goods is not only exposed to the risk of the *goods'* loss, but that they produce the loss of the *narrator* as well. Moreover, it is only from this perspective that the term *evil* appears.[70] Perishable goods are unequivocally evil insofar as they cause one to perish. Note the importance here of the term *enim*.[71] This term does not lead the explanation towards a demonstration of the loss of goods, for this is something that has, in fact, been recognised from the beginning. Rather, it simply enumerates examples of the losses suffered by people who seek such goods. For the first time in the journey, the focus is squarely on the 'I' – not the 'I' of the narrator, however, but the 'I's' of his fellow human beings; beings who, without being named, nevertheless exemplify through their persecution, death, and suffering the reasons one has to be fearful. The consideration of those goods that we were concerned with, and which revealed themselves to be harmful to us, no longer constitutes a valid reason not to devote oneself to the search for the true good. This search is now free to begin. The trajectory thus seems to be complete at the theoretical level. And yet, paradoxically, while everything is now in place for the subject to make their decision, and even if the subject has already begun, in part, to apply this decision, the path has also led to an aporia: the very force of the subject's reasoning seems to undermine its results. If it is now clear that the goods are in fact evil, and if we know all of the reasons why they remain attached to us – even if we are no longer attached to them – then might we not still fear the worst? Are we not condemned, despite ourselves, to remain under the sway of these goods' power – that is, of what appears to us as the height of unhappiness? We feel ourselves retreat as soon as the force of our reasoning weakens. However, this aporetic situation does not prevent us from thinking;[72] indeed, this aporia already constitutes an advance with respect to the preceding situation. Yet what it does prevent us from doing is always being able to reflect, and, when we are no longer reflecting at all, it deprives us of the fruits of our reflection.[73]

The second stage of the decision undoes this difficulty. It does so initially at the practical level. From there, experience moves towards explanation.

---

[70] 'Mala certa pro bono certo omitterem', § 7 G II, p. 6 , ll. 31–2 [*TdIE* 7; *CWS* I, 8]. The term is repeated in paragraph 9: 'haec orta esse mala . . .'.

[71] § 8: 'Permuta enim exstant exempla . . .' [*TdIE* 8; *CWS* I, 9].

[72] This is indicated by the following condition: 'modo possem serio deliberare', which is made explicit by the concession 'quamvis haec mente adeo clare perciperem', § 10, G II, p. 7, ll. 27–8 [*TdIE* 10; *CWS* I, 10]. It is obvious that the narrator would not have been able to say this during the third stage.

[73] 'Non poteram tamen ideo omnem avaritiam, libidinem, atque gloriam deponere', § 10 G II, p. 7, ll. 28–30 [*TdIE* 10; *CWS* I, 10].

Since I perceive, so long as I deliberate, the superiority of the true good, I can thus begin to reflect on the means of reaching it. Now, it just so happens that this operation itself turns me away from the evils I am fleeing, and does so in its very unfolding and for as long as it lasts. A division thus arises at the very heart of the narrator's lived time – not a division between a 'before' and an 'after' separated by a single cut, but between two qualitatively different sorts of moments that alternate in the narrator's life. It is this type of division that is referred to by the term 'intervals',[74] and which occurs in the form of an alternation *quamdiu . . . tamdiu. . . .*[75] In sum, the very act of reflection produces a sort of liberation, which the subject notices before being able to account for it, and which is reinforced in the course of his progression. In turn, an explanation arises: on the one hand, the very fact of relative liberation, which is conditional on the attraction exerted by the 'goods' that have in the subject's own eyes become evil, proves that 'those evils would not refuse to yield to remedies'.[76] In other words, if they are rightfully the object of fear, they are not absolutely so. Indeed, we now have a practical proof of this. On the other hand, however, in continuing to reflect the subject sees that these goods' harmfulness is itself relative (without us knowing *why* this is the case). Just as the life of the narrator is divided between two kinds of moments, the goods are divided between two uses: in the first (their use in light of the true good), they reaffirm their positivity; it is only with respect to their second use (that is, when they are used for themselves) that they are harmful – or, put differently, their positivity, which was given as such in their irreflexive use in the first stage, remains, and it is only the effect they have on the mind that can be said to be good or bad. We are now ready to formulate the decision in its definitive form.

We can now take up the second part of the first phrase – that is, the principal proposition whose subordinate parts we analysed above. I will argue that its structure is strictly symmetrical to those of its subordinate clauses, and that at this level too a parallelism in form translates a conjunction in thought. The principal verb *constitui* has two complements, two indirect interrogative homonyms ('an aliquid daretur?'), just like the two infinitives are linked to two homonymic *omnia*. These two interrogatives are determined once again by two relatives: *aliquid quod . . . et a quo solo . . .; aliquid quo . . .*

---

[74] § 11, G II, p. 8, l. 1 and 3 [*TdIE* 11; *CWS* I, 10].
[75] § 11, G II, p. 7, ll. 31–2 [*TdIE* 11; *CWS* I, 10].
[76] 'Nam videbam illa mala non esse talis conditionis, ut remediis nollent cedere', § 11, G II, p. 7, ll. 33–4 [*TdIE* 11; *CWS* I, 10].

(A) Constitui tandem inquirere;
(B$_1$) an aliquid daretur;
(C$_1$) quod verum bonum et sui communicabile esset;
(C$_1$ bis) et a quo solo, rejectis caeteris omnibus, animus afficeretur;
(B$_2$) imo an aliquid daretur;
(C$_2$) quo invento et acquisito continua ac summa in aeternum fruerer laetitia.

The *imo* introduces, between the two aspects of the subject's quest, a disequilibrium that recalls the one between *postquam* and *cum*. We can therefore expect each of the two aspects to respond to the intention of one of the clauses from the first part of the phrase. This is, indeed, the case. The first subordinate clause referred to the vanity and futility of the goods that were given to the subject; the first interrogative opposed these goods to the true good. Since these *omnia* were given as plural, the unicity of the true good was affirmed at the same time. The second subordinate clause expressed the fears that the narrator experienced during the third stage; the second interrogative responds with the affirmation of joy, which will be the journey's end point. Reality against futility; a feeling of the perishable against a feeling generative of eternity: the whole of the first phrase thus appears to be structured by an extremely rigorous architecture, where all of the elements of the argument find in the language that expresses them an equivalent at the level of rhetoric.

Since the final stage is the one that opposes, as we have just seen, the feeling of the eternal to the fear of the perishable, it is not surprising that we find here an example of a mortal illness: it is suggested by the very movement of the argument. Some have wanted to see in this example a reference to Seneca. Whatever the case may be, the representation of the crises of human life in medical terms is part of a long philosophical tradition.[77] It is more instructive to see what Spinoza does with this tradition: in Seneca, this example is often used to indicate the permanence of a crisis even after it is resolved.[78] Here,

---

[77] It goes back at least to the *Gorgias*, where the analysis of the *technai* explicitly places in parallel the care of the soul and the care of the body. For philosophy in Rome, cf. Groethuysen, *Anthropologie philosophique*, Paris: NRF, 1953, pp. 76–8, and the extracts from texts (as well as on neighbouring themes), pp. 81–3. Note that in the majority of these texts the sickness is a state opposed to a different state, that of philosophical life; in Spinoza, it is a crisis.

[78] Seneca, for example *Letter 72*: 'Hoc, inquam, interest inter consummatae sapientiae virum et alium procedentis, quod iner sanum et ex morbo gravi ac diutino emergentem, cui sanitatis loco est levior accessio: hic nisi adtendit, subinde gravatur et in eadem revolvitur, sapiens recidere non potest, ne incidere quidem amplius.' 'I tell you, there

on the contrary, it serves to sketch out a powerful image of, precisely, its resolution.

3. The Specificity of Spinozan Certainty

It remains for us to draw a double conclusion – a conclusion concerning the meaning and scope of the form of certainty that structures the prologue, and a conclusion concerning the homonymous term that is so decisive in Descartes' work. It is well known that the presence of the same term 'certainty' is one of the main reasons that some interpreters have been led to link the *proemium* with specific Cartesian texts.[79]

---

is the same difference between a man of perfected wisdom and another whose wisdom is in progress, as between the healthy man and one emerging from a serious and prolonged illness; for this man a milder attack is the equivalent of health: if he does not give it attention he will soon be weighed down and sink back into the same condition, but the wise man cannot relapse, nor even fall further into ill-health', *Seneca: Selected Letters*, Oxford: Oxford University Press, 2016, p. 115. O. Proietti refers to this text in his article cited above; but one can already find an analogous movement in *De tranquilitate animi*: 'Quaero mehercules jamdudum, Serene, ipse tacitus, cui talem affectum animi similem putem, nec ulli propius admoverim exemplo quam eorum qui, ex longa et gravi valetudine expliciti, motiunculis levibusque interim offensis perstringuntur et, cum reliquias effugerunt, suspicionibus tamen inquietantur medicisque jam sani manum porrigunt et omnem calorem corporis sui calumniantur. Horm, Serene, non parum sanum est corpus, se sanitati parum assuevit . . .' (§ II); 'I have long been silently asking myself, my friend Serenus, to what I should liken such a condition of mind, and I find that nothing more closely resembles it than the conduct of those who, after having recovered from a long and serious illness, occasionally experience slight touches and twinges, and, although they have passed through the final stages of the disease, yet have suspicions that it has not left them, and though in perfect health yet hold out their pulse to be felt by the physician, and whenever they feel warm suspect that the fever is returning. Such men, Serenus, are not unhealthy, but they are not accustomed to being healthy . . .'.

[79] Cf. for example, Armand Saintes, who refers to 'ce que Spinoza a vraiment emprunté à Descartes', specifically by way of the following question: 'Toujours, à l'entrée du domaine de la philosophie, on devra faire cette demande: Comment puis-je acquérir la certitude?', *Histoire de la vie et des ouvrages de B. de Spinoza, fondateur de l'exégèse et de la philosophie modernes*, Paris: Renouard, 1842, p. 35. Dunin-Borkowski, drawing on works beyond the *TdIE*, goes so far as to produce a schema of interpretation for the biography of the young Spinoza who owed to 'his master Descartes' the fact that he overcame his crisis of scepticism. Thus, the young heterodox appears as if he were essentially seeking – albeit in an unconscious fashion – 'a logic and a theory of knowledge', *Spinoza*, vol. I, *Der junge De Spinoza*, cf. in particular the paragraphs 'Zum Frieden durch Wissen', p. 249 ff. and 'Der Kampf um die Gewissheit', p. 261 ff. See also, more recently, K. Hammacher, 'B. de Spinoza: Gewißheit in Erkenntnis und

As far as the meaning of the word 'certainty' goes, in my view a rigorous analysis leads to the conclusion that there is much that separates the two philosophers. In Descartes, the necessity of certainty is no doubt marked with as much force as it is in Spinoza. Yet, both in the *Discourse* as in the *Meditations*, certainty always belongs to the order of knowledge. The term is associated with the verbs 'connaître' and 'savoir'[80] and is opposed to doubt,[81] with the two terms constituting the two fundamental attitudes of the mind[82] and instituting the essential difference between science and opinion. When Father Bourdin puts the following question to Descartes: 'What if the cunning demon is presenting all these matters to you as doubtful and shaky when in fact they are firm and certain?'[83] Descartes thinks he is able to mark sufficiently clearly the irreducible distinction between his interlocutor and himself by replying: 'This remark makes it quite clear that, as I have pointed out above, my critic regards doubt and certainty as being in the objects rather than our thought.'[84] Finally, the term which best illustrates the anchoring point of the problematic of certainty in Descartes is

Handeln', in *Grundprobleme der großen Philosophen*, ed. von Josef Speck, Philosophie der Neuzeit I, Göttingen: Vandenhoeck & Ruprecht, 1979, pp. 101–38, in particular pp. 103–5. Hammacher marks the necessity of modulating according to the forms of each system the principle that he states at the beginning of his work: 'Das Problem der Gewißheit kennzeichnet in besonderer Weise die neuzeitliche Philosophie.'

[80] In the French translation of the *Meditations* it appears ten times (cf. the index of occurrences in the volume *Cogito 75*, edited by A. Robinet, Paris: Vrin, 1976, p. 74) and always alongside 'connaître', 'savoir', 'connaissance', 'évidence' and 'science'.

[81] 'Now if this conviction is so firm that it is impossible for us ever to have any reason for doubting what we are convinced of, then there are no further questions for us to ask: we have everything that we could reasonably want. [. . .] For the supposition which we are making here is of a conviction so firm that it is quite incapable of being destroyed; and such a conviction is clearly the same as the most perfect certainty' ('quae proinde persuasio idem plane est quod perfectissima certitudo'), *Second Set of Replies*, AT, IX-1, pp. 113–14 [PWD II, 103] (the first occurrence has no equivalent in the Latin text, AT, VII, pp. 144–5). The use is, moreover, traditional: cf. St Thomas 'Dubitatio enim opponitur certitudini', *Summa Theologica*, IIa, IIae, qu. 4, art. 8, 1.

[82] The fact that each term refers to the other has led some to write things like the following: 'Chez Descartes, tant va d'abord le doute, tant va ensuite la certitude', J.-M. Beyssade, 'Certitude et Fondement', in *Le Discours et sa méthode*, ed. N. Grimaldi and J.-L. Marion, Paris: PUF, 1987, p. 343.

[83] 'Quid si catus ille omnia tibi velut dubia et nutantia proponat, cum firma sint, cum certa?', *Seventh Set of Objections with Replies*, AT, VII, p. 470, l. 31; p. 471, l. 1 [PWD II, 316].

[84] 'Hic clare patet, quod supra monui, dubitationem et certitudinem considerari ab illo tanquam in subjectis, non tanquam in nostra cogitatione', *Seventh Set of Objections with Replies*, AT, VII, p. 474, l. 27; p. 475, l. 3 [PWD II, 319].

the adjective *assurée* [*certain*], which can be found both in Descartes' French texts and in the translations of his Latin texts.[85] If certainty consists in being 'certain' [*assuré*] of something, it is indeed because certainty is of the order of knowledge and refers above all to the attitude of the knowing subject.

The meaning of this term 'certainty' should obviously be situated in relation to Descartes' general concern for a philosophy whose aim is to constitute the criteria and content of knowledge. Descartes distinguishes clearly between two registers, the register of 'actions' and the register of 'judgement'.[86] It is the second of these that lies at the heart of his philosophy; and it is to this register – of judgements, truth and knowledge – that the notion of certainty is linked. The key moments in Descartes' system – the exposition of method (the Second part of the *Discourse*), its results (the Fourth and Fifth parts), and the developed chain of certainties (*Meditations*, *Principles*) – are all moments that constitute a logic of certain knowledge. While the letters on morality and the *Passions of the Soul* foreground the analysis of human action, this analysis remains within the context of Descartes' efforts to found his theory on what his other writings have already established.[87] It can therefore be said that the themes at the heart of Descartes' system are all responses to the question: what is true?

With Spinoza, by contrast, at least at the beginning of the *TdIE*, as Gebhardt has shown[88] – even if we are not obliged to accept the reasons advanced by the illustrious editor[89] – the initial question posed concerns

---

[85] Cf. in *Discourse on the Method*, Part One, AT, p. 4, l. 23 [*PWD* I, 113]; p. 10, l. 14 [*PWD* I, 115], Part Two, p. 21, l. 19 [*PWD* I, 121], etc. The opposition with the sceptics is thus summed up as follows: 'my whole aim was to reach certainty' (p. 29, l. 4 [*PWD* I, 125]) and this 'aim' is immediately translated by the effort to 'expose the falsity or uncertainty of the propositions I was examining'.

[86] Likewise, lest I should remain indecisive in my actions while reason obliged me to be so in my judgements . . .', *Discourse on the Method*, AT, VI, p. 22, ll. 24–5 [*PWD* I, 122].

[87] 'Il est facile de situer le *Traité des passions* dans la pensée de Descartes; il n'est pas purement et simplement une œuvre de circonstance; il faut le rapporter à cette tendance scientifique que nous suivons depuis 1628 et dont l'idée directrice est une explication totale de l'univers. Le *Traité des passions* est un chapitre du grand *Traité du Monde*, chapitre qui n'était sans doute pas prévu dans le plan primitif, si ce n'est comme un simple paragraphe dans le chapitre de l'Homme', Gouhier, *La Pensée religieuse de Descartes*, p. 151.

[88] 'Descartes als der große Initiator des modernen Philosophie geht aus von dem Zweifel an den überlieferten Meinungen und stellt an den Eingang seiner Lehre die Frage: was ist wahr? Spinoza beginnt, verzweifelnd an den Scheingütern des Lebens, mit der Frage: was ist gut?', *Spinozas Abhandlung über die Verbesserung des Verstandes*, p. 66.

[89] 'Der rationalistische Franzose, rein von theoretischem Interesse geleitet, sucht vor allem nach einer sicheren Erkenntnis. Der Sephardi geht im Gedanken seines

what is good much more than what is true. In fact, this difference in aim has even become a commonplace among commentators.[90] Yet it is the same term 'certainty' that is made to carry the weight of this question. Here, certainly refers to the availability of things, to their accessibility, or, more profoundly, to the solidity of their inscription in being. Inversely, uncertainty is inaccessibility, or, more fundamentally, the characteristic of being perishable.[91] A certain good is a good that is sought, acquired and enjoyed, and which is also, perhaps, exposed to the possibility of its loss – save when certainty has been redefined precisely as what cannot be lost. The aim, here, is profoundly different to the aim of *The Discourse on Method*, and the context in which this aim is affirmed is more anthropological than epistemological. In Spinoza, what matters is knowing how to act in the midst of uncertain goods, how to strike out on a sure path despite the mutability of things, and how to orient oneself in a world divided by the diversity of human activities. The soil from which this problematic grows resembles the classical theory of fortune as it had been revived by humanists from Salutati to Vossius, much more than it does a mathematical doctrine of the true idea.

religiösen Eudämonismus – wenn es erlaubt ist, zwei anscheinend so weit voneinander liegende Begriffe zu verbinden – darauf aus, das wahre Glück ze bestimmen, darin der große Sohn des Volkes, das von den Zeiten der Propheten bis auf unsre Tage unter den Völkern der Träger des ethischen Gedankens gewesen ist', ibid., pp. 66–7. For the theory of the Jewish people as an ethical link between epochs, see Gebhardt's Preface to his edition of Uriel da Costa.

[90] See Freudenthal, *Die Lehre Spinozas* . . ., p. 96: 'Was ist wahr, was ist gewiß, was ist unbestreitbar [. . .]? Das ist die Frage, mit der Descartes in seinen *Meditationen* seine Philosophie eröffnet. Was ist das *wahre Gut* [. . .]? Damit leitet Spinoza seine *Abhandlung* ein, die die Vorbereitung ze seiner Philosophie enthält'; see also A. Léon, *Les éléments cartésiens de la doctrine spinoziste*, Paris: Alcan, 1907, p. 71; and Martinetti, *Spinoza*, p. 119; and Tejedor Campomames, *Una Antropología del Conocimiento*, p. 21.

[91] A proof *a contrario* is provided by Alquié's reading, which systematically transposes Spinoza's vocabulary into the form of Cartesian expressions. In his commentary on this passage, he begins by noting, correctly, that 'le problème que traite d'abord Spinoza est celui de la certitude et de l'incertitude', *Le rationalisme de Spinoza*, Paris: PUF, 1981, p. 77. But he immediately translates this problem into a problem of the subject, writing, with respect to the true good: 'Spinoza confesse qu'il n'est nullement assuré de l'existence d'un tel bien, ce qui constitue une première incertitude', ibid. This term will return with great frequency: 'Quant au Bien en soi, je ne suis même pas assuré qu'il existe. Et à supposer qu'il existe, je suis encore moins assuré de pouvoir l'atteindre', p. 78; 'il serait ainsi [par le compromis] assurée de ne rien laisser perdre', ibid.; 'nous sommes pourtant assurés que, s'il existe et se révèle accessible, il est, essentiellement et par nature, un bien', p. 80. I noted above that in this passage Spinoza never says 'I am certain'; but an interpretation like Alquié's makes him say it, because it reduces his project to Descartes'.

Symmetrically, could we also call 'doubt' the procrastinations of uncertainty? The term is absent from the prologue to the *TdIE* but can often be found in the writings of its commentators. While on the one hand doubt seems to account for the subject's hesitations and false starts, at the same time as it ties Spinoza to Descartes, on the other hand we should not forget the very clear remarks Spinoza makes against Cartesian doubt, whether in the rest of the *TdIE*[92] or in the *Ethics*.[93] Most importantly, the nature and role of procrastination and doubt in Spinoza are very different. Cartesian doubt, which is second to natural doubt, is voluntary, methodical; it is not Spinozan uncertainty. As for natural doubt itself, it shares with methodical doubt the fact that it is centred on the subject: it suspends the subject's adhesion to the object. In Spinoza, uncertainty is a property of the object, while the mind's hesitations occur as an oscillation between two objects. This hesitation cannot, therefore, be called 'doubt' except by taking the term in its etymological sense, where it names a situation in which the subject is faced with forking paths.[94] In any case, the very absence of the term 'doubt' in the *proemium* confirms the slippage of the meaning of the term 'certainty'.

The meaning of the term 'certainty' is therefore profoundly different from one problematic to the other. Why, then, is the same word used in the two lexicons? Neither Descartes nor Spinoza invent this word: rather, they adapt to their respective projects a word that belongs to a common philosophical vocabulary. This term communicates with a common adjective ('certain'),[95] while its technical meaning is systematised in specialised lexicons. Goclenius, for example, defines certainty as 'the solidity and the immutability of a truth'.[96] He seems thereby to place certainty on the terrain of knowledge. Indeed, the term effectively remains on this terrain, even if Goclenius distinguishes between the certainty that corresponds to the object and the certainty that corresponds to the subject – to the knowing subject. Both are necessary in the passage from opinion to science.[97] The second form of certainty concerns the assent we give to the thing, while the first implies

---

[92] § 77–80, G II, pp. 29–30 [*TdIE* 77; *CWS* I, 34].

[93] *Ethics* II, 43, Schol., G II, pp. 123–4 [*CWS* I, 479].

[94] Cf. E. Benveniste, *Problèmes de linguistique générale*, Paris: NRF, 1966, chap. XXIV: 'Problèmes sémantiques de la reconstruction', pp. 294–5. Note that this reconstruction derives doubt from the semantics of fear.

[95] On the semantics of the word in Descartes and its links with *cernere*, *certamen*, see P.-A. Cahné, *Un autre Descartes. Le philosophe et son langage*, Paris: Vrin, 1980, p. 147–9.

[96] 'Certitudo est firmitas et immutabilitas quaedam veritatis', *Lexicon philosophicum quo tanquam clave philosophiae fores aperiuntur*, Frankfurt, 1613, p. 361.

[97] 'Utraque requiritur in Scientia. Si utraque vel alterutra defuerit, Opinio dicitur', ibid.

that the thing cannot be otherwise.[98] We are witness here to the birth of a conception of certainty that, in isolation, could well be made to correspond to Spinoza's goods. In sum, while Descartes consistently uses certainty in the sense of *certitudo subjecti*, Spinoza, by contrast – or the Spinoza of the prologue to the *TdIE* – derives the *certitudo objecti* from the *certitudo rei*.

Does Spinoza hold true to this use? For the most part, no. It is true that he continues, for example in a few passages from the *TTP*, to speak of uncertain[99] goods and of certain or uncertain evils.[100] In general, however, in his later lexicon, certainty leaves the domain of things and passes into the domain of thought. A glance at the rest of Spinoza's œuvre suffices to show this. It is not surprising that when Spinoza presents Descartes' thought he adopts the latter's terms;[101] elsewhere, however, while he might give a cognitive meaning to certainty, he does so for different reasons and with other implications than Descartes. This is the case in both the *TTP*[102] and in the *Ethics*.[103] It is even the case in the remainder of the

---

[98] 'Estque *Objecti*, id est rei cognitae, quae aliter se habere nequit; vel *Subjecti*, id est, Hominis cognoscentis, hoc est: assensus nostri ad rem, quae cognoscenda proponitur', ibid.

[99] 'ob incerta fortunae bona, quae sine modo cupiunt', Preface, G III, p. 5, ll. 5–6 [*TTP* Praef., 1; *CWS* II, 65]; and no doubt it would be necessary to also read *bona* in 'qui incerta sine modo cupiunt', ibid., ll. 26–7 [*TTP* Praef., 4; *CWS* II, 66].

[100] If we refuse to give to the State the *jus circa sacra* on the pretext of the possible vices of its leaders, one does not correct the evil but on the contrary increases it, 'For denying them this right makes them necessarily impious [and a] harm and evil to the whole Republic, which would have been uncertain and contingent, becomes certain and necessary' ('nam hoc ipso fit, ut necessario [. . .] impii sint, & consequenter ut totius reipublicae damnum et malum ex incerto, & contingente certum, & necessarium reddatur', XIX, G III, p. 236, ll. 21–4 [*TTP* XIX, 47; *CWS* II, 341]. Also, this example seems to be the only one of its kind.

[101] An example: Axiom I from the first part of the *Principia*: 'In cognitionem et certitudinem rei ignotae non pervenimus, nisi per cognitionem et certitudinem alterius, quae ipsa prior est certitudine et cognitione', G I, p. 151, ll. 9–11 [*PP* I; *CWS* I, 240].

[102] The whole section of Chapter II from the *TTP* devoted to the certainty of prophecy and to its mathematical or moral character attests to this. It is announced at the end of the first chapter by a revealing phrase: 'Cum hoc ita sit, cogimur jam inquirere, unde Prophetis oriri potuit certitudo eorum, quae tantum per imaginationem, & non ex certis mentis principiis percipiebant', G III, p. 29, ll. 5–8 [*TTP* II, 48; *CWS* II, 93].

[103] Notably in Book II, Scholium of Proposition 43: 'Nam nemo, qui veram habet ideam, ignorat veram ideam summam certitudinem habere', G II, p. 124, ll. 6–7 [*Ethics* II, 43, Schol.; *CWS* I, 479]; Scholium of Proposition 49: 'idea falsa, quatenus falsa est, certitudinem non involvit' [*Ethics* II, 49, Schol.; *CWS* I, 485], and two other occurrences: G II, p. 131, ll. 11–12, 20 and 22 [*Ethics* II, 49, Schol.; *CWS* I, 485].

TdIE.[104] On this point, then, the *TdIE*'s prologue occupies an exceptional place. With respect to the use of this key term 'certainty', the *TdIE* is Spinoza's most anti-Cartesian text. The term has two different meanings corresponding to two divergent aims.

Is this to say that there is no relation whatsoever between Descartes' project and Spinoza's? Whatever the case may be, there is certainly no relation of simple identity between them. Nevertheless, in the prologue to the *TdIE* Spinoza chooses to use terms that can also be found in Descartes' work. Indeed, he mobilises them – just as Descartes did – in the form of a journey. In reading these two philosophers' works, one is struck by certain similarities – similarities that are not erased by the difference in context.[105] To account for these similarities, but without dismantling the barriers that we have just shown exist between Descartes and Spinoza, we must adopt a slightly different point of view. It is possible that the analysis of the prologue's *meaning* does not exhaust the question of its *scope*. It is undeniable that the content of Spinoza's journey is not inspired by Descartes' philosophy: Spinoza neither reprises Descartes' terms nor their specific meaning. Yet it is no less undeniable that Spinoza is engaged here in the closest possible dialogue with Descartes, at the same time as he takes his distance from him. Spinoza adopts a certain type of approach against a certain type of adversary. By annulling the theoretical meaning of Descartes' foundational journey, he replaces it with a strategy of fortune. It is by way of this substitution that Spinoza can adapt for his own ends those elements that remain equally important to both projects.

Even though they speak of different things, as I believe I have shown, Spinoza and Descartes have much in common when it comes to the way their respective texts progress. The conquest of the sought-after goal occurs by way of a veritable enterprise, an enterprise that goes against the order of the world as it is given (specifically, in Descartes' case, against the world's prejudices, and in Spinoza's case, against the occurrences of fortune). This order is like a tenacious tissue that tends to reconstitute and even strengthen itself as soon as one fails to be vigilant towards it. The sought-after goal is therefore not immediately readable in the world as it is; a detour is necessary

---

[104] 'Certitudo, hoc est idea vera cum non distinctis commiscetur', § 74, G II, p. 28, l. 19 [*TdIE* 74; CWS I, 33].

[105] F. Alquié notes this in a remark that is accurate precisely by virtue of its imprecision: 'Il demeure que les formules de Spinoza ont parfois un ton cartésien', *Servitude et Liberté selon Spinoza*, Paris: CDU, 1971, p. 11.

in order to find it. This detour requires a certain spiritual tension and a return to the foundations of what the subject truly has confidence in. This, then, is the significance of the idea of certainty for both Descartes and Spinoza, whatever variations in meaning it might have. Since both Descartes and Spinoza consider the 'evidence' against which their enterprises are directed to be rooted in what could be called, in a word, 'life', the most appropriate form of philosophical explanation consists in the narrative of how a *gap* can be opened up between oneself and this 'life'.[106] This form is that of the journey. From the same perspective, one could inquire into the parallel between the way Spinoza passes from the first certainty of perishable goods to the more profound certainty of the true good, and the way Descartes passes from the certainty of the *cogito*, a certainty founded on the simplest and most accessible of elements, to the deeper certainty concerning the existence of God – a certainty that alone is capable of giving a guarantee to his argument.[107] Finally, what Spinoza owes Descartes is not some positive content but rather the model of a movement by which one tears oneself away from what is initially given in one's 'life'.

Can we go further? Yes, by advancing the following hypothesis: Descartes and Spinoza share – as others philosophers do – the fact they both begin from the world of fortune, of the philosophy of wisdom, and then place something else at the centre of their thought. But neither of them entirely suppress what they thereby set aside. In both cases, the motif of certainty is a possible indication of the place where this operation occurs.

If we inquire, not into the immediate aims of Descartes' project, but into the perspective that it presupposes, we realise that the distinction between judgement and action, insofar as it is a real distinction, does not entail the exclusion of action from the horizon of this project. Indeed, even in those texts where what is at stake is establishing a foundation for knowledge, action is not excluded. Such epistemological works are in fact grounded in a certain anthropology. The concern for knowledge and truth is itself

---

[106] Stuart Hampshire notes this, albeit without drawing any conclusions: 'In his already quoted autobiographical passage from *On the Correction of the Understanding*, designed as a relatively popular work [sic], he follows Descartes in stating the purpose of his philosophy in terms of the occasion which prompted him to begin his inquiry', *Spinoza*, Harmondsworth: Penguin, 1951, p. 25.

[107] Cf. Beyssade: 'La métaphysique nous apprend que la première proposition qui se présente à celui qui conduit ses pensées par ordre n'est pas la première vérité de la science, qui est conclue à partir d'elle et la garantit rétrospectivement. Le retard accède ici à une forme de nécessité', *La philosophie première de Descartes*, p. 346.

rooted in a search for wisdom – a search that remains irreducible to this very concern.[108] If one seeks out indications in the first pages of *The Discourse on Method* as to how Descartes positions himself with respect to truth, one cannot but be struck by the coexistence, under cover of the biographical *I*, of both propositions on knowledge and statements on the course of the world, with the latter serving either as the stages or goals of a journey,[109] or as points of comparison that serve to better represent what is of the order of knowledge.[110] Furthermore, when questions of knowledge are raised, they are initially raised in anthropological terms, and indeed in a way that accords with a humanist anthropology: the comparison of minds[111] and their relative per-

---

[108] As Baillet argues, the concern of the *Studium Bonae Mentis* was how to 'acquérir la sagesse, c'est-à-dire la science avec la vertu', AT, X, p. 191.

[109] The 'various activities and undertakings of mankind' (AT, VI, p. 3, ll. 15–16 [PWD I, 112]), the search for 'all that is useful in life' (p. 4, l. 24 [PWD I, 113]), the concern for the morals of one's country and one's time (p. 6, ll. 17–30 [PWD I, 113]), the attitude to be taken with respect to glory (p. 9, ll. 7–10 [PWD I 115]), the reading of the great book of the world (p. 9, l. 21 [PWD I, 115]; p. 11, l. 2 [PWD I, 116]). This last theme is crucial for the status of the *Discourse* as it indicates the opening to an 'elsewhere' *qua* experience of the world – an opening that is at once radically insufficient yet fundamentally necessary. This theme thus marks the specifically Cartesian way of thinking of the necessity of the path.

[110] The statement: 'The greatest souls are capable of the greatest vices' is made, for instance, to explain that 'it is not enough to have a good mind; the main thing is to apply it well', AT, VI, p. 2, ll. 12–15 [PWD I, 111]. This principle of comparison will persist, even in texts where the other use of references to the course of the world is no longer present. Take the following negative comparison: 'For a long time I had observed, as noted above, that in practical life it is sometimes necessary to act upon opinions which one knows to be quite uncertain just as if they were indubitable. But since I now wished to devote myself solely to the search for truth, I thought it necessary to do the very opposite . . .', *Discourse on the Method*, Part Four, AT, VI, p. 31, ll. 20–6 [PWD I, 126–7]. And the following positive comparison: 'from time to time I have found that the senses deceive, and it is prudent never to trust completely those who have deceived us even once', *First Meditation*, AT, IX, p. 18 [PWD II, 12]; 'But as for my natural impulses, I have often judged in the past that they were pushing me in the wrong direction when it was a question of choosing the good, and I do not see why I should place any greater confidence in them in other matters', *Third Meditation*, AT, IX, p. 39 [PWD II, 27] – the Latin simply says 'nec video cur iisdem in ulla alia re magis fidam', AT, VII, p. 39.

[111] We find this throughout the *Discourse*. Cf. in the Third Part the repentance of the 'weak and faltering spirits', AT, I, p. 25, l. 16 [PWD I, 123]; in the Sixth Part those 'with only mediocre minds' who use obscurity to argue 'against the most subtle and clever thinkers', AT, I, p. 70, l. 28 ff. [PWD I, 147]; and finally those who, 'the more penetrating and acute they are', are 'the more prone to error [. . .] and the less capable of truth', AT, I, p. 76, l. 26 ff. [PWD I, 150].

fection, and the ethic of self-judgement.[112] One also finds references to the course of the world[113] in the Third Part of *The Discourse on Method*, where the author asks how one should act in the face of the goods of fortune.[114] In sum, the strategy of fortune, which is at the heart of the argument from the beginning of the *TdIE*, is not entirely absent from *The Discourse on Method*. Nevertheless, it is at once contained and relegated to the background. Thus, in both *The Discourse on Method* and the *TdIE* – Descartes' *Meditations*, by contrast, are a different matter[115] – we find the coexistence of two worlds: the world of goods, and the world of the true. Yet the way the two philosophers treat the difference between these worlds is not the same: in Descartes the two worlds are disjunct, while in Spinoza the first is used as a path to the second. What was in the background in Descartes' text returns momentarily to the foreground in Spinoza's and is witness to its own dissipation. We could thus mark the difference between Descartes and Spinoza by saying that the method at work in the opening to the *TdIE* consists in introducing the lexicon and indeed the entire universe of the Third Part of the *Discourse* – the shocks of fortune (which we have described as being of the order of occurrences), goods, and the activities of human beings – into the Fourth Part, with a view to resolving the problems of the First Part. Taking a step back, one could note that in both cases, as in the work of Hobbes and Bacon, the core components of a humanist philosophy – the moral philosophy of fortune, of virtue, and a rhetorical treatment of thought[116] – are repressed

---

[112] 'I know how much we are liable to err in matters that concern us, and also how much the judgements of our friends should be distrusted when they are in our favour', p. 3, ll. 27–31 [*PWD* I, 112].

[113] 'the various occupations which men have in this life', p. 27, ll. 3–4 [*PWD* I, 124], the true goods which are in our power, p. 28, ll. 5–6 [*PWD* I 125], and the comedy of the world, p. 28, l. 25 ff. [*PWD* I, 125], which, as a critical gaze requires, now replaces the book of the world.

[114] 'change my desires rather than the order of the world', p. 25, ll. 21–2 [*PWD* I, 123]. Cf. p. 26, l. 20 [*PWD* I, 124] and p. 27, l. 1 [*PWD* I, 124].

[115] To the degree that they exist exclusively at one or other of the levels that the *Discourse* distinguishes (cf. the end of the *First Meditation*: 'quandoquidem nunc non rebus agendis, sed cognoscendis tantum incumbo', AT, VII, 22 [*PWD* II, 15]).

[116] I cannot analyse here in detail the coherence of this logic with its variations. It will have to suffice to refer to the description provided by Groethuysen, *Anthropologie philosophique*, specifically in the chapters devoted to Petrarch and Erasmus. In Petrarch there emerges a meditation on human life, which takes up the classical theme of Fortune but in order to make it signify, above all, 'l'impression produite par le hasard des conditions de la vie et des rencontres qu l'on y fait', p. 138. As for Erasmus, Groethuysen characterises the modification that he brings to the classical model by the rejection of the therapeutic gaze, a rejection which allows life as such to be at

without being destroyed by a project that follows a scientific model. Spinoza takes from Descartes a model of this repression, at the same time as he puts it to work in an entirely different way.[117]

I have reconstituted the structure of the prologue and shown that it introduces the reader to its theses in the manner of a dramatic narrative. It remains for us to study the dynamic of each of the prologue's actors. As we have seen, the way the prologue progresses is a function of the relations between these 'characters': the narrator (along with his attributes: *animus, mens*), the goods, and the true good. The place these 'characters' occupy in the narrative determines their function: they are, in other words, the 'actants' of classical philosophy.[118] Yet their function is specified by the determinations proper to Spinozist *certitudo*. The foundation of certainty and the narrator's struggle for it refers to the analysis of goods: it is these goods themselves that determine, more so than the narrator, the change of status that certainty undergoes. That these goods are possessed, lost and loved means that they constitute the very objects of certainty. It is therefore with these goods that we must begin.

> the centre of his interpretation: 'Les hommes tels que les conçoit Erasme, sont placés au beau milieu de la vie. Il ne saurait leur suffire qu'on leur donnât simplement les moyens de venir à bout de certaines émotions que l'on peut définir et traiter comme telles selon une méthode appropriée [. . .] Tout ce que l'homme fait et pense s'ordonne ainsi dans le cours d'une vie. C'est le cours de la vie qui devient ce qui importe vraiment', p. 254. A convergent analysis – as far as civil ethics are concerned – can be found in E. Garin, *Scienza e vita civile nel Rinascimento italiano*, Bari: Laterza, 1965, in particular pp. 1–21; and, on the subject of Manetti, *L'umanesimo italiano*, Bari: Laterza, 1952, 1978, p. 69–74. For the place of Fortune as a historical concept, cf. below, Part Two.

[117] I have left aside the possible comparison with the *Regulae*, on the one hand because the text was unpublished when Spinoza was writing, and on the other because the *Regulae* does not present a journey. Such a comparison would therefore be of little interest. For an alternative perspective, see J. D. Sanchez Estop, 'Spinoza, lecteur des *Regulae*. Notes sur le cartésianisme du jeune Spinoza', *Revue des Sciences philosophiques et théologiques*, 1 (1987), pp. 55–66.

[118] I am loosely reprising A. J. Greimas' terminology from his *Sémantique structurale*, Paris: Larousse, 1966, p. 172 ff. Yet just as it might be illuminating to investigate the actants common to classical philosophies, it is also likely impossible to identify them with the actors of such-and-such a philosophy, for individual philosophies are specified by their architectonics and are thus irreducible to each other. As such, the tableau that Greimas proposes on p. 181 (Philosophie / Monde / Dieu / Humanité / Matière / Esprit) seems inapplicable to the study of a determinate problematic.

3

Common Life and Perishable Goods

The analysis of the stages of certainty has thus led us to the goods and to the different degrees of certainty that characterise them. The entire movement of Spinoza's argument is structured by the opposition between the *verum bonum* and the other goods – goods that a certain ethical tradition would call false goods, though Spinoza does not use this term. More generally, with the prologue we seem to be following the well-worn path of the moral tradition, along which we encounter such themes as life, goods, and the choice of the true good. The reader who encountered these themes without determining how the prologue organises them in its own specific way would have the immediate impression of finding themselves on the at once familiar yet indeterminate terrain where, ever since Aristotle, each philosophical school has taken turns to present life lessons, reprimand the reader, or indicate to them what authentic values are. It is not only philosophical schools that have done this, but other discourses as well. For it is in this indeterminate region of the moral tradition that it becomes difficult to distinguish philosophy from other discourses such as impassioned speeches, sermons and even satire. Doctrines on different kinds of life are easily transformed into exhortations, while exhortations naturally tend towards becoming denunciations of the illusory. Should we situate Spinoza within such a tradition? I will now try to show that the most direct effect of the originality of Spinoza's procedure in the *TdIE* is that it strips the terms he uses of any moral meaning they might otherwise have. The text thus reprises what is perhaps one of the more originary aims of Aristotle's work – more originary, that is, than the transformation of Peripateticism into the first (or second) link in the chain of the 'history of moral philosophy'.

Returning to the question of goods, what does the text tell us about them? Their presentation occurs in a number of stages. They are named explicitly in the course of the third stage, where Spinoza will ask what prevents the compromise between the old and the new institution. At this point it becomes necessary to explain what powers the old *institutum* possesses that prevent one from devoting oneself to the new *institutum*. Here, the goods will be referred to as the *haec tria* – pleasure, wealth and honours. However, from as early as the first stage, that of irreflexive life, the first relative clause speaks in the form of a neutral plural of 'everything that regularly occurs in common life . . .'. Are the *haec tria* already being referred to in the words *omnia, quae* . . .? One might think so, in particular if one notes the reprise of the same phrase a little further on[1] – a phrase whose subject speaks of the *haec tria*. Yet one might also conclude that in the first sentence it is a matter of *events* in the proper sense of the term. Is it possible to say of goods that they 'happen'? If this were the case, then we could read the second sentence as saying that events *can be reduced* to these three goods, in the sense that events can be *classed* in terms of the categories indexed by the three goods (*rediguntur* is not equivalent to the verb 'to be'). This distinction is not introduced simply to allow the syntax of these first sentences to be more easily followed: if it is necessary to distinguish between events and goods, it is because their totality forms something like a general category of activity, a category that is irreducible to some temptation external to us, but which, on the contrary, provides Spinoza with the means for analysing human life as a totality.

It is within this totality that Spinoza inscribes the goods that he will subsequently go on to enumerate and whose effects he will describe. It is therefore against the backdrop constituted by these goods that we can read the use Spinoza makes of the topos of the *haec tria*. This is why, in order to know to what degree Spinoza reprises an older discourse and in what sense he transforms it, we must first acquire a general conception of this activity by which events occur and goods are sought: the *communis vita*.

1. The Dimensions and Sequences of Common Life

'They regularly occur in common life': these goods, or the events related to them, are thus referred to in the text before they are defined. This is not unheard of in Spinoza's style of presentation. What identifies these goods most immediately is their insertion in the *communis vita*. But what is 'common life'? This expression is also not defined. However, the use it is put to is equivalent to a description of its structures. We will see that it is characterised by a number of different dimensions: it is *given*, *homogeneous*

---

[1] 'Nam quae plerumquae in vita occurunt, [. . .] ad haec tria rediguntur', § 3, G II, p. 5, ll. 26–8 [*TdIE* 3; *CWS* 7].

and constituted by *elementary sequences* that have a relation to goods. After listing these dimensions, we will be able to return to interrogate the very notion of 'common life' itself and the determinations that it brings to the fore in terms of the semantics of the word 'life'.

A. Koyré translates *communis vita* as 'ordinary life' [*vie ordinaire*], no doubt in opposition to the 'extraordinary', which is often the point of entry into philosophical life. Saisset, for his part, translates it as 'common life' [*vie commune*]. In French as in Latin, 'commun' can mean 'commonplace' [*courant*] or 'ordinary' [*ordinaire*] in the sense of 'shared' [*partagé*]. How should we understand it? Is it a matter of daily life, of routine, or is it what people have in common? In other words, is the accent placed on simplicity or on sociality? The context can help us choose and be more precise. A little further on, the text speaks of the '*ordo et commune meae vitae institutum*'.[2] And this 'ordo' – or, more precisely, the impossibility of changing it – is described as being what 'what regularly occurs in common life . . .'.[3] The word *plerumque* is a clear reprise of the term *frequenter*. Furthermore, as I noted above, the Dutch translation brought the two formulas together by translating *communis* and *plerumque* in an analogous fashion.[4] They effectively refer to the same notion. Simply put, the characteristic 'common' has been transferred from life itself to the *institutum* by which the individual structures their life. We can deduce from this that *common* is not opposed to what is *proper* to the individual, but also that it names something more than what is simply *ordinary*: that is, it refers both to what is ordinary (the habitual course of things, that which takes place in the vast majority of cases) and to the reason it is ordinary: it is that which has no need of change in order to be there. It is the person who wants something else who has to change. This is marked both by the expression of the 'new' *institutum* and, a few lines prior, by the description of the subject's new quest, and then again in paragraph 6 by the phrase *ad novum institutum*.[5] The register of the *communis* is thus the register of what is there 'by default'.[6] Common life is always there. It is unsurpassable. It is not a lifestyle choice. One can perhaps decide to leave it, but not to enter it. It is already there *when* we enter it; it is the spontaneous form of our condition. There is therefore no reason to lament its limits – if it has

---

[2] § 3, G II, p. 5, l. 25 [*TdIE* 3; *CWS* 7].
[3] § 3, G II, p. 5, l. 26 [*TdIE* 3; *CWS* 7].
[4] NS, p. 407: *in't gemeen leven; gemeenlijk*.
[5] § 3, G II, p. 5, l. 24 [*TdIE* 3; *CWS* 7]; § 6, G II, p. 6, l. 25 [*TdIE* 6; *CWS* 8].
[6] Not in the legal sense, but in the sense used by programmers: the program that is there before a command has modified anything.

any – for common life is as it is and cannot be otherwise. This does not mean that it is the foundation of everything else but that it is the first given on the basis of which we seek out a foundation. The *Ethics* will say the same thing, even if it does so in a different language.

We can also find in this sense of the term the other meaning inscribed in 'common' – namely, that which is shared – so long as we understand that sharing is not the result of a decision to conform to the same events, but rather derives, quite simply, from the fact that all events have, by default, the same initial conditions of life.[7] As we will see further on, this sharing of the same behaviours will also contribute to reinforcing their coherence.[8] It is therefore a matter less of sociality in the proper sense than of the identity of the behaviours that lie at the basis of the social.[9]

In vita communi should thus be understood as: in life such as it is given, before it is the object of reflection. We will soon discover that this given is in fact a construct. However, we will have to travel down a long path to come to know this: practically speaking, this path will lead us to Book V of the *Ethics*. I showed above that the first stage of experience arose out of the world of occurrences. The first dimension of the *vita communis*, as the first stage of certainty, is to represent the field of the given.

B. A second dimension completes this description. I noted above that the Dutch version of the *TdIE* translated *communis* by *gemeen* and then reprised this term, through the adverb *gemenelijk*, in order to render *plerumque*. A little further on, *vulgo* and *frequenter* are again translated in the same way.[10] Everything happens as if the field of the *communis* had been maximally extended in order to characterise a number of traits that converge in the description of the situation that precedes the final decision. I do not have total confidence in the Dutch translation,[11] but here it seems to identify in

---

[7] In the *Ethics*, this will be explained through the unicity of the laws of nature and, at the human level, by the fact that all human beings have the same structure. But here this explanation is not needed: it is matter of describing, not explaining.

[8] Cf. the end of paragraph 5.

[9] We will see this reemerge in the Appendix to Book IV of the *Ethics*.

[10] NS, p. 408: 'met het geen te schuwen, dat gemenelijk van de menschen geschuwt word, en met dat te zoeken, 't welk gemenelijk van hen gezocht word'; p. 409: 'Doch alle de dingen, naar de welken wy gemenelijk trachten [. . . zijn] gemeneljk d'oorzaak van d'ondergang der bezitters.' We can see that the phrase receives a more defined architecture since it is modified so that the subject *vulgus* leaves in turn a place for the same adverb.

[11] Cf. Akkerman's study cited above and the work by Mignini on the new edition of the *TdIE*.

the text something that is definitely suggested by it. A translation choice that conflates a number of words from the original can either invite misreadings (and this is no doubt the more common occurrence), or it can bring out more clearly a conceptual relation that is latent in the text. It appears here that the translation only unifies what was waiting to be unified. Common life is indeed the unique field where the events constituting it can be read, and where the search for different types of goods take on their meaning. It is not simply an empty frame or the convenient name for a plurality of varied and irreducible phenomena. It forms a homogeneous ensemble. A second term, *institutum*, demonstrates this point. How should this term be translated? Here, too, the *versio belgica* hesitates to strictly follow the original, but its hesitation has the opposite meaning: it renders the single word *institutum* alternatively as *ooggemerk* (intention) and *gesteltenis* (constitution, disposition).[12] We can thus hesitate between a project (this is Koyré's choice in the French) and a structure. 'Intention' or 'design' [*dessein*] is not impossible in Spinoza's lexicon (we find these words elsewhere with this same meaning),[13] and it might be appropriate for rendering what concerns the new *institutum* – because, precisely, this latter implies a choice.[14] However, when Spinoza speaks in the first person and wants to insist exclusively on the voluntary aspect of a decision, he instead says, using a classical idiom,[15] *propositum*.[16] In *institutum*, on the contrary, we can hear the word *instituere*, which means less deciding and more putting something in place or in order. When used in the

---

[12] 'Ik overwoog dieshalven in mijn gemoed, op het mogelijk zou zijn om tot dit nieu oggemerk, of ten minsten tot de zekerheit daar af, te geraken, zonder d'ordening en gemene gesteltenis des levens te veränderen', NS, p. 407.

[13] 'sed meum institutum est, de sola mente humana agere', *Ethics* IV, 3, Schol., G II, p. 145, ll. 19–20 [CWS I, 498]. 'Verum quoniam meum institutum praecipue est, de iis tantum loqui, quae solam Scripturam spectant, sufficit de lumine naturali haec pauca dixisse', *TTP*, I, G III, p. 16. ll. 19–21 [*TTP* I, 5–6; CWS II, 78]. In other (particularly legal and political) contexts, *institutum* can be opposed to *natura*, but more often we find the phrase *institutum naturae*.

[14] We also find it in Descartes' Latin: 'sed laboriosum est hoc institutum', *First Meditation*, AT, VII, p. 23 [*PWD* II, 15].

[15] With respect to the Sovereign Good, Cicero compares man to an archer who does everything to realise his ends 'ut omnia faciat quo propositum assequatur', *De Finibus*, III, 22.

[16] 'Resumamus jam nostrum propositum', *TdIE*, § 49, G II, p. 18, l. 26 [*TdIE* 49; CWS I, 22]; 'Superest tamen te monere ad haec omnia assiduam meditationem, et animum et propositum constantissimum requiri', Letter 37 to Bouwmeester, 10 June 1666, G IV, p. 189, ll. 10–12 and 24–6 [*Ep*. XXXVII; CWS II, 33]. By contrast, the term does not appear in the *Ethics*.

past tense,[17] *instituere* conveys the idea that the instituted structure perhaps has more importance than the instituting decision – a decision which, moreover, does not exist as part of the subject's old *institutum*. What, then, does this term mean? It refers to the structure, the tissue, the organisation of life.[18] It is not by chance that it is associated with *ordo*. Common life is not formed from a simple juxtaposition of activities: it constitutes a homogeneous tissue. To be fully convinced of this, take the following comparison: at the end of the *Ethics*, Spinoza speaks of 'totum vitae spatium [. . .] percurrere'.[19] The contrast between these two expressions and their contexts is quite clear: the passage from *Ethics*, Book V, presupposes an individual who acts against the indeterminate backdrop constituted by life; the emphasis thus falls on the determination of the individual by themselves. By contrast, in the *TdIE* the individual is not foregrounded as a determining power. Rather, he oscillates between the determinations of one *institutum* and another. It is these two *instituta* that are described, not the individual who moves between them. *Institutum* thus clearly names something more consistent than *spatium*. When described in this way, life is a force field, not a race course.

We have just seen a second dimension, namely homogeneity, a guarantee of consistency, come to characterise the *vita communis* at the same time as this life is described as being *given*. This homogeneity allows us to interpret common life as an ensemble of activities – activities which, as I said above, occur before they are reflected on.

C. But we need to be more precise. What does it mean to reflect on these activities? The following paragraphs show us that in this irreflexive life, quite a bit of reflection actually does occur. This refers us to the difference between *quaerere* and *inquirere*. One reflects on how to obtain honours or pleasures, on how to protect oneself from the blows of fate, and on how to make one's

---

[17] 'Instituta Dei', *TTP*, Chapter 3, G III, p. 49, ll. 10–11 [*TTP* III, 22; CWS II, 116]; 'regis instituta, seu decreta', *TP*, Chapter VI, 18, G III, p. 302, l. 3 [*TP* VI, 18; CWS II, 537].

[18] Here again Otto Pfersmann's study clearly indicates the relevant perspective: the thematisation of the notion of *institutum vitae* occurs in the context of the *Nicomachean Ethics* and refers there to the *ratio vivendi* of the *TTP* and the *Ethics*: 'La spéculation spinoziste s'enracine donc dans une première réduction des données à ce seul aspect de la vie pratique, dont la description en termes aristotéliciens permet un démontage et un développement rigoureux. Le *vitae institutum* désigne un ordre durable des actions par lesquelles se maintient la vie sociale et privée d'un individu', 'Spinoza et l'anthropologie du savoir', in *Spinoza, science et religion*, p. 61.

[19] 'Qui enim ex infante, vel puero, in cadaver transiit, infelix dicitur, & contra id felicitati tribuitur, quod totum vitae spatium mente sana in corpore sano percurrere potuerimus', *Ethics* V, 39, G II, p. 305, ll. 20–4 [CWS I, 614].

fortune. One thus reflects in a manner that is internal to the register of common life. If common life is the life where one does not think about what determines one's actions, various determinations – and indeed potentially contradictory ones – nevertheless still appear there. One can choose between such-and-such an end, or prefer one end to another, without this reducing the characteristics of the givenness or consistency of the *vita communis*. What is common is not uniform. Yet the diversity that emerges from common life always leads back to the same regime of consistency. One can even take charge of one's own life, yet to do so is not necessarily to leave the order of what is common. The proof of this is that when Spinoza mentions taking charge of one's own life (for instance, with respect to honours),[20] he shows that it involves imitating others and conforming to their opinions in order to win their support. It is in this sense that, as we have just seen, the fact of sharing the same behaviours serves to reinforce the coherence of common life. So long as one remains in this register, one's choices conform to what one shares with others. The effort to direct one's own life is thus the height of alienation.

We are now at the point where the first two dimensions of common life show it to be constituted by a multiplicity of determinations, a majority of which do not, however, undermine the consistency of the sensible tissue in which these determinations take on their meaning. How can we identify and analyse these determinations? There are two conceivable ways of doing so. In fact, Spinoza employs both successively. The second and most conspicuous one has often been remarked upon: namely, the classification of goods. It is the most conspicuous since it is one of the pre-existing elements of the moral topos (the reader expects such a classification in a discourse that deals with the true good), but it is also conspicuous because Spinoza explicitly treats it as such. However, this classification is used, indeed useable, only under the jurisdiction of another, more inapparent topos – one without which the effective functioning of the text would become basically unreadable. This is what I shall call the sequences of human activity. These sequences are represented by the following verbs: *quaerere* and its composites, but also 'obtain', 'enjoy', along with 'keep' and 'take'. Finally, there is one particular sequence to which all of the others will be related: the sequence represented by the verb *cogitare*. This division between sequences does not coincide with the division between goods; rather, it runs transversally to it, and indeed allows it to function. It thus represents what is most fundamental in Spinoza's argument.

---

[20] 'Vita necessario ad captum hominum est dirigenda', § 5, G II, p. 6, l. 18 [*TdIE* 5; *CWS* I, 8]. And a moment prior: 'ad quem omnia diriguntur', ibid., ll. 11–12 [*TdIE* 5; *CWS* I, 8].

Spinoza nevertheless does not thematise this division. Yet we see it appear in a practical state as soon as it is a matter of understanding the subject's hesitations in the face of the search for the true good – that is, as soon as Spinoza goes beyond stating, or simply reminding us of, the teachings of experience, and begins to describe situations that are actually experienced. Thus, the first reason that makes Spinoza describe the search for the unique and true good as *inconsultum* is not the simple consideration of honours or wealth; these are not initially given as ends in themselves and as goods whose prestige would be enough to divert the subject from the path of happiness. On the contrary, they are named in the course of a comparative calculation: I see the advantages that honours and wealth allow one to acquire (*acquirere*); I see that the new enterprise will mean I must stop seeking them out (*quaerere*);[21] yet this new enterprise itself consists in seeking (*inquirere*)[22] the true good in order to acquire it (*acquirere*) once I have found it.[23] *Quaerere* and its composites thus refer to an activity that transcends the distinction between the true good and other goods, between the *commoda* and the *aliquid* for which the *commoda* will be sacrificed. This commonality is not the idea of the good in general, but the common movement of the search for, and the procurement of, what is sought. It is this common movement that makes possible the evaluation of different ends by reducing them to a common denominator, and it is these same tools that will serve in the following paragraphs to describe the quest for honours and wealth (*prosequi* will be joined this time to *quaerere*).[24] A number of actions of this kind can, moreover, be linked to each other, with one serving indirectly as the means for obtaining another. Thus, the means for obtaining honours is to seek (*quaerere*) what the crowd seeks.[25] We learn at the same time that the totality of human actions can be characterised by this search; whoever wants to imitate other human beings need do no more than imitate this activity. The ends that the subject seeks can vary, while the movement of seeking is constant. The description of human life thus seems to find its most profound anchoring point in the analytics of *seeking*.[26]

---

[21] 'Videbam nimirum commoda, quae ex honore ac divitiis acquiruntur, et quod ab iis quaerendis cogebar abstinere', § 2 G II, p. 5, ll. 18–19 [*TdIE* 2; *CWS* I, 7].

[22] 'Constitui tandem inquirere . . .', § 1, G II, p. 5, l. 12 [*TdIE* 1; *CWS* I, 7].

[23] 'Quo invento et acquisito . . .', § 1, G II, p. 5, l. 15 [*TdIE* 1; *CWS* I, 7].

[24] 'Honores ac divitias prosequendo non parum etiam distrahitur mens, praesertim ubi hae non nisi propter se quaeruntur', § 4, G II, p. 6, ll. 7–8 [*TdIE* 4; *CWS* I, 8].

[25] 'Et quaerendo quod vulgo quaerunt homines', § 5, G II, p. 6. ll. 19–20 [*TdIE* 5; *CWS* I, 8].

[26] Spinoza's note to paragraph 4 introduces a distinction, but it remains interior to the *quaerere*: 'distinguendo scilicet divitias, quae quaeruntur vel propter se, vel propter

Life, however, is not reducible to the act of seeking. We must also take into account a symmetrical sequence: that of fleeing,[27] a sequence that completes the broad set of actions attributed to the *homine* and which must be imitated by whomsoever seeks men's favour.[28] Additionally, we must also take into account the fact that when we find a good, we acquire it (*acquirere*, but also *assequi*,[29] and further on *consecutio*),[30] we stop seeking other goods out for a time, and we enjoy it (*fruitio* from paragraph 4 again takes up *quiesceret*).[31] Here, too, we encounter a symmetry: we can obtain goods, but we can also have our hopes frustrated.[32] I remarked above on the almost obsessive profusion of terms from the family of *certus* in the preceding paragraph. The same could be said for the verbs composed from *quaerere*[33] and *sequi*.[34] The word 'hope' itself is implicitly defined as what ties the *quaerere* to the *acquirere*.[35] Finally, what has been acquired – possessed – can be lost – can perish. And indeed, one can even lose oneself – that is, one, too, can perish. I noted above that these two modalities of loss were decisive, since they constitute the catalyst for the second and fourth stages of the narrator's path.

All by itself, then, and before we engage in any explicitly ethical considerations, the *vita communis* teaches us to recognise what is at stake in common life: the *fruitio*, the *quiescere in aliquo bono*, the *commoda*, the means for obtaining them – seeking, fleeing, acquiring – and a danger: that of perishing, or of losing what we have obtained. We can thus indicate the series of fundamental sequences that constitute the actions both of the narrator and of people in general: seeking and fleeing; winning; losing; profiting; enjoying; perishing. Together they give us the instruments required for an

---

honorem ...', G II, p. 6, note a [*TdIE* 4; *CWS* I, 8].

[27] An analogous symmetry exists in Descartes: *prosequi/fugere*, Fourth Meditation, AT, VII, p. 57 [*PWD* II, 40].

[28] 'Fugiendo scilicet quod vulgo fugiunt [...] homines', § 5, G II, p. 6, l. 19 [*TdIE* 5; *CWS* I, 8].

[29] 'Ut ipsum assequamur', § 5, G II, p. 6, ll. 17–18 [*TdIE* 5; *CWS* I, 8].

[30] 'Quoad ipsius consecutionem', § 6 G II, p. 6, ll. 3–4 [*TdIE* 6; *CWS* I, 8].

[31] 'Ac si in aliquo bono quiesceret ...', § 4, G II, p. 6, ll. 3–4 [*TdIE* 4; *CWS* I, 8]; 'post illius fruitionem', ibid., 1, 4–5 [*TdIE* 4; *CWS* I, 8].

[32] 'Si autem spe in aliquo casu frustremur ...', § 5, G II, p. 6, l. 15 [*TdIE* 5; *CWS* I, 8].

[33] For *quaerere* and its composites, cf. all of the examples already cited; to these we can add the following: *fixum enim bomum quaerebam* (§ 6); *summis viribus quaerere* (§ 7); *summis viribus cogitur quaerere* (§ 7); *totisque viribus quaerendum* (§ 10); the three *quaeruntur* from paragraph 11; and the substantive *acquisitio* (§ 11).

[34] *Prosequendo* (§ 5); *assequamur* (§ 6); *consecutionem* (§ 6); *omnia quae vulgus sequitur* (§ 7); *ut honorem assequerentur* (§ 8).

[35] § 5, cited above, and § 7.

analysis of common life. It could be argued that we encounter them again, in another form, in Books III and IV of the *Ethics*. For the time being, we can note that by returning to what is most primitive in the narrator's journey, we have revealed these fundamental sequences. These sequences thus constitute the critical threads of the narrator's ethical trajectory. They determine in the final analysis the specificity of Spinoza's approach in the *proemium*.

If we wish to understand the form proper to Spinoza's approach, we have to consider these sequences more closely. They have four characteristics:

— These sequences take the form of individual actions, even if they can have other individuals as their object, whether as models or as conditions. Collective action is not primary. Neither the city, divinity, nor an explicit natural law is present. The sequences of common life constitute so many anthropological episodes that require no transindividual foundation. Certainly, the other is present on their horizon, but they are not given as necessary: the collectivity is a collectivity of repetition and imitation, indeed of competition and exclusion; it does not, however, constitute a foundation. It goes without saying that neither science, nor politics conceived as an analysis of the city (that is, insofar as it is different from an individual search for honours), nor theology appear here. The human being is thus revealed as a site of various actions, none of which are hierarchised with respect to one another. The *praesertim* of paragraph 4 and the *vero* of paragraph 5 both indicate instances, not precedents. We can read in this collection of individual activities something that transcends them, or towards which they tend in order to find their ultimate signification.

In this sense, the tone of the prologue is close to that of Hobbes's anthropology, such as it appears in *De Natura humana*. In this work, Hobbes analyses life as a plurality of activities.[36] Nothing in this plurality institutes a teleological order, a natural rule, or a social law: for Hobbes, while there exists a plurality of people, they do not immediately constitute a State which gives them rules. Indeed, it is this non-hierarchical plurality of activities that allows Hobbes to deny the existence of a Sovereign Good:[37] the finality of

---

[36] For example, Chapter VII, which will introduce the notions of good and evil, begins with definitions of pleasure and pain, which (in addition to their mechanical engendering) are grasped through the consequences they have on human actions: 'This motion, in which consisteth *pleasure* or *pain*, is also a solicitation or provocation either to draw *near* to the thing that pleaseth, or to *retire* from the thing that displeaseth', *EW*, vol. IV, p. 31.

[37] 'But for an utmost end, in which the ancient philosophers have placed felicity, and disputed much concerning the way thereto, there is no such thing in this world, nor way to it, more than to Utopia: for while we live, we have desires, and desire presupposeth

actions exhausts their exercise, without subordinating them to a signification that would structure or transcend them; their only end is the empirical end of their existence – whence the Hobbesian comparison of the passions to the situation of a man in a race:[38] 'To consider them behind, is glory. To consider them before, is humility. [. . .] And to forsake the course, is to die.'

There is nevertheless one difference here with respect to Hobbes. In the latter's work, the subject's originary movements place the other in their immediate vicinity and thus make the relation to the other a constitutive element of human action. Let us begin again with the description of passions that we have just cited. Certainly, in Hobbes's works the subject's acts are not structured in relation to a Sovereign Good. But they are nevertheless organised in a specular manner since their power is refracted through the gaze of another subject. Thus, the race is at the same time a comparison. In the Hobbesian universe, one does not run alone; if the meaning of the race is irreducible to its end, it nevertheless still has a meaning: namely, the distance between the competitors, which is the source of either the happiness or sadness of the runner. This is why it is clear in Hobbes that civil society is not foundational (it is, on the contrary, founded *by* individuals and *with* individuals), while the inter-human dimension nevertheless founds the traits possessed by individuals. The other – my anthropological equal – is already there within me, in the form of the many dimensions of the passions, before being constituted as an adversary in the state of war and as a partner after the institution of a pact. There is nothing of this in the *proemium*: the other is there, and they can either be a rival or an admirer, an occasion for the loss of goods or the object of flattery. But neither rivalry nor admiration are constitutive of the individual.

— Again, as with Hobbes, these sequences are ethically indifferent. It is not possible to say that seeking is good or that fleeing is evil, nor can we say the contrary. In themselves, these sequences to which human life can be reduced have no ethical orientation. They are not given as good or bad; they are profoundly indifferent to good and evil, just as they are indifferent to the various types of goods (including the Sovereign Good). It is this ethical neutrality that gives the opening of the *TdIE* its innovative power. For Spinoza, these goods cannot produce illusions. It is on this point that Spinoza breaks most spectacularly with traditional moral rhetoric: the goods are links in a chain that produce various effects, but none of them is *a priori*

a further end', *EW*, vol. IV, p. 33.
[38] *De Natura humana*, chap. IX, § 21, *EW*, vol. IV, p. 52–3. Cf. my analysis of this anthropology in *Hobbes, science, politique, religion*, Paris: PUF, 1988, pp. 37–9.

negative. At this anthropological level, nothing is to be condemned, if not condemnation itself. The sequences of action allow us to compare and evaluate different goods and to analyse their results, without subordinating them to a preestablished moral ideal. These sequences will then also allow us to go beyond these same goods, without having to introduce anything that is extraneous to the text's logic. It is one and the same play of sequences that, by taking seriously the promise emitted by perishable goods, constructs the model of another good.

We saw in Chapter 2 that the internal transformation of the stages of certainty was the key to the immanence of Spinoza's reasoning: it distinguished the language of experience both from the protreptic and from the conversion narrative. We now see that the self-transformation of certainty is possible only by the concatenation of these neutral segments, the sequences of human activity. Indeed, these sequences are so neutral that they will be used to describe the Sovereign Good. This originary distribution thus remains unsurpassed. It does not characterise some 'before' but rather covers the entire terrain of the description of behaviours. Yet it does so in a manner that is worth noting. Fundamentally, everything that we read about here describes, at a very general level, what is contained in Book IV of the *Ethics*. Certainly: but we should also note that we do not find – not even once – the words *affectus* or *passio*. The description focuses on the effects of the force that guides us towards the goods, without pausing to qualify this force itself, still less to explain it. For the time being the chain of these effects constitutes the sole object of analysis, for this chain suffices – by virtue of what it produces in the form of satisfaction, then in promises, and finally in threats – to legitimate the trajectory that will lead the subject to the final decision.

It is this force that replaces the inter-human play of *De Natura humana*. For the latter work engenders ethics indirectly. In the prologue to the *TdIE*, by contrast, the play of fundamental sequences allows ethics to emerge directly; but it does so only at the price of a reconstitution of the Sovereign Good. But is this not a regression? From a Hobbesian point of view, it most certainly is. But what must be thought here is precisely the following paradox: a Sovereign Good reconstituted on the basis of a world without ends.

— There is another difference with Hobbes that should also be highlighted here. In Hobbes's work, the human being is the support of their activities, and thanks to their internal movement[39] is these activities' found-

---

[39] Recall the definition of pleasure and pain (Chapter VII, § 1): '*conceptions* and *apparitions* are nothing *really*, but *motion* in some internal substance of the *head*; which motion *not stopping* there, but proceeding to the *heart*, of necessity must there either

ing centre, their origin. In Spinoza, by contrast, the human being certainly appears as the support and place of the exercise of these activities; but the human being themselves is not described. Rather, the description presented by the *proemium* constitutes an anthropology without a subject. I will take up further on the question of whether the *animus* can be the site of all of this, at least in part. Let us observe for the moment that the *animus* is not explicitly mentioned in the prologue. Indeed, throughout the text, the *animus* is mentioned only in relation to the effects that events have on it,[40] never as a motor or a principle of choice. The sequences we have described are all given just as common life itself is. But why are *these* sequences the ones given? And why are they described in this way? Man, ultimately, at least in the prologue, is the sum of these sequences, or of their possibility. In Book II of the *Ethics*, the human being will be constructed by way of a physics, while in Books III and IV the plurality of their actions will be reduced to the *conatus*. This is not the case here. Rather, in the prologue we are given only the general means for describing various human behaviours, without these behaviours being assigned a place where they can find the rule of their identity. Likewise, these activities are not essentially related to the goods that come to play the role of object complements to the verbs: each good can be sought, won and lost; the activities always have a correlate which gives them meaning, but their distinction remains of a formal order.

— These first three traits of the fundamental sequences have brought us close to a Hobbesian anthropology. They have allowed us to both bring to light the strong similarities between the two doctrines and to keep them apart at the points where they are clearly distinct – that is, at precisely those points where Hobbes emphasises what separates him from the tradition. It remains for us to ask in what sense Spinoza's argument does not constitute a return to this tradition – a tradition that both thinkers appear to reject. What is common to the different goods is not a general idea of the good; it is rather this description of sequential or substitutable actions (one seeks then one acquires; one keeps then loses), in terms of which all human activities can be described. These actions have a content, yet they are anterior or transversal to their content. As soon as we specify this

---

help or *hinder* the motion which is called *vita*; when it *helpeth*, it is called *delight, contentment* or *pleasure* [. . .] but when such motion *weakened* or *hindereth* the vital motion, then it is called *pain*', *EW*, vol. IV, p. 31. Cf. also the definition of the pleasures of the senses, Chapter VIII, § 1 and 2, ibid., pp. 34–5.

[40] 'nisi quatenus ab iis animus movebatur', § 1; 'quod ab libidinem attinet, ea adeo suspenditur animus . . .', § 4; 'propter illud, quod non amatur [. . .] nullae commotiones animi', § 9, etc.

content, we are in the realm of *one* of the goods. In fact, what is given in this series of verbs is precisely what is required to dissect the efficacy of the different goods. We cannot even distinguish these goods in terms of actions that arise from the soul and actions that arise from the body: these actions concern *both* the body (which, moreover, is never named) *and* the *animus*. The enumeration of this series of actions avoids considering the goods as ends. The goods are, rather, the correlates of actions. It could be said that this is a fine nuance indeed. Nevertheless, it seems to me that if we read this description alongside the one from the *Nicomachean Ethics*, the difference is stark. We see the same thing, certainly, but it is not the same *scene* that is foregrounded. Aristotle begins by taking into account a series of disciplines or forms of action: technē, methodōs, praxis and proairesis. He then states that all of them tend towards a certain good.[41] This inclination is registered in common opinion, while philosophy approves of it. From the outset, then, Aristotle interprets activities in terms of an end.[42] Philosophy then remarks upon a spontaneous hierarchy that emerges between these activities. A movement of multiplication and organisation traverses them, with each activity enlisting itself in the service of another activity that is architectonically superior to it. The schema of the end thus applies not only to the relations between an activity and its good, but also to the relations between activities themselves, and thus between goods and other goods. It is in this way that the Sovereign Good and its science – politics – emerge. There is no need to investigate further to give a clear content to this concept; but it is at the very least necessary to say that the Sovereign Good appears as a given: it is intelligible as the very principle of empirical activities. Dividing human life into the art of making bridles, of riding horses, of strategy, politics, and so on, fundamentally presupposes what it will make appear; it contains a model of intelligibility constituted by the determinate

---

[41] *Nicomachean Ethics*, I, 1, 1094a. 'Every skill and every inquiry, and similarly every action and rational choice, is thought to aim at some good', Aristotle, *Nicomachean Ethics*, trans. Roger Crisp (Cambridge: Cambridge University Press, 2004), p. 3.

[42] 'and so the good has been aptly described as that at which everything aims' (I, 5, 1094a; *Nicomachean Ethics*, p. 3). The next sentence then continues with a reference to the diversity of ends. This link will be confirmed in the analysis of the choice (I, 5, 1097a; *Nicomachean Ethics*, pp. 9–10). Commentators have accentuated this reading by translating it into a mediated identity: 'omnia autem ista ordinantur ad aliquod bonum sicut in finem', S. Thomas Aquinas, *In decem libros ethicorum Aristotelis ad Nichomachum Expositio*, § 8, ed. R. Spiazzi, OP, Rome: Marietti, 1964, p. 4; or an immediate one: 'ergo appetunt bonum, & finem propter quem operantur', Sylvester Maurus, *Aristotelis Opera* [. . .] *Illustrata*, Rome, 1668, vol. II, p. 4.

permanence of a certain number of forms of action that are already filled with a certain content. This is how the good towards which each activity tends is conceived, and it implies from the outset the principle of the revelation of a final good.[43] In Spinoza, by contrast, the formal character of the fundamental sequences makes it impossible for there to be a hierarchy that structures the path towards the ultimate good. This is why, even if it is a paradox, Spinoza is closer than it appears to Hobbes on this question as well: in Spinoza, there is no Sovereign Good that is *given*. A process is required to *construct* it.

We can mark this difference from another perspective as well. We could say that the Aristotelian description is nominal while Spinoza's is verbal. Aristotle evokes a world of ends and asks whether they are hierarchised or not (and he immediately responds in the affirmative). But what are these ends? They are referred to using nouns that immediately indicate their content, however general this content might be. The schema action-end-good is possible, and it becomes meaningful if we understand that action is rational action that aims at a certain end – namely, a good. Spinoza's text remains, not at a level of greater generality, but rather at a prior level of description. It is a matter of apprehending, by way of verbs, the elements of action. To seek or to acquire is above all more fragmentary, and thus more neutral, than strategy, politics or wealth. The nominalising approach of the Aristotelian tradition fundamentally refuses the possibility that there really are neutral elements at the basis of ethics.[44]

In the context of life, and above all of common life, goods do not have meanings that are given once and for all; they are objects that are measured and analysed in a way that transcends their individuality, and by means of those instruments of comparison that are the vital sequences. Their plurality is not reducible to a single foundation called 'man'. The Postulates of Book II of the *Ethics* will try to construct, at least by way of an *exemplar*, such a foundation. Here this is not the case.

We have thus surveyed what the prologue presents as the dimension of the *communis vita*. It is characterised as being given, consistent and organised

---

[43] This is why, despite the presence of a term which is so decisive in Spinoza's system, the Aristotelian definition of the good as 'what all desire' probably marks the point of greatest distance from Spinoza. For Spinoza, it is necessary to say, on the contrary, that the good is what is desired by each individual.

[44] This is the meaning of the first of the *Ethical Problems* of Alexander of Aphrodisias, *Supplementum aristotelicum* (hrg. I. Bruns), vol. II-2, Berlin, 1892, pp. 118–20.

into constitutive sequences. In light of these three characteristics, can we now give a better definition of common life? But first of all, what is life? I have left this word obscure up to this point so as to focus on its determinations. We have concluded that these determinations lead to a conception of human action in terms of three distinctions: a vertical distinction between ordinary life and what is not ordinary life; a horizontal distinction between the three sorts of goods and the activities that tend towards them; and a distinction that runs transversally to the second – namely, between the different sequences of activity: seeking, obtaining, losing, resting. But beyond these distinctions, what is life?

With respect to other parts from the system, we could refer to Sylvain Zac's book.[45] Yet Zac deals almost exclusively (and in a magisterial fashion) with life conceived as a vital power. He completely neglects life as a way of living. It is moreover characteristic that Zac never analyses the text that we are currently studying: he cites it, in whole or in part, at three moments in his thesis,[46] but he never focuses on the term 'life' from this passage and on the perspective that it presupposes. He thus implicitly recognises that it has a different use here, or that it belongs to a different dimension, to the one he himself considers.

The term 'life' in Spinoza's lexicon has a number of meanings – meanings which are not incompatible with one another, and Spinoza takes care to distinguish between them in a number of passages.[47] However, we will see that in the course of making these distinctions, one of the meanings of 'life' – specifically, the fourth – is overlooked by Zac. We can distinguish: (a) life as a biological act, defined by the circulation of blood[48] – a definition which, even outside of this scientific distinction, corresponds to a given of common consciousness: it is the contrary of death. To be alive is a characteristic shared by all animals, to the exclusion of simple material objects. To kill someone is to make them lose their life by stopping their biological mechanisms. By extending it somewhat, this meaning can also include the means for conserving this biological continuity. Paragraph 8 of the *TdIE*

---

[45] *L'idée de vie dans la philosophie de Spinoza*, Paris: PUF, 1963.
[46] See ibid., p. 116 (the task of philosophy), p. 155 (the passage from the level of duration to that of eternity), p. 173 (interrogation of the meaning of life as a point of departure for philosophical reflection).
[47] *Cogitata Metaphysica*, 2nd Part, Chapter 6, G I, p. 260 [CW II; CWS I, 325–6]; TP, Chapter 5, 5, G III, p. 296, ll. 11–15 [TP V, 5; CWS II, 530].
[48] 'Quae [...] sola sanguinis circulatione, et aliis, quae omnibus animalibus sunt communia [...] definitur', TP, Chapter 5, 5, G III, p. 296, ll. 13–15 [TP V, 5; CWS II, 530].

clearly opposes life thus conceived and death in the series of examples illustrating the stupidity of those who devote themselves to perishable goods.[49] A little further on, by contrast, Spinoza speaks of the correct amount of money that allows one to 'conserve life and health'.[50] (b) Life as a power of being alive, the source and cause of the biological act and of what conditions it.[51] The life of a being is identical with its productivity. Fundamentally, what is most living is the dynamism of the laws of Nature – and thus the dynamism of God Himself as the reason for these laws and the immanent cause of all things. If the latter are living, it is 'in the sense that their productivity, their "effort to persevere in being", is a manifestation of the infinite productivity of God'[52] (c) The 'true life', that which is proper to man[53] and which is defined by reason, whose external conditions must be guaranteed by the State, but which an additional effort – that engaged in by the individual – must bring to fruition. (d) Finally, the 'life' that Spinoza sometimes speaks of but which he does not define: namely, common life, which is twice named at the beginning of the *TdIE*. It is that which we 'direct' towards such-and-such a good, that which also implies morals but remains irreducible to them. This is life as the site of human actions. We can see the relations of the first three strata of signification to one another, and all the more easily since the author himself clearly indicates them. Life in the sense of (b) refers to the laws that produce life in the sense of (a). The true life, or (c), is the model, immanent to the human being, of which God in the sense of (b), is the principle.[54] The true life, finally, is distinct from life in the sense of (a), which it nevertheless presupposes as a general condition[55] – that is, it is that which is most worthy of the human being as distinct from what is common to all animals. The fourth strata, by contrast, is never elucidated; nevertheless, I would be

---

[49] 'Ut tandem vita poenam luerent suae stultitiae', § 8, G II, p. 7, ll. 12–13 [*TdIE* 8; *CWS* I, 9].

[50] 'Quantum sufficit ad vitam et valetudinem sustentandam', § 17, G II, p. 9, ll. 31–2 [*TdIE* 17; *CWS* I, 12].

[51] 'Quare nos per *vitam* intelligimus *vim, per quam res in suo esse perseurant*', CM, II, Chapter 6, G I, p. 260, ll. 15–16 [CM, VI; *CWS* I, 326].

[52] Zac, *L'idée de vie dans la philosophie de Spinoza*, p. 20.

[53] 'Vitam humanam intelligo, [...] quae maxime ratione, vera mentis virtute et vita defininitur', TP, 5, G III, p. 296, l. 12 and 14–15 [TP V, 5; *CWS* II, 530]. This definition completes the phrase where the other signification of *vita* is defined, that which is common to all animals. Cf. also TTP, Chapter IV, G III, pp. 66–7 [TTP IV, 41; *CWS* II, 136].

[54] TTP, Chapter XIII, G III, p. 171, l. 22 [TTP XIII, 23; *CWS* II, 262].

[55] Chapter II of the TP links *vitam sustentare* and *mentem colere* (15, G III, p. 281, l. 22 [TP II, 15; *CWS* II, 513]).

tempted to say that it holds the philosophical key to all of the others. In fact, if, rhetorically speaking, we can oppose the 'true life' to purely animal life, it is no less the case that it remains difficult, particularly in a system of thought that refuses finality, to identify directly what is proper to the human being with what is most worthy of them; for not all seek the *vera vita*. The formula from Chapter V of the *Political Treatise* thus cannot be said to give a complete indication of what characterises human life as such. The true life is one of the forms that life can take as a site of actions; it is not opposed to life, no more so than reason is to nature. Moreover, the true life can only emerge against the backdrop constituted by common life. However, life in the fourth sense is not the same thing as biological life. It names the way in which people live biological phenomena, or the way people deploy their biological possibilities. More precisely, when Spinoza speaks of life in this fourth sense, the reader has the impression that the emphasis is being placed on a different aspect of life than its determination by physical causes. The latter exist, no doubt, but when in the present text Spinoza deals with the *events* of life (*omnia quae occurrunt*), or when in other texts he deals with the *use* of life (*usus vitae*),[56] he provisionally abstracts the causes that determine the continuation of life and directs our attention to the fact that something habitually happens in life and that we know what this thing is[57] (even if it is not in a rational fashion).[58] I know (even if I do not know the causes of) what I do, and I know what has taken place. I also see what other people do. Life in this sense is the play of a gaze on human activities. It is not a specification of biological life, of which the true life would be another supplementary specification (moreover, nothing tells us formally that only human beings can have this type of experience).[59] Rather, it should be conceived as a gaze on another gaze – a perspective on reality considered not in its causal determinations, but

---

[56] This is what defines and limits the role of the Prophets (Preface to the *TTP*, G III, p. 9, l. 31 [*TTP* Preface, 21; *CWS* II, 72]; Chapter II, p. 42, ll. 26–30 [*TTP* II, 52; *CWS* II, 109]; Chapter VII, p. 109, ll. 9–11 [*TTP* VII, 56; *CWS* II, 182]) and the field of the notion of the possible, Chapter IV, p. 58, ll. 25–6 [*TTP* IV, 3; *CWS* II, 126].

[57] Hobbes makes an analogous distinction when he remarks in *De Corpore* that we can also know civil philosophy by way of experience, and not only by deducing it causally from moral philosophy (which is knowledge of the movements of the mind), which itself is deduced from physics (*Human Nature*, I, Chapter 6, § 7, p. 121–2. However, in contrast to Spinoza, he does not go as far as to look at experience *directly*.

[58] 'In communi vita verisimillimum, in speculationibus vero veritatem cogimur sequi', Letter 56, G IV, p. 260, ll. 15–16 [*Ep*. LVI [to Hugo Boxel]; *CWS* II, 422].

[59] We are referred here to a problem analogous to the one that Alexandre Matheron treats in his study 'L'anthropologie spinoziste?', *Revue de synthèse*, 99 (1978), pp. 175–88, republished in *Anthropologie et politique au XVIIe siècle*, Paris: Vrin, 1986, pp. 17–28.

directly, as a place where choices are made and maintained. It is the presence of the human being to their actions and to the memory of these actions, as well as to the actions of others.[60] This dimension thus appears as an open field where all are exposed to the other's gaze. This allows us to advance another interpretation of the expression 'common life', which can serve as a foundation for the two other meanings between which we were previously hesitating: common life is also – perhaps by forcing the point a little – the life that makes things common, the life that we project into the public sphere, within the circle of the gaze of others, where everyone can memorialise it. It is in this way that common life becomes the site of experience.

Thus, the *vita communis* appears as the field where experience presents its lessons. It is the place where events occur and the terrain on which certain goods are pursued. Above all, we find here at the level of content what in the previous chapter we considered at the level of form: namely, familiarity. By reflecting on common life we see this familiar décor arise; and it is on its basis – and *only* on its basis – that we can strike a path towards the unknown. In other words, as we will learn elsewhere – though the *proemium* prepares us for this lesson – it is from common life that we depart towards the true life.

2. The 'Summa Felicitas'

The first hesitation arises when one compares the aspiration to the true good with the goods to which one is habituated in common life, along with their familiar advantages. What is at stake is referred to as the *summa felicitas* – a concept which, for the time being, remains empty (since it could refer to either of the two kinds of good). The *summa felicitas* is empty yet still desired. In what sense? And why? Here, too, we find ourselves in the midst of the rhetorical tradition. An entire topos grounds the relation of the human being to ethics in an initial aspiration: 'we want to be happy . . .' – even if this aspiration ends up tending towards an end that was not immediately perceivable by the person who first had this aspiration. Since Plato[61] this has been the common basis for all discourses that concern conduct: each person has the task of determining how to arrive at this happiness and to define what it truly is; each person must assure themselves that they are only proposing to others what they already wanted, albeit confusedly.[62] Here, by contrast,

---

[60] 'nam quae plerumque in vita occurrunt, et apud homines, ut ex eorum operibus colligere licet . . .', *TdIE*, § 3, G II, p. 5, ll. 26–7 [*TdIE* 3; *CWS* I, 7].

[61] Cf. The text of the *Euthydemus* cited above.

[62] It is thus that Epictetus defines the protreptic style: 'To be able to show both to one person and to many the struggle in which they are engaged, and that they think more

we could say that Spinoza replaces the traditional verb with a noun: *felicitas* replaces *volumus*, a term repeated by Cicero,[63] Seneca[64] and Augustine,[65] as well as by Pascal[66] and Malebranche much later.[67] An action in the place of a goal; but an (empty) content in the place of a desire. The only thing that we know about this content is that we enjoy it (*frui*). This term returns in similar contexts in the *Ethics*. It is a matter of enjoying a good, enjoying the Sovereign Good, and so on.

What is remarkable here is that Spinoza insists more on the disquiet that is provoked by the *summa felicitas* than on the legitimation of the concept by people's spontaneous aspirations. But where does the concept itself come from? A clue is perhaps provided by a co-occurrence of this term: each time that the term arises it is linked with the term *sita*. The same term is also an equivalent of *spes*. Why? Hope and happiness are secondary objects, which have their place in an other (cf. the noun *situs*). This distinction does not coincide with the distinction that opposes a real being to a being of reason; rather, it refers to an order. Being a magistrate, a councillor or a banker are primary realities. When a Roman begins a career of honours, his hope refers first to one of these positions, and is then displaced to another once he has obtained the first. Hope is thus less an object than a determination defined in relation to a multiplicity of objects. The same goes for happiness:

---

about anything than about what they really wish. For they wish the things which lead to happiness, but they look for them in the wrong place', *Discourses* (Infomotions, 2000), pp. 121–2.

[63] 'Beati certe omnes esse volumus'; Saint Augustine, in *De Trinitate*, XIII, 4, 7, writes: 'Shall we consider that to be false, therefore, which not even that Academician Cicero doubted (for the Academicians doubt everything) . . .'.

[64] 'Vivere, Gallio frater, omnes beate volunt: sed ad pervivendum quid sit quod beatam vitam efficiat caligant', *De Vita beata*, I ['All men, brother Gallio, wish to live happily, but are dull at perceiving exactly what it is that makes life happy'].

[65] 'Sed censesne quemquam hominem non omnibus modis velle atque optare vitam beatam?' *De libero arbitrio*, I, 14, 30; 'Summo autem bono adsecuto et adepto beatus quisque fit, quod omnes sine controversia volumus', ibid., II, 9, 26, vol. VI, p. 250 and 318.

[66] 'Tous les hommes recherchent d'être heureux. Cela est sans exception, quelques différents moyens qu'ils y emploient', *Pensées*, 148, Lafuma, 425, Br. See the commentary on this text by P. Magnard in the chapter 'Le Désir d'être heureux' from *Nature et histoire dans l'Apologétique de Pascal*, Paris: Belles Lettres, 1975, p. 257 ff., which shows clearly the articulation of this theme with that of the *delectatio victrix*.

[67] 'Car enfin tous les esprits, et les démons mêmes désirent ardemment d'être heureux, et de posséder le Souverain Bien; et ils le désirent sans choix, sans délibération, sans liberté et par la nécessité de leur nature', *Recherche de la vérité*, Livre III, Part I, Chapter 4, § 1, Paris: Pléiade, p. 313.

both suppose a separation between the spontaneous movement of the vital sequences and the reflection on these sequences.

On this point, too, as on that of the elementary forms of moral description, it is necessary to compare Spinoza's text to Aristotle's *Ethics*. But this time we should turn to the *Eudemian Ethics*, which begins with happiness. In the first seven chapters, Aristotle investigates the means for obtaining well-being, as well as his own situation with respect to different kinds of life, along with opinions concerning its nature. But there is one point that is never questioned: namely, the very existence of happiness in its coincidence with an object – even if this object remains to be determined. There is thus one thing whose existence is not doubted,[68] and the entire meaning of the quest consists in identifying this object among the different goods that we know of. By contrast, in paragraphs 2 and 9 of the *TdIE*, the appearance of *felicitas* is there only to tear the search for the good away from an object and to transform it into a question. Far from giving a name to a reality, it serves instead to de-realise what other names refer to.

It is here that our interest in Spinoza's reasoning with regards to *felicitas* lies: insofar as *felicitas* is detached from the *verum bonum*, its essential function is to open up, in the midst of common life, the space necessary for a question. Thanks to it, the goods which up to this point have remained unquestioned as to their essence are submitted to an inquiry that will lead the subject to the determination of their limits. Thus, at the very point where the subject is hesitating, the foundations have been laid for the passage to the following stage: the inversion of certainty.

3. 'Haec Tria'

The main content of the third stage consists in the analysis of what experience teaches us concerning perishable goods and their effects. Since one hesitates between perishable goods – goods that, while close at hand, are patently inadequate – and the promise of another good, a good that is more distant but which promises to be more satisfying (so long as it exists); and since the question of happiness depends on the choice between these two goods, it seems natural to attempt, if possible, a reconciliation between the

---

[68] The first chapter, for example, investigates the identification of the agreeable and the beautiful in happiness, then on the causes and the elements of the happy life (I, 1, 1214, *a-b* [Aristotle, *The Eudemian Ethics*, trans. H. Rackham, Cambridge, MA: Harvard University Press, 1992, pp. 199–205]). For the entirety of this discussion the existence and the notion of the happy life itself are there presupposed.

two: that is, to enjoy the goods that are present while making an effort to obtain the more distant good. Doing so is all the more natural since nothing initially appears to prevent such a compromise from being effected. It is only experience that will show it to be impossible. We are thus in the second stage of experience here, one that can only begin after the subject's initial aspirations, but which draws on elements from before this stage while reorganising them in the light of the new questions that have now been posed. It is the irreducible time of experience that is marked by the term 'at last' from the text's first sentence and which is underscored by the self-citation ('dico: me tandem constituisse') from the second paragraph. This complete upending of life and its reorganisation in terms of the new goal that is now being sought are not the results of an initial exigency. Rather, it is the failure of attempts at conciliation that shows the necessity of doing everything possible to transform aspiration into decision.

Nevertheless, failure alone is not enough to transmit this lesson. Rather, failure only offers up its lesson when one asks *why* these attempts have been made in vain – in other words, when one assesses experience. Now, this assessment comes down to showing in what sense what 'regularly occurs in life' prevents us from thinking about the true good. Above all, since one can always be tempted to make another attempt at compromise, perhaps with different means, it is important to show why this obstacle *necessarily* arises. It is not enough to say: 'I see that up to this point I have failed.' Rather, the difficulty of abandoning the (real) goods from the realm of occurrences is such that I must be able say: 'I understand that I will always fail if I go down this path.' Without this realisation, I could always be tempted to try again. Thus, to move towards the final decision, it is necessary to prepare the terrain by showing that all paths that involve compromise are blocked.

Now, up to this point we have seen goods, or the events of common life, appear in the form of three successive figures: their occurrence, which is always governed to a certain degree by chance; the fact that they disappoint us (we come to the conclusions that, since it is always possible for these goods to disappear, they are universally vain); and their power of attachment, which makes us hesitate to break with them entirely: we thus seek a compromise solution. In none of these three cases is it necessary to undertake a general inventory of kinds of goods: chance, or these goods' own movement, presented them to us; and when their loss affected us, it was doubtless enough to lose some goods – or to know that one could always lose them – to eventually find all of them to be vain, without any need to demonstrate this necessity. On the other hand, it is necessary to move towards a fourth figure: that of universal inhibition. To short circuit any further desire to attempt a compromise solution, this inhibition must be shown to be *necessary*. It is essential to pass by way of a form of experience that mobilises, if not all goods, then at least some goods to which all of the others can be reduced. We thus find ourselves faced with an entirely new task: while up to this point the figures of experience offered up their lessons seemingly effortlessly – indeed, their total signification ('*omnia* . . . *vana et futilia sunt*') was derived empirically from only a few cases – it is now essential to pass by way of a figure of necessary universality. We thus have to arrive at a new *omnia*, one that is stronger than the preceding one. This is a paradox: how can experience provide us with necessary conclusions?[69]

It is life itself that holds the key. Spinoza states that all perishable goods can be reduced to the following three things: wealth, honours and pleasures. We can thus reason on the basis of these three terms and in doing so, totalise experience. But on what basis can we know this? Spinoza does not demonstrate this point; he thus supposes that it will seem clear and sufficiently legitimate to his readers. One of the reasons for this is clearly that the idea of reducing goods to three principal goods is part of a common rhetorico-philosophical culture. I noted above that such a reprise of a common topos is one of the forms of the appeal to experience. Commentators have not failed to notice this. Wolfson in particular sums up Spinoza's procedure by writing that Spinoza 'follows Aristotle'.[70] By contrast, Koyré sees in the

---

[69] Indeed, the *Short Treatise* explicitly highlights the fact that the person who judges by experience cannot be sure that what he experiences in only a few particular cases can constitute a rule for him in all cases: 'want, hoe kan hy doch zeeker zyn, datt de ondervinding van eenige bezondere, hem een regul kan zyn van alle?', KV, M, p. 206 [CWS I, 98]. The remainder of the *TdIE*, by contrast, describes the second mode of knowledge (*experientia vaga*) as inferring universal axioms on the basis of particular cases, and this inference is described by the conjunction of the verbs *to see* and *to conclude* ('alii vero ab experientia simplicium faciunt axioma universale [. . .] et cum vident eundem numerum produci, quem sine hac operatione noverant esse proportionalem, inde concludunt operationem esse bonam ad quartum numerum proportionalem esse inveniendum', § 23, G II, p. 11, l. 25; p. 12, l. 7 [*TdIE* 23; CWS I, 15]). But it does not say if this inference is valid. The accent of the comparison between modes of knowledge falls elsewhere: that is, on choosing the best kind of knowledge, that which leads the understanding to perfection.

[70] Wolfson, *The Philosophy of Spinoza*, vol. II, p. 236: 'He follows Aristotle still further in enumerating three things, outside contemplation, which are generally considered by men as the highest good, namely riches, honor and pleasure' (and he refers to *Nicomachean Ethics* (*EN*), I 5 [equivalent to Chapter 3 of Tricot's translation]).

same passage from the prologue the mark of a 'clearly Stoic'[71] inspiration, yet he refuses to assign it a determinate source since he does not believe 'it is worth seeking a precise model for commonplaces'.[72] Effectively, we find here one of the nodal points of Spinoza's cultural inheritance. Or rather, it would perhaps be more accurate to say that this is one of the points where Spinoza's decisions concerning his conceptual strategy lead him to draw on the culture he shares with his readers. If it is indeed true that his text's content intersects here with a tradition, it is necessary to determine what this intersection signifies – that is, in the sense both of the tradition that Spinoza expects his readers to be familiar with, and the way that he himself reprises this tradition.

Let us pause for a moment over this tradition. I would qualify it as a rhetorical one in the sense that, even if it is taken up in philosophical texts, to a large degree it exceeds them. Moreover, it is a tradition that is made up less of concepts than of commonplaces whose contours are not always easy to define. It is sufficiently vague that it can be found, in slightly modified forms, from one philosophical discourse to the next, irrespective of the differences between systems. From the perspective that interests us, this tradition can essentially be identified with three names: Aristotle, Seneca, Descartes. But it can also be found in various forms in the arguments of almost all those who deal with human life and the choices it involves. The philosophers who mobilise this tradition invariably consider it to be something that goes without saying. Thus, they do not feel obliged to make it explicit. It is important to distinguish this tradition from the topos of different kinds of life, which it partly intersects with,[73] albeit not entirely – for one kind of life is exclusive of others: it is what a specific category of people has chosen, while on the other hand the same person can pursue successively or simultaneously pleasure, honour and wealth. The tradition of the three goods consists less in describing choices than in classifying everything that an individual can seek out.

When he analyses the components of the ethical life, Aristotle provides various classifications for the goods that claim to be the Sovereign Good. In passing,[74] he mentions pleasure, wealth and honours, but without pre-

---

[71] Cf. his translation of the *Treatise on the Emendation of the Intellect*, Paris: Vrin, 1979, p. 97: 'Volupté, richesses, honneurs: lieux communs de la prédication morale; l'inspiration de tout ce debut est nettement stoïcienne.'
[72] Ibid., This refusal is stated against Dilthey, Wolfson, Dunin-Borkowski.
[73] Cf. further on the quotation from *EN*, I, 3.
[74] *EN*, I, 2, 1095a. *Nicomachean Ethics*, pp. 5–6.

senting this tripartite division as the only one possible: 'Most people', he writes, 'agree about what [the good] is called, since both the masses and sophisticated people call it happiness, understanding being happy as equivalent to living well and acting well. They disagree about substantive conceptions of happiness, the masses giving an account which differs from that of the philosophers. For the masses think it is something straightforward and obvious, like pleasure, wealth, or honour . . .'. But just after this he mentions health, wealth again, the admiration for lofty speeches, and those who think of the good that exists by itself; and he adds: 'Examining all the views offered would presumably be rather a waste of time, and it is enough to look at the most prevalent ones of those that seem to have something to be said for them.' It is thus clear that in Aristotle's eyes the three goods mentioned first do not exhaust the list of all of possible goods, nor do they totalise them. They are cited as examples, indeed as essential examples, but not as a compendium. Such a reservation, moreover, coheres with the Aristotelian conception of ethics: given that ethics arises from the world of contingency and approximation, it can hardly be susceptible to definitions as rigorous as those of mathematics. The ethicist is more at ease with an open list of examples.

At the end of the same book, in chapters 8 and 9, after having given his own definition of the Sovereign Good, Aristotle verifies that this definition is confirmed by common opinion, and once again enumerates a series of goods, without the reader being able to reduce these goods to three principal ones. Aristotle cites virtue, pleasures and external goods, among which he includes friends, wealth and political influence.[75] Once again we see that the 'three goods' – those that will go on to be the 'three goods' of the tradition – can be found here, but they are neither present all by themselves, nor as the conclusion to an argument that is supposed to present them deductively. It is common opinion that provides this list – a list at once varied and coherent, but whose coherence does not require an extreme fixity.

At the same time,[76] Aristotle analyses common conceptions of goods as a function of the life one leads: pleasure (for the many); honour (for cultured people who enjoy the active life); and the contemplative life (which he says he will examine later). Aristotle then mentions the life of the businessman, which is oriented towards wealth, before rejecting it on the basis that it is simply a means to a different end.[77] We are thus dealing here with

---

[75] EN, I, 9, 1099a-b. *Nicomachean Ethics*, pp. 14–16.
[76] EN, I, 3, 1095b 14 ff. *Nicomachean Ethics*, pp. 6–7.
[77] Ibid., 1096a 8. *Nicomachean Ethics*, p. 5.

a reflection on different kinds of life.[78] If we wanted to give a title to this chapter from Aristotle's work, the precise formulation would have to be: 'conceptions of happiness according to the three kinds of life, with an annex on wealth'. But the influence of this tripartite division is so strong that in his translation Tricot gives the following title to Chapter 3: 'Les théories courantes sur la nature du bonheur: le plaisir, l'honneur, la richesse'.[79] In other words, the 'standard' theory of the three goods exerts a retrospective influence on Aristotle's text through the intermediary of its translations. It is thus a commonplace that gives Aristotle's text a false coherence that it did not initially possess.

Let us conclude: on the one hand, the division of goods is a movement that can seem quite natural on the part of someone seeking to categorise the ends of activity. However, this division never appears as a strict framework. It is always provisional and capable of being reworked. On the other hand, this division is part of a movement that isolates ends by referring each of them to a specific desire. We should not rush to say that this makes Spinoza similar to Aristotle, for it is perhaps here that they are most distant from one another. In the prologue to the *TdIE*, desire as such does not appear, no more than the act of desiring. Finally, the meaning of the questions that Aristotle puts to the three goods (or to different goods, when the list of goods is longer) can always be determined at the first level of experience. What is said of this stage of experience is identified with whatever common opinion says of it, or it takes root there. This experience is a point of reference on the basis of which discussion in a proper sense can begin.

After Aristotle, the classification becomes – or becomes again – a topos.[80] It is found in the Stoics,[81] then in the oratory tradition. It loses neither its vagueness nor its provisional character, but it does produce rhetorical effects more than analysis. It is thus that Cicero addresses the problem in

---

[78] This is how Sylvester Maurus understands the text: he speaks of *variae hominum classes* and of three *modi vivendi* (*Aristotelis opera* [. . .] *illustrata*, vol. II, pp. 9–10).

[79] Aristotle, *Éthique à Nicomaque*, trans. J. Tricot, Paris: Vrin, 1967, p. 43.

[80] We already find it in Isocrates: 'Thus I assert that everyone does everything for pleasure, profit, or honor. For I do not see that people desire anything apart from these things', Isocrates, 'Antidosis', in *Isocrates I*, trans. David C. Mirhady and Yun Lee Too (Austin: University of Texas Press, 2000), p. 245.

[81] Cleanthes, *Hymn to Zeus*: 'But now, unbid, they pass on divers paths/Each his own way, yet knowing not the truth, – /Some in unlovely striving for renown,/ Some bent on lawless gains, on pleasure some,/Working their own undoing, self-deceived' (trans. E. H. Blakeney).

the *Topica*[82] when he produces a list of all of the questions an orator has to consider: 'But when the question is what something is, one has to explain the notion, the property, and the division and partition. [. . .] Division and partition: are there three types of goods?'[83] He also lists wealth, power and domination, and, with reference to an interpretation of the ring of Gyges,[84] sensual appetite. What was a still-indeterminate instrument of the search has become one formula among others.[85]

It is with Seneca that the tradition acquires the most recognisable rhetorical form by which it is seamlessly transmitted to moral discourse. We find the topos most clearly formulated (even if it is in the form of a simple reminder) in remarks whose purpose is to convince the interlocutor. But this clarity does not represent any progress in the analysis. We are, rather, at a point that is prior to Aristotle. Fundamentally, the determination of the good as an end exhausts its negative effects by producing subtractive comparisons: it serves, in a context of Stoic exhortations, to condemn evil ends on the grounds that they are appearances and illusions, vices and prejudices. It serves to justify after the fact an opposition that already exists between fortune and virtue. Thus, in Seneca's *Letters to Lucilius*, the exhortation frequently makes use of this determination whenever it is a matter of classifying a certain number of goods under the category of chance: 'For all those things over which Chance holds sway are chattels, money, person, position; they are weak, shifting, prone to perish, and of uncertain tenure.'[86] Seneca continues: 'On the other hand, the works of fortune are free and unsubdued, neither more worthy to be sought when Fortune [*Fortuna*] treats them kindly, nor less worthy when any adversary weighs upon them [*aliqua iniquitate rerum*].' One could cite other

---

[82] *Topica*, XXII, § 83: 'Cum autem quid sit quaeritur, notio explicanda est, et proprietas, et divisio et partitio [. . .] Divisio et eodem pacto partitio sic: triane genera honorum sint.'

[83] [Translation by Tobias Rienhardt, Cicero, *Topica* (Oxford: Oxford University Press, 2016), p. 162].

[84] *De Officiis*, III, 9, 39.

[85] Some commentators seem to think that an entire part of the *Hortensius* was structured by the tripartite division of goods. This is the case, for example, in D. Turkowska's work, *L'Hortensius de Cicéron et le Protreptique d'Aristote*, in particular p. 53 ff. It is certain that numerous fragments treat of such-and-such a good, but none of the fragments collected by Ruch and by Grilli attest to the theme of the 'three goods' as playing an explicitly organising role. Perhaps we should see here another example of the retroactive force of the topos.

[86] *To Lucilius*, 66, 23: 'Omnia enim ista, in quae dominium asus exercet, serva sunt, pecunia et corpus et honores, inbecilla, fluida, mortalia, possessionis incertae' [Translation by Richard Gummere, *Seneca's Letters from a Stoic*, Mineola: Dover, 2016, p. 162].

analogous occurrences, whether it is a matter of showing the seduction of vices[87] or the motivational role of prejudices.[88] The most interesting formula can be found in Letter 84: 'Quomodo, inquis, hoc effici poterit? – Adsidua intentione: si nihil egerimus nisi ratione suadente, si nihil vitaverimus, nisi ratione suadente.'[89] The reader would have noticed the *adsidua intentione*: we are not far from the Spinozist formula here, but the meaning is different: it is a matter of a determinate effort, that of choosing one's actions according to the counsel of reason. There then follows the list of what one must renounce: 'relinque divitias, aut periculum possidentium aut onus; relinque corporis atque animi voluptates, molliunt et enervant; relinque ambitum, tumida res est, vana, ventosa, nullum habet terminum'.

On the other hand, in other letters, the tripartite division takes a different form and *gratia* takes the place of the *corpus*, perhaps because in these instances it is more a matter of insisting on social relations. In fact, the distinction between the public and the private is one that governs the foundations of Seneca's philosophical texts. It thus necessarily comes to trouble the division of the *haec tria* with which it overlaps. Let us take an example from Letter 74: 'Picture now to yourself that Fortune is holding a festival, and is showering down honours, riches, and influence [*honores, divitias, gratiam*].'[90]

Seneca's entire body of work is structured by this topos, even if it emerges most clearly in the *Letters*. But we also find it in *De Brevitate vitae*[91] or the

---

[87] *To Lucilius*, 69, 4: 'Nullum sine auctoramento malum est: avaritia pecuniam promittit, luxiuria multas ac varias voluptates, ambitio purpuram et plausam et ex hoc potentiam et quicquid potentia potest' (*Seneca's Letters from a Stoic*, p. 162).

[88] *To Lucilius*, 78, 13: 'Omnia ex opinione suspensa sunt; non ambitio tantum ad illam respicit et luxuria et avarita: ad opinionem dolemus. Tam miser est quisque quam credidit'. ('Everything depends on opinion; ambition, luxury, greed, hark back to opinion. It is according to opinion that we suffer. A man is wretched as he has convinced himself he is', *Seneca's Letters from a Stoic*, pp. 219–20).

[89] *To Lucilius*, 84, 11.

[90] *Seneca's Letters from a Stoic*, p. 196. See also Letter 76: 'quid exspectas? nulli sapere casu obtigit. Pecunia veniet ultro, honor offeretur, gratia ac dignitas fortasse ingerentur tibi: virtus in te non incidet' ('Why do you wait? Wisdom comes haphazard to no man. Money will come of its own accord; titles will be given to you; influence and authority will perhaps be thrust upon you; but virtue will not fall upon you by chance', *Seneca's Letters from a Stoic*, p. 207). These references are given by Proietti, who does not distinguish between the different kinds of tripartite division.

[91] § 7: 'Tot maximi viri, relictis omnibus impedimentis, cum divitiis, officiis, voluptatibus renuntiassent, hoc unum in extremam usque aetatem egerunt, ut vivere scirent'. ['Many very great men, having laid aside all their encumbrances, having renounced riches, business, and pleasures, have made it their one aim up to the very end of life to know how to live', trans. John W. Basmore].

De Constantia Sapientis.[92] Likewise, in the *Consolations to Helvia*, we find the alternative triad, that of *pecunia*, *honores* and *gratia*.[93] How can we describe this new figure? On the one hand, it has an effective tendency to congeal into three terms, but these terms give the impression of being evoked more for the ternary rhythm they produce than to give a complete analysis. On the other hand, their role is less to evoke real differences between the goods than to devalue the functions of life in favour of an already constituted interior life. One can pursue social or civic activities, but only if one is conscious of their derisory nature, of the fact that they escape our control, but also of their externality to the field of what is essential. In short, one must be conscious of the roles these goods make us play. It is in this movement that the reference to the three types of goods henceforth finds its place. From here on, the door is open for describing these goods in terms of the ridiculous (the disorientation of human behaviours), the pernicious and the harmful.

It is in this way that Saint Augustine takes up this topos, for example in *De Utilitate credendi*: 'For I am not afraid that you may think that I was possessed by light at the time that I was entangled in the life of this world, having a darksome hope from the beauty of my wife, from the pomp of riches, from the emptiness of honours and other harmful and destructive pleasures.'[94] Without listing the *haec tria* in an abstract manner, Augustine makes his chosen examples conform to it. He thus accepts this schema as something that is well known and does not consider the list of goods to be exhaustive (*caeterisque*).[95] The role this tripartite division plays in devaluing goods is thus mobilised in the service of a theology that places God in the position of the true good. This hardly modifies its status: failures, vanities, disillusionments – a whole swathe of human existence can, thanks to this division, find itself invested with meaning. These aspects of human existence are brought together only to then be condemned. We can thus

---

[92] § 6: there are four *haec tria*, since Seneca distinguishes between patrimony and riches.
[93] *Consolations to Helvia*, § 5.
[94] *On the Advantage of Believing*, trans. Luanne Meagher, from *The Immortality of the Soul* . . ., p. 394. 'Non eim vereor ne me arbitreris inhabitatum lumine, cum vitae hujus mundi eram implicatus, tenebrosam spem gerens, de pulchritudine uxoris, de pompa divitiarum, de inanitatehonorum caeterisque noxiis et perniciosis voluptatibus.'
[95] Similarly, in the *Confessions*, VI, 6, 9: 'I was eager for fame and wealth and marriage, but you only derided these ambitions. They caused me to suffer the most galling difficulties, but the less you allowed me to find pleasure in anything that was not yourself, the greater, I know, was your goodness to me', Saint Augustine, *Confessions*, Harmondsworth: Penguin, 1961, p. 118.

understand why the reference to the three goods occurs so often in the form of a discourse on false goods.

Thus, in the third book of his *Consolations*, Boethius presents philosophy as providing him with a list of the *falsa bona* in order that he may escape their grasp.[96] Once again, the list is longer than the three principal goods, but it is connected to it: those goods which Boethius surveys include wealth (*divitiae*), honours, the maximum amount of power, celebrity (*honores, summa potentia, claritas*: these three terms develop what the classical triad sums up in a single term), and pleasure (*voluptas*). But the interest of the *Consolations* lies elsewhere: namely, in clarifying the descriptions by which the false goods are disqualified. In the explicit analysis of the relations between false goods and the true or Sovereign Good, 'What all men want, although they seek it by different routes and through different activities, is to be happy.'[97] The latter is defined as the good which, once it has been obtained, leaves nothing more to be desired. And if all goods are directed towards it, albeit along their own specific paths, it is because 'the desire for the true good is naturally inborn in the minds of men, but they are led astray after false goods'.[98] It is thus the very movement towards the true good that leads people towards false goods. The latter are opposed to the true good, but at the same time they present themselves as if they were the true good. Indeed, it seems that they draw all of their force from this imitation. Their very prestige is an avowal of their impotence. The distance from Aristotle's investigations is at once immense and minute: we have gone from an interrogation of human activities that are recognised as being positive, albeit within limits, and whose ends open onto what surpasses them, to a condemnation of worldly goods as illusory and misleading; goods that are called on to give way to the true good whose place they usurp. Yet both this interrogation and this condemnation are founded on the same certainty: the meaning of goods can be immediately determined when they are present to us. At most, the exhortation of the sage or the imprecations of philosophy are needed to reveal them to the gaze.

---

[96] 'Tu quoque falsa tuens bona prius / Incipe colla iugo retrahere', *Consolatio philosophiae*, Book III, first passage in verse, v. 11–12 in Boethius, *Tractates, De Consolatione Philosophiae*, Loeb Classical Library, p. 230. [Anicius Manlius Severinus Boethius, *The Consolation of Philosophy*, trans. David R. Slavitt (Cambridge, MA: Harvard University Press, 2008), p. 60].

[97] 'Omnis mortalium cura quam multiplicium studiorum labor exercet, diverso quidem calle procedit, sed ad unum tamen beatitudinis finem nititur pervenire', ibid., second passage in prose, pp. 230–2. [*The Consolation of Philosophy*, p. 61].

[98] 'Est enim mentibus hominum veri boni naturaliter inserta cupiditas, sed ad falsa devius error abducit', ibid., p. 232. [*The Consolation of Philosophy*, p. 61].

There is no use following the whole, repetitive history of this commonplace.[99] It suffices to identify a stage that is just prior to the one represented by Spinoza's text. Commenting on Seneca's *De Vita beata*[100] – from which this tripartite division is, in fact, absent – Descartes writes: 'we must consider what makes a life happy, that is, what are the things which can give us this supreme contentment. Such things, I observe, can be divided into two classes : those which depend on us, like virtue and wisdom, and those which do not, like honours, riches, and health.'[101] Descartes thus reprises the tripartite division between goods. Yet here it has lost all reference to opinion ('I observe'), and it participates in another vaguely Stoic division (namely, the division between what depends on us and what does not).[102] We can thus see what the situation is at the moment Spinoza is writing: this tripartite division is part of a common pool of references, which one can always suppose the reader to accept; it is based on a presupposition that there exist two categories of objects; and it is in some sense the static version of a theme which, in the Augustinian tradition, is represented in a dynamic form by the metaphor of the path of life.

How do things stand at the beginning of the *TdIE*? It seems to me that it is precisely the goods' insertion into the *communis vita* that allows Spinoza to extract the theme of the three goods from the moral tradition. Thus, Spinoza takes up for his own ends a topos that he empties of its philosophical content in order to make it an instrument of analysis.[103] While in its different forms the tradition presents the three goods as categories of existing objects whose essence is immediately disclosed to the subject, or whose status is

---

[99] In 1453, Aeneas Silvius Piccolomini, now Pope Pius II, writes to the Sultan to persuade him to convert. He explains to him the causes of war by distinguishing those which come from religious conflicts and others, which have to do with the fact that human beings are subject to powerful passions. And he details these passions as follows: 'Illum ambitio exagitat, hunc cupiditas trahit, libido alium impellit', *Epistula ad Mahomatem*, II, edited with translation and notes by Albert R. Baca, Bern: Peter Lang, 1990, Chapter III, § 23, p. 127.

[100] To Princess Elizabeth, 4 August 1645, AT, vol. IV, pp. 263–8 [*CWD* III, 257].

[101] Ibid., p. 264, l. 20.

[102] 'Vaguely' because, as we will see further on, this division in no way serves to elaborate a Stoic conception of the Sovereign Good. The distinction between virtue and wisdom is already an indication of this.

[103] The topos itself can be found in Spinoza: in the *Short Treatise*, while listing perishable goods, he distinguishes between those which have an essence (he only gives one example of these) and those which do not – and he cites 'de Eere, Rykdommen en wellusten', *KV*, M, pp. 226–8. We also find it in the work of his friend Lodewik Meyer, *Philosophia S. Scripturae Interpres*, Amsterdam, 1666, Chapter VII.

immediately revealed by the exhortation, by contrast the *TdIE* submits these goods to a veritable work of transformation, which makes them progressively reveal those of their dimensions that are not immediately apparent in the first experience one has of them. One might be tempted to say that, in some sense, the goods also undergo a journey. But in truth they do not do so by themselves: rather, they are simply called on at different occasions to respond to different questions, which the narrator himself can only pose as a function of the different stages through which his progression leads him.

The goods are there, certainly, from the very beginning, along with the lessons that they teach us; but they develop these lessons only in the course of their successive appearances to the gaze that surveys common life. In their multiplicity, the goods are given to us – indeed they are the sole given of primary experience. However, the *three* goods in their specificity are a construction of secondary experience. Three times, at three different moments of the trajectory, the goods are called upon to bear witness to something that was in them from the very beginning, but which could only be brought out by the twists and turns of the narrator's adventures.

What are these three turning points?

Pleasure, wealth and honours are invoked in order to represent the totality of experience. But they are not invoked as such at the beginning, for they serve neither to devalue experience nor to confront it with a pre-existing 'Sovereign Good'. There is no need here for the tripartite division to produce an aspiration to the true good. The first time it *is* needed, however, is when it is put to a use that appears to be original in the history of the topos: namely, when it is used to show the diversity of ways in which goods make the compromise between perishable goods and the true good impossible. Thus, Spinoza analyses the goods' power and not their impotence, their efficacy and not their illusory nature. Prior to the reference to their division, the goods, irrespective of their different categories, invoke an ontology of the promise that produces an aspiration to the true good by transcending the limits of the goods' positive character. Once the narrator has begun his attempt at a compromise solution and the necessity of giving an account of its failure arises, one and the same positive characteristic of the good is interrogated as to the qualities that made the compromise impossible, but which prevented it only from the perspective of the search for the true good, a project the subject has just formed.[104]

Once this situation of necessary inhibition is established and the compromise itself has been recognised as essentially impossible – and not simply

---

[104] § 3, 4, 5.

as *de facto* impossible – the three goods will take on a second function: in the crisis situation thus created, the narrator will be led to identify them as elements in his perdition by appealing to his memory (the *exempla*).[105] The goods will thus allow him to take a step back and analyse what he already knew but which was not yet legible as experience. Finally, a third question will be put to them: that of the relation between the decision and its effectuation. While theoretical reasoning does not succeed in allowing the narrator to escape the goods' grasp, the practice of meditation brings out those 'intervals' where the power of these goods is diminished. It simultaneously reveals the possibility of using the goods as means[106] – something that will be taken up, in another register (that is, once the narrative is complete), in the rules of the *ratio vivendi* cited in paragraph 17. Far from being a pure epiphany concerning the given, experience is split into three phases where the goods of common life are made to progressively divulge their secrets, and they do so thanks exclusively to the situations that common life constructs.

We should note that in the course of this trajectory, Spinoza presupposes that his reader knows the traits proper to each good – and thus, symmetrically, that the narrator has already experienced these traits by the time the analysis in paragraph 3 begins. These traits are thus not analysed in themselves, but are evoked only in a fragmentary fashion, and only to the degree that the argument requires this in order to show, first, the impossibility of compromise, second, the harmful character of the *haec tria*, and third, the possibility of their neutralisation *tanquam media*. When it comes to understanding each good, Spinoza seems to trust what the reader already knows, including what the reader has learnt from the tradition. For his part, Spinoza is content to reveal at each stage the pertinent traits of the goods in order to advance his construction. We can thus in no way consider the indications encountered in the course of the text as constituting the Spinozist theory of the three goods. What is at stake, rather, is the Spinozist vision of their impact on the search for the true good.

Let us nevertheless begin by identifying what is said of each good. We will then inquire into the three turning points that reveal their efficacy.

— From the third to the eleventh paragraphs, the first good is consistently called the *libido*. The equivalent in paragraph 17 is *deliciae*.[107] What is

---

[105] § 8 and 9.

[106] § 11, reprised further on in paragraphs 15–17.

[107] 'Deliciis in tantum frui, in quantum ad tuendam valetudinem sufficit', § 17, G II, p. 9, ll. 28–9 [*TdIE* 17; *CWS* I, 12].

said of it? That we enjoy it (*frui*).[108] The *libido* is the only one of the three goods for which this term is used.[109] Aside from the *libido*, only the true good and the joy it inspires[110] – and then, later on, the rational life – are associated with this verb. Spinoza also says that we enjoy the *libido* in a way that absorbs the mind. This enjoyment is followed by an extreme sadness (with the succession of states presented in such a way that the connection between enjoyment and sadness appears as both internal and necessary). The example given in paragraph 8 indicates that an excess of *libido* 'hastens death'.[111] The reprise in paragraph 17 seems to relate the regulated use of the *deliciae* to one's health. In both cases, it is a matter of a *direct* relation between health and the body. By contrast, the dangers of wealth and honours are matters of life and death only by the mediation of the situations in which they place people (persecution, perils, suffering). By opposition, the *libido* is thus the direct good of the body, whose use is advantageous to one's health, yet whose excess (and absence) is harmful. That enjoyment is followed by a form of sadness – satiety – is not a new idea with Spinoza: we find the same idea in Boethius[112] and Leo the Hebrew.[113] We will also find it in the *Ethics*.[114] How should we translate the term *libido*? Koyré chooses 'volupté' and 'passion charnelle' (§ 11), which seems quite restrictive. The majority of other French translators choose 'plaisir des sens' or 'plaisir

---

[108] 'Post illius fruitionem'; the verb *frui* is used in paragraph 17 for *deliciae*, G II, p. 9, l. 28 [*TdIE* 17; *CWS* I, 12].

[109] R. Caillois (in a note to the Pléiade translation, p. 1391) and, less clearly, A. Koyré (*Traité de la Réforme*, p. 97), seem to attribute to Spinoza the traditional restriction of the term *frui* to the Sovereign Good by opposition to perishable things, which are only ever used, not enjoyed. On the contrary, Spinoza employs *frui* or *fruitio* both for the true good and for pleasure – and not only here, in paragraphs 4 and 17 of the *TdIE*'s prologue, but also in the *Ethics* [III, 59, Schol.; *CWS* I, 503]. On the other hand, he does not use it for honours or wealth.

[110] 'in aeternum fruerer laetitia', § 1, G II, p. 5, ll. 15–16 [*TdIE* 1; *CWS* I, 7].

[111] Cf. Boethius, who does not go as far: 'Quantos illae [sc: voluptates] morbos, quam intolerabiles dolores quasi quendam fructum nequitiae fruentium solent referre corporibus!', *Consolatione Philosophiae*, III, prose VII.

[112] 'Quid autem de corporis voluptatibus loquar quarum appetentia quidem plena est anxietatis, satietas vero poenitentiae ?', *Consolatione Philosophiae*, III, VII, p. 256.

[113] *Diàlagos de Amor*, texto fixado, anotado e traduzido por Giacinto Manupella, Lisbon: Instituto Nacional de Investigaçao Cientifica, 1983, vol. 1, p. 13: 'Hanno ancor queste cose delettabili tal proprietà che, avute che sono, così come cessa il desiderio di quelle, cessa ancor il più de le volte l'amore, e molte volte si converte in fastidio e aborrizione: perché quel che ha fame o sete, di poi ch'è sazio, non desidera più il mangiare né il bevere, anzi gli viene in fastidio.'

[114] *Ethics* III, 59, Schol., G II, p. 189, ll. 15–28 [*CWS* I, 530].

sensuel'[115] — choices which indeed refer to the general signification of the term. Let us refer once again to Leo the Hebrew. He borrows his examples from food, drink and sexual pleasure. However, there is no reason to end the list here: anything that is a sensual pleasure could be included.[116] Moreover, in the *Ethics*, a longer list will appear: perfumes, plants, finery, music, games and spectacles;[117] and when Spinoza reflects on the reasons for satiety, it is food that will serve as his example.[118]

— Honour is named as early as paragraph 2,[119] alongside wealth and thus prior to the formal reprise of the formula of the three goods. I said above that the advantages honour procures are well known. The term reappears in the singular[120] and in the plural.[121] It is then replaced by *gloria*.[122] After this, it seems to disappear from the rules given in paragraph 17. But it is clear, at least by subtraction, that rule 1 corresponds to it. This rule states the degree to which one must be *ad captum vulgi loqui* and thus do everything that does not prevent us from obtaining our ends.[123] The variety of terms used here alludes to the size of the field typically covered by this second good. Contrary to the choices made by translators — who, no doubt influenced by the tradition of the *topos*, often uniformly translate both the singular and the plural by 'honours' — it seems to me to designate two things that are partly distinct. For the singular form of the term Appuhn suggests esteem [*l'estime*],[124] though I would say 'social relations' — that is, the fact

---

[115] But often by commenting on it using formulations that reserve a particular destiny to sexual pleasure, even if it is to say that it is not the only good aimed at: cf. A. Dominguez: 'En Spinoza, et término libido significa *placer sexual* (*E*, III, DA #48; *KV*, II, 1915), mas también deseo en general (*E*, IV, 17, esc.)', in Spinoza, *Tratado de la Reforma del Entendimiento* . . ., Madrid: Alianza, 1988, p. 300, note 6.

[116] Wim Klever adds drugs (Spinoza, *Verhandeling over de verbetering van het verstand*, p. 113). Why not?

[117] *Ethics* IV, 45, Cor. 2, Schol., G II, pp. 244–5 [*CWS* I, 572].

[118] 'Ex gr. cum aliquid, quod nos sapore delectare solet, imaginamur, eodem frui, nempe comedere cupimus [etc.]', G II, p. 189, l. 20 sq [*Ethics* IV, 59, Schol.; *CWS* I, 530].

[119] G II, p. 5, l. 18 [*TdIE* 2; *CWS* I, 7].

[120] *Honor*: § 3, G II, p. 6, l. 1 [*TdIE* 3; *CWS* I, 7]; § 5, p. 6, l. 9 [*TdIE* 5; *CWS* I, 8] and 17; § 8, p. 7, l. 14 [*TdIE* 8; *CWS* I, 9].

[121] *Honores*, § 4, G II, p. 6, l. 7 [*TdIE* 4; *CWS* I, 8].

[122] From paragraph 10 onwards: *gloriam deponere*, § 10, G II, p. 7, ll. 29–30 [*TdIE* 10; *CWS* I, 10]; § 11, G II, p. 8, l. 5 [*TdIE* 11; *CWS* I, 10].

[123] 'et illa omnia operari, quae nihil impedimenti adferunt, quo minus nostrum scopum adferunt', G II, p. 9, ll. 23–4 [*TdIE* 17; *CWS* I, 12].

[124] We would thus not be far from the definition from the *Korte Verhandeling*: 'De eerste [sc.: de Eere, named at the beginning of the paragraph] is een seeker slach van Blydschap, die een ieder in zig zelfs gevoeld, wanneer hy gewaar word dat zyn doen

of being in communication with others. By contrast, *honours* in the plural stands for power. In this sense honours are one of the forms of the relation to others, and thus one form of what honour – in the singular – refers to (this explains why the singular can stand in for the plural, but not the other way round). In the history of the topos, it is true that the term 'honours' often alludes to a political career (it names the active life, a list of positions or offices that please Romans like Seneca and Boethius). It is also true that it is often doubled – or completed when the list is extended to include four pleasures – by the addition of glory. Moreover, other forms of social communication are noted, like friendship, but the authors do not always have a clear idea of how to class them. If we consider Spinoza's description closely, we have the impression that it flattens these differences in order to give the second term, not the broadest possible meaning but rather the most radical one – that is, the meaning that accounts in a single description for what is common to a large number of experiential phenomena, at the same time as it refuses to explain them causally. What does this description tell us? That, like wealth, honour provides *commoda*. It also tells us that the pursuit of honour is never-ending, and that we fall into sadness when our hopes are disappointed. These characteristics are all traits that are also proper to wealth. A particular trait is added, however, but without Spinoza explaining the consequences of this addition: namely, that whoever seeks honours must habituate themselves to living their life *ad captum hominum* and to imitating people's behaviour. In what sense does imitation stop us from thinking? If we wish to complete these elliptical formulations, we can compare them with those from the *Ethics* on vainglory.[125] The glory founded on the opinion of the *vulgus* is a desperate effort to gain the *summum bonum*. It throws human beings at once into internal torment and interpersonal rivalry, which are easy to conceive of as preventing them from being able to think. The *acquiescentia* tied to glory is effectively a joy, but a provisional one in these conditions, and one that falls back into sadness. The description from the *Ethics*, which is more detailed than the one from the *TdIE*, is thus not incompatible with the latter and helps us understand what it alludes to. However, it is

---

by andere geacht en geprezen word, zonder opzigt van eenig ander voordel of profyt dat zy beoogen' (ed. F. Mignini, L'Aquila: Japadre, 1986, p. 254). 'The first [honour] is a certain kind of joy, which each person feels in himself when he realises that his action is deemed to please others, without him thinking that he draws advantage or profit from it.' The definition from the *KV* aims at the feeling, while the description from the *TdIE* identifies more the external givens that correspond to it.

[125] *Ethics* IV, 58, Schol., G II, pp. 253–4 [*CWS* I, 578. Translator's note: as I said above, Curley speaks of an 'empty' form of 'esteem'].

based on an element that is absent from the *TdIE*: the *acquiescentia in se ipso* is not found in the *TdIE* and indeed cannot be, for a positive notion of the *conatus* would be needed.

The *exemplum* from paragraph 8 is the only one that does not mention death (even if death is not explicitly excluded). Spinoza seems more sensitive to the sufferings one endures in order to win or conserve honour. Perhaps he is thinking here of honours in the political sense of the term. But perhaps, too, we can read here an allusion to the price that has to be paid to engage in social relations (on this point, we could compare the *TdIE* to Uriel da Costa, for whom honour, in a more restricted sense, is the content of natural law). Rule 1 from paragraph 17 reprises neither the word 'honour' nor the word 'glory'; it does not propose any other general substantive, but instead offers a reflection on what could be called different modes of communication with others. The meaning of this communication is dual: on the one hand, the philosopher can find advantages in it; on the other, it prepares others for truth. This is equivalent to saying that one can neither live nor help others to think by refusing the rules of the game in society.[126] Finally, to 'play the game' would be a good translation of *ad captum vulgi loqui*.

— Wealth, too, appears as early as paragraph 2. In addition to the noun *divitiae*, we find wealth in the following expressions: *comparare opes*,[127] *avaritia*[128] and *nummorum acquisitionem*.[129] The reprise in paragraph 17 will speak of *tantum nummorum* by expanding it to include the expression *aut cujuscunque alterius rei*. One can rightly be surprised by the fact that nothing specific appears to be said about wealth that would not also apply to honour. Is Spinoza so confident in what common consciousness has understood that he sees no use in offering any additional characterisation of wealth? In actual fact, he gives us an indication of what, in his eyes, is specific to wealth in

---

[126] This idea can also be found in the chapter on honour and shame in the *Korte Verhandeling*: 'Doch ik wil niet zeggen, dat men zo by de menschen moet leven, als men buyten haar, daar, *Eer en Schaamte* geen plaats heeft, leeven zoude; nemaar in tegendeel staa ik toe dat ons die niet alleen vrystaan te gebruyken als wy die tot nut van de menschen en om haar te verbeteren aandwenden, maar ook het zelve mogen doen met verkortinge van onse (anderzins volkomen en geoorlofde) eigen vryheid', p. 256. 'But I don't mean that one must live among men as one would live without them, where Love of Esteem and Shame have no place. On the contrary, I grant that we are permitted not only to use [these passions] for men's advantage and improvement, but also to do this even if it involves a restriction of our own freedom, which is otherwise complete and lawful' [*CWS* I, 116].

[127] § 8, G II, p. 7, ll. 11–12 [*TdIE* 8; *CWS* I, 9].

[128] § 10, G II, p. 7, l. 29 [*TdIE* 10; *CWS* I, 10].

[129] § 11, G II, p. 8, ll. 4–5 [*TdIE* 11; *CWS* I, 10].

relation to the two other goods. This is found in note *a*. This note makes a distinction between wealth pursued for itself and wealth pursued with a view to obtaining two other goods. The unity of the three sorts of wealth is summed up in the word *propter*. Wealth is a means or a detour for acquiring something else. Thus, it functions as a passage to other goods. It is understood here that an instrument can be used for itself – and that it is in this form that we are most often prevented from thinking of the true good. In any case, such an instance of instrumentalisation is mentioned neither for pleasure nor for honour. Thus, for Spinoza, it is instrumentalisation itself that represents the specific character of the *divitiae*. The latter can lead to death – not directly, as in the case of pleasure, but rather by the perils which it exposes one to. Such a death punishes the *stultitia* (this is the only time Spinoza uses this term) that consists in seeking to accumulate wealth. Finally, paragraph 17 will implicitly reprise the distinction from note *a*. Fundamentally, wealth does not have its measure in itself. It is limited to being a negative measure (it is not pursued as an end in itself) and seeks its measure either in health or honour. For it is indeed these latter that are at stake here: on the one hand, it is necessary to have these *tantum . . . quantum* to sustain one's life and health (this is the good that was noted in rule 2), and on the other hand to imitate the morals of the city in a way that is not entirely incompatible with one's goal. This is what the *Ethics* will call trust.[130] The nuance here comes directly from the nuance contained in rule 1. But above all, what we find here is imitation: we are in the domain of honour.[131] What was inhibiting in the

---

[130] Cf. *Ethics* IV, App., 16, G II, pp. 270–1 [*CWS* I, 590]. One could get the impression that the *Ethics* is more rationalist (Scholium, IV, 37) since it defines *honestas* as what is lauded by people who are governed by reason. But this is not certain: there is no way to exclude the possibility of others accomplishing for different reasons what people who are led by reason accomplish rationally.

[131] An example of this is given in the *Short Treatise*, at the end of the paragraph we have just cited on honour. Its interest lies in distinguishing between two uses of honour (and thus, mediately, of wealth, since it is a matter of expensive clothes): 'Als by exempel: zo iemand zich kostelyk kleed, om daardoor geacht te zijn, deze zoekt een Eere die uyt de liefde syns zelfs hervoorkomt, zonder enige opzicht op syn even mensch te hebben; maar zo iemand syn wysheid (daar door hy aan syn eeven naasten konde vorderlyk zyn) ziet verachten, en met de voet treden, omdat hy een slecht kleed an heeft, deze doet wel dat hy (uyt beweging om haar te helpen) zich met een kleed, daar aan zy haar niet enstooten, verziet, wordende alzo, om syn eeven mensch te winnen, syn eeven mensch gelyk', *KV*, p. 256. 'For example, if someone dresses expensively in order to be honored for that, then he seeks an Esteem that arises from self-love, not from any regard for his fellowmen: But if someone sees that men disdain his wisdom, by which he could be helpful to his fellow men, and trample it under foot

final phrase from paragraph 5 was not imitation in itself – which seems here to be understood as a necessary dimension of social relations – but rather unbridled imitation in the pursuit of power. If we refer this idea of imitation to rule 1, we can deduce from it that speaking *ad captum vulgi* implies less hypocrisy than simple imitation – and that imitation is a characteristic of language. We will have to keep this in mind when we come to the question of *usus*. Note, finally, that the *Ethics* also recognises a measured use of wealth: money is a vice only for those who abuse it.[132]

We can now consider for themselves the three modalities of the work carried out on the goods that helps the narrator progress along his path.

— How do the goods that we habitually seek[133] stop us from thinking of the true good? The answer lies in the play of two prohibitions: occupation and pursuit, to which a third should be added: imitation. But all together these prohibitions are regulated by the fundamental states of joy and sadness, which have the same effect. The play of these fundamental states[134] is

because he dresses badly, then he does well if he provides himself with clothing that will not shock them, thereby becoming like his fellow men in order to win them over and help them' [*CWS* I, 116–17]. The difference between the *KV* and the *TdIE* comes down to the fact that the *KV* explains where the first form of honour comes from ('die uyt de liefde syns zelfs hervoorkomt'); the *TdIE*, at least in its prologue, has no need of doing so.

[132] *Ethics* IV, App., 27–9. 'But this [that is, the fact that money has become the *compendium* of all things] is a vice only in those who seek money neither from need nor on account of necessities, but because they have learned the art of making money and pride themselves on it very much', G II, pp. 273–5 [*CWS* I, 593]. Note that money is reduced to something that maintains the body – it disappears here from social relations.

[133] It is worthwhile indicating how we are dividing up paragraphs 3 to 5: it is clear that paragraph 3 and paragraph 4, right up to *hebetat* (l. 6) refer to the *libido*. The last sentence of paragraph 4 ('Honores, ac divitias [. . .] sumum esse bonum', ll. 7–9) refers initially both to wealth and to honours, and then, from *praesertim* (l. 8), restricts itself to wealth. The first sentence from paragraph 5 ('honore vero [. . .] diriguntur', ll. 9–12) concerns honours alone; the second ('Deinde in his [. . .] summa oritur tristitia', ll. 12–16) refer once again to both honours and wealth. Finally, the last phrase once again concerns honours alone, as it explicitly says ('Est denique honor [. . .] quaerunt homines', ll. 17–20). The only part of this division which requires discussion is the phrase 'Deinde in his . . .': it cannot be a matter here of honour alone since honour is found in the singular form in the proposition that immediately precedes this (as it is, moreover, in what follows). It also cannot be a matter of wealth alone, because of *utriusque*. Thus, *his* refers to the formula from paragraph 4, *honores ac divitias*.

[134] Joy and sadness here are states, effects and indicators; they are not forms of the power of acting, as they will be in the *Ethics* (III, 11, Schol., G II, pp. 148–9 [*CWS* I, 500]).

different in each case, even if the result is constant. It is indeed this difference that justifies giving an account of each good in particular. The general effect of *tristitia* seems to be that it makes us incapable of thinking, at least as soon as it reaches a certain level – that of the *summa tristitia*, which is attained in each of the three cases.[135] The effect of *laetitia* is initially different; in the case of the *libido*,[136] it is in some sense static and initially maximal: it occupies the mind completely, and prevents us from thinking of anything else. It blocks thinking about pleasure in such a way that it can no longer move one towards any other object.[137] In the cases of wealth and honour, joy is, on the contrary, always susceptible to being increased.[138] But precisely for this very reason our mind is kept from thinking of the true good, for joy indicates to thought a repetitive path: new wealth, new honours.[139] Finally, with respect to the pursuit of honours, to self-imitation there is added the imitation of the crowd,[140] which once again absorbs our thought.

Note the variations on the opposition between *laetitia* and *tristitia*: in the *libido*, maximal *laetitia* automatically and immediately provokes *tristitia*. Each singular moment of enjoyment thus ends in a negative state. This is what Spinoza calls, a few lines further on, *paenitentia*.[141] With wealth and honours,

---

[135] Spinoza twice uses this expression: for the *libido* ('post illius fruitionem summa sequitur tristitia', § 4), then for honours and wealth ('tum summa oritur tristitia', § 5). It is in the first case only that he mentions that it stops one from thinking ('si non suspendit mentem, tamen pertubat et hebetat'), but he does not restrict this property to this case alone, and the repetition of the expression *summa tristitia* in the following paragraph suggests that the situation itself repeats – a conclusion that is coherent with the general meaning of the context.

[136] It could be objected that the term *laetitia* is not used explicitly as far as the *libido* is concerned. This is true: however, the state which accompanies *fruitio* is clearly opposed to sadness. Even if one wished to give it a different name – and this would only complicate the analysis – it has the characteristics of *laetitia*.

[137] 'Ea adeo suspenditur animus, ac si in aliquo bono quiesceret; quo maxime impeditur ne de alio cogitet', § 4, G II, p. 6, ll. 3–4 [*TdIE* 4; *CWS* I, 8].

[138] 'Quo plus utriusque possidetur, eo magis augetur laetita', § 5, G II, p. 6, ll. 13–14 [*TdIE* 5; *CWS* I, 8].

[139] 'Et consequenter magis ac magis incitamur ad utrumque augendum', § 5, G II, p. 6, ll. 14–15 [*TdIE* 5; *CWS* I, 8].

[140] 'Vita necessario ad captum hominum est dirigenda', § 5, G II, p. 6, l. 19 [*TdIE* 5; *CWS* I, 8].

[141] We saw in the quotation from Boethius that the term belongs to a traditional vocabulary: it refers simply to the automatic regret that follows this type of joy. It is therefore not necessary to explain it by the definition of the term in the *Ethics* (III, DA #27, G II, p. 197 [*CWS* I, 536–7]), which refers to a belief in *liberum mentis decretum* that is visibly absent here – or which is at least not necessary here. Similarly, the difficulties

by contrast, the mind does not immediately suffer from a negative feeling, but is caught in a cycle of the pursuit of goods of which there are always more to come – hope being the link between what we have and what we seek, and thus the motor that makes us continue without pausing right up to the point where we happen to fall. Sadness is thus no longer the consequence of joy but of hope's frustration. It is no longer automatic in each event but rather aleatory for each event, while also becoming quasi-necessary in the cycle as a whole, to the degree that the cycle will not stop until we encounter sadness.

That pleasure knows satiety, and that the thirst for wealth and power is insatiable, is not a new discovery on Spinoza's part. But Spinoza does not stop here: he supposes that his reader knows this already and that they have learnt it in their personal life or by reading good authors. He leaves this remark precisely at the level of experience, without seeking to explain it.[142] What interests Spinoza, and what is more original with him, is the inclusion of these traits in the argument itself. This inclusion comes down to the following point: in common life, we do nothing but seek, pursue, and all the rest. Thus, even the true life, if it exists, will have to be submitted to these sequences. If the sequence of human activity that leads to the true good cannot take place, the true good will not be obtained. It will not impose itself on its own, and it will not be given to us. Furthermore, it will be acquired only within the anthropological framework within which we acquire and lose common goods. If the latter dissimulate it – not by themselves but through the activities that these goods provoke or prevent – then the quest for the true good will fail. This is why the compromise solution fails, and also why it is necessary to change things at the level of the *institutum*.

— To arrive at the true good, it is necessary to conceive of the three goods as factors in one's perdition. Not only do we lose these goods, they make us lose ourselves. This thesis is stated in two ways and then confirmed by three examples. Let us begin with the two ways in which the goods interact with us: namely, by possessing us or being possessed. Here, too, we find a topos that Spinoza transforms: where others see an opposition,[143] Spinoza goes

---

that commentators encounter when trying to explain that Spinoza does not really say *post coitum animal triste* (Dominguez, 'En Spinoza, et término libido significa', p. 300, note 8; Fernández and Margot, *Tratado de la Reforma del Entendimento y otros escritos*, p. 63, note 4) above all come down to commentators' desire to reconcile this passage with the text of the *Ethics*. In fact, such an interpretation is more partial than false: the thesis of satiety concerns all the pleasures of the senses.

[142] Whereas Leon the Hebrew constructs an explanation founded on the ends of Nature and the theory of the five senses: *Diálogos de Amor*, pp. 40–1.

[143] Aristippus, certainly (who Spinoza knows through Diogenes Laërtius), but also

further. The meaning of the opposition as it is typically understood is about praising self-control. Between the person who possesses and the person who is possessed, the two paths diverge. By contrast, Spinoza does not reason in terms of self-mastery, and the torsion that he makes the habitual presentation of this commonplace undergo reveals a theoretical difficulty internal to the *proemium*. How should we understand Spinoza's argument? That we possess goods is something that we all share. But certain among us are possessed by them in return. We can understand this in two senses: either the strong sense, which will be that of the *Ethics*, in a passage where we find the *haec tria* in their traditional guise: someone devotes themselves exclusively to a single good;[144] or in a weak sense, which is perhaps the surest one here: that of abandoning oneself to goods, even if it is not exclusively to one good. Why would possessing goods and being possessed by them both lead to death? Because at this stage we have no concept of the loss of self other than physical death. In the *Ethics*, we will be able to distinguish between the two.[145] Here we cannot do so because we do not yet have the opposition between action and passion – not that Spinoza has not elaborated it, but that it is impossible to introduce into a purely experiential description like the one that interests us here. The exaggeration is thus necessary as a function of the problematic proper to the *proemium*, which is to bring out the harmful

---

Seneca in the *De Ira*: 'Aristoteles ait affectus quosdam, siquis illis bene utatur, pro armis esse. Quod verum foret, si velut, bellica instrumenta sumi deponique possent induentis abitrio. Haec arma, quae Aristoteles virtuti dat, ipsa per se pugnant, non expectant manum; habent, non habentur'; see the paraphrase by Montaigne, *Essais*, II, 31, *De la Colère*: 'Encore un mot pour clore ce pas. Aristote dit que la cholere sert parfois d'arme à la vertue et à la vaillance. Cela est vray-semblable; toutes-fois ceux qui y contredisent respondent plaisamment que c'est un'arme de nouvel usage: car nous remuons les autres armes, cette-cy nous remue; nostre main ne la guide pas, c'est elle qui guide nostre main; elle nous tient, nous ne la tenons pas', édition S. de Sacy, Paris: Club français du livre, 1962, vol. 1, p. 781, and Augustine, *De Libero Arbitro*, I, 14, 33: 'Cum igitur iisdem rebus alius male alius bene utatur, et is quidem qui male, amore his inhaereat atque implicetur – scilicet subditus eis rebus quas ei subditas esse oportebat . . .' BA, 6, p. 258. 'Hence the selfsame things are used in a good manner by one person and in an evil manner by another. The person who uses them in an evil manner holds fast to them with love and is tangled up with them. That is to say, he is controlled by things that he ought to control', Augustine, *On the Free Choice of the Will, on Grace and Free Choice, and Other Writings* (Cambridge: Cambridge University Press, 2010), p. 28.

[144] IV, 44, Schol., G II, p. 243 [CWS I, 571]. This is what Alexandre Matheron analyses as a 'monoidéïsme catastrophique', *Individu et communauté chez Spinoza*, pp. 116–17.

[145] Cf. the ignorant who 'simulac pati desinit, simul etiam esse desinit', *Ethics* V, 42, Schol., G II, p. 308, ll. 19–20 [CWS I, 616].

character of goods insofar as it is only these goods that are at stake. It is necessary to show – or rather recall – the examples by which each of the goods causes the suffering and death of those who pursue them. We know of these examples before the beginning of the journey, but they remain insignificant since the right question has not yet been put to them. Now, on the contrary, after the birth of the aspiration to the true good and the recognition of the *de jure* impossibility of a compromise between the two *instituta*, they acquire a real power to disqualify circumstantial goods insofar as they are pursued for themselves.

— Finally, why do these goods nevertheless remain? Because they are inscribed in our spontaneous movements: seeking, enjoying and so on. The only way to make the true good triumph will thus be to inscribe it in turn in these movements: it is therefore not only the content of the aspiration that will win out, but its inscription in life. At the same time, we will also discover the possible meanings of the goods as means or as adjuvants (§ 11). Yet it is still necessary to understand the reason why this is the case: this is what the rules from paragraph 17 will do. This question lies outside of our concerns here because Spinoza is content in paragraph 11 to recount experience without describing it, while in paragraph 17 the narration is complete. On the basis of the three rules of the *ratio vivendi*, we can simply suppose in what sense each of the three goods can serve the new quest; but to do so we have had to pass by way of speculative statements that no longer arise from experience: we have thus changed terrain. However, one thing in particular must be underscored: this inscription of the true good in the movements of life is in no way a matter of a middle ground, but of a measure determined by an end (*scopus*). In this sense, the final decision does indeed constitute a rupture with those mixed attitudes *à la* Seneca. To place the goods of common life in the service of the search for the true good is in no way to juxtapose them: the *novum institutum* has indeed effectively replaced the old one.

I believe that I have now clarified the meaning of the text's progression: Spinoza judges his reader to be familiar with the topos, and he leaves them to presuppose experience. All Spinoza requires of his reader is a general impression, drawn from their own life, from observations and from the cultural tradition. But Spinoza takes up these lessons for his own ends, essentially by integrating them into the description of life as sequences of actions. This description undoes the effects of the rhetorical tradition through analysis. On three occasions it is the goods' inscription in life that gives meaning to their action. It is this inscription that selects the functional traits that are retained at each stage, while these stages determine that the three goods function successively as factors of inhibition, of perdition, and as adjuvants of the true good. The first determination arises from experience *in* common life, the second from the experience *of* common life, and the third from the dawning of an experience of the *true* life.

4

The True Good

This whole progression is only meaningful, however, in relation to its absent pole: the true good. The true and not the Sovereign Good: the reader will have noticed that in these eleven paragraphs, the term 'Sovereign Good' is never used in a positive sense. This is not the least of the *proemium*'s paradoxes. This text, which situates itself in a certain sense in the lineage of the innumerable texts that oppose the Sovereign Good to illusory goods, hardly ever speaks of the Sovereign Good in relation to the category of illusion. The *haec tria* are introduced into the text's argument because people 'think [them] to be the Sovereign Good'.[1] Wealth is said to occupy the mind when it is pursued for itself, for then it is 'assumed to be the Sovereign Good'.[2] As for honour, it is said to be simply 'a good through itself'.[3] The true good, by contrast, the good to which one begins to aspire, is never referred to in this way: it is simply called *verum bonum*,[4] and then, by way of metaphor, *remedium*,[5] and finally – after its significance has been better understood – *res aeterna*.[6] Thus, in the course of common life, the idea of the Sovereign Good emerges spontaneously. However, this idea is connected to finite goods and thus, it would seem, cannot be used to characterise the true good as such.[7]

---

[1] 'Apud homines [...] tanquam summum bonum aestimantur', § 3, G II, p. 5, ll. 26–7 [*TdIE* 3; *CWS* I, 7].

[2] 'Quia tum supponuntur summum esse bonum', § 4, G II, p. 6, l. 9 [*TdIE* 4; *CWS* I, 8].

[3] 'Supponitur enim semper bonum esse per se', § 5, G II, p. 6, ll. 10–11 [*TdIE* 5; *CWS* I, 5].

[4] § 1 and § 11.

[5] § 7; the term is reprised in § 11.

[6] § 10, G II, p. 7, l. 24 [*TdIE* 10; *CWS* I, 9].

[7] We can read in the way Spinoza expresses himself here his implicit critique of the idea according to which the Sovereign Good would be directly legible in what is

Likewise, in these eleven paragraphs, Spinoza does not seem to think that it is useful to explain what he means by the good. By contrast, the ethical tradition is always careful to remind the reader of Aristotle's formula: namely, that the good is 'that to which all things tend',[8] or some variant of this[9], even if the text at hand gives this formula a different meaning.[10] Aristotle's formula constitutes something of a point of origin for the different uses of the term 'good' that appear in the many domains through which its use is diffracted. What the *TdIE* brings to the fore, by contrast, are the descriptive sequences.

As I have already noted, the journey of the *TdIE* includes nothing that prefigures what the law is – not a revelation, not a call, not even a master (and not even a master who would be nothing more than nature or consciousness). Everything is immanent: common life seems to provide, at this point, all the means necessary for its overcoming. It is impossible to circumvent common life: there is no other path one can take to escape it but that of common life itself. But is the end of this path given in experience? Its absence at least seems to be. The subject's realisation of the existence of the true good, or rather of the necessity of seeking it out – firstly as a question, then as an aspiration, and finally as a necessity – marks the moment where experience *in* and *as* common life becomes experience *of* common life. A question thus arises: can we say anything about this term, that of the true good, that has us embark on this journey? Can we determine any of its characteristics in a way that is not simply negative?

The response comes down to the positivity of the goods of common life: *if they are in part illusory insofar as we take them to be the Sovereign Good, they also have a degree of positivity; and it is this positivity which prefigures the true good, or rather which gives us an idea of it; for this idea exists on a continuum with the goods' positive features.* What is positive about each of the goods of

---

given; we can also relate this attitude to Spinoza's thesis according to which the God of the imagination is not even an approximation of the true God.

[8] 'that is why some people were right to describe the good as that which everything seeks', *Nicomachean Ethics*, I, 1, 1094a.

[9] 'Est igitur hoc nichil aliud nisi bonum, quod quidem sic dicitur quoniam id omnia boant et clamant', Coluccio Salutati, *De Nobilitate legum et medicinae*, Chapter 14 (*De Nobilitate legum et medicinae. De Verecundia*, ed. E. Garin, Florence: Vallecchi, 1947, p. 100).

[10] Thus Hobbes, in *De Homine*, XI, 3, writes: 'The common name for all things that are desired, insofar as they are desired, is *good*; and for all things we shun, *evil*. Therefore Aristotle hath well defined *good* as that which all men desire. But, since different men desire and shun different things, there must needs be many things that are *good* to some and *evil* to others; so that which is *good* to us is *evil* to our enemies. Therefore *good* and *evil* are correlated with desiring and shunning.'

common life is at once real yet limited. The illusion of the Sovereign Good arises because of this limit; the consistency of the true good is glimpsed in the consistency of what is real and positive in each good. Even though Spinoza does not make this explicit, the prologue puts this idea to work. We thus begin to represent to ourselves the being of the true good on the basis of the promises which the other goods make but do not keep. We should obviously not understand the term 'promise' here as signifying a subjective engagement. Rather, it refers to the benefits bestowed by the three goods, or the qualities that characterise them – qualities which, so long as we are ignorant of the laws of nature governing production and their limits, suffice to give us hope. Then, when we have formed the aspiration that will cause us to begin the journey towards the true good, we will be confronted with the formidable obstacle these goods represent and the danger they pose. Our conception of what the true good is will come about as a result of this movement. Indeed, as we will see, it will be enriched by this experience. After the ontology of the promise there thus follows an ontology of the threat. Finally, when the true good begins to impose itself, at least momentarily, in our mind, it will no longer appear as the rival of the other goods, but as their measure. The characteristics of the *verum bonum* – those which it becomes possible to represent to oneself at the end of the journey – are thus a *result* of the journey itself.

I will leave aside provisionally the prologue's first sentence, which refers to the decision the narrator takes, and study the stages which lead to this decision. We will see that the true good appears in a number of different forms in the course of these stages. We will then see, in the final moment, the double transfiguration that gives the true good an affirmative name, one that is initially metaphorical – the remedy – and then a name all of its own – the eternal and infinite thing.

1. Ontology of the Promise

As I have just noted, in the third stage each of the *haec tria* – or at least one of their aspects – is taken to be the Sovereign Good. We will use this analogy as a thread for us to follow. Besides, this analogy has a real foundation: if, by reference to one of its particular aspects, we take a perishable good to be the true good, it is because this good really does possess a characteristic that it shares with the true good (but we will only come to know this later). It is therefore not illusory at all: it is the identification of the good *as a totality* with this characteristic (or inversely, of this characteristic with the totality of the true good) that generates illusions.

In the first stage, we do not yet have an idea of a true good that is distinct from those goods that are close at hand. In other words, we spontaneously judge, albeit implicitly, that these goods are the true goods. We perhaps do not think to say why this is so, but if we were asked about it, we could no doubt render this judgement explicit: there is no reason to think that spontaneous enjoyment is necessarily ignorant of everything it experiences. It is ignorant of what governs it, but nothing stops it from being able to formulate what it lives. The proof of this is that in the third stage we can formulate in what sense the different goods stop us from thinking about another institution of life. And in order to formulate what these obstacles consist in, we will draw on what we already know of the positivity of each of the *haec tria*. We can, then, from the first stage onwards, form, if not an idea of the good in general, then at least a certain number of positive determinations of this idea.

In the second stage, we encounter limits to our enjoyment of the three goods. By virtue of their very positivity, these goods have made a promise that they have nevertheless failed to keep. Thus, little by little, the idea of the true good is separated from our immediate adhesion to the three types of goods. This limit can certainly be indicated to us in a general manner, but only in a negative way: the true good is what escapes us. But this formulation does not get us very far: it gives us no positive indication of how to form the image of what we aspire to. However, if we consider not the general limit of each one of these three goods but instead its specific way of failing to keep its promises, it will perhaps be possible to give the outlines of the positive content of this aspiration. It is true that Spinoza does not make this reasoning explicit. Nevertheless, here, too, we can seek out these determinations in the description that is given of the three goods in the third stage; for there we are dealing with the same objects, and it seems reasonable to think that it is the ensemble of these determinations that will prevent us from moving towards the Sovereign Good. Thus, the description of those moments where the journey is interrupted can also provide us with the description of the limits encountered by the goods' positive aspects. In sum, we will follow, albeit in a different spirit, the route indicated to us by Boethius: it is a matter less of recognising in each of the goods the trace of the Sovereign Good or the prestige the latter bestows, and more of discerning the positive continuity that unites them.

A. Let us begin with pleasure. As we have seen, this is the only good for which the text uses the word *fruitio*. The very expression by which the text indicates that the mind considers pleasure a good implies that the mind finds a form of rest in pleasure.[11] This, then, is the positive determination of the good that appears through pleasure. The mind is in motion, or is perturbed; when it encounters this good – that is, pleasure – it comes to rest. One of the roles played by this good, or by its positive aspect, is thus to make movement cease, or to still the agitations or disquiet of the mind.[12] This refers us to everything the tradition conveys in the words 'appeasement' or the 'satisfaction of desires'.[13] This determination is valid, then, at least at first glance, for pleasure. More fundamentally still, it is also valid for the true good. It explains that the *animus* spontaneously takes pleasure to be the true good; and, inversely, that it aspires to the true good through this specific characteristic of pleasure.

Yet this determination encounters a limit, which Spinoza calls *paenitentia*. The satisfaction tied to pleasure is followed by hebetude, a form of *tristitia*. Thus, pleasure is both discontinuous in time and, when it ends, is replaced by its contrary. Here, too, Spinoza follows the tradition: it is well known that satiety, disgust, and so on, follow satisfaction. But Spinoza does not linger over the description of these states: he is content to record them using the general term *tristitia* and to specify this description by the terms *perturbat et hebetat*.[14] The satisfaction provided by pleasure troubles the subject and thus annuls the feeling of rest that pleasure had once brought. Pleasure leaves us numb – that is, it makes us incapable, at least provisionally, of seeking anything else. We are left in a state neither of rest nor of positive movement, which would allow us to find another good. We turn in circles. After the *fruitio*, we no longer seek anything, not because we are satisfied but because we have been weakened.

A first aspect of the true good can now emerge: the true good will possess the positivity of the *libido* without its limits, and would thus allow us to enjoy a form of rest[15] that would not be followed by sadness. Such a formula seems, at this stage, to be a contradiction in terms, since the joys of wealth and honours arise, in effect, from another form of continuity: that of repetition and accumulation.

---

[11] 'Ac si in aliquo bono quiesceret', § 4, G II, p. 6, ll. 3–4 [*TdIE*, 4; *CWS* I, 8].

[12] Cf. the terms *movere*, *commotiones* and even *distrahere*.

[13] It is only Hobbes and Pascal (cf. fragment 136 Lafuma, Br. 139, p. 517) who question the thesis according to which the human being spontaneously seeks rest.

[14] § 4, G II, p. 6, l. 6 [*TdIE* 4; *CWS* I, 8].

[15] This expression is also found in the *Short Treatise*, in a formula which, in conformity with the problematic of this text, makes God occupy the place of the Sovereign Good: 'Zo zien wy dan nu hoe wy de liefde krachtig maaken, en ook hoe de zelve alleen in God moet rusten', *KV*, II, 5, § 12, M, p. 230 [*CWS* I, 107]. 'So we see, then, how we make Love powerful, and also how it must rest only on God.'

B. Let us turn now to wealth. Spinoza is very elliptical on this point. He states that here, too, it happens that we take wealth, too, to be the Sovereign Good. But he does not describe, not even briefly, the effects wealth produces. Nevertheless, it is possible, as we saw above, to derive these effects from the text and from the note that accompanies it. The note distinguishes between different uses of wealth: wealth can be sought for its own sake, or for something else.[16] Wealth also refers to other goods: honour, pleasure, health, and so on. The text itself makes clear that it is in terms of the first of these uses that wealth is taken to be the Sovereign Good.[17] We can deduce from this that the Sovereign Good is sought for itself; but this is an insufficient determination. Let us consider instead what the different uses of wealth have in common. What they share is the term *propter* (which is not used to define honour or pleasure; it is therefore by referring to this term that we can find what is proper to wealth). Even the absolute use cannot do without this term, but instead gives it a reflexive form: *propter se*. The characteristic that is common to the different uses of wealth is thus instrumentality: wealth serves to procure something that is useful (including itself); it augments our power. One might object that pleasure and honours do this as well. But they do so only indirectly, while wealth does nothing but this. If everything *can* be pursued in view of another thing, it is the *essence* of wealth to be pursued with a view to something else. Note, therefore, that the model of the final synthesis, which in Aristotle is given as universally valid, is here articulated according to two distinct categories. Wealth is more essentially a means than other means are.

What is its limit? The fact is that wealth does not carry in itself its *paenitentia*, as the *libido* does. In other words, it can be continuous, but its continuity is not a continuity of enjoyment; wealth does not bring us a sense of rest. On the contrary, wealth brings with it an ever-growing hope that leads us to accumulate ever more wealth. If sadness in the case of pleasure takes the form of satiety, wealth, by contrast, makes us insatiable. If, by chance, our hopes are frustrated, we fall into the *summa tristitia*. The same expression that was used for pleasure is thus used again here, but it intervenes in different circumstances: it follows, not a moment of rest, but a frantic movement. It is produced by chance[18] and is not necessarily tied to enjoyment.

---

[16] 'Distinguendo scilicet divitias, quae quaeruntur vel propter se, vel propter honorem, vel propter libidinem, vel propter valetuidenm et augmentum scientiarum et artium ...', note *a*, G II, p. 6 [*TdIE* 4; *CWS* I, 8].

[17] 'Praesertim ubi hae non nisi propter se quaeruntur ...', § 4, G II, p. 6, l. 8 [*TdIE* 4; *CWS* I, 8].

[18] 'Si autem spe in aliquo casu frustremur ...' § 5, G II, p. 6, l. 15 [*TdIE* 5; *CWS* I, 8].

How, then, can we think the true good? By conserving the positive determination of wealth without its limits. This means, to be precise, that the true good directly reaches its goal without referring to anything else. At this point, such an idea seems to be unrepresentable – except, precisely, in the form of wealth that is sought for itself. It is necessary to envisage a true good that suffices by itself to satisfy the soul. The true good will thus have both the sufficiency of pleasure and the absence of any interruption characteristic of the pursuit of wealth. Can we go further and think instrumentality itself as a possible characteristic of the true good? At first glance this seems to be a nonsense, for the idea of an instrument that would be sufficient in itself seems to be a contradiction in terms. And yet, if at the heart of the idea of instrumentality we isolate the idea of a productive power, or potentiality, then perhaps it is possible to discern here, too, another trait of the *verum bonum*. What the true good and wealth have in common is that they both make us powerful. But the power that the true good confers on us cannot be limited in the way that wealth is limited. We will learn further on that the true good is acquired *propter se*, but in this case it is not a matter of the misappropriation of an instrument. On the contrary, it is a case of a pure and non-instrumental power.

C. Finally, what is said of wealth can also be said of honour. Yet honour possesses two additional characteristics: on the one hand, it appears to be a good in itself – that is, it is always an end in itself; it therefore does not have the character of an instrument, as wealth does. In what, then, does honour's positive determination fundamentally consist? In sharing something with others. However, to the degree that one expects to gain positions or rewards – things that cannot be shared – it is necessary to obtain the agreement of other people so that they accept the elevation of a single person. And these others will only do so, in one way or another, if they recognise themselves in that person. Thus, to monopolise power it is necessary to share the tastes and prejudices of those one wishes to dominate. Here we find the limit of honour, tied to its positive determination.

The idea of the Sovereign Good thus consists not only in transforming procurement into enjoyment, as is the case with wealth, but also in dreaming of it being possible for people to share with one another in a way that would be a true form of communication and not just the reverse side of a monopoly. This is one of the dimensions of the true good that Spinoza consistently recognises. The word *communicabile* from the first phrase alludes to this.[19]

---

[19] Perhaps it is in this way that we should understand the *sui* from *sui communicabile*, in opposition to acts of imitation to which we submit our search for honours.

This dimension will be attributed to the *summum bonum* when it finally receives – albeit at the end of the journey – a positive determination: 'That is, it is part of my happiness to take pains that many others may understand as I understand . . .'.[20]

At this point – that is, at the end of the second stage – we find ourselves in possession of a conception of the *verum bonum* that is more than purely negative. We could say, instead, that we now have a *differential* conception of it. This conception consists in imagining a good that conserves the positive determinations of the three types of goods we know of, but without conserving their limits. The problem, now, is that the Sovereign Good is unrepresentable.

In such a conception, the Sovereign Good can only be a rejection of all the other goods. It is represented more as a quantitative augmentation of their positive aspects than as having an altogether different content. One thinks less of the *laetitia* that is proper to the Sovereign Good and more of what separates it from other goods. In this sense the first formula from the first sentence describes quite clearly this differential conception: the Sovereign Good is characterised essentially by a relation to what is external to it. Exclusivity is the form in which plenitude first appears.[21]

2. Ontology of the Threat

In the course of the narrator's hesitations and resolution, the third and fourth stages will lead us to discover other aspects of the true good. In the third stage, it is initially clear that it is necessary to choose between two conceptions of the good, between two ends to be pursued. Now, the true good has two disadvantages that speak against it, and it is these disadvantages that provide the outline for what I characterised above as the true good's unavailability. On the one hand, the true good is not yet envisaged in anything other than a differential manner. It does not appear to our mind except insofar as it is continuous with perishable goods; it is revealed when we experience the weaknesses of these goods. This is why the true good is as weak as the perishable goods' weaknesses are inconsistent. Each time I think of the *commoda* – that is, of the real and positive aspects of common goods – the image of the true good disappears. Spinoza says this clearly: it suffices to see[22]

---

[20] 'De mea felicitate etiam est operam dare, ut alii multi idem atque ego intelligant', § 14, G II, p. 8, l. 29–30 [*TdIE* 14; *CWS* I, 11].

[21] 'et a quo solo, rejectis caeteris omnibus, animus afficeretur', § 1, G II, p. 5, ll. 13–14 [*TdIE* 1; *CWS* I, 7].

[22] This is what the vocabulary itself indicates: *intuitu*, *videre*.

the existential consistency of the true good compared to common goods as they are given to us for the idea of abandoning these common goods with their attendant certainty to seem reckless. On the other hand, the determination of the true good in terms of exclusivity shows that whosoever abandons their old *institutum* risks abandoning the advantages that it brings. The idea of a use being a means (*media*) cannot yet be formulated at this stage – whence the suggestion of a compromise between the two *instituta*.

It is the realisation of the impossibility of this compromise that will provoke a new evaluation of the true good (*cum itaque viderem* . . .).[23] In fact, from this point on, the true good no longer appears simply as continuous with the former goods, as a corrective to their vanity. It now becomes necessary to calculate the force and the consequences of each good, as one would evaluate the strategic reserves of one's adversary in a battle. What was once an opposition becomes a crisis. The narrator finds himself in a situation of constraint: 'I was forced to ask what would be more useful to me.'[24] We once again encounter a term from the family *quaerere*, but this time in the form of a critical use of the term: it is no longer a matter of seeking a good, but of seeking a reason.

This search will take place in two stages, both of which are marked by the sign of constraint.

The first moment (§ 6) resolves the relations between the nature of the goods and the mode of their acquisition. And, for the first time, the positive character of the Sovereign Good is given: it is said to be *fixum*.[25] Note that this has not been said prior to this point. Up to now all of this was confused; henceforth, the distinction between a good's mode of acquisition and its nature forces us to think of the Sovereign Good no longer *differentially* but, at least formally, *in itself*. In fact, it was previously thought that the true good was not ephemeral like the others; it was thus understood in terms of the opposite of acquisition, that is, of loss, and thus implicitly in terms of acquisition *tout court*, with the greater prestige of immediately visible goods determining their superiority over the true good. Now, on the contrary, we are concerned with what grounds this non-ephemeral character of the true good. It is therefore no longer defined negatively but positively. It is true that this positivity still remains very vague, but by giving a positive name to this characteristic, we have changed terrain.

This occurred after only a relatively brief reflection. Now, after assiduous

---

[23] § 6, G II, p. 6, l. 21 [*TdIE* 6; *CWS* I, 8].
[24] § 6, G II, p. 6, ll. 23–4 [*TdIE* 6; *CWS* I, 8].
[25] 'Fixum enim bonum quaerebam', § 6, G II, p. 6, l. 29 [*TdIE* 6; *CWS* I, 8].

meditation, the second moment takes things even further (§ 7, 8, 9 and half of 10). The crux of Spinoza's reasoning, which here allows him to invert the opposition between goods and evils and to justify the image of a mortal illness, is contained in the final phrase of paragraph 7: the site of the meditation shifts to the conservation of the narrator's being and is no longer restricted to the conservation of objects.[26] The goods that are available to him no longer simply disappear: they are themselves a source of disappearance. Examples of this disappearance are given – once again in three moments – in paragraph 8. What remains to be done is to state the law that links perishable goods to the subject who suffers a loss. This happens in three moments, specifically in the series of negative sentiments analysed in paragraph 9 and linked to the 'quality of the object to which we cling in love'. This law is then applied successively to perishable goods and finally to the Sovereign Good. The series of *commotiones animi* alone allows us to pass from the description of effects to the description of causes, and, in the same stroke, from a differential conception to a resolutely affirmative conception of the Sovereign Good.

What do we now know of this Good? That it is eternal and infinite, and that love for it produces a joy without sadness – a superlative joy, a *summa laetitia*. This term is connected to the *summa tristitia* evoked in the prologue's opening paragraphs.

The ontology of the threat contained in perishable goods has thus led to the revelation of a new aspect of the true good. From here on, the relation is reversed: it is the true good which in some sense constitutes the more fundamental term. This does not cancel out the description that was given of it at the first level, but we know more about it now. At the end of the journey, as we will see, we will rediscover the characteristics that the moral tradition attributes to the Sovereign Good. These characteristics are thus not presented as if they went without saying; instead, they are produced by the successive transformations that the gaze of experience makes the goods of common life undergo, and which, in turn, transforms the lessons that the *animus* receives from life. Experience and opinion are therefore not purely and simply identical: what opinion unites in a somewhat haphazard fashion, experience orders into structured strata.

The two propositions from the first sentence from paragraph 1 seem to

---

[26] 'Illa autem omnia, quae vulgus sequitur, non tantum nullum conferunt remedium ad nostrum esse conservandum, sed etiam id impediunt, et frequenter sunt causa interitus eorum qui ea possident, et semper causa interitus eorum qui ab iis possidentur', § 7, G II, p. 7, ll. 5–9 [*TdIE* 7; *CWS* I, 9].

me to correspond clearly to these two stages: the first, with its still exclusive and negative definition; the second, with its affirmative definition. The *imo* which ties them together indicates the progression from one to the other.

In the second proposition, the condition of exclusivity that concerns the acquisition of the true good is suppressed at the level of practice: it is no longer mentioned. It remains to be transformed theoretically. What also remains is the transformation of this conclusion into a decision. These two transformations mutually condition one another.

3. Ontology of the Measure

After having described 'love for an eternal thing', Spinoza returns to the condition that he had posed just prior: 'But not without reason ...'.[27] Everything that has been said up to this point has been said on the following condition: 'if only I could deliberate thoroughly.' If this condition is not respected, the narrator's discoveries lack force. A new difficulty thus reveals itself. Now, one might think that a new paragraph might begin here, and that Bruder and Koyré were wrong when they failed to clearly mark the links in Spinoza's argumentative chain. The three goods continue, in effect, to impose themselves even now that the path has shown them to be evils. We could relate this paradox to the *Ethics*, which often repeats the line: I see the better yet do the worse. This is a truth of experience. It is also a truth of reason. We do the worse because the worse is not nothing; indeed it corresponds to a necessary causal chain (this is what the letters from 1665 to Blijenbergh incessantly repeat).[28] How is this paradox conceived of here? In exactly the same way: if the three goods were 'false goods', they would vanish once they became known as such. If they do not vanish, it is because truth is not the only thing that matters: the goods are evils to the same extent that they are goods. Knowing evil as evil does not make it disappear since it does not suppress the real causes of its attraction; the only way to suppress evil *qua* evil is through the positive progression of the good and the conversion of what is positive in the evil thing.

How does this progression occur? The narrator does not advance any

---

[27] 'Verum non absque ratione', § 10, G II, p. 7, l. 27 [*TdIE* 10; *CWS* I, 10].

[28] In particular the first on the subject of Adam (Ep. 19, G IV, p. 86 ff. [*Ep.* XIX [to Willem Van Blijenbergh]; *CWS* I, 357]) and the third on the subject of Nero (Ep. 23, G IV, p. 144, ff. [*Ep.* XXIII [to Willem Van Blijenbergh]; *CWS* 387]). Cf. G. Deleuze, 'Les Lettres du Mal', in *Spinoza, Philosophie pratique*, Paris: Editions de Minuit, 1981, pp. 44–62.

arguments on this point: rather, he simply makes a statement (the verb *videre* is used three times in paragraph 11 to designate the three remarks that make the action advance). The narrator remarks, on the one hand, and in a positive fashion, that the very fact of thinking begins momentarily (*quamdiu*) to overturn the domination of perishable goods. He thus bears witness, yet without knowing why, to a shift in the relation of forces in his mind. Note that the assiduous meditation is the site of two shifts: the theoretical shift which involves certainty and which by itself is not enough, and the practical shift in attention (*versabatur, aversabatur*), which is essential but which is preceded by the other shift as its condition of possibility. The vocabulary Spinoza uses here makes us think that the *animus* is the agent of the first shift – even if it is a constrained agent (*cogi*). With the second shift, by contrast, the *animus* seems to be a mere spectator (*videre*). This is not because some other agent carries out this inversion without the subject's participation, but rather because the power of the subject's enterprise itself is in the process of being revealed as a power that is irreducible to his consciousness alone.

On the other hand, the goods change status in light of the meditation that has thus occurred: they become in themselves the site of a dichotomy between means and ends. This remark itself then allows us to extend the length of the phases where the goods' domination is overturned. At this moment the journey is complete. However, what also happens at this moment is that the true good acquires a new and previously unknown characteristic: not only does it not exclude the other goods, it organises them in relation to itself. It separates their effectivity from the harm they cause. The true good is therefore their principle of measure; its demands serve to regulate the goods' powers and to restrict them to a tempered use. The true good is therefore no longer the opposite of the perishable goods, but the culmination and criterion of their positivity. We thus see a new possibility emerge, one that is not internal to the journey, but which appears on its horizon: the possibility that the *verum bonum* will, in turn, be thought of in terms of the category – itself redefined – of the *summum bonum*.

4. Transfigurations of the True Good

Promise, threat, measure: these are the three possible figures of the relation between the true good and those that appear successively as its antecedents, its competitors and its instruments. It is in the accomplishment of these figures that, in ever more positive ways, the name of the true good is filled with content; it progressively emerges in an ever clearer form from out of its primordial uncertainty. That this content is not a mere sum of differences or the symptom of a dissatisfaction is also marked by the fact that, in the course of the journey, the true good comes to be designated with ever more resolutely affirmative terms.

An indication of the way in which the idea of the true good is enriched and transformed is the term *remedium*, which Spinoza introduces in order to characterise, or at least refer to, the true good's effects. Certainly, the use of this word in a moral sense is a classical trope,[29] yet here it appears progressively and in a particularly determinate way. It is first mentioned in the comparison with a mortal illness, and in two senses: literal and metaphorical. This is the first and only real metaphor that is ever truly developed in these few pages. It intervenes at the point where the narrator is approaching the most acute moment of his crisis. He has understood that he could not pursue his new aspiration without abandoning the former *institutum*, and he has accepted that the forces that are opposed to the abandonment of the former goods are of a rare power, and that this power is expressed in almost all human activities. He understands, in other words, that he has arrived at a crossroads: the paths in front of him diverge so radically that it is necessary to renounce either one or the other.[30] Henceforth it is clear to him in a radical sense that it is no longer a matter of adding another good to his current life but of choosing between two types of life. It is therefore life itself that is at stake. A first moment in his reflection allows the narrator to readjust the idea of certainty attached to the two kinds of goods.[31] But this is still not enough: the 'assiduous meditation' will show that what he took to be goods

---

[29] For example, Seneca, in Book II of *De Ira*: 'aliis contra iram, aliis contra tristitiam remediis utendum est' (§ 20); 'Maximum remedium irae mora est' (§ 29); in the treatise on passions from the *Summa Theologica*, Thomas Aquinas deals with 'de remediis tristitiae seu doloris' (Ia IIae qu. 38) then 'de remediis contra iram' (ibid., qu. 47). In French, see the end of the *Passion de l'Ame*, in particular art. 203 (AT, XI, p. 481 – also against anger [PWD I, 400]) and art. 211 (AT, XI, p. 485 [PWD I,402]). But all of these examples refer to a very determinate use of the metaphor: it is a matter of remedies against passion, and, more precisely, against specific passions. This is not the case in the first three occurrences of this term in the *TdIE*, and then only partly in the fourth.

[30] 'Adeo esse opposita, ut ab uno, aut altero necessario esset abstinendum', § 6 G II, p. 6, ll. 22–3 [*TdIE* 6; CWS I, 8].

[31] As we saw above, it is essential to distinguish two successive moments in the re-evaluation of goods. First, a re-balancing (first part of paragraph 6), which associates both certainty and uncertainty with the goods: the three goods are certain as to their mode of acquisition, but uncertain in terms of their nature; the true good is certain by nature, but uncertain as to its mode of acquisition. There then occurs an inversion which assumes both that the three goods are, in fact, evils, and that the true good is 'certain', and nothing more.

will appear, in fact, as a series of evils – and, by the same token, that what allows him to escape these evils draws an additional certainty from its quality of hope. It is in this context that the idea of a remedy intervenes three times and with two different meanings. Let us reconstruct the detail of Spinoza's argument:

— The comparison begins with the narrator taking himself as the focus: 'I saw that I was . . .', he says. Up to this point, what he saw were advantages or obstacles.[32] Suddenly, his gaze turns back on himself, and he remarks more forcefully on the danger he finds himself in.[33] We find ourselves here at the point of maximum intensity, which I highlighted in Chapter 1. This intensity is necessary, for it will ensure the inversion of certainty with respect to the true good. If we are in a state of mortal danger, then every chance at salvation is a good, even an absolute good, since we have no choice but to take such a chance. Indeed, any chance is an absolute good even if we are uncertain about whether it will come about; for, in fact, we now have nothing to lose (in contradistinction to what has been assumed up to this point). The new type of certainty that is henceforth linked to the true good is a certainty that is no longer tied to the true good's qualities but rather to the situation in which the subject comes to discover that they must seek this true good. In such a situation, one cannot help being struck once again by the difficulty one faces in acquiring or indeed representing to oneself what is in fact the only possible way of getting out of this situation: the true good. But how does one get to this point in the argument, this point that is the condition of being able to say (against what has been established up to this point): 'I will give up certain evils for a certain good'?[34] Three stages are necessary. Spinoza presents them in a few compact but nevertheless discernible formulations:

— [A] First of all, it is necessary to make present and evident to oneself this *de jure* relationship between a situation without an exit and an absolute aid; that is, one must transform the logic of choice into a logic of catastrophe. This role will be played by the comparison with the mortal illness.

— [B] It is then necessary to advance the claim that we do indeed find ourselves in such a situation of catastrophe. This is the role played by the final phrase from paragraph 7: *now*, it says, everything people do leads them

---

[32] 'Videbam nimirum commoda . . .', § 2, G II, p. 5, l. 18 [*TdIE* 2; *CWS* I, 7]; 'Cum itaque viderem, haec omnia adeo obstare . . .', § 6, G II, p. 6, l. 21 [*TdIE* 6; *CWS* I, 8].

[33] 'Videbam enim me in summo versari periculo', § 7, G II, p. 6, l. 32 [*TdIE* 7; *CWS* I, 9].

[34] I am translating here in a direct style the phrase: '[viderem quod tum . . .] mala certa pro bono certo omitterem', G II, p. 6, ll. 31–2 [*TdIE* 7; *CWS* I, 9]. That what follows states the condition is indicated by *enim* in the following phrase (ibid., l. 32). This *enim* governs the remainder right up to *acceleraverunt* (§ 8, p. 7, l. 16 [*TdIE* 8; *CWS* I, 9]).

to this situation; *thus*, it concludes, implicitly,[35] the true good is the only way out — and it is, for this reason, a certain good.

— [C] All that remains is to cite examples that the narrator is already familiar with to show that, in fact, the goals that people pursue lead to the situation evoked in a *de jure* fashion in [A] and in a *de facto* fashion in [B]. But as these examples are in fact cases of death, persecution or suffering, they are relevant only because in [B] a principle is advanced for the first time that was without doubt operative from the beginning but which was never made explicit: namely, that what conditions our activities, that in which our hope lies, is to 'preserve' our life, or rather 'our being'.

At time [A], a relation of strict equivalence is established with a mortal illness, a relation marked by the repetition of terms: not only of *remedium* but also of *summis*, *viribus*, *cogi* [*cogitur*] and *quaerere*. This last expression is obviously the most cutting response to the former hope for a compromise solution. Can its force be weakened? No: in such a crisis, it is necessary to invest all of one's energy in one single solution. The comparison has an immediate effect (in addition to its visual power — it positions the reader before a spectacle whose emotional intensity engages them much more intensely than an abstract calculation would): it reformulates, without engaging in a long, logical analysis, the terms of the problem. We are no longer in 'common life', where the vanity and advantages of goods give rise to hesitations; we are at a point where, if common life continues, life itself will end. All of a sudden, life's sequences of action no longer appear as indefinitely repeating: they encounter their negation, and in a double form: in the medium term, death, and in the short term, suffering. Such a metaphor goes much further than hebetude, disappointment, or the other forms of *tristitia* that have previously been identified. It is in terms of this logic that the idea of a remedy is introduced. What is a remedy, in the literal sense of the term? It is a medication (or a treatment, if we are speaking of extended cures) that puts an end to an illness. What is the true good as a remedy? It is that which will put an end to the crisis the narrator is traversing. He will be cured. It is no longer a question of enjoyment or of finding rest, but of the narrator saving himself. However, when it is determined in this way, the true good still conserves a quasi-differential meaning: we do not know in what sense it will save us.

---

[35] In fact, this conclusion is the proposition that was stated above: 'Videbam enim me in summo versari periculo, et me cogi, remedium, quamvis incertum, summis viribus quaerere', § 7, G II, p. 6, l. 32; p. 7, l. 2 [*TdIE* 7; CWS I, 9].

The metaphor of the remedy does not go so far as to give us a definition of the true good.

The word remedy appears at time [B], where we can finally give it a positive meaning: the true good is that which preserves our being. This time, in fact, the word 'remedy' is completed by a determination that fills it with a positive meaning. It is no longer only a remedy for an illness, or a remedy for the crisis; it is a remedy 'ad nostrum esse conservandum'.[36] The true good is thus given a positive content and a positive power. How has this become possible? The preceding moment had made sickness and death appear, but as points of comparison. They were compared with the crisis the narrator was traversing. What we had not been told, however, was what concrete form this crisis took. What was the equivalent to the death and suffering of the sick person on the other side of the comparison, that is, on the side of the *animus* in its state of disarray? We now know the response and it is extraordinary: it is *the same thing*, namely, death (*interitus*) and, in the examples given in the following paragraph, suffering. In other words, the comparison is not a comparison at all; or rather, if it is a comparison, then it has the following remarkable feature: its terms are not equivalent but absolutely identical. In the course of the text, the metaphor has been transformed into a description: life, as one of the common goods, is so similar to a mortal illness that it *is* a mortal illness. What threatens the narrator is nothing other than what threatens the person suffering *morbo laethali*. An explanatory discourse would say that it is because the crisis is mortal that it resembles a mortal illness. In the prologue, however, and in conformity with its own descriptive logic, the opposite is the case. The problematic of death has emerged little by little, on the text's horizon and under cover of other questions. Here, all of a sudden, it takes central stage. We find ourselves faced with a veritable heuristics of the occasion. In a stroke, a question that had not yet been posed is suddenly resolved: what is the final end of our actions? Up to this point, our actions had been reduced to a certain number of fundamental sequences, to the pursuit and enjoyment of different goods; we did not ask whether they were all undergirded by an ultimate meaning. This question will continue to be omitted, and for logical reasons: it is not, generally speaking, a part of the horizon of experience. To claim to resolve it in a demonstrative fashion would lead one to think in terms of finality. On the contrary, the process of experience's exposition leads, at the highpoint of the crisis, to the sudden emergence of a response. This response is shown, not justified. The conservation of life is not the object of a discourse that would be able to think this object for itself;

---

[36] § 7, G II, p. 7, l. 6 [*TdIE* 7; *CWS* I, 9].

it is simply the contrary of life, that is, the loss of life, which concentrates the experience of the vicissitudes tied to the three types of goods.

Note that, once gain, when we are no longer dealing with what is immediately given, experience is better at showing the negative aspects of life than it is able to think its positive aspects. What makes experience advance are obstacles, crises and death. But these aspects themselves are an effect on the individual of the power of goods that are external to them. We can draw two methodological conclusions from this: on the one hand, once again, the fragility of the individual appears clearly in the face of the power of things, while knowing the vanity of things in no way diminishes their power; on the other hand, the experiential mode of thought often presents itself as reflecting affirmative traits in the form of negative contents; it advances by encountering these limits. These limits are the effect on the narrator of a positive power and; an explanation would draw out the causes of these powers in their positivity. But the order of experience is felt initially in the fact that the narrator confronts it, encounters it, or sees others do so. This shock of experience is not, however, the final word on the matter: for what the narrator experiences as a negation is at the same time a source of conflict that projects him towards a new perspective, where the same effects and the same possibilities are grasped differently, leading to new resolutions or new hesitations. We could use the term 'dialectic' here on the condition that we adequately establish its meaning. It is not a matter of putting an originary negativity to work, but of bringing out at each stage the still unperceived limitations that cause the productive displacements along the narrator's path.

Thus, the formula 'to preserve our being' will certainly go further than what has just been established. More precisely, it anticipates something more. Just as we saw that pleasure and honour were respectively the first certainty of health and of relations to others, here life is the first certainty of being, that is, its first form of appearance. But at the same time the formula opens up a space such that, in what follows in the description, there can appear the quality of being that it is marked by the disjunction joy/sadness and the opposition perishable/eternal. The second occurrence of *remedium* brings us closer to this meaning. We see how the succession of the first two meanings of the word has allowed us to progress within the ontology of the threat itself. As a result, the dialectic of limitation opens up a path towards a logic of anticipation.

The third meaning arises, finally, during the episode that is characteristic of what I have called the ontology of the measure. The former goods were characterised as evils. It was feared that they could not be overcome. We nevertheless realise, step by step, that as the true good comes to be better known, we can push back against these evils, at least by degrees: these evils are therefore not, as the narrator says, without remedy.[37] There are multiple remedies at stake here. It is no longer a matter of conserving life or being in general, but of being healed of each one of these evils. We thereby enter the reign of a positive and plural therapy, which occurs through knowledge – without us knowing why, nor in detail how, this therapy is to occur. These remedies do not constitute the true good in the strict sense of the term, but are rather the advantages that we draw from the movement leading towards it, at the same time as they are steps along this road. It is the same plural[38] that will be used in the *Ethics* – specifically in the Preface[39] and in the first part of Book V[40] – where Spinoza presents the remedies to the affects. There we will come to know by means of a demonstration in what sense the remedies are tied to knowledge: they consist in the causal knowledge of the affects. There, too, the remedies will not be the true good in the strong sense – that is, the Sovereign Good – but will be both a step on the way towards it and a consequence of this movement. Thus, the third meaning of the word 'remedy' that we encounter is the closest to the systematic meaning: experience at its most fundamental level redefines one of its terms in such a way that it comes to coincide with the signification that, in a quite different manner, the geometrical order will confer upon it.[41]

The expression that characterises the true good is that of the *res aeterna*.[42]

---

[37] 'Ut remediis nollent cedere', § 11, G II, p. 7, l. 34 [*TdIE* 11; *CWS* I, 10].

[38] Except in the Scholium from Proposition 4, but the context shows that it has a collective meaning; in any case, it is indeed a matter of a remedy for the affects. It is written in the singular in order to oppose what produces true knowledge of the affects to every other conceivable remedy: 'Atque hoc [. . .] affectum remedio, quod scilicet in eorum vera cognitione consistit, nullum praestantium aliud, quod a nostra potestate pendeat, excogitari potest', G II, p. 283, l. 33 [*Ethics* V, 4, Schol.; *CWS* I, 598]; p. 284, l. 1 [*Ethics* V, Praef.; *CWS* I, 599].

[39] 'Affectum remedia [. . .] sola Mentis cognitione determinabimus', G II, p. 280, ll. 22–5 [*Ethics* V, Praef.; *CWS* I, 597].

[40] 'Atque his omnia affectuum remedia [. . .] comprehendi', *Ethics* V, 20, Schol., G II, p. 293, ll. 4–6 [*CWS* I, 605]; the formula is reprised at the end of the Scholium, p. 294, l. 19 [*CWS* I, 606].

[41] The proof of this is that the preface to Book V of the *Ethics* will make it clear that these remedies are also known by experience – but that they are insufficiently well discerned or poorly put into practice: 'affectum remedia, quae omnes experiri quidem, sed non accurate observare nec distincte videre credo, sola Mentis cognitione determinabimus', G II, p. 280, ll. 22–5 [*Ethics* V, Praef.; *CWS* I, 597].

[42] 'Amor erga rem aeternam', § 10, G II, p. 7, l. 24 [*CWS* I, 9].

What does this mean? For the reader who has no other knowledge of Spinoza's system but who is familiar with the Christian culture of the Second Reformation, the term will no doubt make them think of the order of time: either of perpetuity, or of an eternal present. If, on the contrary, they are familiar with the *Ethics*, they will think of necessary existence, as opposed to duration.[43] Now, time is not mentioned here; neither are duration nor existence. Let us try, then, to engage with this term by drawing only on what the *proemium* tells us. In its immediate context, the eternal is opposed to the perishable. It is opposed to it less in terms of the nature of the two concepts and more in terms of the effects they produce. What is perishable provokes emotions in our mind and thus induces either a greater sadness in us or a provisional joy – a joy that will end in sadness. What is eternal does not provoke such emotions, but rather engenders a joy that is exempt from sadness. The terms *fixed* or *stable* (*fixum*), which foreshadow the term *eternal* and its associated term the *infinite*, both describe this absence of limitation (through movement or finitude) that engenders in us an untrammelled joy. We thus discover in the very thickness of our experience an unmistakable sign of eternity. This can occur either directly or differentially: *differentially* when we aspire to eternity in opposition to the limits of other forms of joy; *directly* when, momentarily, we grasp this joy itself.[44] Eternity is not only an abstract term at the beginning of the system: it is something which can be felt, in a certain sense, during this journey that presents itself as prior to the system.

Nonetheless, this feeling cannot be identified completely with the concept that is produced geometrically by the system. To be convinced of this, it suffices to compare paragraphs 9 and 10 from the *TdIE* with the Scholium which, in the middle of the final Book of the *Ethics*, develops the same theme.[45] There, the same principle is stated: no one suffers any torments or anxiety except with respect to what one loves;[46] and, in light of this principle, we find the same opposition between love 'for a thing which undergoes

---

[43] 'Per aeternitatem intelligo ipsam existentiam, quatenus ex sola rei aeternae definitione necessario sequi concipitur' [*Ethics* I, Def. 8; CWS I, 409]; and 'per durationem aut tempus explicari non potest', G II, p. 46 [*Ethics* I, Def. 8, Exp; CWS I, 409].

[44] There is no contradiction in the act of grasping an eternal thing in intervals: during each interval the joy is pure and brings no sadness. If following this interval there is a moment where the *mens* turns away from the true good, it again finds the joy mixed with sadness, which is contained in common life. But this sadness is not an effect of the *summa laetitia* itself.

[45] *Ethics* V, 20, Schol., G, p. 292–4 [CWS I, 605–6].

[46] Ibid., p. 294, ll. 3–4 [CWS I, 606].

many changes' and love 'erga rem immutabilem et aeternam'.[47] However, in the *Ethics* the quality of the thing is doubled by a determination that does not appear in the *TdIE*: namely, our mastery of the thing (*compos esse*). Furthermore, the second type of life is not simply opposed to the first: recall that the Propositions that precede this Scholium in the *Ethics* demonstrate how it is engendered by clear and distinct knowledge.[48] The order of the eternal thus appears in the context of a causal discourse, while at the beginning of the *TdIE* what emerges is what experience alone permits.

---

[47] Ibid., p. 294, l. 12 [CWS I, 606].

[48] This Demonstration (which occurs in Propositions 14 and 15 from Book V) refers as to its foundation to Proposition 15 from Book 1, that is, to the very heart of the theory of immanent causality.

5

The 'Animus' and Love

The ultimate distinction between existing goods and the hoped-for or promised good resides in the quality of love that each inspires – that is, in their effects on the *animus* or *mens*.[1] It is therefore to this actor that we must now turn. We must immediately ask what relations the narrator's 'I' has to the *animus* and the *mens*. For in fact, while the individual who undertakes the journey recounts this journey in the first person, he describes the majority of situations as affecting him by way of these two agencies.

We should note in passing that the term *animus*, which seldom appears in the *Ethics*, most often signifies in that work either 'heart' or 'courage', following the Latin use of these terms.[2] In fact, in the *Ethics*, it is *mens* that is typically used to designate the human mind in general.[3] In the *proemium*, by contrast, it is the *animus* that comes to the fore, while *mens* plays only a secondary role, one reserved for everything that concerns properly intellectual operations.[4] That the meanings of *mens* and *animus* partly[5] overlap is also a

---

[1] § 9, G II, p. 7, ll. 16–19 [TdIE 9; CWS I, 9].
[2] This is the way historians and orators use it. Caesar almost constantly uses it in this sense, while Cicero does so in his speeches.
[3] I am leaving aside here the question of translation (that is, of the determination of the semantic field) of *mens* in the *Ethics*. See the classic study by Emilia Giancotti, 'Sul concetto spinoziano di mens', in G. Crapulli and E. Giancotti-Boscherini, *Ricerche lessicali su opere di Descartes e Spinoza*, Rome: Edizioni dell'Ateneo, 1969, pp. 119–84.
[4] It is worthwhile noting that when, in the remainder of the TdIE, reference is made to the soul in its relation to the body (insofar as it is distinct from it, united with it, and so on), Spinoza will use the term *anima* – a term that is absent from the *proemium*, just as the term *corpus* is.
[5] The verb *cogitare*, for example, has for its subject alternatively *mens* (§ 3 and 11) and *animus* (§ 4). We can also note its use in the formula that refers to the attachment that preoccupies the mind, at the beginning of paragraph 4, where the same expression is reprised successively with both *animus* and *mens*.

function of the Latin use of these terms.[6] However, this does not mean that the word *animus* has a purely epistemological value. The context shows that it is also – and even primarily – related to feelings or emotions understood as movements of the mind. In fact, the narrator describes what happens to the *animus* in terms that recall events taking place on a battlefield: he notes the movements that shake it, the impediments or attachments that it succumbs to, and the victories of joy or sadness that it experiences, almost as if the *animus* were the external chronicler of these events. But this externality should not mislead us: each of the actions the narrator performs as an *I* is determined by the *animus*' prior state. This battlefield is at once the site and origin of the narrator's decisions. There is indeed only one, unique character in the text, and the different terms used to refer to him reflect the necessities of experiential analysis, not a real division.

1. The Operations of the 'Animus' and Their Results

Let us begin with an inventory. What is the *animus* capable of besides love? The answers to this question are given in a disorderly fashion in the course of the journey: the *animus* is capable of desire (towards the three types of goods as well as towards the fourth type; it is therefore capable of desiring what is at hand and aspiring to what does not yet seem to be so); of fear; of hesitating or of being uncertain; of joy; of sadness; and, more generally, of *commotiones animi*. Some of these capacities are not explicitly attributed to the narrator's *animus* in the course of his journey; instead, Spinoza refers to them as capacities that are common among people. This is the case with hatred, envy and everything that concerns struggle or rivalry.[7] The *animus* is also capable of making decisions, of meditating and of undergoing various internal scissions. Let us try to inject a bit of order into this multiplicity.

It appears that the *animus*, or the 'I' who speaks of it, can carry out or undergo three processes (further on, we will determine its varying degrees of activity). As for their effects, these processes produce three results.

A. The Three Processes

Throughout the narrator's journey, there are three chief operations undertaken or lived by the narrator and his *animus* (note that the latter is never qualified by a possessive adjective; such a construction conforms to the Latin

---

[6] That is, of the use of these terms in Lucretius' and Cicero's philosophical texts.
[7] § 9, G II, p. 7, ll. 19–22 [*TdIE* 9; *CWS* I, 9].

use of this term, but it again reinforces the effect of anonymity). These operations are thinking, being moved, and meditating.

1. The first process is that of thought. Thought is not defined here as an attribute but is instead conceived as the activity of an individual. The operation of *cogitare* is explicitly ascribed to the *animus*, and especially to the *mens*. Indeed, it is the sole operation attributed to the *mens*. The only other active verb of which *mens* is the subject is found in the phrase 'versare in has cogitationes'. The other occurrences of the term *mens* are either object complements[8] or subjects of verbs given in the passive voice.[9] These verbs refer to the reasons why, or the ways in which, the *mens* is prevented from thinking. We can conclude from this that the *mens* is the part or function of the *animus* charged with representing the *cogitatio*. It is not a distinct agency, only a specification of one. As for the question of determining what part it plays in the constitution of the subject, it is not necessary to know anything about the *mens* for the time being to understand what interests Spinoza here.

What is most important to note is that, for a good portion of the text, the verb *cogitare* stands out above all by its absence. Almost everything that is said of it consists in saying why it is impossible. For instance, the *haec tria* prevent the *mens* from thinking of any other good, while because of the repose the *mens* finds thanks to the *libido* the *animus* is incapable of turning its attention to anything else. Similarly, we do not succeed in thinking of the true good when our *mens* is riven by the quest for wealth or honours, nor when it is preoccupied with imitating others. The term *cogitare* then disappears for a number of paragraphs, but if we assume that these paragraphs develop the reasons why it is impossible to come to a compromise solution we realise that this *cogitare*, which might appear as an autonomous activity of the mind, is indeed present for the quasi-totality of the journey – but ultimately in the optative mode alone: it is what we do not succeed in obtaining, which is impeded, obscured and repeatedly excluded.

We should nevertheless make the following reservation: can we not say that the mind can at least think of other goods? Yes and no. Spinoza only says this using negative formulations, as if *cogitare* in the strong sense could only be said of the true good, and as if the other goods occupied my mind more than my mind has power over them.

Finally, we should note that in the whole of the process of reflection

---

[8] 'Si non suspendit mentem, tamen pertubat et hebetat', § 4, G II, p. 6, ll. 5–6 [*TdIE* 4; *CWS* I, 8].

[9] 'Distrahitur mens', § 3, G II, p. 6, ll. 1 [*TdIE* 3; *CWS* I, 7]; § 4, p. 6, ll. 7–8 [*TdIE* 4; *CWS* I, 8]; § 5, p. 6, l. 10 [*TdIE* 5; *CWS* I, 8].

described in paragraphs 6 to 10 neither the term *cogitare* nor the noun *cogitatio* appear. In its most decisive moments, then, the journey occurs in a different way and with other intellectual instruments.

2. The second process that occurs in the *animus* – the one that appears as the most invasive in the order of the given – is the series of *commotiones animi*. These are fear, hope, sadness, joy and envy. All of these *commotiones animi* had occurred prior to the journey, and they continue to take place as it unfolds and because of it. This list corresponds to one part of the list of the passions enumerated in the *Short Treatise*. It is not these *commotiones* that seem to allow the mind to progress; rather, they slow it down, or, at best, signal to it by a positive state that it is on the right track. But what, then, allows the mind to advance? If *cogitatio* is the sought-after process and *commotio* the process that actually takes place, what process functions as the mind's motor?

3. It suffices to consult the text: without referring to this process using a general noun, Spinoza describes a type of progression – one that he does *not* call 'thought' – and that instead of naming he describes using literary terms and imagery such as 'volvebam animo', 'aliquantulum rei incubueram', 'assidua meditatio' and 'modo possem penitus deliberare'. To this list should be added *consulere*, present in *inconsultum*. What these four or five terms share is the fact that while they certainly allude to thought, they refer to a thought that has more affective thickness than *cogitatio* does; a thought that is more dramatic, indeed more temporalised (as the terms *aliquantulum*, *assidua* and *penitus* indicate; as for *inconsultum*, it explains the term *denique*). This form of thought is, perhaps, the thought proper to experience. If *cogitatio* represents demonstrative thought, the above terms stand, by contrast, for a thought that accumulates, that weighs up different options, and that is swept away by the force of things. It also proceeds by means of examples and bases its convictions on them: 'permulta enim existant exempla', with three illustrations, which each time repeat the word *exempla*. This form of thought is freighted with the lessons of an individual history, not illuminated by the rigour of a theorem. Finally, even in paragraph 11, where we finally arrive at the stage of *cogitatio*, the narrator, in order to describe the state in which he finds himself, prefers the expression *in cogitationes versari*, which again reinforces the experiential character of the situation. The term *quamdiu* also adds the dimension of time, which occurs in *intervalla*. I noted above that the concept of duration does not enter into the *proemium*'s problematic. However, I should add that the process of resolution is embedded in its entirety in the thickness of a concrete duration, one that can be grasped in each of the expressions that describe it.

B. The Results

When the *animus* goes through one of these processes, what results does it obtain? Sometimes the *animus* decides, in others, by contrast, it is constrained. Above all, the *animus* sees.

1. The first result cited in the narrative is of a particularly voluntary nature: *constitui*. The narrator presents himself to the reader as a figure individuated by a decision. Yet, as we have seen, the narrative's order does not reflect the actual chronology of events. The narrator makes his decision only at the end of his trajectory, and as we saw above, if we isolate this decision we get a false image of the relation between the narrator and what happens to him. This false image is, in fact, quite a Cartesian image, one where the voyager is in some sense the master and possessor of the path he is following. However, Spinoza does indeed use the word *constitui*, if only to sum up the end of the trajectory. Moreover, in addition to *constitui* Spinoza uses other terms that evoke the narrator's will, albeit with a slightly different emphasis. These terms – *serio, penitus*,[10] *mutaretur* (negative) and *dare operam* – insist more on the seriousness and tenacity required for the decision and its effectuation; they indicate that it is an 'enterprise'. Does this not make the *constitui* illusory? What is illusory is to take the *constitui* at its word. It describes a real moment, certainly, the final one in the journey, but it does not indicate the causes of this moment. Rather, it describes the representation of the effort required to make the decision more than it describes the decision itself and the process that produced it. We can again find the equivalent of this in the letter to Bouwmeester from June 1666.[11] If we wanted to know more about

---

[10] The NS translates these two terms by *ganschelijk*, a term that today has disappeared but which in the classical age signified 'totally' or 'entirely'. (*Het groot Woordenboek der Nederlandische en fransche taele* . . . attests to it still in the edition of 1793, p. 147). The idea is indeed to devote oneself without reserve to the enterprise one has begun.

[11] No doubt Spinoza is no longer thinking precisely of a procedure strictly identical to the one from the start of the *TdIE*. Moreover, Bouwmeester's question bears directly on method and not on the means for arriving at it. This is why Spinoza responds in terms of the difference between imagination and understanding. But he nevertheless poses the question of knowing what is necessary for this. And he replies that, on the one hand, the description of ideas suffices and that knowledge of the soul by its first cause is not necessary ('non est opus naturam mentis per primam ejus causam cognoscere, sed sufficit mentis sive perceptionum historiolam concinnare': this first condition refers, as the reference to Bacon shows, to the equivalent of what follows in our text); and on the other hand, that 'ad haec omnia assiduam meditationem, & animum, propositumque constantissimum requiri, quae ut habeantur apprime necesse est certum vivendi modum et rationem statuere, et certum aliquem finem praescribere', G IV,

the conditions of possibility of this decision, we would have to engage in the well-known debate on the links between determinism and ethics, but this is not necessary here. What we should retain from all this is the notion that the activity of the *I* is less the proof of an immediately experienced freedom and more an index of the effort required to accomplish the journey.

2. By contrast, other terms show the 'I' in a state of passivity. These terms are, of course, the series of formulations where the narrator admits that he was forced to reflect and to seek a remedy in the same way a sick person is forced to take care of themselves (*cogebar, cogi, cogitur*[12] . . .). We should also count the incapacity of the *I* to overcome certain difficulties: *frustra tentavi, mens suspenditur* and *distrahitur*. Let us take a closer look all the same. The verb 'to constrain' does not imply a general theory of determinism; it indicates only the necessary consequences of a hypothesis. If I do such-and-such, then I am constrained to . . . It will be agreed that this has more to do with the discussion of a situation and its limits than with the affirmation of a constraint that makes any initiative impossible. Finally, the terms 'to tear' and 'to suspend' show the mind's subjection to goods. Here, too, things are not definitive. Nevertheless, the power of adhesion that goods possess is powerfully marked. What should be noted – and this is typical of the language of experience – is that this power does not cease once it comes to be known. We thus find in these pages less a theory of necessity and more the progressive discovery of its determinations (attachments, the formation of desires, the constitution of emotion) by a narrator who initially knows nothing of them, and who is also ignorant of the initially unperceived difficulty of extracting himself from them.

3. Finally, beyond the experience of effort and the coming to consciousness of necessity's determinations, a third result is indicated by the word *videre*. This is

---

p. 189, ll. 5–7 and 10–14 ('all these things require uninterrupted meditation, and a constant mind and purpose. To acquire these it is necessary above all to decide upon a definite way and principle of living, and to prescribe an end for oneself' [*Ep.* XXXVII [to Johannes Bouwmeester]; CWS II, 32]). On the echo of these recommendations in Bouwmeester's preface to his translation of the famous *Hai Ebn-Yokdhan*, see W. Klever, *Spinoza. Verhandeling over de verbetering van het verstand*, pp. 43–4.

[12] Cf. R. Schottländer's study, 'Comment le libéralisme politique de Spinoza est-il compatible avec son déterminisme éthique', *Tijdschrift voor de Studie van de verlichting*, VI (1978), 1–4, pp. 191–203. Cf. also Carla Gallicet-Calvetti, *Spinoza lettore del Machiavelli*, Milan: Vita e Pensiero, 1972, which brings out 'la aporia fra una metafisica deterministica, destinata a recondurre tutto il reale a un sistema necessario e necessitante ed in cui le stesse "proprietà" della umana natura dovrebbero denunciare le leggi condizionanti necessariamente l'umano operare, ed un'etica di liberazione delle passioni e di perfezionamento, costantemente celebrata', pp. 28–9.

the verb that marks, past the obstacles but before the final decision, practically all of the moments of the narrator's reasoning: the stages of the *I* are punctuated by the terms *videbam*,[13] *viderem*,[14] and *vidi*,[15] etc., and also by *perspiciebam*[16] and *perciperem*.[17] The term *videre* is closer to the essence of the *I* than the other verbs or expressions that refer to the processes or results of its actions, for it is this term that governs them: I saw that in order to apply myself seriously to this new enterprise, I had to . . .;[18] I saw that the mind reflected. . . .[19] In fact, the events that occur in the mind or the projects that it forms cannot be perceived by it except through the mediation of this term *videre*. In particular, each time that the verb *cogi* is used, it is used as a complement of the principal verb *videre*, or as a principal verb determined by a causal *videre*.[20] Experience records less the constraint than the perception of the constraint. I noted above that this verb *videre* was typical of the beginning of the *TdIE*. In fact, in the remainder of the text it cedes its place to verbs that refer to the understanding.

It is not difficult to group this verb with the principal indicators of the category of experience. It refers to the outcome of a procedure that is not irrational but that operates with a form of reasoning internal to experience. One weighs up hopes, one lives through situations that one does not yet understand, one perceives more than one demonstrates. This in no way means that the narrator is not rational; it means that in order to undertake this journey there is no need for rationality in the geometrical sense of the term. In sum, *videre* manifests at the linguistic level the same procedure that another sign of the experiential register denotes substantively: the term *exemplum* (here used in the plural: *exempla*).

At the end of this inventory, we can note that experience certainly finds in the *animus* a support, albeit a weak one. Yet it is in the *animus*' weakness that

---

[13] § 2, G II, p. 5, l. 18 [*TdIE* 2; CWS I, 7]; § 7, p. 6, l. 32 [*TdIE* 7; CWS I, 8]; § 11, p. 7, ll. 31 and 33 [*TdIE* 11; CWS I, 10].

[14] § 1, G II, p. 5, l. 9 [*TdIE* 1; CWS I, 7]; § 6, p. 6, l. 21 [*TdIE* 6; CWS I, 8]; § 7, p. 6, l. 30 [*TdIE* 7; CWS I, 9].

[15] § 11, G II, p. 8, l. 4 [*TdIE* 11; CWS I, 10].

[16] 'Perspiciebam, me ea debere carere', § 2, G II, p. 5, l. 21 [*TdIE* 2; CWS I, 7].

[17] 'Nam quamvis haec mente adeo clare perciperem . . .', § 10, G II, p. 7, l. 28 [*TdIE* 10; CWS I, 10].

[18] § 2, G II, p. 5, ll. 18–20 [*TdIE* 2; CWS I, 7].

[19] § 11, G II, p. 7, ll. 31–3 [*TdIE* 11; CWS I, 10].

[20] 'Videbam nimirum [. . .] quod ab iis quaerendis cogebar abstinere', § 2, G II, p. 5, ll. 18–19 [*TdIE* 2; CWS I, 7]; 'Cum itaque viderem haec omnia [. . .] adeo esse opposita, [. . .] cogebar inquirere . . .', § 6, G II, p. 6, ll. 21–4 [*TdIE* 6; CWS I, 8]; 'Videbam enim [. . .] me cogi', § 7, G II, p. 6, l. 32 [*TdIE* 7; CWS I, 8]; p. 7, l. 2 [*TdIE* 7; CWS I, 9].

the strength of the journey lies: the journey is universalisable only because the narrator has hardly any individualised traits and indeed cannot have any. He has too little consistency to be anything more than the receptacle of his own *commotiones animi* and of what the events of his interior life allow him to see. The equilibrium of the *TdIE* is founded on precisely this.

2. Love

What are the characteristics of love? Here we must draw out a paradox that we will encounter again and again in the course of this work: happiness depends on the quality of the object, and yet, as we learn a few paragraphs further on, this object is relative only to us. How can we explain this paradox?

Perishable goods inspire a love that ends with them or with the threat of their disappearance. While the term 'finite' does not appear here, we catch a glimpse of it in its opposite, 'infinite'. What else is there in the idea of the 'finite' that is not contained in the idea of the perishable? The idea that ontological lack is not only a matter of continuity in time. The proof of this is that the very presence of these goods immediately does harm, without there being any need to await their absence. Their presence itself is a promise of absence. Their absence is also an absence for others, and an absence that is part of their very nature. This absence provokes vain efforts, disputes and sadness. It is the horizon that determines the relative certainty of presence, and prevents the *commoda* from being used naively.

By contrast, the eternal and (the term finally appears) infinite good makes joy triumph over sadness. Spinoza says: this eternal good is what is most desirable, what one must seek with all one's might. Let us pause for a moment over these two descriptors. We see a norm appear here for the first time in the text. What justifies this norm? The very structure of the text gives us the answer: this norm does not come – and cannot come – from the outside (for we are within common life), but nor is it the result of a demonstration. It is thus what is 'taught' – by experience. This *laetitia* is the contrary of the *tristitia* tied to the vanity and futility of the goods that occur most frequently in common life. In other words, the norm – even if it is only practical or implicit – is taught by what *is*, or at the very least by what is *given*. By promising and by offering less than what they promised, finite goods are what we seek and what casts a shadow over us; they suggest that there exists a good that does not cast such a shadow and that will satisfy the aspirations of the *animus*. But how do we know of the *animus*' aspirations? For the time being, it seems, it is thanks to experience itself. Thus, if we unpack it a little, we see that the promise of finite goods is double: with respect to these goods as objects (and thus, by extension, with respect to all objects), they promise possession; with respect to the *animus* to which they are addressed, these goods promise satisfaction, constancy and tranquillity. Without being explicitly defined, love is thus given practically as the aspiration to an untroubled form of possession, a promise of constancy in the relation between the *animus* and its object. In contrast to what happens in the *Short Treatise*, nothing is said here regarding the necessity of love: in the *TdIE*, Spinoza is content to confront us with its reality. But the experience that is presented, and the reflection that occurs on its basis, are indeed compatible with the thesis demonstrated in the *Short Treatise*, namely that we cannot live without love (the reason being that, from a certain perspective, it is love that confers upon us a reality).[21] Furthermore, the true question is not 'Should we love?' but: 'Since we necessarily must love, what object is it preferable for us to love?' As we saw above with respect to perseverance in being, we see emerge here a logic of anticipation. The strong thesis – that we live only by virtue of love – is not explicitly stated, but if we are already familiar with it we can recognise it in what begins to emerge in paragraph 9. Having understood the extent to which we are gripped by everyday goods, and thus the extent to which they hold the keys to our existence, the term 'love' now comes to name this general state of adhesion, a state that had previously been glimpsed only in relation to particular questions but which ultimately comes to occupy our entire horizon. In a first stage, when I was occupied exclusively with seeking those goods that presented themselves to me, I could believe in a circumstantial relation of pure exteriority between these goods and myself. In a second stage, however, when I try to reconcile this search with the search for the true good, I realise to what extent each of the goods that I thought were contingent are in fact attached to me by a thousand threads; I also understand the extent to which they prevent me from thinking of anything else, thereby annulling the very possibility of any other kind of search and throwing me back into an ever-renewed quest once I am satisfied, or moving me to imitate others. But if this is the case, then this means that the goods I love penetrate deep into my interiority, model my desires, choose my thoughts and occupy the ideal place that I might have thought was that of an autonomous self. Finally, the *exempla* from paragraph 8 show that this love for goods can go so far as to overwhelm what I am beginning to discover as the core of my existence: my tendency to persevere in my being. Experience shows that some people have identified so strongly

---

[21] Cf. KV, M, II, Chapter 5, p. 53 [CWS I, 105].

with the goods they pursued that they ended up abandoning their life, or at least risking it, in the course of this pursuit. Thus, in three consecutive moments, without the question ever being thematised for itself, the simple progression of experience makes us discover (so long as we decide to reflect on this fact) that the love of perishable goods determines not only our actions but also our desires, and even what is most essential in our sense of self. If we were to formulate an abstract argument about this (something that experience as such obviously does not do), we could ask if it is possible to resist such a power. The description of our actions has already given us the answer: since everything we do is oriented according to sequences of action, would anything remain if we were to suppress these sequences? Since these sequences cannot be suppressed, it is best to change their object. Now, we have seen that these sequences are precisely not determined by their object. It is therefore possible to modify this object, and in doing so modify the results of our relation to the world.

Certainly, experience itself does not reason in this way, nor can it do so. I have reconstituted this argument simply to show that all of its elements are there: the narrator's journey contains all of the lived and felt materials needed to justify a conclusion analogous to the one from the *Short Treatise*. Yet, if this reasoning is not carried out, another equivalent reasoning is outlined: the *animus* experiences itself through its *commotiones*; these are always experienced in relation to changes occurring in perishable things; and thus it appears that there exists a tenacious, albeit non-necessary, link between goods and the *commotiones animi*. It suffices to take away from one what causes its movement, and we will find in the other a content without movement: that is, rest.

Nothing here is demonstrated *debito ordine* and according to the norm of the true idea such as it will be determined in paragraph 44, nor is it presented in the *more geometrico* style. However, something is established, and established according to a procedure that is not that of geometry but that is nevertheless compatible with it (for if this were not the case, how could we articulate the two types of reasoning?). Above all, it is necessary that we begin from this precise point: this is the situation that is given; and there is a path to be cut through and in the midst of what is given. The stages of this path are indicated, as we have seen, by the successive appearances of the verb *videre*, which is the index of this form of the establishment of what is true.

Let us return to the paradox I mentioned at the beginning of this section. The text's progression has shown not the relativity of good and evil in the strict sense – that is, in terms of the sense this relativity has in Spinoza's system – but rather the nature of good and evil in terms of the effects they have on the *animus*. Now, these effects depend neither on the content nor the substance of the object, but rather on its *quality* (that is, on whether it is perishable or eternal). There is therefore nothing contradictory about tying human happiness to an external object, and, simultaneously, affirming the partial relativity of this object. This partial relativity is given twice in experience: in paragraphs 9 and 10, it is experienced in the differential relation between the goods and the narrator, while in paragraph 11 it is experienced in the instrumental relations between goods. Thus, when the journey is complete, all of these obstacles, both theoretical and practical, have been overcome and the decision can finally be made. One of the justifications for this decision, as it is described in the *proemium*'s first sentence, is precisely the thesis of the partial relativity of goods; however, this sentence formulates this thesis differently. Among the various forms of sadness, the narrator's decision confers a particular privilege upon fear. Why? The answer has to do with the two occurrences of the term *felicitas*. If the final decision is taken at the moment we come to know where *felicitas* is to be found,[22] it is because the narrator's uncertainty as to its location had blocked his ability to reason.[23] Now, this uncertainty was indeed a form of fear, even if the term was not explicitly used. In other words, what for a long time deferred the narrator's decision, and functioned as the counterweight to his aspiration to the true good, was without doubt, at a first level, the ensemble of preoccupations tied to his pursuit of the goods of common life – goods that inspired, in addition to limited forms of joys, all of the various kinds of sadness that prevent us from thinking of anything else. But what also deferred his decision was, at a second level, the specific kind of fear that marked the beginning of the progression itself. And it is in fact the resolution of this second problem that allows the narrator to make progress on the first. It is therefore essential to distinguish between the fear of objects and the state of fear.[24] If an object

---

[22] Cf. § 9 and 10: 'quod tota felicitas, aut infelicitas in hoc solo sita est . . .', etc.

[23] Cf. § 2: 'et si forte summa felicitas in iis esset sita [. . .]; si vero in iis non esset sita', etc.

[24] As a hypothesis, it is perhaps not impossible to see in the double formula from the first paragraph a reference to these two levels of fear. Spinoza in fact uses the verb *timere* at once transitively and intransitively: 'Omnia quae timebam' would thus refer to the things or events that I fear spontaneously, as I seek them, flee them, and enjoy them. Here, the accusative designates the object of one of the constitutive sequences of behaviour – sequences that are expressed using transitive verbs throughout the entirety of the *proemium*. By contrast, 'omnia a quibus timebam' would refer to the 'reflexive' fear, born in the course of the journey and which bears upon the journey's results. This fear does not concern one of the objects of common life but rather the state of fear

provokes fear (and the same goes for hatred or envy), it is necessary to change one's object – this is what paragraphs 9 and 10 suggest. If an experience throws us into a state of fear, its outcome will be marked not only by a change in object but by also the appearance of a positive compensatory state: consolation. This is what paragraph 11 explicitly states.[25]

3. The Narrative 'I'

I remarked at the beginning of this work how important the category of singularity is in these paragraphs. Can we now better characterise the narrator's *I*? Notice one significant detail: on two occasions, this 'I' returns to what it has previously said – not in order to contradict itself, but to indicate what is at stake or the reasons for traversing a particular stage: I am referring here to the two self-citations. How should we interpret this figure from the narrative? It is the proof of the articulation between the narrative in the proper sense and a form of explanation that is subordinate to it; it is the mode of calculation proper to action.

How does the *I* guide itself in its journey? It discovers the principles of this journey in the course of undergoing it, in particular in the narrator's search for his own advantage. This formula is obviously absent from our text; it belongs to the *Ethics*, where it represents a universal principle,[26] valid from one end of the doctrine to the other. Here, on the contrary, this principle is produced. We can even identify where this production takes place. Indeed, it is not by chance that the reference to advantages occurs in paragraph 6, and does so in the form of a comparison. This reference occurs at the moment where it has finally become clear that it is absolutely necessary to abandon one or the other of the two *instituta*. Now, at this point in the argument, the narrator does not yet know what he will come to learn in what I have called 'the ontology of measure': namely, that certain advantages can also be found in the new *institutum*, on the condition that they are useful to the true good. Yet, even then they will not all be refound. At this stage, then, we are in a situation that calls for a choice – a choice that, in the eyes of the person choosing, will lead to a real loss. It is thus necessary to choose the lesser of

---

(concerning happiness) I suffer from as I consider the riskiness of the choices I make and of the power of goods insofar as they reveal themselves to be evils – a state that is described by the same verb *timeo* taken in the intransitive sense.

[25] 'quod magno mihi fuit solatio', G II, p. 7, l. 33 [*TdIE* 11; CWS I, 10].

[26] 'Cum Ratio nihil contra naturam postulet, postulat ergo ipsa, ut unusquisque seipsum amet, suum utile, quod revera utile est, quaerat', *Ethics* IV, 18, Schol., G II, p. 222, ll. 17–19 [CWS I, 555].

two evils: whence the question of knowing which is the more advantageous. In the *Ethics*, the principle 'of two evils, choose the lesser' will be a product of reason,[27] which itself is nothing other than the search for one's own advantage. Here the procedure is inverted. The search for the advantageous appears only by way of the determination of *what* is most advantageous – in other words, the principle appears only by being put into practice. Even then, it does not appear immediately: the narrator must travel down a long path to be convinced of the power – including the immanent power – of the goods that arise from the realm of occurrences. Only then is he confronted with the necessity of a choice that he believed he could defer. If at the end of the trajectory, and after having learnt the lessons of its various movements, we ask ourselves what guided the narrator throughout, we must therefore respond: first, in an obscure form, it was the principle of the advantageous in the form of the pursuit of goods; then it was the simultaneous aspiration to the true good and the illusion of compromise; and finally, in a quasi-explicit form, it was the search for what is most advantageous. Once again, we see at work towards the end of the journey a logic of anticipation: the strong thesis that sees both Reason and the good incarnate in the useful appears here in the form of an almost homonymic figure, within the limits of what can be assimilated by experience alone.

This question links up with another: that of the universal and the singular. How is it possible that certain people make the choice of the most advantageous while others do not? Nothing, in the end, distinguishes the *I* who speaks from any other person, if it is not precisely the journey it has taken. The narrator thus constructs the figure of his singularity, not from his own interiority, but on the basis of the adventure of experience. Nothing, however, can explain why the experience that the narrator undergoes was lived by one person and not by another. Without thematising it, the narrator identifies this difference when he says 'men' and not 'me'. Yet, by identifying this difference, he simultaneously indicates the difficulty it implies: namely, that on the basis of what one finds among 'men', the narrator concludes as to what concerns *him* alone. On only one occasion does this difference that slips in between the inalterable identity of the *I* and the universal receive a name. This takes place at the end of the first *exemplum*. Those who die in the course of confronting the dangers they are exposed to because of their thirst for wealth perish as victims of their own stupidity. *Stultitia*: this is the only content that fills this apparently empty difference between those who

---

[27] 'De duobus bonis majus, et de duobus malis minus ex Rationis ductu sequemur', *Ethics* IV, 65, G II, p. 259, ll. 19–20 [CWS I, 583].

have kept seeking what is vain and those who have gone to the end of the journey. In the *Ethics*, this difference is thought on the basis of the difference between individual essences. At the time of the *TdIE*, however, we do not know if Spinoza can conceive of this difference in these terms. In any case, the type of discourse characteristic of the *proemium* excludes this. This difference can only be grasped in terms of its effects – effects which, when seen from the vantage point of the end of the journey, can manifest themselves only as madness.

4. Impotence and Unhappiness

The *I*, the *animus*, the *mens* – these are the three agencies that make up the unique support of the journey. This unicity means that the *I* has more than a simple narrative function: it not only recounts what has happened, it recounts what has happened to *it* – and what has happened to it is also what the *I* has become. In fact, through its confrontation with the successive figures of goods from the realm of occurrences, the *I* takes on traits that are not only related to its act of enunciation or to the simple enjoyment of what is given. The empty neutrality of the speaking *I* has progressively been coloured by the meaning of its own finitude. The more the goods appear powerful and perishable, at once threatening to life and irritating to the mind, the more the *I* who confronts them feels their power within him, both in the form of his desires and as an obstacle to his thought. The more, too, the very uncertainty of these goods and their limitations becomes apparent, the more the narrator feels his own limitations. The narrator is a subject to the degree that he is subjected to these goods. Each of the three goods can reveal to him, within his own interiority, a form of unhappiness. Attached as he is to the love of perishable things, he deciphers in them a triple limitation: in pleasure, he sees the impossibility of making his joy last; in wealth and honours, he sees his propensity to exhaust himself in an indefinite search; and finally, in honours, he witnesses his tendency to construct himself through imitation. This impotence is not a pure nothingness: it is actualised in each of the activities the narrator engages in. His own life thus perpetually engenders it. This impotence is again manifest, and in a striking form, in the very middle of the journey when the narrator is unable to pass from aspiration to decision. It is only by taking this impotence to its extreme (by imagining himself as being in extreme peril, as beset by a malady), and by reflecting on human impotence in general (by recollecting sufferings, persecutions and death), that he will be able to overcome this situation. The solution thus consists not in escaping finitude but in discovering it in a rigorous way. It is this discovery that makes possible the series of salvific choices the narrator makes – so much so that certain commentators have spoken of an 'existential calculation of possibilities'.[28]

Unhappiness and choice: the association between these two terms would seem to transport us to a Pascalian context. I noted in passing that commentators have often been tempted to assimilate the *proemium*'s journey with the argument of the wager. This assimilation is most often invoked only briefly, and without taking into account any of the differences between the two authors[29] (Ferdinand Alquié's work is an exception to this).[30] The furtive nature of this *rapprochement* reflects the markedly little interest that has been shown in the secondary literary for the comparison between Pascal and Spinoza in general.[31] I would nevertheless like to insist on it for a moment, for if a comparison between the fragment 'Infinity Nothingness' from the *Pensées* and the *TdIE* has any theoretical interest, then this can only be revealed through a more sustained treatment. It would be easy to underscore the formal differences between the two texts (one is a dialogue, the other a journey; one is mathematical and a fragment, the other a prologue). But we can leave these differences aside, at least provisionally, for they risk obscuring a partial but real proximity between the two texts' respective procedures.

---

[28] 'Existentiële kansrekening', W. Klever, *Spinoza. Verhandeling over de verbetering van het verstand*, p. 112.

[29] Whether this association is accepted (C. Tejedor Campomanes, *Una Antropologia del Conocimiento* . . ., p. 18) or refused (R. Caillois, notes to his Pléiade translation, p. 1391). C. Gallicet-Calvetti goes so far as to suppose a direct influence – something that seems impossible given that the *Pensées* are only published in 1670: 'Resta ora soltanto da richiamare rapidamente quel motivo che sembra suggerito dal "pari" pascaliano [. . .]. Argomentazione complessa quella del "pari" pascaliano che può aver indotto il filosofo olandese all'osservazionze sopraferita [= the formula "primo enim intuitu inconsultum videbatur", etc.]', *Benedetto Spinoza di fronte a Leone Ebreo*, Milan: CUSL, 1982, p. 31.

[30] *Servitude et Liberté selon Spinoza*, Paris: CDU, 1971, pp. 7–8.

[31] An exception is constituted by the chapter that Brunschvicg devotes to Pascal in *Spinoza et ses contemporains* Paris: PUF, 1951, Chapter IX, pp. 194–211. Brunschvicg nominates as an anchoring point of the comparison the relation of the finite and the infinite, but he restricts his study to the relations between the geometrical order and Revelation: 'Le solitaire de Port-Royal et le Juif de Voorburg avaient tous deux sur leur table de travail la Bible et le *Discours de la Méthode*; sans se connaître, ils se sont en quelque sorte répondu', p. 198. The theme is narrowed again in Maurras' tale *Pascal puni* (Paris: Flammarion, 1953). Since then Pierre Macherey has expanded on the question in his talk at Urbino, 'Entre Pascal et Spinoza: le vide', in *Spinoza nel 350 Anniversario della nascita*, ed. E. Giancotti, Naples: Bibliopolis, 1985, pp. 71–87. He does not, however, take up the thesis we are exploring.

To facilitate this comparison, I will analyse Pascal's argument in terms of the concatenation of three theses: (a) with respect to the crucial choice of knowing whether or not God exists (and of knowing whether we should act as a consequence of this knowledge), we cannot turn to reason; (b) it is nevertheless absolutely necessary to make a choice; and (c) this choice – that is, this wager – structures the categories of certainty and uncertainty in such a way that there is an infinity to win while we only have to take a chance on finitude.

In the fragment 'Infinity Nothingness', the first thesis that traces the possibility of the wager is the thesis of divine incomprehensibility. This thesis excludes a first form of the determination of the choice, namely, the analysis of proofs by reason.[32] We cannot be certain about the existence of God; however, if He did exist, then we could be certain that His existence, like His nature, would escape our knowledge. The same goes for His inexistence. We therefore cannot blame those Christians who fail to provide proofs for their religion, but nor can we refute them.[33] But what about those who are still deciding if they must choose? They must come to a decision concerning the question of whether or not God exists, but not through a form of reasoning that is strictly determined by a proof of reason. Perhaps, though, they can simply refuse to decide? No, for they are committed, and they must therefore wager, for the wager will be the form that this second determination will take. In this wager, they have nothing to lose but their unhappiness and their errors. This is how the third stage begins: 'Let us weigh up the gain and the loss by calling heads that God exists.'[34] In the context of a search for beatitude, this is a true choice, for the player hesitates because he fears losing his happiness should he make the wrong choice. Winning and losing concern real and incompatible goods. Indeed, it is because of this that the calculation has a meaning.

What happens in Spinoza? We also find the same three moments in the construction of the *proemium*. It is clear that in Spinoza the first moment

---

[32] This thesis is strictly homogeneous with Pascal's refusal, expressed on many occasions, of the traditional demonstrations of the existence of God. Cf. fragment 3 Lafuma, Br. 227 and 244.

[33] Whence the indeterminate character of the question from this perspective: 'Votre raison n'est pas plus blessée, puisqu'il faut nécessairement choisir, en choisissant l'un que l'autre', 418 Lafuma, 233, Br., p. 550 ['Your reason is not hurt more by choosing one rather than the other, since you do have to make the choice', *Pensées and Other Writings*, trans. Honor Levi, Oxford: Oxford World's Classics, 1999, p. 154].

[34] *Pensées*, p. 154.

does not refer to the God of the Christians.³⁵ However, we can accept *at the level of their effects* a certain structural equivalence between the incomprehensibility of God and the initial uncertainty in which we find ourselves when faced with the true good. Certainly, the first kind of incomprehensibility is necessary while the other is entirely provisional, but this does not relieve us of having to analyse their consequences in the course of our reasoning. The reservation *inconsultum viebatur* corresponds quite well to Pascal's 'Yes, I must wager. But perhaps I am betting too much.'³⁶ Everything that is deduced from this double hesitation in Spinoza also finds an echo in Pascal's text, in particular the fear of losing *felicitas* so long as we do not know with certainty where *felicitas* is to be found.³⁷ There is thus a real proximity between Pascal and Spinoza at the level of their descriptions of the form this hesitation takes, as well as the motivations for it. But the proximity ends there: as soon as we analyse more closely what is at stake and identify the process that leads to the decision, we see that the content of the two texts is as different as their structures:

— In the third stage, there is no real choice, as Ferdinand Alquié has shown.³⁸ In fact, the end of the journey turns the goods we know of into means in the service of the true good. It could be objected that in Pascal we also lose nothing: 'you will realise in the end that you have wagered on something certain and infinite, for which you have paid nothing'.³⁹ But we only realise this *after* the decision-making process. In the *proemium*, such a realisation is an integral part of the process itself.

— It is above all in the second stage that the difference between the two texts is to be found. To the question: 'Is it possible to not decide?', both Pascal and Spinoza respond that it is impossible. But this shared response takes such different forms that any analogy between the two is illusory.

---

[35] Likewise, Spinoza begins from common life without presupposing any religious language, while in Pascal we can know what is on the 'other side of the cards' by way of the Scriptures and the testimony of others – but this is not essential at this point in the unfolding of the argument.

[36] *Pensées*, p. 154.

[37] On the Spinozist side, the argument from paragraph 2, 'et si forte summa felicitas in iis esset sita . . .', G II, p. 5, ll. 20-4 [*TdIE* 3; *CWS* I, 7]. In the fragment 'Infini rien', the objection is refuted by: 'Car il ne sert à rien de dire qu'il est incertain si on gagnera', p. 551 ['For it is no good saying that it is uncertain if you will win . . .', *Pensées*, p. 155].

[38] 'Car il ne s'agit pas pour Spinoza d'une véritable option [. . .]. En réalité, selon un schéma de pensée que nous retrouvons toujours chez Spinoza, on n'a rien à perdre en abandonnant richesses, honneurs ou plaisirs des sens . . .', *Servitude et Liberté selon Spinoza*, p. 7.

[39] *Pensées*, p. 156.

Pascal responds: it is necessary to wager, for you are committed; and his interlocutor does not seem to object to this.[40] All in all, a glance at the human condition suffices to show that we do not have the choice to make a choice; henceforth, the wager imposes itself. By contrast, the Spinozist response first concerns the refusal to wager: for a long time the narrator seeks a compromise, something no Pascalian player would do, for that would be to attempt to change the rules of the game. Something extraordinary happens in Spinoza's text: the elements of the game themselves make it known that it is impossible to reformulate the rules of the game. In other words, in the *proemium* the narrator comes to the point of choosing after having been subjected to the games' rules much more than he has accepted them. The narrator thus inhabits conditions in which experience has imposed upon him the necessary inversion of his certainties, without there being any real calculation on his part. Moreover, the emphasis is placed on the certainty of the true good and no longer on its mode of acquisition. Thus, in Spinoza's text, we are at the antipodes of Pascalian incomprehensibility.[41]

What Pascal's text and the *proemium* have in common is thus their descriptive aspects, in particular the perspective they take on Man's situation prior to the beginnings of his hesitations (in Pascal's wager, the brief allusion to misery; in the *TdIE*, the terms *vana et futilia*). Above all, they share a moment where both describe the same thing: the hesitations of a mind that no longer adheres to its former certainties but lacks the strength to embrace new ones; a mind that is in some sense more unhappy now, having been divested of its former errors, than it was in its state of naivety. In Pascal, what is felt is not blind misery, but a second kind of misery, one that is revealed to us when we want to be able to believe. What corresponds to this in the *proemium* is what I have called Spinoza's 'tragic' side. However, as soon as we turn to the description or the analysis of what is at stake in the two texts, the two thinkers part ways. We get an even clearer sense of this in a text of Pascal's where such a description is precisely foregrounded. It is not in the *Pensées* that we should seek out such a text but in the pamphlet *On the Conversion of the Sinner*.[42] We find in this text a vocabulary and a procedure,

---

[40] The thesis is then reaffirmed: 'you would have to play (since you must necessarily play', *Pensées*, p. 154.

[41] To complete this analysis, it would be necessary to also take into account the way the obstacles are overcome and to compare this with the *adsidua meditatio*. Cf. P. Magnard, 'Sur les relations entre le pari et le discours de la machine', *Nature et Histoire dans l'Apologétique de Pascal*, p. 216 ff.

[42] *Œuvres complètes*, présentation et notes de Louis Lafuma, Paris: Seuil, 1963, pp. 290–91. Father Guerrier, by whom one of the two manuscripts was transmitted,

both of which possess traits that recall Spinoza's writings. We see how a new aspiration causes the soul to lose 'the repose which it found in the things which made her delight'. If the soul can no longer enjoy itself in this way, it is because experience has taught[43] it that these are 'vain and fragile things'. Henceforth, 'it considers perishable things as perishable and even already perished'. The soul then sets out in 'search of the true good', but at the beginning of its quest feels both fear and bitterness, for it does not know how to choose between the two kinds of objects: 'On one side, the vanity of the visible objects interests it more than the hope of the invisible, and on the other the solidity of the invisible interests it more than the vanity of the visible.' At the end the soul understands that the true good must possess two qualities: 'the one that it shall last as long as herself, and that it cannot be taken away from her except by its consent, and the other that there shall be nothing more lovely'. It sees that in the love it had for the world, it found – or believed it had found – the second quality; but as the world does not possess the first, 'it knows that it is not the Sovereign Good'.[44]

On this point, the two texts clearly diverge, even in terms of their lexicon (the soul begins to seek the Sovereign Good that is 'above it', addresses itself to the Creator, prays ardently to Him, etc.). It remains the case, however, that the entire first half of Pascal's *On the Conversion of the Sinner* – right up to the first occurrence of the term 'Sovereign Good' – takes place in a climate that very much recalls the first pages of the *TdIE*. This can be explained by the fact that Spinoza's text attempts to stay as close as possible to the tradition of conversion narratives, which it tries to synthesise through its description. But we can go further. For Pascal's text above all represents an attempt to group together the descriptive motifs from the Augustinian tradition, albeit without explaining them – whence the constitution of an analytics of aspiration and prevarication that recalls the Spinozist journey. Thus, we can conclude that, within these limits, the aim of the two passages is very similar – in contrast to what we noted concerning Descartes and Spinoza.

And yet, reciprocally, the scope of the two texts is different in every way. The same analysis of hesitation and of the aspiration to the true good is framed in terms of two profoundly different procedures. This distance appears best in the first phrase from the text *On the Conversion of the Sinner*,

---

attributed it to Jacqueline Pascal. Lafuma judged that 'il est incontestablement de Blaise', p. 290.

[43] 'Quand les choses du monde auraient quelque plaisir solide, ce qui est reconnu pour faux par un nombre d'expériens si funestes et si continuelles...', ibid., 290.

[44] Ibid., p. 291.

which we have not yet cited: 'The first thing with which God inspires the soul that he deigns to touch truly is a knowledge and most extraordinary insight by which the soul considers new things and herself in a manner wholly new.' We should note here less the reference to God and His will and more the fact that experience is explained (at least in an indicative fashion) before it is even described. Thus, even though they identify the same traits, Pascal and Spinoza's inscription of the lived forms of human impotence have different meanings. The only common element is the two authors' anti-humanism.[45] The movement from an initial impotence to a secondary impotence is an important aspect of experience, one that will subsequently be opposed in Spinoza's *Ethics* both to the Stoics and to the Cartesians.[46] But in Pascal this movement signals the power of Grace, while for Spinoza it refers to a path that is immanent to the natural possibility of accessing the true good.

In sum, it is less the argument of the wager that brings the two authors together and more the conditions of the wager and what it gestures to (in Pascal's text, this is the allusion to the unhappiness that is to be transcended). This consciousness of unhappiness is made present in the *Apology* by means of procedures that are close to Spinozist experience.[47] This unhappiness presents itself as given, as tied to the vanity of things (even if the explanation given for this property is different), and as readable in the very groove of people's actions – both the actions of others and of the person speaking. For divergent demonstrative ends, Pascal and Spinoza both need to produce a radical description of ethics, with the remainder of their discourse founded on this lived vision of a subject who is riven, impotent and blind. To do this, they both give an intensity and a sense of proximity to

---

[45] With respect to Pascal, cf. H. Gouhier, 'L'Antihumanisme de Pascal', *Revue des travaux de l'Académie des Sciences morales et politiques*, 1962, reprised in *Etudes sur l'histoire des idées en France depuis le XVIIème siècle*, Paris: Vrin, 1980, pp. 49–65, as well as the summary in which Gouhier discusses the Bremondian notion of a 'humanisme dévot', ibid., pp. 177–83.

[46] Perhaps humanism could be defined in terms of the rejection of such a secondary misery. A doctrine that knows of only one form of misery that is natural to the human being and of the means to overcome it is thus opposed to those that highlight how the awareness of, and the will to extract oneself from, the first form of misery leads us to an even greater sense of impotence that can plunge us into a state of at least provisional hopelessness. Descartes, Hobbes and the neo-Stoics are on one side of the divide, Pascal and Spinoza on the other – but they immediately distinguish themselves from each other.

[47] Cf. the formula 'rien n'est plus ordinaire que cela', Lafuma 79, Br. 128, p. 509 ['Nothing is more common than that', *Pensées*, 37].

commonplaces transmitted by the tradition. It is not by chance if Pascal also often has recourse to the *I* – and indeed to an anonymous *I* – in order to produce such an intensity.

I have thus shown that in these few pages, Spinoza, without using the technical concepts of his system, undertakes both to recount his journey and to engage the reader on the path towards philosophy. He has recourse to notions the majority of which can be found elsewhere in his system, and in a way that is compatible with the use that is made of them here. However, he does not use demonstrations of a geometrical or definitional nature, nor does he engage in polemics as we see him do in certain Scholia from the *Ethics*.

However, what is said in the *proemium* is based on a procedure whose purpose is to establish certain results. This procedure can be used because, outside of the *animus* itself, there exists a possibility of learning and communicating. This possibility is experience. To speak of experience is to refer to the world of common life, to everyday language, to acts and aims that are shared by everyone. This not only implicates the individual but also involves a certain relation between the individual and the universal, a relation that insinuates itself into the very singularity of the narrative subject and which, on occasion, casts a shadow over its apparent transparency.

It remains to once again summarise what I believe I have shown regarding the text's content. These few pages, it has been said, are charged with rhetoric. This is true. They are inscribed in an ethical tradition – something that I do not contest. But this rhetoric and this tradition are inserted into a singular order, which brings forth a new figure. On the one hand, it is possible to enumerate a certain number of propositions that concern the way in which the *TdIE*'s prologue is distinct from the tradition on the basis of which it appeals to its reader. On the other, a careful reading of its forms of reasoning allows us to identify a number of procedures that are significant in the prologue's construction.

Let us begin with the propositions that indicate the *proemium*'s originality. I will present them as so many theses by which my interpretation can be seen as distinct from other possible interpretations, which overestimate the weight of the tradition.

- Perishable goods are not 'false goods'.
- They are what is at stake in the sequences of the spontaneous and ethically neutral actions that constitute common life.
- Their illusory aspect consists not in their proper essence but in their structural limit, which makes one consider them as Sovereign Goods.

- The narrator's aspiration turns not to a Sovereign Good that is already given, but towards a 'true good' that is constituted on the basis of the positive aspects of perishable goods.
- The structure of the journey consists in placing the goods of common life in new interrogative situations. Each one of these situations makes the goods reveal new aspects of themselves, thereby determining in an ever richer way the image of the true good.
- None of these situations is constituted freely by the narrator; rather, they come about thanks to the preceding crisis. Each draws its lessons either from the experience of past life, or from present experience.
- The *animus* draws its singularity from the experience that constitutes it, much more so than from its own resources.

Furthermore, we can note a certain number of the narrative's characteristics:

— The motifs that organise the journey are not laid out geometrically, but arise in accordance with their own specific order. This experiential order includes elements that are given at the outset. It also includes elements that emerge in the course of the confrontation between the mind and goods. These elements arise from what we have called a heuristics of the occasion: they appear, as the various levels of experience unfold, in the form of a certain number of questions that are repeatedly raised. They emerge in a practical form, and when they are formulated in a more general way it is only briefly and after the fact.

— Thanks to this procedure there emerges a logic of anticipation: along this Spinozist path we see appear, albeit in a minor key, themes that belong to the system. These themes sometimes appear in a different form and are presented in the course of action and not in the geometrical concatenation that will produce them in the *Ethics*. These themes include: the relativity of good and evil; the necessity of the search for what is advantageous to one's self; self-preservation; the link between thought and the Sovereign Good; the insufficiency of abstract Reason for dominating the passions; progress in the knowledge of the true good as a remedy to the affects; and the presence of the eternal in the world of experience.

It remains for us to analyse what makes these results possible – that is, to determine the effective content of the register of experience – and to find to what extent this form of experience is particular to a certain stage in the development of Spinoza's philosophy.

ANNEX: TABLE OF THE THREE GOODS AND OF THEIR FUNCTIONS

	Pleasure	Honour	Wealth
§ 2		commoda	commoda
§ 3, 4, 5	• fruitio • maxime impenditur • summa tristitia	• distrahitur mens • ad captum • non datur paenitentia • sed magis ac magis • summa tristitia	• distrahitur mens • propter • non datur paenitentia • sed magis ac magis • summa tristitia
§ 7, 8	mortem accelerare	passi sunt	persecutio ad necem
§ 10	non deponere	non deponere	non deponere
§11	tanquam media	tanquam media	tanquam media
§ 17	ad tuendam valetudinem	• ad captum vulgi loqui/operari/scopum • mores civitatis imitare	• ad vitam et valetudinem . . . • ad mores . . . imitandos
Relation with the true good	fruitio	• continuity • power	• continuity • relation with others
Relation with the subject	Impossibility of a continuous joy	• imitation of others • hopes and disappointments	• limitation of power • hopes and disappointments

6

The Circles of Experience

1. The Limit-Point

At the end of paragraph 11, the narrator's journey has led both him and the reader to the following clearly articulated decision: to seek the true good. It has also led him to the three-part knowledge that justifies this decision: the harmfulness of the other goods, the at best intermittent force of a remedy, and the reappearance of perishable goods as means in the service of the sought-after end, the true good. Certainly, these final determinations of the decision remain vague and allusive: the intervals during which thought turns away from certain evils are suggested more than they are described, while the narrator's ever-greater knowledge of the true good emerges quite suddenly, as if it had anticipated its own concept. The same can be said of the enigmatic 'end'[1] to which everything leads and which Spinoza speaks of for the first time here, without giving us much information about it. This 'end' will nevertheless serve as the motor for the organisation of life from paragraph 14 onwards.[2] One might expect the narrator's journey

---

[1] 'Sed contra ad finem, propter quem queruntur, multum conducent', § 11, G II, p. 8, ll. 8–9 [*TdIE* 11; *CWS* I, 10].

[2] In the two forms of *finis* and *scopus*; 'Hic est itaque *finis* . . .', § 14, G II, p. 8, l. 27 [*TdIE* 14; *CWS* I, 11]; 'me omnes scientias ad unum *finem* et *scopum* dirigere velle', § 16, G II, p. 9, ll. 13–14 [*TdIE* 16; *CWS* I, 11]; 'et sic omne illud, quod in scientiis nihil ad *finem* nostrum nos promovet, tanquam inutile erit rejiciendum', § 16, G II, p. 9, ll. 15–17 [*TdIE* 16; *CWS* I, 11]; 'illa omnia operari, quae nihil impedimenti adferunt, quo minus nostrum *scopum* attingamus', § 17, G II, p. 9, ll. 23–4 [*TdIE* 17; *CWS* I, 12]; 'ad mores civitatis, qui nostrum *scopum* non oppugnant, imitandos', § 17, G II, p. 9, ll. 32–3 [*TdIE* 17; *CWS* I, 12]; 'ad emendandum scilicet intellectum, eumque aptum reddendum ad res tali modo intelligendas, quo opus est, ut nostrum *finem* assequamur', § 18, G II, p. 9, l. 35–p. 10, l. 2 [*TdIE* 18; *CWS* I, 12]; and § 25 before distinguishing the modes of knowledge: 'Ut autem ex his optimus eligatur modus percipiendi, requiritur,

to continue and for these allusions to be completed and clarified,[3] right up to the point of giving a total explanation – an explanation that would coincide with the beginning of the system.

And yet, none of this happens. At the beginning of paragraph 12, there is an abrupt change of register: for two paragraphs we are witness to a veritable technical and systematic presentation, one that runs counter to the style hitherto adopted and which is written in the present tense. The narrative is thus complete, truly complete, and not simply interrupted. For what will now be presented (the enumeration of rules for action and forms of knowledge) will no longer be written in the past tense but in the future tense,[4] or in the form of: 'it is necessary . . .' (that is, in the form of *necesse est*[5] or of the equivalent verbal adjective).[6] In paragraphs 12 to 13, Spinoza speaks of man and no longer of the narrator: the universal is thus an object of which the subject is speaking; it no longer lies at the heart of the narrator's position of enunciation. The *I* remains, but it has become an assertive *I* analogous to the one we find in the *Ethics*: 'I say . . .', 'I mean . . .',[7] and 'when I say what I mean, I define . . .'.[8] Finally, the text's vocabulary is itself henceforth

---

ut breviter enumeremus, quae sint necessaria media, ut nostrum *finem* assequamur', G II, p. 12, ll. 14–16 [*TdIE* 25; *CWS* I, 15]. The term *finis* returns with the same meaning in the letter to Bouwmeester on method (G IV, p. 189, l. 14 [*Ep. XXXVII* [to Johannes Bouwmeester]; *CWS* II, 32]).

[3] This appears to be indicated by the subordinate clause 'ut suo loco ostendemus', which comes at the end of paragraph 11. But in the *TdIE* this *locus* is never reached (except if we treat the statements from paragraphs 16–17 as a demonstration).

[4] 'Me accingam . . .' § 18, G II, p. 9, l. 35 [*TdIE* 18; *CWS* I, 12].

[5] 'Necesse est tantum de Natura intelligere [. . .]; deinde formare . . .', § 14, G II, p. 8, l. 32 [*TdIE* 14; *CWS* I, 11]; 'necesse est vivere', § 17, G II, p. 9, l. 20 [*TdIE* 17; *CWS* I, 12].

[6] 'Danda est opera', 'concinnanda est integra Medicina', 'Mechanica nullo modo est contemnenda', § 15, G II, p. 9, ll. 6–10 [*TdIE* 11; *CWS* I, 11]; 'excogitandus est modus medendi intellectus', § 16, G II, p. 9, ll. 10–11 [*TdIE* 16; *CWS* I, 11]. I remarked above that this use of the verbal adjective had begun subtly in paragraph 10 ('quod valde est desiderandum totisque viribus quaerendum'): on this point as on others, the end of the path presents affinities with what comes after – albeit without founding these affinities, and thus without diminishing the impression of a rupture having occurred.

[7] 'Quid per verum bonum intelligam', § 12, G II, p. 8, l. 10 [*TdIE* 12; *CWS* I, 10].

[8] Moreover, the definitions very quickly come to be stated in the passive voice 'bonum et malum non nisi respective dicantur', § 12, G II, p. 8, l. 12 [*TdIE* 12; *CWS* 10]; 'Nihil enim in sua natura spectatum, perfectum dicitur vel imperfectum', ibid., ll. 14–15; 'omne illud [. . .] vocatur verum bonum', § 13, G II, p. 8, ll. 22–3 [*TdIE* 13; *CWS* I, 10].

of a specialised nature: we see the ideas of the perfect and the imperfect appear,[9] along with the order of Nature[10] and its determinate laws.[11] Above all, the notion of the good – which up to this point had been kept within the register of the familiar – becomes the object of a definition and thus makes the transition to philosophy and its lexicon. The same goes for the complex expressions that are linked to it.[12] We are therefore no longer in the domain of simplicity and familiarity that characterised the preceding pages. Paragraphs 12 to 13 thus constitute a theoretical bloc, one that is not entirely separable from the rest of the text, but which is still clearly delimited. The reason these paragraphs are not separable is that Spinoza takes care to say that he is pausing to explain something:[13] what follows is therefore necessary to the progression of his argument, but in making this argument Spinoza has abandoned the form of a narrative. The moment of experience has come to an end.[14]

It is thus time to take the measure of experience, to understand how it has led us to this point. But first it is necessary to consider what, precisely, experience leads us to – specifically, the explanation given in paragraphs 12 to 13, which opens onto the programme of the emendation of the intellect. We will then be able to measure the difference and evaluate the link between the two registers. This difference and this link will also determine the questions we will put to the procedure Spinoza pursues in the first eleven paragraphs.

The explanation that is given immediately after the journey's end brings together three theses, each of which can be found elsewhere in Spinoza's system[15] and whose articulation conditions the meaning of this system's ethical elaborations: the relativity of the good, the construction of an *exemplar*, and the positive definition of the Sovereign Good. These three theses are not presented here in as developed a form as elsewhere, but they can still be clearly recognised. Spinoza proceeds in a number of stages, of which the first

---

[9] 'Eodem modo ac perfectum et imperfectum', § 12, G II, p. 8, l. 14 [*TdIE* 12; *CWS* I, 10].

[10] 'Secundum aeternum ordinem', § 12, G II, p. 8, ll. 16–17 [*TdIE* 12; *CWS* I, 10].

[11] 'Secundum certas Naturae leges', § 12, G II, p. 8, l. 17 [*TdIE* 12; *CWS* I, 10].

[12] *Verum bonum; summum bonum*, § 13, G II, p. 8, ll. 22–5 [*TdIE* 13; *CWS* I, 10].

[13] 'Hic tantum breviter dicam . . .', § 12, G II, p. 8, l. 10 [*TdIE* 12; *CWS* I, 10].

[14] Theo Zweerman has clearly identified this discontinuity, which he describes as a 'manifest transformation of style and content', *Spinoza's inleiding tot de filosofie*, p. 64.

[15] *KV*, I, 6, 8; I, 10 (good and evil are beings of reason), II, 4 (good and evil; the idea of a perfect man); *Pensées métaphysiques*, I, 6; *TTP*, Chapter IV, G III, pp. 59–60 (Sovereign Good) [*TTP* IV, 12; *CWS* II, 128]; *Ethics* IV, Praef. [*CWS* I, 543–6].

two seem, *prima facie*, to be contradictory. The goal of this explanation consists, he says, in defining two of the expressions that have so far been used:[16] *verum bonum* and *summum bonum*. 'To understand this properly', Spinoza writes, we must refer to the notions of *bonum* and *malum* in themselves. We thus expect a definition to be given. Yet this is not what happens. Rather, what we get is an attempt to put all of this into perspective: *bonum* and *malum* can be spoken of 'only in a certain respect'. What should we understand by this? These notions are relative – but to what? The expression *adeo ut*,[17] if we take it to be more than a purely syntactical pivot, expresses the idea that there are degrees of relativity and that good and evil are relative in the strongest sense of the term. The relativity of a good does not concern only one aspect of its being; rather, the being of a good is exhausted by this relation. As a consequence, the properties of good and evil are radically excluded from having a bearing on the deepest consistency of things: nothing can be said to be good 'in sua natura spectata'.[18] The proof of this is that the same thing can be good or evil depending on the different relations it is envisaged as having (*respectus*, which *respective* renders as an adverb). This is a radical thesis, and one that Spinoza expresses with force. No proof is given of it, nor any examples. One might be tempted to search for these in what has been said above: is Spinoza not simply repeating here what he said in paragraph 1[19] or paragraph 11?[20] One might imagine that money, for instance, if it is taken as an end in itself, will lead to ruin, but if, by contrast, it is taken *tanquam medium*, it will be useful (an example of utility is given further on in rule 3). We see how money can be 'good' in a certain way and 'evil' in another. Yet, so long as we remain at this level, we have perhaps not reached the most profound sense of the relativity of good and evil. We remain at a superficial level of relativity. The example cited above suggests that there is an absolute good and an absolute evil: namely, the preservation and loss of life. Furthermore, in this context, describing any given thing as 'good' is valid only because an equivalence has been established between the good and the useful – an

---

[16] 'Quid per verum bonum intelligam, et simul quid sit summum bonum', G II, § 12, p. 8, ll. 10–11 [*TdIE* 12; *CWS* I, 10].

[17] 'Adeo ut una eademque res possit dici bona, vel mala, secundum diversos respectus', § 12, G II, p. 8, ll. 12–14 [*TdIE* 12; *CWS* I, 10].

[18] This expression is only used with respect to the notions of *perfectum* and *imperfectum*, but the context shows that the structure of the reasoning is the same in both cases.

[19] 'Nihil neque boni, neque mali in se habere', G II, p. 6, l. 24 [*TdIE* 6; *CWS* I, 8]. Cf. the remarks on this subject in the following paragraph.

[20] In the distinction between *propter se* and *tanquam media*, G II, p. 8, ll. 4–9 [*TdIE* 11; *CWS* I, 10].

equivalence that would be familiar to readers of the rest of the system, but for which no justification has been given here: neither in what is said in paragraph 12, nor in the journey that precedes it (the only other possibility is given in the brief formula from paragraph 6).[21] I would add here that the content of paragraph 1, which appears identical to the content from paragraph 12, itself an apparent summary of the ultimate conclusions of the journey, was in fact subject to two restrictions that limited its field of application: those things that were feared 'had nothing of good or bad in themselves', but were feared 'only insofar as [the] mind was moved by them'.[22] Moreover, this 'nothing' was nuanced by the phrase 'except insofar as'.[23] This is equivalent to saying that there exists, at least at a certain level, both good and evil, and that these are to be situated in a movement of the mind. This is not the same thing (at least at the point where we find ourselves) as reducing good and evil to a pure relation. Thus, the second preamble to the decision from paragraph 1 does not formulate a universal conclusion concerning relativity in the strong sense of the term – that is, one that would have implications for every good. It only deduces, albeit rigorously, a lesson from what experience has taught us about the relations between the mind and the field of distribution of its fears. Thus, in paragraph 12, the status of the relativity of the goods is quite strange: on the one hand, Spinoza is advancing an argument here for which he does not, and cannot, provide a demonstration (when he does demonstrate this argument, namely in the *Ethics*, it is with the help of concepts that are not yet available); on the other hand, this argument has not been entirely constituted by the preceding experience. As for perfection – a concept whose critique can be found elsewhere in his system[24] – it is given here in a formula that is even shorter and more enigmatic still: 'The same applies to perfect and imperfect.'[25] Thus, we do indeed find a sort of justification for this argument, but it is produced only in light of a future knowledge. Here, too, the system appears to be presupposed in its first two representatives, the terms *bonum* and *malum*. The relativity of the good and the perfect (if we understand relativity in the strong sense that is given to it here) is therefore a thesis that is not drawn from experience. Nor is it demonstrated *more geometrico*.

[21] 'Quid mihi esset utilius', § 6, G II, p. 6, l. 24 [*TdIE* 6; *CWS* I, 8]. Cf. the remarks on this matter in the following paragraph.
[22] 'Omnia a quibus et quae timebam', § 1, G II, p. 5, ll. 9–10 [*TdIE* 1; *CWS* I, 7].
[23] 'except insofar as [my] mind was moved by them', 'nisi quatenus ab iis animus movebatur', §1, G II, p. 5, l. 11 [*TdIE* 1; *CWS* 7].
[24] *Ethics* IV, Praef.; *CWS* I, 543–6.
[25] 'Eodem modo ac perfectum et imperfectum', § 12, G II, p. 8, l. 14 [*TdIE* 12; *CWS* I, 10].

Let us at least concede that this relativity is taken as given in the text, even if no proof is provided for it. However, when Spinoza does establish this thesis, would we not expect to see him reject the notions of the true or Sovereign Good? If every good is relative, how can one of them be said to be 'true' or 'supreme'? If these notions are not rejected out of hand, then they should be reduced to the preservation of life. Such a reduction would be analogous to the procedure followed by Hobbes – something that should not be particularly surprising, given that the critique of the idea of the absolute good is Hobbesian.[26] And yet, this is not at all that happens: Spinoza defines in positive terms both a true and a Sovereign Good, and grounds neither of them exclusively in the preservation of the individual. Everything comes down to the role played by the *humana imbecillitas*, whose thought is incapable of following the necessary order of nature. Thus, man, failing to see the necessary causes that make him what he currently is, compares himself to a model of human nature that is 'stronger than his own' and seeks to bridge the gap between what he is and what he can conceive of.[27] It is in the space defined by such a gap and by the effort made to pass from one side to the other that ethical notions are situated. Let us leave aside the specific content of the stronger nature that is in question here (the knowledge of the mind's union with the whole of Nature):[28] Spinoza explicitly says that this

---

[26] Not only does Hobbes refuse, as I noted above, the very idea of the Sovereign Good; the relativity of the notions of good and evil is a central thesis in his thought: 'But whatsoever is the object of any mans Appetite or Desire; that is it, which he for his part calleth *Good*: And the object of his Hate, and Aversion, *Evill*; And of his Contempt, *Vile*, and *Inconsiderable*. For these words of Good, Evill, and Contemptible, are ever used with relation to the person that useth them: There being nothing simply and absolutely so; nor any common Rule of Good and Evill, to be taken from the nature of the objects themselves; but from the Person of the man (where there is no Commonwealth,) from the Person that representeth it; or from an Arbitrator or Judge, whom men disagreeing shall by consent be set up, and make his sentence the Rule thereof', *Leviathan*, Part I, Chapter 6, pp. 120–1. This does not mean that for him all goods are equal; rather, Hobbes considers self-preservation as a 'first good' ('Bonorum autem primum est sua cuique conservatio', *De Homine*, XI, § 6 – the title in the margin says 'bonorum maximum') and as 'the greatest of goods' the dynamic that carries it to its maximal effect ('Bonorum autem maximum est, ad fines semper ulteriores minime impedita progressio', *De Homine*, XI, § 15).

[27] There is an analogous theme in the *Short Treatise*, II, Chapter IV. Cf. J. Ganault, 'Immanence et Transcendance dans le *Court Traité*', *Archives de Philosophie*, 51/1 (1988), § 4, pp. 35–7.

[28] 'Cognitio unionis quam Mens cum tota natura habet', § 13, G II, p. 8, ll. 26–7 [*TdIE* 13; *CWS* I, 11].

nature cannot be deduced from the present demonstration.[29] What is most decisive is that this 'natura multo firmior' can be conceived by the *imbecillitas*. Confronted with such a procedure, the reader who is unfamiliar with the preceding pages might be surprised. They might ask: should we read here a condemnation of the illusions of human weakness – and, by extension, of the ideas of the true good and the Sovereign Good? Spinoza, however, seems to approve of the effort incarnated in these illusions. Should we therefore admit that it is man's weakness, indeed blindness, in the face of the laws of nature that allows him to progress? That would constitute a kind of negative valorisation. In fact, the analogy with the rest of the system helps us see that the figure of the *imbecillitas* is not a pure negation: it names human impotence, that is, a power that is *de facto* limited and determined. Thus, to understand this thesis, we need something more than what is given to us here, for instance the theory of the *exemplar* such as we find it in the *Ethics*,[30] or at least an equivalent. The path of experience cannot provide what is needed for this construction.

That being said, the effects of this construction retrospectively clarify what has hitherto only been glimpsed: the positive definition of the Sovereign Good allows us to understand both that the aspiration was justified and that the path was possible, while the notion of the true good such as it has now been defined allows us to link together a series of acts judged no longer in terms of their autonomous value (we now understand why this value changes with each different level of experience) but in terms of their relation to the *cognitio unionis*. Everything that was lived and inchoate at the level of experience now finds the concepts that allow it to be understood and presented in an extremely compact fashion.

To sum up, on the one hand the explanation from paragraphs 12 to 13 coheres with the rest Spinoza's system and exhibits some of this system's most striking architectonic effects. On the other hand, it also coheres with the journey from paragraphs 1 to 11, on which it sheds new light and for which it presents a justification from the point of view of the system.

At the same time, however, this explanation is not founded on this journey. Experience leads us to the system, but it does not provide the means

---

[29] He even says this twice: in the text ('ostendemus suo loco') and in the note ('haec fusius suo loco explicantur').

[30] 'Nam quia ideam hominis, tanquam naturae humanae exemplar, quod intueamur, formare cupimus, nobis ex usu erit haec eadem vocabula eo, quo dixi, sensu retinere [...] Deinde homines perfectiores aut imperfectiores dicemus, quatenus ad hoc idem exemplar magis aut minus accedunt', *Ethics* IV, Praef., G II, p. 208, ll. 15–18 and 22–4 [CWS I, 543–4].

for the system's commencement. The examples given suffice to show this: the concepts present in the explanation for the most part exceed what has been established in the preceding paragraphs. Might we not then fear to see a circle appear? If the status of the final certainties acquired in the course of the *animus*' progression is based only on the explanation that follows, and if this explanation fails to provide any proof for what it advances, where does the narrator's certainty come from? The limit-point would thus be the point at which an incoherence is revealed in the passage from experience to systematicity. Commentators have not failed to highlight the fact that what we find here is a 'leap', or at least a rupture.[31]

It seems to me that we can respond to this objection if we mark as clearly as possible the difference in register between these two sections: experience is not the beginning of the system; it is therefore illusory to expect it to found it. In fact, rigorously speaking, the system is founded exclusively on its own architectonic. In the space of this architectonic, the system produces its own beginning. In the *Ethics*, this beginning will be the construction of the idea of God.[32] But the system itself shows us how another beginning can

---

[31] Elbogen, *Der Tractatus de intellectus emendatione und seine Stellung in der Philosophie Spinozas*, p. 43; Gebhardt, *Spinozas Abhandlung . . .*, p. 51; H. H. Joachim, *Spinoza's Tractatus De Intellectus Emendatione: A Commentary*, Oxford: Clarendon Press, 1940, pp. 20–3. This latter writes: 'The explanation is brief, dogmatic, and very inadequate; and in one respect inconsistent verbally with what precedes', p. 21. Finally, P. Di Vona writes: 'Con questa teoria del vero bene [sc. that of paragraphs 1 to 11] sta in contrasto la successiva definizione del *verum bonum* e del *summum bonum*. [. . .] Il contrasto di questa pagina con l'inizio del *Tractatus de intellectus emendatione* crediamo che non possa essere negato', *Spinoza e i Transcendentali*, Naples: Morano, 1977, pp. 224–5.

[32] It would be necessary to discuss here in detail the theses developed on this subject by P. Macherey in his book *Hegel ou Spinoza*, Paris: Maspero, 1979, which has played a crucial role in the history of studies on the reception of Spinozism by presenting an exemplary model of how one can pass from a logic of comparison to one of confrontation. Macherey remarks first of all that the notion of the beginning plays an essential role in the way that Hegel determines Spinoza's theoretical and historical position: Spinozism is at once a philosophy that begins and a philosophy of the beginning (pp. 24–31). Further on, he criticises this affirmation as being tied to a formalist prejudice, one that sees in the beginning of the *Ethics* an 'absolute beginning'. In fact, 'substance, attributs, modes, tels qu'ils apparaissent dans ces principes liminaires, sont justement l'équivalent de ce caillou mal dégrossi dont les premiers forgerons ont eu besoin pour "commencer" leur travail: ce sont des notions encore abstraites, de simples mots, des idées naturelles qui ne prendront véritablement une signification qu'à partir du moment où elles fonctionneront dans des démonstrations, en y produisant des effets réels, exprimant ainsi une puissance dont elles ne disposaient pas au départ', p. 66. Macherey is right so far as the mode of exposition is concerned; it remains no less the case that for Spinoza philosophy has a beginning and that it is important to present

exist – namely, the beginning of the philosopher and not of philosophy; a beginning that explains how the individual sets out from what is given and makes their way towards the rigour of knowledge and freedom. The impression of a leap or a rupture is only the reverse side of this strict disjunction between these two beginnings. Experience, then, is the occasion for philosophy; it is in no way its foundation. In terms of the system's order of reasons, this occasion can be thought rationally, just as any other human fact can be. But in terms of experience's internal order, experience cannot depend on the strong rationality proper to the system. Rather, experience brings together forms of reasoning that are internal to the lived: forms of thought that makes us 'see' or 'find' certain things, along with the pressure exerted by various movements that the mind lives through and that produce certain results. This pressure and these images would be inappropriate as the beginning of a philosophical system. Yet they are perfectly placed at the beginning of an experience situated at heart of the given and of common life.[33]

And yet, if we escape the possibility of a circle in this way, do we not fall into another circle – not a logical circle, but into one of the circles of hell? What, precisely, is the purpose of experience as it is presented to us here, that is, in terms of its own self-suppression? The different moments of experience seem destined to show in ever more intense ways that common life, in which we spontaneously exist, is a site of unhappiness that is comparable to a mortal illness, a source of perdition. Can experience, rooted as it is in common life, only devalue this life – and, in so doing, devalue itself – since it shows the necessity of another kind of knowledge? If this is the case, then the end of the journey is effectively equivalent to a murder. The final and sole lesson that experience can give us is that we must change terrain. As soon as this thought arises, experience appears to have no other purpose than to guide us out of common life by way of a crisis of exceptional intensity. Have we come to recognise the power of common life to teach us lessons through uncommon situations only to be led on a trajectory outside of common life? Certainly, *experientia docuit*, but in experience we turn in circles, and the only lesson it can offer us is the necessity of its own end. One would be justified in thinking that such narrowness is tied to another trait we have already

    this beginning in the most radical way possible, as is shown by Spinoza's repeated efforts to give the maximum amount of power to this exposition.

[33] These remarks concern only the relations of the *proemium* to the system. In terms of the very different problem of the relations of the *TdIE* in its entirety to the *Ethics*, see for example H. D Dijn, 'The Significance of Spinoza's Treatise on the Improvement of the Understanding (*Tractatus de Intellectus Emendatione*)', *Algemeen Nederlands Tijdschrift voor Wijsbegeerte*, 66/1 (1974), p. 1–16, in particular p. 12 ff.

identified: the absence or weakness of the *conatus*. It is perhaps because the limitation of human power is seen as *imbecillitas* (a term that will not return with the same meaning in the *Ethics*) that we can derive nothing from it.

What remains is for us to do is to try and understand how it was possible to arrive at this point – that is, at this point and no other. We must therefore inquire, not into what experience teaches us – the text tells us this very clearly – but into what the narrator's journey was such that it could teach us these lessons.

2. The Effective Content of Experience

The term *experientia* appears only once, at the beginning of the journey. It could therefore be said to concern only the journey's first phase. Nevertheless, I have argued that it characterises the journey as a whole and that one could inscribe under the heading of *experientia* not only the vanity and futility that are explicitly referred to, but also the state of unquestioned certainty that preceded the journey, along with the different moments through which the narrator passed. A certain number of external indicators tell us this is the case: the recurrence of the verb *videre* and analogous expressions; the absence of a geometrical demonstration and of discussions founded on a philosophical lexicon; and the references to life and goods. But my conviction was above all grounded in a single internal proof: namely, the homogeneity in tone between these eleven paragraphs and the text's first sentence. It thus seemed legitimate to me to consider the entirety of this sequence (in opposition to what follows) as arising – as I announced at the beginning of this work, though there I did so in terms of a simple difference with other commentators – from a special register: that of experience. Put differently, this unique term *experientia* is part of a system of other terms and procedures, and has a style that gives a strong unity to this sequence as a whole. I argue that everything that precedes suffices to show this.

A new question now arises: what is the content of this experiential register, such as we encounter it here? In fact, when I put forward this definition, it was for methodological reasons, and I insisted on the *tone* and the *mise en scène* that distinguished the *proemium* from an autobiography or from a purely rhetorical exhortation. Now that the journey has been completed, we can go a little further and ask what its *effective content* is. Let us consider, then, the path that has been followed, less to study its results than to determine from what perspective these results were produced. In doing so we will come to know what this perspective itself consists in. Are we now in a position to say what the experiential order is? This mode of thought has emerged little by little beneath our eyes, through the situations and results it has revealed to us. I identified at the beginning three traits that were signs of the irreducible tone of the experiential register: familiarity, tension and singularity. I then noted at the end three procedures that structured the frontier between the experiential and the systematic dimensions of Spinoza's philosophy: a heuristics of the occasion, a dialectic of limitation and a logic of anticipation. It is these traits and these procedures that will allow us to indicate the principal characteristics of the experiential mode.

A. Description and Demonstration

We can glimpse the first characteristic of the experiential mode if we take into account both the first trait that we identified in the *proemium*'s tone – its familiarity – and the procedure that we have called a heuristics of the occasion.

What is most striking to the reader in these pages is first of all a certain descriptive tone. The feeling of the familiar that grips the reader correlates with a certain attitude adopted by the narrator, an attitude that seeks neither to explain nor to demonstrate but which restricts itself to grouping phenomena together in the light of memory. I noted the abundant use of the verb *to see* in this segment and its quasi-disappearance in the rest of the *Treatise*, where it is replaced by *intelligere*.[34] The verb *to see* does indeed have a relation to this descriptive tone, which itself disappears when the stage of making an inventory of experience has been completed. *To see* involves letting phenomena appear in their purity, presenting them to the narrator and to the reader. Letting these phenomena appear means that they are not explained through their causes, nor reduced to a nature that would stand in for them (something that is a permanent temptation for whosoever speaks of human passions). The only occurrences of the word 'nature' in our text concern goods, not the passions. This presentation implies a certain balance in tone, halfway between a universalising discourse and overly concrete examples. The discourse remains at the superficial level of the visible: when one speaks of feelings, one is referring neither to the pineal gland nor to the imitation of the affects. Spinoza cites neither the explanation that he considers to be the correct one, nor the one he considers false. We are in an entirely different universe to the universe of explanation or demonstration. We are immediately placed in the theatre of civic or personal life. What is

---

[34] Th. Zweerman, *Spinoza's inleiding tot de filosofie*, pp. 51–2.

presented to us is a succession of scenes that stage people who chase after honours, people who are greedy for wealth, and people who suffer or die . . . The order of these spectacles is produced by the imbrication of different past experiences connected by association: I begin by recounting that I aspired to the true good; then, I thought of the advantages that (for a long time) I had drawn from common life; and after this I attempted to bring the two kinds of life together. The discourse of experience is founded on memories. It is not a pure narrative, for it restructures these memories. The past presents itself to memory as divided into different levels, each of which refers to other levels, whether contradictory or complementary. In contrast to the geometrical order, which is a direct presentation of the necessity of the true, presentation by experience is a *re*presentation because it is founded on an effect of memory (as is shown by the fact that the narrative is written in the past tense, and also by the structure of the examples, which assess situations that have previously been lived and known).[35] The various levels of experience succeed one another in an order that cannot be altered. Experience is also a *re*presentation in the theatrical sense of the term: it is a succession of moments where actors take turns to walk the stage of memory and where each one plays a role, whether it be in a duel where blows are exchanged, or to bring new and hitherto unknown information to light. Finally, experience is a *re*presentation in the juridical sense of the term since certain select facts are put forward in order to represent others.

Such a descriptive tone is opposed to the geometrical form taken by the system. But the precise limits of this opposition must be determined. It is not enough to note that the first eleven paragraphs do not use the external apparatus of geometry: after all, neither does the rest of the *TdIE*. It is more important to note that the procedure of these paragraphs is in no way demonstrative, if we take demonstrative to refer to a procedure that consists in exhibiting the necessary link between causes and consequences and which can be expressed otherwise than by theorems. Here the argument does not proceed by way of a causal engendering. This does not exclude the existence of causes, but the latter are not presented in, precisely, a causal order. While the argument progresses, it is not by moving from cause to effect. It proceeds, rather, by bringing to light something that was already there, something that has already been noticed but which has not been designated and remains at the margins rather than at the centre of the frame of experience. The best example of this is the use of the second *colligere* in paragraph 6. After concluding

---

[35] Cf. what is implied by the term *colligere* from paragraph 3, as well as the examples from paragraph 8.

that the sought-after compromise was impossible, the narrator again takes up the question of certainty, and he finds (*inveni*) that to abandon the goods of common life is to abandon goods that are uncertain by nature. But how does he find this out? Not by immediately undergoing a new experience but rather by making an inference from what has already been said.[36] Now, at first glance it seems surprising that Spinoza says that he has shown that goods are uncertain by their very nature. In fact, in paragraphs 4 and 5, he undertook to show that they prevented one from thinking of the true good. But in the following paragraph he passes directly from this assurance to the uncertain character of goods (that is, that they are uncertain in themselves, in opposition to the uncertainty of their acquisition) and then on to the dangers they pose for whoever possesses them or wishes to acquire them. Everything happens as if Spinoza assumes that the elements required to affirm the uncertain character of goods (and even perhaps the danger they represent) had appeared in the margins of the preceding demonstration, which concerned goods but which dealt with a different point. This is a plausible assumption: for example, when we consider how honours prevent one from thinking of the true good, we realise how they make us repeatedly run the same race; thus, we realise the permanent dissatisfaction that honours hide behind each momentary joy they offer us, along with the threat of brutal disappointment that weighs over the hopes they inspire. One might even potentially think of the reasons for this disappointment – that is, for instance, of the rivalries and persecutions that honours lead to. Nevertheless, these causes are not studied in themselves: they appear in the course of the journey under the jurisdiction of another question (namely: is the race to win honours so all-consuming as to prevent one who participates in it from thinking of anything else?). Thus, the same experience presents two levels of meaning that are revealed to two successive perspectives, and the passage from one to the next is not that of cause to consequence. From the first perspective, the uncertainty and the danger posed by goods are certainly grasped by the narrator, yet they are grasped without being designated as such. With respect to the second perspective, the emphasis shifts and the uncertainty of goods, as well as the danger they pose, are designated within the framework of a new chain of experience that begins with a new question. This alternation between grasping and designating defines the rhythm of the evolution of experience.[37] By contrast, in a causal chain, what

---

[36] 'Ut clare ex dictis possumus colligere', § 6, G II, p. 6, ll. 27–8 [*TdIE* 6; *CWS* I, 8].

[37] The recourse to the couple grasping/designating is freely inspired by the use made of it by J.-T. Desanti in a quite different context ('Disparitions, structures et mobilités', in *La Philosophie silencieuse*, Paris: Seuil, 1975, pp. 154–71).

is grasped is designated at the same time, even if it is not immediately named. If it is necessary to consider the conclusion concerning the uncertainty of goods as a by-product of the demonstration of the inhibiting effect they have on the mind, it is because certain essential properties appear not as a function of their causes but rather in the course of the demonstration of other properties. Thus, even when the experiential order indicates a cause, it does so outside of the causal chain. Its order is rather that of the encounter. But the encounter is not an instance of chance: it is the consequence of successive displacements that draw aspects of experience from the periphery towards the centre of our concerns.

This is why it is necessary to insist on the implications of the verb *videre*. That the discovery is a matter of vision does not imply that everything is given in a single stroke: vision occurs by degrees, and the text's vocabulary insists on the forms of reflection proper to these different degrees: *volvebam*, *incubueram*. These terms are chosen in such a way as to designate a rumination more than an instance of active reasoning. They play, so to speak, the role of so many passive expressions of *doceo*. To see in this way is not to know but to learn from a situation and from the effects it has on the mind. This characteristic runs counter to one of the usual senses of the term 'experience': experience is not what is there, given once and for all; it is also what we learn from a particular process. We are closer here to the meaning we find in the expression 'to be experienced'. This expression means someone has discovered, bit by bit, from within the folds of common life, a fabric with designs or patterns that could not be perceived in its totality at first glance.

But how do things unfold in this way? In the movement through the different levels of experience, it is less a matter of falsity than of a lack of determinate limits. Everything is there in front of my eyes; but does this mean that everything is true? What is seen is not given as true; rather, it stuns us by its presence and obscures its individual outline. When this outline comes to the fore, the content of the gaze is modified. This does not, however, make what remains appear as false. To see is to see situations in which a rule is being applied that we are unaware of and whose limits we cannot discern. The thought of the limit (in the sense of a frontier) is a causal thought. In the experiential mode, I do not see at what point a law ceases to apply (on other occasions I do not even see this law itself). This is why seeing in experience is neither true nor false. It is true at its centre, but the centre is not seen as the differential consequence of a rule. The different scenes succeed one other in the form of different *occasions* as the gaze focuses on them; these *occasions* can involve causes, but their unfolding is not fundamentally governed by causality. For example, in the *fruitio* tied to pleasure, a person who enjoys a good identifies this good and its essence with this enjoyment. The feeling of *tristitia*, however, is on the horizon, and the narrator knows, thanks to his previous experiences, or by what he has seen in the experiences of others, that it is waiting at the edge of this experiential series. Yet, so long as it remains on the horizon, its shadow does not obscure the centre of the scene. I know and I do not know what is to come. It is on this basis that the different levels of experience unfold. The occasion is not a product of chance: it articulates in a more subtle manner distance and proximity.

B. Collision and Impact Points

We can glimpse the second characteristic of the experiential mode if we take into account another tonal trait, that of singularity, along with what I have called the dialectic of limitation. Where is experience situated? What constitutes it? It cannot be said to take place within a subject, the narrator, for it initially involves a collision with goods. It is lived by the narrator, but resonates within him thanks only to these impact points. It is the latter that constitute the chain of experience. In this sense it would be wrong to speak of internal experience. Instead, experience occurs much more on the threshold between the narrator and the world.

What takes place at this frontier is not a simple confrontation. The term *adhaeremus*[38] is revealing: the *animus* is not content to seek out goods and to enjoy them; it clings to them – in other words, it loves them. One should not mistake the functional role of different 'feelings': we are not dealing here with a theory of the passions. Love is the category that refers to the general relation of the agent-narrator to things. Joy and sadness, by contrast, are states that function as indicators of the effects of external goods on the mind. In the description there is neither hierarchy nor competition between them: they play different roles. In the *Ethics*, love plays a key role but the general explanation of the affects is built on the basis of joy and sadness. What is at stake here is not a general explanation of the affects; as such, asking what the fundamental passion is would be to replace a Spinozist *description* with a Cartesian (or Spinozist)[39] *question*. Here it is not a matter of explaining but of describing, and to describe one needs diverse instruments or criteria, not all of which play the same role.

---

[38] 'in qualitate objecti, cui adhaeremus amore', § 9, G II, p. 7, ll. 18–19 [*TdIE* 9; *CWS* I, 9].

[39] In the sense that this question refers to the system and not to the experience described in the *proemium*.

The question of love can thus help us think experience's impact point on consciousness. This is a decisive problem since consciousness has no other content than these very experiences. At the same time, the world that this consciousness needs is constituted by the zone of indeterminate goods, which are organised following the journey. Experience's teachings are thus extremely limited, and can lead only to the destruction of experience itself. This is why in the *TdIE* the problem of experience's impact point occupies a particularly prominent place: it is this impact that distributes limits and hides and reveals in turn the various aspects of the goods that successively occupy centre stage. Whence the role of the narrative *I*. Even when the term 'men' is used, it is in terms of the refraction of their activities under the gaze of the *I*. For example, in paragraph 3, men and what one can *colligere* of their actions intervene only through the intermediary of the thoughts that run through the narrator's mind (*volvebam animo*). Experience is allocation. This in no way means that it is a purely subjective operation.

I noted above that in the experiential mode, I do not see where a law ceases to apply. But to this one should add that I feel this limit when I come up against it. The aspiration to the true good initially constitutes an unlimited given. However, when I try to put this aspiration to work I feel that it contradicts the habitual cycle of my life. The attempt at compromise might at first glance seem perfectly possible, but practice teaches me that it ends in failure. Reciprocally, once the power of perishable goods has been perceived, I judge it to be unlimited and I have difficulty seeing how to 'put aside all desire of wealth, pleasure, and glory'. But the practice of attending to the true good makes me see that these limits exist and that these evils are not without remedy. It is thus with each discovery of these limitations that the subject takes form.

All of this inevitably makes one think of the path of consciousness in the *Phenomenology*. There, too, experience is not a simple given but on the contrary involves the transformation of the immediate. There, too, consciousness does not remain immutable in the face of the transformations of what is given, for it has no other content than its experiences. And there, too, we encounter the subject where it is, in the element of the immediate; and it is with its errors, its crises and its development that it is led to knowledge. Nevertheless, we must immediately draw a fundamental line of demarcation: Hegelian experience is nothing other than – and is already – the dialectic.[40]

---

[40] 'Diese *dialektische* Bewegung, welche das Bewußtsein an ihm selbst, sowohl an seinem Wissen als an seinem Gegenstande ausübt, *insofern ihm der neue wahre Gegenstand daraus entspringt*, ist eigentlich dasjenige, was *Erfahrung* gennant wird', Werke, vol. 3,

The ultimate figure of absolute knowledge is, dialectically speaking, identical to the *Meinen*.[41] In Spinoza, an absolute rupture occurs. This is why in Hegel the first and last figures of the odyssey of consciousness mutually found one other. This is in no way the case in Spinoza. It is perhaps for this reason that Hegel can describe each of the different stages of consciousness in the present tense, while Spinoza must do so in the past tense.

C. Opacity and Recurrence

The third characteristic of the experiential mode can be glimpsed if we take into account both the intensity that affects the prologue's tone and the procedure I have called a logic of anticipation.

What first emerges from the detours and interrogations leading to the final decision is the opacity of the journey for the subject who undertakes it: at each moment, he does not know where he will be led. He does not know if his aspirations will give rise to a decision, while his hesitations are based on uncertain calculations. But this very opacity is itself opaque: for when the subject comes close to a position near to one from the system and that contains the solution to his hesitations, he cannot be wholly aware of this, precisely because he is not in possession of the system. It is we who see this for him, or it is he who sees it after the fact in the rear-view mirror of his narrative. We should refer here to the complex set of relations between grasping, designating, grounding, and being conscious of limits. When I state a theorem, I am obscurely conscious of some of the consequences that can be drawn from it – not all of them, of course, but nothing in principle prevents me from drawing such-and-such a consequence. At worst, any difficulties I face are reducible to my limited system of references. In experience, there is always evidently an in principle obstacle, and it lies at the very heart of experience and concerns precisely the point of collision. The limit is situated at the impact point: it is the allocation itself that hides what is to be seen. I know that goods lead to death; I have always known this. It is not at the final moment that I discover, on the basis of the ruin that goods can

---

p. 78; 'this *dialectical* movement which consciousness exercises on itself and which affects both its knowledge and its object, is precisely what is called *experience*', *Phenomenology of Spirit*, p. 55.

[41] '[. . .] daß sie sich zum Geiste läutere, indem sie durch die vollständige Erfahrung ihrer selbst zur Kenntnis desjenigen gelangt, was sie an sich selbst ist', *Werke*, vol. 3, p. 72; 'so that it may purify itself for the life of the Spirit, and achieve finally, through a completed experience of itself, the awareness of what it really is in itself', *Phenomenology of Spirit*, p. 49.

cause, the innumerable examples of this happening. Such examples have accumulated in my memory. But a crisis is necessary, one that can be assimilated to a mortal illness of the mind, for me to know that *I*, too, will die from them. Until a crisis forces me to occupy the place of the subject of the statement, this weighty knowledge feels too light, too transparent to apply to me. To have experience is therefore less to acquire new information than to succeed in modifying their impact point or the effect the goods exert on the impact point.[42]

The meaning of this whole trajectory is only fully revealed in the recurrence of a non-experiential knowledge. This is what constitutes the reason for the apparently illogical leap between paragraphs 11 and 12. Only a gaze informed by the system can release the lessons of experience from their opacity. But then these lessons are precisely no longer experientially known. Experience can lead to the point where it is known as such – to the point of rupture. It cannot dictate its own recurrence. Its opacity remains within it a perpetually constitutive trait.

D. Saturation and Totality

The three characteristics that we have just identified help us to understand a fourth. We have encountered this problem with respect to the question of knowing if the three goods represented the totality of goods. It is time, now, to take up this question again. There are clearly two different approaches to the question of the totality: one that opposes and organises the particular and the universal, and another that reasons in terms of saturation. In other Spinozist texts, we read: 'satis superque'. What we find here in the *TdIE* is of the same order. Things are thus and no one can ask for anything more. What in geometrical reasoning would be a logical fault is here a reaffirmation of what the terms *plerumque* and *frequenter* signified. Saturation (the Dutch translation of this term shows this in the choices it makes) is the crowning achievement of the order of the common.

With respect to experience, the universal is not a *de jure* totality (it is not of the order of necessity) but a *de facto* totality: that is, it is what experience

---

[42] We can see here the obscuring of the difference between the mode of knowledge that constitutes vague experience [*l'expérience vague*] and the form of teaching that is the journey, or experience. From vague experience I have long known that I will die (cf. § 20, G II, p. 10, ll. 24–7 [*TdIE* 20; CWS I, 13]); but a journey is necessary with its conflicts and displacements for me to come to designate the fact that it is I who will die.

has witnessed 'most often'. It is what no occasion can justify not having to take into account. What has not encountered its limit remains master of the field. It is only from a retrospective position that we can pose the question of a *de jure* totality. Here, it is enough to consider that the synopsis is complete. The saturation of motives for action suffices for the teachings of common life.

We have thus surveyed the effective content of the register of experience. I believe I have shown the coherence and originality of this mode of thought and exposition such as it is presented at the beginning of the *Treatise on the Emendation of the Intellect*. Up to this point, we have studied this text in isolation, for both methodological reasons (that is, so as not to suppose its total coherence with Spinoza's other works) and for internal reasons (the way in which it presents itself is irreducible both in terms of its tone and register to other texts in which Spinoza's system is present). But can this experiential mode teach us anything about the system itself? Is it compatible with it? Are there echoes of experience in the system, or must we include the *proemium* among the relics of Spinoza's youthful works? With regards to this question of the status of experience outside of the text where it is clearly foregrounded in its specificity, it is impossible to offer a simple response. I will begin by questioning the other texts from the same period. Let us distinguish, in the first pages from the *TdIE*, the procedure – that is, the specific form of the journey – from the doctrine we find there. This doctrine, of course, is not simply constituted by the few theses that deal strictly with experience; it also includes analyses of notions associated with it: common life, goods and love. We should note the homogeneity of this doctrine with Spinoza's texts from the same period, in particular the remainder of the *TdIE* and the *Short Treatise*, but also the *Principia*, which follows it by only a few years. I have already noted in passing a few points of comparison.[43] I will now return to those that merit a structural and not merely a punctual *rapprochement*.

The principal relation between experience and common life is reaffirmed both in the remainder of the *TdIE* and in the *Principia*. In paragraph 20 of the *TdIE*, after speaking of vague experience, Spinoza remarks: 'And in this way I know almost all the things that are useful in life.'[44] Similarly, in the first part of the *Principia*, Proposition 15, Scholium, we read (with respect to

---

[43] II, 1, § 3, with respect to the relations between experience and universality; II, 5, § 6, with respect to the three goods; II, 12, § 3, with respect to honour.

[44] 'Et sic fere omnia novi, quae ad usum vitae faciunt', § 20, G II, p. 11, l. 3 [*TdIE* 20; *CWS* I, 14].

freedom) in a passage where Spinoza seems to be speaking in his own name more than in that of Descartes: 'And if we also consider what is needed and advantageous in human life, we shall find it absolutely necessary, as daily experience sufficiently teaches everyone.'[45] We thus find an affirmation of the same link between experience and the use of life. But it is necessary to explain the meaning of the term 'vague experience', which appears in the first of these two quotations. I will return to this a little further on.

The second part of the *Short Treatise* develops a theory of goods and of love that is essentially analogous to the one we have just reconstituted on the basis of the *proemium*. Yet, since it is not presented in the form of a journey, in the *Short Treatise* we find laid out in a discursive fashion what the *TdIE* presents in narrative form. It is thus possible in this instance to find explicit definitions and causal deductions. However, no passage is devoted as such to defining experience, but we do encounter the term on a number of occasions,[46] for instance when Spinoza refers to the way in which we progress in liberating ourselves from the love of a finite good or when we discover that the things of the world do not bring us salvation.

Chapter V, titled *Of Love*,[47] begins with a definition: 'Love, then, is nothing but enjoying a thing and being united with it.'[48] Love can thus be divided in terms of the qualities (*hoedanigheden*) of its object. The object can in effect be either perishable or eternal. Up to this point, nothing contradicts the *proemium*, even if we get a more precise definition. Above all, the distinct goods that love can pursue are given simultaneously to reflection: we do not pass from one to the next. We thus see how the two texts use the same theoretical division in different ways. In one, this division is given precisely as an explicit division, where two terms named simultaneously are defined and judged in an explanatory process. In the other, we begin with one of the terms (the perishable one), the one that is known first, even if it is not immediately grasped in terms of all of its determinations, before turning to the other in the very same movement that discloses the previously unperceived dimensions of the first. Similarly, in the *Short Treatise*, love appears first and the goods according to which it is specified appear second, while the *TdIE* only thematises love once it has evoked the goods to which the

---

[45] 'Et si etiam ad usum, & utilitatem vitae humane attendere volumus, id prorsus necessarium reperiemus, ut quotidiana experientia unumquemque satis docet', G I, p. 175, ll. 15–19 [CWS I, 259].

[46] *Ondervinding* or the verb *ondervinden*.

[47] 'Van de lievde', KV, M, p. 224 [CWS I, 104].

[48] 'De Lievde, die niet anders is, als een zaak te genieten en daar mede vereenift te worden', ibid., ll. 3–5 [CWS I, 105].

narrator adheres. We thus see how a doctrine that appears fundamentally identical can be presented differently and, most importantly, can found the possibility of its different modes of exposition. In fact, it is the disequilibrium between the perishable and the eternal that makes it possible for something like the journey to take place. If one comes first and is then the source of disappointment, then the gradual knowledge we gain of its diverse characteristics can be presented in the form of a trajectory. If, moreover, the eternal possesses the characteristics that appear to be lacking from the perishable, then the path down which one advances in the knowledge of the perishable is one that moves *towards* the eternal. It is thus the synchronic analysis presented in the *Short Treatise* that sketches out the space where, at the beginning of the *TdIE*, experience will become a philosophical genre.

Continuing to identify the differences at the beginning of this chapter, note that an additional distinction is created within the category of eternal objects; a distinction that concerns whether they are eternal by virtue of their own force or through what causes them. We should not be surprised that this distinction does not appear at the beginning of the *TdIE*, for it refers to the nature of objects, and can therefore only be made because the second part of the *Short Treatise* is preceded by the entire deduction of God and of infinite modes. In the register of experience, this distinction has no place.

Finally, the only notable difference is the term 'enjoy' (*genieten*), which is used in conjunction with love. This term does not seem to be reserved for one of the three goods. Here, too, the discordance can be explained by reference to the mode of exposition: the emphasis is not placed on the differential description of the various perishable goods; on the contrary, their evocation is limited to the few traits they have in common. It is thus possible that the particular form of acquisition of one of these goods is used to represent globally the acquisition of all, without regard for their specificities. Finally, the definition of love in terms of knowledge[49] might appear more intellectualist than in the *TdIE*, but it is not necessary to understand 'knowledge' in the sense of adequate knowledge. Every form of knowledge is a cause of love, and it is precisely as a cause that it is absent from the *proemium*. On the other hand, what is common to the two texts is the inexistence of a will, appetite or faculty that would be the proper site of love.[50] The *animus*

---

[49] 'Love, then, arises from the perception and knowledge which we have of a thing', *CWS* I, 104 ['De Liefde dan onstaat uyt het begrip en kennisse die wy van en zaake hebben'].

[50] F. Mignini, in his commentary, is right to note this as far as the *Short Treatise* is concerned (*Korte Verhandeling*, pp. 609–10).

adheres by love to the goods that are presented to it, so long as these goods occupy the terrain and are not replaced by a good that is more powerful than them. Experience feels this adhesion, while the demonstrative order explains it genetically in terms of knowledge.

After having defined love and its conditions, the same chapter from the *Short Treatise* poses the question of knowing how to liberate oneself from it.[51] Here, too, we find the same problematic as the *TdIE*, but seen as if from a different angle. There are two ways to liberate oneself from love: either because we know of a greater good,[52] or because through experience (*ondervinding*) we see that the loved object, which we once thought of as tremendously magnificent, brings with it much unhappiness and disaster.[53] If this question is raised at all, it is apparently because liberation from love can be desirable, at least theoretically. But the rest of the chapter continues by showing that this is neither possible nor desirable. We thus once again find ourselves faced with an apparent contradiction, as in paragraph 14 from the *TdIE*. And once again, at this crossroads, we see appear the enigmatic figure of human weakness (*swakheid*). We cannot liberate ourselves from love because we are not strong enough to do so: the solution depends on the object and not on us. The only way to not desire the object would be to have never known it.[54] This thesis, therefore, does not contradict the preceding one: it indicates not that freedom itself is absolutely impossible, but that it is impossible for us to free ourselves. It is not we who succeed in seeing the defects or qualities of the goods, but rather these qualities and these faults which, as soon as they become visible (or comparable to those other goods), provoke the beginning or the extinction of love. In some sense, it is not we who choose goods; they choose us.[55]

Furthermore, our weakness entails that we must attach ourselves to an object. The extinction of one love is the beginning of another. We might

---

[51] KV, M, p. 224, l. 28 [CWS I, 105].

[52] This hypothesis has already been put forward in Chapter III, KV, M, p. 212 [CWS I, 100].

[53] 'Dat de beminde zaak, die voor wat groots ende herlyks gehouden is, veel onheil en ramp met zig sleept', KV, M, p. 224, ll. 30–2 [CWS I, 105].

[54] 'Het welke, soo wy't niet en wilden beminnen, noodzaakelyk van ons tevoren niet en most gekend zyn', KV, M, p. 226, ll. 3–6 [CWS I, 105].

[55] G. Boss sums up this point in an excellent formula: 'C'est un automatisme inhérent à notre nature, que nous expérimentons mais qui reste indépendant de notre volonté, car dès qu'une chose aimable nous apparaît, nous ne pouvons nous empêcher de l'aimer immédiatement', *L'Enseignement de Spinoza. Commentaire du 'Court Tratié'*, Zurich: Editions du Grand Midi, 1982, p. 75.

ask ourselves how to move from a good that is less desirable to one that is more desirable, but by nature we still have to attach ourselves to something, for it is from what we enjoy that we draw our force and unity.[56] We can now understand why the *TdIE*, when it sought to identify the causes of the *commotiones animi*, envisaged only two causes – our adhesion to perishable objects or, on the contrary, to an eternal and infinite thing. The solution for calming the mind that would have consisted in purely and simply giving up on being attached to an external object was not even considered, but it was not said why this was the case. Here, in the *Short Treatise*, we are given the reason. Our weakness is such that we cannot do without this attachment. This weakness is referred to three times;[57] the most powerful expression of our weakness is given in what resembles a parenthesis, but this parenthesis systematises all of the other references: if we knew nothing, we would not be anything.[58] The knowledge at the foundation of love is not only a knowledge: it is a guarantee of our consistency.

While all of the above is coherent, in this chapter on love experience is more mentioned than it is analysed. On the other hand, it is clearly taken into account in two other chapters.

In Chapter 14, Spinoza argues forcefully that there exists no love without a determinate object and that it is this relation that founds the notions of good and evil.[59] In fact, love is determined by the determination of the object. This insistence coheres with Chapter 5 and with the *TdIE*. However, we do not find this thesis in the same form in the *Ethics*. The analysis of sad passions (hatred, sadness, etc.) refers to the fact of loving, not God, but perishable objects. These effects follow as the loved object changes.[60] On the contrary, the human being wins their freedom from the passions when they love the immutable object that is God. Here we glimpse a description hiding behind an explanation: once again the distinction between what is perish-

---

[56] 'Iets [. . .] waar mede wy vereenigt woorden en verstekt', *KV*, M, p. 226, ll. 11–13 [*CWS* I, 105].

[57] *KV*, M, p. 226, ll. 7–8; ll. 10–11; ll. 18–19 [*CWS* I, 105].

[58] 'Want zo wy niets kenden, voor zeeker wy en waaren ook niet', *KV*, M, p. 226, ll. 7–8 [*CWS* I, 105].

[59] 'Om dan noch meer klarheid in alle dez te geven, diend aangemerkt, dat het fundament van alle goed en kwaad is de Lievde vallende op seker voorwerp', *KV*, M, p. 262, ll. 14–16 [*CWS* I, 118].

[60] If we love 'those things which through their own kind and nature are corruptible, there follow necessarily from that hate, sadness, etc., according to the changes in the object loved', *CWS* I, 118. ('die dingen die door eigen aart en natuur vergankelyk zyn (dewyl het voorwep zo veel toevallen, ja de vernietinge zelve onderworpen is) de haat, droefheid, enz., na veranderinge van het geliefde voorwerp', ibid., ll. pp. 20–5).

able and what is eternal is grasped directly by its effect on the mind. Before being a distinction between two concepts, it is given as the opposition between two states, one of which overwhelms us while the other liberates us.

In Chapter 26, the principle of the *suum utile* is formulated more explicitly than in the *TdIE*. In this latter text, the narrator had noted, in the course of one of his conflicts, that he 'was forced to ask what would be more useful to me'.[61] This was neither a general principle nor a restrictive formulation. By contrast, the *Short Treatise* clearly says that in order to find our salvation and our rest, we must only seek our advantage.[62] Now, in this context, what we experience (*ondervinden*) is that, when we seek out sensual pleasures – voluptuousness, the things of the world – we do not find our salvation.[63] It is therefore experience that fills out the framework sketched by the abstract theory of salvation.

It appears, then, that on the points we have examined, the *TdIE* and the *Short Treatise* are on the whole homogeneous with one another, the differences between them being essentially reducible to the registers in which they are written and not to any differences in doctrine. The concept of experience appears on the whole as being situated at the centre of a complex set of notions – goods, life, love, the distinction between the perishable and the eternal – all of which cohere with one another. It is this complex that is at the basis of the particular form taken by the *TdIE*. As such, the most powerful of these notions (from the point of view of their attribution) can only be exhibited in an intense form, as the narrator's journey is.[64]

We can highlight two further characteristics of Spinoza's writings from this period:

— The *Treatise on the Emendation of the Intellect* and the *Short Treatise* both present – as will Book II of the *Ethics* – a theory of the different kinds of knowledge. From the perspective that interests us, the versions of

---

[61] 'Cogebar inquirere, quid mihi esset utilius', § 6, G II, p. 6, ll. 23–4 [*TdIE* 6; CWS I, 8].

[62] 'Soo zien wy dan, day wy, om te bereyken de waarheid van't geene wy voor vast stellen aangaande ons heyl en ruste, geen eenige andere beginzelen van noden hebben als allean dit, namelyk ons eigen voordeel te behartigen, een zaake en alle dingen zeer narurlyk', KV, M, p. 338, II. 23–9 [CWS I, 146–7].

[63] KV, M, p. 338 [CWS I, 147].

[64] It could be asked if, from a certain point of view, the two dialogues inserted into the first part of the *Short Treatise* do not bear witness to the search for such a form. It is often claimed that they pre-exist the *Short Treatise* itself. Mignini affirms – correctly, in my view – that their doctrine does not diverge from the general theses advanced in the *TdIE*. But why not think that the form refers to this aim and not to a difference in date?

this theory contained in these first two pieces of writing diverge on very few points.[65] What I would wish to highlight, however, is that within the theory of the different kinds of knowledge, something else is constituted, something that does not contradict this theory but that shifts the emphasis to a different aspect: namely, to teaching. Now, it is this aspect alone that makes the theory productive. The *TdIE* counts four kinds of knowledge, the *Short Treatise* four, and then three additional ones. The kind of knowledge that occupies the second position[66] is called 'experience': the *Short Treatise* says *ondervinding*[67] while the *TdIE* says 'vague experience',[68] which is occasionally shortened to 'experience'.[69] This kind of knowledge clearly belongs – like knowledge by hearsay and (in the *TdIE*) knowledge by signs – to those that are devalued. When we know by way of these kinds of knowledge, we know the false or at least the non-necessary. This is why the *TdIE* distinguishes this knowledge from what can lead the human being to perfection: 'Apart from the fact that it is a very uncertain thing, and without end, in this way no one will ever perceive anything in natural things except accidents [through vague experience].'[70] Certainly. Nevertheless, the same word 'experience' is consistently valorised in those cases where it is said to teach: that is, in three extremely precise contexts: *TdIE*, § 1; *KV*, II, 5; and *KV*, II, 26. And on each occasion what experience is said to teach is something unique: it orients us towards the true good, or the immutable good. Besides these three incontestable textual examples, the entire logic of the beginning of the *TdIE* and of the corresponding texts from the *Short Treatise*, as we have studied them, seem to me to go in the same direction. How else can we make sense of the fact that the same word 'experience' refers at one and the same time to an inferior kind of knowledge, one that is misleading

---

[65] Martial Gueroult systematically compares the three classifications in appendix No. 16 in his second volume: *Spinoza*, II, *L'Ame*, Paris: Aubier, 1974, pp. 593–608.

[66] Either as the second kind in the *TdIE*, and in the example of the rule of three from the *KV*, or as a second category of the first kind at the beginning of Chapter I and in Chapter II from the second part of the *KV*.

[67] Second Part, Chapter I, *KV*, M, p. 204, l. 15; p. 206, l. 16, l. 31 and note 2 [CWS I, 98].

[68] 'Experientia vaga', § 19, G II, p. 10, l. 11 [*TdIE* 19; CWS I, 12]; § 20, ibid., l. 24 [*TdIE* 20; CWS I, 13].

[69] At least in § 23, G II, p. 12, l. 1 [*TdIE* 23; CWS I, 15]; perhaps in the note from § 27, ibid., p. 13 [*TdIE* 27; CWS I, 16]

[70] A, p. 235. 'Praeterquam quod sit res admodum incerta, et sine fine, nihil tamen unquam tali modo quis in rebus naturalibus percipiet praeter accidentia, quae nunquam clare intelliguntur, nisi praecognitis essentiis. Unde etiam secludendus est', § 27, G II, p. 13, ll. 2–6 [*TdIE* 27; CWS 16]. Appuhn does not include brackets in his translation. In any case, the context clearly shows that it is a matter of *experientia vaga*.

and subject to error, and a form of teaching that orients us towards the true good? Is it a homonymy? The truth is, in fact, that a shift in perspective has occurred. In the interests of clarity, let us distinguish between the kind of knowledge called 'vague experience' and the form of teaching called 'experience' (in other words, let us conform to the distinction that appears to be the one established in the *TdIE*, even if only implicitly and in an inchoate manner).[71] We can then say that experience uses the results that come to be known thanks to vague experience. It uses them and neutralises them; by taking care to not treat them as knowledge, experience is not led astray. These results are present less as knowledge and more as motives in a crisis. They push us to perform an action – and in experience, this is what matters. Of his wealth, the merchant no doubt has knowledge by vague experience – as he has of his 'rule of three'. But this is not what interests us when we ask whether or not he could move towards philosophy. What interests us lies at a different level: what will he make of his life?

— The whole movement of the beginning of the *TdIE*, like the explanations from the *Short Treatise*, tends to constitute a radical ethics – that is, a restricted universe where the conduct of all people is brought back to its roots. In this sense, the procedure of these texts is closest to those of Aristotle or Pascal, where an ethical reflection is grounded in a survey of human activity in its most originary dimensions. This procedure is closer to Pascal than to Aristotle since the origin is given principally in the form of unhappiness. This description also takes the form of a circle. Perhaps there is a precise complicity between radical ethics and circularity. Having just been opened, the domain of experience is immediately closed. In these early writings of Spinoza, experience does not lead to an extensive analysis of human activities. The intensity of experience seems proportional to the narrowness of its field of application.

---

[71] It will be said that 'vague experience' is a term that comes from Bacon. I will deal with this question further on. Let us content ourselves with saying that when he employs this term – that is, in the *TdIE* – Spinoza does not use it in all of the same instances where the *Short Treatise* uses the word experience. This seems to indicate that there are, for him, two different meanings to the word, and that he has recourse to 'vague experience' to describe only one of these meanings – the one that refers to one of the kinds of knowledge. This suffices to give a proper figure to the other meaning, the one that interests us here.

3. The Treatise That Was Not Written

I noted above that a number of the prologue's traits and those of corresponding texts can be illuminated if we refer to human weakness and to the apparent absence of the concept of the *conatus*.[72] There is, certainly, in the *Korte Verhandeling*, a 'particular providence' that consists in the effort (*poginge*) that each thing makes to preserve and perfect itself.[73] But it is mentioned only briefly and plays no explicit role in the description of the passions or of the path towards freedom. On this point, is it possible to determine the evolution of Spinoza's thinking and to draw some consequences regarding experience?

A sign of this evolution can be found in Letter XXX. This letter is of interest to us in that it indicates, following a remark made by Oldenburg, the reasons that lead one to philosophise: the troubles of men (in this case, war) motivate one to better observe human nature. On this point, Spinoza evokes in the past tense the mistakes he made in considering as vain and absurd the things that did not accord with the desires of a philosophical soul.[74] Might we read here an allusion to the beginning of the *Treatise on the Emendation of the Intellect*? The context seems moreover to sketch a portrait of an attitude, now abandoned, that consisted in condemning human madness.[75] What should we understand by this? We find nothing explicitly like

---

[72] The term appears in the *Principia*, III, Definition III, G I, p. 229, l. 21 [PP III, Def. 3; CWS I, 297], and in the *Cogitata*, I, VI, G I, p. 248, l. 7 [CM VI; CWS I, 314]. But there it is not the Spinozist concept as it will be developed in the *Ethics*. Likewise, the *cupiditas* appears briefly in the *TdIE*, § 14, G II, p. 8, ll. 29–31 [TdIE 14; CWS I, 11], but in a very different context from the concept from the *Ethics*. In the *TdIE*, *cupiditas* is twice identified with *intellectus* following a classical tradition (which L. Meyer will denounce in Spinoza's name in the preface to the *Principia*). In the *Ethics*, if it appears in a series, it is with *laetitia* and *tristitia*.

[73] Part I, Chapter V, *KV*, M, pp. 174–6 [CWS I, 84].

[74] '& ex solo hujus cognitionis defectu reperio, quod quaedam naturae, que ita ex parte & non nisi mutilate percipio, & quae cum nostra mente philosophica minime conveniunt, mihi antehac vana, inordinata, absurda, videbantur', G IV, p. 166, ll. 15–18 [Ep. XXX [to Henry Oldenburg]; CWS II, 14]. The interest of this passage obviously has to do with the self-critique that is absent from parallel passages (*TTP*, Chapter XVI, G III, p. 191, ll. 4–10 [*TTP* XVI, 11; CWS II, 284]; *TP*, Chapter II, G III, p. 279, ll. 29–36 [*TP* II, 8; CWS II, 511]).

[75] The term 'madness' does not appear here, but the allusion to Democritus who laughed in the face of the strange actions of men and, by contrast, the decision to now recognise in each person the right to live according to their own nature instead of laughing at them or deploring them, does indeed seem to refer to the traditional opposition between wisdom and madness.

this in the *TdIE*, save for the reference to the *stultitia*. But perhaps such a distinction was a response to the following implicit question: why do certain people follow the path right to the end but others do not? Such a response would fail to take into account necessity and its effects, and would therefore interpret human diversity as a hierarchy of differences in light of a model of wisdom. But is this not what the *TdIE* implicitly does? The reading of the *exemplar* made by the *imbecillitas* (and by the *swakheid* in the *KV*) might lead us to think this. If the content of the essence of the human being is determined only in terms of weakness, then the diversity of human behaviours is not positively thinkable, while the consequences of their actions can be interpreted only as so many kinds of irrationality. Such theses are nevertheless not affirmed as such in Spinoza's early writings. It is more a case of an inflection than of any explicit content. Nevertheless, we can conclude that:

- in the early writings, while the structure of the individual is not denied, it plays a minor role;
- as a consequence, the thesis of universal necessity is lived passively by human beings (this is why in the *KV* we encounter expressions like 'slaves of God', which will later disappear). It could be said that everything that is often interpreted as being 'mystical' in the *TdIE* concerns this weak reading of individuality and the negative reading of necessity that corresponds to it.[76]

How do Spinoza's ideas evolve after this? The evanescence of individuality, the necessity of thinking its consistency only in its relation to an other, whether perishable or eternal, leads the individual to the limits of the ineffable. If we are truly nothing when we know or love nothing, then the human being is a quasi-non-being who receives their qualities from outside of themselves. The logic of such a determination leads to the rejection of most common notions as unthinkable – a point marked by the terms stupidity and absurdity. Such a position contradicts one of the essential principles of Spinozism: that of the total intelligibility of the real.[77] It is thus predictable that the development of the system will lead to the liquidation of this

---

[76] On other aspects of the specificity of the early writings, see A. Negri, *L'Anomalia selvaggia. Saggio su potere e potenza in Baruch Spinoza*, Milan: Feltrinelli, 1981, p. 43 ff.

[77] For the determination of this principle, I refer to the works of Martial Gueroult and Alexandre Matheron. Beyond their detailed analyses, the entire aim of their work consists in drawing this principle out with ever greater force. In particular Matheron's latest studies seem to me to owe their fecundity to the fact that they no longer consider this principle as a foundation but as a programme.

position. The form taken by this liquidation will be, in the *TTP*, the positive analysis of the diversity of human behaviours in terms of *potentia*, *cupiditas* and *appetitus*. These terms will be articulated by way of the concept – which finally appears – of the *conatus* and will be developed in Book III of the *Ethics* and after. Yet, simultaneously, Books I and II will thereby be changed. One might think that the small physics from Book II does not figure among the earlier drafts.[78] And indeed, we find nothing like it in the *Short Treatise*, where in order to explain the functioning of the soul Spinoza seems capable of doing without an explanation of the constitution of the body. What is said in the appendix to the *Short Treatise* on the subject of parallelism[79] does not imply a strong doctrine of individuation. By contrast, when the *Ethics* defines particular things as affections of the attributes of God,[80] it is in a context which interprets in an affirmative register what the *Short Treatise* had advanced in the form of a restriction. Indeed, this thesis immediately leads to an analysis of the productivity of these things themselves and of their determination in terms of necessity.[81] A place is thus established as early as Book I for the construction of a doctrine of desire:[82] if things strive to persevere in their being, it is above all because they express in a determinate form the attributes of God. The consistency proper to the individual thereby also becomes intelligible.

From this perspective, we can begin to understand the distance that separates the Spinoza of the *Ethics* from his former position. This position must have come to seem to him to be on certain points untenable. A proof of this is what becomes of the example of illness. In the *proemium*, this example helped us understand in positive terms the crisis that the narrator was going through. In the *Ethics*, by contrast, this example will be disqualified. We can refer here to the Corollary from Proposition 63 from Book IV: its Scholium opposes the sick person who fears death to the proper man who 'fruitur et gaudet'.[83]

[78] I have placed in the appendix my hypotheses on the different periods of the composition of *Ethics*. The analyses that I am proposing here are relatively independent of these hypotheses. [Translator's note: Moreau is referring here to an appendix that was never written, just like Spinoza's Treatise which he is referring to here].
[79] KV, M, pp. 356–65.
[80] 'Res particulares nihil sunt, nisi Dei attributorum affectiones, sive modi, quibus Dei attributa certo et determinato modo exprimuntur', *Ethics* I, 25, Cor., G II, p. 68, ll. 10–12 [CWS I, 431].
[81] Cf. in particularly Propositions 26 to 29.
[82] Proposition 6 from Book III, which practically introduces the *conatus* (in the form of the verb *conatur*, the substance being found in Proposition 7), constructs its demonstration essentially on this Corollary from Proposition 25 from Book I.
[83] 'Explicatur hoc corollarium exemplo aegri et sani. Comedit aeger id, quod aversatur,

There is therefore now an internal positivity that means there is no need for a crisis as an occasion for entering into the system. We also understand the reasons that make the references to the three goods disappear: in the *Ethics*, these goods play only a marginal role and are never part of a positive argument. This is because there is no longer any need to link thought to objects of desire or love. The study of the internal mechanisms of the desiring or loving being suffices to account for this being and to determine the movement towards salvation.

In the *TdIE*, the finite singularity has a positive but weak structure. This minimal positivity suffices to extract it from the negative traditions of ethical topoi. Yet it borrows this positivity from things – and above all, of course, from the infinite thing. In the *TTP* and even more so in the *Ethics*, the finite singularity has a strong positive structure. It realises in itself, in a limited yet irreducible fashion, the power of the infinite.

This trajectory comes to fruition in the *Political Treatise*. There, the term *conatus* disappears – or almost disappears – but for opposite reasons to its absence in Spinoza's earlier writings. It gives way to pure divine power, which is expressed in the power of the individual.[84] Moreover, this is indicated only at the end of the exposition of this dual power: this is what the *conatus* is.[85] Paradoxically, this total affirmation of the individual is invoked using formulations that are almost identical to those from the *Short Treatise*, but which are advanced in an entirely opposite spirit. The power of individuals is only that of the divine: in this context, this is equivalent to saying not that they are simply the 'slaves of God', but on the contrary that they have the greatest possible ontological consistency.

Does this new situation for finite modes change the status of experience and of what it makes possible? We must first ask if it excludes an introduction to philosophy. In a certain way it does: it excludes the possibility of beginning from human weakness. This is why Spinoza did not reprise the *TdIE*. While not out-dated, the *TdIE* is built on foundations that have now been surpassed. This reason can be added to the pedagogical reasons that Alexandre Matheron has brought to light with respect to the Cartesians.

All the same, it is possible to conceive of another kind of discourse, and

---

timore mortis; sanus autem cibo gaudet, & vita sic melius fruitur, quam si mortem timeret, eamque directe vitare cuperet', *Ethics* IV, 63, Cor., G II, p. 258, l. 31 [*CWS* I, 582]; p. 259, l. 2 [*CWS* I, 583].

[84] 'Ex quo sequitur, rerum naturalium potentiam, qua existunt et consequenter qua operantur, nullam aliam esse posse, quam ipsam Dei aeternam potentiam', *TP*, Chapter II, § II, G III, p. 276, ll. 20-3 [*TP* II, 2; *CWS* II, 507].

[85] Chapter III, § 18, G III, p. 291, ll. 21-7 [*TP* III, 18; *CWS* II, 524].

we know that in 1671 – that is, after the publication of the *TTP* – Spinoza thought of one. He mentions such a discourse in a letter to Jarig Jelles. Spinoza had been left indignant after reading a book titled *Homo politicus*,[86] no doubt because this book seemed to begin with an argument that one could mistake for the foundations of Spinozism itself: namely, self-preservation. But in this work self-preservation is immediately and definitively determined in terms of individual interest – that is, in terms of what one profits from. The Sovereign Good is constituted by honours and wealth (and thus by two of the *haec tria* studied in the *TdIE*). How did Spinoza conceive of refuting this book? With *Homo politicus*, Spinoza was dealing with a discourse that dealt directly with the Sovereign Good.[87] It is only after establishing what the Sovereign Good is that the treatise takes up the question of human misery. According to this treatise, human misery has a dual and conditional form: it concerns, above all, individuals, but also States. An 'insatiable desire' throws the first into agitation and disquiet,[88] and the second into ruin.[89] However, this desire is proper only to those people who do not seek honours or wealth. In other words, the text's procedure is the reverse of the one from the *TdIE*. The treatise begins by determining what the Sovereign Good is, and only then does it direct our attention to 'false goods'. Moreover, the latter no longer give rise to a radical ethics. The problem of conversion is no longer posed, while states are foregrounded at the same time as individuals. This importance that the treatise accords the political should not be analysed as diminishing the individual; on the contrary, it is in fact the proof that the excess in individuals' behaviour directly challenges the structure of the collective ensembles that give them meaning. One might be led to believe that Spinoza's letter presents an *ad hoc* argument, motivated by the attacks

---

[86] *Homo politicus, hoc est consiliarius novus, officiarius et aulicus, secundum hodiernam praxin, auctore Pacifico a Lapide*, 1664, 1668; On this work, cf. Meinsma, *Spinoza et son cercle*, pp. 392–5. Freudenthal, *Spinoza. Leben und Lehre*, I, pp. 179–80.

[87] 'om van ter zijden hier tegen een boekje te schrijven, daar in ik van't opperste goet zou handelen', Ep. 44, G. IV, p. 228, ll. 10–11 [*Ep*. XLIV [to Jarig Jelles]; *CWS* II, 391]; 'ut contra hunc auctorem libellum indirecte conscriberem [. . .] in quo Summum bonum tractarem', [*Ep*. XLIV [to Jarig Jelles]; *CWS* II, 391].

[88] 'D'ongeruste en elendige stant', ibid., 1, 13 [*Ep*. XLIV [to Jarig Jelles]; *CWS* II, 391]; 'inquietam ac miseram [. . .] conditionem', ibid., ll. 31–3 [*Ep*. XLIV [to Jarig Jelles]; *CWS* II, 391].

[89] 'Dat de gemene Staten nootzakelijk door onverzadelijke eerzucht en geltgierigheit vergaan moeten, en vergaan zijn', ibid., ll. 15–17 [*Ep*. XLIV [to Jarig Jelles]; *CWS* II, 391]; 'Respublicas insatiabili Honorum et Divitiarum cupiditate debere interire et interiisse', ibid., ll. 34–5 [*Ep*. XLIV [to Jarig Jelles]; *CWS* II, 391].

against the *TTP*[90] (the beginning in particular might lead one to think this). However, it should be noted to what degree it nevertheless functions as a protreptic, as if it were a small piece of writing in its own right. It is not explicitly directed against the author (and thus Spinoza aims less to engage in a polemic than to indicate the true path), while the very style of the final lines of the project, along with the vocabulary they use (insatiable desire; having to perish and effectively perishing), recall certain passages from the *proemium*. Nevertheless, the story of Thales, on which the letter ends, perhaps evokes or sketches out what the book might have been. The narrative of a wise person who is named as such replaces the anonymity of the first person. Wealth is first thought of under the jurisdiction of its correct use, and knowledge itself is opposed to a sordid and laborious quest, including on the practical terrain. Finally, if Spinoza takes up the classical theme of the community between the Wise and the Gods, is this not a way of thinking the divine determination of the person guided by reason more than human weakness or the vanity of common life?

This treatise was never written.[91] Its project is nevertheless present in the trace of what might have been. This trace shows the displacement undergone by the notion of experience at a point where the system had been reworked on the basis of a stronger conception of individual consistency.

What, finally, can we say about experience in this new context? What does it become in Spinoza's system in its fully developed state? Detached from the journey, it subsists, but is in some sense liberated: there is no longer any radical ethics, no longer any circles of experience. Yet there are open fields

---

[90] This letter is dated 17 February 1671, namely less than a month after to the letter from Lambert de Velthuysen to Jacob Osten (24 January).

[91] Elbogen supposes bizarrely that it was written and inserted at the beginning of the *TdIE*. This text would therefore be made up of pages added in 1671 and that we read as the *proemium*. It is this that explains their disproportionate length (*Der Tractatus . . .*, p. 44 ff.). This thesis is indefensible and Gebhardt is right to reject it in his commentary on letter 44 (Baruch de Spinoza, *Briefwechsel*, Hamburg: F. Meiner, 1914, p. 356). I can add other reasons: Gebhardt remarks that the content of the beginning of the *TdIE* does not correspond to that of the *Homo politicus*. Nor does it correspond to the project described in letter 44. I also cannot accept Pollock's hypothesis, who sees in the *TP* the realisation of this project. With respect to the remarks on lazy people and sumptuary laws from the *TP*, chap. X, 4–8, where Gebhardt himself identifies 'an echo (*Nachwirkung*) of these reflections', these latter concern a very specific subject and do not allude to the Sovereign Good. It is perhaps for this reason that Gebhardt did not take up this comparison in the commentary that he was completing at the moment of his death (*Spinoza Opera*, vol. V, Heidelberg: Carl Winter, 1987, pp. 193–5).

where experience can unfold itself and confirm itself, singularising itself and functioning as the double of a rational discourse to which it is no longer the mere introduction. These fields are constituted by the splintering of Spinoza's first discourse. The tragic closure gives way to a plurality of modes of access to the consistency of the finite and to the diversity that these modes offer people in *their* plurality – a plurality that transcends that of the sole narrative subject. This is what we shall study in the following chapters.

II

Experientia:
Determination and Fields of Experience

7

Determinations and Limits of Experience

1. The Standard Theory

At the beginning of this work, I remarked that the majority of commentators have shown little interest in the concept of experience in Spinoza's work. I should now qualify this statement: not only have they shown little interest in it, those who have made an effort to speak about experience have done so only in order to declare that Spinoza himself took no interest in it. In general, these scholars have said this as a reproach to the author of the *Ethics*. We are therefore dealing, not with a case of a simple omission on the part of the secondary literature, but rather with a situation in which this literature accepts that the category of experience and its attendant procedures are either inexistent or repressed in Spinoza's writings. There are various reasons why commentators have thought that experience is either absent from, or disregarded by, Spinozism. However, the majority of the reasons scholars have advanced in support of this claim can most often be reduced to a single idea, one given clear expression very early on in the writings of Victor Cousin's school. This is not by chance: having resurrected Spinoza studies in France,[1] the school set out to situate Spinozism in the history of philosophy,[2] waged polemics around it,[3] and finally produced the first

---

[1] Including research into Spinoza's milieu. Cf. Cousin's text 'Spinoza et la synagogue des juifs portugais à Amsterdam', *Fragments philosophiques*, Paris, 1838.
[2] Cf. *L'Histoire générale de la philosophie* from 1863, in which Cousin collates older materials.
[3] The first attacks against Cousin, which were extraordinarily violent, never fail to identify him with Spinoza, at the same time as with Hegel, and so include him in their condemnation of these two philosophers. This is the case, for instance, with Goschler's thesis, *Du Panthéisme*, defended in 1839 in Strasbourg under the supervision of Bautain. We should also mention Maret, Bioberti and Gratry.

scholarly instruments for accessing Spinoza's doctrine.[4] The roots of this historiographical enterprise can be found in the school's eclectic spiritualism and its related theoretical positions. Having initially flirted with 'pantheism', and after being attacked on multiple fronts at once, Cousin's school was forced to shift its spiritualism away from Hegel and Spinoza and to make a more strict appeal to a Cartesian heritage[5] – a heritage the school also set out to re-evaluate in a systematic albeit complex manner.[6] I will return briefly a little further on to the stakes of this debate.[7] Let us begin by considering the series of arguments that the historiography of Cousin's School elaborated concerning the status of experience in Spinozism. The advantage of such an approach is that it will help us make explicit certain theses that implicitly govern vast swathes of Spinozist studies to this day.

Rather than turn to Cousin's sparse texts, however, I will seek out the Cousinian interpretation of Spinoza in Saisset's[8] work, which was devoted

---

[4] Emile Saisset presented the first almost complete translation of Spinoza's works in 1843, to which the *Political Treatise* was added in 1861. Twenty years later, another disciple of Cousin, Paul Janet, translated the first volume of the *Short Treatise*, following Schaarschmidt's edition (and also by drawing on the latter's German translation): *Dieu, l'Homme et la Béatitude*, 1878. In the meantime, Damiron's *Mémoire sur Spinoza et sa doctrine* of 1843 appeared, along with studies by Bouillier and Bordas-Dumoulin on the history of Cartesianism, which were produced in the context of the *concours* established in 1839 by the philosophy section of the Académie des Sciences Morales et Politiques (in other words, by Cousin himself). Cf. O. Bloch, 'Damiron et Spinoza', in *Spinoza entre Lumières et Romantisme, Cahiers de Fontenay*, 1985, pp. 229–32.

[5] As the official historiographer of the School Paul Janet notes in *V. Cousin et son œuvre*, Paris: Alcan, 1885, 1893, p. 42, from as early as his voyage of 1817, Cousin had gathered from the Germans 'des idées neuves alors, et que personne ne connaissait en France: l'apologie discrète, mais convaincue, du spinozisme, le rapprochement de Spinoza et de Platon, l'idée d'une immortalité impersonnelle'.

[6] 'La transformation de la philosophie de Cousin a consisté surtout dans le passage de la forme hégélienne à la forme cartésienne, c'est-à-dire dans le retour à la forme française et dans l'abandon de la forme allemande de l'idéalisme', ibid., p. 365; 'l'occasion déterminante de la transformation philosophique de Victor Cousin a été l'accusation de panthéisme dirigée contre lui et contre laquelle il cherche à se défendre dans la préface de 1833, dans la préface de 1838, et dans la préface du rapport sur Pascal en 1842', ibid., p. 372.

[7] Cf. on this point Etienne Gilson's remarks. It is in Cousin's time that it becomes habitual to study the *Discourse on Method* separately to the works that it prefaces. It was thought that this would better bring out the 'spiritualism' that had been 'égaré par le démon des mathématiques', Gilson, *Etudes sur le rôle de la pensée médiévale dans la formation du système cartésien*, Paris: Vrin, 1930, pp. 282–3.

[8] I will not cover here all of the work that Saisset devoted to Spinoza. I have studied this in a separate piece: 'Saisset lecteur de Spinoza', *Recherches sur le XVIIe siècle*, 4 (1980), pp. 85–98.

to the exposition and refutation of Spinozism.[9] This work is the crowning achievement of Saisset's grand labour of translation. In a certain sense, it is the final volume of Saisset's work that gives his project its meaning, since the goal of this text – which Saisset had long been writing – was to determine what, precisely, the pantheism that the spiritualist school had been accused of was, and to present this school's credentials so as to differentiate itself from it.[10] The interest of Saisset's work lies in the fact that it explicitly addresses our theme and even places it at the centre of its reading. In the first part (*Exposition*), the most important elements can be found in the chapter entitled 'La méthode de Spinoza'. I will then follow the development of Saisset's argumentation in the other chapters, from God to politics. In the second part (*Critique*), the most significant elements are to be found in Chapter I, 'Origines du système de Spinoza. Ses rapports avec la philosophie de Descartes'. Paradoxically, as we will see, this critique is already developed in the first part of Saisset's book. In fact, it accompanies the exposition step-by-step. Despite its title, the second part consists, by contrast, in a reasoned analysis of the difference between the Cartesian and Spinozist methods.

At the beginning of the chapter devoted to method, Saisset notes that readers have reproached the *Ethics* for 'all of this geometrical apparatus'.[11] However, as he will go on to observe, the true question does not concern the text's geometrical form but the method that is expressed through it. And indeed, Spinoza himself admits that this is the fundamental question. 'An essentially reflexive genius who was taught at the strict school of Descartes, Spinoza was not ignorant of the fact that in philosophy, there is no problem more fundamental than that of method.'[12] What is important is that in presenting this method, Saisset refers directly to the hierarchy of the different kinds of knowledge.[13] In fact, this hierarchy is quite representative of what

---

[9] *Introduction critique* (= Volume One of *Œuvres de Spinoza*, trans. Eile Saisset, Paris: Charpentier, 1861).

[10] 'J'adorais la philosophie et ne me sentais aucun goût pour le panthéisme. Je voulus savoir si j'allais au panthéisme sans m'en douter, et s'il était vraiment impossible de croire en Dieu et de rester philosophe. Comment faire? Je savais à peine quelques mots d'allemand, et j'étais hors d'état de lire Hegel. Je me mis à lire Spinoza', E. Saisset, *Essai de philosophie religieuse*, Paris: Charpentier, 1859, p. ii.

[11] 'tout cet appareil de géométrie', *Introduction critique*, p. 14.

[12] 'Génie essentiellement réfléchi, élevé à l'école sévère de Descartes, Spinoza n'ignorait pas qu'il n'y a point en philosophie de problème antérieur à celui de la méthode', ibid.

[13] It could be said that in Spinoza the analysis of this hierarchy comes prior to method in the strict sense, and that by identifying these different kinds of knowledge one runs the risk of transforming Spinozism into a methodology of the false idea. We must nevertheless leave aside this question here.

might be called academic Spinozism.¹⁴ Taking the *Treatise on the Emendation of the Intellect* as his guide, Saisset begins by summarising the distinction between 'perception by mere hearsay and perception by vague experience',¹⁵ but he immediately collapses this distinction when it comes to the *Ethics*. He then gives the name 'experience' to the totality of imaginative knowledge. This confusion is not a product of an attempt to simplify Spinoza's language: it supposes from the outset a quite loose notion of experience. In the remainder of Saisset's work, then, we will never know where the frontier between hearsay and vague experience lies – or, more precisely, we will see Saisset treat this frontier as if it were insignificant. Saisset then explains that

> the first kind of knowledge, which is useful for life, has no value for science. It reaches only the accidents, the surfaces of things, and never their essence or depth. Perpetually mobile, the product of fortune and chance and not the internal activity of thought, this first kind of knowledge agitates and preoccupies the mind, but fails to provide any insight. It is the source of sad passions that incessantly obscure the pure ideas of the understanding, tearing the soul away from itself and in some sense dispersing it across external things, and troubling the serenity of its contemplations.¹⁶

This summary mixes Spinozist formulations with others that could be described as Platonic in origin. For example, Saisset takes the term 'accident' from the *TdIE* – a term which is not typically Spinozist¹⁷ – and uses it

---

¹⁴ I noted above that right up until the end of the eighteenth century, those who presented or refuted Spinoza devoted little attention to the theory of the three kinds of knowledge. Yet, from the nineteenth century onwards, it is the opposite that often happens: this theory is at the centre of summaries of Spinoza's doctrine, which relegate to the background the theory of the true idea, the theory of definition and the causal explanation of perceptions.

¹⁵ 'perception par simple ouï-dire et perception par expérience vague', *Introduction critique*, p. 18.

¹⁶ 'le premier genre de connaissance, utile pour la vie, n'est d'aucun prix pour la science. Il atteint les accidents, la surface des choses, non leur essence et leur fond. Livré à une mobilite perpétuelle, ouvrage de la fortune et du hasard, et non de l'activité interne de la pensée, il agite et occupe l'âme, mais ne l'éclaire pas. C'est la source des passions mauvaises qui jettent sans cesse leur ombre sur les idées pures de l'entendement, arrachent l'âme à elle-même, la dispersent en quelque sorte vers les choses extérieures et troublent la sérénité de ses contemplations', ibid.

¹⁷ It appears in the early writings without having a very precise technical meaning. The *Cogitata* explicitly refuse the distinction between substance and accident, while in the *Ethics* the word never appears, save in the expression *per accidens*.

to introduce the notion of an order of mobility and chance that is essentially unintelligible. Still following the *TdIE*, Saisset then examines the degree of scientific value possessed by different species of perception. His first response is the one I cited above:

> Experience, in its dual form [that is, the first two kinds or the first two forms of the first kind of knowledge], cannot give us philosophical knowledge; for it presents us with confused images, while philosophy seeks ideas. It grasps only the accidents of things, but science neglects the accident so as to attain the essence. Experience is therefore absolutely excluded, in an unrestricted and unreserved fashion, from the domain of metaphysics.[18]

The note refers to the *TdIE* and to the letter to De Vries. For the time being I do not intend to discuss the partly implicit interpretation that this statement supposes of the first two texts; but I should note that this proscription of experience, which is immediately attributed to Spinoza as being the most general trait of his method, is affirmed in this chapter only by way of a double or triple amalgamation: between 'experience' and 'vague experience', between 'vague experience' and 'knowledge by hearsay', and finally between the subordination and the exclusion of accidents.[19] Saisset will repeat the idea that this refusal of experience constitutes the general principle of Spinozism right up until the end of his book: for him, it is this principle that constitutes Spinoza's supreme claim;[20] it is also the key position that Saisset himself must contradict each time he wishes to advance.[21]

It is in light of this principle that, in the following chapter, Saisset presents Spinoza's metaphysics. Having outlined the relations between substance,

---

[18] 'L'expérience, sous sa double forme [c'est-à-dire les deux premiers genres ou les deux premières formes du premier genre], ne peut fournir une connaissance philosophique; car elle donne des images confuses, et le philosophe cherche des idées; elle n'atteint que les accidents des choses, et la science néglige l'accident pour s'attacher à l'essence. L'expérience est donc absolument proscrite, sans restriction et sans réserve, du domaine de la métaphysique', ibid., p. 21.

[19] While paragraph 27 from the *TdIE* effectively says that one must abandon knowledge by vague experience, it does not say that philosophy excludes knowledge of accidents; it says that '[accidents] are never understood clearly unless their essences are known first'.

[20] 'C'est la prétention hautement avouée de Spinoza de construire une métaphysique où les données de l'expérience n'entrent pour rien, où tout découle strictement d'une seule idée, l'idée de l'Etre', *Introduction critique*, p. 123.

[21] 'En quoi consiste-t-elle en effet? dans l'emploi de la raison pure et du raisonnement déductif, à l'exclusion de l'expérience', ibid., p. 249.

attributes and modes, Saisset concludes: 'What should above all be noted in this first outline of the system is the effort Spinoza makes to ensure that no empirical element, nothing that is given to consciousness, can penetrate this system. Everything that is there is, in his view, strictly rational, necessary, absolute.'[22] Again referring to the *TdIE*, Saisset then adds: 'Experience has no place here; it could only trouble with its shadows the purity of intellectual intuition and stall, by the force of its impressions and the seductions of its prestige, the progress of metaphysical deduction.'[23] Purity, seduction, prestige: we are here in the domain of the opposition between *episteme* and *doxa*. Whence Saisset's conclusion: 'Like the Platonic dialectic, Spinoza's method excludes all sensible ideas; it begins with ideas, continues with ideas, and it is with ideas that it ends and accomplishes its aim.'[24] For Saisset, we should therefore see in the geometrical method a refusal of everything that is effectively visible to us and which Spinoza condemns in the name of logic. It is this characteristic of Spinoza's method that accounts for the construction of the system: 'If Spinoza had not had the premeditated design to avoid any reference to experience, if he had not, so to speak, put a blindfold over his eyes, would he have constructed his entire system of beings with only these three elements: substance, attributes, modes?'[25]

The reader will have noticed that if, up until this point, the definition of experience remained somewhat confused due to Saisset's initial three-part amalgamation, I have now cited two examples that give content to this term: experience consists in what is given to the senses and to consciousness. It is the second term that most preoccupies Saisset: 'Certainly', he writes,

> if there is an immediately observable reality for man, a reality of which he has the permanent and energetic feeling, then it is the reality of the very

---

[22] 'Ce qu'on doit surtout remarquer dans cette première esquisse du système, c'est l'effort de Spinoza pour n'y laisser pénétrer aucun élément empirique, aucune donnée de la conscience et des sens; tout y est, à ce qu'il lui semble, strictement rationnel, nécessaire, absolu', ibid., p. 33.

[23] 'L'expérience n'a rien à faire ici; elle ne pourra que troubler de ses ténèbres la pureté de l'intuition intellectuelle et arrêter, par la force de ses impressions et la séduction de ses prestiges, le progrès de la déduction métaphysique', ibid., p. 34.

[24] 'Comme la dialectique platonicienne, la méthode de Spinoza exclut toute idée sensible, elle part des idées, poursuit avec les idées, et c'est encore par les idées qu'elle s'achève et s'accomplit', ibid., p. 34.

[25] 'Si Spinoza n'avait pas eu le dessein prémédité de se passer de l'expérience, si pour ainsi parler il ne s'était pas mis un bandeau devant les yeux pour n'y point regarder, aurait-il construit le système entier des êtres avec ces trois seuls éléments: la substance, l'attribut et le mode?', ibid., p. 34.

principle that constitutes him, the reality of the ego. Look for the place of the ego in Spinoza; it isn't there, it *cannot* be there ... The ego is thus banished without hope of return from Spinoza's universe. It is in vain that consciousness demands its place there; a logical necessity, one inherent to the system, pushes it aside and expels it from each and every degree of existence.[26]

This, then, is the apparent touchstone of Saisset's critique: Spinoza's method excludes any and all experience (or almost all experience, as we will see further on); but there is one experience in particular that is missing and whose absence, more than any other, ruins the system. As is well known, in Cousin's philosophy the experience of the ego allows one to elevate oneself, by a sublime and irresistible movement, to the level of the Absolute. The absence of this experience thus signals not only Spinoza's errors in terms of psychology, but also from the perspective of theodicy: the trials of consciousness are missing from both Book I and Book II of the *Ethics*. Spinozism is also destined to encounter problems when it comes to common sense, such as when it affirms that there exists an infinity of attributes even if we can only know two of them:

> But Spinoza is in no way inclined to sacrifice a logical necessity for a fact of observation. Doing so would be a disorder of the mind for him, an inversion of the order of ideas and things. Experience gives us what appears, what happens, what is; logic gives us what should be. It is therefore up to experience to order itself following the necessary laws imposed upon it by this all-powerful logical necessity governing the universe and which consciousness aspires to reflect.[27]

---

[26] 'Certes, s'il est une réalité immédiatement observable pour l'homme, une réalité dont il ait le sentiment énergique et permanent, c'est la réalité du principe même qui le constitue, la réalité du moi. Cherchez la place du moi dans l'univers de Spinoza; elle n'y est pas, elle n'y peut point être ... Le moi est donc banni sans retour de l'univers de Spinoza. C'est en vain que la conscience y réclame sa place; une nécessité logique, inhérente à la nature du système, l'écarte et le chasse tour à tour de tous les degrés de l'existence', ibid., pp. 34–5.

[27] 'Mais Spinoza n'est point homme à sacrifier une nécessité logique à un fait d'observation. C'eût été à ses yeux un dérèglement d'esprit, un renversement de l'ordre des idées et des choses. L'expérience donne ce qui paraît, ce qui arrive, ce qui est; la logique donne ce qui doit être. C'est donc à l'expérience à se régler suivant les lois nécessaires que lui impose cette logique toute-puissante qui gouverne l'univers et que la conscience aspire à réfléchir', ibid., p. 36.

One could nevertheless object to Saisset by saying that Spinoza, even if he does not begin with an irreducible experience of consciousness in the Cousinian sense of the term, nevertheless devotes a number pages from Book II to describing the mechanisms of the human soul. In particular, he attempts to think the soul's unity – not, of course, on the basis of a unique feeling of existence, but in terms of the constitutive relation of individuality. What is remarkable is that Saisset reproaches Spinoza for failing to go far enough in the direction of the denial of the human soul – or rather, for failing to go far enough in terms of the perspective that Saisset thinks is actually Spinoza's. Given that Spinoza fails to take experience into account, and given that this neglect is one of the principles of his philosophy, according to Saisset Spinoza should have reduced the soul to a simple collection of sensations or ideas. Whence the following conclusion: 'this system is thus unfaithful to experience here and to itself'.[28] In other words, Spinoza's generalised refusal of experience is such a central concept in his system that when the system seems to take experience into account, it mistakes its own nature.

If the system is obliged by its own methods to disregard the experience of the ego, by the same token it prevents itself from offering a complete analysis of thought. Its original sin stops it from penetrating very far into the diversity of facts, so swiftly does it seek to dissolve them into the system's principles: 'Forced to give experience its rightful place, Spinoza makes this place as small as possible. He ceaselessly reduces facts to their first principles, and if there is any debate between reasoning and experience, between a fact and a pure idea, it is experience that will be wrong, it is the fact that will have to yield.'[29] Thus, the rigour of the geometrical method undermines the analyses of the thinking thing from Book II, just as it prevents a proper understanding of Being in Book I.

Finally, the same negation of experience can be found in the philosophy of action. In morality, Saisset notes, our consciousness draws on both the feeling of free will and the order of the good. Yet Spinoza refuses both of these: 'This is because free will and the feeling of good and evil are only, after all, facts, and when it comes to a choice between facts and a logical necessity, Spinoza does not hesitate. What remains for us to understand is why, after this stunning denial of the human being's consciousness, Spinoza

---

[28] 'ce système est donc infidèle ici à l'expérience et à lui-même', ibid., p. 114.
[29] 'Forcé de faire à l'expérience sa part, Spinoza la lui fera aussi petite que possible. Il ramènera sans cesse les faits à leurs principes premiers, et si quelque débat s'engage entre le raisonnement et l'expérience, entre un fait et une idée pure, c'est l'expérience qui aura tort, c'est le fait qui devra succomber', ibid., p. 124.

then proposes a morality whose conditions of possibility he has destroyed in advance.'[30]

God, human nature, action: the whole of Saisset's presentation of Spinoza's system is oriented around an axis – the problem of method – and his critique of each one of these domains is based on the same idea: Spinoza prohibits himself from truly understanding morality and metaphysics because in each of these domains he refuses the teachings of experience. This first trait is thus a fundamental trait: it is on its basis that we can understand the essential parts of Spinoza's doctrine in terms of their specific characteristics; it is also on its basis that this doctrine can be critiqued.

Nevertheless, Saisset occasionally concedes that Spinoza has recourse to experience in other domains, for instance when he is operating at some distance from the core of his system. But these concessions concern fields that, in the eyes of a Cousinian, are secondary in nature. They include physics and politics (on this point, the academic French tradition will largely follow the Cousinians). Furthermore, these concessions are formulated in an extremely restrictive way. Let us read one such concession that concerns the *TTP* (and which, moreover, appears only in a note):

> It would not be useless to note here that it is only in the metaphysical domain that Spinoza excludes experience; he is far from denigrating its use in other kinds of research. Here is a passage where the method of observation and induction is described with perfect precision: 'For the method of interpreting nature consists above all in putting together a history of nature, from which, as from certain data, we infer the definitions of natural things' (*The Theologico-Political Treatise*, Chapter XII).[31]

This quotation is based on a passage from the *TTP*[32] in which the word 'experience' does not appear. Moreover, it isolates part of a sentence that

---

[30] 'C'est que le libre arbitre et le sentiment du bien et du mal ne sont, après tout, que des faits et entre les faits et une nécessité logique, Spinoza n'hésite pas. Reste à comprendre qu'après ce démenti éclatant donnée à la conscience du genre humain au nom de la logique, Spinoza vienne ensuite proposer aux hommes une morale dont il a par avance détruit les conditions', ibid., p. 150.

[31] Ibid., p. 124, n. 3.

[32] In fact, it is from the beginning of Chapter VII: 'Nam sicuti methodus interpretandi naturam in hoc potissimum consistit, in concinnanda scilicet historia naturae, ex qua, utpote ex certis datis, rerum naturalium definitiones concludimus', G III, p. 98, ll. 18–21 [*TTP* VII, 6; *CWS* II, 171]. The qualification 'exact' [in Saisset's translation of this passage] must have been added in order to make it seem less geometrical.

deals neither with theology nor politics. The only thing that is mentioned is the recourse to certain data from the phenomena of nature. This seems to restrict the field of application of this remark to physics and thus experience to a method of observation and induction. The most we can conclude from it is that Spinoza's general disregard for experience does not prevent him from recognising the value of the facts of the physical sciences. For Saisset, this does not concern the core of Spinoza's philosophy and is not even a very original thesis.

The second concession concerns politics. In question is the brief judgement that the author of the *Political Treatise* makes of his predecessors. As we know, Spinoza begins by rejecting the utopia and myth of a golden age. He then speaks of those he names 'Political Practitioners' [*les Politiques*]: 'Spinoza shows himself more indulgent towards political practitioners, among whom he gives a special place to Machiavelli.'[33] But the way in which Saisset sums up Spinoza's judgement is itself surprising: 'The mistake of these kinds of minds is to believe that the things of this world occur randomly; they know only the surface of things and are ignorant of the fact that beneath these fugitive accidents, which the common people call caprice, fortune, chance, there reigns a hidden order as certain and inflexible as the geometrical order.'[34] This is not at all what Spinoza says. In fact, in the second paragraph from the first chapter, he says that the Political Practitioners are judged to be 'shrewd rather than wise' and that the means they have recourse to are those of men who 'usually practice more from fear than because they're guided by reason'.[35] In fact, Saisset places in Spinoza's mouth a criticism of the practices of Politicians that comes directly from the formulation he himself has constructed at the beginning of his book on the subject of experience: the terms 'accidents', the 'surface of things', 'fortune' and 'chance' are all explicitly reprised. This allows Saisset to

---

[33] 'Spinoza se montre plus indulgent pour les politiques, parmi lesquels il donne une place à part à Machiavel', *Introduction critique*, p. 202.

[34] 'Le tort de ce genre d'esprits c'est de croire que les affaires de ce monde vont à l'aventure; ils ne connaissent que la surface des choses et ne savent pas que sous ces accidents fugitifs que le vulgaire nomme caprice, fortune, hasard, règne un ordre caché aussi certain, aussi inflexible que l'ordre de la géométrie', ibid., p. 203.

[35] 'At Politici contra hominibus magis insidiari quam consulere creduntur, & potius callidi quam sapientes aestimantur [. . .] homines, magis metu quam ratione ducti', G III, p. 273, ll. 26–7 [*TP* I, 2; *CWS* II, 504] and p. 274, ll. 2–3 [*TP* I, 2; *CWS* II, 504]. Machiavelli is not named in this passage. He is named in Chapter V, and is praised without reserve: he is described as *sapiens, acutissimus, prudentissimus*, and considered as being 'on the side of freedom, and gave very good advice for protecting it', G III, p. 290, l. 30 [*TP* V, 7; *CWS* II, 531]; p. 291, l. 11 [*TP* V, 7; *CWS* II, 531].

conjure a Spinoza who is attempting to find a balance between experience and reason: 'Spinoza's ambition is therefore to hold at an equal distance utopians and empiricists, Morus and Machiavelli; he seeks to satisfy both reason, which alone gives us true principles, and experience, which subjects these principles to the test of the facts.'[36] It is clear that this interpretation is quite removed from the text; but my aim here is not to determine the reasons for this. It is enough to note that the only two domains in which Saisset recognises in Spinoza a certain use of experience are very limited and have no repercussions for the system as a whole. Just as the thesis of the unity of the soul appeared as a kind of oversight, the proofs of Spinoza's attention to the facts of physics or politics seem to be minor concessions made by a systematic thinker who is no longer working at the core of his system.

We can now turn to the second part of Saisset's work – not to find there his critique of Spinozism, which is already complete by this point, but to read the careful line of demarcation that Saisset traces between Spinozism and Cartesianism. For Saisset, Descartes' method is experiential [*expérimentale*] in the sense that it is based on the testimony of consciousness (since Cousin's time, this had been the spiritualist reinterpretation of the *cogito*).[37] Spinoza distinguishes himself from Descartes precisely by prioritising the geometrical order over this testimony: 'Spinoza is the apostle of the contrary method. Never has one professed a more fervent faith in pure reason; never has one believed so firmly in the power of argument; never has one set aside the facts of experience with a more superb disdain.'[38] This is why the *Meditations* and the *Ethics* propose two divergent paths: the first begins with

---

[36] 'L'ambition de Spinoza serait donc de se tenir à égale distance des utopistes et des empiriques, entre Morus et Machiavel; il voudrait satisfaire à la fois la raison qui seule donne de vrais principes et l'expérience qui les met à l'épreuve des faits', *Introduction critique*, p. 204.

[37] For example, Cousin writes: 'L'étude de l'esprit humain s'appelle scientifiquement la psychologie. Nous voilà donc ramené par une autre voie à ce principe qui est l'âme de tous nos travaux, qui constitue le caractère propre et aussi le caractère national de notre philosophie, la rattache à Descartes et la sépare de toute philosophie étrangère, à savoir que la psychologie est le point de départ nécessaire, la suprême condition, la méthode unique de toute saine philosophie, qu'elle seule introduit légitimement dans le sanctuaire de la métaphysique et qu'elle fournit même à l'histoire sa plus sûre lumière', *Histoire générale de la philosophie*, p. 6.

[38] 'Spinoza est l'apôtre de la méthode contraire. Jamais on n'a professé pour la raison pure un culte plus fervent; jamais on n'a cru à la puissance du raisonnement d'une foi plus entière; jamais on n'a écarté les faits de l'expérience avaec un plus superbe dédain', *Introduction critique*, p. 231.

man, with the experience of the feeling of freedom, but then stops before the boundary marking the limits beyond which the human mind cannot go: the *Meditations* consciously resign themselves to noting the mystery instead of mutilating real facts such as these are presented to conscious experience. The *Ethics*, by contrast, aspires without this guardrail to deduce everything and to explain everything. This is why it tends towards pantheism, a danger that can be avoided only by having respect for facts and for the analysis of the ego. In other words, the general principle that constitutes both the method and foundation of Spinoza's system is, at one and the same time, the originary point of demarcation by which it differentiates itself from Cartesianism. The refusal of experience marks the choice of geometry over a Cartesian filiation.

What can be deduced from this is, of course, that if the geometrical method and the refusal of experience lead to pantheism, then the appeal to the testimony of consciousness saves one from this danger. Leibniz is thus wrong to condemn Descartes, while those who see pantheism everywhere are wrong to accuse the spiritualists of it, for the spiritualists are the rightful heirs of Cartesianism. But above all, for Saisset's demonstration to be complete, it is important for him to hold firm on the following point: that the geometrical spirit by itself cannot lead to the immortality of the soul, since this spirit tends to dissolve individuals in the unique substance. Saisset must therefore reject those texts where Spinoza seems to contradict this exclusion. It is once again as a result of an internal incoherency in his thought that Spinoza seems to believe in an experience of eternity. In fact, from Spinoza's point of view – or, again, from the point of view that should be his, according to Saisset – we do not really feel that we are eternal.[39]

Let us sum up what we have learnt from Saisset's work. It is based on three fundamental theses: for reasons of principle, Spinoza sacrifices experience on the altar of deduction; this sacrifice is explicit; and it is this sacrifice that separates him from Descartes and leads to his pantheism. All of these analyses are based on an extraordinarily broad conception of experience. As we have seen, experience is at once vague experience and knowledge by hearsay, the feeling of freedom, of the ego, and the observation of facts and induction. We might be surprised not to find in this selection the more precise meaning of experience that appeared to govern the introduction to the *Treatise on the Emendation of the Intellect*. But let us remain for the time being with what Saisset says. We can read his point of departure and his conclusion in two

[39] Ibid., pp. 261–2.

ways: either in terms of the limited and historical debate between Cousin's school and his adversaries on the topic of Spinoza and Descartes, or by showing that beyond the limits of this historical framework and beyond his own weaknesses, Saisset produced a standard interpretation of the status and role of experience in Spinoza – an interpretation that has remained largely uncontested, indeed has been reinforced, including among those who do not know of or quote from his book.

It is clear what is at stake in these analyses. For Cousin and Saisset, it is Descartes who represents experience, while Spinoza represents a disregard for experience in favour of geometry, or an exaggerated geometry.[40] The function of Saisset's book could thus be summarised as follows: it advances an argument whose purpose is to shield Descartes – and thus the spiritualist school that appeals to him – from the accusation of pantheism. Those who make this accusation – until the middle of the nineteenth century, these were the tenants of the 'philosophie du clergé', while after them it was Foucher de Careil – echo Leibniz's formulation: Spinoza begins where Descartes ends.[41] It is thus important for the 'philosophie de l'Université' to separate these two authors as much as possible by showing that pantheism takes root at precisely the point where Spinoza turns away from Descartes. A number of hypotheses will be put forward on the nature of this point of distinction: while Cousin had chosen to distinguish Spinoza and Descartes mostly in terms of the opposition between experience and geometry, Saisset will adopt this position consistently. In his later years, Cousin, along with Adolphe Franck, drawing on Munk's writings, will then try another way: by referring to Spinoza's Jewish origins.[42] What will be said from this perspective about Spinoza's Judaism will again involve taking a position on the extent of the supposed influence of Descartes on Spinoza. Once again, it will be a matter of identifying Spinoza's pantheism at a point in his system that cannot be found in Descartes'. All of these debates will produce a climate that for a long time will determine the reading of Spinoza in the French university system, including among the opponents of Cousinian historiography. The desire to read Spinoza exclusively in relation to Descartes, whether to

---

[40] Saisset remarks moreover that on certain points Descartes had prepared the terrain for Spinoza by moving away from his own method. Spiritualism thus finds itself defending Cartesianism against Descartes.

[41] Foucher de Careil, *Lettres et opuscules inédits de Leibniz*, Paris: Ladrange, 1854; *Leibniz, Descartes et Spinoza*, Paris: Ladrange, 1862.

[42] Cf. my article cited above for the way in which Damiron and Saisset defend against Cousin the positions Cousin himself had formerly adopted ('Saisset lecteur de Spinoza', pp. 92–6).

find points of continuity, rupture or development, remains alive at least until Léon Brunschvicg[43] and Alain.[44]

It is not enough, however, to determine in this way what is at stake in Saisset's analysis. Let us leave aside Saisset's third thesis and his reading of Descartes, neither of which interest us here, being too close to Cousin's apologetics. Saisset's two other theses – Spinoza's refusal of experience and the explicit nature of this refusal – can be read by and for themselves. It must be said, moreover, that they have hardly ever been refuted. It is no doubt easy to identify obvious weaknesses in certain formulations of these theses, such as Saisset's catch-all notion of experience, the tendency to class as incoherencies those of Spinoza's formulations that do not fit into Saisset's interpretation, and the overly hasty survey of certain texts. But these weaknesses might still appear as the more exaggerated moments of an interpretation that is essentially correct. This is why, despite the historical determinations I mentioned above, Emile Saisset's work can be considered as representative of a sort of common opinion among historians of philosophy concerning the status of experience in Spinoza's system. Indeed, Saisset's work has the advantage of explicitly expressing theses that we encounter everywhere, albeit in an implicit state. If Saisset did not invent all of the themes of this common opinion,[45] he did develop and systematise them in a way that made them both visible and transmissible. The interpretation that he formulates

[43] Thanks to Brunschvicg's influence, in the 1930s the French University will still read Spinoza from this perspective, but this time by seeking out a positive continuity: 'Il était bien entendu qu'il [Spinoza] "accomplissait" Descartes', J.-T. Desanti, *Un destin philosophique*, Paris: Grasset, 1982, p. 119.

[44] In a preface written in 1946 for the second edition of the work he published in 1900, Alain writes: 'Il faut partir de Descartes et mener cette belle doctrine jusqu'à Spinoza. C'est le moyen de ne pas tomber dans la philosophie scolaire et de réveiller l'homme dans le lecteur', Mellotée, 1949, reissued as *Spinoza*, Paris: Gallimard, 1986, p. 11.

[45] We already find – for example, in Léon de Montbeillard's work – the association between a refusal of experience and the unicity of substance: 'C'est que la considération de la substance exerce sur les esprits qu'elle préoccupe la fascination de l'abîme. Une fois sur cette voie, on ne sent plus ni le frein de l'expérience, qui devient impossible, ni celui du bon sens, qui ne sonde pas ces profondeurs', *De l'Ethique de Spinoza*, Paris: Joubert, 1851, p. 56. But the reader will notice that in Montbeillard's presentation it is in some sense the appeal to substance that causes one to reject experience, and not the method that explains the doctrine. To be convinced of this, one need only read the following lines: 'Le monde phénoménal disparaît sous l'analyse, comme devant l'épée de Tancrède les apparitions de la forêt enchantée. On s'encourage, on s'aventure, et, le charme décevant de l'abstraction croissant toujours, on se sent, pris de vertige, glisser, à travers un vide effrayant, jusqu'à l'unicité de substance', pp. 56–7.

has hardly any adversaries. Better still, even on those points where Saisset seems to forgive Spinoza, at least in part, for disregarding experience, others still reproach him. Very early on, for example, Nieuwentijt claimed that the new experimental philosophy being developed in England was better at accounting for facts than geometrical deduction and that the absence of experience rendered Spinoza's system false.[46] Since then, specialists in the history of the sciences have shown how Spinoza, in his discussion with Boyle, was careless in his dealing with facts and lagging behind philosophically[47] because he believed he was able to solve all problems concerning matter via a deductive method.[48] Finally, certain historians of political theory seem to find Spinoza's works even more geometrical than Saisset himself believed they were.[49] Everyone thus seems to agree with Saisset and even occasionally to reinforce the rigour of his interpretation. The main interest of Saisset's book, and more broadly of the Cousinian school, is therefore that it formulates a critique of Spinozism from a unitary perspective, one that could then be exported outside of this school's own problematic.[50]

---

[46] B. Nieuwentijt, *Gronden van Zekerheid*, Amsterdam, 1720, p. 244 ff. We find the essential parts of the fourth part, which contains the critique of Spinozism, in the volume published by R.-H. Vermij in the collection 'Geschiedenis van de wijsbegeerte in Nederland': *Bernard Nieuwentijt: Een zekere, zakelijke wijsbegeerte*, Baarn: Ambo, 1988, pp. 99–115. On Nieuwentijt as a reader of Spinoza, see also Dunin-Borkowski, *Spinoza nach dreihundert Jahren*, Berlin/Bonn: Ferd. Dümmlers Verlag, 1932, p. 130 and M. J. Petry, *Nieuwentijt's Criticism of Spinoza*, MVHS, XL, Leiden: Brill, 1979.

[47] H. Daudin, 'Spinoza et la science expérimentale: sa discussion de l'expérience de Boyle', *Revue d'histoire des sciences*, II, 2 (1949), pp. 179–90. To Boyle, the experimenter, the author opposes 'le philosophe métaphysicien qui n'attribue d'autre rôle à l'expérience que celui de confirmer ses principes', and concludes: 'Les plus grandes doctrines sont prisonnières du passé et les découvertes capitales ne sont pas toujours leur fait.'

[48] A. Rupert and Marie Boas Hall, 'Philosophy and Natural Philosophy: Boyle and Spinoza', *L'aventure de l'esprit*, Mélanges Alexandre Koyré II, Paris: Hermann, 1964, pp. 241–56. The clearest formulation can be found on p. 251 and concerns the difference recognised by the chemistry of the seventeenth century between common salt, nitre and potassium: 'In Spinoza's philosophical hands even this little empirical certainty was dissolving away.' One finds an analogous interpretation in the work of N. Maull, 'Spinoza in the Century of Science', in *Spinoza and the Sciences*, ed. M. Grene and D. Nails, Dordrecht: Reidel, 1986, pp. 2–13.

[49] 'In Holland Spinoza undertook to present his ethics in the form of a geometrical demonstration, with all the paraphernalia of axioms, theorems, scholia and corollaries, and his *Political Treatise*, though lacking the form, was scarcely less rigorous in its procedure', G. H. Sabine, *A History of Political Theory*, London: Harrap, 1948, p. 363. Furthermore, Sabine clearly considers this form a failure. Cf. ibid., pp. 365 and 391.

[50] The originality and productivity of this critique obviously comes down to the desire

If we leave aside certain thoughtless or extreme formulations, the characterisation provided by Saisset and his successors is based on a limited number of incontestable arguments drawn from the texts and structure of Spinozist philosophy:

— The general form of the system does indeed seem to suggest a rationalism without limits. Explaining God and things *more geometrico* can hardly prepare one for the surprises and novelties that experience might introduce into the system. This is why the Spinozist procedure appears to historians of philosophy as synonymous with an *a priori* construction, with the subordination of facts to principles, when it is not purely and simply suppressing these facts. To this we can add the fact that those who do not believe in the consistency of the geometrical method accord greater value to tradition or dissimulation than to experience: this is case with Leo Strauss[51] and Wolfson.[52]

— Spinoza's explicit formulations describe vague experience as the most inferior of the different kinds of knowledge. The text is clear and unavoidable on this point. This is not a marginal note: it is clearly said three times in Spinoza's exposition of the kinds of knowledge.[53] Propositions 41 and 42 from Book II of the *Ethics* draw irreducibly negative consequences from this: 'Knowledge of the first kind is the only cause of falsity, whereas knowledge

---

to simultaneously defend a spiritualism that is based on the analysis of consciousness. It is under the jurisdiction of this analysis that the disjunction between deduction and experience emerges. By contrast, if we consider the German tradition of the critique (and, symmetrically, the defence) of Spinozism, then we find that it is carried out on an entirely different basis. For instance, during the offensive against Wolff, Lange brings together Descartes, Leibniz and Spinoza under the same category of fatalism. Cf. M. Wundt, *Die deutsche Schulphilosophie im Zeitalter der Auflkärung*, Tübingen: Mohr, 1945; Hildesheim: Olms, 1964, p. 240 ff. Similarly, during the pantheism controversy, Jacobi is careful to indicate that 'the path of demonstration leads each time to fatalism' by explicitly grouping Leibniz and Wolff alongside Spinoza. It is faith, and not experience, that he opposes to demonstration. Cf. in the *Letters* the six propositions that follow the letter from 21 April 1785. As for Wolff himself, when he demarcates himself from Spinozism, it is above all on the question of the unity of substance, then on that of fatalism. Cf. J. Ecole, 'La critique wolffienne du spinozisme', *Bulletin de l'Association des Amis de Spinoza*, 5 (1981), pp. 9–19.

[51] Cf. *Persecution and the Art of Writing*, Illinois: The Free Press, 1952, Chapter V.

[52] 'There is thus behind our present *Ethics*, demonstrated in geometrical order, an *Ethics* demonstrated in rabbinical and scholastic order', *The Philosophy of Spinoza*, vol. I, p. 59.

[53] *TdIE*, § 27, G II, p. 13, ll. 1–6 [*TdIE* 27; CWS I, 16]; *KV*, Part II, Chapter II, § 2, M, p. 43 [CWS I, 99–100]; *Ethics* II, 40, Schol. 2, G II, p. 122 [CWS I, 477–8].

of the second and the third kind is necessarily true.'[54] Book V adds: 'The Striving, or Desire, to know things by the third kind of knowledge cannot arise from the first kind of knowledge, but can indeed arise from the second.'[55] It is thus as a rupture that the *Ethics* represents the relation between the first kind of knowledge – of which vague experience forms a part – and the kinds of knowledge that lead to adequate knowledge and beatitude.

— The letter to De Vries, which has the advantage of confronting our problem head on and not in the context of a typology of knowledge, denies almost any role to experience. The 'very learned young man' had asked, no doubt in the name of the study circle that had been formed by the philosopher's friends in Amsterdam, if experience was necessary for knowing if the definition of an attribute were true. Spinoza's response is decisive. Let us recall the well-known terms of the letter: 'we need experience only for those things which cannot be inferred from the definition of the thing [. . .] but not for those things whose existence is not distinguished from their essence, and is therefore inferred from their definition. Indeed no experience will ever be able to teach us this, for experience does not teach the essence of things.'[56] There are two parts to Spinoza's answer: not only is experience not necessary (we *can* do without it), but moreover it is useless (we *should* do without it). Experience does not appear as another path alongside deduction and definition of a geometrical type: it is not a path at all.

Should we give our consent to this very common opinion? Is the case definitively closed? If yes, then we have to consider the beginning of the *Treatise on the Emendation of the Intellect* as a hapax and admit that Spinoza's mature works definitively dismiss the idea that experience can teach us anything – except only occasionally and on points of secondary interest. Yet this

---

[54] 'Cognitio primi generis unica est falsitatis causa, secundi autem et tertii est necessario vera', G II, p. 122, ll. 32–3 [*Ethics* II, 42; *CWS* I, 478]; 'Secundi et tertii, et non primi generis cognitio docet nos verum a falso distinguere', ibid., p. 123, ll. 9–10 [*Ethics* II, 42, Dem.; *CWS* I, 478].

[55] 'Conatus, seu cupiditas cognoscendi res tertio cognitionis genere, oriri non potest ex primo, at quidem ex secundo cognitionis genere', *Ethics* V, 28, G II, p. 297, ll. 25–7 [*CWS* I, 609].

[56] 'Ad hoc respondeo, nos nunquam egere experientia, nisi ad illa, quae ex rei definitione non possunt concludi [. . .] Non vero ad illa, quorum existentia ab eorundem essentia non distinguitur, ac proinde ab eorum definitione concluditur. Imo nulla experientia id unquam nos edocere poterit: nam experientia nullas rerum essentias docet', Ep. X (February or March 1663), G IV, p. 47, ll. 7–9 and 10–13 [*Ep.* X [to Simon de Vries]; *CWS* I, 196].

problem cannot be resolved so easily. In fact, it is possible to formulate a certain number of arguments that go in the opposite direction:

A. Spinoza's reasoning does not always present itself in an exclusively geometrical form. It cannot be said that the *Treatises* deduce all of their theses from their initial definitions. Even in the *Ethics*, the Scholia on the whole hardly resemble a work of geometry; they do more than simply comment on the Propositions and Demonstrations. Certain Scholia are polemical, while others seem to appeal to the world of facts or to what the reader already knows – in short, to an entire body of knowledge that perhaps either confirms or illustrates the geometrical deduction, but which is not known uniquely by virtue of deduction.

B. The following massive fact cannot be avoided: despite everything we have just mentioned, there are numerous passages where experience (and not vague experience) is mentioned in explicitly positive terms, and not as a mistress of error. Let us cite just a few examples: the physics from Book II is justified to the extent that 'all those postulates which I have assumed contain hardly anything that is not established by experience which we cannot doubt'.[57] In the face of those who believe in the absolute power of the soul over the body, it is essential to recall that 'experience teaches all too plainly that men have nothing less in their power than their tongue, and can do nothing less than moderate their appetites'.[58] Furthermore, 'experience itself, no less clearly than reason, teaches'[59] that people who believe themselves to be free do so because they are conscious of their actions but ignorant of the causes that lie behind them. The fact that nothing is more useful to man than man, above all a man governed by reason, 'is also confirmed by daily experience, which provides so much and such clear evidence that this saying is almost in everyone's mouth: man is a God for man'.[60] And finally,

---

[57] 'quandoquidem omnia illa, quae sumpsi, postulata, vix quicquam continent, quod non constet experientia, de qua nobis non licet dubitare', *Ethics* II, 27, Schol., G II, p. 105, ll. 26–8 [CWS I, 464]. The final relative is clarified by an indication ('postquam ostendimus corpus humanum, prout ipsum sentimus existere') to which I will return further on.

[58] 'At experientia satis superque docet, homines nihil minus in potestare habere quam linguam, nec minus posse quam appetitus moderri suos', *Ethics* III, 2, Schol., G II, p. 143, ll. 14–16 [CWS I, 496].

[59] 'Ipsa experientia non minus clare quam ratio doceat . . .', ibid., ll. 29–30 [*Ethics* III, 2, Schol.; CWS I, 494].

[60] 'Quae modo ostendimus, ipsa etiam experientia quotidie tot, tamque luculentis testimoniis testatur, ut omnibus fere in ore sit: hominem homini Deum esse', *Ethics* IV, 35, Schol., G II, p. 234, ll. 2–4 [CWS 563].

'experience also testifies'[61] to the fact that the power of the soul over the affects is proportional to the knowledge of the necessity governing singular things. These examples are all taken from the *Ethics*, the most openly geometrical book in terms of its structure; but we find just as many examples in the *TTP* or the *Political Treatise*.[62] The reader will have noticed the repeated formula, which recalls the first sentence of the *TdIE*, but which is expressed in the present tense this time: 'experientia docet'.[63] Spinoza *never* contradicts this positivity of experience (whereas Descartes, for instance, accepts that experience can be misleading).[64] Even when Spinoza says that experience *seems* to be misleading, it is only when he is communicating the objections of a possible adversary, and in such cases it is once again experience that he opposes to such objections. For example, when he lists the arguments that could be made against his thesis of the identity between the understanding and the will, he expects that an adversary will counter with the experience of the suspension of judgement; and he responds that this suspension is in reality a perception and not a case of free will, as the daily experience of sleep proves.[65]

[61] 'Quo haec cognitio, quod scilicet res necessariae sint, magis circa res singulares, quas distinctius et magis vivide imaginamur, versatur, eo haec mentis in affectus potentia major est, quod ipsa etiam experientia testatur', *Ethics* V, 7, Schol., G II, p. 284, l. 30; p. 285, l. 3 [*CWS* I, 599–600].
[62] *TTP*, Chapter III, G III, p. 47, l. 10 [*TTP* III, 14; *CWS* II, 114]; ibid., p. 56, l. 26 [*TTP* III, 53; *CWS* II, 124]; Chapter V, p. 70, l. 25 [*TTP* V, 7; *CWS* II, 140]; Chapter VI, p. 47, l. 27 [*TTP* VI, 32; *CWS* II, 159]; Chapter XIII, p. 167, l. 14 [*TTP* XIII, 2; *CWS* II, 257]; Chapter XVI, p. 196, l. 30 [*TTP* XVI, 44; *CWS* II, 291]; p. 199, l. 26 [*TTP* XVI, 62; *CWS* II, 294]; etc. *TP*, Chapter I, G III, p. 273, l. 28 [*TP* I, 2; *CWS* II, 504]; Chapter II, p. 278, ll. 1–2 [*TP* II, 6; *CWS* II, 509]; etc. I will not quote these passages here, for a defender of Saisset could claim that this is a secondary field, exterior to the centre of Spinoza's thought, or that these expressions are proper to the style of the *TTP*. I will show further on that this is not the case at all, but for the time being these quotations from the *Ethics* will suffice to establish the presence of positive references to experience in Spinoza's key work.
[63] In the *TTP* and the *TP*, we also find it in the past tense: 'experientia docuit'.
[64] 'Notandum insuper, experientias rerum saepe esse fallaces . . .', *Rule Two*, AT, X, p. 365 [*PWD* I, 12]; cf. J.-L. Marion, *Sur l'ontologie grise de Descartes*, Paris: Vrin, 1975, pp. 42–7. As for Montaigne, if the final chapter of the *Essays* begins by admitting that 'quand la raison nous faut, nous y employons l'expérience', it is to immediately add that it is 'un moyen plus faible et moins digne', Book III, Chapter XIII.
[65] *Ethics* II, 49, Cor., Schol., G II, p. 132, l. 32, sq [*CWS* I, 487]: 'Secundo nobis objici potest, quod experientia nihil clarius videatur docere, quam quod nostrum judicium possumus suspendere, ne rebus, quas percipemus, non assentiamur.' The response is given on p. 134, l. 11 ff. [*Ethics* II, 49, Cor., Schol., *CWS* I, 488]: 'Ad secundum objectionem respondeo negando, nos liberam habere potestatem judicium suspendendi.

C. Finally, we must return to the enigmatic formulation that, as we saw, Saisset rejected and that occupies the middle of the final Book of the *Ethics*: we know and we experience that we are eternal.[66] As difficult as it is to interpret, this formulation exists and one is right to consider that a reading of Spinoza that thinks itself capable of doing without it is forgetting at least one dimension of the system.

Here, then, are a series of indications, drawn from Spinoza's mature works, which permit us to think that Spinoza's method, even in those places where it is employed most systematically, does not exclude recourse to experience – indeed, that in certain cases, it grants experience a strong probative value. We have not come to the end of our efforts, however. The two series of texts cited above are in equal measure works by Spinoza. That the interpretative tradition has privileged the first series should not authorise us, in turn, to neglect it. Furthermore, another tradition has concerned itself with the last of the passages quoted (on experience and eternity) and has most often sought to draw consequences from it that are hostile to the coherence of the system. Should we condemn a passage because of the way it has been hijacked? At what price can we restore its proper meaning? As for the other passages, we cannot rest content with simply juxtaposing them. Either Spinoza is contradicting himself, or these texts are not speaking of the same thing. If we wish to understand Spinoza it is therefore necessary to define and distinguish and no longer be satisfied with random references to facts and induction. We must restore these various indications to the level of the system they belong to, not isolate them by simply citing them. To continue our inquiry, it would be best to determine what experience is, to explain it, and above all to explain what it is not. We must distinguish experience from vague experience, from scientific experimentation and possibly also from other terms that are at least in part homonymic. Since it is articulated with other notions as part of a system, we will have to draw up a catalogue of the full range of its co-occurrences, as we did in the first part of this work. To do this, I will sometimes have to insist on distinctions that Spinoza does not himself explicitly make, but which, it seems to me, are present in a practical state in his writing and forms of reasoning. We will also have to

---

Nam cum dicimus, aliquem judicium suspendere, nihil aliud dicimus, quam quod videt, se rem non adaequate percipere. Est igitur judicii suspensio revera perceptio, et non libera voluntas [. . .] Atque hoc quotidie in somnis experimur.'

[66] 'At nihilominus sentimus experimurque nos aeternos esse', *Ethics* V, 23, Schol., G II, p. 296, ll. 3–4 [CWS I, 607].

analyse the dialogue that he pursues with other doctrines and which alone allows us to exhaustively evaluate the importance of a term or the reasons for the modifications it undergoes. Only then will we be able to judge if, in addition to geometrical reasoning, there remains a place for experiential procedures in Spinoza's thought. Most importantly, in doing so we will be able to understand if the recognition and analysis of the modalities of such an experiential procedure help us to better comprehend Spinoza's texts and system.

2. What Experience Is Not

It seems clear that experience cannot be reduced to the mere reference to facts, nor to simple observation. That said, an analysis is required of vague experience and of scientific experimentation since these notions can also be found in the *Treatises* and the *Ethics*. It will be equally necessary to inquire into mystical experience, since there exists a tradition that interprets Spinoza from this perspective.

A. Experience is Irreducible to Vague Experience

One of the most important reasons why commentators have failed to take an interest in experience is without doubt because they have reduced it to *experientia vaga*. This is a reductive interpretation of the thesis of the three (or four) kinds of knowledge.[67] Indeed, the Spinozist theory of method – or, to use the vocabulary of the *Ethics*, of the soul as a thinking thing – is in no way reducible to the classification of different kinds of knowledge. It could even be argued that any summary of Spinoza's theory of thought that reduces it to this classification – or, alternatively, that presents it only from the perspective of this classification – would fail to comprehend what is most original in the causal theory of adequate ideas. We must therefore return to this classification here.

As I noted above, in Spinoza's early writings there is a tendency to distinguish between experience and vague experience, less as two different objects and more as two perspectives on the same object, with one of these

---

[67] To simplify the terminology, I will henceforth call *kinds* of knowledge the four forms of perception that Spinoza distinguishes in all of his works. This gives us three or four kinds of knowledge depending on whether the first two types are or are not grouped together in a single kind. Even when they are grouped together, however, they are never confused with one another.

perspectives using as its material what the other produces. This difference is not explicitly thematised, but we can still catch a glimpse of it in Spinoza's textual practice. In the *Short Treatise*, a single term is used but in the context of two different problematics; in the *TdIE*, two distinct terms are used. We now have to ask what happens in Spinoza's mature work: with regard to these later works, should the notion of experience be conceived on the basis of vague experience alone? This is what the majority of commentators have done without even posing the question. We saw that Saisset referred to the first two kinds of knowledge using the same term 'experience' and applied what the *TdIE* said about them to the *Ethics*. All of the secondary literature on Spinozism conforms to such an assimilation. The formulations from the Scholium from Proposition 40, along with Propositions 41 and 42 from Book II concerning vague experience, are applied directly to experience *tout court*. Thus, Spinoza seems in practice to exhibit the greatest possible confidence in a type of knowledge that he elsewhere treats theoretically as the unique cause of falsity. Thus, what we have noted concerning the early writings should on the contrary inspire us to be prudent when we approach the *Ethics* and the two great *Treatises*.

It seems to me that three crucial remarks are in order:

— There are very few actual occurrences of the term *experientia vaga*, while its use as a category is limited. It is expressly employed only once in the whole of the *Ethics*, and we never find it in the *TP*, nor in the *TTP*. A few passages from Book II of the *Ethics* deal with it implicitly, as can be seen thanks to the play of references in the second Scholium to Proposition 40. By contrast, there are a large number of texts that refer explicitly to experience *tout court*, and if we judge these references by their contexts, they seem to cohere among themselves. It is at the very least paradoxical to claim that the more common and widely distributed notion should be thought on the basis of a notion whose use is more restricted.

— The contextual distinction between 'experience' and 'vague experience' is clearer in the early writings. The two expressions bring with them a series of different co-occurring terms, which leads the reader to think that within the universe of Spinoza's mature thought these expressions arise from different domains of reasoning.

— Finally, it is clear that in the later works experience borrows its materials from forms of knowledge other than vague experience. For instance, when in the *TTP* Spinoza seeks to justify the usefulness of biblical narratives, he notes that the Scriptures instruct by way of experience and not by reasoning. He thus writes: 'Scripture proves these teachings solely by experience, i.e., by the narratives it relates', and, while not giving any definitions of clear and distinct knowledge, 'still it can teach and enlighten men enough to imprint obedience and devotion on their hearts'.[68] After this demonstration, Spinoza summarises what he believes he has established: it is for the common people that 'acquaintance with [biblical narratives], and faith in them, is most necessary'.[69] This argument as a whole shows clearly that we are not dealing with vague experience here: the usefulness of biblical stories is obviously based on knowledge *ex signis*. The materials from which *experientia* draws its 'teachings' are thus even broader in scope than in the early writings.

At the point at which we find ourselves, it seems therefore that *experientia* is distinguished from vague experience by its field of co-occurrences, its content and its materials. We still have to make sense of this triple difference and to try and better define the two terms.

Let us begin with vague experience. It belongs to the register of kinds of knowledge. I will not deal with this theory in its totality here but will try only to isolate those points that can help us better determine the type of knowledge that interests us, along with its characteristics.[70] The expression *experientia vaga* itself is borrowed from Bacon – a well known yet little studied filiation. If Spinoza takes a formula from the Lord Chancellor, this does not mean that its meaning is the same for the two philosophers, particularly if we recall the reservations Spinoza expresses in the first letter to Oldenburg.[71] At the same time, however, the fact that Spinoza reprises this term, and precisely at a time when he is reading Bacon and reflecting on his contribution to questions of method, suggests that in his eyes there are sufficient affinities, or at least local ones, between certain aspects of their respective approaches to justify borrowing a technical term, even if this means modifying its horizon of reference. The point of commonality between the two as regards the use of this term has to do with the fact that the adjective *vaga* signals the existence of a plurality of possible experiences or of possible uses of experience, which are important to distinguish. If one

---

[68] TTP V, 39; CWS II, 149.
[69] TTP V, 40; CWS II, 149.
[70] On the Spinozist theory of knowledge, see M. Gueroult, *Spinoza*, vol. II, *L'Ame*, passim, in particular pp. 198–487; A. Matheron, *Individu et communauté chez Spinoza*, p. 63–77; L. Teixeira, *A Doutrina dos Modos de Percepçao e o Conceito de Abstraçao na Filosofia de Espinosa*, Sao Paulo, 1954; Raul Landim Fliho, 'La notion de vérité dans l'*Ethique* de Spinoza', in *Méthode et métaphysique*, *Travaux et documents du Groupe de recherches spinozistes*, 2, PUPS, 1989, pp. 121–42.
[71] Ep. II, G IV, pp. 8–9 [*Ep*. II [to Henry Oldenburg]; CWS I, 165–6).

has to say that certain experiences are vague, it is because other experiences are not vague or should not be. Thus, by itself, the word 'experience' is ambiguous. In Bacon, the notion appears in the framework of a two-part description: the analysis of the facts of the human soul and the assessment of pre-existing knowledge. These two aspects are articulated by the fact that the topography of the soul indicates what paths the collective achievements of science must travel down (along with those it has not yet been able to explore). In this topography, experience is the first step to knowledge, on the condition that it is used appropriately:[72] if it is neglected, then this will give rise to scholasticisms, but if one draws on it without taking any precautions, then it can only be decrypted by using the interpretations provided by idols. This is why the philosophical weapon constituted by experience is double-edged and why the discourse on experience must be carefully balanced: without experience, one cannot know the 'real and natural subtlety of things' and their system of differences, which are revealed thanks to the senses.[73] A philosophy that cuts itself off from 'those roots of experience that have allowed it to prosper and grow is a cadaver'.[74] At the same time, the sophist is 'diverted from experience by the variety of common phenomena' or 'parades experience around, distorted to suit his opinions, a captive',[75] while the empiricist deforms the importance of experience by referring only

---

[72] 'L'*experientia* recoupe l'attitude minimale souhaitable d'acceuil des faits observés et recensés, en même temps qu'elle recouvre un champ indéterminé tant que n'est pas intervenue la mise à l'épreuve.' Reduced to its bare bones, experience is 'peu éclairante. Ainsi envisagée, l'*experientia* ne saurait faire autorité', D. Deleule, 'Experientia-experimentum chez F. Bacon', in 'Francis Bacon', *Terminologia e fortuna nel XVII secolo*, a cura di Marta Fattori, Rome: Edizioni dell'Ateneo, 1984, p. 62.

[73] Translator's note: since, to the best of my knowledge, there exists no English translation of Bacon's *Redargutio philosophiarum*, I am translating here from the Latin and French versions, both of which Moreau provides. Moreau's French comes from the translation by G. Rombi et D. Deleule, *Récusation des doctrines philosophiques et autres opuscules*, Paris: PUF, 1987, pp. 138–9. The Latin text that gives the full context of this phrase, and which Moreau also gives, reads: 'postquam verae et nativae rerum subtilitati, et differentiis in experientia signatis et expressis et sensui subjectis aut saltem per sensum in lucme extractis, paululum insuevistis', *The Works of Francis Bacon, Volume III*, collected and edited by James Spedding, Robert Leslie Ellis, and Douglas Denon, The Riverside Press, 1900, p. 92.

[74] 'Quare omnem philosophiam ab experientiae redicibus ex quibus primum pullulavit et incrementum cepit avulsam, rem mortuam esse', 'Cogitata et visa de interpretatione naturae sive de scientia operativa', in *The Works of Francis Bacon, Volume III*, p. 136.

[75] *The New Organon*, Book I, Aphorisms 62 and 63, Cambridge: Cambridge University Press, 2000, pp. 51–2.

to 'the narrow and unilluminating basis of a handful of experiments'.[76] In short, it is just as bad to betray experience as it is to abandon it.[77] The solution consists in proceeding in an orderly fashion. Vague experience is thus experience without order.[78] Yet, in Bacon, this disorder threatens to extend beyond these bounds:[79] the terms *vaga*, *mera*, *quaesita* and *literata* suggest that experience is always at risk of making one fall back into bad habits if one fails to be sufficiently cautious when using it. One might be tempted to say that the entire system of categories established in the *Novum Organum* and *The Advancement of Learning* aims to extract experience from chance and give it, finally, an organised form, without which it cannot fulfil its promise. Bacon's theory of knowledge is a matter of strategy, but it is a strategy that seems to bear upon conquests that are always at risk of being lost.

What happens in Spinoza? One possibility is that, in his early writings, Spinoza reprised the term *experientia vaga* because at the time experience was for him something that lacked order – or was at least something that could not be thought of as possessing an order. The characteristics of vague experience given in the *TdIE* do indeed seem to reprise, at least in part, those belonging to Bacon's conception of vague experience – for instance, that it is not determined by the understanding, and that it emerges from chance.[80] We thus find the ideas of both disorder and restriction. However, this restriction is already being thought differently in Spinoza, at least in an indicative fashion: chance still plays a role, but less in the production of vague experience and more by virtue of the fact that vague experience remains dominant so long as it has not been refuted by any other more powerful experience.[81] Put differently, what is foregrounded in Spinoza is

---

[76] Ibid., Aphorism 64, p. 52.
[77] 'Temporis partus masculus', in *The Works of Francis Bacon, Volume III*, pp. 20–32. The references here are to Paracelsus and Galien respectively.
[78] 'Thus we must seek to acquire a greater stock of experiments, and experiments of a different kind than we have yet done; and we must also introudce a quite different method, order and process of connecting and advancing experience. For casual experience which follows only itself (as we said above) is merely groping in the dark, and rather bemuses men than informs them. But when experience shall proceed by sure rules, serially and continuously, something better may be expected from the sciences', Bacon, *The New Organon* pp. 81–2.
[79] Cf. D. Deleule, 'Experientia-experimentum chez F. Bacon', p. 64.
[80] 'quae non determinatur ab intellectu'; 'quia casu sic occurrit . . .', § 19, G II, p. 10, ll. 12–13 [*TdIE* 19; *CWS* I, 12–13].
[81] 'sed tantum ita dicitur, qui casu sic occurrit, et nullum aliud habemus experimentum, quod hoc oppugnat, et ideo tanquam inconcussum apud nos manet', § 19, G II, p. 10, ll. 12–15 [*TdIE* 19; *CWS* I, 12–13].

a positive thesis concerning the relation of forces between different ideas. Nevertheless, the *TdIE* itself remains at the level of description, noting, for example, the uncertain, non-definitive and superficial character of vague experience. We can now see that Spinoza borrows a noun from Bacon: whatever the reservations he might inspire, Bacon knows how to describe.[82] Now, in terms of the requirements of method, it is precisely not necessary to know the soul by its first causes: it suffices to unfold a *historiola* in the manner of Bacon.[83] Separated from the assessment of the history of the sciences, the topography of the soul can be reimagined through the search for the true good, while the description of facts lays out in advance the landmarks that will retrospectively allow us to see this topography in terms of its effects.

But things happen differently in the *Ethics*. How are we to conceive of the specificity of the classification of kinds of knowledge presented in this work? We can begin by comparing the two phrases that introduce this classification in the two Latin texts. The *TdIE* says: 'the modes of perceiving which I have had up to now for affirming or denying something without doubt'.[84] The *Ethics* says: 'we perceive many things and form universal notions'.[85] There are two differences here: the first concerns the place of the introductory phrase in the argument as a whole; and the second has to do with the fact that in the *Ethics* the notion of the universal comes to the foreground. Both of these phrases refer to a preceding situation, but in the *TdIE* this situation is the history of past perceptions, the flow of lived experience (*hucusque*) that preceded the moment of the aspiration and the decision to seek the true good. In the *Ethics*, the preceding situation is the analysis of imaginative knowledge and then of common notions – the chain of thought (*ex his supra dictis*) made up of the Demonstrations preceding Proposition 40. This means

---

[82] Summarising his critiques for Oldenburg, Spinoza notes that Bacon speaks in a very confused way and proves almost nothing, but that he is content to narrate ('de hac re admodum confuse loquitur, & fere nihil probat; sed tantum narrat', Ep. II, G IV, p. 8, ll. 29–30 [*Ep.* II [to Henry Oldenburg]; *CWS* I, 167]). This suggests that this narration, even if it is insufficient, is not false in itself.

[83] 'Ad haec intelligendum, saltem quoad Methodus exigit, non est opus naturam mentis per primam ejus causam cognoscere, sed sufficit mentis, sive perceptionum historiolam concinnare modo illo, quo Verulamius docet', Ep. XXXVII, G IV, p. 189, ll. 5–8 [*Ep.* XXXVII [to Johannes Bouwmeester]; *CWS* II, 33]. Saisset is wrong to be indignant about the word *historiola*: nothing permits us to say that it is used pejoratively.

[84] 'Quod ut fiat, exigit ordo, quem naturaliter habemus, ut hic resumam omnes modos percipiendi, quos hucusque habui ad aliquid indubie affirmandum vel negandum', § 18, G II, p. 10, ll. 1–3 [*TdIE* 18; *CWS* 12].

[85] 'Ex omnibus supra dictis clare apparet, nos multa percipere, et notiones universales formare', Book II, 40, Schol. 2 G II, p. 122, ll. 2–3 [*CWS* I, 477].

that in the *Ethics* the enumeration of the different kinds of knowledge occurs only after the deduction of their causes and thanks to these causes. When these three kinds of knowledge are named, we already have available to us all of the elements necessary for conceiving of them genetically. In the *TdIE*, by contrast, their only textual support was the project to attain a certain goal (*finis* and *scopus*) for which the narrator was seeking the means. Most importantly, this implied producing an inventory of the modes of perception that had been used up to that point, followed by an attempt to categorise them. We can now better understand why the *TdIE*'s classification could only be descriptive, whereas the one from the *Ethics* is explanatory.[86] What does this properly explanatory approach consist in? It is here that we must introduce the difference between the two introductory phrases: for the *TdIE*, to know is to perceive and to affirm; for the *Ethics*, it is both to perceive and to form universal notions. Contrary to the tradition of the theory of knowledge, the universal is no longer the prerogative of one kind of knowledge; each kind of knowledge is defined by the specific way that it forms universal notions. It is no longer possible to distinguish between knowing in an ordered fashion and knowing without order: each type of knowledge arranges perceptions in a certain order. This is why, as some have rightly said, the most interesting aspect of the theory of knowledge in Spinoza's mature work is the fact that the subject is exposed to it by beginning with a theory of general ideas.[87] We cannot overestimate the importance of this first phrase from the second Scholium to Proposition 40. Indeed, the term 'knowledge' is one of those key terms that Spinoza never defines but which help to define others.[88] Now, this first phrase presents in a practical state, if

---

[86] We could describe this difference by reprising a formula that Alexandre Matheron uses with respect to the 'idea of the idea' in the two texts: 'In the *TdIE*, Spinoza sticks to immediate appearances.' The *Ethics* moves away from this but 'give[s] an account of these immediate appearances that the *TdIE* stuck to', 'Idea, Idea of the Idea and Certainty in the *Tractactus de Intellectus Emendatione* and the *Ethics*'. Matheron, *Politics, Ontology and Knowledge in Spinoza*, trans. F. Del Lucchese, D. Maruzzella and G. Morejón, Edinburgh: Edinburgh University Press, 2020, p. 12. 'Idée, idée d'idée et certitude dans le *Tractatus de Intellectus Emendatione* et dans l'*Ethique*', in *Méthode et métaphysique*, *Travaux et documents du Groupe de recherches spinozistes*, 2, PUPS, 1989, p. 104.

[87] 'O que há de mais interessante na Etica a respeito dos modos de percepçao é que o assunto é exposto tendo como ponto de partida uma teoria das idéias gerais', L. Texeira, *A Doutrina dos Modos de Percepçao e o Conceito de Abstraçao na Filosofia de Espinosa*, p. 111. This is the best study on this question. Martial Gueroult praises it in his own exposition of the kinds of knowledge.

[88] On the status of these terms, cf. P.-F. Moreau, 'Métaphysique des formes et

not a definition, then at the very least a description of knowledge: to know is, at one and the same time, to perceive and to abstract universal notions from this perception. Can we be more precise about the relation between these two aspects? We must first briefly inquire into the meaning of the word *perception*. It has no particular relation to sensation, as is the case in other philosophical lexicons. The terms 'to perceive' and 'perception' are in turn refused then used by Spinoza in the course of one and the same Book from the *Ethics*, Book II. At the beginning of Book II, when he says what an idea is, Spinoza defines it as 'a concept of the soul that the soul forms because it is a thinking thing',[89] and he clarifies this by saying: 'I say concept rather than perception, because the word perception seems to indicate that the soul is acted on by the object. But concept seems to express an action of the soul.'[90] The fact is, however, that if one 'prefers' (*potius*) to use one word rather than another, it is because, fundamentally, one might well have used the other. Furthermore, in what follows, the verb 'to perceive' is used to signify 'having such-and-such an idea' (*hanc vel illam*).[91] It is easy to understand why: the soul is, in one and the same movement, both active and passive. It is active since, in its spontaneity, it forms the concept or idea; and it is passive since this idea most often expresses an encounter that does not depend on laws internal to the individual.[92] To this extent, the soul is passive, if not with respect to the object, then at least with respect to the encounter between the object and the body of which it is the idea.[93] To perceive is therefore first

---

métaphysique de la substance', in *Méthode et métaphysique*, *Travaux et documents du Groupe de recherches spinozistes*, 2, PUPS, 1989, pp. 9–18.

[89] 'Per ideam intelligo mentis conceptum, quem mens format propterea quod res est cogitans', *Ethics* II, Def. III [CWS I, 447].

[90] 'Dico potius conceptum quam perceptionem quia perceptionis nomen indicare videtur, mentem ab objectio pati; at conceptus actionem mentis exprimere videtur', *Ethics* II, Def. 3, Exp. [CWS I, 447].

[91] 'Therefore, when we say that the Soul perceives this or that, we are saying nothing but that God, not insofar as he is infinite, but insofar as he is explained through the nature of the soul, has this or that idea', *Ethics* II, 11, Cor. [CWS I, 456].

[92] 'C'est pourquoi l'idée de l'affection qui correspond à cette rencontre subit l'influence de cette extériorité, soit directement en ce qu'elle enveloppe la nature du corps extérieur' (Proposition 16), 'soit indirectement en ce qu'elle s'enchaîne à d'autres idées suivant les dispositifs de la mémoire', A. Matheron, *Individu et communauté chez Spinoza*, p. 66.

[93] Thus, 'puisqu'une affection passive découle à la fois de la nature de notre corps et de celle du corps extérieure qui nous affecte, son idée enveloppe à la fois ces deux natures. Notre âme, dès lors, doit percevoir non seulement son propre corps, mais tout ce qui, directement ou indirectement, agit sur lui', ibid.

of all to represent to oneself the event of the encounter between our body and another body. Insofar as this encounter occurs following an order that is not the internal order of the soul,[94] we can see why Spinoza uses a term with connotations of passivity. What we find here is thus fundamentally what we have called, in the context of the prologue to the *TdIE*, the order of the given. The entire web of the imagination is initially constituted by reference to this encounter, to this present event, which the function of the imagination will double, multiply and generalise. Without going into the detail of the analysis from Book II, we can already draw two conclusions: on the one hand, knowledge ineluctably begins with a present perception;[95] on the other hand, this perception as such is at this point neither true nor false – or, put differently, its truth is the truth of an automatism.[96]

Yet, as we have seen, knowledge is not limited to perception: in fact, everything happens as if the human soul were so constituted as to be incapable of contenting itself with this punctual given and immediately seeks to insert this given into a system of relations and comparisons. It does indeed seem that in the *Ethics* one can speak of knowledge – and even of false knowledge – only when a perception is taken up by a universal. Moreover, it is this uptake that absolves us from having to add, to this quasi-definition of knowledge, the idea of affirmation. This uptake refers to the various ways in which the soul can treat its own imaginative support. Indeed, knowledge does not always organise what the imagination provides for it into the form of universal ideas in the same way. The first three kinds of knowledge all work directly on what is given by the imagination, and all three draw general ideas from it,[97] albeit in different ways – whether repetitive, associative or comparative. Knowledge by vague experience abstracts from repeated events

---

[94] 'Cf. *Ethics* II, 18, Schol.: 'Dico secundo hanc concatenationem fieri secundum ordinem et concatenationem affectionum corporis humani, ut ipsam distinguerem a concatenatione idearum quae fit secundum ordinem intellectus, quo res per primas suas causas mens percipit, et qui in omnibus hominibus idem est', G II, p. 107, ll. 9–13 [*CWS* I, 466].

[95] Cf. *Ethics* II, 17 and Cor. [*CWS* I, 463–4].

[96] On the epistemological neutrality of images, cf. *Ethics* II, 17, Schol. [*CWS* I, 465]: 'And here, in order to begin to indicate what error is, I should like you to note that the imaginations of the Soul, considered in themselves contain no error, *or* that the Soul does not err from the fact that it imagines, but only insofar as it is considered to lack an idea that excludes the existence of those things that it imagines to be present to it.'

[97] We could also include knowledge by intuitive science in this definition, for it is indirectly based on what is given to the imagination to the degree that is based on knowledge of the second kind. And, while it does not proceed by universal notions, it proceeds by singular adequate ideas of which each one is universally true.

a universal that confusedly isolates these events' similar aspects. Knowledge by signs or *ex auditu* associates the event with other events of which we have heard tell or indeed whose signs have already been engraved in our memory.[98] Both fabricate a universal on the basis of the body's deformation of the positive traits possessed by the perceived object. This universal is the extrapolation of what we could call a negative particularity. For example, if a flame burns my hand, I can draw a universal from this, but in such instances the relation of cause and effect with regard to the flame is blurred by the relation of the effect with my body, which isolates what is inessential. What I feel of the flame is not its definition but its burning. All of this forms a series of processes, each of which exists in itself but whose conjunction constitutes something like a particular negative essence. The negation here is not an internal negation, but is constituted by the mutual limitation of two affirmative singularities.[99] By contrast, knowledge by common notions brings out, against the backdrop of a vast perceptive field, what is common to my body and to the objects that affect it. It can thus adequately grasp what is purely particular neither to one nor the other. Its universal is founded not on a particular limitation but on the absence of essential particularities. Each of these three types of knowledge is thus based on the imagination but works with it productively in different ways. There is therefore no continuity between them, and above all, there is no continuity between the two types of knowledge that constitute the first kind of knowledge by common notions. Altogether this justifies the trenchant formulations cited above[100] on the equivalence between the first kind of knowledge and the register of the false and on the impossibility for this first kind of knowledge to be the origin of the other two. Even if the different kinds of knowledge have a common terrain – namely, the imagination[101] – there must be a rupture between the two types that

---

[98] *Ethics* II, 40, Schol. 2 [CWS I, 477–8]. In this sense knowledge *ex signis* in the *Ethics* does indeed follow knowledge *ex auditu* from the *TdIE*. It simply extends its field. It is possible that the analysis of prophetic knowledge, which Spinoza undertook in the intervening years, played a role in this shift.

[99] If we were to grasp these particularities in the total order of nature – that is, if our understanding were infinite – then we would conceive of them as the intersection of causal series and not as negations.

[100] See *Ethics* II, 41 and 42 [CWS I, 478–9], and *Ethics* V, 28 [CWS I, 609].

[101] We should consider the imagination as such as a negative factor. This is what J. Frohschammer saw, *Ueber die Bedeutung der Einbildungskraft in der Philosophie Kant's unde Spinoza's*, Munich: Th. Ackermann, 1879, p. 117 and 162–72 (and yet, while he showed that the system confers upon the imagination an essential status, he believed that one could only come to it by according it a foundational role in the individuation and the connection between modes). This is above all what C. De Deugd has demon-

belong to the first kind of knowledge and the second kind. While all are based on the same givens of the imagination, knowledge in the proper sense consists in the transformation of this given through processes of connection that are of at least two different orders. Every attempt to diminish or efface this rupture reduces the specificity of Spinozism by minimising the difference between the adequate and the inadequate.

Of course, the contribution of such-and-such a type of connection in a given individual does not arise from free will or attentiveness; it is a function of physical and biographical circumstances that have formed an individual's *ingenium*, as well as the historico-political context in which the individual's thought has developed. It could even be suggested that there are three types of imagination – the lively imagination, the practical imagination and the powerful imagination – according to whether the imagination lends itself more easily to one of three operations. The first, which proceeds by association, produces the prophet; the second, which proceeds by repetition, gives us the empiricist; and the third, which favours comparison, gives us the man of understanding. Spinoza does not systematise these distinctions, but they can help us understand how the dispositions of the different *ingenia* that are more or less favoured by historical circumstances give rise to different kinds of minds.[102]

What becomes of vague experience in this context? It still possesses the characteristics it had in the *TdIE* – that is, it is still without order, uncertain and inadequate. Now, though, we know why: we can understand vague experience from a more comprehensive perspective and explain why it is the way it is.

The first fundamental characteristic of vague experience is the one it shares with the two other fundamental types of knowledge: it is rooted in the present and in my body. There could be no knowledge by vague experience if there did not exist a body which, in each of its encounters, was the occasion for the production of an idea in the mind that corresponded to this body. The present of this encounter is the point of irreducible anchorage that all of the associations, imitations or connections that the imaginative process organises will be attached to.

The second fundamental characteristic has to do with the particular way in which this type of knowledge transcends the present. Its proper object is

---

strated in *The Significance of Spinoza's First Kind of Knowledge*, Assen: Van Gorcum, 1966, and M. Gueroult, *Spinoza*, vol. II, *L'Ame*, pp. 221–3.

[102] On the distinction between the strong and the lively imaginations, cf. Gueroult, *Spinoza*, vol. II, p. 221.

less things than our encounter with things – what we called above negative or limitative singular essences. What vague experience foregrounds of the thing is not its essence but rather what has affected us in the effect the thing has had on us. Now, this effect does indeed manifest the power of the thing, but it does so from a certain angle, or by way of a certain refraction – that is, in terms of how it is limited with respect to our body. For instance, what vague experience retains of the mortal fruit is the scene of agony. This scene is not false, but it is only one consequence of an internal chemical process. If we understood this process and the structure of our body in their positivity, we could deduce what happens in this encounter. However, if we begin by imagining the effect of the encounter – a bundle of consequences without their causes – then we will not be able to trace the thread back to the particular affirmative essences that are the nature of the poison and the structure of our body.

We can now deduce and explain those traits of vague experience that we encountered in the *TdIE* in only descriptive terms:

— Such knowledge is not without order; it is simply ordered in a different way to the understanding. Thus, vague experience no longer represents the ever-present threat of a lack of order; it is the order that arises from everyday life. This is an order that dominates everyday life but that everyday life cannot itself dominate. When our body encounters external bodies, it does so by way of a determinate series of events whose logic escapes us and whose concatenation we call chance. At the same time, the ideas produced by these encounters link up with one another within us following the same order, or following an order that recalls previous encounters. From out of this repetition there can emerge habits that are useful in our lives: for instance, many of those behaviours that involve precaution, prudence or tact can be engendered by these repetitive connections. Nevertheless, we cannot cross the abyss that separates this register from the order of the understanding. When we are operating in the order of the understanding, we possess sufficiently strong chains of adequate ideas that the ideas that express our encounters with the external world take place in accordance with these chains and are no longer inadequate. This is why when this order of the understanding begins to grow within me, the order of exteriority, which I still fail to dominate, appears to me as disordered and as the product of the pure play of chance.

— If knowledge by vague experience is superficial, it is because it foregrounds neither the body nor the thing itself but rather their intersection, with the repetitions highlighting this very intersection. Vague experience does not transcend the disorder of the body and the biography of the individual. It is superficial to the extent that it is individual — in opposition to knowledge by common notions, which is universal (*omnibus hominibus*).¹⁰³

— Finally, vague experience is inadequate to the extent that it is subjected to the disorder of images. This is what makes it uncertain and has it mistake accidents for essences. This explains why its domain is that of the false.

We can see clearly now in what sense this explanation reprises and completes the description from the *TdIE*. By identifying the causes of vague experience, it makes the latter's descriptive traits appear as so many effects. In this sense, Martial Gueroult's¹⁰⁴ formula perfectly applies here.¹⁰⁵ A question nevertheless remains: why continue to call it vague experience now that we no longer believe in its disorder? The reason is that, of all the different kinds of knowledge, vague experience remains the one that is rooted most firmly in the imagination and that has the smallest margin of autonomy with respect to it. Now, 'vague' is precisely the adjective that applies to the imagination, not in the sense that it is imprecise, but insofar as it goes astray.¹⁰⁶ We are therefore no longer dealing with 'vague experience' in the Baconian sense of the term. However, it is also not a matter of a pure homonymy or the mere survival of a noun following the redefinition of its concept. It is likely that in Spinoza's eyes, conserving this term borrowed from Bacon is justifiable to the extent that the theory of the *Ethics* explains why this experience appears

---

[103] *Ethics* II, 28, Schol., G II, p. 119, ll. 6–7 [CWS I, 470].

[104] 'Dans les premiers *Traités*, la classification est purement descriptive et ne suppose pas de genèse, elle est un constat, ou une nomenclature; dans l'*Ethique* au contraire, elle résulte d'une genèse; ce par quoi se trouve précisée sans ambiguïté la caractéristique de chaque genre de connaissance, tandis que se trouve fondée de façon solide, en vertu de leur origine, leur statut propre et leur différence de nature', *Spinoza*, vol. II, *L'Ame*, app., XVI, p. 608.

[105] By contrast, however, Gueroult is thinking of the higher kinds of knowledge. Similarly, at ibid., pp. 594–5, he remains very elliptical as regards the difference between knowledge *ex signis* and random experience. Nevertheless, his formula applies to our description.

[106] 'Imaginatio vaga est et inconstans', *TTP*, Chapter I; the *fluctuatio imaginationis* is opposed to the *concatenatio* of Reason, *Ethics* II, 44, Schol. [CWS I, 480–1]. Wim Klever synthesies these quotations at the end of the first paragraph of his article, 'Remarques sur le *TIE* (Experientia vaga, paradoxa, ideae fictae)', *Revue des sciences philosophiques et théologiques*, 71 (1987), p. 104. He also cites the article *vagus* from Calepin's dictionary, which Spinoza had in his library: 'huc illuc oberrans, incertus, instabilis, inconstans', with the following example from Cicero: 'vaga sententia, id est incerta'.

as, precisely, vague. Moreover, its vagueness is characteristic less of vague experience itself than of the imagination that produces it.[107]

Let us now turn to what we have called experience *tout court*. What does Spinoza mean when he says that experience has taught him such-and-such a lesson? What is essential is neither the cause nor the content, but the result. What Spinoza means to say is: I judge that this is something that everyone knows; and since it is often a matter of refuting a prejudice or an objection, when Spinoza says 'everybody knows' he also means: this should stop one from innocently affirming the preceding thesis. In other words, 'experientia docet' aims to establish or rather recall a fact: such-and-such a thing is known by all. Experience is at once a reminder and a barrier. Obviously, some have learnt such-and-such a thing from a book or a teacher, while others have learnt it by repetition. But that is not what matters (some have even perhaps learnt this lesson through reason, but this is of little importance). The statement 'experientia docet' affirms neither a perception (even if it can refer to many perceptions) nor a universal, at least not in the way that knowledge does. 'Everybody knows' does not mean 'each individual person knows', and even less: 'everybody knows such-and-such a thing adequately'. To say 'there will be vices so long as there are men' does not say how one has learnt this fact: this statement is a result, and a result that is almost external to us, like the objects we seek. Thus, experience lies beyond both the true and the false. Or rather, this statement makes the distinction between the adequate and the inadequate inoperative. In effect, it supposes an existing knowledge and uses it for something else – either to found an action or to oppose a prejudice. This opposition can, moreover, be perfectly inefficacious (we pass our time going against the teachings of experience, just as we go against those of reason). Still, this opposition does not concern the process of the acquisition of knowledge. In this process, we do not go from the particular to the universal. Instead, we possess a stock of truths (however these have been acquired) and use them as materials. For example, if I see a minister engaged in intrigues against a leader of the State, I can add this perception to other, similar perceptions, and will thereby gain knowledge of this event through vague experience. I can also associate it with what the Bible says about obedience to Caesar and I will draw from this a piece of knowledge *ex signis*. In both cases, I can fabricate the idea of vice, which universalises the negative

---

[107] We can add that in grammatical terms Spinoza opposes *vaga* individuals, which are identified using a noun without an article, to *certa* individuals, which are identified by a noun accompanied with a definite article, *Compendium*, Chapter IX, G I, p. 322 [HG 51]. *Vagus* is thus indeed once again synonymous with *incertus*.

traits from these events; I thereby produce for myself a false and inadequate knowledge of human nature. Finally, I can reduce all of this to common notions about human passions by comparing them and thus explain what is going on. So long as I link my perceptions together in this way, I construct a knowledge of one type or the other. But if I say: there will be vices so long as there are men,[108] I am no longer in the process of constructing a universal: I am using a knowledge that I have already acquired (and in a certain sense the status of this knowledge matters little) either to engage in an action within the State or to explain the necessity of such-and-such an institution, or to reject the reveries of a moralist who would wish to organise reality in the name of an ideal that prejudges it. For what is essential is no longer the language in which I formulate this knowledge, but the consequences I draw from it. Whatever the language I use to express myself,[109] experience will help me demonstrate prudence in my actions. Experience draws on what has been gained through different modes of knowledge, but it makes something else out of them. It is a matter of indifference whether these gains are adequate or inadequate: in their reutilisation by common experience, this inadequation is neutralised. It is no longer a matter of knowing but of being educated. And in the totality of our actions, 'being educated' seems to be a sequence that is at least as important and as neutral as those identified in the *TdIE*.

Just as it neutralises the difference between adequation and inadequation, experience neutralises the individualisation of knowledge. To say 'everybody knows' is to be indifferent not only to the way in which each person has learnt such-and-such a thing; it is also to be indifferent to what, in the body – or the *ingenium* – of individuals bears the mark of this gain in knowledge. We here find a trait that we have already commented on in the *proemium* to the *TdIE*: experience draws lessons from life, but the life in question is not my life. Yet this does not mean that experience is situated at the level of the universal. To say 'I judge that everyone knows' in no way means that everyone knows in the same way, as is the case for common notions. People know by experience, or by reading the Bible, that it is necessary to practise justice and charity, but each represents these ideas to themselves as a function of their

---

[108] 'Docuit nimirum eosdem experientia, vitia fore, donec homines', *TP*, Chapter 1, 2, G III, p. 267, ll. 26–7 [*TP* I, 2; *CWS* II, 504].

[109] Instead of saying 'there will be vices so long as there are men', I could say: 'human nature is so constituted that certain effects are constant'. The expression would thus be more in conformity with the geometrical method, but the consequences would be the same.

imagination, just as the prophets do. The difference between individuals, like the difference between the adequate and the inadequate, is relegated to the past. It is not suppressed but rather fades into the background when one says: this is what experience teaches us.

But is what we gain from the past not produced by reason? Reason does indeed produce it, and this is why Spinoza also says: reason teaches us that ... There are therefore four types of knowledge (grouped into three kinds), but there are only two types of teaching. When we simply say *ratio docet*, this means: few people know this; but when we say *experientia docet*, this means: everybody knows this.

We could summarise all of these characteristics by noting that *experientia* is not situated in the present of perception; it supposes that something has been acquired prior to perception. This is why it does not belong to the order of knowledge in the strict sense of the term. Rather, it assesses a piece of knowledge and then applies it in action – or in a new process of knowledge. In these conditions one might be led to think that experience concerns only action. We will see further on that this is not the case.

There remains one question to ask: are we right to use the term experience to refer to all of this? It seems to me that this is a legitimate move for two reasons: (a) common use speaks of 'having experience', or of 'a man of experience',[110] to designate precisely this capacity to draw lessons from the past; and (b) vague experience remains the principal provider of materials for *experientia*, either directly or indirectly – if indeed it is true, as Edwin Curley shows, that knowledge *ex signis* always presupposes vague experience.[111] By using the same word in both expressions, the only difference being the adjective *vaga*, Spinoza, far from risking confusion, built on the promptings of ordinary language, while still taking into account the sources from which experience draws its meaning and its force.

In conclusion, we can say that Spinoza does not disregard experience – so long as we distinguish experience from vague experience. As a mode of knowledge, vague experience is inferior and leads to error and inadequation.

---

[110] In Latin as in French. Judging Drusus and Germanicus to be too young to re-establish order, the Romans think that Tiberius should himself have gone to meet the revolting legions, who would have submitted themselves to a prince who had become strong thanks to their extensive experience ('principem longa experientia'), Tacitus, *Annals*, I, 46.

[111] E. Curley, 'Experience in Spinoza's Theory of Knowledge', in *Spinoza: A Collection of Critical Essays*, ed. Marjorie Grene, Garden City: Anchor Books, 1973, Notre Dame: University of Notre Dame Press, 1979, p. 30 ff.

It has a different foundation to the two superior modes of knowledge and cannot lead to them. It is only in terms of a rupture that we can understand their relation. From this point of view, Spinoza's theses recall those of Bachelard.[112] As a form of teaching, however, experience responds to another question than the one answered by the different modes of knowledge. This is why its revaluation in Spinoza's mature writings does not lead to the revaluation of vague experience. If we do not carefully distinguish one form of experience from the other, we transform Spinozism into an empiricism in which we gradually pass from inferior to superior forms of knowledge.[113] In truth, Spinozism is neither an empiricism nor a pure deductivism; it is, as I hope to show, a rationalism of experience.

B. Experience is Not Experimentation

The rare pages devoted in the secondary literature to the Spinozist notion of experience also often confuse it with scientific experimentation. It is worthwhile pausing over this confusion for a moment, for Spinoza does indeed deal with scientific experimentation explicitly. The way in which Spinoza addresses this topic can help us better understand the place his thought occupies in the development and representation of classical science – which, crucially, was established by constructing experiments that were irreducible to experience as it is given.[114]

We should note first of all that as early as the *Treatise on the Emendation of the Intellect*, a terminological distinction appears in Spinoza's writings, one that is required by the doctrine of method itself. The problem is indicated in a note from paragraph 27. Spinoza has explained for what reason vague

---

[112] *La formation de l'esprit scientifique, contribution à une analyse de la connaissance objective*, Paris: Vrin, 1938.

[113] This is the tendency evinced by I. Franck's study, 'Spinoza's Logic of Inquiry: Rationalist or Experientialist?', in *The Philosophy of Baruch Spinoza*, ed. Richard Kennington, Washington DC: Catholic University of America Press, 1980, pp. 247–72. The emphasis placed on continuity (between body and soul, body and universe, imagination and common notions) leads Franck to derive the second kind of knowledge from the first by a process of critical reprisal. Despite its interest as regards the question of the revaluation of the imagination, C. De Deugd's book, *The Significance of Spinoza's First Kind of Knowledge*, is sometimes guilty of the same confusions, in particular when de Deugd affirms that the distinction between kinds of knowledge is relative and not absolute (p. 188). In fact, there can be no continuity between processes that have such resolutely distinct causes: the difference is indeed absolute.

[114] Cf. G. Bachelard, *Le rationalisme appliqué*, Paris: PUF, 1949, chapters VI and VII; D. Lecourt, *L'Epistémologie historique de Gaston Bachelard*, Paris: Vrin, 1972, pp. 66–9.

experience is not the mode of perception we require to attain our goal. He then adds: 'Here I shall discuss experience somewhat more fully, and examine the Method of proceeding of the Empiricists and of the new Philosophers.'[115] This note is one of a series of programmatic notes from the *TdIE* in which Spinoza announces a development that is to occur or a distinction that is to be made. These notes attest either to Spinoza rereading his text with a view to redrafting it, or to his jotting down thoughts in the course of his first draft in such a way that he could look ahead without interrupting the continuity of his text. In both cases, these are notes that would not have appeared in this form in the final text had the author got to the stage of publication. They would have been replaced by the text they announce. We are therefore correct to consider them as Spinoza's remarks on his own work and as indications of a possible bifurcation. In this instance, Spinoza's reflections on the notion of vague experience draw attention to another theme, one that is not identical with it but to which it is closely related: the apparently novel doctrine of experience found in the 'Empiricists' and the 'new Philosophers'. The first are perhaps doctors or those who perform experiments on nature without referring to existing theories and without introducing any new ones; the second doubtless refer – if we judge by Spinoza's correspondence – to Bacon and Descartes, and more broadly to those philosophers who are part of the general anti-Aristotelian ambience. What kind of 'experience' is at stake here? Spinoza is certainly not speaking of vague experience, for he has said everything there is to say about it – or everything that was necessary for his argument in the *TdIE*, and everything that he could say from the point of view of the description of facts, as the corresponding text from the *Short Treatise* attests. The character of the note and the references to the Empiricists and 'new Philosophers' suggests that experience here is more a matter of experimentation – that is, it is no longer experience as it is given but rather constructed experiments. In this part of the text, however, Spinoza has said nothing about experimentation, and while he can refer to its importance, he cannot transform it into a concept. It is therefore not very surprising that he takes little care to refer to it with a particular name. The term *experientia* still suffices.

[115] 'Hic alquianto prolixius agam de experientia; et Empiricorum et recentium Philosophorum procedendi methodum examinabo', G II, p. 13, note. I am keeping Koyré's translation for *prolixius*. [Translator's note: Moreau's translation is as follows: 'Ici, je m'occuperai un peu plus en détail de l'expérience et l'examinerai la méthode des empiriques et des philosophes nouveaux'.] The term does not appear to have the technical meaning of a reference to the geometers that it will have in the later writings.

There nevertheless exists a second term in the Latin lexicon: *experimentum*. Traditionally, it is quasi-synonymous with *experientia*, save that it can also refer to an act or fact and thus to something momentary, situated at a precise point in time. It refers to what someone has felt, known or suffered personally.[116] Spinoza uses it a few paragraphs prior when defining vague experience. He specifies there that vague experience is so named only because it arises from chance and remains an authority for us only insofar as we have no other *experimentum* that can contradict it.[117] It is clear that in this passage *experimentum* cannot signify 'experimentation'. The word *aliud* clearly shows that the *experientia* that is contradicted and the *experimentum* that contradicts it are of the same nature.[118] If there is a difference, it concerns only the fact that *experientia* refers to a perception that, having not yet been contradicted, has time on its side and remains in the foreground; by contrast, *experimentum* refers to the result of learning some information that will (or rather could) overturn the reign of what had been established up to that point on the basis of chance. But it has no need to be constructed: learning this information might just as well occur by chance. The most

---

[116] Three examples suffice to show this, borrowed respectively from classical, medieval and humanist Latin: when Jugurtha tries to take pity on Metellus, Metellus becomes distrustful, for having experienced the perfidy of the Numides he had learnt the fickleness of their character and their love of change: 'Sed Metello jam antea experimentis cognitum erat genus Numidarum infidum, ingeio mobili, novarum rerum avidum', Sallust, *The Jugurthine War*, Chapter 46. The good and the bad angel now both know that sin leads to the fall, but it is not for the same reason that they have this knowledge: 'Nam quod ille scit ipso sui experimento, hoc iste didicit solo aletrius exemplo', St Anselm, *De Casu Diaboli*, Chapter 25. I have already quoted Petrarch's formula where he states that old age confirms through experience the truths learnt previously in reading: 'Senecta autem corrixit, experimentoque perdocuit verum illud quod diu ante perlegeram', *Lettera ai posteri*, a cura di Gianni Villani, Rome: Salerno Editrice, 1989, p. 34. Note the plural in the first quotation, which individualises each *experimentum*; the opposition with the example in the second, which personalises it; and the reference to time in the third, which situates it in relation to the anterior time of reading. All of these traits allow us to better distinguish, against a common backdrop, the continuity and impersonality that are more traditionally the prerogative of experience.

[117] 'Sed tantum ita dicitur, quia casu sic occurit, et nullum aliud habemus experimentum, quod hoc oppugnat, et ideo tanquam inconcussum apud nos manet', § 19, G II, p. 10, ll. 12–15 [*TdIE* 19; *CWS* I, 12–13].

[118] More precisely, *experientia* is reprised, in the second part of the phrase, by a second and implicit *experimentum*, with which the neutral terms *hoc* and *inconcussum* accord. If one wanted to render the text word for word, it would be necessary to translate it as follows: 'and we have no other *experimentum* that is opposed to that one, and thus that one remains for us solidly established'.

precise way to translate *experimentum* – and staying as close as possible to its status as a substantivised past participle – would therefore be: 'what we have experienced'.

However, the punctual character and the sense of individualisation that the term brings with it in its semantic field prepare it to play the role – as soon as this becomes necessary – of designating scientific experimentation. This is a technical sense that the word already possesses in classical Latin and that we find in the seventeenth century,[119] notably in Bacon's works,[120] where even *experientia* seems ever ready to tip over into experimentation.[121] In fact, a newly accepted meaning of the word 'experience' emerges, one that no longer designates simple observation or the givens of sensible knowledge,

---

[119] We find it for example in the polemics around Galileo. Note, for instance, that P. Grassi uses *experientia* to refer to the common observations on which Aristotelianism is based and *experimentum* to refer to the experimental apparatuses that Galileo proposes. An example: 'cum longa experientia compertum sit, quo rariora corpora fuerint magisque perspicua . . .', *Il Saggiatore*, § 22 (Feltrinelli, a cura di Libero Sosio, p. 141); 'Sed videamus nunc quam verum sit experimentum illud, cui maxime Galilaei sententia innititur [. . .] Ex quibus aliisque experimentis, scio aliquos ingenium Galilaei commendasse plurimum, qui ex rebus levissimis, atque ab oculos positis,facilitate mirabili in rerum difficilimarum cognitionem homines manuduceret', § 40, pp. 211–12. However, in the same passage, to found his own opinions, Grassi returns for coherent reasons to *experientia*: 'Atque haec quidem ab experientia certa sunt; quae tamen experientia si absit, doceat haec quoque ratio ipsas', p. 215. It should be noted that, when commenting on and refuting these passages in Italian, Galileo uses *esperienza* in both cases.

[120] Cf. M. Malherbe, 'L'expérience et l'induction chez Bacon', in *Francis Bacon. Science et Méthode*, Actes du Colloque de Nantes, ed. M. Malherbe et J.-M. Pousseur, Paris: Vrin, 1985, pp. 113–44; M. Le Dœuff and M. Llasera, 'Histoire des sciences et laboratoires imaginaires', in Sir Francis Bacon, *La nouvelle Atlantide*, suivi de *Voyage dans la pensée baroque*, par M. Le Dœueff et M. Llasera, Paris: Payot, 1983, pp. 182–216.

[121] This is why I cannot entirely follow Koyré's judgement, who refuses Bacon any role in the history of scientific experimentation. Cf. *Etudes galiléennes*, Paris: Hermann, 1966, p. 12; *Etudes d'histoire de la pensée scientifique*, Paris: Gallimard, 1973, p. 167; and above all the text cited without reference by G. Jorland, *La Science dans la philosophie. Les recherches épistémologiques d'Alexandre Koyré*, Paris: Gallimard, 1981, p. 275, and which dates from the 1920's: 'L'expérience baconienne, c'est celle d'un homme "qui a de l'expérience", c'est aussi l'expérience d'un homme qui recherche les mystères de la nature, les qualités occultes et secrètes des animaux, des plantes et des germes. Ce sont ces faits, ces vertus et ces qualités magiques qu'il s'agit pour lui d'étudier et évidemment, on ne peut le faire que par expérience, puisque justement elles sont occultes et par conséquent ne peuvent être déduites. Il faut faire des expériences, dit-il, exactement dans le même sens où le diraient ses contemporains, les magiciens et les alchimistes.'

but rather refers to the result of a transformation in sensible knowledge thanks to certain instruments and indeed to special apparatuses set up with the help of these instruments.[122] To refer to this new meaning, a specialised term might be needed. Thus, when at the end of the *TdIE* Spinoza elaborates a theory of the knowledge of changeable things, it is quite naturally this term that he uses. And this time he really does have a concept.

After dealing with the series of fixed and eternal things, Spinoza notes that knowledge of singular things is quite difficult to attain: in fact, their order cannot be deduced from that of eternal things, which are by nature simultaneous, nor from a series of similar things, which give us only extrinsic and circumstantial determinations.[123] It is therefore necessary to have recourse to specific *auxilia*. More precisely, these *auxilia* have two purposes. The first is that they must teach us to use our senses;[124] we therefore find here the opposition between *experimentum* and vague experience in the form that the Baconian tradition had given it.[125] The senses teach but first they must be taught.[126] The second reason is that the *auxilia* will allow us to carry out experiments according to laws and a determinate order.[127] This time we are clearly dealing with constructed experiments. It is not a matter of observing what is given, and perhaps not even of enlarging the field of the given. The verb *facere* clearly implies at the very least the production of an apparatus – if not, indeed, of experimental equipment – while the references to order and to law show that this apparatus must owe nothing whatsoever to chance:

---

[122] It is this shift in the history of observation (or rather this shift that gives observation a history) that explains why Galileo places the Aristotelian principles according to which 'sensate esperienze si devono anteporre ai discorsi umani' alternatively in the mouth of Simplicio, to refute it, and in that of Salviati, who adopts it: in the first case, it is a matter of non-experimental observation (*Dialogo supra I due massimi sistemi del mondo*, Turin: Einaudi, a cura di L. Sosio, 1970, Dialogo primo, pp. 41, 58); and in the second, of observation informed by new instruments (ibid., pp. 63–4, 70): thanks to the telescope, we see something other than what Aristotle saw, and if he had seen what we now see, he would not have advanced the same discourse.

[123] He had already made the same claim a little prior to this, in paragraphs 100 and 101, and the impossibility of knowing the series refers again to human *imbecillitas*.

[124] 'ut nostris sensibus sciamus uti . . .', § 103, G II, p. 37, ll. 22–3 [*TdIE* 103; CWS I, 42].

[125] Cf. M. Malherbe, 'L'expérience et l'induction chez Bacon', p. 118 on the *ministratio ad sensum*. And, on the *auxilia*, J.-M. Pousseur, *Bacon. Inventer la science*, Paris: Belin, 1988, pp. 119–23.

[126] And we could add that we are not far from the idea identified above with respect to Galileo: the historical dimension of perception.

[127] 'et experimenta certis legibus et ordiner facere' (implicit: *scieamus*), § 103, G II, p. 37, ll. 23–4 [*TdIE* 103; CWS I, 42].

we have left the domain of vague experience and can now rightly translate *experimenta* by 'experimentations'. These experimentations 'will suffice to determine the thing we are seeking, so that at last we may infer from them according to what laws of eternal things it was made, and its inmost nature become known to us . . .'.[128]

In fact, the *TdIE* stops a few pages after these sentences, and before reaching this endpoint Spinoza does not deal with *experimenta*. The reader thus remains provisionally disappointed. We will therefore have to seek out in Spinoza's correspondence examples of *experimenta* and the rules for their use. Nevertheless, it is already possible to draw some conclusions from what has just been said. Experiments seem to be governed by three principles:

— First of all, a principle concerning a difference in field. The *experimenta* have a well-defined place in the process of knowledge. They do not concern eternal things but are related to singular and changeable things. Consequently, there are some questions they will never be able to answer — and yet, reciprocally, the fact that they cannot respond to these questions in no way diminishes their value as far as the questions they are appropriate for are concerned. This situation rules out any assessment of Spinoza's thought that could be summarised by a formula like: 'Spinoza is a partisan (or an adversary) of experimentation.' Such a formula would neglect the rigorous distinction between these two fields.

— Next, a principle of instrumentality. The *experimenta* are determined not only in terms of the place they occupy relative to the distinction between the changeable and the eternal, but also, in terms of their functioning, by the *auxilia*. What does this mean? André Lécrivain has a proposed a reading that seems to me to be accurate, in the context of a comparison with the *Principia*[129] and with the meaning that is conferred upon this text by certain developments in Letter XII.[130] With respect to physical objects, these *auxilia* are 'the operational and abstract means that allow us to give a numerical determination and a mathematised expression to things'.[131] The

---

[128] 'quae sufficient ad rem, quae inquiritur, determinandam, ut tandem ex iis concludamus, secundum quasnam rerum aeternarum leges facta sit, et intima ejus natura nobis innotescat', § 103, G II, p. 37, ll. 24–6 [*TdIE* 103; *CWS* I, 42].

[129] A. Lécrivain, 'Spinoza et la physique cartésienne', *Cahiers Spinoza*, I (1977), pp. 235–65.

[130] Time, measure and number as *auxilia imaginationis*, Ep. XII to L. Meyer, G IV, p. 57, ll. 15 and 18; p. 58, ll. 17–18 [*Ep.* XII [to Lodewijk Meyer]; *CWS* I, 203].

[131] 'les moyens opératoires et abstraits qui permettent de les déterminer numériquement et d'en donner une expression mathématisée', A. Lécrivain, 'Spinoza et la physique cartésienne', p. 261.

auxilia thus allow one to insert singular, changeable things into experimental protocols. In other words, experimentation such as Spinoza foresees it is not only something constructed; it is also, to a certain degree, mathematised. While mathematical beings are 'beings of reason' – that is, modes of the imagination – a certain regulated use of the imagination allows one not only to know the laws of nature, but to know by which laws of nature such-and-such an empirical object is determined. Note that this is a *regulated* use: this is what the terms *order* and *laws* allude to. It is therefore not a matter of indistinctly enlisting everything that observation presents us with in the service of science. And yet, as we will see further on, it is perhaps not impossible either that pre-existing observations can relieve us of having to construct an experiment, so long as these observations are such that they can be adapted to the *auxilia*.

— Finally, a principle of discrimination. What does experimentation actually teach us? Not, properly speaking, to know laws, but to choose between them. It is important to appreciate this crucial distinction. An empiricist conception of science, whose fundamental presupposition is that reason is only ever faced with a scarcity of laws (or at least of true laws), would give experience the responsibility of discovering them. By contrast, Spinoza seems persuaded of nature's superabundance. Nature, it seems, can produce the same phenomena through a multiplicity of laws[132] (and of true laws). Experimentation thus serves to decide not between true and false laws but between true laws that are effective in some cases and not in others. By occupying this position, Spinoza inscribes himself within the Galilean-Cartesian movement. Galileo clearly states the principle of the superabundance of nature – in a sense, he places this principle at the beginning of all research: it is only after having convinced oneself of this principle that one can begin working and divest oneself of the noisy assurances of those who project onto nature their own narrow imagination.[133] Descartes

---

[132] Cf. note y in the *TdIE*, which briefly indicates this with respect to astronomical hypotheses (G II, p. 22 [*TdIE* 57; *CWS* I, 26]).

[133] Cf. the famous passage: 'Parmi d'aver per lunghe esperienze osservato tale esser la condizione umana intorno alle cose intellettuali, che quanto altri meno ne intende e ne sa, tanto piú risolutamente voglia discorrerne; e che, all'incontro, la multitudine delle cose conosciute ed intese renda piú lento ed irresoluto al sentenziare circa qualche novità', Il Saggiatore, § 21, p. 126. Isolated, this phrase could seem to be a banal warning against the lack of observation; but it takes on quite a different resonance when one reads the long fable that follows it: namely, the story of a man who raises birds and studies the physical means by which they produce their songs. Living in a solitary place, he believes that this is the only way that nature can produce such

states this in the form of an epistemological programme when he makes a plan for experiments (that is, constructed experiments) in *The Discourse on Method*.[134] Everything happens as if at least one of the essential currents of the science of the classical age placed at the foundation of its justification for experimentation a certain idea of the extraordinary power of Nature, which can produce the same effects by diverse means, all of which are knowable by Reason. Experimentation attests not to the impotence of reason, but rather to the necessity of finding criteria to discriminate between different yet entirely rational means.

Difference in fields, presentation in operational terms, selection between natural laws: such are the principles that govern, according to the concise yet solid formulations of the *TdIE*, the construction of experiments.[135] We now have to consider how these principles are applied in those texts where Spinoza speaks of concrete experiments, whether these experiments are carried out by Spinoza himself or by someone else. The best-known and most instructive of these texts are the set of letters exchanged with Oldenburg on the subject of Boyle's experiments with nitre.[136]

Spinoza's correspondence with Boyle – with Oldenburg operating as

---

songs. The successive encounters with a shepherd who plays the pipe, with a child who uses a string instrument, with a man who makes a glass sing by sliding his finger over the edge, the observation of wasps, mosquitos and cicadas makes him realise that nature possesses a lot of other ways to produce the same effect. Experience here is less of a heuristic than of a programmatic order: it indicates the depth of the field that will have to be explored, without prejudging the means of exploration. It reveals a superabundance of Nature's power, *which surpasses even itself*: 'Io potrei con altri molti esempi spiegar la ricchezza della natura nel produr suoi effetti con maniere inescogitabili da noi, quando il senso e l'esperienza non lo ci mostrasse, la quale anco talvolta non basta a supplire alla nostra incapacità', ibid., p. 128.

[134] 'But I must also admit that the power of nature is so ample and so vast, and these principles so simple and so general, that I notice hardly any particular effect of which I do not know at once that it can be deduced from the principles in many different ways; and my greatest difficulty is usually to discover in which of these ways it depends on them. I know of no other means to discover this than by seeking further observations whose outcomes vary according to which of these ways provides the correct explanation', *Discourse on the Method*, Part Six, AT, VI, pp. 64–5 [*PWD* I, 144].

[135] M. Walther has powerfully emphasised the importance of these paragraphs from the *TdIE*, in which he sees, from a perspective close to the works of Blumenberg, 'ein bedeutsamer Wandel im Begriff der Vernunft', *Metaphysik als Anti-Theologie. Die Philosophie Spionzas im Zusammenhang der religionsphilosophischen Problematik*, Hamburg: F. Meiner, 1971, p. 67 ff.

[136] Translator's note: 'nitre' is a mineral form of potassium nitrate.

their intermediary – has been studied on a number of occasions.[137] Sadly, however, commentators have failed to read it alongside the principles that emerge both from the *TdIE* as from other of Spinoza's epistemological texts. It seems to me that these few pages define an experimental programme that helps us better understand what Spinoza is seeking when he defines or criticises experimental protocols.

The theme of the discussion is well known: Oldenburg sent Spinoza Boyle's *Tentamina*[138] and asked for his opinion on 'the Experiments he has included on Niter, and on Fluidity and Solidity'.[139] Spinoza responds with a detailed critical examination of Boyle's work; his remarks on the experiment with nitre dominate the discussion. Not only does he analyse Boyle's experiments, he proposes a number of other experiments. When Boyle's response gets back to him, again by the intermediary of Oldenburg, Spinoza clarifies his position, albeit more concisely this time.[140] There is no use going

---

[137] In addition to the articles by Daudin and the Halls already cited, mention should be made of the study by E. Yakira, 'Boyle et Spinoza', *Archives de philosophie*, 51/1 (1988), pp. 107–24, and a long note by J.-P. Osier in the new edition of Meinsma, *Spinoza et son cercle*, Paris: Vrin, 1983, pp. 313–15. H. G. Hubbeling offers a very synthetic summary of the exchange of letters in his *Spinoza*, Fribourg/Munich: Karl Alber, 1978, pp. 70–2. [Moreau has in fact not previously cited the Halls' article: A. R. Hall and M. B. Hall, 'Philosophy and Natural Philosophy: Boyle and Spinoza', in *Mélanges Alexandre Koyré*, Paris: Hermann, 1964, published on the occasion of his 70th birthday.]

[138] He had promised to send the work to him as early as his first letter from the 13/26 of August 1661, after insisting on the large number of *experimenta* that proved his theses (Ep. I, G IV, p. 6, ll. 14–20 [Ep. I [from Henry Oldenburg]; CWS I, 164]). He returned to this topic in his second letter of 27 September (Ep. III, G IV, p. 12, ll. 9–13 [Ep. III [from Henry Oldenburg]; CWS I, 170]).

[139] 'Libellum, quem promiseram, en accipe, mihique tuum de eo judicium, imprimis circa ea, quae de Nitro, deque Fluiditate ac Firmitudine inferit specimina rescribe', Ep. V, G IV, p. 14, ll. 28–30 [Ep. V [from Henry Oldenburg]; CWS I, 172].

[140] The whole of the discussion takes a certain amount of time: the letter to Oldenburg is from 11/21 October 1661, Spinoza's first response (which we have in two versions: the copy conserved by the Royal Society and published in facsimile form by W. Meijer in 1902, and the copy from the *Opera Posthuma*) is not dated. Oldenburg confirms reception many weeks later (Ep. VII) but does not communicate Boyle's observations until 3 April 1663 (Ep. XI). Spinoza responds to these observations on 17/27 July (Ep. XIV), and at the beginning of the month of August Oldenburg communicates Boyle's second response to him (Ep. XVI). The discussion thus lasted almost two years. Thus, even if it occurred thanks to Oldenburg's initiative, it cannot be considered something marginal to Spinoza's intellectual activity: he had the time to reflect, he undertook other experiments than those that had been communicated to him, and he reaffirmed his position after a sufficiently long time.

over in detail the narrative of the experiments themselves.[141] It suffices to summarise their essential aspects.[142] By decomposing saltpetre (that is, nitre), Boyle obtains both nitrous gas (vapours of nitrogen peroxide) and 'fixed nitre' (potassium carbonate), along with carbon gas, which he does not observe. Next, he pours nitrous liquid (or water that contains it) into a solution of potassium and obtains saltpetre in crystal form. In Boyle's eyes this double experiment proves that nitre is a body composed of two different elements, for he was able to decompose it into these elements, each of which have characteristic properties, and then to recompose it from them. Boyle is essentially right, with two reservations: the fixed nitre and the nitrous gas are not strictly speaking components of nitre (specifically, the potassium contains carbon that comes from the carbon used in the reaction), and he neglected the role of certain elements in the two reactions (in particular the carbonic gas that is emitted on each occasion).[143]

The core of the discussion concerns the interpretation of this double reaction that Boyle produces. Boyle believed he had decomposed this product into two elements, thereby proving it was a composite. By contrast, where Boyle sees a decomposition, Spinoza discerns a continuity: one of the elements produced (nitrous gas) is in fact the same thing as the original element (nitre) but in a different form. The authors diverge on the same point for the second process: Boyle thought he had succeeded in recomposing (*redintegratio*) nitre by putting the two bodies into which it had been decomposed back together. By contrast, Spinoza argues that he had simply restored the unique element to its original form (just as we get water again when ice melts). A number of other arguments are linked to this central one: if nitrous gas is, according to Spinoza, the same thing as nitre – that is, if there is neither decomposition nor recomposition – then what is the status of the other product found at the end of the decomposition? Spinoza's response is logical: this second element

---

[141] The two experiments are analysed well in Daudin's article, and in a more detailed fashion in the notes to the Akkerman-Hubbeling-Westerbrink edition of the correspondence (Spinoza, *Briefwisseling*, Amsterdam: Wereldbibliotheek, 1977, p. 441 ff).

[142] Cf. *The Works of the Honourable Robert Boyle*, London, 1772, vol. I, p. 359: *A physico-chymical Essay, with some Considerations touching the differing parts and redintegration of Salt-Petre* (the description of the experiment properly speaking can be found in sections 3 to 11); p. 377: *The History of fluidity and firmness*.

[143] On Boyle's conception of the simple and the mixed body, see the very clear pages by H. Metzger, *Les doctrines chimiques en France du début du XVIIe siècle à la fin du XVIIIe siècle*, Paris: A. Blanchard, 1922, p. 252 ff – in particular the following formula that clarifies what is at stake in the problem of *redintegratio*: 'le corps simple semble être pour notre auteur un corps que l'on n'est pas encore parvenu à décomposer', p. 259. This is what pits Boyle against both the Aristotelians and the alchemists.

does not belong to the nature of nitre: it is a simple impurity, one that persists, in part, in nitrous gas. How does Boyle prove the real difference between nitre and nitrous gas? By reference to the difference between their sensible qualities: one is flammable, the other is not.[144] They also do not have the same flavour.[145] To speak in a Spinozist language, this proves that a finite mode is not only constituted by movement or by figures, but – at an intermediary level of reality – by specific qualitative components, which are not simple states of this mode but are *other* to it in the full sense of the term. I will not analyse here the reasons why Boyle undertook these two experiments. However, I will examine the content of Spinoza's theoretical arguments.

First, we should note that in the course of this discussion Spinoza only uses the term *experimentum* and never *experientia*. The systematic nature of this use confirms that, for him, *experimentum* is a technical term that refers not to observation in general but to observations conducted by reference to a theoretical system. The distinction between experience and experimentation, while not thematised, is present in a practical state. It is crucial to insist upon this distinction, for nobody seems to have noticed it, including French translators[146]

---

[144] The question is posed in section 19: does non-flammability require in its components 'a distinct sulphureous ingredient'? (*Works*, p. 367). The question immediately receives a response in section 20: 'Salt-petre (which not only is inflammable, but burns very fiercely and violently) may be produced by the coalition of two bodies, which are neither of them inflammable', ibid.

[145] Ibid., sections 22 and following.

[146] In his translation Appuhn does not distinguish between *experientia* and *experimentum*, translating them both as *expérience* (while in the passage: 'simulque duo aut tria experimenta admodum facilia adjungam ...', G IV, p. 17, l. 12, he renders *experimenta* by 'examples' – it is hardly surprising after this that the reader takes away the idea that Spinoza has hardly any confidence in experimentation!). The Pléiade edition reproduces Appuhn's choices (including for the occurrence on p. 17, l. 12 which is also rendered as 'examples'). As for Saisset, he did not translate letters VI and XIV, remaining content to refer to them in a note. However, foreign translators are more careful (Gebhardt, 'Experiment/Erfahrung', in *Briefwechsel*, Hamburg: F. Meiner, 1914; Droetto, 'Esperimento/esperienza', in *Epistolario*, Turin: Einaudi, 1951; Dominguez, 'experimento/experiencia', in *Correspondencia*, Madrid: Allianza Editorial, 1988; the same choice is made by J. D. Sanchez Estop, *Correpondencia completa*, Madrid: libros Hiperion, 1988, and formerly by O. Cohan in *Obras Completas*, vol. IV, Buenos Aires: Acervo cultural, and A. Wolf, 'experiment/experience', in *The Correspondence of Spinoza*, London: George Allen & Unwin, 1928; the same choice is made by Curley in CWS I). Yet the care taken in translation does not always carry over into clarity in the commentaries. Abraham Wolf, who comments at length on letter VI (*The Correspondence of Spinoza*, pp. 379–88), does not devote a single line to the question.

and commentators.¹⁴⁷ It will be agreed that this lack of attention does not give us the best chance to judge fairly Spinoza's attitude with regards to the experimental sciences.¹⁴⁸ There is, however, a single apparent exception: at the end of the observations on the *redintegratio nitri*, the version of the *Opera Posthuma* uses the term *experientia* once.¹⁴⁹ It should be noted, however, that it is absent from the manuscript version sent to the Royal Society and that it is replaced there by *semel*.¹⁵⁰ We are not dealing, then, with the result of a constructed experiment but with an observation made as if marginally and furtively on the occasion of a construction meant to fulfil another purpose. The word *experientia* thus refers not to a rigorous procedure but to a fact that strikes the operator of the experiment. After these terminological remarks, we can now examine the content of Spinoza's arguments:

— This term *experimentum* refers not only to those experiments that Boyle constructs and which he describes in the *Tentamina*, but also to others that Spinoza opposes to Boyle and that he himself carried out with the greatest of care. Spinoza even reproaches Boyle for having performed experiments in areas where it was not necessary to do so.¹⁵¹ Instead, he affirms that one cannot do experiments on just anything. In the discussion of fluidity, which follows the analysis of the decomposition of saltpetre, Spinoza criticises a remark made by Boyle. Boyle had suggested that it would be difficult to

---

[147] E. Yakira, who is the author of the most philosophically refined commentary on the Boyle/Spinoza discussion, directly applies to the role of the *experimentum* in Letter VI what Letter X says regarding *experientia* ('Boyle et Spinoza', p. 112). This does not mean that it is useless to compare the two texts, but one should doubtless take precautions.

[148] It could be objected that the word 'expérimentation' [experimentation] is overdetermined in French and that it is commonly replaced by 'expérience', without any resulting confusion. Certainly, and we will see that I do so occasionally in the present commentary. It is still important to have at least highlighted the problem if we wish to really avoid confusion. The stylistic reasons are in no way negligible in a work of translation; but they are applied all the better when questions of conceptual distinction have been decided.

[149] 'De hujus phaenomeni causa jam locutus sum; hic tantum addo, me etiam experientia invenisse, guttulis illis salinis particulas salis fixi innatare', G IV, p. 26, ll. 6–8. [*Ep.* VI [to Henry Oldenburg]; *CWS* I, 179].

[150] 'De hujus phaenomeni causa jam locutus sum hic tantum addo me semel invenisse guttulis illis salinis particulas salis fixi innatasse', ibid., 1. 23–5 [*Ep.* VI [to Henry Oldenburg]; *CWS* I, 179].

[151] 'Haec, inquam, consclusio [sc. heterogeneity, that is, the composite character of nitre], ut diceretur bona, videtur mihi adhuc requiri aliquod experimentum, quo ostendatur spiritum nitri non esse revera nitrum . . .' G IV, p. 16, l. 14; p. 17, l. 2 [*Ep.* VI [to Henry Oldenburg]; *CWS* I, 173–4].

believe the extent to which the smallness of the parts of fluid elements contributes to moving them and to keeping them mobile, 'if we were not able to confirm it by chymical experiments'.[152] Spinoza responds by saying that no one will ever succeed in doing so; one can only do so by 'demonstration and computation'.[153] The question here is that of the infinite decomposition of the movement of the particles. The clearest formula can be found in the second exchange of letters. Oldenburg says that Boyle performed this experiment to prove the vanity of 'substantial forms'. Spinoza replies that no experiment will ever demonstrate this.[154] Thus, in his eyes Boyle's error on this point is to fail to know the limits of the field within which experiments are both possible and profitable. We thus see at work here the principle of the difference in fields that we identified in the remarks from the *TdIE*.

— Spinoza again explicitly says that one should not trust the senses as such. This does not mean that he does not take what they can teach into account, but rather that he seeks to explain them instead of treating them as a criterion. Sensible differences do not suffice to prove the real heterogeneity of bodies: two states of the same body can affect the senses in different ways. The difference in flavour of nitrous gas and saltpetre, along with the fact that the second is not flammable while the first is, refers to the structure of the particles and their movement.[155] This is what justifies the demand either for a second experiment, which would take this difference in nature or state as its object, or at least for a more precise quantification, which could make this difference appear. The proportionality proves more than the observable properties. We thus find the principle of instrumentality that we identified in paragraphs 102–103 from the *TdIE*.

— We can also identify this principle of instrumentality in the care with which Spinoza constructs the experiments he proposes. His intervention into the discussion is indeed a case of clarification. It is therefore absolutely

---

[152] 'whereas it would scarce be believed, how much the smallness of parts may facilitate their being easily put into motion, and kept in it if we were not able to confirm it by chymical experiments', section 5, *Works*, p. 380.

[153] 'Nunquam chymicis neque aliis experimentis nisi demonstratione et computatione aliquis id comprobare poterit', Ep. VI, G IV, p. 29, ll. 13–14 [*Ep.* VI [to Henry Oldenburg]; *CWS* I, 182].

[154] Ep. XIII, G IV, p. 64, l. 27 sq [*Ep.* XIII [to Henry Oldenburg]; *CWS* I, 208].

[155] There is a certain bad faith in summarising this objection, as H. Daudin does, by saying: 'Spinoza ne posera, entre l'esprit de nitre et le nitre comme différence nette, que celle qui ressort manifestement de l'expérience commune', 'Spinoza et la science expérimentale', p. 182: The reference to the speed of particles is a Cartesian argument, and not a common experience.

inadmissible to say that he is 'very inattentive to the true nature of scientific experimentation'.[156] He reproaches Boyle for failing to quantify in the way he should have.[157] But it is not a matter of measurement for measurement's sake. Given that Spinoza reproaches Boyle for failing to demonstrate that saltpetre really is a compound, and given also that, in terms of the opposite thesis – his own – fixed salt is a simple impurity, Spinoza determines the theoretical site of the measurable by this difference in hypotheses. If the residue (the fixed salt) is really a component of nitre, its quantity must be proportional to the quantity of saltpetre. If we redo the experiment by increasing the quantity of saltpetre, the mass of the residue should increase proportionally (something that would no doubt be the case if it were a simple impurity). Only this measurement will allow us to decide between the two hypotheses and thus refute the simple hypothesis of the conservation of the nature of a given body. Spinoza thus has very coherent reasons for reproaching Boyle for failing to undertake such a measurement.[158] The reader will have noticed that Spinoza does not refuse *a priori* the law of composition put forward by Boyle, but, judging it to be less realistic than the opposite thesis, he judges Boyle's thesis to be the one that stands in need of proof. Thus, we clearly see at work not only the principle of instrumentality but also the principle of selection that was given alongside it in the *TdIE*. But we also notice, at least in this example, that their application does not suppose an absolute equivalence between hypotheses. More proofs will be demanded of some laws than others.

---

[156] 'très inattentif à la vraie nature de l'expérience scientifique', E. Yakira, 'Boyle et Spinoza', p. 112. Yakira's study is useful in that it does not position itself from a purely empiricist point of view. It distinguishes between observed experience and constructed experience. But Yakira does not seem to realise that Spinoza *also* makes such a distinction, all the while formulating it *differently*. Yakira also assigns to Spinoza a 'jugement sévère' with respect to experimentation by citing the *TdIE* in an incomplete fashion: he refers to the formula from paragraph 101 (there is no point in understanding the *series* of changing singular things) in abstraction from those from paragraphs 102–3 (the *auxilia* allow one to know them otherwise than by this *series*). Yakira's isolation of paragraph 101 is moreover a sort of rite of passage in the Spinozist literature, which permits one to banish the singular into the realm of the ineffable (we already find this argument in another form in the commentary that Theodor Camerer makes on this passage from the *TdIE*, *Die Lehre Spinozas*, Stuttgart: Cotta, 1877, 1914, pp. 130–2). On the other hand, everything that Yakira says on the question of chemical identity is remarkable, 'Boyle et Spinoza', p. 114 ff.

[157] Cf. Wolf, *The Correspondence of Spinoza*, pp. 185–6.

[158] 'Vel ad minimum requirebatur inquirere, an salis fixi, quae in crucibulo manet quantitas, semper eadem ex eadem quantitate nitri, et ex majore secundum proprtionem reperiatur', Ep. VI, G IV, p. 17, ll. 3–6 [*Ep.* VI [to Henry Oldenburg]; *CWS* I, 174].

It can thus be said that, in his discussion with Boyle, Spinoza rigorously applies the principles that he had put forward rather elliptically in the *TdIE*. Reciprocally, this discussion can help us better understand the meaning of these principles as it provides an example of their application. But is this to say that there is nothing more in the letters from 1662–3 than in the *Treatise*? We can glimpse a final trait, indeed an insistent one, which commentators have mostly failed to identify, or which they have taken as a sign of a simple regression to common discourse: Spinoza declares that there exist notions on the basis of which it is useless to construct a complex experiment, for *experimenta satis obvia* demonstrates them. What should we understand by this? It is not a matter of principles in the strict sense – principles that concern essences and thus do not arise from experimentation at all – but rather of principles for which Spinoza seems to consider that an experiment is at once necessary but already available and always ... insufficient. The expression first occurs with respect to the reducibility of tactile qualities to movement alone.[159] Boyle's experiment does not provide 'more illuminating evidence' than others 'which are readily enough available'.[160] Spinoza provides a number of such proofs, which successively concern heat (rubbing two sticks together produces a flame; lime heats up if water is poured onto it); sound (the boiling of ordinary water); colour (we see this in multiple ways among plants); and flavour (wine that is sweet changes into vinegar).[161] This is a remarkable series: in each case, a movement produces a change in a sensible quality. Furthermore, in each case experience is given in daily life, either in the natural world or by way of very simple techniques. We are no longer in the domain of constructed experiments. We are dealing more with what we would call observation than with experimentation. We can see why the logic of Spinoza's reasoning leads him to again speak of *experimenta*. Why? For two reasons, it would seem: the first concerns the pertinence of mathematics for these common events. It is not a matter of knowing if human

---

[159] In fact, Boyle devotes sections 12 to 18 of his essay on nitre to this problem (that is, those that immediately follow the description of the experiment). He summarises his interpretation as follows: 'and first this experiment seems to afford us an instance, by which we may discern, that motion, figure and disposition of parts and such like primary and mechanical affections (if I may so call them) of matter, may suffice to produce those more secondary affections of bodies, which are wont to be called sensible qualities', section 12, *Works*, p. 364.

[160] Or: 'are sufficiently visible for people'. Ep. VI, G IV, p. 25, ll. 9–10 [*Ep.* VI [to Henry Oldenburg]; *CWS* I, 179]. Appuhn's translation of *satis obvis* by 'très banales' does not sufficiently take into account the availability of fundamental *experimenta*.

[161] G IV, p. 25, l. 10; p. 26, l. 2 [*Ep.* VI [to Henry Oldenburg]; *CWS* I, 179].

beings die or if the dog is an animal who barks, but of movement as the cause of sensible qualities. Someone who considers that vague experience informs us only of accidents cannot recognise its pertinence here, for here what is at stake is the essence of natural phenomena. And secondly, each of these observations is read not in terms of the specificity of its process – which, at this level, is uncontrollable – but in some sense in an abstract fashion. The same will go further on for relations between movement and fluidity.

Everything therefore happens as if, for certain fundamental questions, certain observations of a determinate type that are detached from common experience play the role of experimentation. But these are very specific experiments, since Spinoza makes the same reservation with regard to them as he does with regard to Boyle's: in Letter XIII, he reprises an analogous argument and adds: 'as I expressly said, I did not offer these experiments that they might confirm absolutely what I said'.[162] This phrase does not concern all experiments. It isolates a series of *experimenta* that bear upon the most general aspects of Nature (the origin of sensible qualities, the nature of movement, the status of fluids). In fact, all of these questions refer directly to nature and to the power of movement. With respect to all of the problems that concern these notions, Spinoza seems to say: it is useless to construct experiments. What is given suffices, so long as it is interrogated properly. It suffices to set off down the right path, but neither this path nor a constructed experiment will prove anything definitively. Nature, when looked at conventionally, shows everywhere the efficacy of movement. If one wishes to demonstrate Nature's forms and its diverse processes, it is necessary to reason mathematically. We thus see Spinoza assign a *pre-theoretical role* to common experience as far as the principles of Nature are concerned. Here, too, it is worthwhile again recalling a Cartesian thesis: that of the distinction between different experiments as a function of the progress of knowledge. Let us return to a passage from the *Discourse*: 'I also noticed, regarding experiments, that the further we advance in our knowledge, the more necessary they become. At the beginning, rather than seeking those which are more unusual and highly contrived, it is better to resort only to those which, presenting themselves spontaneously to our senses, cannot be unknown to us if we reflect a little.'[163] What should we conclude from this

---

[162] Ep. XIII [to Henry Oldenburg]; CWS I, 210.

[163] AT, p. 63, ll. 18–25 [PWD I, 143]. Translator's note: Dugald Murdoch translates 'expériences' here as 'observations', but notes that this term is close to 'experiments' in the modern sense. I have used 'experiments' to keep the unity of vocabulary in this section. Nevertheless, as Moreau makes clear, it remains worthwhile asking to what

final trait? Spinoza does indeed make a distinction between common experience and scientific experimentation; but this distinction does not completely cover the difference between experience that is given and experience that is constructed – in other words, experiments. As far as the fundamental laws of nature are concerned, the determination of the given suffices for science, so long it is interrogated from a mathematical perspective. It can thus be said that, even in this domain, Spinoza places common experience as such at the foundation of science: if the given is to respond to the questions asked of it, it is necessary that it be deciphered by a mind habituated to reading essential distinctions at the heart of appearances. The pre-theoretical value of what is given to us in nature is thus certain only for the person who seeks the constancy of its forms.

Have we now seen all there is to see as far as Spinoza's opposition to Boyle is concerned? We can now affirm that Spinoza presents a conception of experimentation that differs on certain points from Boyle's, but which is similarly inscribed within the field of interpretations that constitute classical science. We cannot explain their argument by reference to a simple refusal of experimentation on Spinoza's part, with Spinoza apparently opposed to Oldenburg's and Boyle's empiricism.[164] On what points, then, do they actually diverge? Fundamentally, they differ more in terms of ontological questions than epistemological problems. On the one hand, Spinoza refuses the void.[165] On the other hand, his conception of homogeneous matter prevents him from being able to admit that between sensible givens and the mathematical foundation of things (extended particles and movement) there can exist an intermediary degree of intelligibility that accounts for certain quantitative constants. In the Spinozist physics of 1661–3, no more so than in Cartesian physics, there is no place for a chemistry, that is, for a theory of the significant differences between natures that have a certain stability. All

---

degree the concept of 'expérience' covers that of observation as opposed to, or indeed at the same time as, experimentation.

[164] Then again, is Boyle purely and simply an empiricist? If we read his treatises closely, we would be tempted to say that he has two philosophies: one (which is conveyed by Oldenburg) that effectively places experiments at the basis of reasoning by always reserving the right to evaluate them (section 39 from the essay on nitre remarks that it is necessary to judge experiments according to their value and not according to their number); and the second, which seems to guide the choice of a number of experiments, and which is based less on a theory than on the will to combat a theory – in short, the Paracelsian heritage; corpuscular philosophy often seems to be mobilised to counter spagyrism on those points where it claims to be able to replace Aristotle.

[165] Cf. J.-P. Osier, *Spinoza et son cercle*, Paris: Vrin, 1983, p. 314.

of this obviously refers to a certain conception of space and to the Spinozist radicalisation of Cartesian physics.[166] It is very precisely this conception, and not Spinoza's supposed contempt for experience or experimentation, that prevents him from understanding the interest of Boyle's experimental construction. Now, is this conception of space a constant in Spinozism? We are not fully aware of what Spinoza thinks about this ten or fifteen years later. We only know – but this is already an indication – that at this point he explicitly refuses the Cartesian laws of movement, even if he has not yet given an ordered expression to what he himself thinks of extension. At the very least, these terms suggest that Spinoza abandoned all or part of these physical theses from 1661, but we cannot guess what he replaced them with. Above all, however, we can be sure that henceforth he will no longer link his philosophy to a determinate physics.[167]

Let us summarise the lessons we have drawn from the exchange of letters from the years 1661–3:

- In terms of the facts, Spinoza's conclusion concerning the two reactions is false, and incontestably so. Boyle's is too. Contemporary chemistry sees here a more complex reaction than a simple decomposition.
- In terms of method, Spinoza's attitude with regards to experimentation perfectly illustrates the theses from the *TdIE* and clarifies what remained elliptical in them. This attitude is neither a retrograde refusal, nor the source of Spinoza's incomprehension.
- In terms of the status of chemical compounds, despite his error Boyle is on the path of what will become classical chemistry. Spinoza, without excluding this solution *a priori*, refuses it in the name of a conception of space that is not essential to his system but which characterises the version that he gives of it in his writings from the 1660s. Yet, it is characteristic that, even when he refuses certain results by taking a broader perspective, Spinoza admits that he would accept them if an improved experiment in his eyes were able to prove it. We cannot read in his attitude an irreducible refusal tied to an *a priori* conviction.

---

[166] On this theoretical conjuncture, cf. P. Van der Hoeven, 'Over Spinoza's Interpretatie van de cartesiaanse fysica, en de betekenis daarvan voor het system der Ethica', *Tijdschrift voor Filosofie*, 35/1 (1973), pp. 27–86; and I. Filippi, *Materia e scienza in B. Spinoza*, Palermo: Libreria Dario Flaccovio, 1985, in particular pp. 37–64.

[167] We can do no better than to refer to the demonstration of this point by A. Matheron at the colloquium in Thessaloniki in 1987. The text is published in *Cahiers Spinoza*, VI (1991), pp. 83–109.

After the years 1661–3, Spinoza continues to perform experiments, as his correspondence proves. He does so himself (one can find the narrative of one of these experiments in a letter to Jelles in 1669)[168] and he takes an interest in those performed by others (the last of the letters to Oldenburg before the *TTP* asks for information on an experiment that challenges Cartesian laws of motion).[169] In the *Ethics*, however, the term *experimentum* does not appear, though the place for it is marked in the small physics from Book II. If this physics is established by way of Lemmas and Postulates, it is because it does not arise from a purely deductive order. It would be necessary to mobilise this physics if we really wished to determine what the laws of physics and biology were. What the Lemmas state are the abstract laws of individual natures: no experiment can contradict them; on the contrary, these natures will have to be inscribed in the framework set out by this physics. On the other hand, however, these natures will be necessary for giving a content to this framework itself. The Lemmas state the persistence of the individual form beyond the variations of its ways of being affected; but when it comes to the nature of these ways of being affected, as to the nature of their components (and above all of their equivalence in nature), these Lemmas tell us nothing. This is why Gilles Deleuze is right to note that: 'In the sphere of the composition of relations, it is not merely reason that intervenes, but all the resources of the programming of physico-chemical and biological experiments (for example, investigations concerning the unity of composition of animals among themselves).'[170] And Deleuze adds in a note: 'Indeed, unlike the simpler inner essences, which refer to the intuition of the third kind, the composable or decomposable relations refer to all types of processes (second kind). We have no *a priori* knowledge of relations of composition; they require experimentation.' After having compared Spinoza and Geoffroy Saint-Hilaire on this point, Deleuze continues: 'In Spinoza, experimentation plays a very particular role, not only in the *Ethics* but in the form of a presentiment that emerges at the end of the completed pages of the *Treatise*

---

[168] Ep. XLI, G IV, pp. 202–6 [*Ep.* XLI [to Jarig Jelles]; CWS, II, 40–2]. The Dutch original speaks of *ervarenheit* and *onderuinding* – which the OP translate by *experientia* and *experimentum*.

[169] Ep. XXXII, G IV, p. 174 [*Ep.* XXXII [to Henry Oldenburg]; CWS II, 20]. Note that the Latin original carefully distinguishes, at a few lines distance, *experimentum* (that is, experimentation in the form that the Royal Society undertook) and *experientia* (experience has shown me that spherical lenses are better polished by hand than by machine).

[170] *Spinoza: Practical Philosophy*, trans. Robert Hurley, San Francisco: City Lights Books, 1988, p. 116.

on the *Emendation of the Intellect*: a brief but intense call for experiments (§ 103).'[171] Contrary to what a reading like Saisset's would suggest, the goal of the Lemmas is not to be a substitute for experimentation, it is to neutralise the results of experiments. As we have seen, such a neutralisation is proper to *experientia*. It is therefore not surprising that a few lines further on Spinoza affirms the conformity between what he has just said and *experientia*.

We can now conclude our remarks on Spinoza's attitude towards experimentation in the sciences of nature. We could compare Spinoza's account of experiments to that of Bachelard. Both institute a strict rupture between common knowledge and scientific knowledge. Both conceive of experimentation as informed by mathematics and as offering up its lessons only to questions of a theoretical nature. But this comparison finds its limit in the disregard Bachelard shows for experience-as-observation: in science, Bachelard says, everything is constructed, nothing is given.[172] Rationalist materialism always supposes construction; brute facts must be transformed into cultural facts. In Spinoza, if the rupture between the first kind of knowledge and the others is in principle strongly affirmed, if mathematics is necessary for the majority of experiments, there are nevertheless certain observations that can be taken up after the fact in the framework of mathematical questions, as ready-made responses for questions formulated by reason. Finally, certain experiences *satis obvia* – those that I have called pre-theoretical – do not even need to be constructed: they make us feel, without demonstration, the general reduction of the laws of nature to movement. Thanks to them we see the work of common notions in the variety of perceptions.

To account for this difference, and to be convinced that it is not the simple vestige of a 'prescientific' mentality, it is necessary to note that the distinction between the given and the constructed is not one that is traced once and for all. It is constituted historically, and it is this progressive constitution that will liberate the field in which an autonomous practice of experimentation will develop. In Spinoza, as elsewhere in classical physics and philosophy, the question of the birth of experimental science cannot be

---

[171] Ibid., p. 117 n. 12. This is a presentiment because, according to Deleuze, experience is tied to the discovery of common notions and it is this discovery that leads to the abandonment of the *TdIE*. I share Deleuze's opinion on the essential points: the Spinozist theory of experimentation has not changed. On the other hand, the term 'pressentiment' seems to me more problematic, for the inexistence of common notions at the time of the *TdIE* is, in my view, far from certain.

[172] Cf. the trenchant formulations from the opening pages of the *Formation de l'esprit scientifique*.

reduced to the opposition between the given and the constructed, between observation and experimentation. Certainly, such an opposition allows us to account for a certain number of significant differences, but it is overly simplistic as regards the movement of history. In fact, the experience that serves as a basis for the birth of physics is divided into a number of different levels: common experience, or observation; the extension of the latter to new objects or through new instruments, even without constructing experiments: an example of this is the telescope in astronomy (we saw that Galileo's text conceives of the introduction of the telescope as a foundational event); new experiences that are not constructed but that arise as a result of the history of technology;[173] and finally constructed experiments. On the other hand, experience has a number of different functions: inciting, suggesting, verifying, deciding. It is the articulation between these different statuses and functions that allows us to distinguish the diverse ways in which the philosophy of the seventeenth century interprets the relation between reason and the senses and the interrogation of nature. Among these currents, Spinoza is certainly closer to Galileo and to Descartes than to Boyle and Oldenburg. But he occupies a real place in the historical constitution of the spectre of scientific experimentation.

The best way of thinking the unity of these meanings of the term *experimentum* in Spinoza and distinguishing it from *experientia* perhaps consists in defining these meanings in terms of time. If vague experience supposes the present of perception while *experientia* draws on what has been acquired in the past, for its part *experimentum* sketches out a future project. It always takes the form of a programme of construction; or, if it is a matter of a past experience, of a programme of re-reading. Thus, where experience assesses what is given, experimentation projects the form of an interrogation. Likewise, while what is given is given to all, only some – namely, those who adopt a mathematical perspective – can construct an interrogative schema for dividing up the given or for reconstructing it. These few people will accede to the rightful universality of the demonstrable. All of those who 'have experience' remain at the level of the factual universality of what is given. Finally, necessity and clarity mark the results of experimentation, once they are integrated into the certainty of theory. The lessons of experience, by contrast, are shrouded and opaque: everyone knows that such-and-such a

---

[173] G. Canguilhem has shown the link between experience and technology in the domain of the life sciences. Cf 'L'expérimentation en biologie animale', *La connaissance de la vie*, Paris: Vrin, 1971 (2nd edn.), pp. 17–39. It is well known that Koyré has a tendency to minimise this.

thing is the case, but no one knows themselves. *Experientia* is thus as distinct from *experimentum* as it is from vague experience.

There remains another difference to mark, or rather a lack to highlight. Spinoza declares on a number of occasions that he is dealing with passions, morals and societies as lines, planes and volumes. One would thus expect to see him speak of experimentation in psychology as well, not to mention politics and history. Yet this is in no way what he does: the domain of *experimenta* ends at the limits of physics and chemistry. Spinoza does speak of a sort of social experimentation, one that is, moreover, limited[174] – but he calls it *experientia*. How should we explain this difference?

With respect to knowledge of society, everything is there, everything is available. We cannot appeal to experimentation. No doubt we can extrapolate from the *Political Treatise* to Books III and IV of the *Ethics* and explain why there is nothing more to learn. Similarly, with respect to affective phenomena, everything is already given. In sum, the science of complex beings occurs in a domain in which everything already exists; the science of simple beings occurs in a domain where almost everything can and must be reconstructed. Physical phenomena can indeed become complex by way of accumulation, yet they remain simple in the sense that they are reducible to bodies moved by the laws of motion and rest underlying the complex forms these phenomena take. One can thus construct the relevant difference between these laws, and put this difference to the test via an experimental programme where the complexity of singular things will not overwhelm our calculations. On the other hand, there is no place for experimentation when the complexity is too great. The *experientia* thus concern what is immediately visible in complex things. This visibility in no way automatically constitutes a guarantee of truth. The root of experience is to be found in the disproportionate relation between the essential complexity of human phenomena and the simplicity of the perceptions that we have of them.

We cannot leave the question of the relation between Spinoza and science without dealing with a recent interpretation of Spinozism that grants a key role to this concept of experimentation, as well as to other concepts that are tied to it. This interpretation has been developed in the last few years by Wim Klever in a number of articles and conference presentations. We could summarise Klever's main thesis by saying that Spinoza is a physicist: it

---

[174] TP, Chapter I, 3: 'Et sane mihi plane persuadeo, experientiam omnia Civitatum genera, quae concipi possunt [. . .] ostendisse', G III, p. 274, ll. 10–14 [*TP* I, 3; *CWS* II, 504].

is only the science of nature that can guarantee the salvation of man.[175] The positive side of Klever's thesis is that Spinoza performed scientific experiments[176] and his thought in its entirety must be understood from this point of view; the content of his work essentially comes back to the affirmation of determinism.[177] The negative side of Klever's thesis is that we can no longer consider Spinoza a philosopher, to the degree that the science he is developing renders the ideological discourse of philosophy obsolete. This is why the legitimate inheritors of Spinoza are not the philosophers of today, who remain attached to outdated research programmes, but the scientists: physicists, psychologists or economists, all of whom pursue positive researches. It is from this point of view that Klever advances his critique of formalist epistemology[178] and with which he develops his own Spinozist economics.[179] These latter aspects of his work do not interest us here. I will limit myself to discussing the theme of Spinozism understood as a science of nature.

When Klever says that Spinoza is a physicist, he could mean a number of things:

— That Spinoza effectively engaged in physical experiments. This is true,

[175] Klever's commentary on the *TdIE* concludes as follows: 'In een gigantisch denkproces heeft hij laten zien, dat het menselijk heil enkel van een aangehouden en stug doorgezette natuurwetenschap te verwachten valt, en van niets anders', p. 208. [Translator's note: it is unclear which text of Klever's Moreau is referring to here. The text cited previously, however, is 'Remarques sur le *TIE* (Experientia vaga, paradoxa, ideae fictae)'].

[176] 'He discussed in his correspondence the hot items of mathematics and natural science and did experimental works on various fields. He studied a lot of books on anatomy, astronomy and mathematics [. . .] Still Spinoza *loved experiments* and tries to arrange them wherever possible [. . .] His work in optics was likewise built on experimental discoveries [. . .] In general, *experience has a place of paramount importance* in Spinoza's scientific practice and in his theory of science.' W. Klever, 'Anti-falsificationism: Spinoza's Theory of Experience and Experiments', in *Spinoza: Issues and Directions*, ed. E. Curley and P.-F. Moreau, Leiden: Brill, 1990, p. 124.

[177] '*The main assertion of the KV is the simple affirmation of a complete and fullfledged radical determinism.* Other assertions are complementary, subsidiary, preparatory or consequent. That Spinoza's later works do have this message as their central theme, is well known and doesn't need any demonstration.' W. Klever, 'Determinism, the "true belief" according to the *KV*', in *Dio, l'Uomo, la libertà. Studi sul Breve Trattato di Spinoza*, a cura di F. Mignini, L'Aquila-Rome: Japadre, 1990, pp. 193–4. Cf. the first two chapters of his book *Voorbeschikking. De wetenschappelijke filosofie*, Nijmegen: Markant, 1989.

[178] Klever draws on the articulation that he discerns between reason and experimentation in Spinoza to place Spinoza on the side of Bachelard and Cavaillès against Popper (cf. his intervention in the Chicago colloquium in *Spinoza: Issues and Directions*).

[179] *Zuivere economische wetenschap*, Amsterdam: Boom Meppel, 1990.

but it is a precise description of only a minor part of his activity. That said, Klever is right to underscore that it is not only a moment of transition in Spinoza's biography. André Lécrivain has also noted that from the beginning to the end of the correspondence we bear witness to Spinoza's interest in physics in the strict sense of the term.[180] After the experiments on nitre there followed experiments on optics, on gold,[181] and probably others still. This is an aspect of Spinoza's intellectual biography that should not be neglected and that accounts for a background condition of his system, even if his later texts do not explicitly set out to integrate this aspect with the others.

— That Spinoza is informed of the physics of his time and that he frequents physicists. This is also true, and indeed more true than has for a long time been thought. Klever's research, but also that of Keesing, Vermij and Wurtz on Borch's diary,[182] Huygen's letters,[183] Tschirnhaus' circle,[184] or the teachings of Burchard do Volder,[185] have been very useful in shedding light on Spinoza's contacts. Whereas Meinsma's work had emphasised in an overly unilateral fashion the Libertines and the religiously heterodox,[186] it is worthwhile recalling that Spinoza was also part of a vibrant milieu of physical, chemical and technical researchers.[187]

---

[180] 'Spinoza et la physique cartésienne (suite): la partie II des *Principia*', *Cahier Spinoza*, II, Répliques (1978), p. 206.

[181] Cf. the Helvetius affair (Ep. XL, 25 March 1667, G IV, pp. 196–201 [*Ep*. XL [to Jarig Jelles]; CWS II, 37–9]). In 1675 Spinoza is still discussing an analogous experiment (Ep. LXXII, G IV, p. 305, l. 30; p. 306, l. 1 [*Ep*. LXXII [to G. H. Schuller]; CWS I, 465–6]).

[182] *Studia Spinozana*, V, 1989, pp. 311–26.

[183] E. Keesing, 'De gebroeders Huygens en Spinoza', *Bulletin* 121 (1985), pp. 5–10; 'Le frères Huygens et Spinoza', *Cahiers Spinoza*, V (1985), pp. 109–28.

[184] E. W. von Tschirnhaus, *Médecine de l'esprit* . . ., introduction, traduction, notes et appendices par J.-P. Wurtz; R. H. Vermij, De Nederlanse Vriendenkring van E. W. von Tschirnhaus, *Tijdschrift voor de Geschiedenis der Geneeskunde, Natuurweteschappen, Wiskunde en Techniek*, XI/4 (1988), pp. 153–78.

[185] W. Klever, 'Burchard de Volder (1643–1709), a crypto-spinozist on a Leiden cathedra', *Lias*, XV/2 (1988), pp. 191–241.

[186] The same goes for the books by J. C. van Slee, *De Rijnsburger Collegianten*, Haarlem, 1895, reprinted with a preface by S. Zilverberg, Utrecht: HES, 1980; C. B. Hylkema, *Reformateurs*, Haarlem, 2 vol., 1900; Groningen/Amsterdam, 1978; Kolakowski, *Chrétiens sans Eglise*. It is true that we cannot reproach them for their unilateral character, since it is in some sense determined by their subject matter. Nevertheless, if we refer only to them, the studies of Spinoza's horizon will risk seeing their perspective rendered false.

[187] On the ensemble of these milieux, see the studies collected in *Cahiers Spinoza*, VI (1991).

— That he drew inspiration from physics. This is more contestable. It is more precise to say that for Spinoza physics and ethics are both inspired by mathematics, which provides them at once with a norm of truth and a model of exposition.[188] But the domain proper to each activity presents specificities that prevent one from considering this connection as a pure and simple continuity. Mathematics proceeds by composing beings of reason. Physics interrogates relatively simple objects, where the intervention of an artefact can reveal essential relations: this is what delimits the place of experimentation. Ethics (and its psychological and sociological foundations) reasons on complex objects, where the relevant difference is precisely not easily constructible, while the figures it treats are available in experience. At this level, experience and practice suffice, as we saw above. Furthermore, ethics as a domain of knowledge depends, in terms of its order, on principles that are treated in other domains: this is what Spinoza says in response to Blijenbergh.[189] But in this context it is not only physics that ethics presupposes, but also metaphysics.[190]

— That all of his philosophy (if we can still use this word) is an extension of physics. This thesis is indefensible. In fact, the *Ethics* in its final stages privileges Reason. Not only can reason understand everything, and any given person can stop (and legitimately so) on his path,[191] the *Ethics* is

---

[188] On the aptitude of geometry alone – and the inaptitude of physics – to provide a model of philosophy, see the pages that M. Gueroult devotes to the comparison between the three disciplines, *Spinoza*, vol. II, *L'Ame*, pp. 471–3.

[189] In letter XXIV, Blijenbergh asks Spinoza about error, freedom and the will, the structure of the soul, the relation between knowledge of God and virtue. He adds that, without getting a response to these questions, he cannot understand the foundations of the thought of his interlocutor. Spinoza responds: 'those things do not make for a solution of your first problem, but that, on the contrary, most of them depend on [the solution of] that problem. So it is far from being the case that you cannot understand my opinion regarding the necessity of things without the solution of these new questions, because the solution of the latter, and what pertains to them, cannot be perceived unless one first understands that necessity', *Ep.* XXVII [to Willem Von Blijenbergh]; CWS I, 395.

[190] 'Sed etiam magnam Ethices partem, quae, ut cuivis notum, Metaphysica et physica fundari debet' ('maar ook van een groot deel van de Ethica, die gelyk een ieder weet op de metaphisica en de phisica gegront moet werdern'), G IV, pp. 160–1 [*Ep.* XVIII [to Willem Von Blijenbergh]; CWS I, 395].

[191] This is why for each individual we can speak of a certain 'flourishing' [*épanouissement*] (a term Appuhn uses to translate *gaudere* and *gaudium*) as a function of their nature, *Ethics* III, 57, Schol., G II, p. 187, ll. 12–14 [CWS I, 528]. 'Quamvis itaque unumquodque individuum sua, qua constat, natura, contentum viveat eaque gaudeat [. . .].' This does not prevent these *gaudia* from being very different (cf. the remainder of the same Scholium).

written from the point of view of a completely unfolded Reason. This is why, moreover, Spinoza can still use the terms 'philosopher' and 'philosophy'[192] in a non-pejorative sense: it indicates the line of demarcation that passes between those who believe in the imagination and those who refer to the understanding.[193]

Taken as a whole, the *Ethics* is neither a physics, nor a psychology, nor a sociology, nor the sum of these three. Certainly, it is based on these three disciplines, which produce knowledge of the power of Nature and how the latter produces Reason. It is also true that, once constituted, Reason asks for nothing that is contrary to Nature. Finally, it is also true that both the madman and the person guided by Reason are equally necessary[194] (and thus equally justified) from the point of view of natural causality. But the *Ethics* is not limited to constructing a science of behaviour that discloses the conduct of the mad and of those governed by Reason; it is not even content to indicate why the second are to be privileged over the first.[195] It elects a certain point of view, and it is this choice that forms the basis of its philosophical position. Spinoza explicitly says that his project is to lead us as if by the hand to the knowledge of Beatitude,[196] and he determines the themes that he will deal with in the *Ethics* as a function of this choice.[197] He

---

[192] In fact, in the *Ethics*, Spinoza still uses *philosophus* and the verb *philosophari* (in the expression *ordo philosophandi*, which is used positively, since he reproaches others with not observing this order). The word *philosophia* does not appear (no more so than does *ethica*, outside of the title), but it is still used right up until the last letter. Cf. on this point my presentation at the colloquium of Urbino on Hobbes and Spinoza, in D. Bostrenghi, *Hobbes e Spinoza: scienza e politica: atti del Convegno internazionale: Urbino, October 14–17*, Naples: Bibliopolis, 1992.

[193] 'Denique ex praecedenti propositione sequitur, non parum etiam interesse inter gaudium, quo ebrius ex. gr. ducitur, et inter gaudium, quo potitur philosophus, quod hic in transitu monere volui', *Ethics* III, 57, Schol., G II, p. 187, ll. 18–21 [*CWS* I, 528].

[194] Cf. *TTP*, Chapter XVI, G III, p. 189, l. 30 [*TTP* XVI, 4; *CWS* II, 283]; p. 190, l. 10 [*TTP* XVI, 6; *CWS* II, 283].

[195] 'Ex quibus apparet, quantum Sapiens polleat, potiorque sit ignaro, qui sola libidine agitur', *Ethics* V, 42, Schol., G II, p. 308, ll. 15–17 [*CWS* I, 616].

[196] 'Sed ea solummodo quae nos ad mentis humanae ejusque summae beatitudinis cognitionem, quasi manu, ducere possunt', *Ethics* II, Praef., G II, p. 84, ll. 10–12 [*CWS* I, 446].

[197] Explaining in a Scholium from Book III that he cannot lay out in detail the multitude of affects, which are as numerous as their objects, he then adds that even if it were possible, it would not be necessary ('nec, si possem, necesse est'). For a general definition of the affects suffices to pursue his agenda, namely to 'determine the power of the affects and the power of the Soul over the affects' ('Nam, at id, quod intendimus,

thus chooses to provide answers to certain questions and to help the reader advance along a certain path,[198] as arduous as it is. That these questions and this path, like physics, suppose neither freedom nor will nor finality, does not suffice to make them a simple extension of physics. I will return to this. Let us be content for the time being with remarking that we have found such notions for the first time at the beginning of the *TdIE*, in a text where it was a question of experience and not of experimentation.[199] It is not for nothing that Spinoza chooses to give his great work the title, not of *Philosophy*, but of *Ethics*.[200]

Thus, the interpretation of Spinozism as a whole as a science of nature seems to me to have the definite advantage of bringing to light a culture, references and a partial model that are decisive for understanding Spinozism. Yet, because it generalises this model, because it understands experience almost exclusively from the perspective of experimentation, this interpretation misses one of the foundational dimensions of Spinozism: its character as a philosophical system and its grounding in human experience.

C. *Experience is Not Mystical Experience*

We must now deal with a final equivocation that, while not central to the subject we are treating, is nevertheless present in the work of some commentators and which adds a certain dose of confusion to the vocabulary. Does

nempe ad affectuum vires, et Mentis in eosdem potentiam, determinandum, nobis sufficit, uniuscujusque affectus generalem habere definitionem'). And he clarifies that, whatever the differences are, for instance, between the various forms of love, hatred or desire, 'nobis tamen has differentias cognoscere, et affectuum naturam et originem ulterius indagare, non est opus', *Ethics* III, 56, Schol., G II, p. 185, l. 33 [CWS I, 527]; p. 186, l. 10 [CWS I, 527]. Similarly, a little further on, he clearly indicates that his choice is guided by utility; the goal of ethics is not to know everything that exists, it is to make known what leads us to our goal: 'ad meum institutum praecipuos [sc.: *affectus*] tantum enumeravisse sufficit: nam reliqui, quos omisi, plus curiositatis quam utilitatis haberent', *Ethics* III, 59, Schol., G II, p. 189, ll. 13–15 [CWS I, 530].

[198] *Ethics* V, 42, Schol., G II, p. 308, ll. 23–8 [CWS I, 617].
[199] The limitation in terms of *utilitas* indicated in the Scholium to Proposition 59 from Book III is itself clearly an echo of paragraph 16 from the *TdIE*: 'Unde quisque jam poterit videre, me omnes scientias ad unum finem et scopum velle dirigere, scilicet, ut ad summam humanam, quam diximus, perfectionem perveniatur; et sic omne illud, quod in scientiis nihil ad finem nostrum nos promovet, tanquam inutile erit rejiciendum', G II, p. 9, ll. 12–17 [*TdIE* 16; CWS I, 11].
[200] For an interpretation of this choice, cf. W. Bartuschat, 'Metaphysik als Ethik. Zu einem Buchtitel Spinozas', *Zeitschrift für philosophische Forschung*, 28/1 (1974), pp. 132–45.

there exist in Spinoza's work a mystical form of experience? This question is all the more legitimate since mysticism is one of the domains in which the idea of 'experiential knowledge' has traditionally been developed. The existence since German Romanticism of an entire tradition that interprets Spinoza in mystical terms makes this question all the more impossible to avoid,[201] even though in France it has become a minority position.[202] I do not intend to deal here with the question of whether Spinoza's doctrine contains elements of mysticism. In effect, the answer depends to a large degree on one's definition of this term. Some refuse to see Spinoza as a mystic because they define this term in a way that excludes Reason.[203] To the extent, however, that others call 'mysticism' any intellectual or spiritual affirmation that is formulated with a certain intensity, they come to call mysticism exactly what others call rationalism.[204] There are insufficient differences between the two interpretations to justify a true confrontation between them. But we can formulate the question of Spinoza's mysticism in a way that lends itself more easily to discussion. Just as the question is vague and remains susceptible to diverse interpretations so long as we remain at the level of the word 'mysticism', so too does it become precise and deter-

---

[201] It develops during the *Pantheismusstreit* on the basis of certain remarks by Jacobi. We also find it in Novalis. On this period, see Herman Timm, *Gott und die Freiheit. Studien zur Religionsphilosophie der Goethezeit*, Frankfurt: Vittorio Klosterman, 1974. This type of interpretation enjoyed a second life in Germany at the beginning of the twentieth century in Anna Tumarkin, Georg Mehlis, and even Gebhardt's work, in the form of a 'mysticism of Reason' or of a polarisation between mysticism and rationalism. Fritz Mauthner concluded with 'eine gottfremde, gottlose Mystik' (*Spinoza. En Umriß seines Lebens und Wirkens*, Dresden: Reissner, 1922, p. 156) after correcting Novalis's formula ('Zu den gotttrunkenen Mystikern gehörte Spinoza night; er war nur alltrunken'). See the critique of this current in Heinz Pflaum, *Wissenschaft und Geistesgeschichte*, IV, 1926, pp. 127–43, reprinted in *Texte zur Geschichte des Spinozismus* (hrsg. V. N. Altwicker), Darmstadt: Wissenschaftliche Buchgesellschaft, 1971, pp. 216–31.

[202] It appears in a marginal form in Cousin's work, where it serves to distinguish Spinozist pantheism from materialist pantheism. Its existence is suggested, yet without being demonstrated, through analogies – Spinoza the Indian Wise Man, Spinoza the Persian Mouni – that will all come to be rejected both by Cousin's rivals such as Foucher de Careil and disciples like Saisset. Later on, we find a very different version of this thesis in Daumal.

[203] M. Gueroult, *Spinoza*, vol. II, *L'Ame*, p. 464: on the opposition between Spinoza's intuitive science and the 'ineffable fusion with the Infinite' of affective mysticism.

[204] Elsewhere, Gueroult himself uses the expression 'mystique sans mystère' to refer to absolute rationalism, where 'le désir mystique s'assouvit dans sa plénitude par le simple épanouissement de la raison', *Spinoza*, vol. I, *Dieu*, Paris: Aubier, 1968, p. 9.

minate when we speak of 'mystical experience'. For instance, in a work that compares Ruysbroeck and Spinoza, H. G. Hubbeling affirms that there exist in both thinkers elements that can be described as mystical, but that the line of demarcation between their respective doctrines concerns the presence in one and the absence in the other of mystical experiences in the proper sense of the term.[205] Hubbeling's demonstration nevertheless remains elliptical: he limits himself to correctly noting the absence in Spinoza of images tied to the highest state of knowledge. Yet this is precisely the question that must be posed: an interpretation of Spinozism in terms of mysticism has only a relative interest – that is, can only be an object of discussion – if it supposes the existence of just such an experience and claims to discover it in the exposition of the system. I will therefore take mystical experience to mean experience of contact with the Absolute,[206] and I will ask if the *Ethics* refers to such a situation. This is the point of view adopted by the majority of the great works on the history of mysticism in the classical age.[207]

I will limit the discussion to Jon Wetlesen's theses. Wetlesen's reading of Spinoza represents the most coherent and well-argued expression that can be given of such an interpretation. While little-known in France,[208] Wetlesen's work has been central to the renewed interest in traditional questions that were once asked of Spinozism, and for this reason it merits a particular discussion.[209] I will approach it here from a limited perspective: the question of experience. While comparisons between Spinoza and oriental wisdom typically occur without any demonstrations,[210] the comparisons made by Wetlesen are based on an extremely rigorous discussion of Spinoza's doctrine. One of the strengths of his analysis consists in distinguishing between

---

[205] *Logica en Ervaring in Spinoza's en Ruusbroecs mystiek*, MVHS 31, Leiden: Brill, 1973.
[206] 'Ephapsathai', as Plotinus says, *Enneads*, V, 3.
[207] Cf. H. Delacroix, *Etudes d'histoire et de psychologie du mysticisme*, Paris: Alcan, 1908, in particular p. 345 (the imbrication of experience and system amongst the great Christian mystics); J. Baruzi, *Saint Jean de la Croix et le problème de l'expérience mystique*, Paris: Alcan, 1924, p. 225 ff. (the relation between experience and meditation on Scripture). See also the discussion by L. Kolakowski at the beginning of *Chrétiens sans Eglise*, p. 37 ff.
[208] See, all the same, the summary given by A. Matheron, *Bulletin de l'Association des Amis de Spinoza*, 2 (1979), pp. 15–16.
[209] J. Wetlesen, *The Sage and The Way: Spinoza's Ethics of Freedom*, Assen: Van Gorcum, 1979. See also the discussion between Wetlesen and Arne Naess in *Spinoza's Philosophy of Man*, Proceedings of the Scandinavian Spinoza Symposium 1977, ed. Jon Wetlesen, Oslo: Universitetsforlaget, 1978, pp. 136–58 and 204–10.
[210] There is one exception: Michel Hulin, 'Spinoza l'Oriental', *Cahiers Spinoza*, IV (1983), pp. 139–70.

two 'strategies of liberation' in the *Ethics*: the first is gradual, as it passes by way of the knowledge and mastery of the affects, and resembles the traditional philosophical education of human beings by Reason; and the second is instantaneous, for here intuitive knowledge intervenes. This second 'strategy' brings Spinoza closer to – among others – the illumination that certain Buddhist schools conceptualise. It is in this context that Wetlesen affirms the presence in Spinoza's doctrine of a number of experiences that are irreducible to habitual experience. Wetlesen does not use the adjective 'mystical' to describe them, even though he does use this term elsewhere. As we will see, however, these experiences correspond to what is normally understood by the term 'mystical'. For Wetlesen, the third kind of knowledge is accompanied by the experience of a concrete or 'lived' duration, to use a term borrowed from Bergson. In the third kind of knowledge, we know the singular essence of the body and the mind. Now, this singular essence is the body and mind's actual essence, that is, their effort to persevere in their being.[211] The awareness of this 'concrete duration' is part of the instantaneous strategy of liberation, and, as such, constitutes 'a gateway to eternity'.[212] We thus feel that we are eternal at precisely the moment where we abandon the gradual strategy, which is situated in time, and suddenly become aware of the concrete duration in which we participate in the very life of God.

As we can see, we are at some distance here from Saisset. Not only is the Scholium from Proposition 23 from Book V not repressed, on the contrary it dominates a large part of the interpretation.[213] We can only be grateful to Wetlesen for taking into account a text that for so long has been rejected. Similarly, the second part of Book V, which is usually neglected, receives in Wetlesen's work a favourable treatment. It appears as the site of the instantaneous strategy. Wetlesen's interpretation is seductive both because it restores a meaning to key texts and because it uses these texts to construct this interpretation instead of using any external affirmations. Nevertheless, three criticisms can be made of Wetlesen's reading:

— It makes experience appear as a privileged instant, reserved only to some people, or to some people at certain moments. Wetlesen clearly states

---

[211] 'What is more, and here we come to a crucial point, when this conation is experienced and felt from the viewpoint of eternity, it is adequately conceived as a concrete duration. It is felt and experienced as a living duration (durée vécue), to use the expression of Henri Bergson, and in so far as it is conceived adequately through the power of God as its immanent and adequate cause, it is understood to be participating in the very life of God', J. Wetlesen, *The Sage and the Way*, p. 313.
[212] Ibid.
[213] Moreover, Wetlesen makes it the exergue to his book.

that experience is linked to the flourishing of the third kind of knowledge. It appears when we succeed in adopting the point of view of eternity. Then, through the 'eyes of the soul', we know that the eternal essence of our soul is constituted by adequate knowledge. We know it not only in a general and discursive fashion, but also in a singular and intuitive way, thanks to the third kind of knowledge. Thus, the knower and the known are one and the same thing, and they feel and experience that they are eternal.[214]

In my view, this reading is impossible, and for two complementary reasons. On the one hand, Spinoza never speaks of experience as something that would be reserved for certain individuals, or that would be attained through effort. Experience is what everyone knows, and it cannot be said that everyone succeeds in developing the third kind of knowledge. When Spinoza says 'we', he never means 'we the wise'. Rather, he means 'all people'. We thus cannot interpret *sentimus experimurque* in the Scholium as applying exclusively to those who have arrived at a certain stage of the journey of salvation. Moreover, a later Scholium explicitly says that all are conscious of their eternity, but that the majority interpret this experience poorly.[215] Furthermore, Spinoza always speaks of conceiving from the point of view of eternity, never of experiencing from this perspective. It is therefore impossible to draw an equivalence between 'experiencing that we are eternal' and 'conceiving from the point of view of eternity'.

— Wetlesen represents this experience as a sort of irruption of eternity into time. Such an irruption implies a break between the first and the second parts of Book V.[216] Furthermore, he interprets this irruption in terms of instantaneity.[217] Such an irruption is necessary because of the incommensurability between eternity and time.

Paradoxically, this interpretation means conceiving of eternity as another present, one that would be separate to the movement of duration. Wetlesen warns his reader against such a 'temporalising' conception of this irruption. Yet, in fact, his only way of extracting this irruption from time consists in distinguishing it from the idea of continuity. Wetlesen thus presents it

---

[214] 'The cognizer and the cognition are here one, and he feels and experiences that he is eternal (CP 5, p. 23, sch., p. 36, sch)'; and Wetlesen continues: 'Both Spinoza and the Mahayan Buddhists agree that when a person sees himself from the viewpoint of eternity in this manner, he sees that in his essential being he is uncreated, immutable and imperishable', *The Sage and the Way*, p. 308.

[215] *Ethics* V, 34, Schol. [CWS I, 612].

[216] 'There is no common measure between time and eternity, and therefore it is futile to set out to approach eternity through a process of time', *The Sage and the Way*, p. 305.

[217] Cf. the final paragraph, ibid., p. 309.

as an instant without a past. This is not necessarily false: Spinoza himself remarks that it is difficult to speak of eternity without having recourse to the language of time. But this means making experience, at least in this case, a dimension that is thinkable only in terms of the present.

If we consider the mode of reasoning Spinoza uses in the Scholium to Proposition 23, it appears on the contrary that his entire effort consists in comparing this experience to that of the past – and to showing that it is, of course, not identical to it. Yet he does refer to the past, albeit in negative terms, on three occasions: existence that precedes the body, the questions of traces, and memory.[218] On each occasion Spinoza states that this is not what is at stake, but the whole movement of the Scholium seems to prove that the past is at the very least the only dimension he can refer to so as to make this distinction. We could summarise the situation by saying that the experience of eternity is given as the impossible equivalence with a past, and not as the substitute of a present. It is not the instant of illumination; it is constituted by a feeling which, in temporal terms, would correlate with memory.

— We cannot imagine God. And yet, in one way or another, experience is always founded on the imagination. The experience mentioned here comes down to imagining God, either directly or indirectly. It is effectively reducible to making something of God – specifically, our union with him – appear as present, if not in a vision, then at least in a conscious experience that is tied to our body. If we feel ourselves participating in the very life of God, then it is because this life can be known through images and we can reach God in the midst of duration. Now, Spinoza explains that while we imagine our relation with the *rectores naturae*, we can only *think* our relation with God. It is impossible to discover an experience that goes further than Reason, as the classic analyses of Heinz Pflaum demonstrated a long time ago.[219]

We can now see in what sense experience in the Spinozist sense is distinct from any mystical experience: it does not manifest the absolute; it is not the prerogative of a superior stage of knowledge; and it is not a shortcut to knowledge. Certainly, experience can involve a journey, as we have seen in the *TdIE*, while the *Ethics*, too, speaks of a path. But this journey leads to

---

[218] 'Nec tamen fieri potest, ut recordemur nos ante corpus exstitisse, quandoquidem nec in corpore ulla ejus vestigia dari possunt, nec aeternitas tempore definiri [...] Quamvis itaque non recordemur, nos ante Corpus exstitisse, sentimus tamen [...]', G II, p. 295, l. 31; p. 196, l. 8 [*Ethics* V, 23, Schol., CWS I, 607].

[219] H. Pflaum, *Texte zur Geschichte des Spinozismus*, pp. 224–31.

something other than an experience, even if it begins with experience and occasionally draws on it. It leads to knowledge. Wanting to see it lead to an experience means wanting to place the image at the end of the idea. Yet this is impossible without a regression to the level of the imagination. The transfigurations of the true good do not lead to the figuration of God. There is no Mount Tabor of substance.

3. What Experience Is

We have now reviewed a few common meanings of the word experience, both from everyday language and from the works of commentators. What we have gained from this is the ability to dissipate a certain number of confusions, and also, through differentiation, to better grasp what constitutes common experience, or what Spinoza calls experience *tout court*. We can now respond one by one to Saisset's arguments and to those of other critics. Save for one exception, these arguments have not resisted analysis. It is true that Spinoza makes a clear distinction between vague experience and Reason, but this rupture does not apply to *experientia* insofar as it is distinct from vague experience. It is not true that Spinoza is dismissive of scientific experimentation, though it is true that the latter has no place in the *Ethics*. But again, *experientia* is not scientific experimentation. Finally, *experientia* is characteristic of all people, who interpret it in terms of the past. It is thus distinct from the exceptional and particular event called mystical experience. The reader will have noticed that in the course of our argument we have seen the positive traits of *experientia* emerge on the basis of these successive demarcations. We must now consider *experientia* itself in positive terms, such as it appears in the *Ethics* and the *Treatises*. The simplest way of doing so is to begin with the letter to Simon De Vries, since it constitutes the only remaining piece from the standard theory. I will refer to it alongside other texts in which this theory appears in a practical state.

Allow me first of all to offer a translation of letter X:

You ask me whether we need experience to know whether the Definition of any Attribute [NS: any thing] is true. To this I reply that we need experience only for those things which cannot be inferred from the definition of the thing, as, for example, the existence of Modes (for this cannot be inferred from the definition of the thing); but not for those things whose existence is not distinguished from their essence, and	Tu me demandes si nous avons besoin de l'expérience pour savoir si la définition d'un attribut est vraie? A cela je réponds que nous n'avons jamais besoin de l'expérience sinon pour ce qui ne peut se conclure de la définition d'une chose, par exemple l'existence des modes: cette existence en effet ne peut se conclure de la définition d'une chose. Mais nous n'en avons pas besoin pour ce dont l'existence ne se

therefore is inferred from their definition. Indeed no experience will ever be able to teach us this, for experience does not teach any essences of things. The most it can do is to determine our mind to think only of certain essences of things. So since the existence of the attributes does not differ from their essence, we will not be able to grasp it by experience.[220]

distingue pas de l'essence, et par suite, se conclut de leur définition. Bien plus: cela, aucune expérience ne pourra jamais nous l'enseigner. En effet l'expérience ne nous enseigne jamais l'essence des choses; mais le plus qu'elle puisse faire est de déterminer notre esprit à penser à certaines essence des choses seulement. C'est pourquoi, pusique l'existence des attributs ne diffère pas de leur essence, aucune expérience ne pourra nous la faire saisir.

We can now comment on it.

What immediately strikes one in reading this letter is its negative tone. It is the only text in which Spinoza seems to take sides against experience. He insists on its weakness and its impotence, and advances arguments that at first glance seem repetitive. If, as Saisset does, and as a whole tradition after him has done, we read this letter as Spinoza's declaration on the nature of experience, then it seems insuperably difficult to reconcile its tone with the confidence shown in experience in other passages.[221] We must either eliminate these other passages on the grounds of their insignificance (this is what Saisset does), or content ourselves with noting the incompatibility between the texts. However, if we study these phrases closely, we realise that the letter's content is less negative than its tone. This tone can very easily be explained: it concerns the status of the letter. The letter is responding to a question from De Vries, but De Vries has not asked what experience is. What he has most probably asked Spinoza is whether experience is useful for knowing if the definition of an attribute is true.[222] In other words, De Vries has asked Spinoza not about the *nature* of experience but about its *function*. More precisely, he has asked about a function that experience cannot perform. Spinoza's response is thus inevitably negative; and as the smallest uncertainty on this point would put in question the comprehension of his doctrine, one should not be surprised that Spinoza insists on experience's negative character. Yet we would be wrong to confuse this characteristic of experience's function with the nature of experience itself, which Spinoza does not speak of here. We would also be wrong if we failed to see that the content of his response is more nuanced than the tone, and that it sketches a theory of the diversity of experience's functions. Indeed, even if Spinoza insists with some vehemence on what experience cannot do, his concessions

---

[220] Ep. X, G IV, p. 47, ll. 6–17 [*Ep.* X [to Simon De Vries]; *CWS* I, 196].
[221] Those that we have cited at the end of the first section of this chapter.
[222] This is what is indicated by the first sentence from the translated passage.

and comparative clauses lead him to also say what experience can do. It is up to us to paint a picture of experience's functions and to seek examples that illustrate it.

Spinoza's response to De Vries is wholly structured by three verbs: 'to need'/'to not need'; ['to teach']/'to not teach'; and 'to determine to think'. These verbs will allow us to draw out three functions of experience:

— Spinoza affirms that we do not need experience to know if the definition of an attribute is true. If Spinoza had limited himself to making just this affirmation, then we could not know if experience is necessary for other things, or if it is never necessary. But Spinoza is not content to simply affirm: he gives an explanation and this explanation traces a line of demarcation. The attributes are indifferent to experience because their existence is not distinct from their essence (which one arrives at from their definition), and experience is not necessary for knowing what follows from the definition of a thing. On the other hand, experience is necessary for what does not follow from this definition. We can deduce from this that there exist fields in which experience is constitutive: for all things whose existence is distinct from their essence – that is, for all of the modes – experience will be necessary to us.

— After affirming that we do not need experience to judge the definition of an attribute, Spinoza doubles down: we can also never learn anything from experience. How should we understand this insistence? If it is not a pure repetition, it means that, in all of those domains where experience is not constitutive, we can distinguish between two subsets of experience: those where experience can still teach us something, and those where it cannot. The second domain includes at the very least the definition of the attributes, and, more generally, of the essence of things. The first, if it is not an entirely empty subset, can thus include what is not the essence of a thing but follows from its definition – that is, certain properties. In other words, to know these properties, we do not need experience in the strict sense – that is, it is not necessary, since the thing's properties follow from its definition – but we can also learn of these properties from experience. Without being constitutive, experience is confirmative.

— Let us restrict ourselves finally to the domain in which experience is neither constitutive nor confirmative. Here, it plays no role – this, at least, is what we would expect to read. However, after offering this series of negative formulations, even here Spinoza still grants experience a function, albeit what is certainly a minor one: it can 'determine our mind to think only of certain essences of things'. In short, experience does not play an internal role in thought, but it does have an indicative function.

It remains to take up these functions one by one. By analysing them alongside the content of the texts that illustrate them, we can identify the levels of experience and the modalities according to which these levels function.

A. The Three Functions of Experience

— Experience is *confirmative* or *substitutive* in those domains where its teachings can produce results that are equivalent to those of Reason. Thus, we can rationally deduce the effects of the passions, but the Scholia from Books III and IV of the *Ethics* appeal for the most part to our experience to confirm what has been deduced. Almost all of the effects of the passions are things that we already know, even if we do not know their causes. Similarly, Chapter V from the *TTP* also remarks that 'If someone wants to persuade or dissuade men of something not known through itself, to get them to embrace it he must deduce it from things which have been granted, and convince them either by experience or by reason.'[223] We can demonstrate the necessity of justice and charity, but experience, too, can teach us this – and in a way that is simpler for the multitude. Biblical narratives also serve to transmit an experience: without passing by way of causal deduction, they establish the teachings of Scripture, which are of a speculative order. 'Scripture proves these teachings solely by experience, i.e., by the narratives it relates. It does not give any definitions of these things, but accommodates all its words and arguments to ordinary people's power of understanding.' Whence the difference between making known and teaching: 'And although experience cannot give any clear knowledge of these things, or teach what God is, and how he sustains and directs all things, still it can teach and enlighten men enough to imprint obedience and devotion on their hearts.'[224] In all of these domains, there are two ways to be taught. We see the weaknesses of instruction by experience: since it does not allow us to know causes, it fails

---

[223] 'Si quis hominibus aliquid suadere, vel dissuadere vult, quod per se notum non est, is, ut id iidem amplectantur, rem suam ex concessis deducere, eosque experientia vel ratione convincere debet', G III, p. 76, ll. 30-2, A, p. 109-10 [*TTP* V, 35; CWS II, 147].

[224] 'Atque haec scriptura sola experientia comprobat, nempe iis, quas narrat, historiis, nec ullas harum rerum definitiones tradit, sed omnia verba et rationes captui plebis accomodat. Et quamvis experientia nullam harum rerum claram cognitionem dare possit, nec docere, quid Deus sit, et qua ratione res omnes sustentet & dirigat, hominumque curam habeat, potest tamen homines tantum docere et illuminare, quantum ad obedientiam & devotionem eorum animis imprimendum sufficit', G III, p. 77, l. 29; p. 78, l. 1, A, p. 110 [*TTP* V, 39; CWS II, 148-9].

to indicate when these causes cease to operate. In other words, experience does not disclose the limits of the application of the results about which it otherwise teaches us. But we also perceive its advantages: all can profit from experience, not only a few; and even for the person who learns by Reason, experience is useful for life prior to their arriving at the end of the process of scientific knowledge.

— If we can clearly see in what sense experience is confirmative, it is perhaps less easy to grasp the importance of its *constitutive* function. The latter comes into play when certain facts cannot be shown to follow from the definition of a thing. Certainly, with respect to the existence of a mode, insofar as its existence does not follow from its definition, we need experience to be able to affirm whether or not it does in fact exist. But this might seem a quite modest achievement: experience seems to be of use only to signal the existence of an individual — an individual which, once it exists, will have its existence determined by laws that are deduced from its definition or from Nature.[225] In fact, things are more complicated. On the one hand, the existence of an individual is regulated not only by laws that can be deduced from its essence, but also by those that can be deduced from the essence of the other individuals it encounters and confronts — individuals that it determines and that determine it in turn. Now, the concrete proportion according to which such-and-such a law is acting rather than some other law is largely determined by the relations of force between individuals, and above all by the very fact of their existence.[226] On the other hand, what is true of the individual is true of entire fields of reality. Certainly, the general laws of nature apply, but in a form that depends on the configuration of each field. The conjunction of a certain number of individual facts can modify this configuration and henceforth experience is necessary to know what concrete forms these general laws will take. What are the fields in question? Let us reread letters 82 and 83 from and to Tschirnhaus. The latter asks how

---

[225] And this really is the case for *corpora simplicissima* or for objects subject only to simple physical laws. This is why experience, as it is defined here, is neither useful nor possible — except when one limits oneself to stating the brute fact of these objects' existence. The rest is directly knowable by laws, and thus deducible.

[226] An example: the laws of human nature necessarily produce a certain number of passions; we can know this before even knowing if such-and-such a singular individual exists concretely. Certain of these passions are activated by theocracy, others by democracy. Also, when such-and-such a singular individual comes into the world, the (empirical) fact that the country where they are born and whose constitution will influence them, whether theocracy or democracy, is something that we must know so that we can know the affective laws that will be at work in the individual's life.

'the variety of things can be shown a priori from the concept of Extension' and Spinoza responds that it is impossible to deduce the diversity of things by beginning with the sole idea of extension.[227] Spinoza even affirms that he has demonstrated this: he does not simply state this impossibility, but establishes it in his system itself.[228] It is clear that Tschirnhaus is thinking of physics, but Spinoza's response can be applied to other domains too, and above all to more complex ones. We can think, first, of history – though not insofar as it is the site of biblical lessons, but rather as the site of the evolution of human affairs; we can think of language, the site of communication between human beings; and we can think of the passions, which is the site of their imaginative relations. In all of these fields, nothing will happen to human beings that will make them an *imperium in imperio* – the same laws of Nature will apply in each case. Yet, for a finite understanding that cannot reconstitute the lines of causality that are operative in these cases, a certain number of structures and relations cannot be known except by experience. Others will be known by deduction and confirmed by experience. These fields will thus be the privileged site where the confirmative and constitutive functions of experience will be manifest.

— What about experience's *indicative* function? Experience cannot teach us anything in mathematics or in metaphysics – that is, in those fields where the essence of things is identical with their existence. But it can determine the mind to apply these essences. It thus plays a role in the orientation of the *cogitare*. Is this not what we saw in the *proemium* to the *TdIE*? We can now better account for what we named there a logic of anticipation. Experience itself could not resolve the problem of the relation to an eternal thing, but the journey in its entirety showed how experience could orient the mind towards searching for it.[229]

---

[227] G IV, pp. 333–5 [*Eps.* LXXXII, LXXXIII, LXXXIV [from and to Walther Von Tschirnhaus]; CWS II, 484–5].

[228] This is why Hubbeling does not go far enough when he says that Spinoza 'acknowledges' that this derivation is impossible (*Spinoza's Methodology*, Assen: Van Gorcum, 1964, p. 23). Formulated in this way, the thesis seems like a concession (a concession that moreover refers to an anticipated derivation by the deductive method). Spinoza does not 'acknowledge' this point, he positively demonstrates the irreducibility of the *varietas* to the sole concept of extension.

[229] On the ensemble of these functions of experience, the author who seems to me to have best perceived the problem, without for all that being able to develop it (recall that his is an unfinished work) is Piero Martinetti, *Spinoza*, Naples: Bibliopolis, 1987, pp. 158–61.

B. The Levels of Experience

I noted above that experience is present most often in the form of an assessment of the past. Spinoza does not innovate as far as such a determination is concerned. It is also in this way that experience is understood in common language. Hobbes understands it in this way as well. Moreover, Hobbes defines experience in such a way as to include within its domain a non-mathematical form of experimentation.[230] Hobbes was inscribing himself in the Aristotelian tradition that articulates experience and memory.[231] But neither Aristotle nor Hobbes drew the same consequences from this definition of experience as Spinoza does. This tradition insists on the multiplicity of things that the memory takes up and synthesises in the form of a unity of a larger number of sensations.[232] Spinoza's perspective is, once again, quite different: he considers less the fact of the multiplicity of things and more the equivalence between them.

What are the different levels at which this assessment of the past is carried out? We find here certain of the components of experience that we discovered in the *TdIE*. All the same, the list of these components and their respective importance has been somewhat modified:

— Personal experience and the experience of others: as in the *TdIE*, we once again find these two levels. But here the importance of the *I* has been considerably diminished. Instead, the impersonality of the narrative of experience has come to the fore. The individual nevertheless remains, and they are still stripped of their particularities. The *I* appears more as a subtractive effect. Everyone knows that things are thus, but each person excepts

---

[230] 'Memoria multarum rerum experientia dicitur', *Leviathan*, Chapter II, OL, vol. 3, p. 9: 'Experience: The remembrance of a succession of one thing to another, that is, of what was antecedent, and what consequent, and what concomitant, is called an experiment; whether the same be made by us voluntarily, as when a man putteth any thing into the fire, to see what effect the fire will produce upon it; or not made by us, as when we remember a fair morning after a red evening. To have had many experiments, is that we call experience, which is nothing else but remembrance of what antecedents have been followed by what consequents', *Human Nature*, Chapter IV, § 6, *EW*, vol. 4, p. 16.

[231] 'Now, experience accrues to men from memory; for repeated acts of memory about the same thing constitute the force of a single experience . . .', Aristotle, *Metaphysics*, A, 1, 980b; 'experientia fit ex multis memoriis', Saint Thomas, *Summa Theologica*, Ia, qu. 54, art. 5.

[232] Cf. Aristotle, ibid., and the *Posterior Analytics*, II, 19, 100a 3. It is this process that allows experience to be at the origin of *technè* and science. This is an impossible derivation in Spinoza.

themselves from this state of affairs. I remarked above on this opacity of experiential reflection when analysing the first pages of the *Treatise on the Emendation of the Intellect*. It is now explicit. It seems to bring together two of the traits from the first pages of the *TdIE*: familiarity and a transformed sense of singularity. On the other hand, the tension that had constituted the third trait is no longer effective: experience presents its lessons in a state of serenity. There is only one exception, which we will find at the end of this work.

— We can also note that on a number of occasions, when Spinoza summarises what experience teaches, he does so using a well-known maxim: for example, that man is a God for man,[233] or 'So many heads, so many attitudes'.[234] After the Latin formula there follows the Dutch proverb: there is no heretic without a text.[235] Everything happens as if experience took the form of proverbs, quotations and memorable formulations. Language presents itself as a refuge for its lessons, and carries them anonymously. Experience thus takes the form of a tradition.

To this anonymous tradition can be added what one acquires though reading. The contrast is striking between, on the one hand, Spinoza's geometrical texts, where he uses a sober and stripped-back style,[236] and on the other his more persuasive passages whose style is woven from citations and allusions. He explicitly cites Curtius Rufus, Tacitus, but also others without referencing the author's name. It has been shown that certain scenes that are never explicitly cited (for instance, the Catilinarian conspiracy)[237] literally haunt Spinoza's text. They provide a bridge between his thought and the reader's culture, just like the references to impersonal experience provide a link to common life – that is, to the life that the reader lives, the life that he sees. Historians, poets, comics and satirists all come together in

---

[233] 'Quae modo ostendimus, ipsa etiam experientia quotidie tot tamque luculentis testimoniis testatur, ut omnibus fere in ore sit: hominem homini Deum esse', *Ethics* IV, 35, Schol., G II, p. 234, ll. 1–3 [*CWS* I, 563].

[234] 'hoc omnes satis experti sunt. Omnibus enim in ore est, quot capita, tot sensus, suo quemque sensu abundare, non minora cerebrorum quam palatorum esse discrimina', *Ethics* I, App., G II, p. 83, ll. 4–7 [*CWS* I, 445].

[235] 'Unde apud Belgas dudum in usum Proverbii abierit: geen ketter sonder letter', *TTP*, Chapter XIV, G III, p. 173, ll. 16–17 [*TTP* XIV, 2; *CWS* II, 264].

[236] 'Auch jene Darstellungsweise, deren Schmuck das Schmucklose ist, und der eigentliche Ausdruck, der immer die Sache trifft, sind Tugenden, welche dem geometrischen Vorbilde entsprechen', A. Trendelenburg, *Ueber Spinoza's Grundgedanken und dessen Erfolg*, Historische Beiträge zur Philosophie, vol. II, Berlin: Bethge, 1855, pp. 31–111, p. 47.

[237] O. Proietti, '*Adulescens luxu perditus*. Classici latini nell'opera di Spinoza', *Rivista di Filosofia neoscolastica*, 2 (1985), pp. 210–57.

Spinoza's humanist education and in the education his public has had, with the heritage of Latin culture standing ever ready to serve as a common point of reference – and not only Latin philosophers but also those who wrote histories and described morals. Cicero and Seneca are present, but more for their descriptions than for their philosophical theories. And, in addition to this storehouse of proverbs, we must not forget such baroque images as the somnambulist, the forgetful poet and the Brazilian from the dream.

— Finally, the *TTP* and the *TP* present collective memory in a form that was absent from Spinoza's early writings: namely, as historical experience. We see here the way in which human beings have organised themselves. The history of societies acquires a depth that it did not possess in the *TdIE* or in the *Short Treatise*.

C. The Modalities of Experience

Can we go further in our description of experience? Spinoza never defines experience, but by considering the texts in which it appears we can identify the modalities of its functioning.

— *Experience classifies*. It subtracts from the individual what is purely individual. Can it be said that it thus proceeds as reason does, in the sense that reason draws out common notions from the multiplicity of imaginative perceptions? No, for common properties in the Spinozist sense of the term are above all what is common to my body and to the bodies it encounters; the resulting common notions are thus adequate to the extent that this communion of bodies prevents the interference of heterogeneous effects. Nothing of the sort happens in experience: instead, experience draws out 'common notions' in the pre-Spinozist sense of the term. It grasps only what is common insofar as it is immersed in the multiplicity of perceptions – whence the preference experience has for examples, emblems and proverbs.

From this there follows a surprising effect: experience makes the traits it recognises circulate, while being reluctant to recognise this. What I see in others, I know that this also exists in me. What the weak say, the strong will say when they are weak. What is significant to the people is also significant to the nobility. Experience states all of these equivalences, but it perpetually defers their application. It could be said that it functions following the double principle of the displaced exception (what seems to be an exceptional case is only the application of the rule in exceptional circumstances) and the deferred rule (I know that things are thus, but I except myself from this fact, or I except the present moment, or some surprising example). Spinoza's critical reappraisal of experience will thus often consist in suppressing the second principle so as to make the first function to its full extent.

— *Experience functions as a point of closure or a barrier.* Spinoza often appeals to experience when he wishes to end a discussion: experience has shown 'enough and more than enough' that things are thus.[238] In this instance the function of experience is therefore to reject certain arguments as arising from now out-dated controversies. At the same time, it bars the route to other arguments: someone claims such-and-such a thing, but experience has shown that it is impossible. This is a particularly interesting case for it shows how, while it is not knowledge per se, experience can free up the path towards true knowledge by suppressing those arguments that would otherwise prevent the truth from manifesting itself. In such contexts, experience uses for its materials ideas that are certainly confused and inadequate, but whose existence alone suffices to close off certain paths to reflection. It also prevents certain hypotheses from being made by disclosing their evident absurdity. At the same time, experience does not make its materials adequate (for then it would become an instance of the second kind of knowledge), no more than it can be qualified as inadequate in itself (for then it would be an instance of the first kind of knowledge): in fact, experience neutralises the inadequation of knowledge – in the same way that a well-constructed State neutralises the vices of its citizens.

— *Experience instructs.* This implies that it never leads us astray. Experience is always real. What is false is the interpretation that is given of it. In such cases, it is reason that is used poorly. I cited above the example of the belief in the domination of the mind over the body. This possible belief is one of

---

[238] *Satis superque*: this is one of Spinoza's preferred expressions, *Ethics* II, 42, Schol., G II, p. 124, l. 36 [*CWS* I, 480]; Book III, 2, Schol., p. 143, l. 14 [*CWS* I, 495]; Book V, Praef., p. 280, l. 21 [*CWS* I, 597]; *TTP*, Preface, G III, p. 12, l. 7 [*TTP* Praef., 33; *CWS* II, 75]; Chapter II, p. 42, l. 26 [*TTP* II, 52; *CWS* II, 109]; Chapter II, p. 49, ll. 22–3 [*TTP* II, 25; *CWS* II, 117]; Chapter III, p. 52, l. 13 [*TTP* III, 37; *CWS* II, 119]; Chapter V, p. 72, l. 26 [*TTP* V, 15; *CWS* II, 142]; Chapter XI, p. 195, l. 24 [*TTP* XI, 37; *CWS* II, 290]; p. 196, ll. 30–1 [*TTP* XI, 44; *CWS* II, 291]; TP, Chapter II, 2, G III, p. 278, ll. 1–2 [*TP* II, 6; *CWS* II, 509]; Chapter XI, 2, p. 359, l. 11 [*TP* XI, 2; *CWS* II, 602]; Ep. LVIII, G IV, p. 266, ll. 26–7 [*Ep.* LVIII [to G. H. Schuller]; *CWS* II, 428]. With a few variants: experience has shown this *satis* (*TTP*, Chapter V, p. 70, l. 25 [*TTP* V, 7; *CWS* II, 140]), *plus quam satis* (Chapter XVI, p. 199, l. 26 [*TTP* XVI, 61; *CWS* II, 294]), *abunde* (Chapter XVII, p. 202, l. 31 [*TTP* XVII, 9; *CWS* II, 298]), *clarissime* (p. 201, ll. 21–2 [*TTP* XVII, 3; *CWS* II, 296]), *quam clarissime* (p. 203, ll. 13–14 [*TTP* XVII, 13; *CWS* II, 298]; p. 215, ll. 21–2 [*TTP* XVII, 82; *CWS* II, 314]), *quotidianis exemplis* (Chapter XX, p. 244, ll. 25–7 [*TTP* XX, 33; *CWS* II, 350]), *tam clare* (Ep. LII, G IV, p. 244, l. 1 [*Ep.* LII [to Hugo Boxel]; *CWS* II, 409]).

the consequences of the opacity of experience: everything is given to me, but I do not make use of it. A good example of this situation is provided by the preface to the *TTP*. There, with respect to the relation between fear and superstition, Spinoza puts forward two epistemologically essential theses:

- 'I judge that no one is ignorant of such-and-such a thing' (thesis A);
- 'All the same, I believe that the majority of people are ignorant of themselves' (thesis B).[239]

Arguably, these two theses frame the entirety of the Spinozist use of experience. In contrast to geometry, experiential discourse is manifest in the register of the already-there. When we begin to discuss with someone, he has perhaps never heard tell of the mathematical laws (or of the laws constructed on the model of mathematics) that we will demonstrate to him. This is no impediment so long as he knows of and accepts the rules of the mathematical game. Yet, he has necessarily already heard of what experience teaches, and has reflected on this himself (in this instance, it is the laws of fortune; but it could also be: that the lover returns to the coquette despite his promises; that the drunk or the chatterbox speaks despite their will; that no one is so vigilant that he does not occasionally fall asleep; that young people, if they are not careful, are attracted by what is fashionable and by the prestige of the foreign; that loyalty often leads counsellors to their doom . . .). This knowledge is not an illusion. Nevertheless, people are mistaken, and mistaken often ('Quamvis centies fallat'). Why? On the one hand, it is because they graft onto experience all sorts of ideologies or mythologies that interpret it and extend it in artificial ways; on the other hand, it is because they fail to draw lessons from it; in particular, they fail to apply the lessons that they draw from the experiences of others to their own case, or fail to apply in situations of adversity those maxims that they learnt or elaborated in a situation of tranquillity. The conditions of experience determine that it is opaque to its own lessons. Whence the following paradox: nobody is ignorant of experience's lessons, save that he is ignorant of himself. When Spinoza says that in days of prosperity each person is full of wisdom, he is hardly being ironic: the propositions in which this wisdom is formulated (those of neo-Stoicism, to be exact) might well be precise, but they do not take into account the thickness of human situations and are therefore mere *dictamina* that will be difficult to apply in

---

[239] 'Atque haec neminem ignorare existimo, quamvis plerosque se ipsos ignorare credam', G III, p. 5 [*TTP* Praef., 2; CWS II, 66].

those situations – which are in no way impossible to foresee – where reason is overwhelmed.

— *Experience leads to a serene pessimism*, to a disabused resignation, as foreign to utopian optimism as to satire. There will be vices so long as there are people. This is the pessimism of Latin rhetorical culture. We cannot draw any conclusions from this concerning a possible pessimism as far as Spinoza's system is concerned, for the system begins after the reception of experience, and it organises the incontestable traits that experience presents in a different way.

If this mode of reasoning is so specific, it must have its own language. I noted above that the expression *satis superque* was characteristic of experience. We should add to it those trenchant formulations where Spinoza states, without any demonstration, that 'everyone knows',[240] or, better still, that 'no one does not know'.[241] We find here – albeit in a different form – saturation as a figure of effective totalisation, which we identified in the early writings. There also belong to this register those formulations that refuse to pause over certain points 'because they are sufficiently well known'.[242] If these points were said to be 'known in themselves', one could hesitate between thinking that Spinoza is using either an axiomatic or an experiential argument;[243] but the term *satis* leaves no room for doubt. The regime of examples is also characteristic of experience: when Spinoza reasons mathematically, he often gives an example and analyses it.[244] When he reasons experientially, he

---

[240] 'Cujus rei causam omnibus patere existimo', *TTP*, Chapter XX, G III, p. 239, l. 32 [*TTP* XX, 5; *CWS* II, 345].

[241] *TP*, Chapter VII, 14, G III, p. 314, l. 3 [*TP* VII, 14; *CWS* II, 551], Chapter VIII, 31, p. 337, ll. 4–5 [*TP* VIII, 31; *CWS* II, 578]; *TTP*, Preface, G III, p. 5, ll. 9–10 [*TTP* Praef., 2; *CWS* II, 66]; 'nemo dubitet', *TTP*, Chapter XIV, p. 176, l. 35 [*TTP* XIV, 22; *CWS* II, 268].

[242] 'utpote satis nota', *TTP*, Chapter VII, G III, p. 20, l. 10 [*TTP* VII, 20; *CWS* II, 83]; 'Satis nota sunt', Chapter VIII, p. 12, l. 32 [*TP* VIII, 12; *CWS* II, 570]; 'nimis noti sunt', *Ethics* IV, 57, Dem., G II, p. 251, l. 29 [*CWS* I, 577]. There are occurrences that bring together *satis* and *omnes*: 'sed, quandoquidem haec apud omnes satis vulgata esse existimo, iisdem supersedeo', *TTP*, Preface, p. 6, ll. 16–17 [*TTP* Praef., 6; *CWS* II, 67]; 'nisi putarem ea omnibus esse satis nota', *TTP*, Chapter I, p. 20, ll. 11–12 [*TTP* I, 20; *CWS* II, 83]; 'quod omnibus satis esse notum existimo', *TTP*, Chapter III, p. 50, ll. 13–14 [*TTP* III, 27; *CWS* II, 117].

[243] Cf. A. Rivaud, 'Les *Per se nota* dans l'*Ethique*', *Chronicon spinozanum*, II (1922), pp. 138–54.

[244] I cannot enter here into the analysis of the problems posed by the functioning of scientific models. It will have to suffice to refer to two fundamental works, those of

tends rather to mention that there are innumerable examples of what he is talking about,[245] or to insist on their ready availability.[246] In this context, *testimonia* can be replaced by *exempla*.[247] Finally, certain verbs participate in this experiential register: *docere*, of course, but also *suadere*,[248] *comprobare*,[249]

J. Bernhardt, 'Infini, substance et attributs', *Cahiers Spinoza*, II, Répliques (1978), pp. 53–92, and D. Parrocchia, 'Physique pendulaire et modèles de l'ordre dans l'*Ethique* de Spinoza', *Cahiers Spinoza*, V, Répliques (1985), pp. 71–92, as well as 'Sur quelques modèles scientifiques de la métaphysique spinoziste, *Travaux et documents du GRS*, 2, PUPS, 1989, pp. 47–65.

[245] '& quamvis experientia in dies reclamaret, ac infinitis exemplis ostenderet', *Ethics* I, App., G II, p. 79, ll. 23–4 [*CWS* I, 441]; 'et ad hunc modum perplurima adferri possent exempla, quae quam clarissime id ipsum ostendunt', *TTP*, Preface, G III, p. 6, ll. 10–12 [*TTP* Praef., 6; *CWS* II, 67]; 'quae omnia hic multis exemplis illustrare possem', *TTP*, Chapter IX, p. 139, ll. 4–5 [*TTP* IX, 51; *CWS* II, 221]; 'cujus rei exempla omnia viderunt saecula', *TTP* Chapter XIX, p. 235, ll. 23–4 [*TTP* XIX ; *CWS* II, 340]; 'cujus rei exempla omnia viderunt saecula', *TP*, Chapter III, 10, G III, p. 289, 7–8 [*TP* III, 10; *CWS* II, 522]; 'ut innumera ostendunt exempla', Chapter VII, 14, p. 314, ll. 12–13 [*TP* VII, 14; *CWS* II 552]; 'et praeter haec plurima exempla in historiis leguntur', Chapter VII, 24, p. 318, ll. 6–7 [*TP* VI, 24; *CWS* II, 556]. Recall that the opening of the *TdIE* showed the harmful character of the goods of common life by way of *exempla permulta, non pauciora, innumeranda*, G II, p. 7, ll. 9–10, 13. 15 [*TTP* 10; *CWS* II, 68–9]. Finally, to show clearly the coherence of the lexicon and of the experiential process, let us cite a passage that ties the number of examples, the uselessness of citing them, and the formula *satis nota* together: 'Et ad hujus exemplar multa possem adferre exempla ex Sacris Literis, nisi putarem ea omnibus esse satis nota', *TTP*, Chapter I, p. 20, ll. 10–12 [*TTP* I, 20; *CWS* II, 83].

[246] 'Exempla praesto sunt; nec opus mihi est ea longe petere' (before giving Amsterdam as an example of a free city), *TTP*, Chapter XX, G III, p. 245, ll. 34–5 [*TTP* XX, 39; *CWS* II, 351].

[247] 'Quae modo ostendimus, ipsa etiam experientia quotidie tot tamque luculentis testimoniis testatur [. . .]', *Ethics* IV, 35, Schol., G II, p. 234, ll. 2–3 [*CWS* I, 563]. *Testimonium* is, furthermore, the technical term used regularly in the *TTP* to refer to the examples drawn from Scripture – and thus to indicate an operation that chapters V and VII refer to precisely as experiential.

[248] *Ethics* IV, 39, Schol., p. 240, l. 22 [*CWS* I, 569].

[249] *Ethics* III, 2, Schol., p. 141, l. 32; p. 142, l. 1 [*CWS* I, 494]; DA 27, p. 197, ll. 19–20 [*CWS* I, 537]; *TTP*, Chapter V, p. 77, ll. 23 and 29 [*TTP* V, 38, 39; *CWS* II, 148]; Chapter VI, p. 92, l. 22 [*TTP* VI 55; *CWS* II, 165]; Chapter XIX, p. 231, l. 30 [*TTP* XIX, 19; *CWS* II, 336]; cf. also *confirmare*, *TTP*, Chapter V, p. 77, l. 14 [*TTP* V, 37; *CWS* II, 148]; Chapter XIII, p. 167, l. 14 [*TTP* XIII, 2; *CWS* II, 257]; Chapter XVI, p. 200, l. 19 [*TTP* XVI, 66; *CWS* II, 295]; *confirmare* is furthermore the quasi-technical term used by Spinoza when in the *TTP* he passes from a demonstration founded on reason to proofs drawn from Scripture – that is, as we will see further on, founded on an historical form of experience.

testari,²⁵⁰ *reclamare*²⁵¹ – with this latter clearly playing the role of the barrier that I referred to above. *Docere* and *suadere* are used with other subjects (*ratio*, certainly, but also *appetitus*,²⁵² *superstitio*²⁵³ and *scriptura*),²⁵⁴ while *comprobare*, *testari* and *reclamare* appear to be reserved for the functions of experience. The subjects of other verbs are the people who undergo certain experiences: *experiri*,²⁵⁵ *sentire*²⁵⁶ and sometimes *percipere*. When it is a matter of referring to what a person could see had they accepted the lessons of experience – that is, had they succeeded in dissipating its opacity – the term *consulere* that is used.²⁵⁷ Finally, we should note the reference to daily repetition that often marks the lessons of experience.²⁵⁸

---

²⁵⁰ *Ethics* IV, 35, Schol., p. 234, l. 2 [*CWS* I, 563]; Book V, 6, Schol., p. 285, l. 3 [*CWS* I, 599]; *TTP* Chapter VI, p. 87, l. 27 [*TTP* VI, 32; *CWS* II, 159]; Chapter XVI, p. 199, l. 26 [*TTP* XVI, 62; *CWS* II, 294]; Chapter XVII, p. 202, l. 31 [*TTP* XVII, 9; *CWS* II, 298] and p. 215, l. 22 [*TTP* XVII, 82; *CWS* II, 314].

²⁵¹ *Ethics* I, App., p. 79, l. 24 [*CWS* I, 441]; Book V, Praef., p. 277, l. 22 [*CWS* I, 595].

²⁵² *TP*, Chapter II, 8, G III, p. 279, l. 24 [*TP* II, 8; *CWS* II, 511].

²⁵³ *TTP*, Chapter VII, G III, p. 97, ll. 32–3 [*TTP* VII, 4; *CWS* II, 170].

²⁵⁴ *TTP*, Chapter VII, G III, p. 98, ll. 14–15 [*TTP* VII, 6; *CWS* II, 171]

²⁵⁵ This verb is also tied to the substantive *experientia* by a proximity that is not only etymological but also contextual, as is shown by the phrase that introduces the reflection on children's imitative practices in Book III of the *Ethics*: 'Denique, si ipsam experientiam consulere velimus, ipsam haec omnia docere experimur', 32, Schol., G II, p. 165, ll. 17–18 [*CWS* I, 513]. The *Ethics* uses it almost exclusively in the Scholia from Books III and IV to confirm what the theorems have demonstrated. An occurrence in the Preface to Book V clearly indicates the division between the fields of experience and knowledge: 'affectuum remedia, quae omnes experiri quidem, sed non accurate observare nec distincte videre credo . . .' G II, p. 280, ll. 22–4 [*CWS* I, 597]. Lastly, I will return in the final part of this work to the occurrence from the Scholium to Proposition 23.

²⁵⁶ *Sentire* in fact possesses three semantic domains: (1) to estimate or to notice (with respect to the group *existimatio, despectus, abjectio, superbia*; *Ethics*, Book II 26, Schol.; App., Def., 21, 22, 28, 29; Book IV, 49 and 57); (2) to have an opinion; and (3) to feel. It is this last sense that experiential givens translate; it runs throughout Book II; and it is this sense that is often associated with *percipere*.

²⁵⁷ *Ethics* III, 32, Schol., G II, p. 165, ll. 17–18 [*CWS* I, 513]; *TP*, Chapter XI, 4, G III, p. 359, l. 35 [*TP* XI, 4; *CWS* II, 603].

²⁵⁸ Cf. the formulations we have already cited a number of times: 'quamvis experientia in dies reclamaret [. . .]', *Ethics* I, App., p. 79, l. 24 [*CWS* I, 441]; 'ipsa etiam experientia quotidie tot tamque luculentis testimoniis testatur [. . .]' *Ethics* IV, 35, Schol., G II, p. 234, ll. 2–3 [*CWS* I, 563]. And also: 'atque hoc quotidie in somnis experimur [. . .]', *Ethics* II, 49, Schol., p. 134, ll. 21–2 [*CWS* I, 489]; he who draws glory only from the opinion of the crowd 'quotidiana cura [. . .] experiatur', *Ethics* IV, 58, Schol., p. 253, ll. 16–17 [*CWS* I, 578]; as for the general experience of the excessive affects (those that we observe easily, in opposition to *hilaritas*, which, more balanced but more rare,

It should be noted that, if we leave aside the letter to De Vries (and take into account the reservations about its status), then Spinoza does not write any theoretical texts on experience. The reason for this is no doubt that he borrows this concept and its characteristics from ordinary language and common rhetoric. This will also be the case for those notions that we will soon see associated with experience: *usus, ingenium, fortuna*. If we wish to go further than the positive determinations of experience that can be derived from its limits, we will have to look to the chapters where these notions are found in a practical state.

Can we measure the path travelled since the *TdIE*? What is clear is that the circles of experience have disappeared. Experience opens onto a very large variety of fields. We will now study some of them: language, the passions, history.

---

is instead conceived of by demonstration and not perceived by experience), it will be summarised as follows: 'nam affectus, quibus quotidie conflictamur [. . .]', *Ethics* IV, 44, Schol., p. 243, l. 9 [CWS I, 571]. We find this *experientia quotidiana* in the *Principia* (PP I, 15, Schol., G I, p. 175, l. 17 [CWS I, 259]), in letter XIII (G IV, p. 66, l. 6 [*Ep.* XIII [to Henry Oldenburg]; CWS I, 207]) and in the *TTP* (Chapter XVI, p. 200, ll. 19–20 [*TTP* XVI, 66; CWS II, 259] and 'experientia quotidianis exemplis docet', Chapter XX, p. 244, ll. 25–7 [*TTP* XX, 33; CWS II, 350]).

8

Fields of Experience: Language

None of Spinoza's works, not even a special chapter, is devoted to the philosophy of language. Nevertheless, language is a theme that consistently returns in each one of his writings. Spinoza often alludes to the philosophy of language as to something that his readers are already familiar with. He goes beyond advancing a few theoretical theses on the nature of words or the relation between language and thought. Among his works we thus find various approaches to what today we would call the sciences of language. For instance, Spinoza produced a grammar (the *Compendium Grammatices Hebraeae Linguae*), a study of rhetoric and an analysis of genres (outlined in a number of passages in the *TTP*), and a hermeneutics, or at the very least an analysis of the act of interpretation (not only of the Holy Scriptures but also of profane authors; thus, Spinoza asks both: 'What did Moses mean to say?',[1] and: 'What is the meaning of Machiavelli's writings?'[2]). Furthermore, despite the conscious sobriety of his Latin, Spinoza was able to mobilise an extreme variety of styles and forms, from mathematical exposition to dialogues, textual commentaries, the analysis of historical examples, and letters that either discuss or polemicise,[3] and so on. It is therefore essential to note a persistent and varied attention in Spinoza's work to the problems posed by particular languages [*les langues*] and by language in general [*le langage*]. It is also this diversity that we must take into account when reconstituting Spinoza's doctrine on these matters. We will therefore have to consider both the theoretical status that Spinoza assigns language and the

---

[1] *TTP*, Chapter VII, G III, p. 100–1 [*TTP* VII, 18–22; *CWS* II, 174–5]
[2] Cf. the *TP*, Chapter V, 7, G III, pp. 296–7 [*TP* V, 7; *CWS* I, 531].
[3] The two genres should be distinguished, for nothing is more distant than the style of the letters addressed indirectly to Boyle or the violent critiques directed towards Albert Burgh.

way he analyses its concrete effects when faced with practical problems concerning classification, ambiguity, grammar and rhetoric. These two points of view are not necessarily contradictory, but the second will perhaps offer us a different angle of approach to the first.

1. The Theoretical Status of Language

A. Critique: Words and Adequation

In the *Cogitata metaphysica*, when speaking of beings of reason, Spinoza remarks that it is unreasonable to divide being into real being on the one hand and beings of reason on the other, for this entails dividing being into being and non-being. He then adds: 'Nevertheless, I do not wonder that Philosophers preoccupied with words, or grammar, should fall into such errors. For they judge the things from the words, not the words from the things.'[4] In a single stroke, Spinoza makes a triple cut: between words and things (with words seeming to possess hardly any ontological purchase at all); between the method that begins with things and the method that begins with words (the ontological void thus becomes an epistemological trap); and finally between two different philosophies. The way he refers to his adversaries here as philosophers who are 'verbales sive grammaticales' seems to indicate that language – or these philosophers' attachment to language – is the fundamental source of their errors. The *TdIE* argues that certain errors made by the soul arise from the same source: that is, if a person evokes in their memory both the word 'soul' and some corporeal image, then they will easily come to believe that they are imagining and configuring a corporeal soul: 'he does not distinguish the name from the thing itself'.[5] For the same reason, Spinoza dismisses the division of divine attributes into those that are communicable and those that are not,[6] while he rejects the debate on the distinction between the possible and contingent in the following way: 'I am not accustomed to dispute about words.'[7] Everything

---

[4] 'Attamen non miror philosophos verbales sive grammaticales in similes errores incidere: res enim ex nominibus judicant, non autem nomina ex rebus', CM, I, 1, G I, p. 235, ll. 6–9 [CM I; CWS I, 301].

[5] 'Quia nomen a re ipsa non distinguit', *TdIE*, § 58, G II, p. 22, Note z [*TdIE* 58; CWS I, 27].

[6] 'Divisio magis nominis quam rei', CM II, XI, G I, p. 274, l. 31 [CM I; CWS I, 340].

[7] Possibility and contingency are defined as two different faults – and this is the only thing that Spinoza asks that we accord him. Furthermore, he introduces a distinction between the two terms, but 'quod si quis id, quod ego *possibile* voco, *contingens*, et

involving words and language thus appears to be marked by a negative sign, while the distinction between good and bad philosophy is grounded in the interest a philosophy shows for language. In truth, we can recognise here a quite common anti-scholastic argument that we find in Bacon when he denounces the idols of the marketplace;[8] in Descartes when he identifies language as one of the sources of our errors;[9] in Arnauld and Nicole when they define, following Descartes, the causes of the confusion in our thought and speech;[10] in Locke when he addresses the issue of the imperfection and abuse of words;[11] in Leibniz when he criticises 'psittacism';[12] and in Malebranche when he explains that 'what is evident in itself is not evident for everyone'.[13] The whole of the classical age is characterised by this discrediting of words, which are said to be responsible at once for the prejudices of the common people and for those false philosophies that must be rejected. But this argument, which is common to the whole of the seventeenth century, takes on a particular importance in Spinoza because it is linked in his thought to the

---

contra id, quod ego *contingens, possibile* vocare velit, non ipsi contradicam: neque enim nominibus disputare soleo', CM, I, III, G I, p. 242, I, 20–3 [CM I; CWS I, 307].

[8] 'Plainly words do violence to the understanding, and confuse everything; and betray men into countless empty disputes and fictions', *The New Organon*, p. 42. Cf. also aphorisms 59 and 60. Thus, 'great and solemn controversies of learned men often end in dispute about words and names', ibid., p. 48.

[9] *Principia*, First Part, § 74: 'The thoughts of almost all people are more concerned with words than with things; and as a result people very often give their assent to words they do not understand, thinking they once understood them, or that they got them from others who did understand them correctly', AT, IX-2, p. 61 [PWD I, 220].

[10] 'Nous avons déjà dit que la nécessité que nous avons de signes extérieurs pour nous faire entendre, fait que nous attachons tellement nos idées aux mots, que souvent nous considérons plus les mots que les choses', *Logique* of Port-Royal, First Part, Chapter XI.

[11] *An Essay Concerning Human Understanding*, Book III, Chapters 8 and 9.

[12] Cf. the remark on the best and the worst: 'We often reason in words, with the object itself virtually absent from our mind', Leibniz, *New Essays on Human Understanding* (Cambridge: Cambridge University Press, 2012), p. 186. Whence the abrupt formula from Chapter I, which recalls the following formula from Spinoza: 'But if someone uses terms differently, I would not argue about words', ibid., p. 78.

[13] 'L'on est accoutumé à se payer de mots et à en payer les autres [. . .] Le don de la parole est le plus grand des talents, le langage d'imagination le plus sûr des oyens et une mémoire remplie de termes incompréhensibles paraîtra toujours avec éclat, quoique les cartésiens en puissent dire', *XII Eclaircissement*, Paris: Pléiade, 1979, p. 942. What follows indicates the necessity of this illusion in the here-below: 'Quand les hommes aimeront uniquement la vérité, alors ils prendront bien garde à ce qu'ils disent [. . .] Mais quand sera-ce que les hommes aimeront uniquement la vérité? [. . .] Cela n'arrivera jamais en cette vie', ibid., pp. 942–3.

theory of the imagination and to the doctrine of parallelism. It could thus be said that, while he certainly did not invent all of the themes of his critique of language, Spinoza did give them an original articulation that considerably modifies their meaning as well as their effects. It is only by studying such modifications that we can come to understand why Spinoza's conception of language leads him to, among other things, the biblical lessons from the *TTP* and the defence of freedom of speech.

Words are corporeal movements. Since there is no interaction between the body and the soul, strictly speaking these movements have nothing to do with ideas, which, insofar as they arise from thought, imply no notion of extension. Words are images that are produced in the body on the occasion of encounters in the corporeal order. This is what both the *TdIE* and the *Ethics* affirm. The *TdIE* begins with the statement that words are part of the imagination, and immediately translates this into the thesis that many of our concepts come about through the disordered (*vage*) composition of our memory of words, which itself results from some disposition of the body.[14] The concepts that are thereby formed are obviously not adequate ideas. The word thus appears as the bearer of inadequation. It is linked to the chains formed by images – that is, to the order of exteriority. To this first argument, Spinoza adds a second: words are formed 'according to the pleasure and power of understanding of ordinary people'.[15] This supplementary determination reinforces the effect of the imagination: the collective dimension of language makes any attempt by an individual to escape it and to make language conform to the understanding utterly inefficacious.[16] Spinoza gives as an example of this determination such positive and negative words as 'finite' and 'infinite', 'corporeal' and 'incorporeal'. In each case, the notion that is most important from the perspective of the understanding is expressed using a negative term, as if it were only the negation of its opposite. Thus, language seems to suggest that it is more natural, or more thinkable, to be finite than to be infinite, to be corporeal than to be incorporeal. Spinoza is not

---

[14] 'Deinde cum verba sint pars imaginationis, hoc est, quod, prout vage ex aliqua dispositione corporis componuntur in memoria, multos conceptos fingamus [. . .]', *TdIE*, § 88, G II, p. 33, ll. 8–10 [*TdIE* 88; *CWS* 38].

[15] 'Adde quod sint constituta ad libitum et captum vulgi', § 89, G II, p. 33, l. 113 [*TdIE* 89; *CWS* I, 38].

[16] Here again Spinoza is close to Bacon: 'Men associate through talk; and words are chosen to suit the understanding of the common people. And thus a poor and unskilful code of words incredibly obstructs the understanding. The definitions and explanations with which learned men have been accustomed to protect and in some way liberate themselves, do not restore the situation at all', *The New Organon*, p. 542.

content here to simply state that the distribution of these words is arbitrary and goes against the rational order.[17] He simultaneously identifies the reason for this lack of reason: it is indeed the order of imaginative encounters that determines this aspect of words. Since we encounter in ordinary life neither the infinite nor the incorporeal, neither the uncreated nor the independent, we give the primary and positive names to perceived realities, and only then do we forge their opposites, which thus appear as derivative and as negative.[18] Thus, the person who reasons on the basis of words, once these are constituted, will be spontaneously induced to believe that the finite is prior to the infinite. Language thus conserves the order of daily life and surreptitiously grants it the legitimacy of what is natural.

Spinoza develops similar arguments in the *Ethics*. There, language is related in a comparable way to memory, while memory is related to the links between the modifications of the body. These links differ from those that arise according to the order of the understanding and by virtue of which the soul perceives things through their first causes, which is the same for all people. Language is thus marked from the beginning by the modifications of the body and by the body's particularity. A Roman, hearing the word *pomum*, will immediately pass to the thought of a fruit. Now, the fact is that there exists no internal relation between this fruit and this word. Nevertheless, a relation does indeed exist, one that explains why the Roman immediately thinks of a fruit and indeed does so whenever he hears the word *pomum* – but this relation, the reproductive root of meaning, does not reside in the thing: it resides in the body of the Roman. For this Roman, habit has ordered the images of things in his body.[19] The foundational link of language is therefore neither the identification of a real similarity, nor an instituting act: it is an effect of association. This effect of association is as valid for language as it is for any other system of signs, whether voluntary or not:[20] for the soldier, the traces of a horse on the sand evoke the image of a horseman, then that of war; for the peasant, they evoke the image of the plough and of a field. What the biography of each person has inscribed in his body as links between images structures in advance what he will read in the silence of the sign. Seen in this way, the word appears to be as silent as any

---

[17] This is what Descartes does with the same example: Cf. Letter to Hyperaspistes August 1641, AT, III, p. 427 [PWS III, 192].

[18] *TdIE*, § 89, G II, p. 33, l. 15–22 [*TdIE* 89; *CWS* I, 38].

[19] 'Et sic unusquisque ex una in aliam cogitationem incidet, prout rerum imagines uniuscujusque consuetudo in corpore ordinavit', *Ethics* II, 18, Schol., G II, p. 107 [*CWS* I, 466].

[20] For Spinoza as for Hobbes, the idea of the sign does not bring with it the idea of intention. Cf. *De Natura humana*, Chapter, IV, § 9.

other sign. We should pause for a moment over the term 'a Roman'. Is one a Roman as one is a soldier or a peasant? We will see further on that this is a special determination that Spinoza indicates only indirectly here. We will have to return to this point when we analyse the relations between language and the universal – for not everyone speaks Latin.

Not only does language belong along with memory and the order of the body, to the same register of inadequation, it lies, moreover, at the root of a particular type of error: that of misunderstanding. This error arises from the fact that the same words do not always have the same meaning. 'And indeed, most errors consist in our not rightly applying names to things.'[21] Misunderstandings are the source of controversies: two people who in reality think the same thing say different things and thus come to think that they are opposed to one another. Disagreements can even arise within the self: whoever commits an error in calculation has other numbers in mind than those that are on the paper. Language thus appears powerful enough to confuse the native power of the understanding. The inadequation of language is such that it can extend error well beyond the adequacy of ideas. It can even go so far as to force into existence words that appear to be contradictions in terms, and which, moreover, cannot even be represented by the imagination: the person who speaks of a square circle thus succeeds in deceiving the understanding and the imagination all at once.[22]

Finally, language plays a role in the constitution of general ideas: it is the erasure of differences between things that permits us to concentrate in a word an inadequately affirmed image of a large number of singular beings, which alone are real in the strict sense of the word.[23] Words thus help us to forge general ideas that are, in fact, nothing at all – an additional reason to be suspicious of them. What is often called Spinoza's nominalism above all concerns the role that language plays in creating imaginative connections.[24]

---

[21] 'Et profecto plerique errores in hoc solo consistunt quod scilicet nomina rebus non recte applicamus', *Ethics* II, 47, Schol., G II, p. 128, ll. 23–5 [*CWS* I, 483].

[22] 'Circulum quadratum verbis quidem exprimimus, imaginari autem nullo modo, et multo minus intelligere possums', *Cogitata metaphysica*, I, Chapter III, G I, p. 241, ll. 12–14 [CM III; *CWS* I, 307]. The example of the square circle is reprised on multiple occasions, precisely because of the impossibility of thinking it. (*TdIE*, G II, p. 25, ll. 1–3 [*TdIE* 54; *CWS* I, 29]; CM, II, Chapter X, G I, p. 272, ll. 11–13 [CM X; *CWS* I, 338]; *Ethics* I, 11, Dem. 2, G II, p. 53, ll. 3–5 [*CWS* I, 417]; *Ethics* I, 15, Schol., G II, p. 58, ll. 29–34 [*CWS* I, 423]).

[23] *Ethics* II, 40, Schol. [*CWS* I, 475–7].

[24] 'For nominalists, words are unimportant. Spinoza does not care about words either. They are the product of imagination', H. Hubbeling, *Spinoza's Methodology*, p. 21.

All of these criticisms are summed up in the Scholium where Spinoza deals with the question of the will. The imagination creates the general idea of the will by effacing the difference between volitions. We believe in the autonomy of the will because we can – at least in speech – affirm or deny something that runs counter to our feelings.[25] We can reject these prejudices so long as we attend to the nature of thought, which does not encompass the concept of extension: the idea, as a mode of thought, cannot consist in words: the 'essence of words and of images is constituted only by corporeal motions, which do not at all involve the concept of thought'.[26] That language is anchored in the imaginary, and thus in the realm of the inadequate; that it misrecognises the singular; that it possesses an illusory sense of autonomy and generates illusions – all of these are reasons to be suspicious of language, and to suppose that such suspicion is the beginning of wisdom.

In the final analysis, what constitutes the properly Spinozist basis for the critique of language is his analysis of the imagination[27] – or, more precisely, of the constrained necessity of the imagination. The suspicion of words that is manifested by the well-known analyses I have just cited is neither a simple effect of the 'ambience' of the rationalist philosophy of the seventeenth century, nor is it a product of a series of remarks made in passing that supposedly show, for instance, Spinoza's contempt for the body. It refers to the separation, which Spinoza explicitly affirms, between extension and thought, as well as to the submission of extension to laws over which the soul has no power. Spinoza's distrust of language is indeed articulated with the essential points of his system by way of the inscription of language not in the body

---

[25] 'Deinde, qui verba confundunt cum idea, vel cum ipsa affirmatione, quam idea involvit, putant se posse contra id, quod sentiunt, velle; quando aliquid solis verbis contra id, quod sentiunt, affirmant aut negant', *Ethics* II, 49, Schol., G II, p. 132, ll. 12–15 [*CWS* I, 486].

[26] 'Verborum namque, et imaginem essentia, a solis motibus corporeis constituitur, qui cogitationis conceptum minime involvunt', ibid., I, pp. 19–21 [*Ethics* II, 49, Schol.; *CWS* I, 486].

[27] On this fundamental point, we can compare Spinoza's analysis of language with Hume's. I am referring here to the comparison undertaken by G. Boss, *La différence des philosophes. Hume et Spinoza*, Zurich: Editions du Grand Midi, 1982, vol. II, pp. 756–83. Besides, Boss also rightly underscores that this anchorage in the imagination has a different meaning in the two doctrines. In Spinoza there is no privileging of a habitual or original meaning that would supposedly be closer to perception. On this basis, two different strategies emerge: for Hume, a return to the primary meaning; for Spinoza, a fashioning of language so as to produce as best as possible a language that is proper to the understanding.

but in the necessary effects of the encounter between the body and things that are external to it. This critique of language is all the more important given that any instance of communication between human beings occurs precisely by way of the body and its effects.[28] For this reason, it is essential to evaluate the consequences of this critique for the presentation of the system itself. This is what certain commentators have done, sometimes by highlighting the difficulties that this thesis presents. On this point, two studies, which have now become classic, are worth mentioning: Savan's work with its radical conclusions; and, more recently, Chiereghin's more fine-grained analyses, which are of interest because they tie Spinoza's critique of language to an evaluation of the geometrical method.

For Savan, 'Spinoza's views on words and language make it impossible for him to hold that his writings (or anyone else's) can be a direct or literal exposition of philosophical truth.'[29] Since words are nothing other than corporeal movements, nothing of what they express can claim the status of adequate knowledge. Their confused and imaginative character cannot be explained by simple ignorance, and thus cannot be eliminated by knowledge. In sum, it is impossible to pass from an erroneous language to a true language. Spinoza separates words from adequate ideas in such a radical way that it is difficult to give language any philosophical function at all.[30]

Similarly, Chiereghin argues that, if language is a prisoner of the imagination, then not only will it always be inadequate for expressing true ideas: the very inadequation of language itself with respect to truth becomes difficult to express.[31] This difficulty is all the more serious given that in the geometrical method language replaces the traditionally discredited content of mathematical knowledge: number and quantity. Everything happens, then, as if imagination threatened all the means for the expression of truth. This is why if the true idea that is the source of knowledge cannot be expressed adequately, 'inadequation radically invests the very possibility of expressing absolute knowledge'.[32]

---

[28] When citing Deuteronomy, 'face to face God spoke to you', Spinoza adds: 'as two men usually communicate their concepts to one another, by means of their two bodies', *TTP*, Chapter I, G III, p. 18, ll. 16–18 [*TTP* I, 14; CWS II, 80].

[29] David Savan, 'Spinoza and Language', *The Philosophical Review*, 67 (1958), pp. 212–25.

[30] 'So sharply does Spinoza separate words from adequate ideas that it is difficult to make out for language any useful philosophical function at all', ibid., p. 63. Savan adds: 'It is no more possible for us to discover and express true knowledge through language than it is for a somnambulist to communicate intelligently with the waking world.'

[31] F. Chiereghin, 'Introduzione a Spinoza. La critica al sapere matematico e le aporie del linguaggio', *Verifiche*, 5 (1976), p. 21.

[32] Ibid., p. 22.

Spinoza's critique of language thus seems to be so strong that it exceeds its own aims. Does it not risk leading to the ineffable? This would indeed be a paradox for a thought set on denouncing each and every *asylum ignorantiae*. How can we get out of this impasse? How can we conserve the gains of Spinoza's critique of language, all the while authorising ourselves to understand what other people say and to make propositions that we can claim to be true?

B. The Imagination Reordered

We should note first of all that Spinoza nowhere says that language makes philosophy impossible. Even when he is highlighting the difficulties created by verbal expression, he does not seem to think that these difficulties are insurmountable. For example, in the *TdIE* Spinoza issues the following warning about language: 'it is not to be doubted that words, as much as the imagination, can be the cause of many and great errors, unless we are very wary of them'.[33] He thus seems to suppose that this effort is possible, and that this is something that goes without saying. But we must explain why he thinks this is the case.[34] To do this, we must also explain what language is in its positivity for Spinoza, for up to this point all of the quotations and examples we have given have served only to place language within a more general category. To say that language is of the order of the imagination, and thus of extension, is to say the same thing of language that is said of sensible images, of geometrical figures, or of the physiological roots of the passions. This allows Spinoza to warn his reader against confusing certain words with ideas or to indicate certain effects, but it hardly helps the reader make any progress in the precise understanding of what language itself is.

The problem I am raising here consists, in fact, in the juxtaposition of two difficulties: one that concerns the status of the imagination and its relation to adequate ideas (this is a difficulty that does indeed concern more than words); and a difficulty that arises from the particular type of images that words are. On the one hand, is it true that the imagination is always irreducible to the order of the understanding? On the other hand, if the imaginary

---

[33] 'ideo non dubitandum, quin etiam verba, aeque ac imaginatio, possint esse causa multorum magnorumque errorum, nisi magnopere ab ipsis caveamus', § 88, G II, p. 33, ll. 10–12 [*TdIE* 88; *CWS* I, 38].

[34] G. H. R. Parkinson has criticised Savan's theses in a study published in the same volume, 'Language and Knowledge in Spinoza', *Spinoza: A Collection of Critical Essays*, ed. M. Grene, pp. 73–100. He refutes Savan's arguments one by one, but does not bring out the positive structure of language.

can constitute links that follow the order of the understanding, how can these links be represented in the specific case of language?

Some have tried to solve the first difficulty by opposing the free imagination to the constrained imagination. This, for example, is what Sylvain Zac does in an article[35] where he begins by recalling the difficulties tied to language, before seeking a solution in the Scholium from the *Ethics* that defines the imagination[36] and in Spinoza's letter to Peter Balling. According to Zac's interpretation, the language of the true is based on a free imagination 'which would depend only on the nature of the soul, that is, only on the nature of the body of which it is the idea, of the body as it is in itself and not as it has been modified by external causes'.[37]

It seems to me that we should clearly distinguish between these two texts. The Scholium from Proposition 17 notes that the imagination would be free were this faculty to depend on its nature alone. But this is neither an affirmation nor the statement of an effective division of the imagination into two distinct species. The fact is that it is impossible for the *imaginandi facultas* to depend on its nature alone.[38] Furthermore, Spinoza writes the sentence in question in the irreality of the present tense. Spinoza's intention in this passage is only to highlight the fact that the imagination as such contains no error. To imagine is to contemplate bodies, not in terms of these bodies' natures, such as these are revealed to us through adequate ideas, but rather in terms of the effects these bodies have on us – effects that are disclosed to us by the ideas of the affections of our body. In particular, to imagine is to represent to oneself as present things that are not present, but whose corresponding ideas arise through association following the order of the affections of our body. This representation itself is not an error: it is an effect of the productive power of the soul. Error begins (and in truth it has always, already begun) with the fact that we do not possess any adequate ideas that exclude the presence of these imagined things. This distinction of Spinoza's is not a hypothesis that belongs to a particular school of philosophy. Rather,

---

[35] 'Spinoza et le langage', *Giornale critico della filosofia italiana*, July–December 1977, pp. 612–33.
[36] *Ethics* II, 17, Schol. [CWS I, 464–5].
[37] 'qui dépendrait de la seule nature de l'âme, c'est-à-dire de la seule nature du corps dont elle est l'idée, du corps tel qu'il est en lui-même et non tel qu'il est modifié par des causes extérieures', 'Spinoza et le langage', p. 618.
[38] Cf. M. Gueroult, *Spinoza*, vol. II, *L'Ame*, p. 222: 'Il apparaît bien qu'elle ne l'est pas [free], puisque, loin de relever de la seule nature de l'Ame, elle dépend avant tout de la suite infinie des choses qui causent les affections du corps, c'est-à-dire de l'ordre commun de la Nature.'

it should be considered as the transposition of a meditation on the laws of optics: if I see an object in the mirror, I necessarily represent it to myself as being behind the mirror; but I am only mistaken if I do not know, in addition to this, that it is in fact on my side of the mirror. The fabrication of the image is a positive consequence of the laws of reflection. The thesis that Spinoza defends in this passage is thus a thesis concerning the imagination's neutrality. The imagination's apparent freedom is only a supposition whose purpose is to make the main argument easier to understand.

By contrast, the letter to Balling explicitly evokes a reality, and indeed a reality that is known by experience. 'The effects of the imagination', Spinoza says, 'arise from the disposition of either the Body or the Soul'.[39] Spinoza shows this by reference to experience, and he does this for each of the two causes that he cites. He thus begins with the body – something that in principle teaches us nothing new as far as the *TdIE* and the *Ethics* are concerned. Fevers and other illnesses cause hallucinations, while those with overly thick blood imagine struggles and murders. The only thing that is worthy of note in these examples is that, as in the *TTP* and in certain Scholia from the *Ethics*, Spinoza illustrates the laws of the normal imagination by reference to the most visionary effects of the extraordinary imagination.[40] What about the second proof? The phrase gives no precise examples: 'We see that the imagination is also determined by the constitution of the soul alone; for as we find by experience, it follows the traces of the intellect in everything and links its images and words together in order, as the intellect does its demonstrations, so that we can hardly understand anything of which the imagination does not form some image from a trace.'[41] This text thus recognises in positive terms the possibility of organising images according to the order of the understanding (and its experiential status implies that everyone can recognise this). If this reading

---

[39] 'Effectus imaginationis ex constitutione vel corporis vel mentis oriuntur', Ep. XVII, G IV, p. 77, ll. 9–10 [*Ep*. XVII [to Pieter Balling]; CWS I, 353]. I am correcting Appuhn's translation by making *constitutio* 'disposition', following Gueroult's remarks. [Translator's note: I have accordingly modified Curley's translation, which renders *constitutio* as 'constitution'].

[40] These examples do not imply an action of the body on the mind, as J. D. Sanchez Estop seems to suppose in an otherwise very suggestive study: 'Des présages à l'entendement: notes sur les présages, l'imagination et l'amour dans la lettre à P. Balling', *Studia spinozana*, IV (1988), pp. 68–9.

[41] 'Videmus etiam imaginationem tantummodo ab animae constitutione determinari; quandoquidem, ut experimur, intellectus vestigia in omnibus sequitur, et suas imagines ac verba ex ordine, sicuti suas demonstrationes intellectus, concatenat et invicem connectit', Ep. XVII, G IV, p. 77, ll. 15–19 [*Ep*. XVII [to Pieter Balling]; CWS I, 353].

is correct, then what is valid for each image is valid for the particular form of images that are words.

On this point, Gueroult seems to refuse this possibility. But this is because he adopts a perspective from which the term 'disposition' is understood to be synonymous with 'cause'. We are thus effectively returned to Cartesianism and to the interaction of the soul with the body.[42] But if this is the case, then we are reading a text by Spinoza that is not yet Spinozist. Gueroult is thus entirely correct to warn against a 'causalist' reading of this letter. But was this reading Spinoza's own? It might be thought that the date 1664 is a little late to call this letter a work of Spinoza's youth.[43] Can it be read differently? Book V offers us another possibility. Images can be understood as being linked together, not under the *influence* of the intellect, but nevertheless following the *order* of the intellect, even if it is the images' own movement that so arranges them. Proposition 10 from Book V outlines just such a possibility: 'So long as we are not torn by affects contrary to our nature, we have the power of ordering and connecting the affections of the Body according to the order of the intellect.'[44] In advancing this proposition, Spinoza is in no way thinking of an interaction between the soul and the body. He notes only that the body always attempts to accomplish those actions that follow from its nature and lead to its preservation. These actions are provoked by images that are explained in part by the order of the heterogeneous (that which exclusively manifests the order of exteriority) and in part by the order of the homogeneous (those properties that are common to our body and to external bodies). Once they have been imprinted on us, these images can be associated with one another in one of two ways: either according to the relations between those of their various aspects that cannot be explained solely by our nature, or on the contrary

---

[42] 'Cette thèse [...] semble bien plutôt de nature cartésienne et se référer au libre arbitre. Elle s'accorde avec ce préjugé commun qui conduit les hommes à se figurer que le corps est à la disposition de l'Ame', M. Gueroult, *Spinoza*, vol. II, *L'Ame*, p. 572. Furthermore, Gueroult points out that the expression *vestigia intellectus* echoes the expression 'vestiges de la pensée pure' that Descartes uses in a letter to Arnauld from 28 July 1648, ibid., p. 573.

[43] Nevertheless, the possibility cannot be excluded that, in addressing himself to a correspondent who belongs to the milieu of what has been called the 'Cartesian-Spinozists', and having chosen – as he himself underscores – to not provide a rigorous demonstration, Spinoza has formulated his own thesis in a Cartesian-like language to make its essential content more easily accessible to his interlocutor.

[44] 'Quamdiu affectibus, qui nostrae naturae sunt contrarii, non conflictamus, tamdiu potestatem habemus ordinandi et concatendandi corporis affectiones secundum ordinem ad intellectum', *Ethics* V, 10, G II, p. 287, ll. 4–7 [CWS I, 601].

according to the relations that emerge from those of their aspects that can be explained by our nature alone. In the first case, we obtain a juxtaposition that, properly speaking, is of the order of the body, or the order of the imagination – that is, the order of exteriority. In the universe of the given, it is obviously this order that is the more common one. In the second case, we obtain logical links between bodies – that is, links that are 'the physical equivalent of rational deduction'.[45] We thus see how it is possible to link together the affections of the body *ad intellectu.*

What is valid for images is valid for language as well, at least negatively: we can no longer say that the simple association of language with the imagination suffices to make language a definitive agent of inadequation. We need only affirm that, in the order of the given, language is most often the vehicle of inadequate ideas, and that, moreover, it helps forge new inadequate ideas – all of which amply justifies the critique that is made of it. But it is also not impossible for the imagination to organise itself by expressing the order of adequation, by way of the play of the *conatus*. It is only that this is a very weak possibility in the order of the given, one that can be reinforced only by the common transformation of the body and the soul in the course of the extension of reason's power.

C. The Double Image

We still need to determine how this transformation occurs in the case of language. Yet, this is more than a matter of understanding how a philosophical language is constituted. If philosophers can make language capable of expressing adequate ideas, it is by taking up and transforming an instrument that has been created by others.[46] What we must first understand, then, is how the language of the crowd is itself constituted, in particular because important information is transmitted by this language, and because its inadequation can be limited and neutralised. Finally, we must also determine how it is possible for people to understand one another, for if language is tied to the body of each individual, it must be marked to such a degree by this body's individuality that it becomes necessary to explain how, despite everything, it can fulfil its communicative function.[47]

---

[45] 'l'équivalent physique de la déduction rationnelle', A. Matheron, *Individu et Communauté chez Spinoza*, p. 559. For everything concerning Proposition 10, I am following very closely Matheron's luminous commentary, ibid., pp. 557–60.

[46] 'Vulgus vocabula primum invenit, quae postea a philosophis usurpantur', CM, I, Chapter VI, G I, p. 246, ll. 18–19 [CM I; CWS I, 312].

[47] Among those who have written on Spinoza and language, it is A. Dominguez who has most clearly highlighted the importance of this question of language as an instrument

We must therefore examine more closely the relations between language, the imagination and adequation. This is all the more necessary since the critiques of language that I enumerated above remain largely descriptive. It is not enough to affirm that words belong to the register of the imagination if we wish to understand why, precisely, they remain attached to it, why they reinforce it, and by what means they contribute to the formation of general ideas – not to mention in what way misunderstandings can arise, indeed contradictions in terms. So long as we fail to answer these questions, we will remain in the order of *historiola*. We might even wonder if these critiques are coherent among themselves.[48]

To respond to these questions, we need to first know what particular type of image language is. Spinoza nowhere gives us an answer to this question – and indeed he does not need to, since his goal in the *Ethics* is not to construct a specific theory of language.[49] But we can try to reconstitute it on the basis of the examples that he does give. Let us reread the double illustration from the Scholium on memory.[50] We will thus be putting a question to the text that is not the same as the one Spinoza is himself addressing. It is not illegitimate to pose this question, since Spinoza deals with it in passing; but by bringing this question to the fore, we will be separating what Spinoza himself unifies, and it is this act of dislocation that will prove to be instructive for us. Memory links ideas together according to the order of the body's affections. It thus presupposes above all the following trait, which is common to every imaginative effect: the relation between an image (the affection of the body, that is, its modification by an external thing) and an idea (the idea of this affection, which must not be confused with the adequate idea of the external thing). This is not the place to demonstrate that this relation is not causal in nature. The problem that Spinoza wants to illustrate at this juncture is the following one: how can two ideas be joined together in the

---

of communication. Cf. his study 'Lenguaje y hermeneutica en Spinoza', *Miscelanea Comillas*, XXXVI/69 (1978), pp. 301–25, in particular pp. 302–7.

[48] For example, it does not go without saying that it is legitimate to criticise a phenomenon by asserting both that it is tied to the necessity of the order of images and that it produces certain effects (the *circulus quadratus*) that are, properly speaking, unimaginable. It might be thought that it is possible to get around this problem by rejecting the quotation from the *Cogitata* in the Cartesian-like early writings. The persistence of the example in other contexts seems to me to prevent this. We will see moreover that this is not necessary.

[49] Cf. the beginning of Book II: 'Non quidem omnia . . .', G II, p. 84, l. 8 [*Ethics* II, Praef.; CWS I, 446].

[50] 'Hinc clare intelligimus, quid sit memoria', *Ethics* II, 18, Schol., G II, p. 106, l. 35 [CWS I, 465].

soul of an individual following the order, not of what is currently happening to the body, but of what has long since happened to this body. A Roman who hears the word *pomum* thinks of a fruit. A soldier or a peasant who sees the trace of a horse in the sand thinks either of war or of work in the field. The two examples are tied together in the Scholium by an explanation that is valid for both (namely, habit) and they are assimilated by means of the expression 'And in this way each of us . . .'.[51] In the eyes of the author, then, the two examples appear to say the same thing: all of the characters cited associate one image with another, because their bodies have previously and often been affected by the two images at the same time. However, if we look more closely, a number of traits allow us to distinguish between the two examples. The peasant who associates the image of a horseshoe on the sand with that of a plough links two different images that he himself recognises as being different and which, in his soul, evoke two different things. This is the case even if his life and his work have constituted him such that he links them. The Roman who associates the phonic image constituted by the word *pomum* with the visual image of the fruit links together two images that for him are not different and that correspond to a single idea. Certainly, it is possible to think of the word separately, to inquire into its sonorous character or, if it is a written word, to investigate the form of the letters composing it. At that point, however, we would be dealing with a metalanguage and the word would no longer be playing its role as a word. When it does play this role, it corresponds to no other idea besides the idea of the thing that the visual image represents to us. A modification of our body (the word) is associated by habit with another modification of our body (the image of the thing), which it evokes and refers to. Language thus has the particularity of not only tying together an idea and an image: it ties together an idea with *two* images.[52]

[51] 'Et sic unusquisque', etc., ibid., p. 107, l. 21 [*Ethics* II, 18, Schol.; *CWS* I, 466].

[52] It might be objected that because of parallelism, there corresponds to the external extended thing an idea in the attribute Thought, and that to this thing that is equally external and extended – the word that is said – there corresponds another idea in the attribute Thought. This is perfectly correct, but what these ideas *are* does not condition the ideas that we *have* (just as there exists a difference between the idea that is our soul and the idea that we have of our soul in the order of the given). We could displace this objection and note that to the modification of our body by the external thing there corresponds an idea that we possess, whereas to the modification of our body by the extended word there corresponds another, which is distinct. In principle this is correct, but it can happen that these ideas are not distinct for us, and this authorises us to consider them as a unique (and certainly inadequate) idea. The same cannot be said, obviously, for the horse and war in the mind of the soldier.

The word is thus like the image of an image.[53] This suffices to distinguish it from other effects of the imagination.[54] This also suffices to radically distinguish Spinoza's theses from those of all other theoreticians of language. For the latter, words represent things (this is the case for Vossius[55] and, in part, for Leibniz)[56] or the ideas of things (this is the case for Aristotle).[57] For Spinoza, words represent the affections of the body. It is only by the intermediary of these affections that they can have any relation to things or ideas.[58] This does not prevent words from being misleading (we have seen ample evidence of this above), but it does pose in a quite different way the problem of their nature and of how to understand them – and thus the problem of linguistic error and its correction.

A second difference also appears if we read the text attentively. Spinoza begins by stating in a general way that in the chains of images, or the chains of thought that follow the order of images, we pass 'from the thought of one thing, immediately [. . .] to the thought of another, which has no likeness to the first'.[59] The absence of *similitudo* thus characterises all of these sequences. This negative characteristic is the counterpart of a positive characteristic: habit. However, when Spinoza gives examples, we notice that he does not strictly hold to this principle in the two cases. In fact, with the example of

---

[53] Rigorously speaking, this expression is imprecise. The word that is heard is the image in our body of the word that is pronounced. But it fulfils its function only if it appears to us as the image of the other modification of our body, which it accompanies and refers to, before referring to it then evoking it.

[54] With respect to these other effects of the imagination, there can also exist connections between images, but these are not constitutive. On the contrary, there is language only if there is a connection between these two modifications of the body.

[55] 'Verba, rerum symbola', *De philologia*, Amsterdam, 1660, p. 30. On the question of what Spinoza might have imbibed of the theory of language from the humanist culture of his time and in particular from Vossius, see the remarkable summary by F. Biasutti, *La dottrina della scienza in Spinoza*, Bologna: Pàtron, 1979, pp. 140–5.

[56] Cf. *New Essays On Human Understanding*, Book III, Chapter 9: the knowledge of languages makes possible the knowledge of things since 'their properties are often reflected in their names (as can be seen from the names of plants among different nations)', p. 343.

[57] 'Words spoken are symbols or signs of affections or impressions of the soul', Aristotle, *On Interpretation*, Chapter I, 16a.

[58] When he calls them *signa rerum*, it is to clarify that 'they are only signs of things as they are in the imagination, but not as they are in the understanding', *TdIE*, § 89, G II, p. 33, ll. 13–15 [*TdIE* 89; *CWS* I, 38].

[59] 'Cur mens ex cogitatione unius rei statim in alterius rei cogitationem incidat, quae nullam cum priore habet similitudinem', G II, p. 107, ll. 14–16 [*Ethics* II, 18, Schol.; *CWS* I, 466].

the *pomum*, he explicitly repeats the statement of principle and speaks of 'the thought of the fruit, which has no similarity to that articulate sound'.[60] By contrast, he no longer alludes to this principle in the second example. Is this an ellipsis, or an irrelevant point? What it shows above all is that, from this perspective as well, the two cases are very different. If we understand *similitudo* in the very strict sense of an identity of forms, or an identity of causes, it is true that all of the links between images lack *similitudo*. In this sense, the horseman does not resemble his horse, and neither do the images of war. This justifies the general affirmation stated prior to the two examples. On the other hand, if we understand *similitudo* in a less precise sense as the relation between two images that belong to the same register, or that possess points of commonality, then we can see that the two examples are not situated at the same level: there are common points between the horse and its plough, or between the horse, the horseman and war – an identity of functions, the integration into a common category made up of various facts that are often tied together. These facts possess internal determinations that make it legitimate to associate them with the same universe. But there is nothing of this type between the articulated sound and the physical thing that is seen or felt. This is not a question of degree: in one case, the relation is purely arbitrary, and this is why Spinoza repeats his formula by clarifying the difference in nature between the thing and the phonic image; in the other, by contrast, the absence of similarity does not imply a total heterogeneity.

There is a third difference as well. When Spinoza speaks of the inscription of habit in the body, he gives a general rule that is valid for all imaginative effects. Yet, once again, the consideration of the two examples shows that he applies this rule in very different ways. If the peasant and the soldier associate different images with the traces left by the horse, it is because they do not have the same biography. The body in which memory is inscribed is thus an individual body. We can certainly group individuals together in the same categories and even describe collective imaginaries, but in principle these are always on the verge of fragmenting: individual history remains the criterion for the learning and deciphering of signs. By contrast, the Roman who hears the word *pomum* hears something that was constituted before him – something that others had pronounced and heard in an identical form. If his body is often affected by the same sound at the same time as by another thing, it is because the association of one with the other is already constituted as a collective fact before he has even gained access to it. In other

---

[60] 'Qui nullam cum articulato sono habet similitudinem', ibid., ll. 17–18 [*Ethics* II, 18, Schol.; CWS I, 466].

words, the criterion for learning and deciphering words is a fundamentally collective phenomenon.

I have thus identified three differences that ground the specificity of words within the general category of images. The first is the difference that means that signification links two images that refer to the same idea. The second and third are obviously complementary: the link between these two images is arbitrary, and it can subsist despite this arbitrariness thanks only to a collective consistency that takes the place of biographical homogeneity.

Having arrived at this point, we can now draw two conclusions. The first is that if one accepts what has just been demonstrated, then it is possible to explain and unify the different negative effects of language that we have encountered above in a descriptive state.

We can now understand how language transmits and perpetuates the errors of the imagination. As we know, the imagination is essentially variable to the degree that the body is submitted to all kinds of fluctuations. This variability is one source of the unhappiness of the life of the passions, but at the same time it has a positive side: common notions are all the more easily distinguished from the fluid backdrop of inadequate ideas. By indexing an image to an unchanging phonic image, the word produces multiple effects of memory and thus helps the imagination resist common notions. We can now also understand how language contributes to the mechanisms of the formation of general ideas. Such ideas are constituted only by erasing differences between singular beings. How can these differences continue to exist in the face of specific singular things that make a powerful impression on our body? A name chosen arbitrarily allows these things to reappear more easily each time they are summoned; it thus reinforces the impression of obviousness that general categories possess. Finally, we can also better understand how an expression like 'square circle' can come about: it puts into relation two images that are habitually associated at the phonic level with two distinct visual images whose characteristics are mutually exclusive. As a complex phonic image, the 'square circle' is not internally contradictory: it merely concatenates three syllables, that is all. It is therefore not physically impossible to form it.[61] From the understanding's point of view, it is not contradictory either: it simply signifies nothing. To what extent can we say that, while existing in the form of a word, the 'square circle' is unimaginable? The obstacle that the visual imagination comes up against is the fact that each element of the 'square circle' necessarily summons, by a simultaneous

---

[61] And there is obviously in thought an idea of the words 'square circle'. But it is not an idea *of* the square circle.

connection, a visual image that excludes another. We are thus dealing here with a case of *fluctuatio imaginationis*. There is no adequate idea that corresponds to this formula, but there is an unstable inadequate idea – an idea as unstable as the image that this fluctuation produces.

Consequently, with respect to the three major effects that link the word to inadequation, we can now move from the descriptive to the explanatory level. However, at the same time as the critique of language is grounded, it is simultaneously limited, for we can also understand that the mechanisms in question do not wholly prevent communication; we can thus seek out the means for mastering these mechanisms. This is why it is not unthinkable for Spinoza to juxtapose his critique of words with a work *on* language (specifically on the comprehension of language and of Scripture), along with a work *of* language (that is, an elaboration of a philosophical language), both of which presuppose an at least partly positive relation with the order of words.

Thus, the second consequence of what we have just established is that we are now able to begin envisaging the practical problems that Spinoza confronts with respect to language, and to understand the perspective from which he confronts them. Spinoza himself gives us an indication of this when he evokes with respect to Scripture those words whose meaning has been lost.[62] The relation between words and ideas is therefore not exhausted by the question of adequation. This relation is also temporal. In the relation between the first image (and thus also the idea) and the phonic or written image, there is a before and an after. The thickness of duration inserts itself into the relations between words and their meaning. Now, as we know, the receptacle of the past is experience, and it is also experience that permits the neutralisation of inadequation. If there exists at the root of language something irreducibly arbitrary, but about which time can teach us, then we sense that the opposition between adequation and inadequation is no longer entirely pertinent. This opposition accounts for one aspect of language (that which concerns the question: to what degree does language translate ideas?), but language brings with it other dimensions too (those that concern questions like: what meaning does such-and-such a language confer upon a word? Or: how should we understand the words that have been transmitted to us?). Here, it is less a matter of knowledge than of noting that certain equivalences have for a long time been present and known. We thus find ourselves on the terrain of existing facts, and, insofar as we are unable to deduce these facts from an *a priori* essence, we are consequently on

---

[62] 'Sed si postea usus ita pereat, ut verba nullam habeant significationem . . .', *TTP*, Chapter XII, G III, p. 160, ll. 24–5 [*TTP* XII, 1; *CWS* II, 250].

the terrain of experience. If words can be associated with multiple images, it will not be impossible to make a list of these associations. Indeed, as we will see, arguing on the basis of such lists is for Spinoza a fundamental requirement for the study of language. Here again it is experiential reasoning that will dictate the method required to constitute such lists and decide between the solutions they propose.

We can now relativise the critique of words with which we began. This critique is incontestably valid, but only within certain limits: those of the sphere of geometrical reasoning. Outside of these limits, there opens up the domain of work on language, which allows us to develop an archaeology of meaning, an analytic of texts, and even a reflection on natural languages. As for knowing what the dimension of experience represents with respect to the question of language, it is useless to seek it on our own, as Spinoza himself provides an answer to this question. In fact, he elaborates a theory of the *use* of language that represents his attempt to account for the existence of entities in the domain of meaning.

It is thus the articulation between the deductive and the experiential modes that helps us understand why Spinoza can at once develop the critique of language that we referred to above while also signalling his interest in empirical languages and in everything they transmit. Spinoza can – and indeed must – construct instruments to approach these languages in their irreducible materiality.[63] These languages are therefore in no way considered as equivalent to one other. Thus, the work on *Hebrew Grammar*, the 'philological' or 'hermeneutical' chapters from the *TTP* and other scattered reflections on language and the meaning of names, no longer appear as juxtaposed to the activity of the philosopher. They constitute an integral part of this activity; and their modes and status are indicated by the system itself.

---

[63] From this perspective Spinoza distinguishes himself from Descartes: the letter to Mersenne from 20 November 1629 only envisages as an effective work on languages the construction (which is *de jure* thinkable but *de facto* impossible) of a universal language founded on the order of notions – in opposition to empirical languages where 'les mots que nous avons n'ont quasi que des significations confuses, auxquelles l'esprit des hommes s'étant accoutumé de longue main, cela est cause qu'il n'entend presque rien parfaitement'. Similarly, Hobbes, in the chapter 'Of Speech' (I, V) from the *Leviathan*, mentions Babelian diversity in passing, but draws no consequences from this: his analysis of the uses and abuses of language occurs entirely at the deductive level, and, thirty chapters later, the philological and hermeneutical analyses of the words 'spirit', 'angel', 'God's word', etc., occur in abstraction from any specific reference to an empirical language.

2. Use of Life, Use of Language

What now remains to be done is to consider how Spinoza deals practically with words and language. How does he name the realities he studies? How does he organise those effects of language that are the materials of Scripture? What argumentative strategies does he use when studying grammar or rhetoric? We will thus come to know whether we are dealing with reason or experience, and in what form.

A. *The Names of the Passions*

A persistent question runs throughout Book III of the *Ethics*: that of the names of the passions. Spinoza is dealing with a subject – the passions – which he did not invent. He deals with this subject in Latin, an already constituted language replete with a stock of denominations in this domain. Both philosophers and common language have already constituted lists of the passions. Whoever writes on this subject cannot ignore these lists: a ready-made nomenclature exists; and while it might be possible to modify it, it is not possible to suppress it.[64] Now, with regards to this pre-existing nomenclature, Spinoza constantly refers to two traits: first, that this nomenclature is both insufficient (there are more passions than names) but also that it is occasionally redundant (certain passions have multiples names); and second, that it is organised not according to the nature of the passions themselves but by reference to their effects – that is, to the way that they form part of the use of life. Neither the first nor the second of these two remarks contradicts the critique of language we analysed above, though Spinoza's approach does inflect this critique in a new direction.

That there are more passions than names for them is not surprising if we consider that the imagination cannot grasp a large number of individual differences. Thus, the complex passions remain for the most part anonymous.

---

[64] Cf. Gertrud Jung, *Spinozas Affektenlehre*, Diss., Berlin 1926, in particular p. 63, where she notes, with respect to the influence of Descartes on the definition of the passions in the *Short Treatise*: 'Sie [= die Affektbestimmungen] sind jahrundertealtes Erbgut. Ihr sprachliches Gewandt ist – als Ausdruck immer gleicher Erfahrungen – nicht auf eine bestimmte Mode und auf eine bestimmte Person zugeschnitten. Es ist zeitlos und unpersönlich. Nur durch geschickten Ausputz wird es dem Geschmack des Trägers und dem Stil seiner Zeit angepaßt.' Jung in fact distinguishes within this heritage Aristotle, the Stoics, Saint Thomas, Vivès and Descartes. On the question of Descartes' influence in particular, see S. H. Voss, 'How Spinoza Enumerated the Affects', *Archiv für Geschichte der Philosophie*, 63 (1981), pp. 167–79.

When wonder is joined to fear, to prudence, anger or love, the tradition places only a few names at our disposal. But if it is joined to hatred, to hope or confidence, 'we can deduce more Affects than those which are usually indicated by the accepted words'.[65] Similarly, the Definition of the Affects in the last part of Book III ends with the following restrictive remark: 'I pass over in silence the definitions of Jealousy and the other vacillations of the soul, both because they arise from the composition of affects we have already defined, and because most of them do not have names.'[66] This preconstituted language is therefore less rich than natural reality is. Yet, inversely, on other points, this preconstituted language appears to be superabundant. Thus, at the beginning of the same definitions of the affects, after having surveyed desire, joy and sadness, Spinoza adds the definitions of wonder and disdain; and he says that even though he in no way considers wonder and disdain to be affects[67] he is obliged to speak of them given linguistic use: 'I have spoken of Wonder only because it has become customary for some to indicate the affects derived from these three by other names when they are related to objects we wonder at.'[68] Once again, it is linguistic use that makes it necessary to distinguish emulation from imitation, while from a genetic perspective there is only one single thing: 'not because we know that emulation has one cause and imitation another, but because it has come about by use that we call emulous only him who imitates what we judge to be honorable, useful, or pleasant'.[69] Whoever engages with the Latin description

---

[65] 'Et ad hunc modum concipere etiam possumus odium, spem, securitatem et alios effectus admirationi junctos; adque adeo plures affectus deducere poterimus, quam qui receptis vocabulis indicari solent', *Ethics* III, 52, Schol., G II, p. 180, ll. 27–30 [*CWS* I, 524]. Similarly, for mockery: 'Possumus denique amorem, spem, gloriam et alios affectus junctos contemptui concipere atque inde alios praeterea affectus deducere, quos etiam nullo singulari vacabulo ab aliis distinguere solemus', ibid., p. 181, ll. 14–17 [*CWS* I, 524].

[66] 'Definitiones zelotypiae et reliquarum animi fluctuationum silentio praetermitto, tam quia ex compositione affectuum, quos jam definivimus, oriuntur, quam quia pleraeque nomina non habent', *Ethics* III, DA #48, Exp., G II, p. 203, ll. 16–19 [*CWS* I, 542].

[67] These are simple modifications (*affectiones*) of the soul, and not *affectus*, as is indicated by the Scholium from Proposition 52.

[68] 'Nec alia de causa verba de admiratione feci, quam quia usu factum est, ut quidam affectus, qui ex tribus primitivis derivantur, aliis nominibus indicari soleant, quando ad objecta, quae admiramur, referuntur', *Ethics* III, DA #4, Exp., G II, p. 192, ll. 8–11 [*CWS* I, 532].

[69] Whoever flees or is scared because they see others flee or be fearful, 'eum imitari quidem alterius affectum, sed non eumdem aemulari dicemus ; non quia aliam aemulationis, aliam imitationis novimus causam, sed quia usu factum est, ut illum tantum vocemus aemulum, qui id, quod honestum, utile, vel jucundum esse judicamus, imitatur', *Ethics*

of the passions thus finds themselves faced with a language that, sometimes through excess and sometimes through lack, fails to precisely coincide with the nature of the objects it speaks of. However, this absence of coincidence is not unthinkable. There is a reason for it, or at least a name for this reason, one that we have already encountered twice: use.

This use of language is not arbitrary, and it has its own cause: the use of life. This is because the effects of certain passions are more important since they attract our attention and occupy a more prominent place in the lexicon. While a purely scientific terminology would be established on the basis of the nature of the affects alone, common language is based on the consequences of the affects in our lives. Here we find the play of encounters that distributes the various roles of the imagination. Thus, in the Scholium that refers to the anonymity of the many composites of wonder, Spinoza immediately adds: 'So it is clear that the names of the affects are found more from the ordinary use [of words] than from an accurate knowledge [of the affects].'[70] The definitions of the affects will repeat this point with regards to erroneous oppositions: 'We are, nevertheless, accustomed to oppose Humility [and not, as should be the case, despondency] to Pride.'[71] And if impudence wrongly passes for its opposite, namely prudishness, it is because 'the names of the affects are guided more by use than by nature'.[72] Lastly, on the topic of those fluctuations of the soul that also remain anonymous, Spinoza adds: 'it is sufficient for practical purposes to know them only in general'.[73] The use of language is thus conditioned by the use of life, and the latter reveals both the way language functions and its interests.

If this is so, then we can no longer quite represent the various discordances between words and things solely as an effect of the power of the imagination. They certainly are effects of the imagination, but such effects obey laws and

---

III, DA #33, Exp., G II, p. 200, ll. 12–19 [CWS I, 539]. The terms *dicemus*, *vocemus*, clearly indicate that it is a matter of a pure problem of language. [Translator's note: I have replaced Curley's term 'usage' with 'use', both here and in every other instance, for reasons of uniformity.]

[70] 'Unde apparet, affectuum nomina inventa esse magis ex eorum vulgari usu, quam ex eorumdem accurata cognitione', *Ethics* III, 52, Schol., G II, p. 180, ll. 30–2 [CWS I, 523].

[71] 'Solemus tamen saepe superbiae humilitatem opponere, sed tum magis ad utriusque effectus quam naturam attendimus', *Ethics*, III, DA #19, Exp., G II, p. 198, ll. 26–7 [CWS I, 538].

[72] 'Sed affectuum nomina (ut jam monui) magis eorum usum quam naturam respiciunt', *Ethics* III, DA #31, Exp., G II, p. 19, ll. 16–18 [CWS I, 538].

[73] 'Quod ostendit ad usum vitae sufficere, easdem in genere tantummodo noscere', *Ethics* III, DA #48, Schol., G II, p. 203, ll. 19–20 [CWS I, 542].

refer to a specific reality, not to a source of irrationality. The general tonality of Spinoza's reflections on the language of the passions refers less to the impossibility of speaking adequately of them, and more to the recognition of a specific resistance or solidity that is proper to the linguistic level. Prior to being an instrument or an obstacle, language is a reality that has its own systematic structure with its own causes that exist before we begin to speak it and which we have to take into account. To demand that language be purely and simply transparent, or to complain that it is not, would be to make it an *imperium in imperio*.

As such, we can expect that in other texts Spinoza will analyse this linguistic reality and its singular consistency for itself. Now, this consistency presents two interesting traits. On the one hand, it presupposes in each person a foundation in their biography and, at the level of the collective, in a history. This consistency presents itself as an unsurpassable inheritance from the past. On the other hand, a word refers less to the idea or to the image (that is, to a process of knowledge) than it does to the system of oppositions, derivations or vital marks that tie it to other words. The two traits proper to language – as the culmination of a history and as the site of our insertion into the common world – cannot but recall what we know of experience. We can thus expect language to present the positive traits that we are familiar with in experience: for example, to bar the route to certain errors, to neutralise inadequation, and to transcend the corporeal individual.

This is indeed what happens in the *TTP*. Spinoza speaks frequently of language in this book – not to denounce language, but rather to use it as an instrument in the service of his research.[74] In the *Treatise* as in the *Hebrew Grammar*, use has many positive functions, none of which contradict the theoretical critique of the status of words. On the whole, however, these positive functions outline an historical field that is irreducible to the sole problem of error.

B. Use as the Guardian and Interpreter of a Language

If we consider the arguments that underwrite Spinoza's textual critique, we realise that it is essential to begin by establishing a distinction between meaning [*sens*] and signification [*signification*]. Spinoza does not always mobilise this distinction explicitly, but the necessity of this distinction appears if we compare the different texts in question. This distinction is more fundamental in Spinoza than the distinction between meaning and truth or

---

[74] S. Zac already noted this in his article cited above, 'Spinoza et le langage', p. 613.

between literal meaning and metaphor. Note first of all that Spinoza always speaks of signification in the singular while he often speaks of meaning in the plural, and that when he uses the singular of sense – *sensus* – it is often by qualifying it with an adjective,[75] thus suggesting that it refers to one meaning [*sens*] among many. Put differently, a word has one signification but it can have many meanings. Elsewhere Spinoza occasionally opposes the signification of words to the meaning of texts.[76] The context shows that this opposition refers, on the one hand, to the (more or less fixed) series of a word's possible meanings, and on the other hand to the general meaning that emerges from a text on the basis of the organisation of its words. A word's signification is thus like a fan of meanings between which one must choose relative to the appropriate context. But the context does not create the meaning from nothing: the signification is in some sense the ensemble of possible meanings.[77] It is thus predetermined prior to the reading or interpretation of a text. With reference to this principle, we can reconcile apparently contradictory formulas such as those where Spinoza says that we can[78] and cannot[79] change the signification of a word. In the second case, it is a matter of changing the meaning that prevails within the bounds of this signification. To this end, Spinoza uses the formula *certa significatio*, which should be understood as referring to a text's meaning [*sens*] as the determination of its signification.[80] In sum, the means by which Spinoza expresses this distinction are sometimes unstable, but the distinction itself seems to be fundamentally rigorous.

Why does the signification of a single word have a plurality of meanings? It is quite easy to reconstruct the reasons for this. Because of metaphor or association, the word slips from one image to another, from the concrete to the abstract, and indeed from historical allusions to everyday points of reference. There is nothing surprising about this if we remember that, by virtue of its very constitution, a word can be linked to many different images – and thus to the ideas that correspond to them. It could thus be said that

---

[75] 'Wind' is the *sensus genuinus* of *ruagh*, in opposition to other meanings that are 'mind', 'will' and 'passion', etc., *TTP*, Chapter I, G III, p. 21, l. 31 [*TTP* I, 26; *CWS* II, 85].

[76] *TTP*, Chapter VII, G III, p. 105, l. 33; p. 106, l. 5 [*TTP* VII, 40; *CWS* II, 179].

[77] Thus, when Spinoza asks, in the middle of the first chapter, 'quid significat vox hebraea ruagh', he enumerates a series of *sensus* that respond to this question. He then does the same for the fact of relating a thing to God, then for the expression 'the mind of God'.

[78] *TTP*, Chapter VII, G III, p. 105 [*TTP* VII, 40; *CWS* II, 179].

[79] *TTP*, Chapter XII, G III, p. 160 [*TTP* XIII, 11; *CWS* II, 250].

[80] *TTP*, Chapter XII, G III, p. 160, ll. 21–2 [*TTP* XIII, 11; *CWS* II, 250].

the first experience we have of signification is not of its obscurity, but of the paradoxical connection between its clarity and its uncertainty. We can perfectly well understand the signification of a word while at the same time being uncertain with regards to what it means. 'The Spirit of God was hovering over the water' is a sentence that is perfectly clear: it is well-constructed, and each of its words has a signification. Nevertheless, so long as I am unaware of the plurality of meanings of the word 'spirit' and do not know how to choose between them, I cannot understand with precision what the author of this phrase means. Reciprocally, two expressions that have different significations ('the house of God' and 'the house of iniquity') can refer to the same object – that is, can possess the same meaning.[81] This is why it is necessary to go so far as to say that for Spinoza clear phrases pose more problems than obscure ones. In fact, if a phrase is definitively obscure, it is lost as far as its meaning is concerned.[82] Yet, with respect to an entire book, this loss does not necessary affect the meaning of the whole.[83] On the other hand, a clear sentence offers an abundance of possibilities between which one must choose.

How can we come to know all of these possibilities and decide between them? Reason can warn us of the possibility of a plurality of meanings. When the content of this plurality is known – that is, when we possess the list of the different meanings a given word has in a certain language – reason can, by drawing on the context and other criteria, determine which meaning is the correct one within the phrase at hand. But it is not reason that will dictate the predetermined list of meanings of a word in a language. Spinoza's position on this point is very clear: only use can teach us this.[84] It might well be possible to predict that a given metaphor is possible, but use alone will be able to show us that such a meaning actually exists. What matters is that the analysis of the stock of meanings possessed by a word is in principle anterior to the analysis of a text. Now, this analysis does not arise from reason; it arises from experience. And for good reason, for in conformity with what Letter X says, this analysis concerns things that exist.

It is these distinctions that are at work in the numerous passages where Spinoza offers concrete analyses of texts and above all of the facts of language that they constitute. In these passages, *usus* seems to fulfil three functions:

---

[81] *TTP*, Chapter XII, G III, p. 160, 1. 14–20 [*TTP* XII, 10; *CWS* II, 250].
[82] *TTP*, Chapter VII, G III, p. 106, 1. 24 ff. [*TTP* VII, 45; *CWS* II, 180].
[83] *TTP*, Chapter VII, G III, p. 111, 1. 8 ff. [*TTP* VII, 65; *CWS* II, 185].
[84] 'Verba ex solo usu certam habent significationem', *TTP*, Chapter XII, G III, p. 160, ll. 21–2 [*TTP* XII, 11; *CWS* II, 250].

it is the interpreter of words, the witness to history, and the guardian of language.

The Interpreter of Words. One could cite here all of the discussions where Spinoza seeks to establish the multiple significations of words – prophet,[85] spirit,[86] life[87] – while exegetes isolate only one meaning, making it imaginarily *the* meaning. The procedure is always the same: the first error committed by Spinoza's adversaries is to inflate a single meaning of a word with the plenitude of signification. Occasionally, however, Spinoza explains the method he is using. In Chapter VII of the *TTP*, he ask what the 'meaning' of the Scriptures signifies, and he insists that it is necessary to distinguish meaning from truth. This is a classical distinction. Yet Spinoza renews it precisely by taking as his primary object the meaning of words as distinct from their signification, and by invoking the notion of *usus* as a way of deciding between meaning and signification. To seek the truth of things is to ask oneself what a thing really is, or, if it is an event, whether it really happened. By contrast, to seek the meaning of a phrase is only to ask oneself what the author meant to say with these words. But in order to know how the author was using these words, we first have to know the list of possible empirical meanings for these words in his language. When Moses says: 'God is a fire', or 'God is jealous', it is by referring to use that we can know what meanings these words can have in Hebrew.[88] Thus, the expression offers a handful of possible meanings, but it is use that allows us to choose between them so as to determine what the author meant. We then see that what he wanted to say was above all what he was able to say. Against those who would immediately seek to interpret these lines as if they were metaphorical – such people would say that it's impossible for God to be a fire or to be jealous – Spinoza refuses to accept that the key alternative is between the literal and the figural. Rather, the most important alternative is between the possible and the impossible meanings of a word or phase in a given language. Only *usus* will tell us if a given metaphor really exists in Hebrew. If it does exist, then Reason will be able to include it in its interpretation. If it does not exist, then it will be necessary to read the word in terms of its literal meaning. There is thus something irreducible about linguistic material that Reason must recognise – just as Reason recognises the existence of passions of or atmospheric phenomena – but about which only use can teach us.

---

[85] *TTP*, Chapter I, G III, p. 15 [*TTP* I, 1; *CWS* II, 76].
[86] *TTP*, Chapter I, G III, p. 21 ff. [*TTP* I, 26; *CWS* II, 85]
[87] *TTP*, Chapter IV, G III, p. 66, ll. 27–8 [*TTP* IV, 41; *CWS* II, 136].
[88] *TTP*, Chapter VII, G III, pp. 100–1 [*TTP* VII, 18, 19, 20, 21, 22; *CWS* II, 173–5].

The Witness to History. The inventory of a word's meanings might lead one to believe in a static conception of signification. Indeed, the majority of Spinoza's examples seem to suppose that the list of a word's meanings remains stable, the reason being that this stability is the surest guarantee against the arbitrariness of those who would wish to interpret texts according to their own fantasies and without any linguistic criteria. But there is at least one text of Spinoza's where we see use intervene to attest to an historical evolution: the analysis of the expressions 'the house of God' and 'the house of iniquity'. It is use alone that shows us that these two formulas refer to the same object. In fact, they refer to different moments in history: the first to Jacob's prayer, and the second to the time of the sacrifices made to false idols.[89] In this example, the historical nature of the change in meaning is mentioned but without being foregrounded. However, immediately after this it returns to the spotlight: Spinoza envisages the possibility that the meanings of words can purely and simply disappear, or indeed change into their contrary. Spinoza gives no examples of this, for the object of his reflections here is not of a purely linguistic order: he is only concerned to prove that the same words (or the same verbal envelope) can lead, following the changes in meaning that they undergo, to piety or not – and thus whether or not they merit the epithet 'sacred'. Spinoza thus evokes linguistic change not for itself but as an occasion for judging the book that contains these words. Nevertheless, Spinoza does make an effort to explain how words can change their meaning: either they lose their meaning if their use is lost, or they take on an opposite signification if the use of this opposed signification 'prevails'.[90] Thus, when he takes historical change into account, Spinoza does not contradict his initial statements. Both the identification of change and the inventory of diachronic meanings follow a single rule: *usus*. The modification of meaning is not given as the result of an individual initiative – even if it can have such an initiative as its occasion – for in order to conquer its own consistency, it must pass into the tissue of collective associations constituted by use.

The Guardian of Language. When it comes to the evolution of a language, the power of a single individual is thus limited. This is why there are two kinds of tradition: the tradition that transmits teachings or facts through the intermediary of language; and the tradition that is constituted by the use of language itself. While the first can be doubted, the second can be trusted. In the classical age, the orthodox defenders of Scriptural invariability insisted

---

[89] *TTP*, Chapter XII, G III, p. 160, ll. 14–19 [*TTP* XII, 9; *CWS* II, 250].
[90] *TTP*, Chapter XII, G III, p. 160, ll. 20–30 [*TTP* XII, 11; *CWS* II, 250].

on and became indignant about the first thesis. Spinoza – and with him the entire lineage that runs from Saumur to Richard Simon – introduced into sacred philology all of the findings of textual critique, thereby challenging the supposed inalterability of the biblical text. But this first thesis masked a second thesis, which was its limit and condition: changes in language cannot be thought in terms of alteration, and the linguistic material itself resists any attempt to bend it to a conscious design.

It is thus impossible to change a language voluntarily. The fortune of the theme of the imposter is well known in the seventeenth and eighteenth centuries. Spinoza imposes a limit on this theme: there are things that cannot be altered and it is precisely use that guarantees this. The theme of the imposter supposes a voluntaristic conception of human action. However a text might be corrupted (and there are innumerable ways for this to happen, since to modify a manuscript, whether voluntarily or through a lack of attention, is a matter of individual activity), one must suppose, in contrast to this, a tradition that is pure of all corruption. This tradition is language itself. There are two reasons for language's purity: on the one hand, 'it could never be to anyone's advantage to change the meaning of a word; but it could often be to someone's advantage to change the meaning of an utterance';[91] on the other hand, even if someone wanted to change a word's meaning, they would be faced with an almost impossible task since it would be necessary to falsify all of the texts by all of the authors who had ever used this word according to its received meaning. This last clarification helps us better understand what operation Spinoza is referring to when he speaks of 'changing the meaning of a word', an operation that he says is impossible: it is not a matter of adding a new meaning to this word – something that is indeed possible if the collective practice of the language produces at a certain time such-and-such an innovation, or borrows from a foreign language; rather, it is a matter of retroactively transforming the meaning that a word once possessed in past texts, thereby modifying after the fact the constitutive series of significations. What prevents this generalised falsification is obviously the fact that the signification of names remains in use. Use thus appears as the guarantor of a language's texture. A language can evolve, but its evolution does not efface its past.

---

[91] 'Nam nemini unquam ex usu esse potuit, alicujus verbi significationem mutare, at quidem non raro sensum alicujus orationis', *TTP*, Chapter VII, G III, p. 105, ll. 27–9 [*TTP* VII, 40; *CWS* II, 179]. The presence of the expression 'ex usu' in this passage offers us an opportunity to clarify that the word *usus* has three meanings in Spinoza: linguistic use; the use of life; and utility (this is the case here; it is also the case in all of the passages on inter-human relations at the end of Book IV of the *Ethics*).

These three functions of use clearly refer to the same dimensions of language: that it essentially transcends individual initiative, while the creation, conservation or discovery of the meaning of words is not a matter of reason, but instead requires experience. We can confirm this by considering the inverse situation. Is it possible for the meaning of a word to be lost, not only in history (that is, when it stops being used) but also in the context of a tradition (that is, when the word is no longer remembered as having such-and-such a meaning)? Of course it is – but this is not a matter of individual choice. The use of language can on certain occasions be lost, and the loss is in such cases irremediable. Henceforth, it is no longer possible to find for each text the ensemble of its possible meanings.[92]

On the other hand, when we possess the set of a word's significations, use places a limit on our interpretations. Each time Spinoza refers to this situation he says that the Scriptures teach such-and-such a thing *expressimis verbis*.[93] When he uses this formula, this means that the discussion is closed. We thus find here one of the characteristics of the register of experience: *expressimis verbis* is the equivalent in the domain of use of the formula *satis superque*.

The use of language thus plays a regulative function. It imposes limits on interpretation. To 'twist the words' of a text (an expression that Spinoza often uses)[94] is nothing other than to separate it from *usus*. It is not a matter of going against reason, for the text might well say unreasonable things. Thus, when confronting certain commentators, Spinoza evokes the limit that the customs of speakers places on these commentators' hermeneutical licence. We do not read the Bible against the Hebrews: their relation to their language sets the limits of interpretation. To cross these limits is to plunge into madness. '[These commentators] invent many other things

---

[92] 'Non itaque semper poterimus, ut desideramus, omnes uniuscujusque orationis sensus, quos ipsa ex linguae usu admittere potest, investigare, et multae occurrent orationes, quamvis notissimis vocibus expressae, quarum tamen sensus obscurissimus erit, et plane imperceptibilis', *TTP*, Chapter VII, G III, p. 106, ll. 29–33 [*TTP* VII 46; *CWS* II, 180].

[93] 'Expressimis verbis docere', *TTP*, Chapter IV, G III, p. 67, l. 3 [*TTP* IV, 42; *CWS* II, 136]; Chapter XIII, p. 171, l. 1 [*TTP* XIII, 18; *CWS* II, 267]; Chapter XIV, p. 176, l. 10 [*TTP* XIV, 18; *CWS* I, 267]; note that when he presents R. Jehuda Alpakhar's rule, Spinoza modifies the formula and says: 'expressimis verbis affirmare', Chapter XV, p. 181, l. 12 [*TTP* XV, 5; *CWS* II, 273]; p. 182, l. 29 [*TTP* XV, 13; *CWS* II, 275].

[94] 'Verba Scripturae torquere', *TTP*, Chapter II, G III, p. 35, l. 29 [*TTP* II, 25; *CWS* II, 100]; Chapter VIII, p. 123, ll. 8–9 [*TTP* VIII, 25; *CWS* II, 198]; 'mentem Scripturae torquere', Chapter VII, p. 101, l. 24 [*TTP* VII, 22; *CWS* II, 175]; 'Scripturam torquere', Chapter VII, p. 114, l. 9 [*TTP* VII, 77; *CWS* II, .188].

of this kind. If these things were true, I would say, without qualification, that the ancient Hebrews were completely ignorant both of their own language and of how to tell a story in an orderly way. I wouldn't recognise any principle or standard for interpreting Scripture. Instead, we could invent anything we like.'[95] What must be understood here is the importance of the collective dimension of language. Behind a language there lies a community. This community lives and speaks according to the immanent laws of its own existence, while ignorance of these laws leads to the reconstruction of an imaginary language, just as doing politics in ignorance of the laws of human nature leads one to dream of a Golden Age or of the Kingdom of Utopia. If one constructs meanings following one's own preferences, then the dangers of personal interpretation reappear. Whoever does so gives priority to their own individuality over the common experience of language. We should note, finally, that this reference, which is apparently a matter of simple common sense, to the fact that a people knows its own language, refers neither to knowledge by causes nor to the guarantee that such words or uses will not be lost. The appearance here of the norm constituted by the 'ancient Hebrews' simply indicates Spinoza's position in the debate on the *veritas hebraïca*,[96] which had flared up after the Renaissance. At the same time, Spinoza's procedure here attests to a certain confidence in the weight of language. This weight can be found elsewhere, notably in politics, where it will determine the singular traits that define a people.

Thus, *usus* governs the signification of words. It opens language up to history. It prevents one from believing that this domain arises only from Reason. This limit placed on Reason is in no way irrational. It is an acquiescence to experience. Certainly, all of the causes that have meant that a given word has taken on such-and-such a meaning within a given language are rigorously determined. Yet we do not know the detail of this process of formation, which implies many different laws (the majority of which are not linguistic) and brings into play many individual phenomena. Once again, we find ourselves confronted with a play of existing properties that cannot be automatically deduced from essences. In principle, it is not impossible to construct, with the help of common notions, a traditional etymology, but in

---

[95] 'Et ad hunc modum plura alia fingunt, quae si vera essent, absolute dicerem antiquos Hebraeos & linguam suam & narrandi ordinem plane ignoravisse, nec ullam rationem neque normam Scripturas interpretandi agnoscerem, sed ad libitum omnia fingere liceret', *TTP*, Chapter IX, G III, p. 134, l. 32; p. 135, l. 1 [*TTP* IX, 28; *CWS* II, 216].

[96] On this problem, cf. M. Bataillon, *Erasmus et l'Espagne. Recerches sur l'histoire spirituelle du XIVe siècle*, Paris: Droz, 1937, Chapter I, pp. 1–75.

reality we can only explain a very small number of things using this method, while the rest will be known by vague experience or will not be known at all. Recourse to experience – that is, in this instance, to use – thus allows us to neutralise this uncertainty and to secure our footing on this shifting terrain.

C. *Grammar and Rhetoric*

Words are nevertheless not the only domain where use plays a key role. This is above all because a language is not only made up of a series of juxtaposed words, nor it is reducible to a list of names. Rather, a language also includes a grammar and indeed a rhetoric, even if it is true that not all natural languages use the same tropes.

It might be surprising to see these disciplines appear here. When Spinoza speaks of language 'as a philosopher', he seems to equate (as almost all of his contemporaries do, except Leibniz)[97] language with words so closely that it is difficult to remember that there is a place for other questions. If one adopts a perspective that asks if the word corresponds to the thing, the image or the idea, it can be difficult to then inquire into the relations that words have among themselves and with broader units of signification – except if one treats these latter as derivate of logical relations between ideas. The situation is very different, however, when we turn to Spinoza's own linguistic practice, even outside of the *Compendium*.[98] We see Spinoza turn his attention to the form of words, to the regularity and irregularities of their formation, and even to the influence of syntax on morphology – something that could well appear as the most extreme case of the subordination of the study of the word to that of a broader totality.[99]

Is it possible to find in these other aspects of language an important role for use to play? This is a question that has rarely been studied[100] in works

---

[97] On the many aspects of Leibniz's thought, see Sigrid von der Schulenbourg, *Leibniz als Sprachforscher*, Frankfurt: V. Klostermann, 1973.

[98] It is well known that the first to become interested in the *Compendium Grammatices Hebraeae Linguae* was the great philologist Jacob Bernays (who, alas, is all too often neglected these days in favour of his niece who married a young neurologist with a promising future). His study appears in an annex (pp. 195–204) of the work of C. Schaarschmidt, *Des Cartes und Spinoza*, Bonn: Marcus, 1850.

[99] *Compendium*, Chapter XXI [HG 105–6]. We are dealing here with an anticipatory note, since the work ends before it deals with syntax.

[100] Adolph Chajes, *Ueber di hebräische Grammatik Spinozas*, diss., Breslau: F. W. Jungfer, 1869; J. M. Hillesum 'De spinozistische spraakkunst', *Chronicon spinozanum*, I (1921), pp. 158–77; N. Porges, 'Spinozas Compendium der herbräischen Grammatik', *Chronicon spinozanum*, IV (1924–6), pp. 123–59; M. Ben-Asher, 'Hgal hadikhdukh

on Spinoza's grammar. Some commentators have certainly wanted to find in this work a parallel between Spinoza's metaphysical theses and his description of the Hebrew language.[101] In particular, the fact that Spinoza reduces all Hebrew words to a single category – that of the noun[102] – has traditionally been related to the doctrine of the unity of substance.[103] Similarly, some commentators have sought to identify in the *Compendium* an effort on Spinoza's part to present grammar *more geometrico*, but this approach neglects at least one of the work's dimensions. It is interesting to note, on the one hand, that certain phenomena are registered by Spinoza as belonging exclusively to the category of language, and on the other hand that for different phenomena, he attempts to draw a distinction between what can be rationally explained and what escapes such an explanation.

In Hebrew, Spinoza remarks, for certain reasons use 'often' requires that a letter placed between two vowels be doubled.[104] Thus, the *daguesh* is justified only by reference to use, but use is not given as being absolutely consistent. Spinoza then notes that in this instance rules concerning gutturals (for instance, that one cannot double an *r* or a guttural but must instead extend the vowel that precedes it) do not apply universally. It is use, too, that makes us consider as feminine certain 'neutral' substantives because

---

hahgivri leBaruk Spinoza', in *Spinoza 300 shanah lemoto*, University of Haifa, 1978, pp. 187–96. More recently, see the discussion by Z. Lévy and A.-J. Klijnsmit on the question of normativity, *Studia spinozana*, III, pp. 351–90 and IV, pp. 305–14.

[101] To the extent that the work does not entirely resemble what one would normally expect from this perspective, Bernays has sought to explain this feature: written for friends, the *Compendium* does not present the definitive form that it would have had if Spinoza had decided to publish it. It does not present us with the Spinozist conception of the essence of language; however, we can gain access to this essence by way of a virtual systematicity: 'Aber auch durch die nachgiebigere Darstellung blickt noch erkennbar genug der strenge, das Viele in die Einheit sammelnde Systematiker; ja noch mehr, man gewahrht bald, dass in dem *Compendium* dem gegebenen Sprachstoff der Stempel desjenigen Systems aufgeprägt wird, welches in der Ethik entwickelt ist', J. Bernays, *Gesammelte Abhandlungen*, Berlin: W. Hertz, 1885, p. 343. It seems to me on the contrary that the *Nachgiebigkeit* is also constitutive of Spinoza's grammar.

[102] A. Chajes, *Ueber di hebräische Grammatik Spinozas*, p. 11, following Bernays.

[103] Ibid., p. 13; M. Ben-Asher, 'Hgal hadikhdukh hahgivri leBaruk Spinoza', p. 108. Commentators do not seem to have noticed that Spinoza states this categorical unity for a single language, namely Hebrew, by distinguishing it explicitly on this point from Latin. Also, unless he were making Hebrew a sacred language, it is hard to see the interest of finding a homology (that Spinoza, for his part, does not mention) between *a* language and the structure of being.

[104] 'Exigit saepe usus, ut litera aliqua iner duas vocales ob certas causas duplicari debeat', *Compendium*, Chapter III, G I, p. 291, ll. 24–5 [HG 13].

of their declension.[105] There is even a passage where, on the topic of the constructed nature of terms like *mavèt*, Spinoza comes up with a concept of a kind of theoretical use: he begins by indicating what constructed form these words should have *ex communi linguae usu*, but then remarks that in reality another use has prevailed.[106] There exists, then, in the morphological structure of the language, a whole series of phenomena that can only be identified after the fact. If these phenomena possess a regularity, then it is a regularity internal to each one of them, from one biblical text to the next. One might sometimes attempt to predict this regularity (this is what 'common use' is), but this prediction can be contradicted by the facts. The same arbitrariness that governs the signification of words thus also governs their sonorous structuration and formal variations. We are therefore still in the world of existences, where only experience can teach us what has really happened.

We cannot remain at this level, however. Spinoza thus attempts to discover regularities, even if these are at first glance inapparent, before, in certain cases, attempting to explain them by relating them to what seems to constitute the general laws of the human mind. This poses the question of the relations between reason and grammar. If grammar is reducible in its entirety to reason, then there must be a universal language. As is well known, this is a question that is raised throughout the seventeenth century[107] and represents the reprise, in the classical age, of the ancient identification *hebraea mater linguarum*.[108] In both instances it was thought that it was possible to account for the divergences between singular languages simply by referring to their difference from a common model. The only distinction in the classical age is that Reason, as a general abstract language, replaces the model provided by a particular language. For his part, the method Spinoza employs leads him to effectively break with such an aim. I will now describe his procedure on the basis of three examples: the table of verbs he constructs, the gender of the names of inanimate objects, and the study of prepositions and adverbs.

---

[105] 'non nisi usu factum est, ut substantiva quae neque mares neque foeminas exprimunt, ad genus foemininum semper referantur, quando in he vel tav desinunt', *Compendium*, Chapter VIII, G I, p. 313 [HG 41].

[106] Chapter VIII, G I, p. 320 [HG 48].

[107] On the horizon of these problems, see A. Robinet, *Le langage à l'âge classique*, Paris: Klincksieck, 1978, and M. A. Slaughter, *Universal Languages and Scientific Taxonomy in the Seventeenth Century*, Cambridge: Cambridge University Press, 1982.

[108] Cf. A. J. Klijnsmit, 'From *Seemly* to *Nature* to *Un-*, Grammatical Opinions on Hebrew (1500–1700)', presentation at the colloquium 'John Wilkins (1614–1672), Language, religion and science in the seventeenth century', Oxford, September 1990.

The domain in which Spinoza's efforts to unify the rules governing the formation of words are most vigorous is without doubt the morphology of the verb. Faced with the profusion of attested forms, Spinoza proceeds by way of a double reduction in two different directions. On the one hand, he does not hesitate to eliminate hapax if they do not conform to an attested model; he considers them to be copyists' errors. It might be said that he is less careful in this domain than he is in the *TTP* when it comes to respecting the signification of words, but these erasures occur in the name of the coherence of other forms present in the texts, not in the name of some external rationality. On the other hand, Spinoza completes the traditional table of the seven verbal forms with a 'passive reflexive' form that most grammarians were unaware of up to that point and of which there are only a few attested examples. Nevertheless, the rules of this 'passive reflexive' form can be reconstructed by analogy with the passive forms of the simple and the intensive and can help us understand a certain number of other forms that had hitherto been considered irregular. Spinoza then goes a step further: he constructs a general theory of the passive form, which is supposedly always indicated by the prefix *nun* – even though in reality this prefix appears only in the simple passive form and in certain cases in its passive reflexive form (though this disappearance itself can be explained by what could be called the law of sufficient differentiation).[109] We are dealing here with an extreme case where it seems possible to reconstitute laws whose combination produces observable phenomena, including in their apparent irregularities – all without practically appealing to use. It should nevertheless be noted that Spinoza registers a key fact in this classification but does not explain it: the particular value of the passive in Hebrew. This verbal form has a more limited extension in Hebrew than in Latin since it is not the simple inverse of the active but can only indicate an action where the patient is named and not the agent. This difference has obvious consequences for the distribution of the meanings of the four active verbal forms and their corresponding four passive forms. This distinction is immediately related to the way in which the Hebrew language used (*utuntur*) this verbal form.[110] There is another trait, and an even more fundamental one, where the nation that is the bearer of this language makes its appearance. This is the response to the question: why are there four fundamental forms? Spinoza seems to accept as

---

[109] 'Denique quia hoc passivum vocalibus satis ab activo distinguitur, ideo littera nun characteristica scilicet passivi in hac conjugatione saepissime negligitur', Chapter XVII, G I, p. 357, l. 28; p. 358, l. 2 [HG 96]. Chapter XXI generalises this indication.
[110] Chapter XXI, p. 364, ll. 5–8 [HG 105].

a general linguistic necessity that there exist a simple verb and an intensive verb (he cites the Latin examples *videre/visitare* and *frangere/confringere*). Hebrew merely transformed this occasional alteration into a generalised grammatical alteration. The existence of the reflexive is given as a fact that is proper to the Hebrews, who thereby transform a frequently attested logical relation into a grammatical one.[111] Finally, the existence of the causative is given as a consequence of the mentality specific to the Hebrews.[112] Spinoza implicitly reprises here a remark from the *TTP*;[113] however, in that work this remark concerned rhetoric, not morphology. We thus move from use to regularity only to find, at the core of regularity, the particularly of the community of the speakers.

The use of the masculine and the feminine to designate neutral nouns is explained, at least hypothetically, not by a law of reason but by a law of the imagination. Spinoza notes that people have a tendency to confer human attributes on all things. Right after saying 'people', he adds: 'and principally the Hebrews'.[114] This clarification is revealing since there exists in Latin a neutral form that does not characterise all neutral nouns. Spinoza thus finds himself having to explain why the attribution of animate traits to inanimate objects is more systematic in one language than in another. He has the choice of relating it simply to different uses, or, alternatively, of identifying behind use a law of the human mind. In the latter case, however, it would be necessary to remark that this law applies more to one people than to another. Thus, like in the case of the passives, and perhaps more clearly still, at a certain point the attempt to rationally organise the irregular verbs – whether by reference to laws internal to language or by external laws – encounters the appearance of national particularism.[115]

---

[111] 'Sed quia saepe evenit, ut agens, et patiens una eademque persona sit, necesse fuit Hebraeis novam et septimam Infinitivorum speciem formare [. . .]', Chapter XII, G I, p. 342, ll. 12–14 [HG 75–6]. If this fact is a necessity for the Hebrews, it is because of the absence of the reflexive pronoun, which Spinoza simply notes.

[112] 'Solent praeterea Hebraei actionem ad causam principalem referre, quae scilicet efficit, ut actio aliqua ab aliquo fiat, vel ut res aliqua suo officio fungatur', Chapter XII, G I, p. 341, ll. 18–20 [HG 75].

[113] 'Sed hic apprime notandum, quod Judaei nunquam causarum mediarum, sive particularium faciunt mentionem, sed religionis ac pietatis, sive (ut vulgo dici dolet) devotionis causa, ad Deum semper recurrunt', *TTP*, Chapter I, G III, p. 16, l. 33; p. 17, l. 1 [*TTP* I, 8; *CWS* II, 78].

[114] 'Solent deinde homines, et praecipue Hebraei rebus omnibus humana attributa dare [. . .]', Chapter V, G I, p. 304, ll. 17–19 [HG 29].

[115] Similarly, the schema of tense in Hebrew (Spinoza interprets, in a classical fashion, the opposition between the accomplished and unaccomplished as past and future) is

We see this in a third example where Spinoza attempts to explain the plural form of prepositions. Here, we see him clearly mark out the different territories belonging to reason and use, which he again does by way of a reflection on the difference between languages. The fact of this difference is immediately apparent: prepositions, which are invariable in Latin, are variable in Hebrew. Spinoza places more emphasis on this point here than he does elsewhere. He immediately anticipates the expected reaction from his Latinate readers: some of them, he says, will find this absurd.[116] And he attempts, with a rhetorical intensity that is rare for this treatise, to justify the Hebrew language: why would the prepositions not have a plural form? After all, they are nouns, just as substantives are.[117] They are nouns because they express not only relations between things but real effects such as place, time, intensity and accomplishment – all of which are susceptible to having plural forms. There is thus a justification for this within the language itself. By contrast, however, Hebrew knows nothing of the intensity of adverbs, as Latin does. Spinoza does not say that this trait of Latin is absurd; rather, he says that it would have appeared absurd to the Hebrews. Absurdity is thus the mirror of the other's reason. One can find reasons within a language for that language, but these reasons refer in the final analysis to a use of use, which differentiates one language from the others.

In these conditions, is it possible to conceive of a universal grammar? The text[118] in which Spinoza comes closest to such an idea – and where we see in the clearest possible form what distinguishes his work from this idea – is

---

reduced to the way in which the Hebrews represented time as a line, or the present as only a point (Chapter XIII).

[116] Why does Spinoza anticipate this surprise here, but not in the preceding examples? In the case of genders, he knows that his 'Latin' readers also speak common languages where the situation is varied: some have two genders like in Hebrew, others three like in Latin. The fact that the verb can present nominal flexions is no less or more thinkable for these other languages (there exists a personal infinitive in Portuguese, for instance). On the other hand, none of these languages has a flexion for the prepositions: the radical difference in the case of Hebrew thus has every chance of being interpreted as an absurdity.

[117] 'At quod plurales etiam habeant numerum, multis forsan absurdum videbitur; sed quidni, cum revera sint nomina?', Chapter X, G I, p. 327, l. 28; p. 328, l. 1 [HG 58].

[118] There are others too. At the beginning of Chapter XI, before giving, with hardly any commentary, the table of pronouns in Hebrew, Spinoza remarks: 'What a pronoun is and into how many classes it is divided is known to all' [HG 61] – which could mean: the pronouns have the same definition and the same categories in Hebrew as in Latin. It could also mean: there is a universal 'pronoun' function that is realised in the same way in Hebrew and in Latin.

the text where he reasons on cases and modes. He seems to say, in Chapter XIII, that there exist universal logical necessities (the cases of nouns, the modes of verbs) and that natural languages choose from among these necessities those that they will explicitly express. Thus, Latin chooses to express cases grammatically, while Hebrew does not. Latin expresses more modes than Hebrew, but certain (interrogative) modes are expressed in neither language, nor indeed by 'any language', at least as far as Spinoza knows. Natural languages thus represent existing choices within a system of a larger field of possibilities represented by logical necessities.[119] But Spinoza is far from reproaching these languages for being inadequate from this perspective: he does not seem to think that it is necessary to realise all of these logical possibilities by grammatical means. On the contrary, he notes that the absence of certain of these possibilities does not create any ambiguity. He thus seems to think that a natural language that would render explicit all of these logical rules would be weighed down with redundancies, and that it suffices for a language to express what is necessary for comprehension. We thus find here the same criterion of sufficient differentiation that we found in the case of the passives. Once again, the difference between the domain of essences and the domain of existences appears – a difference that marks the site of experience's instauration. But this time we discover a new effect: that of economy. A single essence can give rise to a plurality of properties. Here, however, a plurality of laws of essence can be economically represented by a single distinction between existing things. Those different determinations that can be deduced geometrically come together and are concentrated in a single instance of experience. This is why languages have a relative freedom in the concrete forms they offer the logical laws of language. On this point, Spinoza seems to think that Latin does too much, but that Hebrew sometimes does too little. There is thus no ideal language. Natural languages exist amidst their differences.[120]

---

[119] And what a language expresses by grammar, another language can express by its lexicon or by another grammatical level. This is the case for the alternative between reflexive pronouns and the reflexive form of the verb. This is also what the following remark from the *TTP* seems to indicate: 'all these defects of Tenses and Moods could easily – indeed, with the greatest elegance – have been made up by certain rules deduced from the foundations of the language...', Chapter VII, G III, p. 107, ll. 26–8 [*TTP* VII, 50; *CWS* II, 181]. A theory of translation could be founded on this remark.

[120] On this point, I cannot share the opinion of A. J. Klijnsmit, who argues that Spinoza defended a *Goropian* view of language (this is a reference to Goropius Becanus, who was one of the first to contest the logical and chronological primacy of Hebrew – to the detriment of Dutch), 'From *Seemly* to *Nature*...', p. 19, and 'Spinoza on

Do these differences arise from experience or reason? Spinoza seems to indicate that in the final analysis they are rational, but that it is only by referring to use that can we learn about them. A language cannot be deduced *a priori*. Differences between languages exist, without us being able to deduce them.

Finally, what is proper to a language is not only a matter of its vocabulary and grammar: it is also what is stylistically[121] and rhetorically proper to it.[122] Its singularity thus refers to the sprit of the people who speak it, or to the group of people for whom it is a part of their lives. In this latter sense biblical Hebrew has remained the language, not of the Jews, but of the Hebrews: that is, of an integral nation. Once again, in taking account of one aspect of language, if this aspect is to take on its full meaning one must refer to the following historical reference point: the particularity that constitutes the identity of a people.

D. Language and Culture

Thus, we see that each time we try to determine the relative contribution of use and reason to grammar, we are referred back to the identity of each natural language and to their distinction from one another. I noted above how the term 'a Roman' explicitly introduced this dimension into the *pomum* example. We can now see all of the implications of this. In the *TTP* Spinoza often highlights the specificities of Hebrew, this time at the stylistic level. However, nowhere does he define by way of deduction the *ingenium* of the Hebrews.[123] In certain respects, this *ingenium* seems to be a condensation of one of the forms of the *ingenium* of people in general; in others it is similar to the *ingenium* of barbarous peoples; while in others still it is formed by the history of a nation. Thus, when we attempt to exhaustively identify the constitutive traits of a language, we come up against what does indeed seem to be another category of experience: the *ingenium* of a people.

---

the Imperfection of Words', in P. Schmitter, *Essays Toward a History of Semantics*, Münster: Nodus Publikationen, 1990.

[121] Chapter IX, G I, p. 325 [HG 55].

[122] Spinoza notes that speech also expresses the affections of the soul and regrets that writing does not (*Compendium*, beginning of Chapter IV [HG 18]). L. Meyer makes the same observation (*La Philosophie interprète de l'Ecriture sainte*, Chapter III, § 24).

[123] 'Solent deinde hoines, et praecipue Hebraei rebus omnibus humana attributa dare, ut *terra audivit, auscultata est*, etc. Et forte hac aut alia de causa omnia nomina rerum in masculina et foemininia diviserunt', *Compendium*, Chapter V, G I, p. 304, ll. 17–21 [HG 29].

For Spinoza, then, a language, such as he understands it, resembles in many respects what we would today call a culture. A language brings together its own materiality with facts relating to culture and institutions that arise from the spirit of the people who speak it. There is therefore a spirit of the language. But the spirit of the language can run counter to the materiality of the language. This is the case when Hebrew emerges within Greek.[124] Inversely, the spirit that appears in the book of Job, which is nevertheless transmitted in Hebrew, is not that of the Hebrews. For Spinoza, this indicates that the Book was composed in another language.[125] Taking the relevant precautions, we could relate this permanence of the spirit beyond its materiality to the permanence of a body beyond the change of its component parts, so long as its fundamental ratio is respected.[126]

Thus, when Spinoza declares that he is ignorant of a language, he does not mean that he is ignorant of its words and structures. He means that he is not familiar with the culture and the entire system of references that are proper to this language. In reading the *TTP* we see that he claims to know Hebrew. What he means by this is that he knows how to place a word in the language's proper context, how to recognise its institutions, and how to analyse the different styles present in the Bible. It might be supposed that he thinks that he knows Latin, not only because he can read and write this language but because he is very familiar with the history of Rome, both its institutions and its culture; and that, impregnated by Latin literature, his memory immediately has at its disposal quotations from Roman poets and historians. On the other hand, however, when he declares that he does not know enough Greek to examine the books of the New Testament,[127] he does not mean that he is entirely ignorant of Greek.[128] What he means is that he is much less familiar with the Greek culture that underwrites this language than he is with Latin or Hebrew cultures.[129] And if he nevertheless some-

---

[124] Ep. LXXV, G IV, p. 315 [*Ep.* LXXV [to Henry Oldenburg]; *CWS* II, 473].

[125] *TTP*, Chapter X, G III, p. 130 [*TTP* X, 6, 7, 8, 9; *CWS* II, 208–9].

[126] Cf. *Ethics* II, Lem. 4, 5 and 6 [*CWS* I, 461].

[127] 'Jam autem tempus esset libros etiam Novi Testamenti eodem modo examinare. Sed [. . .] quia tam exactam linguae graecae cognitionem non habeo, ut hanc provinciam suscipere audeam [. . .] ideo huic negotio supersedere malo', *TTP*, G III, Chapter X, p. 150, l. 30; p. 151, l. 1 [*TTP* X, 48; *CWS* II, 239].

[128] It should nevertheless be noted that his Latin is much less full of Greek words than his contemporaries' is. In particular, Spinoza recoils from putting το before the substantivised infinitive, which is common in the Latin of the seventeenth century; we only encounter this once or twice in the *Hebrew Grammar*, in places where it effectively facilitates comprehension.

[129] His library attests to this, as does his choice of historical examples. As for Alexander,

times permits himself to comment in detail on certain passages, it is precisely because he identifies Hebrew-isms in them, which attest either to the texts in question not having been written in Greek but having been translated into Greek from a Semitic language,[130] or to the fact that the mentality of their authors still carries the categories of the Hebrew language (what I called above their 'spirit') while nevertheless being expressed in Greek.[131]

We thus see in what sense language refers not to a geometrical but to an experiential order. Since language always and everywhere concerns existence and not essence, it can only be based on the constitutive role of experience. Thus, philosophy will have to take a detour past experience to understand language – and indeed to work on language to make itself understood.

Before turning to a close study of this work, we must pause for a moment to determine in what sense a system can employ for its own specific ends a common distinction. It is clear that Spinoza does not invent the idea of 'use': it is drawn from the common well of reflections on the origin of words and grammar, both in its explanatory function and its normative temptations (the 'proper use' of a language). But Spinoza gives this notion of 'use' a central role, building upon it a whole series of themes that involve the positivity of language in its entanglements with the accidents of history, the liberties of interpretation and the weight of natural languages. The function of use as the representative of experience allows Spinoza to mobilise around it a mode of reasoning that completes the deductions that occur *more geometrico* and that clarifies those zones that the geometrical method leaves obscure. In the end, *usus* allows Spinoza to totalise both the procedures of rationalist philosophy, whose model is mathematics, and the labour of philology and of the sciences of language that engage with the material diversities of the signifier. If one wished to be convinced of Spinoza's originality – and above all to understand *where* this originality is to be found – one should note that we find, for instance in Descartes, the same essential role of *usus* for determining

---

who appears on multiple occasions in the *TTP*, Spinoza knows him by the mediation of the Latin historian Quintus-Curtius Rufus.

[130] Cf. *Adnotatio*, XXVI: 'Syriaca enim versio (si quidem versio est, quod dubitari potest, quandoquidem nec interpretem novimus, nec tempus quo vulgata fuit, et Apostolorum lingua vernacula nulla alia fuit quam Syriaca) [. . .]', G III, p. 262, ll. 10–13. I am leaving aside here the problem that arises from the fact that Spinoza assimilates Syriac and Armenian.

[131] 'And although John wrote his Gospel in Greek, he still hebraizes', Ep. LXXV, G IV, p. 315, ll. 16–17 [*Ep*. LXXV [to Henry Oldenburg, December 1675 or January 1676]; *CWS* II, 473].

the meaning of words. The words that we use, 'having been invented at the beginning, have since then been corrected and softened by use, and indeed continue to be so every day. In such matters, use does more than the understanding of a great mind could do.'[132] Yet, since Descartes does not elaborate a positive theory of experience, this *usus* has no theoretical echo. This is why if the negative status of language appears in Descartes' texts, as it does in Spinoza's, it is not counterbalanced by the alternate tendency that we have just analysed. The economy of Descartes' system does not require this. By contrast, Spinoza's system mobilises, in its very constitution, this notion of *usus* that is carried both by rhetorical knowledge and common experience.

3. Writing and Experience

The majority of commentaries on the *TTP* begin with the following statement, which they suppose to be justified: what Spinoza says of the Holy Scriptures is shot through with contradictions and absurdities. Commentators are then divided according to whether they consider these contradictions as minor weaknesses, as signs of hypocrisy, or as proof of the operation of a superior and Machiavellian intelligence. I would suggest that we not rush to consider as contradictory formulations that do not necessarily speak of the same thing.

There is no question here of giving an overall reading of Spinoza's hermeneutics.[133] I will envisage this hermeneutics solely from the perspective of its relation to language and experience. This will suffice, I hope, to bring out a few points that are generally neglected. Let us simply recall that the Spinozist reading of the Holy Scriptures brings together a number of different procedures.[134] To read is not, in fact, a simple operation: it is necessary

---

[132] Lettre à Mersenne, 4 March 1630, AT, I, p. 126. [Translator's note: this translation is my own, as the English translation of Descartes' letters, found in volume three of *The Philosophical Writings of Descartes*, does not include this part of the letter.]

[133] I have already laid out the elements of such a study in a number of works: 'La méthode d'interprération de l'Ecriture sainte: déterminations et limites', in *Spinoza, Science et Religion*, Actes du Colloque de Cerisy-la-Salle, organised by R. Bouveresse, Paris (Vrin) and Lyon (IIES), 1988, pp. 108–14; 'Louis Meyer entre Descartes et Spinoza', in L. Meyer, *La Philosophie interprète de l'Ecriture sainte*; 'La lecture de la Bible dans le cercle de Spinoza (en collabration avec J. Lagrée), in *Le Grand Siècle et la Bible*, sous la direction de J.-R. Armogathe, Paris: Beauchesne, 1989, pp. 97–116; 'Les principes de la lecture de l'Ecriture sainte dans le *TTP*', in *L'Ecriture sainte au temps de Spinoza et dans le système spinoziste, Travaux et documents du GRS*, 4, PUPS, 1991.

[134] Cf. my detailed analysis in the article from *La Grand Siècle et la Bible*, cited above, pp. 110–15.

to distinguish what the biblical text says from what it teaches at an ethical level. Furthermore, in addition to its ethical teachings, the text can be the bearer of information that can be used in the construction of an up-to-date science of the State or of human passions. To read the Holy Scriptures is thus both to understand what they say, to draw out what they teach, and, at the political level, to learn from what their experience presents us with. Three questions must therefore be put to the Scriptures:

— First, a general question of fact: 'What do the Scriptures say?' – in the totality of their passages. The analysis of this totality can occur only in terms of a differential archaeology that patiently reconstitutes the available materials of knowledge relative to each author, period and institution. Philology, the history of society, and the history of mentalities together constitute the elements of this archaeology. This is a foundation that is absent from the two authors who are nevertheless habitually compared with Spinoza, namely Hobbes and Ludowijk Meyer.

— Second, a *de jure* question: 'What do the Scriptures teach insofar as they are the Word of God?' Spinoza makes a clear distinction between the Scriptures in their totality and what he calls theology, which, while perhaps not separate to the Scriptures, can nevertheless be separated from them. What Spinoza calls theology is not the discourse of the theologians[135] but the sacred elements of biblical texts. To this question Spinoza responds with a didactics of the divine word that leads to what we could call a minimal *credo*.[136]

— Third, a more limited question of fact: 'What elements from biblical narratives can be used politically?' In the face of those who wish to turn the State of the Hebrews into a universally applicable model,[137] Spinoza is not content to simply refute this abusive pretention; he also draws from the text

---

[135] The term *theologian* in Spinoza is always pejorative: it refers to a passionate, sectarian and superstitious person, ready to quarrel with his peers and to whip up crowds against good citizens, and indeed against magistrates when he does not obtain their support in his struggle against these good citizens. This is a figure that we find in the polemical literature (Meyer, L., Antistius Constans, etc.) with the same characteristics. The term *theology*, by contrast, is always positive and never refers to a theory, even a true one, elaborated by a philosopher (Spinoza never calls the doctrine from the beginning of the *Ethics*, *De Deo*, a 'theology'): it is synonymous with the 'Word of God' in the sense that Spinoza understands it – that is, it refers to the teachings of piety such as these are contained in the Scriptures.

[136] Cf. J. Lagrée, *La Raison ardente*, Paris: Vrin, 1991.

[137] On this question, see the works by F. Laplanche and A. Ligota in the collection cited above, *L'Ecriture sainte au temps de Spinoza et dans le système spinoziste*, Travaux et documents du GRS, 4, PUPS, 1991.

an analysis of the Mosaic constitution and its evolution that he will use to illuminate his theory of the structure of civil societies – a theory that goes beyond the determinations of a theocracy.

It is crucial to distinguish between these questions if we do not wish to weigh Spinoza's text down with contradictions that are in no way inherent to it – something that is otherwise easy to do. I will leave aside here the third question, but we will return to some aspects of it further on when we deal with political passions. I will limit myself to examining the method by which Spinoza engages with the first two questions. I will try to show that what has just been established with respect to use as an experiential category in the field of language allows us to resolve certain difficulties that are commonly attributed to Spinoza's reading of the Holy Scriptures. I will also indicate other functions of experience that are internal to this reading.

A. *The Archaeology of Scripture*

Spinoza states that as a general principle it is necessary to interpret Scripture on its own terms. He presents a number of different applications of this principle in various passages. At least one of these applications opposes this principle to another principle that would consist in interpreting Scripture on the basis of reason or philosophy: this is the well-known passage where he critiques Maimonides.[138] In other passages, by contrast, Spinoza strongly insists on the role of reason in the interpretation of Scripture.[139] Finally, when he deals with miracles, he clearly treats reason as a judge of what is said in the Scriptures.[140] From the very beginning the juxtaposition of these theses has shocked certain readers.[141] How should we make sense of all this?

We must begin by situating this problem concerning the criteria for interpretation in the context of the debate that had raged since the Renaissance on the clarity and obscurity of the Scriptures.[142] In this debate, Spinoza occupies a radically original position. Let us recall in schematic terms the stakes

---

[138] The end of Chapter VII, G III, pp. 113–14 [*TTP* VI, 75; *CWS* II, 187–8].

[139] For example in the critique of Alfakhar in Chapter XV, G III, pp. 182–3 [*TTP* XV, 13, 14, 15, 16, 17, 18; *CWS* II, 275–7].

[140] *TTP*, Chapter VI [*TTP* VI; *CWS* II, 152–69]. Cf. S. Zac's analyses on this topic, *Spinoza et l'interprétation de l'Ecriture*, Paris: PUF, 1965, pp. 199–207.

[141] This is one of the themes of the letter from Lambert de van Velthuysen to Jacob Osten, G IV, pp. 207–18 [*Ep.* XLII; *CWS* II, 374–85].

[142] Cf. F. Laplanche, *L'Ecriture, le Sacré, l'Histoire. Erudits et politiques protestants devant la Bible au XVIIe siècle*, Maarsen: APA/Lille: PU, 1986.

of this debate. For Protestant exegetes, the Bible is fundamentally clear. It can and must explain itself by itself, with its clear passages providing the key to its obscure passages (the principle here is that of analogy and of faith). For the Catholics, the Bible is often obscure by itself; this, then, implies the necessity, if one is to properly understand its teachings, of having recourse to tradition and to majesty. Thus, Suárez comes up with a long list of difficulties that await the reader who is not sufficiently educated.[143] Fundamentally, however, both Protestants and Catholics agree that the ultimate clarity of reading is necessary for interpretation. We could even add that this ultimate clarity is also what is sought, at least as an ideal, by the modern editors of texts, whether sacred or profane. This is an essential exigency of the philological enterprise, but one that is doubled by the divine guarantee of the intelligibility of the sacred text. After so many other exegetes, then, Spinoza confronts the difficulties of Scripture. We should note, however, that the notion of *difficulty* does not entirely cover that of *obscurity*. A text that is philologically obscure is a text where a word is unknown to us, where the meaning of an expression remains uncertain, or where a lesson is unclear. A difficult text can be difficult either because it is obscure or because its clarity subverts what we were expecting it to say, for example if it attributes to God a bodily being or passions that we judge to be excluded from the concept of God; if it seems to praise an action that we consider to be a fault; or if it seems to affirm theses that we know scientifically to be false. In such cases, a hermeneutical obscurity is doubled by a properly philological obscurity. Under the name of 'criteria for interpretation', these two problems are in fact identical, and it is their identification that structures the hermeneutical field in the classical age.

Now, Spinoza occupies an entirely atypical position in this field:

— He recognises that certain passages in the Bible are obscure. It might be thought that Spinoza is closer to the Catholics on this point, but two differences annul this comparison: the majority of these obscurities are, in Spinoza's mind, irremediable. Spinoza also adds that in the final analysis, these points of obscurity are not important. There is perhaps no more radical a condemnation of a certain conception of the sacred than Spinoza's admission that this loss is insignificant. This is a more serious desacralisation than the one that consists in accepting that there exist partial corruptions of the biblical text. Even from the perspective of textual critique, there is no doubt not a single passage in the whole of the *TTP* where Spinoza claims to clarify,

---

[143] Cf. P.-F. Moreau, 'Ecriture Sainte et contre-Réforme: la position suarézienne', *Revue des sciences philosophiques et théologiques*, 64/3 (1980), pp. 349–54.

in the strict sense of the term, a passage that had remained obscure before him. This is quite striking given that the *TTP* is a work that is often considered to be the foundational text of a new kind of exegesis. But our sense of surprise disappears when we note that Spinoza does not seek – and nor does he require – the transparency of the totality of the text for his exegesis. Rather, he is more concerned to rigorously delimit what is known and what is not known.

— As for those passages that are clear but nevertheless difficult, how should they be understood? If they are resolutely clear from the perspective of their signification, the question arises as to how one should choose between their possible meanings. Should one appeal to reason? To political authority? To the authority of majesty or the authority of tradition? To Scripture itself? The first response is that of Maimonides and Meyer – and it is also, *grosso modo*, the response of those 'Cartesian Cocceins' [*coccéiens cartésianisants*] like Velthuysen or Vogelsang. The second response is that of Hobbes; the third is that of the Catholics or of those that Spinoza names the Pharisees; and the last is that of both Reformists and Spinoza himself.[144]

For Spinoza, the question is not that of knowing whether it is necessary or not to use reason in reading Scripture. Of course it is necessary to use reason to the extent that one can. The question is rather: when should reason be introduced as a criterion? There are in fact two successive stages involved in reading: first, establishing the meaning of words and of texts in order to understand what is being said; and second, judging what has thereby been understood.

The first stage is that of archaeology. It is a question of treating the Bible as the science of philology would treat any other text – and, more generally, as the science of Nature would treat Nature. In this sense, to interpret Scripture on the basis of Scripture itself means abstaining from bringing our own beliefs or preferences (even if they are rational) to bear on the object we are studying. When Moses declares that God is a fire or that God is Jealous, the archaeologist will not introduce what he himself thinks of these nominations: he will abstain from saying – in the name of truth, for instance – that God is immaterial and impassive; he will also abstain, in the name of probability, from saying that a man like Moses could not have been under

---

[144] For good measure, we should add individual inspiration, which is not the same thing as Reason. This is the solution of a certain number of sectarians in the eighteenth century. Amongst the Socinians, for instance, natural light is mixed with inspiration from the Holy Spirit.

the sway of these illusions. The argument that would make the archaeologist read these passages – whether in the name of truth or probability – as either additions to the text or as allegories would lead him to confuse his own preferences with those evinced by the object itself. Symmetrically, the Libertine who would pre-emptively judge that these propositions must be read literally – given that they are propositions often made by common people or the ignorant – would also be prioritising his own judgement over the analysis of the text. He would thus not be reading Scripture on its own terms, but in terms of his condemnation of it. Spinoza's solution consists in putting forward an objective criterion that allows us to decide in each individual case – albeit as a function of a universal principle – whether or not the passage in question is allegorical. This criterion is that of the comparison of texts with each other – not directly but by way of a triage of the meanings of words and the reconstitution of the mentalities that these texts contain. Given that the other passages where Moses speaks show that he believed in an immaterial God – the totality of his attitude also shows this – the formula 'God is a fire' must be taken in a figurative sense. On the other hand, given that when one uses the same procedure to show that the idea of divine impassivity is foreign to Moses, as it generally was to the ancient Hebrews, it is necessary to read 'God is jealous' in its literal sense. Thus, there can be no pre-established solution: it is the analysis of the language and thought of the authors of the Holy Scriptures that allows us to come to a decision in each textual situation.

It remains to determine why Spinoza uses the Protestant formula *scriptura sola* to refer to this procedure. We might suspect that this is neither a simple homonymy nor a ruse to seduce a reader who is a believer. In the end, there exists between the Protestant principle of the comparison of texts and the Spinozist principle of the comparison of words and mentalities the same relation that exists between the inadequate and the adequate. The first can be conceived as the mutilation of the second. It is therefore not illegitimate to give them an identical name, following the method that Spinoza himself adopts in the *Cogitata metaphysica*.

In the second stage of archaeology, it is necessary to use reason directly. Once we have understood what the actors and authors of the sacred texts are saying and thinking, we must ask to what extent what they say is truthful, and then what we should retain from it. This is the meaning of Spinoza's critique of Alfakhar: 'It's certainly true that Scripture ought to be explained by Scripture, so long as we're only working out the meaning of the statements and the Prophets' intention. But once we've unearthed the true meaning, we must, necessarily, use judgement and reason to give it our assent.'[145] In sum, if Scripture is the interpreter of meaning, reason is the interpreter of truth.

Let us now return to the procedure that consists in interpreting Scripture by itself in order to understand its meaning. What we discover is that this procedure consists, precisely, in having recourse to experience. Experience cannot contradict reason: it can confirm it, anticipate it or concretise it. We will now see how experience is operative in the different strata that constitute Spinoza's analyses.

— A first level of archaeology consists in drawing on use in order to establish meaning and signification. It is here that we find the theoretical site of Spinoza's discussion with Maimonides. If we wish to know with precision what the Spirit of God signifies, or the Word of God, it is necessary to analyse the series of passages in which these expressions or their components appear – and not to ask what meaning reason or philosophy give these formulas. Now, as I noted in the previous section, the analysis of these passages is constituted entirely by an inventory of language use.

— Another level of archaeology is that of the mentality of authors. Now, one quickly realises that mentality is not the same as intention, and that it is not always of an individual order. To clarify the text by reference to its author (that is, its actor, if it is a matter of words attributed to some individual, or a gesture whose meaning we wish to decipher) is not to ask what the author meant (for this would be to beg the question) but to reconstitute what the structure of their mind, so far as we can know it, should have made them say. Now, this structure cannot be known deductively. Only experience can teach us about singular things. Experience, here, refers to those conclusions that we can draw from the other passages where we see this same actor appear.[146] Take the example of Joshua. To know how to read the passage in which Joshua is said to have stopped the sun in its course,[147] Spinoza begins by establishing that the text is indubitably clear: it effectively says that the sun stopped and that Joseph believed that it did. We thus find ourselves

---

[145] 'Verum quidem est Scripturam per Scripturam explicandam esse, quamdiu de solo orationum sensu & mente Prophetarum laboramus, sed postquam verum sensum eruimus, necessario judicio et ratione utendum, ut ipsi assensum praebeamus', *TTP*, Chapter XV, p. 181, l. 33; p. 182, l. 4; A., p. 251 [*TTP* XV, 8; *CWS* II, 274].

[146] It has perhaps not been sufficiently remarked upon that for Spinoza, the fundamental units of the Bible are neither the books nor even the authors: they are the actors. He thus shows clearly that the author of the Pentateuch is Ezra and not Moses, but it is Moses' mentality that interests him.

[147] *TTP*, Chapter II, G III, p. 35, l. 33; p. 36, l. 19 [*TTP* II, 26–7; *CWS* II, 101].

with a situation that is typical of Spinoza's reading practices: what is most important is showing that the text is not difficult in itself. What causes us difficulties is the disparity between what we expected the text to say and what it does effectively say. But why do we seek to torture the text to make it say something else? The answer is that while we know that the sun cannot stop, the biblical text seems to imply that it did. Spinoza must now struggle on two fronts: on the one hand, against the obscurantist theologian who would seek to make astronomy submit to the text's logic (and here, the use of reason as an interpreter of truth is enough to reject this pretention); and on the other hand against the Concordist theologian, who seeks to reconcile as best as he can the biblical text with the rigour of astronomy.[148] What is Spinoza's positive response? That Joshua was a solider and was therefore not required to know astronomy. What decides the question, then, is Joshua's *ingenium*, and this *ingenium* is not read as a function of an individual's traits, but rather of their profession.

The description that Spinoza gives of mentalities is sometimes individual (this is the case for Moses), but more often than not it is linked to a group — a social category, a type of prophet, and so on. Here again we encounter the following question, a question we encountered with respect to a people, but applied this time to an individual or group: what is their *ingenium*? Here again, we come up against a category that brings together a certain number of traits that cannot be known deductively. We will have to return to this notion of the *ingenium*, in which an entire dimension of experience is concentrated: that which characterises the determinations of an individual.

— When Spinoza explores the meaning of Scripture from an experiential perspective, he also engages in literary analysis. The same content, when recounted in a different way, signifies something different. For example, Spinoza distinguishes between narrative passages and those that convey lessons. But he also distinguishes within the category of narratives an interesting example that brings together Ariosto, Ovid and the Bible. We can read the same story in the three texts, and each time it has a different signification. Samson and Delilah present the same marvellous traits as Roland and Perseus.[149] However, while the stories are similar at the level of their narrative material, the authors' intentions mean that they insert this material into narrative wholes that have different tonalities, whether novelistic, political

---

[148] That the problem remains a contemporary one can be shown by referring to the fact that this is the subject of the quarrel between Velthuysen and Voetius.

[149] *TTP*, Chapter VII, G III, p. 110, ll. 9–23 [*TTP* VII, 2–3; CWS II, 170].

or sacred.[150] It could be said that Spinoza is operating here on the terrain of poetics, which was so important to theoreticians of literature in his time, particularly in the Netherlands.[151] Yet, in Spinoza's work this analysis is not an *a priori* deduction: it is, once again, based on what arises from experience.[152] In fact, Spinoza does not put forward a topography of different ways of writing: rather, he records irreducible differences in the expression of thought. The analysis of literary genres thus becomes the analysis of discursive genres.

At the beginning of Chapter XI of the *TTP*, Spinoza distinguishes between the Apostles and the prophets. What is extremely interesting here is that this distinction is not based on what the Apostles think of themselves. Rather, it is founded on an objective external criterion: namely, the way that the prophets write, which for Spinoza reveals their way of thinking. It is possible to distinguish the style of the prophet from that of the apostle[153] in terms of the way they address their respective audiences: the prophet speaks with authority, for he feels himself invested with a divine mission, while the apostle speaks in a courteous way[154] for he has only his natural reason at his disposal and is only expressing his personal opinion. This is why Paul excuses himself for being too imperious.[155] It is therefore not only the content of the

---

[150] Proeitti suggests that we should read 'poetical' as 'political' when it comes to Ovid. He is no doubt right. In any case, if Spinoza is thinking of a political meaning in Ovid's text (perhaps the programme of reform under Augustus?), he does not say what it is.

[151] Vossius wrote a Poetics. This was not only the obsession of a grammarian: one of the tasks effectively carried out by the society led by L. Meyer and Bouwmeester, *Nil Volentibus Arduum*, was to constitute a theory of theatrical genres, drawing on, amongst other things, the theory of passions. Cf. G. van Suchtele, 'Nil Volentibus Arduum: les amis de Spinoza au travail', *Studia Spinozana*, III (1987), pp. 391–404, and the volume *Onderwys in de toneel-poëzy. De opvattingen over toneel van het Kunstgenootschap Nil Volentibus Arduum*, published with an introduction and notes by A. J. E. Harmsen, Rotterdam: Ordeman, 1989.

[152] I cannot develop here the relation between Spinoza and poetic creation. I will have to be content with referring to the beautiful pages written by F. Mignini, *Ars Imaginandi. Apparenza e rappresentazione in Spinoza*, Naples: Edizioni Scientifiche Italiane, 1981, p. 213 ff.

[153] 'Verum si ad earum [sc.: Epistolarum] stylum attendere volumus, eum a stylo Prophetiae alienissimum inveniemus', *TTP*, Chapter XI, G III, p. 151, ll. 17–19 [*TTP* XI, 2; *CWS* II, 240].

[154] '[Epistolas] nihil continere praeter fraternas monitiones mixtas urbanitate (a qua sane prophetica authoritas plane abhorret)', *TTP*, Chapter XI, G III, p. 153, ll. 20–2 [*TTP* XI, 8; *CWS* II, 243].

[155] 'Paulo audacius scripsi vobis, fratres', Romans 15:15, cited by Spinoza, *TTP*, Chapter XI, G III, p. 153, ll. 24–5 [*TTP* XI, 8; *CWS* II, 243].

apostle's declarations that shows that they base what they say on natural light and Revelation: it is also their way of speaking and teaching.[156] We see emerge here the outlines of a hermeneutics of social life.[157] Note, moreover, that what Spinoza analyses in this way is indeed a structure of discourse and not a particularity of the person who mobilises it. For the Apostles were also prophets, but they were not prophets when they were writing their letters. Inversely, prophets are not perpetually in a state of revelation; but they are when they write.[158]

On this point, too, it should also be noted that Spinoza gives philosophical importance to an argument that he himself does not invent. For example, Hobbes, too, when reflecting on language, outlines an analysis of the genres of discourse and reduces this diversity to certain fundamental traits of the human mind.[159] But he rarely uses this classification when dealing with biblical texts.

Following *usus* and the *ingenium*, the third appearance of experience in the interpretation of Scripture is thus the perception of styles and genres. Up to this point we have presented the way experience functions in the establishment of the text. It remains to show how the consideration of this distinction allows us to eliminate certain apparent contradictions in Spinoza's own work. It is not only in the *TTP* that Spinoza speaks of the Bible. He also mentions it in some detail in the *Ethics* and in the *Correspondence*. And in these works he sometimes seems to forget what he said about the Bible in the *TTP*. Thus, in Book IV of the *Ethics*, Proposition 68, he states: 'If men were born free, they would form no concept of good and evil so long as they remained free.' And the Scholium continues: 'This, and the other things I have demonstrated seem to have been indicated by Moses in that story of the first man.'[160] There are two reasons to be surprised by this: first, Moses

---

[156] 'Tam modi loquendi quam disserendi', *TTP*, Chapter XI, G III, p. 153, l. 17 [*TTP* XI, 7; *CWS* II, 243].

[157] Cf. what R. Piepmeier says with respect to Book III of the *Ethics* (Scholium to Proposition 51): 'Das bedeutet, daß di Bedingungen der Hermeneutik alltäglicher Praxis an die Lieblichkeit des Menschen gebunden sind', 'Baruch de Spinoza: Vernunftanspruch und Hermeneutik', in U. Nassen (hrsg.), *Klassiker der Hermeneutik*, Paderborn: UTB Schöning, 1982, pp. 9–42, p. 13.

[158] This double distinction is explicitly formulated in the first lines of the chapter, G III, p. 151, ll. 8–17 [*TTP* XI, 1; *CWS* II, 240].

[159] *Leviathan*, Part I, Chapter VIII: 'Of the Vertues commonly called Intellectual; and their contrary Defects': classification of poetry, history, praise and invective as a function of the genre according to which the speaker (and not only the writer) expresses themselves allows the listener to know what kind of criteria to use to judge it.

[160] *Ethics* IV, 68, Schol.; *CWS* I, 584.

appears here as the author at the very least of Genesis, which the *TTP* denies is the case; and second, the biblical narrative is being interpreted here as a sort of allegorical double of what the *Ethics* shows rationally. In other words, Spinoza is engaged in a procedure that he elsewhere reproaches Maimonides for following. We cannot avoid this problem by supposing that the text in question belongs to one of the oldest drafts of the *Ethics*, for the fact is that the definitive work that Spinoza left us and that he was most likely getting ready to publish in 1675 contains this passage written in this way. We must therefore account for it as it is presented to us, whatever the date of its effective redaction, as Spinoza did not judge it to be incompatible with the rest of his book.

Now, it must be asked if this divergence does not refer in fact to a difference in status. Indeed, readers of the first chapters of the *TTP* might have the impression that the Bible is prophecy: the study of prophecy begins, in effect, with the study of the Bible; and the Bible serves as a paradigm for thinking the idea of revelation. In this respect, Spinoza's procedure is quite classical. And yet, if we attend closely to the following chapters, we realise that for Spinoza prophecy is only one biblical discourse among others. There exist at least four more: *statements of natural reason*; *historical narratives*; *texts of law*; and *parables*.

— The remarks attributed to Solomon constitute examples of the *discourse of natural reason*. As such, they are in no way related to those properties that characterise prophecy as an imaginative genre. On the other hand, however, Solomon's remarks are recorded in Hebrew and with the stylistic characteristics proper to ancient or oriental languages. In these conditions, part of what was said regarding prophetic discourse – specifically, its mode of expression – applies here as well. This incites one to reread the first chapters to discern, regarding prophecy, what applies in both cases. Similarly, elsewhere, for instance in what Spinoza says of Hebrew and of the mentality that undergirds this language, it is necessary to distinguish what is absolutely proper to Hebrew and what applies to all ancient languages.

— *Historical narratives*. There are two analyses in the *TTP* that deal with two different questions by referring to historical narratives: first, the necessity of faith (Chapter V), and second the utility of reading these narratives (Chapter IV). Faith in historical narratives is necessary for the ignorant or the common people, because it gives them knowledge of the 'word of God' in the form of experience. Put differently, understanding the word of God does not only mean listening to the exhortations of a prophet; it also means reading the lessons incarnated in action. Reading historical narratives is also useful for everyone since it provides knowledge of people's customs. Two chapters (IV and V) from the *TTP* highlight the usefulness of narratives in terms of experience, but it is not the same tonality of experience that is in play in the two cases. In the second, it is also not a matter of a narrative incarnation of the Divine Word, but rather of an experience tied to Reason that occurs in the context of civil society. In this context, biblical narratives have the same use as the narratives of Livy or Tacitus. There is nevertheless an imbalance between this duality of functions, since Scripture composes its narratives in its own style, which is not that of political historians: Scripture makes its narratives tend towards piety and the encouragement of justice (this, moreover, is what determines that its narratives merit the title of Holy Scripture; but it also means that they pose a risk if one wishes to read them directly as models).

— *The Laws.* If the laws are no longer considered as models, then in some respects they become part of the category of narratives. It is nevertheless worthwhile noting the particular type of approach that is manifest in certain of Spinoza's analyses (for example those from chapters XVII and XVIII). The law, being at once a statement and a functional principle, determines that its study will have to take into account both the text of the law and what the historical narrative reveals of the consequences of its functioning. In that case, however, the historical narrative in question is not necessarily a biblical narrative. To judge the *effects* of Moses' construction, Spinoza authorises himself to seek out information in Tacitus or Flavius Josephus. In doing so, however, he does not believe himself to be breaking the rule of *Sola Scriptura*.

— *The Parables.* We must note first of all that each time Spinoza speaks of the parables, it is to point out an uncertainty – not an uncertainty that is his alone, but rather an uncertainty that exists between his adversaries and himself: neither party can agree on what *genre* the text of the parables belongs to. It is this disagreement that governs his discussion of them. For example, at the end of Chapter II, with respect to the Book of Job, Spinoza initially interprets this Book as a narrative in which God speaks to Job by making himself visible. Spinoza then adds that this would indeed be the correct interpretation 'if [. . .] the author [of that book] was concerned to narrate a history, [and] not, as some believe, to embellish his conceptions . . .'.[161] In the first version, we are dealing with a language of the imagination in

---

[161] *TTP* II, 55; *CWS* II, 110. [Translators note: I have had to add a number of syntactical and logical links to this sentence relative to Moreau's original, simply to restore what I think he means to say, but which he expresses here in a particularly elliptical form. I have also altered slightly the quote from the *TTP* to better fit this new formulation.]

the prophetic sense of the word: that is, with a series of images that do not depend on the will of the prophet. In the second, we are dealing with a conscious allegory, where the author uses images to translate a rational intention. Once one has made a decision about which of the two versions is the correct one, there follows, according to the principles of the *TTP*, the usefulness – or not – of inquiring into the speculative meaning of the text. We find the same uncertainty (but in a contrary sense) with respect to the story of Adam and the fruits of the tree of good and evil. Three texts refer to this: the Scholium from the *Ethics*, Book IV, Proposition 68, cited above; Chapter IV from the *TTP*; and two letters to Blijenbergh. Chapter IV from the *TTP* even deals with this story twice: the first time as a narrative in which we see the difference between a law understood in itself and a law conceived as a commandment; and the second time as a parable on the necessity of seeking the good for itself and not because of fear or because it is the contrary of evil. 'It would not be difficult to explain that whole story, *or* parable, of the first man from this foundation.' However, Spinoza omits this explanation precisely because of the divergence between readers on the status of this passage ('most people will not grant that this story is a parable, but maintain without qualification that it is a simple record of fact').[162] Note that Spinoza does not advance such hypotheses concerning books that recount the history of the Hebrews: these must appear to him as being on the whole grounded in the collective tradition of the Hebrew people since Moses. On the other hand, the stories of Adam and Job do not fit this framework – whence the temptation to consider them as fables that have been placed in the Bible for a rational purpose.

With respect to the archaeology of the Bible, we can thus conclude that the experiential nature of language appears here much more as a resource than as a difficulty. When Spinoza condemns the recourse to reason, what he is condemning are misunderstandings of this kind. This in no way means that he rejects reason. What leads us to experience is itself a rational decision.

B. Theology

In the context of this multifaceted archaeology, Spinoza's method runs an obvious risk, one that it shares with all forms of biblical science developed in the classical age: that of erecting a barrier between the sacred text and its readers. If, on the one hand, the text is presented as a mediation between

---

[162] *TTP* IV, 39; CWS II, 135.

the absolute and the believer, but on the other hand is said to be readable only with the help of an entire apparatus of specialised sciences – if it is necessary to know history, oriental languages and psychology – then the question arises of who can be saved. Such an accumulation of conditions obviously does not satisfy the requirements of Protestantism, since it cuts the believer off from their access to Scripture. But we could also question its conformity with Catholicism, for with Spinoza it is the job of scientists and not of the magisterium to confer rights upon biblical interpretation.[163] There is no doubt that it is just such a transformation of the Bible into an object of specialised study that will play a role in the development, at the end of the classical age and after, of those religiosities of the heart or of conscience that will attempt to put an end to this proliferation of scientific exegeses. If the believer is dispossessed of the Bible, they will go and seek truth from some other source. It is possible to consider Hobbes's position as already being a response to this question, and Meyer's as well: what solves the difficulties tied to the archaeology of the letter is, in the first case, the intervention of the Sovereign, and in the second the intervention of reason.

Spinoza is perfectly conscious of this problem; in fact he formulates it explicitly. He also seeks to respond to it with the distinction he establishes between Scripture and theology. As a totality, Scripture is what the Bible says; it is the product of archaeology. Theology, as the word of God in the strict sense, is the product only of what each and every individual understands of the Bible. If Spinoza's solution to this problem is clear, its conditions are perhaps less so. Should we see this solution as one that reduces the obstacles posed by language? But if this obstacle can also be a resource, how does this solution avoid the ambiguity and the dangerous effects of the imagination?

What is perhaps most troubling is the suggested comparison with Euclid. Both the Bible and Euclid, Spinoza tells us, can be understood irrespective of the difficulties of translation they pose because they are speaking of the simplest and most common problems. How should we understand these terms relative to these two cases?

What characterises the fundamental teachings of Scripture is that they remain comprehensible beyond the multitude of problems posed by Scripture's archaeology. In other words, Scripture is at once very difficult and very simple. It is very difficult at the level of the text as a whole, for only extensive and serious work, along with a series of specialises sciences,

---

[163] Cf. what is said about this with respect to Maimonides, but that can also be applied elsewhere, *TTP*, Chapter VII, G III, p. 114, ll. 24–31 [*TTP* VII, 79; *CWS* II, 188–9].

can consolidate its clarity. But it is also very simple in terms of the essence of what it teaches, for what is most common is most easily conceived. It remains to explain why this is so.

At this point one might be tempted to ask: is it not possible to separate the essential text from the total text? The answer must be both yes and no. No, because the crowd understands Scripture only by means of stories. What is essential to the Bible is thus not presented in the form of a conclusion that can always in principle be separated from a text that remains irreducible to it. The essence of Scripture is separable more than it is intrinsically separated. Theology, or the word of God, is not a text, but it is presented to the reader only to the degree that it is inserted into the text of Scripture. This text is not some shell that needs to be taken off. Rather, it is the necessary support for the lessons of experience. But the answer is also yes since Spinoza seems to admit that biblical teachings evolved towards ever greater clarity. It is obvious that for Spinoza the prophets are closer to the essence of Scripture than Moses was. Finally, the specificity of Christ's teachings has to do with the fact that they say nothing new.[164] The proof that the answer to the question posed above is both yes and no is that Spinoza sets out to summarise theology's teachings in the form of a minimal *credo* – a *credo* that was never summarised in this way in the Bible itself. When Spinoza does this, he takes care to indicate that the different variations – or the matrices of possible variations – are functions of the *ingenium* of each individual. And he states that each person is required to adapt this *credo* to their own *ingenium*. If, then, the essential teachings of the Bible are comprehensible in all languages, it is because they can be represented using many different images.

What about mathematics? The objects mathematics deals with are beings of reason,[165] but the imagination still plays a role here as the auxiliary of reason in the figuring of certain properties of things. In mathematical demonstrations, the truth of the demonstration depends not on the imagined figure but on the real property that is thereby being figured. The names used by Euclid are borrowed from common language (they are homonymous with those of the corresponding imagined objects) but they serve simply as indicators that focus the mind on such-and-such a being of reason and communicate to others what has been demonstrated. The process of geometrical demonstration is sufficiently rigorous to exclude all imaginary deviations caused by names. The notions used by Euclid are common and simple insofar as they are practically separated from the names that indicate them. While

---

[164] Cf. A. Matheron, *Le Christ et le salut des ignorants*, Paris: Aubier, 1971.
[165] Cf. M. Gueroult, *Spinoza*, vol. I, *Dieu*, Appendix I.

the ensemble of theological notions is characterised by their perceptive richness, mathematical notions are characterised by their poverty.[166]

Thus, on the one hand, the common character of Euclid's teachings is a common that is separated; the common character of the teachings of theology is a common that is separable. This is why, strictly speaking, if each individual can grasp what is essential in Scripture, it is nevertheless preferable that they have a good text at their disposal and that they be given guidance. This is why Spinoza no doubt undertook to translate the Pentateuch. The role of the learned is no longer that of constituting a new Church but to produce a text that is sufficiently readable for it to engage people's piety.

Let us take three examples: to know if the sum of the angles of a triangle is equal to two right-angles, it matters little what language I can read, for the images on which the demonstration is based are neutralised by adequate ideas. To know whether Moses believed that God was jealous or not, I need linguistic, historical and philological knowledge. To know if the Bible teaches that that there exists a God who models the true life, I do not need to know any of this: reading the Bible in Dutch will show me a sufficient number of stories where this God intervenes. As such, what is essential will remain. The images on which the demonstration is based are not neutralised; they produce equivalent images. They respond to experience – to questions posed by experience. Note that these are the same questions that Meyer believes are posed by the Bible. It is well known that at the end of his book *Philosophy as the Interpreter of Holy Scripture*, where he establishes that the field of theology is the same as that of philosophy, Meyer asks: what use is the Bible? He answers: to awaken in us questions that we would otherwise have never asked. It could be said that Spinoza takes the opposite approach. The final Spinozist meaning appears instead to be that the Bible, as theology, responds to pre-existing questions. If we make a list of these questions – that is, if we conceive the minimal *credo* as a system of responses – then we basically obtain the list of questions that Spinoza had posed in the *proemium*: How should we think of the true life? Towards what end should we direct our actions? Will we perish? Will we seek out an eternal thing to the exclusion of others? Does the choice of certain actions bring punishment? And so on.

In sum, if the Bible contains theological answers, it is above all because there exist theological questions – questions that we all pose, at least confusedly. Without these questions, the Bible's answers would be of no interest

---

[166] What is valid for number is not valid for figures (cf. Gueroult, ibid.) But, in fact, Spinoza considers Euclid to be a geometer.

to us. These are not questions invented by theologians, but questions that arise spontaneously within us and against the backdrop of our activity and our situation. At this point we cannot yet explain why they arise, but we do have to attest to their existence. Let us give them the following provisional name: the questions of finitude.

4. The Work of Language

A first aspect of Spinoza's work on language – one that is not theorised as such – seems to be to tied to language's relation to culture. If language can concentrate a cultural heritage, if it can concentrate experience, then to think and transmit thoughts is also to take up the language of others. This is the reason for Spinoza's multifaceted practice of quotation by which he reprises the anonymous materials of proverbs and the memorable formulas of poets or orators. This is not a cultural tic on Spinoza's part, nor an outgrowth of his scholastic culture: it is an attitude that is grounded in his system itself – specifically, in the system's theses concerning language.

Thus, as we saw above, those formulas of Spinoza's where he condenses experience knowingly take up proverbial forms of speech. The numerous quotations of Tacitus or Terence, of Seneca or Ovid, mark what everyone has always, already known concerning the *ingenium* or fortune, the passions or human affairs. I will give a few examples of this knowledge in the follower chapter on the theory of the passions.

But what about when Spinoza seeks to rigorously define those concepts on which his properly deductive procedure will be based? Let us return for a moment to the names of the affects in the *Ethics*. We saw above that Spinoza takes note of the nature of language, rooted as it is in the use of life and thus irreducible to any purely rational lexical decisions. Faced with this consistency proper to language, what does he do? Will the philosopher who constructs a rational theory of the passions, grounded in their nature and not their effects, create an entirely new terminology, one that deliberately ignores this pre-existing terminology? No, he will not. Instead, he will allow his theses to flow into the mould of the existing language, while occasionally modifying it. There are three possible cases:

— Sometimes Spinoza is content to signal a divergence between what the study of the nature of passions dictates and what use suggests. This is the case with respect to timidity and overestimation. Thus he conforms to use when it comes to the name of the affect, but diverges with respect to the procedure that this name suggests. Spinoza thus takes use into account in a negative way, and he is careful to alert the reader to this.

— On other occasions, Spinoza conforms to use right up to the point of accepting its consequences. This is the case with wonder and the complex passions that derive from it. In the section on the affects Spinoza also goes so far as to deal with both surprise and contempt since these are affects that are commonly referred to. In these cases, then, Spinoza allows use to make a positive contribution to his philosophy.

— Finally, in very rare cases Spinoza goes against use, but once again he does not fail to signal this fact. 'I know', he says, 'that in their common use these words mean something else. But my purpose is to explain the nature of things, not the meaning of words. I intend to indicate these things by words whose usual meaning is not entirely opposed to the meaning with which I wish to use them.'[167] It is obviously this last case that is most interesting. We should note first of all that whenever Spinoza reworks use, he tells the reader what he is doing.[168] There is nothing furtive about this act of redefinition. Moreover, it is indeed a matter of redefining words and not an act of creation or of total change. Spinoza underscores that the definition he requires for his system is not too distant from the common meaning. It is thus necessary to conserve use insofar as it constitutes a common terrain with the reader. We once again find ourselves here in a situation that we have become familiar with since the first pages of the *TdIE*. Shared experience is the point of departure for the journey of philosophy.

Use thus constitutes something of a springboard even for those who wish to distance themselves from it. There is a strategy behind the construction of a philosophical language: this language is not made out of nothing. Even the history of a word can help us gain access to the historical meaning of a notion. We see Spinoza engage in just such an operation of philosophical etymology in the *Cogitata* with respect to the word *true* or the term *life*. He does the same in the introduction to Book IV of the *Ethics* on the topic of the notion of *perfection*, and in the *TTP* on the topic of the word *law*. Let us take the example of the 'true' since it is the most detailed. The philosopher

---

[167] 'Haec nomina ex communi usu aliud significare scio. Sed meum institutum non est, verborum significationem, sed rerum naturam explicare, easque iis vocabulis indicare, quorum significatio, quam ex usu habent, a significatione, qua eadem usurpare volo, non omnino abhorret', *Ethics* III, DA #20, Exp., G II, p. 195, ll. 19–23 [CWS I, 535–6].

[168] The same goes for the redefinition of compassion (DA #24): it is preceded, in the explanation to Definition 23, by the following warning: 'Invidiae opponitur communiter misericordia, quae proinde, invita vocabuli significatione, sic definiri potest', G II, p. 196, ll. 12–13 [*Ethics* III, DA #24, CWS II, 536].

who wishes to know the first meaning of a word must begin by asking himself what this word means for the common people, since it is the common people who invent the words that philosophers then take up. In Spinoza's eyes, this 'first meaning' does not possess any normative value. While it is often the most concrete, nothing requires that it possess more 'truth' than any other meaning. The fact that its meaning is easier to reconstitute effectively avoids the ambiguities inherent in a philosophical lexicon. In the case of the word 'true', this first signification 'seems to have had its origin in stories: a story was called true when it was of a deed that had really happened, and false when it was of a deed that had never happened'. Then, by way of metaphor, philosophers have used the same term to refer to ideas that are 'narratives or mental histories of nature'.[169] There is thus nothing in the history of the word that justifies that we apply it to the same things or to being.

But if this is so, then we must distinguish between two types of modification: on the one hand, the modification that surreptitiously inflects the history of a term, leading to error; and on the other hand, the modification that is consciously introduced, is based on use but modifies it just enough to make the word apt for expressing adequate ideas. The clearest case is no doubt the analysis of the word 'perfect' at the beginning of Book IV of the *Ethics*, where Spinoza explains precisely in what framework he will use the word and which of its successive extensions he will then analyse. Such a work on language is in principle always possible, since we can imagine anything. Even God, who is not an object of the imagination, can find names on the basis of His power.[170]

The work of transforming language can also be more brutal. For instance, it can occur by way of redefinitions, as in the *Short Treatise*.[171] Similarly, in the *TTP*, Spinoza sometimes circumvents the complex schema that we have just described.[172] Finally, numerous Spinozist formulations, based on *seu* or *sive*, represent a similar work on language performed within a common theoretical sequence. The common foundation of all of these procedures is the following: the *prima significatio* and the ones that follow refer to something

---

[169] CM VI; CWS I, 312.
[170] On other approaches to the same problem of the names of God, cf. G. Deleuze, *Expressionism in Philosophy: Spinoza*, New York: Zone Books, 1990, Chapter 3, pp. 53–68; J.-L. Marion, 'Spinoza et les trois noms de Dieu', in *Herméneutique et ontologie. Hommage à Pierre Aubenque*, sous la direction de R. Brague et J.-F. Courtine, Paris: PUF, 1990, pp. 225–45 (on the basis of Proposition 11 from Book I).
[171] Cf. the definitions of providence, predestination, etc.
[172] Cf. in Chapter III, for 'God's guidance', 'God's aid (both external and internal)', 'God's choice', 'fortune', TTP III, 7; CWS II, 112.

inadequate; but an inadequate idea is a mutilated adequate idea; thus, there is no simple relation of homonymy between the two. Similarly, we occasionally take philosophical theses 'literally'.[173] All of this can help us think what the expression *ad captum vulgi* – according to the crowd's understanding – means, it being understood that the learned can be part of the crowd as well. This expression does not refer to a pious lie or to a prudent dissimulation, and for two reasons: first, Spinoza explicitly excludes lies from the work of philosophy; and second, can we call a lie a partial truth to which we are immediately given the interpretative key?

It should be noted that, in all of these cases, Spinoza's work on language occurs out in the open. It is more or less rapid, more or less detailed, but it is never hidden. For this reason it can in no way be identified with a 'double language'. A double language, like the one that the Libertines practised, consists in separating the interior from the exterior, 'the judgement from the hand', as Charron's famous formula says.[174] By contrast, Spinoza's work on language consists in explicitly clarifying one by the other.

This is why the rules of reading proposed by Leo Strauss seem to me to be unacceptable.[175] They suppose, first of all, that there exists no work on language. In Strauss's reading, this work is replaced by the superimposition of two different languages that do not communicate with one another, with the first functioning simply to hide the second, save to some elite reader to whom its existence is signalled by its purposeful contradictions. Such a

---

[173] A. Matheron has shown this in the cases of Grotius and Hobbes ('Spinoza et la problématique juridique de Grotius', in *Anthropologie et politique au XVIIe siècle*, pp. 81–101).

[174] 'Il adviendra souvent que le jugement et la main, l'esprit et le corps se contrediront & que le sage fera au-dehors des choses qu'il juge en son esprit qu'il serait beaucoup meilleur de faire autrement, il jouera un rôle au-dedans et un autre dehors, il le doit ainsi pour la révérance publique et n'offenser personne, ce que la loi, la coutume, la cérémonie du pays porte et requiert & encore qu'il ne soit en soi ni bon ni juste', 'Petit Traité de sagesse', in *Toutes les œuvres de P. Charron*, P. Villery, 1635, p. 205. On this principle and its applications, see the update by F. Charles-Daubert, 'Le libertinage et la recherche contemporaine', *XVIIe siècle*, Special Edition, 149 (1985), 'Le libertinage érudit', p. 413.

[175] Rather than engaging in a complete evaluation of Leo Strauss's positions, I will refer to the studies of Y. Belaval, 'Pour une sociologie de la philosophie', *Critique*, 77 (1953), pp. 852–66 and of E. Harris, *Is There An Esoteric Doctrine in the 'Tractatus Theologico-Politicus'?* MVHS, XXXVIII, Leiden: Brill, 1978. I will return to this at greater length in a commentary on the *TTP*. Here, I will only deal with this evaluation from the point of view of the relations between the work of language and experience.

hypothesis is a product of a failed rationalist reading of the *TTP*. At root, it is an inversion of Meyer's reading: one begins with the principle that everything in language is reducible either to transparency or to wilful obscurity; and since one then sees that language is not immediately transparent, one deduces that it is purposefully hiding what it wants to say. By contrast, by giving experience a place in his philosophy, Spinoza's absolute rationalism also has the means to think what escapes the immediacy of Reason.

This obviously does not imply that Spinoza's work cannot be read from a Libertine perspective. However, if it is, then it loses one of its essential dimensions.[176]

Let us conclude this section on the work on language. For Spinoza, to constitute a philosophical language does not mean returning to a blank slate and erasing common language. Rather, it is a matter of being conscious of the imaginative value of words and transforming them into quasi-conceptual instruments. If every language is a fact of experience, the quasi-conceptual word is the condensation of this experience, and it works thanks to the laws of association that bring this experience to mind. What the word allows the understanding to do, then, is not to extract what is adequate from the inadequate (only the process of knowledge can do this), but to recognise the common consequences of the adequate and the inadequate, which prior to that point had been registered as facts but that are henceforth known as effects.[177]

Certainly, this process is never perfect (whence formulations like 'to depart from the literal meaning as little as possible'), but ultimately what Spinoza does with language recalls the image he uses in the *TdIE* when speaking of the topic of material and intellectual instruments: we improve them bit by bit in practice.

5. Experience of Speech and Freedom of Speech

It is well known that Spinoza distinguishes himself from Hobbes in politics, in particular by his defence of freedom of speech.[178] Two doctrines of the

---

[176] On what happens in the *Traité des trois imposteurs*, it is necessary to refer to the works of F. Charles-Daubert and to those of R. Popkin, as well as to the work of F. Niewöhner, *Veritas sive Varietas. Lessings Toleranzparabel und das Buch Von den drei Betrügern*, Heidelberg: Verlag Lambert Schneider, 1988.

[177] On all of these questions of the reinvestment of language in philosophical discourse, see the detailed analyses of F. Biasutti, *La Dottrina della Scienza in Spinoza*, pp. 167–72.

[178] 'Impossibile esse libertatem hominibus dicendi ea, quae sentiunt, adimere', *TTP*,

State, so close on so many points, give rise to opposite conclusions on this issue. While Spinoza's and Hobbes's distinct conclusions are familiar to us, scholars have typically spent much less time studying the divergent processes of reasoning that lead to them. In fact, Spinoza's argument is striking in that he in no way simply enumerates abstract rights but rather adopts the point of view of the Prince himself. For Spinoza, it is in the Sovereign's interest to recognise freedom of speech. Why is it that what ordinarily appears either as a concession or as a recognition of an other's inalienable right is conceived by Spinoza as a mere fact or as one of the Sovereign's interests? If we seek out the reasons for this, what we find is, precisely, the experiential dimension of language that we have just identified.

In Hobbes, at least in politics, language is transparent. Outside of politics, it is homogeneous with thought, since reason is nothing other than calculations performed on names.[179] In the City, this homogeneity is instead interpreted as an absence of obstacles. To hold one's tongue is something that seems to be within everybody's power.[180] This is why the question of subjects' freedom seems reducible to their freedom to act; and there is no freedom at all, save in the domain that is explicitly or tacitly accorded by the Sovereign. Freedom of thought does not pose a problem, since it is not possible to control others' thoughts[181] (at best we can subjugate their judgement, which is another matter entirely). As for freedom of speech, it is not an intermediary case: it falls within the category of acts, and thus arises in its entirety from the regime of acts.[182] The true frontier passes between what is internal (thought) and what is external (acts and speech).[183] What is internal escapes the sphere of human justice, while what is external is part of it.[184] Thus, I can think what I want so long as I keep it to myself, but as a

---

Chapter XX, G III, p. 246, ll. 26–7 [*TTP* XX, 43; *CWS* II, 352].

[179] Cf. *Leviathan*, Part One, Chapters IV and V.

[180] *Leviathan*, Part One, Chapter VI: 'speaking' is given as an example of voluntary movement, just after 'walking'.

[181] Can a prince, for instance, prohibit someone from believing in Christ? 'To this I answer, that such forbidding is of no effect, because Beleef and Unbeleef never follow mens Commands', ibid., p. 527.

[182] 'Profession with the tongue is but an externall thing, and no more than any other gesture whereby we signify our obedience', ibid., pp. 527–8.

[183] We could compare this distinction with the one that is implicit in the *proemium* to the *Agricola*: after evoking the spying which, under Domitian, prevented everything including 'loquendi audiendique commercium', Tacitus adds: 'Memoriam quoque ipsam cum voce perdidissemus, si tam in nostra potestate esset oblivisci quam tacere', Chapter II.

[184] 'For internal faith is in its own nature invisible, and consequently exempted from human jurisdiction', in contrast to 'the words and actions that proceed from it',

good citizen I must do and say what the prince has commanded. This is at once necessary and possible – and Hobbes does not seem to doubt this for an instant. Each person is responsible for their thoughts before God alone. They are accountable for what they say or do to the Sovereign.

In Spinoza, by contrast, it is important to distinguish between freedom of acts and freedom of speech. The drive to speak appears as absolutely irrepressible. It is all the more strong that people claim to be unaware of it. Each individual believes themselves to be the master of their tongue. Two opposite situations arise from this: in the first, the person who has not yet spoken believes that they are capable of not speaking; in the second, he who does speak believes that he does so freely – even if, absurdly, in doing so he manifests his servitude. The tyrant's belief – that he can contradict the speech of others – is here only the mirror image of this belief shared by others. Here, as is so often the case, the person who seems to be exceptional is content to apply the common rule in exceptional circumstances. The drunk, the gossip, the chatterbox, or the childish person are all so many miniature tyrants since they too believe in the dictatorship of thought over language.

It is worthwhile following Spinoza's arguments closely. These arguments can be found in the Scholium where he affirms that the body moves without the intervention of the soul. The preceding Proposition had affirmed that neither the soul nor the body are determined by one another.[185] But only one aspect of this affirmation seems to interest the supposed contradictor, so strongly persuaded are they that the body obeys the commands of the soul. Among the causes of this persuasion, it seems to this contradictor that experience clearly teaches 'that it is in the Soul's power alone to both speak and be silent'.[186] Spinoza responds that, certainly, the affairs of human beings would go much more smoothly if it was in their power to be silent; but the fact is that experience daily proves the contrary: 'experience teaches all too plainly that men have nothing less in their power than their tongue'.[187] The demonstration does not end there, however: experience is also able to show why people fail to believe it. When they have just spoken, or repent for having done so, or when they say that they will regret what they are

Leviathan, p. 560.
[185] 'Nec corpus mentem ad cogitandum, nec mens corpus ad motum, neque ad quietem, nec ad aliquid (si quid est) aliud determinare potest', *Ethics* III, 2, G II, p. 141 [CWS I, 494].
[186] 'Deinde se experiri, in sola mentis potestate esse, tam loqui quam tacere', ibid., Schol., G II, p. 142, ll. 23–4 [CWS I, 495].
[187] 'At experientia satis superque docet, homines nihil minus in potestate habere quam linguam', G II, p. 143, ll. 14–15 [CWS I, 496].

saying – that is, when they show that their body acts without the decree of their soul – people still continue to persuade themselves that they are free. In truth, everyone knows that they are not free, but they only seem to know this as far as others are concerned, or at least certain others whose circumstances make the absence of freedom particularly flagrant. 'So the drunk believes it is from a free decision of the Soul that he speaks the things he later, when sober, wishes he had not said. So the madman, the chatterbox, the child, and a great many people of this kind believe they speak from a free decision of the Soul, when really they cannot contain their impulse to speak.'[188] Why does Spinoza offer these examples? Because they clearly show the opacity of experience for the person who, precisely, experiences it. For the spectator, it is obvious that the drunk is under the sway of their body; the same goes, but for different reasons, for the person who lacks strength for reasons of illness or natural weakness.[189] But what about the spectator themselves? They see clear signs of corporeal determination in others, and, confusing these signs with this determination itself, exempt themselves from determinism. Note that the example of delirium reprises the example from the letter to Balling. For the purposes of our own analysis, note that, once again, Spinoza treats language as an example and not as an object of analysis: it is the illusion of the power of the soul over the body that he is concerned to refute. But to refute it experientially, the detour by language is necessary. This choice is no doubt necessary because language shows in a particularly striking way the coincidence between the consciousness that we have of an action of the body and the ignorance of its cause. Our soul might well have decided that we will not speak – yet we speak all the same. Worse still, at the moment we speak, our soul is the victim of an illusion that determines it to believe that its speech is free. We are all the more subjected that we believe in our capacity to govern our speech. Note here a first specificity of the *impetus loquendi* in contrast to other acts: it more easily gives the (false) impression of freedom, no doubt because we have the impression that no physical power is opposed to speech. I feel the wall that prevents me from

---

[188] 'Ebrius deinde credit, se ex libero mentis decreto ea loqui, quae postea sobrius vellet tacuisse: sic delirans, garrula, puer, et hujus farinae plurimi ex libero mentis decreto credunt loqui; cum tamen loquendi impetum, quem habent, continere nequeant...', G II, p. 143, ll. 25–9 [CWS I, 496].

[189] Natural weakness is the weakness of the child, or a characteristic of the *ingenium*, just as the propensity to loquacity is. This latter is referred to in the feminine (*garrula*) but in a letter with parallel content from 1674 or 1675, Spinoza speaks of a *garrulus* (Letter LVIII to Schuller). Some have thought that it was the correspondence exchanged in Autumn of 1674 with Hugo Bosel that had suggested to him this change of sex.

going forward, or the container that stops me from taking an object, but speech does not encounter this experience of resistance: of all our gestures, it is the most diaphanous. What Spinoza demands of experience is above all that it restore to language its materiality. The conclusion to this text is in no way some improbable right to freedom of speech, but rather the recognition of our general impotence as regards language. The experience of the body confirms what use teaches us: that language hardly belongs to us at all.

What is remarkable is that it is precisely this incapacity that will form the hard kernel of Spinoza's arguments for the necessity of freedom of speech. It is because people are incapable of holding their tongue that it is necessary to recognise their right to express themselves. And when, in Chapter XX, the final chapter of the *TTP*, Spinoza explains this necessity, we see the line of fracture with Hobbes's conception appear. But this fracture was present much earlier on as well: for instance, in the *TTP* and on the question of the relations between the soul and language, it was visible from Chapter XVII onwards. The two Chapters echo each other via their symmetrical formulations, and deal, each in their own way, with the blurring of the strict boundary between the internal and the external.

The first part of this argument runs as follows. One does not command souls as one does tongues,[190] Spinoza says first in Chapter XVII, citing Curtius Rufus.[191] He thus seems to provisionally accept that we can make laws about what is said (and in fact, this is true: Spinoza will never revise this thesis, but he will contest the efficacy of these laws and show the high cost they incur for power). Spinoza thus begins with the position affirmed by Hobbes, yet immediately nuances it in the case of souls. Certainly, it is not possible to command souls directly (*directo mandato*); nevertheless, the Sovereign has the means to influence them in various ways: he can make it so that people believe what he wants – and thus he can manipulate their hatred and their love. If one objected to this argument with the claim that certain people with a critical spirit do not allow themselves to be convinced to believe just anything, Spinoza could respond that, statistically, this does not prevent the social effect of belief from being manifest. This is why he speaks of 'a very large number of people' (*permagna pars*). As for the existence of these means,

---

[190] 'Deinde, quamvis non perinde animis, ac linguis imperari possit [. . .]', *TTP*, Chapter XVII, G III, p. 202, ll. 26–7 [*TTP* XVII, 9; *CWS* II, 298].

[191] 'Jovis filium non dici tantum se sed etiam credi volebat, tanquam perinde animis imperare posset ac linguis' (Quintus-Curtius, VIII, 5), cited by Leo Strauss, 'Beiträge zur Quellen-Analyse des *Tract. Theol.-pol* und des *Tract. pol.*', in *Die Religionskritik Spinozas als Grundlage seiner Bibelwissenchaft*, Berlin: Akademie Verlag, 1930; Darmstadt: WB, 1981, p. 272.

Spinoza makes no effort to demonstrate this point: experience has sufficiently proven it. The tyrant has more powers than Hobbes himself believed.

The second part of this argument is found in Chapter XX. Spinoza begins by provisionally accepting as well known the proposition that he had gone to such lengths to nuance in Chapter XVII: namely, that it is not as easy to command souls as it is to command tongues. In fact, Spinoza only accepts this because it helps him introduce a notion that is indispensable to Hobbes: that of the degree of violence a government is permitted. If it were as easy to command souls as it is tongues, then no government would be violent, for each sovereign would automatically obtain the security and obedience of his citizens since each citizen would accept as a system of values precisely the system that power itself has established. But since reality is not like this, each time a government attempts to bring about such a situation – and this situation does not arise automatically – it will have to vanquish a resistance, and to this extent it will be held to be violent. Hobbes's purely juridical analysis leaves no place between being and not-being the Sovereign. Spinoza's analysis in terms of the passions reveals that there remains something to be thought in the execution of sovereignty. One can be absolutely sovereign, and also be and not be violent, and to different degrees. Once this concept is introduced, Spinoza is free to once again add nuance to the idea that we cannot command souls. Using different terms, he reintroduces the idea of indirect commandment that he had elaborated in Chapter XVII. He also does this from a more general perspective: he no longer restricts the Sovereign's possible acts to those involving the domination of the opinion of others; the emphasis is no longer placed on the means that power gives itself but on the use of prejudices, to which those who are not the Sovereign have recourse: 'I confess that someone can get prior control of another person's judgement in many ways, some of them almost incredible. So though that person does not directly command the other person's judgement, it can still depend so much on what he says that we can rightly say that to that extent it is subject to his control.'[192] Formulated in this way, the power of

---

[192] 'Fateor, judicium multis, et paene incredibilibus modis praeoccupari posse, atque ita, ut, quamvis sub alterius imperio directe non sit, tamen ab ore laterius ita pendeat, ut merito eatenus ejus juris dici possit', *TTP*, Chapter XX, p. 239, ll. 19–22 [*TTP* XX, 4; *CWS* II, 344]. We could interpret the phrase in a different way than does Appuhn and link *multis* to *modis*. This is how Gebhardt understands it ('auf mannigfache und beinahe unglaubliche Weisen', ed. F. Meiner, p. 299) and Dominguez ('de muchas y casi increíbles formas', ed. Alianza, p. 409) and not without some plausibility. But this does not change the general meaning since it can be thought that the multitude of means work on a large number of people, as is indicated in Chapter XVII.

souls can also be applied, for instance, to the cases of theologians, sectarian prophets, or the leaders of factions hostile to magistrates. In sum, if we consider a large enough crowd, the majority of its members will to varying degrees be habituated to thinking in a different way while they are part of it than they do when they are by themselves. But this is precisely the point: the diversity of leaders, these difference in degrees, and no doubt the difference in circumstances too, all reintroduce differences in opinion. Thus, as far as the result is concerned, the alleged absolute impossibility of commanding souls and the analyses of the real means for subjugating them lead to the same conclusions. Spinoza shifts the question from the autonomy of the point of departure to the diversity of the point of arrival. Finally, it matters little that people form their thoughts by themselves or through others: as they undergo various influences and to different degrees, we end up with an inextricable diversity in what exists. This is why experience teaches us that 'so many men' means 'so many minds' [autant de têtes, autant de sens].

But if this is so, then we have to return to the possibility of commanding tongues – and we see that it is just as problematic. It is impossible to contain the expression of this diversity of opinions, precisely because of the human weakness that Book II of the *Ethics* had identified: 'Not even the wisest know how to keep quiet, not to mention ordinary people.'[193] Human beings even speak against their own interests, and do so even when it would be useful for them to remain silent: 'It's a common vice of men to confide their judgements to others, even if secrecy is needed.'[194] This does not mean that that it is impossible to prevent people from speaking for at least some time, but simple orders or interdictions will not suffice. A greater degree of violence is thus necessary. We thus once again find the category that had emerged from Spinoza's attempt to refine the Hobbesian tradition. Now, this higher level of violence engages the Sovereign's authority. In a situation of force against force, it will not necessarily be the Sovereign who will prevail. Thus, it is clear that it is not in the Sovereign's interest to risk such a confrontation. We see, rather, that it is because there exists a double impotence – for some, an impotence to master themselves, for others an inability to contain those who cannot master themselves – that it is necessary to grant freedom of speech.

It should be noted that this argument is valid for speech and for speech

---

[193] 'Nam nec peritissimi, ne dicam plebem, tacere sciunt', *TTP*, Chapter XX, G III, p. 240, ll. 20–1 [*TTP* XX, 8; CWS II, 345].

[194] 'Hoc hominum commune vitium est, consilia sua, etsi tacito opus est, aliis credere', *TTP*, Chapter XX, G III, p. 240, ll. 21–2 [*TTP* XX, 9; CWS II, 345].

alone; it is not valid for any other acts. By means of the social contract, people renounce acting by their own decree. We are thus confronted with a second specificity of speech. Apparently, the drive to act is not as irrepressible as the drive to speak, either because people do not react as violently when they are prevented from acting as when they are prevented from speaking, or perhaps because we more immediately identify our speech with consciousness of our freedom.

To such an argument, two objections could be raised.[195] The first is that while this argument permits everything, certain speech acts are nevertheless dangerous for the City.[196] The second is that this argument will submerge the City in useless speech acts. To the first objection, Spinoza responds by invoking a limit (namely, speech that engenders harmful acts). We thus see appear a third specificity of speech relative to acts: its limit of acceptability lies less in itself than in the acts it induces – that is, in the concrete content of the representations it suggests. We can find here an analogy with the special constitution of the particular type of image that speech is.

As for the second objection, true ideas do not cause free discussion, but they can result from it. The same thing happens with the expression of speech as it does for signification. A production that is initially left to chance can, in certain cases, be oriented towards the good. The beneficial character of discussion is affirmed in the *TTP* and explicitly justified in the *TP*. To those who object to the length of public deliberations,[197] Spinoza responds:

> Some will remind us of the saying, 'while the Romans deliberate, Saguntum is lost'. On the other hand, when the few decide everything, simply on the basis of their own affects, freedom and the common good are lost. For human wits are too sluggish to penetrate everything right away. But by asking advice, listening, and arguing, they're sharpened. When people try all means, in the end they find ways to the things they want which everyone approves, and no one had ever thought of before.[198]

---

[195] On the problem posed by the 'fundamental rule' that distinguishes speech and actions, see E. Balibar, *Spinoza et la politique*, Paris: PUF, 1985, pp. 35–42.

[196] 'Still, we can't deny that majesty can be harmed by words as well as by deeds', *TTP*, Chapter XX, G III, p. 240, ll. 25–6 [*TTP* XX, 10; *CWS* II, 346].

[197] This is one of Hobbes's arguments against democracy, in the chapter from *De Cive* devoted to the comparison between the three types of government (Part 2, Chapter X).

[198] *TP*, Chapter IX, §XIV, G III, p. 352 [*TP* IX, 14; *CWS* II, 594], translation by P.-F. Moreau, Paris: Répliques, 1979, p. 169. The example of Saguntum comes from Livy,

We thus see how, from the point of view of the system, such a formula is justified as far as ideas are concerned: on the one hand, in the very interiority of vague experience, which is so useful in practical life (and political decisions form part of this life), the comparison of and the choice between solutions are better informed if they have a larger field of perception at their disposal; on the other hand, the multitude of ideas presented allows one to better distinguish common notions against the backdrop of these ideas. And it is from these common notions that adequate ideas will arise. Discussion, while it does not, strictly speaking, engender ideas, nevertheless allows one to overcome obstacles to their development. What, then, happens to speech? Is it justified only if it is the bearer of adequate or useful ideas? We must remember that speech is an index: it also helps clarify ideas.

This defence of freedom of thought is expressed in the following memorable phrase: 'everyone should be granted the right to think what he wants and to say what he thinks'.[199] After everything that has been said, it will come as no surprise that this defence of individual expression is an almost word-for-word reprise of Tacitus.[200]

ANNEX: QUESTIONS OF TERMINOLOGY

In the opening sections of this chapter, I used, without any additional explanation, the terms 'idea' and 'image' as they appear in particular in Book II of the *Ethics*. These terms have a strict meaning, which Spinoza nevertheless does not present for itself. It will perhaps be worthwhile summarising the principal choices that form the basis of this terminology.

Recall first the double process that this lexicon refers to. The image is a bodily transformation. An idea is the mental correlate of this modification, a modification Spinoza sometimes calls an *imaginatio mentis* and which constitutes the inadequate idea of the external body insofar as it refers to this external body. The idea is not representative: it is the idea of the image that is representative. In sum, four items can be distinguished:

The History of Rome: 'Dum ea Romani parant consultantque, jam Saguntum summa vi oppugnabatur', XXI, Chapter VII.

[199] 'Et sentire, quae velit, et quae sentiat, dicere, concedatur', *TTP*, Chapter XX, G III, p. 247, ll. 20–1 [*TTP* XX, 46; *CWS* II, 353].

[200] When he evokes the happy kingdoms of Nerva and Trajan: 'rara temporum felicitate, ubi sentire quae velis et quae sentias dicere licet', *Histoires*, I, 1. To the best of my knowledge, no commentator has remarked on this save Chaim Wirzubski in his Hebrew translation of the *TTP*, *Maamar théologi-médini*, Jerusalem: Magnes Press, 1961, p. 216.

1. In extension, the thing (for example: a flame).
2. In extension, the encounter between my body and this thing (I burn myself) induces a modification of my body (not only the trace on my skin, but also and above all the trace in my brain). This is the image. This image can then be reactivated independently of the thing each time that the disposition of my body reactivates the trace. (This is the chain of images. It can arise either from an activity of the body that makes it possible to reactivate the trace, or from the automatic association of images.)
3. In thought, the idea of this image. If I consider this idea as the idea of the flame, then it is an inadequate idea (that is, it makes me think of the flame in relation to my burning skin, which informs me of the flame's effects, or more precisely of its effects on me, but not of its nature). It is not false *per se* (it is true that I was burned), but it is false so long as I take this idea for an idea that truly represents the flame as it is. Now, the natural order of the world necessarily determines that I will initially represent the flame to myself according to the order of these encounters. It is this idea that is in my mind when, in extension, my body encounters the flame. Thus, the idea which, in thought, is the idea of the encounter between the flame and my body, appears, in the mind that corresponds to this body, as the idea of the flame.
4. In thought, there exists an (adequate) idea of the flame. This idea is not (in this adequate form) in my mind. It can only be produced in my mind on the basis of the common notions of space, movement, and so on, which will allow me to come up with the relevant physics and the theory of the causes of heat and finally to account for what happens in my body when I touch the flame.

In this context, we can summarise Spinoza's lexicon as follows:

— An image is a modification of the body; Spinoza says this very clearly on many occasions (for example, in *Ethics* Book II, Proposition, 36, Corollary, Demonstration; Book II, Proposition 49, Scholium; Book III, 32, Scholium).

— An imagination is an idea, the idea that corresponds to this modification of the body. Spinoza makes the subject of the verb 'to imagine' the soul and not the body. The word *imaginatio* thus has two meanings, which can easily be distinguished by reference to the context (and rendered in English using definite or indefinite articles): it can refer either to the 'faculty' that produces the ideas of images, or to a particular image.

— In fact, Spinoza does not use the expression 'the idea of the image' (though Gueroult does[201] by identifying it with the *imaginatio mentis*), but he does occasionally use the term 'image' in a loose sense to refer simultaneously to the image and to its idea.

— While in the philosophical lexicon of the classical age, to imagine is to form images, rigorously speaking this is not the case in Spinoza. The soul imagines when the body forms images and considers external bodies according to the ideas it forms of these images.

---

[201] *Spinoza*, vol. II, *L'Ame*, p. 224.

9
Fields of Experience: The Passions

In studying the field of language, we twice encountered a notion that, while seemingly marginal in Spinoza's system, we can nevertheless find there as soon as we locate the point where deduction comes to an end. This was the notion of the *ingenium*. Like history,[1] both grammar and rhetoric refer in the final analysis to the *ingenium* that is proper to a people.[2] Understanding a text, once the meaning of individual words has been determined, is impossible without knowing the *ingenium* of the person who wrote it or whose words the text is communicating.[3] What, then, does the term *ingenium* mean, this term that seems to mark the fundamental ground of the differences between communities or singular individuals?

1. The *Ingenium* and the Passions

At first glance, what could be called, using a modern term, Spinozist psychology does not lend itself easily to the analysis of experience or individuality.

---

[1] Mosaic law is not universal: it is 'maxime ad ingenium & singularem conservationem unius populi acommodata', *TTP*, Chapter IV, G III, p. 61, ll. 16–18 [*TTP* IV, 17; *CWS* II, 129]. The moral precepts contained in the Pentateuch are not laid down there as teachings that are common to all people 'sed tanquam mandata ad captum & ingenium solius Hebraeae nationis maxime accomodata', *TTP*, Chapter V, G III, p. 70, ll. 19–20 [*TTP* V, 7; *CWS* II, 140]. Moses joins to his commandments the threat of punishment 'quae pro ingenio uniuscujusque nationis variare potest et debet, ut experientia satis docuit', ibid., ll. 24–5 [*TTP* V, 7; *CWS* II, 140].

[2] Thus Paul's language can be explained by reference to the way he adapts to the speech of *ingenio plebis*, *TTP*, Chapter IV, G III, p. 65, ll. 18–20 [*TTP* IV, 35; *CWS* II, 134].

[3] 'Eo facilius verba alicujus explicare possumus, quo ejus genium et ingenium melius noverimus', *TTP*, Chapter VII, G III, p. 102, ll. 2–4 [*TTP* VII, 24; *CWS* II, 175].

If the ultimate object of knowledge is the individual, then this knowledge is possible only by identifying causal series that chiefly concern the specific essence of individuals. This knowledge seeks to demonstrate laws that apply, as mathematical laws do – and indeed the model here is, precisely, mathematics – to all individuals. It is a matter of listing and explaining those passions that constitute the foundation, as well as the cause of the torments, of the human condition.

In certain chapters of the *TTP* and in Books III and IV of the *Ethics*, Spinoza presents, among other things, a theory of life.[4] These works respond in a certain way to the questions: What is human life? What can be analysed in a human life?

Yet they do so, precisely, *in a certain way* – that is, by adopting a certain perspective and admitting in advance that there exists a preferred mode of discourse that effectively excludes other perspectives or marginalises them. In the classical age and in the tradition that precedes it, we can identify the following different ways of approaching human life:

The Biography of the Hero. This is the tradition of Plutarch. Here, the individual is at the heart of life, and they appear in their immediacy in the story that stages this life. If one inquires in this tradition into the passions or the vices, it is by referring to events from which one seeks draw lessons. Such a method lends itself to moral considerations but is not particularly concerned with identifying laws. Does Curtius Rufus' biography of Alexander, so omnipresent in Spinoza's work, belong to this genre? Whatever the answer, Curtius Rufus' book tends strongly towards being a moral work where the hero's life is merely the support for a series of reflections, for instance on superstition. Indeed, it is in this form that Spinoza uses it. It is true that the *TTP* evokes a few individual figures: not only Alexander but also Moses or Hannibal.[5]

---

[4] On the particular situation of the *Short Treatise* with respect to this question, cf. Ch. Ramond, 'Les mille et une passions du *Court Traité*', *Archives de la philosophie*, 51/1 (1988), pp. 15–27; W. Riese, *La théorie des passions à la lumière de la pensée médicale du XVIIe siècle*, Basel/New York: Karger, 1965, pp. 59–66.

[5] What Spinoza says of Hannibal is moreover read through a transformed Machiavellian schema. This is another indication that the individual as such is not the immediate subject of the reflection (*Discorsi*, III, 21: 'nel suo esercito, ancoraché composto di varie generazioni di uomini, non nacque mai alcuna dissensione, né infra loro medesimi, né contro di lui. Il che non potette dirivare da altro, che dal terrore che nasceva dalla persona sua: il quale era tanto grande, mescolato con la riputazione che gli dava la sua virtù, che teneva i suoi soldati quieti ed uniti.' There is a parallel text in *The Prince*, Chapter XVII: 'inumana crudeltà'; *TP*, Chapter V, 3: 'Unde Hannibali merito eximiae virtuti ducitur quod in ipsius exercitu nulla unquam seditio orta fuerit' [*TP*

But as soon as it comes to explaining their behaviour, Spinoza appeals to his theory of the passions. If he uses biographies or autobiographies,[6] it is to draw upon the materials they provide.

Character. This is the tradition of Theophrastes, which La Bruyère reprises. Here the empirical individual is transcended in favour of a fictional individual who is structured by a fundamental passion: one person is jealous, another avaricious, and a third ambitious. There is a greater degree of abstraction here relative to the biographical genre, and which prevents one from becoming too attached to empirical differences. At the same time, however, one loses the concrete richness of the person: the multiplicity of the individual's traits, if these still exist, simply become multiple examples of a single thesis.[7] However, in both cases it is still the individual, whether singular or typical, who takes centre stage.

The Passions. In the seventeenth century, this is the solution adopted by most moralists and philosophers. This tradition dates back at least to Aristotle's *Rhetoric*,[8] but in the classical age it takes on autonomous forms that make it a discipline in its own right. The individual, whether empirical or abstract, no longer occupies centre stage. They cede their place to movements of the soul that are described, explained,[9] and for which examples are sought. In a certain way, the analysis of the passions contains the truth of the biographical genre or the treatises on character: the passion that appeared in passing there as a motive for the hero's actions or for those of his adversaries, or which was uniquely incarnate in a given character, is here immediately foregrounded; having become the proper object of analysis, it is studied in terms

---

V, 3; CWS II, 350]. Terror and cruelty have disappeared: 'inhumana crudelitas' comes from Livy, XXI, 4 – that is, just before the episode at Saguntum).

[6] For example, the works of Antonio Pérez. Cf. H. Méchoulan, 'Spinoza lecteur d'Antonio Pérez', *Ethnopsychologie*, 29/4 (1974), pp. 289–301. It is from Antonio Pérez's work that Spinoza came to know of the example of Aragon's constitution.

[7] These days we could find an equivalent in Julien Green's novelistic aesthetics: 'Une passion par personne, ça suffit' (*Léviathan*, end of Chapter VIII, p. 71 from the édition de poche). Thus: curiosity in Madame Londe (who is the object of this theorem), avarice in Mrs Fletcher from *Mont-Cinère*, and envy in Germaine, the sister of Adrienne Mesurat.

[8] Book II. The use Hobbes makes of this is well known.

[9] The explanation is a necessary condition of these movement's regulation: 'S'il est besoin de connaître les maladies pour les guérir, il n'est pas moins nécessaire de connaître les passions pour les régler, et de savoir celle qui nous attaque avec plus de fureur', J-F. Senault, *De l'usage des passions*, 1639, Paris: Fayard, 1987, p. 60.

of its origins, its conflicts with other passions, and its relations to reason. The individual's life is thus treated less as the development of a character and more as the field of conflict or of composition between different passions. Such a perspective does not exclude moral judgement (one can, for instance, consider these passions as vices), but more often than not this genre studies the passions, at least at a certain level, as morally neutral behaviours.[10] This perspective also allows for an inter-individual analysis: if the same passions, or analogous passions, are encountered by turns in different individuals, it is because these passions are not entirely reducible to the determinations proper to these individuals. Studying them can therefore allow the laws that govern these individuals to be identified. Such a procedure lends itself more easily than the description of character to a reading concerned with the causal underpinnings of the passions, for instance with their physiological foundations.[11] The first part of the *Leviathan*, or the *The Passions of the Soul*, belong to this register. From such a perspective, one can move from individual conduct to the rules by which people are governed;[12] and, without having to limit oneself to the question of the means of government, one can identify the very consistency of social life as a chain of passions.[13]

It is this last possibility that Spinoza adopts in his work. The individual in their unity is effaced when we read the series of theorems from Books III and IV and another object comes to the fore: a specific affect. The passions are at once intra- and inter-individual: multiple passions coexist in the same individual, while identical passions are active in different individuals.[14] But what, then, is the individual? Are they an ensemble or succession of affects? Are they the abstract site that serves as a backdrop to this succession? Yes, insofar as it is a matter of studying the production of the passions in an abstract sense. Following this there remains the possibility of analysing the form that the affects take in a singular individual. By means of this deduction, the human being in their immediacy becomes something *derived*. There

---

[10] Senault explains that passions are the fruit both of virtues and vices (First Part, Fourth Treatise, ibid., pp. 117–26).

[11] Cf. W. Riese, *La théorie des passions*, p. 19 ff. (on Cureau de la Chambre).

[12] Thus, in Senault's work, the fifth treatise from the first part is devoted to the power of the passions over the will of men: in the arts (II) but also in politics (III, IV: love and fear as means of the prince's power).

[13] Cf. A. Matheron, *Individu et Communauté*, p. 83 ff.; K. Hammacher, 'La Raison dans la vie affective et sociale selon Descartes et Spinoza', *Etudes philosophiques* (January–March 1984), pp. 73–82.

[14] On the condition that we take into account what the final propositions from Book III indicate. See below.

exists no presumptive constancy in an individual's character[15] though such a constancy can emerge when certain circumstances are maintained. At this point, however, this constancy becomes a sort of madness: if, for one reason or another, an affect is said to be stable, then one is said to fall into the 'madness' of money, power or pleasure.[16] That said, in normal circumstances, the same person will, at different moments, react differently – something that is proven by reference both to history and to vague experience. It is remarkable that Spinoza – who in his mature work does not use the distinction between wisdom and madness and considers the passions and vices from the perspective of the necessary consequences of human nature – here reintroduces the notion of madness to refer to those who are possessed by a *single* passion.

Different people, submitted to the same pressures, will react *to a certain degree* in the same way: man for man, as Brecht says, and as Spinoza might have said, at least as far as the first stage of his argument is concerned. Individuality, then, is no longer anything but a certain way of conjugating and actualising the laws of essence. The individual is defined in the final analysis by the proportion according to which these laws are mixed with one other. But these laws are articulated together in the individual in an irreducible way. This is why, after having been relegated to the background, the individual can return to the foreground when the perspective changes and we inquire into the following existential fact: their individuality. If we now wish to interrogate experience, it will be necessary to do so in two stages: first with respect to the causal theory of the passions, and second when it comes to bringing to the fore this knot of passions that is the concrete individual. We will discover that experience plays a key role at each of these levels, but with different functions.

A. *The Confirmative Function: The Passions*

Books III and IV of the *Ethics*, along with large parts of Book V and the *Treatises*, are thus devoted to showing, by way of the protracted procedures of the geometer, how it is possible to explain the passions on the basis of a few fundamental affects. To explain the passions means explaining their

---

[15] Different configurations of the passions can succeed each other in the same individual: 'et unus idemque homo ab uno eodemque objecto potest diversis temporibus diversimode affici', *Ethics* III, 51, G II, p. 178, ll. 18–19 [CWS I, 522]. Cf. also the Scholium: 'Videmus itaque fieri posse ut [. . .] unus idemque homo jam amet, quod antea oderit, et ut jam audeat, quod antea timuit, etc', ibid., ll. 30–3 [CWS I, 522].

[16] *Ethics*, IV, 44, Schol. [CWS I, 571].

nature, their different characteristics, their conflicts with each other and with Reason, and finally the means by which they can in a certain manner be governed.[17] Thus, in principle – or so long as we remain in a deductive mode – Spinozist psychology initially excludes individual differences. Indeed, this is the condition of its scientificity. It is the price that must be paid so that human behaviours can be considered in the same way as lines, surfaces and solids.[18] The different passions will thus be demonstrated on the basis of their causes: the *conatus* and its actualisations in the form of desire, joy and sadness. Each will be derived from these three affects by the mechanisms of transference, association and, in the case of inter-individual passions, the exigency of reciprocity.[19] We thus learn in the *Ethics* in a genetic manner what was lived and described in the *TdIE*. Thus, the role of the imitation of the vulgar, which had formerly been identified as one of the conditions for the pursuit of honours, as well as one of the things that impeded the search for the true good, is now explained in the framework of Ambition, as part of the deduction of inter-human passions.[20] Does this mean that experience does not appear here? On the contrary, it appears at each point in its confirmative role: references to the poets or to what has long been well known by all are interspersed throughout Books III and IV of the *Ethics*.[21] This confirmative function is manifest in various forms:

— In the form of a *pure and simple confirmation*, which establishes by other means what the deduction has just shown. In this case there is a sort of parallelism between the two methods. Thus, Propositions 27 to 32 from Book III examine the principle of the diverse forms that the imitation of the affects can take. Once these demonstrations are complete, Spinoza adds that we can know these properties of human nature by different means, and that proof of this is already in front of us: 'Finally', he writes, 'if we wish to consult experience, we shall find that it teaches all these things, especially if we attend to the first years of our lives. For we find from experience that

---

[17] 'Affectum naturam et vires, et quid contra mens in iisdem moderandis possit', *Ethics* III, Praef., G II, p. 137, ll. 24–5 [*CWS* I, 491].

[18] 18: 'Et humanas actiones atque appetitus considerabo perinde, ac si quaestio de lineis, planis aut de corporibus esset', *Ethics* III, Praef., G II, p. 138, ll. 26–7 [*CWS* I, 492].

[19] Cf. A. Matheron, *Individu et Communauté*, Chapter V: 'Fondement et déploiement de la vie passionnelle', pp. 81–222.

[20] *Ethics* III, 29, Schol. [*CWS* I, 510].

[21] J. Bennett remarks that, if we are convinced by the laws established in Book III, 'it must be by our observations of the human scene', *A Study of Spinoza's Ethics*, Cambridge: Cambridge University Press, 1984, p. 277. He adds that the demonstrations themselves are not conclusive – but this is a topic that lies outside of our subject.

children, because their bodies are continually, as it were, in a state of equilibrium, laugh or cry simply because they see others laugh or cry. Moreover, whatever they see others do, they immediately desire to imitate. And finally, they desire for themselves all those things by which they imagine others are pleased.'[22] Studying childhood thus allows us to see, in an almost unmediated form, what has just been demonstrated mathematically. Reciprocally, the demonstration *more geometrico* gives us reasons for something that we have always known – the pleasure that children take in imitating others – but that we did not know how to explain, and that, perhaps, we did not even take into account because we could not grasp what was going on. In this sense, if such an experience confirms the demonstration, then for its part the demonstration makes experience appear as meaningful. We could find analogous examples of such simple confirmations by direct parallelism in the cases of suicide,[23] the role of education in the formation of values,[24] and the origins of superstition.[25]

— A more complex procedure is constituted by what could be called *displaced confirmation*. An example of this is given by the Scholium to Proposition 47 from Book III: 'The Joy which arises from our imagining that a thing we hate is destroyed, or affected with some other evil, does not occur without some Sadness of soul.' Let us leave aside the difficult relation between the proposition and its two demonstrations, which does not interest us here.[26] Let us consider only the second demonstration (the one that

---

[22] 'Denique, si ipsam experientiam consulere velimus, ipsam haec omnia docere experiemur; praesertim si ad priores nostrae eatatis annos attenderimus. Nam pueros, qui eorum corpus continuo veluti in aequelibrio est, ex hoc solo ridere vel flere experimur, quod alios ridere vel flere vident; et quicquid praeterea vident alios facere, id imitari statim cupiunt, et omnia denique sibi cupiunt quibus alios delectari imaginantur', Ethics III, 32, Schol., G II, p. 165, ll. 17–23 [CWS I, 513].

[23] Ethics IV, 20, Schol. [CWS I, 557].

[24] Ethics III, DA #27, Exp. [CWS I, 537].

[25] Ethics III, 50, Schol. [CWS I, 521–2]. We know, in fact, that there exist superstitions, that human beings are anxious to know the future and that the manifestations of superstition are at once varied and subject to fluctuations (cf. the Preface of the *TTP*, which records these givens without explaining them, thus registering them as parts of experience). Now, Propositions 25 and 50 explain to us why fear and hope engender superstitions, specifically by the play of circumstances that we interpret as signs of the future, while the Scholium indicates, without going into detail about it, the root of their fluctuations.

[26] The difficulty comes down to the fact that, contrary to appearances, the Proposition seeks to establish not the relation of causality, but the *fluctuatio animi* that characterises all instances of *Schadenfreude*. The first demonstration is valid for a particular case –where the object of hatred is another person – and the cause of our sadness is the evil

makes up the beginning of the Scholium) and the appeal to experience that extends it. The deductive argument establishes, on the basis of Proposition 17 from Book II, that each time we remember a thing we hate, we imagine it to be present. Thus, we consider it with the same sadness as if it were really present. In the case of a thing that has disappeared or been destroyed, we also consider it as if it were really present. But the memory of its destruction is imprinted in us and is produced by the evocation of the thing, with which it is henceforth associated in our mind. Thus, the joy tied to the destruction of what threatened us appears and reduces the sadness. The Scholium could end here since the demonstration is complete. But Spinoza continues: 'This is also the cause of men's rejoicing when they recall some evil now past, and why they enjoy telling of dangers from which they have been freed.'[27] It is clear that this is an appeal to experience, even if the term is not used here. This is a situation that does not need to be demonstrated (it is a fact) nor proven historically (it is not a singular fact, but a situation of common life). It is a fact that former combatants like to recount their wars and seamen their shipwreck. This is something that we have all seen, indeed experienced. There then follows the explanation, which applies the law that has just been demonstrated to this common fact.

What, precisely, is the role of experience here? We do indeed see it playing its confirmative role. But experience does not confirm in the way that a biblical narrative does, which proves the rational deduction by different means; nor does it do so in the manner of the proof by reference to children's imitations, which directly shows the principle of the imitation of the affects, a thesis that has has just been demonstrated geometrically. For in its isolated form, this common fact does not establish the Proposition. Nor is it a simple example: it is not limited to illustrating the law, but instead contains something more. The significance of this example has to do with the fact that the law, which is itself not paradoxical – or at least not explicitly so in its present form – nevertheless clarifies a fact that is. Fundamentally, the argument begins with a fact that we are all familiar with and that nevertheless should surprise us: people like to recount how they were fearful; and in doing so, they become fearful again. We know this well. What pleasure do they take

---

that we see him undergo, and thus the sadness by which he is affected. The second is thus part of a more general case, and the cause of our sadness is the evil that the thing threatens to make us suffer or has threatened to make us suffer.

[27] 'Atque haec eadem est causa, cur homines laetantur, quoties alicujus jam praeteriti mali recordantur, et cur pericula, a quibus liberati sunt, narrare gaudeant', *Ethics* III, 47, Schol., G II, p. 176, ll. 16–18 [*CWS* I, 520].

from this? We can easily understand that they take pleasure from recalling agreeable situations, but what about disagreeable situations? This seems to contradict the law that says that we seek to avoid those imaginations that diminish our power to act.[28] Experience here takes the form of a question: we regularly notice what we take to be bizarre features of human nature. The law, as it has been deductively established, explains this bizarre feature: it shows that pleasure is born from a joy that pushes back against the sadness, and that, in some sense, people only get scared in order to subsequently reassure themselves. The pleasure of the catastrophic narrative is one use of the *fluctuatio animi*. We could draw from this example both aesthetic laws and ideological consequences that Spinoza himself does not draw here.[29] Let us restrict ourselves to noting that the relation of confirmation is at the same time a relation of displacement. What we go through in experience is indeed the same thing that we can demonstrate by reference to laws, but the emphasis has shifted. Whence the effect of recognition that occurs when this law is contradicted. With respect to the preceding example, we said that the law reveals as a phenomenon a common fact that we had registered without understanding it. This time the law integrates a fact of common life that surprises us without us being able to deny its reality. The law raises to the level of obviousness an experience that was at first glance obscure. We will often find in Spinoza's proofs this same displaced confirmation.

Sometimes, even what is given in experience seems provisionally to undermine the law or to give us reasons for hesitating (*scrupulus*): it thus helps us to reformulate the law with more precision by taking different circumstances into account. Proposition 55 from Book III states that 'When the Soul imagines its own lack of power, it is saddened by it.' The first Corollary to the Scholium develops the consequences of this thesis with respect to relations with others: people are sad when they are together and when they imagine that their actions, compared to the actions of others, are weaker.[30] They therefore seek to avoid this sadness by interpreting the actions of others falsely. This explains why they are inclined to hatred, as well as to envy, both by nature and by educational reinforcement.[31] Now, that things are thus is

---

[28] 'Hinc sequitur, quod Mens ea imaginari aversatur que ipsius et corpori potentiam minuunt vel coercent', *Ethics* III, 13, Cor., G II, p. 151, ll. 2–3 [CWS I, 502].

[29] It would not be impossible to construct a Spinozist theory of tragedy, where this effect would replace the Aristotelian theme of catharsis.

[30] 'Et contra contristabitur, si suas, ad aliorum actiones comparatas, imbecilliores esse imaginetur', G II, p. 183, ll. 17–19 [*Ethics* III, 55; CWS I, 525].

[31] 'Apparet igitur homines natura proclives esse ad odium, & invidiam, ad quam accedit ipsa educatio', ibid., ll. 21–3 [*Ethics* III, 55, Schol.; CWS I, 526]. Note the attention

something that is well known – but now we are no longer surprised, or no longer indignant, in the face of these waves of negative emotions that we have had ample occasion to notice. At this point the deduction intersects with a lesson from experience. Previously, experience had appeared in its confirmative guise in its simplest possible form. But now there arises another experience that seems to undermine the same thesis: 'not infrequently we admire and venerate men's virtues'.[32] How can we reconcile this fact that we also know well with the propensity to envy that has just been deduced and identified? How can it happen that in the face of other peoples' strengths we do not feel diminished and affected with sadness? Whence the necessity of adding a second Corollary, which clarifies and limits the Demonstration: 'No one envies another's virtue unless he is an equal.' In other words, when we venerate a man, we imagine that his virtues belong to him singularly, and, as a consequence, we do not consider them as ways of being that are common to human nature. This relieves us of having to compare ourselves with him to our disadvantage. Thus, these two givens of experience, which at first glance appeared contradictory, both receive a place in the theory, once we have taken care to consider all of the circumstances that modulate it. Experience, here, forces us to consider the detail of the law.

— Finally, experience can appear in the form of *recourse to tradition*, in particular to Latinate culture. The characters of the avaricious person, the lover,[33] the parasite[34] and the military man,[35] along with so many others that

---

Spinoza gives in many of his examples to education and to the relation between parents and children. Cf. also *Ethics* IV, App., 13 [*CWS* I, 589–90]; *TTP*, Chapter, XVI, G III, p. 195, ll. 5–15 [*TTP* XVI, 35; *CWS* II, 289] (the comparison between paternal law and the law of the master). This interest can be explained in various ways, including by the fact that these relations provide the experience of an inter-human relation that, while certainly not isolated from political relations, has its own relatively autonomous intelligibility.

[32] 'Sed scrupulus forsan remanet, quod non raro hominum virtutes admiremur, eosque veneremur', G II, p. 183, l. 25–6 [*Ethics* III, 55, Schol.; *CWS* I, 526].

[33] *Ethics* III, 55, Cor., Dem., Schol., G II, pp. 183–4 [*CWS* I, 525–6].

[34] *Ethics* IV, 57, Schol., where, on the topic of parasites and flatterers, Spinoza adds the following revealing incision: 'horum definitiones omisi, qui nimis noti sunt', G II, p. 251, ll. 28–9 [*CWS* I, 578]. Why are they so well known as not have to been defined geometrically? Because of everyone's experience and even more so because of the literary tradition that has made them into characters.

[35] Leopold remarks that the example from Chapter 13 from the Appendix to Book IV (those young people who sign up to the army to flee paternal authority) is made up of terms borrowed from Terence (*Adelphoe*, v. 385) and, he adds, 'facile etiam argumentum quoddam comicum agnoscas', *Ad Spinozae Opera Posthuma*, p. 35.

seem to have emerged from a Latin comedy, people the Scholia. Similarly, a number of facts and traits are evoked in the same terms as classical authors. The definition of ambition cites Cicero in order to lambast those philosophers who write books on the contempt for glory but do not forget to inscribe their own names on them.[36] The impotence of Reason is expressed with the help of a formula borrowed from Ovid.[37] The effort by which we attempt to share our loves and hatreds is also illustrated by two verses from Ovid.[38] To these explicit citations there are added familiar expressions, where the language of historians and poets comes to serve as a substrata to Spinoza's own. While he has just demonstrated that repentance is not a virtue – that is, that

[36] 'Optimus quisque, inquit Cicero, maxime gloria ducitur. Philosophi etiam libris, quos de contemnenda gloria scribunt, nomen suum inscribunt', *Ethics* III, DA #44, G II, p. 202, ll. 16–18 [*CWS* I, 541]. The reference is to *Pro Archia* (11) and, more assuredly still, to *Tusculanes*, I 15, § 34: 'Quid nostri philosophi? nonne in iis libris ipsis quos scribunt de contemnenda gloria sua nomina inscribunt?'

[37] 'Video meliora proboque, deteriora sequor', *Metamorphosis*, VII, 20. It is Medea who is speaking, at the point where she is failing to rid her heart of her growing love for Jason:

> Excute virgineo conceptas pectore flammas
> Si potes, infelix. Si possem, sanior essem;
> Sed trahit invitam nova vis; aliudque cupido,
> Mens aliud suadet. Video meliora proboque,
> Deteriora sequor.

The formula is explicitly given as a quotation in the Scholium to Proposition 17 from Book IV. The Preface from the same book said the same thing already but without a reference: 'ut saepe coactus sit, quanquam meliora sibi videat, deteriora tamen sequi', and the Scholium from Proposition 2 from Book III noted that we know by experience that 'nosque saepe, quando sc. contrariis affectibus conflictamur, meliora videre et deteriora sequi'. We also read the following in letter LVIII to Schuller: 'Nam, quamvis experientia satis superque doceat, homines nihil minus posse, quam appetitus moderari suos, & quod saepe, dum contrariis affectibus conflictantur, meliora videant, & deteriora sequantur, se tamen liberos esse credunt ...', G IV, p. 266, ll. 26–30 [*Ep. CWS* I, 428]. For Spinoza, this quotation thus concentrates one of the more general lessons of experience. He gives as a synonymous expression a citation from Ecclesiastes, as if to insist on the fact that all traditions have perceived this fact. Note that Clauberg uses the same citation from Ovid in Chapter IX of his *Initiatio Philosophi* (*Dubitatio Cartesiana*) to explain the *me invito* from the end of the *First Meditation* (*Opera Philosophica*, Amsterdam: Blaeu; Hildesheim: Olms, 1968, vol. II, p. 1196).

[38] 'Speremus pariter, pariter metuamus amantes, Ferreus est, si quis, quod sinit alter, amat', *Amores*, II, 19, v. 4–5. In this quotation (*Ethics* III, 31, Cor. [*CWS* I, 512]), as in the preceding one, Ovid is called the Poet. On the different solutions proposed by the translators for understanding this Corollary and what it contains, see the important note by Otto Baensch in his translation *Die Ethik, nach geometrischer Methode dargestellt*, Hamburg: F. Meiner, 1905, pp. 308–9.

its origin is not in Reason – Spinoza adds in passing that as far as unreasonable people are concerned, repentance is nevertheless more useful than not, just as hope and fear are in general terms. Spinoza concludes from this that the prophets were right to preach repentance. Now, the geometrical demonstration of the utility of repentance is not carried out in detail; it is replaced by a brief evocation that draws on what we all know already, namely that if people did not fear anything and were ashamed of nothing, how could they be disciplined? Indeed, the crowd is terrible when it is without fear.[39] This description is all the more persuasive in that its very terms seem to be those of a maxim. Its rhetorical elements come from Terence,[40] then from Tacitus.[41] It is thus a Latin poet and a Latin historian who justify the behaviour of the prophets.[42] In other passages still, we hear the words of Terence mixed with proofs from experience. The inclusion of the positive description of the pleasures of life is accompanied by a statement taken from the *Adelphoe*: 'My account of the matter, the view I have arrived at.'[43] The description of

---

[39] 'Nam si homines animo impotentes aeque omnes superbirent, nullius rei ipsos puderet, nec ipsi quicquam metuerent, qui vinculis conjugi constringique possent? Terret vulgus nisi netuat', *Ethics* IV, 54, Schol., G II, p. 250, ll. 13–16 [CWS I, 576].

[40] *Adelphoe*, V. 84–5:

> Quem neque pudet
> Quicquam nec metuit quemquam neque legem putat
> Tenere se ullam.

[41] 'Nihil in vulgo modicum; terrere, ni paveant', *Annals*, I, 29. Spinoza also cites this phrase in Chapter VII from the *TP*, 27, G III, p. 319, ll. 26–7 [*TP* VII, 27; CWS II, 558]. In this last passage, the citation is placed in the mouth of the adversaries of freedom, whose position Spinoza is critiquing. But it is precisely here that we find a good illustration of the status of experience and of its opacity: when Spinoza takes up the words in his own name, he does not refute the idea itself, but refuses to limit it to the *vulgus*. Once again, those who gather the truths of experience forget to apply them to themselves. 'Moreover, [the reason] "there's no moderation in the common people", [the reason] "they're terrifying, unless they themselves are cowed by fear", is that freedom and slavery are not easily combined' ('Nihil praeterea in vulgo modicum, terrere, nisi paveant: nam libertas et servitium haud facile miscentur', ibid., p. 320, ll. 3–5 [CWS II, 559].

[42] We could even add that the phrase that introduces this reflection – 'in istam partem potius peccandum' – also comes from the *Adelphoe* (v. 174, cf. O. Proietti, 'Adulescens luxu perditus. Classici latini nell'opera di Spinoza', pp. 224–5).

[43] 'Mea haec est ratio, et sic animum induxi meum', *Ethics* IV, 45, Schol. [CWS I, 572]. Cf. *Adelphoe*, V. 68: 'Mea sic est ratio et sic animum induco meum.' Spinoza has already said that 'sed mea haec est ratio' in the preface to Book II, in a similar contextual situation: there, he was referring to his project of treating geometrically what others consider as vain, absurd and worthy of horror.

the proud person is clarified by reference to an argument from the *Eunuchus*: the flatterers 'make a madman of a fool'.[44] In the same Scholium, a proverb evokes the alleviation of sadness that occurs when the passionate person considers the vices of others.[45] More generally, beyond any specific citation, various scenes evoked by the Scholia recall the world of Latin comedy.[46] We could explain the purpose of these similarities by saying that they are mere ornaments or serve a communicative function (by creating a common terrain with those readers who are impregnated with the same culture), or indeed we could explain them by reference to Spinoza's biography.[47] But we could also assign them a theoretical status: these quotations or uses of Terence, these appearances of conventional characters – almost all belong to analogous contexts, contexts that perhaps have something to do with the constitutive structure of the comic universe. But what is this constitutive structure? Most often, this structure involves scenes where an individual is performing an action under the guidance of their will, but where subsequent events (determined at once by the decisions they have made, their character, and by the habitual course of things, which escapes them – including in the form of their own behaviour) lead them to a result that is the contrary of what they claimed to be doing or seeking. Now, this outcome could have been foreseen to the extent that, while it is disconcerting for the agent, it is not abnormal for the spectator who could expect to see this outcome given what they know of the human condition. Each person blindly believes that he is especially capable of escaping this, and the pleasure of the spectator consists precisely in seeing this hope disappointed and having confirmed in front of him what he had always suspected. One of the mechanisms of the

---

[44] 'Et ex stulto insanum faciunt', *Ethics* IV, 57, Schol., G II, p. 252, ll. 14–15 [*CWS* I, 577]. Cf. *Eunuchus*, 251.

[45] 'Solamen miseris socios habuisse malorum', *Ethics* IV, 57, Schol., G II, p. 252, ll. 21–2 [*CWS* I, 578].

[46] Leopold, in his classic study 'De Spinozae elocutione dicendique genere', remarks that Spinoza seems to have borrowed from Latin comedy not only its language but even its universe: 'Immo (ut plane dicam, quae sentiam), non tantum vocabula et versus in suam rem facientes interdum a comico mutuatus esse videtur philosophus, sed haud raro etiam res ipsas et argumenta fabularum respexisse, ita ut hic illic non tam suae aetatis homines et instituta quam res antiquae et ante oculos versatae esse et pro experientia, quae vocatur, fuisse videantur, une ea, quae theoretice deduxisset, illustraret vel probaret', *Ad Spinozae Opera Posthuma*, p. 33. This is entirely correct, but one should add that the people and the institutions of Antiquity provide, in Spinoza's eyes, an experience that is still valid, *mutatis mutandis*, in his own time, since nature is one and the same.

[47] I refer here to the works of Akkerman on Spinoza and Van den Enden.

theatre of Menander and Terence concerns the juxtaposition of these series: whatever happens, the old man will be taken advantage of, the stupid slave will be dealt blows, the lover will have to revisit his faults. This double denegation is found in the Scholia where each time it reveals the irony of the life of the passions. The fact that these traits of experience are well known and are already inscribed in literary memory (*decantati*) only makes the blindness with which we throw ourselves into their illusory negation all the more flagrant, and all the more cruel the way in which reality reasserts its rights. It should be added that what with the poets is a case of irony becomes with the historians a disabused consideration;[48] we could also account in this way for a significant part of Spinoza's rhetoric of citation.[49]

To this repertoire we should add the evocation of whole scenes where the Scholia transform themselves into spectacles and present us with Seneca[50] opening his veins following the tyrant's orders, or with the Spanish poet forgetting the comedies he had composed.[51] In these cases, it is not words that are cited, nor a conventional situation; it is a particular historical example, which serves simply to illustrate a variant of a thesis that has already been demonstrated. In these two evocations, the resonance is more dramatic, and the themes of suicide and madness recall Baroque theatre.[52] But the complexity of experience is weaker: in these two cases it is simply a matter of adding an example to a series. Why does Spinoza insert these two examples here? The reference to a singular historical character adds nothing at the level of theoretical content. It creates a reality-effect whose purpose is to help overcome the reader's incredulity in the face of a thesis that is too

---

[48] E.-L. Etter has underscored that it is through Tacitus that Spinoza thinks to what extent citizens, even oppressed ones, remain the principal peril for the City (*Tacitus in der Geistesgeschichte des 16. und 17. Jahrhunderts*, Basel-Stuttgart: Verlag von Helbing & Lichtenhan, 1966, p. 149). She remarks that his vision of Tacitus is determined by Spinoza's reading of Justus Lipsius (cf. also the whole chapter 'Die Bedeutung des Tacitus für di Niederlande', pp. 115–49).

[49] 'Per nervature piú o meno evidenti il lettore colto dell'Europa e, ancor più, dell'Olanda del Seicento, dopo Lipsio e con Grozio, terra e tempo d'elezione per la fortuna di Tacito, era ricondotto alla lettura di quel classico', as O. Proeitti notes, '*Aduelscens luxu perditus*. Classici latini nell'opera di Spinoza', p. 213, on a highly overdetermined phrase from the *TP*, G III, p. 312, ll. 29–34 [*TP* VII, 12; CWS II 549].

[50] *Ethics*, IV, 20, Schol. [CWS I, 557].

[51] *Ethics* IV, 39, Schol. [CWS I, 569].

[52] On Spinoza and the Baroque, see Gebhardt's well-known work, 'Spinoza/Judentum und Barock', in *Vier Reden*, Hiedelberg: Carl Winter, 1927, and Dunin-Borkowski, *Spinoza*, vol. II, 1933, p. 322–44, as well as the more reserved analyses of A. Negri, *L'anomalia selvaggia*, pp. 100–5.

opposed to his spontaneous convictions (the heteronomy of suicide, the succession of human identities in a single body).

Simple confirmation, displaced confirmation, ironic confirmation. All of these instances of experience arise from what could be called a particular anthropology. Each of them illustrates or reveals a situation involving the passions. But there are other occurrences that have a supplementary interest since they bring out a general anthropology. The end of Book III is revealing on this point. Spinoza begins by saying that in the preceding Propositions he has 'explained and shown through their first causes the main affects and vacillations of soul'.[53] We are thus in the domain of a genetic explanation: the Demonstrations have established how these fluctuations are born from the three primitive affects. The language itself in which this result is summarised has a geometrical allure to it ('to explain', 'to show', 'causes'). But if the demonstration has explained to us *why* our soul is fluctuating, do at this point that we learn *that* it fluctuates – or were we already aware of this? The following phrase gives us a double response: by its content it states that it appears that we are prey to external causes 'in many ways' and that our life is governed by contradiction and ignorance. Yet, as such, this phrase insists only on the necessary character of this proof. By its tone, on the other hand, it clearly subtracts itself from the geometrical demonstration: 'we are driven about in many ways by external causes, and [. . .] like waves on the sea, driven by contrary winds, we toss about, not knowing our outcome and our fate'.[54] We recognise here the rhetoric of the experiential procedure. This is the same as saying that the perception of the fluctuation comes first and that the role of the Demonstration is not to show this perception but to demonstrate its causes and explain its necessity.

The Scholium that closes the first section of Book IV completes this general anthropology by bringing impotence and inconsistency together as the most general traits of the condition of the passions.[55] Here again, the deduction demonstrates the causes of the situation, but Spinoza seems to think that the very fact that these are the most general traits of the passions

---

[53] 'Atque his puto me praecipuos affectus, quae ex compositione trium primitivorum affectuum, nempe Cupiditatis, Laetitiae, et Tristitiae oriuntur, explicuisse, perque primas suas causas ostendisse', *Ethics* III, 59, Schol., p. 189, ll. 1–4 [CWS I, 530].

[54] 'Ex quibus apparet, nos a causis externis multis modis agitari, nosque perinde ut maris undae, a contrariis ventis agitatae, fluctuari, nostri eventus atque fati inscios', ibid., ll. 4–6 [CWS I, 530].

[55] 'His paucis humanae impotentiae et inconstantiae causas, et cur homines Rationis praecepta non servent, explicui', *Ethics* IV, 18, Schol., p. 222, ll. 10–11 [CWS I, 555].

is known to us. Now, this fact is not a particular fact: it constitutes the most universal experience of the human condition. Impotence, inconsistency, internal division: this seems to be the backdrop against which particular passions come to the fore. We have always felt this, without knowing the reasons why; and because we do not know the reasons, we do not know the necessity of what we feel. We are therefore still operating under the illusion of being able to escape these passions – an illusion that is repeatedly undermined but always reborn. What is specific to the *Ethics*, then, is that it confirms experience by explaining it, thereby destroying even the illusion that prevents us from rigorously drawing its consequences.

We have just quoted two texts in which this general anthropology is developed. But there are numerous other passages where it seems as if this anthropology is presupposed or quoted as if it went without saying; passages that refer to a situation that everyone is familiar with and that is to be explained and no longer simply shown.[56] Let us add to these passages the formula from Ovid[57] that is so often repeated: it is given as a well-known lesson of experience (two of the sentences where it is introduced begin with *saepe*,[58] while another is marked by the phrase 'experientia satis superque docet'[59]). The quotation from Ovid perfectly sums up the most general formula of our impotence in the very domain where reason begins to affirm itself.[60] This general anthropology reveals what we called, with respect to

---

[56] Thus, the preface to Book III reproaches the moralists for not understanding the causes of human impotence. It is thus a good thing that all – the moralists, Spinoza, and the readers that both are addressing – know well that this impotence exists. They know it only too well. The divergence bears upon the causes that should be assigned to it.

[57] It is also found in Paul, Romans 7:19, and before this in Euripides, *Medea*, vv. 1078–80. It is not particularly surprising that Spinoza does not mention Euripides: he hardly cites any Greek authors. Why, on the other hand, is he silent on Paul, one of the authors that elsewhere he cites the most, when he seeks an equivalent in the Ecclesiastes? Perhaps it is because the Epistle to the Romans inserts this remark in a theological reflection on sin that renders it too particular.

[58] 'Ut saepe coactus sit, [. . .],' *Ethics* III, Praef. [CWS I, 491]; 'nosque saepe [. . .]', *Ethics* III, 2, Schol. [CWS I, 494]. The variant from Book IV (Proposition 18, Schol.) is preceded by the same *saepe* at one line's interval.

[59] 'Quamvis experientia satis superque doceat [. . .]', Letter LVIII to Schuller [*Ep*. LVIII; CWS II, 428].

[60] Spinoza willingly calls upon Ovid to underscore contradictions of this type, for example between desire and its prohibition. (*Amores*, III, 4, v. 11 and 17, whose echo we hear in the *TTP*, G III, respectively p. 243, ll. 12–14 [*TTP* XX, 22; CWS II, 348] and p. 216, ll. 25–6 [*TTP* XVII, 91; CWS II, 316], then in the *TP*, p. 355, l. 28 [*TP* X, 5; CWS II, 599]. Cf. O. Proietti, '*Adulescens luxu perditus*. Classici latini nell'opera di Spinoza', p. 256.

the *TdIE*, a radical ethics. It has the same depth and the same appearance of saturation. It presents almost all of the same characteristics, except one: circularity. It forms the backdrop of our life, but without preventing us from seeing what's in the foreground. It makes us feel our finitude – and thus, perhaps, in a differential way (even if this is not said), it makes us aspire to eternity, just as at the beginning of the *TdIE* the vanity and futility of the goods and events of common life did.

B. The Constitutive Function: The *Ingenium*

But this is not all: what insists is, precisely, individuality. On the one hand, the passions themselves are diversified according to individuals, just as individuality is itself diversified according to its objects.[61] On the other hand, certain properties of individuals in general concern their particularity; these are, among others, those properties that concern these individuals' politics and religion. When it comes to characterising the way in which the prophets are distinct from other men, and thus to marking their difference, this difference is not something that can be deduced: it can only be noted. It is thus experience that reveals the concrete form of individuality that governs the expression of justice and piety. Can this individuality be thought for itself? When it comes to indicating the spontaneous rule of men's behaviour towards others, we cannot say that such-and-such a passion triumphs: each person has a spontaneous tendency to want to regulate others according to their own complexion. Thus, even if it is within inter-human relations that the passions are operative, determining the laws of the passions cannot answer all of the possible questions we might have. What we need are the means for designating what, at the level of the passions, is proper to the individual.

The way in which this notion is introduced in Book III of the *Ethics* is quite instructive. The Corollary to Proposition 31 had demonstrated that each person, as much as they can, seeks for everyone to love what they themselves love and to hate what they themselves hate. Put in this way, the theorem seems to bear upon two passions only, namely love and hate. But it is based on Proposition 31, which also named desire, and there is no reason not to think that desire is not implicated in the Corollary as well. Better still, the Scholium reformulates the Corollary by replacing the names of the

---

[61] 'Quilibet uniuscujusque individui affectus alterius tantum discrepat, quantum essentia unius ab essentia alterius differt', *Ethics* III, 57, G II, p. 186, ll. 11–14 [CWS I, 528]. For the differentiation between objects, cf. the preceding proposition.

passions with a much more general expression: 'And so we see that each of us, by his nature, wants the others to live according to his complexion [*ingenium*].'⁶² Why this change? No doubt because the rule is so constant that it applies not only to the primitive passions (desire, joy through love, sadness through hatred) but also to those that are derived from them. It is therefore all of the passions that each person seeks to share with the others. Is, then, the *ingenium* simply a collective noun for the totality of passions? If this were the case, Spinoza's argument would gain nothing from the Scholium, besides a little brevity. But this is not so. The key is provided by the passage from the 'we' of the Proposition and from the Demonstration to the 'each of us' from the Corollary and the Scholium. By saying 'we', the geometrical order aims at human nature in its system of causes. Its object is the passions, and it is applicable to each of them through the intermediary of the fundamental affects. Yet, when we speak of 'each person', we aim at the precise complex of passions that constitutes each individual; and this complex is different for each individual, even if individuals are constituted by the same components. In one individual such-and-such a passion is dominant, while another individual is associated, for biographical reasons or for reasons of the environment that weighs on them, with some other passion; another passion again takes on certain characteristics because of the specific structure of the individual's body or of such-and-such a preferential object of their personal history. In another individual the same elements are organised differently, in a whole with a different tonality. Only experience can teach us about these existential givens. But the geometrical order begins by stating a law that experience exemplifies. Paradoxically, individuality, whose mathematical law does not give us its content, is summoned by the same law that regulates this very content to determine this law's application. We thus require a concept that refers to this irreducible knot of passions, whose site is designated by geometry, but without geometry being able to assign it a determinate figure. It is this site that the term *ingenium* refers to.

This is not a novel concept.⁶³ It plays a central role in humanist texts, and

---

⁶² 'Atque adeo videmus, unumquemque ex natura appetere, ut reliqui ex ipsius ingenio vivant', G II, p. 164, ll. 28–9 [*Ethics* 31, Schol.; CWS I, 512].

⁶³ The term is common in classical Latin, but it rarely has a conceptual status. Sallust often uses it to refer either to the temperament or the 'nature' of an individual, or to the qualities of the spirit as opposed to those of the body. Catalina was 'ingenio malo pravoque' (*Conjuratio*, Chapter V); the senators' bodies had been weakened by the passing years, but their spirit had been fortified by wisdom, 'corpus annis infirmum, ingenium sapientia validum', ibid., Chapter VI.

then, in the classical age, in the works of Vives,[64] Huarte,[65] Gracián[66] and Cervantes.[67] It takes on a new dimension in these works to the extent that it provides a link to the humanist reflection on individual differences. It oscillates between two meanings: it either marks the diversity of minds or the superiority of some among them. It can signify what is 'natural' in a given individual as opposed to others, or it can refer to the genius or mind that characterises some individuals more than others.[68] In both cases, it clearly marks the fact that the human mind is not reducible to reason. In Vives' work, the *ingenium* is the ensemble of creative capacities that go beyond the simple understanding. In Spinoza, this duality is less clearly marked: the first meaning becomes essential, while the second is only thought, when it appears, under the jurisdiction of the first. To be talented is to have one possible complexion, one possible nature.[69] We thus move from a reflection on originality to a meditation on diversity.

From this perspective, Spinoza is incontestably closer to the tradition of Huarte.[70] In Huarte's work, the notion of the *ingenio* is introduced to

---

[64] Cf. E. Hidalgo-Serna, 'Ingenium and Rhetoric in the Works of Vives', *Philosophy and Rhetoric*, 16/4 (1983), pp. 228–41.

[65] *Examen de los Ingenios*. The concept is cited in one of the annotations on the example of Florence. Cf. I Sonne, 'Un manoscritto sconosciuto delle "adnotationes" al trattato teologico-politico di Spionza', *Civiltà moderna*, 5 (1933), pp. 305–12; G. Totaro, 'Un manoscritto inedito delle "adnotationes" al *Tractatus theologico-politicus* di Spinoza', *Studia Spinozana*, V (1989), pp. 205–24.

[66] E. Hidalgo-Serna, 'The Philosophy of Ingenium: Concept and Ingenious Method in Baltasar Gracián', *Philosophy and Rhetoric*, 13 (1980), pp. 245–63. Spinoza had the *Criticon* in his library.

[67] Cf. H. Weinrich, *Das ingenium Don Quijotes. Ein Beirtrag zur literarischen Charackterkunde*, Munster: Aschendorff, 1956. Spinoza possessed a copy of the *Nouvelles exemplaires*.

[68] This duality of meaning makes it difficult to translate it into a language other than Italian or Spanish. E. Hidalgo-Serna remarks on this on the topic of Germanic languages ('Ingenium and Rhetoric in Vives', p. 240, note 32), but this is also the case for French. I borrow Appuhn's term 'complexion'.

[69] Spinoza sometimes uses the word in this non-conceptual sense and without precision: the theologians wanted to prove their talent (*ingenium ostentare*) by giving ends to things, *Ethics* I, App., G II, p. 80, ll. 30-1 [CWS I, 443]. Similarly, Descartes, with his theory of the *affectus*, has done nothing but show his great talent (*magni sui ingenii acumen*), *Ethics* III, Praef., G II, p. 138, ll. 4–5 [CWS I, 492].

[70] As is well known, scholars have also sought to identify this tradition in Descartes as well: G. A. Pérouse supposes that Descartes had at least read the first prologue to the *Examen* on the specialisation of minds. *L'Examen des esprits du docteur Juan Huarte de San Juan. Sa diffusion et son influence en France aux XVIe et XVIIe siècles*, Paris: Belles Lettres, 1970, pp. 144–52.

explain why, while all souls are equal, individuals and nations have such diverse capacities in both knowledge and practical activities.[71] The diversity of *ingenios* is in turn rooted in the diversity of the dispositions of the body[72] – that is, in the irreducible ways Nature has, for each singular individual, applied its laws. What in Huarte's work refers to the mixture of the four humours, in Spinoza supposes an equation in terms of rest and movement. Yet in both cases it is indeed a matter of forging a concept to identify the diversity of individuals and to think this diversity in relation to their corporeal determinations.[73]

Most importantly, the advantage of this notion is that it allows one to characterise individuals *a posteriori*, without taking a detour past geometrical deduction. Each individual is determined by a certain proportion of motion and rest. This proportion could be known by an infinite understanding, which would master the system of the totality of laws by which a complex individual is constituted. A finite understanding can certainly master this system when they study very simple individuals, where very few components are involved. As soon as it is a matter of more complex individuals, the same process is by rights always possible, but in actual fact never occurs. Does this prevent one from having any access to the individual and to their relation to the other, or does it limit us to accessing them only inadequately? Here again experience provides an answer. Without knowing the essential composition of a given individual, we can say that all can recognise this composition: frequenting the individual gives us a solid knowledge of them – a knowledge that is not that of causes, certainly, but one that is still sufficiently certain to prevent some ideas from being entertained and to mark specific limits. Just as we recognise the traits of the individual's face, so do we recognise the traits of their mind. These traits are not reducible to how far they have advanced down the path of rationality, even if this can play a role in our perception

---

[71] *Examen de los ingenios*, Chapter XI ff., in the volume *Obras escogidas de filosofos*, Biblioteca de Aurores españoles, vol. 65, Madrid, 1953, p. 447 ff.

[72] Ibid., Chapter VIII, p. 433 ff.

[73] This proximity is generally neglected. Cf. M. Iriarte's book, *El doctor Huarte de San Juan y su Examen de los ingenios*, Madrid: CSIC, 1948, which devotes several chapters to Huarte's influence but does not mention Spinoza. Reciprocally, Spinoza specialists have rarely taken an interest in Huarte. Dunin-Borkowski, who cites whole libraries, does not name him on a single occasion. It is true that the comparison is only of interest if it brings out the decisive role of the *ingenium* in Spinoza. There is another point of comparison too: the analysis of miracles as a function of the crowd's *ingenium* (*Examen*, Chapter IV, pp. 418–19. It is to this passage that marginal note 42 refers to and that I. Sonne identifies, 'Un manoscritto sconosciuto', pp. 6–7).

of the whole. Rather, they are a knot of passions, or the way in which the passions are modulated and imbricated in a singularity.

What are the characteristics of the *ingenium*? These characteristics can be enumerated by way of two apparently contradictory moments – moments that can, in fact, be deduced from one another. The irreducible individuality of the *ingenium* is manifest initially as a rule of diversity among individuals. It is then manifest in each individual as a principle of judgement and thus functions as a rule of assimilation. The paradoxical conjunction of these two rules dictates a spontaneous strategy in inter-human relations.

The Rule of Diversity. Spinoza repeats this insistently: 'men vary greatly in their mentality, because one is content with these opinions, another with those, and because what moves one person to religion moves another to laughter'.[74] He repeats this point just before presenting the universal *credo*, and this time explicitly uses the following formula, which is characteristic of experience: 'No one doubts that the common mentality of men is extremely variable, and that not everyone is equally satisfied by all things. Opinions govern men in different ways: those which move one person to devotion, move another to laughter and contempt.'[75] Of course, the form proper to each individual can be explained by the ensemble of laws that are combined to produce them and to give them a biography, and so on. But, if we take a sufficiently large number of people, we can be sure, even before we have examined them, that we will find among them an extreme diversity of complexions. Once again, with the *ingenium* we encounter a concept that allows us to reduce inadequation by neutralising its effects. The *ingenium* affirms the irreducibility of individuals while simultaneously taking into account their variety. This variety can be reduced to degrees of understanding.[76] But it can also refer to differences in courage, in compassion,[77] in the capacity to

---

[74] 'Quia hominum ingenium varium admodum est, et alius his, alius illis opinionibus melius acquiescit, & quod hunc ad religionem, illum ad risum movet [. . .]', *TTP*, Preface, G III, p. 11, ll. 1–4 [*TTP* Praef.; *CWS* II, 73].

[75] '& nemo dubitet, commune hominum ingenium varium admodum esse, nec omnes in omnibus aeque acquiescere, sed opiniones diverso modo homines regere, quippe quae hunc devotionem, eae ipsae alterum ad risum, & contemptum movent', *TTP*, Chapter XIV, G III, p. 176, l. 35 [*TTP* XIV, 22; *CWS* II, 268].

[76] The Hebrews leaving Egypt are *rudis ingenii*. The same term is opposed, in Chapter III, to *homines prudentes*, whose complexion and whose vigilance is *non mediocris*.

[77] The interpretation that Spinoza gives of Josiah's procedure, after the discovery of the Book of Law (*TTP*, Chapter II, G III, p. 33 [*TTP* II, 98]), makes us think that the *ingenium muliebre* is, at least in the eyes of the king, more inclined to compassion (and in fact neither 2 Chronicles 34, nor the parallel text in 2 Kings 22, attribute to Josiah the

endure adversity, and to force of mind. It can also concern stubbornness.⁷⁸ This real diversity is built on an irreducible foundation. Yet, as we will see, the very play of the *ingenium* will precisely lead to the imaginary reduction of this diversity.

The Rule of Assimilation. This diversity has repercussions for conceptions of the world. In fact, each person bases the judgements they make on their *ingenium*: they judge good and evil by the sovereign right of nature, while their interest is informed by their complexion.⁷⁹ This judgement is not wrong; rather, it spontaneously generalises and makes the individual believe that what is valid for them is also valid for others. When an individual's complexion is dominated by a single passion, and when they judge according to their *ingenium*, that judgement is based on that passion. 'So the Greedy man judges an abundance of money best, and poverty worst. The Ambitious man desires nothing so much as Esteem and dreads nothing so much as Shame. To the Envious nothing is more agreeable than another's unhappiness, and nothing more burdensome than another's happiness.'⁸⁰ This is proof that 'characters' are readable only as the extreme points of passions: they are given here as uni-dimensional *ingenia*. But above all, people, even when they have a richer complexion, necessarily judge the complexions of others through the lens of their own: they effectively interpret their own actions according to a finalistic schema that expresses *their* specific complexion and not that of the other, no more than it does reality. Thus, when they attempt to interpret the behaviour of others, if they have no other means of knowing this behaviour, they apply this schema to it.⁸¹ Of course, this procedure applies equally to imaginary beings and to real beings. This is why, when

---

choice of the prophetess. But Spinoza could legitimately have thought that his servants were carrying out his intentions). A formula from the *Ethics* seems to subscribe to this characterisation (*Ethics* IV, 37, Schol. 1: 'muliebri misericordia', G II, p. 236, l. 35 [CWS I, 566].

⁷⁸ Before Mosaic law, the *ingenium* of the Hebrews was 'contumax', *TTP*, Chapter V, G III, p. 75, l. 15 [*TTP* V, 28; CWS II, 145].

⁷⁹ 'Atque adeo summo naturae jure unusquisque judicat, quid bonum, quid malum sit, suaeque utilitati ex suo ingenio consulit', *Ethics* IV, 37, Schol. 2, G II, p. 237, ll. 22–4 [CWS I, 566–7].

⁸⁰ *Ethics* III, 39, Schol. [CWS I, 516–17]. That this is in fact a thesis on the *ingenium*, even if the word is not pronounced in this Scholium, can be deduced from the fact that the preceding demonstration cited refers to it.

⁸¹ 'Nihil iis restat, nisi ut ad semet convertant, et ad fines, a quibus ipsi ad simila determinari solent, reflectant, et sic ex suo ingenio ingenium alterius necessario dijudicant', *Ethics* I, App., G II, p. 78, ll. 26–8 [CWS I, 440].

people forge *rectores naturae* to explain the phenomena that surprise them, they conceive the *ingenium* of these *rectores* on the model of their own[82] and invent a cult to them, with each person doing so, once again, on the basis of their own *ingenium*.[83] The diversity of *ingenia* thus explains the diversity of cults and superstitions.[84] Instead of being indignant about this or deploring it, we should take note of its necessity.

The paradox of the *ingenium* will engender a *spontaneous strategy*. At each moment, reality undermines one's spontaneous beliefs. Given this, each person will attempt to transform reality so that it becomes adapted to their beliefs, at the same time as they refuse to others this irreducibility of the *ingenium*, which they cannot help but demand for themselves. Each person will try to make their imaginary reduction pass into the real. They will make an effort so that others live like them, or, at the very least, conform to their criteria for life. This is perhaps the phrase that Spinoza repeats most often when it comes to explaining inter-human relations.[85] This spontaneous strategy is not limited to politics: it also concerns religion[86] and even, for example, intra-social relations, education, and so on.

This spontaneous strategy might recall Hobbes's state of nature. We should nevertheless note that in its concrete application this rule does not imply a 'war of all against all' in the strict sense. It is in fact tied up with another fundamental principle of Spinozist psychology: that of the imitation

---

[82] 'Atque horum ingenium, quandoquidem de eo numquam quid audiverant, ex suo judicare debuerunt', ibid., p. 79, ll. 5–6 [*CWS* I, 441].

[83] 'Unde factum, ut unusquisque diversos deum colendi modos ex suo ingenio excogitaverit', ibid., p. 79, ll. 8–10 [*CWS* I, 441].

[84] 'Circa religionem maxime errare solent homines, & pro ingeniorum diversitate multa magno certamine fingere [. . .]', *TTP*, Chapter XVI, p. 199, ll. 24–6 [*TTP* XVI, 62; *CWS* II, 294].

[85] 'Videmus, unumquemque ex natura appetere, ut reliqui ex ipsius ingenio vivant', *Ethics*, III, 31, Schol., G II, p. 164, ll. 28–9 [*CWS* I, 512]. 'Cum natura humana ita comparatum esse ostendimus, ut unusuisque appetat, ut reliqui ex ipsius ingenio vivant', *Ethics* V, 4, Schol., p. 283, ll. 21–3 [*CWS* I, 598–9]. 'Unusquisque solus omnia se scire putat, & omnia ex suo ingenio mederari vult', *TTP*, Chapter XVII, G III, p. 203, ll. 21–2 [*TTP* XVII, 15; *CWS* II, 299]. 'Demonstravimus [. . .] unumquemque appetere, ut reliqui ex suo ingenio vivant', *TP*, Chapter I, 5, G III, p. 275, ll. 4–8 [*TP* I, 5; *CWS* II, 505].

[86] 'We see that almost everyone peddles his own inventions as the word of God, concerned only to compel others to think as he does, under the pretext of religion' [*TTP* VII, 1; *CWS* II, 170]. Here, at the beginning of Chapter VII from the *TTP*, the word *ingenium* is absent, but we recognise the theme.

of the affects.[87] The mechanisms of this principle explain why, while tending to want to impose their complexion on others, people are at the same time led to identify – at least for a certain time and to a certain degree – with the complexions of others. We can thus understand why certain *ingenia* serve as relays to others and how factions or ideological groups can be constituted, their members at least partially sharing the same passions, and drawing from these shared passions a greater force that can then be imposed on those who resist. The joint application of these two principles helps us understand the following truth of experience that escapes Hobbes:[88] namely, that we never encounter complete anarchy but rather a struggle between constituted groups.

It is on the foundation of these characteristics of individuality that Spinoza will build his politics of relations with others. To this spontaneous strategy, Spinoza will oppose a reflexive strategy; but this reflexive strategy will always have to take into account the necessity of the first. This reflexive strategy operates according to a double distinction: between the individual and the State on the one hand, and between thoughts and actions on the other. This strategy culminates in the tracing of complex lines of demarcation. To see this, it suffices to compare Spinoza's conclusions with those by which Hobbes concludes a similar reflection that begins from the same premises. In *De Cive*, when it comes to defining the notion of sin, Hobbes remarks: 'Human nature is such that each man calls what he wants for himself *good*; what he avoids, he calls *bad*; because men's passions differ, what one calls *good*, another calls *bad*.'[89] This statement parallels Spinoza's, but Hobbes draws quite different consequences from it. From the effective diversity of opinions and the fundamental equality between men, Hobbes immediately concludes that it is necessary for the State to make an authoritarian intervention to give these opinions some order. By themselves, these opinions cannot give rise to any spontaneous order. Spinoza's conclusions are more nuanced.

On the one hand, despite the tendency of each person to judge everything according to their own complexion and to want to govern others as a function of this complexion, nobody is naturally forced to live according

---

[87] *Ethics* III, 37, ff. [CWS I, 515].

[88] Hobbes also feels the need to explain the formation of groups united by the same passion, but only in the case of seditions. Since he does not have available to him a doctrine of the imitation of the affects, he is obliged to produce an impoverished equivalent: eloquence, by which the ambitious bring out the stupidity of the vulgar. *De Cive*, Chapter XII, § 12 and 13.

[89] *De Cive*, Part II, Chapter XIV, § 17.

to the other's complexion,⁹⁰ nor to accept from others the rule of their judgements – that is, to judge on the basis of an *ingenium* that is different to their own.⁹¹ On the other hand, it is necessary to allow people to have this margin of individuality: the State must do this; it must give each person the power to interpret the foundations of faith on the basis of their own complexion. ⁹² Indeed, the State cannot do otherwise:⁹³ if it tries to, it will fall into a cycle of violence that will sweep it away. This type of strategy is thus both desirable and possible. This is, moreover, what happens in the Netherlands,⁹⁴ while the reasonable person also does it on their own account.⁹⁵

But can the City allow each person to live (and not only think and be affected) according to their own complexion? Certainly not, or not entirely: for the person who lives by their own complexion is a creature entirely of their own right and not that of the City.⁹⁶ Thus, if a City allows someone to live as a function of their own *ingenium*, it cedes its own right⁹⁷ – something that is impossible to do without splitting the State.⁹⁸ It is also impossible to allow citizens to interpret the Law in their own way, for this

---

⁹⁰ 'Nemo jure naturae ex alterius ingenio vivere tenetur, sed suae unusquisque libertatis vindex est', *TTP*, Preface, G III, p. 11, ll. 15–17 [*TTP* Praef., 29; *CWS* II, 74].

⁹¹ 'Nemo jure naturae alteri, nisi velit, morem gerere tenetur, nec aliquid bonum aut malum habere, nisi quod ipse ex suo ingenio bonum aut malum esse, decernit', *TP*, Chapter II, 18, G III, p. 282, ll. 15–18 [*TP* II, 18; *CWS* II, 514–15].

⁹² 'Concludo, unicuique sui judicii libertatem, & potestatem fundamenta fidei ex suo ingenio interpretandi relinquendam' and to not judge piety and impiety except on the basis of works alone, *TTP*, Preface, G III, p. 11, ll. 4–6 [*TTP* Praef., 28; *CWS* II, 73].

⁹³ 'Quantumvis igitur summae potestate jus ad omnia habere, & juris et pietatis interpretes credantur, nunquam tamen facere possunt, ne homines judicium de rebus quibuscunque ex proprio suo ingenio ferant, et ne eatenus hoc, aut illo affectu afficiantur', *TTP*, Chapter XX, G III, p. 240, ll. 1–5 [*TTP* XX, 6; *CWS* II, 345].

⁹⁴ 'Cum itaque nobis haec rara foelicitas contingerit, ut in Republica vivamus, ubi unicuique judicandi libertas integra, & Deum ex suo ingenio colere conceditur [. . .]', *TTP*, Preface, G III, p. 7, ll. 21–3 [*TTP* Praef., 12; *CWS* II, 69].

⁹⁵ 'Unumquemque ex suo ingenio vivere sino', Ep. XXX, G IV, p. 166, ll. 18–19 [*Ep.* XXX [to Henry Oldenburg]; *CWS* II, 14].

⁹⁶ 'Unusquisque eatenus sui juris est quatenus ex suo ingenio vivere potest', *TP*, Chapter II, 9, G III, p. 280, ll. 2–5 [*TP* II, 9; *CWS* II, 510–11].

⁹⁷ 'Si Civitas alicui concedat jus, et consequenter potestatem [. . .] vivendi ex suo ingenio, eo ipso suo jure cedit, et in eum transfert, cui talem potestatem dedit', *TP*, Chapter III, 3, G III, p. 285, ll. 8–11 [*TP* III, 3; *CWS* II, 517–18].

⁹⁸ 'Atque adeo sequitur, nulla ratione posse concipi, quod unucuique civi ex civitatis instituto liceat, ex suo ingenio vivere', ibid., ll. 16–18 [*TP* III, 3; *CWS* II, 518].

would also mean letting them live according to their own *ingenium*.[99] We are thus once again referred back to a distinction between the internal and the external.

Nevertheless, such a distinction between the internal and the external is not always a simple one: we have already seen this in the case of language. Whence a sort of ruse of Reason with respect to the State and the *ingenium*: it is necessary to lead people in such a way that each one believes they are not being led but are instead obeying their own *ingenium*.[100] In other words, it could perhaps be said that the ultimate lesson of Spinoza's politics – once the line of demarcation between actions and thoughts has been traced – comes down to inciting governments to manage peoples' actions as if they were thoughts.

What about the person led by reason? The reasonable person does not have the same motives the State has for intervening in the actions of others. Yet, if they repress their tendency to spontaneously reduce others to their own complexion, do they not then risk leaving the field open to the imitation of the affects alone? Spinoza remarks that it is difficult to determine an appropriate line of conduct in this way. The diversity of human beings means that one must exert a singular power over oneself to accept them all with their own *ingenium* and at the same time avoid imitating their affects.[101] The solution to this problem will consist in continuing to pursue, to a certain extent, the spontaneous strategy – that is, in attempting to guide others towards reason, which thus plays the role of the *ingenium* of the reasonable man.

One particular form of this strategy concerns what is necessary for educating men, or simply speaking to them. Spinoza says that it is necessary to speak *ad captum vulgi*, or that Scripture be taught *ad captum vulgi* – that is, according to the crowd's understanding. What does *captum* mean? The term is sometimes interpreted as proof of the existence of a 'double language' in Spinoza. In truth, it has, at least in part, the same semantic distribution as

---

[99] 'Praeterea concipere etiam non possumus, quod unucuique civi liceat Civitatis decreta, seu jura interpretari. Nam si hoc unucuique liceret, eo ipso sui judex esset; quandoquidem unusquisque facta sua specie juris nullo negotio excusare, seu adornare posset, & consequenter ex suo ingenio vitam institueret, quod [...] est absurdum', *TP*, Chapter X, 4, G III, p. 285, l. 32; p. 286, l. 2 [*TP* X, 4; *CWS* II, 518].

[100] 'Homines ita ducendi sunt, ut non duci, sed ex suo ingenio, et libero suo decreto vivere sibi videantur', *TP*, Chapter X, 8, G III, p. 356, ll. 26–7 [*TP* X, 8; *CWS* II, 599].

[101] 'Sunt enim homines varii [...] Unumquemque igitur ex ipsius ingenio ferre et sese continere, ne eorum affectus imitetur, singularis animi potentiae opus est', *Ethics* IV, App., 13, G II, p. 269, ll. 16–22 [*CWS* I, 589–90].

the term *ingenium*. It refers to the ensemble of each person's opinions, the frame through which they receive discourse.[102] It is not an epistemological term; but rather refers to what constitutes in the individual the conditions for knowledge. The receiver of discourse has a body and a complexion that corresponds to this body. When the receiver is a people, their frame of comprehension is formed by their national *ingenium*.[103]

The *ingenium*, such as we find it in these texts, is of a constitutive and not a confirmative order. We cannot demonstrate *a priori* that the mind of a given individual will have certain characteristics. Only experience can teach us this. Furthermore, we cannot consider this individual's *ingenium* to be a mere residue of ignorance, or, inversely, a pure equivalent of knowledge. It insists beyond the acquisition of knowledge. Spinoza speaks in effect of the *ingenium* of the person led by reason,[104] at the same time as he speaks of their *vivendi ratio*.

What happens when we turn to those ensembles of people called cities? We will see these two aspects of experience come into play successively: the confirmative aspect as regards the formation of the State, the constitutive aspect for the maintenance of its individuality.

2. The Passions and the State

In letter L, dated 20 June 1674, Spinoza responds to a question posed by his friend Jarig Jelles: what difference is there between his politics and that of Hobbes? Before we deal with Spinoza's answer, it is worthwhile pausing over Jelles' question. Why does Jelles – a cultured merchant concerned with his salvation and a member of a collegial circle that constituted a heterodox and dynamic minority within or on the margins of Calvinism – pose such a question? Why, rather than ask Spinoza about a particular aspect of his own political doctrine, does he demand that he situate himself in relation to another philosopher, namely Hobbes?

Jelles no doubt has in mind one of the burning issues facing the Dutch society he lives in. He thus he expects Spinoza to respond to *this* issue. It also happens that this issue is partly linked to Hobbes. The question at hand is in fact that of the *Jus circa sacra*. This question principally concerns knowing

---

[102] Cf. *TTP*, Chapter XIV, G III, p. 173 [*TTP* XIV, 1, 2, 3, 4; CWS II, 263–4].

[103] Cf. *TTP*, end of Chapter XI: the Apostles adapted the evangelical message to the *ingenium* of the people of their time, Paul to that of the Greeks, the others to that of the Jews (G III, p. 158 [*TTP* XI, 247]).

[104] *Ethics* IV, 66, Schol., G II, p. 260, l. 28 [CWS I, 584].

who has authority over religious institutions, and, indissociably, over the expression and predication of the beliefs that found these institutions. In these times of division between confessions, it is not only a matter of knowing if the State can or must support a Church: the question is also to what extent the State can or must intervene in the Church's own organisation, indeed in the determination of its teachings. In the terms of such a debate, Church and State do not appear as two entities that are wholly external to and independent of one another. On the contrary, what is at stake is the very status of each institution, which has to prove its right to exist. This is why, when we look beyond pamphlets and invectives, we see a second question come into view that is linked to this first one: that of the legitimacy and the conditions of the State's perpetuation. This second question is obviously less immediate than the first, less tied to a contemporary controversy. But it determines the first question because it provides the conditions for its resolution.

With regards to the first question, there exists in the Netherlands a double tradition, or rather a polemical tradition.[105] On the one hand, Calvinist orthodoxy says that when the salvation or the good of the faithful is at stake, the State must serve the decisions made by the spiritual authority (concretely, this could mean, for example, banning books that are condemned by the Synod, or punishing those individuals who pastors denounce to the State).[106] On the other hand, for more than a century the regents of Amsterdam and other cities most often defended the independence of civil power, as well as the right of civil power to dominate and control the Church. The ideologists of this lineage[107] did not, in fact, dissociate the independence *of* the State from its authority *over* the Church. They seemed to think that a total separation between these two instances was illusory and impossible. Either the Church dominated the State or the State dominated the Church. If there was no middle ground, this was because pastors wielded great power over souls, and thus, if these pastors disagreed with magistrates, they could always excite the passions of the people and awaken the hatred of the multitude against the Sovereign, with all of the attendant dangers this entailed for the stability of the State. This is why the Sovereign must,

---

[105] Cf. D. Nobbs, *Theocracy and Toleration: A Study of the Disputes in Dutch Calvinism from 1600 to 1650*, Cambridge: Cambridge University Press, 1938; L. Mugnier-Pollet, *La Philosophie politique de Spinoza*, Paris: Vrin, 1976.

[106] The first version is given by Walaeus, against whom Vossius directs his theses. Later in the century, Voetius formulates Calvinist theses more clearly.

[107] The stage prior to the importation of Hobbesian theses is represented by Vossius' *Epistolica Dissertatio* or Grotius' *De Imperio Summarum Potestatum circa sacra*.

for his own security and thus for the security of all, keep close watch over the ecclesiasts and their teachings.[108] Those who held these positions found in Hobbes, when they read him, something of a theoretical guarantee:[109] his theory of the state of nature and of the social pact provided reasons and arguments to defend these theses since it showed that the natural play of individuals and their passions led to the death of all if it was not transcended and organised by a pact that both founded the legitimacy of the Sovereign and prevented each individual subject (in particular the ecclesiasts) from elevating themselves to the level of judges with civil authority. This is why, from 1650 onwards, Hobbes's thought played an ever more important role in the United Provinces.[110]

Jelles' question should therefore come as no surprise. By asking Spinoza 'What is the difference between you and Hobbes?', he is in fact asking: how do you conceive of the substance of the State and the force it possesses for resisting human passions? It is precisely on these points that Spinoza responds. He says:

1. I always maintain natural right (which is equivalent to saying that Hobbes does not).
2. With respect to the City, I only recognise the Sovereign's right over his subjects to the extent that he is more powerful than them (this relation is thus a relation of force, implying that in Hobbes it is not a relation of force, or no longer is).
3. All of this occurs within the state of nature.[111]

---

[108] To complete this list, we should also mention the impact of these questions on a third institution: the university. See for example the analysis provided by P. Dibon of the purification which, in Leiden, followed the Synod of Dordrecht and which affected teachers as famous as Bertius, Barlaeus, Jacchaeus and even Vossius (*La philosophie néerlandaise au siècle d'Or*, vol. I, New York: Elsevier, 1954, pp. 80–9).

[109] This is the case for example with L. Antistius Constans, *De Jure Ecclesiasticorum*, 1665, who develops of a theory of the pact, one that is certainly modified from but impossible without Hobbes. Cf. Nobbs, *Theocracy and Toleration*, pp. 245–50; P.-F. Moreau, 'Spinoza et le *Jus circa sacra*', *Studia spinozana*, 1 (1985), pp. 335–44 and the translation of Constans' work by V. Butori, J. Lagrée, P.-F. Moreau, 1991.

[110] Cf. C. Secrétan, 'Partisans et détracteurs de Hobbes dans les Provinces-Unies du temps de Spinoza', *Bulletin de l'Association des Amis de Spinoza*, 2 (1979), pp. 2–13; 'Première réactions néerlandaises à Hobbes au XVIIe siècle', *Annales d'histoires des facultés de Droit*, 3 (1986), pp. 137–65. See also the works of G. Jongnneelen concerning the influence of Hobbes on Koerbagh, in particular 'La philosophie politique d'Adriaan Koerbagh', *Cahiers Spinoza*, VI (1991), pp. 247–67.

[111] 'Quantum ad Politicam spectat, discrimen inter me & Hobbesium, de quo interro-

Before moving on to a detailed analysis, we can immediately note the unity of this response: it seems to indicate that the line of division between the two philosophies concerns the fact that what Hobbes separates, Spinoza unifies. While Hobbes thinks of the state of nature, natural right, and relations of power as interrupting one another, Spinoza treats them as continuous. This leads us to the following question: how can the state of nature continue to exist?[112] If the state of nature and civil society are the same thing, why retain the notion of the state of nature?[113]

A. Time and the Pact

What is the foundation of the theory of the pact in Hobbes? For Hobbes, the universe is natural through and through. This, moreover, is the necessary condition for knowing it scientifically. There is therefore no region of being that escapes the laws of nature, and no possibility of supernatural intervention. Each substance is corporeal and from this totally corporeal world nothing can escape that could found another domain. The human being has nothing within them that is heterogeneous to the system of the laws of nature.

However, the insistent critique that Hobbes makes of Aristotle's politics comes down to the following point: Aristotle did not see the difference between the state of nature and civil society. Now, the human, and what is most human in him – namely, the City – are not thinkable outside of this fundamental difference. This is an indication that, despite everything, there does exist some human specificity. Moreover, this specificity does not separate the state of nature from civil society: it is differentially refracted in both domains and distinguishes both from animal nature, which is subject to laws of necessity. What, then, is this difference that is nevertheless grounded

gas, in hoc consistit quod ego naturale Jus semper sartum tectum conservo, quodque supremo Magistratui in qualibet Urbe non plus in subditos juris, quam juxta mensuram potestatis, qua subditum superat, competere statuo, quod in statu naturale semper locum habet', Ep. L, G IV, pp. 238–9 [*Ep.* L [to Jarig Jelles]; CWS II, 406].

[112] Spinoza uses the expression *sartum tectum*; the Dutch version of the *Nagelate Schriften* (which Gebhardt takes to the be the original, *Textgestaltung*, p. 417) says simply: *in zijn geheel*, in its totality.

[113] On the letter L and more generally on the relations between Hobbes and Spinoza, the reader can consult M. de Souza Chaui, 'Direito natural e direito civil em Hobbes e Espinosa', *Revista latinoamericana de Filosofía*, 6/1 (1980), pp. 57–71; J.-P. Osier, 'Hobbes et Spinoza devant le canon de l'Ecriture', *Cahiers philosophiques*, 14 (1983), pp. 19–29; J. Lagrée, 'Du magistère spirituel à la *medicina mentis*: Grotius, Hobbes, Constans, Spinoza', in J. Saada (ed.), *Hobbes, Spinoza, ou les politiques de la parole*, Lyon: ENS Editions, 2009.

in nature and supposes neither reason (which is not primary) nor free will (which does not exist)? Something must be found in nature that extracts the human being from nature.

The solution is provided by time.[114] The human being is a body, certainly, as are all other existing beings, but they are a body that lives in time, and this natural trait suffices to extract them from nature, to construct an explanation of society, and to found both the science of politics and the legitimacy of the State. In fact, while animals live in a continuity without memory, human beings, through the power of inscription, can supplement the silence of nature. In seeking to orient their lives, animals are at the mercy of external chance, which traps them in a cycle of repetition. Having observed this fault, man has imagined placing 'visible or other sensible mark[s], the which, when he seeth [them] again, may bring to his mind the thought he had when he set [them] up'.[115]

Hobbes then deduces a series of four consequences from this: the first two concern the development of the individual, while the last two establish the system of the individual's relations with others:

- A *static series*: time makes language possible, which then produces reason and founds the possibility of science.
- A *dynamic series*: man's inscription in time allows him to develop the sense of the new, which lies at the origin of the taste for adventure, the development of civilisation, and the reality of science.
- A *series of passions*: the existence of time allows for the prolongation of desire, and thus for the constitution of the passions, which are themselves multiplied by language.
- A *juridical series*: the representation of the future allows for the instauration of a new language, that of the promise; at this point, both right

---

[114] The principle of the analysis that follows is developed in P.-F. Moreau, *Hobbes. Philosophie, science, religion*, Paris: PUF, 1989, pp. 53–67.

[115] 'The experience we have thereof, is in such brute beasts, which, having the providence to hide the remains and superfluity of their meat, do nevertheless want the remembrance of the place where they hid it, and thereby make no benefit thereof in their hunger: but man, who in this point beginneth to rank himself somewhat above the nature of the beasts, hath observed and remembered the cause of this defect, and to amend the same, hath imagined or devised to set up a visible other sensible mark, the which, when he seeth it again, may bring to his mind the thought he had when he set it up', *Human Nature*, V, 1, *EW*, Vol. IV, pp. 19–20. The interest of this text lies in the fact that what Hobbes refuses to animals is not mere memory, but the memory of thought: in the absence of sensible differences in things, animals cannot re-find the thought they had formed on the first occasion.

and the State can be developed, the two of them resting solely on the possibility of the pact.

It is these last two series that will determine both the misery and happiness of man. The reader will note that both series engage one of the consequences of man's temporal life, namely language, that multiplier, which itself is made possible by temporality. This double key suffices to constitute both the state of nature and civil society. In fact, the play of the passions is enough to make people's lives unliveable so long as they are not united and contained by a State. For it is not hunger or need that provokes the war of all against all; it is much rather the obsession people have with comparing their situation to that of others and their tendency to express the result of this comparison, to either boast of it or to complain about it. The struggle between human beings is not dictated by nature: it is produced by their passions. The exit from this state of perpetually present or impending war is made possible by the series of juridical consequences: because the human being is an animal capable of making promises, humans can commit to respect the will of the Sovereign, to whom they abandon their rights in exchange for other subjects doing the same. Of course, Hobbes knows that people can lie when making promises, or quite simply decide after the fact to not keep them. But he seems to have confidence in the Sovereign's force once it is constituted to repress such thoughts of disobedience. We are here in the paradigmatic dimension of classical juridical space: a logic of obedience founded on the articulation of commitment and force.

In these conditions, is it true that for Hobbes natural right ceases when civil society is created, as Spinoza says? We can offer two elements of an answer to this question:

— If we envisage the problem by isolating the juridical and the passionate dimensions, what does natural right signify in the state of nature? It refers both to an operation and to an effect, both of which have their source in the individual's forces. From the fact that there exists neither Good nor Evil in themselves (on this point, we can see in Hobbes an inheritor of the Sceptics' criticisms and of the tenth trope of Aenesidemus – but we should note that he adapts this heritage in a quite particular way since he replaces the empirical analysis of the diversity of norms by the statement of the principle of juridical nominalism), it follows that there exists no extra-human value or rule of conduct, nor, above all, any extra-individual one. Each person must persevere in their being, ensuring that they have everything that is necessary to achieve this end – which amounts to saying that they have the right to everything they can have or want to have. But this absolute right is a weak right since the right of each person is combated and limited by the rights of all others. Moreover, there is obviously no possible negotiation between these claims since there is no common terrain: the will of each person can at each moment dissolve the effects of an agreement so long as none have the power to constrain others to respect it. In civil society, there is still no transcendent Good and Evil: it is the will of the Sovereign that fixes the line of distinction between the just and the unjust. In sum, in terms of its operation, natural right is concentrated in a single individual. What happens is concentration and not disappearance. As for the effect of natural right, it remains the same since each person finds in the laws thus created both their salvation and their prosperity – that is, what they sought, albeit in vain, in the state of nature. Hobbes thus cannot be accused of making a trivial point since, if the dangerous effects of natural right cease with the constitution of civil society, it is not because of some miracle but because the commitment of each individual makes it possible for them to find another means to persevere in their being (to live in the security of society is more efficacious than living in the elements under the perpetual threat of others), and because the force of the Sovereign is there to remind those who forget their commitments. The abandonment of the right of each individual to all things is in fact this right's continuation by other means: the renunciation of the illusory possession of everything – which is always threatened and always defeated – is the condition of property, certain and protected, over a limited number of objects and over one's own life. In this sense, Spinoza is wrong: it is not true, strictly speaking, that for Hobbes natural right ceases absolutely in civil society.

— But we can also pose the problem in a different way: when Spinoza speaks of natural right, he is not speaking of exactly the same thing as Hobbes: he is in fact speaking simultaneously of right and of the theory of the passions. It is this fusion that constitutes his principal critique of Hobbes: it is not because he is confused that he speaks of both at once. The fact is that for Spinoza, the power of the passions constitutes the effective reality of right. Spinoza's critique of Hobbes's conception of right consists in saying that it is too formal, too separate from the natural reality of the passions. Hobbes takes this reality into consideration in the state of nature and forgets it as soon as the pact is constituted, whereas for Spinoza the pact in no way interrupts it *because natural right is fundamentally nothing other than a complex of passions*. It is in this thesis that the entire meaning of letter L resides. The analysis of a few passages from the *TTP* will suffice to convince us of this.

B. The Foundations of the State and Fundamental Passions

In Chapter XVI of the *TTP*, Spinoza poses the question of the foundation of the State (in terms of the progression of his argument, this is the necessary condition for examining methodically the problem of freedom of thought).[116] Like Hobbes, he begins by dealing with the natural right of the individual, and he defines it using formulations that have a certain Hobbesian allure: 'each individual has a supreme right to do everything it can, *or* that the right of each thing extends as far as its determinate power does'; and: 'each individual has the supreme right to do this, i.e. (as I have said), to exist and have effects as it is naturally determined to do'.[117] Spinoza then deduces from this – and Hobbes would not disagree with him here – that natural right is not essentially defined by Reason. He also excludes from the outset that one must refer to the State or to religion to understand its operation (we are thus indeed in a situation like the state of nature, where it is only the forces and ends of individuals that can found the process of legitimation).

However, even if these formulations have a certain Hobbesian ring to them, they are established on the basis of a problematic of power that is in no way Hobbesian. On the one hand, natural right is defined by reference to man's insertion in nature, and not, as in *De Natura humana* or the *Leviathan*, in terms of man's extraction from nature. This is why it seems logical in Spinoza's lexicon to speak of the natural right of animals and things, an expression that obviously lacks all meaning in the typical logic of the theory of the *Contract*. On the other hand, even the absolute right of the state of nature is immediately translated into a 'determined power'. This power is certainly still too extensive with respect to what the rule of sociability can accept; it will therefore have to recognise the supplementary limits imposed by laws. It is nevertheless significant that even what will have to be abandoned is not described using the two extreme terms of the absolute and the inapplicable, terms which are systematically negative, but rather with terms that imply a determinate positivity. And what determines this power is the system of each individual's 'rules of nature'.

Spinoza's way of thinking thus allows him to formulate a definition and a framework of reasoning that are locally analogous to Hobbes's and that will in part produce the same effects: an analysis of the isolated individual; the recognition of their insufficiency; the necessity of constructing civil society;

---

[116] Cf. A. Matheron's magisterial analysis, *Individu et Communauté chez Spinoza*, p. 290 ff.
[117] G III, p. 189; A, p. 262 [*TTP* XVI, 4, 5; CWS II, 282–3].

the institution of the pact. But from this first stage onwards, Spinoza also marks a reservation that could be expressed as follows: natural right is nothing other than the power that arises from the laws of the individual's own operation. Now, these laws of operation are the passions. The passions thus constitute the effective content of natural right.

At this point it is necessary to underscore the distance separating Hobbes from Spinoza when they say the same thing: when Hobbes refuses to define the human being by Reason, it is because, for him, language is prior to Reason and the temporal power of marks is more fundamental than language, which is only one particular application of such marks. Yet, since Hobbes is nevertheless seeking to found the City on the specificity of the human being, the refusal of Reason is only a methodological precaution – certainly a decisive one, but one that in the final analysis will remain provisional. Reason remains in the background here since the temporal effort made to persevere in one's being implies Reason and represents it even before its effective constitution. Reason is effective in the contract in the form of its representative: fear. More than a passion, fear is, in fact, an eminently rational sentiment since it is the first calculation by which the individual defends their life. It is only that in the state of nature the efficacy of fear is combated by the passions, in particular those involving comparison, which lead the individual to their ruin. The individual is thus defined by their effort to preserve their life, an effort represented by fear and ruled by the passions. The power of the Sovereign that is implemented by the pact allows fear to quieten the passions, or to orient them in a useful way. These passions consequently do indeed play a subordinate role. They do not define man, properly speaking. They serve in a direct form as obstacles, and indirectly as motors.

Things are different in Spinoza. When Spinoza refuses to define natural right by Reason, it is not as a methodological precaution. The presence of nature in man, and not only of human nature, is extended by the presence of the passions in the domain of right, at once before Reason and then alongside it once it is constituted. The passions define natural right in the strong sense: that is, they engender consequences that determine the conduct of individuals when they are not limited by the power of the State. The passions do not determine natural right *completely*, for they encounter in their path the adverse power of external nature, whether of fortune or of other individuals. They also do not determine it in an *adequate* fashion, for the passions manifest the presence of exteriority in the interiority of individuals' being. But they do determine natural right in a *positive* fashion: before the appearance of Reason – and even, to a large extent, after – the specific content of individuals' actions receives from the passions its specific figure.

Moreover, it should be noted that when Spinoza signals the individual motivations for human actions, he does so more in terms of tendencies than interests ('trahit sua quemque voluptas').[118] It is thus necessary to say that 'disputes, hatreds, anger, deceptions'[119] are not obstacles or breaks on natural right; they are its effective content. The analysis of the constitution of the City will henceforth involve taking apart a number of affective mechanisms that play different and articulated roles, and of which right is the result: the passions of inter-human conflict, the passionate aspiration to the benefits of the life of reason, and the affective kernel of antipolitics.

The first principle of Spinoza's conception of natural right can be formulated as follows: as soon as people exist, there is conflict, hatred, anger and aversion — or at the very least the mechanisms for engendering these passions. And if this is true as soon as there are people, it is true so long as they exist.[120] Thus, conceiving of natural right means conceiving of the following principle: the first and most constant experience of humanity is this climate of inter-human conflict. In Chapter XVI, Spinoza does not seek to reduce these 'vices' — that is, these phenomena — to a poor understanding of the *conatus*. It is not (or not only) because we do not see what our interests are that we throw ourselves into hatreds or moments of anger that can lead to our ruin. A natural effect is not an insufficiently rational judgement. To believe this would be to believe that the only laws of Nature that exist are the laws of human Reason. Yet the laws of Nature are prior to the laws of Reason, including in man. It is thus necessary to learn about these laws through the experience that enumerates them, or rather (as in Book IV of the *Ethics*), through Reason — and not through the Reason that judges these laws, but rather through the Reason that knows them through their causes.

Is this to say that the form of Reason that issues injunctions has no place here? It does have a place, and for two reasons that have different statuses: a rational representation, and passionate aspiration (both of which have

---

[118] TP, Chapter II, 6, G III, p. 278, ll. 8–9 [*TP* II, 6; *CWS* II, 509]. 'Unusquisque a sua voluptate trahitur', *TTP*, Chapter XVI, G III, p. 193, l. 2 [*TTP* XVI, 22; *CWS* II, 286]. Cf. Virgil, *Eclogues*, II, 65.

[119] *TTP*, Chapter XVI, G III, p. 190; A, p. 263 [*TTP* XVI, 9; *CWS* II, 284. Translation modified].

[120] The *TP* says: 'as long as there are men, there will be vices' [*TP* I, 2; *CWS* II, 503]. This is, moreover, a citation from Tacitus, from Cerialis' speech (*Histories*, IV 74), as noted by F. Akkerman, who also identifies the same citation in a more complete form in the letter to Oldenburg (Ep. XXIX. Cf. Akkerman, 'La pénurie de mots de Spinoza', *Travaux et documents du Groupe de recherches spinozistes*, 1, PUPS, 1989, p. 18 [*Ep.* XXIX [to Henry Oldenburg]; *CWS* II, 11]).

a negative side and a positive side that Spinoza evokes in less detail). On the one hand, it is true that it is much more useful for human beings to live rationally (and this is something we can all know long before we have become completely rational; among the vast majority of passionate people, Reason exists enough to formulate this idea, even if it is not sufficiently strong to force its realisation). On the other hand, the climate of inter-human conflict is completely intolerable. In other words, we spontaneously aspire to escape it[121] – even if, at the same time, we are constantly part of its production. There is thus in each person a *passionate aspiration to the advantages of Reason*. To this negative aspiration should be added a positive one: people, however lazy they might be, whatever their spontaneous egotism, wish to live as best as possible, and thus to profit from the advantages of civilisation. On this point too, nascent Reason, while still impotent, suggests to them the utility of uniting and of living rationally.

The rational representation of the benefits of the rational life lived in common must be quite extensive, since the passionate character of the majority of people does not exclude a certain presence of Reason. But by itself this representation is incapable of taking people from the state of nature to the advantages of peace, that is, to civil society, so great in them are the forces opposed to this – forces that are necessarily at work as soon as they exist and that work against their interests, including against their own conscious interests (we see here, once again, that it is illusory to simply oppose interests that are well or poorly understood). We thus find ourselves in an analogous situation to the one described, at the level of individual life, in *Ethics*, Book IV, and which is summed up in the quote 'video meliora proboque, deteriora sequor'.[122] However, this representation, while it lacks force, is not without utility, for it will serve in the confrontation between the two complexes of passions just cited: the one that provokes inter-human conflict, and the passionate aspiration to the benefits of Reason. More pre-

---

[121] 'There's no one who does not desire to live securely, and as far as possible, without fear. But this simply can't happen so long as everyone is permitted to do whatever he likes, and reason is granted no more right than hatred and anger. There is no one who lives among hostilities, hatreds, anger and deceptions, who does not live anxiously, and who does not strive to avoid these things, as far as we can', *TTP*, Chapter XVI, G III, p. 191, A, p. 263 [*TTP* XVI, 13; *CWS* II, 284].

[122] As A. Matheron remarks, if rational representation sufficed, that is, if people were integrally rational, there would precisely be no need for a State. Cf. also on this point W. Eckstein, 'Zur Lehre vom Staatsvertrag bei Spinoza', *Zeitschrift für öffentliches Recht*, XIII/3 (1933), pp. 356–68, reprinted in *Texte zur Geschichte des Spinozismus* (hrsg. v. N. Altwicker), pp. 362–76.

cisely, this confrontation will oppose two types of passions, the first of which is broader than the type that opposes individuals to each other. Spinoza does not give us a detailed analysis here, but the short phrase in which he cites these passions shows that it is necessary to include them – in addition to those that have already been mentioned and that are summed up in the term 'hatred' – among those individual vices that tend simply to prevent work or collaboration with others. Spinoza writes: 'Everyone is drawn by his own pleasure. Most of the time the soul is so filled with greed, love of esteem, envy, anger, etc., that there's no room for reason.'[123] Why did he not cite these passions prior to this? Quite simply because this second series is not enough to make life intolerable. It is therefore unnecessary to mention them when one is speaking of the reasons that move one to leave the state of nature. However, these passions do indeed prevent the concrete act of civil construction (and, as we will see, they continue to make their effects felt in the time after this construction). This is why it makes sense to mention them during the analysis of the pact. These passions regularly reproduce in the individual the tendency to prevent the constitution of society, and to leave it once it is constituted. And since one cannot, in fact, escape society, these passions make society function poorly to the degree that this is possible (and circumstances sometimes permit the individual to extend the scope of this possibility). I will henceforth call these passions the affective kernel of antipolitics.

The presence of this affective kernel has two consequences: one is *direct* – each person, despite their desire to benefit from the advantages of society, recoils from having to take up the task personally, that is, to do the work of disciplining their anger and hatred, of accepting institutions that are not perfectly suited to them, and so on. The second is *indirect* – each person, knowing that the others are made in the same way as them, fears having to contend with their stupidity if they enter into society with them. And they are right: it would be stupid of them if they were to simply have confidence in the good faith of others since, without even mentioning wilful trickery, people's very nature leads them to fail to keep their promises as soon as one demands of them something that goes against their interests and above all against their tendencies. It is therefore reasonable to constitute a new agency that constrains people to observe a minimum of rationality, at least on the outside. The common reference to Reason in its normative guise is thus indeed a requirement of the passions. The necessity for there to exist a power over each person is a guarantee for each person. The difference with

---

[123] *TTP*, Chapter XVI, G III, p. 193; A, p. 265 [*TTP* XVI, 22; *CWS* II, 286].

the *Leviathan* is clear here: it is not only a matter of defending one's life. It could be said that civil right as such emerges here in Spinoza's thought, with Spinoza taking into consideration the indirect consequences of these affective kernels. It is only that this detour requires – but requires absolutely – the intervention of the State.

The remainder of Chapter XVI shows how these affective complexes engender the following result: the pact. There is no use analysing this sequence in detail,[124] nor in showing its relations with the other forms of the constitution of society that we find in the *Ethics* or the *Political Treatise*.[125] Yet it could be asked if, as in Hobbes, a common terrain is thereby created. The response will concern the status of the Sovereign power that is thereby constituted: this power must necessarily be strong enough for it to be in the interests of each person to hope that the others will be punished if they break the pact. This formulation is moreover only partially correct, for here, as is often the case, Spinoza presents a general law of operation on the occasion of its first appearance by signalling for the time being only what characterises, precisely, this first appearance. What is at stake is the power of Sovereignty over the minds of its subjects. We will see further on that it has at least four modes to it: fear, hope, love and admiration. Only the first mode is mentioned here because it is the most immediate and the one to which we return in the most brutal fashion at a time of crisis. But the Sovereign who would use only this form of subjugation would be heading for his downfall.[126]

It is still the case that Reason and the passions together determine that each individual enters into society if and only if the operation of this society is not left to the good faith of each person – that is, if society is given the means to constrain all those who enter into it to respect certain rules. The mobilisation of these means of subjugation is thus the very condition of the existence of a civil society. One might prefer certain of these rules to others, but one cannot wish for there to be none at all. Whoever sees a civil society where these means of subjugation are weakened, or indeed do not exist at all, must rationally say to themselves, not 'I would be more free', but 'I would perish'.

---

[124] On its conditions, cf. Chr. Lazzeri, 'Les Lois de l'obéissance: sur la théorie spinoziste des transferts de droit', *Etudes philosophiques* (October–December 1987), pp. 409–38.

[125] A. Matheron does this in *Individu et Communauté*. He has returned to this topic in a later study, 'The Problem of Spinoza's Evolution: From the *Theologico-Political Treatise* to the *Political Treatise*', in *Politics, Ontology and Knowledge in Spinoza*, pp. 163–78.

[126] Cf. what we said about this above on the topic of freedom of expression, in the last section of the preceding chapter of the present work.

C. The Continuation of the State of Nature

The essence of Chapter XVII is devoted to the study of the Hebrew State as it was constituted by Moses. This analysis is introduced as one of two possible responses[127] to a question that could be formulated as follows: given the affective kernel of antipolitics, and supposing it to be permanently present, how can we ensure the security of the Sovereign and avoid civil war, thus guaranteeing the security of the State's citizens?

That this kernel is permanently present is something that is proven by experience. Spinoza employs a dichotomy here that he has recourse to whenever he seeks to remind us of this type of truth: the opposition between theory and practice. What he has just shown, he says, is only an approximation: 'still, it will never happen that this view does not remain, in many respects, merely theoretical'.[128] The reason for this gap is that the person who transfers their right cannot transfer it in its entirety, on pain of no longer being a person. It is obvious that it is not a matter here of an exigency of human dignity but of a purely physical impossibility. To reprise an expression from the *TP*, there are certain things that are just as impossible for a person to do as it is impossible for a table to eat grass. Even when a person might want to, they cannot absolutely give up their passions, for they constitute the person. They can renounce certain of their consequences or the satisfactions they bring; but the mechanism that engenders them is the system of natural laws that are constitutive of the person's being and their individuality. Spinoza is thus led to draw up a list of those passions that resist any authoritarian suppression. These passions can be grouped into two blocs, which Spinoza examines separately because they produce different effects.

The first group is an affective kernel of elementary defence that is constitutive of individuality and its threshold of tolerance towards abuse. What we are dealing with here is a certain number of primary reactions, at once limited in their field of application and particularly tenacious in nature. The reader will notice that by themselves these reactions do not constitute a direct danger to the public; but if the Sovereign attacks these passions and leaves no

---

[127] The other being the direct sacralisation of the royal person.
[128] *TTP*, Chapter XVII, G III, p. 201; A, p. 278 [*TTP* XVII, 1; *CWS* II, 296].

recourse other than the impossible direct abolition of these reactions or the revolt against civil society, he will put civil society in danger on the occasion of a confrontation. 'The supreme power would act in vain if he commanded a subject to hate someone who had joined the subject to himself by a benefit, or to love someone who harmed him, or not to be offended by insults, or not to desire to be freed from fear, and many other things of this kind, which necessarily follow from the laws of human nature.'[129] However, this kernel of elementary defence is not entirely inalterable. What is irreducible is its mechanism of production. It is nevertheless possible, perhaps, to shift this mechanism. Spinoza does not say that it is impossible for a person to hate their benefactor; he says that it is impossible to simply command them to do so. In other words, hate is such a strong passion that it would be necessary to mobilise something other than fear alone to reduce it. Furthermore, Spinoza does not valorise these reactions from a moral perspective. Nevertheless, he does say that they are a guarantee against the abuse of power. 'Admittedly', he notes, 'if men could be so deprived of their natural right that subsequently they could do nothing, except by the will of those who held the supreme Right, then the latter would be permitted to reign over their subjects most violently and with absolute impunity.'[130]

The second group of passions is once again the affective kernel of antipolitics. In contradistinction to the previous group, its effect consists in immediately challenging the solidity of the State. The enumeration that is made on this occasion of this kernel's content is more detailed than in Chapter XVI: 'All men, whether they rule or are ruled, tend to prefer pleasure to difficult work'; the multitude are 'easily corrupted either by greed or by extravagant living'; each individual 'thinks that he alone knows everything, and wants everything to be done according to his mentality', while 'From love of esteem, he disdains equals, and will not put up with being ruled by them. From envy for the greater praise or better fortune someone else receives – these things are never equal – he wishes the other person ill, and is delighted when bad things happen to him.' Finally, this content is summed up in one of those formulas with which Spinoza typically appeals to experience: 'Everyone knows how it goes – a disgust with the present, a craving to make fundamental changes, uncontrolled anger, a scorn for poverty – these affects lead men to wickedness. Everyone knows how much they fill and disturb men's hearts.'[131] We are at a point here where it appears

---

[129] *TTP*, Chapter XVII, G III, p. 201; A, p. 277 [*TTP* XVII, 2; *CWS* II, 296].
[130] *TTP*, Chapter XVII, G III, p. 201; A, p. 278 [*TTP* XVII, 4; *CWS* II, 297].
[131] *TTP*, Chapter XVII, G III, p. 203, A, p. 280 [*TTP* XVII, 14, 15, 16; *CWS* II, 298–9].

that each individual is perpetually and continually an enemy of society, and that this is so not because he is evil or ignorant of his duties, but because of the necessary effect of affective mechanisms that function in him insofar as he is a man. Civil society not only does not suppress these mechanisms by some miracle at the moment of its foundation; on the contrary, it must perpetually confront them and defend itself against them. We can even deduce from these tendencies (this is what the rest of Chapter XVII does) that a significant element in the structure of institutions is precisely the way they respond to this affective kernel of antipolitics. Thus, once it has been identified, this kernel provides us with a principle for interpreting history – a principle that has two sides to it: a whole series of human actions cease to appear as madness or as crises involving instances of inexplicable individual disobedience, now that we can envisage them as so many possible solutions, elaborated more or less consciously, to the problem posed by this perpetual germ of destruction that is carried at the heart of the State and by the very same people who constitute it. Thus, Alexander's attempt to make himself a god appears less as the caprice of a tyrant and more as an attempt to combat through religious reverence the temptation to escape from the bonds of Sovereignty.[132] Similarly, Mosaic law, which governed the first Hebrew State, can be analysed according to a strategy that identifies, first for the rulers and then for the ruled, those procedures that counterbalance each of the passions of this elementary kernel.[133]

We can now identify more clearly the meaning of the opposition that Spinoza perceives between himself and Hobbes. If in Spinoza natural right remains *sartum tectum*, it is because the passions that constitute it are, to an extent, as hostile to the continued existence of civil society as they are to its initial constitution. It is also because the Sovereign can struggle against these passions by mobilising other passions, namely those that function in the individual like the receptacle, or indeed the transmitter, of the four modes of subjugation. When in his letter to Jelles Spinoza says that the Sovereign only has rights over his subjects to the degree that he is more powerful than them, he is not referring to an abstract problematic of force but rather to the implementation of these four modes of subjugation. From this

---

[132] 'For the majesty of the state is the guardian of its safety . . .' (Quintus-Curtius, VIII, 4, cited by Spinoza).

[133] On the analysis of this functioning, then on its decadence in the 'Second State of the Hebrews', see S. Zac, 'Spinoza et l'Etat des Hébreux', *Revue philosophique*, 2 (1977), then *Philosophie, théologique, politique dans l'œuvre de Spinoza*, Paris: Vrin, 1979, pp. 145–76, in particular pp. 166–72.

perspective we can effectively say that natural right ceases in Hobbes with the pact. We can also explain why seditions, civil wars and disobedience are thought by Hobbes in terms of what is inadmissible or regrettable – as the *Behemoth* proves: the separation between rights and passions paradoxically makes the author of the *Leviathan*, as realist as he is with respect to the state of nature, one of those thinkers who are content, when faced with human actions, to either deplore or curse them.

We can now summarise the role of experience in this process of the establishment and conservation of the State. Spinoza himself poses the question once he has demonstrated in the *Ethics* that 'men most agree in nature, when they live according to the guidance of reason'.[134] We could deduce a double 'rationalist' position from this: men who are not led by Reason cannot be useful to other men; only Reason itself (in the deductive mode from the *Ethics*) can establish this utility. Now, the Scholium that follows will show precisely that Reason is not alone in establishing this: 'What we have just shown is also confirmed by daily experience, which provides so much and with such clear evidence that this saying is in almost everyone's mouth: man is a God to man.'[135] Thus, people have always, already known what Spinoza has just proven. Indeed, this is even one of those things that they know best – for otherwise, how could societies even exist? The remainder of the Scholium insists on the independence of this lesson with respect to its demonstration: the novelty of the *Ethics* consists in making this lesson known through its causes, and not by purely and simply revealing it. It is rare for people to live by the conduct of Reason; instead, they are envious and cause each other pain. If this is the way things are (and the ensemble of Books III and IV have shown that things are effectively like this), then we would expect to see people live a solitary life to avoid those disagreeable things that are born from the company of their counterparts. We would expect this all the more since an entire ideology directly or indirectly argues in favour of a solitary life: such a life is lived by satyrs, theologians and melancholics – that is, by all those who interpret human weakness in terms of a reinforcement of the sad passions. And yet, this expectation is disappointed: human societies exist all the same. There are two reasons for this paradox: on the one hand, there is the question of objective interest; and on the

---

[134] 'Quatenus homines ex ductu Rationis vivunt, eatenus tantum natura semper necessario conveniunt', *Ethics* IV, 35, G II, p. 232, ll. 29–30 [CWS I, 563].

[135] 'Quae modo ostendimus, ipsa etiam experientia quotidie tot tamque luculentis testimoniis testatur, ut omnibus fere in ore sit: hominem homini Deum esse', ibid., Schol., p. 234, ll. 2–4 [CWS I, 563].

other hand, there is the experiential recognition of this interest. Faced with the dangers and needs of life, people experience (*experientur*) – even if they cannot rationally demonstrate – the utility of mutual aid and the conjunction of their forces.[136] Two consequences follow from this: people who are not guided by Reason can nevertheless agree[137] (and the necessity of this agreement will lead them to act, at least in part, as if they were reasonable: the entirety of objective right consists precisely in the administration of this 'as if'); and the knowledge of this necessity is most often established – and for the majority of people – by experience.

At this point, it will come as no surprise to see the *TTP* refer to the teachings of experience in various ways as soon as it is a question of identifying affective kernels and the responses to them:

— The *TTP* refers to experience as such: when a pact has ceased to be useful or to preserve one from danger, it ceases to be at the same time as it ceases to be founded, and 'Experience also teaches this, as clearly as one could wish.'[138] The analysis of the *jus circa sacra* begins with the principle that it is in matters of religion that people normally err the most and that the difference between *ingenia* engenders among them a competition between vain fictions, 'as experience testifies only too well'.[139] When we contract with people from a different religion, we are bound to obey them and to respect their sovereignty, including when it comes to rites: 'This is also confirmed by daily experience',[140] for example by the conduct of the Christian Sovereigns when they send their subjects among the Turks or the Japanese. The list of the elements of the affective kernel of elementary defence is founded on the laws of human nature – yet to be conscious of this it is not

---

[136] 'Experientur tamen homines mutuo auxilia ea, quibus indigent, multo facilius sibi parare, & non nisi junctis viribus pericula, quae ubique imminent, vitare posse', ibid., ll. 13–16 [*CWS* I, 563].

[137] Reciprocally, a person who lives under the guidance of Reason can find something useful in a society of the ignorant. This is why, if they avoid their favours, it is only to the extent that this is possible, for 'quamvis homines ignari sint, sunt tamen homines, qui in necessitatibus humanum auxilium, quo nullum praestabilius est, adferre queunt', *Ethics* IV, 70, G II, p. 263, ll. 13–15 [*CWS* I, 586].

[138] 'Quod fundamentum si tollatur, pactum ex sese tollitur; quod etiam experientia satis superque docet', *TTP*, Chapter XVI, G III, p. 196, ll. 29–31 [*TTP* XVI, 44; *CWS* II, 291].

[139] 'Sed quia circa religionem maxime errare solent homines, & pro ingeniorum diversitate multa magno certamine fingere, ut experientia plus quam satis testatur', *TTP*, Chapter XVI, p. 199, ll. 24–6 [*TTP* XVI, 62; *CWS* II, 294].

[140] 'Quod etiam experientia quotidiana confirmatur', *TTP*, Chapter XVI, p. 200, ll. 19–20 [*TTP* XVI, 66; *CWS* II, 295].

necessary to know these laws genetically, that is, by way of a demonstration of Reason. In fact, the list concludes with these words: 'I think experience teaches this very clearly.'[141] Sovereigns often have the means of influencing the sentiments of people, as 'experience abundantly testifies'.[142] The conservation of the State depends above all on the fidelity and virtue of its subjects, as 'Both reason and experience teach, as clearly as can be.'[143] The entire efficacy of these affective kernels, along with the ways human activity responds to them, can thus be known just as well by the teachings of experience as they can by the demonstrations of Reason.

— The *TTP* uses well-known formulas from the Latin rhetorical tradition. These formulas concentrate in their own way centuries of experience; and since the minds of the *TTP*'s readers are impregnated with them, these formulas facilitate access to the lessons of human life as these have been accumulated by history. The majority of expressions by which the *TTP* establishes the register of the passions are, once again, quotations or half-quotations from Terence,[144] Sallust,[145] Cicero[146] and

---

[141] 'Frustra enim subdito imperaret, ut illum odio habeat [cf. the complete quotation above] & alia perplurima hujusmodi, quae ex legibus humanae naturae necessario sequuntur. Atque hoc ipsam etiam experientiam clarissime docere existimo', *TTP*, Chapter XVII, G III, p. 201, ll. 17–22 [*TTP* XVII, 3; *CWS* II, 296].

[142] 'Ut experientia abunde testatur', *TTP*, Chapter XVII, p. 202, l. 31 [*TTP* XVII, 10; *CWS* II, 298]. This is the argument that was analysed above, on the topic of the determinations of freedom of speech.

[143] 'Quod imperii conservatio praecipue pendeat a subditorum fide, eorumque virtute et animi constantia in exequendis mandatis, ratio et experientia quam clarissime docent', *TTP*, Chapter XVII, G III, p. 203, ll. 12–14 [*TTP* XVII, 13; *CWS* II, 298].

[144] 'Omnes namque tam qui regunt, quam qui reguntur, homines sunt ex labore scilicet proclives ad libidinem', *TTP*, Chapter XVII, G III, p. 203, ll. 16–17 [*TTP* XVII, 14; *CWS* II, 298]. Cf. *Andria*, vv. 77–8: 'ingeniumst omnium hominum ab labore proclive ad libidinem'.

[145] Everything that Spinoza says about the taste for novelty seems to be inspired at the thematic level by the *Conjuration of Catalina*: 'omnino cuncta plebes, novarum rerum studio, Catilinae incepta probabat. Nam semper incivitate, quis opes nullae sunt, bonis invident, malos extollunt; vetera odere, nova exoptant; odio suarum rerum mutari omnia student; turba atque seditionibus sine cura aluntur, quoniam egestas facile habetur sine damno', 37. Cf.: 'norunt quippe omnes, quid sceleris fastidium praesentium et rerum novandarum cupiditas, quid praeceps ira, quid contemta paupertas frequenter suadenant hominibus, quantumque eorum animos occupent agitentque', *TTP*, Chapter XVII, G III, p. 203, ll. 26–30 [*TTP* XVII, 15; *CWS* II, 299]. With respect to the idea according to which each person prefers commanding to obeying, the *Political Treatise* refers explicitly to Sallust (*TP*, Chapter VII, 5, G III, p. 303, ll. 26–9 [*TP* VII, 5; *CWS* II, 539]).

[146] 'Salus populi suprema lex esto', *De Legibus*, III, 3. Spinoza will cite this exact expres-

Seneca[147] – and indeed from proverbial expressions as well.[148] In saying this, I do not mean that Spinoza bases his reflections on their authority but that, whenever it is a matter of establishing and recalling truths that are known by all, formulas from classical culture appear beneath his pen and build a bridge between the experience of the reader and the received experience of tradition.

— The *TTP* refers to particular historical examples, but to ones that are well known – the first two come from the scholastic tradition, and the last from the Bible. The fact that the State is threatened more by its citizens than by its external enemies is established, for example, by reference to Tacitus' account of the Roman Republic, then by the example of Alexander as narrated by Curtius Rufus. The same two authors then serve to illustrate the first solution found to respond to this danger: the sacralisation of kings. Finally, Spinoza engages in a long analysis of the Hebrew State. While Spinoza refuses to give this state the status of a model – a status those who speak in the name of the Bible in politics confer upon it[149] – he does not stop himself from seeking in this example proofs of questions posed by the affective complexes and by the possible responses to them that history has revealed.[150] In Chapter XVII, Spinoza thus studies, first, the principles of theocracy insofar

sion in the *TP*. In the *TTP*, he first integrates it into a more complex phrase: 'in Republica & imperio, ubi salus totius populi, non imperantis, summa lex est [. . .]', Chapter XVI, pp. 194–5 [*TTP* XVI, 34; *CWS* II, 288–9]. Then he condenses it into 'leges, hoc est populi salus', Chapter XVII, p. 218, ll. 11–12 [*TTP* XVII, 97; *CWS* II, 318]. In any case, it has become a maxim of political theory: we also find it in Hobbes, *De Cive*, Chapter XIII, § 2: 'Imperantium autem officia omnia hoc uno dicto continentur: salus populi suprema lex', cf. *Elements of Law*, 28, 1; *De Corpore politico*, 9, 3; and *Leviathan*, 30, 1.

[147] 'Violentia enim imperia, ut ait Seneca, nemo continuit diu', *TTP*, Chapter XVI, G III, p. 194, ll. 15–16 [*TTP* XVI, 29; *CWS* II, 288]. Cf. *Trojans*, V, 258.
[148] 'Homo homini deus' has had, since Cecelius, a long history, which Erasmus summarises (at the same time as he summarises the history of expression 'homo homini lupus') in his *Adagia* (I, 1, 69). Hobbes cites them in his dedicatory Epistle from *De Cive*. Bacon used them to compose a unique phrase from the *Augmentis*, VI, 3.
[149] Cf. the beginning of Chapter XVIII: 'Quamvis Hebraeorum imperium, quale ipsum in praecedenti capite concepimus, aeternum esse potuerit, idem tamen nemo jam imitari potest, nec etiam consultum est', G III, p. 221, ll. 16–18 [*TTP* XVIII, 1; *CWS* II, 322]; and the entire demonstration that follows, ll. 19–29 [*TTP* XVIII, 1, 2; *CWS* II, 322–3].
[150] 'Verumenimvero, tametsi in omnibus imitabile non sit, multa tamen habuit dignissima, saltem ut notarentur, & quae forsan imitari consultissimum esset', ibid., ll. 29–31 [*TTP* XVIII, 3; *CWS* II, 323]. In other words, it does not constitute a general model, but it can provide examples of them, indeed partial examples.

as these constitute a solution to the problem of the relations between the State and the sacred[151] (that is, insofar as they resolve, but in a different way, the problem that Augustus and Alexander were confronted with), and second how the constitution that is thus created moderates, on the one hand, the soul of the rulers,[152] and on the other the soul of the ruled[153] – that is, how the constitution responds to the questions posed by the affective kernel of antipolitics. And each one of these points, by virtue of the response that they give to an objective question posed by the affective kernels, contributes to improving our knowledge of them. Spinoza thus concludes these references with a phrase that records all of the results he has just enumerated under the dual sign of Reason and experience: 'reason, I say, teaches, and experience itself has been a witness, how much all these things would strengthen the hearts of the Hebrews to bear everything with special constancy and virtue, for the sake of their Country'.[154]

We should note that the level of experience that these three kinds of references imply is perhaps not quite the same level. The one that is recorded in the expression *experientia docet* is constituted by those lessons that are most universally readable in human life – namely, those lessons that are known by all, and that a simple glance at the life of each person, or at their general memory, suffices to recall clearly. On the other hand, when Spinoza introduces material from Latin culture, it is to draw out principles that are a little less visible to the naked eye, and which have had to be worked on to reduce them to the form of lessons. Thus, after mentioning that Reason and experience clearly show the importance of the fidelity of subjects in the conservation of the State, Spinoza adds: 'But it's not so easy to see how they must be led so that they constantly maintain their loyalty and virtue.'[155] Just after this he begins to enumerate in a more precise way the different elements of

---

[151] *TTP*, Chapter XVII, p. 205, l. 15 [*TTP* XVII, 26; *CWS* II, 301; p. 212, l. 3 [*TTP* XVII, 61; *CWS* II, 310].

[152] Ibid., p. 212, l. 3 [*TTP* XVII, 61; *CWS* II, 310]; p. 214, l. 16 [*TTP* XVII, 64; *CWS* II, 311].

[153] Ibid., p. 214, l. 16 [*TTP* XVII, 64; *CWS* II, 311]; p. 215, l. 16 [*TTP* XVII, 81; *CWS* II, 314].

[154] 'Quantum autem haec omnia [. . .] quantum, inquam, haec Hebraeorum animos firmare valuerint ad omnia singulari constantia & virtute pro Patria tolerandum, ratio quam clarissime docet, et ipsa experientia testata est', *TTP*, Chapter XVII, G III, p. 215, ll. 16–22 [*TTP* XVII, 82; *CWS* II, 314].

[155] 'Qua autem ratione iidem duci debeant, ut fidem et virtutem constanter servent, non aeque facile est videre', *TTP*, Chapter XVII, G III, p. 203, ll. 14–16 [*TTP* XVII, 13; *CWS* II, 298–9].

the affective kernel of antipolitics, for it is this kernel that interposes itself between general necessity and the necessity, which is more broadly recognised (including by those who are most rebellious), of the subjects' fidelity and the effectivity of this fidelity. Now, it is in the course of this analysis that Spinoza's language begins to use those formulas with which Latin historians and poets identified the necessities of human nature. Finally, the study of the history of the Romans, the Macedonians and the Hebrews presents us in only an indirect way with the same fundamental experience, this time through the concrete answers that each of these peoples have invented to respond to these necessities. The description of institutions is therefore not performed for itself but is oriented towards the experiential capture of the same laws insofar as these laws are inserted into concrete contents. But these concrete contents are not simply examples: in each of them we see the inflexions of laws as a function of the circumstances from which they draw their forms of existence.

In any case, we can note in passing that it is impossible to reduce Spinoza's reflections in the *TTP* to a confrontation between a philosophy that is already constituted on the basis of demonstrations and a reprise or *détournement* of biblical Revelation. As soon as we consider a specific text closely – here chapters XVI and XVII – we realise that things are more complex, to the extent that the system combines very different methods of approach, each of which possesses its own level of intervention, scope and limits. In the chapters in question we see rational analysis linked with three experiential modes, while the consideration of the State of the Hebrews as the Bible[156] presents it to us is introduced only as one of the materials from the third of these modes (and certainly the one that is, from a quantitative perspective, the most important one).

Thus, the foundations of the State suppose the passions and, at least in part, through the passions, experience in its confirmative function. We will now see that the knowledge and continuation of a given State appeals, moreover, through the intermediary of the *ingenium*, to experience in its constitutive function.

---

[156] We should be more precise: such as the Bible principally teaches us about it. In fact, Tacitus is also called upon to characterise the capacity of resistance that the Hebrews had to foreign domination, *TTP*, Chapter XVII, G III, p. 215, ll. 27–31 [*TTP* XVII, 83; CWS II, 314–15].

3. The *Ingenium* of the People and the Soul of the State

We have seen what makes a people a people. But what makes a people *this* people, or *such-and-such* a people?

The entire argument of Contract theorists is formulated in such universal terms that we can hardly see how one State rather than another is thereby constituted. The only possible and thus thinkable differences between States concern the variety of forms of government that emerge from the different modalities of the initial pact or in what immediately follows its institution: monarchy, aristocracy and democracy.[157] The rest falls into the domain of the accidental. This radical search for the foundations of the State thus leaves totally obscure the identity of each State or people. In effect, the theoretical deduction of civil society applies to *all* civil societies. We thus see no reason why the society that is thereby founded would be France rather than England, or the inverse. Does the same go for Spinoza? The deduction of the passions, even if it is confirmed by experience, applies like the pact to all passionate people. It thus seems to organise the same abstract civil society, which is independent in principle from time and place. Is there nevertheless a means for thinking or representing the individuality that is proper to a given people? We will, in fact, find, at the collective level this time, the same foundation that we discovered previously at the individual level. Not only is it possible to think the individuality of a people, it is absolutely necessary to do so as soon as we wish to understand the form taken by a people's laws.

A. *The Complexion of a People*

Alongside Spinoza's argument concerning the passions, we also find the concept of the *ingenium* – not the *ingenium* of an individual, but of a group. As Spinoza uses it, the term itself has nothing exclusively individual about it. In different passages from the *TTP*, we see that the term *ingenium* can be applied to an entire nation, or to the common people in general.[158] We

---

[157] Hobbes, *De Cive*, Chapter VII; Locke, *Second Treatise*, Chapter X; Pufendorf, *Droit de la Nature et des gens*, Book VII, Chapter V; Rousseau, *Contrat social*, Book III, Chapters III–VII (Chapter VIII does give a cause for variation in governments, but this cause only concerns a theory of climates: it does not imply a particular figure of a people).

[158] 'At ipsum vulgus [. . .] pro imbecillitate ejus ingenii', *TTP*, Chapter V, G III, p. 79, ll. 4–9 [*TTP* V, 44; *CWS* II, 150]; 'qui tantum varium multitudinis ingenium experti sunt', ibid., Chapter XVII, p. 203, l. 18 [*TTP* XVII, 14; *CWS* II, 298].

also clearly see that that this application is not without consequences, for it will be by referring to this *ingenium* that the effective content of a nation's laws will be determined. In other words, as soon as we go beyond the general exigency of peace and security, as soon as it is necessary to concretely organise people's lives, we cannot neglect the particular figure of the people who are thereby organised into a given society. If we seek to both make laws and to understand them, then the traits of the singular must return to the foreground.

The *TTP* affirms this by developing a series of arguments that reject the idea of election. Mosaic law is not universal: it is adapted to the complexion of a determinate people.[159] Now, this thesis plays a decisive role in the economy of the *TTP* since it prevents us from considering the Hebrew example as a political paradigm that still possesses a contemporary force. Symmetrically, this thesis also implicitly rejects the Christian reading of the relation between the ancient law and the new law in terms of prefiguration and accomplishment.[160] What particularises Mosaic law is not its limitation to a certain epoch of the history of salvation;[161] it is its accommodation to a specific people. This situation is obviously not particular to the Hebrews: each State has laws that are proper to it, and Spinoza rigorously distinguishes these laws from the law concerning true virtue, of which the Book of Job and Paul speak and which is given to all. Each of the laws of a State is adapted to the *ingenium* of a unique nation.[162] Each group of people possesses irreducible and durable traits, which are united in this people's complexion and which must be taken into account both to create laws for this people and to understand their legislation once it comes into existence. The *ingenium*, far from

---

[159] 'Quamvis non universalis, sed maxime ad ingenium & singularem conservationem unius populi accomodata fuerit [. . .]', *TTP*, Chapter IV, G III, p. 61, ll. 16–18 [*TTP* IV, 17; *CWS* II, 129].

[160] This is why Christ in no way abrogated Mosaic law, *TTP*, Chapter V, G III, p. 71, ll. 2–3 [*TTP* V, 9; *CWS* II, 140]. Moreover, the religion of Christ has nothing new in it: its only novelty is that it is revealed to those who do not know it, *TTP*, Chapter XII, G III, p. 163, ll. 14–17 [*TTP* XII, 24; *CWS* II, 253] (from John 1:10: 'in mundo erat et mundus non novit eum'). On the other hand, for the Christian reading of the relation between the two laws, cf. Thomas Aquinas, *Summa Theologica*, Ia, IIae, qu. 103, art. 32: the ancient law is, as far as ceremonies are concerned, abrogated by the new law, which accomplishes its figures; qu. 107, art. 1: the law of Christ is truly new.

[161] 'Deus igitur et legem, et alia beneficia specialia illi populo exhibuit propter promissionem eorum Patribus factam, ut ex eis Christis nasceretur', *Summa Theologica*, Ia, IIae, qu. 98, art. 4, resp.

[162] 'Lex quae ad ingenium unius nationis accommodatur', *TTP*, Chapter III, G III, p. 54, ll. 19–21 [*TTP* III, 44; *CWS* II, 121].

being rejected into the realm of the accidental, contributes to defining the figure proper to the State.

This notion of a collective *ingenium* allows us to interpret the history of bodies of law. When the Aragonese consulted the Pope on the topic of a king, the Pope (and Spinoza approves of this) counselled them to first of all give themselves the institutions that were appropriate to their complexion.[163] When Spinoza lists the measures that, in an aristocracy, prevent citizens from being contemptuous of the customs of the country, he gives a few general rules, then adds: 'Besides these [devices], in each state we can think of others which are agreeable to the nature of the place and the mentality of the people . . .'.[164] In the *Political Treatise* the positivity of the *ingenium* thus allows a specific reading of each individual State: it avoids interpreting these States from the outside in terms of the schema of the three kinds of government, just as it avoids, in the *TTP*, reading the content of bodies of law from the perspective of the primacy of the Hebrews' election. We are thereby able not only to think the consistency of civil society in general – as with the theoreticians of the pact – but also the figure proper to each civil society.[165] The reference to the *ingenium*, with its appeal to historical experience, thus ensures a broader unfolding of reason.

All of this implies that there exists an *ingenium* for each nation. Also, just as each person spontaneously regulates themselves according to their own *ingenium*, the State functions best when its institutions are adapted to the *ingenium* of the nation in question. How can we know what this *ingenium* is? Spinoza nowhere constructs a specific theory of the national *ingenium* of the Romans, the Hebrews, the Greeks or the ancient peoples. These differences never constitute a distinction that concerns the true life, for this life concerns only individuals.[166] But beyond the question of the true life, some constitutive traits can be identified. Can we deduce these traits using Reason, or can they only be identified by experience? I am again posing the same question that I put to grammar. We will see that the response is anal-

---

[163] 'Nisi institutis prius satis aequis, & ingenio gentis consentaneis', *TP*, Chapter VII, 30, G III, p. 321, ll. 24–5 [*TP* VII, 30; *CWS* II, 561].

[164] 'Et praeter haec alia in quocunque imperio cum natura loci, & gentis ingenio consentanea excogitari possunt', *TP*, Chapter X, 7, p. 356, ll. 20–2 [*TP* X, 7; *CWS* II, 599].

[165] In Hobbes, for example, we do indeed find stated recommendations for legislation (*De Cive*, Chapters XII–XIII; *Leviathan*, the entire end part of Part 2), but they are of a universal order and ultimately the laws of such-and-such a country will not draw their consistency from the will of the Sovereign who founds them.

[166] *TTP*, Chapter III, G III, p. 50, ll. 24–9 [*TTP* III, 30; *CWS* II, 118].

ogous: certain general traits can be rationally reconstructed, but as soon as we wish to identify the specific weight and consequences of these traits, it is necessary to have recourse to the individual history of each people. Let us take an example. The analysis from the *Ethics* shows that the natural laws of the affects produce in each person the possibility of being hateful, envious and jealous. This possibility is translated into a tendency to commit violent acts, but this tendency does not necessarily become effective, for the fear of retaliation prevents individuals from going too far down this road. If this tendency exists in each individual, it is also in the crowd and is manifest there in an analogous form.[167] Also, when the beliefs or institutions of a people set up a system of punishments (for example, a highly developed civilisation, or a belief in just gods who are sufficiently powerful to mete out punishments), violence will certainly become manifest sporadically, but it will not become a dominant a force in society. By contrast, when the historical circumstances that have formed a people have habituated it to expect anything and everything from this violence, and if their institutions and mentality reinforce it, violence will constitute an essential part of this people's *ingenium*.

I will now give a few examples of such *ingenia*. In listing them we must proceed carefully, for Spinoza does not construct a comparative historical tableau: he cites such-and-such a trait when he needs to do so in his reasoning, without preoccupying himself with indicating that the characteristic mentioned is proper to a given people or whether it is common to others.[168] We are thus left with having to unify these traits when he cites them and to evaluate them by means of a comparison between texts. This is the only way for us to show exactly who they apply to and to what extent. For example, what is said of the Hebrews – the people most often cited – does not always concern the Hebrews alone. More generally, everything that is revealed to be existentially true for one nation supposes a possibility inscribed in the laws of human nature, but which history has not brought to the fore for another.[169]

---

[167] Cf. 'terreat vulgus, nisi metuat', *Ethics* IV, 54, Schol., G II, p. 250, ll. 16 [*CWS* I, 576]. As for the inconstancy of this crowd, 'multorum tumultuum, & bellorum atrocium causa fuit', *TTP*, Preface, G III, p. 6, ll. 29–30 [*TTP* Praef., 8; *CWS* II, 68].

[168] He sometimes indicates this. Cf. *TTP*, Chapter I, G III, p. 24, ll. 9–10: 'non tantum Judaei, sed etiam Ethnici' [*TTP* I, 31; *CWS* II, 88].

[169] In making this list, I will draw on the pages devoted to these different people written by Alexandre Matheron in his work *Le Christ et le salut des ignorants*, Chapter I (cf. also *Individu et Communauté*, p. 356, ff.). In the course of his analysis, Matheron underscores the role of serendipitous events that have constituted different bodies

The ancients, in general, are characterised by their ignorance of natural causes. This is not a matter of an inadequacy that is particular to individuals: all people (including those who live among more developed peoples) are born ignorant of causes.[170] They can only – or at least certain of them can – modify this state if the science of their time lends itself to this task. The poor development of the sciences – even if there are exceptions to this – was not enough to combat this natural ignorance. A trait that is constitutive of human nature as such is thus found in the form of a durable trait proper to the *ingenium* of the first peoples. This ignorance of causes is joined to admiration or wonder in the face of natural phenomena and produces the belief in miracles,[171] oracles, and more generally in the many interventions of the divine. This rule obviously applies to the treatment of individuals: every instance where one person surpasses another is related to God, and this mechanism not only functions among the Hebrews but also among all of the ancients.[172] We can thus deduce that when Spinoza remarks that the Hebrews do not know of certain intermediate causes,[173] he is describing a mode of mental functioning that is not specific to them, but which the Hebrews perhaps carry to its paroxysm.[174] We should add that

---

of law and that to different degrees have allowed them to respond to universal exigencies (that is, exigencies that are deducible from the laws of human nature). This is quite correct to the extent that Matheron thereby shows that Spinoza does not read the history recounted by the Bible – or by Tacitus, or Quintus-Curtius – from a providential perspective. Yet it seems to me that we can shed light on another aspect of this history by analysing the relations between the *ingenium* of each people and its system of laws, as Spinoza himself invites us to do. Henceforth the part accorded to chance diminishes and cedes its place to determinations that are at once specific and necessary, even if they are wholly knowable for us only through historical experience.

[170] 'Omnes homines rerun causarum ignari nascuntur', *Ethics* I, App., G II, p. 78, ll. 15–16 [*CWS* I, 440].

[171] 'Certum est, antiquos id pro miraculo habuisse, quod explicare non poterant eo modo, quo vulgus res naturales explicare solet, recurrendo scilicet ad memoriam, ut alterius rei similis quam sine admiratione imaginari solet, recordetur; tum enim vulgus rem aliquam se satis intelligere existimat, cum ipsam non admiratur', *TTP*, Chapter VI, G III, p. 84, ll. 7–11 [*TTP* IV, 14; *CWS* II, 155].

[172] Spinoza gives examples from the Hebrews, the Egyptians, the Babylonians and the Latins: 'Quare id absolute omne, quo aliquis reliquos excellebat, ad Deum referre solebant antiqui, non tantu Judaei, sed etiam Ethnici; Pharao enim ubi somnii interpretationem audivit, dixit, Josepho mentem Deorum inesse, & Nabucadonosor etiam Daniëli dixit, eum mentem Deorum Sanctorum habere. Quin etiam apud Latinos nihil frequentius', *TTP*, Chapter I, G III, p. 24, ll. 8–13 [*TTP* I, 31; *CWS* II, 88].

[173] *TTP*, G III, p. 16, l. 33; p. 17, l. 8 [*TTP* I, 8; *CWS* II 78].

[174] Just as in grammar the existence of the factitive is not proper to the Hebrew language.

as a consequence both of ignorance and of the taste for the extraordinary, the vulgar have a tendency to hold common knowledge in contempt.[175] In situations where common knowledge is not sufficiently developed to yield certain fruits that make it widely respected, we can expect this trait to be found in the *ingenium* of ancient nations, more or less modified as a function of their other characteristics. Spinoza refers to all of this as to so many lessons of history that at this degree of generality could be demonstrated by purely rational reflection. We should add that it is possible, in other passages, to understand 'ancients' to be opposed to 'civilised'. This latter term refers more to the development of luxury than to the development of the sciences. In this sense, we can say that before being softened by luxury, human beings are more innocent, at least as far as language is concerned, and call a cat a cat – something that will shock their descendants.[176]

When it is a matter of distinguishing between the different ancient peoples, it is necessary to suppose this common foundation and to expect to learn from history the detail of its variations. For example, an irreducible given in the case of the Hebrews is their monotheism. This suffices to distinguish them from other nations – Romans, Egyptians, Babylonians – with whom they share an ignorance of causes and a wonder in the face of natural phenomena.[177] Since devotion towards the divine, which is the automatic consequence of this wonder, is oriented in the Hebrews' case towards a unique being, the intensity of this devotion will be stronger and will infuse the whole of their lives. Their *ingenium* will thus be more strongly characterised by this sentiment of divinity than the *ingenium* of other peoples. This is why it can be doubted whether the Book of Job was not originally written in Hebrew, since the Book's ambience is so marked by polytheism.[178] Similarly, if all peoples hold common knowledge in contempt, the Hebrews do so more intensely because of their belief in their election.[179] We can clearly see with

---

Yet this language generalised the use of this tense through the creation of a special form that is applicable to all verbs (cf. our discussion on this point above, Chapter 8).

[175] *TTP*, Chapter I, G III, p. 27 [*TTP* I, 41; *CWS* II, 91]; and the formula cited above: 'For the common people think they understand a thing well enough when they do not wonder at it', VI, p. 84 [*TTP* VI, 14; *CWS* II, 155].

[176] *TTP*, Chapter IX, G III, p. 137, l. 33; p. 138, l. 5 [*TTP* IX, 44; *CWS* II, 220].

[177] 'Their difference from the Pagans was just that they believed it was God, not Aeolus, who was the ruler of the winds', *TTP*, Chapter I, G III, p. 23, ll. 32–4 [*TTP* I, 30; *CWS* II, 87].

[178] *TTP*, Chapter X, G III, p. 144, l. 10 ff. [*TTP* X, 16; *CWS* II, 230]. This is why Spinoza tends to agree with those who suppose that this Book has an original non-Hebrew version (cf. also Chapter VII, p. 110, ll. 34–5 [*TTP* VII, 64; *CWS* II, 184]).

[179] 'Quia cognitio naturalis omnibus communis est, non tanti ab hominibus, ut jam

this last example how a typical trait (the belief in election, which is nothing other than the practical form of monotheism)[180] produces another trait proper to the Hebrews by intensifying a common trait of human nature (the contempt for common knowledge). The Hebrews' rhetoric itself is marked by this trait since a trait that for other peoples would only be a literary ornament is with the Hebrews a mark of devotion.[181]

Let us now reprise the characteristics of the different ancient peoples.

A. Spinoza tells us that he does not know enough Greek, and I have noted that this also applies to his knowledge of Greek culture. This is why he speaks very little of the Greeks (the examples that Spinoza borrows from Greece are few in number, not only in comparison to the Hebrews but also with respect to the Romans). But the little that Spinoza does say of the Greeks suggests that the most original trait of their national mentality is their philosophical and polemical chatter. Let me explain this point. The Greeks rose to a quite high degree of civilisation by no longer being able to accept, as the Gentiles did, the divinisation of man.[182] Spinoza tells us nothing about the causes of this degree of civilisation, which he restricts himself to simply marking in the form that historical experience presents it to us. This assumption accords, moreover, with what each reader believes they know, at least vaguely, about Greek civilisation. This corresponds quite closely to the habitual status of experience. Such a development was due no doubt to favourable circumstances from which other peoples were unable to profit.[183] If they favoured peace and security, the Greeks had to fight to push back against superstition, at least in its religious form. In fact, when he speaks of the Greeks, Spinoza never speaks of their Gods as objects of

---

diximus, aestimatur, & praecipue ab Hebraeis, qui se supra omnes esse jactabant, et consequenter scientiam omnibus communem, contemnere solebant', *TTP*, Chapter I, G III, p. 27, ll. 29–33 [*TTP* I, 41; *CWS* II, 91].

[180] On other aspects of this notion, which we cannot engage with here, see the beautifully written pages on this topic by Stanislas Breton, *Spinoza, théologie et politique*, Paris: Desclée, 1977, p. 64 ff.

[181] 'Sed tantum hoc in genere notare velim, Hebraeos his phrasibus non tantum consuevisse ornate, sed etiam, et quidem maxime, devote loqui', *TTP*, Chapter VI, G III, p. 94, ll. 16–18 [*TTP* VI, 63; *CWS* II, 166–7].

[182] Cf. the explanation of the refusal of the Macedonians (visibly assimilated with the Greeks) to adore Alexander, *TTP*, Chapter XVII, G III, pp. 204–5 [*TTP* XVII, 23, 24; *CWS* II, 300–1].

[183] A. Matheron suggests that this is thanks to merchant democracy (*Le Christ et le salut des ignorants*, pp. 51–2).

belief.[184] This trait was able to engender among certain individuals an attitude that Spinoza considers to be truly philosophical, in the positive sense of the term. But these individuals – Thales in the case of morality, Democritus and Epicurus for the causalist vision of the world, Euclid for mathematics – were exceptions. In the nation as a whole, ignorance of causes remained rife, along with all of its typical consequences. Yet, because of the weakening of 'official' polytheism, this ignorance took a particular form: instead of being transformed into a devotion for *rectores naturae*, it was transformed into a search for abstract 'final causes', a search that came to constitute a veritable secular mythology. Founded on the imagination, this mythology was as distant from reason as imaginative religions are: the majority of Greece's philosophers believed in trifles,[185] and their thought referred to fictions[186] that were needlessly complicated.[187] Furthermore, their theses led to madness.[188] More than this, imagination implies division between men, since each person can invent an imaginative explanation of the world on the basis of his own corporeal structure. When this tendency towards division is not kept in check by a religious rule that is unanimously accepted,[189] it is given free reign in the form of polemics and sterile discussions, in particular those directed against reason: Platonists and Aristotelians were made blind with envy in the face of the atomists.[190] Philosophical opinions are associated with the same theological fury that other peoples manifest with respect to their Gods: the war of sects among the Greeks led to the war of religions. The Greek's *ingenium* thus takes the form of infinite chatter and a pseudo-explanatory madness. When Spinoza notes that the Greeks are, at

---

[184] This does not mean that the Greeks as a whole knew the true religion, nor that they became atheist. But Spinoza does seem to consider mythology as having become a mere reservoir of poetic fictions. This in no way prevents religious behaviour, which, in the case of Alexander, oscillated between practical atheism and a frantic recourse to oracles.

[185] 'Eos, qui qualitates occultas, species intentionales, formas substantiales, ac mille alias nugas commentis sunt', Ep. LVI, G IV, p. 261, ll. 33–5 [*Ep.* LVI [to Hugo Boxel]; *CWS* II, 423]; 'nugas aristotelicas', *TTP*, Chapter I, G III, p. 19, l. 31 [*TTP* I, 19; *CWS* II, 82].

[186] CM, II, Chapter VI, G I, p. 259 [*CM* II; *CWS* I, 325].

[187] This is what expressions like 'lofty speculations, or philosophical matters' suggest, *TTP*, Chapter XIII, G III, p. 167 [*TTP* XIII, 4; *CWS* II, 257], in opposition to the *res simplicissimas* that are necessary for salvation.

[188] 'Cum Graecis insanire', *TTP*, Preface, G III, p. 9, l. 6 [*TTP* Praef., 18; *CWS* II, 71].

[189] As is the case, for some time, among the Hebrews, cf. *TTP*, Chapter XVIII, G III, p. 222, l. 14 ff. [*TTP* XVIII, 6; *CWS* II, 323]

[190] Letter LVI, G IV, p. 262 [*Ep.* LVI [to Hugo Boxel]; *CWS* II, 423].

least in Paul's time, so impregnated with philosophy that whoever addresses them must use this language,[191] it is clear that philosophy does not mean something uniquely positive in this case[192] but also refers to the tendency towards disputes and divisions into sects.[193]

B. The Romans' complexion is characterised by its violence, both internal and external. Spinoza considers the Romans to be a factious and blasphemous people.[194] What should we understand by this? Historians and orators say that the Romans were blasphemers. Yet this is a trait that could in fact be deduced rationally from the Romans' overly large number of gods. Polytheism prevents devotion from attaining a sufficient intensity, since it is dispersed across a large number of figures. However, it does produce superstition.[195] If among the Romans the monarch does not begin by taking on a divine aspect, then this is not a proof of civilisation, as it is with the Greeks; rather, it is simply that the brutality of the Romans' institutions did not lend itself to such divinisation.[196] We can thus conclude that the divinisation of the monarch is present among the Romans in a latent state: as soon as a new institution lends itself to this divinisation, it will reappear. Indeed, this is what happens with Augustus.[197] The Romans are factious in that they assassinate their kings and do not know how to construct peaceful institutions. Perhaps it is necessary to see here the prolongation of Rome's foundational situation, even if Spinoza does not mention this: Romulus gathers together people who have escaped from many different cities, or he creates Rome by means of a crime (the murder of Remus). This initial brutality is perpetuated because it is contained neither by monotheistic devotion, as is it is in the

---

[191] *TTP*, Chapter XI, G III, p. 158 [*TTP* XI, 23; CWS II, 247].

[192] On the different senses of the term 'philosophy' in Spinoza, see my contribution to the Urbino colloquium.

[193] The proof of this is that it is this Greek heritage that produces heresies and schisms in Christianity. Here Spinoza takes his own singular position on the question to which Hobbes responded, after all of the anti-Aristotelians. Cf. *Leviathan*, Chapters XLV and XLVI.

[194] 'Utpote ex seditiosis & flagitiosis hominibus conflatus', *TTP*, Chapter XVIII, G III, p. 227, ll. 26–7 [*TTP* XVIII, 35; CWS II, 330].

[195] Only some individuals escape from this, for instance Caesar, as Suetonius says, who Spinoza cites in a letter to Boxel, Ep. LIV, G IV, p. 254 [*Ep*. LIV [to Hugo Boxel]; CWS II, 416].

[196] The Romans were not yet habituated to obedience. They themselves elected their kings, and killed one in three. *TTP*, Chapter XVIII, G III, p. 227, ll. 25–9 [*TTP* XVIIII, 35; CWS II, 330]. It is difficult to adore as gods leaders who are submitted to such conditions.

[197] *TTP*, Chapter XVII, G III, p. 204, ll. 18–21 [*TTP* XVII, 21; CWS II, 300].

case of the Hebrews, nor by the sacralisation of the king, as is it is with the Persians,[198] nor by a certain degree of culture, as it is with the Greeks. After the fall of the kings, Rome's institutions create multiple tyrants and not only one.[199] The situation is so intolerable that the only means for getting rid of this popular violence is to make it flow outwards towards the exterior: whence the long history of wars that make up the history of Rome.[200] The extension of the Empire does not resolve this problem, however; it only makes the solution more necessary. Whence the instauration of an authoritarian power, which ends up re-establishing both the tyranny of a single person and the divinisation of the Sovereign that was potential since the beginning. Despite this, Rome will always remain at the mercy of the violence of its own citizens.[201] How should this long identification of a people with violence be explained? As we noted above, this violence is rooted in human nature. But the circumstances that presided over the existence of the Roman people allowed this common characteristic to come to the fore and to attain a higher degree of effectivity than in other nations.

C. The case of the Hebrews is particularly interesting. In Chapter V of the *TTP*, Spinoza sets out to show the link between the Hebrews' laws and the complexion proper to this people. In terms of this complexion, he seems to emphasise two particular elements: devotion and insubordination. Devotion, for its part, can be read in biblical laws and their effects. The very language of the Hebrews, their rhetoric, along with their way of living, attest to their great piety. But this piety is given to them by laws that institute monotheism and govern life in its entirety in a religious fashion. In sum, if reason teaches us that the ancient people were naturally oriented towards an at least minimal devotion, experience shows that the Hebrews gave themselves structures that conferred upon this devotion the greatest intensity and the broadest possible extension. As for insubordination, it plays a dual role in their history: at the beginning, when Moses is constructing the State; and then in the process that leads to the ruin of this State. Is

---

[198] *TTP*, Chapter XVII, G III, p. 205, ll. 6–12 [*TTP* XVII, 24; CWS II, 301].
[199] 'Tamen nihil aliud fecit, quam loco unius, plures tyrannos eligere', *TTP*, Chapter XVIII, G III, p. 227, ll. 28–9 [*TTP* XVIII, 35; CWS II, 330].
[200] 'Qui ipsum externo, & interno bello misere conflictum semper habuerunt', ibid., ll. 30–1 [*TTP* XVIII, 35; CWS II, 330–1].
[201] 'Invictissima ab hostibus Romanorum respublica, toties a suis civibus victa et miserrime oppressa', *TTP*, Chapter XVII, G III, p. 204, ll. 1–3 [*TTP* XVII, 18; CWS II, 299].

this insubordination something natural for all peoples[202] (as we can deduce from the affective kernel of antipolitics), or is it a particularly intense trait of the Hebrew people? Spinoza seems to accept,[203] then deny,[204] the idea of a particular insubordination. He cannot do otherwise than accept it, at least in part, since it is something taught by experience – specifically, in this instance, by the Bible, which shows repeated examples of this[205] and attributes the statement of the Hebrew's insubordination to God himself.[206] This trait is even reprised by a tradition that makes it a particularity that explains the Hebrews' misfortunes.[207] Yet, even if he accepts it as a given of history, Spinoza must at the same time deny it as a natural phenomenon. It is thus necessary to explain it by specific causes that have to do with laws and morals.[208] The second occurrence of insubordination is explained by the dangerous effects of a specific institution: that of the Levites. But what about

---

[202] 'Constantiam vulgi contumaciam esse' (at the same level as fear and superstition), *TTP*, Preface, G III, p. 12, l. 12 [*TTP* Praef., 33; *CWS* II, 75].

[203] 'Ingenium et animum contumacem', *TTP*, Chapter III, G III, p. 53, l. 24 [*TTP* III, 42; *CWS* II, 121] (as early as Moses' time, even before the Law): 'populi scilicet ingenium contumax', Chapter V, p. 75, l. 15 [*TTP* V, 28; *CWS* II, 145].

[204] When it comes to explaining why the Hebrews defected so many times from the Law, and why their State finally succumbed: 'At forsan hic aliquis dicet, id evenisse ex gentis contumacia. Verum hoc puerile est: nam cur haec natio reliquis contumacior fuit?', *TTP*, Chapter XVII, G III, p. 217, ll. 17–19 [*TTP* XVII, 93; *CWS* II, 317]. G. Brykman makes some useful remarks on this question in 'De l'insoumission des Hébreux', *Revue de l'enseignement philosophique*, 34/2 (1982), pp. 3–9.

[205] As early as the exodus from Egypt the Hebrews complain in the face of each obstacle (Exodus 15:24; 16:2–3; 17:2) and Moses underscores that this recrimination is directed against God (Exodus 16:8). Finally, 'the Lord said to Moses: "How long will you refuse to keep my commands and my instructions"' (Exodus 16:28).

[206] At the time of the episode of the golden calf: '"I have seen these people", the Lord said to Moses, "and they are a stiff-necked people"' (Exodus 32:9; repeated in 33:3; 33:5; 34:9; Deuteronomy 9:6; 9:13; etc.).

[207] Cf. the Midrashic commentary on Exodus 2:14: when Moses says 'What I did must have become known', he means: 'Maintenant s'éclaire pour moi le problème qui me tourmentait: en quoi Israël a-t-il péché plus que les soixante-dix nations et qui lui vaut d'être écrasé sous une cruelle servitude? Mais je vois qu'il le mérite.' In Rachi, *Commentaire sur le Pentateuque*, Paris: Fondation Lévy, 1977, vol. II, p. 10; translated by I. Salzer, p. 11. A whole swathe of Christian anti-Judaism is also founded on this idea of insubordination, from the Epistle of Barnabas and his commentary on the episode of the golden calf.

[208] 'Si igitur concedendum esset, quod Hebraei super reliquos mortales contumaces fuerint, id vitio legum vel receptorum morum imputari deberet', *TTP*, Chapter XVII, G III, p. 217, ll. 24–6 [*TTP* XVII, 94; *CWS* II, 317]. Cf. the rule posited by the *TP*: 'subditorum vitia, nimiaque licentia, & contumacia Civitati imputanda sunt', Chapter V, 3, G III, p. 295, ll. 31–2 [*TP* V, 3; *CWS* II, 529].

the first occurrence, that is, the insubordination that is already manifest at the very beginning? It cannot arise from the Hebrews' laws, which do not yet exist. It is thus necessary to reduce it to the morals and circumstances that contributed to the formation of these laws. Now, this is indeed what the text of the *Treatise* suggests. The foundational event is the exit from Egyptian oppression.[209] The Hebrews' complexion is characterised at the moment of their exit from Egypt by vulgarity, superstition and exhaustion due to servitude[210] – and by a particular kind of insubordination. This situation has two symmetrical effects: on the one hand, it makes the Hebrews hate all oppression, all rules imposed by man[211] (it will be said that this is the case for all peoples, since we are dealing here with a component of the fundamental affective kernel; but among the Hebrews this tendency attains a particular vigour because of the previous oppression they experienced). The insubordination that is natural in every individual is thus reinforced among the first Hebrews by the situation from which they emerge. On the other hand, servitude made the Hebrews vulgar and dis-adapted to freedom. One cannot appeal to their reason to make them accept laws[212] (on this point too, the same could be said of any person; but here the destructive effect of a long-term oppression has reinforced this mechanism). Thus, Moses, because he knew that their complexion was marked by these characteristics, understood that he could not organise them if they were not disciplined by divine aid.[213] Only divine power could force them into a state of obedience that would nevertheless not be experienced as a human oppression.[214] The

---

[209] 'Ab intoleranda Ægyptorium oppressione liberati', TTP, Chapter XVII, G III, p. 205, ll. 18–19 [TTP XVII, 27; CWS II, 301]. It is clear that for Spinoza the history of the Hebrews begins with Moses and not with Abraham. On the other hand, they do have a prehistory: slavery in Egypt. In this latter characterisation, Spinoza does nothing but follow the Biblical text itself, which calls Egypt 'the house of servitude'.

[210] 'Homines supersitionibus Ægyptorium assueti, rudes et miserrima servitute confecti', TTP, Chapter II, G III, p. 40, l. 35; p. 41, l. 2 [TTP II, 46; CWS II, 106–7]; and 'rudis fere ingenii omnes erant, et misera servitute confecti', Chapter V, p. 75, ll. 4–5 [TTP V, 26; CWS II, 145].

[211] In Chapter V, the expression already cited 'populi scilicet ingenium contumax' is clarified by '(quod sola vi cogi non patitur)', p. 75, l. 15 [TTP V, 28; CWS II, 145].

[212] 'Attamen ad nihil minus erant apti, quam ad jura sapienter constituendum, & imperium penes sese collegialiter retinendum', TTP, Chapter V, G III, p. 75, ll. 3–4 [TTP V, 27; CWS II, 145].

[213] 'Sed res est, postquam Moses novit ingenium, & animum suae nationis contumacem, clare vidit, eos non sine maximis miraculis, & singulari Dei auxilio externo, res inceptas perficere posse', TTP, Chapter III, G III, p. 53, ll. 24–6 [TTP III, 41; CWS II, 121].

[214] 'Hac igitur de causa Moses virtute & jussu divino religionem in rempublicam

generalisation of religion that theocratic monotheism allows has the following double effect: it replaces Egyptian servitude by another servitude, but one that is less cruel, so long as it remains consistent. It submits people to it completely and in every aspect of their lives,[215] but it allows no person to be oppressed by another.[216] Everything thus happens as if the particular solution found by Moses for the Hebrews had its source in a particularity of their *ingenium* – a particularity that was itself linked to their history. Once constituted, the mental expression of this solution (intense and monotheistic devotion – intense *because* monotheistic) was in turn destined to colour the other traits of the Hebrew's collective complexion. Thus, historical experience explains both the Hebrew's dominant trait and the dominant aspects of other traits. In particular it can be shown that the idea of a jealous God and the theology of election, far from being a particularity of the Hebrews, expresses a necessary tendency of human nature when its laws apply to an anthropomorphic monotheism.[217] On the other hand, the Hebrews are not essentially characterised by their violence,[218] nor by an aptitude towards philosophical chatter: both are nevertheless part of the givens of human nature and will thus be found in the affective stock of each individual. Yet the accidents of history have not elevated them to the status of essential components of the Hebrews' *ingenium* as a nation, as happened in the first case for the Romans, and in the second case for the Greeks.

Spinoza thus seems once again to have confidence in a constitutive expe-

---

introduxit, ut populus non tam ex metu, quam devotione suum officium faceret', *TTP*, Chapter V, G III, p. 75, ll. 19–21 [*TTP* V, 29; *CWS* II, 145–6]; 'suum jus in neminem mortalium, sed tantum in Deum transferre deliberaverunt', *TTP*, Chapter XVII, G III, p. 205, ll. 23–5 [*TTP* XVII, 27; *CWS* II, 301].

[215] 'Denique, ut populus, qui sui juris esse non poterat, ab ore imperantis penderet, nihil hominibus scilicet servituti assuetis ad libitum agere concessit', *TTP*, Chapter V, G III, p. 75, ll. 25–7 [*TTP* V, 30; *CWS* II, 146].

[216] In this sense, the fact that at a certain time theocracy was *magis opinione quam re* does not mean that it did not exist: if Moses is recognised as a leader, then it was in the name of the divine virtue that raised him up above the others.

[217] Cf. *Ethics* I, App., G II, p. 79, ll. 10–12 [*CWS* I, 441]; *Ethics* III, 35 and Schol., pp. 166–7 [*CWS* I, 514].

[218] Cf. *TTP*, Chapter III, G III, p. 57, ll. 3–4 [*TTP* III, 55; *CWS* II, 124]. How can we reconcile this text with Tacitus' argument, cited by Spinoza, on the irreducible tenacity of the Hebrews (Chapter XVII, G III, p. 215, ll. 27–31 [*TTP* XVII, 83; *CWS* II, 314–15])? The response is to be found in the same chapter of the *TTP*, a few lines above: 'While the city was still standing . . .'. In other words: their institutions repress violence and channel it towards a single function: defending their State. Once this State no longer exists, the first effect subsists.

rience, that of history, to bring out the irreducible individuality of a people. We thus find ourselves in a situation that recalls the status of *usus* with regards to the meaning of words. There nevertheless exists a difference: in the case of use, Spinoza, in contrast to his contemporaries, does not appear to accord any special privilege to the original meaning of words. With respect to the *ingenium*, by contrast, he does indeed seem to think that what happens at the beginning places a definitive stamp on a people. This is one of the traits that constitutes what could be called Spinoza's historical conservatism. In the case of the Romans, the violence that characterises their beginnings seems to unfold across the entirety of their history. Spinoza, who is so profoundly marked by Latin culture, is in no way impressed by the duration of the Roman Empire: he sees in its long history the same sound and the same fury.[219] In the case of the Hebrews, what makes their laws efficacious continues to function despite the upheavals that occurred in the initial disruption they suffered (the substitution of the Levites by sacerdotalism, which had initially been envisaged), despite the restriction of power by the Pontiffs at the time of the Second Temple, and, finally, despite the destruction of their State. The Dutch are determined by the incomplete revolution that allowed the empty place of the Count to remain.[220] In all of these situations, the previous moments appear interpretable less in terms of their own structure than as an echo of initial situations. Moreover, with respect to the Hebrews Spinoza employs a formula that also seems to fit these other cases: their second Empire was only the shadow of the first. To know the *ingenium* of a people is thus to know this people's beginnings. How can we explain this difference with respect to what happens in the case of language, where all epochs seem to enjoy an equal epistemological dignity? The word, as we saw, was a simple association of images. The *ingenium* dictates institutions where, it could be said, this *ingenium* becomes objectivised: henceforth, institutions regularly reproduce it.[221] It is therefore not by way of an origin myth but by a regular and circular reproduction of the beginning that States are naturally conservative. Even deviations are brought back to

---

[219] In Spinoza's writings the references to Roman history are almost always pejorative, whereas he praises the peace that, at certain times, the Hebrews knew (*TTP*, Chapter XVIII, G III, p. 210 [*TTP* XVIII, 54, 55; *CWS* II, 308–9].) He characterises the peace the Romans knew by reprising the formula of the German rebels: 'ubi solitudinem faciunt, pacem appellant'.

[220] *TP*, Chapter IX, 14, G III, pp. 351–2 [*TP* IX, 14; *CWS* II, 594–5].

[221] 'Ex his duobus, legibus scilicet et moribus, tantum oriri potest, quod unaquaeque natio singulare habeat ingenium, singularem conditionem et denique singularia praejudicia', *TTP*, Chapter XVII, G III, p. 217, ll. 21–4 [*TTP* XVII, 92; *CWS* II, 317].

the norm: whether tyranny in Rome, or the monarchy in the Netherlands, both return to occupy a place that was provisionally left empty. Whence the extreme importance of foundational moments. It is a matter less of the role of a hero[222] than the institution of a structure that retrospectively characterises the people in their entirety and reinforces the traits of their *ingenium*.

B. The State as an Individual

Up to this point, by attributing to each people an *ingenium*, we have followed the suggestions provided by Spinoza's texts and proceeded on analogy with the case of the human individual's complexion. We have implicitly admitted that each State is, in a certain way, an individual, with recognisable and, at least to a certain extent, constant traits. This raises the broader question of the State's status as an individual. Must we consider the individuality of the State or the nation as a real individuality, a natural one, in the sense that Spinoza's system defines it both for the simplest bodies as for ever more complex categories of individuals?[223] Or should we, on the contrary, consider it as derivative, indeed as metaphorical, as the language of the contract would tend to suggest? Is the State artificial or not? Spinoza does not raise this question when elaborating his theory of individuality. He is content to say that there exist ever more composite individuals, and among these very complex individuals he cites only the human being and Nature in its entirety[224] – without mentioning or explicitly excluding any

---

[222] This is why R. McShea's thesis seems to me to be indefensible: 'Spinoza adopts the classical, and Machiavellian, concept of the hero-founder [. . .] his only account of the formation of a national character consists of a detailed application of the hero-founder thesis to a Biblical narrative', *The Political Philosophy of Spinoza*, New York: Columbia University Press, 1968, p. 95. As for the text of the *TP*, I, 3, it is clear that it refers not to 'foundational heroes' but to experienced politicians who, in the course of centuries, have leant their equilibrium to the institutions of the City.

[223] Cf. the physics from Book II, in particular the definition that follows axiom II and the Scholium that follows Lemma VII. On this theory of individuality, see A. Rivaud, 'La physique de Spinoza', *Chronicon spinozanum*, IV (1926), pp. 24–57, in particular pp. 38–50; M. Gueroult, *Spinoza*, vol. II, *L'Ame*, pp. 143–89; and A. Matheron, *Individu et Communauté*, pp. 37–61.

[224] Commenting on these texts, A. Rivaud remarks that 'Spinoza semble d'ailleurs avoir tenu pour des individus des réalités d'un autre ordre, par exemple les groupes sociaux les plus importants, comme la famille, l'Etat, l'Eglise, la Nation. La notion d'harmonie ou d'accommodation réciproque est très large et permet les généralisations les plus hardies', 'La physique de Spinoza', p. 43.

other.[225] As far as the State is concerned, we must seek an answer to this question by referring to scattered textual indications, and, above all, to the logic of the system. There are two opposing theses on this question:

- A 'naturalist' thesis, which Alexandre Matheron defends and which considers that the State is an individual in the physical sense of the term.[226] The State thus has both a *mens*[227] and a *conatus*.[228] In line with the schema of the physics from Book II, it is composed of other individuals. In Spinoza, there is no place for a distinction between nature and artifice. We can thus define the individuality of the State in physical terms, as we can for any other natural individual.
- An 'artificialist' thesis, which is that of Den Uyl and Rice: the State is not an individual;[229] it has no *mens*;[230] it is artificial. We can

[225] M. Gueroult remarks (*Spinoza*, vol. II, pp. 169–70): 'Enfin, puisque l'on doit concevoir, entre l'Individu du premier degré et la Nature entière une série infinie d'individus de complication croissante, on devrait concevoir entre le corps humain et le corps de la Nature une série infinie de corps de plus en plus complexes, et, par conséquent, entre l'Ame humaine et l'idée de ce corps, une série d'Âmes de plus en plus parfaites. Cependant cette vue – propre à Leibniz – n'apparaît pas ici, expressément du moins.' This is not surprising precisely because Spinoza himself indicates that his exposition is purposefully elliptical: 'Atque haec, si animus fuisset [van de stoffe of] de corpore ex professo [en bezonderlijk] agere, prolixius explicare et demonstrare debuissem. Se jam dixi me aliud velle...', G II, p. 102, ll. 14–16 [*Ethics* II, Lem. 7, Schol.; CWS I, 462]. Gueroult adds as a note: 'Les sociétés civiles sembleraient devoir être comptées parmi ces individus plus élevés.' He gives as references passages from the *TP* that include the expression *una veluti mente* as well as the Scholium from Proposition 18 from Book IV of the *Ethics*.

[226] 'L'Etat est un système de mouvements qui, fonctionnant en cycle fermé, se produit et se reproduit lui-même en permanence [...] L'Etat est donc, très exactement, un Individu au sens spinoziste du mot', *Individu et Communauté*, pp. 346–7.

[227] 'Du côté de l'Attribut Pensée, l'âme de l'Etat coïncide sinon avec celle du Souverain, du moins avec une partie des idées qui la composent ou qui composent celle de ses membres', ibid., p. 347. Whence the designation in the *TP* of the Sovereign as 'Imperii veluti mens', with the *veluti* referring to a partial coincidence.

[228] 'L'*imperium*, pas plus que l'homme, n'est un empire dans un empire; mais comme l'homme et comme n'importe quel être, il constitute une totalité fermée sur soi et douée, pour cette raison, d'une autonomie relative: même déformé par l'action du milieu, c'est son *conatus* qui le fait agir', ibid., p. 348.

[229] 'The proper way to view either the civitas or its government is not as an individual, but rather as an organised set of relations. Unity in Spinoza's political thought is a matter of harmony, not of individuation', D. Den Uyl, *Power, State and Freedom: An Interpretation of Spinoza's Political Philosophy*, Assen: Van Gorcum, 1983, p. 80. See A. Matheron's discussion in *Studia Spinozana*, I (1985), pp. 422–6.

[230] 'If individual bodies can make up another individual body, why not consider a group

only consider the human being as a constitutive part of the State metaphorically.[231]

I do not intend to study all aspects of this problem here. But we must at least deal with certain among them. In fact, the importance and role of the *ingenium* depends on the response to this question. If the State is, like each person, an individual, then it is logical to attribute to it a recognisable complexion that externally manifests the laws of its individual nature. If, on the contrary, it is only an artificial grouping without any real ontological consistency, then it has no internal laws, and we might fear that it has no necessary singularity that can serve as a support for durable and recognisable traits in experience. Let us examine the details of the case.

A. Spinoza's naturalist logic militates in favour of Matheron's thesis. Moreover, there exists at least one passage in the *Ethics* where Spinoza explicitly envisages people joining their forces in such a way as to form a single individual.[232] It can also be noted that the *Political Treatise* no longer reasons in terms of a contract, but directly considers the existence of the State as a given. That the State has a soul is not surprising in a system where all things have a soul.[233] The true question is rather: what sort of soul does the State possess, and what relation does it have with the souls of individual humans?

Moreover, it could be added, the idea of artifice is nowhere to be found in Spinoza's work. On the contrary, we find the critique of such an idea – one suggested by the 'logic of use'.[234]

---

of individual minds as making up one individual social mind? This analogy fails, however. [...] Spinoza considers the mind as nothing other than the idea of the body. Spinoza's parallelism would thus require that the *social mind* be the idea of an individual *social body*; yet nowhere does he speak of society as being a corporeal unity', Den Uyl, *Power, State and Freedom*, p. 79.

[231] Lee C. Rice, 'Individual and Community in Spinoza's Social Psychology', in *Spinoza: Issues and Directions*, p. 279. This article tracks the history of this discussion.

[232] He states this initially as a general thesis: 'Si enim duo ex. gr. ejusdem prorsus naturae individua invicem junguntur, individuum componunt singulo duplo potentius', *Ethics* IV, 18, Schol., G II, p. 223, ll. 6–8 [CWS I, 556]. Then he applies it to the case of men, ibid., l. 8 ff. [CWS I, 556].

[233] 'Reliqua Individua [...] quae omnia, quamvis diversis gradibus, animata tamen sunt', *Ethics* II, 13, Schol., G II, p. 96, ll. 27–8 [CWS I, 458]. On this question, cf. P. Cristofolini, 'Aliarum rerum mentes', *Bulletin de l'Association des amis de Spinoza*, 10 (1983) (and *La Scienza intuitiva di Spinoza*, Naples: Morano, 1987, pp. 47–53), as well as the work of R. Bouveresse, *Spinoza et Lebniz. L'idée d'animisme universel*, Paris: Vrin, 1992.

[234] Cf. A. Tosel, *Spinoza ou le crépuscule de la servitude*, Paris: Aubier, 1984, pp. 35–9; M. Schewe, *Rationalität contra Finalität*, Frankfurt: Peter Lang, 1987, pp. 125–43.

B. However, those who conceive of political institutions in terms of artifice seem to be able to base their conclusions on a certain number of points of textual evidence. Let us leave aside the *contract* form, which is not essential to the argument (Den Uyl does not give it a central place; but the idea of artifice is common to him as it is to the contract theorists).[235]

— It is true that Spinoza does not use the term *conatus* with respect to society. He does not seem to speak without restriction of the *mens* of the State. On the contrary, each time that he deals with this question, he notes that citizens must be united 'as if (*veluti*) by one soul'[236] or that the right of the Sovereign is like 'the soul of the State'.[237] The *veluti* exceeds a naturalist interpretation.[238] Similarly, the passage from the *Ethics* on the union of human individuals adds the prefix 'quasi-' when it says that the bodies and souls of each individual compose a single body and a single soul.[239]

— While it might be true that Spinoza does not speak of artifice, he does seem to carefully distinguish what is natural from what is not. For otherwise, why would he highlight the fact that nature does not create peoples and that it creates only individuals? He says this at least twice in the *TTP*. In Chapter III, to explain in what sense the Hebrew nation was elected, Spinoza distinguishes three possible objects of an honest desire: knowledge by causes, virtue, and the healthy and secure life. After noting that only the third object concerns States, he adds: 'The only thing which distinguishes one nation from another, then, is the social order and the laws under which they live and by which they are directed.'[240] The same question is posed again in Chapter XVII in another context, which we have analysed above. Here it is a question of knowing why the Hebrews so often defected from the Law, thus leading to their ruin. Among the possible responses, there is one that is suggested by the Bible itself and by tradition: namely, that the Hebrews were an insubordinate people. Spinoza rejects this solution by asking how a nation

---

[235] Den Uyl, *Power, State and Freedom*, pp. 63–4.
[236] 'Una veluti mente', *TP*, Chapter II, 16, G III, p. 281, ll. 32–3 [*TP* II, 16; *CWS* II, 514]; 21, p. 283, ll. 15–16 [*TP* II, 21; *CWS* II, 515]; Chapter III, 5, p. 286, ll. 6–7 [*TP* III, 5; *CWS* II, 519]; etc.
[237] 'Imperii veluti mens', *TP*, Chapter IV, 1, G III, p. 291, l. 31 [*TP* IV, 1; *CWS* II, 525].
[238] As Den Uyl correctly notes, *Power, State and Freedom*, p. 79.
[239] 'Omnes in omnibus ita conveniant, ut omnium mentes et corpora unam quasi mentem, unumque corpus componant', G II, p. 223, ll. 11–12 [*Ethics* IV, 18, Schol.; *CWS* I, 556].
[240] 'Per hoc igitur tantum nationes ab invicem distinguuntur, nempe ratione societatis, & legum sub quibus vivunt et diriguntur', *TTP*, Chapter III, G III, p. 47, ll. 26–7 [*TTP* III, 16; *CWS* II, 114].

is distinguished from others. He replies: nature does not create nations; it creates only individuals, which are differentiated into nations by the diversity of languages, laws and morals.[241] Thus, even if the Hebrews were more insubordinate than other peoples, this characteristic is to be imputed to their laws and morals. This implies that nature is not at fault.

— Similarly, Spinoza explicitly says that human beings are not born citizens but that they become citizens.[242] What better proof that the State is not a natural thing but only constitutes an ensemble of relations between natural things?

Such are the arguments that can be invoked on both sides of the debate. How can we decide between these two interpretations? We must begin by making two preliminary remarks that will allow us to better focus our question:

— The fact that Spinoza does not speak of the State's soul and body (at least not without the restriction *veluti*) is not enough to disprove Matheron's thesis. The simple textual absence of an expression can serve as an indication, but it cannot by itself constitute a proof against the logic of the system. In any case, it is necessary to recognise that Spinoza does indeed speak without any qualifications of the body and soul of the State. He says explicitly – rarely, it is true, but there is textual evidence of this – that the State has a body and that it has a *mens*.[243] Given this, the reservation introduced by the term *veluti* in the phrase 'the sovereign is the like the soul of the state'[244] cannot bear upon the very existence of

---

[241] 'Verum hoc puerile est; nam cur haec natio reliquis contumacior fuit? an natura? haec sane nationes non creat, sed individua, quae quidem in nationes non distinguuntur, nisi ex diversitate linguae, legum & morum receptorum, & ex his duobus, legibus scilicet et moribus, tantum oriri potest, quod unaquaeque natio singulare habeat ingenium, singularem conditionem & denique singularia praejudicia', TTP, Chapter XVII, G III, p. 217, ll. 18–24 [TTP XII, 93; CWS II, 317].

[242] 'Homines enim civiles non nascuntur, sed fiunt', TP, Chapter V, 2, p. 295, ll. 21-2 [TP V, 2; CWS II, 529].

[243] There exists at least one incontestable occurrence of this: 'totius imperii corpus et mens', TP, Chapter III, 2 [TP III, 2; CWS II, 517]. The one from Chapter VII is debatable, 3: 'imperium seu Civitas una semper eademque mente constet' [TP VII, 3; CWS II, 546], to the extent that we could understand *mens* in the sense of 'opinion'. As for the expression *imperii corpus* (without *veluti*), it too appears elsewhere: TP, Chapter III, 5, G III, p. 286, l. 6 [TP III, 5; CWS II, 519].

[244] I will return further on to the meaning of *veluti* in the occurrences of the form *una veluti mente*.

this soul, but concerns only its direct assimilation with the Sovereign.[245] As for the absence of the term *conatus* as applied to the State, it can be explained by the term's inexistence in the lexicon of the *TTP* and (with one exception) the *TP*,[246] as well as by its inexistence as far as individuals and any other individual thing are concerned. On the other hand, the *Ethics* does indeed speak of the *conatus* of each thing (*res*).[247] We are thus led back to the question: is the State a thing?

— That nature does not create peoples does not mean that peoples or States are artificial realities. When put back into their context, these formulations aim to exclude the possibility that the characteristics proper to the State are rooted in the individuals that compose it. Individuals are not naturally members of a State and do not naturally possess characteristics that are found in a people or in one specific people alone. Likewise, a formula like 'men are not born citizens, but become citizens' does not mean that the City is an artifice but rather that the adjustment of individuals to the State is not something that occurs automatically. It is the effect of the structure of the City itself. Furthermore, this formula is largely compensated for by other formulas like the equation 'civiles seu humani'.[248] In a certain fashion, human beings are born social, otherwise they would never become it. But there is nothing in the physical structure of a human being (and in the idea that corresponds to them) that makes them a citizen of one State rather than another: human nature is one and the same.[249]

---

[245] As far as the *quasi* is concerned, which seems to introduce a reservation into the Scholium to Proposition 18 from Book IV, Gueroult remarks: 'On notera le *en quelque sorte*. Il y a donc là une simple analogie. De plus, il s'agit là non d'un fait, mais d'un *dictamen Rationis*; cependant, celui-ci exprime une nécessité présente dans la nature des choses, le *debet* étant toujours fondé dans un *esse*', *Spinoza*, vol. II, *L'Ame*, p. 170, n. 78.

[246] Cf. on this point the last section from Chapter VI of the first part of this work. If one accepts my conclusion according to which the notion of *potentia* replaces that of *conatus*, we can only note that Spinoza speaks abundantly of *potentia imperii*, and, of course, of *jus imperii*, exactly as he speaks of the power and the right of human individuals.

[247] 'Conatus, quo unaquaeque res in suo esse perseverare conatur, nihil est praeter ipsius rei actualem essentiam', *Ethics* III, 7, G II, p. 146, ll. 20–1 [*CWS* I, 499].

[248] *TP*, Chapter X, 4, G III, p. 355, ll. 20–1 [*TP* X, 4; *CWS* II, 598]. Certainly, this is not a thesis on the absolute equivalence between being a human being and being a member of a civil society. It is a question of affirming that people are all the more human (or better actualise their humanity) when they profit from the advantages of civil society.

[249] The phrase 'homines civiles non nascuntur sed fiunt' is followed, moreover, by: 'Hominum praeterea naturales affectus ubique iidem sunt', *TP*, Chapter V, 2, G III, p. 295, ll. 22–3 [*TP* V, 2; *CWS* II, 529].

Once this terrain has been cleared, there no longer remains, it seems, any obstacle to considering the State as an individual. It is subject to the laws of Nature, both in terms of its construction and its conservation. The objection that consists in saying that if States were natural beings, then we would encounter at least some in the state of nature,[250] does not hold. This is because, in an absolute sense, the state of nature did not exist historically, while in a relative sense – that is, insofar as the idea of the state of nature allows one to represent individuals that are not united by laws – we obviously do encounter such things: in terms of their relations among themselves, States are indeed, here and now, in the state of nature.[251] This is something that Spinoza affirms, just as the entire history of natural right does.[252] The question that is thereby posed is rather: what sort of individual is the State (and what sort of individual is the nation or the people)?

What sort of individual is the State? First, a simple response: it is a very complex individual. This response remains absolutely inadequate, for there certainly exist many types of complexity, and the complexity of the State is not necessarily the same as that of the human organism or Nature in its entirety. Now, if we fail to define the status of the State more precisely, we will be led to think of it implicitly on the model of the complexity of the human organism. In fact, because of a long tradition, this organism spontaneously suggests itself as a paradigm of individuality; furthermore, Spinoza does not give us – not even in an abstract form – any analysis of a complex individual save for a single example, which is precisely that of the human body.[253] Relative to the human body, however, the State has at least two particularities: on the one hand, its complexity is in some sense doubled: it is an ensemble of men, but also an ensemble of institutions; on the other hand, if it is the State that makes a people a people, it is not yet certain that these two notions are perfectly identical. We thus encounter two problems that do not seem to arise when we consider the linear reconstruction of the individual-organism. We will thus have to proceed by first delimiting them.

Whatever the difficulties might be, we have two reasons to examine more closely the type of complexity that the State-individual implies. First of all, it is this examination that will help us understand the specific problems of

---

[250] Den Uyl, *Power, State and Freedom*, p. 70.
[251] 'Duo imperia ad invicem sese habere, ut duo homines in statu naturali', *TP*, Chapter III, 11, G III, p. 289, ll. 18–19 [*TP* III, 11; *CWS* II, 522].
[252] Cf. Hobbes, *Leviathan*, end of Chapter XIII.
[253] In the postulates to Book II, in Propositions 38 and 39 from Book IV and in Letter XXXII to Oldenburg, 20 November 1665.

survival the State encounters. In effect, like all complex individuals, the State is ceaselessly threatened in its continuity. This obviously does not contradict the principle stated at the beginning of Book III, namely that no individual tends towards its own destruction.[254] But complex individuals, while they might have no internal contradictions, nevertheless spend their time interiorising external ones. It is thus indeed from the inside that the fatal blow will come.[255] Now, the State presents the following specificity: this threat bears in particular upon its unity and identity. The second reason is that this analysis will help us understand the illusion of autonomy. It is not enough to say that nothing artificial exists or that everything is natural; it is also necessary to explain by what mechanism certain categories of natural beings appear to us as artificial.

To analyse the nature of the State-individual, it is necessary to proceed at three successive levels: *association*, *integration* and *adhesion*.

A. The first level consists in considering the State in terms of what it presents: a whole formed by human individuals. This is a conception that Spinoza seems to adopt as his own in at least one of the definitions we cited above.[256] What, then, is the status of an association of men? From this perspective, no distinction will be drawn between a State and a people. In fact, there exist no peoples outside of a State. The Hebrews, whether in Egypt or Babylon, lived under Egyptian[257] or Babylonian[258] laws. Similarly, the patriarchs obeyed the laws of the State in which they lived and to which they were bound.[259] In a sense, it is perfectly precise to say that it is living

---

[254] 'Nulla res, nisi a causa externa, potest destrui', *Ethics* III, 4, G II, p. 145, l. 22 [*CWS* I, 498].

[255] The axiom from Book IV indicates this clearly: one of the essential determinations of finitude is that each thing can and must encounter what will destroy it. But in the case of the simplest bodies, this destruction is and appears external. In the case of complex bodies, while it is still external, it often takes on an internal appearance since it proceeds by the dissolution of the bodies' unity.

[256] When he says: nature creates individuals that are distinguished into peoples . . .

[257] 'Dum enim inter alias nationes, ante exito ex Ægypto vixerunt, nullas leges peculiares habuerunt, nec ullo, nisi naturali jure, & sine dubio, etiam jure Reipublicae, in qua vivebant, quatenus legi divinae naturali non repugnabat, tenebantur', *TTP*, Chapter V, G III, p. 72, ll. 29–32 [*TTP* V, 15; *CWS* II, 142–3].

[258] 'Non amplus sui juris [. . .] sed Regis Babiloniae erant, cui in omnibus (ut Cap. XVI ostendimus) obedire tenebantur', *TTP*, Chapter XIX, G III, p. 231, ll. 3–5 [*TTP* XIX, 14; *CWS* II, 335]; 'postquam autem imperium amiserunt, & Bablioniam captivi ducti sunt, Jeremias eosdem docuit, ut incolumitati (etiam) illius civitatis, in quam captivi ducti erant, consulerent', ibid., p. 233, ll. 21–3 [*TTP* XIX, 30; *CWS* II, 338].

[259] *TTP*, Chapter V, G III, p. 73, ll. 5–6 [*TTP* V, 16; *CWS* II, 143].

in a State that makes a people a people. Yet, we are also familiar with other kinds of human associations besides States, for instance religious sects, commercial societies, or even societies of lovers of theatre or of tulips. How can we characterise the individuality of such associations?

An association like a State forms a complex individual composed of other complex individuals. It presents a superior degree of composition to theirs, exactly as the biological individual presents a superior degree of composition to that of its organs, or Nature a superior degree of composition to all other individuals. However, if we remain at this level, we do not yet grasp what particular type of complexity the State represents. In effect, its complexity is not reducible to a complexity of composition.[260] The richness of its effects also has to do with the richness of the relations between its component parts – relations that allow the State to maintain a relation with the external world.[261]

Here there appears the first difference between an association of human beings and a biological body. In the case of the human body at least, this richness is tied to the diversity of its component parts.[262] We can thus say that the superiority of the human body over many other bodies has to do not only with its higher degree of composition but also – and perhaps above all – with its higher degree of integration founded on its differentiation. We are thus faced with a case of spontaneous integration, which concerns the fact that the individuals composing the organism begin by being very different. This integration based on differences allows the corresponding soul to be apt for multiple perceptions.[263] Thus, the *mens* will be richer, more perfect,[264] and no doubt more conscious.[265] Above all, the constitutive differences between the elements of the whole will do no damage to the identity of the

---

[260] Cf. A. Matheron, *Individu et Communauté* . . ., pp. 57–8: degree of composition and degree of integration.

[261] Cf. *Ethics* II, Post. 64, after Proposition 13, G II, p. 103, ll. 4–5 [CWS I, 462].

[262] Ibid., Postulates 1 and 3, p. 102, ll. 20–8 [CWS I, 426].

[263] 'Mens humana apta est ad plurima percipiendum, et eo aptior, quo ejus corpus pluribus modis disponi potest', *Ethics* II, 14 [CWS I, 462].

[264] 'Hoc tamen in genere dico, quo corpus aliquod reliquis aptius est ad plura simul agendum, eo ejus mens reliquis aptior est ad plura simul percipiendum', *Ethics* II, 13, Schol., G II, p. 97, ll. 7–9 [CWS I, 458].

[265] Spinoza never defines what he means by *conscius* and *conscientia*, but it is clear that (1) it is most often a matter of being conscious of one's *own* acts, *own* desires and *own* causes (cf. *Ethics* I, App., G II, p. 78, ll. 16–20 [CWS I, 440]; *Ethics* II, 35, Schol., p. 117, ll. 14–15 [CWS I, 473]; *Ethics* III, 9, Dem. and Schol., p. 147, ll. 15–17, 24–25, p. 148, ll. 2–3 [CWS I, 499–500]), etc.; and (2) that consciousness does not necessarily imply adequate perception, cf. A. Matheron, *Individu et Communauté* p. 63–78.

whole. There are no divergences between the ideas of the organs and the idea of the body.²⁶⁶ Certainly, the body is subject to external aggressions since it is itself a part of Nature. But if illness and other disequilibriums lead to violations of the general order of the body, leading to its destruction,²⁶⁷ they do not prevent it from having an identity, save in exceptional cases.²⁶⁸

It is clear that on this point, human individuals united in a State can in no way be assimilated with the organs of a body. Where bodily organs are integrated to the precise degree that they are differentiated, men, as members of the State – as of any other association – are, on the contrary, essentially the same. Such a similarity does not prevent the union of bodies: in fact, Spinoza takes care to tell us that it actually makes it possible. But this union occurs according to a different model: that of suitability and no longer of differentiation.²⁶⁹ The unity of the collective body is based on a conjunction of multiple *conatus* that are geared towards producing an analogous effect. This is obviously the case for a group of sectarians who together seek salvation by means of their rituals, or for a society of amateur theatre-goers who meet to devise rules for dramaturgy or for staging comedies. This is also the case for those who live in a single State, although the goal here – namely, peace and security – is more complex and requires the implementation of means that are more numerous and more difficult to determine and unify. It can be said that, from the perspective of diversity, the State or any other human association is a poor composite. As a consequence, the *mens* that corresponds to such a body will be poorly differentiated and possess very little spontaneous consciousness. More generally, we can expect the soul of an association of human beings to present a weak identity, one more or less centred on the idea that expresses the unique goal of all the identical and conjugated efforts that make up the group's constituent parts. This explains, moreover, the

---

²⁶⁶ This rule is true at each level: all the parts of the blood are under the domination of the same nature, as in its turn the blood is a part governed by the laws of the whole body (cf. Ep. XXXII, G IV, pp. 170–3 [*Ep.* XXXII [to Henry Oldenburg]; CWS II, 18–20]).

²⁶⁷ Cf. *Ethics* IV, 39 and Dem. [CWS I, 568–9].

²⁶⁸ This is the case of the Spanish poet mentioned in the Scholium to Proposition 39. Even in this case, identity is replaced rather than undermined: before and after his illness the amnesiac knows nothing of the division of the soul. Spinoza does not give any examples of a doubling of the personality.

²⁶⁹ Cf. the characterisation that the Scholium from Proposition 18 from Book IV gives. It is suitability, in the preferred form of similarity, that regulates in this instance the possibility of forming a unique individual. Cf. the Appendix to the same Book: 'Nihil magis cum natura alicujus rei convenire potest, quam reliqua ejusdem speciei individua', 9, G II, p. 268, ll. 20–1 [CWS I, 589].

facility with which people pass from one superstitious sect to another: seeing the attachment and violence with which they defend their beliefs, one could be led to think that these beliefs are durable. In fact, it is their violent character alone that is durable, and these people pass easily from one belief to another – which supposes that no belief has sufficient individuality for its believers to identify with it in a durable fashion.[270]

This leads us to a second difference, which has to do with the relative autonomy of human individuals and the State. We can express this relative autonomy as follows: each one of the component parts of the State has a desire. To the extent that human beings are conscious of their appetites, these appetites take the form of desires and are expressed in the soul of each individual.[271] This soul, which is closely integrated with and conscious of its appetites, does not necessarily have any immediate reason to recognise itself in the soul of the State. It can be led by its own passions in an opposite direction. Above all, even if an elementary calculus shows that its interests lie in being part of society, why should this soul swear allegiance to one State rather than another? Why accommodate itself to the State's current structure and not invest all of its hopes in another? If many component individuals reason in this way, the identity of the State is threatened.[272] The risk of the State losing what constitutes it as a State is thus given at the outset in its specific type of composition. Each of the *mentes* that belong to the individuals who compose the State can function as a centrifugal element. This is true of the State; it is also true of other complex ensembles: non-political

---

[270] 'Quam itaque facile fit, ut homines quovis superstitione capiantur, tam difficile contra est efficere, ut in uno eodemque perstent', *TTP*, Preface G III, p. 6, ll. 24–6 [*TTP* Praef., 8; CWS II, 68]. In certain respects, Spinoza's entire body of work is defined by the concern with what could be called a psycho-sociology of sects. It will be said that he was witness to many, as he was to conversions and controversies as well. Yet – to return to a problem that we dealt with on the topic of the alleged biographical materials that lay behind the *TdIE* – it is not prohibited to think that Spinoza's reflections on the structures of identity fail to give us instruments for truly thinking the intellectual history of the Second Reformation and the spiritual disturbances of the classical age, rather than them appearing as a collection of irrational behaviours or as a repertoire of 'sources' for philosophical and theological discussions.

[271] *Ethics* III, 9, Schol.; DA #1 and Schol. [CWS I, 531].

[272] In the passage cited above concerning superstitions, Spinoza continues as follows: 'imo quia vulgus semper aeque miserum manet, ideo nusquam diu acquiescit, sed id tantum eidem maxime placet, quod novum est, quodque nondum fefallit, quae quidem inconstantia multorum tumultuum, et bellorum atrocium causa fuit', *TTP*, Preface, p. 6, ll. 26–30 [*TTP* Praef., 8; CWS II, 68]. This appeal of novelty is also true for political structures – cf. Chapters XVI and XVII.

associations, gangs of dogs or packs of wolves. It is not true of the human individual or of the barking dog. These latter individuals are not constituted by centrifugal elements. The liver or the heart have ideas that correspond to them in the attribute thought; irrespective of whether we can call these ideas *mentes*,[273] we cannot attribute to them a desire that would tend to efface or attenuate the identity of the *mens* of the integrated whole of which they are parts.[274] There is thus a *mens* of the State and a *mens* of individuals, one that is highly differentiated and thus highly conscious. These *mens* can thus enter into conflict.[275]

But in this case the unity of the State comes down to the efficacy of the relations between its centrifugal elements. The problem proper to the State is therefore: how can we make each person identify maximally with the *mens* of the State? In other words: how can we make it so that all human beings are, despite the autonomy of their *mens*, led *una veluti mente*? It has perhaps not been sufficiently remarked that each time Spinoza uses this expression, he does so in a phrase where it is a question not of *composing* something like a common soul but of making it so that all are *led* as if by a common soul. It is not a matter of creating the *mens* of the State; this *mens* is given as soon as the State exists. It is a matter of making this *mens* the point of reference for the *mentes* of human individuals. If the *mens* of the State is given as soon as there is a State, the union of hearts[276] is in no way given. Spinoza clearly affirms this in the passage from the *Political Treatise* where he shows the power of Reason at work both in the case of the human individual and in that of the City.[277] All people have a *mens*, but not all are guided by Reason,

---

[273] If we accept that a single idea of a thing is a *mens*, and reserve the term *res* for fragments of extension that have a certain autonomy, that is, a system of internal laws. It seems to me that this is how Spinoza uses these words, even if he does not render this explicit in a systematic fashion. In any case, it matters little: even if we were to call 'thing' every fragment of extension, and '*mens*' every idea of a thing, it would be no less the case that the ideas of non-autonomous fragments would have little consciousness.

[274] The beehive or the anthill that are dear to political theorists are thus rather on the side of the organism than on the side of human beings or wolves.

[275] Whence the insistence on repeating that a State is always more threatened by its citizens than by external enemies. The same cannot be said of the human body.

[276] I am translating *animus* here by 'heart' to distinguish it from *mens*.

[277] 'sicuti in statu naturali ille homo maxime potens, maximeque sui juris est, qui ratione ducitur, sic etiam illa civitas maxime erit potens, & maxime sui juris, qua ratione fundatur et dirigitur. Nam civitatis jus potentia multitudinis, quae una veluti mente ducitur, determinatur. At haec animorum unio concipi nulla ratione posset, nisi civitas id ipsum maxime indendat, quod sana ratio omnibus hominibus utile esse docet', TP, Chapter III, 7, G III, p. 287, ll. 4–11 [TP III, 7; CWS II, 520].

which gives them maximal power. Similarly, every State has a *mens*, but it does not necessarily make effective the *animorum unio* that would give it maximal power. To ensure that people are guided *una veluti mente*, one must produce a union of hearts.[278] Thus, the existence of a soul for the State refers to the fact of composition; the union of the souls of citizens refers to the process of integration.[279] This is a process because it is necessary to put mechanisms in place that ensure that the bodies of the State will be able to forge for themselves the identity possessed spontaneously by the biological body. This is why the naturalness of the State does not prevent it from having legislators and indeed politicians who seek empirically to realise the best possible equilibrium between its institutions.

Two remarks remain to be made:

— This distinction between different sorts of complex beings appears to the imagination without the causes that produce it. It is thus given as a distinction between 'natural beings' and 'artificial beings'. This distinction, along with the ideology of artifice and of the *contract* – the latter being a specification of this ideology – is is no way due to individual arbitrariness. It constitutes the imaginary of the State in general. This is why the image that the concept of Right produces of the State is precisely that of an association.[280]

— One might object that in our analyses we are confusing references to the *Political Treatise* and references to the *TTP*. But it seems to me that Spinoza's doctrine in these two *Treatises*, at least in terms of the problem that concerns us here, is not fundamentally different. What differs is the perspective taken, and for an important reason: the *TTP* takes the imaginary of the State at its word and thus proceeds as if society were constituted on the basis of individuals; the *TP* abandons this imaginary and passes directly to the study of mechanisms of integration.[281]

---

[278] The reader will notice the parallelism in the vocabulary with Book IV of the *Ethics*. The individual is more free so long as they are led (*ductus*) by Reason. The State functions better so long as its component parts are led (*duci*) as if by a single soul.

[279] This integration will itself be optimal when the City seeks 'id ipsum quod sana ratio omnibus hominibus utile esse docet'. Reason itself ensures the link by suitability between similar people. This does not require that people themselves be reasonable. We will see this further on.

[280] In this sense, strictly speaking, the analysis proposed by Den Uyl does not seem false to me. It rigorously describes this imaginary of the State.

[281] On the topic of the evolution between the *TTP* and the *TP*, this work has already been done in the inaugural article by A. Menzel, 'Wandlungen in der Staatslehre Spinoza's', *Festschrift für J. Unger zum 70. Geburtstage*, Stuttgart, 1898, pp. 51–86 – in particular on the 'juridico-constructive' form in which the origin of the State is still

B. We can now move on to the second level, that of integration by suitability. What are the means of this integration? What has just been said is valid for every human association – not only for the State, but also for a sect of fanatics, an association of theatre actors, or the crew of a ship. All are united in a common effort, all have a soul that translates this effort, all are threatened by the desires of individual souls. But between these human groups, can we not again establish a distinction at the level of forms of complexity? Such a distinction can be provided by the tenor of the associative relation. For what actually stops these groups from exploding? In the case of the group of sectarians or actors, it is a unique trait, one that is the same for all. Whoever ceases to share the common faith, or be interested in dramatic art, immediately leaves the group (things are not so simple, of course, but abstractly we can consider this to be true). Such an association is thus a simple group of complex parts united by a simple relation. The soul of this group is thus quite poor, only minimally differentiated, and, while it can momentarily unite the souls of its component individuals, this is thanks only to the liveliness of a passion that makes these individuals forget their differences.[282] The soul of the individual only identifies with the soul of the group at the time and to the extent that its efforts are identical to the common effort. What about the State? Its situation is different. It does not aim at a unique trait, one that can be easily defined. It aims at peace and security, and indeed at more than this[283] – that is, it aims at something that engages the entire life of men. To subsist, human beings must necessarily cooperate and distribute tasks,[284] creating a multitude of functions and institutions that are like the organs of the State. What links a judge to a military person, a private individual or a priest, are very different functions, along with relations of money and justice, and so on. The State is thus a simple group of complex parts united

---

being thought in the *TTP* and its replacement by a 'psychological realist' form in the *Ethics* and the *TP*. But Menzel clearly underscores the minor character of these variations with respect to the continuity of a solid *Gedankenkern*, which he characterises in terms of utilitarianism and positivism.

[282] *Mutatis mutandis*, we find here the distinction between richness and vivacity that we found in the analysis of the imagination.

[283] 'Non tantum ad secure ab hostibus vivendum, se etiam ad multarum rerum compendium faciendum', *TTP*, Chapter V, G III, p. 73, l. 14 [*TTP* V, 18; *CWS* II, 143].

[284] Spinoza describes this in the *TTP*, Chapter V, p. 73, ll. 17–24 [*TTP* V, 18; *CWS* II, 143], after having summarised this point by way of the expression *operam mutuam dare*. On the precise meaning of this expression, in this passage and in the Appendix to Book IV of the *Ethics*, cf. U. Goldenbaum's discussion, 'Zu einer vermintlichen Textlücke in Spinozas *Ethica ordiner geometrico demonstrata*, *Deutsche Zeitschrift für Philosophie*, 32/11 (1984), pp. 1036–40.

by complex relations. Its richness, which here is not given by the differentiation of its component parts, is given by the variety of their relations. At this point the soul of the State can begin to become more differentiated. In a certain way, this play of relations can even be foregrounded, and instead of saying that the components of the State are individuals, we can say that they are institutions: this is why Spinoza uses both definitions.[285] Thus, the citizen's soul can identify with the soul of the State, not in the precarious unilaterality of a single effort, but in the durable expression of a complex play of tasks and interests.

What allows for the neutralisation of individuals' centrifugal tendencies is without any doubt violence. But it is obviously also, and even more so, the mechanisms of different economic and political interests.[286] These mechanisms help citizens minimise their hostility to the State. Commercial exchanges, the election and delegation of magistrates, the circulation of money, all contribute to making the associations of bodies, which tend towards peace and security, a truly integrated structure, with the bodies reciprocally communicating their movements following fixed and regulated laws.[287] These mechanisms thus constitute, with respect to the human community, the concrete form of a union of forces. In contrast to the human body, which represents an integration by differentiation, we find here a form of integration by constitution. This process takes place in extension and obviously has its corresponding side in thought. Thus, to the extent that they have an adequate representation, or a moderately adequate one, of their own interests, citizens will defend the State and their soul will identify with the State's soul by means of clearly delineated processes.[288] Moreover, it is when he is describing these mechanisms that Spinoza most often uses the expression *una veluti mente*. Thus, in an aristocracy, it is necessary to institute laws that bind responsible patricians to authority in such a way that they cannot stray from this authority, all the while remaining equal among themselves. The key institution of the guilds will serve to maintain these laws. In this way, something like a unique body can be formed, governed

---

[285] Whence, for the distinction between nations, the variant *ratione societatis et legum*, which does not engage individuals, *TTP*, Chapter III, G III, p. 47, ll. 26–7 [*TTP* III, 16; *CWS* II, 114].

[286] Cf. *TTP*, Chapter V, G III, p. 73, l. 35; p. 74, l. 8 [*TTP* V, 21, 22; *CWS* II, 144].

[287] Cf. my analysis above of the responses to the affective kernel of antipolitics, as well as the already cited studies by S. Zac, 'Spinoza et l'Etat des Hébreux', and *Philosophie, théologie, politique dans l'œuvre de Spinoza*, pp. 145–76.

[288] Cf. *Ethics* III, 19–26 and 45 [*CWS* I, 505–7, 519].

by a single soul.²⁸⁹ Such a gathering, if it is sufficiently large, will have more of a chance of conforming to Reason, which in turn will help the assembly from being enslaved to the Plebs. In fact, the minimal appearance of Reason in desires is necessary to lead a large group of people as if by a single soul.²⁹⁰ This appearance is not identical to Reason itself but is rather some common passion (hatred, fear, a common desire for vengeance) that pushes people to naturally agree and to accept being led as if by a single soul.²⁹¹

The State is not only an association with a strong composition but a weak integration. Its institutional system can give it a stronger degree of integration, where the physical differentiation between component parts is replaced by a differentiation of tasks and a multiplication of organs, which people accept because this differentiation serves to better ensure the satisfaction of their common needs. Their souls should then be able to quieten the irreducibility of their desires and seek recognition in the soul of the State, at least to the degree that this is necessary for the common effort.

C. 'Should' and not 'must' . . . For in fact, a difficulty remains. To function, the preceding system of integration requires a minimum of adequate representation on the part of the State's citizens. This is why Spinoza sometimes says that the man guided by Reason knows that nothing is more useful to man than other men. Yet, as we have seen, individuals necessarily possess an inadequate relation to the City. They know the City in the same way they know their external body: the idea that they form of the City is more the idea of the encounter between themselves and the effects that the City produces (for instance, a particular benefit, an inconvenience or a momentary passion) and less the adequate idea of the totality of the City's functioning. In these conditions, the play of political and economic interests that joins citizens together in a single body does not immediately give rise to a clear identification of their souls with the soul of the State. How, then, can we prevent a relative erasure of the necessity of the State, and above all of citizens' identification with *this* State? For it is only the necessity of the

---

²⁸⁹ 'Ut unum veluti corpus, quod una regitur mente, componant', TP, Chapter VIII, 19, p. 331, ll. 27–8 [TP VIII, 19; CWS II, 572].

²⁹⁰ 'Nam concilii adeo magni voluntas non tam a libidine, quam a raione determinari potest; quippe homines ex malo affectu diverse trahuntur, nec una veluti mente duci possunt, nisi quatenus honesta appetunt, vel saltem quae speciem honesti habent', TP, Chapter VIII, 6, G III, p. 326, ll. 17–21 [TP VIII, 6; CWS II, 567].

²⁹¹ 'Multitudinem non ex rationi ductu, sed ex communi aliquo affectu naturaliter convenire et una veluti mente convenire', TP, Chapter VI, 1, G III, p. 297, ll. 14–16 [TP VI, 1; CWS II, 532].

passions that can make citizens desire another State, another government, the appeal of the foreign. We thus find ourselves faced with a third problem: in addition to the association between human beings and the mechanisms of integration, it is necessary to determine how the soul of each person can positively represent their relation to the totality in the absence of an adequate representation of this totality.

Machiavelli said that it was necessary, at regular intervals, to reduce the State to its principles.[292] Spinoza repeats this claim after him – but to Machiavelli's political solution he prefers a passionate or imaginary solution. He deals with this question in the *Political Treatise* on the topic of the risk of decadence in an aristocracy. He begins by identifying as a danger a tendency towards the loss of national identity: what is foreign comes to be preferred over ancestral traditions. Spinoza sees here a natural tendency of souls that have been relieved of fear. The authority of the guilds (to which Spinoza accords a function that corresponds to that of the Roman dictator, minus the dangers) can put an end to those vices that fall under the sword of the law. It will not be able to prevent the infiltration of 'vices the law can't prevent'.[293] Yet these vices are often the cause of the State's ruin. 'In peace, when fear has been set aside, men gradually change from being savage and warlike to being political *or* civilized, and from being civilised, they become soft and lazy. One tries to surpass another, not in excellence, but in arrogance and extravagant living. As a result, they begin to treat their native customs with disdain, and take on foreign fashions – that is, they begin to become slaves.'[294]

Why is following foreign traditions the same as habituating oneself to slavery? Because not only will one no longer resist in the case of a foreign war, above all one will always be ready to cede to internal disorders, which come from citizens, mercenaries or a government that seeks to transform itself into a tyranny. All of these disorders lead to a violent modification of the play of equilibrium that constitutes the State's individuality – that is, to destroying it. The loss of the State's identity thus precedes and prepares its loss in the proper sense.

Against this loss of national identity, negative measures have no efficacy.

---

[292] *Discorsi*, III, 1. Spinoza cites him at the beginning of Chapter X of the *TP*.

[293] 'Sed nequaquam efficere poterit, ne vitia, quae leges, prohiberi nequeunt, gliscant', *TP*, Chapter X, 4, G III, p. 355, ll. 17–18 [*TP* X, 4; *CWS* II, 598].

[294] 'Homines enim in pace deposito metu paulatim ex ferocibus et barbaris civiles, seu humani, & ex humanis molles & inertes fiunt, nec alius alium virtute sed fastu & luxu excellere studet; unde patrios mores fastidire, alienos induere, hoc est servire incipiunt', ibid., ll. 19–23 [*TP* X, 4; *CWS* II, 598–9].

They excite contempt; more than this, they excite citizens' desires: we want what is refused us.[295] The only solution is to counterbalance these measures with positive mechanisms of attachment to the State – that is, mechanisms that determine that people can recognise themselves in it.

In fact, even if citizens do not *know* the State and its advantages adequately, they can *recognise* them thanks to those traits that make up the State's *ingenium* and that constitute their relation to its *ingenium*. The problem this time consists in concretising the State's *mens* – in making it appear in such a way that it is acceptable to and recognisable by the *mentes* of individuals. It is here that the symbolic comes into play. It is not a matter of 'creating' a people, but of giving to a people, by way of laws, morals and language, a specific configuration. It is necessary to create ideas that attach the souls of individuals to the souls of the State. Now, alongside these ideas there must necessarily exist a corresponding element in extension – a point of linkage, which, in the corporeal order, represents imaginarily the individuality of the State: an image associated with all of the State's advantages; an image or chain of images that represents the totality for each individual. We are as close here as it is possible to get to the necessary root of the symbolic order.

A first response to this problem is given by rites, or ceremonies. In truth, these are ambiguous. It could be said that the rite is an anthropological necessity, logically prior to the State to the extent that when a person thinks of divinity, or of *rectores naturae*, they make use of rites to motivate their devotion or to appease the *ingenium* that they supposes the *rectores* to possess.[296] At this level, the rite is an extension of the image. At a second level, the drive towards ritual is used by the State as well, which employs it for its own purposes and interests – for instance, in the case of the Hebrews, to reinforce the Hebrew people's devotion and to constantly remind them of it. At this level, the rite responds to the second but also the third level that we identified above in the individualisation of the State. But the rite is then a law of the State.[297] As a law, it has power and contributes to maintaining the State's equilibrium. Finally, we can envisage rights that are no longer laws but that continue to subsist as means for private devotion, albeit without any political validity. However, if such rites subsist in a group, it is because the group still considers itself the bearer of a certain identity; it

---

[295] TP, Chapter X, 4, G III, pp. 355–6 [*TP* X, 4; CWS II, 598–9].
[296] *Ethics* I, App. [CWS I, 439–46]; *TTP*, Chapter V, p. 72, l. 3; p. 73, l. 2 [*TTP* V, 16; CWS II, 143].
[297] This is the meaning of Chapter 5 of the *TTP*.

still has a collective memory in the context of which the rite can take on a meaning.

But we can go further than the rite – namely, to the symbol. In what sense are are these two distinct? Spinoza opposes the external rite to the sign.[298] But why is the sign internal? Because it interpellates the individual as such and makes them directly conceive of their relation to the people of which they are a member. Spinoza gives a number of examples of this symbolic order: circumcision among the Hebrews, braids among the Chinese, fringes among patricians. I will return further on to his analysis of these examples. It is first necessary to note that Spinoza gathers all of these from experience, or at least that he in no way deduces their singular existence. It could be said that circumcision is tied to the belief in God's choice of Israel, but Spinoza does not mention this; he is content to cite circumcision as an example of a sign. The braids of the Chinese are also cited as a simple fact, without any attempt at historical explanation.[299] Finally, Spinoza proposes the fringe of patricians' clothing as an element of the typical States described in the *Political Treatise*. Once again, we notice the articulation between reason and experience: rational deduction can demonstrate the necessity of a symbolic order for making citizens adhere to their community; only experience can teach us what sign has played this role and if it has truly succeeded in doing so.[300]

We should note that with this politics of adhesion, Spinoza goes beyond the framework of the classical theory of the State. The theories of the pact, whatever their variations, all come down to a conjunction between commitment (juridical or quasi-juridical) and force. They are logics of obedience. When Spinoza begins to reflect on the symbolic conditions of individuals' adhesion, he displaces the question of this logic of obedience. He thus identifies a problem that will have to wait a long time before it is thematised by reflections on the State.[301]

---

[298] The Jews are distinguished 'non tantum ritibus externis, ritibus caeterarum nationum contrariis, sed etiam signo circumcisionis', *TTP*, Chapter III, G III, p. 56, ll. 23–5 [*TTP* III, 52; *CWS* II, 124].

[299] It is in fact less old than Spinoza believes. But this is of no importance for the argument.

[300] That the hatred provoked by separation (that is, by the conservation of identity) sufficed to conserve the Jews, 'id jam experientia docuit', *TTP*, Chapter III, G III, p. 56, ll. 25–6 [*TTP* III, 53; *CWS* II, 124].

[301] This is not the place to deal with this question, though it seems to me that this logic of adhesion and identity will have to wait for the twentieth century, from Arendt to Habermas, to find a space in which it becomes intelligible again. This space

C. The Affective Root of the Symbolic and Its Effects

The logic of adhesion reveals where the most fundamental consistency of a symbolic order lies. This order does not arise out of nothing. We have just seen in what sense it is useful; we will now identify how it is rooted in the play of the affects, while its material is rooted in the productive mechanisms of language.

The foundation of such a theory of collective identity is given implicitly in Book III of the *Ethics*. There, Spinoza identifies the mechanisms by which we associate an entire group with our love or hatred.[302] Through the dynamics of transference, interpersonal feelings are produced by the imitation of the affects. Spinoza says this in the context of discussing groups that are foreign to us. But his reasoning is just as valid for groups we belong to. In fact, he makes this point in just this way in the *Political Treatise*, on the occasion of advancing a particular argument – an argument he nevertheless gives as if it were a universal rule: namely, that we aspire to a group identity. Each person wants to be distinguished from others by reference to their community: 'everyone is so constituted by nature that he wants to be reckoned as belonging to his own kind, and to be distinguished from the rest by his origin'.[303] There thus exists within the play of our affects an affective material that serves as a foundation for the symbolic. As for the support of this distinction, it can have diverse origins: it can be borrowed from a rite, from an historical particularity, or it can be invented.

The material that serves to carry this collective identity is the productive mechanisms of signs, which we saw at work in the case of language. The sign is not necessarily a word. Here, it is an anchoring point in the body or an ornament of clothing. Why? Perhaps because such a relation produces a greater force of immediacy.[304] The word is common to all because it is not

---

falls short, moreover, in many respects, of the possibilities opened up by Spinoza's interrogations.

[302] 'Si quis ab aliquo cujusdam classis sive nationis a sua diversae, laetitia vel tristitia affectus fuerit, concomitante ejus idea, sub nomine universali classis vel nationis, tanquam causa: is non tantum illum, sed omnes ejusdem classis vel nationis amabit vel odio habebit', *Ethics* III, 46, G II, p. 175, ll. 13–17 [CWS I, 520] Cf. Matheron, *Individu et Communauté*, pp. 208–9.

[303] 'Omnes natura ita comparati sunt, ut unusquisque generi suo adscribi velit, et stirpe a reliquis internosci', TP, Chapter VII, 18, G III, p. 309, ll. 22–4 [TP VII, 18; CWS II, 553].

[304] On gestural and bodily signifiers, cf. M. Bertrand, *Spinoza et l'imaginaire*, Paris: PUF, 1983, pp. 121–2 and p. 144.

appropriated by anyone. The symbol is common to all only because it marks each person.

It remains to determine what different effects the symbolic produces. It is these traits that make a people a people and allow each individual to recognise themselves in the community, which itself is marked by a specific individuality. In sum, not only does experiential reasoning lead Spinoza to think the notion of the *ingenium* so as to identify the visible individuality of a given human being or people; the same logic leads him to once again seek out in history those signs that each human being recognises in themselves insofar as they belong to a people. The perspective Spinoza takes here on a people is no longer quite the same as the one he takes on the question of Right or the theoretical construction of the State. By following the thread of these questions, we see examples and reflections appear that considerably nuance the State-centred logic of his general argument – not by putting it in question but by aligning its conclusions with the existential diversity history presents us with. This is why to the question 'Can there be a people without a State or a State without a people?', a Spinozist response will have to be nuanced. The people and the State are logically constitutive of one another – as is the case in theories of the pact. Yet, if, in the strict sense, there can be no State without a people, what can happen is a degradation of the mechanisms of a people's identification with a State. This is what risks happening in the case of the patricians cited above. It is also what happened in the Netherlands, and it explains how easy it was for the form of the State to be disrupted: the people no longer recognised this structure. In the theoretical case of aristocracy, Spinoza responds with a proposition that is clearly formulated in terms of identity: all of the patricians distinguish themselves by special clothing;[305] when the young people arrive at the required age, they receive 'a mark of honour',[306] and Spinoza concludes a little further on by saying: 'they'll never desire foreign dress, or scorn that of their native land, if the law establishes that the Patricians, and those who seek offices, are distinguished by special clothing'.[307]

Conversely, there can be no people without a State in the strict sense, that is, in a veritable state of nature or a society without institutions. But we can conceive of two situations that come close to this possibility: the first is either a situation of catastrophe, whether positive or negative, which strips a people of any State authority for a brief period. We know of at least three examples of this, all of them violent acts: the Hebrews in the desert,

---

[305] *TP*, Chapter VIII, 45, G III, p. 345, ll. 31–2 [*TP* VIII, 45; CWS II, 587].
[306] *TP*, Chapter VIII, 25, G III, p. 333, l. 35; p. 334, l. 1 [*TP* VIII, 25; CWS II, 574].
[307] *TP*, Chapter X, 7, G III, p. 356, ll. 18–20 [*TP* X, 7; CWS II, 599].

the Dutch when they chased out the Spaniards, and the Aragonese when they chased out the Maures. But even in such cases there is no absolute creation: the people already possess certain traits, which come to them from their prior history: the Hebrews were made into beasts by the Egyptians, the Dutch were familiar with a certain kind of State.

The second case corresponds to what happens when a people loses its State identity, either by dispersion or conquest. It is remarkable that nobody in the classical age poses the question in this way. The question of the right of conquest is dealt with, but not the identity of the vanquished.[308] Now, Spinoza is interested in, precisely, this problem of identity, which is one of the blind spots of the theory of the pact. He gives two examples of this problem at the end of Chapter III from the *TTP*. In asking a *quaestio vexata* – why did the Jews subsist after the loss of their State? – the *TTP* introduces a number of elements of a response to this question. The response subtly modifies the question. Note first that Spinoza in no way inquires into the survival of beliefs. His problem is the continuation of a recognisable community. This community has survived not because it needed its laws – once it was integrated into another State, it drew its life from this second State's laws and was thus required to obey them – but rather because it had a sense of identity that determined that its ancient laws, or certain of these laws, now transformed into pure rites, had subsisted independently of their foundation in the State.[309] The first explanation is hatred – a mark of difference. But this hatred, which comes from others, must also be explained. It is here that the role of the symbol intervenes as a factor in separation – that is, in the delimitation of a people: the feeling of recognition, tied to circumcision. Here, then, is a symbol that responds to the affective drive towards identity. It could even, Spinoza adds, lead to the reconstitution of the State.[310]

---

[308] Hobbes, *Leviathan*, Part II, Chapter XX.

[309] Many years after the *TTP*, the letter to Albert Burgh returns to this question (Ep. LXXVI, G IV, p. 321 [*Ep.* LXXVI [to Albert Burgh]; CWS II, 476]). It reaffirms the essential: namely, the fact – 'de non interrupta succcesione'; and the condition – it is not the law of the State that accounts for this continuity, but only the force of superstition. The letter does not analyse the means of this force, but this is because the problematic in which this question appears is different: it is about knowing if the duration of the Catholic Church is a proof of its truth, and above all if it is unique.

[310] In parts of the preceding analysis, we are close to the positions of Ze'ev Levy, *Baruch or Benedict: On Some Jewish Aspects of Spinoza's Philosophy*, Frankfurt: Peter Lang, 1989. However, Levy seems to restrict the problem by not asking about the affective root of the symbolic. Furthermore, the affirmation according to which for Spinoza the Jews could only reconstitute their State by abandoning their religion contradicts the letter of the text.

It will be noted that this explanation contradicts the two traditional rival explanations of the survival of the Jews: the Christian notion of a people of witness,[311] and the Jewish conception of protection by election.[312] We see here the concept of a people or nation in a form that is distinct from the concept of the State. This is all the more important to highlight since the general thrust of the argument is rather 'statist', and Spinoza does not yield at all on this point. After the end of the Hebrew State, the Jews are *bound* to nothing:[313] it is not laws that remain. What, then, maintains their belonging to a community? Their rites and ceremonies do not suffice; moreover, the latter lose their legal value: these rites subsist only as a function of a choice made by a group of individuals who carry out these rites as part of their sense of identity.[314]

When Spinoza speaks of the reconstitution of the State of the Hebrews, it is as an irreality. But take the following historical fact: the Chinese braid. The Chinese are in an analogous situation to the Hebrews, save that they are not dispersed when they lose their State. They are deprived of it on their own territory by an invader who makes them its subjects and governs them. Logically, the Chinese should disappear and dissolve into the new dominant population. Yet it is the opposite that happens. Why? Because the symbol of their braid allows them to conserve a stronger identity than that of their vanquishers.

---

[311] The classic expression of this is Augustine, *De Civitate Dei*, Book XVIII, Chapter 46, where the theme of witnessing conditions that of dispersion, from Psalm LIX. Cf. J. Isaac, *Genèse de l'antisémitisme*, Paris: Calmann-Lévy, 1956, p. 168 ff.; F. Lovsky, *L'Antisémitisme chrétien*, Paris: Cerf, 1970, p. 179 ff.

[312] Saul Levi Mortera, *Tratado da Verdade da lei de Moises, escrito pelo seu proprio punho em português em Amsterdao 659–1660*, ediçao facsimilada e leitura do autografo, introduçao e comentario por H. P. Salomon, Coimbra Acta Universitatis Conimbrigensis, 1988, for example chapters XI–XII, XVI, XXI: Mortera's whole project is to show the continuity of divine attention for Israel, each one of the miracles of Exodus having its correlate in the modern epoch.

[313] 'To be bound' in all of these texts has a technical meaning: it is a matter of what we must do to preserve our being. It is therefore about the way that the laws of nature justify our obedience to a human law, however we learn it (by revelation, by the passions, by Reason). It is also necessary to note that to no longer be bound to a law does not signify that one is not allowed to follow it. One can do so to the extent that it does not contradict the law of the City.

[314] We should mention here Hermann Cohen's critiques, who identifies a Christian perspective in this thesis on the end of Jewish laws. I have shown above that this is in no way the case. The end of the Law is tied to the end of the State. Spinoza never ties one or the other to the coming of Christ. Cf. S. Zac, *La philosophie de H. Cohen*, Paris: Vrin, 1984.

Thus, on two occasions, Spinoza identifies in historical experience the subsistence of the identity of a people, without this people conserving their State authority. In sum, while the demonstrative argument seeks to establish natural laws that concern the State – for what reasons and in what conditions human beings live grouped into States; how the State regulates civil life; what freedoms it grants its citizens – experiential analysis brings to light the concrete ways in which each people uses common affective materials to forge an identity. This analysis never contradicts the demonstrative reasoning: it occurs within its limits. Note that the symbols by which a people recognises itself have been given to it by their State, even if these symbols survive the State. Note also the insistence with which Spinoza recalls that one is not obliged to follow a law when it has no more legal value. But this reflection itself leads him to inquire more precisely into the moment when the laws cease to apply. When do the laws of the State end? Eleazar was right to combat 'while his country was still standing as best it could'.[315] The adverb here does not refer to sovereignty in the strong sense of the term: rather, it is probable that the fragments of sovereignty had held together thanks to beliefs and symbols that had remained intact.

What has just been said is valid for all States. Would it not, then, also be valid for other groups? Spinoza begins to respond to this question as regards the rites of the early Christian Church. 'Moreover', Spinoza says, 'after the Gospel began to be preached also to other nations, who were bound by the legislation of another Republic, the Apostles set aside ceremonies.'[316] This statement coheres with what comes before: so long as the Apostles preach only to Jews, they submit to the laws of the Hebrew State – and thus to the ceremonies that are part of it. When they preach to others, they abandon these laws. However, it can be noted that the early Christians instituted new ceremonies. It is thus necessary to explain their status. Here, Spinoza admits to being uncertain as to their origin: do they come from Christ or from the Apostles? There is no clear answer. In any case, we must first define these ceremonies negatively: they are external (Spinoza says this twice) and thus contribute nothing to beatitude; they are not political (they are not instituted by a Church-State, nor by another State) and thus seem to correspond to none of the three honest goals of human conduct. The response is: they are external signs of the universal Church. The adjective 'universal' should not be misunderstood. If a Christian lives in a State where these signs are

---

[315] 'Stante adhuc utcunque Patria', *TTP*, Chapter XVI, p. 200, ll. 15–16 [*TTP* XVI, 66; *CWS* II, 295].
[316] *TTP*, Chapter V [*TTP* 14; *CWS* II, 142].

prohibited, he will have to abstain from them. This universality is submitted to the jurisdiction of political singularities. But even with such a restricted status, what we see here is that the Church possesses a social status in an embryonic state. It is quite rare to read such an indication in the writings of one of the defenders of sovereignty. On this point, experiential analysis identifies a strata of social reality that the discussion of the *jus circa sacra* had tended to obscure.[317]

We can now summarise what we have said above. By interrogating the Spinozist theory of the affects, I have shown that it is not reducible to a deductive demonstration. This perspective also allows us to understand how Spinoza can address, at the margins of his text, questions that are barely visible to the theory of the passions and the theory of right of his time. Experience teaches us the laws of the passions, both for the individual as for society. It thus redoubles the lesson of the demonstrations. As for the individuality of the human being as of a people, experience allows us to grasp it or to include it in the argument, at the very point where the demonstration by itself lets this singularity escape. Finally, by repeatedly identifying certain irreducible givens of history, it allows us to exit the geometry of the pact and begin to think the problems that this geometry masks: collective identity, the threat of the State's dissolution, the identification of the individual – an entire logic of adhesion that, outside of Spinozism, the classical age hardly knew.

---

[317] Here, too, it would be necessary to go further by reference to the indications from the letter to Albert Burgh. But these aim less to construct a theory than to refute a panegyric.

10

Fields of Experience: History

When one has rejected the categories of election and of the direct intervention of the Absolute in history, does there remain a field for historical experience? At the very least, one still has to explain how individuals and Cities confront not only their own passions but also what they cannot predict: the pure power of exteriority. It is in this exposure to exteriority that Spinoza identifies the historicity of man, in abstraction from any figure of providence as from any historical finality.[1]

1. Fortune

As its Preface announces, the whole of Book IV of the *Ethics* is devoted to explaining a *de facto* state of affairs. This state of affairs is one that we are all familiar with; Spinoza is simply reminding us of it. He does so in the following terms: 'Man's lack of power to moderate and restrain the affects I call Bondage. For the man who is subject to affects is under the control, not of himself, but of fortune, in whose power he so greatly is that often, though he sees the better for himself, he is still forced to follow the worse.'[2] We are dealing here with each individual person taken in isolation. But if we are seeking an explanation for superstition, which leads both the great and the common astray, we should read the first sentence from the *TTP*: 'If men could manage all their affairs by a definite plan, or if fortune were always

---

[1] I will deal more fully with the Spinozist problematic of history in a forthcoming commentary on the *TTP*. I will only indicate in the present chapter what is useful for completing our survey of the fields of experience.

[2] 'Humanam impotentiam in moderandis et coercendis affectibus servitutem voco; homo enim affectibus obnoxius sui juris non est, sed fortunae, in cujus potestate ita est, ut saepe coactus sit, quanquam meliora sibi videat, deteriora tamen sequi', G II, p. 205, ll. 7–12 [*Ethics* IV, Praef., CWS I, 543].

favorable to them, no one would be in the grip of superstition.'³ Both of the great treatises that Spinoza devotes to human conduct open with a reference to fortune. What is this mythological goddess, this incarnation of chance, doing in a rationalist system? I would like to show that fortune occupies a precisely delimited space: it represents the form that experience takes when it is applied to the history of a human life or to the history of Cities. It thus refers both to the description of the condition of human beings who are prey to external forces, as well as to the play of circumstances to which virtue is opposed.

A. *The Experience of Exteriority*

The power of external forces can be clearly seen in the mechanism that engenders superstition. Let us begin by translating the analysis with which, on the the first page of the *TTP*, Spinoza accounts for this experience.⁴

If men could manage all their affairs by reference to a definite viewpoint,⁵ or if fortune were always favorable to them, no one would be in the grip of superstition. But often they are in such a tight spot that they cannot decide to adopt any such viewpoint. Then they usually vacillate wretchedly between hope and fear, desiring immoderately the uncertain goods of fortune, and ready to believe anything whatever. While the mind is in doubt, it's easily driven this way or that – and all the more easily when, shaken by hope and fear, it comes to a standstill. At other times, it's over-confident, boastful and presumptuous. Everyone, I think, knows this, though most people, I believe, do not know themselves. For no one who has lived among men has failed to see that when they are prospering, even if they are quite inexperienced, they are generally so full of their own wisdom that they think themselves	Si les hommes pouvaient régler toutes leurs affaires suivant un avis arrêté, ou encore si la fortune leur était toujours favorable, ils ne serait jamais en proie à aucune superstition; mais ils en sont souvent réduits à une telle extrémité qu'ils ne peuvent s'arrêter à un avis et que, la plupart du temps, du fait des biens incertains de la fortune, qu'ils désirent sans mesure, ils flottent misérablement entre l'espérance et la crainte; c'est pourquoi ils ont l'esprit si enclin à croire n'importe quoi: lorsqu'il est poussé par la crainte ou l'espérance – alors qu'à d'autres moments il est gonflé d'orgueil et de vantardise. Cela j'estime que nul ne l'ignore, bien que la plupart, à ce que je crois, s'ignorent eux-mêmes. Personne en effet n'a vécu parmi les hommes sans remarquer que la plupart, si grande soit leur inexpérience, regorgent tellement de sagesse aux jours de prospérité que ce serait leur faire injure que de leur donner un avis; dans l'adversité

---

³ 'Si homines res omnes suas certo consilio refere possent, vel si fortuna ipsis prospera semper foret, nulla superstione tenerentur', G III, p. 5, ll. 2–4 [*TTP* Praef., 1; *CWS* II, 65].

⁴ Translator's note. Again, I will place Moreau's original translation of this text alongside a slightly modified version of Curley's translation.

⁵ Translator's note: Curley uses the term 'plan', but as Moreau discusses below, this is not entirely appropriate.

wronged if anyone wants to give them advice[6] – whereas in adversity they don't know where to turn, and beg advice from everyone. They hear no advice so foolish, so absurd or groundless, that they do not follow it. Now they hope for better things; now they fear worse, all for the slightest reasons. If, while fear makes them turn this way and that, they see something happen which reminds them of some past good or evil, they think it portends either a fortunate or an unfortunate outcome; they call it a favorable or unfavorable omen, even though it may deceive them a hundred times.[7]	en revanche ils ne savent où se tourner, ils sollicitent un avis de chacun, et il n'en est aucun qui soit trop stupide, absurde ou vain pour être suivi. Enfin, les plus légers motifs leur redonnent des espérances ou les font retomber dans la crainte. Car si, lorsqu'ils sont dans la crainte, ils voient arriver quelque chose qui leur rappelle un bien ou un mal passés, ils croient y trouver l'annonce d'une issue heureuse ou malheureuse, et pour cette raison, bien que déçus cent fois, ils le nomment présage heureux ou malheureux.

I have already commented on a number of phrases from this text in an attempt to draw out some of the most general characteristics of experience.[8] I am returning to this passage now to identify what is most specific to historical experience: namely, that it shows both how human beings behave in a world that does not depend on them, and, above all, how they affectively engage with this world and the circumstances it imposes upon them – circumstances they interpret as a destiny. This experience presents itself in three forms: variability, opacity and affective productivity.

The first form of this experience (a form at once constitutive of its structure and primary – or almost primary – in its perception) is its temporal variability. Spinoza also identifies the rhythm of this variability: episodes of prosperity, of adversity, and reversals of fortune. If we can speak here in a certain sense of pessimism, or the insight afforded the disillusioned, then we should hasten to add that this pessimism or this absence of illusions concern only the *form* (the stability of a given situation) and not the *content* of situations (misery is no more or less certain than happiness). By way of this variability, the inconstancy that the passions provoke in us finds its symmetrical partner – and often its occasion – outside of us. It should also be

---

[6] Translator's note: The term 'advice', by which Curley here translates the Latin *consilium*, is rendered by Moreau as 'avis' – the same term used in this passage's opening sentence and which I have translated as 'viewpoint'. To the best of my knowledge, there is no English word that can give the sense both of an opinion or viewpoint and advice like the French term 'avis' can. However, readers should note that by using 'avis', Moreau is able to produce an echo between the different iterations of the term 'avis', even while their meaning shifts in interesting ways – as he will explain below.

[7] *TTP*, Preface, G III, p. 5, ll. 2–19 [*TTP* Praef., 1, 2, 3; CWS II, 65–6].

[8] Cf. above, Chapter 7, Section 3: 'What Experience Is'.

noted that this experience is repetitive,[9] both in the life of an individual and from one individual to another. No destiny is continuous: each person can come to know both these alternations and reversals, and no doubt will do so many times over. Finally, this experience is independent of us: each moment is imposed on us without us having chosen it. Fortune is the expression of the fact that we cannot govern our affairs according to a belief that has been fixed once and for all: in other words, our business is not our business. This is the same thing as saying that the primary figure of history is historical chance, insofar as it weighs upon us and prevents us from perfectly coordinating our aims and actions. Inconstancy, impotence, circulation between individuals – we find here, once again, and this time in the rhythms of history, the constitutive dimensions of all experience.

After variability, a second condition of experience immediately appears: the very forms this impotence takes are opaque to its victims. I have already identified the formula 'Everyone, I think, knows this, though most people, I believe, do not know themselves' as describing a constant dimension of the structure of experience. It is not insignificant that it is with respect to fortune that this structure is most clearly manifest. Spinoza also marks here the specific form that this opacity takes in the case of our submission to external laws. In other fields, this opacity takes the form of my ignorance of the causes of my inability to prevent myself from speaking (while at the same time I do not doubt the determinations that constrain others to speak), or of the belief (which is always undermined) according to which I could escape the consequences of my passions. In the case of fortune, this opacity is manifest as an inverted use of judgement. The term 'opinion' (*consilium*) is quite significant. This term, which is repeated four times,[10] structures the entire text. Impotence in the face of circumstances is a factual given. To recognise this is not a proof of madness. On the contrary, the most rational conduct would consist in determining what is possible given the circumstantial limits of each situation. Thus, one could take fortune for what it is: a distribution of events that we do not control. Now, human beings do

---

[9] Cf. 'nam quamvi centies fallat': this is a hope provoked by this situation, but the situation itself also repeats.

[10] This is one of the reasons that I have retranslated this text: the typical translation, which renders *consilium* successively by 'design' and 'counsel', breaks the unity of its meaning and, in so doing, prevents us from seeing its decisive role in this passage. Certainly, the *consilium* is at once the decision that we take and the counsel that we ask for; but it is because these two ideas constitute only one concept, which has diverse appearances according to the moments of fortune, that we can explain how we pass from impotence to superstition.

not succeed in thinking exteriority and its different consequences as if these consequences were so many aspects of one single condition. This is why they behave in opposing ways according to whether fortune is favourable or unfavourable to them. In periods of prosperity, without knowing the limits of their action, they believe that fortune depends only on them, and they refuse the opinions of others. Their illusory autonomy prevents them from asking for advice that could help them rationally choose the most salutary actions. In periods of adversity, they feel that something is escaping them and they immediately want to replace this something by something equivalent. When they believed that they were able to form their opinions all by themselves and to remain faithful to them, they did not dream of evaluating the opinions of others, save for disdaining them or feeling offended when others offered them advice. But in periods of adversity they are too distraught to even form a judgement. At this point they no longer take the time to decide and blindly follow everything that is proposed to them. It is this appeal to the *consilium* that is the cradle of superstition.

Thus, one of the strongest proofs of people's irrationality is that they seek reasons where none exist. They seek intention in chance and since they know full well that chance does not manifest *their* intention, they suppose that it manifests the intention of some other. Put differently, one of the aspects of people's domination by fortune is that they refuse, when they experience fortune, to accept its brute reality. They hope to find a content beneath its form and thus they misrecognise it. They try to explain the things that escape them (and that escape both their mastery and their understanding) by seeking behind them an historical intention.[11] Consequently, they have a spontaneous tendency to anthropomorphise history, just as they anthropomorphise nature. If we read the preface to the *TTP* closely, we realise that it is the perfect parallel to texts like the Appendix to the first part of the *Ethics*, which explains finalistic illusions in the case of natural things. Just as there exists a finality 'in space', there also exists a finality 'in time'. This temporal finality is equally necessary since it is rooted both in experience and in the spontaneous interpretation of experience. It takes the elementary form of the belief in signs and omens (the equivalents in history of miracles in nature), but these forms and these simple imaginary materials can also be combined to constitute a theory of Election or Providence.

A third condition of experience appears in the same text: this historical

---

[11] 'Si quid enim, dum in metu versantur, contingere vident, quod eos praeteriti alicujus boni, vel mali memores reddit, id exitum aut foelicem aut infoelicem obnunciare putant...' G III, p. 5, ll. 17–19 [*TTP* Praef., 3; CWS II, 66].

variability, far from being insignificant, actually produces the essence of human behaviour, precisely to the degree that it is tied to opacity. If fortune did not exist, there would be no superstition. Indeed, there would also be no superstition if fortune was always favourable. But it is of the essence of fortune to be neither always favourable nor always unfavourable. This is why the situations that it is tied to are marked by a strong affective productivity: they perpetually engender both hope and fear. These two feelings are named respectively three and four times in the brief opening passage to the *TTP*, which we have just cited. They are linked to time and to the grasp – indeed the illusory grasp – that we have on time. This is why they always appear when we feel time's uncertainty most strongly. They are a means for governing people precisely to the extent that the Sovereign controls people through fortune in all of its various forms. The 'goods of fortune' are also part of this same theoretical scenery: through our passions, these 'goods' enchain us to the order of exteriority.

However, this initial subordination introduces a spark of hope, a final possibility – one that has not yet been realised to this day – of change: if one day there were to be constituted (for the moment it matters little how this would happen) conditions of life that would push back against the variability of fortune, then superstition would retreat as well. It might be said that a major part of the *TTP* and, later on, of the *TP*, is a development of this second idea.

At this point, we can say that Spinoza describes experience in history without referring immediately to his system. The reader of the preface is not expected to already be familiar with it. Spinoza thus appeals to a feeling that is obscurely shared by his readers: without having realised it, each of them has experienced that both himself and others see the effects of their actions escape them. Each person has also seen how people – and above all other people – behave in such conditions. Once again, experiential description allows us to *recognise* the effects of necessity without it being necessary to *know* the laws that produce them.

And, as always, this description is based on a tradition. Indeed, fortune is not an unknown quantity for Spinoza's readers. It was the object of discussions in classical philosophy,[12] it runs through the rhetoric of antiquity,[13] and it constitutes a centrepiece of the arguments of historians, in particular Polybius, Tacitus and Curtius Rufus. In Polybius, it provides both the plan

---

[12] Cf. the controversies between Aristotelians and Stoics in J. Moreau, *Aristote et son Ecole*, Paris: PUF, 1962, p. 119, 225, 273–6.

[13] See for example, on reversals of fortune, Cicero, *Verrine V*, Chapter 50, § 131–2.

of history and the plan of the historian.¹⁴ In Tacitus, it loses this status of a representative of a secret finality in events and indicates what actually happened in each singular situation, such as this can be read retrospectively in history.¹⁵ In Curtius Rufus, finally, it governs the way we think of the course of those human actions that reason cannot account for.

Spinoza rarely situates himself with respect to the philosophical tradition. For example, Aristotle's classic text on the *tychē* inserts the *tychē* in the system of causes and of finality. Most importantly, Aristotle thinks of *tychē* under the sign of that which is infrequent.¹⁶ Spinoza is more concerned with the descriptive power of the idea of fortune, and, from this perspective, far from seeing it as a rare effect, he is sensitive to the fact that it constitutes the universal rhythm of people's actions.¹⁷ It is therefore in the work of historians rather than philosophers that we should seek points of comparison and significant differences. Spinoza reads a lot of historians' work, and the Dutch humanism of his time is marked by meditations on ancient historians. This, for example, was the contribution of Vossius to classical studies.¹⁸ Polybius is not in Spinoza's library, not even in a Latin translation. Tacitus can be found there, however,¹⁹ but he does not seem to play a role in the formation of the Spinozist notion of fortune. The preface to the *TTP* refers precisely to the authority of Curtius Rufus to confirm the argument that Spinoza makes concerning the relations between reversals of fortune, fear, hope and suspicion. Two explicit references to Curtius Rufus allow us to establish that Alexander fell into suspicion only when he became fearful of fortune (one page further on, a third citation from the same author makes the link

---

[14] 'Just as Fortune made almost all the affairs of the world incline in one direction, and forced them to converge upon one and the same point; so it is my task as an historian to put before my readers a compendious view of the part played by Fortune in bringing about the general catastrophe', Polybius, *The Histories of Polybius*, Vol. 1., Book I, trans. Evelyn S. Shuckburgh (Greenwood Press Publishers, 1962), p. 4.

[15] That destiny has reserved the empire for Vespasian, 'post fortunam credidimus', *Histories*, Book I, Chapter 10. The person called Pison Licinianus (assassinated along with Galba, before being able to prove himself), overcame his fortune, 'fama meliore quam fortune', Chapter 48.

[16] *Physics*, Book II, 6 (195b–198a)

[17] At the end of Chapter V, Aristotle mentions good and bad fortune, which will have a decisive importance in the rhetorical tradition (197a 25); he cites the topos that 'good fortune is unstable'; but this is not the heart of his analysis.

[18] Cf. his famous inaugural harangue to the illustrious school of Amsterdam, as well as his two books on Greek and Latin historians.

[19] In the Lipsius' edition and in the Boxhorn editions.

between superstition and the government of the multitude).[20] We can thus expect to find this common theory of fortune in the *History of Alexander the Great*. It is worthwhile recalling that in the seventeenth century, among those authors who were part of a critical or sceptical tradition, Curtius Rufus enjoyed a reputation as an enemy of superstition, and all the more so since he dealt with a subject that broadly lent itself to it.[21] It is thus not surprising that Spinoza chose him as a mediator between himself and his reader to introduce his own theses in a pre-philosophical manner: he was certain to encounter an at least vague agreement as a basis of discussion. It remains to determine what this argument and this lexicon refer to and the choices that their philosophical treatment, properly speaking, entail.

We will restrict ourselves to Book V, the first that is cited here. It recounts the events following the battle of Arbelus: the surrender of Babylon, the capture of Suez, and, on the Persian side, Darius' flight, the betrayal of the Bactrian leaders, and finally the series of intrigues that led to the arrest and death of the Great King (the final chapters, which recount the assassination itself, are missing). What is remarkable is that the term fortune, while it often appears in the text, indicates more often what happens to the Persians than the Greeks, when it is not directly placed in the mouth of Darius. In paragraph 4, which Spinoza cites, it is not explicitly said that Alexander doubts fortune, but the preceding lines (at the end of paragraph 3) clearly highlight the opposition between two historical sequences: one, in the past, where Alexander seems to be able to do anything and everything ('invictus ante eam diem fuerat, nihil frustra ausus'), and the other, in the present, where he seems to come up against obstacles and where his constant joy up to that point ends with him cornered ('tunc haesitabat deprehensa felicitas'). Thus, having had to retreat thirty stadia, before finding a guide who could help him go around and encircle the enemy troops, Alexander consults the seers in a spirit of superstition.[22] Thus, while the word does not appear,

---

[20] Curtius Rufus, Book V, § 5; Book VII, § 7, Book IV, § 10.

[21] Bayle notes regarding Curtius Rufus' article: 'l'auteur a eu même la sagesse d'aller au-devant du reproche de crédulité qu'il avait à craindre', and he cites La Mothe Le Vayer (*Jugement des principaux historiens*): 'Pour faire voir bien clairement avec quelle circonspection cet historien a toujours traité les choses dont on se pouvait défier, je mettrai ici les terms dont il accompagne la narration de ce chien qui se laissa couper les membres pièce à pièce au royaume du Sophite, plutôt que de démordre et lâcher la prise du lion: equidiem, dit-il, plura transcribo quam credo. Nam nec affirmare sustineo quibus dubito, nec subducere quae accepi.'

[22] 'Non consultare modo quid agendum esset, sed vates quoque adhibere coepit a superstione animi', V, 3.

there are indeed characteristics here that are associated with the idea of fortune; even the common idea that an excessive number of reversals of fortune enrages the victim is present. For Alexander's army is not simply made to fail, it is caught in a labyrinth where its soldiers die without even being able to land any blows – the most miserable situation for courageous men.[23] To the insolence of past happiness there thus corresponds this supplementary unhappiness that renders one impotent at the very moment of fortune's reversal. This idea of opposing excesses is tied to the theme of *ludibria fortunae*, the ironies or mockeries that so fascinate the human imagination.[24]

Let us turn now to Darius' side. As the vanquished, it is to be expected that Darius meditates more on fortune than the victor does, and indeed we see him at the beginning and at the end of the book oppose his past grandeur, as well as that of his ancestors, to his present trials. But another way of speaking appears: Darius speaks of *his* fortune and says to his companions: 'If Fortune had joined me with cowards, and with those who regard life on any terms as preferable to a noble death, I would keep silent rather than waste words to no purpose' (V, 8). Here, fortune is no longer the abstract distribution of goods and evils but instead refers to the series of goods and evils attached to each person; indeed, it refers to a predictable series such that we could translate 'fortune' by 'destiny' or 'fate' and no longer by 'chance'.[25] It is no longer variability but on the contrary individual constancy that comes to the fore. The extreme version of this constancy is the intention that destines a person to suffer a certain end: at this stage, Fortune no longer has to be named to be considered a person who must be placated for fear of irritating them. Thus, in the preceding book, the mother of the Great King, upon receiving the news – which, moreover, is false – of victory, 'remained in the same attitude as before. Not a word escaped her, neither her colour nor her expression changed; she sat unmoved – fearing, I suppose, by premature rejoicing to offend Fortune.'[26]

The common notion of *fortuna* presented to the reader by Curtius Rufus thus includes three different levels:

- The variability of human affairs; the states of fear and superstition into which the reversals of fortune throw men; men's relative forgetfulness

---

[23] 'Nec id miserrimum fortibus viris erat, sed quod inulti, quod ferarum ritu, velut in fovea deprehensi caederentur. Ira igitur in rabiem versa . . .', V, 3.

[24] Examples IV, 16; V, 12 (Darius chained with golden chains).

[25] One would have to take into account as well fortune in the sense of 'bad fortune, misfortune', for example in the case of the Greeks tortured by the Persians, V, 5.

[26] 'Praecoci gaudio verita irritare fortunam', IV, 15.

when their prosperity returns; the feeling of impotence in the face of the unexpected, which serves as the backdrop to the actions of history's agents.
- The series of events that happen to an individual; the idea that this series constitutes a destiny for them.
- And finally, the personalisation of the intentions that lie behind these highs and lows. While this personalisation is only a rhetorical device in the work of the historian, the historian does not hesitate to attribute to his characters a real belief in this person.

This ensemble of traits can give us an idea of what readers from the seventeenth century find in Curtius Rufus. This is not a strong model of the intelligibility of History, as a theory of Providence or Destiny would be, nor is it a causal explanation like a theory of climates or a law about the decadence of governments. What we do have is a rule that reminds readers of the diversity of human situations, their frequent unpredictability, and it also presents a remembered scene that brings together a certain number of typical behaviours in the face of these situations: impotent fury, superstition, prudence . . . All of these can be grasped by means of examples given in the course of the narration; no separate theory is required. Spinoza supposes that all of this is well known, while expecting each person not to apply it to themselves.

Given this, how can we address the lessons of historical experience in this double context of ignorant knowledge? By distinguishing between what is a lesson of experience properly speaking ('experientia docet . . .') and mythology: we can thus note that Spinoza's use of the term 'fortune' reduces it as much as possible to its formal aspects, which I enumerated above. There is no reference to individual fortune,[27] and even to less to its personalisation. Spinoza also asserts his own style by modifying the common theory of fortune so as to openly integrate those aspects that this theory renders opaque: thus, the preface to the *TTP* insists on the universal character of the reactions of fear and hope and on the apparent exceptions that are constituted by stable periods. We thus find the movement we have already identified in grammar: namely, to formulate laws such that even exceptions are instances of these laws in the form of particular cases. It could be said that the common theory of fortune identifies two types of periods and, in its more cultivated forms, characterises these periods by the presence or absence of an ideology

---

[27] Save perhaps in a passage from the *TP* where, in characteristic fashion, it is not so much some specific individual's fortune that is referred to, but rather the fortune of each person in general (Chapter XI, 2).

(superstition) and its affective root (fear and hope); and that Spinoza links all of this to a critical theory of fortune that identifies two ideologies and not a single one: superstition in troubled times, and the illusion of remaining sheltered from fortune in moments of certainty. The inaugural knowledge of the *TTP*, the minimum necessary to have a rational – but not geometrical – discussion with the reader, resides in the application of the second of these series to the first.

We can now discover the content of the critical theory of fortune as Spinoza formulates it. A certain number of passages define it restrictively, by taking care to limit what is registered by experience (whence the *nihil aliud*, the *hoc est* and the *sive*, which signify in this context: only this and nothing else). Chapter III from the *TTP* clarifies this: 'by fortune I understand nothing but God's guidance, insofar as it directs human affairs through external and unforeseen causes'[28] – it being understood that God's guidance is 'the fixed and immutable order of nature, *or* the connection of natural things'.[29] In the following chapter, to think the divine law, Spinoza opposes internal to external divine aid: the man who develops his natural understanding depends 'not [. . .] on the rule of fortune (i.e. on God's external aid), but chiefly on his internal excellence (i.e. on God's internal aid)'.[30] Finally, in a passage from the *Ethics*, in a language that renders singular causes more explicit, Spinoza expresses the same idea by insisting on what arises from the efficacy of our own nature and what escapes it: Spinoza mentions 'matters of fortune, *or* things which are not in our power, i.e. concerning things which do not follow from our nature'.[31] Whatever the register being used, fortune indeed refers in each case to a necessity over which we have no control. The experience of impotence and the feeling of the unexpected are thus conserved in the Spinozist use of the term, but they are separated from any interpretation in terms of intention or malignity.

This is what explains the fact that as far as external affairs are concerned, the prudent and the stupid often obtain the same success and suffer the same setbacks.[32] If Fortune is not a being with a will, it practises neither

---

[28] 'Denique per fortunam nihil aliud intelligo quam Dei directionem, quatenus per causas externas & inopinatas res humanas dirigit', *TTP*, Chapter III, G III, p. 46, ll. 22–4 [*TTP* III, 11; *CWS* II, 113].

[29] *TTP*, Chapter III, G III, pp. 45–6, ll. 34–5 [*TTP* III, 7; *CWS* II, 112].

[30] 'Non ab imperio fortunae (hoc est Dei auxilio externo) sed a sua interna virtute (sive Dei auxilio interno)', *TTP*, Chapter IV, p. 68, ll. 6–8 [*TTP* IV, 46; *CWS* II, 137].

[31] 'Res fortunae, sive quae in nostra potestate non sunt, hoc est [. . .] res quae ex nostra natura non sequuntur', *Ethics* II, 49, Schol., G II, p. 136, ll. 7–9 [*CWS* I, 490].

[32] 'At media, quae ad secure vivendum, & corpus conservandum inserviunt, in rebus

recompense nor irony. What arises from fortune is certainly produced by laws, but these laws do not take our human laws into account. Their coincidence or lack of coincidence with our judgements – even our well-founded judgements – has no meaning whatsoever.

Finally, fortune is diverse, not only in the life of a single man, but also in what it bestows upon different men: whence superstition, as we have seen, but also the belief in election,[33] and, in other cases, envy.[34] These last two reactions are born from the consideration of goods obtained by some but refused to others.

However, while Spinoza refuses to grant an intention to fortune, he clearly affirms the force with which fortune leads us far from our own ends. We do not know if the future will be happy or sad, but we nevertheless can be sure that by becoming attached to the goods of fortune, we will lose our power over ourselves: indeed, even while we are prosperous, fear and hope distance us from Reason. This is why at the beginning of the *TTP* Spinoza cites the desire for such goods as one of the causes of the miserable fluctuations of which people are the victims. Further on, he praises Solomon to the extent that Solomon saw the vanity of these goods. We thus find here, albeit in a different light, one of the themes presented by experience at the beginning of the *Treatise on the Emendation of the Intellect*. It should also be noted that if the link between fear and superstition is a commonplace,[35] it takes on a quite distinct meaning given Spinoza's perspective: fortune's roots in experience give it a stronger anthropological foundation and explain its perpetual reproduction. If fear is not only fear of the unknown, if it is above all a reaction to the unexpected; if it is the expression of impotence more than ignorance; and if, finally, impotence is felt all the more painfully since our desires are attached to goods that by nature can only one day escape us,

---

externis praecipue sita sunt; atque ideo dona fortunae vocantur, quia nimirum maxime a directione causarum externarum, quam ignoramus, pendent: ita ut hac in re stultus fere aeque foelix & infoelix, ac prudens sit', *TTP*, Chapter III, G III, p. 47, ll. 3–7 [*TTP* III, 13; *CWS* II, 114].

[33] 'Ideo Judaei et omnes, qui non nisi ex dissimili rerum humanarum statu & impari hominum fortuna Dei providentiam cognoverunt, sibi persuaserunt, Judaeos Deo dilectiores reliquis fuisse', *TTP*, Chapter VI, G III, p. 88, ll. 31–4 [*TTP* VI, 38; *CWS* II, 160].

[34] 'Prae invidia melioris laudis, et fortunae, quae nunquam aequalis est, malum alterius cupit, eoque delectatur', *TTP*, Chapter XVII, p. 203, ll. 24–6 [*TTP* XVII, 15; *CWS* II, 299].

[35] 'Primos in orbe deos fecit timor', Statius, *Thebaid*, III, 661. Hobbes cites this in Chapter XII from the *Leviathan* ('On Religion') and the *Theophrastus redivivus* in the chapter on the origin of the Gods (Edizione prima e critica a cura di G. Canziani e G. Paganini, Florence: La Nuova Italia, 1981, vol. I, p. 59).

then we can understand why superstition is not some remnant of the distant past; it is human life in all its normality that daily reproduces the foundations of superstition.[36]

Everything that forms part of the register of experience thus finds its demonstrative justification when we turn to the system and its order of reasons. The situation described under the name of fortune appears this time as a consequence of an argument and not as its source: on the basis of Books I and II of the *Ethics* we can demonstrate that our own life necessarily escapes us, that we are submitted to laws, at once physical and physiological, which we cannot master, and that we are confronted through the intermediary of our body by an order of external encounters, some of which harm us and some of which are useful to us. Hope and fear can thus be explained by reference to the confrontation between fundamental passions and time: they are no longer apprehended in the irrefutable but confused movements of experience but are instead deduced from the force by which the images of past and future things impose themselves on our mind.[37] But this theory is not present in the *TTP*, even if the *TTP* does not contradict it: what Spinoza elsewhere demonstrates on the basis of his system's premises, in the *TTP* he shows by reference to the kernel of truth that lies in what everyone always, already knew; or he reminds us of this kernel by referring to the rhetorical culture that has long since registered it and condensed it.

From the perspective of the geometrical order, the fact is that in the final analysis there is no historical contingency. The system demonstrates the full necessity of what happens in each human life. But the contingent still exists for us: there is something unexpected, and it occurs precisely when we least desire it. The term 'fortune' refers to the chance-like consequences of this absence of chance. The necessary laws that govern natural things, including human actions, do not bear the mark of an intention. But our ignorance of these laws and our inability to deduce them from singular events determine, on the one hand, that we live these events in the form of temporal and repetitive chance, and on the other that we are tempted to assign them a will or an irony that surpasses us. It is at this point that we find the roots of the natural tendency to sacralise History.

---

[36] For example, in the chapter cited above, Hobbes certainly mentions good and bad fortune ('good or evill fortune, *Leviathan*, pp. 54 and 55), but without showing us in what sense human behaviour subjects people to these forms of fortune. He prefers to relate people's concern for the future to their desire to know and to the search for causes, which are rooted in something specific to human beings: the perspective on time.

[37] *Ethics* IV, 18, Schol., G II, pp. 222–3 [CWS I, 555–6].

Thus, by constructing his critical theory of fortune, Spinoza extracts from the common theory what is positive in it (and which takes, in fact, the form of a negation: that of uncertainty regarding singular events); and he subtracts from this theory what could give rise to a teleological elaboration.[38] Without the reader knowing what causes it, Spinoza allows them to directly recognise the movement of a general situation whose necessary causes can only be revealed by the geometrical order.

B. Fortune and Virtue

It is not enough to describe the situation characterised by the oscillations of fortune and people's habitual behaviours with respect to it. It is also necessary to propose another way of acting, one that takes into account the lessons of experience or those of Reason. The second aspect of Spinoza's use of fortune is the opposition between *fortuna* and *virtus*. As is well known, this opposition was forged in the context of humanist thought: as the medieval conception of the 'wheel of fortune' weakened – that is, of fortune as an auxiliary of divine providence – there emerged another conception, one that, without immediately breaking with the first, introduced a reflection on those experiences where circumstances tested people's virtue.[39] This conception takes on a first form in the writings of Petrarch,[40] who devotes his treatise *Remedies for Fortune Fair and Foul* to it.[41] After traversing the thought of humanism and of the Renaissance,[42] it comes to fruition in Machiavelli, where fortune appears as what provides an individual's virtue with the occasion for both forging and manifesting itself.[43] It is clear that the meaning of the term *virtue* changes between the two. In Petrarch, virtue is certainly admirable, but it remains in the background: it is the path towards happi-

---

[38] On other aspects of this problem of fortune, which I will not deal with here, one should refer to the remarkable article by F. Mignini, 'Theology as the Work and Instrument of Fortune', in proceedings of the Amsterdam conference 1982, *Spinoza's Political and Theological Thought*, Amsterdam: North Holland, 1984, pp. 127–36.

[39] A. Doren, 'Fortuna im Meittelalter und in der Renaissance', in Bibliothek Warburg, Vorträge 1922–1923, I, Teil. Leipzig: Teubner, 1924, pp. 71–144; K. Reichert, *Fortuna oder die Beständigkeit des Wechsels*, Frankfurt: Suhrkamp, 1985.

[40] K. Heitmann, *Fortuna und Virtus. Eine Studie zu Petrarcas Lebnsweisheit*, Cologne: Böhlau Verlag, 1958.

[41] *De Remediis utriusque Fortunae*, written between 1354 and 1366.

[42] Boccaccio, Salutati, Poggio Braccionlini, all devote works to this theme.

[43] G. Nicoletti, 'Caso-causa o fortuna nel machiavellismo', in the edited collection *Il Tema della Fortuna nella letteratura fancese e italiana del Rinascimento. Studi in memoria di Enzo Giudici*, Florence: Olschki, 1990, pp. 343–53.

ness, without being happiness itself. The meaning of Petrarch's treatise consists above all in describing the goods of fortune, such as beauty or glory, as a kingdom of shadows, and in warning the reader against the illusions of prosperity by reminding them that nothing can resist time.[44] It is thus a matter of teaching people to not be surprised, and thus defeated, by either side of fortune. But precisely, in the context of this problematic of the remedy, Petrarch's description of the experience of variation and unexpected occurrences, of disappointment and the force of virtue, can appear in the form of a condemnation of human illusions. In Machiavelli's writings, virtue comes to the fore and is treated more as a power to act than as a matter of conforming to an ethical exigency. It is virtue that makes history, within the context presented by fortune. The latter thus appears as the *occasio* and not only as a *casus*. Fortune refers more to a possibility of being active in history and less to the attested fact that one is subject to history.[45]

The problematic of remedies to fortune is present in Spinoza's work, where virtue also plays the principal role. We even find in passing the phrase and the idea of 'fortune both good and bad'.[46] But such themes take on quite a different force in a system where virtue consists in living under the guidance of Reason, and where doing so is its own reward.

The main form this problematic takes is manifest in the opposition between 'obeying fortune' and 'obeying oneself'. The first possibility comes down to abandoning oneself to the laws of the external world, and thus to

---

[44] 'Gaudium: Forma corporis eximia est. – Ratio: Nichil firmior est illa quam tempus: cum eo veniens, cum eodem fugit. Siste, si potes, tempus: poterit forsan et forma consistere. – Gaudium: Forma corporis egregia est. – Ratio: Fragili niteris fundamento. Corpus ipsum umbre in morem preterit', *De Remediis*, I, 2, in Francesco Petrarca, *Prose*, a cura di G. Martellott, P. G. Ricci, E. Carrara and E. Bianchi, Milan and Naples: Ricciardi, 1955, p. 612; 'Ratio: Cave ne, quam gloriam veram putas, imago falsa sit. In rebus hominum multa regnat illusio', I, 92, p. 634; 'Ratio: Sentio quam felicitatem dicis. Aut felix igitur errore tuo es, ut ait ille – que felicitas, ut dixi, miseria est – aut virtute animi felix. Que nec ipsa felicitas plena est, quamvis sit ad felicitatem via', I, 108, p. 640.

[45] Cf. in particular the beginning of the second book of the *Discourses on Livy*, where Machiavelli polemicises against Plutarch's treatise *On the Fortunes of the Romans*. Finally, if fortune can still function as providence, it is in some sense at a second level, by choosing to govern people whose virtue corresponds to its designs (cf. ibid., II 29, pp. 188–90). As for the short poem *Di Fortuna*, pp. 976–9, it translates elements of the traditional vision into images, albeit by occasionally reorganising them (a system of wheels replaces the single wheel) in such a way that these elements gesture towards the theory of the *Discorsi*.

[46] 'Utramque fortunae faciem aequo animo expectare & ferre', *Ethics* II, 49, Schol. G II, p. 136, ll. 9–10 [CWS I, 490].

unhappiness, even if we believe that we will find our happiness there; the second, by contrast, comes down to living according to the laws of one's own nature, which is the very definition of virtue. This opposition structures the theorems that, in Book IV, compare 'what is useful to man and what is harmful to him'; it appears in the final Scholium to Book II, which announces these theorems; and it also reappears in Book V with regards to those whose virtue is not real, but only inspired by the fear of the beyond.[47] Spinoza insists that he who lives according to virtue does not need the help of Fortune;[48] such a person even commands Fortune – 'so much as is possible'.[49] This is not a matter of regressing to the illusion of autonomy. Nevertheless, it is true that whoever practises virtue strives to make themselves less dependent on hope and to free themselves from fear: such a person thereby escapes the affective consequences of external chance.

This opposition between virtue and fortune is so strong that we even find it at a level higher than that of the individual: when Spinoza mentions the problem posed by Machiavelli (namely, how to periodically reduce the State to its principles), he remarks that, if this is not done, the State 'won't be able to last by its own excellence, but only by good luck'.[50] Already in the *TTP*, Spinoza posited as a principle that, to found a society, one needs an extraordinary complexion and degree of vigilance. Thus, civil societies are more or less subject to fortune depending on whether or not people who engage with them are more or less virtuous.[51]

All of these expressions, while they conform to Spinoza's system, nevertheless strike a note that undeniably recalls humanist morality and its rhetoric of virtue. What is the reason for these formulations? As we have seen, in the *TTP* what is at stake is describing people's behaviour without appealing to geometrical deduction. In the *Ethics*, it is also a matter of showing that the consequences of geometrical reasoning join up with and justify, at least in part, what the ethical tradition teaches us about the relation between

---

[47] 'Et fortunae potius quam sibi parere vellent', *Ethics* V, 41, Schol., G II, p. 307, ll. 19–20 [*CWS* I, 616].
[48] 'Et fortunae auxilio quam minime indiget', *Ethics* IV, 46, Schol., G II, p. 245, l. 25 [*CWS* I, 573].
[49] 'Quo itaque magis ex ductu Rationis vivere conamur, eo magis spe minus pendere, et metu nosmet liberare, et fortunae, quantum possumus, imperare conamur, nostrasque actiones certo Rationis consilio dirigere', *Ethics* IV, 47, Schol., G II, p. 246, ll. 14–17 [*CWS* I, 573].
[50] 'Non poterit imperium sua virtute, sed sola fortuna permanere', *TP*, Chapter X, 1, G III, p. 353, ll. 18–19 [*TP* X, 1; *CWS* II, 596].
[51] *TTP*, Chapter III, G III, p. 47, ll. 7–18 [*TTP* III, 13, 14; *CWS* II, 114].

virtue and fortune. In sum, we can clearly see experience performing in its first function here, at once confirmative and substitutive: in the *Ethics*, experience accompanies the statement of necessary laws, while in the *TTP* it is a substitute for this statement of these laws. In the *TTP*, it is a matter of directly describing those dimensions of human life that the author has chosen not to explain at this point.

2. The End of History

When Spinoza thinks history, it is on the basis of this theory of fortune:[52] no other rationality for States or individuals exists. It is by reference to these same constraints of exteriority, of opacity, of the force of the imaginary, that we can account for both collective life and individual life.[53] There exists neither a general course of history nor any providential intention governing individuals' lives. At most we can compare different Cities, indeed class them into a few essential types. Even those texts of Spinoza that sketch out a schema of evolution do so only with respect to an individual City: there is nothing that resembles a theory of the succession of Empires. The units of history are the political constitutions of States.

The first chapter of the *Political Treatise* states that this history is closed: experience has sufficiently shown all of the kinds of Cities that are possible and also the means by which the multitude must be led.[54] Once again, experience marks the closure of reasoning, and constitutes a barrier to any utopian constructions. However, Spinoza permits himself to describe model States – not because he believes that he is able to invent new forms, but because he seeks to identify the means that are empirically present in such-and-such an historical figure. He can thus better reconstruct these States on the basis of the elements presented by history. Reciprocally, only history allows one to identify such-and-such a figure of a national State: here again, only experience can teach us how Venice combined an aristocratic constitution with that element from the monarchy, the Doge.[55] We thus

---

[52] 'La fortune est le visage de l'histoire comme possible', writes A. Tosel accurately in his study 'Y a-t-il une philosophie du progrès historique chez Spinoza?', in *Spinoza: Issues and Directions*, p. 320.

[53] Louis Althusser remarked that Spinoza was 'le premier à proposer à la fois une théorie de l'histoire et une philosophie de l'opacité de l'immédiat', in L. Althusser, E. Balibar, *Lire Le Capital*, Paris: Maspero, 1973, vol. I, p. 14.

[54] *TP*, Chapter I, 3, G III, p. 374, ll. 10–22 [*TP* I, 3; CWS II, 504–5].

[55] Cf. P.-F. Moreau, 'Spinoza et l'Italie: le modèle vénitien', *Les langues néolatines*, 76/2 (1982), pp. 87–92.

see experience at work here performing its second function: its constitutive dimension allows us to draw up a balance sheet of the individual traits of an existing individual. This constitutive dimension even acquires, for once, an active form, when Spinoza gives us the following unique synonym for *experientia* in his work: *experientia sive praxis*.[56] This clarification is no doubt thinkable only on the basis of the final form that human power takes in the *Political Treatise*. It nevertheless remains limited: it refers neither to a possible future nor to Spinoza's own theoretical construction. It marks only the action of politicians within the quite narrow limits that the laws assign them, as well as the echoes of this action in historical memory.

Yet, while it might be *theoretically* possible to reorganise people's lives on more rational foundations, is this *actually* possible? Does experience itself not teach us that, as we have just seen, fortune always provokes superstition and negative feelings in people? Must we conclude, then, that the final word of this philosophy of history is the impossibility of change? That Spinoza is content to secularise sacred history and to refuse – or even to dissolve – the various philosophies of Providence? This meditation on fortune would thus lead to the simple reaffirmation of the vanity of, and the absence of meaning in, human conduct: being eternal, human nature eternally engenders the same effects. We cannot escape the cycle of history, which is made up of barbarism, civilisation and decadence.[57]

A different path is nevertheless opened up: the theory affirms the existence of an eternal anthropological foundation to history, even if we do not, perhaps, know all of its possible effects. We can identify in human nature a small number of fixed laws that explain sufficiently well the space of variations in which the successes and catastrophes of individuals and societies occur. Despite the variety of individuals and the irreducible character of each person's *ingenium*, there exists a possible description of the human species and of its behaviours that corresponds to constant motifs.

Yet, we always know these motifs in an already socialised form: there exists no individual who really lives in the state of nature. Thus, even if individual psychology appears to be the foundation of history, the latter unfolds in such a way that the effects of this psychology are always imbricated in the acquisition of morals and laws that people acquire from their earliest childhood.

---

[56] 'Experientia sive praxi', TP, Chapter I, 3, G III, p. 274, l. 14 [TP I, 3; CWS II, 504]. The term returns ten times in the TP.

[57] On these questions and on the importance Spinoza accords to the time in which he is writing, see the recent works of A. Tosel and E. Balibar; on the theory of history, see Matheron, *Individu et Communauté*.

What becomes now of the effects of fortune? Are they immutable? They are indeed immutable to the extent that fortune itself is immutably variable; they are immutable even if this variability includes, through chance circumstances that are not impossible to conceive, a long period of individual stability. For, as we have seen, the individual will perhaps be provisionally distanced from superstition, but they will not be able to tear up the roots of superstition, which are perpetually reproduced by the ideological apparatuses put in place during periods of fear and insecurity. But what would happen if, following a series of circumstances that are initially due to chance, an entire society came to enjoy security? At this point, not only will superstition retreat, in the long term we will see the installation of institutions able to make it retreat even further, or able to develop civilisation and commerce to such a degree that it will effectively retreat. We will thus escape, at least in part, the ineluctable play of fear and hope and their consequences, and will do so on the basis not of some mysterious disappearance of human nature, or an atonement for corruption, but on the contrary through the very play of the same necessary laws in other conditions. The production of these conditions is indeed originally the work of what for us is the same contingency; these conditions are then reproduced by the effects they have engendered, namely civilisation, reason, and even the philosophical perspective on society that leads, in the Holland of the seventeenth century, to the struggle for freedom of conscience.

At this point, we can conclude that the critical theory of fortune elaborated in the *TTP* is also a means of collectively escaping the hazards of fortune. It is part of the strategy that will allow us to escape, without ignoring the cycles of history, history in its cyclicity.

However, beyond these possibilities, Spinoza's perspective on history presents us with an even more powerful experience. Whatever we can hope for from a possible organisation of States according to the best models, it is a fact that the majority of empirical States are indeed victims of their own internal weaknesses. Even the Hebrew State, which could have lasted for all eternity,[58] carried within it an initial flaw – the situation of the Levites – that led it to its downfall. This is not all: even when internal stability is assured, even when the Machiavellian problem of the return to principles is resolved, 'not only will [the State] not fall by its own defect, it will fall

---

[58] Spinoza uses the term at least twice: *TTP*, Chapter XVII, G III, p. 220, ll. 31–2 [*TTP* XVII, 112; CWS II, 321]; Chapter XVIII, p. 221, ll. 16–17 [*TTP* XVIII, 1; CWS II, 322].

only by some inevitable fate'.[59] But who can postpone the inevitable, that is, the necessity tied to finitude? Despite everything, history thus seems to culminate in the lesson that all Empires will perish – if not from within, then from without. Just as the general anthropology developed with reference to the passions imprisons human beings in servitude – that is, in the impotence and inconstancy caused by the affects – so that which governs in the final instance Spinoza's statements on history seems indeed to be the feeling that everything is perishable in the face of the blows of fortune. The experience of the person who considers the history of States gives this person the idea of eternity in the form of an aspiration – and not, precisely, as a characteristic of historical objects, even the best constructed ones.

---

[59] 'Non poterit ipsum suo vitio, sed solummodo inevitabili aliquo fato cadere', *TP*, Chapter X, 1, G III, p. 353, ll. 20–1 [*TP* X, 1; *CWS* II, 594].

III
Aeternitas: The Experience of Eternity

11

A Metaphysical Experience?

In his letter to Simon de Vries, Spinoza envisaged three possible functions for experience: comparative, constitutive and indicative. We have seen the fields in which the first two are operative – namely, where existence is separated from essence. Yet a question remains: where can we find the third function in the system's operation? Can we speak of a metaphysical experience, one that would serve neither to confirm a demonstration nor complete it but to 'determine our mind to think only of certain essences of things'?[1]

It would seem logical to place the experience of eternity, which Book V speaks of in such enigmatic terms, in this third category. But this experience cannot be understood without first determining the framework set by the system's fundamental principles and by the experience of the self. Thus, I will examine successively the theory of necessity presented in Book I, the theory of the soul developed in Book II, and the theory of the eternity of souls from Book V.

In addressing this question, we will find ourselves in a quite different situation to the preceding chapters. In fact, up to this point, in speaking of experience I have dealt with themes that on the whole have rarely been studied in Spinoza scholarship: scholars have either ignored them, or they have explicitly denied their interest. By contrast, I will now address themes that scholars have written on extensively. With respect to eternity, this theme has been of the greatest interest not only to commentators, but also,

---

[1] 'Sed summum, quod efficere potest, est mentem nostram determinare, ut circa certas tantum rerum essentias cogitat', Ep. X, G IV, p. 47, ll. 9–10 [*Ep.* X [to Simon de Vries]; CWS I, 196]. Translator's note: throughout this chapter, I will consistently use the term 'soul' in those contexts where Curley would use 'mind'. This is because, as Moreau mentions in his introduction, in the context of the *Ethics* in particular, he chooses to use the term 'âme' as opposed to 'esprit'.

and above all, to those first readers of Spinoza who wrote either to refute or – as was much less often the case – to defend Spinozism. Whenever these polemics or studies addressed Book V, it was often to highlight the inconsistency between this final Book's theses and those from the preceding Books, in particular as regards the principle of parallelism. By contrast, I will try to show that these texts cohere with one another and that what we have learnt about experience from the other Books of the *Ethics* and from the *Treatises* provides us with an approach that permits a better understanding of certain aspects of Book V and allows us to better trace certain lines of division.

1. An Experience of Forms?

Book I does not refer to experience in the sense that we have defined it in the preceding chapters. The word 'experience' never appears there, nor does any term associated with it – save in those passages that anticipate the material of the following Books.[2] This situation is perfectly understandable: the theoretical dryness of the subjects dealt with in Book I leaves no place for those objects whose essence is separated from their existence, while the formal grammar of the attributes can be based only on a geometrical deduction. Likewise, the Scholia are of a more explicative or polemical order, and are not principally geared towards providing examples for the Demonstrations. There thus appears to be nothing in this first Book that is tied to what everyone already knows, to that register of the past that is always a shared past, or to the neutralisation of the inadequate – all of which are signs that we have learnt to associate with the register of experience. We are, it would seem, firmly situated in the order of demonstrative deduction.

However, we come up against a paradox here, one that the system's adversaries have not failed to highlight: if Spinoza's reasoning is valid solely by virtue of its geometrical force, from where does the self-evidence of its demonstrations derive? What guarantees are we given that we should accept the system's definitions and primitive axioms? Is there not a sophism at the very heart of the demonstrative order, one that is hidden behind its appearance of rigour? This was a question posed by the very first of Spinoza's

---

[2] The word *experientia* appears in the appendix to Book I, where Spinoza anticipates his theory of error. It is also only in the Appendix that we find the verb *experior*. *Sentire* never appears.

correspondents[3] and repeated by authors who sought to refute his system.[4] This is an objection that is not lacking in force since it takes the system at its word as regards its own internal rigour. If Spinoza had failed to respond to this objection, he would have exposed himself to those who contested not only one particular proof from his system but rather the root of all his proofs. Now, it just so happens that Spinoza did respond to this objection, and his response is a consistent one: these theses, he argues, are sufficiently clear for whoever is a philosopher[5] – or, more precisely, for whoever knows how to draw the necessary distinctions. The serene unfolding of the theorems thus presupposes a fundamental division, one that is already present when the argument gets underway. The affirmation of self-evidence refers above all to those who are witness to it. Such a response is not without its own problems: how do we recognise that someone is a 'philosopher'? Is this not simply a way of avoiding the objection by referring to something ineffable? Everything depends on whether or not Spinoza presents a coherent criterion of demarcation. If there exists a primordial difference whose identification indicates one's aptitude to read the *Ethics*, what is its content?

A. The Line of Demarcation

We therefore have to seek out the principle that separates legitimate readers from illegitimate ones. This fundamental demarcation cannot be

---

[3] See Oldenburg, as early as Letter III (27 September 1661): 'Haec igitur Axiomata, cum apud me non videantur extra omnem dubitationis aleam posita [. . .]', G IV, p. 11, ll. 14–16 [*Ep.* III [from Henry Oldenburg]; CWS I, 169].

[4] Cf. Wittichius, *Anti-Spinoza*, Amsterdam, 1690 (on the first definition). See W. Schmidt-Biggeman's analysis of this question in 'Spinoza dans le cartésianisme', *Travaux et documents du Groupe des recherches spinozistes*, PUPS, 1991. Dom François Lamy makes an analogous argument: 'Spinoza avait entrepris de démontrer qu'il n'y avait qu'une unique substance dans la Nature, que Dieu est cette unique substance, que toutes choses ne sont que des manières d'être cette substance, et que tout ce qui peut tomber sous l'entendement n'est qu'une suite nécessaire de la nature divine. Or il est visible que Spinoza suppose tout cela dans la sixième définition', *Le nouvel athéisme renversé, ou réfutation du sistême de Spinosa* [. . .] , par un religieux bénédictin de la congrégation de Saint-Maur, Roulland, 1696, p. 252. Lamy wanted his argument to be all the more decisive that he reconstructed, in addition to the 'common' refutation, a 'geometrical' refutation destined to make Spinoza fall into the trap of his own radicality.

[5] 'Rationem vero hujus differentiae etiam in memorato Scholio satis clare, ni fallor, proposui, praecipue Philosopho. Supponitur enim non ignorare differentiam, quae est inter fictionem & inter clarum et distinctum conceptum', Ep. IV, G IV, p. 13, ll. 8–11 [*Ep.* IV [to Henry Oldenburg]; CWS I, 170].

demonstrated in the strict sense. If it could, it would appear as a theorem existing prior to the theorems, and would lead only to the exigency of rewriting Book I. It therefore cannot be a Proposition. Rather, it is a matter of a certain perspective on reality. Yet, this demarcation is not something ineffable, for Spinoza explicitly formulates it. It consists in distinguishing between those who judge in a confused way and those who know by reference to causes.

This line of demarcation is briefly defined in the second Scholium to Proposition 8, which takes up and develops the affirmations from Letter IV to Oldenburg: 'I do not doubt that the demonstration of P7 will be difficult to conceive for all who judge things confusedly, and have not been accustomed to know things through their first causes – because they do not distinguish between the modifications of substances and the substances themselves, nor do they know how things are produced. So it happens that they fictitiously ascribe to substances the beginning which they see that natural things have.'[6] Note that the 'confusion' mentioned here does not refer to a confused idea, but to the fact that two ideas are being confused with one other.[7] The term 'confusion' refers, in short, to a fiction. The demarcation thus concerns the 'origin' and 'production' of things: different people fail to perceive these things in the same way. Those who are not – or are not yet – philosophers confuse substance and natural things; but at the same time they also mistake the origin of natural things. In this way, the entire functioning of causality in principle escapes them. There is thus indeed something like a preparation for the exercise of the demonstration, a training that the reader must undergo, one that, in truth, proves nothing as far as essences are concerned but predisposes the reader to consider these very essences.

This philosophy of the difference between fiction and knowledge by causes is presented in a more detailed form in other texts. The confusion bears upon what governs origin and production, or upon what Spinoza refers to on a number of occasions using the following lapidary term: the forms. Indeed, the remainder of the Scholium immediately speaks of these forms: 'those who do not know the true causes of things confuse everything and without any conflict of soul feign that both trees and men speak,

[6] 'Non dubito quin omnibus, qui de rebus confuse judicant, nec res per primas suas causas noscere consueverunt, difficile sit, demonstrationem 7. prop. concipere; nimirum quia non distinguunt inter modificationes substantiarum et ipsas substantias, neque sciunt, quomodo res producuntur. Unde fit, ut principium, quod res naturales habere vident, substantiis affingant', G II, p. 49, ll. 26–31 [*Ethics* I, 8, Schol. 2, CWS I, 412–13].

[7] Essentially, these are the same thing; but it is not the same aspect that is being foregrounded.

imagine that men are formed both from stones and from seed, and that any form whatever is changed into any other'.⁸ The line of demarcation is thus clearly affirmed. To confuse is to mix forms. This distinction comes into effect with respect to the capacity to forge fictions.⁹ It is therefore necessary to compare it to those passages from the *Treatise on the Emendation of the Intellect* where Spinoza analyses fictions. In that work we find the same opposition between the world of metamorphoses and the world of the regularity of forms.¹⁰ Thus, 'the less men know Nature, the more easily they can feign many things, such as, that trees speak, that nothing becomes something, that even Gods are changed into beasts and into men, and infinitely many other things of that kind'.¹¹ Similarly, a few pages further on, the second type of false idea is illustrated by reference to analogous examples: 'such perceptions must always be confused, composed of different confused perceptions of things existing in nature – as when men are persuaded that there are divinities in the woods, in images, in animals, etc.; or that there are bodies from whose composition alone the intellect is made; or that corpses reason, walk, and speak; or that God is deceived, and the like'.¹² The kinship between these two texts is thus evident, and their coherence is reinforced by a shared singularity: the sudden appearance of a series of descriptive images in the midst of some of the most abstract passages in Spinoza's writings. This series of images is, moreover, of a particularly determinate nature. Note that the first of these two citations from the *TdIE* focuses the reader's attention on transformations, as does the Scholium from the *Ethics*: the unregulated passage from the form of one

---

⁸ 'Qui enim veras causas ignorant, omnia confundunt, et sine ulla mentis repugnantia tam arbores quam homines loquentes fingunt, et homines tam ex lapidibus quam ex semine formari, et quascunque formas in alias quascunque mutari imaginantur', G II, p. 49, ll. 31–5 [*Ethics* I, 8, Schol. 2; *CWS* I, 413].

⁹ Cf. *affingunt, fingant* in the Scholium cited above.

¹⁰ Cf. on this point P.-F. Moreau, 'Métaphysique de la substance et Métaphysique des formes', *Travaux et documents du Groupe de recherches spinozistes*, 2, 'Méthode et Métaphysique', PUPS, 1989, pp. 9–18.

¹¹ 'Quo minus homines norunt Naturam, eo facilius multa possunt fingere; veluti, arbores loqui, homines in momento mutari in lapides, in fontes, apparere in speculis spectra, nihil fieri aliquid, etiam Deos in bestias et homines mutari, ac infinita ejus generis alia', *TdIE*, 58, G II, p. 22, ll. 21–5 [*TdIE* 58; *CWS* I, 27].

¹² 'Tales perceptiones necessario semper sunt confusae, compositae ex diversis confusis perceptionibus rerum in Natura existentium, ut cum hominibus persuadetur, in silvis, in imaginibus, in brutis, et caeteris adesse numina; dari corpora, ex quorum sola compositione fiat intellectus; cadavera ratiocinari, ambulare, loqui; Deum decipi et similia', *TdIE*, § 68, G II, p. 26, ll. 4–9 [*TdIE* 68; *CWS* I, 30].

being to another (men changing into stone, gods changing into beasts), or, most radically, the passage from non-being to being (the nothing becoming something). We recognise here the world of Ovid – that is, the world of the nymph who is hunted and who changes into a spring, or the god who transforms Philemon and Baucis into trees. Thus, the philosophical principle that is traditionally opposed to creation (namely, that nothing comes from nothing)[13] appears here as a particular case of the confusion of metamorphoses. Yet, in these metamorphoses, what is scandalous for the philosopher, constituting an obstacle for him, is not change in itself but rather the absence of laws governing change and thus limiting it – that is, determining its power. In fact, in these lines Spinoza does not deny the possibility of transformation: one thing can be born from another, so long as it has the same form; and even forms can be transformed, albeit not *in any way whatsoever*.[14] The term 'seed' should not mislead us: what is at stake here is expressing the fact that all transformations occur by laws. If the rule of transformations is opposed to the chaos of metamorphoses, it is because the true line of demarcation is drawn by the recognition that all power is determined by laws. This is why in the second quotation Spinoza does not foreground the change in forms; instead, this quotation refers to affirmations that attribute properties to certain beings that these beings do not actually possess (corpses that can walk, a God who makes a mistake). In such a context, it becomes useless to ask what a form is.[15] The term refers less to a concept than to an exigency – that of the constancy and omnipresence of laws. This is why, for instance, the determination of form is not opposed to an indeterminate element which form would come to shape.[16]

---

[13] We find a discussion of this principle in L. Meyer, *Philosophia S. Scripturae Interpres*, Chapter VIII, § 2, trans. Lagrée and Moreau, Paris: Intertextes, 1988, p. 141 ff.). As is well known, this will constitute one of the axes of the discussion between Kuyper and Bredenburg in the polemic that begins in 1684 (cf. Kolakowski, *Chrétiens sans Eglise*, Chapter IV, in particular p. 270; L. van Bunge, *Johannes Bredenburg (1643–1691). Een Rotterdamse Collegiant in de ban van Spinoza*, Rotterdam: Erasmus Universiteit, 1990, pp. 207–9).

[14] Cf. the repeated expression 'quascunque formas' used to characterise the imagination, G II, p. 49, ll. 26–31 [*Ethics* I, 8, Schol. 2; *CWS* II, 413].

[15] For the main conceptual fields of this term, cf. the study cited above, 'Métaphysique de la substance et Métaphysique des formes', pp. 9–18.

[16] The term 'matter' is practically absent from Spinoza's lexicon. We should understand in a similar way the dismissive terms used to refer to 'substantial forms' ('doctrinam illam puerilem et nugatoriam', Ep. XIII, G IV, p. 64, ll. 19–30 [*Ep.* XIII [to Henry Oldenburg]; *CWS* I, 208]; 'plane inepta', CM, Chapter I, G I, p. 249, l. 34 [*CM* I; *CWS* I, 316], etc.).

The metaphysics of forms is the institution of the reign of necessity. It is in this sense that it gives us access to the metaphysics of Substance.

This central affirmation of the constancy of the forms and laws of nature cannot but remind us of one of the most consistent theses of Epicureanism. Paradoxically, Spinoza has been reproached for representing almost all of the ancient philosophies,[17] save for Epicureanism[18] – no doubt because his readers have been hypnotised by the question of the void and the atoms.[19] But if Spinoza defends Epicurus and Lucretius in his final letter to Hugo Boxel,[20] and if he reproaches his correspondent for not having named them,[21] it is no doubt because he feels a kinship with Epicurus and Lucretius grounded in their intense commitment to unmasking phantoms.[22] This kinship can perhaps above all be discerned in their shared insistence on refuting the world of metamorphoses, which they do with the help of analogous arguments and principles – arguments and principles which, without referring to ends, affirm the absolute unity of the universe in terms of its intangible natural laws.

The principles from the *Letter to Herodotus* and from Book I of *De Natura Rerum* are founded on the axiom 'nothing comes from nothing'. Now, this

---

[17] Platonism: C. Gebhardt, 'Spinoza und der Platonismus', *Chronicon spinozanum*, I (1921), pp. 178–234; L. Brunschvicg, 'Le platonisme de Spinoza', *Chronicon spinozanum*, III (1923), pp. 253–68; A. Hart, *Spinoza's Ethics, Part I and II: A Platonic Commentary*, Leiden: Brill, 1983; Aristotelianism: O. Hamelin, 'Sur une des origines du spinozisme', *L'année philosophique*, XI (1900), pp. 115–28; F. Chiereghin, 'La Presenza di Aristotele nel Breve Trattato di Spinoza', *Verifiche*, 16 (1987), pp. 325–41; Stoicism: B. Carnois, 'Le désir selon les Stoïciens et selon Spinoza', *Dialogue*, 19 (1980), pp. 255–77, R. Schottlaender, 'Spinoza et le stoïcisme', *Bulletin de l'Association des amis de Spinoza*, 17 (1986), and many others; Scepticism: P. di Vona, 'Spinoza e lo scetticismo classico', *Rivista critica di Storia della Filosofia*, XIII (1958), pp. 291–304; R. Popkin, *History of Skepticism from Erasmus to Spinoza*, Berkeley: University of California Press, 1979, pp. 229–48.

[18] With the exception of J.-M. Guyau, *La morale d'Epicure et ses rapports avec les doctrines contemporaines*, 1878, 3rd edition, 1886, Book IV, Chapter III, pp. 226–37.

[19] A good example can be found in the article 'Democritus' from the *Dictionnaire historique et critique*, note R (republished in the volume P. Bayle, *Ecrits sur Spinoza*, choisis et présentés par F. Charles-Daubert et. P.-F. Moreau, Paris: Berg International, 1983, p. 123; cf. also p. 27).

[20] *Ep*. LVI, G IV, pp. 258–62 [*Ep*. LVI [to Hugo Boxel]; *CWS* II, 420–4].

[21] 'Miratus fuissem si Epicurum, Democritum, Lucretium, vel aliquem ex Atomistis, atomorumque defensoribus protulisses [. . .]', ibid., p. 261, ll. 31–3 [*Ep*. LVI [to Hugo Boxel]; *CWS* II, 423].

[22] Lucien's pamphlet *Alexander the False Prophet* provides abundant evidence of the Epicurean's committed struggle against superstition.

axiom should not only be read in a material sense. It must also be understood in a formal sense: everything occurs according to laws; everything comes from a seed that perpetuates itself through it. If this were not the case, 'anything would have arisen out of anything, standing as it would in no need of its proper seeds';[23] 'Men from the sea / Might rise, and from the land the scaly breed, / And, fowl full fledged come bursting from the sky; [. . .] Nor would the same fruits keep their olden trees, / But each might grow from any stock or limb / By chance and change'.[24] On the contrary, 'But, since produced from fixed seeds are all, / Each birth goes forth upon the shores of light / From its own stuff, from its own primal bodies'.[25] Furthermore, other passages insist on the coherence and causality that govern these necessary series: 'Nor is the flame once wont to be create / In flowing streams, nor cold begot in fire'.[26] Thus, in the wake of the Epicurean tradition Spinoza takes up the theme of the constancy of the laws of nature and makes it a determinate criterion in the consideration of things. This is a doctrine of necessity that can be discerned each time it emerges by reference to the affirmation of the constancy of natural forms. This is why those authors who have sought to refute Spinoza and who have associated him with Epicurus[27]

---

[23] Epicurus, *Letter to Herodotus*, 38, French translation by J. Bollack, M. Bollack and H. Wismann, *La Lettre d'Epicure*, Paris: Editions de Minuit, 1971, p. 75. Cf. their commentary: 'La naissance à partir du non-être priverait les choses de leurs origines distinctes, de leurs semences. Elles seraient nées du hasard, sans demander en plus (pros-deomenon) du fait de naître, une cause de leur naissance', ibid., p. 174.

[24] 'E mare primum homines, et terra possit oriri
squamigerum genus, et volucres erumpere caelo; [. . .]
Nec fructus idem arboribus constare solerent
sed mutarentur; ferre omnes omnia possent' (Book I, vv. 161–2 and 165–6).

[25] 'At nunc seminibus quia certis quaeque creantur,
inde enascitur atque oras in luminis exit
materies ubi inest cuiusque et corpora prima (vv. 169–71).

[26] 'Usque adeo sequitur res rem, neque flamma creari
fluminibus solita est, neque in igni gignier algor' (Book III, vv. 622–3).

[27] Isaac Jacquelot, *Dissertation sur l'Existence de Dieu où l'on démontre cette vérité par l'histoire universelle de la première antiquité du monde, par la réfutation du système d'Epicure et de Spinoza, par les caractères de divinité qui se remarquent dans la religion des Juifs et dans l'établissement du christianisme* [. . .], The Hague: Foulques, 1697; the entirety of the 2nd Dissertation, 'Où l'on prouve que le monde a été formé par une cause intelligente et non par un hasard' (pp. 315–460) is explicitly directed against Epicurus, but chapters XII–XIII, devoted to Spinoza, begin by noting that Spinoza has been sufficiently refuted by what has come before. Furthermore, a large number of pages noted the proximity between Lucretius and Spinoza (on freedom, pp. 381–2, pp. 393–4; on the explanation of the word by the movement of matter, p. 414, ff.). 'Je suis persuadé que

have perhaps been more perspicacious than those who have neglected this proximity.

Taking this proximity into account can help us better identify the meaning of the line of demarcation that Spinoza so strongly affirms. We cannot content ourselves with saying that there is a difference between the understanding and the imagination. For on the one hand, this latter difference is internal to each human soul and thus cannot distinguish between souls; and on the other hand, the imagination takes many forms and produces a number of different effects. The paradigm of the metamorphoses is the particular effect that is opposed to the apprehension of necessary causality. In the topography of the imaginary, it is the imagination that must be reduced so that 'true knowledge of things'[28] can be constituted.

B. *The Critical History of Knowledge*

We now have an idea of what in Spinoza's eyes can serve as a propaedeutic to Book I and to the *Ethics* in general. What separates the 'philosopher' from the 'vulgar' is not knowledge of a determinate demonstration, nor is it an experience in the sense we have understood experience up to this point: it is an apprehension of forms. When readers approach the Definitions and the Axioms, they have already left the world of the imagination. We have thus found the answer to the question formulated by Spinoza's contradictors. But this answer engenders another question: how is all of this possible? How do we arrive at the point where at least some people can approach metaphysical questions with a ready-made idea of eternal necessity?

In the passages cited above, this distinction is given only as a result. It remains for us to understand how it is produced. In fact, the opening to Book II does indeed seem to indicate that all people are from the outset necessarily subject to the imagination. The apprehension of forms, as a means of access to the reign of causality, is therefore not something spontaneous. But how does this apprehension occur? Does the system mention it at some point in its development? It seems to me that this is indeed the case, specifically in the second part of Book II.

---

ce qu'Epicure appelait hasard et ce que Spinoza appelle nécessité est la même chose', La Placette, *Eclaircissements sur quelques difficultés*, Amsterdam: Etienne Roger, 1709, p. 317 (cited by P. Vernière, *Spinoza et la pensée française avant la Révolution*, Paris: PUF, 1954, p. 71); symmetrically, Fénelon refutes Epicurus and Spinoza in the two parts of his *Traitée de l'Existence de Dieu*, 1713, édition critique établie par J.-L. Dumas, Paris: Editions Universitaires, 1990, pp. 73–88, and 119–26.

[28] 'Vera rerum cognitionem', *Ethics* I, App., G II, p. 80, l. 1 [CWS I, 442].

In the first of the two passages from the *TdIE* cited above, Spinoza provides a clue: the knowledge of nature. Most importantly, he inserts this clue into one of those revealing formulations of proportion that we encounter at the most decisive points[29] in his work: 'the less men know Nature, the more easily they can feign many things'.[30] In other words, the 'philosophical' soul develops as natural knowledge grows. It is therefore by studying the process by which this knowledge emerges in an individual soul[31] that we will be able to understand how, after initially being dominated by the imagination, certain people can acquire the aptitude to distinguish the necessity of laws.

This progression is illustrated by developments from Book II. The theoretical history of knowledge that is implicit here casts the theses from Book I in a different light. In Book I, the characteristics of things are stated as such, while the Scholia allude to the difference between their perception by Reason and their perception by the imagination. In Book II, by contrast, what is analysed is the production of ideas, and what happens is that the historical order of their development in the individual coincides in large part with their logical order.[32] The way the characteristics of things are perceived is dealt with in the derivative theorems, corollaries and scholia. We can thus address the question of forms from a different perspective: no longer as a sign of separation, but as a process of acquisition. The distinction is given not as a result, but in its very process of production. There are three implicit moments in this critical history of knowledge: knowing things as necessary; thinking them under the category of necessity; and forming the idea of eternity itself.

If the passage from the non-philosophical conception to the philosophical conception occurs in proportion to the growth of knowledge about Nature, one might be tempted to attribute to mathematics the development

---

[29] Cf. for example the Corollary to Proposition 39 from Book II, which establishes the foundations of the second genre of knowledge: 'Hinc sequitur, quod mens eo aptior est ad plura adaequate percipiendum, quo ejus corpus plura habet cum aliis corporibus communia', G II, p. 119, l. 32, p. 120, l. 2 [*Ethics* II, 39, Dem., Cor.; CWS I, 475].

[30] 'Quo minus homines norunt Naturam, eo facilius multa possunt fingere', *TdIE*, § 58, G II, p. 22, l. 21 [*TdIE* 58; CWS I, 27].

[31] Cf. Lee C. Rice, 'The Continuity of *Mens* in Spinoza', *The New Scholasticism*, XLIII/1 (1969), pp. 75–103.

[32] Certainly, as a matter of principle, everything is always, already there: the common notions and the idea of God are present in the constitution of each soul, whatever it is, just like the disposition to produce inadequate ideas. However, there exists something like a theoretical chronology: we begin by living under the rule of the inadequate, and common notions then engender only knowledge of the second kind.

of the paradigm of causality and of necessity. Famous texts by Spinoza underscore the fact that mathematics seeks essences and properties, not ends, and that, in contrast to the imagination, mathematics indicates 'another standard of truth'.[33] Mathematics would thus be tasked with 'conditioning' the soul to approach philosophy. This is why, moreover, philosophy must be written *more geometrico*. This is no doubt part of the answer, but it must be nuanced: on the one hand, mathematics deals only with beings of reason, while on the other hand Spinoza seems to refuse to identify the philosopher with the mathematician – indeed, he explicitly underscores the fact that Solomon was ignorant of geometry,[34] and he no less explicitly considers the texts attributed to Solomon as containing a philosophy that is more or less equivalent to his own.[35] There are therefore other ways of being initiated into knowledge. Furthermore, the Appendix to Book I says: 'And besides Mathematics, we can assign other causes also.'[36] Yet, if mathematics can serve as a model, it is because it gives us the best indication of the aspiration towards the recognition of necessity. Freudenthal was the first to highlight this point: 'Mathematics', he noted, 'not only gives us an example of a science that contains a system of incontestable truths; it is the deepest foundation of Spinozism that pushes it to use the same Method to which mathematics owes its admirable structure. Philosophy seeks to know the internal links between things.'[37] It is these 'internal links' that constitute the proper object of Reason, and all knowledge that reveals these links is an incursion onto the terrain previously occupied by the imagination since it replaces the imagination's arbitrary games with the causal reign of laws. This

---

[33] 'Nisi mathesis, quae non circa fines, sed tantum circa figurarum essentias & proprietates versatur, aliam veritatis normam hominibus ostendisset', *Ethics* I, App., G II, p. 79, ll. 32–4 [CWS I, 441].

[34] 'Quia enim non tenemur credere Salomonem Mathematicum fuisse, licet nobis affirmare, eum rationem inter peripheriam, et circuli diametrum ignoravisse, et cum vulgo operariorum putavisse, eam esse, ut 3 ad 1', *TTP*, Chapter II, G III, p. 36, ll. 27–31 [*TTP* II, 29; CWS II, 102].

[35] *TTP*, Chapter II: 'Nec ullus in Vetere Testamento habetur, qui magis secundum rationem de Deo locutus est, quam Salomon, qui lumine naturali omnes sui saeculi superavit [. . .]', G III, p. 41, l. 17 ff. [*TTP* II, 48; CWS II, 107].

[36] 'Et praeter mathesin alia etiam adignari possunt causae', *Ethics* I, App., G II, p. 79, ll. 34–5 [CWS I, 441].

[37] 'Die Mathematik aber liefert uns nicht bloß das Beispiel einer Wissenschaft, die ein System unbestreitbarer Wahrheiten enthält; der innerste Grund des Spinozismus drängt ihn zu derselben Methode, der die Mathematik ihre bewundernswerte Fassung verdankt. Die Philosophie will den Zusammenhang der Dinge erkennen', Freudenthal, *Die Lehre Spinozas*, p. 110.

is why, in Proposition 44 from Book II, after having described the second kind of knowledge, Spinoza characterises this knowledge as follows: 'It is of the nature of reason to regard things as necessary, not as contingent.'[38] In other words, each piece of rational knowledge brings with it, as one of its components, the idea of necessity. The demonstration is founded on the fact that Reason makes us perceive things as they are in themselves – that is, as governed by a necessity that expresses the necessity of substance.[39] If, from the moment it appears in history, mathematics has a privileged place, it is because it exhibits this necessity in an apparently pure way, and thus shows the soul its own capacity for rationality. Those souls that mathematics has formed are thus partially prepared for the decisive philosophical demarcation. But others who are unfamiliar with mathematics, by applying their reason to human activities or to the examples of fate, have also arrived at the same feeling of necessity.

How can we isolate this necessity? How can we pass from knowing a thing as necessary to grasping the root of this necessity itself? The knowledge of laws leads to the identification of the idea of necessity, then of universal necessity. This latter then receives the name eternity. This is why the Corollary to Proposition 44 continues as follows: 'It is of the nature of reason to perceive things under a certain species of eternity.'[40] Note that there are two Demonstrations for this Corollary: in the first, the necessity of things refers, according to Proposition 16 from Book I, to the eternal necessity of divine nature; in the second, since they are common notions, the principles of Reason do not explain the essence of any singular thing – and thus they exclude any relation to time.[41] Eternity is therefore introduced here at once positively and negatively, in the form of what founds necessity as well as what necessity excludes. There is thus something like a movement of the transformation of the soul, which in the process of knowledge makes the soul pass from the consideration of the necessity of a thing or of a Proposition to the necessity of what founds them. This is why, in the text cited above, Freudenthal is very logically led to identify necessity with eternal order.[42] To conceive of things by way of their forms

---

[38] 'De natura Rationis non est, res ut contingentes, sed ut necessarias contemplari', *Ethics* II, 44, G II, p. 125, ll. 6–7 [CWS I, 480].

[39] Cf. the reference to *Ethics* I, 29 [CWS I, 433].

[40] 'De natura Rationis est, res sub quadam aeternitatis specie percipere', *Ethics* II, 44, Cor. 2, G II, p. 126, ll. 20–1 [CWS I, 481].

[41] This is what the references to Propositions 37 and 38 indicate.

[42] 'Die Ethik Spinozas will uns die Ezige Ordnung der Dinge in ihrer unverrückbaren Notwendigkeit kennen lehren und in dieser Erkenntnis uns durch die Macht des

is to conceive them *sub specie aeternitatis*.⁴³ Gueroult remarks on this with respect to Proposition 44 from Book II: the scientist knows the eternity of laws in an at least negative fashion – that is, insofar as they escape time. It is still necessary to pass from this perspective to the positive expression of eternity, 'that is, to the eternal nature of God, which the *Ethics* deduces as that from which these necessary laws follow'.⁴⁴ This movement is not given immediately in each scientific proposition: certainly, divine necessity is implied in every affirmation of the necessity of things, but whoever makes the second claim is not necessarily conscious of the first.⁴⁵ In fact, it is this gap that allows the existence, in the classical age, of philosophies that in Spinoza's eyes are irremediably flawed.⁴⁶

Gueroult's remark leads us to a final question. How do we pass from these laws to their principles? Certainly, each proposition produces a piece of knowledge under the category of eternity. But how do we pass from knowledge *sub species aeternitatis* to *aeternitas* itself? It might be objected that it is hard to see how the knowledge of a great number of singular scientific propositions prepares us for reading Book I. The response is in the *TTP*: we work our way backwards from what is manifest to what manifests itself. 'But since (as we've already shown) the laws of nature extend to infinitely many things, and we conceive them under a certain species of eternity, and nature proceeds according to them in a definite and immutable order, to that extent they indicate to us God's infinity, eternity and immutability.'⁴⁷ This does not mean that the idea of God is given to us when we apprehend

---

Denkens zur Freiheit und zur Glückseligkeit führen', *Die Lehre Spinozas*, p. 111.

⁴³ This second Corollary to Proposition 44 will be the axis used in Proposition 29 from Book V to pass from the first to the second perspective on the eternity of souls.

⁴⁴ 'c'est-à-dire à la nature éternelle de Dieu que l'*Ethique* déduit comme ce dont ces lois nécessaires procèdent'. M. Gueroult, *Spinoza*, vol. II, *L'Ame*, p. 413.

⁴⁵ 'La notion de la nécessité des choses n'étant rien d'autre que celle de la nécessité de la nature de Dieu, cette dernière notion *doit* être présente en toute Âme qui a la notion de la nécessité des choses. [. . .] Toutefois, en fait, il ne suffit pas d'avoir la notion de cette nécessité pour avoir du même coup conscience que cette nécessité est celle de la nature éternelle de Dieu. Le savant, en tant seulement que savant, prenant la nécessité des choses comme leur propriété commune, n'a pas nécessairement conscience de leur fondement métaphysique', ibid.

⁴⁶ Cf. A. Donagan, *Spinoza*, New York: Harvester Wheatsheaf, 1988.

⁴⁷ 'At quoniam Naturae leges (ut jam ostendimus) ad infinita se extendunt, & sub quadam specie aeternitatis a nobis concipiuntur, & natura secundum eas certo, atque immutabili ordine procedat, ipsae nobis eatenus infinitatem, aeternitatem et immutabilitatem aliquo modo indicant', *TTP*, Chapter VI, G III, p. 86, ll. 13–17 [*TTP* VI 25; *CWS* II, 158].

forms. However, such an apprehension does allow this idea that was always present in us – albeit unperceived – to emerge. No proposition arising from the second kind of knowledge can by itself lead us to the third kind of knowledge. But the progression internal to the second kind can give us something like a habit for these forms, meaning that at each instant we are within a kind of horizon of causality: each new proposition is inscribed in the anticipation of this lawfulness and thus little by little there emerges the idea, no longer of singular necessity, but of infinite necessity. Spinoza affirms nothing less when, highlighting the fact that natural knowledge merits the name of divine knowledge, he adds: 'Anyone who has tasted the certainty of the intellect must have experienced this in himself.'[48] The fact of 'experiencing' or of 'tasting' this certainty is identified with no particular demonstration, with none of the necessary causal relations that have come to be known; it marks the way in which the soul has been transformed by a certain number of acts of the understanding, which on each occasion have put it in the presence of necessity and of what grounds it.[49]

There thus comes to be constituted in us a sort of past of Reason that determines that each time a new event occurs, the philosopher and the common person do not react in the same way. When faced with a surprising incident, one sees a miracle while the other supposes that it has a still unknown cause. When faced with the diversity of phenomena, one reacts by referring to the paradigm of metamorphoses, the other by seeking out laws. Thus, even before beginning the approach to metaphysics, there has been constituted in the philosopher something like a habit of Reason, which has educated their gaze in their search for Necessity.

C. Semantics of Eternity

The theoretical history of Reason thus culminates in the idea of eternity. We have to pause here for a moment. We know that the term eternity and its uses have made a lot of ink flow in the secondary literature. It is not my purpose to deal with all of the different functions that eternity has in

---

[48] 'Qui certitudinem intellectus gustavit, apud se, sine dubio expertus est', *TTP*, Chapter I, G III, p. 16, ll. 18–19 [*TTP* I, 5; *CWS* II, 78].

[49] The importance of this passage was clearly highlighted in a small piece of writing from 1767, which is no doubt falsely attributed to Boulainvilliers (*Doutes sur la Religion, suivies* [sic] *de l'analyse du 'Traité théologico-politique' de Spinoza*, par le Compte de Boulainvilliers, London, 1767, p. 70). The work in no way merits the contempt that Renée Simon and P. Vernière show it, for it demonstrates a quite fine-grained understanding of the system.

Spinoza's architectonic. Nevertheless, we must draw a few distinctions that are necessary for dealing with the precise problem we are faced with here. I will leave aside for the moment the question of the eternity of human souls, to which I will return below.

The task of understanding the idea of eternity itself involves three difficulties: the apparent paradox of eternity's definition; the various possible contents that the texts seem to suggest for eternity; and the rupture with parallelism that Book V seems to imply.

— The simplest approach would consist, it seems, in reprising the definition that Spinoza gives of eternity at the beginning of Book I: 'By eternity I understand existence itself, insofar as it is conceived to follow necessarily from the definition alone of the eternal thing.'[50] But it appears that this definition has not sufficed to clarify the concept of eternity for commentators. To them it seems particularly paradoxical to define eternity by the eternal.[51] Martial Gueroult sums up the difficulties that have traditionally been identified as follows: in Definition 8, eternity is less defined than presumed to already be known; it is more a matter of elucidating 'on what conditions we can attribute an existence to this property, which is known by all and commonly attributed to essences and truths',[52] and of indicating 'that the word eternity will henceforth refer to any existence that satisfies this condition'.[53] Gueroult, in fact, refuses this solution, and rewrites the definition of eternity (eternity is the property of a thing that exists by itself). He then adds that we can see here 'a sin against terminological rigour'[54] when Spinoza extends the term eternity to anything other than substance and its attributes.

— Beyond this definition, the different texts that use the notion of eternity have suggested quite different interpretations to Spinoza's commentators. One might be tempted to define the notion of eternity by 'sempiternity':

---

[50] 'Per aeternitatem intelligo ipsam existentiam, quatenus ex sola rei aeternae definitione necessario sequi concipitur', *Ethics* I, Def. 8, G II, p. 46, ll. 13–15 [CWS I, 409].

[51] The tone is set by Poiret as early as 1685: 'addit & absurdissimam tautologiam, intrudendo in sua definitione ipsum definitum, de quo quaeritur: Est, inquit, *existentia, quatenus ex sola rei aeternae definitione* ... Sed, heus tu! Dic prius uid sit *res aeterna*. Quid est *res aeterna*? Est *res praedita aeternitate*. Atqui *aeternitas* est hoc ipsum nescio quid, quod nescis, & quod quaeris!', *Fundamenta Atheismi Eversa*, Sectio prima, in *Cogitationes rationales de Deo, Anima et Malo*, 1685, 2nd edition, 1715, 3rd edition, Hildesheim: Olms, 1990 (introduction by M. Chevallier), p. 867.

[52] 'à quelle condition on peut attribuer à une existence cette propriété connue de tous, couramment accordée aux essences et aux vérités'.

[53] 'que le mot d'éternité désignera désormais toute existence satisfaisant à cette condition'.

[54] 'un péché contre la rigueur terminologique'.

this is quite a commonly accepted meaning of the term. In the classical age, it was the meaning explicitly intended by Hobbes.[55] This is why certain commentators have defined eternity by the totality of time.[56] This definition has the advantage of encapsulating a quite vague but clear meaning: to be eternal is to always exist, with neither end nor beginning – in opposition to what is mortal and exists only for a certain duration. One can thus account for the following trivial yet incontestable fact: an eternal law of physics, for example, does indeed have as one of its characteristics, among others, to always be true – in the time of Solomon as in the time of Huygens. By contrast, other commentators see in eternity the total absence of a relation to time and to duration. These latter commentators base their conviction on a number of strong and insistent formulas in Spinoza's writing: eternity is defined neither by duration, nor by time, and so on.[57] Spinoza even takes care to explicitly exclude an indefinite duration.[58] This is why, if one is absolutely set on identifying eternity with the totality of time, it will be necessary to admit that Spinoza failed to perfectly understand himself.[59] But one can object to this 'atemporalist' reading by referring to other texts, whose lexicon incontestably articulates eternity and duration.[60] The defenders of the 'atemporalist' thesis are thus obliged to read these other texts as moments of inattention or as metaphors. Furthermore, to place identity 'outside of

---

[55] *Leviathan*, Chapter XLVI.

[56] Martha Kneale, 'Eternity and Sempiternity', *Proceedings of the Aristotelian Society*, 69 (1968–9), pp. 223–38, republished in *Spinoza: A Collection of Critical Essays*, ed. M. Grene, pp. 227–40. Kneale even comes to characterise Spinoza's position (which extends beyond her interpretation of Spinoza) as follows: 'I would go so far as to say that it is true that to-day two and two have been four for a day longer than they were yesterday and similarly that, if God exists, he has existed a day longer to-day than he had existed yesterday', p. 231.

[57] 'Absque ulla temporis relatione, sed sub quadam aeternitatis specie', *Ethics* II, 44, Cor. II, Dem., G II, p. 82, l. 31 [CWS I, 481]; 'nec aeternitatis tempore definiri, nec ullam ad tempus relationem habere potest', *Ethics* V, 23, Schol., p. 296, ll. 2–3 [CWS I, 608].

[58] 'Tametsi duratio principio et fine carere concipiatur', *Ethics* I, Def. 8, Exp., G II, p. 46, l. 19 [CWS I, 409]. He had already said in the *Cogitata*: 'quamvis eorum duratio utroque creat fine', II, Chapter 1, G I, p. 252, ll. 19–20 [CM I; CWS I, 318].

[59] This is what Kneale does at the end of her article ('Eternity and Sempiternity', pp. 238–40), not only with respect to the *Cogitata* (in particular passage II, Chapter 1, p. 250, which explicitly denies that the essence of the circle or the triangle, as an eternal truth, has lasted longer now than in the time of Adam), but also with respect to the internal coherence of the *Ethics*.

[60] 'Quae ad mentis durationem sine relatione ad corpus pertinent', *Ethics* V, 20, Schol., G II, p. 294, ll. 23–4 [CWS I, 606]; 'sed ejus aliquid remanet, quod aeternum est', *Ethics* V, 23, G II, p. 295, l. 15 [CWS I, 607].

time' seems to make it difficult to think (or to reduce to an illusion) the fact that what is eternal always exists. Finally, other interpreters, leaving aside time and duration, insist more on the idea of necessity. This is what is suggested by the argument from Book II. Other passages bring these two notions together.[61] But here the difficulty comes from the fact that everything is necessary while not everything is eternal. Thus, the question arises as to whether it is possible to find a way of making such divergent texts agree with each other.

— The third difficulty has to do with the fact that the attribution of eternity to certain modes of thought appears to break the parallelism between the attributes affirmed at the beginning of Book I. If it is true that 'The order and connection of ideas is the same as the order and connection of things',[62] how is it possible that certain ideas are eternal while the body that corresponds to them is perishable? It thus seems necessary to accept that in the course of his work, Spinoza redefines his conception of the relation between the attributes.[63]

Is it possible to resolve these difficulties? Note that commentators borrow all of these possible definitions (sempiternity, eternity's exteriority to time, necessity) from the philosophical tradition that precedes Spinoza, and that in this tradition these definitions succeed one another and sometimes coexist in the work of one and the same author. Similarly, these definitions are also more-or-less mixed in common opinion. It is thus less a matter of identifying such-and-such an inherited trait in Spinoza's language and more of discovering how he organises them. Thus, to identify the connections and distinctions in Spinoza's work, it is important to delimit the uses and the semantic fields of the different terms.

A first remark is necessary: in Spinoza's language, 'eternity' and 'duration' do not refer to different universes between which beings are distributed

---

[61] 'Necessitatem sive aeternitatem . . .', *Ethics* I, 10, Schol., G I, p. 52, ll. 12–13 (on the attributes) [CWS I, 416]; 'sub eadem aeternitatis seu necessitatis specie', *Ethics* IV, 62, Dem., p. 257, ll. 5–6 [CWS I, 581]. Also in Book IV, the Scholium from Proposition 50 reaffirms the link between divine necessity and the eternity of natural laws.

[62] 'Ordo et connexio idearum idem est, ac ordo et connexio rerum', *Ethics* II, 7, G II, p. 89, ll. 21–2 [CWS I, 451].

[63] This is D. Steinberg's position: noting that her interpretation 'is vulnerable to the criticism that it ignores the basic metaphysical guidelines (specifically E, II, 7)', she responds: 'To this I have no answer but that the text of Book V seems to indicate that Spinoza himself ignores them', 'Spinoza's Theory of the Eternity of the Mind', *Canadian Journal of Philosophy*, 11 (1981), p. 53.

(these terms cannot be considered as representing a Spinozist version of the 'beyond' or the 'here-below'). They are modes of existence – that is, characteristics of things.[64] The proof of this is that Spinoza hardly speaks of duration in general: he speaks of the duration of such-and-such a thing.[65] There is therefore a certain semantic imprecision when we say that we live in the world of duration, as commentators sometimes do. For we then predetermine the relations between eternity and duration as relations between two different universes. Similarly, it is not a matter of fundamentally temporal terms conceived negatively: it is only when Spinoza polemicises against other interpretations that he foregrounds eternity and duration's relation or absence of relation with time. This does not prevent us, however, from inquiring into the temporal dimensions of these notions.

On this point, we must first observe that as far as the relations between time, eternity and duration are concerned, Spinoza's texts are not as contradictory as some have wanted to believe. It suffices to be attentive to the way these terms are used and to pose them the questions that are specific to them.

— It is certain that eternity can be defined neither by duration nor by time: Spinoza's affirmations on this point are formal.[66] We therefore cannot consider eternity to be equivalent to sempiternity. This is why, for instance, even if the world is sempiternal (that is, if it has a duration with neither

---

[64] The *Cogitata* used the term 'attribute' under which we conceive the existence of a thing: '[aeternitatem] esse attributum sub quo infinitam Dei existentiam concipimus. Duratio vero est attributum, sub quo rerum creatarum existentiam, prout in sua actualitate perseverant, concipimus', I, Chapter IV, G I, p. 244, ll. 17–20 [CM IV; CWS I, 301]. This expression disappears in the *Ethics* because the term *attribute* receives a more restricted technical meaning. But we do find its equivalent. The same goes for Letter XII: 'Ex quo oritur differentia inter Aeternitatem et Durationem: per Durationem enim modorum tantum existentiam explicare possumus; Substantiae vero per Aeternitatem, hoc est, infinitam existendi, sive, invita latinate, essendi, fruitionem', G IV, p. 54, l. 17; p. 55, l. 3 [*Ep.* XII [to Lodewijk Meyer]; CWS I, 202].

[65] 'Duratio rerum', *Ethics* II, 31, G II, p. 115, l. 15 [CWS I, 472]; *Ethics* IV, Introduction, p. 209, l. 6 [CWS I, 546]; *Ethics* IV, 62, Schol., p. 257, l. 17 [CWS I, 581]; 'duratio nostri corporis', *Ethics* II, 30, p. 114, l. 29 [CWS I, 471]; *Ethics* II, 31, Dem., p. 115, l. 24 [CWS I, 472]; 'mentis durationem', *Ethics* V, 20, Schol., p. 294, l. 23 [CWS I, 606], etc. In fact he hardly ever uses the word *duratio* except in negative phrases to say what it is not or what it does not do. As for Definition 5 from Book II ('Duratio est indefinita existendi continuatio'), it is clarified by an Explanation that immediately refers to the *res existens* (G II, p. 85, ll. 10–14 [CWS I, 447]).

[66] Cf. the texts cited above: *Ethics* II, 44, Cor. 2, Dem. [CWS I, 481]; *Ethics* V, 23, Schol. CWS I, 607–8].

beginning or end), it is not eternal.[67] But we should not misunderstand the meaning of this refusal. On the one hand, to not be eternal does not mean: to have begun in time — Spinoza's position is not a response to the theses of the Averroists or the Libertines.[68] On the other hand, this is not enough to exclude every relation between eternity and duration. Spinoza does indeed admit that an eternal law is always true; it is only that this 'always' is not a part of the *definition* of eternity but is only a *consequence* of it. Note that from this point of view, Spinoza nowhere says that eternity has *no relation* to duration; he only says that it is not *defined* by duration, which is quite different. It is with time that eternity has no relation — but time, in the technical sense given to it by the system,[69] is only the quantitative register of duration.[70] Thus, we cannot say that eternity is totally 'outside of duration': it is not defined by duration, but it does have effects on it. For this reason we can, in a certain manner, say of an eternal thing that it exists sempiternally, on the condition that we clarify that its eternity does not consist in this sempiternal existence. We can thus consider as legitimate — but not as essential — the common conception of eternity: namely, that an eternal thing exists for the totality of time,[71] without being subjected to the accidents of time. This justifies a phrase like: 'God's omnipotence has been actual from eternity and will remain in the same actuality to eternity.'[72]

— In these conditions, can we speak of the duration of an eternal thing? Yes, to the extent that it has one. Its eternity has effects on its duration.

---

[67] This is the thesis of the *Cogitata Metaphysica*, II, Chapter I, G I, p. 251, l. 15 [CM V; CWS I, 317]. Spinoza does not return to it explicitly in the *Ethics*.

[68] Cf. for example the entirety of the *Second Treatise* from the *Theophrastus*, 'Qui est de Mundo' — which is in fact 'de aeternitate mundi', *Theophrastus Redivivus*, vol. I, pp. 173–337. On the history of this debate, see L. Bianchi, *L'Inizio dei Tempi. Antichità e novità del mondo da Bonaventura a Newton*, Florence: Olschki, 1987.

[69] 'Haec [duratio] autem ut determinetur, comparamus illam cum duratione aliarum rerum, quae certum et determinatum habent motum, *haecque comparatio tempus vocatur*', CM, I, Chapter IV, G I, p. 244, ll. 23–5 [CM IV; CWS I, 310]; 'Praetera nemo dubitat, quin etiam tempus imaginemur, nempe ex eo, quod corpora alia aliis tardius, vel celerius, vel aeque celeriter moveri imaginemur', *Ethics* II, 44, Cor. 1, Schol., G II, p. 125, ll. 24–7 [CWS I, 480].

[70] Cf. the remarks by A. Donagan, 'Spinoza's Proof of Immortality', in *Spinoza: A Collection of Critical Essays*, ed. M. Grene, pp. 241–59, which are based in particular on the first Corollary to Proposition 44 from Book II.

[71] By giving to the word 'time' its common meaning, not its technical meaning.

[72] 'Dei omnipotentia actu ab aeterno fuit, et in aeternum in eadem actualitate manebit', *Ethics* I, 17, Cor. 2, Schol., G II, p. 62, ll. 19–20 [CWS I, 426]. It is characteristic to see Appuhn recoil in the face of the future tense and translate this as 'et demeure pour l'éternité', A, p. 61.

Does this imply that we can speak of the duration of God? Certainly not. The only mode of God's existence is eternity. This is why, when Spinoza uses 'temporal' expressions to refer to eternal things, he does so only with respect to the eternity of modes. A finite eternal mode is of the order both of duration and of eternity. The consequences of its eternity can be translated into its duration. This is why it is not contradictory to speak of 'what remains' after the death of the body or of the 'duration of the soul' outside of its relation to the body.[73] This is neither a case of inattentiveness nor of metaphor. On the other hand, this articulation is meaningful only with respect to divine eternity. God has effects on the duration of nature in its entirety and on each thing in particular, but he does not have his own duration.[74] We can thus argue that, with respect to all of these questions, Spinoza's language is at once rigorous and less distant from the exigencies of common opinion than is frequently admitted. The coherence proper to the system imprints its order on these traditional terms, all the while responding to the questions they raise.

Up to this point we have simply eliminated the causes of uncertainty linked to the use of temporal terms. We have not made any headway, however, as far as the proper content of eternity is concerned. What is this content? The way in which we saw it introduced in Book II suggests that eternity coincides with necessity. But if eternity is necessity, the question arises as to why we require a second term to refer to a single thing. Everything might well be necessary – but not everything is eternal.

We also need to know why it seems to go without saying that eternity should be defined as necessity. Here, too, the language of philosophy comes up against an exigency of common consciousness, one that, moreover, Spinoza is well aware of. We have just encountered a first aspiration of this common consciousness concerning eternity: its equal presence at all moments in time. It seems contradictory to Spinoza to say that something is eternal and that it *is not* at each instant, or that it is at one instant and not at another. In this sense, the three solutions proposed above (sempiternity as essence; the absence – which is necessarily equal at all moments – of a

---

[73] Cf. the texts cited above, *Ethics* V, 20, Schol. [*CWS* I, 605–6]; *Ethics* V, 23 [*CWS* I, 607].

[74] A. Donagan, 'Spinoza's Proof of Immortality', remarks that Spinoza uses three technical concepts: eternity, the duration of a thing, and time, but that he has no term to refer to what is commonly called time as the unfolding of the totality of events. In fact, there is no need for a supplementary concept: this unfolding is the duration of Nature as a whole.

relation to time; and sempiternity as a consequence of eternity) all respond, each in their own way, to this exigency. A second dimension of this diffuse conception of eternity could be characterised by dissatisfaction in the face of the perishable. In this sense, the eternal is not only what does not perish (this would mean that it refers simply to the temporal grounding of one's gaze on eternity), but is also, and above all, what cannot perish; it is that which is such that it cannot perish. Here, the focus is no longer on time but on the force of existence. The constitution of the notion of eternity supposes that people see that everything around them becomes more or less corrupted in the long term and that they aspire to encounter something that escapes this corruption. Time, if it still appears from this perspective, is less a rule of succession than a power of erosion. Spinoza registers this common dissatisfaction in the face of the perishable in the penultimate objection to the Appendix to Book I: 'if all things followed from the necessity of God's most perfect nature, why are there so many imperfections in nature? why are things so corrupt to the point where they stink? so ugly that they produce nausea? why is there confusion, evil, and sin?'[75] Not only is Spinoza familiar with this aspiration of common consciousness (an aspiration that is sufficiently strong to make this consciousness retreat in the face of the idea of universal necessity), he also makes an effort to show that his own philosophy responds to it. When he speaks of God as eternal, he often takes care to associate this adjective with another adjective that marks not the relation to time but precisely the dimension of the inalterable: God is an 'immutable and eternal'[76] thing; the love of God is 'constant and eternal'.[77] In such qualifications, there is more than the idea of sempiternity: immutability and constancy mark the force that resists the erosion of time.

If this is so, then the first content of the idea of eternity is the power to exist. Not the simple fact of existing, but the affirmative plenitude of existence. Each time that Spinoza takes as his object the notion of eternity for itself,[78] he is not content to simply mention the idea of necessity: he also

---

[75] 'Unde ergo tot imperfectiones in natura ortae? Videlicet rerum corruptio ad foetorem usque, rerum difformitas quae nauseam moveat, confusio, malum, peccatum, etc.', G II, p. 83, ll. 19–21 [CWS I, 446].

[76] 'Rem immutabilem et aeternam', *Ethics* V, 20, Schol., p. 294, l. 12 [CWS I, 606].

[77] 'In constanti et aeterno erga Deum amore', *Ethics* V, 36, Schol., p. 303, ll. 3–4 [CWS I, 612].

[78] And not with respect to Reason, as is the case in Book II, in the second Corollary to Proposition 44. There, as we have seen, Spinoza only effectively mentions necessity. We will see a little further on why.

always introduces the idea of existence.[79] We can now better understand the three characteristic traits of his approach.

A. For a thing to be eternal, it must not only be necessary; its necessity must not encounter anything that prevents it from existing. Eternity is thus not only necessity but a certain conjunction of existence and necessity. We can say that everything is necessary, but that some things draw their necessity from the web of laws and external things of which they are a part, while for others necessity is the immediate manifestation of the first principle of all existence. However, even what arises from only the first type of necessity is linked by the network of laws to this principle. Thus, while everything might not be eternal, everything that is known necessarily is known under the category of eternity.

B. We can also now understand why Definition 8 reduces eternity to an 'eternal thing'. For a thing to be eternal is for it to immediately draw its existence from the power to exist of this first principle. It is therefore normal to define eternity on the basis of this first principle – which is God.[80] Eternity is not a general property of certain beings that is applied to God among other things. Spinoza is therefore not being inconsistent at the level of his terminology by speaking of the eternity of certain modes, since these modes owe this property very precisely to the essence of this eternal being (and not to their own essence).

C. We can now explain in what sense duration and sempiternity constitute a consequence of this conjunction. The mutual limiting of beings translates into their reciprocal succession and determination in duration. Thus, what is never prevented by another thing from existing simply always exists – without this 'always' being a part of its definition. What is prevented by others does not yet exist; what is no longer prevented from existing exists presently; what exists now but will be prevented from existing no longer exists. The different aspects of duration and even indefinite duration can thus be deduced from the confrontation that follows from the existence of

---

[79] 'Par aeternitatem intelligo ipsam existentiam, quatenus ex sola rei aeternae definitione necessario sequi concipitur', *Ethics* I, Def. 8, G II, p. 46, ll. 13–15 [CWS I, 409]. He says this again in Book V: 'Aeternitats est ipsa Dei essentia quatenus haec necessariam involvit existentiam', *Ethics* V, 30, Dem., p. 299, 10–11 [CWS I, 610].

[80] As is shown clearly by the reference from the Demonstration to Proposition 30 from Book V to Definition 8 from Book I.

finite things. We are thus indeed in the register of what has been called a 'logic of war'.[81]

It is not enough, however, to state that existence is articulated with necessity. It is also necessary to determine how the forms taken by this articulation allow us to think the status of different modes, and, in particular, that of the human soul. To do this, we will have to make a supplementary distinction, or rather identify one in the texts. If we consider Spinoza's textual usage, we notice that he always distinguishes between two expressions: 'to be eternal' and 'to be an eternal truth'. One might be tempted to say that these are the same thing, since 'to be an eternal truth' is on the one hand 'to be true' and on the other 'to be eternal'. In such an interpretation, 'to be an eternal truth' would be the sum of two simpler properties, truth and eternity. However, Spinoza does not reason in this way. He does not consider these two expressions to be equivalent; moreover, for him, 'to be an eternal truth' constitutes the simpler expression since he uses it to demonstrate the other. If we wish to delve more deeply into his problematic, we will in turn have to deploy this distinction by attempting to grasp its implications. We must therefore distinguish between at least three categories: things that are not eternal truths (the existence of finite modes); eternal things (God; the infinite modes; certain ideas); and finally things that are eternal truths but are not themselves eternal (the essence of finite modes). It is on this final category that we must focus our attention. In fact, Spinoza says explicitly – and on many occasions – not that the essences of things are eternal[82] but that they are eternal truths.[83] It is on this distinction that the coherence between Books I and II depends, as well as the second part of Book V.

---

[81] G. Albiac, *La Sinagoga vacía. Un estudio de las fuentes marranas del espinosimo*. Madrid: Hiperión, 1987, p. 359: 'el conatus, el esfuerzo, no es sino la relacíon agonal de unos seres con otros en el infinito escenario de encuentro (*i.e.*: of shock) que es la naturaleza'; p. 360: 'una lógica de las potencias en conflicto, que es una lógica de la guerra'.

[82] B. Rousset correctly insists on this in *La perspective finale de l'*'Ethique' *et le problème de la cohérence du spinozisme*, Paris: Vrin, 1968, Chapter I, in particular p. 31: 'Il n'est jamais question de l'eternité de l'essence, contrairement à ce qu'une lecture hâtive pourrait laisser croire: certes, Spinoza fait appel, dans sa preuve de l'éternité, à l'essence du corps et à celle de l'esprit, mais ce n'est pas pour affirmer leur éternité'. M. Guéroult suggests on a number of occasions that the essences of finite things are eternal (*Spinoza*, vol. I, p. 327, 331), but he almost immediately gives this affirmation a restrictive interpretation. Matheron says very precisely: 'toutes les essences sont des vérités éternelles', *Individu et Communauté*, p. 574.

[83] In the first part, the Scholium to Proposition 17 states that if a person can be the cause of the existence of another person, they cannot be the cause of their essence, 'est enim

Let us examine the meaning and field of application of these two expressions by taking into account the additional fact that there exist two sorts of eternal truths: those that are nothing outside of thought,[84] and those which, by contrast, are things.[85]

— An eternal truth of the first kind (an axiom like 'nothing comes from nothing' or 'the whole is greater than the part') is a necessary truth; its necessity is immediately eternal in the sense that nothing hinders it. But this does not suffice to make of it a thing, and thus to confer upon it an existence in the strong sense of the word.

— What becomes, now, of things? Each thing has an essence and an existence. The essence of a thing is an eternal truth of a second kind: this means that it possesses an internal coherence that makes it knowable in a necessary way. For example, if the circle of the radius AB exists, it is necessarily produced by the rotation of a segment AB around the point A. This rotation constitutes its essence, and it is eternally true that I can produce the circle in this way (and also know it by reconstituting the process of its production). To be an eternal truth in this sense is to be able to be known under the category of eternity. Of course, the circle can very easily be drawn or not drawn, but each time that it is drawn it will instantiate this law. To say that an essence is an eternal truth means, therefore, that it has an internal necessity that suffices for us to be able to formulate its laws. But

---

haec aeterna veritas', G II, p. 63 [CWS I, 427]. The Explanation to Definition 8 can be understood in the same way. The Scholium to Proposition 8 says that the existence of substance is an eternal truth, just as its essence is; the structure of the phrase clearly indicates that since the emphasis is placed here on the cause of existence, then this is because, as far as essence is concerned, the characteristic of being an eternal truth applies to all things. Letter X affirms without limitations (*omnio*) that things and their effects are eternal truths (G IV, p. 47, ll. 19–20 [*Ep.* X [to Simon de Vries]; *CWS* I, 196]); it adds that we nevertheless avoid giving them this name so as not to confuse them with eternal truths in the common sense as 'a nihilo nihil fit' (a distinction like this one is at work in Letter IX, p. 43, ll. 12–15 [*Ep.* IX [to Simon de Vries]; *CWS* I, 194]). One might be led to think that this last example proves too much since it also includes the affects. Spinoza no doubt means to say: to the degree that they are deducible from essence.

[84] 'Haec, inquam, similesque propositiones vocantur absolute aeterna veritates, sub quo nihil aliud significare volunt, quam quod talia, nullam sedem habent extra mentem', Ep. X, G IV, p. 47, ll. 22–4 [*Ep.* X [to Simon de Vries]; *CWS* I, 196].

[85] That a thing can be a truth is not surprising in certain lexicons from the eighteenth century. E. Powell, *Spinozas Gottesbegriff*, Halle, 1899, Hildesheim: Olms, 1980, p. 57, then G. Huan, *Le Dieu de Spinoza*, Arras: Schoutheer, 1913, p. 273, also note that what Heerebord understood by 'aeterna veritas' was 'aliquid reale extra intellectum', *Meletemata*, I, 307.

by itself this internal necessity is not enough to confer upon it an effective right to exist.

— Why is the essence of a thing not eternal? Precisely because it does not necessarily imply existence.[86] Certainly, it tends towards existence, but its necessity must confront others that counteract it and that it counteracts in turn, and that define its relation to duration and its acquisition of a limited part of this duration. Its essence is not a plenitude of existence. In the example cited, someone is needed to draw the circle, while someone else can efface it. This is why Spinoza refuses to say that the essence of a finite thing is eternal,[87] all the while granting that it is an eternal truth.[88] Here the second figure of necessity intervenes: namely, external necessity, which only brings to fruition the right to existence of these non-eternal essences. As this

---

[86] B. Rousset correctly notes that even if the eternity of essences seems to go without saying for the philosophical tradition, it is incompatible with the problematic that emerges from Definition II from Book II. The essence 'n'est pas un autre être, qui pourrait jouir d'une existence nécessaire et immuable par opposition à l'être contingent et périssable, mais c'est la définition propre de l'être en question, fût-il contingent et périssable; aussi est-il impossible d'attribuer une veritable éternité à ce qui constitue la nature de la chose existante, quand on la refuse à la chose existante elle-même', *La perspective finale de l'Ethique*, p. 29.

[87] As Rousset notes, in the only two texts – in the *Cogitata* – where Spinoza seems to attribute eternity to essences, he considers this doctrine as external to his own, and he accepts with reservations that this is due to the inadequacies of language ('atque hoc sensu [the formal essence depends only on the existence of divine essence] iis assentimur, qui dicunt essentias rerum aeternas esse', CM, I, Chapter II, G I, p. 239, ll. 3–4 [CM II; CWS I, 305]; and: 'assueti sumus, propter defectum verborum aeternitatem etiam rebus, quarum essentia distinguitur ab earum existentia, tribuere [. . .] atque etiam essentiis rerum, quamdiu ipsas non existentes concipimus; eas enim tum aeternas vocamus', CM, II, Chapter I, p. 251, ll. 12–17 [CM I; CWS I, 317]). In the *Ethics*, even this weak sense disappears. On the other hand, I cannot follow Rousset in his explanation of Definition 8 and of the letter to De Vries, which is obscured by the fact that he does not distinguish between eternity and eternal truth (but in an inverse sense from that of other commentators).

[88] Despite some uncertainties in his vocabulary, G. Huan clearly saw the problem: 'Une essence peut être, en effet, une vérité éternelle sans developper d'une manière nécessaire sa propre existence; car l'essence d'une chose est exprimée par une définition adéquate (Ep. 9 et 10, *De Int. Em.*, p. 29 [= § 95]), et une définition adéquate est une vérité éternelle, c'est-à-dire que, si elle est affirmative, elle ne pourra jamais être négative (*De Int. Em.*, p. 16, note 3 [= § 54, n. 1]); or, une définition n'enveloppe et n'exprime rien que la nature ou l'essence de la chose définie, et, par suite, la cause de l'existence de cette chose doit être donnée en dehors de sa définition (*Ethique*, I, 8, scolie II) ou comprise dans sa définition comme le principe générateur de son essence [which is not true for substance]', *Le Dieu de Spinoza*, p. 272.

necessity is external, it can either coincide or not with internal necessity. This is why corruption, becoming and the fragility of things are nevertheless compatible with the rigour of the laws they manifest.

— What happens when a thing is eternal? In this instance not only is its essence eternal, its existence is as well. In this case, its internal necessity is strong enough to suffice for its existence.[89]

Thus, the principal difficulties tied to the notion of eternity can be undone when we think of eternity as something proper to existence and when we reconstitute from this perspective the various concepts the system uses to think the different relations of things to their principles. It is worthwhile recalling that one of Spinoza's first readers had clearly underscored this link between existence and eternity – namely, Boulainvillers, who in his *Essai de métaphysique* recomposed the themes of the *Ethics* on the basis of a meditation on existence.[90] From this he derived a Spinozism that one might find heterodox, but which attests to a confident recognition of the structures of the system.

We can now return to the question of parallelism and of its alleged rupture. Without exploring all aspects of this question, we must note that the Demonstration to Proposition 7 from Book II essentially refers to causality.[91] The Proposition thus in no way affirms that the mode of existence of things (of extension or of any other attribute) is the same as that of ideas. It affirms that the connection of their causes is the same. This connection of causes in

---

[89] For reasons of facility I am using here the opposition *internal* and *external* because it is traditional. But for this opposition not to be misleading, it is necessary to recall that an internal necessity is not always a necessity proper to a thing: when it is a matter of an eternal thing that is not God, it is divine necessity within a modal essence.

[90] 'Or de toutes les propriétés des êtres dont j'ai connaissance, la plus simple et la plus générale me paraît être celle de l'existence. Mais comme je ne pourrais pas raisonner sur cette propriété, la concevant attachée à certains sujets et dépendante d'eux sans les connaître eux-mêmes auparavant' (it is necessary to consider being in general and the necessity of its existence), 'je suis donc convaincu par ma raison qu'il y a un être absolu et nécessaire; et par sentiment qu'il y en a plusieurs particuliers, qui ne sont ni absolus ni nécessaire et qui toutefois existent les uns après les autres dans un certain ordre dont la disposition ne m'est pas connue', published in the volume *Réfutation de Spinoza*, Bruxelles: Foppens, 1731, pp. 7–8.

[91] 'Nam cujuscunque causati idea a cognitione causae, cujus est effectus, dependet', G II, p. 89, ll. 24–5 [*Ethics* II, 7, Dem.; CWS I, 451]. Cf. also the example from the Scholium: 'Nec ulla alia de causa dixi, quod Deus sit causa ideae ex. gr. circuli, quatenus tantum est res cogitans, & circuli, quatenus tantum est res extensa [. . .]', ibid., p. 90, l. 18, ff. [*Ethics* II, 7, Schol.; CWS I, 451].

each attribute thus takes on the disposition proper to that attribute.[92] Thus, if this disposition allows it, it is quite possible for there to correspond to a perishable mode an eternal mode, so long as the connection of their causes remains unchanged. Now, this just so happens to be the case, thanks to the characteristics specific to the attribute Thought. The idea of a finite existing thing, insofar as it is finite, needs other ideas to exist, and in the order of their succession. On the other hand, the idea of an eternal truth – in particular that of an essence – is eternal. It does not need succession to exist. In other words, the same reality is manifest here in two different forms: on the side of extension, the essence of a finite mode is not eternal, but it does constitute an eternal truth; on the side of thought, the idea of this essence is not only an eternal truth: it is an eternal mode. This is what founds the difference of possibilities that Alexandre Matheron has rightly named a 'distortion'[93] and that allows the mortality of bodies to be juxtaposed with the partial eternity of souls – without, for all that, there being a rupture of the unity in the connection of causes.

Let us summarise what we have said so far. What makes certain people apt to read the *Ethics* is their apprehension of the necessity of the laws of Nature, which is identified with the immutability of forms. This apprehension is rooted in the necessity of each law, without it being confused with any of them in particular. It culminates in the apprehension of divine necessity, which opens the *mens* up to the consideration of Eternity.

It remains for us to ask why Spinoza does not use the term experience to refer to this apprehension of forms. Moreover, we find in Book I no terms that are related to the language of experience. However, a certain number of common points can be identified with the status of what we have named experience in the journey of the *TdIE*, or indeed with respect to language, the passions, or history. The apprehension of necessity is inscribed in the

---

[92] This is, moreover, why the term 'parallelism', which is not Spinoza's, is not very well chosen: it suggests the idea of a perfect isomorphy.

[93] 'Sans doute, de la Pensée à l'Etendue, la structure formelle d'un individu donné reste-t-elle identique à elle-même; mais le type d'activité selon lequel elle se déploie n'en change pas moins du tout au tout. D'où une distorsion dont les conséquences sont capitales', *Individu et Communauté*, p. 25. The demonstration can be found on pp. 27–8 for bodies, pp. 31–5 for ideas. The double mode of existence of ideas is deduced from two characteristics possessed by the attribute Thought: it is not spatialising as Extension is (and thus its modes are eternal); it is representative (and thus its modes correspond to the nature of their idea). It could be objected to such an explanation that it 'imports' the duration of Extension into Thought while Spinoza does not do this. Matheron responds that when Spinoza 'étudie une forme quelconque de séparation dans la Pensée (la passion, en particulier), il l'explique toujours en se référant au corps', p. 34.

past of each demonstration. This apprehension is not to be confused with demonstrative knowledge itself. Why not, then, consider this apprehension as if it were like the third type of experience that Letter X spoke of – that which, without teaching us the essence of things, determines our soul to think of this essence?

One possible response has to do with the non-universality of this experience: all possess the idea of God, but not all develop their Reason to the point that this necessity appears to them in itself. Thus, we do not find here the circulation between individuals that is always characteristic of experience. Furthermore, this perspective on eternity is not at all anchored in the singular – in the I. This is the core of the difference between the *Ethics* and the beginning of the *Treatise on the Emendation of the Intellect*. Finally, it is clear that the idea of necessity is an adequate idea. Its inadequate variation (the pseudo-causality of miracles) is on the contrary characteristic of the logic of metamorphoses, which the philosopher must purge themselves of. Experience neutralises the difference between adequation and inadequation, since it can use what the imagination has acquired to teach without having to concern itself with the imagination's epistemological status. The differences are thus more important than the analogies.

Thus, in Book I and at the end of Book II, we do indeed have an apprehension of eternity, but Spinoza does not qualify it as an experience. And following the logic of his lexicon and of his system, he is right not to describe it in this way.

2. The Soul and the Body

Book II from the *Ethics* is devoted to the soul, and its first Propositions deal in particular with the relations between the soul and the body. Can we read here something like an experience of the self – an experience that, in different forms, has become constitutive of modern philosophy? The canonical approach of modern philosophy often articulates the analysis of the power of thought with the identification of a material tied to the body (perception, memory) and its malfunctionings (errors of meaning, dreams, somnambulism). It is such an experience of the self, understood as an analysis of consciousness, that Saisset, as we saw above, judged to be decisive for elaborating a metaphysics. As we know, Saisset reproached Spinoza for misunderstanding the import of this analysis. But what is this experience precisely? In a Cartesian and post-Cartesian context, a first form of the experience of the self would be the evidence of the 'I think'. Cartesian experience could be said to be a radical experience in the sense that it is at once immediate (there are no conditions for experiencing it; doubt serves to bring it about in its purity, even if it pre-exists this doubt) and irreducibly true (it is at once experience and knowledge). The conjunction of these three characteristics confers on such an experience an authenticity in which presence and effectivity are indissociable.[94] This is not the case in Spinoza. From the *Principia* onwards, Spinoza refuses to accord any experiential character to the *Cogito*. At the beginning of this work, which claims to present the principles of Cartesian philosophy, the 'I think, I am', is in fact the object of a demonstration.[95] It is obviously not a question here of a mere problem of exposition. The divergence is situated at the level of principles: an experience cannot be confused with foundational knowledge. This distance will again be reinforced in the *Ethics*, where the human soul is a complex whole that cannot be given in a unique and immediate experience.[96] Whatever the importance Spinoza attaches to the description of the affects of the soul, of its knowledge of the body, of the phenomena of perception, this identification of the self cannot lead to the transcendence of an *I*.

A. The Memorial Dimension of Experience

Is this to say that there is no experience of the self? There is such an experience, but it is above all one of dependence and not of foundation: in Book II, it is given as an opaque experience tied to the body. However, this opacity in no way prevents it from playing a key role in the argument. Analysing it allows us to bring out the memorial structure of the experience of the soul. This is why, while some have argued that 'according to Spinoza, consciousness is above all an *illusion* as regards the mode of transparency that it attributes to itself',[97] we must add that this illusion brings with it a necessary attestation of Reason. The vocabulary of these passages draws, moreover, on the same lexicon that we have identified concerning the confirmative and

---

[94] 'Adeo ut, omnibus satis superque pensitatis, denique, statuendum sit hoc pronuntiatum, Ego sum, Ego existo, quoties a me profertur, vel mente concipitur, necessario esse verum', *Second Meditation*, AT, VII, 25.

[95] Cf. M.-H. Belin, 'Les *Principes de la philosophie de Descartes*: Remarques sur la duplicité d'une écriture', *Archives de philosophie*, 51 (1988), cahier 1, p. 104.

[96] With respect to Proposition 15 ('The idea that constitutes the formal being of the human mind is not simple'), which is described as a 'capital qualification', Gueroult highlights the following point: 'On voit, en tout cas, combien on est loin ici du Cogito cartésien, être simple, indivisible, etc.', *Spinoza*, vol. II, *L'Ame*, p. 193.

[97] 'selon Spinoza la conscience est d'abord *illusion* sur le mode de transparence qu'elle s'attribue', J. Lacroix, *Spinoza et le problème du salut*, Paris: PUF, 1970, p. 11.

constitutive modes of experience: we encounter the term *experientia*[98] itself but also the terms *sentire* and *percipere*;[99] reference is made to a multitude of examples;[100] and the experience is based on a feeling present in all people and that can be recalled using the first person plural pronoun.[101]

The axial formula is Proposition 13, which culminates in the following principle: the body exists as we feel it. This conceptual knot ties together two levels of experience.[102] The first level refers to the presence of the corporeal, and opens up a space for the feeling of the self – but this is a neutral and universal feeling. On this basis, the second level refers to the variety of the corporeal register, and allows us to introduce the play of differences at the heart of the universality of souls.

The first level records the minimum necessary for identifying the composition of the singular mode that is man; but this identity will only be acquired after the work of the Demonstration on this experiential nucleus. The axioms began by positing what everyone knows: that the human being thinks; that we have perceptions of a body. It is the human being that

---

[98] 'Omnia illa, quae sumpsi, postulata vix quicquam continent quod non constet experientia, de qua nobis non licet dubitare [. . .]', *Ethics* II, 17, Schol., G II, p. 105, ll. 27–8 [*CWS* I, 464].

[99] 'Nos corpus quoddam multis modis affici sentimus', *Ethics* II, Ax. 4, G II, p. 86, ll. 4–5 [*CWS* I, 448]; 'Nullas res singulares, praeter corpora, & cogitandi modos, sentimus nec percipimus', *Ethics* II, Ax. 5, G II, p. 86, ll. 6–8 [*CWS* I, 448]; 'corpus humanum, prout ipsum sentimus, existere', *Ethics* II, 13, Cor. G II, p. 96, ll. 19–20 [*CWS* I, 457]. The terms of this Corollary are recalled in the Scholium to Proposition 17 to justify the 'de qua nobis non licet dubitare', p. 105, ll. 28–9 [*CWS* I, 464].

[100] 'Multis exemplis explicui', *Ethics* II, 16, Cor. 2, G II, p. 104, l. 16 [*CWS* I, 463].

[101] Cf. *sentimus, percipimus*, in the passages that have just been cited (Axioms 4 and 5, Corollary to Proposition 13).

[102] Here I am following J.-T. Desanti's demonstration from his *Introduction à l'Histoire de la philosophie*, Paris: Les Essais de la Nouvelle Critique, 1956: he shows clearly how Propositions 11 and 13 from Book II constitute the point of departure for the theory of the soul, and he divides the Demonstration to Proposition 11 into two moments: on the one hand, what constitutes the actual being of the soul is an idea; on the other hand, this idea is that of a singular thing. He notes: 'La première partie de la démonstration utilise des données immédiates de l'expérience commune, données que Spinoza a pris soin de réunir au début de la deuxième partie sous le nom d'axiomes', p. 112. He then underscores the similarity with Descartes: Spinoza appeals to the testimony of conscience: 'Seulement son originalité vient de ce qu'il ne s'en tient pas là. L'intimité que la pensée possède à l'égard d'elle-même ne suffit pas à ses yeux à montrer la nature de l'âme', pp. 112–13. This is why Spinoza introduces, to then apply it to the givens of experience, his general conception of nature: this is the meaning of the reference to the Corollary to Proposition 8.

thinks, not an I who thinks.[103] A body, not our body. The first thirteen Propositions of the Book will be necessary, not for arriving at the body proper, but simply for understanding that it is possible to ask this question. The axiom should not mislead us: it is a matter of recording a presence, not an evident and necessary truth.

Can we nevertheless come to know more about the experiential tenor contained in these axioms? To do this, it suffices to identify, in the following Propositions, the different facts that the geometrical order is tasked with explaining. Among these facts, it is necessary to underscore the particular status of external bodies. Their role is decisive, but they exert their influence only in an oblique manner. What counts is less their existence than their presence, that is, their capacity to impose themselves on us. This is why the feeling of external bodies is not cited as such in the minimal conditions identified by the opening axioms. In fact, these bodies are perceived to the degree that they modify our body.[104] Reciprocally, to feel our body is above all to feel the affections of the body; these affections are the modifications of the body by external bodies.[105] External bodies are themselves perceived as 'existing in act' or as 'present to the Soul' ('sibi praesens'),[106] and this perceived presence in no way implies their effective presence. This, moreover, is the originary given of experience: the gap between presence and effectivity.[107] We are familiar with this gap: it often happens that we consider as present what does not, in fact, exist.[108] The soul, finally, is not content to perceive its body and other bodies: it also perceives itself[109] (which in no way means that it knows itself adequately). Finally, the soul perceives duration – of things, of bodies, of itself. None of these givens is indicated with certainty as being the source of the others. These givens impose themselves on us with the force of presence – but nothing in this force confers upon these givens any theoretical validity. This is all we can know clearly through experience

---

[103] Why does Axiom 2 say 'Homo cogitat' and not 'modos cogitandi sentimus'? In fact, this last formula is present in Axiom 5 and it can be found in almost the same form in the Dutch version of Axiom 2 ('De mensch denkt; of anders, wy weten dat wy denken' – with, in the margin, the annotation: 'modi cogitandi').
[104] Cf. Proposition 16, Corollary 2.
[105] Cf. Proposition 16.
[106] Cf. Proposition 17.
[107] Cf. Proposition 17, Corollary. The Scholium clearly indicates that we know all this by experience, and that it is only a matter of explaining it: 'Videmus itaque qui fieri potest ut ea, quae non sunt, veluti praesentia contemplemur, ut saepe fit'.
[108] Cf. Proposition 17, Scholium.
[109] Cf. Propositions 20–3.

at the moment when geometrical reasoning begins. At the same time this is what geometrical reasoning must account for: not only what we feel and perceive, not only the possible errors in these perceptions, but also the reason for this force of presence. Finally, the traditional function of closure is not lacking: Axiom 5 fulfils it perfectly.

It is with these givens that the demonstrative order will get to work. Propositions 1 to 10 construct a general schema of relations between the two attributes that are in question here; Proposition 11 states that the object of the human soul is a singular thing; Proposition 12 demonstrates that everything that happens to this singular thing is perceived (without saying that this perception is adequate); and Proposition 13, finally, returns to the body that had emerged only in Axiom 4. The Corollary can thus conclude as follows: 'man consists of a Soul and a Body, and that the human Body exists, as we are aware of it'.[110] Note that 'as we are aware of it' does not mean 'adequately'. What do we know, then? That this soul that we feel is our own, and that the body whose affections we feel is ours as well. This is a lot, but also not much at all: it is a lot, because in this way the experience that comes to us through the feeling of the body is given legitimacy (and while it is not necessary for there to correspond to this experience any adequate ideas, we still know that everything that happens in this experience gives rise to an idea, and that these ideas concern only what happens in this experience); and it is very little, for on the one hand, nothing proves to us that the consciousness of affections is authentic[111] (and in fact, what comes next will show both that it is not authentic, but that it nevertheless possesses a lot of power to make us believe that it is), while on the other hand nothing of what has been said is specific to the human being – every soul that feels a body is in the same situation.[112] And nothing allows us to draw a distinction between different people. In sum, at the stage marked by Proposition 13, the first strata of experience has attained the limits of what it can contribute to the argument. It forces us to notice something that is given and that reason can justify on the basis of the principles from Book I. Yet this given, justified in this way, cannot found an ethics – that is, a reflection on significant differences, for instance between the human soul and other souls, between

---

[110] 'Hinc sequitur, hominem mente et corpore constare, et corpus humanum, prout ipsum sentimus, existere', *Ethics* II, 13, Cor., G II, p. 96, ll. 19–20 [CWS I, 457].

[111] In the sense that authenticity implies that there is no disjunction between presence and effectivity.

[112] 'Nam ea, quae hucusque ostendimus, admodum communia sunt, nec magis ad homines quam ad reliqua individua pertinent, quae omnia, quamvis diversis gradibus, animata tamen sunt', *Ethics* II, 13, Schol., G II, p. 96, ll. 26–8 [CWS I, 458].

different human souls, or between the imperfection and perfection of an individual soul. With respect to the relations of the soul to the body, this experience presents us with a point of view that could be characterised as absolute, the reason being that it does not refer to such-and-such a particular determination of the soul or of the body but is rather true for all souls and all bodies. Yet, the reverse side of the universality of this point of view is its poverty.

It is thus necessary to change perspective and to introduce differential elements. It is here that the analysis of the soul begins. As the Scholium to Proposition 13 shows, this analysis passes by way of the analysis of the body, since the differences between ideas are identical to the differences between bodies.[113] A science of the soul can only be constituted to the degree that the science of the body is already constituted for itself. One might be surprised to see such a consequence being drawn: if the two orders of difference are identical, why not go immediately to the science of the soul? A first, external response is possible: Spinoza wants to constitute a psychology, and he already has a physics in his possession. It is thus a matter of the knowledge of thought catching up, following a historical delay, to the knowledge of extension. But a second response is necessary – one that, moreover, accounts for the first: the movements of the soul are known only by those of the body. There cannot exist a direct knowledge of the soul by itself. This will be demonstrated in what follows, but the principle is already posited in the statement from Proposition 13: the object of the human soul is the body *and nothing else* – in particular, it is not the soul itself.[114] Furthermore, a rational knowledge is founded on common notions and we do not possess common notions about the domain of thought, since the recognition of a common property supposes the encounter of two individuals – that is, it supposes an attribute where things exist *partes extra partes*. All of this explains why the true knowledge of the soul must presuppose a minimal physics. Now, this knowledge is not explicitly cited in the *Ethics* for itself. The Scholium that affirms its necessity simultaneously makes a claim as to why it can be omitted: 'I cannot explain this here, nor is that necessary for the things I wish to demonstrate.'[115] We must now, then, appeal to the second level of experience, which explains and determines the first: what sort of body, and

---

[113] G II, p. 96, l. 32–p. 97, l. 6 [*Ethics* II, 13, Schol.; CWS I, 458].

[114] It is this distinction that governs the theory of the *idea ideae*. Cf. Proposition 21 and Scholium, and Gueroult's commentary, vol. II, pp. 245–56.

[115] 'Eam autem hic explicare non possum, nec id ad ea, quae demonstrare volo ncesse est', *Ethics* II, 13, Schol., p. 97, l. 6–7 [CWS I, 458].

thus soul? It is a knowledge that Spinoza himself declares to be experiential[116] that will allow us to constitute the minimum necessary for knowing, not the functioning of the body, but those characteristics which, among other things, will allow us to understand how the soul perceives the body, and how it perceives at the same time both external objects and itself. Now, this experience is one that 'we cannot doubt, after we have shown that the human Body exists as we are aware of it'.[117] Two things result from this: on the one hand, we will learn how the complexity and stratification of our body is the occasion in us for consciousness and for diverse forms of knowledge; and on the other hand, we will learn the reasons why we represent to ourselves what is not present as if it were present. The reason for this is the memorial structure that lies at the base of our consciousness: our body is so constituted that it retains traces of what it has encountered, and it reanimates these traces by associative processes even when the bodies that left them are absent. External bodies, which were not mentioned in the axioms, now reappear in full force; but they reappear with this force thanks only to our own constitution. The structure of our body is such that it reminds the soul, which takes the body as its object, of their presence, even in their effective absence. It is this particularity that governs the way we perceive our body, and concomitantly the way in which we perceive our soul. In other words, the memorial structure that organises our relation to the external world has repercussions for our relation to our internal world. In effect, it produces the totality of our experience of duration. This is why we are not conscious of the duration of our soul by itself, except to the extent that our body exists and is in contact with external objects. For this reason, it appears that the tripartite experience of duration as such cannot be an adequate form of knowledge.

The experience of the self is thus both positive and negative: thanks to my body, I know that the body exists, that it feels, and that it has relations with the external world. I know that I exist, that I perceive myself and the world. But the knowledge produced by these points of contact is more often than not inadequate. It can become adequate as reason develops, but, on the one hand, no sort of immediacy is a guarantee of authenticity – in this sense, then, there is no foundational experience – while on the other hand

---

[116] 'Omnia illa, quae sumpsi, postulata vix quicquam continent, quod non constet experientia', *Ethics* II, 17, Schol., p. 105, ll. 27–8 [CWS I, 464].

[117] 'Experientia, de qua nobis non licet dubitare, postquam ostendimus corpus humanum, prout ipsum sentimus, existere', *Ethics* II, 17, Schol. [CWS I, 464]. The differential perception goes beyond absolute perception, but it presupposes it as its condition.

the inadequate comes first in my personal history. However, what is inadequate as knowledge is still an attestation of experience: I am always, already conscious of existing and of entering by means of my body into relation with the world. Of course, this experience that concerns 'my' body is applicable to all; it is thus universal to the same degree that it is singular. It has already begun when we feel a particular sensation. It thus has all of the characteristics of experience such as we have identified them with respect to language, the passions or history.

B. The Negative Dimension of Experience

The negative form of the experience of the self is more decisive than in the other fields of experience. In fact, if we draw all of its consequences, then we can identify the most central illusion of all: that of the autonomy of the self, behind which we find the question of freedom. Yet, if this experience is invested with a pre-established belief in free will, then the illusion of freedom is perpetually reproduced by appearing to be self-evident. This is why we have to work to examine what experience really teaches us, precisely so that we can reject such illusions. This negative lesson is studied closely in a discussion from the beginning of Book III, as well as in a letter to Schuller, which develops the same arguments in often identical terms.[118] These two cases show that the objection confronted in the *Ethics* does indeed correspond to a real objection, one that has been raised even by those close to the philosopher. Note the surprising disequilibrium between the opening Propositions to Book III. Where about ten lines suffice for the entirety of the Propositions that precede the establishment of the *conatus*, along with their Demonstrations, five pages are assigned to a single Scholium – that of Proposition 2. This is because Spinoza identifies here a major point of disagreement between himself and his adversaries. The point concerns in particular the relation between the soul and the body. The Proposition states that there is no interaction between them[119] (and thus, implicitly, that each arises from a causality proper to its corresponding attribute). The Demonstration geometrically proves the Proposition – essentially by referring to Book II. The beginning of the Scholium sketches out two other demonstrations, which also refer to Book II. On this point, there exist three

---

[118] *Ep.* LVIII, G IV, pp. 265–8 [*Ep.* LVIII [to G. H. Schuller]; CWS II, 427–30].

[119] 'Nec corpus mentem ad cogitandum, nec mens corpus ad motum, neque ad quietem, nec ad aliquid (si quid est) aliud determinare potest', G II, p. 141, ll. 6–8 [*Ethics* III, 2; CWS I, 494].

ways of establishing through demonstrative reason what happens to be the case. The reader should thus be convinced. But will the reader allow themselves to be persuaded? Spinoza notes that, 'although these things are such that no reason for doubt remains',[120] still the majority of people will refuse to examine them without prejudice. As Spinoza does not take this precaution everywhere, we can deduce from this that we are faced with a key point of resistance to the Demonstration. But what is most important is that Spinoza names at once the knot of the prejudice and the nerve of its refutation: experience. The reason people are so sure of themselves on this point is that they believe they have experienced what they are affirming.[121] And one can refute them by referring to experience itself.[122] This is one of the rare places in the *Ethics* where Spinoza opposes experience to experience, or rather (for he does not seem to concede that experience can contradict itself), one lesson to another from a single experiential field.

There are three moments to the argument. We will see that it does not have the same object as the proposition. In refuting in principle the theses of his adversaries, Spinoza deals only with one of the possible ways of denying Proposition 2 (the affirmation of an action of the soul on the body) and leaves aside entirely the second possibility (the action of the body on the soul). There are many reasons for this, including the fact that the adversaries cited do not claim to experience the determinant action of the body, and that it is therefore useless to inquire into it. The first movement consists in reversing the charge of proof regarding the action of the soul on the body; the second discusses the interpretation of the positive experiences that these adversaries refer to; and the third raises the question of freedom that was from the beginning in the background to the discussion, unperceived yet present.

The first movement begins by stating the thesis of Spinoza's adversaries: 'They are so firmly persuaded that the Body now moves, now is at rest, solely from the Soul's command, and that it does a great many things which depend only on the Soul's will and its art of thinking.'[123] The question being

---

[120] 'Quamvis haec ita se habeant, ut nulla dubitandi ratio supersit', G II, p. 141, ll. 31–2 [*Ethics* III, 2, Schol.; *CWS* I, 494].

[121] 'At, dicent, [. . .] se tamen experiri', G II, p. 142, ll. 20–2 [*Ethics* III, 2, Schol; *CWS* I, 495].

[122] 'Nisi rem experientia comprobavero', G II, p. 141, l. 32; p. 142, l. 1 [*Ethics* II, 2, Schol.; *CWS* I, 494]; 'sed, quod ad primum attinet, ipsos rogo, num experientia non etiam doceat', p. 142, ll. 25–6 [*Ethics* III, 2, Schol.; *CWS* I, 495].

[123] 'Adeo firmiter persuasi sunt, corpus ex solo mentis nutu jam moveri, jam quiescere plurimaque agere, quae a sola mentis voluntate et excogitandi arte pendent', G II, p. 142, ll. 2–4 [*Ethics* III, 2, Schol.; *CWS* I, 495].

posed here is, at the most obvious level, that of the power of the soul over the body. But at the same time, another question hovers in the background, one that will only come to the fore at the end of the Scholium: that of the relation between necessity and freedom. For those who say that the soul acts on the body do not mean that the soul makes its own determinations felt at the level of the body; they mean that the soul is not determined at all. The corollary of the introduction of a vertical causality is the suppression of all horizontal causality.

Spinoza's response elucidates the difference between the experience of facts and the experience of causes. It is extraordinarily concentrated and its levels of detail can only be glimpsed by relating Spinoza's response to what follows, indeed by identifying within it allusions to controversies from the classical age. A first level of the discussion consists in saying: I affirm the internal causality of the world of bodies, yet it so happens that I cannot show this causality in detail ('And of course, no one has yet determined what the Body can do').[124] You, on the other hand, affirm external causality, that is, of the soul on the body – but you cannot show this causality either. We thus find ourselves faced with an admission of ignorance on both sides. You do not have sufficient means to refute my thesis, even if you are right to say that experience does not offer any arguments in my favour.[125] Stated in this way the argument seems weak if it is a matter of establishing what the proposition is advancing. But something entirely different is at stake, and in both cases. Faced with a corporeal phenomenon, we cannot say: 'I know (or feel) clearly how it is caused.' While we certainly experience these phenomena, we do not experience their causality. On the other hand, as far as science is concerned – and Spinoza does not speak of it here – we have the beginnings of a mechanical science which, while it might not explain all of the details of the action of bodies, is already able to explain a part of it to us. But for the moment it is not at the level of science that Spinoza is situating himself. It is only a matter (but in a radical sense) of effacing the impression of self-evidence given by this prejudice.

However, within the argument about 'what a body can do', Spinoza does not limit himself to making this concession. He adds a second sentence, which prevents his adversaries from assuming even the positive part of the

---

[124] 'Etenim, quid corpus possit, nemo hucusque determinavit', G II, p. 142, ll. 4–5 [*Ethics* III, 2, Schol.; *CWS* I, 495].

[125] It is indeed experience that is in question here: the preceding phrase is immediately clarified by: 'hoc est, neminem hucusque experientia docuit [. . .]', ibid., ll. 5–6 [*Ethics* III, 2, Schol.; *CWS* I, 495].

theme. Spinoza cites three examples of complex phenomena: the structure of the human body; the impressive actions of animals; and the acts of sleepwalkers. And he concludes that 'This shows well enough that the Body itself, simply from the laws of its own nature, can do many things which its Soul wonders at.'[126] What is the crux of this argument? It consists in drawing from common experience certain facts that the partisans of the action of the soul cannot claim have been produced by the soul. The implicit lemma here is: if we accept that such-and-such a fact is not produced by the soul, then it is produced by the laws of corporeal nature alone. The demonstration is completed by an implicit argument *a fortiori*: these facts, which you recognise do not need the soul to be produced, are in reality more complex (and thus more difficult to produce) than those for which you claim the action of the soul is necessary.

Let us begin with the final example, for it is the most explicit. The sleepwalker accomplishes while sleeping things that he would not dare attempt while awake.[127] It can be supposed that even if his soul guides his body while awake, it does not do so during sleep. But if we accept the duty of explaining the sleeper's acts by reference to the body alone, then he who can do the most can do the least, and the supposition of the action of the soul on the body during the state of wakefulness is useless. The actions of animals[128] refer to the debate regarding their soul. In the face of such an argument, the Cartesian – and only the Cartesian – has their backs to the wall.[129] If one refuses to grant animals a soul, and if one claims that all of their actions can be explained in mechanical terms, then the action of the soul is useless for explaining people's behaviour by applying the same principle. In these two cases, then, Spinoza implicitly shows, not that we have an experience of the internal action of bodies, but that his adversaries experience situations where, according to their own principles, they accept the sufficiency of intra-corporeal explanation. What about the first of the three examples? The structure of the body is so complex that no person can (up to the present) explain all of its

---

[126] 'Quod satis ostendit, ipsum corpus ex solis suae naturae legibus multa posse, quae ipsius mens admiratur', G II, p. 142, ll. 12–14 [*Ethics* III, 2, Schol.; *CWS* I, 495].

[127] G II, p. 142, ll. 11–12 [*Ethics* III, 2, Schol.; *CWS* I, 495].

[128] G II, p. 142, ll. 10–11 [*Ethics* III, 2, Schol.; *CWS* I, 495].

[129] An Aristotelean or a sceptic who grants a soul to animals will not be obliged to explain their behaviour, including their most surprising behaviour, by reference to mechanics alone. Cf. for example Cureau de la Chambre, *Traité de la connaissance des animaux*, 1645, réédition par O. Le Guern, Paris: Fayard, 1989.

functions.[130] Should we recognise here the argument by design?[131] Obviously not. This example is also a response to the question of interaction and must therefore be understood as follows: even the partisans of the action of the soul must admit that the human soul has not constructed the human body. Experience thus places before our eyes a very complex object, which was produced by corporeal laws alone.[132]

We can now conclude the first movement: the action of the soul on the body is a name for our ignorance. Above all, it is at play in those cases where we find nothing to be surprised at. We should note the role played by surprise throughout this part of the discussion. One will also note the very particular status of experience: it is present, but in an inverted form: 'it was not able to teach us such-and-such a thing . . .'. Or, in the specifics of Spinoza's language: 'no one up to this point has been able to . . .'. We thus again find the reference to the past and the saturation that is typical of experiential discourse, but here their purpose is to refer to what for a long time *we did not know*. This is a sign that in this domain, the limits that have long been identified with the experiential register must come to the fore, for the discourse of Spinoza's adversaries is based on forgetting these limits.

The second movement, in contradistinction to the first, begins with Spinoza's adversaries appealing to experience. There are two aspects to this appeal. We experience that the body is inert when the soul is unable to think; we feel that it is in the power of the soul to speak or to be silent. The meaning of this argument is immediately experiential, and it takes account of the refutation of the prejudice by the preceding argument (all the while believing that it has short-circuited it by a new impression of self-evidence): certainly, says the interlocutor, I do not know concretely how the process occurs, but I have the concrete, undeniable feeling of my power over my body. We thus find here the principle of authenticity that Spinoza refuses from the outset.

---

[130] 'Nam nemo hucusque corporis fabricam tam accurate novit, ut omnes ejus functiones potuerit explicare', G II, p. 142, ll. 8–10 [*Ethics* III, 2, Schol.; *CWS* I, 495].

[131] This argument was criticised in the Appendix to Book I of the *Ethics*.

[132] In my reading, the word 'body' in the two occurrences 'what a body can do' and 'structure of the body' (*fabrica corporis*) therefore do not have quite the same meaning. There is no equivalence between the two formulations, as Gilles Deleuze says (*Spinoza and the Problem of Expression*, Chapter XIV). There is a relation of causality. If I understand the meaning of the argument correctly, then it signifies: we do not know what the laws of corporeal nature can do (they can do more than is commonly believed); they can even construct this very complex figure that is the human body (or any other complex natural body). A *fortiori*, they can thus construct more simple things (for example, the paintings or the edifices that will be mentioned in the course of the second movement).

Spinoza responds separately to each one of these two proofs, and in doing so even adds a supplementary response to a reformulation of the first proof:

— Those who invoke the experience of simultaneous inertia must concede that the proof runs in both directions. Two arguments show this: that of sleep, and that of the 'reawakening' of images. Spinoza thus does not refuse the interlocutor's appeal to experience; he even adds other similar appeals. But the only thing he concedes to his adversary is simultaneity. If we begin by interpreting this simultaneity in terms of causality, certain examples seem to militate for the action of the soul on the body, while others militate for the action of the body on the soul. Here again we see that Spinoza does not operate *stricto sensu* in the order of geometrical demonstration, for if he did, he would quite simply be in the process of proving the existence of a double interaction and not the inexistence of a unilateral action. In sum, he would be reprising Lucretius' conclusions[133] so as to complete (and not refute) Descartes' arguments. However, the question that is being posed here is not this particular question but is rather: do we have the immediate experience of the power of the soul over the body? If we think we have this experience, then we have to concede that it is neither radical nor irreducible.

— Here the imagined interlocutor attempts to reintroduce a criterion of distribution: that of creativity. He seems to say: I accept your argument for simple actions, but past a certain degree of complexity it is necessary to suppose the action of the soul on the body to explain corporeal phenomena. This is the argument that the Cartesians use to show (with respect to language in particular) that other subjects are irreducible to purely mechanical laws and that I have to suppose a soul behind their manifestations.[134] Spinoza's response invokes two of the preceding examples: the actions of sleepwalkers, the structure of the human body. Why recall them? Because, in a certain sense, the interlocutor's argument is repetitive, even if it has changed levels. Previously he had said: I know well that the human soul can govern the body; he now says: I feel clearly that indeed it does govern it, and that without it the body could not achieve all that it does.

To these two examples, Spinoza adds a reference to a geometrical demonstration, that is, to the theory of power from Book I. It is logical that he does

---

[133] Cf. *De Natura Rerum*, Book III.
[134] This is the principle that Chomsky places at the foundation of 'Cartesian linguistics'.

not develop it ('not to mention that I have shown [this] above'),[135] for it is not situated at the same level.

— Spinoza then moves on to the refutation of the second argument: is it in people's power to speak or to be silent? He addresses this refutation in two ways: first by distinguishing what is desirable from what is real; then by showing that people only formulate this alleged experience under the rule of a theory they have spontaneously formed. They do not dare to say that we are always free to speak or to be silent: everyone knows that, even when it comes to stating what they claim to feel, too many examples prove the contrary. They thus fabricate a theory of a division, which is tasked with accounting for the contradiction between experiences. Spinoza will also make use of this division, but will do so differently. It is undeniable that we see the child ask for the milk, the drunk reveal his secrets, and that we know the causes of their actions. Everyone has always, already known these causes in both cases. How can we juxtapose these two kinds of knowledge? The interlocutor articulates them according to a specific mode of experience – that is, by excluding himself from what he sees. And as he does not dare divide the world into two categories of men, he divides the sites of enunciation into two categories: either I am strongly determined, and then I am not free; or I am affected only lightly, and can thus conserve my freedom. Freedom thus occurs when affection is absent. The drunk, the chatterbox, etc., are determined only because their affection is strong, or stronger than themselves. What, by contrast, is the line of division that Spinoza proposes? It consists in identifying one's ignorance of oneself that lies behind the self-assurance of one's act. The interlocutor's rule neglects the following fact: what he wants to justify is the feeling of the non-causality of the soul; now, this feeling is neither stronger nor more authentic among some people than among others, or in certain situations rather than in others. The drunk believes themselves to be as free as the philosopher. Thus, the proposed line of demarcation is invalid since it fails to provide a criterion for distinguishing the true determination from the false. On the contrary, the distinction concerns whether one is ignorant or not of the causes of one's actions. Ultimately, Spinoza does not deny the internal experience of freedom: he takes it into account but refuses to take it at its word. He notes its presence in us, but without considering it as a guarantee of legitimate evidence: he thus lays the foundations for his causal explanation. Spinoza offers an interpretation that puts him in agreement

---

[135] 'Ut jam taceam quod supra ostenderim: ex natura, sub quovis attributo considerata, infinita sequi', G II, p. 143, ll. 10–11 [*Ethics* III, 2, Schol.; CWS I, 496].

with external experiences of determination, and that suppresses the zone of individual opacity proper to all experiential evidence.

It is here that the third movement begins. As the preceding movement progressed, we saw the question of freedom little by little substitute for the power of the soul over the body. It will now be taken up for itself. Spinoza will use two interlinked arguments: that of memory and that of dreaming. The first argument begins with the principle that 'we can do nothing from a free decision of the Soul unless we recollect it'.[136] This phrase can seem obscure, but the example of the word makes it comprehensible: we cannot say a word unless we remember it. This obviously does not mean that our action is merely a repetition, but that at least a part of it is exerted on images that memory presents to us. Spinoza does not deny verbal creativity here. He simply reminds us of the necessity that there be a support for the representation. We cannot object to him that he is reasoning with reference to a substrata that mixes what his own doctrine distinguishes – namely, actions and representations – since he is situating himself here on the terrain of his adversary. Moreover, it is not very difficult to translate this argument into a purely Spinozist language. The first conclusion is thus that the freedom of the soul is not complete: it does not create from out of nothing the material on which it reasons (or on which it acts, if we are speaking here in terms of its influence on the body). Now, the disposition of this material (memory, forgetting) does not depend on the soul. We thus return here to the memorial structure of the body and to the status of use in language: both prohibit absolute autonomy in the manipulation of our ideas.

There now comes the second moment. The interlocutor seems to retreat and say: certainly, the soul does not constitute from nothing its substrata of memories, images and words. But once a memory is presented to it, the soul at least enjoys a minimal degree of freedom: it can accept or refuse what it remembers – accepting to speak of it or deciding to be silent about it; daring or not to say something. It is now the task of the argument of the dream to dissociate this experience from its self-evidence. The procedure will be the same as with the drunk and the chatterbox: it will be a matter of showing that an experience knows nothing of the limits that we falsely impose upon it. The two sides of the dream are like the two sides of drunkenness: nothing allows us to say that an experience is more pure or authentic than another.

It is worthwhile noting what material Spinoza has recourse to here in this Scholium: sleep, sleepwalking and dreams – all of which are Baroque

---

[136] *Ethics* III, 2, Schol. [*CWS* I, 497].

metaphors concerning the idea of life being a dream, an idea that is also used, albeit more briefly and to different ends, by Descartes.[137] Beyond the Baroque, this is a philosophical argument that refers to the arguments of the sceptics and the Epicureans: Lucretius' discussions of the body and the soul employ these same arguments, as does his discussion of catalepsy. The classical age in turn mobilises them. This ensemble of references tends to be constituted as an obligatory field of reference when it comes to the experience of the self. Like others, Spinoza has recourse to them, but he does so for his own ends: far from serving to reveal the ultimate freedom of the Subject, these same examples, these same facts known by all and recorded in philosophical memory, contribute to establishing our originary impotence and opacity.

These analyses reveal a number of traits of the experience of the self:

— The feeling of the body is a particular form of experience. It has all of the characteristics of experience – including negative ones (opacity, inadequation). But because of the particular metaphysical implications of this experience, these characteristics tend to be foregrounded in the discussion. This does not mean that experience by itself can refute the illusion of free will: a demonstration is necessary. But when properly analysed, experience can at least be an obstacle to the impression of self-evidence that the defenders of the action of the soul on the body refer to.

— The feeling of the soul is based on the feeling of the body. The experience of the soul has a memorial structure: the soul is in effect conscious of its past to the degree that it is conscious of the modifications of the body. Its imaginary relation to itself supposes the presence of its corporeal correlate. On the other hand, it does not suppose any necessary knowledge of what constitutes this correlate. I do not need to know biology to be conscious that I exist. Even what is false – the dream – also provides me with this consciousness.

— Is the feeling of individuality thus tied to the body? The feeling that is manifest here is tied to the existence of the body and to its affections. This existence translates an essence that, for the time being, is not given to us in any other form. Nevertheless, this does not suffice to prove that it does not exist in other forms. When we recognise the *ingenium* of an individual, this means that their singularity – which is produced by causes linked to their essence – is manifest in a physical and psychological fashion and with sufficient clarity that we can recognise it without needing to know its causes. These manifestations are obviously subjected to the body and to

---

[137] For example in the *First Meditation*.

what corresponds to the body in the soul. The disappearance of the body makes these marks of individuality disappear. But nothing for the time being proves to us that these are the only possible marks of individuality; they are simply the only things that we have encountered.

Our conclusion here is in some sense the opposite to the conclusion from the preceding section: with respect to the questions raised at the beginning of Books II and III, Spinoza speaks of experience, and he is right to do so since the feeling of the ego that is analysed in these texts presents all of the characteristics that we have encountered up to this point in experiential analyses. But this feeling is tied to the duration of the body; it does not make us experience the order of the necessary but rather concerns the memory of affections: it is not an experience of eternity.

3. The Experience of Eternity

Book V is divided into two parts: after having dealt with the power of the soul over the affects, Spinoza announces that he will move on to another subject: the duration of the soul in the absence of its relation to the body. In this second part of the Book, three successive questions are linked together concerning the third kind of knowledge, the intellectual love of God and beatitude. In the course of Spinoza's treatment of these questions, on a number of occasions the problem of the eternity of souls appears. Almost all of the passages where this problem is dealt with are written in a demonstrative style and are in part integrated into the geometrical argument. However, on at least one occasion, eternity appears in the form of an experience.

We can now address the Scholium to Proposition 23 from Book V, the only text where Spinoza explicitly speaks of an experience of eternity. Let us begin by translating it in its entirety:

P23: The human Soul cannot be absolutely destroyed with the Body, but something of it remains which is eternal.	Proposition 23. – L'âme humaine ne peut être absolument détruite avec le corps, mais quelque chose d'elle demeure, qui est éternel.
Schol.: There is, as we have said, this idea, which expresses the essence of the body under a certain species of eternity, a certain mode of thinking, which pertains to the essence of the Soul, and which is necessarily eternal. And though it is impossible that we should recollect that	Scolie. – Comme nous l'avons dit, cette idée qui exprime l'essence du corps sous la catégorie de l'éternité est un mode déterminé du penser, qui appartient à l'essence de l'âme. Il est impossible pourtant que nous nous souvenions d'avoir existé avant le corps, puisqu'il ne peut y avoir dans le

we existed before the Body – since there cannot be any traces of this in the body, and eternity can neither be defined by time nor have any relation to time – still, we feel and know by experience that we are eternal. For the Soul feels those things that it conceives in understanding no less than those it has in the memory. For the eyes of the soul, by which it sees and observes things, are the demonstrations themselves. Therefore, though we do not recollect that we existed before the body, we nevertheless feel that our soul, insofar as it involves the essence of the body under a species of eternity, is eternal, and that this existence it has cannot be defined by time *or* explained through duration. Our soul, therefore, can be said to endure, and its existence can be defined by a certain time, only insofar as it involves the actual existence of the body, and to that extent only does it have the power of determining the existence of things by time, and of conceiving of them under duration.[138]	corps aucune trace d'une telle existence, et que l'éternité ne peut se définir par le temps, ni avoir aucune relation avec le temps. Et néanmoins nous sentons et nous éprouvons que nous sommes éternels. Car l'âme ne sent pas moins ces choses qu'elle conçoit dans le fait de comprendre que celles qu'elle possède dans la mémoire. Car les yeux de l'âme, par lesquels elle voit et observe les choses, sont les démonstrations elles-mêmes. C'est pourquoi, bien que nous ne nous souvenions pas d'avoir existé avant le corps, nous sentons pourtant que notre âme, en tant qu'elle implique l'essence du corps sous la catégorie de l'éternité, est éternelle et que cette sienne existence ne peut se définir par le temps ni s'expliquer par la durée. L'âme donc ne peut être dite durer, et son existence ne peut être définie par un temps déterminé que dans la mesure où elle implique l'existence actuelle du corps et c'est seulement dans cette mesure qu'elle a la puissance de déterminer par le temps l'existence des choses et des les concevoir dans la durée.

To understand this text, it is first necessary to clarify the terms that it uses. It is not a question of treating in detail everything that concerns the eternity of souls in Spinoza's system, nor of analysing the whole structure of Book V. This would require much more extensive developments. These problems have, moreover, been dealt with in a number of recent studies.[139] I will only deal with what is necessary for clarifying our topic. To reconstitute Spinoza's procedure, it is first of all necessary to make a few distinctions. In fact, these highly elliptical pages speak successively from different points of view. The argument progresses by articulating at least five themes: immortality; the foundation of eternity; the differential reality of eternity; knowledge of eternity; and finally the feeling that emerges in the Scholium to Proposition 23. Even a brief analysis of these notions will allow us to leave aside certain

---

[138] *Ethics* V, 23, Schol. [CWS I, 607–8].

[139] B. Rousset, *La perspective finale de l''Ethique'*; A. Matheron, 'Remarques sur l'immortalité de l'âme chez Spinoza', *Etudes philosophiques*, 3 (1972), pp. 369–78; K. Hammacher, *Spinoza und die Frage nach der Unsterblichkeit*, MVHS, XLIII, Leiden: Brill, 1981; Gueroult, *Spinoza*, vol. I, *Dieu*, pp. 77–83, pp. 300–8; vol. II, *L'Ame*, pp. 404–14, 609–15.

positions that are far too distant from the properly Spinozist meaning of the text. This last section of the *Ethics* is in effect at once condensed and rigorous. If we wish to avoid too hastily identifying 'contradictions' or 'paradoxes', we have to take into account the fact that Spinoza broaches using a single substantive a number of different themes. His procedure, nevertheless, is not ambiguous, since the initial definition of eternity still remains valid. The different themes effectively concern the same concept, but seen as if from different perspectives. Finally, these themes are distinguished in a rigorous way by their place and role in the structure of the argument.

A. *Eternity of Modes and Immortality*

Some readers of this final section of Book V have on occasion sought to see Spinoza rallying here to common beliefs, whether Jewish or Christian, and thus abandoning without rigour what he had established most securely up to this point.[140] Alternatively, some have read it, if not as a sincere return to religiosity, then as a discourse of pure concession destined to protect the heterodoxy of his work.[141] This last reading presupposes that Spinoza uses a double language that his very doctrine renders impossible. But is our only choice between incoherence and dissimulation? All of these confusions are founded on an implicit or explicit identification between eternity and immortality: the very question, in fact, can only be posed if we accept that the last twenty Propositions essentially defended a doctrine of the immortality of the soul. Yet, Spinoza distinguishes these notions in a very rigorous fashion.

---

[140] This is Siegfried Grzymisch's conclusion: the phrases that attribute to the soul an eternal duration 'machen nur dem gemeinen Glauben und dem religiösen Bedürfnisse Spinozas selbst ein Zugeständnis, und durchbrechen ihnen zuliebe die strenge Folgerichtigkeit des Systems, lassen aber zugleich ahnen, wie fest und tief die gewöhnliche Unsterblichkeitslehre in unserem Denker gelebt haben muss, wenn sie noch hier, in der *Ethik*, eine lang fortgesetzte Reihe von Gedanken plötzlich aufhalten und am pflichtgemässen Vorwärtsschreiten hindern konnte', *Spinoza's Lehren von der Ewigkeit und der Unsterblichkeit*, Breslau, 1898, pp. 28–9. More recently, A. Darbon developed similar considerations (*Etudes spinozistes*, Paris: PUF, 1946, p. 150 ff.).

[141] Thus Lamy notes that Spinoza follows the consequences of his system when he affirms that the soul is mortal. He adds: 'Cependant dans la crainte qu'elles n'effraient trop le monde, il essaie de les adoucir, en disant que si après la destruction du corps, Dieu n'en voit plus l'existence, il en voit encore l'essence, et que l'idée qu'il a de cette essence est quelque chose qui appartient à la nature de l'âme, et qu'ainsi il n'y a qu'une partie de l'âme qui périt pendant que l'autre subsiste', *Le nouvel athéisme renversee*, p. 28.

The *Short Treatise* certainly used the term immortality,[142] but gave it a content that already implied a very clear demarcation between immortality and the idea of duration.[143]

The *Ethics*, for its part, clearly distinguishes between the eternity of souls and immortality. At the level of its terminology, in this text Spinoza never uses the word 'immortality'; he only once uses the adjective 'immortal', and it is in a very vague and negative sense.[144] With respect to content, he says very precisely that people confuse the survival of memory and of the imagination after the death of the body with eternity.[145] If Spinoza notes this confusion, then it is to distance himself from it. The central theme in question at the end of the *Ethics* is thus indeed eternity, both the term and its meaning. It is necessary to do violence to the text to read in it at the surface level a doctrine of the immortality of the soul. This does not exclude a certain form of immortality in the system – that which corresponds to the survival of the understanding without the imagination.[146] But it has a limited and specific signification, and it is impossible for it to exhaust the sense of the word eternity. In any case, it does not concern the totality of the soul: it thus cannot be assimilated to the traditional religious conception of immortality. It is also necessary to reject the identification of eternity with the immortality of one part of the soul.[147] Such a reading immediately

---

[142] *Van des Ziels onsterfelykheid*, Part 2, Chapter XXIII, KV, M, p. 322 [CWS I, 140].

[143] On the difficulties of this chapter, see Mignini's excellent commentary, pp. 720–4.

[144] 'Vel, quia videt mentem non esse aeternam seu immortalem, ideo amens mavult esse et sine Ratione vivere', *Ethics* V, Proposition 41, Schol., G II, p. 307, ll. 23–4 [CWS I, 616]. At stake here is the description of a behaviour that is described as absurd. The person in question thus does not make a conceptual distinction between eternity and immortality: he simply sees that they escape him and also (wrongly) that they ruin his present life, since he represents piety as a burden that only another life could compensate him for or justify.

[145] 'Si ad hominum communem opinionem attendamus, videbimus, eos suae mentis aeternitatis esse quidem conscios, sed ipsos eamdem cum duratione confundere, eamque imaginationi seu memoriae tribuere, quam post mortem remanere credunt', *Ethics* V, 34, Schol., G II, p. 301, l. 30; p. 302, l. 2 [CWS I, 611–12].

[146] Matheron has very precisely shown what form it would take in his article from 1972, and above all has indicated its limits. Partial eternity is not immortality 'au sens ordinaire', 'puisqu'elle n'a rien de commun avec une durée indéfinie' (p. 369); ideas that remain in our soul after death 's'y trouvaient avant la naissance' (p. 377); 'notre participation à l'éternité est proportionnelle à la capacité qu'a notre corps de soumettre ses affections à la domination de ses propres lois' (p. 378, with reference to Proposition 34).

[147] This is how Wolfson understands it, who thereby assimilates Spinoza with the Aristotelean-Averroist tradition. But in truth this assimilation occurs in Wolfson's

obliterates the specific signification of the term eternity[148] so as to reduce Spinozism to a sort of late branch of the Aristotelian tradition. It leaves aside Spinoza's insistence on the rootedness of the soul's eternity in the essence of the body, and makes of it a sort of eternal intellect by nature.[149]

Above all, the eternity of souls, such as we encounter it in Book V, refers to what we already knew about eternity. It is based on the concept of eternity that has already been defined with respect to divine eternity. This is why it cannot be identified either with total immortality (which is impossible), nor with partial immortality (which is real but derived). The eternity of the soul is not defined more by immortality than eternity in general is defined by sempiternity. On the other hand, just as eternity in the general sense implies sempiternity as one of its consequences (but not as part of its definition), so does the partial eternity of souls imply immortality as one of its consequences (but not as part of its definition).[150]

It is nevertheless not enough to distinguish between immortality and the soul's eternity. To understand the precise status of the latter, we must analyse how it is introduced into the argument. In fact, it is introduced twice, and according to two clearly distinct perspectives, but whose articulation alone allows us to think the complete concept of beatitude: an absolute perspective and a differential perspective.

without any discussion: it is presupposed from the beginning; never in the whole chapter that Wolfson devotes to this question does he use the word 'eternity' (Chapter XX is moreover entitled 'Love, Immortality and Blessedness' and paragraph 3 is entitled 'Immortality and Intellectual Love of God'). We thus learn that the thinking essence of the soul 'comes from above' (p. 291), then 'returns to unite itself with the attribute of thought whence it came' (p. 293). There then follows a series of misunderstandings (for example: the soul as eternal knows neither its body nor other bodies) that culminate in a historiographical nonsense: Book V of the *Ethics* would exist side by side with Samuel da Silva and Menasseh ben Israel to defend the tradition of the immortality of the soul against Uriel da Costa (p. 323).

[148] Certainly, the question of knowing to what extent the Spinozist system displaces and transforms, on its own terrain, questions inaugurated by the Aristotelean tradition is far from being devoid of interest. Hamelin dealt with this question in an inaugural article. Yet, if one poses this question, it is still necessary to distinguish the two terms. The pure and simple identification between eternity and immortality, whether partial or total, prevents us from understanding the Spinozist system, and thus from comparing it with any other.

[149] Reciprocally, it has lead to the neglect of parallelism: thus Wolfson writes that during its life the soul is found *in* the body (p. 302).

[150] It is important to clarify the vocabulary here: by 'total' and 'partial' I mean: 'that which concerns the totality (or only a part) of the mind'. Eternity as such knows nothing of parts.

B. The First Perspective: The Foundation of the Eternity of Souls

The first approach can be found in Propositions 21–23. It aims to establish the foundation for the affirmation of eternity. It could be described as an absolute or a universal approach.

If the soul is eternal, it is because something to do with the body is conceived under the category of eternity.[151] In this case, it is the body's essence that is at stake. We have seen that, if the essences of things are not eternal, they nevertheless constitute eternal truths, while the ideas that correspond to them in the attribute Thought present this characteristic of being eternal in the strict sense of the term. In the second part of Book V, Spinoza will base his argument precisely on this characteristic insofar as it applies to a particular thing: namely, the human body.

We thus find here a first approach to eternity, which grounds the eternity of one part of the soul in the essence of the body. This point must be firmly reinforced: if this foundation did not exist, nothing in what remains of Spinoza's argument would hold. This is because the soul is the idea of an eternal truth that is itself eternal. It is here that beatitude – which is nevertheless not reducible to this idea – finds its first point of anchorage and its first condition.

But it is also necessary to indicate the limit of this demonstration from the perspective of salvation: what is said here is absolutely *not* specific to human beings. The argument is founded on a trait that is common not only to all bodies, but indeed to all things and all attributes.[152] This foundation is common to all things, and thus to all souls. This suffices to distinguish

---

[151] Following Matheron (*Individu et Communauté*, p. 576), I am reprising L. Brunschvicg's translation. For the critique of Appuhn's translation, see Gueroult, *Spinoza*, vol. II, Appendix 17, pp. 609–15.

[152] Proposition 22 concerns the human body, but its demonstration refers uniquely to Book I and to Proposition 3 of Book II, which does not concern the human being specifically: God is the cause of the existence and of the essence of things (Proposition 25); this essence must necessarily be conceived by the knowledge of its cause (Axiom 4), that is, by the very essence of God; this production and its knowledge are inscribed in an eternal essence (Proposition 15); finally, as there is necessarily in God an idea both of his essence and of everything that necessarily follows from his essence (Book II, Proposition 3), everything that Proposition 22 says of the human body can be said of anything whatsoever: there necessarily exists in God an idea that expresses the essence of this thing under the category of eternity. Of course, this thesis is true not only of extended things, but also of all the others, including of the human soul. But the point is precisely, as Rousset correctly remarks, that Spinoza does not refer to this characteristic in his demonstration.

Spinozist eternity from the classical thesis of the separation of the agent intellect. It is no more the case here than anywhere else in the system that the human being is neither a kingdom within a kingdom, nor a State within a State. Even with respect to eternity, there is no radical difference between natural things. The only distinction that can be made here concerns a specific application of universal laws. Yet it is not enough to note that the argument does not only apply to human souls; to the degree that it does apply to them, it applies to all equally. It is thus impossible from this perspective to distinguish between the wise and the ignorant, just as it is impossible to distinguish between human beings and other finite modes.

Furthermore, this common foundation of eternity is hardly capable of constituting all by itself something like salvation or beatitude. This eternal something can be very weak, and even, so to speak, inexistent.[153] Since all things have a soul, this eternity is, for the majority of souls, an eternity to which they are blind. It is hardly something that can be considered as salvific, so long as we wish to conserve a strong meaning for the term salvation. It is now necessary to pose a new question: how can human beings – or certain human beings – go beyond this common eternity? We will thus have to introduce a second point of view, one that explains what the human soul possesses above and beyond other souls, and also, potentially, what certain people possess more than others. Finally, we will also have to explain how certain moments in people's lives transcend others. We must therefore turn, now, from the fundamental to the differential perspective.

The reader will notice the analogy between this question and the one that was raised at the end of Proposition 13 from Book II. There, this question was used to justify the exposition of a physics, the purpose of which was to help us think, by reference to common laws, the specificity of the human body.

C. The Second Perspective: Salvation as Self-Knowledge, of God and of Things, and as a Greater or Lesser Part of Eternity

Here, by contrast, eternity is no longer defined in relation to the essence of the body, but in relation to the knowledge that the soul has of God, of things and of itself. This second perspective is proportional and differential (the vocabulary itself indicates this: see, among others, the term *quo magis*).

---

[153] Spinoza declares this explicitly for the ignorant ('simulac pati desinit, simul etiam esse desinit', Proposition 42, Schol., G II, p. 308, ll. 19–20 [CWS I, 616–17]). This is true *a fortiori* for non-human things.

It is no longer a matter of affirming that every soul has something eternal in it, but of accounting for the greater or lesser dimension of the eternal part of the soul.

We must nevertheless note that we once again encounter the body here. But not in its essence; instead, in the greater or lesser multiplicity of its capacities. The entirety of this argument is governed by the effects of Proposition 13 from Book II and of its Scholium, to which Proposition 34 from Book V responds.[154]

The structure of the argument is worth noting. The bloc of Propositions 21–23 establishes the foundations of eternity. The Propositions that follow abandon this question and move on to another matter: that of the development of the third kind of knowledge. It is because we are positioned here on the terrain specific to the human soul – namely, knowledge – that we will be able to leave the common and impoverished register that serves as a universal foundation for the eternity of the soul. Proposition 29 is a junction between the two chains of the argument, but it seems to rewrite the set of Propositions from 21 to 23. In fact, it restricts itself to drawing unperceived consequences from them – consequences that derive from the decisive Proposition 13 from Book II. The argument is also based on the character of reason: to conceive things under the category of eternity (Spinoza refers us here to the second Scholium to Proposition 44 from Book II). Thus, in order to pass from the first to the second perspective on eternity, we see the two branches of the argument that we had identified previously come together: on the one hand, the meditation on eternity and on the knowledge of necessity; and on the other hand, the experience of the self on the basis of the presence and then of the differential capacity of the body. This time we begin with what is specific to the human soul: namely, knowledge. The more that knowledge of the third kind develops, the more the eternal part of the soul grows; and we pass from an eternity that is in some sense passive and common to all the ideas of essences, to an active eternity where the soul directly expresses, by way of its own power of thinking, divine necessity.

D. The Knowledge of Eternity

Salvation is not in the strict sense the knowledge of eternity, but it is accompanied by it. The final Scholia show this clearly: the wise person knows

---

[154] 'Qui corpus ad plurima aptum habet, is mentem habet, cujus maxima pars est aeterna', G II, p. 304, ll. 32–3 [CWS I, 614].

that the greatest part of his soul is eternal.[155] To the degree that he knows himself, he knows this too. We are obviously dealing here with adequate knowledge. We thus cannot say that finding the path of salvation consists in becoming conscious of eternity; this coming to consciousness, to the degree that it accompanies the growth in knowledge of the third kind, is a consequence and not a principle.

We can now return to the feeling of eternity, such as it appears in this Scholium. We should first observe that it is not to be confused with any of the four preceding themes.

A. It is not to be confused with immortality, even if some have assimilated them. Spinoza explicitly distinguishes eternity and immortality; and he twice remarks on their confusion: first in the Scholium that we are studying, then in the Scholium to Proposition 34. That the vulgar assimilate eternity and survival in duration is not, moreover, an affirmation specific to the *Ethics*. We also find it in the Preface to the *TTP*.[156]

B. It is not identical to the foundation of eternity that emerges from the first perspective: it has a more restricted field. The reasons we are eternal are not applicable to human beings alone; and yet Spinoza says 'we' or 'men' when speaking of the feeling of eternity. It thus seems to concern all human beings and humanity alone.

C. It is not to be confused with the proportion of eternity that we can obtain in the second perspective. In effect, it has a larger field of application and, it seems, one that is equal for all. Now, as we have seen, this differential perspective allows salvation for certain human beings only, and in a way that conceives of this salvation in terms of proportion. In sum, this feeling of eternity says too much for the second perspective while not enough for the first. Moreover, Spinoza never says that the feeling of eternity is tied to the body (contrary to what certain commentators have suggested). It is tied neither to its essence (as from the absolute perspective), nor to its greater or lesser aptitude (as from the differential perspective). On the contrary, it is the translation of this feeling into a corporeal language that means that many people, all the while possessing it, interpret this feeling in a false way.

---

[155] 'Mentes [. . .] quarum maxima seu praecipua pars est aeterna', *Ethics* V, 39, Schol., G II, p. 305, ll. 15–17 [*CWS* I, 614]. All people can, in principle, have such souls; but only some attain this level.

[156] 'Vulgus (superstitioni addictum, et quod temporis vestigia supra ipsam aeternitatem amat)', G III, p. 10, ll. 22–3 [*TTP* Praef., 25; *CWS* II, 73].

D. Finally, it is clear that this feeling of eternity is not at all an adequate knowledge and that it therefore cannot be identified with the knowledge of the wise mentioned in the final Propositions. The expression 'coming to consciousness' of eternity can thus be a source of confusion, to the degree that it refers both to the adequate and to the derived knowledge that the wise man possesses, as well as to the confused feeling that is found in all people.

The experience of eternity is thus indeed a fifth theme, which is certainly tied to the four preceding ones but whose exact articulation we must determine if we wish to understand the texts in which it appears – and, above all, if we wish to grasp what role it plays in the system.

To understand this role and this articulation, we now have to return to the Scholium to Proposition 23.

What should first be noted is that this Scholium is clearly written in the language of experience. We recognise here the words and the turns of phrase that we have grown accustomed to recognising as the expression of experience.[157] By itself, this would already suffice to distinguish this Scholium from a number of other passages from the second part of Book V – those precisely where the four other themes concerning eternity are dealt with.

The second trait to note is the adversarial structure of this text. We cannot understand this text if we do not see in it an implicit dialogue. It is structured by an alternation. This alternation refers to the double definition of the soul and its implications. It is like a dialogue with a Spinozist interlocutor – a Spinozist who would have understood the second part of the *Ethics* and would have tried to apply its rules to this new field that has since been opened up for him. The first phrase states what has just been established by the block of Propositions 21 to 23: 'this idea, which expresses the essence of the body under a species of eternity, a certain mode of thinking, which pertains to the essence of the Soul'.[158] The interlocutor recalls what has been said of the soul in Book II and is tempted to apply it to this new part of the soul. What had then been established?

- That the soul feels and experiences that it has a body, so long as this body exists;
- that this experience is not necessarily the object of an adequate idea; and that, in general, it is in fact the object of an inadequate idea;

---

[157] Cf. *sentimus, experimur*, etc.
[158] *Ethics* V, 23, Schol. [CWS I, 607].

- that this experience takes place thanks to the senses and to duration, through the intermediary of memory. It is because the body has a memorial structure that experience can take place; and its inadequation does not prevent it from attesting to this. Each instant has a past that the constitution of the body keeps active and through which what effectively exists can alone be perceived.

The interlocutor thus asks if we can apply these three conclusions to the part of the soul whose existence has just been discovered. Spinoza responds by refusing the third thesis: the particular conditions that characterise this part of the soul prevent the memorial structure, and thus at least this type of experience. This is what is indicated by the phrase that begins with *tamen*: 'it is impossible that we should recollect that we existed before the Body – since there cannot be any traces of this in the body, and eternity can neither be defined by time nor have any relation to time'.[159]

Logic would thus also have us abandon the two preceding conclusions, since they are conditioned by the third. We can thus imagine the interlocutor, basing himself on the logic of Book II, saying: without a memorial structure, there is no experience; thus, we do not have an experience of this eternity of a part of our soul.

To this conclusion, Spinoza responds with a second restriction: *nihilominus* – we feel and experience that we are eternal. In other words, there is nevertheless an experience of this part of the soul. How is this possible? This can only be the case if there exists something that plays, *mutatis mutandis*, the same role as the memorial function of the body. This affirmation requires an explanation: can the soul feel things that it conceives through the understanding? The explanation is given in the sentence that begins with *nam*: yes, there is a sensation of intellection, which is the equivalent of memory. There thus exist, in this strict sense, eyes of the soul. These eyes, Spinoza says, are the demonstrations themselves. It is this formula that constitutes the core of the difficulty.

Let us read the conclusion (*itaque*): even though we do not remember having existed before the body (this is a reminder of the invalid nature of thesis 3), we nevertheless feel (*tamen*) that our soul is eternal (thus, thesis 1 is valid).

Let us return to the difficulty: it concerns the dual aspect of the demonstrations.

— On the one hand, everything seems to confirm thesis 2: Spinoza never

---

[159] *Ethics* V, 23, Schol. [*CWS* I, 607].

speaks of *knowledge*; rather, he says *to feel* or *to experience*.[160] The term 'to feel' returns three times: this cannot be by chance. What follows will confirm that the form of comprehension tied to experience is far from adequate: the Scholium to Proposition 34 will note that, if all people are conscious of the eternity of their soul, they translate this eternity inadequately in terms of immortality. This idea is thus just as inadequate in us as the idea of the flame or of our own hand burning: in one case we confuse the thing with the encounter; in the other we confuse the thing with its projection in time. There does indeed exist a quasi-memorial structure, but we do not know yet what it is, even if we can note some of its empirical effects.

— On the other hand, this quasi-memorial structure, which plays an equivalent role to that of the past, resides only in the demonstration. Is this not to deny everything that we have learnt about experience? Or rather should we not admit that experience takes a different perspective on the demonstration than the demonstrative perspective? But how is this possible?

At this point in our analysis, the entire problem of the experience of eternity comes down to the following question: is it possible to describe a structure that would be wholly internal to the soul and that would nevertheless have analogous effects to those of the body and so produce a feeling? What is this quasi-memorial structure? How can the soul *feel* demonstrations? The response seems to me to have to do with the fact that even the knowledge of necessity does not abolish in the soul pre-existing perceptions and feelings, which form something like a backdrop such that the soul feels the difference between what it demonstrates and the rest of what it lives. Certainly, each time that the soul operates with a demonstration, it obtains first of all a result that is not of the order of feeling. It understands the necessity of each demonstration. But at the same time this necessity stands out against the backdrop of what is not necessary. The soul thus perceives, in the same movement, this difference. It cannot be said that the soul knows what is not necessary; but what is not necessary serves as a backdrop against which necessity emerges. Besides the *knowledge* of what is necessary, there is thus a differential perspective that constitutes the *experience* of necessity. It is

---

[160] Translator's note: Curley's translation nevertheless has the phrase 'know by experience', which, as Moreau is claiming, is not to be confused with 'knowing' pure and simple. As the reader can see above, Moreau translates *experimurque* as 'éprouver', which is usually translated as 'to experience'. Given the awkwardness of a phrase like 'to feel and experience by experience that we are eternal', I have retained Curley's phrase 'know by experience', despite the potentially misleading reference to knowledge.

thus indeed the demonstration that makes this experience felt, by the fact that the demonstration separates itself from what constitutes a register of uncertainty – finitude – and without which the demonstration would have exclusive dominion. Thus, it is the existence of finitude that allows necessity to be the object not only of adequate knowledge, but also of a feeling.

Is it possible for all to have this experience? Spinoza does not say that all possess knowledge of the third kind. Nevertheless, the 'we' of the Scholium is without qualification. This is possible because:

A. Each person possesses the point of departure for the third kind of knowledge. Each develops it to a greater or lesser degree (precisely as they develop the common notions to a greater or lesser degree). But from the point of view of the weight of the quasi-memorial – of the idea of the idea in its experiential dimension – what counts is not the length of the chain but its consistency.

B. What gives this chain its consistency? The answer is its difference from everything else. Its intensity comes from this difference and not from any intellectual power. The testimony of experience is proportional to this intensity. How is this difference manifest? Through the feeling of finitude. The feeling of finitude is the condition for the feeling of eternity – indeed, in a certain sense, it *is* the feeling of eternity. It is by one and the same movement, namely by gaining access to necessity and by becoming conscious of all that is not immediately necessary, that the soul sees its impotence and aspires to escape from contingency, which takes on the figure of external necessity. In its very limitations, finitude thus plays an intensely positive role: it sketches out the lineaments of the necessary and incites us to assume its eternity. All souls are finite and in part eternal, but not all have the feeling of finitude, and thus of eternity.[161]

The feeling of finitude, which plays a major role in the determination of the experience of eternity, is not something unknown: we have already encountered it four times in our survey of the experiential regions of Spinoza's system.

— At the beginning of the *TdIE*, we saw that in the flux of our daily activities, there emerged a sense of dissatisfaction that did not come from the outside but from the very promises made by these activities. What this sense of dissatisfaction made us tend towards already had the name of 'eternity'. The

---

[161] It can be said that God does not have the feeling of eternity, and that we would not have it were we born free – and the same goes for the true knowledge of good and of evil.

feeling of finitude was the vector for the aspiration to eternity. In the movement of the *proemium*, it was often the negative aspects (prohibition, crisis, death) that made the *animus* advance by forcing it to come up against limits that it subsequently had to displace. These negative aspects were, moreover, the effect on the individual of positive powers that their finitude prevented them from grasping in any other way. Moreover, the solution consisted less in escaping finitude than in discovering it in a rigorous fashion.[162]

— In what we have called the general anthropology: we are torn by the affects, are impotent and inconstant. This dimension characterises the entirety of our life. But it also seems to distinguish us from other beings, even though Spinoza does not mention this explicitly. It is therefore not only knowledge that gives us the differential experience of necessity: it is each moment of our affective life. It is as the very heart of this splitting and this inconstancy that we feel that we are eternal, since the demonstrations, as minimal and embryonic as they are, give us the form of a world that contrasts violently with this other world. But since we do not succeed in representing to ourselves this contrast in any other way than as a succession in time, we translate this feeling and imagine this eternity as a form of survival in a better world.[163]

— In the aspiration to the minimal *credo* or to salvation: we have thus seen that if the *credo* has a meaning, it is because there already exists in each person an aspiration to salvation, a consciousness of their erring and a dissatisfaction with their finite life such as it is given to them.[164]

— In history: each State is destined to perish, whether from the inside or under the effect of external forces. This general destruction under the blows of Fortune also gives us the feeling of finitude — and thus, if our analysis is correct, it also gives us the experience of eternity.[165]

That this impotent being, inconstant and perishable, is capable of necessary knowledge suffices to give it the feeling of eternity — and thus the aspiration to develop this feeling; an aspiration called the desire for salvation.

One might be surprised to see a positive role conferred on finitude here. But this positivity is present in Spinoza almost from the first, or at least in his reading of Descartes. When Lodewijk Meyer notes in the preface to the *Principia* that there exist divergences between Descartes and Spinoza, he

---

[162] Cf. above, Part I.
[163] Cf. above, Chapter 9.
[164] Cf. above, Chapter 8.
[165] Cf. above, Chapter 10.

gives as an example – in addition to the question of free will – the Spinozist refusal of the thesis according to which 'this or that surpasses the human understanding'.[166] Our author, he says, judges on the contrary 'all those things, and even many others more sublime and subtle, can not only be conceived clearly and distinctly, but also explained very satisfactorily – provided only that the human Intellect is guided in the search for truth and knowledge of things along a different path from that which Descartes opened up and made smooth'.[167] Nothing is therefore in itself incomprehensible, and we can elevate our understanding 'to the pinnacle of knowledge'.[168] This is an extremely important thesis that indicates clearly where the divergence passes between Descartes on the one hand and Spinoza (and Meyer) on the other:[169] namely, along the lines draw by the theory of finitude, which is a key element of the two doctrines, but which is perceived and oriented in a totally different way in one and the other. In Descartes, finitude constitutes one of the directive schemas in the order of reasons; it governs both the first proof of the existence of God and the distinction between understanding and conceiving; and it is what allows us to determine in what sense Cartesian rationalism is, so to speak, self-limiting: the philosopher's refusal to deal with certain subjects is neither a concession nor a protective move but is rather grounded in the articulation of the first principles of the doctrine. In Spinoza, by contrast, finitude – which is just as present and just as strongly marked and just as continuously thought – never leads to a limitation of the capacity of our soul. On the contrary, by positively founding the finite in the infinite, finitude ensures that our power to think (like that of acting) is the very power of God. It is indeed from such a perspective that Meyer situates himself, both when he presents his own work as when he refers to Spinoza's. Such an ontology of positive finitude explains *both* the enthusiasm for Descartes as a destroyer of prejudices, a restorer of knowledge and an initiator of new sciences, *and* Spinoza's reservations in the face of what appears as Descartes' timidity and inconsistency. In this problematic, what in Descartes is an impossibility becomes a limit to be breached, the possible extension of a movement that has refused to posit from the outset any limit to its effort. At root, a 'Cartesio-Spinozism' that rejects the Cartesian thesis of finitude is necessarily led to interpret as two juxtaposed domains existing

---

[166] 'Hoc aut illud captum humanum superare', G I, p. 132, l. 27 [*PP* I; *CWS* I, 230].
[167] [*PP* I; *CWS* I, 230].
[168] [*PP* I; *CWS* I, 230].
[169] In fact, it also applies to the *Interpres* of this latter and explains the heterodox use that he makes of Cartesianism.

in a single field of knowledge what in Descartes, and for no less necessary reasons, constitute two distinct domains between which communication is impossible. This is why the horizon of such a Cartesio-Spinozism is an exit from Cartesianism, so long as the latter is conceived in terms of the rigour of its fundamental proofs. What appears as a limitation is only the limited form of a resolutely affirmative power. The effects of this limitation are lived as impotence, misery, contingency. But they are also, as such, the bearers of a positivity that manifests itself in the rupture they provoke and the path that they incite us to take towards other forms of the same power.

We now have to return to a question that we left aside in the second section of this chapter: that of the individualisation of experience. One could raise the following objection to the preceding explanation: Spinoza says 'We feel and know by experience that we are eternal', and not 'we feel and we experience that necessary (or eternal) truths exist'. How does the interpretation that we have just given of the feeling of finitude and of the feeling of eternity imply that it is *we* who feel it? Not only that we, human beings, are eternal; but also that each one of us is eternal *as ourselves*? The only form that we know of the feeling of individuation seems to be tied to the body and to memory.[170]

The experience of our eternity refers neither to knowledge of the affects of the body, nor to knowledge of the essence of the body. Either could serve as the adequate knowledge of eternity (that is, of consciousness of eternity in the sense that Spinoza understands this at the end of Book V). It is the demonstrations that make us feel the eternity of the soul – of *our* soul. Now, Spinoza says: the demonstrations are the eyes of the soul. It is thus the demonstrations that are the organs that put us in contact with things and, on the occasion of this contact, give us this feeling of ourselves. Spinoza had already used the same expression in the *TTP*: 'Invisible things, and those which are the objects only of the soul, can't be seen by any other eyes than by demonstrations. Someone who doesn't have demonstrations doesn't see anything at all in these things. If they repeat something they've heard about them, it no more touches or shows their soul than do the words of a Parrot or an automaton, which speaks without a soul or without meaning.'[171] This metaphor has a long history,[172] but Spinoza uses it in an irreducible way.

---

[170] The problem does not concern knowledge of individuation: knowledge of the third kind is precisely an adequate knowledge of singular essences. It does indeed concern feeling.

[171] TTP, Chapter XIII, GIII, p. 170, ll. 9–15; A, p. 213 [*TTP* XIII, 17; *CWS* II, 260–1].

[172] It goes back, certainly, to Plato (*The Republic*, VII, 519b, 533; *The Sophist*, 254a), but

In our contact with corporeal things, we feel our body and, in so doing, we also feel our soul. In our contact with theoretical things, we feel our power to demonstrate, and, in this way, we feel our soul, in which this power of demonstration is rooted. This is what we have called the quasi-memorial structure. What characterises the first feeling is the configuration proper to the body; what characterises the second is the configuration proper to the power to demonstrate. Is this power nevertheless not the same for all? Does it not distinguish individuals only in terms of the greater and the lesser? It also arises from the form proper to individuality insofar as it is against the backdrop of *such-and-such* a finitude, of *such-and-such* a limitation, that I feel the necessity that characterises the demonstration. The content of the demonstration is thus the same for all, but the feeling that accompanies it is obscurely singular. It is obscure because nothing implies an adequate consciousness of the individual; it is also not this feeling that validates the demonstration, which is always sufficient in itself. The singular is much more subjected to knowledge than it is its subject.[173]

I experience my finitude, and thus my eternity. Furthermore, the very error people commit by interpreting their experience of eternity as a promise of immortality is itself indicative of a dimension of experience. Up to this point we have seen that the experiential mode is always constituted by reference to the gaze of others and the heritage of a tradition. In this sense, the religious practices of others, as inadequate as they are, confirm by their very presence that these others have the very same feelings as me, even if they necessarily interpret them poorly. Once again, experience is grounded in the circulation between its three fundamental dimensions.

This does not mean that Spinoza rallies here to some proof by universal consent. The feeling of eternity is experienced. It proves nothing. Only the geometrical order can prove something. Experience plays another role: it does not demonstrate, but incites. By experiencing that we are eternal – that is, that the necessity that we discover matters to us – we aspire to live this necessity from within. This experience thus forces us to set out on a quest for this eternity, which is at once promised and given – that is, to take the path that will lead us towards knowledge and beatitude.

perhaps the Augustinian reference is more important for Spinoza, even though there mathematics are first envisaged then rejected (*Soliloquia*, the whole of Book I).

[173] J.-C. Fraisse, who is right to warn us against various false interpretations, and who clearly underscores the differences between the *Ethics* and the *KV*, comes to restrict the experience of eternity to the refusal of the loss of individuality. He thus ties it to the third kind of knowledge, since the second leads only to non-individual knowledges. *L'œuvre de Spinoza*, Paris: Vrin, 1978, pp. 280–1.

Thus, we see that at the end of Book V, the apprehension of eternity links up with the feeling of the self to constitute this unique feeling and this irreducible experience of eternity. This feeling has a role to play in the system: it encourages us to pass from the absolute perspective to the differential perspective.

Conclusion: The Constitution of Spinoza's System

In the first part of this work, I analysed the beginning of the *Treatise on the Emendation of the Intellect* by seeking to account for its singularity and to understand what, in these few short pages, was effectively at stake. It was a matter of understanding a certain kind of perspective, which could initially be identified by reference to a certain tone. The perspective suggested by this tone, as well as by the generic framework and the situations described, resembled neither those which organise the remainder of the *Treatise*, nor the geometrical order with which we are used to identifying Spinoza's procedure. This perspective is nevertheless neither a case of pure rhetoric, nor is it a simple declaration destined to vanish into the system. I believed that it was possible to describe this perspective on the basis of the notion of experience. This latter term appears only once, in the text's first line, but what it refers to governs the text in its entirety. By articulating what derives from each person's life, what each person can see of the lives of others, and what they receive from the literary tradition, this procedure unifies under the heading of the 'common' certain givens that initially escape demonstrative reasoning but which allow us to enter into the system in the proper sense. Thought takes the form of a journey where the goods of common life suggest their own overcoming; where from crisis to crisis the narrator moves towards a true good that he was ignorant of at the beginning; and where the logic of certainty leads one to change the institution of life itself.

Such a path does not occur in the same clear order as that of geometric reasoning: it supposes the half light of first discoveries, hesitations, moments of ignorance about oneself, and steps forward that occur under the pressure of events. These forms of exposition use singular procedures: the heuristics of the occasion; the dialectics of limitation; the logic of anticipation. The justification for these procedures lies in the effort they make to give a meaning to things which must disappear – but which will disappear thanks only to a meaning that these procedures will ultimately help discover. The intensity of the text comes down to the irreducible way it engages with a problematic that is also present in the *Short Treatise*, and which derives an individual's weakness from the power of the goods that are the object of their love.

The second question that I posed was that of the continuation of this experiential mode in Spinoza's mature works. Against the majority of interpreters, it seemed to me that experience played a decisive role, or rather many roles, in the *Ethics* and in the *Treatises*. So long as we distinguish it from vague experience, from physical experimentation and from mystical experience, *experientia* appears in effect as one of the principal forms for apprehending reality, at the same time as it is an essential means for understanding Spinoza's reflections on language, the passions and history. It is no longer limited to presenting a journey, but rather allows the exploration of entire territories of the human world: in a confirmative mode when it teaches us in a different way what the geometrical order has demonstrated; and in a constitutive mode when the play of existences extends the laws of nature into the networks of the singular.

Usus, ingenium, fortuna: these are the categories that govern the different fields of experience. They have scarcely been examined up to this point in the scholarship.[1] They nevertheless appeared to me as the specific forms of intelligibility proper to experience when it is a matter of taking stock of the way in which people relate to words and to texts, to passions and to the figure of the State, to the shocks of circumstance and to what is unexpected in one's historical destiny. Through these categories, the effective work of Spinozism begins. We have seen how experience registers what at first glance seems to escape the grasp of Reason, and how by taking a detour past these domains experience can neutralise inadequation and the partiality that is indissociable from what is consigned to the archives of common life, or perpetually reimposed by the latter's reproduction. We now know why the Spinozist philosopher can be a linguist, an exegete, a psychologist and an historian, and how he can do so without ceasing to be a Spinozist and a philosopher.

Thus, the unity of the system seems to me to be even stronger now thanks to the fact that it itself distributes the different modes of its construction and exposition. What does not arise directly from the geometrical order is not a by-product or a pedagogical derivation: it is of a different order, one

---

[1] None of these three terms appears in the title of an article or a book devoted to Spinoza – if we exclude Mignini's study 'Theology as the Work and Instrument of Fortune'.

whose relations with the geometrical order are thinkable in terms of the architectonic rigour of the system. This experiential order itself possesses a strong internal coherence: in addition to the difference between fields, we were able to recognise regularities in its operation. Everywhere we find the imbrication of the *I*, the relation to others and to tradition, albeit without the tension that marks the journey of the *TdIE*. Everywhere the body and the imaginary provided this order with its materials, yet they never made it incapable of a certain form of universality, even if they excluded this universality from the consideration of causes and of necessity. Everywhere there also reigned the same opacity in the way that experience was lived. This opacity took diverse forms: the displaced exception (what seems an exceptional case is only the application of the rule in exceptional circumstances); the deferred rule (I know that things are thus, but I except myself from them, or I except the present moment, or the example that surprises me); and the denial of embeddedness (I do not want to know that my choice expresses my complexion, that my satisfaction betrays my prosperity). Lastly, the texts revealed to us a specific lexicon, whose simple appearance sufficed to distinguish the experiential mode from the geometrical mode. Thus, a new universe became visible to us: there where we saw only appendices, scattered remarks, 'applications' or illustrations, indeed incoherencies, there now emerges a mode of teaching governed by constant principles and covering the majority of human activities.

In contrast to the procedures of the *TdIE*, these principles do not suppose that the experience which these principles have come to characterise disappears. They are not effaced when we approach the threshold of beatitude; they dependably organise our relation to the world, and, if recognising them can also help the conduct of the person guided by Reason, their status is not limited to being a propaedeutic. The perspective of experience safeguards the habits of language, provides rules of conduct in life and maxims for the government of States. However, on the margins of this exercise, or in its background, we discover a constant: the dual aspect, both affirmative and limiting, of human finitude.

Finally, the letter to Simon de Vries led us to ask about the indicative role that experience can play in metaphysics. Here we could not but encounter the famous and little understood phrase: *sentimus experimurque nos aeternos esse*. I supposed that one of the sources of this incomprehension had to do with the fact that commentators had failed to interpret what register this phrase was written in. The order of experience being invisible to them, they did not think to apply its rules to what they read in the Scholium to Proposition 23. By contrast, I accepted that to understand this Scholium, it was was necessary to consider the lexicon of experience as univocal: if eternity is given to us in an experiential mode, this means that, *mutatis mutandis*, we can apply to this phrase what we learnt in other forms of experience. Among the different possible readings, I could thus reject those that did not satisfy this requirement of this univocity. Furthermore, I reconstituted the semantic sphere of Spinoza's eternity and the different themes that it articulates in the geometry from the end of Book V. In the organisation of these themes, what we know of the experiential mode allowed us to determine how the feeling of eternity finds its place in the argument. It plays a precise role: it bears witness, in each person, to the presence of a consciousness of necessity at the heart of finitude, which alone can orient this person towards more powerful forms of this necessity.

What remains to be done is to once again underscore the fact that experience understood in this way cannot be opposed to Reason. Franco Biasutti has noted[2] that experience according to Spinoza in no way represents a defeat of Reason nor a submission to givens that would impose themselves in spite of it. Biasutti insists on the fact that the results of experience are taken up by the intellect and that it is this reprise that gives these results both consistency and solidity. But we must go further: it is true that Spinoza rejects empiricism; nevertheless, Biasutti's formulation suggests that a full recognition of experience would involve the retreat of rationalism. On the contrary, experience is the mode of intervention proper to rationalism in those fields where reason has no direct access. It maintains the order of necessity in its full extension: everything, by rights, arises from Reason; but there where the finitude of human understanding is at pains to reconstitute the series of singular causes, experience assumes the role of a relay that allows us to gather together in a different mode what cannot yet be adequately known. Thus, nothing is rejected from the sphere of the thinkable. This is why we can affirm without paradox that it is because Spinozism appeals to experience that it merits the name of an absolute rationalism: in effect, experience allows the system to complete the work of Reason so that all of the domains in which the rationality of the real is manifest are taken into account – that is, precisely, the real in its totality.

---

[2] 'In ultima analisi, secondo il punto di vista spinoziano, non è tanto la razionalità ad avere bisogno dell'esperienza comme puntello delle proprie operazioni, quanto, all'opposto, sono i dati empirici che necessitano del soccorso dell'intelletto e della ragione per acquistare solidità e consistenza', *Prospettive su Spinoza*, Trento: Pubblicazioni di Verifiche, 1990, p. 55.

How is something like experience possible? Spinoza does not say, and it is not experience itself that can tell us. By speaking of itself, as of any other thing, experience can only indicate its own presence and effects. It is thus conceivable that the question of its cause is not posed: the experiential procedure is so common in shared opinion and in the rhetorical tradition that when one has recourse to it, it is useless to inquire into its causes. We can nevertheless risk a hypothesis on the way in which we could account for experience from the systematic perspective: experience is nothing other than the manifestation of the particular power of the human body. Human bodies are at once capable of a number of different actions and are relatively similar to each other. Whence the gathering in the soul of numerous ideas – even and above all inadequate ones – on which associative mechanisms function in two ways: first, a rare process (but which will most develop the power of thinking) that draws out common notions and that is the origin of knowledge by adequate ideas; and a more common process (that of the imagination), which confuses typical notions, fabricates inadequate ideas, general ideas, universals, and so on. Yet the *modi cogitandi* are not only ideas, even if all other ideas are founded on them. This is why a third process is possible, one that is not of the order of knowledge but which is without doubt the same as that which founds the imitation of the affects: because of our resemblance to others,[3] we share in a certain sense what we see happen to them. The ideas that are common to the most frequent encounters in our life and in the lives of others can thus be brought together and thought, certainly, in the individuated form of our body, of our imaginary, but with a specific nuance that allows them to appear to us as essentially concerning both ourselves and others. The special tonality that affects these ideas is at the origin of the feeling of common life and of experience. The cause of experience is thus the complexity and similarity of human beings' power.

It thus appears logical for the status of experience to develop, in the history of the system, in parallel with that of power: we can distinguish a first stage, where it marks both the weakness of the subject and the possibility of the subject's relation to what gives it meaning; a second stage, that of the *Ethics* and the *TTP*, where it unfolds at the rhythm of the activities of the *conatus*; and finally, the ultimate stage of the *Political Treatise*, where, becoming active (... *sive praxis*), at least within certain limits, it marks the full unfolding of divine power at the heart of a positive finitude.

---

[3] *Ethics* III, 27 [CWS I, 508].

I indicated at the beginning of this work that I hoped that through it we could come to understand how a philosophy constitutes its relation to its outside, and, in doing so, how it situates itself. It is time to return to this question.

— Spinoza's philosophy is an architecture. We know what this implies: a philosophy is not reducible to a central intuition, but constitutes a rigorous structure that organises this intuition or this plurality of intuitions and confers upon them its force. If things were otherwise, we would be faced with wisdom and not with philosophy. In the case of Spinozism, this structure seems, moreover, to present itself in an external form, which is that of the geometrical order.

— But how does this architecture give itself the means for its own operation? In other words, how does the system constitute itself? This is not the same question as 'How is it formed?' or 'How does it unfold its forms of rationality?'[4] Unless we accept that the system creates its own concepts, proofs and modes of demonstration out of nothing, it is indeed necessary to explain how it can establish a dialogue with its potential reader. We have already encountered this problem in the first part of our work, in the form of a question that derives from it: that of the protreptic. But prior to the question of the protreptic we find the question of the constitution of the system, which is its condition. How can the architectonic of a thought integrate its relation to what is external to it?

The range of responses is well known. We find a discussion of them, for example, in Martial Gueroult's 'dianoématique'. There are three extreme possibilities. One can explain a philosophy by the criticism that it undertakes of previous systems; a philosophy would thus be a new formulation of a philosophical tradition, born of the dissatisfaction induced by its predecessors, or produced by a mixture of a plurality of influences. Yet it has often been remarked that the clearest traits of a system of thought are already formed prior to its reception of it predecessors. Furthermore, if the impression of unity produced by a system is not illusory, it must be recognised that its consistency has different foundations than a mere series of variations or juxtapositions that derive from what precedes the system. One can also read the system as a direct description of reality – but why, then, do so many

---

[4] Cf. P.-F. Moreau, 'Biographie intellectuelle et règles d'interprétation', in *Spinoza's Political and Theological Thought*, ed. C. De Deugd, Amsterdam: North Holland, 1984, pp. 137–42.

systems exist?⁵ Above all, one is then led to underestimate the role of the architectonic and the reworking that it imposes on the real. Finally, to avoid these dangers, we can strongly emphasise the difference between the interior and the exterior. We thus insist, and rightly so, on the fact that the core of a system's intelligibility resides above all in its own structures. The 'common real' thus ends up receding before disappearing entirely.⁶ This is Gueroult's tendency, who considers that social, scientific and religious factors cling only 'fugitively' to systems: they constitute a sort of periphery whose variations are not determining.⁷

We cannot resolve these questions here in a general sense. But perhaps the work we have just completed can allow us to see things more clearly as far as the case of Spinozism is concerned.

A first answer consists in identifying the sectorial disciplines and their own languages: that of physics, law and the theory of the passions. Like other philosophies, Spinozism is the inheritor of these disciplines just as it reorganises them, but without creating them from nothing. It thus finds itself on a common terrain, where its argumentation is elaborated on the basis of pre-philosophical givens – certainly to transform them, but without being able to ignore them. Reciprocally, its capacity to convince the reader will rest on its ability to resolve pre-existing problems, or to clarify their solutions. This is the case in the classical age for the problems of extension and movement, of the legitimation of the State, of the domination of the passions, or of the interpretation of the Scriptures. It will be said, however, that these are precisely the 'periphery' of the system.

But we can also find a second response by noting that all of the terms that make up the order of experience in Spinoza's thought – *experientia, usus, ingenium, fortuna* – have a common point: they belong to a larger lexicon than that of philosophical language. They crystallise points of view, examples and arguments carried by pre-philosophical discourses, from the orators and historians of Rome right up to the moralists of the Renaissance. The system thus shares certain of its boundaries with a rhetorical tradition: these boundaries are manifest predominantly in those notions that are closest to human experience and can thus from the outset be interpreted outside of a specialised approach. These borders provide the philosopher and the reader with a common terrain that itself seems to call for a metaphysical

---

⁵ M. Gueroult, *Philosophie de l'histoire de la philosophie*, Aubier, 1979, p. 60
⁶ 'Cessant de vouloir se fonder par rapport à un réel common extérieur à elles, elles [= philosophies] découvrent en elles-mêmes le fondement de leur réalité', ibid., p. 106.
⁷ Ibid., p. 138.

interpretation. It is therefore not a 'common real' determined once and for all that forms the ground of the system: it is an experience that has already been reflected on, or is part of a tradition of reflection and that orients the way that facts are interpreted by those who live them. Certainty, this tradition is determined historically – the different levels that compose it can be identified – but it has become anonymous and constitutes something like an interpretative backdrop for ordinary life, which many systems can account for, each according to its own norms.

In this sense, there is much to learn from the way that the great rationalist philosophers of the seventeenth century were immersed in what was once the humanistic thought of experience and of fortune – sometimes to draw inspiration from it, but often to displace or invert its concepts. What is proper to Spinozism is that it founds these notions, which are at once inherited and familiar to each person, on a way of approaching reality that introduces pre-philosophical preoccupations into the very heart of the system. Experience is not, therefore, the system's periphery: it is the point at which the exterior becomes the interior.

An Infinite Internal to the Finite:
An Interview with Pierre-François Moreau on
Experience and Eternity in Spinoza

Experience and its Vicissitudes

Robert Boncardo: *Experience and Eternity in Spinoza* is the first of your books to be translated into English. However, for almost five decades now, your work has been read across the world – in particular in Europe – and has been translated into German, Italian, Spanish and Dutch. We'll return to this international context of reception a little further on, but to begin with, could you give us a general idea of what you were hoping to achieve in *Experience and Eternity in Spinoza*? What are the work's main arguments in your eyes?

Pierre-François Moreau: I'd make two points to begin with. On the one hand, at the level of content, my aim was to insist on the presence of experience in Spinoza, and on the fact that Spinozism is a thought of practice. In the history of French philosophy, as well as in the history of Spinoza's reception in France, these are important claims; for ever since the work of Victor Cousin, a doxa has existed in France that has held that Spinoza neglected experience. In the nineteenth century, French spiritualism was founded on the idea that true philosophy was to be found in the heritage of Descartes, and that Descartes himself was good when his philosophy was close to experience, and less good when he turned away from experience – in other words, whenever he did mathematics. This doxa also held that Spinoza wasn't any good at all, or rather that he was at once fascinating and dangerous. When Spinoza left the ground of experience, he went in the direction of either materialism or mysticism. Thus, an entire ideology and nomenclature was established by Victor Cousin before being reprised by Émile Saisset, Spinoza's first translator; and this ideology has subsisted through a whole series of transformations and transfigurations, even when philosophers have forgotten that it was Victor Cousin who invented this interpretative machine. If you did your studies in France, you would often hear people say: 'Spinoza is a rationalist; he's not interested in experience.' Furthermore, in France as elsewhere, including in the Anglo-Saxon world, there was this old idea of an opposition between continental rationalism on the one hand and Anglo-Saxon empiricism on the other. When you take a closer look, however, you realise that things are a lot more complicated: those we call empiricists give reason an important role to play, and vice versa. In other words, it's not a good explanatory framework. But above all, I had the impression that thinking that Spinoza was against experience had the effect of obscuring what was essential in his thought. It was this idea that had meant that Spinoza's readers were less interested in the *Political Treatise* or the *Theologico-Political Treatise*. It also obscured many of the Scholia from the *Ethics*, for in these Scholia Spinoza speaks of real people, of their activities. Think of the son who has gotten into an argument with his father and who has left to join the army, or of the scorned lover whose mistress has betrayed him and who speaks ill of women, but who's ready to return to her as soon as she calls for him. The *Ethics* is teeming with life, with a life that we either experience ourselves, that we see in others, or that we learn about from the literary tradition, which functions as a kind of condensation of collective experience. I was struck by the fact that all of this was massively present in Spinoza. It wasn't present in the form of some kind of concession or compulsion or afterthought; rather, it was at the very heart of Spinoza's thought. When Spinoza is reasoning about things that are apparently abstract or rational, all of this is there in the form of examples, of material, of living flesh, underneath his thought's structures. Thus, there are at once the structures of thought, which are incontestably rationalist, and then there is a flesh, a material to these structures. That was my first goal: to show that Spinoza was a philosopher of experience, of practice. I wouldn't go so far as to say that he was a philosopher of 'lived experience', because in France 'lived experience' often has a very loose, very irrational meaning. I'm being a bit harsh in saying that, but when you've spent some time in the French university system, you know what 'lived experience' means.

Robert Boncardo: Were there any other aims to your work beyond re-establishing the centrality of experience in Spinoza's thought?

Pierre-François Moreau: The second goal of the book, after showing that Spinoza was a thinker of experience, was to demonstrate that it was possible to do the history of philosophy by articulating it with the history of ideas. I wanted to both confirm that the great philosophers were systematic philosophers, and that their systems were developed and expressed within conditions of production that are those studied by the history of ideas. We have known ever since Delbos and Hamelin that these philosophers were systematic. In the French university system, it was traditional to write books like 'Aristotle's System', 'Plato's System', 'The Thought of Descartes', or 'Descartes According to the Order of Reasons', and so on. Gueroult was at once the theoretician and the supreme representative of this structural history. Thus, in a sense, when structuralism arrived in the 1960s, historians of philosophy weren't at all shocked since they'd been working in a 'structuralist' way for a century. What they did best was precisely to analyse the structures of philosophy. Just as Lacan analysed the structures of the unconscious, or Lévi-Strauss the structures of kinship or myth, we studied the structures of philosophy. The problem with this structural history was obviously that we were less interested in those philosophers who seemed less systematic. There was no place for Kierkegaard, no place for Jean-Jacques Rousseau. There exists an absolutely catastrophic article by Gueroult on Rousseau where he concludes that what's best in Rousseau's thought is whatever Fichte did with it, since Fichte turned it into a system. As far as Rousseau himself was concerned, he wasn't systematic, and thus he wasn't a proper object of thought. The second negative effect was that this structural history wasn't interested in the biography of philosophers, with their intellectual biography. Rousseau is precisely someone who doesn't use the word 'nature' in his early writings in the same way he does in his later writings. You might suppose that it would be interesting to study this process of transformation, but precisely for someone like Gueroult, it's a scandal: Gueroult wanted a system that could be flattened out once and for all. Finally, the third fault of this structural history was that, fundamentally, it wasn't interested in the texts themselves. This is a very French fault, one that doesn't just concern structural history. When you say to a French student – I wouldn't dare say a French colleague, so let's take a student – 'We're going to study Pascal', for instance, what do they do? They go to a library and they take the Pascal volume off the shelves. And for them, Pascal is there in that volume. They never ask: 'What edition do I have in my hand?', or 'Who decided to publish the *Pensées* in this order?' I'm obviously using the example of Pascal because the *Pensées* are available in the Brunschvicg and the Lafuma editions, along with some other more recent ones; and the *pensées* are precisely not published in these different editions in the same order. If you place two pensées one after the other, you obtain a structure that is not the same as the structure that would have resulted had they been placed at opposite ends of the book. Generally speaking, French philosophers never pose the question of how one goes from the author's manuscript or the author's thought to the book that they find in the bookstore. The philological, even epigraphic, side of things is passed over in silence. When you publish a book, you realise that there are people who intervene in the constitution of your book, who decide to add a paragraph, a semicolon, quotation marks – and all of this changes the meaning. If you're careful, it doesn't change the meaning much, but if you're not, it changes it a lot. Thus, when you work on someone's posthumous writings – and this is the case for Pascals' *Pensées*, Spinoza's *Ethics*, Descartes' correspondence, and for a significant portion of Hegel's writings – you are confronted with works that have been published by people who aren't the author themselves and where many decisions involving structure, organisation, presentation – everything that is essential for the book's structure – have been taken by others and for reasons that arise from individual predilection or the norms of the publishing world, the university, or a group. Think of Pascal's sister or of Nietzsche's sister. Structural history wasn't really concerned with any of this. My aim was to bring the history of philosophy together with the history of the real conditions of production of thought: the generative, collective ground of thought, philosophers' biographies, and forms of writing. I certainly wanted to reaffirm, as structural historians had done, the essential role of systematic thought. Thus, for instance, when you find the word 'will' in Descartes and the word 'will' in Spinoza, what's important is not that the same word has been used twice but rather that the word 'will' draws its meaning in the first case from Descartes' system and in the second from Spinoza's system. On this point I'm in perfect agreement with Gueroult: you ultimately have to consider the two words as homonymic. You can't explain the word 'will' as it's used in Spinoza by the word 'will' in Descartes, or you at least have to make a huge effort to explain why you can. Thus, I was in favour of structural history, so long as it was at the same time articulated with, or completed by, an analysis of the author's evolution and their intellectual biography. Now, there were people in France who did this, and there was one in particular who did it exceptionally well: Henri Gouhier. Henri Gouhier was concerned with intellectual biography as an object of philosophy, while for Gueroult intellectual biography was a matter of doxa, of 'doxography'. Thus, I tried to articulate this structural history of philosophy with the history of ideas, intellectual biography and philology. It was a big project! I'm not sure I was entirely successful, but I do think I succeeded at least in part. All the same, *Experience and Eternity in Spinoza* is a work that's centred on structural history; it's an analysis of certain structures of thought in Spinoza that commentators hadn't previously seen. However, I did so by way of occasional excursuses on the tradition of the protreptic before Spinoza, on the conversion narrative, on the theory of fortune before Spinoza, and so on. I did so not by reference to influences but by demarcating differences and frontiers. That's perhaps a military language: the idea of seeking demarcations, dialectics, conflicts, and so on.

From French Spinozism in the 1960s and Early 1970s . . .

Robert Boncardo: We can perhaps return to these questions of method further on. For now, and before we engage with the details of your text, since we're not particularly familiar with your intellectual trajectory in the Anglophone world, could you tell us a little bit about your philosophical career? In 1975, almost twenty years before *Experience and Eternity in Spinoza*, you published a book titled simply *Spinoza*. Before that, you did two theses: a master's thesis and a *thèse de troisième cycle*. Could you explain how you came to study philosophy? Who were your teachers? What did these first two works of research involve?

Pierre-François Moreau: I'm not sure if it's interesting in and of itself, but I began by wanting to study mathematics. When I was in the final year of high school, I was readying myself to go to the preparatory class in the sciences. At the beginning of the year, we didn't have a philosophy teacher. By Easter, we were starting to worry about our exams. Then, two months before the final exams, a teacher arrived, Yvon Letourneur, who all of a sudden spoke to us students who had never heard of philosophy before – in France, you only study philosophy in your final year – about Husserl, Kant and Marx in a clear and fascinating way. And I said to myself: that's what I want to do. And so I didn't go to the preparatory class in the sciences but instead I went to the preparatory class in letters. In this class you did much more literature, history and classical languages than philosophy. So I had to study Latin, Greek, French, but also philosophy. It was at that moment that I read Sylvain Zac's book *La morale de Spinoza* and began to be interested in Spinoza and not only in Kant, Marx or Descartes. And from that point on I had in the back of my mind the idea that one day I would have to work on Spinoza. I did my first master's thesis on the theory of crises in *Capital*, precisely at the time of the great financial crisis of 1970 when everyone thought that capitalism was going to collapse. In '68, we thought that the people were challenging capitalism politically, while in 1969–70, it was as if capitalism was collapsing financially. All of a sudden the markets went mad. And so I studied the theory of crisis in volume two of *Capital*, the theory of crises of overproduction, of circulation, and so on. I had read the first volume of *Capital* in *khâgne*, and I noticed that each time that Marx explains what's specific about his work, what makes him different, he always proceeds in the same way: he presents a classicism, a standard theory, and it's in relation to this standard theory that he affirms his own positions. First, he explains that there are those thinkers who are the offcuts of this theory – he calls these the vulgar economists – and he says that there's no point wasting your time with these people. It's better, he says, to critique the standard theory itself. Here he's using 'critique' in the classical sense of the term: you take what you can and cut off what you have no use for. For Marx, this standard theory is represented by Adam Smith and even more so by Ricardo. And each time that he analyses this classical theory of political economy, he finds what he calls Ricardo's 'mad error'. So, after passing the *agrégation* exams, I began my *thèse de troisième* cycle, and I wanted to focus on the question of the difference between Ricardo and Marx, or rather, more precisely, to the extent that Ricardo is not an idiot, what makes him unable to see what Marx sees through him. Marx never claimed to have discovered anything all by himself. He was obviously trained as an economist, but he claims to read over Ricardo's shoulder what Ricardo has written but not read. What is it in Ricardo's text that begins to sketch out something that Ricardo hasn't seen? The answer that I came up with was that it was what I called a 'theoretical space', a 'classical theoretical space'. This is something that begins with William of Ockham and is developed by the theoreticians of natural right, by Locke, Hobbes and Rousseau. It's not the content of their theories but a certain way of thinking the relations between the individual and society, the difference between the present and the origin of the present, and the relation between 'is' and 'ought'. It's a series of scissions that determine that each object is considered as having two sides: active citizenship and passive citizenship, universal humanity and less-than-universal humanity. This refers to a division between the form or the receptacle, which is something that is universal and equal for all (and this idea is not false; indeed it's an immense progress to say this), and a content that is not supposed to have any importance in the argument considered in its universal validity, but which in fact counts for quite a lot and determines the effects and the forms of existence of the universal. With Kant, it's very clear that he wants to explain why women cannot vote: they may be completely human at the universal level, but at the same time they have properties that mean they cannot be citizens in the proper sense of the term. He gives a similar explanation for why everyone has the right to vote, but why those who don't have any property nevertheless don't have this right, and so on. There is always this dual schema, this figure with two levels, which we also find in Ricardo's work on economics. And so, I was interested in Ricardo, certainly, but above all in what was beyond Ricardo, namely what I called the 'classical theoretical space'. So, when I finished my *thèse de troisième* cycle, I said to myself that I should either analyse this 'space' for itself, or study what resists this 'space'. And it was at that point that Spinoza returned. I had the impression that Spinoza was someone who didn't fit into this dual schema. So I had the idea of undertaking a project that would be at once a detailed analysis of the classical theoretical space, the Spinozist theoretical space, and the Marxist theoretical space. At the time, doing a *thèse d'État* meant beginning with a huge project and then, under the constraints of time and the necessities of analysis, reducing its size bit by bit – this is also true for more recent theses, even if they're shorter. In time, the project became more and more modest. I began by getting rid of everything that wasn't Spinoza, and within Spinoza I got rid of more and more things, such that the book that is now called *Experience and Eternity in Spinoza* was initially meant to be the introduction to my thesis. When I got to page 700 or 800, I said to myself: 'I should stop.' Logically, however, the thesis was meant to begin after that with an analysis of each work. But I said to myself: 'I can't take another twenty years to complete my thesis; I have to stop.'

Robert Boncardo: In listening to you, what strikes me is that your thesis, or rather your thesis project, was inscribed within a sort of Althusserian problematic. We know that Althusser was profoundly interested in Spinoza. We also know that at that time in France, there was a resurgence of interest in Spinoza's philosophy. Deleuze published his two famous works, the two monumental volumes of Gueroult's work appeared, and Matheron published his crucial book. What were the links between your own thought and the other thinkers who were interested in Spinoza at that time?

Pierre-François Moreau: I'd begin by saying that, as I mentioned above, the first bit of reading I did that led me to Spinoza was of Sylvain Zac's book. This was before the publication of Gueroult's or Matheron's books. In *La morale de Spinoza*, Zac approached the problems raised by Spinoza's oeuvre in a rigorous and clear manner. He made you feel the power of a coherent and efficacious system behind a small number of questions that were rooted in life and in the most common of experiences. After Zac came Althusser and the problem of structural causality. From Althusser, an entire generation learnt, or believed they learnt, that in order to understand the complexity of causes in a totality (a society, for instance), it was necessary to avoid both the error that sees only the action of one individual on another, or of a singular event on another (this is Descartes' error), and the symmetrical error that consists in thinking you can explain everything by the expressive action of a totality (this is Leibniz's error). Spinoza was the one who allowed us to think of the construction of a complex causality with many different levels. This was no doubt a simplistic and possibly fantastical vision, but it had the efficacy and the relative truth of a 'solid error'. I would also add that in the atmosphere of the 1960s and '70s, Gueroult and Matheron's readings of Spinoza were joined in our minds – even if it's hard to explain why – with the tradition of historical epistemology of Bachelard, Canguilhem and the early Foucault, but also of Koyré (who nevertheless held different theoretical positions) or Cavaillès. The most revealing link, if you like, was the quote from Cavaillès saying that his reflections on mathematics, like his antifascist actions as part of the Resistance, were both tied to Spinoza. Beyond this reference, there was the demand for a rigorous reading that would occur in parallel with the history of the sciences and the history of texts and systems. At a more personal level, my relation was obviously first of all to Althusser. I had just left the Ecole Normale Supérieure and become a high-school teacher when Althusser asked me to return to teach Spinoza to those who were studying for the *agrégation*. This was at the time I published my first little book. When the journal *Cahiers Spinoza* was founded, Matheron wrote to Althusser to ask him if he wanted to write an article and he replied that since I was on the editorial committee, it would suffice for me to write an article since my thought was close to his own and that I knew what he wanted to say about Spinoza.

Robert Boncardo: How was your own first book on Spinoza received?

Pierre-François Moreau: The book was translated into German in 1978 by some German Althusserians, who gave the book the title *Marx und Spinoza*, which was a bit of an exaggeration given that I'd only written a few lines on Marx. After the appearance of the book in 1975, my Dutch friends (Guido van Suchtelen in particular), while supportive of the book's basic arguments, made clear to me what my limitations were at the philological and historiographical levels. It was true that, at the time, I wrote like a French philosopher (of that time: I hope today that my students do a better job): that is, by showing a perfect indifference to the linguistic and editorial underpinnings of Spinoza's work, to the minute work of erudition, and to the concrete reality of the historical context (even though we always talked about historical context in France, we did so in the form of generalities).

After 1975, I set out to explore everything that I was missing, and took up those instruments that I lacked – instruments that my entire generation, in fact, lacked (or, worse, whose utility we didn't even perceive). Also, before teaching the history of philosophy at the Sorbonne, for a few years I taught the rudiments of the human sciences and the history of pedagogy and social work in Institutes that taught students who weren't students of philosophy. This also helped me enlarge my horizon. Thus, in the course of my work as a teacher and as a journalist (I used to write a lot, not in newspapers, but in human sciences magazines: this allowed me to engage with current practices outside of the history of classical philosophy), I studied the history of materialism, the historical of classical political ideas, the history of utopia and of heterodox religious figures; and I learnt to read texts more closely – their words, their connections, everything that is 'under' the system's structure. It was after all of these detours that I wrote my *thèse d'État*, Experience and Eternity in Spinoza.

Robert Boncardo: During this period there were others who were also working on Spinoza. I'm thinking for instance of Pierre Macherey.

Pierre-François Moreau: Yes. I never spoke much to Macherey about Spinoza. In fact, Macherey became interested in Spinoza at a time when I was no longer seeing him. We met up again many years later when we were both invited by the Italians to Urbino, to Rome, and so on. When the *Cahiers Spinoza* were put together, there was Matheron, and there was André Lécrivain, who was interested in Spinoza's physics and who published a very long article in two editions on Spinoza and Descartes' physics; a very meticulous article. It was pure Gueroult. There was also Monique Schneider, who I came to know when she was teaching at the ENS in Sèvres and was training to be a psychoanalyst. She wrote very interesting texts on Spinoza and Freud. Later on I founded a collection with another editor and I asked her to write a book on feminism and witchcraft and on Freud's texts on femininity and witchcraft. She analysed the Loudun possessions in the seventeenth century, where the nuns said that they were possessed and where the priest ended up being burnt. She analysed the priest's texts from a psychoanalytic perspective. She was halfway between Freud and Spinoza. In France, interest in Spinoza either takes the form of Spinoza and Marx or Spinoza and Freud.

... to Dutch, German and Italian Spinozisms in the late 1970s

Robert Boncardo: There was also a resurgence of interest in Spinoza at the international level at that time too.

Pierre-François Moreau: At the international level, there were Spinozists in all the different countries, but they didn't know each other. The turning point was 1977. Since the Second World War, Spinozists had been isolated within their national traditions. It was as if the ties that existed before 1940 – or rather before 1933 – had been broken. However, in 1977, the 300th anniversary of Spinoza's death, a number of conferences were held that allowed everyone to begin the dialogue again. We all met in Paris, Amsterdam, Leiden and Rome. Many works published after this bear the marks of our discussions from the time. Hubbeling was there, the great Dutch Spinoza specialist, along with his student Akkermann, who wasn't a philosopher but rather a philologist. It was thanks to Akkermann that I all of a sudden discovered philology – the fact that the material support of texts is just as important as anything else. For instance, Spinoza writes in a certain Latin, not just any Latin. There was also Manfred Walther and Wolfgang Bartuschat from Germany, and a whole series of Italians, for instance Filippo Mignini and Omero Proietti, who was a fascinating person. Proietti knew by heart all of Terence's plays and so when reading Spinoza could say: 'Here are two words from such-and-such a play', or: 'Here's a sentence that's the transformation of such-and-such a verse from the *Adelphoe*', or: 'Here's an allusion to what Sallust said but modified using a phrase from Terence.'

Robert Boncardo: There are traces of all this in your book.

Pierre-François Moreau: Yes indeed. There was also the great Emilia Giancotti Boscherini, the queen of Italian Spinozism, who had composed the monumental two volumes of the *Lexicon Spinozanum*, where all of Spinoza's vocabulary was recorded. In Padua there was also a school of Hegelian Spinozists, including Chiereghin, who had come to Spinoza from Hegel and from what Hegel says about Spinoza. He sought the foundations of Hegel's dialectic in Spinoza's thought. There's always been a tradition of Spinoza studies in Italy, one that, importantly, has always been philological in inspiration. While the Germans had lost their philological and historiographical tradition – represented by Freudenthal and Gebhardt – the Italians analysed the linguistic and literary structures of texts. For instance, when Mignini went to the Netherlands to study the *Korte Verhandeling*, he was brought the manuscript and noticed that the previous reader had been Gebhardt at the beginning of the century! No one else had asked to see it. There was also Piero di Vona, an absolutely fascinating Neapolitan who knew by heart the whole of late scholasticism. He could explain Spinoza and Descartes to you by showing you what they owed to the Dominicans and Jesuits and others besides. When you read the *Cogitata Metaphysica*, you can see that there is a part of Spinoza that is indeed rooted in this history of scholastic ontology. And when you read Descartes' discussion in the Objections and Replies, you see that it, too, is rooted in this late scholasticism. I spent a month in Rome as a member of the CNRS, where I spent my time in the Gregoriana, their extraordinary library, and I realised that throughout the twentieth century the Italians had worked on Machiavelli and Spinoza, Marx and Spinoza, and so on. The Italians are much more sensitive to philological questions than the French, as well as to the circulation of texts and of notions. Thus, for them, Spinoza is always immediately 'Spinoza and . . .'.

Robert Boncardo: So was your task to synthesise these approaches, the Dutch, French, German and Italian?

Pierre François Moreau: It was to articulate them. You'd have to be really, really talented to synthesise them. Fundamentally, I tried to inherit from these traditions: the Italian and Dutch philological tradition, and the systematic tradition of the French. But in fact, once I become a university professor, I was able to openly defend the history of ideas and to encourage my students to engage in it as well, and to protect them when they did so.

Philosophy and the History of Ideas in France

Robert Boncardo: Was there a sort of prohibition against the history of ideas at that time in France?

Pierre-François Moreau: Among philosophers it was considered as something only literature scholars did. I remember that when I wanted to found a series in the history of ideas at Presses Universitaires de France, I spoke about my project to the President of the publisher, and he said to me: 'Hold on, since this is about philosophy, I'd prefer to ask the opinion of philosophers.' And so he asked some philosophers what they thought and they all told him: 'No, this is not a serious, it's vulgar.' And so he said to me: 'Listen, I'm sorry; all of your colleagues are saying that the history of ideas isn't serious.' So I founded the series elsewhere. I think that now, twenty years later, you can no longer say that. Thirty years ago, in 1994, when I published my thesis, philosophers would react by saying: 'No, that's not proper philosophy.' Studying Spinoza alongside a minor heterodox protestant, or studying Kant alongside a materialist from the eighteenth century – these things just weren't done. There were certainly those who did the history of ideas without any shame, namely literary scholars. They did the history of ideas but without being systematic about it; the challenge was to show how it could be done with reference to solid structures. In fact, among literary scholars there were some great and successful examples of the history of ideas, in particular when it came to identifying continuities (I'm thinking of Curtius), or stylistic questions (I'm thinking of Spitzer), or constructing histories of reception. I've been deeply interested in clandestine manuscripts and I currently edit a journal called *La Lettre Clandestine*, which is devoted to the materialists of the eighteenth century and to the libertines of the seventeenth century, as well as to all the clandestine manuscripts that have been circulating for centuries. It's said that the classical age is the age of reason, of orthodoxy, of Bossuet, and so on; but at the same time in seventeenth- and eighteenth-century France there were piles of anti-Christian, materialist and occasionally republican manuscripts that circulated. Obviously none of them were published, or if they were it was in the Netherlands, which they entered as contraband; selling these manuscripts would make booksellers rich. In this tradition, there are philosophical concepts that circulate and which impregnate the works of published philosophers. So, you have ideas that circulate in official philosophy, as well as in secret philosophy. The clandestine philosophers don't have systematic structures, but they do have what I would call structures of intensity. Their ideas aren't organised in an articulated way, via theorems, as is the case with Spinoza, but they cluster together in different ways. It's extremely interesting. I dived into all of this, and I was a bit scandalised by the contemptuous attitude of philosophers who would say: 'No, no, it's not proper, you shouldn't do that.' Thus, when I published a collection of my articles called *Problèmes du spinozisme*, I wrote a preface where I said that the university doesn't like the history of ideas, but that it's the university that's wrong. Since then I've noticed that there are now many theses that are defended, on subjects other than Spinoza, and the students quote page two, and it's that sentence that they quote. I have the impression that that sentence liberated them. They say: 'Oh! We do have the right to do the history of ideas! We can do it! Moreau has said it's the university that is wrong.' It's amusing.

Robert Boncardo: Do you have any memories of philosophers' reaction to *Experience and Eternity in Spinoza*?

Pierre-François Moreau: Yes, but since my book was a structural book, they were really in a bind. They couldn't say: you're wrong. In a sense, from the moment I defended my thesis – and on the jury I had people like Deleule, Matheron and Desanti, who were all very well-respected in the university world – I was untouchable. They all had the impression that I was henceforth the owner of Spinoza – alongside Matheron, of course, but since Matheron agreed with me, no one could criticise me anymore. And so from that moment on I could encourage my students to work on the history of ideas; I had legitimised them. I suppose I contributed to the introduction of the history of ideas into philosophy. However, if I can now say that the history of ideas is the right way to go, it's because, paradoxically, I wrote a classical, structural book.

Robert Boncardo: You've just mentioned the name of Jean-Toussaint Desanti, who was your supervisor for both your first and second theses. Could you tell us about your relation to Desanti, who is someone we don't know particularly well in the Anglophone world, but who has been hugely important in France?

Pierre-François Moreau: Desanti was important above all because, until 1956, he was one of the official philosophers of the French Communist Party. He left the Party discretely, while others left by slamming the door on their way out. There were many on the Right in the university system who hated him for a long time. Nevertheless, he became a professor at the Ecole Normale Supérieure de Saint-Cloud, which is now in Lyon. He trained generations of young philosophers. Since Desanti did epistemology, he gave his students a sense of mathematical rigour, and he reprised the tradition of Bachelard, Canguilhem and Cavaillès. At the same time, he used to say something that I repeat a little too often: 'Position yourself in the midst of positivities.' Canguilhem used to say that any material whatsoever is appropriate for philosophy. It's the same thing. It means that philosophy shouldn't turn around in a circle, but should be done by investigating biology, the history of life, and so on. For Desanti, doing the philosophy of mathematics wasn't about saying a priori what mathematicians should do; it was about placing yourself in the midst of the history of the functions of real variables in the nineteenth century and seeing how philosophers tried such-and-such a theory, and how they tried another when that didn't work. It's an empirical matter in one sense – seeing mathematicians' concrete practices, their efforts and errors – but it's also mathematics itself. It's about the real work of scientists, their actual practice. Thus, Desanti trained philosophers who went on to study linguistics, ethnology, the hard sciences, and so on; they positioned themselves in the midst of the positivities of these sciences. It was very important to work with Desanti since he encouraged you to go and take a look at what was happening outside of philosophy, as a way of doing philosophy. That was something that was extremely important. Moreover, he had a way of thinking that consisted in taking a problem and looking at it from all sides. For example, I remember a really impressive two-hour seminar he gave on time for the *agrégation* exam. Desanti arrived with his hands in his pockets, with neither notes nor books. He took out a piece of chalk and in the middle of the blackboard drew a large circle, and on this circle he made twelve marks, added a point in the middle, a big hand a little hand: it was a clock. And for two hours, on the basis of this simple drawing, Desanti constructed an entire philosophy of time. It was fascinating. You can see the influence of phenomenology here. But Desanti had a very materialist conception of phenomenology: you renounce what's in the *Cartesian Meditations*, you renounce Husserl's idealist and subjectivist turn, and you transform phenomenology into a materiology.

Robert Boncardo: So into a more Sartrean phenomenology?

Pierre-François Moreau: Yes, though Desanti didn't begin with an internal analysis of consciousness; he went straight to very concrete things.

Robert Boncardo: You wrote an afterword to the 2006 edition of his work *Introduction à l'histoire de la philosophie*.

Pierre-François Moreau: Yes. When the ENS was moved from Saint-Cloud to Lyon, the Dean, Sylvain Auroux, who had been a student of Desanti was both a philosopher and linguist, invited Desanti's students to a conference on his work. And when Desanti died in 2002, we created the Desanti Institute, one of whose aims was to republish his works with additional texts. Desanti was someone who published quite rarely, and his books are for the most part either interventions or dialogues or collections of articles. Dominique Desanti, his wife, gave us his manuscripts, and we scanned them and began to republish his old books with additional texts. His book on Spinoza, for instance, now has an additional section that was to be the second volume but which was never published. We also found other texts that we published as well. We've just published a volume called *Mathesis et historicité*, which is a collection of articles on mathematics, and we're currently working on a collection of articles on the history of philosophy. The afterword you're referring to is part of this attempt to re-read his works and to show their underlying logic.

Robert Boncardo: If I'm not mistaken, in that afterword you explain that Desanti's insight was that in trying to understand the history of philosophy – or in studying philosophy historically – one always has to contend with a plurality of causal forces and never with a single explanatory principle.

Pierre-François Moreau: I'd note in passing that that's what Althusser used to call overdetermination.

Robert Boncardo: Yes, yes – once again, an Althusserian problematic! What struck me in reading that afterword was that in *Experience and Eternity in Spinoza* you explain that for Spinoza, experience names, precisely, a domain where there is an always singular interweaving of various determinations.

Pierre-François Moreau: In fact, in listening to your question, I've realised something that I wasn't aware of, which is that when I read Desanti or comment on him, I seek out in his texts what brings him closest to Althusser. Since it was Althusser who had sent me to Desanti, it's something like an ouroboros.

Robert Boncardo: Is it the same thing when you study Spinoza? You seem to find overdetermination in him as well.

Pierre-François Moreau: Yes, indeed. Recently I wrote a series of articles on the *Theologico-Political Treatise* and on a certain number of objects that Spinoza deals with therein, such as prophecy, Christianity, insurrections, and so on. I realised that Spinoza constructs his objects on the basis of various materials, from the Bible to Roman historians, and he mixes all of this with his analyses of the passions. Together all of this constitutes and overdetermines the concrete objects that are insurrections, the meaning of Christianity and the history of the prophets.

Robert Boncardo: So it's a way of re-thinking singularity, or individuality?

Pierre-François Moreau: Yes. The idea that's at the foundation of all of this – and it wasn't me who invented it – is that the simple is not at the origin of things. In theories of the social contract, indeed in the entire history of liberal ideology, you always find the idea that the simple comes first and then becomes more complex. But it's not true. The simple comes last and is the product, the articulation, the synthesis of very complex things.

Re-reading the *Treatise on the Emendation of the Intellect*

Robert Boncardo: Let's turn now to the book *Experience and Eternity in Spinoza* itself. Almost the entirety of the first half of the book is devoted to a microscopic analysis of the first eleven paragraphs of the *Treatise on the Emendation of the Intellect*. This is a text that has been commented on many times throughout the centuries and which forms part of the philosophy curriculum in France. Why did you choose to study such a well-known text in such detail?

Pierre-François Moreau: There was a kind of proverb that used to circulate in the 1960s, inspired either by Roland Barthes or Althusser: 'What is well known is badly known.' It's almost always true. What is well known is too well known and thus misunderstood. The idea is that when everyone has talked about a certain text, what you should do is ignore what's been said and look at the text itself. Gueroult had a student, Victor Goldschmidt, who was a specialist of Antiquity but who had also written on Rousseau and Kant. Whenever students posed the classic question of how they could do something original, Goldschmidt would reply: 'Read the texts and you'll be original.' I think Goldschmidt was right. In the French university system, the *Treatise on the Emendation of the Intellect* was read widely but for bad reasons, such as that it was a short text that was convenient for use in exams. It's easier than reading the *Ethics*. For the same reason, we give students the *Discourse on Method* rather than the *Principles of Philosophy*, Marx's *Introduction to the Critique of Political Economy* rather than *Capital*, or the *Manifesto* rather than *Capital*. There is a kind of automatic pressure exerted by the institution in favour of short texts. Secondly, the *Treatise on the Emendation of the Intellect* is also a text that can apparently be detached from Spinoza's corpus. The university likes such detachable texts; it avoids students having to learn the entire system. At the same time, when structural historians of philosophy like Gueroult approach this text, they cite it, but they crush it beneath the weight of the system. In Gueroult's work, the *Treatise on the Emendation of the Intellect* isn't studied on its own terms. Gueroult sometimes cites it in his footnotes when he's commenting on the *Ethics*. The text's specificity isn't taken into account; it's present only insofar it agrees with the *Ethics* or illuminates it. I set myself the challenge of reading the text on its own terms. I didn't want to detach it from Spinoza's system, but at the same time I didn't want it to be lost beneath the *Ethics*. I wanted to ask: 'What question was Spinoza asking in this text?' Moreover, it's a good introduction to the role of experience since its first sentence is precisely: 'After experience had taught me . . .'. This philosopher who is supposedly uninterested in experience begins his first text by saying: 'After experience had taught me . . .'. Moreover, the sentence continues: 'that everything that regularly occurs in common life . . .'. Here is someone talking at once about experience and about what happens in common life. This doesn't really correspond to the image of a rationalist cut off from the real world or from practice. Thus, the prologue to the *Treatise on the Emendation of the Intellect* was a good point of entry into Spinoza's philosophy.

Robert Boncardo: You show that there's an underlying structure to this text, which is articulated around different stages of certainty. Before you, scholars hadn't seen this structure. What did you want to show by making this visible?

Pierre-François Moreau: First of all, that this structure is perfectly visible, in particular on the basis of the text's vocabulary itself. People hadn't been particularly attentive to the very rigorously structured vocabulary that Spinoza uses. You realise that in reality the text doesn't speak of very general issues of method; it doesn't say: 'I've lived for a long time, so now I can warn you of such-and-such a thing . . .'. Rather, it's very carefully constructed so as to lead the reader precisely from common life towards a rupture with common life itself. That's what I wanted to show.

Robert Boncardo: And it's a real rupture, isn't it?

Pierre-François Moreau: It's an immanent rupture – that is, it's not a revelation that comes from the outside. It's for this reason that it's not a conversion. It's fundamentally common life itself that produces dissatisfaction with common life. There is thus a process of sublation. Hegel's terms aren't really appropriate, however, since nothing is conserved, or rather what is conserved is conserved in a different form. You're forced to pose questions about the fields of experience, about fields such as history, language and the passions where *experientia* is at work.

Lived Experience, Spinozist Experience: The Case of Althusser

Robert Boncardo: After studying this text for about 200 pages, you move on to a sort of genealogy of the repression of the question of experience in Spinoza. We've already spoken a little about Émile Saisset and Victor Cousin and his school. You sketch a history of the marginalisation of experience in Spinoza in French. If I'm not mistaken, you trace this history right up to Alain. The question I wanted to ask was whether we could continue to speak of a marginalisation of experience in the work of French Spinozists throughout the twentieth century. What about Althusser's critique of lived experience, where experience is at the level of illusion, of the imaginary?

Pierre-François Moreau: You can interpret Althusser partly in that way, but not only in that way. For Althusser, experience becomes two different things. He doesn't speak of things explicitly in this way, but let's admit that he does. Experience comes on the one hand from practice, and on the other hand from the imaginary. The first thing to say is that the imaginary isn't really marginalised. Yes, it's the contrary of science, above all in the early Althusser, but at the same time it's absolutely essential: we live within it, and there are even ideological state apparatuses whose function is to reproduce this imaginary. Thus, if you meant to say that experience qua imaginary is something negative in the sense of being the opposite of science, then yes. But experience is something that's very much present in Althusser's work; indeed, you could say that the whole of Althusser's thinking was geared towards analysing how this imaginary experience is not only produced but regularly reproduced, and how it summons individuals and makes subjects of them. In this sense, it's essential. The other side of experience, however, is practice, and Althusser first tried to think practice as theoretical practice – even if this led to a dead end, as we all know, for it meant he was going round and round in circles. He then tried to think practice as the representation of politics within theory. At another moment he attempt to enumerate a number of different practices – scientific and political practices, for instance. In a sense, what he tried to do is more interesting than what he succeeded in doing. He shows us that philosophers have never succeeded in constituting an anthropology, that is, a description of forms of human conduct organised as practices. In contrast to German philosophers, French philosophers haven't at all been interested in philosophical anthropology. In Germany, from Feuerbach to Max Scheler all the way to certain Husserlians, there's an entire tradition of philosophical anthropology that asks 'What is Man?', 'How does Man act?', and which is in dialogue with anthropologists, historians of prehistory, and biologists. In France, this wasn't taken seriously. For instance, Scheler was translated before the First World War, then he disappeared. The French are now starting to become interested in all this again. The only person who played a role in all of this was Merleau-Ponty. Since interest in Merleau-Ponty has begun to grow again, this aspect of his work has been rediscovered. In fact, Blumenberg's philosophical anthropology has just been translated. In Germany, Blumenberg is the culmination of a century and a half of work and reflection on what Man is, and which has included negative answers. I'm thinking of someone like Gunther Anders for whom the only way to respond to the question 'What is Man?' is to not respond. Man is what perpetually flees when one seeks to analyse him. I'm editing with a colleague an anthology of this history of German anthropology, from Feuerbach to Blumenberg; I've also published a book on Anders with other colleagues. It's interesting to see that there are both positive responses such as 'Man is the one who works', or 'Man is a sexed being', as well as negative responses: 'Man is what can't be defined', or 'Man is not only what escapes civilisation but what civilisation is in the process of destroying.' In other words, despite often interesting and detailed descriptions, the analysis is often caught in a circle and ends with abstract definitions. All of this is absent from the work of French philosophers. It's now returning, but it's also taking the form of abstract definitions: 'Man is such-and-such.' Thinking in terms of practice, as Althusser sought to do, is to refuse abstract definitions. As soon as you start saying 'Man is such-and-such', you lose access to the reality of human practices. This is why the Althusserian critique of humanist anthropology is without doubt the best or the only way to constitute a veritable anthropology.

Robert Boncardo: In other words, if we don't follow Althusser, we lose sight of human diversity.

Pierre-François Moreau: Linguistics, ethnology and anthropology, for instance, never seek to respond to the question: 'What is Man?' As soon as you begin to do linguistics seriously, the question 'What is Man?' disappears, just as the question of the origin of language disappears. The so-called human sciences were constituted by leaving aside metaphysical and ideological questions – questions that are tied, precisely, to 'lived experience'. It's my belief that when Althusser distinguishes between the imaginary and ideology, on the one hand, and practice on the other, he is trying – he doesn't succeed but he tries – to chart a course between the two, that is, between this imaginary discourse and a kind of false consciousness of the lived.

Robert Boncardo: Do you understand *Experience and Eternity in Spinoza* to be part of this Althusserian lineage?

Pierre-François Moreau: I understand it to be an attempt to see what Spinoza has to say on the matter. The first thing to do was to determine if Spinoza really did have anything to say about all of this. You know, before *Experience and Eternity in Spinoza*, not many people had really written anything about language in Spinoza. Before publishing my book I wrote an article on Spinoza and language, and I can remember a colleague, who wrote a summary of the journal in which my article appeared, saying: 'My friend Moreau deals with a problem that doesn't exist: that of language in Spinoza.' By contrast, now everyone thinks that this problem exists. Lorenzo Vinciguerra's book *Spinoza et le signe* finally convinced them. At the time of *Experience and Eternity in Spinoza*, however, when I said that I was going to study experience in Spinoza in the fields of language, history and the passions, people were sceptical. They were ready to accept that there was a relation between experience and the passions, but in the other domains, not so much.

Experience in Language, the Passions and History

Robert Boncardo: Let's turn to language then, because the first of the three long chapters that make up the heart of *Experience and Eternity in Spinoza* is devoted to language. The concept of 'use' is at the centre of this chapter. Could you say what the relation between 'use' and experience is?

Pierre-François Moreau: I would say that use is the stand-in for experience in the domain of language. This was something I discovered in a two-stage process. First, I noticed that Spinoza quite often cites the notion of *usus* – not only use in language, but use in human practices – and that he does so at essential points in his argument. Just as he speaks of *ratio* and *experientia* in the system, when it comes to language he speaks of *ratio* and *usus*. I initially said to myself: this is a real discovery; no one who has written on Spinoza has examined the couple *ratio/usus*. And then when I started to read the grammarians, I realised that what I thought was a discovery was in fact a banality. All of the grammarians distinguish between *ratio* and *usus* and they explain the history of language by the equilibrium and disequilibrium between *ratio* and *usus*. In other words, what I thought was a discovery relative to Spinoza was in fact a case of Spinoza appropriating a prior history that I wasn't aware of because I hadn't studied the history of grammar. What makes this particularly embarrassing is that I was born at an intellectual moment when everyone was talking about linguistics. For us, linguistics was Saussure. But when you discover that linguistics had existed for 2,000 years before Saussure and that it dealt with things that we no longer talk about, you say to yourself: 'What a miracle!' But also: 'How stupid could I have been?' If I now had to offer a criticism of my work, it would be to say that while I discovered the importance of *usus* in Spinoza's work on language, I should have persevered and gone further since *usus* is important to Spinoza well beyond the domain of language. The concept of use is relevant to customs and dispositions; there is also a concept of use in relation to the passions. Furthermore, while he doesn't use the term explicitly, there is a relation to be determined between use and usury. In politics, for instance, institutions 'wear out' [*s'usent*]. Why is a dictatorship necessary from time to time in Rome? To restore order to institutions that have a tendency to become worn out and to lose their force. Thus, use itself creates usury, and at the end of a certain period of time an effort is required to put things back in place. I should have analysed all of this a little more closely, but I didn't.

Robert Boncardo: In the second chapter of this central part of the book, you turn to a study of the passions. It could be said that the passions are what's closest to experience. However, in the *Ethics*, Spinoza deals with the passions in a deductive mode, which seems quite distant from experience. Yet you show that there is a kind of back-and-forth between experience in a familiar sense and the geometrical method in Spinoza's construction of the passions.

Pierre-François Moreau: What's fascinating about the geometrical method is that it's so simple: at the beginning of your deductions, you begin with almost nothing. This purposeful minimalism is something that one could devote an entire book to. Imagine that on an unknown planet there exists a race of beings that can't be described but that we can nevertheless see with the help of a telescope. We don't know how these beings are constructed – they may be bipeds or they may not be – but we do know that they have relations with the external world around them and that they are capable of influencing this external world. They're not the only beings who can do this on the planet – other living beings also exist – but they have more relations with the world than the others, and the world can affect them more in turn. Then, one also supposes that these beings have mechanisms within their bodies that allow them to conserve the trace of the impressions the world makes on them. That's all you begin with. I find that fascinating. This multiplicity of relations with the external world, and the trace in these beings' minds of this external world's impressions – memory, in other words – is all you need in order to produce joy, sadness, hatred, love, jealousy, ambition: everything! After this come institutions, wars, finance, courts, and so on. There is something fascinating in the geometrical order. You begin with almost nothing – but this almost-nothing is, if I may say so, a quite powerful almost-nothing. With this powerful almost-nothing you can construct, from Proposition 14 in Book II of the *Ethics* onwards – that is, after you have all of the postulates on the human body – the three kinds of knowledge, desire, joy, sadness and their composite forms. You can also construct one other thing, whose provenance Spinoza doesn't clearly explain but which plays an essential role, namely the capacity to imitate. Thus, like everyone in the seventeenth century, Spinoza constructs a list of the passions and attempts to explain their role and origin. But in contrast to other seventeenth-century thinkers, he adds another element, the imitation of the affects. Thus, not only are there mechanisms within me that produce love, joy, hate, and so on, but I also have a mechanism that determines that when I see someone who is happy I feel happy as well. When this happens with someone who I at the same time hate, there is a mechanism that's stronger than or as strong as my hatred that makes me enjoy what they enjoy. I'll have a dual relation to this person, since to see them is to become sad, but at the same time, I become joyful. I'll be split between these two passions – whence all of the psychiatric problems one can imagine. The geometrical method consists in constructing the maximum number of passions on the basis of a minimal number of conditions. Now, at the same time, alongside this deductive construction, it just so happens that you're already familiar with this multiple world of the passions. You see it all around you in Amsterdam, in particular in your role as a merchant, when you see people shouting in the street selling tulips, and so on. You've also read about it in Juvenal's satires, in Terence's comedies. There is a correspondence between this concrete world and what you've just reconstructed axiomatically. What one should do is read one after the other Descartes' *Passions of the Soul* and the last three Books of Spinoza's *Ethics*. When you read the chapter titles, the impression you get is that the two works are exactly the same. The chapter titles are the same. They're not in exactly the same order, but they're the same: pride, hatred, jealousy, and so on. Now, Spinoza had read the Latin version of Descartes' works. This explains – among other things – why Spinoza sometimes puts two passions where Descartes puts only one. The reason is that the Latin translator had used a different term, and Spinoza is thus obliged to find a content for the two terms. It's fascinating. I explain this kind of thing in my edition of the *Ethics*. When you look closely, you realise that you can better understand what Spinoza means when you refer, not to Descartes in the French, but to Descartes in the Latin. Thus, if you take a look at the titles of the paragraphs in Descartes and the theorems in Spinoza, you see that they're the same. But when you look at the Scholia – or at the paragraphs in Descartes that to some degree resemble Scholia – you realise that Descartes gives very few examples. There's about ten all up. For instance, when it comes to smell, you have the Cartesian knight who smells a rose. There's the governor of a city whose honour rests on protecting that city that the king has conferred upon him. There is the young noble who defends himself against brigands with his sword. Thus, Descartes' world is a world of young nobles who smell roses, protect cities and defend themselves against the little people. But Spinoza's world is one of prostitutes, soldiers, shopkeepers . . .

Robert Boncardo: Poets . . .

Pierre-François Moreau: No, not poets – things that poets talk about!

Robert Boncardo: I was thinking of the Spanish poet from the *Ethics*.

Pierre-François Moreau: Exactly – *mad* poets! There are madmen in Spinoza. There are misers, boastful soldiers, people who love telling tales about former military campaigns. It's a picaresque world. It's the world that Spinoza is familiar with from Latin comedies but also from picaresque Spanish novels. When you read certain passages from Cervantes, or from those novels that recount stories about beggars and thieves, you realise that this is Spinoza's world. It's the world that he knew, but also the world that he recognised in the literature that interested him. It's a much more sordid and suggestive world than that of Descartes. And the experience of that world is present in the background to the theorems from the *Ethics*.

Robert Boncardo: And what is the epistemological status of this experience? You make an important distinction between *experientia vaga* and *experience tout court*. Could you talk a little about this distinction, perhaps in reference to these examples?

Pierre-François Moreau: In my view, Spinoza reprises Bacon's term *experientia vaga* but without giving it much importance. He uses it to characterise the first kind of knowledge. When he speaks of experience in the strong sense, it's of something that instructs us. He often says: *experientia docet*, 'experience has shown that . . .'. For him, reason and experience are different modes of teaching; they help us make our way in the world. By 'vague experience', I can know that if my apartment has a gas supply, the flame is extinguished when there's no more gas. Experience in the strong sense is something different: it's what tells us that when I breathe in too much gas I will die, or that when I leave my apartment I should turn the gas off. Experience is much closer to the practice of common life – the 'common life' of the *Treatise on the Emendation of the Intellect* – and to the world of my experience, the experience of others, but also the experience that I find in a condensed form in literature.

Robert Boncardo: And which has an epistemological status that Spinoza doesn't neglect.

Pierre-François Moreau: No indeed. There are things that only reason can teach us. But experience can at the very least show us where to look.

Robert Boncardo: And what paths not to follow.

Pierre-François Moreau: Experience can tell us that it's necessary to study such-and-such a thing, for instance. Althusser used to say that ideology at least had the advantage of indicating a site of possible research. After that, it's the concept that will do to work.

Robert Boncardo: The final chapter of this central part of the text is on history and the concept of fortune. You study the way in which the concept of experience is linked to the way Spinoza thinks of history and the constitution and de-constitution of States. Could you speak a little about the relation between experience and fortune?

Pierre-François Moreau: Fortune represents experience in the guise of the unpredictable. Reason can come up with laws of history. Theological reason, for its part, comes up with false laws, the laws of providence. But it's also possible to establish true laws. However, the problem is that reason always seeks that which is predictable. But in the experience of history, things that we didn't expect to happen, happen. This is what the mythology of fortune tries to explain. Spinoza learnt this from humanist thought; there's also a philosophy of fortune in Petrarch and Erasmus, the myth of the wheel of fortune, with the king who is on top but who then finds himself crushed by the wheel. Fundamentally all of this is an imaginary way of talking about the unpredictable nature of historical causality. At the same time, it allows one to critique providentialist versions of historical laws. Spinoza reprises from time to time, without giving them too much significance, the expressions 'fortune' and 'virtue', and so on. He reprises them not because of some automatism that leads him to quote from humanist thought, but because it allows him to institute a secular conception of history, just as Machiavelli had done. When Machiavelli uses the term 'fortune' and when he writes his *Discourses on Livy*, the idea of fortune allows him to set aside the idea of providence. It's the same for Spinoza. But also, in Spinoza, you have the desire to constitute a science of history. This isn't his concern in the *Ethics*, but it's partly the problem he addresses in the *Treatises*, such as when he reconstitutes the history of the Hebrew people. He supposes that his readers are familiar with the history of Rome, and he's writing at a time when there still exist humanist writers such as Vossius, who wrote an *ars historica*. Spinoza tries to think rationally everything that happened from Moses to the fall of the Hebrew empire; he tries to think the golden age of Christianity; and he tries to think the history of Rome. He even poses questions regarding what travellers have seen of China and Japan. Now, in dealing with all of this material, he doesn't cite exempla – he doesn't believe in history as a genre that can construct models for life, and he doesn't draw any moral judgements – but instead he tries to make points of historical comparison. In this instance, he acts as if it were possible to construct a rational science of the successive facts of history. He thinks that rules of historical evolution exist. For example, when he says that Esdras didn't put the books of the Bible in the right order, he says that if it's a profane book, then one would never accept that it's a work of history. In other words, he supposes that his readers already know what a work of history is – namely, a collection of documents, the organisation of these documents in a certain order, and the identification of a certain number of laws. Spinoza is thus the contemporary of the birth of the science of history, and he supposes that his reader is as well.

The Experience of Eternity

Robert Boncardo: Your book culminates in a long and quite traditional chapter, philosophically speaking, which comments on the phrase: 'We feel and know by experience that we are eternal.' This is another text that's been the subject of innumerable commentaries. You study it conceptually and show that the use of the word 'experience' here is systematic in nature, and that it's homogeneous even with the first sentence from the *Treatise on the Emendation of the Intellect*. You explain that the experience of eternity is in fact the experience of a difference – of a difference internal to the finite itself. We are finite, we feel that we are finite, yet we also have the capacity to access the infinite. And that's the experience of eternity. It's not the experience of a thing, but the experience of a difference, a rupture, a wound even.

Pierre-François Moreau: But which is internal to the finite. There's not the finite on one side and the infinite on the other. Desanti used to give an example of this: when I carry out the demonstration of a mathematical theorem – that is, not when I simply read it but when I make the effort to perform the demonstration and to follow it – and if I have the requisite mathematical knowledge, at the end I come to the same conclusion as Euclid. And yet, I'm a finite being. This theorem existed before me, human history existed before me, all of culture, including mathematical culture, existed before me, and when I die it will continue to exist without me. But at the moment where I identify with the knowledge of this theorem, I know it exactly as Euclid knew it. There is nothing in the theorem that exceeds my finitude. Thus, the infinite is present in the finite, just as, at the beginning of the *Treatise on the Emendation of the Intellect*, the aspiration to leave common life is born from common life itself.

Robert Boncardo: What led you to this reading? Did you deduce it from your analysis of experience? Or was it that, in re-reading the prologue to the *Treatise on the Emendation of the Intellect*, you had a sort of revelation?

Pierre-François Moreau: I don't really know. As far as I can remember, my approach was to eliminate a certain number of possible interpretations. And the one I came up with was the one that remained. All of the other possible interpretations presupposed that the word 'experience' changed meaning between the experience of history and the experience of eternity. So I said to myself – in part against Leo Strauss, or against all those who try to find hidden meanings behind a text's contradictions – that before trying to determine what Spinoza's presuppositions are, it's important to know if such contradictions exist in the first place! I began from the principle that what Spinoza says about experience in the *Ethics* is the same as what he says about it elsewhere. This meant I had to work out what he said about experience in the rest of his work – hence the huge amount of work on the experience of history, of the passions, of language. But it turned out that the meaning of experience is the same for the experience of eternity. A member of my thesis defence jury, who I won't name, said: 'Look at what you've done! After all of those pages about things that aren't philosophical, you finally succeed in saying something interesting, something that's really philosophical!' I was devastated since the whole purpose of my thesis was to say that this final part was meaningful only insofar as it rested on what came before. Thus, if that jury member admired the last part but disconnected it from the rest, then in my eyes the thesis no longer had anything to admire in it.

Robert Boncardo: Why didn't you also inquire into the meaning of *sentimus*, and not just *experientia*? Does *sentimus* belong to the same register as experience?

Pierre-François Moreau: Yes, it does. *Sentimus* is the most immediate, most perceptive part of experience. *Sentimus* is what we ourselves feel. I'd say that if experience is what we feel, what we see in others, and what we learn from literature, then *sentimus* is the first layer of experience, the most originary layer. But experience itself is broader. The two other strata give us a guarantee against the subjective nature of the first. If there is no *experior* and only *sentire*, then we risk confusing this form of experience with free will, dreams, and so on.

Robert Boncardo: You also show that there is a universality to this experience of eternity, that it's possible for everyone to experience it.

Pierre-François Moreau: And therefore that it's not mystical experience.

Robert Boncardo: And that there's no contradiction between the singular and the universal at this level either. Everyone is finite, everyone has singular experiences, but there remains a difference between this finite singularity and the infinite.

Pierre-François Moreau: Spinoza does indeed say 'we'. He doesn't say 'some people'. Now, there is a tradition that speaks of eternity and that says: 'The wise know that . . .', or says that there are three sorts of people: those who aren't rational, those who are beginning to be rational, and those who are wise. But Spinoza says precisely that everyone experiences eternity, even if we sometimes interpret it badly and obscure it through the imaginary.

The Literary Being of Philosophy

Robert Boncardo: I wonder if we could return now to some more methodological questions. What was particularly interesting for me in your book was that you study Spinoza's work using tools that in part come from literary criticism. My question is therefore: how do you see the link between the methodology that you used and the idea that philosophy is an autonomous discourse with its own rules, and which, for this very reason, cannot be approached using tools from any other domain, such as literary theory? Do you see a contradiction or a tension between a literary approach, an historical approach, and a philosophical, conceptual approach?

Pierre-François Moreau: A contradiction, yes, but not an antagonism. On the one hand, as we were saying before, a philosophy is always nourished by what is outside of it, chiefly by four things: politics, religion, plastic systems such as literature, and the sciences. Philosophies are bound to these four domains but also construct links or modes of passage between things that are ordered in a certain way in the sciences and other things that are found in theology, for example. On the other hand, philosophy, if it is to communicate what it has to say – and so long as you're not Socrates, who doesn't write, or Christ, who isn't a philosopher – then it must be written down. I've never met Immanuel Kant, I've met the writings of Immanuel Kant. At a certain point in time, Kant had to pose the question of how to write the *Critique of Pure Reason*. As he says, he gave up making it a popular book. In other words, he chose a certain type of writing. He could have written it otherwise – in verse, for instance, like Lucretius – but he chose to write it in prose. And he chose to use terms like anticipation, analogy of perception, and so on – in other words, terms that are a little abstract. Sometimes Kant gives examples; thus, even this philosopher, who is sometimes as abstract as Spinoza, presents a whole array of examples. In other texts by Kant such as the *Anthropology* or the *Observations on the Beautiful and the Sublime*, we see the text devolve into a whole series of descriptions that mix observations with anecdotes that come from travellers, along with pure ideology: the day is beautiful, the night sublime, women's virtue is beautiful, man's sublime. There are whole pages of rich examples. You get the impression that on the whole, they form a poem. Every philosopher thus uses literary forms of expression to present themselves as a philosopher. There are very few philosophical texts written in the form of treatises. We're accustomed to think that there are lots of them since in the university world we're used to writing theses. But in the history of philosophy, there are, for instance, lots of dialogues. Descartes writes dialogues, Spinoza writes dialogues; there are also poems, as well as philosophical novels like Diderot's *Jacques le fataliste*. Diderot's *Le Rêve d'Alembert* is also a philosophical text, albeit written in the form of a literary dialogue. There are therefore many forms in which philosophy is written. I think that if tomorrow I were to write a dialogue, my colleagues would be surprised; nevertheless, there are some who write dialogues; there's even a resurgence of dialogues in philosophy today. The dialogue is an interesting philosophical genre since it's a theatrical dialogue, but one without much action. There are gestures; the protagonists can smile or blush, but they can't stab each other, as in a tragedy. Thus, philosophers borrow forms from literature but they adapt them, and it's interesting to study how they modify them. I think that the way they modify these forms is a function of the content of their system. This is something one could reproach the structural study of philosophy for not doing. For someone like Gueroult, such questions are totally alien. I spoke about Goldschmidt earlier. Now, if you read Goldschmidt's book, *Les dialogues de Platon*, at no point do you learn that Plato wrote dialogues. What interested Goldschmidt was the dialogues' content, not the fact that this content was distributed between at least two interlocutors. When Goldschmidt comes to a myth, obviously he ignores it; such myths don't interest him since they're not philosophy. But it's interesting when philosophers use myths. Leibniz was still using myths. Something that's essential to philosophy is its literary being, its written being.

Contemporary Spinozisms

Robert Boncardo: What also struck me about your book, in addition to the methodology that you use, is that unlike many other readers of Spinoza, you don't seek to enlist Spinoza's thought in a political or theoretical project – something that's arguably not the case for Althusser, for Negri, or today for Lordon. I therefore wanted to ask you how you conceived of your work, since it seems to me that it's above all a work of pure scholarship, and that you had no intention of enlisting or instrumentalising Spinoza.

Pierre-François Moreau: I'm not sure that Althusser 'enlisted' Spinoza. He above all used him as a sign, as a way of saying: there's something here that we need to study, and Spinoza can show us how to do so. That's not quite an 'enlistment'. It's less direct than what Negri does, for instance. Moreover, it seems to me that there's something more interesting going on in the work of Spinoza's readers, including Negri and Lordon. For instance, my student Jacques-Louis Lantoine's work is based on a confrontation between Spinoza and Bourdieu. What Lantoine tries to show is that Spinoza thought deeply about the notion of disposition, and that it's by analysing Spinoza's thoughts on disposition that we can clarify, not Bourdieu's work itself, but rather the object of Bourdieu's work, namely the reason why people believe that they're freely doing something that they've been taught to do. That's precisely what Bourdieu calls a habitus, and Spinoza a disposition. Now, if he hadn't read Bourdieu, Lantoine wouldn't have discovered that this notion is in Spinoza too. Thus, reading contemporary authors in the human sciences or asking political questions can help us identify things in Spinoza's thought that are marginal, and we can then develop them. Furthermore, in my view what's interesting in the political or sociological use of Spinoza is not so much pasting a bit of Spinoza over the top of a contemporary problem, for instance by asking if the Yellow Vests can be thought using Spinoza. I recently wrote an article on the thought of insurrection in Spinoza. And it's true that at the time I was thinking about the Yellow Vests movement. But I wasn't interesting in enlisting Spinoza; I was seeking instruments of thought in his work that could help us think our current reality. Thus, you can find in Marx, Lucretius, or any number of other thinkers, instruments of thought that we can take up, either to develop them or perfect them, and which we can use to analyse contemporary topics. But it's not possible to directly superimpose one over the other.

Robert Boncardo: So you'd refuse my metaphor of 'enlistment'?

Pierre-François Moreau: I'd say that if it's valid, then it's valid more for Negri or Lordon than Althusser. I'd absolutely refuse its validity for Althusser, since he never tried to enlist Spinoza. Machiavelli, on the other hand . . .

Robert Boncardo: It's been over twenty-five years since the publication of *Experience and Eternity in Spinoza*. Do you have any reflections on the reception of the book and on the influence that it might have exerted on other works, or on the meaning and importance the book might have today?

Pierre-François Moreau: I'd say that my work, along with those of Laurent Bove and Chantal Jaquet, have exerted something of a collective influence. I don't think that I've had any personal influence, but I've played a role in a collective. When people talk about experience in Spinoza, that's because of me, but when they talk about the strategies of the conatus, that's Bove. I think that in the history of Spinoza studies in France, there have been a few different stages. There was first of all the Spinoza renaissance that occurred after an almost seventy-five-year-long void, with the works of Zac, Gueroult, Matheron and Deleuze, all of whom sought to re-read Spinoza's system. This was the case for Deleuze as well, since even for him what was important was discovering the properly structural, philosophical or, to use Gueroult's terms, architectonic nature of the system. It was absolutely necessary to pass through this stage. If we hadn't, we would have remained at the level of a kind of impressionistic conception of philosophy. There are still books being published in this vein today. For example, there's a recent book called *Le miracle Spinoza*, where the author tells to you how to be happy. He has previously written on yoga and on Buddhism. Why not, if that's what makes him happy? But to write books like that, it's absolutely not necessary to have read Gueroult. If you really want to do philosophy seriously, however, you have to pass through Gueroult. The second stage of Spinoza's recent reception in France is made up of the works of Chantal Jaquet, Laurent Bove, and myself, and then a little latter of Lorenzo Vinciguerra and Pascal Sévérac. These are all people who considered the structural study of Spinoza as a baseline, and went on to study different notions, themes and problematics. For me it was all of the forms of experience in Spinoza; for Laurent Bove, it was the conatus and its strategies; and for Chantal it was everything to do with the body. In Chantal's case, she doesn't enlist Spinoza, but by using Spinoza's writings she has gone on to publish a book on the body, on perfume, on smell, and so on. Now, Spinoza hardly ever speaks about these last couple of things. For Chantal, it's not a matter of enlisting Spinoza, but of being infused by his thought. This second stage, after the first stage dominated by Gueroult, ran from 1990 to 2010. There's now a new stage that's principally made up of my own doctoral students, as well as those of Chantal and Laurent. These students also consider what we did as a baseline; they don't contest it but they also don't take it up in an identical form; in any case, there's no point in them repeating it. They draw on what we did and apply it to different questions. For instance, Lantoine applies our insights to questions of habit and political disposition – questions that Bourdieu asked from a sociological perspective. There's also Pascal Sévérac, who was interested in the relation between activity and passivity in Spinoza, and little by little that has led him to write about disability and childhood. Sévérac doesn't enlist Spinoza, but rather uses the instruments forged by his reading of Spinoza to analyse contemporary problems around childhood disability; he's also been led to rediscover the Soviet psychologists from the 1930s who asked similar questions. There's also someone like my colleague Yves Clot, for example, who has worked with Sévérac and has engaged with the question of work in the light of Spinoza's thought. I also have students from a Christian background who work on the *Theologico-Political Treatise* in order to re-think religion on the basis of Spinoza. Thus, today there are people who draw inspiration from what my generation did, and use these instruments to think contemporary problems.

Robert Boncardo: And what interests you outside of France?

Pierre-François Moreau: Last year in June I marked a thesis written by an Italian who had reprised Proietti's approach, but differently. She analysed Spinoza's political texts in terms of how he cited sections from Tacitus and Livy. She went much further than we had previously believed possible. She was also someone who used Genette's work to show that there are two or three different ways of citing, and how Spinoza uses these different forms of reference to Latin historians. The Italians are absolutely unsurpassable when it comes to these sorts of things. They are really, really good at studying Spinoza's relation to these writings from the past. I remember once that Macherey said that the Italians were antiques salesmen. There's something true about that; it's not a pejorative statement. They certainly do have an historicist sensibility, and not only for Spinozism. As for the Americans, at the beginning there was only Curley, then Rice. The true Spinozist renaissance in America came from two kinds of people: on the one hand, from those who were interested in the history of the sciences and who came to study philosophy from that direction; and on the other hand, from those who were interested in Descartes or the Cartesians and for whom Spinoza was one Cartesian among many. When you look at their bibliographies, you notice that they write a thesis on Descartes, then a book on Malebranche, a book on Spinoza – or they write a theses on Descartes and then a book on minor Cartesian philosophers or articles on Spinoza and Malebranche. We're obviously in dialogue with them, but in a sense they're people who are only now rediscovering structuralism and reading Gueroult. I feel much more affinity with them than I do with analytic philosophers.

Robert Boncardo: I'd like to leave you the last word, if there's something else you might like to add.

Pierre-François Moreau: I think that one of the lessons of Spinozism is that there is no final word! It's important to leave individual readers with the task of drawing what they can from my work, and to find things that I can't foresee. What's of interest is for them to do something that I can't predict – in other words, something creative.

Paris, 6 January 2020

Bibliography

I have limited the following list to works cited in this book and to a few others that deal with related problems or that have had a significant impact on my research. For an exhaustive bibliography, the reader can refer to the bibliographies cited in I(a), in particular to the *Bulletin de bibliographie spinoziste* for an analysis of the most recent works.

I. Instruments of Research

(a) Bibliographical Resources

Bulletin de bibliographie spinoziste, since 1979 (each annual edition appears in cahier 4 of the *Archives de philosophie*).

Garoux, Alain, *Spinoza: Bibliographie 1971–1977*, Université de Reims, Centre de Philosophie Politique, 1981.

Kingma, J. and Offenberg, A. K., 'Bibliography of Spinoza's Works Up to 1800', *Studia Rosenthaliana*, 11 (1977), pp. 1–32. This was published as a separate edition by van Gorcum in 1977.

Leone, Adele, 'Bibliografia spinoziana 1972–1979', *Verifiche*, 11 (1982), pp. 59–97.

Oko, A. S., *The Spinoza Bibliography*, compiled by Adolph S. Oko, published under the auspices of the Columbia University Libraries, Boston: G. Hall & Co., 1964.

Préposiet, J., *Bibliographie spinoziste, Répertoire alphabétique – Registre systématique – Textes et documents: Biographies de Lucas et de Colerus, article 'Spinoza' du Dictionnaire de Bayle, inventaire de la bibliothèque de Spinoza*, etc., Paris: Belles Lettres, 1973.

Santinelli, Cristina, *Spinoza in Italia. Bibliografia degli scritti italiani su Spinoza dal 1675 al 1982*, Urbino: Università degli studi di Urbino, 1983.

Totok, W., *Handbuch der Geschichte der Philosophie*, IV, *Frühe Neuzeit, 17. Jahrhundert*, unter Mitarbeit von Erwin Schadel, Ingrid Dietsch und Helmut Schröer, Frankfurt: Klostermann, 1981, pp. 232–96.

Ueberweg, F., *Ueberwegs Grundriss der Geschichte der Philosophie. Dritter Teil, Die Philosophie der Neuzeit bis zum Ende des XVIII. Jahrhunderts*, völlig neubearbeitet von M. Frischeisen-Köhler und W. Moog, Berlin: Mittler & Sohn, 1924, pp. 269–94.

Van der Linde, Antonius, *Benedictus Spinoza*, Bibliografie, The Hague: M. Nijhoff, 1871, new edn, Nieuwkoop: B. de Graaf, 1961.

Wetlesen, J., *A Spinoza Bibliography. Particularly on the Period 1940–1967*, Oslo: Universitetsforlaget, 1968, Id., 1971. 2nd rev. edn arranged as a supplementary volume to Oko's Spinoza bibliography.

(b) **Linguistics and Lexicographies**

Akkerman, F., *Spinoza's tekort aan woorden. Humanistische aspecten van zijn schrijvershap*, Leiden, 1977, Mededelingen vanwege het Spinozahuis, 36. French translation by A. van de Lindt and J. Lagrée, 'La pénurie de mots de Spinoza', *Travaux et documents du Groupe de recherches spinozistes*, I, 'Lire et traduire Spinoza', PUPS, 1989, pp. 9–37.

Bouveresse, R. and Moreau, P.-F., 'Index informatique', in Spinoza, *Tractatus politicus/Traité politique*. Latin text. Translated by P.-F. Moreau. 'Index informatique' by P.-F. Moreau and Renée Bouveresse, Paris: Répliques, 1979.

Crapulli, G. and Giancotti Boscherini, E., *Ricerche lessicali su opere di Descartes e Spinoza* (Lessico intellettuale europeo, 3), Rome: Ed. dell'Ateneo, 1979.

Giancotti Boscherini, E., *Lexicon Spinozanum*, The Hague: M. Nijhoff, 1970, 'Archives Internationales d'Histoire des Idées', 28 (2 vols).

Guéret, M., Robinet, A., and Tombeur, P., *Spinoza. Ethica. Concordances, index, listes de fréquences, tables comparatives*, Louvain-la-Neuve: CETEDOC, 1977.

Her groot Woordenboek der Nederlandsche en fransche Taele, getrocken uyt verscheyde soo Nederlandsche als Fransche Schryvers, naementlijk uyt den genen van P. Richelet, Brussels, 3rd edn, 1739.

Kajanto, I., 'Aspects of Spinoza's Latinity', *Arctos, acto philologica fennica*, 13 (1979), pp. 49–83.

Leopold, J. H., *Ad Spinozae Opera Posthuma*, The Hague: M. Nijhoff, 1902.

II. Texts and Translations

Original Editions

Renati Des Cartes Principiorum Philosophiae Pars I et II More Geometrica demonstratae per Benedictum de Spionza Amstelodamensem. Accesserunt ejusdem Cogitata Metaphysica, Amsterdam: Riewerts, 1663.

Tractatus theologico-politicus, continens dissertationes aliquot, Quibus ostenditur libertatem philosophandi non tantum salva Pietate, & Reipublicae Pace posse concedi: sed eandem nisi cum Pace Reipublicae, ipsaque Pietate tolli non posse, Hamburg: Künrath, 1670.

B. D. S. *Opera Posthuma, Quorum series post Praefationem exhibetur*, s. 1., 1677.

De Nagelate Schriften van B. D. S. Als Zedekunst, Staatkunde, Verbetering van't Verstant, Breiven en Antwoorden, uit verscheide Talen in de Nederlandsche gebragt, s. 1., 1677.

Reference Editions

Benedicti de Spinoza Opera quotquot reperta sunt, ed. J. van Vloten et J. P. N. Land, Leiden: Nijhoff, 2 vols, 1883; 3 vols, 1895; 4 vols, 1914.
1. Tractatus de Intellectus Emendatione. Ethica. Tractatus politicus. Tractatus theologico-politicus.
2. Tractatus theologico-politicus (continued). Letters.
3. Korte Verhandeling. Principia. Cogitata metaphysica. Stelkonstige reeckening van den regenboog – Reeckening van kanssen. Compendium grammatices linguae hebraeae.

Spinoza Opera. Im Auftrag der Heidelberger Akademie der Wissenchsaften herausgegeben von Carl Gebhardt. Carl Winter: Heidelberg, 1925. 2. Auflage Heidelberg, 1972, 4 vols. Unveränderter Nachdrunk der Ausgabe von 1925.
1. Korte verhandeling van God, de mensch en des zelfs welstand – Renati Des Cartes principiorum philosophiae, pars. I, II – Cogitata metaphysica – Compendium grammatices linguae hebraeae.
2. Tractatus de intellectus emendatione – Ethica.
3. Tractatus theologico-politicus – Adnotationes ad Tractatum theologico-politicum – Tractatus politicus.
4. Epistolae – Stelkonstige reeckening van den regenboog – Reeckening van kanssen.

Spinoza Opera V. Im Auftrag der Heidelberger Akademie der Wissenchaften herausgegeben von Carl Gebhardt, Carl Winter: Heidelberg, 1987.
    5. Supplementa. Kommentar zum Tractatus theologico-politicus. Kommentar zu den Adnotationes ad Tractatum theologico-politicum. Kommentar zum Tractatus politicus. Einleitung zu den beiden Traktaten.

Complete Works

Werken van B. de Spinoza. Uitgave onder auspiciën van de Vereniging Het Spinozahuis, Amsterdam, 3 vols, 1977–1982.
    1. Briefwisseling. Vertaald uit het Latijn en uitgegeven naar de bronnen alsmede van een inleiding en van verklarende en tekstkritische aantekeningen voorzien door F. Akkerman, H. G. Hubbeling en A. G. Westerbrink, 1977.
    2. Ethica. Uit het Latijn vertaald en van verklarende aantekeningen voorzien door Nico Van Suchtelen. Nieuwe uitgave, herzien en ingeleid door Guido Van Suchtelen, 1979.
    3. Korte geschriften. Bezorgd door F. Akkerman, H. G. Hubbeling, F. Mignini, M. J. Petry en N. en G. Van Suchtelen, 1982. René Descartes, De Beginselen van de zijsbegeerte – Korte verhandeling van God, de mensch en deszelvs welstand – Vertoog over de verbetering van het verstand – Stelkonstige reeckening van den regenboog – Reeckening van kanssen.

Œuvres de Spinoza, traduites par Emile Saisset, avec une introduction du traducteur, Paris: Charpentier, 2 vols. 1842. Edition revue et augmentée, 3 vols, 1861.
    1. Introduction critique.
    2. Vie de Spinoza. Traité théologico-politique. Traité politique.
    3. Ethique. De la Réforme de l'Entendement. Lettres.

Œuvres de Spionza, traduites et annotées par Charles Appuhn, Paris: Garnier, s.d., réédition Garnier-Flammarion, 4 vols, 1964–66.
    1. Traité de la Réforme de l'Entendement. Court Traité. Les principes de la philosophie de Descartes. Pensées métaphysiques, 1964.
    2. Ethique, 1965.
    3. Traité théologico-politique, 1965.
    4. Traité politique. Lettres, 1966.

Œuvres complètes, texte traduit, présenté et annotée par Roland Caillois, Madeleine Francès et Robert Misrahi, Paris: Gallimard, La Pléiade, 1954, 1978.

Sämtliche Werker in sieben Bänden [*und einem Ergänzungsband*]. In Verbindung mit Otto Baensch und Artur Buchenau herausgegeben und mit

Einleitungen, Anmerkungen und Registern versehen von Carl Gehbardt. Leipzig: Felix Meiner, 'Philosophische Bibliothek', 7 vols, 1905–1914; new edition, 8 vols, Hamburg, 1965–1984.

1. *Kurze Abhandlung von Gott, dem Menschen und seinem Glück*. Herausgegeben von Carl Gebhardt, 1965, Nachdruck der 4. Auflage 1922.

2. *Die Ethik nach geometrischer Methode dargestellt*, Übersetzung, Anmerkungen und Register von Otto Baensch, 1905; 1910 (2nd edn). Einleitung von Rudolf Schottlaender, 1967. Nachdruck mit erneut ergänztem Literaturverzeichnis, 1976. Auswahl-Bibliographie von Wolfgang Bartuschat, 1989.

3. *Theologisch-politischer Traktat*, Auf der Grundlage der Übersetzung von Carl Gebhardt (1908) neu bearbeitet, eingeleitet und herausgegeben von Günter Gawlick, 1976, 2. durchges. Auflage, 1984.

4. *Descartes' Prinzipien der Philosophie auf geometrische Weise begründet* mit dem 'Anhang, enthaltend metaphysische Gedanken', Übersetzung von Artur Buchenau (1907), Einleitung und Anmerkungen von Wolfgang Bartuschat, 5. Auflage, 1978.

5. *Abhandlung über die Verbesserung des Verstandes. Abhandlung vom Staate*, Übersetzung, Anmerkungen und Register von Carl Gebhardt (1907), Einleitung von Klaus Hammacher, 5. Auflage, 1977.

6. *Briefwechsel*, Übersetzung und Anmerkungen von Carl Gebhardt (1914), 2. durch weitere Briefe ergäntze Auflage mit Einleitung und Bibliographie von Manfred Walther, 1977.

7. *Lebensbeschreibungen und Gespräche* (Jelles, Lucas, Kortholt, Bayle, Colerus, Stolle-Hallmann), Einleitung, Übersetzung und Anmerkungen von Carl Gebhardt (1914), Nachdrunk mit einer Bibliographie von Manfred Walther, 2. Auflage, 1977.

Ergänzungsband. Algebraische Berechnung des Regenbogens – Berechnung von Wahrscheinlichkeiten, Übersetzung, eingeleitet und mit Anmerkungen herausgegeben von Hans-Christian Lucas und Michael John Petry, Niederländisch-Deutsch, Felix Meiner Verlag, 1982.

Opera – Werke, Lateinisch und Deutsch. Darmstadt: WB, 2 vols.

1. Tractatus theologico-politicus: Theologisch-politischer Traktat. Herausgegeben von Günter Gawlick und Friedrich Niewöhner, 1979.

2. Tractatus de intellectus emendatione – Ethica: Abhandlung über die Berichtigung des Verstandes – Ethik. Herausgegeben von Konrad Blumenstock, 1967, 1978, 1980.

Obras completas, I–V. Prologada por Abraham J. Weiss y Gregorio Weinberg, traducciones de Mario Calés y Oscar Cohan, Buenos Aires: Acervo Cultural, 1977.

1. Breve Tratado. Los Principios de la Filosofia de Descartes. Pensamientos metafisicos.
2. Tratado teologico-politico. Tratado politico.
3. Etica.
4. Tratado de la Reforma del Entendimiento. Epistolario.
5. Gramatica hebrea. Tratado sobre el arco iris. Tratado sobre el calculo de posibilidades.

The Collected Works of Spinoza, vol. I, edited and translated by Edwin Curley, Princeton: Princeton University Press, 1985. [Treatise on the Emendation of the Intellect. Short Treatise on God, Man, and his Well-Being. Letters 1–16. Principles of Philosophy. Letters 17–29. Ethics.]

The Collected Works of Spinoza, vol. II, edited and translated by Edwin Curley, Princeton: Princeton University Press, 2016. [Letters 29–41. Theological-Political Treatise. Letters 42–84. Political Treatise.]

Treatise on the Emendation of the Intellect

Traité de la Réforme de l'entendement et de la meilleure voie à suivre pour parvenir à la vraie connaissance des choses, texte, traduction et notes par A. Koyré, Paris: Vrin, 1937, 1969 (4th edn), 1974 (5th edn), 1979 (6th edn).

Traité de la Réforme de l'entendement, préface de B. Rousset, présentation et commentaire de B. Huisman, Paris: Nathan (Les intégrales de philo), 1987.

Traité de la Réforme de l'entendement, introduction, texte, traduction et commentaire par Bernard Rousset, Paris: Vrin, 1992.

Traité de la Réforme de l'entendement, préface, traduction et commentaires de André Scala, Paris: Agora, 1990.

Tratado de la Reforma del entendimiento y otros escritos, traducción, notas y comentario de Lelio Fernández y Jean-Paul Margot, Universidad nacional de Colombia, 1984.

Tratado de la Reforma del entendimiento. Principios de Filosofia de Descartes. Pensamientos metafisicos, introducción, traducción y notas de Atilano Dominguez, Madrid: Alianza Editorial, 1988.

Tratado da Reforma do Entendimento, trad. Abilio Queiros, Lisbon: Ediçoes 70, 1987.

Verhandeling over de verbetering van het verstand, introduction, translation and commentary by Wim Klever, Baarn: Ambo, 1986.

Ma'amar al tikkun hasekhel, translated by Nathan Spiegel, introduction and notes by Joseph Ben-Shlomo, Jerusalem, 1972, 1976 (2nd edn).

Short Treatise

Korte Verhandeling, van God, de Mesch, en deszelvs Welstand, Breve Trattato su Dio, l'Uomo, e il suo Bene, introduzione, edizione, traduzione e commento di Filippo Mignini, L'Aquila: L. U. Japadre editore, 1986.
Tratado breve, traducción, prologo y notas de Atilano Dominguez, Madrid: Alianza Editorial, 1988.

Ethics

Etica, demostrada segun el orden geométrico, edicion preparada (introdución, tradución y notas) por Vidal Peña Garcia, Alianza Editorial: Madrid, 1975, 1979 (2nd edn), 1980 (3rd edn), 1984 (4th edn).
Etica, a cura di Emilia Giancotti, Rome: Editori Riuniti, 'Biblioteca del pensiero moderno', 1988.
Ethique, texte original et traduction nouvelle par Bernard Pautrat, Paris: Seuil, 1988.
Ethique, introduction, traduction, notes et commentaire de Robert Misrahi, Paris: PUF, 1990.
The Ethics and Selected Letters, translated by Samuel Shirley, edited, with an introduction by Seymour Feldman. Indianapolis: Hackett, 1982.
Ethics, edited, with a revised translation, by G. H. R. Parkinson, London: Dent & Sons, 1989.

Theological-Political Treatise

Tractatus theologico-politicus, translated by Samuel Shirley, with an introduction by Brad S. Gregory, Leiden: Brill, 1989.
Trattato teologico-politico, introduzione di Emilia Giancotti Boscherini, traduzione e commenti di Antonio Droetto ed Emilia Giancotti Boscherini, Turin: Einaudi, 1972, 1980 (2nd edn).
Tratado teologico-politico, introducción, traducción, notas, indices de Atilano Dominguez, Madrid: Alianza Editorial, 1986.
Tratado Teologico-Politico, trad., introd. e notas de Diogo Pires Aurélio, Lisbon: Imprensa Nacional/Casa da Moeda, 1988.

Political Treatise

Traité politique, texte latin, traduction par P.-F. Moreau, index informatique par P.-F. Moreau et Renée Bouveresse, Paris: Répliques, 1979.

Tratado politico, translation, introduction, analytic table of contents and notes by Atilano Dominguez, Madrid: Alianza Editorial, 1986.

Hoofdstukken uut de Politieke Verhandeling, introduction, translation and commentary by Wim N. A. Klever, Amsterdam: Boom Meppel, 1985.

Tratado politico, introducción, traducción, notas, index latinus translationis y bibliografia: Humberto Giannini y Isabel Flisfisch, Santiago du Chili: Editorial Universitaria, 1989.

Politischer Traktat, translation by Gerhard Güpner from the Gebhardt edition, completed with an extract from Chapter 16 of the *TTP* and an appendix by Hermann Klenner (chronology, notes, bibliography and an essay on Des Bento/Baruch/Benedictus realistiche Utopie, pp. 137–56), Leipzig: Reclam, 1988.

Correspondence

Epistolario, a cura di A. Droetto, Turin: Einaudi, 1951, 1974 (2nd edn).

Correspondencia completa, traducción, introducción, notas e indices de Juan Domingo Sanchez Estop, Madrid: Libros Hiperion, 1988.

Correspondencia, introducción, traducción, notas e indices de Atilano Dominguez, Madrid: Allianza Editorial, 1988.

Letter to Louis Meijer

Brief van Spinoza aan Lodewijk Meijer, 26 juli 1663, Uitgegeven door A. K. Offenberg, Amsterdam: Universiteitsbibliotheek, 1975.

Letter from Spinoza to Lodewijk Meijer, 26 July 1663, ed. by A. K. Offenberg, in *Speculum spinozanum* (1978), pp. 426–35. Id: *Philosophia*, 7 (1977), pp. 1–13.

Lettre de Spinoza à Lodezijk Meijer, 26 juillet 1663, éditée par A. K. Offenberg, traduction par Michèle Miny-Chustka, *Revue philosophique de la France et de l'étranger*, 102 (1977), pp. 273–84.

III. Journals and Collections Devoted to Spinoza

Chronicon spinozanum, Hagae Comitis, curis Societatis Spinozanae, 5 vols. 1921–1927.

Mededelingen vanwege het Spinozahuis, Leiden: Brill, since 1934; puis Eburon, Delft, from number 59, 1989 (cited as MVHS).

Cahiers Spinoza, Répliques, 6 volumes since 1977.

Bulletin de l'Association des Amis de Spinoza, since 1978.

Bulletin de bibliographie spinoziste, in *Archives de philosophie*, since 1979.
Studia Spinozana, 6 volumes since 1985.
Travaux et documents du Groupe de reherches spinozistes, Presses de l'Université Paris-Sorbonne, 4 volumes published since 1989.
Guest Lectures and Seminar Papers on Spinozism, Rotterdam, Erasmus Universiteit, since 1986.

IV. Studies and Commentaries

Abraham, R. D., 'Spinoza's Concept of Common Notions. A Functional Interpretation', *Revue internationale de philosophie*, 31 (1977), pp. 27–38.
Adler, Jacob, 'Divine Attributes in Spinoza: Intrinsic and Relational', *Philosophy & Theology*, IV/1 (1989), pp. 33–52.
Akkerman, F., 'L'édition de Gebhardt de l'*Ethique* de Spinoza et ses sources', *Raison présente*, 43 (1977), pp. 37–51.
Akkerman, F., 'Vers une meilleure édition de la correspondance de Spinoza?', *Revue internationale de philosophie*, 31 (1977), pp. 4–26.
Akkerman, F., *Studies in the Posthumous Works of Spinoza. On Style, Earliest Translation and Reception, Earliest and Modern Edition of Some Texts* [Th.], Groningen: Rijksuniversiteit Groningen, 1980.
Akkerman, F., 'Le caractère rhétorique du *Traité théologico-politique*', in *Spinoza entre Lumières et Romantisme, Cahiers de Fontenay*, 36–38, Fontenay-aux-Roses, 1985.
Akkerman, F. and Hubbeling, H. G., 'The Preface to Spinoza's Posthumous Works, 1677, and its Author Jarig Jelles (c. 1619/20–1683)', *LIAS sources and documents relating to the early modern history of ideas*, 6 (1979), pp. 103–73.
Akkerman, F. and Glazemaker, J. H., 'An Early Translator of Spinoza', in *Spinoza's Political and Theological Thought*, Amsterdam: North Holland, 1984, pp. 23–9.
Alain (pseudonym of Emile Chartier), *Spinoza*, Paris: Delaplane, 1901; Mellottée, 1949; Gallimard, 1972.
Albiac, Gabriel, 'Maledictus', *El Pais*, 27 July 1985.
Albiac, Gabriel, *La sinagoga vacia. Un estudio de las fuentes marranas del espinosismo*, Madrid: Hiperion, 1987.
Albrecht, E., 'Was hat uns Spinoza heute noch zu sagen? Festvortrag aus Anlaß des 300. Todestages des großen holländischen materialistischen Philosophen', *Greifswalder Universitätsreden*, 36 (1977), pp. 1–13.
Aldrich, V., 'Categories and Spinoza's attributes', *Pacific Philosophical Quarterly*, 61 (1980), pp. 156–66.

Alexander, S., 'Lessons from Spinoza', in *Chr. sp.* V, 1927.
Allendesalazar, Mercedes, *Spinoza, Filosofia, pasiones y politica*, Alianza Universidad, 1988.
Allison, Henry, E., *Benedict de Spinoza*, Boston: Twayne, 1975.
Allison, Henry, E., *Benedict de Spinoza: An Introduction*, New Haven: Yale University Press, rev. edn, 1987.
Alquié, Ferdinand, *Le rationalisme de Spinoza*, Paris: PUF, 1981.
Alquié, Ferdinand, *Servitude et Liberté selon Spinoza*, Paris: CDU, s.d., 'Les Cours de Sorbonne', 1967.
Althusser, Louis, *Eléments d'autocritique*, Paris: Hachette, 1974; 1979.
Altkirch, E., *Spinoza im Porträt*, Jena: Eugen Diederich, 1913; reprint London, 1980.
Appuhn, Charles, *Spinoza*, Paris: Delpeuch, 1927, 'Civilisation et Christianisme, X'.
Arnaldez R., 'Spinoza et la pensée arabe', *Revue de synthèse*, 99 (1978), pp. 151–72.
Assoun, P. L., 'Spinoza, les libertins français et la politique 1665–1725', *Cahiers Spinoza*, 3 (1980), pp. 171–207.
Atkins, D., *George Eliot and Spinoza*, Salzburg: Salzburg Studies in English Literature, 1978.
Auerbach, Berthold, *Spinoza. Ein Denkerleben*, Stuttgart: Gottascher Verlag, 1860; Nachdrunk: Tübingen, 1980.
Aurelio, Diogo Pires, 'O Deus dos Attributos', *Analise*, 1 (1984), pp. 49–70.
Auvray, P., 'Richard Simon et Spinoza', in *Religion, Erudition et Critique à la fin du XXVIIe siècle et au début du XVIIIe*, Université de Strasbourg, Bibliothèque des Centres d'études supérieurs spécialisées, Paris: PUF, 1968, pp. 201–14.
Avenarius, Richard, *Über die beiden ersten Phasen des Spinozischen Pantheismus und das Verhältnis der zweiten zur dritten Phase. Nebst einem Anhang: Über Reihenfolge und Abfassungszeit der älteren Schriften Spinoza's*, Leipzig: Eduard Avenarius, 1868; reprint: London, 1980.
Avila, Crespo Remedios, 'Finalidad, deseo y virtud. Spinoza y Nietzsche', *Anales del Seminario de Metafisica*, 20 (1985), pp. 21–45.
Ayrault, Robert, *La genèse du romantisme allemand. Situation sprituelle de l'Allemagne dans la deuxième moitée du XVIIIe siècle*, Paris: Aubier, 1961. (Cf. volume II: *La Querelle du spinozisme: le Dieu de Goethe et de Herder*, pp. 511–28.)
Balibar, Etienne, *Spinoza et la politique*, Paris: PUF, 1985.
Balibar, Etienne, 'Spinoza: la crainte des masses', in Giancotti, Boscherini,

E. (ed.), *Spinoza nel 350° anniversario della nascita. Atti del congresso internazionale Urbino 4–8 ottobre 1982*, Naples: Bibliopolis, 1985.

Balibar, Etienne, 'Spinoza, politique et communication', *Cahiers philosophiques*, 39 (1989), pp. 17–42.

Balling, Pieter, *Het Licht op den Kandelaar*, s. 1., 1661; republished C. Gebhardt (*Chr. sp.*, IV, 1924–1926).

Banfi, Antonio, *Spinoza e il suo tempo. Lezioni e scritti a cura di L. Sichirollo* (Socrates, 6), Florence: Vallecchi, 1969.

Baraz, Michael, *La Révolution inespérée: Constantin Brunner*, Paris: José Corti, 1986.

Barret-Kriegel, Blandine, 'Liberté et égalité chez Spinoza ou le traitement d'une antinomie', *Cahiers philosophie politique et juridique*, 8 (1985), pp. 97–106.

Barthelemy, D., 'Critique et Prophétie selon Spinoza, Simon et Bossuet', *La vie de la Parole dans l'Ancien Testament*, études d'exégèse et d'herméneutique offertes à Pierre Grelot, Paris: Desclée, 1987, pp. 319–22.

Bartuschat, Wolfgang, 'Metaphysik als Ethik. Zu einem Buchtitel Spinozas', *Zeitschrift für philosophische Forschung*, 28 (1974), pp. 132–45.

Bartuschat, Wolfgang, 'Neuere Spinoza-Literatur', *Philosophische Rundschau*, 24 (1977), pp. 1–44.

Bartuschat, Wolfgang, 'Selbstsein und Absolutes', *Neue Hefte für Philosophie*, 12 (1977), pp. 21–63.

Bartuschat, Wolfgang, 'Spinoza in der Philosophie von Leibniz', in *Spinozas Ethik und ihre frühe Wirkung*, Wolfenbüttel: Herzog August Bibliotek, 1981, pp. 51–66.

Bartuschat, Wolfgang, 'The Ontological Basis of Spinoza's Theory of Politics', in *Spinoza's Political and Theological Thought*, Amsterdam: North Holland, 1984, pp. 30–6.

Bartuschat, Wolfgang, 'Über Spinozismus und menschliche Freiheit bein frühen Schelling', in H.-M. Pawlowski, S. Smid and R. Specht (eds), *Die praktische Philosophie Schellings und die gegenwärtige Rechtsphilosophie*, Stuttgart: Frommann-Holzboog, 1989, pp. 153–75.

Baruch de Spinoza 1677–1977. Werk und Wirkung, Katalog der Ausstellung von 21. Februar zum 30. April 1977 in der Herzog-August Bibliothek gezeigt. zusammengest. u. eingel. von W. Schmidt-Biggemann. Wolfenbüttel: Herzog August Bibliotek, 1977.

Bastien, M., 'Dom Deschamps et Spinoza', *Recherches sur le XVIIe siècle*, 1 (1976), pp. 111–24.

Bauer, Emmanuel, J., *Das Denken Spinozas und seine Interpretation durch Jacobi*, Bern: Peter Lang, 1989.

Bayle, Pierre, *Dictionnaire historique et critique*, Rotterdam: Leers, 1697.
Bayle, Pierre, 'Lettres sur Spinoza', *Bulletin de l'association des amis de Spinoza*, 9 (1982), pp. 1–10.
Bayle, Pierre, *Ecrits sur Spinoza*, ed. F. Charles-Daubert et P.-F. Moreau, Paris: Berg, 1984.
Belaief, G., *Spinoza's Philosophy of Law*, The Hague: Mouton, 1971.
Belaval, Y., 'Note sur l'emploi par Leibniz de l'expression spinoziste d'idée adéquate', *Archivio di filosofia* (1978), pp. 121–32.
Belaval, Y., 'Leibniz lecteur de Spinoza', *Archives de philosophie*, 46 (1983), pp. 531–52.
Bell, David, *Spinoza in Germany from 1670 to the Age of Goethe*, London: Institute of Germanic Studies, University of London, 1984.
Bellangé, Charles, *Spinoza et la philosophie moderne*, Paris: H. Didier, 1912.
Bennett, J., *A Study of Spinoza's Ethics*, Cambridge: Cambridge University Press, 1984.
Bent, Victor, *Spinoza, el limite humano*, Caracas: Mediciencia, 1987.
Bernhardt, J., 'Infini, substance et attributs: sur le spinozisme (à propos d'une étude magistrale)', *Cahiers Spinoza*, 2 (1978), pp. 53–92.
Berti, Silvia, '*La vie et l'esprit de Spinoza* (1719) e la prima traduzione francese dell'*Ethica*', *Rivista Storica italiana*, 98/1 (1986), pp. 5–46.
Bertrand, M., *Spinoza et l'imaginaire*, Paris: PUF, 1983.
Bertrand, M., 'Spinoza: le projet éthique et l'imaginaire', *Bulletin de l'association des amis de Spinoza*, 14 (1984), pp. 1–12.
Biasutti, Franco, 'Aspetti della critica spinoziana alla religione', *Verifiche*, 7 (1977), pp. 731–54.
Biasutti, Franco, 'L'idea di Dio e il problema della verità in Spinoza', *Verifiche*, 6 (1977), pp. 240–74.
Biasutti, Franco, 'Uomo e natura in Spinoza', in *Atti del XXVI congresso nazionale di filosofia*, 1978, pp. 152–60.
Biasutti, Franco, *La dottrina della scienza in Spinoza*, Bologna: Pàtron, 1979.
Biasutti, Franco, 'Verità e certezza nella epistemologia spinoziana', *Verifiche*, 17 (1988), pp. 61–79.
Billecoq, Alain, 'Spinoza et les spectres: l'autorité', *Revue de l'enseignement philosophique* (December 1985), pp. 20–32.
Blom, H. W., 'Politieke wetenschap in de Gouden Eeuw. Kritiek, geschiedenis en theorie in het Nederlandse zeventiende eeuwse politieke denken', *Acta Politica*, 13 (1978), pp. 305–30 (pp. 318–24: 'Spinoza's wetenschappelijke politiek').
Blom, H. W., 'Spinoza précurseur de la méthode analytique dans les sciences sociales', *Il Pensiero politico*, 18/1 (1985), pp. 18-38.

Blom, H. W., *Spinoza en De la Court. Politieke wetenschap in de zeventiende eeuw*, Leiden: Brill, 1981; Mededelingen vanwege het Spinozahuis, 42.

Bolton, M. B., 'Spinoza on Cartesian Doubt', *Nous*, 19 (1985), pp. 379–95.

Bonger, H., *Spinoza en Coornhert*, Leiden: Brill, 1989; Mededelingen vanwege het Spinozahuis, 57.

Bordoli, Roberto, 'Spinoza politico nella critica francese contemporanea', *Critica marxista*, 6 (1989), pp. 115–51.

Borges, Anselmo, 'Spinoza e a quastao de Deus', *Humanistica e Teologia*, 2 (1987), pp. 175–94.

Boss, Gilbert, *L'enseignement de Spinoza. Commentaire du 'Court traité'*, Zurich: Editions du Grand Midi, 1982.

Boss, Gilbert, *La différence des philosophies. Hume et Spinoza*, Zurich: Editions du Grand Midi, 1982.

Boss, Gilbert, 'La conception de philosophie chez Hobbes et Spinoza', *Archives de philosophie*, 48/2 (1985), pp. 311–26.

Bossers, Anton, *'Nil Volentibus Arduum*: Lodewijk Meyer en Adriaan Koerbagh', in *Opstellen over de Koninklijke Bibliotheek en andere Studies*, Hilversum: Verloren, 1986, pp. 374–83.

Bostrenghi, Daniela, 'Immaginazione e Ragione nella teoria Spinoziana della conoscenza e degli affetti: un progetto problematico', *Istituto di Filosofia Annali Due* (1987), pp. 5–67.

Bouiller, Fancisque, *Histoire de la philosophie cartésienne*, Paris: Delagrave, 3rd edn, 1868, 2 vols (Spinoza: I, chap. XV–XIX, pp. 315–428).

Bourel, Dominique, 'La purification du spinozisme chez Mendelssohn', *Archivio di filosofia* (1978), pp. 133–45.

Bourel, Dominique, 'Leibniz et Spinoza: un essai de conciliation chez Moses Mendelssohn', in *Theoria cum praxi. Zum Verhältnis von Theorie und Praxis im 17. und 18. Jahrhundert*, Akten des III, internationalen Leibnizkongresses, Hannover, 12. bis 17. November 1977, vol. 2: *Spinoza*, Wiesbaden: Franz Steiner, 1981, pp. 104–9.

Bourel, Dominique, 'Spinoza en Allemagne: jalons', *Bulletin de bibliographie spinoziste*, 2 (191), pp. 1–4, in *Archives de philosophie*, 44 (1981).

Brann, H. W., 'Schopenhauer and Spinoza', *Journal of the History of Philosophy*, 10 (1972), pp. 181–96.

Breton, Stanislas, 'Ame spinoziste, âme néo-platonicienne', *Revue philosophique de Louvain*, 71 (1973), pp. 210–24.

Breton, Stanislas, 'Les fondements théologiques du droit chez Spinoza', *Archives de philosophie du droit*, 18 (1973), pp. 93–105.

Breton, Stanislas, *Politique, religion, écriture chez Spinoza*, Lyon: Profac, 1973.

Breton, Stanislas, 'Origine et principe de raison', *Revue des sciences philosophiques et théologiques*, 58 (1974), pp. 41–57.
Breton, Stanislas, *Spinoza. Théologie et politique*, Paris: Desclée, 1977.
Breton, Stanislas, 'Hegel ou Spinoza. Réflexions sur l'enjeu d'une alternative', *Cahiers Spinoza*, 4 (1983), pp. 61–87.
Breton, Stanislas, 'Grammaire, langage, expression chez Spinoza', *Bijdragen*, 45 (1984), pp. 170–82.
Brochard, Victor, 'Le Dieu de Spinoza', *Revue de métaphysique et de morale*, 1908.
Brown, Norman, O., 'Philosophy and Prophecy, Spinoza's Hermeneutics', *Political Theory*, 14/2 (1986), pp. 195–213.
Brunner, Constantin, *Spinoza gegen Kant und die Sache der geistigen Wahrheit*, Berlin, 1910 (trans. H. Lurié, *Spinoza contre Kant et la cause de la vérité spirituelle*, Paris: Vrin, 1933).
Brunschvicg, Léon, *Spinoza*, Paris: Alcan, 1894; *Spinoza et ses contemporains*, 1923; Paris: PUF, 1951.
Brunschvicg, Léon, 'Sur l'interprétation du spinozisme', *Chr. sp.*, I, 1921.
Brunschvicg, Léon, 'Le platonisme de Spinoza', *Chr. sp.*, III, 1923.
Brunschvicg, Léon, 'Sommes-nous spinozistes?', *Chr. sp.*, V, 1927.
Brykman, Geneviève, *La judéité de Spinoza*, Paris: Vrin, 1972.
Camerer, Th., *Die Lehre Spinozas*, Stuttgart: Cotta, 1877 (2nd edn, 1914).
Camerer, Th., *Spinoza und Schleiermacher*, Stuttgart: Cotta, 1903.
Campana, Gilberto, *Liberazione e salvezza dell'uomo in Spinoza*, Rome: Città Nuova, 1978.
Campana, Gliberto, 'Presentazione del *TTP* di B. Spinoza', *Per la filosofia*, 2/4 (1985), pp. 72–86.
Campana, Gilberto, 'Libertà e salvezza laica in Spinoza', *Per la filosofia*, 2/5 (1985), pp. 44–51.
Carnois, B., 'Le désir selon les Stoïciens et selon Spinoza', *Dialogue*, 19 (1980), pp. 255–77.
Charles-Daubert, F., 'Le *TTP*, une réponse au *Traité des trois Imposteurs?*', *Etudes philosophiques: Spinoza*, 4 (1987).
Chenoufi, Ali, 'Les théories de l'interprétation et les crises d'autorité', *Revue tunisienne des études philosophiques*, 4 (1984), pp. 39–46.
Chiereghin, Franco, 'Introduzione a Spinoza. La critica al sapere matematico e le aporie del linguaggio', *Verifiche*, 5 (1976), pp. 3–23.
Christ, Kurt, *Jacobi und Mendelssohn. Eine Analyse des Spinozastreits*, Würzburg: Königshausen & Neumann, 1988.
Clair, P., 'Spinoza à travers les journaux en langue française à la fin du XVIIᵉsiècle', *Cahiers Spinoza*, 2 (1978), pp. 207–39.

Clair, P., 'Hétérodoxie et déisme chez J. Toland', *Recherches sur le XVIIe siècle*, 4 (1980), pp. 127–44.
Cohen, Gustave, *Le séjour de Saint-Evremond en Hollande et l'entrée de Spinoza dans le champ de la pensée française*, Paris: Champion, 1929.
Colombero, C., 'Andrea Cesalpino e la polemica anti-aristotelica e anti-spinoziana', *Rivista critica di storia della filosofia*, 35 (1980), pp. 343–56.
Comte-Sponville, André, 'D'un silence à l'autre', *La Liberté de l'esprit*, 9–10 (1985), pp. 20–56.
Comte-Sponville, André, 'Jean Cavaillès ou l'héroïsme de la raison', *La Liberté de l'esprit*, 16 (1987), pp. 43–69.
Corsano, A., 'Bayle e Spinoza', *Giornale critico della filosofia italiana*, 56 (1977), pp. 319–26.
Corsi, M., *Politica e saggezza in Spinoza*, Naples: Guida Editori, 1978.
Couchoud, P. L., *Benoît de Spinoza*, Paris: Alcan, 1902 (2nd edn, 1924).
Courtois, G., 'Le *jus sive potentia* spinoziste', *Archives de philosophie du droit*, 18 (1973), pp. 341–64.
Courtois, G., 'La loi chez Spinoza et saint Thomas d'Aquin', *Archives de philosophie du droit*, 25 (1980), pp. 159–89.
Courtois, G., 'Le rationalisme de Spinoza', *Les études philosophiques* (1982), pp. 461–72.
Cousin, Victor, 'Spinoza et la Synagogue des Juifs portugais à Amsterdam', in *Fragments philosophiques pour faire suite au cours de l'histoire de la philosophie*, 5th edn, 1866, vol. II.
Cramer, K., Jacobs, W. G. and Schmidt-Biggeman, W. (eds), *Spinozas Ethik und ihre frühe Wirkung*, Woflenbüttel: Herzog August Bibliotek, 1981.
Cramer, Konrad, 'Gedanken über Spinozas Lehre von der All-Einheit', in Henrich Dieter (ed.), *All-Einheit. Wege eines Gedankes in Ost und West*, Stuttgart: Klett-Cotta, 1985, pp. 151–79.
Cremaschi, S., *L'automa spirituale. La teoria della mente e delle passioni in Spinoza*, Milan: Universita Cattolica del Sacre Cuore, 1979.
Cristofolini, Paolo, *Cartesiani e sociniani. Studio su Henry More*, Urbino: Argalia, 1974 (pp. 118–25: 'Il primo incontro con Spinoza').
Cristofolini, Paolo, 'I due/infiniti attributi in Spinoza', *Annali della scuola normale superiore di Pisa*, 9 (1979), pp. 1175–88.
Cristofolini, Paolo, 'Labriola e Spinoza', *Paradigmi*, 2/5 (1984), pp. 271–80.
Cirstofolini, Paolo, 'Amor erga rem immutabilem et aeternam', *Guest Lectures and Seminar Papers on Spinozism*, 3 (1986).
Cristofolini, Paolo, *La Scienza intuitiva di Spinoza*, Morano: ETS, 1987.
Cristofolini, Paolo, 'Tschirnhaus, Spinoza e l'Italia', *Discorsi*, 1 (1986), pp. 24–42.

Cuchetti, Carlos, 'Baruch Spinoza: un filosofo ebrio de Dios', *Anales de la Academia nacional de ciencias morales y politicas*, 15 (1987), pp. 419–22.

Curley, Edwin, *Behind the Geometrical Method*, Princeton: Princeton University Press, 1988.

Da Costa, Uriel, *Die Schriften des Uriel da Costa, mit Einleitung, Übertragung und Regesten*, hrsg. v. Carl Gebhardt, Curis Societatis Spinozae, Amsterdam: M. Hertzberger, 1922, Bibliotheca Spinozana, vol. II.

Da Sila, Joao Esteves, 'Espinosa e Marx – sobre o processo do conhecimento', *Filosofia*, 2 (1985), pp. 125–35.

Damiron, Jean Philibert, 'Mémoire sur Spinoza et sa doctrine' [février 1843, lu à l'Académie des Sciences morales et politiques], *Mémoires de l'Académie des Sciences morales et politiques*, Paris: Didot, 1844, 2nd series, vol. IV, pp. 1–63.

Darbon, André, *Etudes spinozistes*, Paris: PUF, 1946.

Dascal, M., 'Spinoza. Pensamiento e linguagem', *Revista latinoamericana de filosofia*, Buenos Aires, 3 (1977), pp. 223–36.

Daudin, A., 'Spinoza et la science expérimentale: sa discussion de l'expérience de Boyle', *Rev. hist. des Sciences*, 2/2 (1949), pp. 179–90.

De Carvalho, Jaoquim, *Orobio de Castro e o Espinosismo* (Memorias da Academia das Ciências de Lisboa, Classe de Letras, vol. II), Lisbon: Lisbon Academy of Sciences, 1937.

De Deugd, Cornelis, *The Significance of Spinoza's First Kind of Knowledge*, Assen: Van Gorcum, 1966; Wijsgerige teksten en studies, XV.

De Dijn, Herman, 'Spinoza's geometrische methode van denken', *Tijdschrift voor filosofie*, 35 (1973), pp. 707–65.

De Dijn, Herman, 'Adriaan Heereboord en het Nederlands cartesianisme', *Algemeen Nederlands tijdschrift voor wijsbegeerte*, 75 (1983), pp. 56–78.

De Dijn, Herman, 'Conception of Philosophical Method in Spinoza: Logica and Mos geometricus', *Review of Metaphysics*, 40 (1986), pp. 55–78.

De Dijn, Herman, 'Spinoza als bevrijdingsfilosoof. Omtrent Antonio Negri's Spinoza-interpretatie', *Tijdschrift voor Filosofie*, 48 (1986), pp. 619–30.

De Dijn, Herman, 'Negri's spinozisme. Een nieuwe bevrijdingsphilosophie?', *Bijdragen*, 48 (1987), pp. 41–50.

De Flaviis, Giuseppe, *Kant e Spinoza*, Florence: Sansoni, 1986.

De Olaso, Andrieu, E., 'Feijoo lecteur de Spinoza', in *Spinoza entre Lumières et Romantisme*, Cahiers de Fontenay, Fontenay-aux-Roses, 1985.

De Souza, Chaui, M., *Introduçao à leitura de Espinoza* [Th.], Sao Paulo, 1971.

De Souza, Chaui, M., 'Problema da linguagem em Espinosa', *Discurso, Faculdade de filosofia, letras e ciencias humanas. Universidade de Sao Paul*, 2 (1972).

De Souza, Chaui, M., A nervura do real. Espinosa e a questao da liberdade [Diss.], Sao Paulo, 1977.

De Souza, Chaui, M., 'Do obra espinosana ao espinosismo. Correspondência entre Dortous de Mairan e o reverendo padre Malebranche', *Almanaque*, 7 (1978), pp. 12–25.

De Souza, Chaui, M., 'Matematica, experiéncia e politica', *Almanaque*, 9 (1979), pp. 30–52.

De Souza, Chaui, M., 'Politica e profecia', *Discurso, Faculdade de filosofia, letras e ciencias humanas. Universidade de Sao Paulo*, 10 (1979), pp. 111–59.

De Souza, Chaui, M., 'Direito natural e direito civil em Hobbes e Espinosa', *Revista latinoamericana de filosofia*, 6 (1980), pp. 57–71.

De Souza, Chaui, M., 'Linguagem e liberdade. O contradiscurso de Baruch Espinosa', in *Da realidade sem mistérios ao mistério do mundo. Espinosa, Voltaire, Merleau-Ponty*, Brasiliense: Sao Paulo: Brasiliense, 1981, pp. 10–103; 1983 (3rd edn).

De Vet, J. J. V. M., 'Was Spinoza de auteur van *Stelkonstige reeckening van den regenboog* en van *Reeckening van kanssen*?', *Tijdschrift voor filosofie*, 45 (1983), pp. 602–39.

de Vries, Theun, *Baruch de Spinoza in Selbstzeugnissen und Bilddokumenten*, Reinbek bei Hamburg: Rowohlt, 1970; 1981; 1983.

de Vries, Theun, *De Gezegende*, Amsterdam: Querido, 1985.

Delahunty, R. J., *Spinoza*, London: Routledge & Kegan Paul, 1985.

Delbos, Victor, *Le spinozisme*, cours professé à la Sorbonne en 1912–1913, 3rd edn, Paris: Vrin, 1950.

Deleuze, Gilles, *Spinoza: Practical Philosophy*, trans. Robert Hurley, San Francisco: City Lights, 1988.

Deleuze, Gilles, *Expressionism in Philosophy: Spinoza*, trans. Martin Joughin, New York: Zone Books, 1990.

Den Uyl, D. J., *Power, State and Freedom: An Interpretation of Spinoza's Political Philosophy*, Assen: Van Gorcum, 1983.

Den Uyl, D. J., 'Passion, State and Progress: Spinoza and Mandeville on the Nature of Human Association', *Journal of the History of Philosophy*, 25/3 (1987), pp. 369–95.

Deregibus, A., *Bruno e Spinoza. La realtà dell'infinito e il problema della sua unità*; vol. 2: *La dottrina di Spinoza sull'infinito*, Turin: Giappichelli, 1981.

Desanti, Jean-Toussaint, *Introduction à l'histoire de la philosophie*, Paris: Les Essais de la Nouvelle Critique, 1956.

Desanti, Jean-Toussaint, 'Inflexible Spinoza', *Le Monde*, 11 March 1977.

Descartes et le cartésianisme hollondais. Etudes et documents, Editions françaises d'Amsterdam, Paris: PUF, 1950 (E. J. Dijksterhuis, C. Serrurier, P. Dibon, H. J. Pos, J. Orcibal, C. Thijssen-Schoute, G. Lewis).

Descartes, R., *The Philosophical Writings of Descartes, Volume I*, trans. Cottingham, J., Stoothoff, R., Murdoch, D., Cambridge: Cambridge University Press, 1985.

Descartes, R., *The Philosophical Writings of Descartes, Volume II*, trans. Cottingham, J., Stoothoff, R., Murdoch, D., Cambridge: Cambridge University Press, 1984.

Descartes, R., *The Philosophical Writings of Descartes, Volume III, The Correspondence*, trans. Cottingham, J., Stoothoff, R., Murdoch, D., Kenny, A., Cambridge: Cambridge University Press, 1991.

Deschepper, J.-P., 'Le spinozisme', in Y. Belaval (ed.), *Histoire de la philosophie*, vol. 2, *De la Renaissance à la révolution kantienne*, Paris: Pléiade 1973, pp. 483–507.

Di Luca, Giovanni, *Critica della Religione in Spinoza*, L'Aquila: Japadre, 1982.

Di Noi, G. B., *Lo spinozismo critico di Léger-Marie Deschamps*, Lecce: Milella, 1985.

Di Vona, P., *Baruch Spinoza*, Florence: La Nuova Italia Editrice, 1975.

Di Vona, P., 'La definizione dell'essenza in Spinoza', *Revue internationale de philosophie*, 31 (1977), pp. 39–52.

Di Vona, P., *Spinoza e i transcendentali*, Naples, 1977.

Dibon, Paul, *La philosophie néerlandaise au Siècle d'Or*; tome I: *L'enseignement philosophique dans les Univresités à l'époque précartésienne (1575–1650)*, Paris/Amsterdam/London/New York: Elsevier, 1954 (publ. de l'Inst. fr. d'Amsterdam, Maison Descartes).

Dominguez, A., 'Reflexiones en torno al método de Spinoza', *La ciudad de dios*, 188 (1975), pp. 18–45.

Dominguez, A., 'La religion chez Spinoza', *Guest-Lectures and Seminar Papers on Spinozism*, 4 (1987).

Donagan, Alan, *Spinoza*, New York: Harvester Wheatsheaf, 1988.

Dos Penedos, Alvaro, 'Acerca do direito natural, direito civil e libertade no Tratado Teologico-politico de Spinoza', *Ensaios. Historia da Filosofia* (1987), pp. 95–108.

Doz, A., 'Remarques sur les onze premières propositions de l'*Ethique* de Spinoza. A propos du Spinoza de Martial Gueroult', *Revue de métaphysique et de morale*, 81 (1976), pp. 221–61.

Doz, A., 'Réponse à Mlle Dreyfus à propos de Spinoza de Martial Guéroult', *Cahiers Spinoza*, 3 (1980), pp. 209–37.

Dreyfus, G., 'L'analyse des structures de l'*Ethique* par Martial Gueroult', *Kant-Studien*, 66 (1975), pp. 483–99.
Dreyfus, G., 'Sur le Spinoza de Martial Guéroult. Réponses aux objections de M. Doz', *Cahiers Spinoza*, 2 (1978), pp. 7–51.
Duchesneau F., 'Modèle cartésien et modèle spinoziste de l'être vivant', *Cahiers Spinoza*, 2 (1973).
Dufour-Kowalska, G., *L'origine. L'essence de l'origine. L'origine selon l' 'Ethique' de Spinoza*, Paris: Beauchesne, 1973.
Dufour-Kowalska, G., 'Un itinéraire fictif. Le *Traité de la réforme de l'entendement et de la meilleure voie à suivre pour parvenir à la vraie connaissance des choses*', *Studia philosophica*, 35 (1975), pp. 58–80.
Dunin-Borkowski, Stan. von., *Spinoza nach dreihundert Jahren*, Berlin/Bonn: Dümmler, 1932.
Dunin-Borkowski, Stan. von, *Spinoza*, Münster: Aschendorf, 1933–1936 (4 vols: I Der junge de Spinoza; II. Aus den Tagen Spinozas, Das Entscheidungsjahr 1657; III. Aus den Tagen Spinozas, Das neue Leben; IV. Aus den Tagen Spinozas, Das Lebenswerk).
Ecole, J., 'La critique wolffienne du spinozisme', *Bulletin de l'Association des Amis de Spinoza*, 5 (1981), pp. 9–19.
Eisenberg, P. D., 'How to understand *De intellectus emendatione*', *Journal of the History of Philosophy*, 9 (1971), pp. 171–91.
Elbogen, Ismar, *Der Tractatus de Intellectus Emendationie Spinozas und seine Stellung in der Philosohie Spinozas. Ein Beitrag zur Entwicklungsgeschichte Spinozas* [Diss.], Breslau, 1898.
Erdmann, Joh (ed.), *Malebranche, Spinoza und die Skeptiker und Mystiker des 17 Jahrhunderts*, Riga, 1836.
Etudes philosophiques: Spinoza, 4 (1987).
Faller, A., 'Anatomie und Philosophie: Niels Stensen (1638–1686) und sein Jugendfreund B. de Spinoza (1632–1677)', *Gesnerus*, 43/1–2 (1986), pp. 47–60.
Fell, Margaret, *A Loving Salutation*, ed. R. H. Popkin and M. A. Signer, Assen: Van Gorcum, 1987.
Fernandez, Garcia Eugenio, *Potencia y Razon en B. Spinoza*, Madrid: Editorial de la Universidad Complutense de Madrid, 1988.
Feuer, Samuel Lewis, *Spinoza and the Rise of Liberalism*, Boston: Beacon Press, 1958, 1966; and London: Mayflower Publ., 1960.
Filippi, Ignazio, *Materia e Scienza in B. Spinoza*, Prefazione di Gieuseppe Semerari, Palermo: Libreria Dario Flaccovio, 1985.
Filosofia, publicaçao periodica da sociedade portuguesa da filosofia, No. 2 (December), *Sobre Espinosa*, Lisbon, 1985.

Foucher de Careil, Louis Alexandre (ed.), *Leibniz, Descartes et Spinoza, avec un rapport par M. Victor Cousin*, Paris: Ladrange, 1862.

Foucher de Careil, Louis Alexandre (ed.), *Réfutation inédite de Spinoza par Leibniz*, Paris: Brière, 1854.

Fraisse, J.-C., *L'œuvre de Spinoza*, Paris: Vrin, 1978.

Frances, Madeleine, *Spinoza dans les pays néerlandais de la second moitié du XVIIe siècle*, Paris: Alcan, 1937.

Frankfurt, Harry, G., 'Two Motivations for Rationalism: Descartes and Spinoza', in A. Donagan (ed.), *Human Nature and Natural Knowledge*, Dordrecht: Riedel, 1986, pp. 47–62.

Freudenthal, J. (ed.), *Die Lebensgeschichte Spinoza's in Quellenschriften, Urkunden und nichtamtlichen Nachrichten*, hrsg. von. J. Freudenthal, Leipzig: Veit, 1899, XVI; reprint: London, 1980.

Freudenthal, J., *Spinozas Leben und Lehre. I. Das Leben Spinozas von J. Freudenthal*, 2. Auflage, hrsg. v. Carl Gebhardt. II, *Die Lehre Spinozas*, auf Grund des Nachlasses von J. Freudenthal, bearb. v. Carl Gebhardt; 'Bibliotheca Spinozana', vol. V, Curis Societatis Spinozanae, Heidelberg: Carl Winter, 1927.

Friedman, Joel, 'How the Finite Follows From the Infinite in Spinoza's Metaphysical System', *Synthèse*, 69/3 (1986), pp. 371–407.

Fuks, L. 'A propos de la bibliothèque de Spinoza', *Revista de archivos, bibliotecas y museos*, 80 (1977), pp. 55–61.

Gabaude, J.-M., *Liberté et raison. La liberté cartésienne et sa réfraction chez Spinoza et Leibniz*; vol. 2: *Philosophie compréhensive de la nécessitation libératrice*, Toulouse: Publication de la Faculté des Lettres et des Sciences Humaines de Toulouse, 1972.

Gallicet, Calvetti Caral, *Spinoza, i presupposti teoretici dell'irenismo etico*, Milan: Vita e Pensiero, 1968 (publ. Università Cattolica del Sacro Cuore, Scienze filosofiche, XII).

Gallicet, Calvetti Carla, *Spinoza lettore del Machiavelli*, Milan: Università Cattolica del Sacro Cuore, 1972.

Gallicet, Calvetti Carla, 'Spinoza interprete del *Principe*', in *Studi in onore di A. Chiari*, vol. 1, Brescia: Paideia, 1973, pp. 549–66.

Gallicet, Calvetti Carla, 'Due testi chiave di Spinoza su Hobbes', in *Studi di filosofia in onore di G. Bontadini*, vol. 1, Milan: Vita e Pensiero, 1975, pp. 439–70.

Gallicet, Calvetti, Carla, 'In margine a Spinoza lettore del De Cive di Hobbes', I and II, *Rivista di filosofia neo-scolastica*, 73 (1981), pp. 52–84; 235–63.

Gandini, Sergio 'Linee di tendenza della critica francese del '900 intorno a Spinoza', *Rivista di Storia della filosofia*, 4 (1987), pp. 737–46.

Garcia, Leal. J., 'Fisica y Ontologia in Spinoza', *Revista de Filosofia*, 8 (1985), pp. 253–80.
Garniron, P., 'La substance spinoziste d'après les manuscrits d'auditeurs des cours de Hegel d'histoire de la philosophie à Berlin', *Raison présente*, 43 (1977), pp. 81–106.
Garniron, P., 'Hegel: deux leçons sur Spinoza (textes); Leçon de 1823–1824; Leçon de 1825–1826', *Cahiers Spinoza*, 4 (1983), pp. 89–116.
Gebhardt, Carl., *Spinozas Abhandlung über die Verbesserun des Verstandes*, Eine entwicklungsgeschtliche Untersuchung von C. Gebhardt, Heidelberg: Carl Winter, 1905.
Gebhardt, Carl., 'Spinoza und der Platonismus, *Chr. sp.* I, 1921, pp. 178–234.
Gebhardt, Carl, 'Juan de Prado', *Chr. sp.*, III, 1923.
Gebhardt, Carl (ed.), *Leone Ebreo, Dialoghi d'Amore. Hebraïsche Gedichte*, hrsg. mit einer Darstellung des Lebens und des Werkes Leones, Bibliographie, Register ze den Dialoghi, Uebertragung der hebräischen Texte, Regesten, Urkunden und Anmerkungen v. C. Gebhardt, Curis Societatis Spinozanae', Heidelberg: Carl Winter, 1929; 'Bibliotheca Spinozana', vol. III.
Gelhaar, Sabine, *Prophetie und Gesetz bei Jehudah Hallevi, Maimonides und Spinoza*, Bern: Peter Lang, 1988.
Geismann, Georg, 'Spinoza jenseits von Hobbes und Rousseau', *Zeitschrift für philosophische Forschung*, 43/3 (1989), pp. 405–31.
Gentile Giovanni, 'Leone Ebreo e Spinoza', in *Studi sul Rinascimento*, Florence: Valsecchi, 1923 (2nd edn, Florence: Sansoni, 1936).
Giancotti, Boscherini Emilia, 'La question du matérialisme chez Spinoza', *Revue internationale de philosophie*, 31 (1977), pp. 174–97.
Giancotti, Emilia, *Baruch Spinoza 1632–1677. La ragione, la libertà, l'idea di Dio e del mondo nell'epoca della borghesia e delle nuove scienze*, Rome: Editori Riuniti, 1985.
Gilead, Amihud, 'Spinoza's *principium individuationis*, and Personal Identity', *International studies in philosophy – Studi internazionali di filosofia*, 15 (1983), 1, 45–57.
Gilead, Amihud, 'The Order and Connexion of Things', *Kant-Studien* (1985), pp. 72–8.
Gilead, Amihud, 'The Problem of Immediate Evidence: The Case of Spinoza and Hegel', *Hegel-Studien*, 20 (1985), pp. 145–62.
Gilead, Amihud, *Darkha shel torat Spinoza leshitah filosofit* (The Journey of Spinoza's Doctrine Towards a Philosophical System), Jerusalem: Bialik Institute, 1986.

Gilli, M., 'L'influence de Spinoza dans la formation du matérialisme allemand', *Archives de philosophie*, 46 (1983), pp. 590–610.
Giovannangeli, Daniel, 'Spinoza et le problème de l'analogie', *Cahiers internationaux du Symbolisme*, 51–2 (1985), pp. 55–71.
Glazemaker 1682–1982. Catalogus bij een tentoonstelling over de vertaler Jan Hendriksz Glazemaker in de Universiteitsbibliotheek van Amsterdam, M. Keyser (hrsg.), Amsterdam, 1982 (pp. VIII–XIII: F. Akkerman, *Glazemakers wijze van vertalen*).
Goggi, Gianluigi, 'Spinoza contro Rousseau: un commento ad alcuni passi di Diderot e di D'Holbach', *Annali di Ca' Foscari*, 25 (1986), pp. 133–59.
Goldenbaum, Ursula, 'Zu einer vermeintlichen Textlücke in Spinozas Ethica', *Deutsche Zeitschrift für Philosophie*, 32/1 (1984), pp. 1036–40.
Goldenbaum, Ursula, 'Spinozas Überwindung des Naturrechts durch eine utilitaristische Gesellschaftsauffassung', in M. Buhr and W. Förster (eds), *Aufklärung – Gesellschaft – Kritik*, Berlin: Akademie Verlag, 1985, pp. 277–97.
Goldschmidt, V., 'La place de la théorie politique dans la philosophie de Spinoza', *Manuscrito*, 2 (1978), pp. 103–22.
Goschler, Isidore, *Du panthéisme* [Th. Lettres], Strasbourg: Université de Strasbourg: 1840.
Grange, Joseph, 'Spinoza's Scientia Intuitiva', *Philosophy and Theology*, 2 (1988), pp. 241–57.
Grene, M. (ed.), *Spinoza: A Collection of Critical Essays*, Garden City, NY: Anchor, 1973; reprint Notre Dame (Ind.), 1979.
Groen, J. J., *Ethica en ethologie. Spinoza's leer der affecten en de moderne psycho-biologie*, Leiden: Brill, 1972; Mededelingen vanwege het Spinozahuis, 29.
Gründer, K. and Schmidt-Biggemann, W. (eds), *Spinoza in der Frühzeit seiner religiösen Wirkung*, Heidelberg: Lambert Schneider, 1984.
Grünwald, Max, *Spinoza in Deutschland*, Berlin: Calvary, 1897; Aalen: Scientia Verlag, 1986.
Gueroult, Martial, *Spinoza*, Paris: Aubier; Hildesheim, Olms; 1968–1974; vol. 1, *Dieu (Ethique, 1)*, 1968; vol. 2, *L'Ame (Ethique, 2)*, 1974.
Gueroult, Martial, 'Spinoza, tome 3 (Introduction générale et première moitié du premier chapitre)', *Revue philosophique de la France et de l'étranger*, 102 (1977), pp. 285–302.
Guigue, Bruno, 'De Machiavel à Spinoza, l'émergence de l'Etat moderne', *La liberté de l'Esprit*, 13 (1986), pp. 41–64.
Guzzo, Augusto, *Il pensiero di B. Spinoza*, Florence: Vallecchi, 1924 (2nd edn, Turin: Edizioni di Filosofia, 1964).

Haddad-Chamakh, F., *Philosophie systématique et système de philosophie politique chez Spinoza*, Tunis: University of Tunis, 1980.
Haitsma, Mulier, E. O. G., *The Myth of Venice and Dutch Republican Thought in the Seventeenth Century*, Assen: Van Gorcum, 1980.
Hall, A. Rupert and Hall Marie Boas, 'Philosophy and Natural Philosophy: Boyle and Spinoza', in *Mélanges Alexandre Koyré*, publiées à l'occasion de son 70e anniversaire; tom I: *L'aventure de la science*; tome II: *L'aventure de l'esprit*; Paris: Hermann, 1964 (coll. 'Histoire de la pensée', XII–XIII), vol. II, pp. 241–56.
Hallet, H. F., *Aeternitas: A Spinozistic Study*, Oxford: The Clarendon Press, 1930.
Hallet, H. F., *Benedict de Spinoza: The Elements of His Philosophy*, London: Athlone Press, 1957; Fair Lawn: Essential Books, 1957.
Hallet, H. F., *Creation, Emanation and Salvation: A Spinozistic Study*, The Hague: M. Nijhoff, 1962.
Hamelin, Octave, 'Sur une des origines du spinozisme', *L'Année philosophique*, XIe année, 1901, pp. 15–28.
Hamelin, Octave, 'La théorie de la certitude dans Spinoza', cours inédit, ed. F. Turlot, *Bulletin de l'association des amis de Spinoza*, 8 (1982), pp. 1–10.
Hammacher, Klaus, *Spinoza und die Frage nach der Unsterblichkeit*, Leiden: Brill, 1981, Mededelingen vanwege het Spinozahuis, 43.
Hammacher, Klaus, 'La raison dans la vie affective et sociale selon Descartes et Spinoza', *Les études philosophiques* (1984), pp. 73–81.
Hammacher, Klaus, 'Ist Spinozismus Kabbalismus? Zum Verhältnis von Religion und Philosophie im ausgehenden 17. und beginnenden 18. Jahrundhert, *Archivio di Filosofia*, 53/2–3 (1985), pp. 29–50.
Hampshire, S., *Spinoza*, Harmondsworth: Penguin, 1951; 1981.
Harmsen, A. J. E., *Onderwys in de tooneel-poëzy (Nil Volentibus Arduum)*, with a summary in French, Rotterdam: Ordeman, 1989.
Harris, E. E., *Salvation From Despair: A Reappraisal of Spinoza's Philosophy*, The Hague: M. Nijhoff, 1973.
Hart, A., *Spinoza's Ethics, part I and II. A Platonic Commentary*, Leiden: Brill, 1983.
Hecker, K., *Spinoza's allgemeine Ontologie*, Darmstadt: WB, 1978.
Heimbrock, H.-G., *Vom Heil der Seel. Studien zum Verhältnis von Religion und Psychologie bei Baruch Spinoza. Zugleich ein Beitrag zur Vorgeschichte der modernen Religionspsychologie* [Diss.], Frankfurt/M., 1981.
Henrad, R., *Nietzsche en Spinoza, vreemde verwanten*, Leiden: Brill, 1989; Mededelingen vanwege het Spinozahuis, 56.

Herer, M., *Spinoza, die Philosophie der Wahrheit und der Erkenntnis*, Jerusalem: Israel Universities Press, 1971.

Hermosa, Andujar Antonio, *La teoria del Estado de Spinoza*, Seville: Universidad de Sevilla, 1989.

Hessing, Siegfried (ed.), *Spinoza: Dreihundert Jahre Ewigkeit, Spinoza-Festschrift, 1632–1932*, 2. verm. Auflage, The Hague: M. Nijhoff, 1962.

Hirsch, P., *Bloch over Spinoza. Een poging tot verheldering van de plaats van Spinoza's wijsbegeerte, belicht vanuit de historische en sociaaleconomische kontekst van zijn tijd, in de geschiedenis van de filosofie*, [Th.] Huizen, 1978.

Hobbes, Thomas, *Leviathan*, London: Penguin Classics, 2017.

Hoffheimer, Michael H., 'The Four Equals: Analysing Spinoza's Ideal of Equality', *Philosophia*, 15 (1985), pp. 237–49.

Hoffheimer, Michael H., 'Locke, Spinoza and the Idea of Political Equality', *History of Political Thought*, 7 (1986), pp. 341–60.

Hong, Han-Ding, *Spinoza und die deutsche Philosophie*, Aalen: Scientia Verlag, 1989.

Hubbeling, H. G., *Spinoza's Methodology*, Assen: Van Gorcum, 1964 (2nd edn, 1967); Philosophia Religionis, Bibliotheek van geschriften over de godsdienstwijsbegeerte, XI.

Hubbeling, H. G., *Logica en ervaring in Spinoza's en Ruusboecs mystiek*, Leiden: Brill, 1973; Mededelingen vanwege het Spinozahuis, 31.

Hubbeling, H. G., 'La méthode axiomatique de Spinoza et la définition du concept de Dieu', *Raison présente*, 43 (1977), pp. 25–36.

Hubbeling, H. G., *Spinoza*, Freiburg: K. Adler, 1978.

Hubbeling, H. G., 'Spinoza's axiomatische methode en zijn definitie van God', *Algemeen Nederlands tijdschrift voor wijsbegeerte*, 70 (1978), pp. 18–28.

Hubbeling, H. G., 'La morale de Spinoza: une vision ouverte encadrée par une argumentation stricte', *Bulletin de l'Association des Amis de Spinoza*, 4 (1980), pp. 15–17.

Huisman, B., 'L'inaliénable et l'imprescriptible. Autour d'une rencontre peu fortuite entre Spinoza et Hegel', *Cahiers Spinoza*, 4 (1983), pp. 117–26.

Hungisto, Markku and Oittinen Vesa, 'Potentia hominis: Spinoza, Hegel, Marx, über das meschliche Wesen', *Annalen der Internationalen Gesellschaft für dialektische Philosophie*, Societas Hegeliana, 3 (1986), pp. 170–8.

Hylkema, C. B., *Réformateurs. Geschiedkundige Studiën over de godsdienstige bewegingen uit de nadagen onzer gouden eeuw*, Haarlem, 1900–1902, 2 vols. Groningen/Amsterdam: Herdruk Bouma's Boekhuis/Bert Hagen, 1978, 1 vol.

Igoin, A., 'De l'ellipse de la théorie politique de Spinoza chez le jeune Marx', *Cahiers Spinoza*, 1 (1977), pp. 213–28.

Irrlitz, G., 'Spinoza, die Ethik in der *Ethik*', *Deutsche Zeitschrift für Philosophie*, 30 (1982), pp. 285–313.
Jacob, M., *The Radical Enlightenment: Pantheists, Freemasons and Republicans*, London: Allen & Unwin, 1981.
Jacobs, Wilhelm G., 'Spinozas Theologisch-politischer Traktat und das Problem der Geschichte', in Wolfgang Kluxen (ed.), *Tradition und Innovation*, Hamburg: Felix Meiner, 1988, pp. 82–9.
Jelles, Jarig, *Belydenisse der algemeenen en Christelyken geloofs, vervaltet in een brief aan N. N., door Jarig Jelles*, Amsterdam: Jan Rieuwertsz, 1684.
Joachim, Harold H., *Spinoza's Tractatus de Intellectus Emendatione. A Commentary*. Preliminary Note by Elisabeth Joachim and Preface by W. D. Ross, Oxford: The Clarendon Press, 1940; republished New York: Russell & Russell, 1964.
Jung, Gertrud, *Spinozas Affektenlehre* [Diss.], Berlin, 1926.
Jungmann, Albert, *Goethes Naturphilosophie zwischen Spinoza und Nietzsche*, Bern: Peter Lang, 1989.
Kaplan, Francis, 'Les définitions de la substance et du mode par Spinoza', *Etudes philosophiques*, 1 (1989), pp. 21–37.
Kaplan, Y., 'A propos de la signification historique du phénomène hétérodoxe dans les communautés séfarades occidentales au XVIIe siècle', *Bulletin de l'Association des Amis de Spinoza*, 4 (1980), pp. 1–14.
Karppe, Salomon, 'L'idée de nécessité chez Averroès et Spinoza', in *Essais de critique et d'histoire de la philosophie*, Paris: Alcan, 1902, pp. 109–17.
Karppe, Salomon, 'Richard Simon et Spinoza', in *Essais de critique et d'histoire de la philosophie*, Paris: Alcan, 1902.
Kashap, S. P. (ed.), *Studies in Spinoza: Critical and Interpretative Essays*, Berkeley: University of California Press, 1972.
Kashap, S. Paul, *Spinoza and Moral Freedom*, New York: State University of New York Press, 1987.
Kennington, R. (ed.), *The Philosophy of Baruch Spinoza*, Washington DC: Catholic University of America Press, 1980.
Kibrick, S. (ed.), *Homenaje a Baruch Spinoza. Con motivo del tricentenario de su muerte*, Buenos Aires: Museo Judio, 1976.
Klever, Wim N. A., *Dialektiek contra axiomatiek. Een confrontatie tussen Spinoza en Hegel onder methodologisch opzicht*, Leiden: Brill, 1974; Mededelingen vanwege het Spinozahuis, 33.
Klever, Wim N. A., 'Nieuwe argumenten tegen de toeschriving van het auteurs – chap van de *Stelkonstige reeckening van de regenboog* en *reeckening van kanssen* aan Spinoza', *Tijdschrift voor Filosofie*, 47/3 (1985), pp. 493–502.

Klever, Wim N. A., 'Burchard de Volder (1643–1709). A cryptospinozist on a Leiden cathedra', *Lias*, XV/2 (1986), pp. 191–241.

Klever, Wim N. A., *De Methodologische Functie van de Godsidee*, Leiden: Brill, 1986; Mededelingen vanwege het Spinozahuis, 48.

Klever, Wim N. A., 'De Spinozistische prediking van Peter Balling', *Doopsgezinde Bijdragen*, 14 (1988), pp. 55–85.

Klever, Wim N. A., 'Het Koppelingsbeginsel in Spinoza's politicologie', *Acta politica*, 3 (1988), pp. 359–77.

Klever Wim N. A., *Voorbeschikking. De wetenschappelijke filosofie*, Nijmegen: Markant, 1989.

Klijnsmit, Anthony, J., 'Spinoza over taal', *Studia Rosenthaliana*, XIX/1 (1985), pp. 1–38.

Klijnsmit, Anthony, J., *Spinoza and Grammatical Tradition*, Leiden: Brill, 1986; Mededelingen vanwege het Spinozauis, 49.

Klijnsmit, Anthony, J., 'Spinoza on "the imperfection of words"', *Cahiers voor taalkunde*, 1 (1989).

Koerbagh, J., and Koerbagh, A., *Een ligt schijnende in duystere plaatsen*, ed. H. Vandenbossche, Bruxelles: Vrije Universiteit Brussel, 1974.

Kogan, B. S. (ed.), *Spinoza: A Tercentenary Perspective*, Cincinnati: Hebrew Union College, 1979.

Kopper, Joachim, 'Einige Bemerkungen zur Bedeutung von Ewigkeit und Dauer in Spinozas Ethik', *Zeitschrift für philosophische Forschung*, 43 (1989), pp. 432–48.

Kortholt, Christian, *De tribus impostoribus magnis liber, cura editus Christiani Kortholti*, Kiloni, 1680 (2nd edn, Hamburgi, imprimebat Joachimus Reumann, 1700; 3rd edn, 1701).

Kortholt, S., 'Sur la vie de Spinoza; préface au De tribus Impostoribus', *Bulletin de l'Association des Amis de Spinoza*, 7 (1982), pp. 1–5.

Kreimendahl, L., *Freiheitsgesetz und höchstes Gut in Spinozas Theologisch-politischen Traktat*, Hildesheim: Olms, 1983.

Lachterman, D. R., 'The Physics of Spinoza's *Ethics*', in R. W. Shahan and J. I. Biro (eds), *Spinoza: New Perspectives*, Norman: University of Oklahoma Press, 1978; reprint, 1980, pp. 71–111.

Lagrée, Jacqueline, 'De quelques références spinozistes chez Sartre', *Bulletin de l'Association des Amis de Spinoza*, 15 (1985).

Lagrée, Jacqueline, 'Une traduction française du *Traité théologico-politique* de Spinoza au XVIIIe siècle', *Travaux et documents du Groupe de recherches spinozistes*, 1, PUPS, 1989, pp. 109–23.

Lagrée, J. and P.-F. Moreau, 'La lecture de la Bible dans le cercle de Spinoza', in *Le Grand Siècle et la Bible*, sous la direction de J.-R. Armogathe (BTLT, vol. VI), Paris: Beauchesne, 1989, pp. 97–116.

Laplanche, François, *L'Ecriture, le sacré, l'histoire. Erudits et politique protestants devant la Bible en France au XVIIᵉ siècle*, Amsterdam: APA, Holland University Press/Presses universitaires de Lille, 1986, pp. 97–116.

Lauth, R., 'Spinoza vu par Fichte', *Archives de philosophie*, 1 (1978), pp. 27–48.

Lazzeri, C., 'Les lois de l'obéissance: sur la théorie spinoziste des transferts de droit', *Etudes philosophiques: Spinoza*, 4 (1987).

LeClerc, Jean, *Epistolario*, vol. I, 1679–1689, a cura di Mario Sina, Florence: Leo Olschki, 1987.

Lécrivain, A., 'Spinoza et la physique cartésienne', I et II, *Cahiers Spinoza*, 1 (1977), pp. 235–65; (1978), pp. 93–206.

Lefèbvre, J.-P., 'Heine, Hegel et Spinoza', *Cahiers Spinoza*, 4 (1983), pp. 211–29.

Lenoble, M., 'L'état civil selon Hobbes et selon Spinoza', *Cahiers de philosophie politique et juridique*, 3 (1983), pp. 113–21.

Léon, A., *Les éléments cartésiens de la doctrine spinoziste sur les rapports de la pensée et de son objet*, Paris: Alcan, 1907.

Lermond, Lucia, *The Form of Man*, Leiden: Brill, 1988.

Les premiers écrits de Spinoza, Acts du colloque organisé par le Groupe de recherches spinozistes au CNRS du 9 au 11 avril 1986, *Archives de philosophie*, 51/1 (1988).

Les premiers écrits de Spinoza, Actes du colloque organisé par le Groupe de recherches spinozistes au CNRS du 9 au 11 avril 1986, *Revue des sciences philosophiques et théologiques*, 71/1 (1987).

Levinas, E., 'Avez-vous relu Baruch?', in *Difficile liberté*, Paris: Albin Michel, 2nd edn, 1976, pp. 148–59.

Levinas, E., 'Le cas Spinoza', in *Difficile liberté*, Paris: Albin Michel, 2nd edn, 1976, pp. 142–7.

Levy, Ze'ev, 'Hermeneutik und Esoterik bei Maimonides und Spinoza', *Schleiermacher-Archiv*, 1 (1985), pp. 541–60.

Levy, Ze'ev, 'The Relation of Spinoza's Concept of Substance to the Concept of Ultimate Reality', *Ultimate Reality and Meaning*, X/3 (1987), pp. 186–201.

Lewis, Christopher E., 'Baruch Spinoza: A Critic of Robert Boyle. On Matter', *Dialogue*, 27 (1984), pp. 11–22.

Liepert, A., 'Der Spinozismus Lessings', *Deutsche Zeitschrift für Philosophie*, 27 (1979), pp. 59–70.

Liepert, A., 'Über Lessings Spinoza-Rezeption', in H. Seidel (ed.), *Marxismus und Spinozismus. Materialien einer wissenschaftlichen Konferenz*, Leipzig: Karl-Marx Universität, 1981, pp. 180–8.

Lo spinozismo ieri e oggi, M. M. Olivetti (ed.), special edition of *Archivio di filosofia*, 1 (1978).

Loewenhardt, S. E., *Benedictus von Spinoza in seinem Verhältnis zur Philosophie und Naturforschung der neueren Zeit*, Berlin, 1872.

Loptson, Peter, 'Spinozist Monism', *Philosophia*, 18 (1988), pp. 19–38.

Lucas, H.-C., *Spinoza in Hegels Logik*, Leiden: Brill, 1982; Mededelingen vanwege het Spinozahuis, 45.

Lucas, H.-C., 'Causa sive ratio', *Cahiers Spinoza*, 4 (1983), pp. 171–204.

Lucas, H.-C., 'Hegel et l'édition de Spinoza par Paulus', *Cahiers Spinoza*, 4 (1983), pp. 127–38.

Lucas, H.-C., 'La légitimation de la peine (Réflexions sur la conception de la liberté chez Spinoza)', *Les études philosophiques* (1984), pp. 83–96.

Lucash, F. S., 'The Mind's Body: The Body Self-Awareness', *Dialogue*, 23 (1984), pp. 619–33.

Maccone, Sina M. G., 'Le *Apologie de Spinoza* di Languenes', *Nouvelles de la République des Lettres*, 2 (1984), pp. 117–37.

Machado de Abrea, Luis, 'Uma apologia de Spinoza – o prefacio as obras postumas', *Revista da Universidade de Aveiro/Letras*, 2 (1985), pp. 293–329.

Machado de Abreu, Luis, 'O Regresso de Spinoza. A proposito de um coloquio do CNRS', *Revista da Universidade de Aveiro/Letras*, 3 (1986), pp. 311–13.

Macherey, Pierre, *Hegel ou Spinoza*, Paris: Maspero – La Découverte, 1979; 1990.

Macherey, Pierre, 'De la médiation à la constitution: description d'un parcours spéculatif', *Cahiers Spinoza*, 4 (1983), pp. 9–37.

Madanes, Leiser, 'Spinoza y la libertad de expresion', *Revista de filosofia y teoria politica*, 26–7 (1986), pp. 279–83.

Magliano, F., *Il diritto nel sistema di Spinoza*, Milan: Bocca, 1946.

Malet, André, *Le Traité théologico-politique de Spinoza et la pensée biblique*, Paris: Les Belles Lettres, 1966 (publications de l'Université de Dijon, XXXV).

Marcus, Ruth Barcan, 'Spinoza and the Ontological Proof', in A. Donagan (ed.), *Human Nature and Natural Knowledge*, Dordrecht: Riedel, 1986, pp. 153–66.

Maréchal, G., 'Les retombées de la *Vie de Philopater* dans la République néerlandaise de la fin du XVIIe siècle', *Etudes philosophiques: Spinoza*, 4 (1987).

Maret, H., *Essai sur le panthéisme dans les sociétés modernes*, Paris: Fulgence, 1840.
Marion, Jean-Luc, 'Le fondement de la *cogitatio* selon le *De intellectus emendatione*, essai d'une lecture des paragraphes 104–105', *Les études philosophiques*, 47 (1972), pp. 357–68.
Marion, Jean-Luc, 'De la création des vérités éternelles au principe de la raison: remarques sur l'anticartésianisme de Spinoza, Malebranche, Leibniz', *XVIIe siècle*, 147 (1985), pp. 143–64.
Mark, T. C., 'A Unique Copy of Spinoza's Nagelate Schriften', *Journal of the History of Philosophy*, 13 (1975), pp. 81–3.
Martinetti, Piero, 'La dottrina della conoscenza e del metodo nella filosofia di Spinoza', *Rivista di Filosofia*, 1915–1916.
Martinetti, Piero, 'La dottrina della libertà in B. Spinoza', *Chr. sp.*, IV, 1926, pp. 58–67.
Martinetti, Piero, *Spinoza*, a cura di Franco Alessio, Naples: Bibliopolis, 1987.
Marx, Karl, 'Le *Traité théologico-politique* et la *Correspondance* de Spinoza: trois cahiers d'études de l'anée 1841', *Cahiers Spinoza*, 1 (1977), pp. 29–157.
Marx, Karl and Engels, F., *Exzerpte und Notizen bis 1842*, Berlin: De Gruyter Akademie Forschung, 1976, 2 vols: *K. Marx und F. Engels Gesamtausgabe*, Vierte Abteilung, Bd. 1.: 1. *Text*, pp. 233–76: 'Exzerpte aux Benedictus de Spinoza: Opera ed. Paulus'; 'Spinoza's Theologisch-politischer Tractat'; 'Briefe'; 2. *Apparat*, pp. 773–818: 'Entstehung und Überlieferung'; 'Übersetzung der lateinischen Textteile'.
Mason, R. V., 'Spinoza on Modality', *Philosophical Quarterly*, 36 (1986), pp. 313–42.
Mason, R. V., 'Spinoza on the Causality of Individuals', *Journal of the History of Philosophy*, 24 (1986), pp. 197–210.
Matheron, Alexandre, *Individu et communauté chez Spinoza*, Paris: Les Editions de Minuit, 1969.
Matheron, Alexandre, *Le Christ et le Salut des ignorants chez Spinoza*, Paris: Aubier-Montaigne, 1971.
Matheron, Alexandre, 'Remarques sur l'immortalité e l'âme chez Spinoza', *Les études philosophiques* (1972), pp. 369–78.
Matheron, Alexandre, 'Femmes et serviteurs dans la démocratie spinoziste', *Revue philosophique de la France et de l'étranger*, 102 (1977), pp. 181–200.
Matheron, Alexandre, 'Le *Traité théologico-politique* vu par le jeune Marx', *Cahiers Spinoza*, 1 (1977), pp. 159–212.
Matheron, Alexandre, 'Spinoza et le pouvoir', *La nouvelle critique*, 109 (1977), pp. 45–51.

Matheron, Alexandre, 'Spinoza et la sexualité', *Giornale critico della filosofia italiana*, 56 (1977), pp. 434–57.
Matheron, Alexandre, 'L'anthropologie spinoziste?', *Revue de synthèse*, 99 (1978), pp. 175–85.
Matheron, Alexandre, 'Spinoza et la décomposition de la politique thomiste: machiavélisme et utopie', *Archivio di filosofia* (1978), pp. 29–59.
Matheron, Alexandre, 'Spinoza et la propriété', *Tijdschrift voor de studie van de Verlichting*, 6 (1978), pp. 96–110.
Matheron, Alexandre, 'L'anomalie sauvage d'Antonio Negri', *Cahiers Spinoza*, 4 (1983), pp. 39–60.
Matheron, Alexandre, *Anthropologie et politique au XVIIe siècle (études sur Spinoza)*, Paris: Vrin, 1986.
Matson, Wallace, I., 'Spinoza on Beliefs', *Guest Lectures and Seminar Papers on Spinozism*, 7 (1989).
Mauro, Letterio, 'Cristo nel pensiero di Spinoza', *Verifiche*, 6 (1977), pp. 789–809.
Mauro, Letterio, 'Nota sulla teologia filosofica di Spinoza', *Sugkrisis, Testi e studi di storia e filosofia del linguaggio religioso*, a cura di C. Angelino, E. Salvaneschi, 1983, pp. 103–13.
Maxwell, Vance, 'The Formalist Treatment of Spinoza', *Dialogue*, 25 (1986), pp. 337–47.
Maxwell, Vance, 'The Philosophical Method of Spinoza', *Dialogue*, 25 (1988) pp. 89–110.
Mazzoli, Lisci, A. L., 'Baruch Spinoza: un marrano della ragione', *Rassegna mensile di Israel*, 49/5–8 (1983), pp. 531–42.
Méchoulan, Henri, 'Spinoza lecteur d'Antonio Perez', *Ethnopsychologie, revue de psychologie des peuples*, 29 (1974), pp. 289–301.
Méchoulan, Henri, 'Morteira et Spinoza au carrefour du socinianisme', *Revue des études juives*, 135 (1976), pp. 51–65.
Méchoulan, Henri, 'Quelques remarques sur le marranisme et la rupture spinoziste', *Studia Rosenthaliana*, 11 (1977), pp. 113–25.
Méchoulan, Henri, 'Spinoza face à quelques textes d'origine marrane', *Raison présente*, 43 (1977), pp. 13–24.
Méchoulan, Henri, 'Quelques remarques à propos du marranisme: un concept à tout faire', *Ethnopsychologie, revue de psychologie des peuples* (1978), pp. 83–100.
Méchoulan, Henri, 'Le herem à Amsterdam et l'"excommunication" de Spinoza', *Cahiers Spinoza*, 3 (1980), pp. 117–34.
Méchoulan, Henry, *Hispanidad y Judaismo en tiempos de Espinoza*, Edicion

crítica de la *Certeza del Camino* de Abraham Pereyra, Salamanca: Ediciones Universidad de Salamanca, 1987.

Meckenstock Günter, *Deterministische Ethik und kritische Theologie*, Berlin/New York: de Gruyter, 1988.

Meijer, Jaap, *Om de verloren zoon. Spinoza weerspiegeld in het geschiedbeeld der nederlandse Joden, 1840–1940* (Balans der Ballingschap, VIII–IX), Heemstede: J. Meier, 1986.

Meijer, Jaap, *Om de verloren zoon. Supplementum sefardicum neerlandicum* (Balans der Ballingschap, XIII), Heemstede: J. Meier, 1988.

Meijer, Jaap, *Beeldvorming om Baruch. Supplementum sefardicum historicum* (Balans der Ballingschap, XIV–XV), Heemstede: J. Meier, 1989.

Meininger, J. V., and Sucthelen, G. van., *Liever met wercken, als met woorden. De levensreis van doctor Franciscus Van den Enden, leermeester van Spinoza, complotteur tegen Lodewijk de Veertiende*, Weesp: Heureka, 1980.

Meinsma, K. O., *Spinoza en zijn kring. Historisch-kritische studiën over Hollandsche vrijgeesten*, 's-Gravenhage, 1896; Herdruk: Utrecht, 1980 (German translation, *Spinoza und sein Kreis*, Berlin: Schnabel, 1909; French translation, *Spinoza et son cercle. Etude critique historique sur les hétérodoxes hollondais*, Paris: Vrin, 1983).

Meli, F., *Spinoza e due antecedenti italiani dello spinozismo*, Florence: Sansoni, 1934.

Menasseh ben Israel, *Espérance d'Israel*, introd., trad. et notes par H. Méchoulan et G. Nahon, Paris: Vrin, 1979.

Menasseh ben Israel and his World, ed. Yosef Kaplan, Henry Méchoulan and Richard H. Popkin, Leiden: Brill, 1989.

Meozzi, A., *Le dottrine politiche e religiose di B. Spinoza. Parallelo con T. Hobbes*, Pisa: Vallerini, 1914 (2nd edn, Arezzo: Sinatti, 1915; 4th edn, Florence: Gonnelli, 1917).

Meur, Angès, 'Spinoza et l'imaginaire', *Raison présente*, 81 (1986), pp. 121–7.

Meyer, Ludowijk, *Philosophia S. Scripturae Interpres*, Amsterdam: Eleutheropoli, 1666, *La philosophie interprète de l'Ecriture Sainte*, traduction du latin, notes et présentation par Jacqueline Lagrée et Pierre-François Moreau, collection 'Horizons', Paris: Intertextes éditeur, 1988.

Mieth, G., 'Einige Thesen zu Hölderlins Spinoza-Rezeption', *Weimarer Beiträge*, 24/7 (1978),pp. 175–80.

Mignini, Filippo, 'Per la datazione e l'interpretazione del *Tractatus de intellectus emendatione* de B. Spinoza', *La Cultura*, 17 (1979), pp. 87–160.

Mignini, Filippo, 'Un documento trascurato della revisione delle opere di Spinoza', *La Cultura*, 18 (1980), pp. 223–73.

Mignini, Filippo, *Ars imaginandi. Apparenza e rappresentazione in Spinoza*, Naples: Edizione Scientifiche italiane, 1981.
Mignini, Filippo, 'Il sigillo di Spinoza', *La cultura*, 19 (1981), pp. 351–89.
Mignini, Filippo, *Introduzione a Spinoza*, Rome: Laterza, 1983.
Mignini, Filippo, 'Données et problèmes de la chronologie spinozienne 1656–1665', 'Les premiers écrits de Spinoza', *Revue des sciences philosophiques et théologiques*, 71/1 (1987).
Mignini, Filippo, 'L'intendere è un puro patire (*KV* 2/15, 5)', *La Cultura*, 1 (1987), pp. 1–151.
Mignini, Filippo, 'La cronologia e l'interpretazione delle opere di Spinoza', *La Cultura*, 26 (1988), pp. 339–60.
Mignini, Filippo, 'Lo *Spinoza* di Piero Martinetti', *Rivista di Filosofia*, LXXX/1 (1989), pp. 127–52.
Minazzi, Fabio, 'Juvalta intepret delle dottrine morali di Spinoza', *Rivista di Storia della Filosofia*, 41 (1986), pp. 619–27.
Mirri, F. S., *Richard Simon e il metodo storico-critico di B. Spinoza. Storia di un libro e di una polemica sullo sfondo delle lotte politico-religiose della Francia di Luigi* XIV, Florence: Le Monnier, 1972.
Mitsui, Y., 'Essai sur l'article Spinoza dans le *Dictionnaire historique et critique* de Pierre Bayle', *Etudes de langue et littérature française*, 38 (1981), pp. 36–48.
Montag, Warren, 'Spinoza: Politics in a World Without Transcendence', *Rethinking Marxism*, II/3 (1989), pp. 89–103.
Moreau, Joseph, *Spinoza et le spinozisme*, Paris: PUF, 1971; 1977.
Moreau, Joseph, 'L'argument ontologique chez Spinoza', *Les études philosophiques*, (1972), pp. 379–83.
Moreau, Joseph, 'Spinoza et la création', *Giornale di metafisica*, 32 (1977), pp. 487–505.
Moreau, Joseph, 'Nature et individualité chez Spinoza et Leibniz', *Revue philosophique de Louvain*, 76 (1978), pp. 447–56.
Moreau, Pierre-François, *Spinoza*, Paris: Seuil, 1975.
Moreau, Pierre-François, '*Jus et lex*: Spinoza devant la tradition juridique, d'après le dépouillement informatique du *Traité politique*', *Raison présente*, 43 (1977), pp. 53–61.
Moreau, Pierre-François, 'L'indexation du *Tractatus politicus*', *Cahiers Spinoza*, 1 (1977), pp. 229–33.
Moreau, Pierre-François, 'Spinoza et Victor Cousin', *Archivio di filosofia*, 1 (1978), pp. 327–31.
Moreau, P.-F., 'Spinozisme et matérialisme au XIXe siècle', *Raison présente*, 52 (1979), pp. 85–94.

Moreau, Pierre-François, 'Saisset, lecteur de Spinoza', *Recherches sur le XVIIe siècle*, 4 (1980), pp. 85–98.
Moreau, Pierre-François, 'Spinoza et l'Italie: le modèle vénitien', *Langues néo-latines*, 76 (1982), pp. 87–92.
Moreau, Pierre-François, 'Les premiers écrits: problèmes et ressources', 'Les premiers écrits de Spinoza', *Revue des sciences philosophiques et théologiques*, 71/1 (1987).
Moreau, Pierre-François, 'Nouveaux documents sur Spinoza', *Etudes philosophiques: Spinoza*, 4 (1987).
Moretti, Costanzi, T., *Spinoza*, Rome: Editrice Universitas, 1946.
Moretto, G., 'Prometeo contro Spinoza?', in *Etica et storia in Schleiermacher*, Naples: Bibliopolis, 1979, pp. 175–84.
Morichère, B., 'L'objet transcendental et la question du 'spinozisme' de Kant', *Cahiers philosophiques* (CNDP), 3 (1980), pp. 33–48.
Morrison, James C., 'The Ethics of Spinoza's *Ethics*', *Modern Schoolman*, 63 (1986), pp. 173–91.
Morteira, Saul Levi, *Tratado da Verdade de lei de Moises, escrito pelo seu proprio punho em português em Amsterdao 1659–1660*, ediçao facsimilada e leitura do autografo, introduçao e comentario por H. P. Salomon, Coimbra: Acta Universitatis Conimbrigensis, 1988.
Moura, Zaza, 'Dificil libertade – aspectos da filosofia de Espinosa em *The Fixer* de Bernard Malamud', *Filosofia*, 2 (1985), pp. 136–42.
Mugnier-Pollet, L., 'Esquisse d'une axiologie de Spinoza', *Les études philosophiques*, 3 (1972), pp. 385–97.
Mugnier-Pollet, L., *La philosophie politique de Spinoza*, Paris: Vrin, 1976.
Naess, Arne, 'Limited Definiteness of "God" in Spinoza's System. Answer to Heine Siebrand', *Neue Zeitschrift für Systematische Theologie und Religionsphilosophie*, 28/2 (1986), pp. 275–83.
Nahon, G., 'Amsterdam, métropole occidentale des Séfarades aux XVIIe siècle', *Cahiers Spinoza*, 3 (1980), pp. 15–50.
Negri, A., *L'anomalia selvaggia. Saggio su potere et potenza in Baruch Spinoza*, Milan: Feltrinelli, 1981.
Niccolo Stenone, 1638–1686, Florence: Olschki, 1988.
Nieuwentijt, Bernard, *Gronden van zekerheir. ter wedelegging van Spinosaas denkbeeldig samenstel*, Amsterdam, 1720.
Nieuwentijt, Bernard, *Een zekere, zakelijke wijsbegeerte*, introduction and notes by R. H. Vermij, Baarn: Ambo, 1988.
Niewöhner, Friedrich W., 'Ein schwieriges Maimonides-Zitat im *Tractatus theologico-politicus* und Hermann Cohens Kritik an Spinoza', *Zeitschrift für philosophische Forschung*, 31 (1977), pp. 618–26.

Niewöhner, Friedrich W., 'Maimonides und Spinoza', *Guest Lectures and Seminar Papers on Spinozism*, 1 (1986).

Niewöhner, Friedrich W., *Veritas sive varietas, Lessings Toleranzparabel und das Buch von den drei Betrügern*, Heidelberg: Lambert Schneider, 1988.

Norena, Carlos G., 'Suarez and Spinoza: The Metaphysics of Modal Being', *Cuadernos salmantinos de Filosofia*, 12 (1985), pp. 163–82.

Nourrisson, Jean-Félix, *Spinoza et le naturalisme contemporain*, Paris: Didier, 1866.

O'Higgins, J., *Yves de Vallone: The Making of an Esprit-fort*, The Hague: M. Nijhoff, 1982.

Offenberg, A. K., 'Spinoza's Liberty: The Story of a Reconstruction', *Quarendo, a quarterly journal from the low countries devoted to manuscripts and printed books*, 3 (1973), pp. 309–21.

Oittinen, Vesa, 'Idea adaequata und imaginäre Realitäten. Zur Spinoza-Rezeption der Althusser-Schule', *Aufklärung und Franzöische Revolution*, I, hrg. Juha Manninen, Oulu, 1986, pp. 151–231.

Olivetti, M. M., 'Da Leibniz a Bayle: alle radici degli 'Spinozabriefe'', *Archivio di filosofia* (1978), pp. 147–99.

Osier, J.-P., 'Judaïsme et hétérodoxie au siècle du Spinoza: les argument de Léon de Modène', *Bulletin de l'Association des Amis de Spinoza*, 5 (1981), pp. 1–3.

Osier, J.-P., *D'Uriel da Costa à Spinoza*, Paris: Berg International, 1983.

Osier, J.-P., 'Sur un inédit de Feuerbach relatif à Spinoza (texte "Sur le système spinoziste")', *Cahiers Spinoza*, 4 (1983), pp. 205–10.

Otto, R., 'Herder auf dem Wege zu Spinoza', *Weimarer Beiträge*, 24/10 (1977), pp. 165–76.

Pacchiani, C., *Spinoza tra teologica e politica*, Padua: Francisci, 1979.

Paganini, G., *Analisi della fede e critica della ragione nella filosofia di Pierre Bayle*, Florence: La Nuova Italia, 1980.

Parkinson, G. H. R., *Spinoza's Theory of Knowledge*, Oxford: The Clarendon Press, 1954.

Peña, Etcheverria F. Javier, *La Filosofia politica de Espinosa*, Vallodolid: Universidad de Vallodolid, 1989.

Peña, Garcia V. I., *El materialismo de Spinoza. Ensayo sobre la ontologia spinozista*, Madrid: Biblioteca de filosofía, 1974.

Perrot, Maryvonne, 'Spinoza, Rousseau et la notion de *dictamen*', *Les Etudes philosophiques* (1972), pp. 399–410.

Petitdemange, G., 'Les traversées de la fin. Spinoza, Kant, Derrida', *Recherches de science religieuse*, 68 (1980), pp. 358–90.

Petry, M. J., *Nieuwentijt's Criticism of Spinoza*, Leiden: Brill, 1979; Mededelingen vanwege het Spinozahuis, 40.

Philosophie et réception: Spinoza, Revue de métaphysique et de morale, 2 (1988).

Pietarinen, Juhani, 'Possible and Necessary Existence in Spinoza', *Annalen der Internationalen Gesellschaft für dialektische Philosophie*, Societas Hegeliana, 3 (1986), pp. 150–3.

Piguet, Jean-Claude, *Le Dieu de Spinoza*, Geneva: Labor et fides, 1987.

Pines, Shlomo, 'Note sur la conception spinoziste de la liberté humaine, du bien et du mal', *Bulletin de l'Association des Amis de Spinoza*, 6 (1981), pp. 13–25.

Pines, Shlomo, 'Nietzsche: Psychology vs. Philosophy, and Freedom', in Y. Yovel (ed.), *Nietzsche as Affirmative Thinker*, Dordrecht: M. Nijhoff, 1986, pp. 147–59.

Pires, Aurelio Diogo, 'Uriel da Costa: o discurso da vitima', *Analise*, 1 (1985), pp. 5–33.

Pires, Aurelio Diogo, 'Imaginaçao e razao face au contrato', *Analise*, 8 (1988), pp. 99–109.

Piro, Franceso, 'La differenza tra *in se esse* e *per se concipi*. Sulla critica leibniziana a Spinoza', *Instituto di Filosofia Annali Due* (1987), pp. 69–111.

Pitassi, Maria Cristina, *Entre croire et savoir, le problème de la méthode critique chez Jean le Clerc*, Leiden: Brill, 1987.

Pitassi, Maria Cristina, 'Un manuscrit genevois du XVIIIe siècle: *La Réfutation du système de Spinoza par M. Turrettini*', *Nederlands Archief voor Kerkgeschiedenis*, 68 (1988), pp. 180–212.

Pitts, Edward I., 'Spinoza on Freedom of Expression', *Journal of the History of Ideas*, 47 (1986), pp. 21–35.

Poch y Gutierrez de Cavedes, Antonio, 'Nexos hispanicos de Benito Espinosa', in *Estudios de filosofia del derecho y ciencia juridica en memoria y homenaje al catedratico don Luis Legaz y Lacambra*, vol. 2, Madrid: Centro de Estudios Constitucionales, 1985, pp. 251–64.

Pollock, Frederick, *Spinoza: His Life and Philosophy*, London: Kegan Paul, 1880 (new edn 1912, reprint of the 2nd edn, New York: American Scholar Publications, 1966).

Popkin, Richard H., 'Hume and Spinoza', *Hume Studies*, 5 (1979), pp. 65–93.

Popkin, Richard, H., *The History of Scepticism from Erasmus to Spinoza*, Berkeley: University of California Press, 1979.

Popkin, Richard H., 'Spinoza, the Quakers and the Millenarians, 1656–1658', *Manuscrito*, 6 (1982/1983), pp. 113–33.

Popkin, Richard, H., 'Spinoza a-t-il pu connaître le *Colloquium Heptaplomeres* de Bodin?', *Bulletin de l'Association des Amis de Spinoza*, 15 (1985).

Popkin, Richard H., 'Spinoza and Samuel Fischer', *Philosophia*, XV/3 (1985), pp. 219–36.
Popkin, Richard, H., 'Un autre Spinoza', *Archives de philosophie*, 48/1 (1985), pp. 37–58.
Popkin, Richard H., 'Serendipity at the Clark: Spinoza and the Prince of Condé', *The Clark Newsletter*, 10 (1986), pp. 4–7.
Popkin, Richard H., *Isaac La Peyrère (1596–1676): His Life, Work and Influence*, Leiden: Brill, 1987.
Popkin, Richard H., 'Some Seventeenth-Century Interpretations of Spinoza's Ideas', in C. Augustin et al. (eds), *Kerkhistorische opstellen aangeboden aan Prof. Dr. Jan van den Berg*, Kampen: Kok, 1987, pp. 63–74.
Popkin, Richard, H., 'The First Published Discussion of a Central Theme in Spinoza's Tractatus', *Philosophia*, 17 (1987), pp. 101–9.
Porges, N., 'Spinozas Compendium der hebräischen Grammatik', *Chr. sp.*, IV, 1924–26.
Portugueses em Amsterdao 1600–1680, red. por Renée Kistemaker e Tirtsah Levie, Amsterdams Historisch Museum/De Bataafsche Leeuw, Amsterdam, 1988.
Pousseur, J.-M., 'La première métaphysique spinoziste de la connaissance', *Cahiers Spinoza*, 2 (1978), pp. 287–314.
Préposiet, J., 'Remarques sur la doctrine de la double nécessité dans le spinozisme', *Revue internationale de philosophie*, 31 (1977), pp. 135–44.
Proietti, Omero, 'Sul problema di un assioma inutile in Spinoza', *Rivista di filosofia neo-scolastica*, 75 (1983), pp. 223–42.
Proietti, Omero, '*Adulescens luxu perditus*: classici latini nell'opera di Spinoza', *Rivista di Filosofia neoscolastica*, 2 (1985), pp. 210–57.
Puchet, E., 'Autoridade teologica e livre pensamento em Spinoza', *Discurso, faculdade de filosofia letras e ciencias humanas*, 12 (1981), pp. 83–97.
Radchik, Laura, 'La Beatitud en Baruch Spinoza', *Logos*, 14 (1986), pp. 95–102.
Ramond, Ch., 'La question de l'origine chez Spinoza', *Etudes philosophiques: Spinoza*, 4 (1987).
Ravoux, Jean-Philippe, 'Rêverie sur un inachèvement', *Revue de l'enseignement philosophique*, 37/3 (1985), pp. 12–30.
Ravven, Heidi M., 'Notes on Spinoza's Critique of Aristotle's Ethics: From Teleology to Process Theory', *Philosophy & Theology*, IV/1 (1989), pp. 3–31.
Raymond, Pierre, 'La générosité', *Cahiers philosophiques*, 35 (1988), pp. 7–21.
Redl, Karoly, 'Spinoza und Lessius', *Annales Universitatis Roland Eötvös*, sectio philosophica, 17 (1983), pp. 327–45.

Rensi, G., *Spinoza*, Rome: Formiggini, 1929 (Milan: Bocca, 1942).
Revah, I. S., 'Aux origines de la rupture spinozienne: nouvel examen des origines, du déroulement et des conséquences de l'affaire Spinoza-Prado-Ribera', *Annales du Collège de France*, 70 (1969/70), pp. 562–8; 71 (1970/71), pp. 574–89; 72 (1971/72), pp. 641–53.
Revah, I. S., 'Aux origines de la rupture spinozienne. Nouveaux documents sur l'incroyance dans la communauté judéo-portugaise d'Amsterdam à l'époque de l'excommunication de Spinoza', *Revue des Etudes juives*, 1964, III, fasc. 3, 4, pp. 359–431.
Revah, I. S., *Spinoza et le Dr. Juan de Prado*, Paris/The Hague: Mouton & Cie, 1959.
Revue philosophique, 2 (1985), 'Hobbes et Spinoza'.
Ribeiro, Ferreira Maria Luisa, 'A "outra parte" da Etica', *Filosofia*, 2 (1985), pp. 92–108.
Ribeiro, Ferreira Maria Luisa, 'Consideraçoens sobre o Deus de Espinosa: o itinerario da substância a Deus', *Ao Encontro da Palavra*, Homenagem a Manuel Antunes, Lisbon: Faculté des Lettres, 1986, pp. 87–121.
Rice, L. C., 'Spinoza on Individuation', *The Monist*, 55 (1971), pp. 640–59.
Rice, L. C., 'Emotion, Appetition, and *Conatus* in Spinoza', *Revue internationale de philosophie*, 31 (1977), pp. 101–16.
Rice, L. C., 'Spinoza's Account of Sexuality', *Philosophy Research Archives*, 10 (1985), pp. 19–34.
Rice, Lee C., 'Spinoza, Bennett, and Teleology', *The Southern Journal of Philosophy*, 23/2 (1985), pp. 241–53.
Rickman, H. P., *The Adventure of Reason: The Uses of Philosophy in Sociology*, Westport: Greenwood Press, 1983.
Riesinger, P., 'Hölderlin zwischen Fichte und Spinoza oder der Weg zu Hegel', in H. Bachmeier, Th. Retsch (hrsg.), *Poetische Autonomie? Zur Wechselwirkung von Dichtung und Philosophie in der Epoche Goethes und Hölderlins*, Stuttgart: Klett-Cotta, 1987.
Rivaud, Albert, *Les notions d'essence et d'existence dans la philosophie de Spinoza*, Paris: Alcan, 1906.
Robinet, A., 'Considerations lexicales sur "attribute" (*Ethica* 77)', *Raison présente*, 43 (1977), pp. 63–80.
Robinet, A., 'Expression ou expressivité selon *Ethica* 77', *Revue de synthèse*, 99 (1978), pp. 223–69.
Robinet, A., *Le langage à l'âge classique*, Paris: Klincksieck, 1978.
Robinet, A., 'Modèle géométrique et critique informatique dans le discours spinozien', *Studia leibnitiana*, 12 (1980), pp. 96–113.

Robinet, A., 'Ethica 77: premiers résultats informatiques sur le dépouillement lexical de l'Ethica de Spinoza (Substantia)', Recherches sur le XVIIe siècle, 4 (1980), pp. 67–84.

Robinet, A., 'Res et nihil dans Ethica 77', in Res. Atti del III colloquio internazionale del Lessico intellectuale europeo 1980, Rome, 1982.

Robinet, A., 'Theoria et praxis chez Spinoza et Leibniz', in Theoria cum praxi, vol. 2: Spinoza, Wiesbaden: Franz Steiner, 1981, pp. 20–30.

Robinet, A., 'Spiritus/esprit chez Spinoza et Malebranche', in Spiritus, a cura di M. Fattori e M. Bianchi, Rome, 1984, pp. 333–43.

Rodis-Lewis, Geneviève, 'Le monde philosophique contemporain de Spinoza', Revue de synthèse, 99 (1978), pp. 7–17.

Rodis-Lewis, Geneviève, 'Questions sur la cinquième partie de l'Ethique', Revue philosophique, 2 (1986), pp. 207–21.

Rohs, Peter, 'Transzendentalphilosophie als spatio-temporaler Spinozismus', in Gisela Müller und Thomas M. Seebohm (eds), Perspektiven transzendentaler Reflexion. Fetschrift Gerhard Funke, Bonn: Bouvier Verlag, 1989, pp. 99–108.

Roldan, Panadero Concha, 'Critica de Leibniz al determinismo absoluto de Spinoza', Revista de Filosofia, 7 (1984), pp. 327–38.

Rotenstreich, Nathan, 'Moses Hess – ein Jünger Spinozas?', Archiv für Geschichte der Philosophie, 71/2 (1989), pp. 231–47.

Rotenstreich, N. and Schneider, N. (eds), Spinoza: His Thought and Work. Interviews in Jerusalem, 6–9 September 1977, Jerusalem: Israel Academy of Sciences & Humanities, 1983.

Roth, Leon, Spinoza, Descartes and Maimonides, Oxford: The Clarendon Press, 1924 (New York: Russell & Russell, 1963).

Rottner, E., Spinoza in Israel. Eine kritische Betrachtung, Nieuwkoop: Heureka, 1979.

Rousset, Bernard, La perspective finale de l''Ethique' et le problème de la cohérence du spinozisme. L'autonomie comme salut, Paris: Vrin, 1968.

Rousset, Bernard, 'Homo homini deus. Anthropologie et humanisme dans une conception spinoziste de l'Etre', Cahiers de Fontenay, 39–40 (1985), pp. 133–9.

Rousset, Bernard, 'L'être du fini dans l'Infini selon l'Ethique de Spinoza', Revue philosophique, 2 (1986), pp. 223–47.

Rousset, Bernard, 'Le Spinoza d'Alain', in Alain lecteur des philosophes, présenté par Robert Bourgne, Paris: Bordas, 1987, pp. 83–94, discussion pp. 225–9.

Rousset, Bernard, 'Actualité du spinozisme à la fin du XXe siècle', Cahiers philosophiques, 35 (1988), pp. 23–38.

Rubel, M., 'Marx à la rencontre de Spinoza', *Cahiers Spinoza*, 1 (1977), pp. 7–28.
Russell, John M., 'Freedom and Determinism in Spinoza', *Auslegeng*, 11 (1984), pp. 378–89.
Saccaro Battisti, Giuseppa, 'Le origini della metafisica di Spinoza nell'Abbozzo del 1661', *De homine*, 42–3 (1972), pp. 19–142.
Saccaro Battisti, Giuseppa, 'Democracy in Spinoza's Unfinished *Tractatus Politicus*', *Journal of the History of Ideas*, 38 (1977), pp. 623–34.
Saccaro Battisti, Giuseppa, 'Sistemi politici del passato e del futuro nell'opera di Spinoza', *Giornale critico della filosofia italiana*, 56 (1977), pp. 506–49.
Saccaro Battisti, Giuseppa, 'Spinoza politico tra due rivoluzioni', *Archivio di filosofia* (1978), pp. 61–95.
Saccaro Battisti, Giuseppa, 'Spinoza, l'utopia e le masse: un'analisi dei concetti di *plebs, multitudo, populus e vulgus*', *Rivista critica di storia della filosofia*, 39 (1984), pp. 61–90; pp. 452–74.
Saccaro Battisti, Giuseppa, 'Herrera and Spinoza on Divine Attributes', *Italia*, 4 (1985), pp. 21–58.
Saccaro Battisti, Giuseppa, 'La cultura filosofica del Rinascimento italiano nella *Puerta del Cielo* di Abraham Cohen Herrera', *Italia Judaica* (1986), Atti del Il Convegno Internazionale, Genova 10–15 June 1984, pp. 295–334.
Sacksteder, William, 'Simples Wholes and Complex Parts', *Philosophy and Philosophical Research*, 45 (1985), pp. 393–406.
Saint-Sernin Bertrand, 'Une épistémologie du concept: Georges Canguilhem', *Cahiers philosophiques*, 23 (1985), pp. 7–14.
Saintes, Amand, *Histoire de la vie et des ouvrages de B. de Spinoza, fondateur d'exégèse et de la philosophie moderne*, Paris: Renouard, 1842.
Saisset, Emile, 'Sur la philosophie des Juifs: Maïmonide et Spinoza', *Revue des Deux Mondes*, XXXVI (1862), pp. 296–344.
Salazar, Freddy, *Marx y Spinoza. Problemas del Metodo y del conocimiento*, Antioquia: Universidad de Antioquia, 1986.
Sandys-Wunsch, J., 'Spinoza, the First Biblical Theologian', *Zeitschrift für alttestamentliche Wissenschaft*, 93 (1981), pp. 327–40.
Sanen, Hans, 'Baruch de Spinoza', in *Neuzeit: Von der Konfessionskriegen bis zur Aufklärung* (Pipers Handbuch der politischen Ideen, 3, chap. 8: *Die Vertragstheoretiker und deren Kritiker*), Munich/Zurich: Piper, 1985.
Santinelli, Cristina, 'La storiografia spinoziana contemporanea in Italia 1945–1969', *Istituto di Filosofia Annali Uno* (1986), pp. 57–120.
Santinelli, Cristina, 'Studi sul pensiero di Spinoza in Italia', *Cultura e scuola*, 97 (1986), pp. 87–103; and 99 (1986), pp. 115–37.

Sasso, R., 'Parcours du *De Deo* de Spinoza (*Ethique*, 1). Un exemple des fonctions de la systématicité dans la constitution du discours philosophique', *Archives de philosophie*, 44 (1981), pp. 579–610.

Savater, Fernando, 'Imaginacion religiosa y teologia politica en Spinoza', *Er*, 1/2 (1985), pp. 35–46.

Schaefer, Alfred, *Spinoza, Philosoph des europäischen Bürgertums*, Berlin: A. Spitz, 1989.

Schaub, M., 'Spinoza ou une philosophie politique galiléenne', in F. Châtelet (ed.), *Histoire de la philosophie*, vol. 3, Paris: Hachette, 1972, pp. 162–95.

Schaub, M., 'Philosophie politique en France et spinozisme', *Recherches sur le XVIIe siècle*, 2 (1978), pp. 140–8.

Schleiermacher, *Jugendschriften 1787–1796*, ed. G. Meckenstock, Berlin: de Gruyter, 1984 ('Spinozismus'; 'Kurze Darstellung des Spinozistischen Systems'; 'Ueber dasjenige in Jacobis Briefen und Realismus, was den Spinoza night betrifft, und besonders über seine eigene Philosophie').

Schmidt-Biggemann, W., 'Spinoza, Spionzismus, Geschichtlichkeit. Ein NachWort', in K. Cramer, W. G. Jacobs and W. Schmidt-Biggeman (eds), *Spinozas Ethik und ihre frühe Wirkung*, Wolfenbüttel: Herzog August Bibliotek, 1981, pp. 117–29.

Schmidt-Biggemann, W., 'Veritas particeps Dei. Der Spinozismus im Horizont mystischer und rationalistischer Theologie', in K. Gründer and W. Schmidt-Biggemann (eds), *Spinoza in der Frühzeit seiner religiösen Wirkung*, Heidelberg: Lambert Schneider, 1984, pp. 65–91.

Schneider, Monique, 'Le fini, l'autre et le savoir chez Spinoza et chez Freud', *Cahiers Spinoza*, 1 (1977), pp. 267–319.

Schobinger, J.-P., 'La portée historique des théories de la lecture', *Revue de théologie et de philosophie*, 112 (1980), pp. 43–56.

Schottlaender, Rudolf, 'Spinoza: ein Meister der Freiheit', *Zeitschrift für philosophische Forschung*, 31 (1977), pp. 511–26.

Schottlaender, Rudolf, 'Comment le libéralisme politique de Spinoza est-il comaptible avec son déterminisme éthique?', *Tijdschrift voor de studie van de Verlichting*, 6 (1978), pp. 191–203.

Schottlaender, Rudolf, 'Spinoza et le stoïcisme', *Bulletin de l'Assocation des Amis de Spinoza*, 17 (1986), pp. 1–8.

Schrader, Fred E., *Substanz und Begriff: Zur Spinoza-Rezeption Marxens*, Leiden: Brill, 1985; Mededelingen vanwege het Spinozahuis, 47.

Schrijvers, M., 'Johannes Müller, admirateur de Spinoza', *Bulletin de l'Association des Amis de Spinoza*, 9 (1982), pp. 11–13.

Schröder, Winifried, *Spinoza in der deutschen Frühaufklärung*, Würzburg: Königshausen & Neumann, 1987.

Schütt, Hans-Peter, 'Spinozas Konzeption der Modalitäten', *Neue Hefte für Philosophie*, 24/25 (1985), pp. 165–83.
Schwartz, Joël, 'Liberalism and the Jewish Connexion: A Study of Spinoza and the Young Marx', *Political Theory*, 13 (1985), pp. 58–84.
Scruton, Roger, *Spinoza*, Oxford: Oxford University Press, 1986.
Secrétan, Catherine, 'Partisans et détracteurs de Hobbes dans les Provinces-Unies du temps de Spinoza', *Bulletin de l'Association des Amis de Spinoza*, 2 (1979), pp. 2–13.
Secrétan, Catherine, 'Premières réactions néerlandaises à Hobbes au XVIIe siècle', *Annales d'histoire des facultés de droit*, 3 (1986), pp. 137–65.
Secrétan, Philibert, 'Du salut sans la grâce', in *Paradigmes de théologie philosophique*, Freiburg: Editions universitaires, 1983.
Seidel, H., 'Marxismus und Spinozismus', *Deutsche Zeitschrift für Philosophie*, 25 (1977), pp. 46–61.
Seidel, H. (ed.) *Marxismus und Spinozismus. Materialien einer wissenschaftlichen Konferenz*, Leipzig: Karl-Marx Universität, 1981.
Semarari, G., 'L'idea della scienza in Spinoza', *Quaderni di filosofia*, 1 (1978), pp. 9–23.
Semerari, G., 'L'ontologia della sicurezza in Spinoza', *Paradigmi*, 1 (1983), 1, pp. 33–55.
Shahan, R. W. and Biro, J. I. (eds), *Spinoza: New Perspectives*, Norman: University of Oklahoma Press, 1978; 1980.
Sheldon, M. 'Spinoza, Imagination and Chaos', *The Southern Journal of Philosophy*, 17 (1979), pp. 119–32.
Shimizu, R., 'La méthode et le donnée', in S. Hessing (ed.), *Speculum spinozanum 1677–1977* (1978), pp. 455–74.
Shimizu, R., 'Excommunication and the Philosophy of Spinoza', *Inquiry*, 23 (1980), pp. 327–48.
Siebrand, Heine J., 'Dutch Cartesianism and Spinozism, an Introduction', *Guest Lectures and Seminar Papers on Spinozism*, 2 (1986).
Siebrand, Heine J., 'Is God an "Open Place" in Spinoza's Philosophy of Religion?', *Neue Zeitschrift für systematische Theologie und Religionsphilosophie*, 28/3 (1986), pp. 261–74.
Siebrand, Heine J., *Spinoza and the Netherlanders: An Inquiry Into the Early Reception of his Philosophy of Religion*, Assen: Van Gorcum, 1988.
Siena, Robertomaria, 'Sull'antropologica e l'etica di Spinoza', *Sapienza*, 39 (1986), pp. 337–43.
Simonutti, Luisa, *Arminianismo e tolleranza nel seicento olandese, il carteggio Ph. van Limborch – J. Le Clerc*, Florence: Leo Olschki, 1984.

Slyomovics, Peter, 'Spinoza: Liberal Democratic Religion', *Journal of the History of Philosophy*, 23 (1985), pp. 499–513.

Snel, Robert, *Het hermetisch universum. Nietzsches verhouding tot Spinoza en de moderne ontologie*, Delft: Eburon, 1989; Mededelingen vanwege het Spinozahuis, 60.

Sonne, I., 'Un manoscritto sconosciuto delle *adnotationes* al *Trattato teologico-politica* di Spinoza', *Civiltà moderna*, 3–4 (1933).

Speculum spinozanum 1677–1977, numéro spécial de *Revue internationale de philosophie*, 31/119–20 (1977).

Spinoza entre Lumières et Romantisme, Actes du colloque tenu du 19 au 24 septembre 1983 à l'ENS de Fontenay, à l'initiative de Pierre-François Moreau, Michèle Crampe-Casnabet et Michèle Le Dœuff, Cahiers de Fontenay, 36–38 (March 1985), Fontenay-aux-Roses, 1985.

Spinoza herdacht 1677, 21 februari, 1977, Assen: Van Gorcum, 1977.

Spinoza in Soviet Philosophy, a series of essays selected and translated with an introduction by G. L. Kline. London, 1952; reprint: Westport, 1981.

Spinoza nel 350° anniversario della nascita. Atti del congresso internazionale Urbino 4–8 ottobre 1982, a cura di Emilia Giancotti, Naples: Bibliopolis, 1985.

Spinoza on Knowing, Being, and Freedom. Proceedings of the Spinoza Symposium at the International School of Philosophy in the Netherlands (Leusden, September 1973), ed. J. G. van der Bend, Assen: Van Gorcum, 1974.

Spinoza's Political and Theological Thought. International Symposium under the auspices of the Royal Netherlands Academy of Arts and Sciences. Commemorating the 350th Anniversary of the Birth of Spinoza, Amsterdam 24–27 November 1982, C. de Deugd (ed.), Amsterdam: North Holland, 1984.

Spinoza, Sciences et Religion, De la méthode géométrique à l'interprétation de l'Ecriture Sainte, Actes du colloque de Cerisy la Salle, 20–27 September 1982, IIEE, Lyon, Paris: Vrin, 1988.

Spinoza. Troisième centenaire de la mort du philosophe. Catalogue de l'exposition mai-juin 1977, Paris: Institut néerlandais, 1977.

Sprigge, T. L. S., *The Significance of Spinoza's Determinism*, Leiden: Brill, 1989; Mededelingen vanwege het Spinozahuis, 58.

Starobinski-Safran, Esther, 'Histoire et appartenance culturelle: le cas de Spinoza', *Cahiers internationaux du symbolisme*, 56–58 (1987).

Steenbakkers, Piet, *Over kennis en ideologie hij Louis Althusser. Een materialistische kritiek*, Groningen, 1982.

Steenbakkers, Piet, *Opera minora van Spinoza. Een bespreking en aantekeningen*, Amsterdam: Richard Tummers boekverkoper, 1988.

Steinberg, Diane, 'Spinoza's Ethical Doctrine and the Unity of Human Nature', *Journal of the History of Philosophy*, 11 (1981), pp. 35–68.

Steinberg, Diane, 'A Note on Bennett's Transattribute Differentiae and Spinoza's Substance Monism', *Southern Journal of Philosophy*, 24/3 (1986), pp. 431–45.

Steinberg, Diane, 'Necessity and Essence in Spinoza', *Modern Schoolman*, 64 (1987), pp. 187–95.

Strauss, Leo, *Die Religionskritik Spinozas als Grundlage seiner Biblewissenschaft. Unterschungen zu Spinozas Theologisch-politischen Traktat*, Berlin: Akademie-Verlag, 1930.

Strauss, Leo, 'How to Study Spinoza's Theologico-political Treatise', *Proceedings of the American Academic for Jewish Research*, XVII (1948), pp. 69–113 (reprinted in *Persecution and the Art of Writing*, pp. 142–201).

Strauss, L., *Persecution and the Art of Writing*, Glencoe: Free Press, 1952; reprint: Westport, 1973.

Studi sul Seicento e sull'immaginazione, a cura di Paolo Cristofolini, Pisa: Scuola Normale Superiore di Pisa, 1985.

Teensma, B. N. 'Sefardim en Portugese Taalkunde in Nederland', *Studia spinozana*, XIX/1 (1985), pp. 39–74.

Teixeira, Livio, *A doctrina dos modos de percepçao e o conceito de abstraçao na filosofia de Espinoza*, Sao Paulo: Fac. de Filos., 1988 (1954).

Tejedor, Campomanes, C., *Una antropologia del conocimiento. Estudio sobre Spinoza*, Madrid: Universidad Pontificia Comillas, 1981.

Texte zur Geschichte des Spinozismus, ed. N. Altwicker, Darmstadt, 1971.

Theoria cum praxi. Zum Verhältnis von Theorie und Praxis im 17. und 18. Jahrhundert. Akten des III. internationalen Leibnizkongresses, Hannover, 12. bis 17. november 1977, vol. 2: *Spinoza*, Wiesbaden: Franz Steiner, 1981.

Thijssen-Schoute, Caroline Louise, *Nederlands Cartesianisme*, Amsterdam, 1954; Utrecht: HES uitgevers BV, 1989.

Thiry, B., 'Désutopie et transition: l'actualité de la politique spinoziste selon A. Negri', in G. Labica and M. Delbraccio, *De Marx au marxisme*, Paris: CNRS, 1986, pp. 167–80.

Tilliette, Xavier, 'Foi et savoir dans le conflit des autorités', *Les études philosophiques*, 2 (1977), pp. 157–67.

Tilliette, Xavier, 'Spinoza devant le Christ', *Nouvelles de l'Institut catholique de Paris*, 2 (1977), pp. 2–17.

Tilliette, Xavier, 'Spinoza préromantique. Aspects de la première renaissance', *Archivio di filosofia* (1978), pp. 217–29.

Tilliette, Xavier, 'Schelling et Spinoza', *Bulletin de l'Association des Amis de Spinoza*, 22 (1989).

Timm, Hermann, *Gott und die Freiheit. Studien zur Religionsphilosophie der Goethe-zeit*, vol. 1, *Die Spinozarenaissance*, Frankfurt: Klostermann, 1974.

Timm, Hermann, 'Amor Dei intellectualis. Die teleologische Systemidee des romantischen Spinozismus', *Neue Hefte für Philosophie*, 12 (1977), pp. 64–91.

Todorov, T., *Symbolisme et interprétation*, Paris: Seuil, 1978, pp. 125–38 and 157–9.

Tognon, G., 'Leibniz, Toland et Spinoza. Une lettre inédite à propos des Lettres à Serena', *Bulletin de l'Association des Amis de Spinoza*, 12 (1984), pp. 2–11.

Tombeur, P., 'L'analyse par ordinateur du vocabulaire de l'*Ethique* de Spinoza: méthodes et résultats', in *Theoria cum praxi*, vol. 2: *Spinoza*, Wiesbaden: Franz Steiner, 1981, pp. 189–202.

Tosel, André, 'Résumé de sa thèse de doctorat d'Etat sur *Religion, politique, philosophie chez Spinoza*', *Bulletin de l'Association des Amis de Spinoza*, 8 (1982), pp. 14–19.

Tosel, André, *Spinoza ou le crépuscule de la servitude. Essai sur le 'Traité théologico-politique'*, Paris: Aubier, 1984.

Tosel, André, 'La marxisme au miroir de Spinoza', *Guest Lectures and Seminar Papers on Spinozism*, 6 (1988).

Totaro, Giuseppina, 'Spinoza nei *classici della filosofia moderna*. Per una storia dell'edizione gentiliana dell'*Ethica*', *Giornale critico della filosofia italiana*, 45/2 (1986), pp. 273–83.

Totaro, Giuseppina, 'Perfectio e realitas nell'opera di Spinoza', *Lexicon philosophicum*, 3 (1988), pp. 71–113.

Touati, C., 'L'excommunication de Spinoza', *Annales de l'Ecole pratique des hautes études*, 80–81 (1974), pp. 221–3.

Touati, C., 'Croyances vraies et croyanes nécessaires (Platon, Averroes, philosophie juive et Spinoza)', in *Hommage à Georges Vajda*, Louvain: Peeters, 1980, pp. 169–82.

Troisfontaine, Claude, 'Liberté de pensée et soumission politique selon Spinoza', *Revue philosophique de Louvain*, 84 (1986), pp. 187–206.

Troisfontaine, Claude, 'Maurice Blondel et Victor Delbos', *Revue philosophique de la France et de l'étranger*, 111 (1986), pp. 467–83.

Trompetter, L., 'Spinoza: A Response to De Vries', *Canadian Journal of Philosophy*, 11 (1981), pp. 525–37.

Trouillard, J., *L'action chez Spinoza*, Paris: Institut catholique, 1972.

Trouillard, J., *Procession et conversion chez Spinoza*, Paris: 1972.

Trouillard, J., 'Le quiétisme de Spinoza', *Nouvelles de l'Institut catholique de Paris*, 2 (1977), pp. 18–21.

Trouillard, J., 'Proclos et Spinoza', *Bulletin de l'Association des Amis de Spinoza*, 6 (1981), pp. 1–12.

Tschirnhaus, E. W. von., *Médecine de l'esprit, ou préceptes généraux de l'art de découvrir*, introduction, traduction, notes et appendices par J.-P. Wurtz, Paris: Ophrys, 1980.

Tschirnhaus, E. W. von, *Medecina Mentis*, Naples: Guida, 1987.

Ueno, Osamu, 'Le reste (les autres collectifs) – Spinoza et le paradoxe du contrat social de Hobbes', *Cartesiana*, Mémoires du département I de Philosophie et d'histoire de la Philosophie de la Faculté des Lettres d'Osaka, 8 (1988), p. 27 sq. (in Japanese; summary in French); French version in *Cahiers Spinoza*, VI (1990).

Van Balen, Petrus, *De verbetering der gedachten*, Uitgegeven, ingeleid en van aantekeningen voorzien door M. J. van den Hoven, Baarn: Ambo, 1988; Geschniedenis van de wijsbegeerte in Nederland, 11.

Van den Hoven, M. J., *Petrus van Balen en Spinoza over de verbetering van het verstand*, Leiden: Brill, 1988; Mededelingen vanwege het Spinozahuis, 55.

Van der Hoeven, P., *De cartesiaanse fysica in het denken van Spinoza*, Leiden: Brill, 1973; Mededelingen vanwege het Spionzahuis, 30.

Van der Hoeven, P., 'Over Spinoza's interpretatie van de cartesiaanse fysica, en de betekenis daarvan voor het systeem der Ethica', *Tijdschrift voor filosofie*, 35 (1973), pp. 27–86.

Van der Tak, W. G., 'De Ludovico Meyer', *Chr. sp.*, I, 1921.

Van der Wal, G. A., *Politieke vrijheid en demokratie bij Spinoza*, Leiden: Brill, 1980; Mededelingen vanwege het Spinozahuis, 41.

Van Heemst, Jean, 'Omnis determinatio negatio est? Hegels lezing van Spinoza polemisch getoetst door Pierre Macherey', *Algemeen Nederlands Tijdschrift voor Wijsbegeerte*, 77 (1985), pp. 222–34.

Van Peursen, C. A., *Eindigheid bij Spinoza*, Leiden: Brill, 1977; Mededelingen vanwege het Spinozahuis, 37.

Van Slee, J. C., *De Rijnsburger collegianten*, Haarlem, 1895; Utrecht: Herdruk, 1980.

Van Suchtelen, Guido (ed.), *Spinoza's sterfhuis aan de Paviljoensgracht. Levensbericht van een Haags monument 1646–1977*, The Hague, 1977.

Van Suchtelen, Guido, 'François van den Enden, précepteur de Spinoza', *Bulletin de l'Association des Amis de Spinoza*, 1 (1979), pp. 3–14.

Van Suchtelen, Guido, 'Une lettre de Spinoza inédite en français', *Bulletin de l'Association des Amis de Spinoza*, 10 (1983), pp. 1–5.

Van Suchtelen, Guido, K. O. 'Meinsma en de kring van Spinoza', *Tijdschrift voor de studie van de verlichting*, I (1985), pp. 69–75.

Vandenbossche, H., *Adriaan Koerbagh en Spinoza*, Leiden: Brill, 1978; Mededelingen vanwege het Spinozahuis, 39.

Vandenbossche, J., 'Quelques idées politiques de Koerbagh', *Tijdschrift voor de studie van de Verlichting*, 6/1–3 (1978).

Vandenbossche, H., 'Le spinozisme d'Adriaan Koerbagh: une première analyse', *Bulletin de l'Association des Amis de Spinoza*, 1 (1979), pp. 15–36.

Vaz Dias, A. M., *Spinoza and Simon Joosten De Vries*; Van der Tak, W. G., *Jarich Jellesz' Origins*; *Jellesz' Life and Business*, Delft: Eburon, 1989; Mededelingen vanwege het Spinozahuis, 59.

Vaz Dias, A. M. and van der Tak W. G., *Spinoza Mercator et Autodidactus. Oorkonden en andere authenticke Documenten betreffende des Wijsgeers jeugd en Diens betrekkingen*, The Hague: M. Nijhoff, 1933; *Spinoza Merchant and Autodidact*, Assen: Van Gorcum, 1982.

Vazquez, Juan, 'El limite de conocimiento en la filosofia de Spinoza', *Dianoia*, 30 (1984), pp. 111–21.

Vazquez, Rodolfo, 'El proceso de la religion en Lutero, Spinoza y Bayle', *Estudios*, 10 (1987), pp. 43–66.

Vermij, R. H., 'De Nederlands Vriendenkring van E. W. von Tschirnhaus', *Tijdschrift voor de Geschiedenis der Geneeskunde, Natuurweteschappen, Wiskunde en Techniek*, 11 (1988), pp. 153–78.

Vernière, Paul, *Spinoza et la pensée française avant la Révolution*, Paris: PUF, 1954.

Vieira, Jordao Franciso, 'Iluminismo e tradiçao do texto religioso em Espinosa', *Tradiçao e crise*, 1 (1986), pp. 186–243.

Viguier, A., 'Vielles outres et vins nouveaux, penseurs nouveaux et langus anciennes', *Cahiers de littérature du XVIIe siècle*, 6 (1984), pp. 433–49.

Vink, H. J., *Plotiniaanse en spinozistische elementen in de esthetische opvattingen van de kunstpedagog Bremmer*, Leiden: Brill, 1988; Mededelingen vanwege het Spinahuis, 54.

Vinti, C., *La filosofia come 'vitae meditatio'. Una lettura di Spinoza*, Rome: Città Nuova, 1979.

Vinti, C., 'Possibilità di una antropologia in Spinoza. Due posizioni a confronto', in *Vetera novis augere. Studi in onore de Carlo Giacon per il 25o convegno degli assistenti universitari del movimento di Gallarate*, Rome: La Goliardica, 1982, pp. 265–77.

Vinti, C., 'Recherches sur Spinoza en Italie 1945–1979', *Cahiers Spinoza*, 4 (1983), pp. 243–71.

Vinti, C., *Spinoza. La conoscenza come liberazione*, Rome: Studium Roma, 1984.

Violette, R., 'Méthode inventive et méthode inventée dans l'introduction au *De intellectus emendatione* de Spinoza', *Revue philosophique de la France et de l'étranger*, 102 (1977), pp. 303–22.

Voss, S. H., 'How Spinoza Enumerated the Affects', *Archiv für Geschichte der Philosophie*, 63 (1981), pp. 167–79.

Vuilliaud, Paul, *Spionza d'après les livres de sa bibliothèque*, Paris: Chacornac, 1934.

Walker, Ralph C. S., 'Spinoza and the Coherence Theory of Truth', *Mind*, 94 (1985), pp. 1–18.

Walther, Manfred, 'Die gesellschaftliche Begründung der Vernunft bei Spinoza', in G. H. R. Parkinson (ed.), *Truth, Knowledge and Reality. Inquiries into the Foundations of Seventeenth Century Rationalism*, Wiesbaden: Franz Steiner, 1981, pp. 44–55.

Walther, Manfred, *Metaphysik als Anti-Theologie. Die Philosophie Spinozas im Zusammenhang der religionsphilosophischen Problematik*, Hamburg: F. Meiner, 1971.

Walther, Manfred, 'Spinoza als Kritiker der Neuzeit? Bestimmungen der Aktualität Spinozas in der neuren Literatur', *Philosophische Rundschau*, 28 (1981), pp. 274–300.

Walther, Manfred, 'Spinozas Religionsphilosophie als Gesellschaftstheorie. Zu Stanislas Breton: Spinoza Théologie et politique 1977', *Studia leibnitiana*, 14 (1982), pp. 48–55.

Weischedel, W., *Der Gott der Philosophen*, vol. 1, Munich: Lambert Schneider, 1971; 1979 (pp. 175–183: 'Die philosophische Theologie bei Spinoza').

Wenzel, A., *Die Weltanschauung Spinozas*, vol. 1: *Spinozas Lehre von Gott, von der menschlichen Erkenntnis und von dem Wesen der Dinge*, Leipzig, 1907, Aalen: Scientia, 1983.

Wernham, A. G., 'Le contrat social chez Spinoza', *Revue de synthèse*, 99 (1978), pp. 69–77.

Wetlesen, J., 'Recherches récentes sur Spinoza en Norvège', *Cahiers Spinoza*, 2 (1978), pp. 315–18.

Wetlesen, J. (ed.), *Spinoza's Philosophy of Man: Proceedings of the Scandinavian Spinoza Symposium 1977*, Oslo: University of Oslo Press, 1978.

Wetlesen, J., *The Sage and the Way: Spinoza's Ethics of Freedom*, Assen: Van Gorcum, 1979.

Wiedmann, F., *Baruch de Spinoza. Eine Hinführung*, Würzburg: Königshausen & Neumann, 1982.

Wiehl, R., *Die Vernunft in der menschlichen Unvernunft. Das Problem der Rationalität in Spinozas Affektenlehre*, Göttingen, 1983.

Wienpahl, P., *The Radical Spinoza*, New York: New York University Press, 1979.

Wilbur, J. B. (ed.), *Spinoza's Metaphysics: Essays in Critical Appreciation*, Assen: Van Gorcum, 1976.
Williams, Forrest, 'Some Reflections on Spinoza's Ethics as Edifying Ontology', in E. Casey (ed.), *The Life of the Transcendental Ego*, Albany, NY: SUNY Press, 1986, pp. 95–110.
Wolfson, H. A., *The Philosophy of Spinoza: Unfolding the Latent Process of his Reasoning*, Cambridge, MA: Harvard University Press, 1934; 1983, 2 vols in one.
Wollgast, Siegfried, *Ehrenfried Walter von Tschirnhaus und die deutsche Frühaufklärung*, Berlin: Akademie-Verlag, 1988.
Wurtz, Jean-Paul, 'Tschirnhaus et l'accusation de spinozisme: la polémique avec Christian Thomasius', *Bulletin de l'Association des Amis de Spinoza*, 1 (1979), pp. 37–50.
Wurtz, Jean-Paul, 'Tschirnhaus et Spinoza', in *Theoria cum praxi*, vol. 2: *Spinoza*, Wiesbaden: Franz Steiner, 1981, pp. 93–103.
Wurtz, Jean-Paul, 'L'éthique et le concept de Dieu chez Tschirnhaus: l'influence de Spinoza', in *Spinoza's Political and Theological Thought*, Amsterdam: North Holland, 1984, pp. 230–42.
Wurtz, Jean-Paul, 'Über einige offene oder strittige, die *Medicina Mentis* von Tschirnhaus betreffende Fragen', *Studia Leibnitiana*, 20/2 (1988), pp. 190–211.
Wurzer, W. S., *Nietzsche und Spinoza*, Meisenheim a. Glan: Hain, 1975.
Yakira, Elhanana, 'Etudes spinozistes en Israël', *Cahiers Spinoza*, 3 (1980), pp. 271–7.
Yerushalmi, Yosef Hayim, *De la Cour d'Espagne au ghetto italien*, Paris: Fayard, 1987.
Yovel, Yirmiyahu, 'Bible Interpretation as Philosophical Praxis: A Study of Spinoza and Kant', *Journal of the History of Philosophy*, 11 (1973), pp. 189–203.
Yovel, Yirmiyahu, 'Why Spinoza Was Excommunicated', *Commentary*, 64/5 (1977), pp. 46–52.
Yovel, Yirmiyahu, 'Marranisme et dissidence. Spinoza et quelque prédéesseurs', *Cahiers Spinoza*, 3 (1980), pp. 67–99.
Yovel, Yirmiyahu, 'Heinrich Heine and the Message of Pantheism', *Jerusalem Quarterly*, 35 (1985), pp. 101–11.
Yovel, Yirmiyahu, 'Nietzsche and Spinoza: Amor Fati and Amor Dei', in Y. Yovel (ed.), *Nietzsche as Affirmative Thinker*, Dordrecht: M. Nijhoff, 1986, pp. 183–203.
Yovel, Yirmiyahu, *Spinoza vekoufrim akherim* (Spinoza and other heretics),

Tel-Aviv: Sifriat Paolim, 1988; *Spinoza et d'autres hérétiques*, trad. par J. Lagrée et E. Beaumatin, Paris: Seuil, 1991.

Zac, Sylvain, *La Morale de Spinoza*, Paris: PUF, 1959, 1972.

Zac, Sylvain, *L'idée de vie dans la philosophie de Spinoza*, Paris: PUF, 1963.

Zac, Sylvain, *Spinoza et l'interprétation de l'Ecriture*, Paris: PUF, 1965.

Zac, Sylvain, *Philosophie, théologie, politique dans l'œuvre de Spinoza*, Paris: Vrin, 1979.

Zac, Sylvain, *Essais spinozistes*, Paris: Vrin, 1985.

Zac, Sylvain, *Spinoza en Allemagne. Mendelssohn, Lessing et Jacobi*, Paris: Méridiens Klincksieck, 1989.

Zuber, R. 'Spinozisme et tolérance chez le jeune Papin', *Dix-huitième Siècle*, 4 (1972), pp. 217–27.

Zuber, R., 'Isaac Papin lecteur de Spinoza', *Bulletin de l'Association des Amis de Spinoza*, 11 (1983), pp. 1–14.

Zubimendi, Martinez Julian, 'La teoria de la distinctiones en Espinosa', *Pensamiento*, 41 (1985), pp. 257–79.

Zweerman, T. H., *Spinoza en de hdendaagse kritiek op het humanisme als idologie*, Leiden: Brill, 1975; Mededelingen vanwege het Spionzahuis, 34.

Zweerman, T. H., *Spinoza's inleiding tot de filosofie. Een vertaling en structuuranalyse van de inleiding der Tractatus de intellectus emendatione; benevens een commentaar bij deze tekst*, Leuven: Catholic University of Leuven, 1983.

Index of Names

Alquié, Ferdinand, 191, 193
Althusser, Louis, ix, 575–6, 583, 584, 586–8, 597
Antoninus, Marcus Aurelius, 54, 58, 74
Aristippus, 74, 153–4n143
Aristotle, xi, 23, 42n79, 48n94, 59, 113, 135, 136, 142, 158, 162, 225, 309, 333, 419, 483
   Eudemian Ethics, 133
   Nicomachean Ethics, 126, 127, 136–8
   Rhetoric, 392
Augustine of Hippo, 34n51, 36, 38n67, 38n70, 39n72, 39n73, 40, 77, 132, 141–2

Bachelard, Gaston, 271, 290
Bacon, Francis, 58, 111, 257, 258–60, 267, 272, 274, 320, 321n16, 591
Boethius, 142, 146, 148, 160
Boyle, Robert, xiv, 249, 278–91

Cicero, Marcus Tullius, 43, 68, 132, 138–9, 177n6, 311, 400, 434
Cousin, Victor, xiv, 236–7, 241, 242, 247, 298n202, 569–70, 586
Curtius Rufus, Quintus, 310, 383, 391
   History of Alexander the Great, 484–6

De Vries, Simon, 303–4, 499
Delbos, Victor, 60, 74, 571
Deleuze, Gilles, xx, 289–90, 575, 598
Desanti, Jean-Toussaint, viii–ix, 3–4, 581–3, 594

Descartes, René, xiii, xiv, xvii, 24, 54, 57, 58, 60, 67n153, 69–72, 95, 102–12, 117n14, 121n27, 136, 143, 195, 196n96, 237, 245, 247, 248, 250n50, 271, 272, 277–8, 288, 291, 320, 337n63, 348, 538, 541, 555–7, 569, 572, 584, 591, 596
   Meditations, 70, 71, 87, 111, 244, 245
   The Discourse on Method, 54, 56, 95, 110, 111, 278, 286
   The Passions of the Soul, 590, 600

Epicurus, 58, 505, 506
Euclid, 372–4, 594

Galilei, Galileo, 274, 275n122, 275n126, 277, 291
Gebhardt, Carl, 3, 49, 54, 55, 69, 104
Gueroult, Martial, xx, 57n128, 61, 225n65, 227n77, 267, 329, 389, 511, 513, 565, 566, 571, 572, 575, 576, 584, 597, 598, 599, 600

Hegel, Georg Wilhelm Friedrich, xiii, 47n90, 236, 237n10, 572, 585
   The Phenomenology of Spirit, 215–16
Hobbes, Thomas, xiii, xvii, 53, 54, 96, 111, 122, 123, 124, 125, 127, 161n13, 196n46, 205, 309, 337n63, 360, 363, 368, 372, 379–91, 383, 384, 392n8, 394, 416–24, 431–2, 514, 574

Behemoth, 432
De Corpore, 130n57
De Cive, 413
De Homine, 158n10, 205n26
De Natura humana, 122–3, 124–5, 423
Leviathan, 205n26, 393, 423, 427

Jelles, Jarig, 416–18

Klever, Wim, 292–7
Koyré, Alexandre, 84, 86, 115, 117, 135–6, 146, 167

Leibniz, Gottfried Wilhelm, 60, 246, 247, 250n50
Leo the Hebrew, 146, 147
Lucretius, 177n6, 505, 538, 541, 596, 598
  De Natura Rerum, 505–6

Malebranche, Nicolas, 132, 320
Macherey, Pierre, 207n32, 577
Machiavelli, Niccolò, 244, 245, 468, 490, 492, 495, 593, 598
Maimonides, 361, 363
Matheron, Alexandre, viii–ix, xx, 3, 4, 49, 64, 227n77, 229, 453, 454, 525, 575, 576, 598
Meyer, Lodewijk, 363, 372, 374, 379

Ovid, 68n155, 366, 400, 405, 504

Pascal, Blaise, xiii, 74, 132, 161n13, 191, 225, 571, 572
  On the Conversion of the Sinner, 194–5
  Pensées, 191–4
Plato, 131
  Euthydemus, 43, 47–8
  Gorgias, 101
Polybius, 482–3

Saisset, Emile, xiv, 115, 236–49, 254, 256, 290, 300, 303, 304, 526, 569, 586
Sallust, 434, 578
Schopenhauer, Arthur, x, 21, 22, 52
  The World as Will and Representation, 19–20
Seneca, xi, 43, 56–7, 59, 68, 101, 132, 136, 139–41, 148, 154n143, 155, 169n29, 311, 375, 403, 435
Solomon, 94, 369, 488, 509, 514
Strauss, Leo, 250, 378, 594

Tacitus, Publius Cornelius, 310, 375, 387, 401
Terence, 375, 434
  Adelphoe, 394n35, 401, 578

Wetlesen, Jon, 299–303

Zac, Sylvain, 32, 128, 327, 573, 575, 598

Index of Concepts

Animus, 125, 126, 168, 172, 177–90, 198
affects, 338–41, 393–5
   and experience 394–406

Bible *see* Scripture
body, 526, 533–42
   relation to the soul, 533–42

certainty, 75–112
common life (*communis vita*), 114–19, 127–31
common notions, 264–6, 269, 290, 311

eternity, 510, 511, 512–25, 544–59; *see also* experience of eternity
experience (*experientia*), x–xv, 1–2, 65–8, 72, 202–32, 303–16, 499–500, 525, 527–8, 560–7, 569–70, 593–5
   and affective kernels, 433–52
   of eternity, xviii–xix, 1, 499, 542–59
   and history, 477–96
   in the history of Spinoza scholarship, 236–48
   and mystical experience, 297–303
   of the self, 533–42
   see also fortune; language; vague experience
experimentum, 273–4; *see also* Boyle

fortune, 477–90, 592
   and history, 493–6
   and virtue, 490–3

haec tria, 114, 133–56, 199; *see also* honours; pleasure; wealth
Hebrew State, 429, 431, 437, 443, 447–50, 451, 455–6, 469, 470, 474, 495
history *see* fortune
honours, 118, 119, 129, 147–9, 163–4, 173, 178

ingenium, xvi–xvii, 265, 373, 390
   of the individual, 406–21
   of peoples, 416–52
imagination, 263–8, 277, 321, 324, 326–30, 335

Knowledge, 255, 256, 260–9

language
   and freedom of speech, 379–87
   and the imagination, 326–30, 335
   as a specific kind of image, 330–6
   Spinoza's critique of language, 319–26
   see also Scripture
life, 128–31

natural right, 419–52

passions *see* affects
pleasure, 118, 145–7, 160–1, 173, 178

remedium, 169–76

scientific experimentation, 271–92, 303
   Spinoza's discussion with Boyle, 279–92

Scripture, 256, 268, 269, 306, 318, 336, 345–79
  and biblical hermeneutics, 359–75
  see also language
Sovereign Good, 157, 158, 159, 160, 162, 166, 197–8, 202, 205, 206
State
  as individual, 452–70
  separation of Church and State, 416–19
  see also natural right

true good, 157–76

vague experience (*experientia vaga*), xiv, 238, 239, 246, 255–68, 270–1, 303, 394, 591–2
  in Bacon's work, 258–60

wealth, 120, 149–51, 157, 162–3, 178

Index Locorum

Cogitata Metaphysica 238n17, 364, 376
- I   319–20, 330, 504, 514, 523
- II   319, 445, 523
- III   324
- IV   226, 516, 523
- V   517
- VI   377
- X   323

Descartes' Principles of Philosophy 218, 276, 527, 555
Preface by Meyer 556

I
- Ax. 1   107
- 15 Schol.   317

III
- Def. 3   226

Ethics xii, xiii, xiv, xxi, 3, 9, 28, 29n42, 31, 50, 55, 60, 61, 64, 116, 127, 196, 207, 237, 238n17, 245, 256, 261, 289, 296, 299, 303, 321, 328, 369, 395, 524–6, 533, 561, 564, 570, 585, 590, 594

I
- Def. 8   175, 513, 520
- Ax. 4   528, 547
- Ax. 5   528
- 8 Schol. 2   28, 502–4
- 10 Schol.   515
- 11 Dem.   323
- 15   176, 547
- 15 Schol.   323
- 15 Schol. 2   28
- 16   510
- 17 Schol.   521, 528
- 17 Cor. 2 Schol.   517
- 25   547
- 25 Cor.   228
- 26   228
- 27   228
- 28   228
- 29   228, 510
- App.   310, 315–16, 408, 411, 442, 450, 460, 469, 481, 500, 507, 509

II
- Praef.   296, 331
- Def. 3   262
- Ax. 2   529
- Ax. 4   528–9
- Ax. 5   528–9
- 1   530
- 2   530, 533
- 2 Schol.   534
- 3   530, 547
- 4   530
- 5   530

6	530
7	515, 530
7 Dem.	524
7 Schol.	524
8	530
8 Cor.	528
9	530
10	530
11	528, 530
12	530
13	528, 531, 548–9
13 Cor.	528, 530
13 Schol.	454, 460, 530–1, 549
Lem. 4	357
Lem. 5	357
Lem. 6	357
Lem. 7 Schol.	453
15	527
16	529
16 Cor. 1	529
16 Cor. 2	528–9
17	529
17 Cor.	263, 529
17 Schol.	263, 327, 528–9, 532
18 Schol.	263, 322, 331–4
20	529
21	529, 531
21 Schol.	531
22	529
23	529
27 Schol.	252
28 Schol.	267
30	516
31	516
35 Schol.	460
36 Cor. Dem.	388
37	510
38	510
39 Dem. Cor.	508
40 Schol.	323
40 Schol. 2	250, 256, 260, 264
41	241, 256, 264
42	241, 251, 256, 264
42 Dem.	251
42 Schol.	310
43 Schol.	106–7
44	510–11
44 Schol.	267, 549
44 Cor. 1 Schol.	517
44 Cor. 2	510–11
44 Cor. 2 Dem.	516
47 Schol.	323
49 Schol	324, 388, 487, 491
49 Cor. Schol.	107, 253, 316, 487, 492
61	250
62	250

III
Praef.	395, 405, 408
2	381, 405, 533
2 Schol.	252, 315, 381–2, 533–40
4	459
6	228
7	228, 457
9 Dem.	460
9 Schol.	460, 462
11 Schol.	151
13 Cor.	398
19–26	466
27	564
29 Schol.	395
32 Schol.	316, 396
35	450
35 Schol.	450
37	413
39 Schol.	411
44 Schol.	394
45	466
46	471
47 Schol.	397
50 Schol.	396
51	394
52 Schol.	339–40
55	398
55 Cor. Dem. Schol.	399
55 Schol.	398–9
56 Schol.	296–7

III (*cont.*)
57	406
57 Schol.	295–6
59 Schol.	146, 297, 404
DA #4 Exp.	339
DA #19 Exp.	340
DA #20 Exp.	376
DA #23 Exp.	376
DA #24 Exp.	376
DA #27 Exp.	152, 396
DA #31 Exp.	340
DA #33 Exp.	340
DA #44 Exp.	400
DA #48	147, 339
DA #48 Exp.	339–40

IV
Praef.	202, 204, 206, 477
3	88
3 Schol.	117
4	88
18 Schol.	188, 404, 454, 455, 489
20 Schol.	396
26	97
27	97
35	432
35 Schol.	252, 310, 315, 316, 432
36 Schol. 1	94
37 Schol. 1	94, 411
37 Schol. 2	150
39 Schol.	315, 403
39 Dem.	461
44 Schol.	154, 317
45 Schol.	401
45 Cor. 2 Schol.	147
46 Schol.	492
47 Schol.	492
54 Schol.	441
57 Dem.	314
57 Schol.	399, 402
58 Schol.	94–5, 148, 316
59 Schol.	147
62 Schol.	516
62 Dem.	515
63 Cor.	228–9
65	189
66 Schol.	416
68 Schol.	368
70	433
App.	116
App. 13	399, 415
App. 16	150
App. 29	51
App. 27–9	151

V
Praef.	174
4 Schol.	174, 412
7 Schol.	253
9 Dem.	97
10	329
14	176
15	176
20 Schol.	174–6, 514, 516, 518
21	547, 549, 553
22	547n., 549, 553
23	vii, 515, 518, 542, 543, 547, 549, 553
23 Schol.	254, 300, 302, 516, 542–3, 551–2
25	547
28	251, 264
29	511, 549
30 Dem.	520
34	549
34 Schol.	301, 545, 550, 553
39	118
39 Schol.	550
41 Schol.	492, 545
42 Schol.	154, 296–7, 548

Hebrew Grammar 318, 337, 341, 391
III	350
IV	30
V	353
VIII	351

IX	268n107	§ 9	414
X	354	§ 15	129
XII	353	§ 16	455
XIII	354	§ 18	414
XVII	352	§ 21	455
XXI	349, 352		

Letter III 501

Letter IV 502

Letter X 257, 303–6, 317, 343, 526

Letter XII 276

Letter XIII 286

Letter XXIV 295

Letter XVII 328

Letter XXX 95, 226

Letter XXXVII 181n11

Letter XLIV 230–1

Letter L 416–19

Letter LXXXII 307–8

Letter LXXXIII 308–8

Political Treatise 227, 256, 292, 428–9, 454, 464, 470, 564, 570

I
- § 2   244, 253, 425, 253, 269, 425
- § 3   292, 493
- § 5   412
- § 6   253

II
- § 6   229, 253, 314, 425
- § 8   226, 316

III
- § 2   456
- § 3   414
- § 5   455, 456
- § 7   463
- §11   315, 414, 458

IV
- § 1   455

V 130, 244
- § 2   456–7
- § 3   392, 448
- § 5   128–9
- § 7   244, 318

VI
- § 1   467
- § 18 118
- § 24 315

VII
- § 3   456
- § 5   434
- § 12 403
- § 14 314–15
- § 18 471
- § 27 401
- § 30 440

VIII
- § 12 314
- § 6   467
- § 19 467
- § 25 472
- § 31 314
- § 45 472

IX
- § 14 386, 451

X
§ 1   492, 496
§ 4   457, 468–9, 415, 457
§ 5   405
§ 7   244, 440, 472
§ 8   415

XI
§ 2   312
§ 4   316

Short Treatise 72n167, 180, 186, 218, 225, 229, 256, 272, 311, 377

II
§ 2   224
§ 3   135n69

III
§ 5   221

V 219
§ 1   104, 220
§ 2   221
§ 3   185, 222
§ 4   219, 222
§ 6   221
§ 12   107, 161n15

XII
§ 3   149n126, 150–1n131

XIV
§ 4   222

XXVI
§ 5   223
§ 6   223

XXXIII
§ 1   545

Appendix II   228

Theologico-Political Treatise x, 17, 25, 28, 50, 59, 228–31, 256, 321, 328, 337, 341, 352, 391, 464, 562, 570

Preface
§ 1   107, 478, 479
§ 2   66, 313–14, 479
§ 3   479, 481
§ 4   66, 107
§ 6   314–15
§ 8   441, 462
§ 12   414
§ 18   445
§ 21   130
§ 25   550
§ 28   414
§ 33   312, 448

I
§ 1   344
§ 5   117, 512
§ 6   117
§ 8   353, 442
§ 14   325
§ 19   29, 445
§ 20   314–15
§ 26   342, 344
§ 30   443
§ 31   441–2
§ 41   443–4

II
§ 24   347
§ 25   312
§ 26   365
§ 27   365
§ 29   509
§ 40   449
§ 48   94, 107, 509
§ 49   107
§ 52   130, 312
§ 98   410

III
§ 7   29, 487
§ 11   487
§ 13   488, 492
§ 14   253, 493

§ 15	253	§ 63	444
§ 16	455–6	§ 75	361
§ 22	118		
§ 27	314	VII	
§ 30	440	§ 1	412
§ 37	312	§ 2	366
§ 41	449	§ 3	366
§ 44	439	§ 4	316
§ 52	470	§ 6	243, 316
§ 53	253, 470	§ 13	10
§ 55	450	§ 16	10
		§ 18	318, 344
IV		§ 19	318, 344
§ 3	130	§ 20	314, 318, 344
§ 12	202	§ 21	318, 344
§ 14	442	§ 22	318, 344, 347
§ 17	390, 439	§ 24	390
§ 35	390	§ 40	342, 346
§ 41	129, 344	§ 45	343
§ 42	347	§ 46	347
		§ 50	355
V		§ 56	130
§ 7	253, 312, 390	§ 64	443
§ 9	439	§ 65	343
§ 14	475	§ 77	347
§ 15	312, 459	§ 79	372
§ 16	459, 469		
§ 18	465	VIII	
§ 21	466	§ 25	347
§ 22	466		
§ 26	449	IX	
§ 27	449	§ 28	348
§ 28	411, 449	§ 44	443
§ 29	450		
§ 30	450	X	
§ 35	306	§ 6	357
§ 306	315	§ 7	357
§ 38	315	§ 8	357
§ 39	257, 315	§ 9	357
§ 40	257	§ 16	443
§ 44	438	§ 48	357
		§ 51	315
VI			
§ 25	511	XI	
§ 32	253, 316	§ 1	368
§ 38	488	§ 2	367
§ 55	315	§ 7	368

XI (cont.)		§ 22	425, 427
§ 8	367	§ 29	435
§ 23	446	§ 34	435
§ 37	312	§ 35	399
§ 44	312	§ 44	253, 433
		§ 61	312
XII		§ 62	253, 316, 412, 433
§ 1	336		
§ 9	345	§ 66	315, 317, 433, 457
§ 11	343, 345	§ 82	316
§ 24	439		
§ 93	456	XVII	
		§ 1	429
XIII		§ 430	
§ 2	253, 315	§ 3	312, 434
§ 4	445	§ 4	430
§ 10	343	§ 9	312, 383
§ 11	342, 345	§ 10	434
§ 17	557	§ 13	312, 434, 436
§ 18	347	§ 14	430, 434, 438
§ 23	129	§ 15	412, 430, 434, 488
XIV		§ 16	430
§ 1	416	§ 21	446
§ 2	310, 416	§ 23	444
§ 3	416	§ 24	444, 446
§ 4	416	§ 26	436
§ 18	347	§ 27	449–50
§ 22	314, 410	§ 61	436
		§ 64	436
XV		§ 81	436
§ 5	347	§ 82	312, 436
§ 8	365	§ 83	437, 450
§ 13	347, 361	§ 93	448
§ 14	361	§ 94	448
§ 15	361	§ 97	435
§ 16	361	§ 112	495
§ 17	361		
§ 18	361	XVIII	
		§ 1	435, 495
XVI		§ 2	435
§ 4	296, 423	§ 3	435
§ 5	423	§ 6	445
§ 6	296	§ 18	447
§ 9	316, 425	§ 35	446–7
§ 11	226	§ 54	451
§ 13	426	§ 55	451

§ 91	405	§ 6	27, 76, 77, 91, 98, 115, 121, 165, 169, 170, 199, 203, 204, 212, 223
§ 92	451		
XIX			
§ 14	459		
§ 19	315	§ 7	26, 27, 74, 76, 99, 121, 166, 170, 171, 172, 183, 199
§ 30	459		
§ 47	107		
XX		§ 8	26, 99, 121, 129, 144, 149, 170, 199
§ 4	384		
§ 5	314		
§ 6	414	§ 9	26, 27, 91, 96, 144, 177–8, 187, 199, 214
§ 8	385		
§ 9	385		
§ 10	386	§ 10	27, 41, 61, 99, 147, 149, 157, 167, 187, 199
§ 22	405		
§ 33	312, 317		
§ 39	315	§ 11	100, 121, 144, 149, 157, 174, 177, 183, 188, 199–201, 203
§ 43	379		
§ 46	387		

Treatise on the Emendation of the Intellect ix–xiii, 7–232, 263, 266, 267, 269, 278, 283, 285, 308, 309, 319, 328, 526, 554, 560–6, 584–8, 594		§ 12	201–4
		§ 13	79, 201–2, 205
		§ 14	164, 200–1, 226
		§ 15	145
§ 1	7, 26, 75, 76, 82, 87, 89, 120, 146, 157, 164, 183, 199, 204	§ 16	145, 200–1
		§ 17	129, 145–7, 199, 200–1
		§ 18	200–1, 260
§ 2	26, 76, 77, 87, 96, 120, 147, 170, 183, 187, 199	§ 19	224
		§ 20	217
		§ 23	135, 224
§ 3	62, 76, 77, 86, 87, 89, 91, 97, 114, 115, 131, 144, 147, 157, 177, 179, 193, 199	§ 25	200–1
		§ 27	224
		§ 49	117
		§ 57	277
		§ 58	503, 508
§ 4	26, 120, 121, 144, 152, 157, 161, 177, 179, 199	§ 68	503
		§ 74	108
		§ 77	106
§ 5	27, 119, 120, 121, 144, 147, 152, 157, 162, 179, 199	§ 88	321
		§ 89	321–2
		§ 103	275–6

EU representative:
Easy Access System Europe
Mustamäe tee 50, 10621 Tallinn, Estonia
Gpsr.requests@easproject.com

www.ingramcontent.com/pod-product-compliance
Lightning Source LLC
Chambersburg PA
CBHW052052300426

44117CB00013B/2093